37$\underline{^{25}}$

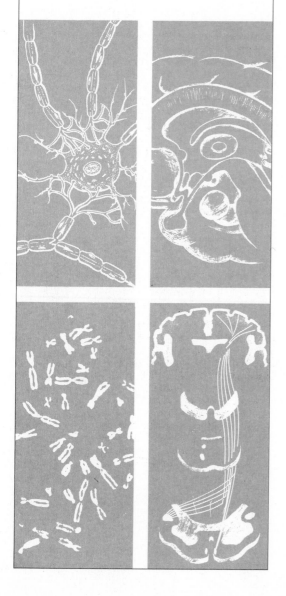

Physiology of Behavior

THIRD EDITION

Neil R. Carlson

University of Massachusetts

ALLYN AND BACON, INC.

Boston • London • Sydney • Toronto

This book is dedicated to the memory of my mother,
Alice Janson Carlson,
1913–1984.

Managing Editor: Bill Barke
Developmental Editor: Allen Workman
Composition Buyer: Linda Cox
Manufacturing Buyer: Andrew Rosenau
Production Coordinator: Kazia Navas
Text Designer: Deborah Schneck
Cover Coordinator: Linda Knowles-Dickinson

Library of Congress Cataloging-in-Publication Data
Carlson, Neil R., 1942–
  Physiology of behavior.

  Bibliography: p. 374
  Includes index.
  1. Psychology, Physiological.   I. Title.
[DNLM: 1. Behavior—physiology.   2. Nervous
System—physiology. 3. Psychophysiology. WL 102
C284p]
QP360.C35   1985   152   85-13475
ISBN 0-205-08501-6
ISBN 0-205-08649-7 (international ed.)

Printed in the United States of America
10 9 8 7 6 5 4   90 89 88 87

Contents

17
Physiology of Mental Disorders 679

Preface

The third edition of a book, I am told, often represents a watershed: does the writer still have the spark necessary to turn out a fresh piece of writing, or has the project gotten stale? Researchers have been very busy in their laboratories during the years since the previous edition of *Physiology of Behavior* came out. Thus, they have provided me with many new things to write about. If my writing still seems fresh, it is largely because of the efforts of these researchers. Their research reports gave me new facts and ideas to think about and write about.

In the preface to the second edition, I mentioned some of the new techniques, such as the horseradish peroxidase method, amino acid autoradiography, radioactive 2-DG autoradiography, and methods to assay receptors, that had been developed to help investigators study the physiology of behavior. These techniques, and many others, have become almost commonplace and have been fruitful, indeed. More and more, researchers are combining techniques that converge upon the solution to a problem. In the past, individuals tended to apply their particular research method to a problem; now they are more likely to use many methods, sometimes in collaboration with other laboratories.

I have made some changes to the outline of the book, as a reader familiar with the previous edition will discover. Some of these changes were made in response to new directions in research efforts, and some were made in response to suggestions of students and colleagues concerning pedagogy. The first part of the book is concerned with foundations: the history of the field, the structure and functions of neurons, neural communication, neuroanatomy, and research methods. The second part is concerned with inputs and outputs: the sensory systems and the motor system. The third part deals with classes of species-typical behavior: reproduction, sleep, ingestion, and aggression. The fourth part deals with learning: reinforcement, the anatomy of learning, and the physiology and biochemistry of learning. The final part deals with human communication, both verbal and nonverbal, and mental disorders. Because I combined several pairs of small chapters, the book consists of seventeen chapters rather than twenty.

Besides updating my discussion of research, I have updated my writing. Writing is a difficult, time-consuming endeavor, and I find that I am still learning how to do it well. I have worked with copy editors who have ruthlessly marked up my manuscript, showing me how to do it better the next time. I keep thinking, "This time there will be nothing for the copy editor to do," but I am always proved wrong: the amount of red pencil on each page remains constant. But I do think that each time the writing is better organized, smoother, and more coherent. If I have at least partly achieved my goal, readers will find that I have no particular writing "style," and yet they can understand what I have said and will remain interested in what they are reading. I agree with Graves and Hodge (1947), who say ". . . good English is a matter not merely of grammar and syntax and vocabulary, but also of sense: the structure of the sentences must hold together logically. . . . [Even] phrases which can be justified both grammatically and from the point of view of sense may give [the] reader a wrong first impression, or check his reading speed, tempting him to skip." "Readability" is not to be determined by counting syllables in words or words in sentences; it is a function of the clarity of thought and expression.

Good writing means including all steps of a logical discourse. My teaching experience has taught me that an entire lecture can be wasted if the students do not understand all of the "obvious" conclusions of a particular experiment before the next one is described. Unfortunately, puzzled students sometimes write notes feverishly, in an attempt to get the facts down so they can study them — and understand them — later. A roomful of busy, attentive students tends to reinforce the lecturer's behavior. I am sure all my colleagues have been dismayed by a question from a student that reveals a lack of understanding of details long since passed, accompanied by quizzical looks from other students that confirm that they too have the same question. Painful experiences such as these have taught me to examine the logical steps between the discussion of one experiment and the next, and to make sure they are explicitly stated. A textbook writer must address the students who will read the book, and not simply address the colleagues who are already acquainted with much of what he or she will say.

Because research on the physiology of behavior is an interdisciplinary effort, a textbook must provide the student with the background necessary for understanding a variety of approaches. I have been careful to provide enough biological background early in the book so students without a background in physiology can understand what is said later, while students with such a background can benefit from details that are familiar to them.

I designed this text for serious students who are willing to work. In return for their effort, I have endeavored to provide a solid foundation for further study. Those students who will not take subsequent courses in this or related fields should receive the satisfaction of a much better understanding of their own behavior. Also, they will have a greater appreciation for the forthcoming advances in medical practices related to disorders that affect a person's perception, mood, or behavior. I hope that students who carefully read this book will henceforth perceive human behavior in a new light.

■ ACKNOWLEDGEMENTS

Although I must accept the blame for any shortcomings of the book, I want to thank colleagues who helped me by sending reprints of their work, suggesting topics that I should cover, sending photographs that have been reproduced in this book, and pointing out deficiencies in the previous edition. I thank:

Huda Akil, David Asdourian, Ross J. Baldessarini, Richard H. Bauer, Walter K. Beagley, William W. Beatty, James D. Belluzzi, Theodore W. Berger, K.J. Berkley, Steven E. Brauth, S. Marc Breedlove, Rebecca M. Cherire, Ronald M. Clavier, Lowell T. Crow, William C. Dement, J. Anthony Deutsch, A. Ehrlich, Linda Enloe, Alan N. Epstein, Carl J. Erickson, Hans C. Fibiger, Mark I. Friedman, Albert M. Galaburda, Charles R. Gallistel, Judy L. Gibbons, Karen K. Glendenning, Richard Gold, Robert W. Goy, Paul Greengard, Sebastian P. Grossman, Michael Guile, Elizabeth L. Hillstron, J. Allan Hobson, Bartley G. Hoebel, Susan A. Hoppe, James Horel, David H. Hubel, Arnold Hyman, Barry Jacobs, K.W. Jacobs, Wesley P. Jordan, Eric R. Kandel, G.L. Kandel, Raymond P. Kesner, Daniel P. Kimble, Kenneth R. King, Richard A. King, F. Scott Kraly, Neil Krieger, Sara F. Leibowitz, Michael Leon, William B. Levy, John C. Liebeskind, Joel F. Lubar, Gary Lynch, Helen Mahut, Morrill J. May, Albert McCormick, T.J. McCrystal, Bruce S. McEwen, Mortimer Mishkin, Gordon J. Mogenson, Frank Morrell, Vernon B. Mountcastle, Enrico Mugnaini, William Neff, Ralph Noble, Steve Noble, Donald Novin, George A. Ojemann, David S. Olton, Thomas Parisi, Jack H. Peck, Ron Peters, Donald W. Pfaff, Edward I. Pollak, Joseph H. Porter, Rick Rayfield, John Renfrew, Bruce E. Rideout, David O.

Robbins, Terry E. Robinson, J. Peter Rosenfeld, John A. Ross, Aryeh Routtenberg, Evelyn Satinoff, Paul Sawchenko, Susan J. Schumacher, Don Scott, Lester M. Sdorow, Jerome M. Siegel, Dennis A. Silva, John B. Simpson, Robert F. Smith, Solomon H. Snyder, Paul R. Solomon, Tam M. Spitzer, Larry R. Squire, Janice R. Stevens, Jeffrey S. Stipling, Robert Sturgeon, Philip Teitelbaum, Elliot S. Valenstein, Cornelius H. Vanderwolf, Gerald S. Wasserman, Wilse B. Webb, Frank M. Webbe, Norman M. Weinberger, Paul J. Wellman, Ian Q. Whishaw, Torsten N. Wiesel, R.C. Wilcott, and Bonnie S. Wright.

Several colleagues reviewed the manuscript of parts of this book and made suggestions for improving the final drafts. I thank:

William W. Beatty, North Dakota State University
Ilene Bernstein, University of Washington
David B. Cohen, University of Texas
Barry Jacobs, Princeton University
Richard A. King, University of North Carolina
Donald Novin, University of California, Los Angeles
Edward I. Pollack, West Chester University
Robert F. Smith, George Mason University
Bruce Svare, State University of New York at Albany
John W. Wright, Washington State University

Leanna Standish and Elizabeth Swearengen, Department of Psychology, Smith College, have prepared a student workbook to accompany this text. We all know how important active participation is in the learning process, and this workbook provides an excellent framework for guiding the student's study behavior. Leanna and Elizabeth are fine teachers, and their combined experience has permitted them to make this edition of the workbook even better than the last one.

I also want to thank the people at Allyn and Bacon. Bill Barke, my editor, provided assistance, support, and encouragement. Lauren Whittaker, an editorial assistant, helped me gather comments and suggestions from colleagues who have read the book. Kazia Navas, the production editor, demonstrated her masterful skills of organization. Few people realize what a difficult, demanding, and time-consuming job a production editor has with a project such as this, with hundreds of illustrations and an author who tends to procrastinate, but I do, and I thank her for all she has done. Nancy Newman was my copy editor. Her attention to detail surprised me again and again; she found inconsistencies in my terminology, awkwardness in my prose, and disjunctions in my logical discourse, and gave me a chance to fix them before anyone else saw them in print. Leslie Galton provided invaluable assistance with obtaining permissions to use figures previously published elsewhere. Mark Lefkowitz, medical illustrator; Vantage Art; and Horvath and Cuthbertson, Illustrators, did a superb job on the art, as you can easily see.

I must also thank my family for their assistance. My daughter Kerstin helped me cut and paste illustrations and find references. My son Paul ran errands for me and patiently accepted that I was often busily engaged in reading or writing in my study. My wife Mary typed the entire second edition into my computer so I could use it to prepare this edition, found missing references, and prepared the author index. But even more important than this assistance was the moral support and encouragement that my family provided me.

I was delighted to hear from many students and colleagues who read previous editions of my book, and I hope that the dialogue will continue. Please write to me and tell me what you like and dislike about the book. My address is: Department of Psychology, Tobin Hall, University of Massachusetts, Amherst, Massachusetts 01003. When I write, I like to imagine that I am talking with you, the reader. If you write to me, we can make the conversation a two-way exchange.

Introduction

Physiological psychologists, like other psychologists, try to explain behavior. What we know about the causes of behavior is certainly less than complete. The study of the physiology of behavior is thus very much an ongoing quest for answers. This book is much more a description of that quest than a list of answers. Its objective is to introduce you to what has been learned about the physiology of behavior and to describe the methods used to investigate this topic.

Investigation of the physiology of behavior has a long history, with roots in philosophy and biology. Philosophers asked how we perceive and understand reality and posed the mind-body question, which remains with us still. They also devised the scientific method —a set of rules that permits us to ask questions about the natural world with some assurance that we will receive reliable answers. Biologists devised experimental physiology, which provides the tools we use to investigate the workings of the body. They also developed the framework needed to integrate findings from diverse species — the principles of natural selection, evolution, and genetics.

Our knowledge about the physiology of behavior has been obtained through the efforts of psychologists, neurophysiologists, neurologists, cell physiologists, molecular biologists, biochemists, neuroanatomists, and endocrinologists. No single academic discipline can claim the field as solely its own, which accounts for the diversity of titles used to describe it. The names *physiological psychology, biological psychology, psychobiology, biopsychology, behavioral physiology,* and *behavioral neuroscience* all have approximately the same meaning.

■ PHILOSOPHICAL ROOTS OF PHYSIOLOGICAL PSYCHOLOGY

Philosophy ("love of wisdom") originally concerned itself with the basis of human knowledge and thought. Philosophers soon realized that in order to understand the basis of knowledge, they must understand the nature of reality, which led them to develop "natural philosophy," the predecessor of modern physical and biological science.

One of the most universal human characteristics is a need to *explain* things. In ancient times, natural phenomena were commonly explained as being the results of animating spirits. All moving objects—animals, the wind and tides, the sun, moon, and stars— were assumed to have spirits that caused them to move. For example, stones fell when they were dropped because their animating spirits wanted to be reunited with Mother Earth. As our ancestors became more sophisticated and learned more about nature they abandoned *animism* in favor of physical explanations for inanimate moving objects. But they still used spirits to explain human—and sometimes animal—behavior.

From the earliest historical times, people have believed they possess souls. This belief stems from the fact that each person is aware of his or her own existence. When we think or act, we feel as if something inside us is thinking or deciding to act. It is natural to assume that other people have similar experiences —that *they* feel something inside them, too. Because we cannot directly examine these "things" people have inside them, we conclude that they are made of something different from that of our physical bodies.

Dualism

Early philosophers believed that reality was divided into two categories: the material and the spiritual. According to this belief, humans had physical bodies and nonphysical spirits, or souls. The belief that humans possess both mind and body is called *dualism*. But if the physical and spiritual aspects of our nature are independent, as this model suggests, then what is the purpose of having both, or in what way are they related? If the body functions independently of the soul, then what does the soul do?

The concept of soul is the cornerstone of religion; philosophers were therefore unwilling to dispense with it. Instead, they suggested that the soul controls the body. The soul and body interact: hence the term *interactionism*. Because the eyes and ears — the primary windows to the soul — are located in the head, the probable location of the soul was presumed to be the brain. Moreover, damage to the head can lead to unconsciousness or paralysis, which suggested that the soul moved the body by controlling the operations of the brain.

In the seventeenth century, the French philosopher and mathematician René Descartes attempted to explain how the soul could control the body. (See **Figure 1.1.**) Descartes believed that animals other than humans were machines. If we could understand how their parts were put together, we should be able to understand them completely. The *bodies* of humans were also machines and operated on exactly the same principles. However, unlike other animals, we had a God-given soul. The soul received information about the world through the body's senses, thought about what it perceived, and made decisions about actions. When it wanted to move the body, it did so by acting on the brain, which in turn moved the muscles.

Descartes formulated the first physiological model of behavior. He based his model on the mechanism that activated the statues in the Royal Gardens. As a young man, he was fascinated by the hidden mechanisms that would cause the statues to move and dance when people visiting the gardens stepped on hidden plates. The statues were moved by hydraulic cylinders powered by water pressure. Descartes believed that the muscles of the body also worked hydraulically. When we

FIGURE 1.1
René Descartes (1596–1650), French philosopher and mathematician, at the court of Queen Christina of Sweden. Descartes's particular form of dualism (interactionism) stimulated interest in the relation between mind and body. (Courtesy of the Granger Collection.)

exert a force with our limbs, our muscles appear to get larger. Descartes concluded that this enlargement occurs because fluid is pumped into the muscles through the nerves. When nerves are cut, a liquid oozes out; hence, the nerves must be hollow.

What is the source of the fluid that gets pumped into the muscles? According to Descartes, it was the *cerebral ventricles* — the hollow, fluid-filled chambers of the brain. He concluded that the mechanism that directed the pressurized fluid into the appropriate nerves was the *pineal body,* a small organ situated on top of the brain stem. The pineal

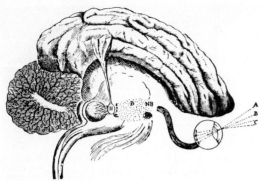

FIGURE 1.2
Descartes believed that the soul controlled the movements of the muscles through its influence on the pineal body. His explanation is modeled on the mechanism that animated statues in the Royal Gardens. More recent attempts to explain the physiology of behavior are modeled on newer devices, such as computers. (Courtesy of Historical Pictures Service, Chicago.)

body acted like a little joystick: when it was tilted slightly in various directions, it opened pores that permitted fluid to enter the nerves and inflate the muscles. (See **Figure 1.2.**)

Because animals lacked souls, Descartes believed that this model completely explained their behavior. Of course, the details would have to be worked out through further study. Humans, however, possessed souls as well as bodies. The pineal gland, which controlled the movements of the pressurized fluids through the nerves to the muscles, provided the place for the soul to interact with the body. When the soul desired a particular action, it tilted the pineal gland appropriately, and the muscles needed to carry out the action became inflated.

As philosophers have subsequently noted, Descartes's theory, like all interactionistic theories, contains a built-in contradiction. If the soul or mind is conceived as nonmaterial, then it cannot (by definition) exert a force

that moves physical objects. Thus, it cannot interact with matter. If the soul or mind possesses material properties that permit it to interact with the body, then it, like the body, is physical. Of course, we could conclude that no contradiction exists, but the issue is beyond human understanding.

However, the spirit of human inquiry is not so easily stifled. Some philosophers after Descartes concluded that his conception of the body as a physical machine was correct as far as it went — but that it should go further. For example, the nineteenth-century British philosopher James Mill agreed that the body was a machine but concluded that the mind was simply a part of the machine. As such, it was subject to the same physical laws as the rest of nature.

Monism

The belief that reality consists of a unified whole — and thus that the mind is a phenomenon produced by the workings of the body — is called *monism*. Modern scientists take a monistic approach to studying the physiology of behavior. That is, we believe that the physiological basis of behavior will be completely understood once we know all the details of the working of the body, especially of the nervous system. Of course, a complete understanding of behavior also requires an analysis of the environment and its effects on the organism. But the reality we deal with is entirely physical in nature. When we study the causes of behavior, we consider only physical events in the environment and in the organism's physiology. What we call "mind" is a consequence of the functioning of the body and its interactions with the environment. The mind-body problem thus exists only as an abstraction.

What can a physiological psychologist say

about human self-awareness? We know that it is altered by changes in the structure or chemistry of the brain; therefore, we conclude that consciousness is a physiological function, just like behavior. We can even speculate about the usefulness of self-awareness: Consciousness and the ability to communicate seem to go hand in hand. Species like ours, with our complex social structures and enormous capacity for learning, are well served by our ability to express intentions to one another and to make requests of one another. This communication makes cooperation possible and permits us to establish customs and laws of behavior. Perhaps the ability to make plans and to communicate these plans to others is what was selected for in the evolution of consciousness. Even if these speculations are true (and I think they are at least reasonable), we have no idea why the complex assemblage of nerve cells that constitutes the human brain gives rise to self-awareness. What properties of the circuits of neurons in my brain allow me to know who I am? The answer to this question will not come quickly.

The question of human consciousness suggests another issue: *determinism* versus *free will.* Self-awareness seems to bring with it a feeling of control; most people believe their minds choose to make their brains do what they do. In other words, they believe that they act of their own free will. But our physiological research is limited to those things that can be measured by physical means — matter and energy. We have no tools that permit us to study nonmaterial entities. Therefore, in our research, we act like determinists, looking for the physical causes of behavior. That is, we assume that behavior can be explained (at least in principle) to the last detail by completely understanding its physiology. My qualifying phrase "at least in principle" must not be taken lightly, however. Even if we

someday discover all there is to know about behavior, we will not always be able to predict a particular person's behavior on a particular occasion. In applying the physical laws governing behavior, we would have to know *everything* that is presently going on in a person's body in order to predict what he or she will do next.

From our present perspective, this knowledge seems impossible to obtain, which means that for all practical purposes, physiological psychology will never take all the mystery out of an individual's behavior. Even physical scientists have to confront the difference between understanding general laws and predicting the behavior of complex systems. Although it is impossible to predict where a feather will fall if it is dropped from a tall building during a windstorm, no reasonable person would assert that the landing place is affected by free will on the part of the feather. A determinist would maintain that free will in humans is a myth that is bolstered by two aspects of our nature: the complexity of the human brain, which is far greater than the forces that act on a falling feather, and our own consciousness, which makes us feel that our minds control our bodies, rather than the reverse.

I am sure that many of you do not agree with the determinist position; you may feel that you are in control of your own behavior, and you can point out — correctly — that I cannot prove otherwise. Fortunately, the issue is a philosophical and religious one that can be divorced from the scientific investigation of the physiology of behavior. If a person believes in his or her own free will, that is fine, as long as he or she acts like a determinist in the laboratory. We must limit the scope of our hypotheses to the methods of investigation that we have at hand. Because our techniques are physical, our explanations must also be physical. If organisms do have nonphysical minds or souls that control their behavior, the methods of physiological psychology will never detect them.

■ BIOLOGICAL ROOTS OF PHYSIOLOGICAL PSYCHOLOGY

Not all modern philosophers are monists, and not all believe that the human mind is based on physiological functioning. Yet scientists who study the physiology of behavior trace their intellectual ancestry to the monistic, deterministic school of philosophy. This school encouraged the development of natural scientists, who first studied living organisms in the world around them and eventually applied their techniques and principles to the study of human behavior.

Although such early natural philosophers as Aristotle speculated about the causes of behavior, René Descartes's physiological model provides a good starting place for a discussion of the biological roots of physiological psychology. His model was completely wrong, but it was a reasonable hypothesis, considering the physiological information available to him. Others soon tested its predictions and found them incorrect. For example, experiments showed that the volume of a muscle does not actually increase when it contracts, as it would if it were inflated with fluid. In fact, Luigi Galvani, an Italian physiologist, found that stimulation of a frog's nerve caused the muscle to which it was attached to contract. Contraction occurred even when the nerve and muscle were detached from the rest of the body, so that pressurized ventricular fluid obviously could not be responsible for the contraction. (Alessandro Volta identified the stimulating event as electricity.) The value of Descartes's physiological model did not lie in whether it was right or wrong; rather, it served to focus the efforts of those

who followed him on performing experiments. Thus, knowledge of the physiology of behavior began to accumulate.

Experimental Physiology

One of the most important figures in the development of experimental physiology was Johannes Müller, a nineteenth-century German physiologist. Müller was a forceful advocate of the application of experimental techniques to physiology. Previously, the activities of most natural scientists were limited to observation and classification. Although these activities are essential, Müller insisted that major advances in understanding the workings of the body would be achieved only by experimentally removing or isolating animals' organs, testing their responses to various chemicals, and otherwise altering the environment to see how the organs responded. His most important contribution to the study of the physiology of behavior was his *doctrine of specific nerve energies.* Müller observed that although all nerves carry the same basic message—an electrical impulse—we perceive the messages of different nerves in different ways. For example, messages carried by the optic nerves produce sensations of visual images, while those carried by the auditory nerves produce sensations of sounds. How can different sensations arise from the same basic message?

The answer is that the messages occur in different channels. The portion of the brain that receives messages from the optic nerves interprets the activity as visual stimulation, even if the nerves are actually stimulated mechanically. (For example, when we rub our eyes, we see flashes of light.) Because different parts of the brain receive messages from different nerves, the brain must be functionally divided: Some parts perform some functions, while other parts perform others.

Müller's advocacy of experimentation and

the logical deductions from his doctrine of specific nerve energies set the stage for performing experiments directly on the brain. Indeed, Pierre Flourens, a nineteenth-century French physiologist, did just that. Flourens removed various parts of animals' brains and observed their behavior. By seeing what the animal could no longer do, he could infer the function of the missing portion of the brain. This method is called *experimental ablation* (from the Latin *ablatus,* "carried away"). Flourens claimed to have discovered the regions of the brain that control heart rate and breathing, purposeful movements, and visual and auditory reflexes.

Soon after Flourens performed his experiments, Paul Broca, a French surgeon, applied the principle of experimental ablation to the human brain. Of course, he did not intentionally remove parts of human brains to see how they worked. Instead, he observed the behavior of people whose brains had been damaged by strokes. In 1861 he performed an autopsy on the brain of a man who had had a stroke that caused him to lose the ability to speak. Broca's observations led him to conclude that a portion of the cerebral cortex on the left side of the brain performs functions necessary for speech. Other physicians soon obtained evidence supporting his conclusions. As you will learn, the physiological basis of speech is not localized in a particular region of the brain. Indeed, speech requires many different functions, which are organized throughout the brain. Nonetheless, the method of experimental ablation remains important to our understanding of the brains of both humans and laboratory animals.

Luigi Galvani used electricity in the eighteenth century to demonstrate that muscles contain the source of the energy that powers their contractions. In 1870 the German physiologists Gustav Fritsch and Eduard Hitzig used electrical stimulation as a tool for understanding the physiology of the brain. They applied weak electrical shocks to the exposed surface of a dog's cerebral cortex and observed the effects of the stimulation. They found that stimulation of different portions of a specific region of the cortex caused contraction of specific muscles on the opposite side of the body. We now refer to this region as the primary motor cortex, and we know that nerve cells there communicate directly with those that cause muscular contractions. We also know that other regions of the brain communicate with the primary motor cortex and thus control behaviors. For example, the region that Broca found to be necessary for speech communicates with the portion of the primary motor cortex that controls the muscles of the lips, tongue, and throat that we use to speak.

One of the most brilliant contributors to nineteenth-century science was the German physicist and physiologist Hermann von Helmholtz. Helmholtz devised a mathematical formulation of the law of conservation of energy, invented the ophthalmoscope (used to examine the retina of the eye), devised an important and influential theory of color vision and color blindness, and studied audition, music, eye movements, geometry, allergies, and the formation of ice. Although Helmholtz had studied under Müller, he opposed Müller's belief that human organs are endowed with a vital nonmaterial force that coordinates their operations. Helmholtz believed that all aspects of physiology are mechanistic, subject to experimental investigation.

Helmholtz was the first scientist to attempt to measure the speed of conduction through nerves. Scientists had previously believed that such conduction was identical to the conduction that occurs in wires, traveling at approximately the speed of light. But Helmholtz found that neural conduction was much slower — only about 90 feet per second. This measurement proved that neural conduction was more than a simple electrical message, as we will see in the next chapter.

Twentieth-century developments in experimental physiology include many important inventions, such as sensitive amplifiers to detect weak electrical signals, neurochemical techniques to analyze chemical changes within and between cells, and histological techniques to see cells and their constituents. Because these developments belong to the modern era, they are discussed in detail in subsequent chapters.

Functionalism: Natural Selection and Evolution

In discussing the biological roots of physiological psychology, I have provided a brief history of the contribution of experimental physiology. Müller's insistence that biology must be an experimental science provided the starting point for an important tradition. However, other biologists continued to observe, classify, and think about what they saw, and some of them arrived at valuable conclusions. The most important of these biologists was Charles Darwin. Darwin formulated the principle of *natural selection,* which revolutionized biology. He noted that individuals spontaneously undergo structural changes. If these changes produce favorable effects that permit the individual to reproduce more successfully, some of the individual's offspring will inherit the favorable characteristics and will themselves produce more offspring.

Darwin's theory emphasized that all of an organism's characteristics — its structure, its coloration, its behavior — have functional significance. For example, eagles have strong talons and sharp beaks because they permit the birds to catch and eat prey. Caterpillars that eat green leaves are themselves green because this color makes it difficult for birds to see them against their usual background.

Mother mice construct nests because their offspring will be kept warm and out of harm's way. *Functionalism* assumes that characteristics of living organisms perform useful functions, or at least functions that were useful at one time in the history of the species. To understand the physiological basis of various behaviors, we must first understand the significance of these behaviors. We must therefore understand something about the natural history of the species being studied, so that the behaviors can be seen in context.

To understand the workings of a complex piece of machinery, it helps to know what its functions are. This principle is just as true for a living organism as it is for a mechanical device. However, an important difference exists between machines and organisms: Machines have inventors who had a purpose when they designed them, whereas organisms are the result of a long series of accidents. Thus, strictly speaking, we cannot say that any physiological mechanisms of living organisms have a *purpose*. But they have *functions,* and these we can try to determine.

The cornerstone of evolution is the principle of natural selection. Briefly, here is how the process works for sexually reproducing multicellular animals: Every organism consists of a large number of cells, each of which contains chromosomes. Chromosomes are large, complex molecules that contain the recipes for producing the proteins that cells need to grow and perform their functions. In essence, the chromosomes contain the blueprints for the construction (that is, the embryological development) of a particular member of a particular species. If the plans are altered, a different organism is produced.

The plans do get altered; mutations occur from time to time. Mutations are accidental changes in the chromosomes of sperms or eggs that join together and develop into new organisms. For example, a cosmic ray might strike a chromosome in a cell of a parental testis or ovary, thus producing a mutation that affects the offspring. Most mutations are deleterious: the offspring either fails to survive or survives with some sort of deficit. However, a small percentage of mutations are beneficial, and confer a *selective advantage* to the organism that possesses them. That is, the animal is more likely than those without the mutation to live long enough to reproduce and hence to pass on its chromosomes (with their alteration) to its own offspring. Many different kinds of traits can confer a selective advantage. Examples include resistance to a particular disease, the ability to digest new kinds of food, more effective weapons for defense or for procurement of prey, and even a more attractive appearance to members of the opposite sex (after all, one must reproduce in order to pass on one's chromosomes).

Naturally, the traits that can be altered by mutations are physical ones; chromosomes make proteins, which affect the structure and chemistry of cells. But the *effects* of these physical alterations can be seen in an animal's behavior. Thus, the process of natural selection can indirectly act upon behavior. For example, if a particular mutation results in changes in the brain that cause an animal to stop moving and freeze when it perceives a novel stimulus, that animal is more likely to escape undetected when a predator passes nearby. This tendency makes the animal more likely to survive to produce offspring and pass on its genes to future generations.

Other mutations are not immediately favorable, but because they do not put their possessors at a disadvantage, they get inherited by at least some members of the species. As a result of thousands of such mutations, the members of a particular species possess a variety of genes and are all at least somewhat different from one another. Different environments provide optimal habitats for different kinds of organisms. When the environment changes, species must adapt or run the risk of

becoming extinct. If some members of the species possess assortments of genes that provide characteristics permitting them to adapt to the new environment, their genes will soon dominate, and the species will undergo changes. Thus, many mutations that do not cause immediate changes in the genetic composition of a species may at some future time provide the genetic variability that permits at least some individuals to take advantage of environmental changes.

An understanding of the principle of natural selection plays some role in the thinking of every person who undertakes research in physiological psychology. Some researchers explicitly consider the genetic mechanisms of various behaviors and the physiological processes upon which these behaviors depend. Others are concerned with comparative aspects of behavior and its physiological basis; they compare the nervous systems of animals from a variety of species in order to make hypotheses about the evolution of brain structure and the behavioral capacities that correspond to this evolutionary development. But even though many researchers are not directly involved with the problem of evolution, the principle of natural selection guides the thinking of all physiological psychologists. We ask ourselves what the selective advantage of a particular trait might be. We think about how nature might have used a physiological mechanism that already existed to perform more complex functions in more complex organisms. When we entertain hypotheses, we ask ourselves whether a particular explanation makes sense in an evolutionary perspective.

■ CONTRIBUTIONS OF MODERN PSYCHOLOGY

The field of physiological psychology grew out of psychology. Indeed, the first textbook of psychology, written by Wilhelm Wundt, was titled *Principles of Physiological Psychology*. In recent years, with the explosion of information in experimental biology, scientists from other disciplines have become prominent contributors to the investigation of the physiology of behavior. The united effort of physiological psychologists, physiologists, and other neuroscientists has come about because of the realization that the ultimate function of the nervous system is behavior. The nervous system performs other functions, such as perceiving stimuli and controlling internal physiological processes, but these functions support the basic one: control of movement. The function of perception is to permit events in our environment to control our behavior appropriately; perception without the ability to act is useless, and natural selection does not favor useless characteristics. We maintain our internal physiological processes so that we can live *and move.*

The modern history of investigating the physiology of behavior has been written by psychologists who have combined the methods of experimental psychology with the methods of experimental physiology and have applied them to the issues that concern psychologists in general. Thus, we have studied perceptual processes, control of movement, sleep and waking, reproductive behaviors, ingestive behaviors, aggressive behaviors, learning, and language. In recent years, we have begun to study the physiology of human pathological conditions, such as mental disorders.

The Goals of Research

The goal of all scientists is to explain the phenomena they study. But what do we mean by "explain"? Scientific explanation takes two forms: generalization and reduction. Most psychologists deal with *generalization*. They explain particular instances of behavior as ex-

amples of general laws, which they deduce from their experiments. For instance, most psychologists would explain a pathologically strong fear of dogs as an example of classical conditioning. Presumably, the person was frightened earlier in life by a dog. An unpleasant stimulus was paired with the sight of the animal (perhaps the person was knocked down by an exuberant dog or was attacked by a vicious one), and the subsequent sight of dogs evokes the earlier response — fear.

Most physiologists deal with *reduction.* They explain phenomena in terms of simpler phenomena. For example, they may explain the movement of a muscle in terms of the changes in the membranes of muscle cells, the entry of particular chemicals, and the interactions among protein molecules within these cells. By contrast, a molecular biologist would explain these events in terms of forces that bind various molecules together and cause various parts of the molecules to be attracted to one another. In turn, the job of an atomic physicist is to describe matter and energy themselves and to account for the various forces found in nature. Practitioners of each branch of science use reduction to call on more elementary generalizations to explain the phenomena they study.

The task of the physiological psychologist is to explain behavior in physiological terms. But physiological psychologists cannot simply be reductionists. It is not enough to observe behaviors and correlate them with physiological events that occur at the same time. Identical behaviors may occur for different reasons and thus may be initiated by different physiological mechanisms. Therefore, we must understand "psychologically" why a particular behavior occurs before we can understand what physiological events made it occur.

Let me provide a specific example. Mice, like many other mammals, often build nests. Behavioral observations show that mice will build nests under two conditions: when the air temperature is low and when the animal is pregnant. A nonpregnant mouse will not build a nest if the weather is warm, whereas a pregnant mouse will build one regardless of the temperature. The same behavior occurs for different reasons. Thus, it should not be surprising that these behaviors are initiated by different physiological mechanisms. Nest building can be studied as a behavior related to the process of temperature regulation, or it can be studied in the context of parental behavior.

Sometimes physiological mechanisms can tell us something about psychological processes. This relationship is particularly true of complex phenomena such as language, memory, and mood, which are poorly understood psychologically. For example, damage to a specific part of the brain can cause very specific impairments in a person's language abilities. The nature of these impairments suggests how these abilities are organized. When the damage involves a brain region that is important in analyzing speech sounds, it also produces deficits in spelling. This finding suggests that the ability to recognize a spoken word and the ability to spell it call upon related brain mechanisms. Damage to a certain other region can produce extreme difficulty in reading unfamiliar words by sounding them out, but does not impair the person's ability to read words with which he or she is already familiar. This finding suggests that reading comprehension can take two routes: one that is related to speech sounds and another that is primarily visual, bypassing acoustic representation.

In practice, the research efforts of physiological psychologists involve both forms of explanation — generalization and reduction. Ideas for experiments are stimulated by the investigator's knowledge both of psychological generalizations about behavior and of physiological mechanisms. A good physiolog-

ical psychologist must therefore be both a good psychologist and a good physiologist.

■ ORGANIZATION OF THIS BOOK

Outline

The physiology of behavior means, in large part, the role of the nervous system in the control of behavior. Thus, this book begins with the fundamentals of neurophysiology, neurochemistry, neuropharmacology, and neuroanatomy. Chapter 2 describes the cells of the nervous system and explains how neurons send messages along their axons (nerve fibers). Chapter 3 describes communication between neurons, which is almost always accomplished chemically. The release of the chemical transmitter is explained, as well as the effects it has on the cell receiving the message. Because almost all drugs that have behavioral effects produce them by influencing chemical communication between neurons, the effects of these drugs are also covered in Chapter 3. As you will see, drugs have become important tools in our attempts to understand the nature of brain mechanisms.

Chapter 4 outlines the anatomy of the brain and its interactions with the endocrine system. A necessary step in understanding how the brain carries out its functions is to determine which neural circuits perform which functions. Thus, in order to understand the results of research in physiological psychology, one must know at least some essentials of neuroanatomy. Chapter 5 describes the basic research methods of physiological psychology, including neuroanatomical methods, experimental ablation methods, electrical recording methods, electrical stimulation methods, and neurochemical methods.

The second section of the book describes

the physiology of perception and movement. Chapter 6 discusses vision, and Chapter 7 discusses the other sensory modalities: audition, the vestibular senses, the somatosenses, gustation, and olfaction. Chapter 8 describes the neural control of movement.

The third section of the book deals with species-typical behaviors, which are of special importance to motivation. Chapter 9 describes the physiology of sleep and waking, including sleep disorders and the control of biological rhythms. Chapter 10 describes the physiology of sexual development and reproductive behaviors, including mating and the care of offspring. Chapter 11 describes the control of eating and drinking and the internal physiological processes related to water balance and metabolism. Chapter 12 describes the neural and hormonal control of aggression.

The fourth section of the book deals with the physiology of learning. Chapter 13 discusses the neural basis of reinforcement, the process by which the consequences of a behavior cause the organism to perform the behavior more frequently. Chapter 14 deals with the anatomy of learning, attempting to answer the question "Which parts of the brain are essential for the learning of which kinds of behavior?" Chapter 15 describes research on the physiology and biochemistry of learning —the actual nature of the structural and biochemical changes that take place in the brain as a result of experience.

The final section of the book describes the anatomy and physiology of human communication and of disorders of thought and mood. Chapter 16 discusses what we have learned about the neural organization of various types of communication: listening, speaking, reading, writing, and expressing and perceiving emotions. Chapter 17 describes research on the physiology of serious mental disorders: schizophrenia and the affective disorders.

Some Mechanical Details

I have tried to integrate the text and illustrations as closely as possible. In my experience, one of the most annoying aspects of reading some books is not knowing when to look at an illustration. When reading complicated material, I have found that sometimes I look at the figure too soon, before I have read enough to understand it, and sometimes I look at it too late and realize that I could have made more sense out of the text if I had just looked at the figure sooner. Furthermore, after looking at the illustration I often find it difficult to return to the place where I stopped reading. Therefore, in this book you will find the figure references in boldface (like this: **Figure 5.6**), which means "stop reading and look at the figure." I have placed these references in the locations I think will be optimal. If you look away from the text then, you will be assured that you will not be interrupting a line of reasoning in a crucial place and will not have to reread several sentences to get going again. You will find sections like this: "Figure 4.1 shows an alligator and a human. The alligator is certainly laid out in a linear fashion; we can draw a straight line that starts between its eyes and continues down the center of its spinal cord. (See **Figure 4.1.**)" This particular example is a trivial one and will give you no problems no matter when you look at the figure. But in other cases the material is more complex, and you will have less trouble if you know what to look for before you stop reading and examine the illustration.

You will notice that some words in the text are *italicized* while others are printed in **boldface italics.** Italics mean one of two things: either the word is being stressed for emphasis and is not a new term, or I am pointing out a new term that I do not think is necessary for you to learn. On the other hand, a word in boldface italics is a new term that you should try to learn. Most of the boldface italicized terms in the text are part of the vocabulary of the physiological psychologist. Often, they will be used again in a later chapter. As an aid to your studying, I have listed all of the boldfaced terms at the end of each chapter (except this one), along with the page number on which the term was first used.

The end of the text contains a glossary. The glossary provides definitions for important terms that are used throughout the book. If a term is used only once and is not one that you will encounter later in the text, it is probably not included in the glossary. Its definition will be found where it is first introduced in the text. But if you encounter a scientific term that is not in boldface italics, it was probably introduced earlier. If you need to refresh your memory, the easiest place to find a definition is in the glossary. In addition, a comprehensive index at the end of the book provides a list of terms and topics, with page references.

The physiology of behavior is a complex subject, and this book contains many concepts and descriptions of experiments that will be new to you. At the end of each major section I have included an *interim summary,* which provides a place for you to stop and think again about what you have just read, in order to make sure that you understand the direction the discussion has gone. Taken together, these sections provide a detailed summary of all the information introduced in the chapter.

I hope that in reading this book you will come not only to learn more about the brain but also to appreciate it for the marvelous organ it is. The brain is wonderfully complex, and perhaps the most remarkable thing is that we are able to use it in our attempt to understand it.

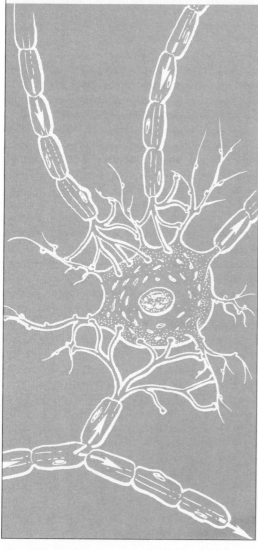

Structure and Functions of Cells of the Nervous System

The functions of the nervous system depend on the properties of its elements: neurons and the cells that support them. This chapter describes the structure of these cells. It also discusses the process of neural integration, the means by which neurons control the activity of other neurons, and the nature of the action potential, which conveys messages from one end of a nerve fiber to the other. These messages represent the information that flows from the environment to the nervous system, from place to place within the nervous system, and from the nervous system to the muscles.

■ CELLS OF THE NERVOUS SYSTEM

Neurons

The neuron (nerve cell) is the information-processing and information-transmitting element of the nervous system. Before describing the particular characteristics of neurons, I will describe the structures and properties these cells have in common with other cells of the body.

Structures of Cells

Figure 2.1 illustrates a typical animal cell. (See **Figure 2.1.**) The ***membrane*** defines the boundary of the cell. It consists of a double layer of lipid (fatlike) molecules in which float a variety of protein molecules that have special functions. The membrane is an exceedingly complex structure; it is far more than a bag holding in the contents of the cell. It is an active part of the cell, keeping in some substances and keeping out others. It even uses up energy by actively extruding some substances and pulling in others. Some of the proteins that float in the membrane detect substances outside the cell (such as hormones) and pass information about the presence of these substances to the interior of the cell. Because the membrane of the neuron is especially important in the transmission of

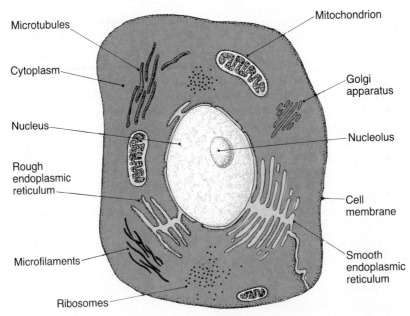

FIGURE 2.1
The principal structures of an animal cell.

information, its characteristics will be discussed in more detail later in this chapter.

The bulk of the cell consists of **cytoplasm.** Cytoplasm is complex and varies considerably across types of cells, but it can be most easily characterized as a jellylike, semiliquid substance that fills the space outlined by the membrane. Cytoplasm is not static and inert; it streams and flows.

Mitochondria (singular: mitochondrion) are important in the energy cycle of the cell; many of the biochemical steps involved in the extraction of energy from the breakdown of nutrients take place on the *cristae* of mitochondria. Mitochondria are shaped like oval beads and are formed of a double membrane. The inner membrane is wrinkled, and the wrinkles make up a set of shelves (cristae) that fill the inside of the bead.

Endoplasmic reticulum appears in two forms: rough and smooth. Both types consist of membranes that are continuous with the outer membrane of the cell. Cell biologists believe that endoplasmic reticulum is concerned with the transport of substances around the cytoplasm and provides channels for the segregation of various molecules involved in different cellular processes. Rough endoplasmic reticulum may be differentiated from the smooth type in that it contains **ribosomes.** These structures are the sites for protein synthesis in the cell. The protein produced by the ribosomes attached to the rough endoplasmic reticulum is destined to be transported out of the cell. For example, the hormone insulin (a protein) is manufactured there in certain cells of the pancreas. Unattached ribosomes are also distributed around the cytoplasm; the unattached variety appears to produce protein for use within the cell.

The **Golgi apparatus** also consists of membrane. This structure serves as a wrapping or packaging agent. For example, secretory cells (such as those that release hormones) wrap their product in a membrane

produced by the Golgi apparatus. When the cell secretes its products, the container migrates to the outer membrane of the cell, fuses with it, and bursts, spilling the product into the fluid surrounding the cell. As we will see, neurons are secretory cells; they communicate with each other by secreting chemicals by this means.

The **nucleus** of the cell is round or oval and is covered by the nuclear membrane. The **nucleolus** and the **chromosomes** reside here. The nucleolus manufactures ribosomes. The chromosomes, which consist of long strands of **deoxyribonucleic acid (DNA),** contain the organism's genetic information. When they are active, portions of the chromosomes **(genes)** cause production of another complex molecule, **messenger ribonucleic acid (mRNA).** The mRNA leaves the nuclear membrane and attaches to ribosomes, where it causes the production of a particular protein. (See **Figure 2.2.**)

Proteins are important in cell functions. As well as providing structure, proteins serve as **enzymes,** which direct the chemical processes of a cell by controlling chemical reactions. Enzymes are special protein molecules that act as catalysts; that is, they cause a chemical reaction to take place without becoming a part of the final product themselves. Because cells contain the constituents needed to synthesize an enormous variety of compounds, the ones they actually do produce depend primarily on the particular enzymes that are present. Furthermore, there are enzymes that break molecules apart as well as put them together; the enzymes present in a particular region of a cell thus determine which molecules remain intact. For example,

$$A + B \underset{Y}{\overset{X}{\rightleftharpoons}} AB$$

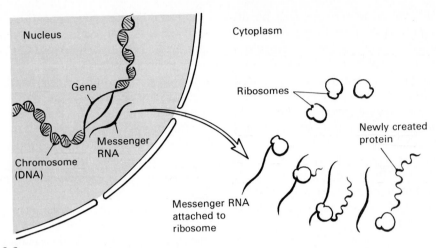

FIGURE 2.2
An overview of the process of protein synthesis, controlled by the genes.

In the case of this reversible reaction, the relative concentrations of enzymes X and Y determine whether the complex substance AB, or its constituents, A and B, will predominate. Enzyme X makes A and B join together, while enzyme Y splits AB apart. (Energy may also be required to make the reactions proceed.)

Arranged throughout the cell are **microfilaments** and **microtubules.** These long, slender, hairlike structures serve as a matrix, or framework, into which are embedded the various components of the cytoplasm. As we will see, they also assist in transporting molecules and structures from place to place within the cell and play an essential role in communication between neurons.

Structures of Neurons
Neurons come in many shapes and varieties, according to the specialized jobs they per-

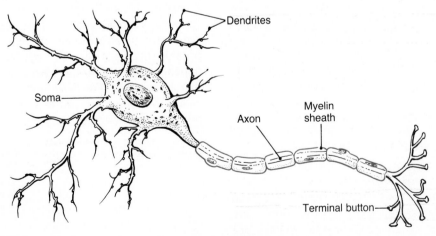

FIGURE 2.3
The principal structures or regions of a multipolar neuron.

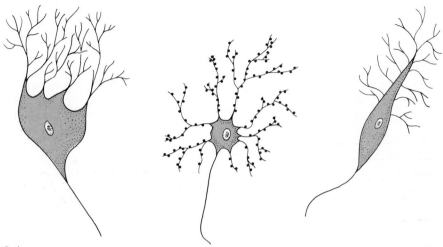

FIGURE 2.4

A sample of the variety of dendritic shapes of various types of neurons.

form. They usually have, in one form or another, the following four structures or regions: (1) cell body, or soma; (2) dendrites; (3) axon; and (4) terminal buttons.

Soma. The **soma** (cell body) contains the nucleus and much of the machinery that provides for the life processes of the cell. (See **Figure 2.3.**) Its shape varies considerably in different kinds of neurons.

Dendrites. *Dendron* is the Greek word for tree, and the **dendrites** of the neuron look very much like trees. (See **Figure 2.3.**) Dendrites vary in shape even more widely than do real trees; a glance at Figure 2.4 shows some of the many forms they can take. (See **Figure 2.4.**) Neurons "converse" with one another, and dendrites serve as important recipients of these messages. The messages that pass from neuron to neuron are transmitted across the **synapse**, a junction between the terminal buttons (described below) of the sending cell and a portion of the somatic or dendritic membrane of the receiving cell. The word *synapse* derives from the Greek *sunaptein,* "to join together."

Synapses on the dendrites of many neurons occur not on the branches or twigs but on little buds known as **dendritic spines.** Figure 2.5 illustrates a terminal button of the sending cell and a dendritic spine of the receiving cell. (See **Figure 2.5.**) Synapses occur not only between a terminal button and a den-

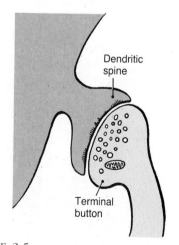

FIGURE 2.5

A synapse of a terminal button of one neuron with a dendritic spine of another.

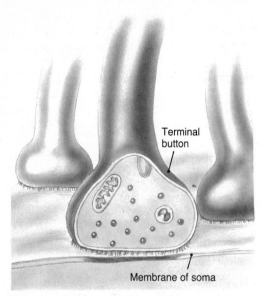

Terminal
button

Membrane of soma

FIGURE 2.6
A synapse of a terminal button of one neuron
with the somatic membrane of another.

dritic membrane but also between a terminal
button and a somatic membrane. In most
cases, there are no spines on the membrane of
the soma; the terminal button just meets the
smooth surface of the membrane. (See **Figure
2.6.**) Communication at a synapse proceeds
in only one direction; a terminal button transmits messages to the receiving cell but does
not receive messages from it.

Axon. The dendritic and somatic membranes receive messages from other cells —
in some cases, from hundreds of other cells.
These messages affect the activity of the
neuron, which as a result may or may not
transmit messages down its ***axon*** to other
cells — those cells to which *this* neuron
transmits messages. (See **Figure 2.7.**)

The axon is a long, slender tube. It carries
information away from the cell body to the
terminal buttons. The message is electrical in

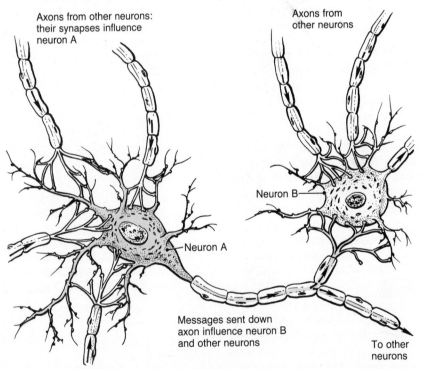

Axons from other neurons:
their synapses influence
neuron A

Axons from
other neurons

Neuron B

Neuron A

Messages sent down
axon influence neuron B
and other neurons

To other
neurons

FIGURE 2.7
An overview of the synaptic connections between neurons.

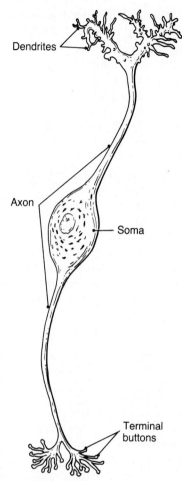

FIGURE 2.8
A bipolar neuron, primarily found in sensory systems (for example, vision and audition).

matic membrane gives rise to one axon but to the trunks of many dendritic trees. ***Bipolar neurons*** give rise to one axon and one dendritic tree, at opposite ends of the soma. (See **Figure 2.8.**) These neurons are usually sensory in nature. Their dendrites are located outside the CNS, where they receive information from specialized cells that detect environmental stimuli. Their axons convey messages to the CNS. In mammals, these neurons transmit visual, auditory, and vestibular (balance, from the inner ears) information.

The third type of nerve cell is the ***unipolar neuron.*** (See **Figure 2.9**) It has only one stalk

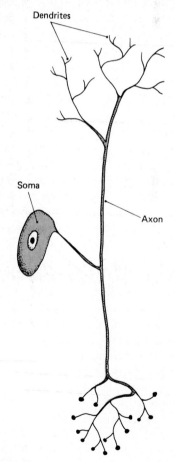

FIGURE 2.9
A unipolar neuron, found in the somatosensory system (touch, pain, etc.).

nature, but, as we will see, it is not carried down the axon the way a message travels down a telephone wire. Like dendrites, axons and their branches come in different shapes. There are three principal types of neurons, classified according to the way in which their axons and dendrites leave the soma.

The neuron depicted in Figures 2.3 and 2.7 is the most common type found in the central nervous system (CNS); it is a ***multipolar neuron.*** In this type of neuron, the so-that leaves the soma and divides into two branches a short distance away. Both ends of these branches arborize (divide up like the branches of a tree—for some reason they "arborize" in Latin rather than "dendritize" in Greek). The unipolar cell, like the bipolar cell, transmits information from the environment into the CNS. The arborizations farther from the CNS are dendrites; the arborizations within the CNS end in terminal buttons. Unipolar neurons receive sensory information directly from the environment, primarily from stimuli applied to the skin.

Terminal Buttons. The axon divides and branches a number of times. At the ends of the twigs are found little knobs called **terminal buttons,** which have a very special function; when a message is passed down the axon, the terminal buttons of the transmitting cell secrete a chemical called a **transmitter substance.** This chemical (there are many different ones in the CNS) affects the receiving cell. The effect it produces excites or inhibits the receiving cell and thus helps determine whether this cell will send a message down its axon to the cells with which it communicates. Details of this process will be described later in this chapter and in Chapter 3.

Supporting Cells of the CNS

Glia

Neurons constitute only about half the volume of the CNS. The rest consists of a variety of supporting cells, the most important of which is the **neuroglia,** or "nerve glue." **Glia,** or **glial cells** (as they are usually called) do indeed glue the CNS together, but they do much more than that. Neurons lead a very sheltered existence; they are physically and chemically buffered from the rest of the body by the glial cells. Glial cells surround neurons and hold them in place, controlling their supply of some of the chemicals they need to

exchange messages with other neurons; they insulate neurons from one another so that neural messages do not get scrambled and they even act as housekeepers, destroying and removing the carcasses of neurons that are killed by injury or that die as a result of old age.

There are several types of glial cells, each of which plays a special role in the CNS.

Astrocytes (Astroglia). Astrocyte means "star cell," and this name accurately describes the shape of these cells. Astrocytes **(astroglia)** are rather large, as glia go, and provide physical and nutritional support to neurons. Together with microglia, they also clean up debris within the brain. Finally, they chemically buffer the fluid surrounding neurons, a function that will be discussed later in this chapter.

Some of the astrocyte's *processes* (the arms of the star) are wrapped around blood vessels; other processes are wrapped around parts of neurons, so that the somatic and dendritic membrane of neurons is largely surrounded by astrocytes. (See **Figure 2.10.**) This arrangement suggested to the Italian histologist Camillo Golgi (1844 – 1926) that astrocytes supply neurons with nutrients from the capillaries and dispose of their waste products (Golgi, 1903). He thought that nutrients passed from capillaries to the cytoplasm of the astrocytes, and then through the cytoplasm to the neurons, with waste products following the opposite route. As Figure 2.10 shows, this hypothesis is plausible. However, despite the age of the hypothesis, we still lack evidence to confirm it.

There is good evidence from the peripheral nervous system, though, that the satellite cells *do* transport substances to neurons. Lasek, Gainer, and Przybylski (1974) found that in the peripheral nervous system of the squid, neurons take up proteins that are synthesized in adjacent satellite cells. Further-

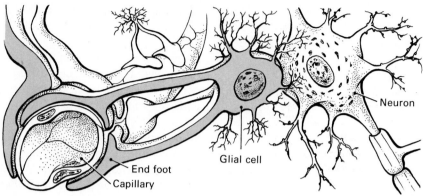

FIGURE 2.10

Structure and location of astrocytes, whose processes surround capillaries and neurons of the central nervous system. (Adapted from Kuffler, S.W., and Nicholls, J.G. *From Neuron to Brain*. Sunderland, Mass.: Sinauer Associates, 1976.)

more, some neurons lose their ability to produce the transmitter substance if the surrounding satellite cells are destroyed (Patterson and Chun, 1974).

Besides a possible role in transporting chemicals to neurons, astrocytes serve as the matrix that holds neurons in place. They also surround and isolate synapses, apparently minimizing the dispersion of transmitter substances that are released by the terminal buttons. Thus, astrocytes provide each synapse with an isolation booth, keeping the neurons' conversations private.

Neurons occasionally die for unknown reasons or are killed by head injury, infection, or stroke. Certain kinds of astrocytes (along with the microglia) then take up the task of cleaning away the debris. These cells are able to travel around the CNS; they extend and retract their processes (*pseudopodia,* or "false feet") and glide about the way amoebas do. When they contact a piece of debris from a dead neuron, they push themselves against it, finally engulfing and digesting it. We call this process *phagocytosis,* and cells capable of doing this are called *phagocytes* ("eating cells"). If there is a considerable amount of injured tissue to be cleaned up, astrocytes will divide and produce enough new cells to do the task. Once the dead tissue is broken down, a framework of astrocytes will be left to fill in the vacant area, and a specialized kind of astrocyte will form scar tissue, walling off the area.

Microglia. *Microglia* are smaller than the other types of glia. They serve as phagocytes, along with the astrocytes.

Oligodendroglia. *Oligodendroglia* are residents of the CNS, and their principal function is to provide support to axons and to produce the *myelin sheath,* which insulates most axons from one another. (Some axons are not myelinated and lack this sheath.) Myelin is made of lipid (70–80 percent) and protein (20–30 percent). It is produced by the oligodendroglia in the form of a tube surrounding the axon. This tube does not form a continuous sheath; rather, it consists of a series of segments, with a small portion of uncoated axon between the segments. This bare portion of axon is called a *node of Ranvier,* after its discoverer. The myelinated axon, then, resembles a string of elongated beads. (Actually, the beads are very much elongated, their length being approximately 80 times their width.)

A given oligodendroglial cell produces only one segment of myelin covering a given axon, but it may provide one segment for each of several different axons. During the development of the CNS, oligodendroglia form processes shaped something like canoe paddles. Each of these paddle-shaped processes then wraps many times around a segment of an axon and, while doing so, produces layers

of myelin. Each paddle, then, becomes a segment of an axon's myelin sheath. (See **Figure 2.11.**)

Unmyelinated axons of the CNS are not actually naked; they are also covered by oligodendroglia. However, in this case the glial cells do not manufacture myelin; the axons are covered in a different way. Instead of being wrapped in segments by the processes of the oligodendroglia, unmyelinated axons pass right through the cell bodies of the glial cells. (See **Figure 2.12.**) Each oligodendroglial cell provides support for several axons.

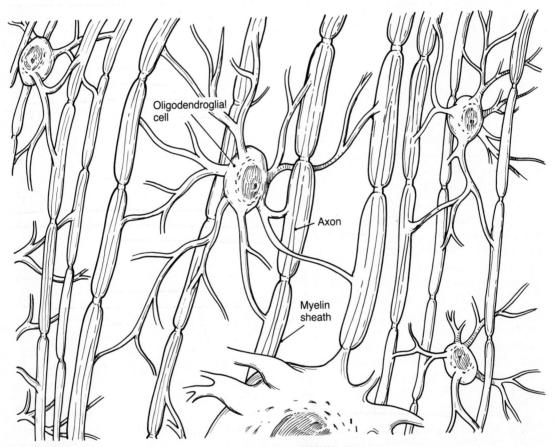

FIGURE 2.11
Oligodendroglia form the myelin that surrounds many axons in the central nervous system. Each glial cell forms one segment of myelin for several adjacent axons.

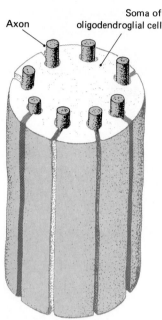

Axon

Soma of
oligodendroglial cell

FIGURE 2.12

Oligodendroglia provide support for
unmyelinated axons in the central nervous system.

Other Cells of the CNS

Besides neurons and glia, a few other kinds of
cells also reside in the CNS: *ependymal* cells
that line the hollow, fluid-filled *ventricles* in
the brain; the cells that make up the blood
vessels that serve the brain; and, of course, the
red and white blood cells within the blood
vessels. Other cells form a set of membranes
that surround the brain and spinal cord.
This lining (the *meninges*) is discussed in
Chapter 4.

Supporting Cells of the PNS

The supportive function served by glia in the
CNS is served by their counterparts in the peripheral nervous system (PNS), the *satellite
cells.* These cells provide physical support to
the neurons located outside the CNS, in sense
organs and in *ganglia* ("knots" of nerve cell

bodies). The structure of ganglia will be discussed in Chapter 4.

In the CNS, oligodendroglia support axons
and produce myelin. In the PNS, *Schwann
cells* perform the same functions. Most axons
in the PNS are myelinated. The myelin sheath
occurs in segments, as it does in the CNS; each
segment consists of a single Schwann cell,
wrapped many times around the axon. In the
CNS, the oligodendroglia grow a number of
paddle-shaped processes that wrap around a
number of axons. In the PNS, a Schwann cell
provides myelin for only one axon, and the
entire Schwann cell — not merely a cellular
process — surrounds the axon.

A way to visualize the relationship of
Schwann cells to an axon is to picture a series
of fried eggs, the yolks representing the nuclei of the Schwann cells, wrapped around a
rope. (I find this analogy helpful, if unappe-
tizing.) Figure 2.13 schematizes the process
by which a Schwann cell wraps around an
axon. (See **Figure 2.13.**)

Schwann cells also differ from their CNS
counterparts, the oligodendroglia, in an important way. If damage occurs to a peripheral
nerve (which consists of a bundle of many
myelinated axons, all covered in a sheath
of tough, elastic connective tissue), the
Schwann cells aid in the digestion of the dead
and dying axons. Then the Schwann cells ar-
range themselves in a series of cylinders that
act as guides for regrowth of the axons. The
distal portions of the severed axons die, but
the stump of each severed axon grows
sprouts, which then spread in all directions.
If one of these sprouts encounters a cylinder
provided by a Schwann cell, the sprout will
quickly grow through the tube (at a rate of up
to 3 – 4 mm a day), while the other, nonpro-
ductive sprouts wither away. If the cut ends of
the nerve are still located close enough to
each other, the axons will reestablish connections with the muscles and sense organs
they previously served.

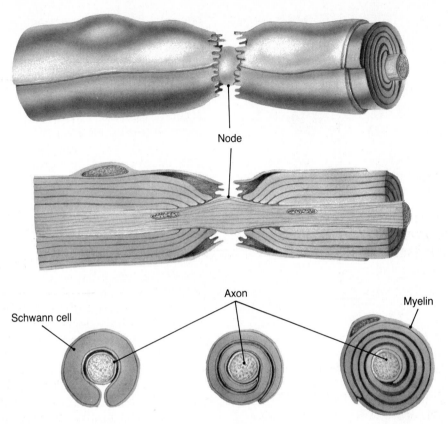

Node

Axon

Myelin

Schwann cell

FIGURE 2.13
During development, Schwann cells tightly wrap themselves many times
around an individual axon in the peripheral nervous system and form one
segment of the myelin sheath.

On the other hand, if the cut ends of the nerve are displaced, or if a section of the nerve is damaged beyond repair, the axons will not be able to find their way to the original sites of innervation. In such cases, neurosurgeons can sew the cut ends of the nerve together, if not too much of the nerve has been damaged. (Nerves are flexible and can be stretched a bit.) If too long a section has been lost, and if the nerve was an important one (controlling hand muscles, for example), a piece of nerve of about the same size can be taken from another part of the body. Because nerves overlap quite a bit in the area of tissue they innervate, neurosurgeons have no trouble finding a branch of a nerve that the patient can lose without ill effect. The surgeon, using a special microscope and very delicate instruments, grafts this piece of nerve to the damaged one. Of course, the axons in the excised and transplanted piece of nerve die away, but the tubes produced by the Schwann cells guide the sprouts of the damaged nerve and help them find their way back to the hand muscles.

Unfortunately, the glial cells of the CNS are not so cooperative as the supporting cells of the PNS. If axons in the brain or spinal cord are damaged, new sprouts will form, as in the PNS. However, the budding axons encounter scar tissue produced by the astrocytes, and they cannot penetrate this barrier. Even if they could get through, the axons would not reestablish their original connections without guidance similar to that provided by the Schwann cells of the PNS. Thus, the difference in the regenerative properties of the CNS and PNS results from differences in the characteristics of the supporting cells, not from differences in the neurons.

INTERIM SUMMARY

All organs of the body consist of cells which contain a quantity of clear cytoplasm, enclosed in a membrane. Embedded in the membrane are protein molecules that have special functions, such as the transport of particular substances into and out of the cell. The cytoplasm contains the nucleus, which contains the genetic information; the nucleolus (located in the nucleus), which manufactures ribosomes; the ribosomes, which serve as sites of protein synthesis; the endoplasmic reticulum, which serves as a storage reservoir and as a channel for transportation of chemicals through the cytoplasm; the Golgi apparatus, which wraps substances that the cell secretes in a membrane; microfilaments and microtubules, which compose the internal "skeleton" of the cell and provide the motive power for transporting chemicals from place to place; and the mitochondria, which serve as the location for most of the chemical reactions through which the cell extracts energy from nutrients.

Neurons receive messages directly from the environment (for example, sights, sounds, smells, and tastes) or from other neurons. Messages from other neurons are received through synapses, junctions between the terminal buttons of the transmitting neurons and the membrane of a dendrite or the soma of the receiving neuron. Terminal buttons are located at the ends of the axons.

Neurons are supported by the glial cells of the central nervous system and the satellite cells of the peripheral nervous system. Within the CNS, astrocytes provide the primary support and also remove debris and form scar tissue in the event of tissue damage. Microglia remove debris. Oligodendroglia form myelin, the substance that insulates axons, and also support unmyelinated axons. Within the PNS, support and myelin are provided by the Schwann cells.

■ THE BLOOD-BRAIN BARRIER

If trypan blue, a dye, is injected into an animal's bloodstream, all tissues except the brain and spinal cord will be tinted blue. However, if the same dye is injected into the ventricles of the brain, the blue color will spread throughout the CNS. This experiment demonstrates that a barrier exists between the blood and the fluid that surrounds the cells of the brain — the ***blood-brain barrier.***

This blood-brain barrier is selectively permeable. Some substances can cross (permeate) this barrier; others cannot. There appear to be two components to the blood-brain barrier: the endothelial cells that line the walls of the capillaries, and the astrocytes that surround them. In most of the body, the ***endothelial lining*** of the capillaries is perforated with small holes, and this perforation permits the free exchange of most substances between blood plasma and the fluid outside the blood vessels that surrounds the cells. Because the capillaries of the brain lack these perforations, many substances cannot get out of them. Others can get past the endothelial lining but are blocked by the astrocytes.

The blood-brain barrier is not uniform throughout the nervous system. In several places the barrier is relatively permeable, allowing substances excluded elsewhere to cross freely. For example, the ***area postrema*** is a part of the brain that controls vomiting. The blood-brain barrier is somewhat weaker there, permitting this region to be more sensitive to toxic substances in the blood. A poison that enters the circulatory system from the stomach can thus stimulate this area to initiate vomiting. If the organism is lucky, the poison can be expelled from the stomach before it causes too much damage.

To a certain extent, the blood-brain barrier works both ways. That is, there is also a *brain-blood barrier.* Proteins present in the fluid bathing the cells of the brain cannot enter the blood supply and hence are not recognized by the body's immune system as belonging to that organism. Indeed, when protein is extracted from CNS myelin and is injected into an animal's blood supply, the immune system reacts by attacking tissue in the CNS as if it were foreign. The disease thus produced is called *experimental allergic encephalomyelitis,* which resembles multiple sclerosis (Einstein, 1972).

Some investigators believe that multiple sclerosis results from virus-produced damage to the blood-brain barrier, which allows myelin protein to enter the blood supply. This invasion of a "foreign protein" mobilizes the immune system against the CNS myelin. With the insulation gone, messages being carried by the axons are no longer kept separate, and the scrambling of messages results in sensory disorders and loss of muscular control. As the disease progresses, the axons themselves are destroyed.

■ NEURAL COMMUNICATION: AN OVERVIEW

Neurons communicate through synapses. The message transmitted by a particular synapse has one of two effects: excitation or inhibition. Excitatory effects increase the likelihood that the neuron receiving them will send a message down its axon; inhibitory effects decrease this likelihood. Thus, the rate at which a neuron sends messages down its axons depends on the excitatory and inhibitory effects that are caused by neurons whose terminal buttons form synapses with it. For

example, in Figure 2.14 neuron A can be excited by the terminal buttons of some neurons (labeled *E*) and inhibited by the terminal buttons of others (labeled *I*). The rate at which neuron A sends messages down its axon is determined by the relative activity of the excitatory and inhibitory synapses on the membrane of its soma and dendrites. A high rate of activity in the excitatory synapses will normally increase the rate at which neuron A sends messages down its axon, but this effect can be canceled by a high rate of activity in the inhibitory synapses. (See **Figure 2.14.**) As far as we know, a particular neuron produces either excitatory or inhibitory effects on other neurons, but not both. Thus, all terminal buttons of a given neuron produce either excitatory or inhibitory effects on the neurons with which they form synapses.

The message that is transmitted down the axon, from the cell body to the terminal buttons, is electrical in nature. Normally, there is an electrical charge across the membrane. The activity of excitatory synapses causes a disturbance in this charge, which triggers an abrupt change in the membrane potential at the *axon hillock,* the junction between soma and axon. This abrupt change is transmitted down the axon to the terminal buttons. When the terminal buttons receive this message, they release a chemical that has either an excitatory or an inhibitory effect on the neurons with which they form synapses. And there the process begins again.

In order to appreciate the operation of this process, consider a simple assembly of three neurons. The first neuron is a sensory receptor that detects painful stimuli. When its dendrites are stimulated by a pinprick, it sends messages down the axon to the terminal buttons, which are located in the spinal cord. (You will recognize this cell as a unipolar neuron: see **Figure 2.15.**) The terminal buttons of the sensory neuron release a chemical that excites the somatic and dendritic mem-

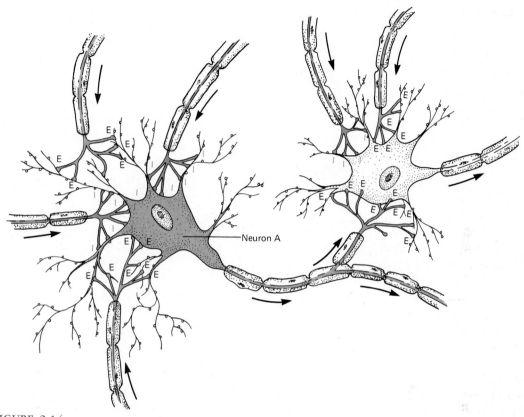

FIGURE 2.14
Terminal buttons may excite *(E)* or inhibit *(I)* the neuron with which
they form synapses. The excitatory and inhibitory messages control the rate
of activity of the axon of neuron A.

brane of the second neuron (the inter-neuron), causing it to send messages down its axon. In turn, its terminal buttons release a chemical that excites the third neuron (the motor neuron), which sends messages down its axon. The terminal buttons of the motor neuron synapse with the cells in a muscle. When they release their chemical the muscle cells contract, causing a part of the body to move. This scheme represents a simplified version of what happens when a pinprick on the end of a finger causes a person to react by reflexively moving his or her arm away from the source of the pain. (See **Figure 2.15.**)

So far, all of the synaptic effects have been excitatory. Now let us complicate matters a bit to see the effect of inhibitory synapses. Suppose you are carrying a bunch of roses from your garden. As you walk, the thorns begin to prick your fingers. The pain receptors stimulate a withdrawal reflex like the one shown in Figure 2.15, which tends to make you open your hand and let go of the roses. However, because you do not want to drop your flowers, you manage to hold onto them until you have a chance to get a better, less painful, grip on them. The message not to drop the roses comes through the axon of a

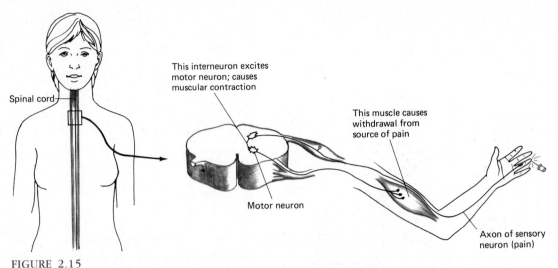

FIGURE 2.15
A withdrawal reflex, a simple example of a useful function of the nervous system.

neuron located in the brain. The terminal buttons at the end of this axon form synapses with an inhibitory neuron in the spinal cord. The terminal buttons of the inhibitory neuron release a chemical that inhibits the activity of the motor neuron. Thus, messages from the

brain prevent the withdrawal reflex from operating. (See **Figure 2.16.**)

Of course, reflexes are more complicated than this description, and the mechanisms that inhibit them are even more so. Yet this simple model, demonstrating one example of

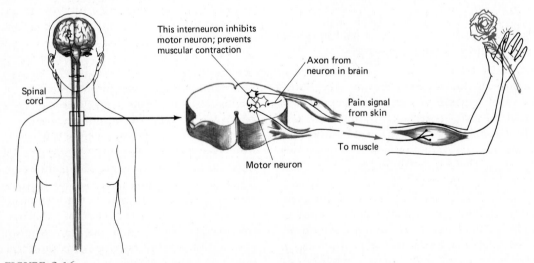

FIGURE 2.16
Inhibitory signals arising from the brain can prevent the withdrawal reflex from causing the person to drop the rose.

the importance of excitation and inhibition, provides an overview of the process of neural communication, which is described in more detail in this chapter and the next.

■ COMMUNICATION WITHIN A NEURON

The details of synaptic transmission — the communication between neurons — will be described in Chapter 3. The rest of this chapter deals with communication within a neuron — the way in which a message is sent from the cell body down the axon. This message is electrical in nature, but the axon does not carry it the way a wire transmits electrical current. Instead, the message is transmitted by means of alterations in the membrane of the axon that cause exchanges of various chemicals between the axon and the fluid surrounding it. These exchanges produce electrical currents.

Forces That Move Molecules

To understand the entire process, we must first examine some of the forces that are involved. These forces are described in a series of simple, imaginary experiments.

Diffusion

When a spoonful of sugar is carefully poured into a container of water, it settles to the bottom. After a time, the sugar dissolves, but it remains close to the bottom of the container. After a much longer time (probably several days), the molecules of sugar distribute themselves evenly throughout the water, even if no one stirs the liquid. The process whereby molecules distribute themselves evenly throughout the medium in which they are dissolved is called *diffusion.*

Diffusion is characterized by movement of molecules down a *concentration gradient.* Once the sugar dissolves, it is located in highest concentration at the bottom of the container. The concentration of sugar molecules

is the lowest at the top. Thus, there is a gradient (or metaphorical "hill") in the concentration of sugar molecules, which goes from highest (at the bottom) to lowest (at the top).

When there are no forces or barriers to prevent it, molecules diffuse down their concentration gradient; that is, they travel from regions of high concentration to regions of low concentration. Molecules are constantly in motion, and their rate of movement is proportional to the temperature. Only at absolute zero (0° Kelvin $= -273.15°$ C $= -459.7°$ F) do molecules cease their random movement. At all other temperatures they move about, colliding and veering off in different directions. The result of these collisions, in the example of the sugar water, is to produce a net movement of water molecules downward and of sugar molecules upward. (Just as there is a concentration gradient for sugar molecules, there is also one for water molecules; initially, water is most concentrated at the top of the container and least concentrated at the bottom.)

Imagine an experiment that could be performed in the absence of gravity (for example, in a manned satellite orbiting the earth) where we will have to contend with only one force. This experiment uses a glass container with a vertical piece of nylon mesh dividing the vessel into two equal chambers. We pour a 10-percent sugar solution into the left side and a 5-percent sugar solution into the right. Because the nylon mesh barrier is permeable to both sugar and water molecules (i.e., it lets them both pass through freely), the container soon has a 7.5-percent sugar solution on both sides. This is merely another example of diffusion. (See **Figure 2.17.**)

Osmosis

Next, suppose that we replace the barrier with a thin piece of uncoated cellophane (not the usual kind, which is coated to make it waterproof). Uncoated cellophane has pores

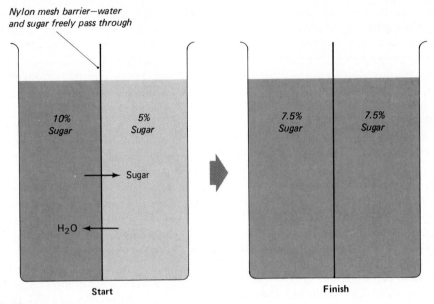

FIGURE 2.17
Diffusion. Both water and sugar molecules readily diffuse through the
nylon mesh, moving down their concentration gradients.

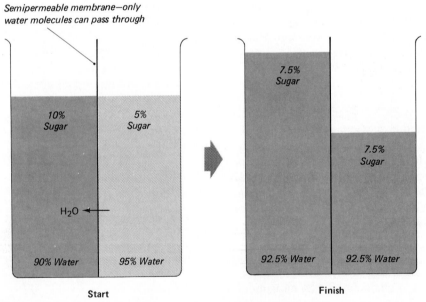

FIGURE 2.18
Osmosis. In the absence of gravity, molecules of water (but not sugar)
diffuse through the semipermeable membrane, moving down their
concentration gradient. Osmotic equilibrium is thus achieved.

large enough to allow water molecules to pass through, but the pores are too small to permit passage of sugar molecules. Again we pour a 10-percent sugar solution into the left compartment and a 5-percent solution into the right one, creating concentration gradients for sugar and water molecules. But this time, because sugar molecules cannot pass through the cellophane membrane, there will be no movement of sugar.

However, water molecules can pass through the barrier, so after a period of time there will be a 7.5-percent sugar solution on both sides of the barrier. (See **Figure 2.18.**) Another way of describing the process is to say that we started with a 95-percent "water solution" on the right and a 90-percent solution on the left. Water moved down its concentration gradient, reducing the concentration of water molecules on the right and increasing the concentration on the left until the concentrations on both sides were equal. Note

that although the concentrations are equal now, the volumes are not. The levels of liquid on each side of the cellophane are different. (See **Figure 2.18.**) This disparity causes no trouble in the gravity-free environment where we conducted the experiment, but things would not be so simple on earth, as will soon be apparent.

The phenomenon just described is called ***osmosis;*** it is defined as diffusion of a fluid through a semipermeable membrane.

Hydrostatic Pressure
Imagine performing another experiment with the container, again using the cellophane barrier. However, this time we will conduct the experiment on earth. We will fill both chambers with pure water: 100 ml in the left one and 50 ml in the right. Water starts flowing from the left-hand container to the right-hand one until each side contains 75 ml. (See **Figure 2.19.**) Because we used pure

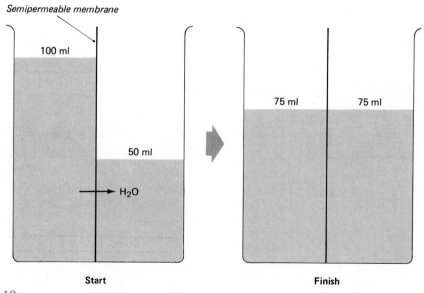

FIGURE 2.19
Hydrostatic pressure. In the presence of gravity, molecules of water are forced by gravity across the semipermeable membrane until the levels of liquid on both sides of the container are equal.

water, osmosis is not observed. Instead, the water volumes become equal because of the effects of hydrostatic pressure, supplied by the force of gravity. We all know that water runs downhill, so no one should be surprised by the results of this experiment. Although hydrostatic pressure is not one of the forces responsible for the membrane potential, its clear-cut role in the next experiment provides a good model for the balance of forces that exist across the membrane of an axon.

Dynamic Equilibrium: Putting the Forces Together

So far, we have seen examples of two different forces (osmotic pressure and hydrostatic pressure) that bring a system from an initial state of *disequilibrium* to one of *equilibrium*. (*Libra* means "balance," so a system is

at disequilibrium when the forces are unbalanced, and at equilibrium when they are balanced.)

To complicate matters just a bit, imagine performing the osmosis experiment on earth. We place equal volumes of sugar solution in the container, a 10-percent solution in the left and a 5-percent solution in the right. Initially, only one force is present—osmotic pressure, which causes water molecules to move from right to left. But this movement of water molecules soon produces a difference in the height of the solution on each side of the membrane; thus, hydrostatic pressure starts pushing water from left to right. Eventually, the forces reach a standoff, so that the movement of molecules going left and right is equal. (See **Figure 2.20.**) Equilibrium is reached, but in this case it consists of a balance between two equal and opposing forces:

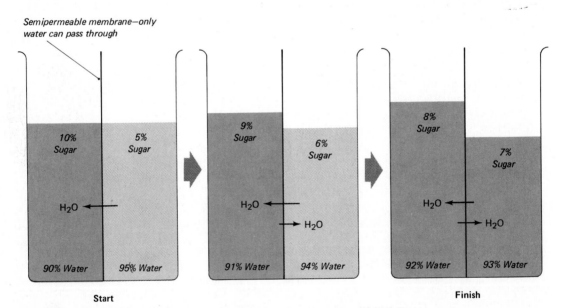

FIGURE 2.20

Dynamic equilibrium. Molecules of water move from right to left, down their osmotic gradient, but as water accumulates on the left side of the container, hydrostatic pressure begins to cause a movement of water toward the right. Eventually a point of equilibrium is reached where there is no net movement of water.

hydrostatic and osmotic pressure. We call this phenomenon *dynamic equilibrium.*

Another Force: Electrostatic Pressure
The membrane of the axon, like the uncoated cellophane barrier, is semipermeable, and it is part of a system that is normally at equilibrium. However, several different substances are dissolved in the cytoplasm of neurons and in the fluid surrounding them, and each contributes osmotic pressure. Just as osmotic pressure was balanced by hydrostatic pressure in the last experiment, the osmotic forces in the axon are balanced by *electrostatic pressure.*

When dissolved in water, many substances split into two parts, each with an opposing electrical charge. Substances with this property are called *electrolytes;* the charged particles into which they decompose are called *ions.* Ions are of two basic types: *cations* have a positive charge, and *anions* have a negative charge. For example, when sodium chloride (NaCl, table salt) is dissolved in water, many of the molecules split into sodium cations (Na^+) and chloride anions (Cl^-). (I find that the easiest way to keep the terms *cation* and *anion* straight is to think of the cation's plus sign as a cross, and remember the superstition of a black *cat* crossing your path. Little mnemonic devices like this often come in handy.)

As you have undoubtedly learned, particles with the same kind of charge repel each other (+ repels +, and − repels −), but particles with different charges are attracted to each other (+ and − attract). Thus, anions repel anions, cations repel cations, but anions and cations attract each other. The force exerted by this attraction or repulsion provides electrostatic pressure. Just as osmotic pressure moves molecules from regions of high concentration to regions of low concentration and water runs downhill, electrostatic pressure moves ions from place to place: cations

are pushed away from regions with an excess of cations, and anions are pushed away from regions with an excess of anions.

The Membrane Potential

Constituents of the Extracellular and Intracellular Fluid
The fluid within cells *(intracellular fluid)* and the fluid surrounding them *(extracellular fluid)* contain different ions. The osmotic and electrostatic forces contributed by these ions give rise to the *membrane potential.* The message that an axon carries consists of a brief change in the membrane potential of the axon, starting at the end nearest the soma and traveling to the terminal buttons at the other end. The term *potential* refers to a stored-up source of energy — in this case, electrical energy. For example, a flashlight battery that is not connected to an electrical circuit has a *potential* charge of 1.5 volts between its terminals. If we connect a light bulb to the terminals, the potential energy is tapped and converted into light energy. Similarly, if we place one wire inside an axon and another wire outside and connect them to a very sensitive voltmeter, we will convert the potential energy to movement of the meter's needle. Of course, compared with a flashlight battery, the potential electrical energy of the axonal membrane is very weak. (See **Figure 2.21.**)

The actual charge across the membrane (the membrane potential) is approximately 70 mV (millivolts, thousandths of a volt). The inside is negatively charged, and the outside is positively charged. By convention, the membrane potential is expressed in terms of the charge *inside* the cell; thus, the membrane potential is said to be at −70 mV.

Because the membrane potential is produced by a balance between osmotic and electrostatic pressures, to understand what produces this potential we must know the concentration of the various ions in the extra-

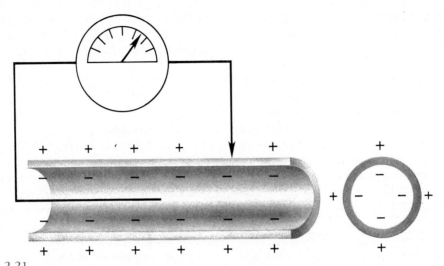

FIGURE 2.21

The means of recording the membrane potential of an axon.

cellular fluid and intracellular fluid. There are four important ions: protein anions (symbolized by A⁻), chloride ions (Cl⁻), sodium ions (Na⁺), and potassium ions (K⁺). The Latin words for sodium and potassium are *na-*

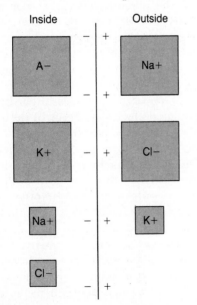

FIGURE 2.22

The relative concentration of some important ions inside and outside the cell.

trium and *kalium;* hence, they are abbreviated *Na* and *K*, respectively. Protein anions (A⁻) are found in the intracellular fluid. Although the other three ions are found in both the intracellular and extracellular fluids, K⁺ is found predominantly in the intracellular fluid, whereas Na⁺ and Cl⁻ are found predominantly in the extracellular fluid. (See **Figure 2.22.**) The easiest way to remember which ion is found where is to recall that the fluid that surrounds our cells is similar to seawater, which is predominantly a solution of salt, NaCl. The other two ions, A⁻ and K⁺, are inside the cell.

Electrostatic and Osmotic Pressure Across the Axonal Membrane

Let us consider the ions in Figure 2.22, examining the osmotic and electrostatic pressure exerted on each, and reasoning why each is located where it is. We can quickly dispense with A⁻, the protein anion, because this ion is too large to pass through the axonal membrane; therefore, although its presence within the cell affects the other ions, it is located where it is because of membrane impermeability. The potassium ion, K^+, is concentrated within the axon. Because its osmotic gradient goes from inside to outside the axon, osmotic pressure tends to push it out of the cell. However, the outside of the cell is charged positively with respect to the inside, so electrostatic pressure tends to force the cation inside. Thus, the two opposing forces balance, just as osmotic and hydrostatic pressure did in the last of our "experiments." (See A in **Figure 2.23.**)

The chloride ion, Cl^-, is in greatest concentration outside the axon. Osmotic pressure pushes it inward, down its concentration gradient. However, because the inside of the axon is negatively charged, electrostatic pressure pushes the anion outward. Again, two opposing forces balance each other. (See B in **Figure 2.23.**)

The sodium ion, Na^+, is also in greatest concentration outside the axon, so it, like Cl^-, is pushed into the cell by osmotic pressure. But unlike chloride, the sodium ion is *positively* charged. Therefore, electrostatic pressure does *not* prevent Na^+ from entering the cell; indeed, the negative charge inside the axon *attracts* Na^+. (See C in **Figure 2.23.**)

Why is Na^+ in greatest concentration in the extracellular fluid, despite the tendencies of both osmotic pressure and electrostatic pres-

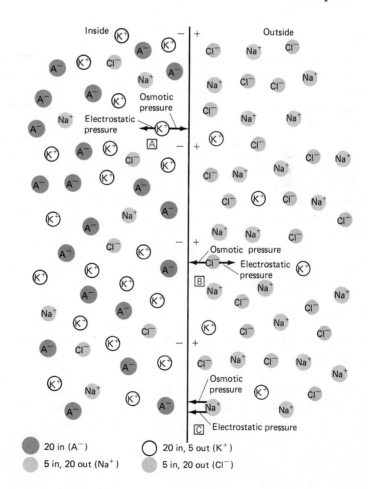

FIGURE 2.23

Electrostatic and osmotic forces acting on some important ions.

20 in (A^-)

20 in, 5 out (K^+)

5 in, 20 out (Na^+)

5 in, 20 out (Cl^-)

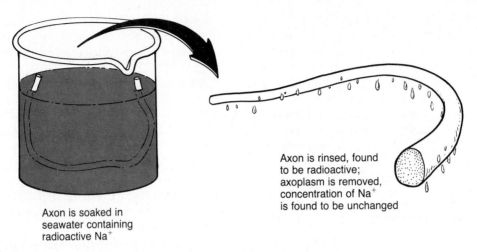

Axon is soaked in
seawater containing
radioactive Na^+

Axon is rinsed, found
to be radioactive;
axoplasm is removed,
concentration of Na^+
is found to be unchanged

FIGURE 2.24
Experimental demonstration that the axonal membrane is permeable to Na^+.

sure to force it inside? The simplest explanation would be that the membrane is impermeable to Na^+, as it is to A^-, the protein anion. This possibility can be tested. Although axons found in mammalian nervous systems are difficult to study, being small and impossible to separate from their associated oligodendroglia or Schwann cells, nature has provided the squid (and therefore the scientist) with an axon of relatively large diameter. The giant squid axon (the giant axon of a squid, not the axon of a giant squid) is about 0.5 mm in diameter, hundreds of times larger than the largest mammalian axon. Studies of the electrical and chemical properties of axons have been performed with giant squid axons.

The following experiment can determine whether the axonal membrane is permeable to Na^+. A giant squid axon is placed in a dish of seawater containing some radioactive Na^+, is allowed to sit awhile, and is then removed and washed off. The axon is now found to be radioactive, which shows that Na^+ *can* pass through the membrane, because some of the radioactive Na^+ in the seawater found its way into the axon. (See **Figure 2.24**.) Subsequent

analysis of the *axoplasm* (the cytoplasm within the axon) finds that the concentration of Na^+ is still normal. This analysis indicates that although Na^+ entered the axon, an equal amount left again, keeping the concentration constant. But as we know, osmotic and electrostatic gradients tend to force the Na^+ into the cell. It is easy to understand why the axon became radioactive—osmotic and electrostatic pressure forced in some radioactive Na^+ molecules. But what force pushed an equal number of Na^+ ions out again, against osmotic and electrostatic pressure?

The answer is this: Another force, provided by the *sodium-potassium pump,* continuously extrudes Na^+ from the axon. The sodium-potassium pump consists of complex molecules situated in the membrane, driven by energy provided by the mitochondria as they metabolize the cell's nutrients. These molecules exchange Na^+ for K^+, pushing three sodium ions out for every two potassium ions they push in. (See **Figure 2.25**.) Because the membrane is not very permeable to Na^+, the sodium-potassium pump very effectively keeps the intracellular concentration of Na⁺ low. By pumping K⁺ into the cell, it also increases the intracellular concentration of K⁺ somewhat. The membrane is approximately 100 times more permeable to K⁺ than to Na⁺, so the increase is slight. The sodium-potassium pump uses considerable energy: up to 40 percent of the neuron's metabolic resources are used to operate it. Neurons, muscle cells, glia — in fact, most cells of the body — have a sodium-potassium pump in their membrane.

The Action Potential

Now that we understand what causes the membrane potential, we can examine its role in the transmission of information in the nervous system. As we will see, changes in membrane permeability to Na⁺ and K⁺ produce the electrical message that is carried down the axon.

Measurement of Changes in the Axonal Membrane Potential

First we will examine the nature of the message. To do so, we place an isolated giant squid axon in a dish of seawater and use an

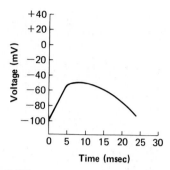

FIGURE 2.26
An oscilloscope can be used to produce a graph of voltage as a function of time, such as this one.

oscilloscope to record electrical events from the axon. A more detailed description of this device can be found in Chapter 5; it suffices here to say that an oscilloscope, like a voltmeter, measures voltages, but it also produces a record of these voltages, graphing them as a function of time. For example, Figure 2.26 shows a curve drawn by an oscilloscope. The voltage started at − 100 mV, changed rapidly to − 50 mV (in about 5 milliseconds, or 5/1000 of a second), and then more slowly changed back to − 100 mV. (See **Figure 2.26.**)

We attach the oscilloscope to the axon via two wires that serve as *electrodes.* (Electrodes are electrical conductors that provide a path for electricity to enter or leave a medium.) We place one electrode outside the membrane and insert the other into the axoplasm. Because the membrane potential of the axon is approximately − 70 mV (the inside is negative), the oscilloscope draws a straight horizontal line at − 70 mV, as long as the axon is not disturbed. This electrical charge across the membrane is called, quite appropriately, the *resting potential.* Now let us disturb the resting potential and see what happens. To do so, we will use another device — a shocker that allows us to alter the membrane potential at a specific location. The shocker can pass positive or negative cur-

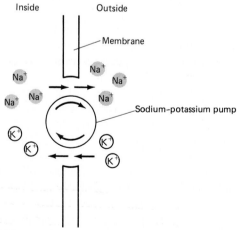

FIGURE 2.25
The effects of the sodium-potassium pump.

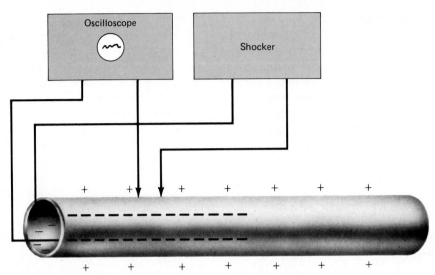

FIGURE 2.27
The means by which an axon can be shocked while its membrane potential
is being recorded.

rent through the electrode on the outside of
the axon, thus increasing the membrane potential in that region (making it more positive
outside) or decreasing it (making it less positive). (See **Figure 2.27.**) Positive shocks,
which increase the membrane potential, produce **hyperpolarization** (more polarization). Negative shocks, which decrease the
membrane potential, produce **hypopolarization** (less polarization). However, to be
consistent with other writers, I will use the
term **depolarization** instead of hypopolarization, although this term is not really correct. (Depolarization literally means *removal* of polarization.)

Triggering the Action Potential
Let us see what happens to an axon when we
artificially change the membrane potential at
one point. Figure 2.28 shows a graph drawn
by an oscilloscope monitoring the effects
of brief depolarizing and hyperpolarizing
shocks. The graphs of the effects of these separate shocks are superimposed on the same
drawing so that we can compare them. The

shock intensity is labeled in arbitrary units
from 1 to 5, with 5 representing the highest
intensity, + representing hyperpolarizing
pulses, and − representing depolarizing
pulses. (See **Figure 2.28.**)
    As you can see, successively stronger hy-
perpolarizations (+ shocks) produce successively larger disturbances in the membrane
potential. The changes in the membrane potential last considerably longer than the very
brief shocks. The reasons for this phenomenon (having to do with the resistive and ca-
pacitive properties of the membrane and axoplasm) need not concern us here. Figure 2.28
also shows the effects of the depolarizing
shocks. The results in this case are different;
the effects of the low-intensity shocks (− 1 to
− 3) mirror those of the hyperpolarizing
shocks, but once the membrane potential
reaches a certain point (approximately − 65
mV for most axons), it suddenly reverses itself, so that the outside becomes *negative*.
Then the potential quickly returns to normal.
The whole process takes about 2 milliseconds. (See **Figure 2.28.**)

This phenomenon, a very rapid reversal of the membrane potential, is called the ***action potential.*** It constitutes the message carried by the axon from one end to the other. The voltage level that triggers an action potential is called the ***threshold of excitation.***

Ionic Events During the Action Potential

As we saw, both osmotic pressure and electrostatic pressure tend to force Na^+ into the cell. However, the membrane is not very permeable to this ion, and the sodium-potassium pump continuously extrudes Na^+, keeping the intracellular level of Na^+ low, even though a little manages to leak in. If something were to cause the membrane suddenly to become permeable to Na^+, it would rush into the cell. This sudden influx of positively charged ions would drastically change the membrane potential. Indeed, experiments have shown that this mechanism is precisely what causes the action potential: A transient drop in the membrane resistance to Na^+ (allowing these ions to rush into the cell) is immediately followed by a transient drop in the membrane resistance to K^+ (allowing these ions to rush out of the cell).

The process of ionic flow occurs in the following sequence:

1. As soon as the threshold of excitation is reached, the membrane barrier to Na^+ drops (actually, to one-eighth of its normal value), and Na^+ rushes in, down its electrostatic and osmotic gradients. The influx of cations produces a rapid change in the membrane potential, from -70 mV to $+50$ mV. At about the time the action potential reaches its peak (in approximately one millisecond) the mem-

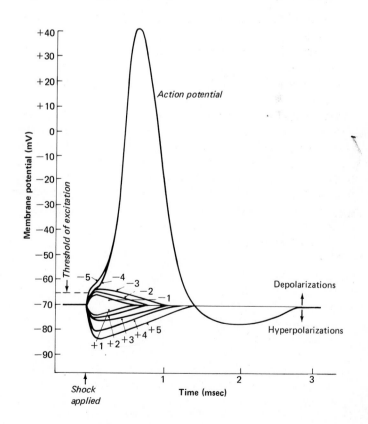

FIGURE 2.28
The results that would be seen on an oscilloscope screen if depolarizing and hyperpolarizing shocks of varying intensities were delivered to the axon shown in Figure 2.27.

brane once again becomes resistant to the flow of Na$^+$.

2. The membrane resistance to K$^+$ now falls. This resistance was not extremely high to begin with, but now it is quite low. At the peak of the action potential, the inside of the axon is now *positively* charged, so that K$^+$ is driven out of the cell, down osmotic and electrostatic gradients. This efflux of cations causes the membrane potential to return toward its normal value. As a matter of fact, the membrane potential overshoots its resting value (−70 mV) and only gradually returns to normal. (See **Figure 2.29.**) You will recall that the sodium-potassium pump manages to keep more K$^+$ inside the cell than there would

otherwise be. With the temporary drop in the membrane resistance to K$^+$, some extra K$^+$ can leak out and make the inside even more negative, hyperpolarizing the membrane.

3. Finally, the K$^+$ resistance of the membrane goes back up to its normal level. The sodium-potassium pump removes the Na$^+$ that leaked in and retrieves the K$^+$ that leaked out.

How much ionic flow is there? When I say "Na$^+$ rushes in," I do not mean that the axoplasm becomes flooded with Na$^+$. Because the drop in membrane resistance to Na$^+$ is so brief, and because diffusion over any appreciable distance takes some time, not too many

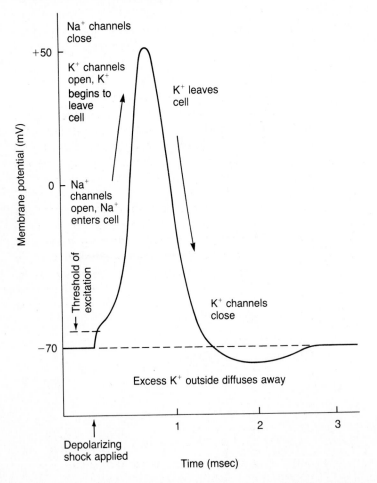

FIGURE 2.29

The ionic fluxes during the action potential.

Na⁺ molecules flow in, and not too many K⁺ molecules flow out. At the peak of the action potential, a very thin layer of fluid immediately inside the axon becomes full of newly arrived Na⁺ ions; this amount is indeed enough to reverse the membrane potential. However, not enough time has elapsed for these ions to fill the entire axon. Before this event can take place, the Na⁺ barrier goes up again, and K⁺ starts flowing out. Experiments have shown that an action potential temporarily increases the number of Na⁺ ions inside the giant squid axon by 0.0003 percent. Although the concentration just inside the membrane is high, the total number of ions entering the cell is very small, relative to the number already there. On a short-term basis, the sodium-potassium pump is not very important. The few Na⁺ ions that manage to leak in diffuse into the rest of the axoplasm, and the slight increase in Na⁺ concentration is hardly noticeable. Of course, the sodium-potassium pump is important on a long-term basis, but even if the pump were stopped, it would take many action potentials to cause any serious gain of Na⁺ within the cell.

The situation is different for the smallest unmyelinated axons in the mammalian CNS, which are approximately 0.1 micrometer (0.0001 mm) in diameter. When these axons fire, their intracellular Na⁺ concentration increases by 10 percent, so to them the sodium-potassium pump is important even on a short-term basis.

So far, we have seen what produces the membrane potential and how changes in this potential, initiated by depolarization of the membrane to around −65 mV (the threshold of excitation), result in action potentials. Now let us examine the characteristics of the membrane responsible for the action potential.

Ion Channels: Membrane Structures That Control Ionic Fluxes. I said earlier that the membrane consists of a double layer of lipid

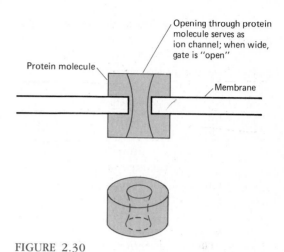

FIGURE 2.30
An ion channel.

molecules in which float many different kinds of protein molecules. One class of protein molecules provides a way for ions to enter or leave the cells. These molecules constitute *ion channels,* which contain gates that can open or close. When a particular gate is open, ions can flow through the channel and thus can enter or leave the cell. (See **Figure 2.30.**) Studies have shown that most ion channels permit only one species of ion to pass, but how the channels recognize the appropriate ion is still not understood. Neural membranes contain many thousands of ion channels. For example, the giant squid axon contains from 100 to 600 sodium channels in each square micrometer of membrane. Thus, the permeability of a membrane to a particular ion is determined by the number of ion channels that are open.

The ionic movements during the action potential are controlled by *voltage-dependent ion channels.* These channels control the movement of Na⁺ and K⁺ through the membrane. (Another class of ion channel, operated by special chemicals, is discussed in Chapter 3.) When the membrane potential is depolarized to the threshold of excitation, the gates in the voltage-dependent sodium channels open, permitting Na^+ to enter. This event further depolarizes the membrane potential, which causes still more sodium channels to open. As the membrane potential continues to depolarize, the gates of the voltage-dependent potassium channels begin to open, allowing potassium to leave the cell. We do not know what causes the gates of the voltage-dependent sodium channels to close again, permitting the membrane potential to return to normal. The voltage-dependent potassium channels close when the membrane potential returns to the resting state.

Propagation of the Action Potential

Conduction by Cable Properties. Now that we have a basic understanding of the resting membrane potential and the production of the action potential, we can consider the movement of the message down the axon, or *propagation of the action potential*. To study this phenomenon, we again make use of the giant squid axon. We attach one shocker to an electrode in the axoplasm and another to an electrode on the outside of the membrane, at one end of the axon. We record membrane potentials with an oscilloscope, which is also attached to two electrodes, one in the axoplasm and the other touching the outside of the axonal membrane. The external electrode is movable, so that recordings can be made from any location along the surface of the axon. (See **Figure 2.31**.)

We produce a subthreshold depolarizing shock (too small to produce an action potential) at one end of an axon and record its effects from a point near the site of stimulation. We repeat this procedure, recording farther and farther down the axon. We find that the shocks produce disturbances in the membrane potential that diminish in intensity as the recording electrode moves farther away from the point of stimulation. Yet there is no noticeable delay in the onset of these disturbances; transmission is almost instantaneous. (See **Figure 2.32**.)

The very rapid transmission of the subthreshold depolarization is *passive*. The axon is acting like a cable, carrying along the current started at one end. This property of the

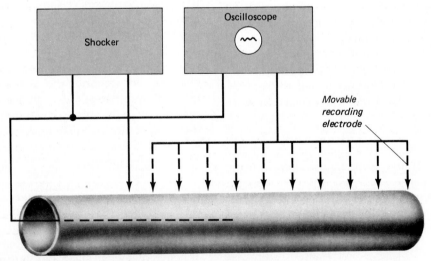

FIGURE 2.31
The means by which shocks can be delivered to one end of an axon while recording the membrane potential at various locations.

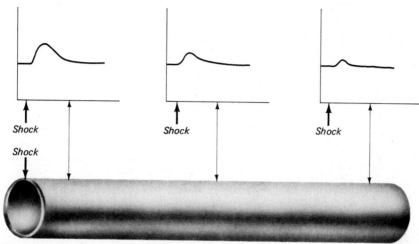

FIGURE 2.32

Decremental conduction. When a subthreshold shock is applied to the
axon, the disturbance in the membrane potential is largest near the
stimulating electrode and gets progressively smaller at farther distances
along the axon.

axon follows laws discovered in the nineteenth century that describe conduction of
electricity through submarine telegraph
cables laid along the ocean floor. Submarine
cables degrade an electrical signal because of
leakage through the insulator, resistance in
the wire, and capacitance between the wire
and the conductor (seawater) surrounding it.
If a large pulse is initiated at one end, a much
smaller signal is received at the other. Because the signal decreases in size (decrements), it is referred to as ***decremental conduction.*** We say that the transmission of
subthreshold depolarizations follows the
laws that describe the ***cable properties*** of the
axon — the same laws that describe the electrical properties of a submarine cable. Because hyperpolarizations never elicit action
potentials, these disturbances, like subthreshold depolarizations, are also transmitted via the passive cable properties of an
axon.

***All-or-None Conduction of the Action Poten-
tial.*** To study the propagation of the action

potential, we produce a number of supra-
threshold (above-threshold) depolarizing
shocks to the end of the axon and record their
effects at successively greater distances from
the site of stimulation. This time, we record
an action potential at each point along the
axon. But conduction of the action potential
is much slower than that of the subthreshold
depolarizations, which are transmitted by
means of the passive cable properties of
the axon. The action potential arrives later
and later at points successively farther away
from the stimulating electrode. (See **Figure
2.33.**)

This experiment establishes a basic law of
axonal transmission: the ***all-or-none law.***
This law states that an action potential either
occurs or it does not occur; once it has been
triggered, it is transmitted down the axon to
its end. It always remains the same size, without growing or diminishing. In fact, the axon
will transmit an action potential in either direction, or even in both directions if one is
started in the middle of its length. However,
because action potentials in intact organisms

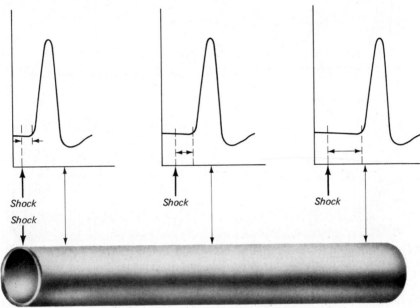

FIGURE 2.33

Nondecremental conduction. When an action potential is triggered, its size remains undiminished as it travels down the axon. The speed of conduction can be calculated from the delay.

always start at the end attached to the soma, axons normally carry one-way traffic.

Conduction in Unmyelinated Axons. The propagation of an action potential in unmyelinated axons is a straightforward process. For the sake of simplicity, consider that the axon is divided into segments. These segments are hypothetical ones, not the actual ones that occur in myelinated axons. (See **Figure 2.34.**) We stimulate the segment at the left end, triggering an action potential there. This potential spreads, via passive cable properties, to the next segment. It may decline in size, but it will still be large enough to depolarize the next segment past the threshold of excitation, triggering an action potential there. This action potential is then transmitted via passive cable properties to the next segment, and . . . well, I think you get the picture. Of course, the naked axon is not really divided into segments; propagation of

the action potential is a smooth, continuous process.

Conduction in Myelinated Axons. You will recall that most axons are myelinated; segments of them are covered by a myelin sheath produced by the oligodendroglia of the CNS or the Schwann cells of the PNS. These segments are separated by portions of naked axon, the nodes of Ranvier. Myelinated axons really *are* segmented, and they transmit the action potential in the way I just described for the hypothetically segmented axon. Suppose we shock one end of a myelinated axon and then record the membrane potential at various places underneath the Schwann cell covering one segment. We use extremely thin electrodes that can pierce the Schwann cell without substantial damage. (See **Figure 2.35.**) Note that the ''action potential'' gets smaller as it passes along the membrane wrapped by the Schwann cell. Why did I write

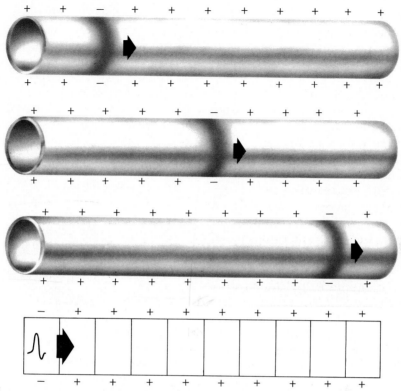

FIGURE 2.34
Propagation of an action potential down an unmyelinated axon.

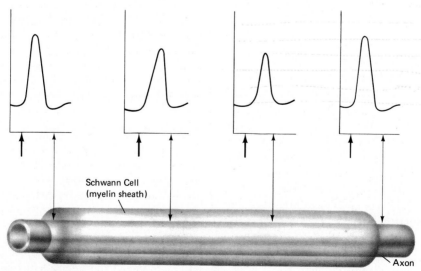

FIGURE 2.35
Propagation of an action potential down a myelinated axon.

"action potential" rather than *action potential?* Because the disturbance only looks like an action potential — it really is not one. If it were, we would have to repeal the all-or-none law.

Schwann cells (and the oligodendroglia of the CNS) wrap tightly around the axon, leaving no measurable extracellular fluid between them and the axon. The only place where a myelinated axon comes in contact with the extracellular fluid is at a node of Ranvier, where the axon is naked. In the myelinated areas, there can be no inward flow of Na^+ when the resistance of the membrane to Na^+ drops, because there *is* no extracellular sodium. How, then, does the "action potential" travel along the area of axonal membrane covered by myelin sheath? You guessed it — cable properties. The axon passively transmits the electrical disturbance from the action potential to the next node of Ranvier. The disturbance gets smaller, but it is still large enough to trigger an action potential at the next node. The action potential gets re-triggered, or repeated, at each node of Ranvier and is passed, via the cable properties of the axon, along the myelinated area to the next node. Its transmission, hopping from node to node, is called **saltatory conduction,** from the Latin *saltare,* "to dance."

There are two advantages to saltatory conduction. First, it is faster than continuous conduction down an unmyelinated axon. The fastest myelinated axon can transmit action potentials at a speed of 100 meters per second (around 224 miles per hour). The increased speed of conduction occurs because the transmission between the nodes is by means of the axon's cable properties, a method that is extremely fast. A delay is introduced at each node, of course, as the action potential is regenerated. The second advantage is an economic one. Energy must be expended by the sodium-potassium pump to get rid of the excess Na^+ that leaks into the axon during the

action potential. The pump is given work to do all along an unmyelinated axon, because Na^+ leaks in everywhere. But because Na^+ can leak into a myelinated axon only at the nodes of Ranvier, much less gets in, and consequently much less has to be pumped out again. Therefore, a myelinated fiber expends much less energy to maintain its sodium balance.

INTERIM SUMMARY

In most organs, molecules freely diffuse between the blood within the capillaries that serve them and the extracellular fluid that bathes their cells. The molecules pass through pores between the cells that make up the endothelial lining of the capillaries. The walls of the capillaries of the CNS lack these pores; consequently, fewer substances can enter or leave the brain across the blood-brain barrier.

Neurons communicate by means of synapses. When a message is sent down an axon, the terminal buttons secrete a chemical that has either an excitatory or an inhibitory effect on the neuron with which it communicates. Ultimately, the effects of these excitatory and inhibitory synapses cause behavior, in the form of muscular contraction.

The message transmitted down an axon is called an action potential. The membranes of all cells of the body are electrically charged, but only axons can produce action potentials. The resting membrane potential occurs because various ions are located in different concentrations in the fluid inside and outside the cell. The extracellular fluid (like seawater) is rich in Na^+ and Cl^-, and the intracellular fluid is rich in K^+ and various protein anions, designated as A^-.

The cell membrane is freely permeable to water, but its permeability to various ions — in particular, Na^+ and K^+ — is regulated by ion channels. When the membrane potential is at its resting value (-70 millivolts), the gates of the voltage-dependent sodium and potassium channels are closed. The experiment with the radioactive seawater showed us that some Na^+ continuously leaks into the axon but is promptly forced out of the cell

again by the sodium-potassium pump (which also forces potassium *into* the axon). When a shocker depolarizes the membrane potential of the axon so that it reaches the threshold of excitation, voltage-dependent sodium channels open and Na$^+$ rushes into the cell, driven by its concentration gradient and by electrostatic pressure. The entry of the positively charged ions reduces the membrane potential and, indeed, causes it to reverse, so that the inside becomes positive. The opening of the sodium channels is temporary; they soon close again. The depolarization and reversal of the membrane potential caused by the influx of Na$^+$ activates voltage-dependent potassium channels, and K$^+$ leaves the axon, down its concentration gradient. The efflux of K$^+$ quickly brings the membrane potential back to its resting value.

The action potential normally begins at one end of the axon, where the axon attaches to the soma. It travels continuously down unmyelinated axons, remaining constant in size, until it reaches the terminal buttons. (When the axon divides, the action potential continues down each branch.) Ions cannot flow through myelinated axons except at the nodes of Ranvier, because the axons are covered everywhere else with myelin, which isolates them from the extracellular fluid. Thus, the action potential is transmitted from one node of Ranvier to the next by means of passive cable properties. When the electrical message reaches a node, voltage-dependent sodium channels open, and the action potential reaches full strength again. This mechanism saves a considerable amount of energy, because sodium-potassium pumps are not needed along the myelinated portions of the axons.

Concluding Remarks

Like all other organs of the body, the central nervous system consists of specialized cells, each with its particular functions. The basic task of the nervous system is to detect events occurring in the environment and to respond with appropriate behaviors. The detection is accomplished by sensory neurons, and the behaviors are accomplished by muscles, which contract when told to do so by the neurons that communicate with them. Simple organisms detect only a few kinds of events and automatically respond with only a few kinds of behaviors. The nervous system of complex organisms such as mammals contains a large number of neurons that receive messages from sensory neurons and communicate with motor neurons and with each other. Thus, the complexity of our perceptions, memories, feelings, and behaviors depends on the numbers of our neurons and the complexity of their interconnections.

This chapter has considered the important features of neurons, the cells that provide their support, and the action potential, the message transmitted down the axon. The next chapter describes the nature of the message transmitted across synapses and the way in which excitatory and inhibitory influences from synapses can interact.

NEW TERMS

action potential p. 41
all-or-none law p. 45
anion p. 35
area postrema p. 27
astrocyte, astroglia p. 22
axon p. 20
axon hillock p. 28
bipolar neuron p. 21
blood-brain barrier p. 27

cable properties p. 45
cation p. 35
chromosome p. 17
concentration gradient p. 31
cytoplasm p. 17
decremental conduction p. 45
dendrite p. 19
dendritic spine p. 19
deoxyribonucleic acid (DNA) p. 17

SUGGESTED READINGS

KANDEL, E.R., AND SCHWARTZ, J.H. *Principles of Neural Science.* New York: Elsevier/North Holland, 1981.

KUFFLER, S.W., AND NICHOLLS, J.G. *From Neuron to Brain,* second edition. Sunderland, Mass.: Sinauer Associates, 1984.

SHEPHERD, G.M. *Neurobiology.* New York: Oxford University Press, 1983.

Neural Communication: Physiology and Pharmacology

Chapter 2 discussed the resting membrane potential and described how a small decrease in this potential produces an action potential that travels down the axon to the terminal buttons. This chapter discusses the nature of communication among neurons and the ways in which drugs facilitate or interfere with this communication. The interactions among neurons constitute the means by which our nervous system functions.

■ SYNAPTIC TRANSMISSION

As we saw in Chapter 2, neurons communicate by means of synapses, and the medium used for these one-way conversations is the chemical released by terminal buttons. These chemicals, called *transmitter substances* or *neurotransmitters,* diffuse across the gap between the terminal buttons and the membranes of the neurons with which they form synapses. The transmitter substances cause a brief alteration in the membrane potential of these neurons, which produces either an excitatory or an inhibitory effect on the rate of firing of their axons.

I begin our discussion of synaptic transmission by describing the structure of synapses. Most of this section then covers the steps involved in the process of synaptic transmission, from release of the transmitter substance to termination of the postsynaptic potential. The role played by autoreceptors in the process is explained in the last portion of this section.

Structure of Synapses

Synapses are junctions between the terminal buttons at the ends of the axonal branches of one neuron and (usually) the somatic or dendritic membrane of another. Because a message is transmitted in only one direction, the membranes on the two sides of the synapse are named in relation to the synapse; the membrane of the terminal button (transmitting neuron) is the *presynaptic membrane,* and that of the receiving neuron is the *postsynaptic membrane.* As Figure 3.1 shows, these membranes are separated by a small gap, which varies in size from synapse to synapse but is usually around 200 Å wide. (An Ångström unit is one ten-millionth of a millimeter.) The space, called the *synaptic cleft,* contains extracellular fluid, through which the transmitter substance diffuses. (See **Figure 3.1.**)

As you may have noticed in Figure 3.1, two prominent structures are located in the cytoplasm of the terminal button: mitochondria and *synaptic vesicles.* Many of the biochemical steps in the extraction of energy from glucose take place on the cristae of the mitochondria; hence, their presence near the terminal button suggests that certain processes that occur there require energy. Synaptic vesicles are small, rounded objects in the shape of spheres or ovoids. They appear to be packages that contain transmitter substance (the term *vesicle* means "little bladder"). They are produced in the soma and transported through the axoplasm to the terminal buttons. They are also produced locally, in the *cisternae,* which are specialized forms of the Golgi apparatus. (See **Figure 3.1.**) Actually, as we will soon see, the cisternae are recycling plants rather than manufacturing plants. They make synaptic vesicles not out of raw material but out of the membrane of old vesicles that have expelled their contents into the synaptic cleft.

Evidence that the soma produces synaptic vesicles comes from a very simple experiment. If a nerve is ligated ("tied") with a bit of thread and is later examined under an electron microscope, a collection of vesicles — along with a lot of other material — will be found on the proximal (closer to soma) side of the obstruction. These vesicles are presumably produced in the Golgi apparatus, the

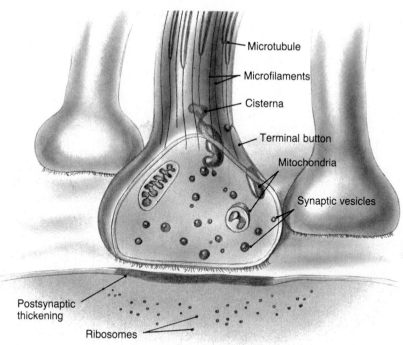

FIGURE 3.1
Details of a synapse.

packaging plant of the cell, and are sent down to the terminal buttons via *axoplasmic transport,* an active process by which substances are propelled along microtubules and microfilaments that run the length of the axon. These fibers also run through the terminal buttons, presumably transporting substances within them.

The postsynaptic membrane under the terminal button is somewhat thicker than the membrane elsewhere. As we will see, it contains specialized protein molecules that detect the presence of transmitter substances in the synaptic cleft and initiate the changes in the membrane potential that excite or inhibit the rate of firing of the cell's axon. Ribosomes are found in the cytoplasm near the postsynaptic membrane. Because ribosomes are needed for protein synthesis, their presence near the postsynaptic membrane implies that protein synthesis is important for some aspect of the process of receiving messages from terminal buttons.

Release of Transmitter Substance

When an axon fires (propagates an action potential), a number of synaptic vesicles filled with a transmitter substance migrate to the presynaptic membrane, adhere to it, and then rupture, spilling their contents into the synaptic cleft. (See **Figure 3.2.**)

The evidence for this process comes from several different kinds of experiments. Clark, Hurlbut, and Mauro (1972) removed a muscle from a frog, along with a length of nerve that innervated it. They infused the muscle and terminal buttons with venom of the black widow spider, which causes transmitter substance to be released from the terminal but-

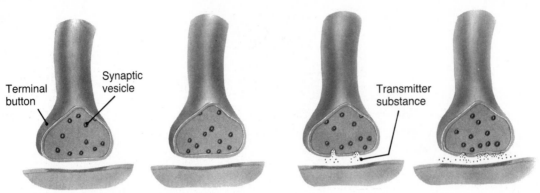

FIGURE 3.2
The release of a transmitter substance into the synaptic cleft from the
terminal button of an axon.

tons that synapse on the muscle fibers. When
they examined the terminal buttons under an
electron microscope, they found that the synaptic vesicles were gone. In addition, the terminal buttons were larger than normal, as if
additions had been made to the membrane,
perhaps from the expended vesicles.

Heuser and colleagues (Heuser, 1977;
Heuser, Reese, Dennis, Jan, Jan, and Evans,
1979) obtained even more direct evidence.
Because the release of transmitter substance is
a very rapid event, taking only a few milliseconds to occur, special procedures are needed
to stop the action so that the details can be
studied. They electrically stimulated the
nerve attached to an isolated frog muscle and
then dropped the muscle against a block of
pure copper that had been cooled to 4° K
(approximately −453° F). Contact with the
supercooled metal froze the outer layer of tissue in 2 milliseconds or less. The ice held the
components of the terminal buttons in place
until they could be chemically stabilized and
examined with an electron microscope.

Figure 3.3 shows a portion of the synapse
in cross section; note the vesicles that appear
to be fused with the presynaptic membrane,
forming the shape of an omega (Ω). (See **Figure 3.3, top.**) The lower two photographs
show an end view of the surface of the termi-

nal button, as the postsynaptic membrane
would see it. The middle picture shows a presynaptic membrane that was frozen 3 milliseconds after the nerve was shocked, which is
too soon for the synaptic vesicles to burst
open. (See **Figure 3.3, middle.**) The bottom
photograph shows a presynaptic membrane
that was frozen 2 milliseconds later; note the
vesicles, caught in the act of emptying their
contents into the synaptic cleft. (See **Figure
3.3, bottom.**)

A study by Heuser and Reese (1973) outlined the means by which the membrane used
in synaptic vesicles is recycled. As the synaptic vesicles fuse with the presynaptic membrane and burst open, their membrane becomes incorporated into that of the terminal
button, which consequently becomes larger.
Therefore, to maintain the proper size of the
terminal button, some membrane must be removed. At the point of junction between the
axon and the terminal button, little buds of
membrane pinch off into the cytoplasm, in a
process called *pinocytosis*. The buds of
membrane migrate to the cisternae and fuse
with them, adding to their membrane. Then
new synaptic vesicles are produced as pieces
of membrane break off the cisternae and are
filled with molecules of transmitter substance. (See **Figure 3.4.**)

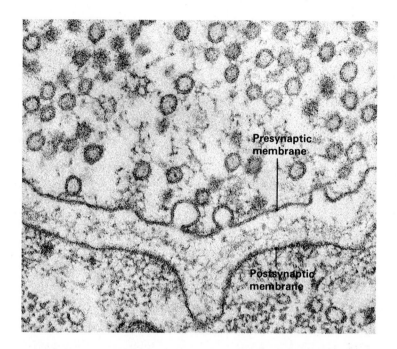

Presynaptic
membrane

Postsynaptic
membrane

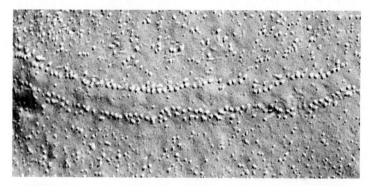

FIGURE 3.3
Photomicrographs of the
fusion of synaptic vesicles with
the membranes of terminal
buttons that form synapses
with frog muscle. *Top:* A cross
section through a terminal
button. *Middle and bottom:*
Views of the surface of
terminal buttons. The dimples
are synaptic vesicles in the
process of fusing with the
membrane (see text). (From
Heuser, J.E., In *Society for
Neuroscience Symposia,
Volume II,* edited by W.M.
Cowan and J.A. Ferrendelli.
Bethesda, Md.: Society for
Neuroscience, 1977; and
Heuser, J.E., Reese, T.S.,
Dennis, M.J., Jan, Y., Jan, L.,
and Evans, L. *Journal of Cell
Biology,* 1979, *81,* 275–300.)

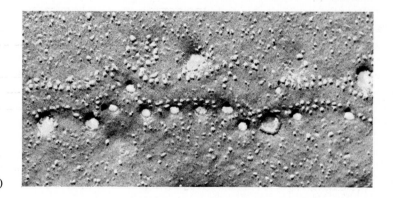

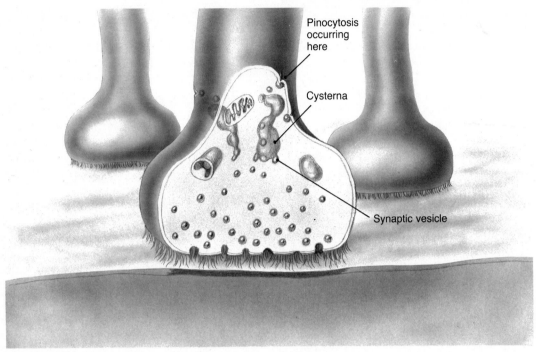

FIGURE 3.4
Recycling of the membrane of synaptic vesicles that have released
neurotransmitter into the synaptic cleft.

In their experiment, Heuser and Reese used a chemical with the unlikely name ***horseradish peroxidase.*** As we will see, this enzyme, extracted from the horseradish plant, is useful to neurochemists and neuroanatomists. Heuser and Reese placed a frog muscle and attached nerve in a solution of horseradish peroxidase and electrically stimulated the nerve, causing the axons to fire. Shortly thereafter, they removed the muscle and nerve from the solution and treated them with chemicals that react with horseradish peroxidase, producing black spots, which are visible under a microscope wherever the chemical is present in the tissue. When they chemically treated and examined the nerve tissue soon after placing it in the horseradish peroxidase solution, they found black spots inside small vesicles in the cytoplasm near the junction of the axon and terminal button.

When they waited a longer time before chemically treating the tissue, they found black spots in the cisternae. When they waited even longer, they found them in the synaptic vesicles themselves. The horseradish peroxidase, which was taken into the cell with a bit of extracellular fluid when buds pinched off the axonal membrane during pinocytosis, was transported to the cisternae and then into the newly made synaptic vesicles.

The force that moves the synaptic vesicles toward the presynaptic membrane appears to be supplied by a process similar to that of axoplasmic flow. The membrane of synaptic vesicles is coated with a protein. The protein coating of the vesicles interacts with that of the microtubules, causing the microtubules to propel the vesicles to the presynaptic membrane. Once the vesicles reach the presynaptic membrane, their protein coating interacts with a protein coating on the inside of the presynaptic membrane, which is similar to that of the microtubules. This interaction tears open the synaptic vesicles, and the transmitter substance spills into the synaptic cleft.

As we will see in Chapter 8, the interaction of two proteins, actin and myosin, provides the force that contracts muscle fibers. They interact and cause a contraction when calcium ions (Ca^{2+}) enter the cell. Similarly, the entry of Ca^{2+} appears to be the event that causes synaptic vesicles to migrate to the presynaptic membrane and rupture. If the extracellular fluid is artificially depleted of Ca^{2+}, the terminal button no longer releases transmitter substance when its axon is stimulated. Studies have shown that when an action potential reaches a terminal button, voltage-dependent calcium channels open their gates and the membrane temporarily becomes permeable to Ca^{2+}. The Ca^{2+} enters the cytoplasm of the terminal button, moving down its electrostatic and osmotic gradients. The entry of Ca^{2+} causes the microtubules to propel the synaptic vesicles to the presynaptic membrane. A calcium pump, similar in operation to the sodium-potassium pump, later removes the intracellular Ca^{2+}.

Activation of Receptors

Transmitter substances affect the membrane potential of the postsynaptic neuron by activating special molecules attached to the postsynaptic membrane. These molecules, which are made of protein, are called ***postsynaptic receptors.*** When a molecule of a transmitter substance diffuses across the synaptic cleft and meets a postsynaptic receptor, it attaches to the receptor in the manner of a key fitting a lock. Once it attaches, the postsynaptic receptor opens the gate of a ***neurotransmitter-dependent ion channel.*** Thus, the transmitter substance permits particular ions to pass through the membrane, changing the local membrane potential.

Neurotransmitters open ion channels by at least two different means. The best-known example of the first method is the acetylcholine receptor. (Acetylcholine is a transmitter substance that will be discussed in more detail later in this chapter.) This receptor has been studied in the organ that produces electrical current in *Torpedo,* the electric ray, where it occurs in great number. Acetylcholine receptors open the gates of the ion channels that permit sodium ions to enter the cell. The structure of the acetylcholine receptor is shown in Figure 3.5. Acetylcholine molecules attach to two sites located on the part of the molecule that projects into the synaptic cleft. When *both* sites are occupied by acetylcholine, the ion channel widens, permitting sodium ions to pass through. (See **Figure 3.5.**)

The second method is more complicated. Some receptors do not open ion gates directly but instead cause the production of the so-called second messengers — substances known as ***cyclic nucleotides.*** Attached to receptors in the postsynaptic membrane at some synapses are molecules of an enzyme called ***adenylate cyclase.*** When this type of receptor is occupied by a molecule of the appropriate transmitter substance, the adenylate cyclase becomes active and causes ***adenosine triphosphate (ATP)*** to be converted into ***cyclic adenosine monophosphate (cyclic AMP).*** Some neurons — in particular, photoreceptors in the retina — use another cyclic nucleotide. In these cells, *guanosine triphosphate (GTP)* becomes *cyclic guanosine monophosphate (cyclic GMP).* The principle of operation is the same, however.

Cyclic AMP activates enzymes called ***protein kinases;*** when activated, these enzymes cause changes in the physical shape of the proteins that control the gates of the ion channels in the postsynaptic membrane. (*Kinase* translates roughly as "enzyme that causes movement.") A protein kinase makes

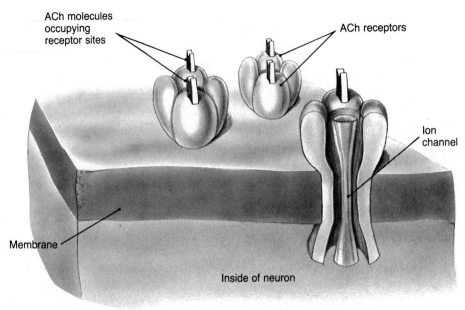

FIGURE 3.5
The acetylcholine receptor, an example of a neurotransmitter-dependent
ion channel. (Adapted from Changeux, J.-P., Devillers-Thiéry, A., and
Chemouilli, P. *Science,* 1984, *225,* 1335–1345.)

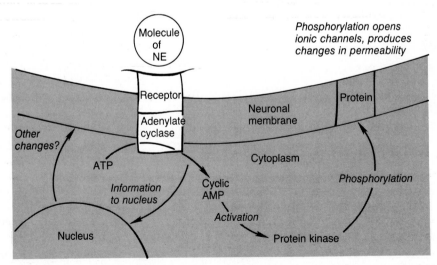

FIGURE 3.6
Many neurotransmitter receptors control ion channels indirectly, by
means of a second messenger, such as cyclic AMP.

the protein change its shape by causing it to be *phosphorylated*—to gain a phosphate ion. The change in the protein's shape opens the gate and permits ions to cross the membrane. As a consequence, the local membrane potential is altered. (See **Figure 3.6.**)

The second messengers, cyclic AMP and cyclic GMP, play a role in other processes besides the production of postsynaptic potentials. For example, they provide the means by which some kinds of hormones, detected by receptors in the membrane, trigger changes in the cell's protein synthesis. To do so, the cyclic nucleotides travel to the nucleus, where they phosphorylate proteins attached to the DNA. Some of the other effects of the cyclic nucleotides will be discussed in later chapters.

Cyclic nucleotides are destroyed soon after they are produced by an enzyme called *phosphodiesterase.* Thus, a drug that inhibits the activity of phosphodiesterase allows cyclic AMP to accumulate and keeps the ion gates open for a longer-than-usual time. In fact, many people daily dose themselves with a phosphodiesterase inhibitor, *caffeine.* This drug increases synaptic activity at some neurons, producing behavioral effects of activation and wakefulness.

Postsynaptic Potentials

When molecules of a transmitter substance are liberated by a terminal button they attach to the postsynaptic receptors and produce a brief change in the membrane potential of the postsynaptic neuron. These changes can either excite or inhibit the postsynaptic neuron; they are thus referred to as *excitatory postsynaptic potentials (EPSPs)* and *inhibitory postsynaptic potentials (IPSPs).* EPSPs are small depolarizations; IPSPs are small hyperpolarizations. Our discussion here concerns the physical and chemical changes that produce EPSPs and IPSPs. A

later section on neural integration discusses the interaction of these two types of postsynaptic potentials on the somatic and dendritic membrane.

Because the *postsynaptic potentials* can be either depolarizing (excitatory) or hyperpolarizing (inhibitory), the alterations in membrane permeability must be caused by the movement of particular species of ions. The sodium-potassium pump maintains a large electrostatic and osmotic gradient for the sodium ion (Na^+). As we saw in Chapter 2, when voltage-dependent sodium channels open during an action potential, Na^+ rushes into the cytoplasm, causing the membrane to depolarize. The sodium-potassium pump also maintains a small osmotic gradient for the potassium ion (K^+). If the membrane becomes more permeable to K^+, some of these cations will follow this gradient and leave the cell. Because K^+ is positively charged, its efflux will hyperpolarize the membrane. Indeed, the influx of Na^+ and the efflux of K^+ are primarily responsible for EPSPs and IPSPs, respectively.

Let us first consider EPSPs. Experiments have shown that when postsynaptic receptors at excitatory synapses are activated by molecules of transmitter substances, they make the postsynaptic membrane more permeable to both Na^+ and K^+. It appears that EPSPs are caused by the opening of ion channels in the membrane that permit both Na^+ and K^+ to cross the membrane. Therefore, during EPSPs, Na^+ enters the cell and K^+ leaves it. Because the driving force behind Na^+ is much stronger than the driving force behind K^+, the quantity of Na^+ that enters is much larger than the quantity of K^+ that leaves; thus, the net effect of the movements of these ions is depolarizing. (See **Figure 3.7.**)

When postsynaptic receptors at inhibitory synapses are activated by molecules of transmitter substances, they open the gates of potassium channels, permitting K^+ to leave the

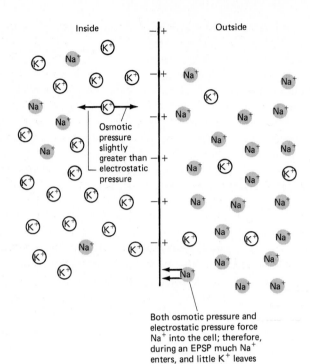

Both osmotic pressure and electrostatic pressure force Na$^+$ into the cell; therefore, during an EPSP much Na$^+$ enters, and little K$^+$ leaves

FIGURE 3.7
During excitatory postsynaptic potentials (EPSPs), the influx of Na$^+$ is much larger than the efflux of K$^+$; thus, the membrane depolarizes.

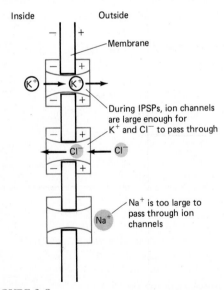

FIGURE 3.8
Inhibitory postsynaptic potentials (IPSPs) at many synapses occur when potassium channels permit K$^+$ to leave the cell, thus hyperpolarizing it.

cell, down its concentration gradient. This outward migration of cations hyperpolarizes the membrane potential. (See **Figure 3.8.**) At many synapses, the neurotransmitter also opens the gates of chloride channels. The effects of the increased permeability to chloride ions (Cl$^-$) are somewhat more complex. The most important effect occurs when the activity of nearby excitatory synapses has already slightly depolarized the membrane. If chloride channels then open, they will permit the anion to enter the cell, at least partially neutralizing the depolarization. (See **Figure 3.9.**)

Termination of the Postsynaptic Potential

Postsynaptic potentials are brief depolarizations or hyperpolarizations caused by the activation of postsynaptic receptors with mole-

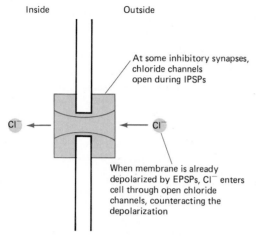

Inside   Outside

At some inhibitory synapses, chloride channels open during IPSPs

Cl⁻

Cl⁻

When membrane is already depolarized by EPSPs, Cl⁻ enters cell through open chloride channels, counteracting the depolarization

FIGURE 3.9

At some inhibitory synapses, the neurotransmitter opens chloride channels. If the membrane is already somewhat depolarized because of the activity of nearby excitatory synapses, Cl⁻ enters, restoring the membrane potential back toward its resting level.

cules of a transmitter substance. They are kept brief by two mechanisms: re-uptake and enzymatic deactivation.

The postsynaptic potentials produced by almost all transmitter substances are terminated by *re-uptake.* This process is simply an extremely rapid removal of transmitter substance from the synaptic cleft by the terminal button. The transmitter substance does not return in the vesicles that get pinched off the membrane of the terminal button; instead, the membrane contains a pumplike mechanism that draws on the cell's energy reserves to force the transmitter substance from the synaptic cleft directly into the cytoplasm. When an action potential arrives, the terminal buttons release a small amount of transmitter substance into the synaptic cleft and then take it back, giving the postsynaptic receptors only a brief exposure to the transmitter substance.

Enzymatic deactivation is accomplished

by an enzyme that destroys the transmitter molecule. As far as we know, postsynaptic potentials are terminated in this way for only one transmitter substance — *acetylcholine (ACh).* Transmission at synapses on muscle fibers and at some synapses between neurons is mediated by ACh. Postsynaptic potentials produced by ACh are short-lived because the postsynaptic membrane at these synapses contains an enzyme called *acetylcholinesterase (AChE).* AChE destroys ACh by cleaving it into its constituents, choline and acetate. Because neither of these substances is capable of activating postsynaptic receptors, the postsynaptic potential is terminated once the molecules of ACh are broken apart. AChE is an extremely energetic destroyer of ACh; one molecule of AChE will chop apart more that 64,000 molecules of ACh each second!

Autoreceptors

Postsynaptic receptors detect the presence of a transmitter substance in the synaptic cleft and initiate excitatory or inhibitory postsynaptic potentials. But the postsynaptic membrane is not the only location of receptors that respond to transmitter substances. Many neurons also possess receptors that respond to the transmitter substance that *they* release, called *autoreceptors.*

Autoreceptors can be located on the membrane of any part of the cell: terminal button, axon, soma, or dendrite. In general, these receptors do not control ion channels; when stimulated by a molecule of the appropriate transmitter substance, they do not initiate changes in the local membrane potential. Instead, they regulate internal processes, including the synthesis and release of transmitter substance. In most cases, the effects are inhibitory; that is, the presence of the transmitter substance in the extracellular fluid in the vicinity of the neuron causes a decrease in the rate of synthesis or release of the transmitter substance. Most investigators believe that autoreceptors are part of a regulatory system that controls the amount of transmitter substance released.

The presence of autoreceptors complicates the interpretation of the behavioral effects of drugs. As we will see, some drugs exert their effects by stimulating or blocking receptors. For example, a drug may block postsynaptic receptors that respond to a particular transmitter substance, thus preventing the transmitter substance from having an effect on the postsynaptic cell when it is released. In addition, the drug may block presynaptic autoreceptors as well. Because the effect of the autoreceptors is usually inhibitory, blocking them causes the presynaptic neuron to release more transmitter substance.

Thus, the drug has contradictory effects. However, if the postsynaptic receptors and presynaptic autoreceptors differ in shape so that the drug affects one kind of receptor better than the other, the net effect of the drug would then be either to block or to facilitate transmission at the synapse. (See **Figure 3.10.**)

INTERIM SUMMARY

Synapses consist of junctions between the terminal buttons of one neuron and the membrane — usually the somatic or dendritic membrane — of another. When an action potential is transmitted down an axon, the terminal buttons at the end release a transmitter substance, a chemical that produces changes in the postsynaptic membrane.

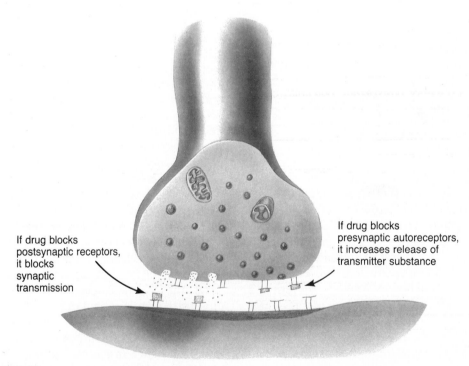

If drug blocks postsynaptic receptors, it blocks synaptic transmission

If drug blocks presynaptic autoreceptors, it increases release of transmitter substance

FIGURE 3.10
Postsynaptic receptors and presynaptic autoreceptors have different effects on synaptic transmission.

Transmitter substances are stored in synaptic vesicles, small sacs of membrane located in the cytoplasm of terminal buttons. When an action potential reaches the terminal button, the sudden depolarization causes voltage-dependent calcium channels in the membrane to open, and Ca^{2+} enters the cytoplasm. This ion catalyzes chemical reactions that propel synaptic vesicles along the microtubules to the inner surface of the presynaptic membrane. The vesicles fuse with the membrane and burst, spilling their contents into the synaptic cleft. The transmitter substance that is thus released diffuses through the extracellular fluid in the synaptic cleft and reaches the receptors in the postsynaptic membrane.

When they are activated by molecules of a transmitter substance, postsynaptic receptors open neurotransmitter-dependent ion channels. They do so directly (as in the case of acetylcholine receptors) or indirectly, through second messengers. Two types of cyclic nucleotides, cyclic AMP and cyclic GMP, act as second messengers, activating protein kinases that cause proteins in the membrane to change their shape, opening the gates of ion channels.

The activation of postsynaptic receptors by molecules of a transmitter substance causes the ion channels to open, resulting in a postsynaptic potential. Excitatory postsynaptic potentials occur when Na^+ enters the cell (and a little K^+ leaves). Inhibitory postsynaptic potentials occur when K^+ leaves the cell. (In some cases, chloride channels open as well.) The next section of this chapter discusses the interaction of postsynaptic potentials.

Postsynaptic potentials are normally brief. They are terminated by two means. In the case of acetylcholine, the enzyme acetylcholinesterase, which is attached to the postsynaptic membrane, deactivates the transmitter substance, breaking it down to choline and acetate. In all other cases (as far as we know), molecules of the transmitter substance are removed from the synaptic cleft by means of a special mechanism in the membrane that pumps them back into the cytoplasm, where they can be used again. This retrieval process is called re-uptake.

Neurons also recycle the membrane of the synaptic vesicles that participate in synaptic transmission. When the membranes of synaptic vesicles fuse with the membrane of the terminal button, the latter increases in size. Small pieces of membrane pinch off into the cytoplasm at the junction of the axon and terminal button and travel to a cisterna, which serves as a reservoir for extra membrane. Pieces of the cisternae break off to form synaptic vesicles, which are filled with the transmitter substance as they migrate toward the presynaptic membrane.

The presynaptic membrane, as well as the postsynaptic membrane, contains receptors that detect the presence of a transmitter substance. Presynaptic receptors, also called autoreceptors, monitor the quantity of transmitter substance that a neuron releases and apparently regulate the amount that is synthesized or released.

■ NEURAL INTEGRATION

The interaction of EPSPs and IPSPs on the somatic and dendritic membranes of a neuron determines the rate at which its axon fires. This interaction is called *neural integration* (*integration* means "to make whole," in the sense of combining two functions). To illustrate this process, we can perform an experiment similar to one we did in Chapter 2.

We isolate a giant squid axon in a dish of seawater and place a recording electrode on the membrane. We attach electrodes from two shockers to the end of the axon; one delivers brief positive shocks (hyperpolarizations) and the other delivers brief negative shocks (depolarizations) to the outside of the membrane. (See **Figure 3.11.**)

We saw in Chapter 2 that if a depolarizing shock brings the membrane potential of an axon to the threshold of excitation, an action potential occurs. Subthreshold depolarizations and all hyperpolarizations produce graded potentials that will be propagated down the axon according to its passive cable properties. This sort of transmission, decremental conduction, contrasts with the nondecremental conduction of the action potential, which is transmitted without decrease in amplitude.

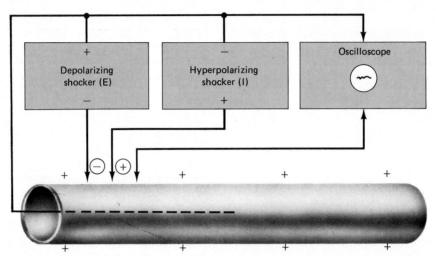

FIGURE 3.11

The means by which an axon can be stimulated with both negative and positive shocks. E = excitatory; I = inhibitory.

The depolarizing (excitatory) shocker is set at a level just sufficient to trigger an action potential. If we deliver a pulse from the hyperpolarizing (inhibitory) shocker just before delivering an excitatory shock, we find that we prevent the occurrence of the action potential. That is to say, we *inhibit* the action potential. The inhibitory pulse increases the membrane potential, so that the effects of the excitatory pulse no longer bring it to the threshold of excitation. (See **Figure 3.12**.) Thus, we see how a hyperpolarizing shock can block the effect of a depolarizing shock.

Let us examine another phenomenon. This time, we administer a small, subthreshold, excitatory pulse. Before the effects of this one are over, we shock the membrane again, and again. After several shocks, the axon fires. (See **Figure 3.13**.) The effects of closely spaced subthreshold excitations are cumulative; a number of small excitations achieves the same effect as a single large one. This process, involving the additive effect of small excitations across time, is called ***temporal summation.***

Let us examine one more phenomenon. If

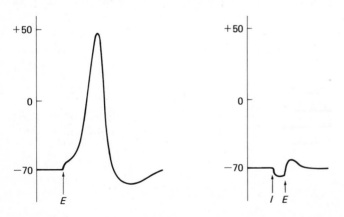

FIGURE 3.12

A depolarizing (excitatory) shock that normally produces an action potential can be inhibited by a previously produced hyperpolarizing (inhibitory) shock. E = excitatory; I = inhibitory.

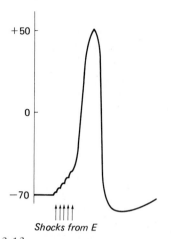

FIGURE 3.13
Temporal summation occurs when subthreshold depolarizations are presented in rapid succession. *E* = excitatory shocker.

we simultaneously deliver excitatory shocks from two different electrodes placed on the axonal membrane, the effects of these shocks add together. Two subthreshold shocks delivered simultaneously at two different locations can summate and trigger an action potential. This additive effect on the membrane potential of shocks applied to various parts of the membrane is called ***spatial summation.*** (See **Figure 3.14.**)

Of course, there are no electrodes on the axons of neurons in intact animals. Instead, there are the terminal buttons of other neurons, arranged on the somatic and dendri-

tic membranes of these cells, which are capable of producing EPSPs and IPSPs. The spatial and temporal summation of these postsynaptic potentials constitutes neural integration.

In most neurons, the membranes of dendrites and soma are not capable of producing an action potential; only an axon can do that. The membrane potential at the axon hillock is what determines whether the axon will fire. This region, the junction between soma and axon, is capable of producing an action potential. If it does so, an impulse is propagated down the axon. Before reaching the axon, the EPSPs and IPSPs that occur at synapses on the soma and dendrites are transmitted decrementally, according to the passive cable properties of the neural membrane. These postsynaptic potentials integrate at the axon hillock; whenever the membrane potential at the axon hillock exceeds the threshold of excitation, the axon fires. If many excitatory synapses on a neuron fire at a high rate, the cell's axon will also fire at a high rate. If inhibitory synapses then begin firing, the rate of axonal firing will decline. Thus, the relative numbers of EPSPs and IPSPs that occur on a neuron's dendritic and somatic membranes determine the rate at which its axon fires.

It is important to note that *neural* inhibition (that is, an inhibitory postsynaptic potential) does not always produce *behavioral* inhibition. For example, suppose a group of neurons inhibits a particular movement. If

Excitatory shocks
administered simultaneously

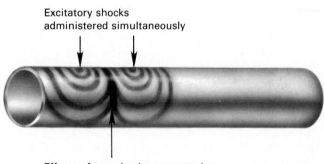

FIGURE 3.14
Spatial summation occurs when subthreshold depolarizations are presented simultaneously at more than one location.

Effects of two shocks summate here
and trigger action potential

these neurons are inhibited, they will no longer suppress the behavior. Thus, inhibition of the inhibitory neurons makes the behavior more likely to occur. Of course, the same is true for neural excitation. Neural *excitation* of neurons that *inhibit* a behavior suppresses that behavior. Neurons are elements in complex circuits, and without knowing the details of these circuits one cannot predict the effects of the excitation or inhibition of one set of neurons on an organism's behavior.

■ OTHER TYPES OF SYNAPSES

So far, my discussion of synaptic activity has referred only to the effects of postsynaptic excitation or inhibition. These effects occur at **axosomatic synapses** or **axodendritic synapses** (synapses between the terminal buttons of axons with somatic or dendritic membrane, respectively). Other kinds of synapses exist as well.

Axoaxonic Synapses

A junction between a terminal button and an axon of another cell is referred to as an **axoaxonic synapse.** This type of synapse does not directly contribute to neural integration, as do the axosomatic and axodendritic synapses discussed in the previous section. Instead, axoaxonic synapses alter the amount of transmitter substance liberated by the terminal buttons of the postsynaptic axon.

The release of a transmitter substance by a terminal button is initiated by an action potential. Experiments have shown that the amount released (and hence the size of the resulting postsynaptic potential) depends on the magnitude of change in the membrane potential. (Normally, this change is from -70 mV to $+50$ mV, or a total of 120 mV.) Furthermore, the transition in potential must be rapid. A slow change in the membrane potential will not release transmitter substance.

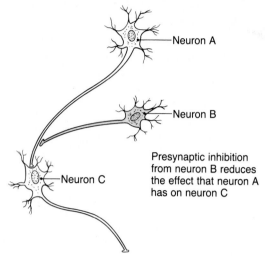

Presynaptic inhibition from neuron B reduces the effect that neuron A has on neuron C

FIGURE 3.15
An axoaxonic synapse.

Here, then, is how presynaptic inhibition works. The axon of cell B fires, and its terminal button releases a transmitter substance, which depolarizes the membrane of axon A. (See **Figure 3.15.**) This depolarization is too small to produce an action potential in axon A and is therefore conducted to the terminal button by means of passive cable properties. Because the change in the membrane potential is relatively slow, no transmitter substance is released by the terminal button of axon A. If an action potential comes down axon A while the terminal button is still slightly depolarized, the membrane potential will quickly shoot up to $+50$ mV and then drop back down. But because transmitter substance is released in proportion to the magnitude of change in the membrane potential, less than the normal amount will be released. The action potential occurs in a less-than-normally polarized terminal, so that the total change in the membrane potential will be smaller than usual. (See **Figure 3.16.**)

Axoaxonic synapses obviously have an effect only if the postsynaptic axon is actually firing. As an example of how these synapses might be useful, let us consider neuron B, which can exert presynaptic inhibition on neuron A through an axoaxonic synapse. When this inhibition occurs, the effect of neuron A on neuron C (with which it has an axosomatic synapse) is reduced. However, neuron C remains sensitive to the effects of other axons. (See **Figure 3.17.**)

Dendrodendritic Synapses

Many very small neurons have extremely short processes and apparently lack axons. These neurons form ***dendrodendritic synapses,*** or synapses between dendrites. Because these neurons lack long axonal processes, they do not transmit information from place to place within the brain. Most investigators believe that they perform regulatory functions, perhaps helping to organize the activity of groups of neurons. Because these neurons are so small, they are difficult to study; thus, little is known about their function.

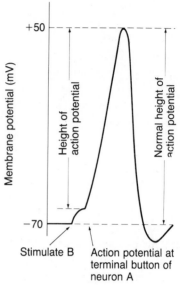

FIGURE 3.16

Presynaptic inhibition. The action potential is recorded from the terminal button of neuron A, shown in Figures 3.15 and 3.17. The small depolarization that precedes the action potential is produced by the activity of the axon of neuron B.

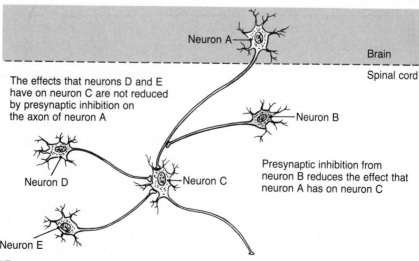

FIGURE 3.17

An example of the advantage of presynaptic inhibition.

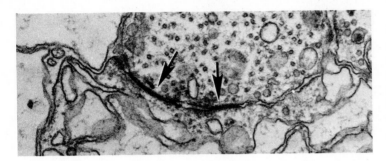

FIGURE 3.18
A gap junction, which permits direct electrical coupling between the membranes of adjacent neurons. (From Bennett, M. V. L., and Pappas, G. D. *The Journal of Neuroscience*, 1983, *3*, 748–761.

Some larger neurons, as well, form dendro-dendritic synapses. Some of these synapses are chemical in nature, indicated by the presence of synaptic vesicles in one of the juxtaposed dendrites and a postsynaptic thickening in the membrane of the other. Other synapses are *electrical*; the membranes meet and almost touch, forming a *gap junction*. (See **Figure 3.18**.) The membranes on both sides of a gap junction contain channels that permit ions to diffuse from one cell to another. Thus, changes in the membrane potential of one neuron induce changes in the membrane of the other. Although most gap junctions in vertebrate synapses are dendro-dendritic, axosomatic and axodendritic gap junctions also occur. Gap junctions are common in invertebrates; their function in the vertebrate nervous system is not known.

postsynaptic potentials from a single synapse, closely spaced in time. Spatial summation refers to the additive effects of postsynaptic potentials produced by the simultaneous activity of several synapses. The occurrence of an action potential is determined at the axon hillock; whenever the membrane there reaches the threshold of excitation, an action potential is triggered.

Axosomatic and axodendritic synapses are not the only kinds found in the nervous system. Axoaxonic synapses produce presynaptic inhibition by depolarizing the membrane of a terminal button enough so that an action potential, if it occurs, produces a smaller change in the polarization of the membrane. The result of this effect is to cause the terminal button to release a smaller quantity of its transmitter substance. Dendrodendritic synapses also occur, but their role in neural communication is not yet understood.

■ **TRANSMITTER SUBSTANCES**

Because transmitter substances have two general effects on the postsynaptic membrane — depolarization (EPSP) or hyperpolarization (IPSP) — one might expect that there would be two kinds of transmitter substances, excitatory and inhibitory. Instead, there are many different kinds. While some do appear to be exclusively excitatory or inhibitory, others can produce either excitation or inhibition, depending on the nature of the postsynaptic receptors. Table 3.1 lists compounds that are believed to be transmitter substances, their distribution in the nervous system, and their hypothesized effects on postsynaptic cells. (See **Table 3.1**.)

INTERIM SUMMARY

As we saw in the first part of this chapter, the release of a transmitter substance by a terminal button produces a postsynaptic potential by activating neurotransmitter-dependent ion channels in the postsynaptic membrane. These postsynaptic potentials, consisting of depolarizations or hyperpolarizations, are propagated decrementally, by means of passive cable properties, over the surface of the somatic and dendritic membranes. The rate at which the axon fires is determined by the algebraic addition of the postsynaptic potentials, a process called neural integration. Temporal summation refers to the additive effects of a series of

T A B L E 3.1   Probable transmitter substances

Probable Transmitter Substance	Location	Hypothesized Effect
Acetylcholine (ACh)	Brain, spinal cord, autonomic ganglia, target organs of the parasympathetic nervous system	Excitation in brain and autonomic ganglia, excitation or inhibition in target organs
Norepinephrine (NE)	Brain, spinal cord (see Figure 9.24), target organs of sympathetic nervous system	Inhibition in brain, excitation or inhibition in target organs
Dopamine (DA)	Brain (see Figure 13.12)	Inhibition
Serotonin (5-hydroxytryptamine, or 5-HT)	Brain, spinal cord	Inhibition
Gamma-aminobutyric acid (GABA)	Brain (especially cerebral and cerebellar cortex), spinal cord	Inhibition
Glycine	Spinal cord interneurons	Inhibition
Glutamic acid	Brain, spinal sensory neurons	Excitation
Aspartic acid	Spinal cord interneurons, brain (?)	Excitation
Substance P	Brain, spinal sensory neurons (pain)	Excitation (and inhibition?)
Histamine, taurine, other amino acids; peptides such as oxytocin and endogenous opiates; many others	Various regions of brain, spinal cord, and peripheral nervous system	(?)

Acetylcholine

The transmitter substance at synapses on skeletal muscles of vertebrates is acetylcholine (ACh). (These synapses are said to be *acetylcholinergic* in nature. *Ergon* is the Greek word for "work.") ACh is also found in the ganglia of the autonomic nervous system and at the target organs of the parasympathetic branch of the autonomic nervous system (discussed in more detail in Chapter 4). Because ACh is found outside the central nervous system in locations that are easy to study, this transmitter substance has received much attention. ACh is also found in the brain. In fact, it is an important transmitter substance there; some investigators believe that the death of acetylcholinergic neurons is the primary cause of Alzheimer's disease, a fatal degenerative disorder. (This disease is discussed in Chapter 15.)

ACh is produced by means of the following reaction:

Choline acetyltransferase
↷

Acetyl CoA + choline → acetylcholine + CoA

Choline, a substance derived from the breakdown of lipids, is taken into the neuron from the general circulation. ***Coenzyme A (CoA)*** is a complex molecule, consisting in part of the vitamin pantothenic acid. It is a ubiquitously useful substance, taking part in many reactions in the body. All substances that enter the Krebs cycle (citric acid cycle), where they are metabolized to provide energy, are first converted to acetate and joined with CoA to form acetyl CoA. Similarly, in the synthesis of ACh, CoA acts as a carrier for the acetate ion, which in the process gets attached to choline to make acetylcholine (ACh). Acetyl CoA is thus composed of CoA with its attached acetate ion. In the presence of the enzyme ***choline acetyltransferase,*** the acetate ion is transferred from the CoA molecule to the choline molecule, yielding a molecule of ACh and one of plain old CoA. A simple analogy illustrates the role of coenzymes in chemical reactions. Think of acetate as a hot dog and choline as a bun. The task of the person (enzyme) who operates the hot dog vending stand is to put a hot dog into the bun (make acetylcholine). To do so, the vendor needs a fork (coenzyme) to remove the hot dog from the boiling water. The vendor inserts the fork into the hot dog (attaches acetate to CoA) and transfers the hot dog from fork to bun.

You will recall that after being released by the terminal button, ACh is deactivated by the enzyme acetylcholinesterase (AChE), which is present in the postsynaptic membrane. The deactivation produces choline and acetate from ACh. Because the amount of choline that is picked up by the soma from the general circulation and is sent to the terminal buttons by means of axoplasmic flow is not sufficient to keep up with the loss of choline by an active synapse, choline must be recycled. After ACh is destroyed by the AChE in the postsynaptic membrane, the choline is returned to the terminal buttons by means of re-uptake. There, it is converted back into ACh.

Sometimes excess ACh is produced—more than can be stored in the synaptic vesicles. For this reason, AChE is also present in the cytoplasm of the terminal buttons. This AChE cannot destroy the ACh that is stored in the vesicles, but it can—and does—destroy any transmitter substance produced by the cell that exceeds the storage capacity of the synaptic vesicles.

There are two different types of ACh receptors, with different molecular shapes. These receptors were identified when investigators discovered that different drugs activated or inhibited them. One class is stimulated by nicotine, the other by muscarine. Consequently, they are referred to as ***nicotinic receptors*** and ***muscarinic receptors,*** respectively. Muscle fibers contain nicotinic receptors, exclusively, but both kinds of receptors are found in the central nervous system.

Norepinephrine

Norepinephrine, dopamine, and serotonin are three transmitter substances that belong to a family of compounds called ***monoamines.*** Because the molecular structures of these substances are similar, some drugs affect the activity of all of them, to some degree.

T A B L E 3.2   Classification of the
monoamine transmitter substances

Monoamines	
Catecholamines	**Indolamines**
Norepinephrine	Serotonin (5-HT)
Dopamine	

The first two, norepinephrine and dopamine, belong to a subclass of monoamines called *catecholamines.* (See **Table 3.2.**)

Because *norepinephrine (NE)*, like ACh, is found in neurons in the autonomic nervous system, this neurotransmitter has received much experimental attention. I should note that *Adrenalin* and *epinephrine* are synonymous, as are *noradrenalin* and *norepinephrine*. *Epinephrine* is produced by the adrenal medulla, the central core of the adrenal glands, which are small endocrine glands located above the kidneys. (It also serves as a transmitter substance in the brain, but is of minor importance, compared with norepinephrine.) *Ad renal* is Latin for "toward kidney." In Greek, one would say *epi nephron* ("upon the kidney"), hence the term *epinephrine.* The latter term has been adopted by pharmacologists, probably because the word *Adrenalin* was appropriated by a drug company as a proprietary name; therefore, to be consistent with general usage, I will refer to the transmitter substance as *norepinephrine.* The accepted adjectival form is *noradrenergic; norepinephrinergic* just never caught on.

Most noradrenergic synapses in the central nervous system produce IPSPs. By contrast, at the target organs of the sympathetic nervous system (discussed in Chapter 4) norepinephrine usually has an excitatory effect. A technique discovered by Falck, Hillarp, Thieme, and Torp (1962) provided a method for precisely locating certain kinds of transmitter substances in the brain. These investigators discovered that when fish brain tissue was exposed to dry formaldehyde gas, noradrenergic neurons would fluoresce a bright yellow color when the tissue was examined under ultraviolet light. The technique was refined and applied to the other monoamines, and investigators drew "maps" showing the distribution of the monoaminergic neurons in the central nervous system. A noradrenergic map is shown in Figure 9.24. Once the location of particular types of neurons is known, it becomes possible to investigate their function. As we will see in Chapter 9, studies have shown that noradrenergic neurons play a role in arousal and alertness.

Neurons that release norepinephrine do not do so through terminal buttons on the ends of axonal branches, as most other neurons release their transmitter substances. Instead, norepinephrine is released through *axonal varicosities,* beadlike swellings of the axonal branches. These varicosities give the axonal branches of noradrenergic neurons the appearance of beaded chains. (See **Figure 3.19.**)

The synthesis of norepinephrine is somewhat more complicated than that of ACh, but each step is a simple one. The precursor molecule is modified slightly, step by step, until it achieves its final shape. Each step is controlled by a different enzyme, which adds a small part or takes one off. The precursor for both of the catecholamines (dopamine and norepinephrine) is *tyrosine,* an essential amino acid that we must obtain from our diet. Tyrosine receives a hydroxyl group (OH — an oxygen atom and a hydrogen atom) and becomes *L-3,4-dihydroxyphenylalanine (L-DOPA).* The enzyme that adds the hydroxyl group is, appropriately enough, called *tyrosine hydroxylase.* L-DOPA then loses a carboxyl group (COOH — one carbon atom, two oxygen atoms, and one hydrogen atom) through the activity of the enzyme *DOPA decarboxylase* and becomes dopamine. Fi-

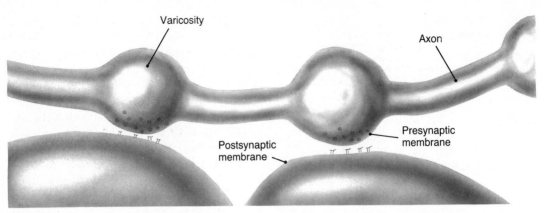

FIGURE 3.19
Noradrenergic axons release their neurotransmitter through varicosities
instead of terminal buttons.

nally, the enzyme *dopamine β-hydroxylase*
attaches a hydroxyl group to dopamine,
which becomes norepinephrine. These reactions are shown in **Figure 3.20.**

Most transmitter substances are synthesized in the cell body, packaged in synaptic
vesicles, and transported down the axon to
the terminal buttons. However, in the case of
norepinephrine, the final step of synthesis
occurs inside the vesicles themselves. The
vesicles are filled with dopamine. There, the
dopamine is converted to norepinephrine
through the action of dopamine β-hydroxylase.

There are several types of noradrenergic
receptors, identified by their differing sensitivities to various drugs. In the central nervous system, *β₁ noradrenergic receptors*
and *α₁ noradrenergic receptors* are found
primarily in postsynaptic membranes, while
α₂ noradrenergic receptors serve primarily
as presynaptic autoreceptors. In addition, *β₂*
noradrenergic receptors are found in the
central nervous system but are apparently associated with glia and muscles in the walls of
blood vessels. All four kinds of receptors are
also found in various organs of the body besides the brain.

Just as the AChE in the terminal buttons of
acetylcholinergic neurons destroys ACh that
is produced in excess of the amount that can
be stored in the synaptic vesicles, the production of the catecholamines is regulated by an
enzyme called *monoamine oxidase (MAO).*

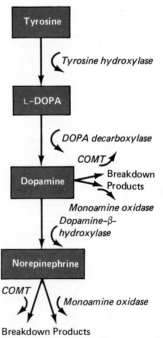

FIGURE 3.20
Biosynthesis of the catecholamines.

This enzyme is also found in the blood, where it deactivates amines that are present in foods such as chocolate and cheese; without such deactivation, these amines would cause dangerous increases in blood pressure.

Dopamine

Like the other catecholamine transmitter substance (norepinephrine), ___dopamine (DA)___ appears to produce IPSPs. Its distribution in the central nervous system has been mapped by histofluorescence techniques. (A dopamine "map" is shown in Figure 13.12.) Dopamine is one of the more interesting neurotransmitters because it has been implicated in several important functions, including movement, attention, and learning; thus, it is discussed in Chapters 8 and 13. Degeneration of dopaminergic neurons that connect the substantia nigra in the brain stem with the caudate nucleus in the forebrain causes ***Parkinson's disease,*** a movement disorder characterized by tremors, rigidity of the limbs, poor balance, and difficulty in initiating movements. The substantia nigra is so called because it is naturally stained black with melanin, the substance that gives color to skin. This compound is produced by the breakdown of dopamine. People with Parkinson's disease are given L-DOPA, the precursor to dopamine. Increased levels of L-DOPA in the brain cause more dopamine to be synthesized and released by the remaining dopaminergic neurons, and the patients' symptoms are alleviated.

Dopamine has been implicated as a transmitter substance that might be involved in schizophrenia, a serious mental disorder (psychosis) characterized by hallucinations, delusions, and disruption of normal, logical thought processes. Drugs that block the activity of dopaminergic neurons alleviate these symptoms; hence, investigators have speculated that schizophrenia is produced by their overactivity. In fact, symptoms of schizophrenia are an occasional side effect of L-DOPA in patients with Parkinson's disease. Fortunately, these symptoms can usually be eliminated by reducing the dose of the drug. The physiology of schizophrenia is discussed in Chapter 17.

We have already seen the biosynthetic pathway for dopamine in Figure 3.20; this transmitter is the immediate precursor of norepinephrine. Excess dopamine in the terminal buttons is destroyed by monoamine oxidase, the same enzyme that regulates norepinephrine.

Two types of dopamine receptors have been identified: D_1 ***dopamine receptors*** and D_2 ***dopamine receptors.*** It appears that D_1 receptors are exclusively postsynaptic, whereas D_2 receptors are found both presynaptically and postsynaptically in the brain.

Serotonin

The inhibitory transmitter substance ***serotonin*** (also called ***5-hydroxytryptamine,*** or ***5-HT***) has also received much experimental attention. Its precursor is the amino acid ***tryptophan.*** The enzyme ***tryptophan hydroxylase*** adds a hydroxyl group, producing ***5-hydroxytryptophan (5-HTP).*** The enzyme ***5-HTP decarboxylase*** removes a carboxyl group from 5-HTP, and the result is 5-HT (serotonin). Figure 3.21 illustrates these reactions. (See **Figure 3.21.**)

The regional distribution of 5-HT in the central nervous system has been studied with the advent of specific staining techniques. Serotonergic neurons in various hindbrain locations send axons to the spinal cord and into forebrain regions.

Besides producing neural inhibition, the behavioral effect of serotonin is also generally inhibitory. Serotonin plays a role in the regulation of mood, in the control of eating, sleep, and arousal, and in the regulation of pain.

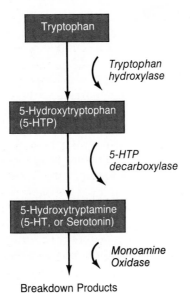

FIGURE 3.21
Biosynthesis of serotonin (5-hydroxytryptamine, or 5-HT).

Drugs that excite serotonergic neurons suppress dreaming, whereas drugs that inhibit them (such as *lysergic acid diethylamide,* or *LSD*) increase dreaming or even cause hallucinations while the person is awake. Investigators believe that LSD inhibits serotonergic neurons by *activating* presynaptic autoreceptors, thus decreasing serotonin synthesis and release.

Amino Acid Transmitter Substances

So far, all of the transmitter substances I have described are synthesized within neurons: acetylcholine from choline, the catecholamines from the amino acid tyrosine, and serotonin from the amino acid tryptophan. Some neurons secrete simple amino acids as transmitter substances. Because amino acids are used for protein synthesis by all cells of the brain, it is difficult to prove that a particular amino acid is a transmitter substance. However, investigators believe that at least

eight amino acids serve as transmitter substances in the mammalian central nervous system. (See **Table 3.3.**) The more important of these amino acids — glutamic acid, gamma-aminobutyric acid (GABA), and glycine — are discussed in this section.

Glutamic Acid

Because **glutamic acid (glutamate)** and gamma-amino butyric acid (GABA) are found in very simple organisms, many investigators believe that they are the first neurotransmitters to have evolved. Besides their effects on postsynaptic receptors, they have direct excitatory effects (glutamic acid) and inhibitory effects (GABA) on axons. The presence of direct effects suggests that these substances had a general modulating role even before the evolutionary development of specific receptor molecules.

Glutamic acid is found throughout the brain. Its precursor, α-*ketoglutaric acid,* is available in abundant quantities from the Krebs cycle. Chinese food also provides glutamic acid in the form of monosodium glutamate (MSG), the sodium salt of glutamic acid. It appears to be the principal excitatory neurotransmitter in the brain.

GABA

Gamma-aminobutyric acid (GABA) is produced from glutamic acid by the removal of a carboxyl group through the action of the enzyme **glutamic acid decarboxylase**

TABLE 3.3   The principal amino acid transmitter substances

Excitatory	*Inhibitory*
Aspartic acid	β-alanine
Cysteic acid	Gamma-aminobutyric acid (GABA)
Glutamic acid	Glycine
Homocysteic acid	Taurine

(GAD). GABA is an inhibitory transmitter substance, and it appears to have a widespread distribution throughout the gray matter (cellular areas) of the brain and spinal cord.

GABA has been implicated in a serious hereditary neurological disorder, Huntington's chorea. This disease is characterized by involuntary movements, depression, progressive mental deterioration, and ultimately death. The disease, which apparently results from the degeneration of GABAergic neurons in brain structures concerned with motor control, is discussed in Chapter 8.

Glycine

The amino acid *glycine* appears to be the inhibitory neurotransmitter in the spinal cord and lower portions of the brain. Little is known about its biosynthetic pathway; there are several possible routes, but not enough is known to decide how neurons produce glycine. The bacteria that cause tetanus (lockjaw) release a chemical that blocks the activity of glycine synapses; the removal of the inhibitory effect of these synapses causes muscles to contract continuously.

Peptide Neurotransmitters

Recent studies have discovered that a large variety of *peptides* serve as transmitter substances. Peptides consist of two or more amino acids that are synthesized by the ribosomes according to instructions contained on the chromosomes in the nucleus. Large peptides, containing over 100 amino acids, are called *proteins,* while those that contain between 10 and 100 are called *polypeptides.*

Table 3.4 lists peptides that are believed to be released by neurons. Some of these peptides probably serve as transmitter substances, whereas others serve as neuromodulators (described in the next section). For example, peptides appear to play a role in

T A B L E 3.4 The principal peptide neurotransmitters and neuromodulators

Adrenocorticotropic hormone (ACTH)	Luteinizing hormone releasing hormone (LHRH)
Angiotensin II	Melanocyte-stimulating hormone (MSH)
Angiotensin III	
Cholecystokinin (CCK)	Peptide E
Dynorphin A	Somatostatin
Dynorphin B	Substance P

Endorphins
  β-Endorphin
  α-Neo-endorphin
  β-Neo-endorphin
	Vasoactive intestinal polypeptide

	Vasopressin (also called antidiuretic hormone)

Enkephalins
  [Leu]enkephalin
  [Met]enkephalin	

Note: Several peptides (such as angiotensin and cholecystokinin) were first discovered in other organs; thus, their names do not reflect their function in the brain.

controlling sensitivity to pain, regulating species-typical defensive behaviors, and increasing eating and drinking. I will have more to say about the behavioral effects of several peptides in later chapters. (See **Table 3.4.**)

Recently, experimenters have discovered that many peptides are released in conjunction with a "classical" neurotransmitter (one of the ones I just described). That is, some synaptic vesicles contain not just one compound, but two. We do not understand the reason for this co-release. Some investigators speculate that the peptide serves to regulate the sensitivity of presynaptic or postsynaptic receptors to the neurotransmitter.

Because the synthesis of peptides is complex and must take place in the soma, these chemicals must be delivered to the terminal buttons by axoplasmic flow. Once they are released, they are deactivated by enzymes; they are not returned to the terminal buttons and recycled. All of the peptides that have been studied so far are produced from a small number of precursor molecules. These precursors are large polypeptides that are broken into pieces by special enzymes; a particular neuron manufactures the enzymes that it needs to break the precursor apart. The pieces of the precursor that a particular neuron uses are stored in synaptic vesicles, and the other ones are destroyed.

Research on peptides released by neurons is presently very active. Because the synthesis of these chemicals is controlled by genetic mechanisms, the gene-splicing techniques of microbiologists make it possible to synthesize them in vitro and to test their effects on animals. It is also possible to produce antibodies to a specific peptide, link these antibodies to a dye, inject it into animals' brains, and stain the particular neurons that contain the peptide. Thus, even though peptide-secreting neurons are relatively few in number, techniques are available to localize them precisely.

Neuromodulators

As we saw in the section on autoreceptors, not all receptors in neural membranes are confined to synapses; others are located on the axons, soma, and dendrites. The extrasynaptic receptors that respond to the transmitter substance that a neuron releases are called *autoreceptors.* But other kinds of receptors exist outside of the synapse as well. For example, many of the peptides released by neurons are believed to act on other neurons at a considerable distance from their site of release. The principles of release and receptor activation for these substances are the same as for the "classical" neurotransmitters. The only differences are the distance the chemical travels before it encounters a receptor and the kinds of effects that the activated receptors produce in the cells that contain them.

In a sense, these chemicals act like hormones whose effects are confined to the brain. They are released, diffuse through the extracellular fluid, and are conveyed throughout the brain by blood vessels. When they encounter the appropriate receptors, they activate them and initiate physiological changes in neurons. The nature of these changes is not known, but investigators presume that they include alterations in the synthesis and release of transmitter substances, and perhaps changes in excitability that make the cells more or less responsive to messages received from synapses with other neurons.

Neuromodulators, as these long-distance neurotransmitters are called, presumably regulate various behavioral functions and apparently affect mood as well. For example, a class of tranquilizing drugs called *benzodiazepines,* such as diazepam (Valium) and chlordiazepoxide (Librium), appear to exert their antianxiety effects by stimulating receptors on GABAergic neurons. When these receptors are activated, they increase the sensitivity of the neurons' GABA receptors. Because GABA is an inhibitory transmitter substance, the effect of this increased sensitivity is to increase neural inhibition. Although investigators have not yet identified the chemical the brain secretes that activates these receptors, the existence of these receptors is undoubtedly not coincidental. Presumably, some neurons in the brain of an organism that is under stress secrete a benzodiazepine-like chemical that activates these receptors, thus reducing anxiety that might otherwise interfere with performance of the appropriate behaviors.

The endogenous opiates, peptides that produce effects similar to those of morphine, heroin, and related drugs, constitute an important category of neuromodulators. I will discuss these substances in detail in later chapters.

INTERIM SUMMARY

The nervous system contains a variety of transmitter substances, each of which interacts with a specialized receptor. Those that have received the most study are acetylcholine and the monoamines: dopamine, norepinephrine, and 5-hydroxytryptamine (serotonin). The synthesis of these transmitter substances is controlled by enzymes. Several amino acids also serve as transmitter substances, the most important of which are glutamic acid (glutamate), GABA, and glycine. Glutamate serves as an excitatory transmitter substance while the others serve as inhibitory transmitter substances. Peptide transmitter substances consist of chains of amino acids. Like proteins, peptides are synthesized at the ribosomes according to sequences coded for by the chromosomes.

Transmitter substances affect only the receptors in the vicinity of the synapse. However, some neurons produce and secrete substances that have more widespread effects. These substances, called neuromodulators, alter the excitability of circuits of neurons in distant parts of the brain and affect behavior, mood, and appetite. Pharmacologists have discovered drugs that mimic or block the effects of some of the neuromodulators.

■ PHARMACOLOGY OF SYNAPSES

Investigators have discovered many drugs that affect the production, storage, release, deactivation, or re-uptake of transmitter substances or that stimulate or block postsynaptic receptors. Many of these drugs are used to study the functions of the nervous system, and some are used to treat disorders. Drugs that affect synaptic transmission are classified into two general categories. Drugs that block or inhibit the postsynaptic effects are called *antagonists,* while drugs that facilitate them are called *agonists.* (The Greek word *agon* means "contest." Thus, an *agonist* is one who takes part in the contest.) Some investigators use the word *agonist* to refer only to a drug that directly stimulates neurotransmitter receptors, but I use it here in a more general sense. Figure 3.22 illustrates the ways in which drugs can act as agonists or antagonists.

First, the transmitter substance must be synthesized from its precursors. In some cases, the rate of synthesis and release of a neurotransmitter is increased when a precursor is administered; in these cases the precursor itself serves as an agonist. As we saw, L-DOPA serves as a dopamine agonist. (See step 1, **Figure 3.22.**)

The steps in the synthesis of transmitter substances are controlled by enzymes. Therefore, if a drug inactivates one of these enzymes, it will prevent the transmitter substance from being produced. For example, the drug *α-methyl-p-tyrosine (AMPT)* blocks the enzyme tyrosine hydroxylase and thus prevents synthesis of the catecholamines, dopamine and norepinephrine. Thus, the drug is a catecholamine antagonist. (See step 2, **Figure 3.22.**)

Transmitter substances are stored in synaptic vesicles, which are transported to the presynaptic membrane, where the chemicals are released. One drug, *reserpine,* makes the membrane of monoamine-containing synap-

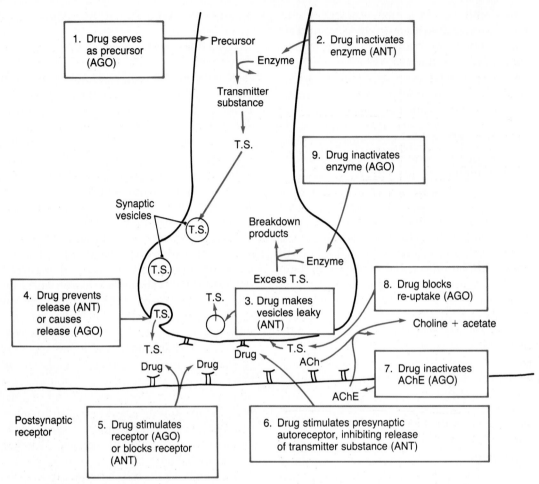

FIGURE 3.22
The most important ways in which drugs can affect synaptic transmission.
AGO = agonist; ANT = antagonist; T.S. = transmitter substance.

tic vesicles become "leaky." The transmitter substances escape into the cytoplasm of the terminal button, where they are destroyed by MAO; hence nothing is released when the vesicles rupture against the presynaptic membrane. Reserpine is a monoamine antagonist. (See step 3, **Figure 3.22.**)

Some drugs act as antagonists by preventing the release of transmitter substances from the terminal button; for example, ***botulinum***

toxin, produced by bacteria that can grow in improperly canned food, prevents the release of ACh. Other drugs act as agonists by stimulating the release of a neurotransmitter. As we saw earlier in this chapter, the venom of the black widow spider causes acetylcholinergic terminal buttons to release ACh. (See step 4, **Figure 3.22.**)

Once the transmitter substance is released, it must stimulate the postsynaptic receptors.

Some drugs serve as agonists by binding with and activating the receptors directly, mimicking the effects of the transmitter substance. For example, ***nicotine*** activates one class of acetylcholine receptor. (Another class is activated by a different drug, ***muscarine.***) Other drugs bind with the postsynaptic receptors but do *not* activate them. Because they occupy the receptors without activating them, they prevent the transmitter substance from exerting its effect, and hence act as antagonists. These drugs are called ***receptor blockers.*** By analogy, a key that fits into a lock but does not turn it prevents it from opening, because the proper key cannot enter the lock so long as it is occupied. (See step **5**, **Figure 3.22.**)

The presynaptic membranes of some neurons possess autoreceptors, which apparently regulate the amount of transmitter substance that is released. Because stimulation of these receptors reduces the release of the transmitter substance, drugs that selectively activate them, but do not activate the postsynaptic receptors, act as antagonists. For example, LSD stimulates serotonergic autoreceptors and thus inhibits serotonin release. As we will see in Chapter 9, the activity of serotonergic terminal buttons suppresses a variety of behaviors, including dreaming. Some investigators believe that LSD and other serotonin antagonists act as hallucinogens because they remove this inhibition, permitting dreamlike activity to occur while a person is awake. (See step 6, **Figure 3.22.**)

The next step after stimulation of the postsynaptic receptor is termination of the postsynaptic potential by enzymatic deactivation or re-uptake of the transmitter substance. A drug that deactivates AChE permits ACh to remain intact longer than usual. Thus, this drug serves as an agonist. An example is ***physostigmine,*** one of a class of drugs called *organophosphates.* Many organophosphates

are used as insecticides. (See step 7, **Figure 3.22.**)

The postsynaptic activity of transmitter substances other than ACh is terminated by active uptake mechanisms in the terminal button. Drugs that block or retard the re-uptake process serve as agonists, because they permit the transmitter substance to remain in the synaptic cleft for a longer time, where it produces a prolonged postsynaptic potential. For example, ***amphetamine*** and ***cocaine*** are potent catecholamine agonists because they retard the re-uptake of these transmitter substances. (See step 8, **Figure 3.22.**)

Certain destructive enzymes are present within the cytoplasm of the terminal button, where they appear to destroy any extra transmitter substance that the cell produces. Drugs that inactivate these enzymes allow excess transmitter substance to be released when the axon fires. An example is ***iproniazid,*** which selectively blocks the particular form of MAO that destroys serotonin; thus it is a serotonin agonist. (See step 9, **Figure 3.22.**)

Many of the drugs that were mentioned in this chapter have been used by neuroscientists to investigate functions of the nervous system. Rather than provide a list, I have included some of the more important drugs in five figures that illustrate acetylcholinergic, noradrenergic, dopaminergic, serotonergic, and GABAergic synapses. These figures may prove useful to you when you encounter a drug later in the text. The format is similar to that of Figure 3.22. Solid lines represent facilitation, dashed lines represent inhibition or blocking. (See **Figures 3.23–3.27.**)

INTERIM SUMMARY

As we have seen in this chapter, the process of synaptic transmission entails the synthesis of the transmitter substance, its storage in synaptic vesi-

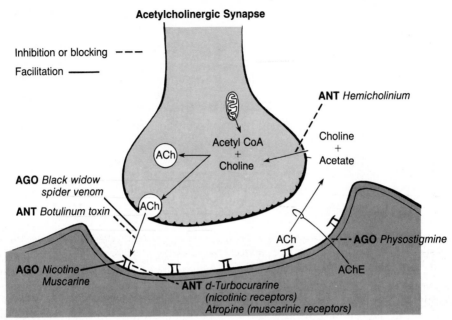

Acetylcholinergic Synapse

Inhibition or blocking — — —

Facilitation ———

ANT *Hemicholinium*

Acetyl CoA
+
Choline

Choline
+
Acetate

ACh

AGO *Black widow
spider venom*

ANT *Botulinum toxin*

ACh

ACh

AGO *Physostigmine*

AGO *Nicotine
Muscarine*

AChE

ANT *d-Turbocurarine
(nicotinic receptors)*
Atropine (muscarinic receptors)

FIGURE 3.23
An acetylcholinergic synapse, with some drugs that can affect its activity.
AGO = agonist; ANT = antagonist.

cles, its release into the synaptic cleft, its interaction with postsynaptic receptors, and the consequent opening of ion channels in the postsynaptic membrane. The effects of the transmitter substance are then terminated by enzymatic deactivation (in the case of acetylcholine) or re-uptake into the terminal button.

Each of the steps necessary for synaptic transmission can be interfered with by drugs, and a few can be stimulated. Thus, drugs can increase the pool of available precursor, block a biosynthetic enzyme, make the synaptic vesicles become leaky, stimulate or block the release of the transmitter substance, stimulate or block postsynaptic receptors, retard re-uptake, or deactivate enzymes that destroy the transmitter substance postsynaptically (acetylcholinesterase) or presynaptically (monoamine oxidase). Drugs have been used to treat neurological and psychiatric disorders, and, as we will see throughout the rest of this book, they have

served as very important tools for investigating the functions of various classes of neurons.

Concluding Remarks

In this chapter, I have described the process of synaptic transmission, including the production, release, and postsynaptic effects of substances thought to serve as neurotransmitters. We have also seen the ways in which drugs can selectively affect the production and activity of these substances. Subsequent chapters describe the ways in which neuroscientists have used drugs to study how the brain controls behavior.

So far, the focus of discussion has been on the properties of individual neurons. We know that perceiving, learning, and behaving depend on the activity of neurons, including the mechanisms de-

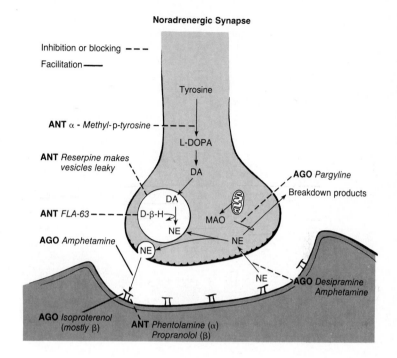

FIGURE 3.24
A norepinephrine-secreting synapse, with some drugs that can affect its activity. AGO = agonist; ANT = antagonist.

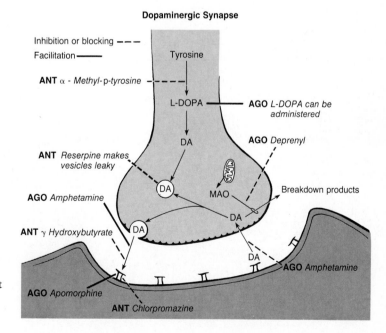

FIGURE 3.25
A dopamine-secreting synapse, with some drugs that can affect its activity. AGO = agonist; ANT = antagonist.

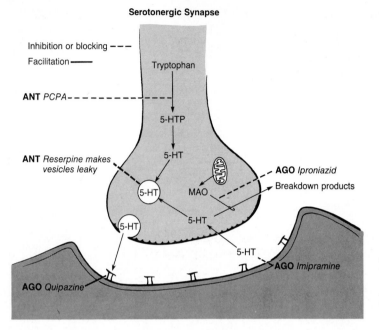

FIGURE 3.26
A serotonin-secreting synapse, with some drugs that can affect its activity. AGO = agonist; ANT = antagonist; PCPA = parachlorophenylalanine.

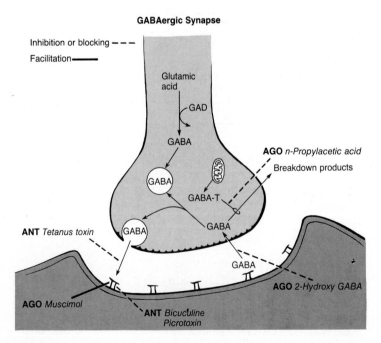

FIGURE 3.27
A GABA-secreting synapse, with some drugs that can affect its activity. AGO = agonist; ANT = antagonist.

scribed in this chapter and in Chapter 2. However, most research on the physiology of behavior deals with the functions of *circuits* of neurons, not with the details of their synaptic communications. Thus, the focus of discussion must shift to the functions of neural circuits. The groundwork for this discussion will be laid in Chapter 4, which describes the anatomy of the nervous and endocrine systems.

NEW TERMS

acetylcholine (ACh) p. 61

acetylcholinesterase (AChE) p. 61

adenosine triphosphate (ATP) p. 57

adenylate cyclase p. 57

agonist p. 77

amphetamine p. 79

AMPT p. 77

antagonist p. 77

autoreceptor p. 61

axoaxonic synapse p. 66

axodendritic synapse p. 66

axonal varicosity p. 71

axoplasmic transport p. 53

axosomatic synapse p. 66

benzodiazepine p. 76

botulinum toxin p. 78

caffeine p. 59

catecholamine p. 71

choline acetyltransferase p. 70

cisterna p. 52

cocaine p. 79

coenzyme A (CoA) p. 70

cyclic adenosine monophosphate (cyclic AMP) p. 57

cyclic nucleotide p. 57

dendrodendritic synapse p. 67

L-3,4-dihydroxyphenylalanine (L-DOPA) p. 71

DOPA decarboxylase p. 71

dopamine (DA) p. 73

dopamine β-hydroxylase p. 72

D_1 dopamine receptor p. 73

D_2 dopamine receptor p. 73

enzymatic deactivation p. 61

epinephrine p. 71

excitatory postsynaptic potential (EPSP) p. 59

gamma-aminobutyric acid (GABA) p. 74

gap junction p. 68

glutamic acid, glutamate p. 74

glutamic acid decarboxylase (GAD) p. 74

glycine p. 75

horseradish peroxidase p. 56

5-HTP decarboxylase p. 73

5-hydroxytryptamine (5-HT) p. 73

5-hydroxytryptophan (5-HTP) p. 73

inhibitory postsynaptic potential (IPSP) p. 59

iproniazid p. 79

α-ketoglutaric acid p. 74

L-DOPA p. 71

lysergic acid diethylamide (LSD) p. 74

α-methyl-p-tyrosine (AMPT) p. 77

monoamine p. 70

monoamine oxidase (MAO) p. 72

muscarine p. 79

muscarinic receptor p. 70

neural integration p. 63

neuromodulator p. 76

neurotransmitter p. 52

neurotransmitter-dependent ion channel p. 57

nicotine p. 79

nicotinic receptor p. 70

α_1 noradrenergic receptor p. 72

α_2 noradrenergic receptor p. 72

β_1 noradrenergic receptor p. 72

β_2 noradrenergic receptor p. 72

norepinephrine (NE) p. 71

Parkinson's disease p. 73

peptide p. 75

phosphodiesterase p. 59

phosphorylation p. 59

physostigmine p. 79

pinocytosis p. 54
postsynaptic membrane p. 52
postsynaptic potential p. 59
postsynaptic receptor p. 57
presynaptic membrane p. 52
protein kinase p. 57
receptor blocker p. 79
reserpine p. 77
re-uptake p. 61
serotonin p. 73

spatial summation p. 65
synaptic cleft p. 52
synaptic vesicle p. 52
temporal summation p. 64
transmitter substance p. 52
tryptophan p. 73
tryptophan hydroxylase p. 73
tyrosine p. 71
tyrosine hydroxylase p. 71

SUGGESTED READINGS

COOPER, J.R., BLOOM, F.E., AND ROTH, R.H. *The Biochemical Basis of Neuropharmacology,* fourth edition. New York: Oxford University Press, 1982.

KANDEL, E.R., AND SCHWARTZ, J.H. *Principles of Neural Science.* New York: Elsevier/North Holland, 1981.

KUFFLER, S.W., AND NICHOLLS, J.G. *From Neuron to Brain,* second edition. Sunderland, Mass.: Sinauer Associates, 1984.

SHEPHERD, G.M. *Neurobiology.* New York: Oxford University Press, 1983.

Structure of the Nervous System and Endocrine System

4

So far, we have studied the structure and function of neurons and their supporting cells and have seen how neurons communicate and interact. Now it is time to begin discussion of some functional systems of the brain, which first requires an acquaintance with the structure of the nervous system.

In this chapter, I will not present a course in neuroanatomy. I would rather present less material and have you learn most of it than present a lot of material and have you try to figure out what is important enough to remember. I will try to keep the number of terms introduced here to a minimum (as you will see, the minimum is still a rather large number). In later chapters dealing with specific behaviors, I will discuss more of the relevant anatomy. With the framework you will receive from this chapter, you should have no trouble learning the new information. This scheme permits me to distribute the anatomical details a bit more (minimizing the probability of neuroanatomical information overload) and allows me to discuss structure and function together. Anatomy is always more interesting (and easier to learn) when it is presented in a functional context.

The nervous system consists of the brain and spinal cord, which make up the *central nervous system (CNS)* and the cranial nerves, spinal nerves, and peripheral ganglia, which constitute the *peripheral nervous system (PNS).* The CNS is encased in bone: the brain is covered by the skull, and the spinal cord resides within the vertebral column.

■ DIRECTIONS AND PLANES OF SECTION

When describing topographical features (hills, roads, rivers, etc.), we need to use terms denoting directions (for example, the road goes north and then turns to the east, as it climbs the hill). Similarly, in describing structures of the nervous system and their interconnecting pathways, we must have available a set of words that define geographical relations. We could use the terms *in front of, above, to the side of,* and so on, but then different terms would have to be used to describe the same set of neural structures in animals like humans, who walk erect and whose spinal cord is oriented at right angles to the ground, and in animals like the rat, whose spinal cord is normally parallel to the ground. To make it easier to describe anatomical directions, a standard set of terms has been adopted.

Directions in the nervous system are normally described relative to the *neuraxis,* an imaginary line drawn through the spinal cord up to the front of the brain. For simplicity's sake, let us consider an animal with a straight neuraxis. Figure 4.1 shows an alligator and a human. This alligator is certainly laid out in a linear fashion; we can draw a straight line that starts between its eyes and continues down the center of its spinal cord. (See **Figure 4.1.**) The front end is *anterior,* and the tail is *posterior.* The terms *rostral* (toward the beak) and *caudal* (toward the tail) are also employed; I will more often use these latter terms. The top of the head and the back are part of the *dorsal* surface, while the *ventral* surface faces the ground. (You could also say, then, that the spinal cord is dorsal to the abdominal surface and ventral to the surface of the animal's back.) These directions are somewhat more complicated in the human; because we stand upright, our neuraxis bends. When describing structures in the human brain, the terms *superior* and *inferior* are often used. The superior structure is above (dorsal to) the inferior one. The frontal views of the alligator and the human illustrate the terms *lateral* and *medial,* toward the side and toward the midline, respectively. (See **Figure 4.1.**)

To see what is in the nervous system, we have to cut it open; to be able to convey information about what we find, we slice it in a

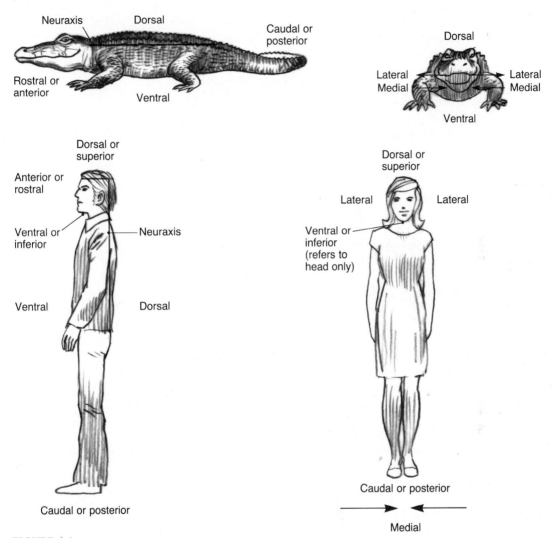

FIGURE 4.1
Side and frontal views of an alligator and a human, showing the terms used to denote anatomical directions.

standard way. Figure 4.2 shows the nervous system of an alligator and that of a human. Again, let us consider the alligator first. We can slice the nervous system in three ways: (1) transversely, like a salami, giving us ***cross sections*** (also known as ***transverse sections, frontal sections,*** or ***coronal sections***); (2) parallel to the ground, giving us

horizontal sections; and (3) perpendicular to the ground and parallel to the neuraxis, giving us ***sagittal sections.*** It is unfortunate that so many terms are used to refer to the first plane of section; I will try to use only two in the text: frontal sections through the brain and cross sections through the spinal cord. (See **Figure 4.2.**)

CNS of Alligator

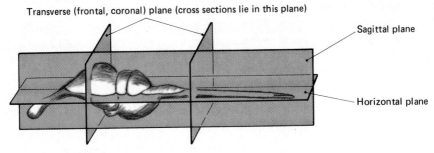

CNS of Human

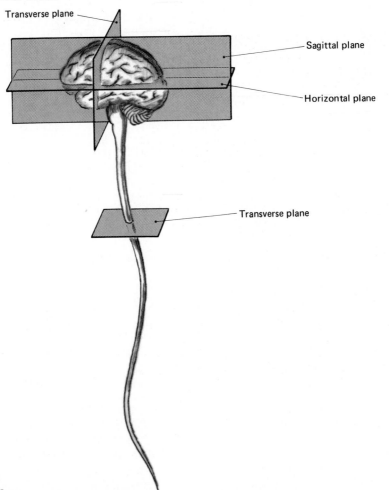

FIGURE 4.2
Planes of section as they pertain to the central nervous system of an alligator and a human.

I should mention one type of section that you will encounter several times in this text: the ***midsagittal section.*** If you slice the brain down the middle, dividing it into its two symmetrical halves, you will have cut it through its ***midsagittal plane.*** If you then look at one half of the brain with its cut surface toward you, you will have a ***midsagittal view.***

■ **GROSS FEATURES OF THE BRAIN**

Figure 4.3 illustrates the relation of the brain and spinal cord to the head and neck of a human. Do not be concerned with unfamiliar labels on this figure; these structures will be described later. (See **Figure 4.3.**) The brain is a large mass of neurons, glia, and other sup-

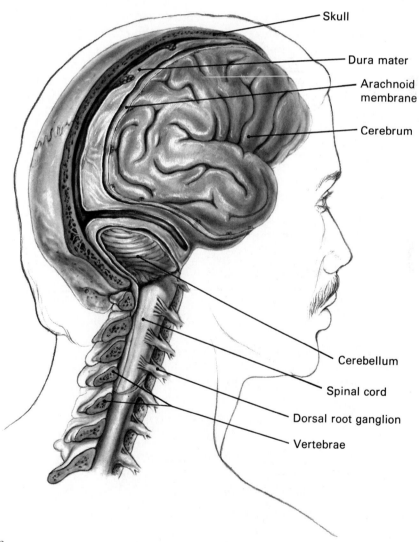

FIGURE 4.3
The relation of the brain and spinal cord to the head and neck.

porting cells. It is the most protected organ of the body, encased in a tough, bony skull and floating in a pool of cerebrospinal fluid. The brain receives a copious supply of blood and is chemically guarded by the blood-brain barrier.

Blood Supply

The brain receives approximately 20 percent of the blood flow from the heart, and it receives it continuously. Other parts of the body, such as the skeletal muscles or digestive system, receive varying quantities of blood depending on their needs, relative to those of other regions. But the brain always receives its share. The brain cannot store its fuel (primarily glucose), nor can it temporar-

ily extract energy without oxygen as the muscles can; therefore, a consistent blood supply is essential. A one-second interruption of the blood flow to the brain uses up much of the dissolved oxygen; a six-second interruption produces unconsciousness. Permanent damage occurs within a few minutes.

Circulation of blood in the body proceeds from arteries to arterioles to capillaries; the capillaries then drain into venules, which collect and become veins. The veins travel back to the heart, where the process begins again. Figure 4.4 shows a bottom view of the brain and its major arterial supply. (The spinal cord has been cut off, as have the left half of the cerebellum and the left temporal lobe.) Two major sets of arteries serve the brain: the *vertebral arteries,* which serve the caudal portion of the brain, and the *internal ca-*

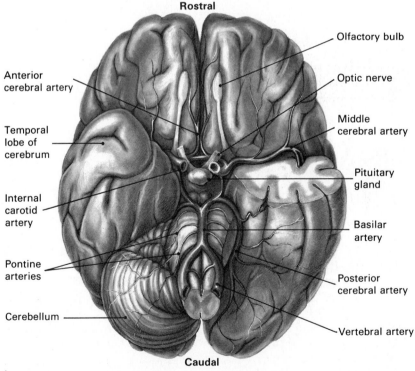

Rostral

Olfactory bulb

Anterior cerebral artery

Optic nerve

Middle cerebral artery

Temporal lobe of cerebrum

Pituitary gland

Internal carotid artery

Basilar artery

Pontine arteries

Posterior cerebral artery

Cerebellum

Vertebral artery

Caudal

FIGURE 4.4
Arterial blood supply to the brain, viewed from beneath.

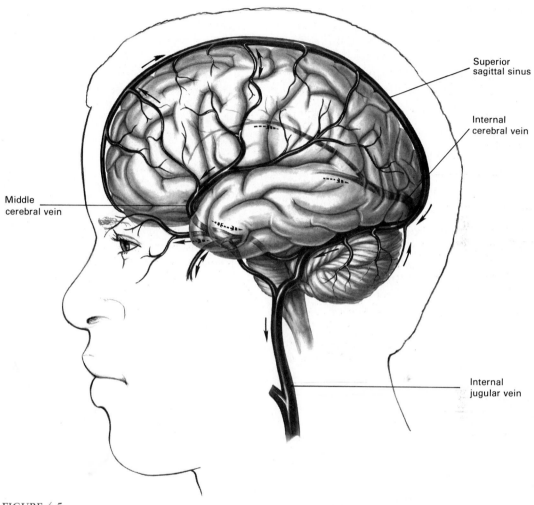

FIGURE 4.5
Venous drainage of the brain.

Superior
sagittal sinus

Internal
cerebral vein

Middle
cerebral vein

Internal
jugular vein

rotid arteries, which serve the rostral portion. (See **Figure 4.4.**) You can see that the blood supply is rather peculiar; major arteries join together and then separate again. Normally, there is little mixing of blood from the rostral and caudal arterial supplies, or, in the case of the rostral supply, from that of the right and left sides of the brain. But if a blood vessel becomes blocked (for example, by a blood clot), blood flow can follow alternative routes, reducing the probability of loss of blood supply and subsequent destruction of brain tissue.

Venous drainage of the brain is shown in Figure 4.5. Major veins, like major arteries, are interconnected, so that blood in some veins can flow in either direction (shown by double-ended arrows), depending on intracerebral pressures in various parts of the brain. (See **Figure 4.5.**)

Meninges

The entire nervous system — brain, spinal cord, cranial and spinal nerves, autonomic ganglia — is covered by tough connective tissue. The protective sheaths around the brain and spinal cord are referred to as the _**meninges.**_ The meninges consist of three layers, as shown in Figure 4.6. The outer layer is thick, tough, and flexible but unstretchable; its name, _**dura mater,**_ means "hard mother." The middle layer of the meninges, the _**arachnoid membrane,**_ gets its name from the web-like appearance of the _**arachnoid trabeculae**_ that protrude from it (_arakhnē_ means "spider"). The arachnoid membrane is soft and spongy and lies beneath the dura mater. Closely attached to the brain and spinal cord, and following every surface convolution, is the _**pia mater**_ ("pious mother"). The smaller surface blood vessels of the brain and spinal cord are contained within this layer. Between the pia mater and arachnoid membrane is a gap called the _**subarachnoid space.**_ This space is filled with _**cerebrospinal fluid (CSF),**_ and through it pass large blood vessels. (See **Figure 4.6.**)

The peripheral nervous system is covered with two layers of meninges. The middle layer (arachnoid membrane), with its associated pool of CSF, covers only the brain and spinal cord. Outside the CNS, the outer and inner layers (dura mater and pia mater) fuse and form a sheath that covers the spinal and cranial nerves and the autonomic ganglia.

In the first edition of this book, I said that I did not know why the outer and inner layers of the meninges were referred to as "mothers." I received a letter from medical historians at the Department of Anatomy at UCLA that explained the name. (Sometimes it pays to proclaim one's ignorance.) A tenth-century Persian physician, Ali ibn Abbas, used the Arabic term _al umm_ to refer to the meninges. The term literally means "mother" but was used to designate any swaddling material, because Arabic lacked a specific term for the word _membrane._ The tough outer membrane was called _al umm al djāfiya,_ and the soft inner one was called _al umm al rigīga._ When the writings of Ali ibn Abbas were translated into Latin during the eleventh century, the translator, who was probably not familiar with the structure of the meninges, made a literal translation of _al umm._ He referred to the membranes as the "hard mother" and the "pious mother" (_pious_ in the sense of "delicate"), rather than using a more appropriate Latin word.

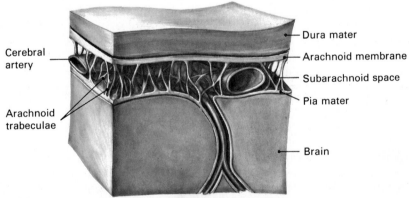

FIGURE 4.6
The meninges: dura mater, arachnoid membrane, and pia mater.

The Ventricular System and Production of CSF

The brain is very soft and jellylike. The considerable weight of a human brain (approximately 1400 gm), along with its delicate construction, necessitates that it be protected from shock. A human brain cannot even support its own weight well; it is difficult to remove and handle a fresh brain from a recently deceased human without damaging it.

Fortunately, the intact brain within a living human is well protected. It floats in a bath of CSF contained within the subarachnoid space. Because the brain is completely immersed in liquid, its net weight is reduced to approximately 80 gm; thus, pressure on the base of the brain is considerably diminished. The CSF surrounding the brain and spinal cord also reduces the shock to the central nervous system that would be caused by sudden head movement. Before the advent of the CAT scanner (described in Chapter 5), a particular diagnostic procedure required the removal of CSF from the ventricles. After the fluid was removed, people would experience painful headaches whenever they moved their heads. These headaches attest to the value of CSF as a shock-absorbing medium. (Fresh CSF is subsequently produced, and the headaches disappear.)

The brain contains a series of hollow, interconnected chambers that are filled with CSF. These chambers, known as *ventricles,* are connected with the subarachnoid space by means of small openings *(foramens),* and they are also continuous with the narrow, tubelike *central canal* of the spinal cord. (See **Figure 4.7.**) The largest chamber is the paired set of *lateral ventricles.* The lateral ventricles are connected by the *foramen of Monro* to the *third ventricle.* The third ventricle is located at the midline of the brain; it is a single structure, and its walls divide the local region of the brain into symmetrical halves. A bridge of neural tissue (the *massa intermedia*) crosses through the middle of the third ventricle. The *cerebral aqueduct,* a long tube, connects the third ventricle to the *fourth ventricle,* which connects at its caudal end with the central canal of the spinal cord. The lateral ventricles constitute the first and second ventricles, but they are never referred to as such. (See **Figure 4.7.**)

Cerebrospinal fluid is manufactured by a special vascular structure called the *choroid plexus,* which protrudes into each of the ventricles and produces CSF from blood plasma. The CSF is produced continuously; the total volume of CSF is approximately 125 ml, and the half-life (the time it takes for half of the CSF present in the ventricular system to be replaced by fresh fluid) is about three hours. Therefore, several times this amount is produced by the choroid plexus each day. The continuous production of CSF means that there must be a mechanism for its removal; Figure 4.8 illustrates the production, circulation, and reabsorption of CSF. (See **Figure 4.8.**)

The illustration shows a slightly rotated midsagittal view of the central nervous system, so that both lateral ventricles, one located on each side of the brain, cannot be shown. (To visualize the lateral ventricles, refer back to Figure 4.7.) (See **Figures 4.7 and 4.8.**) The CSF is produced by the choroid plexus of the lateral ventricles, and it flows through the foramen of Monro into the third ventricle. More CSF is produced in this ventricle, and it then flows through the cerebral aqueduct to the fourth ventricle, where still more CSF is produced. The CSF leaves the fourth ventricle via the *foramen of Magendie* and the *foramens of Luschka* and collects in the subarachnoid space surrounding the brain. All CSF thus flows into the subarachnoid space around the central nervous system, where it is reabsorbed into the blood supply through the *arachnoid granula-*

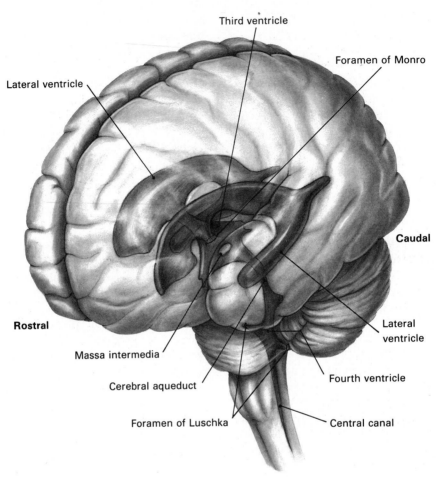

Third ventricle

Foramen of Monro

Lateral ventricle

Caudal

Rostral

Lateral
ventricle

Massa intermedia

Fourth ventricle

Cerebral aqueduct

Foramen of Luschka

Central canal

FIGURE 4.7
The ventricular system of the brain.

tions. These pouch-shaped structures protrude into the ***superior sagittal sinus,*** a
blood vessel that drains into the veins serving
the brain. (See **insert, Figure 4.8.**)

Figure 4.8 also illustrates a fold of dura
mater, the ***tentorium,*** which separates the
cerebellum from the overlying cerebrum.
(See **Figure 4.8.**) This tough sheet of connective tissue extends to the top of the brain
stem, leaving an opening (the ***tentorial
notch***) through which the brain stem passes.
Another fold of dura mater, called the ***falx
cerebri*** (*falx* means ''sickle''), protrudes

down between the dorsal parts of the cerebral
hemispheres. Swelling of the brain from a
tumor or an injury to the head can cause the
brain to ***herniate*** past these folds of dura
mater, causing serious brain damage. One
side of the brain can squeeze underneath the
falx cerebri, or the brain stem can squeeze
through the tentorial notch. (See **Figure
4.9.**)

The meninges, skull, and vertebral column
encase the CNS in a rigid container of fixed
volume. This situation means that any growth
in the mass of the brain must result in dis-

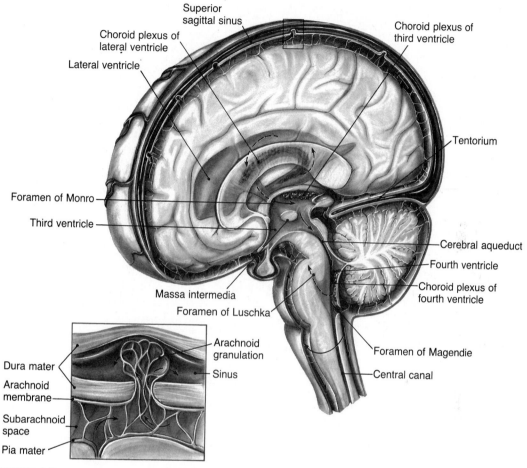

FIGURE 4.8

Production, circulation, and reabsorption of cerebrospinal fluid.

placement of the fluid contents of the container. Hence, growth of a brain tumor, depending on its location, will often deform the walls of the ventricular system, as the invading mass takes up volume previously occupied by CSF. (It is quite fortunate that these hollow ventricles exist; the only other fluid-filled spaces are the blood vessels, which would be constricted by a growing tumor if there were no ventricles in the brain.)

Occasionally, the flow of CSF is interrupted at some point in its route of passage. For example, the cerebral aqueduct may be blocked by a tumor. This occlusion results in greatly increased pressure within the ventricles, because the choroid plexus continues to produce CSF. The walls of the ventricles then expand and produce a condition known as *hydrocephalus* (literally, "water-head"). If the obstruction remains, and if nothing is done to reverse the increased intracerebral pressure, blood vessels will be occluded, and permanent — perhaps fatal — brain damage will occur. The optic nerves, serving the eyes, are covered with meningeal layers, including the flexible but unstretchable dura mater. In-

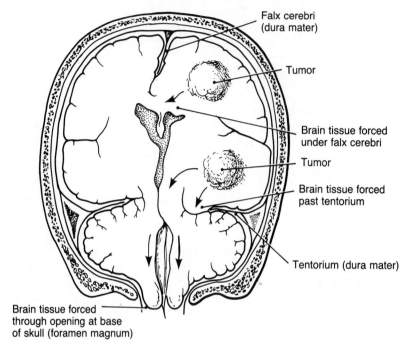

FIGURE 4.9
Swelling of part of the brain can cause herniation of brain tissue under the
falx cerebri or tentorial notch or through the foramen magnum, causing
serious damage.

creased intracerebral pressure is thus transmitted through the contents of the optic
nerve, in the way that water pressure can be
transmitted through a hose. The pressure
causes the **optic disk** (the exit point of the
axons that leave the eye and join the optic
nerve) to bulge forward into the fluid cavity
of the eye. Physicians can detect this bulging
by examining the back of the eye with an
ophthalmoscope.

■ THE MAJOR PARTS OF THE BRAIN

The major divisions of the brain are the **forebrain, midbrain,** and **hindbrain.** These
areas are further subdivided; Table 4.1
presents these subdivisions, along with the

principal structures found in each region.
(See **Table 4.1.**)

Structures of the Forebrain

Telencephalon
The **telencephalon** ("end brain") includes
most of the two symmetrical cerebral hemispheres that comprise the cerebrum. The cerebral hemispheres are covered by the cerebral cortex and contain the basal ganglia and
the limbic system. The latter two sets of structures are primarily located within the deep,
or **subcortical,** portions of the brain.

    Cerebral Cortex. *Cortex* means "bark,"
and the **cerebral cortex** surrounds the cere-

TABLE 4.1 Anatomical subdivisions of the brain

Major Division	Subdivision	Principal Structures
Forebrain	Telencephalon	Cerebral cortex Basal ganglia Limbic system
	Diencephalon	Thalamus Hypothalamus
Midbrain	Mesencephalon	Tectum Tegmentum
Hindbrain	Metencephalon	Cerebellum Pons
	Myelencephalon	Medulla oblongata

bral hemispheres like the bark of a tree. In humans, the cerebral cortex is greatly convoluted; these convolutions, consisting of *sulci* (small grooves), *fissures* (large grooves), and *gyri* (bulges between adjacent sulci or fissures), greatly enlarge the surface area of the cortex, compared with a smooth brain of the same size. The cerebral cortex consists mostly of glia and the cell bodies, dendrites, and interconnecting axons of neurons. Because cells predominate, giving the cerebral cortex a grayish brown appearance, it is referred to as *gray matter*. Beneath the cerebral cortex run millions of axons that connect the neurons of the cerebral cortex with those located elsewhere in the brain. The large concentration of myelin gives this tissue an opaque white appearance — hence the term *white matter*.

The surface of the cerebral hemispheres is divided into four lobes, named after the bones of the skull that overlie them. The *frontal, parietal, temporal,* and *occipital lobes* are visible on the lateral surface and are shown in Figure 4.10. The *central sulcus* divides the frontal lobe from the parietal lobe, and the *lateral fissure* divides the temporal lobe from the overlying frontal and parietal lobes. (See **Figure 4.10.**)

The midsagittal view in Figure 4.11 shows the inner cortical surface of the right cerebral hemisphere. The cerebral cortex that covers most of the surface of the cerebral hemispheres is called the *neocortex* (because it is of relatively recent phylogenetic origin). Another form of cerebral cortex, the *limbic cortex,* is located around the edge of the cerebral hemispheres (*limbus* means "border"). The *cingulate gyrus,* an important region of the limbic cortex, can be seen in this figure. (See **Figure 4.11.**)

Figure 4.11 also shows the *corpus callosum,* which is the largest *commissure* (cross-hemisphere connection) in the brain. The corpus callosum consists of axons that connect the cortex of the two cerebral hemispheres. The axons unite *homotopic,* or geographically similar, regions (*homo* means "same"; *topos* means "place"). In order to prepare a midsagittal view of the brain, one must slice through the middle of the corpus callosum. The *calcarine fissure* ("spur shaped") can be seen on the medial surface of the occipital lobe. (See **Figure 4.11.**)

The actual appearance of part of the corpus callosum is shown in Figure 4.12. Some of the cerebral cortex has been dissected away to reveal bundles of fibers that interconnect homotopic regions. A fine sheet of gray matter (nerve cell bodies) called the indusium griseum ("gray tunic") covers the medial part of the corpus callosum. (See **Figure 4.12.**)

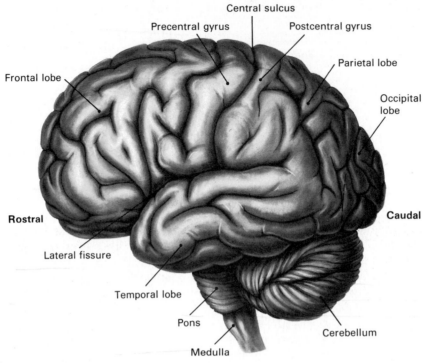

FIGURE 4.10
A lateral view of the left side of the human brain.

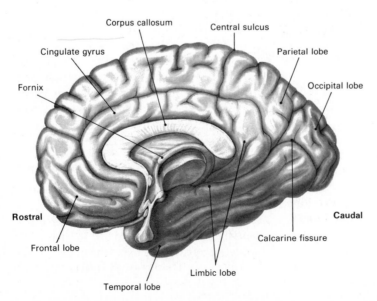

FIGURE 4.11
A midsagittal view of the
human brain, showing the
right hemisphere.

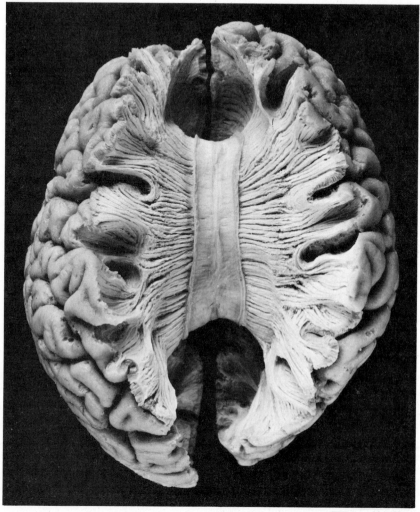

FIGURE 4.12
A dorsal view of a human brain, showing the appearance of the corpus
callosum. (From Gluhbegovic, N., and Williams, T.H. *The Human Brain:
A Photographic Atlas.* Hagerstown, Md.: Harper & Row, 1980.)

The frontal lobes are specialized for the planning, execution, and control of movements. The ***primary motor cortex,*** immediately rostral to the central sulcus, contains neurons that participate in the control of movement. (See **Figure 4.13.**) If an experimenter places a wire on the surface of the primary motor cortex and stimulates the neurons there with a weak electric shock, the current will cause movement of a particular part of the body. Moving the wire to a different spot causes a different part of the body to move.

The posterior lobes of the brain (the parietal, temporal, and occipital lobes) are specialized for perception. The ***primary somatosensory cortex*** lies immediately caudal to the central sulcus, right behind the primary

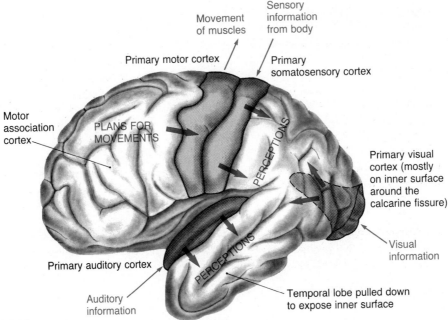

FIGURE 4.13

The primary sensory and motor areas of the neocortex communicate with the association areas.

motor cortex. This region of cerebral cortex receives information about the somatosenses ("body senses": touch, pressure, temperature, and pain). The ***primary visual cortex*** lies at the back of the occipital lobes along the calcarine fissure, mostly hidden between the two cerebral hemispheres. As its name implies, it receives visual information. The ***primary auditory cortex*** lies in the temporal lobes, mostly hidden in the lateral fissure. (See **Figure 4.13.**)

The rest of the neocortex is referred to as ***association cortex.*** The association cortex in the frontal lobes is involved in the planning of movements; thus, neurons there control the activity of those in the primary motor cortex, which in turn control muscular movements. The association cortex in the posterior lobes receives information from the primary sensory areas and is involved in perception and memories. The primary somatosensory cortex sends information to the somatosen-

sory association cortex, the primary visual cortex sends information to the visual association cortex, and the primary auditory cortex sends information to the auditory association cortex. (See **Figure 4.13.**)

If people sustain damage to the somatosensory association cortex, their deficits are related to somatosensation and to the environment in general; for example, they may have difficulty perceiving the shapes of objects that they can touch but not see, they may be unable to name parts of their bodies, or they may have trouble drawing maps or following them. If people sustain damage to the visual association cortex they will not become blind, but they may be unable to recognize objects by sight, although they can often recognize them if they feel them with their hands. If people sustain damage to the auditory association cortex, they may have difficulty perceiving speech or even producing meaningful speech of their own. If people sustain damage to regions of the association cortex at the junction of the three posterior lobes, where the somatosensory, visual, and auditory functions overlap, they may have difficulty reading or writing.

Limbic System. The *limbic system* consists of a set of interconnected structures including several regions of the limbic cortex, the *hippocampal formation* (often referred to as the *hippocampus*), the *amygdaloid complex* (usually called the *amygdala*), the *septum,* the *anterior thalamic nuclei,* and the *mammillary body.* (The latter two structures are actually part of the diencephalon, not the telencephalon, but they are generally considered to be part of the limbic system.)

Figure 4.14 illustrates these structures and their interconnections. An important bundle of axons, the *fornix* ("arch"), connects the hippocampus with both the anterior thalamic nuclei and the mammillary bodies. (See **Figure 4.14.**) The limbic system is involved in emotional behavior, motivation, and learning; details of its structure and function will be discussed in later chapters.

Basal Ganglia. The *basal ganglia* (the *globus pallidus, caudate nucleus,* and *putamen*) are shown in Figure 4.15. (See **Figure 4.15.**) The basal ganglia are an important part of the motor system (described in more detail in Chapter 8). For example, Parkinson's disease is characterized by degeneration

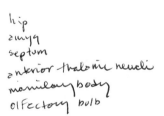

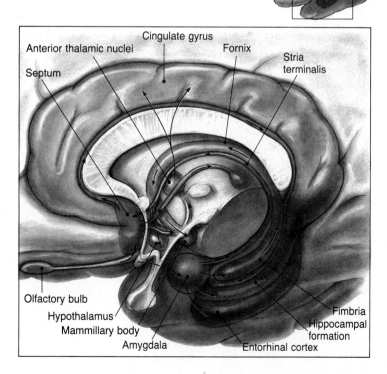

FIGURE 4.14
A schematic, simplified drawing of the limbic system.

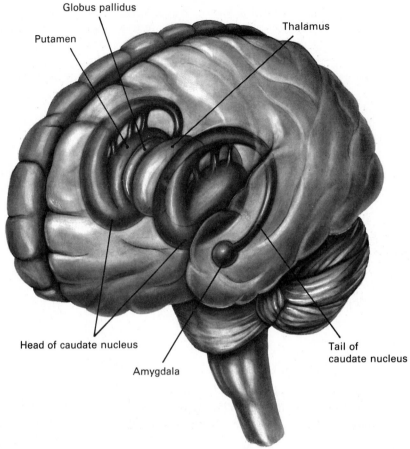

FIGURE 4.15
The location of the basal ganglia in a human brain.

of dopaminergic cells that send axons to the caudate nucleus. As we will see in Chapter 14, the basal ganglia may play a role in learning.

The amygdala ("almond-shaped structure"), considered by some anatomists to be part of the basal ganglia, is located within the temporal lobe near its rostral tip. As we already saw, the amygdala is an important component of the limbic system. As we will see in later chapters, destruction of various parts of the amygdala inhibits the performance of defensive responses and affects reproductive behaviors.

Diencephalon

The ***diencephalon*** ("interbrain") is situated between the telencephalon and the midbrain. (See **Figure 4.16.**) Its two most important structures are the thalamus and hypothalamus.

Thalamus. The ***thalamus*** (from the Greek *thalamos,* "inner chamber") is located in the dorsal part of the diencephalon. It is a large structure with two lobes, connected by a bridge of gray matter called the *massa intermedia,* which pierces the middle of the third ventricle. (You already encountered the massa intermedia in Figure 4.7. See **Figure 4.16.**) The massa intermedia is probably not an important structure, because it is absent in the brains of some apparently normal people.

Most neural input to the cerebral cortex is received from the thalamus; indeed, much of the cortical surface can be divided into regions that receive projections from specific parts of the thalamus. ***Projection fibers*** are sets of axons that arise from cell bodies located in one region of the brain and synapse on neurons located within another region (that is, they project to these regions). Figure 4.17 shows the appearance of some of the projection fibers from the thalamus to the cerebral cortex. Even a gross dissection such as this one reveals how massive the thalamocortical projections are. (See **Figure 4.17.**)

The thalamus is divided into a number of ***nuclei,*** which are groups of neurons of similar shape. Some of these nuclei ***(sensory relay nuclei)*** receive sensory information from the terminal buttons of incoming axons. The neurons in these nuclei then relay the sensory information to specific sensory projection areas of the cerebral cortex. For example, the ***lateral geniculate nucleus*** projects to the primary visual cortex, the ***medial geniculate nucleus*** projects to the primary auditory cortex, and the ***ventral posterior nucleus*** projects to the primary somatosensory cortex. (See **Figure 4.18.**)

Other thalamic nuclei project to specific regions of the cerebral cortex, but they do not relay primary sensory information. For example, the ***ventrolateral nucleus*** receives information from the cerebellum and projects to the primary motor cortex, and the anterior

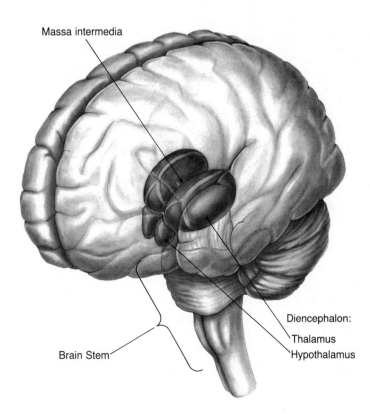

FIGURE 4.16
The location of the human diencephalon, which includes the thalamus and hypothalamus.

Massa intermedia

Diencephalon:
Thalamus
Hypothalamus

Brain Stem

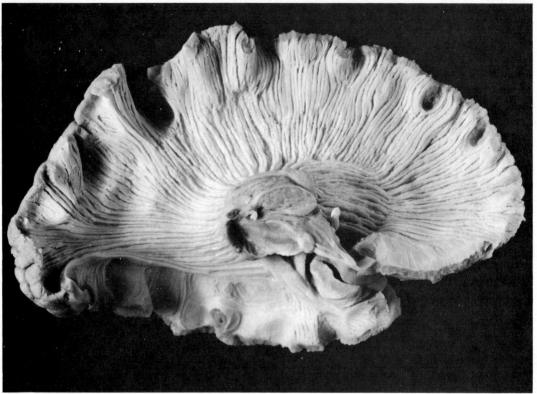

FIGURE 4.17

A lateral view of a partially dissected human brain, showing projection
fibers from the thalamus to the neocortex. (From Gluhbegovic, N., and
Williams, T.H. *The Human Brain: A Photographic Atlas*. Hagerstown,
Md.: Harper & Row, 1980.)

nuclei (already mentioned in the section on
the limbic system) receive information from
the mammillary bodies and project to the cingulate gyrus. Other thalamic nuclei (for example, the *midline nuclei* and the *reticular
nuclei*) project diffusely to widespread regions of the cerebral cortex and to other thalamic nuclei. (See **Figure 4.18.**)

Hypothalamus. The **hypothalamus** lies at
the base of the brain, under the thalamus. Although it is a relatively small structure, it is an
important one. It controls the autonomic nervous system and the endocrine system and organizes behaviors related to survival of the

species — the so-called four F's: fighting,
feeding, fleeing, and mating.

The hypothalamus is situated on both sides
of the inferior portion of the third ventricle.
As its name implies, it is located beneath the
thalamus. The hypothalamus is a very complex structure, containing many nuclei and
fiber tracts. Figure 4.19 indicates its location
and size. Note that the pituitary gland is attached to the base of the hypothalamus via the
pituitary stalk. Just in front of the pituitary
stalk is the *optic chiasm,* the place where
half of the axons in the optic nerves (from the
eyes) cross from one side of the brain to the
other. Above and in front of the optic chiasm

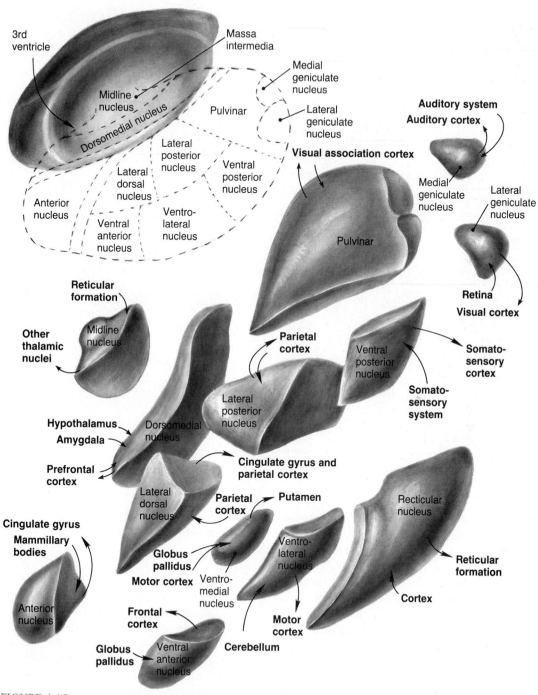

FIGURE 4.18

The thalamus, showing the location and principal inputs and outputs of individual thalamic nuclei. Interconnections also exist among many thalamic nuclei.

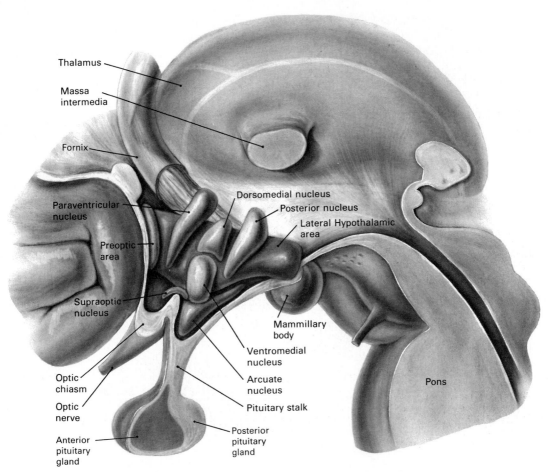

FIGURE 4.19
The regions of the hypothalamus in a human brain.

(and not technically part of the hypothalamus) is an important region called the **preoptic area.** Neurons in the preoptic area play a role in reproductive behaviors. (See **Figure 4.19.**) The role of the hypothalamus in the control of the four F's (and other behaviors, such as drinking and sleeping) will be considered in several chapters later in this book.

Structures of the Midbrain (Mesencephalon)

The **mesencephalon,** or midbrain, is the most rostral portion of the **brain stem** (which also includes the pons and medulla oblongata, discussed later). The mesencephalon consists of two major parts: the tectum and the tegmentum.

Tectum

The **tectum** ("roof") is located in the dorsal portion of the mesencephalon. Its principal structures are the **superior colliculi** and **inferior colliculi** (collectively referred to as the **corpora quadrigemina,** or "quadruplet bodies"). Figure 4.20 illustrates a dorsal and ventral view of the brain stem, with the overlying cerebrum and cerebellum removed.

The four bumps on the dorsal surface are the superior and inferior colliculi (*colliculus* means "small hill"). (See **Figure 4.20.**) The inferior colliculi are a part of the auditory system. As you will see in Chapter 7, all fibers conveying auditory information synapse in or pass through the inferior colliculi on the way to the medial geniculate nucleus and primary auditory cortex. The superior colliculi are part of the visual system. In mammals they are primarily involved in visual reflexes and reactions to moving stimuli.

Tegmentum

The **tegmentum** ("covering") consists of the portion of the mesencephalon beneath the tectum. It includes the rostral end of the reticular formation, several nuclei controlling eye movements, the periaqueductal gray matter, the red nucleus, the substantia nigra, and the ventral tegmental area. (See **Figure 4.21.**)

The **reticular formation** is a large structure consisting of many nuclei (over ninety in all). It is also characterized by a diffuse, interconnected network of neurons with complex

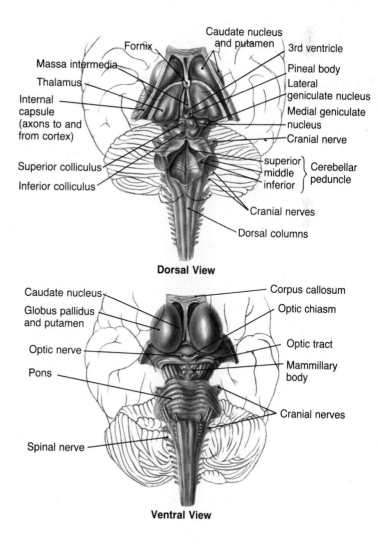

Dorsal View

Ventral View

FIGURE 4.20
Two views of the human brain stem.

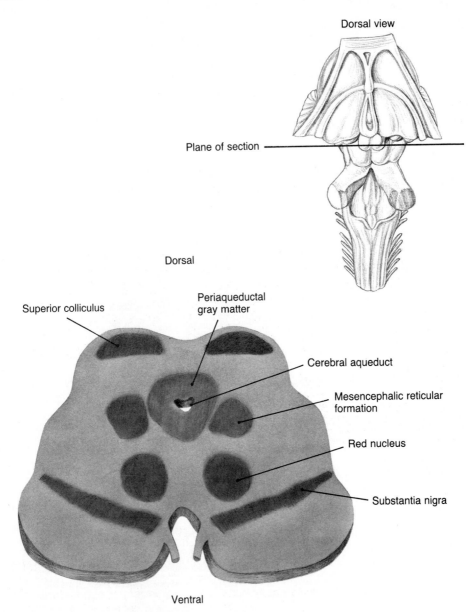

FIGURE 4.21
A cross section through the human tegmentum.

dendritic and axonal processes. (Indeed, *reticulum* means "little net"; early anatomists were struck by the netlike appearance of the reticular formation.) The reticular formation occupies the core of the brain stem, from the lower border of the medulla to the upper border of the midbrain. The reticular formation receives sensory information by means of various pathways and projects axons to the cerebral cortex, thalamus, and spinal cord. It plays a role in sleep and arousal, attention, muscle tonus, movement, and various vital reflexes. Some of these functions will be described more fully in later chapters.

The ***periaqueductal gray matter*** is so called because it consists mostly of cell bodies of neurons ("gray matter," as contrasted with the "white matter" of axon bundles) that surround the cerebral aqueduct as it travels from the third to the fourth ventricle. The opening of the cerebral aqueduct lies just posterior to the corpora quadrigemina. The periaqueductal gray matter contains neural circuits that control sequences of movements that constitute species-typical behaviors, such as fighting and mating. As we will see in Chapter 7, opiates decrease an organism's sensitivity to pain by stimulating neurons located in this region.

The ***red nucleus*** and ***substantia nigra*** ("black substance") are important components of the motor system. A bundle of axons that arises from the red nucleus constitutes one of the two major fiber systems that bring motor information from the brain to the spinal cord. The substantia nigra contains dopamine-secreting neurons that project to the caudate nucleus. As we have seen, degeneration of these neurons causes Parkinson's dis-

ease. The ***ventral tegmental area*** also contains dopamine-secreting neurons; these neurons project to the basal forebrain and cortex, and have been implicated in learning (Chapter 13) and schizophrenia (Chapter 17).

Structures of the Hindbrain

Metencephalon

The ***metencephalon*** ("behind-brain") consists of the pons and the cerebellum.

Cerebellum. The ***cerebellum*** ("little brain") resembles a miniature version of the cerebrum. It is covered by ***cerebellar cortex*** and has a set of ***deep cerebellar nuclei*** that project to its cortex and receive projections from it, just as the thalamic nuclei connect with the cerebral cortex. Figure 4.22 shows the brain stem with the cerebellum dissected away on one side to illustrate the superior, middle, and inferior ***cerebellar peduncles*** ("little feet"), bundles of white matter that connect the cerebellum to the pons. (See **Figure 4.22.**)

Damage to the cerebellum impairs standing, walking, or performance of coordinated movements. (A virtuoso pianist or other per-

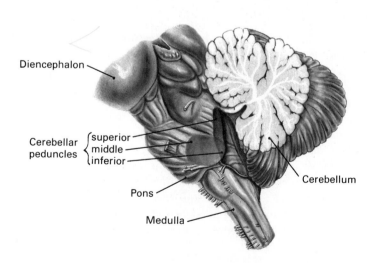

FIGURE 4.22
The attachment of the cerebellum to the human brain stem. Only the right cerebellar hemisphere is shown; the left has been removed to show the cerebellar peduncles.

Diencephalon

Cerebellar peduncles { superior middle inferior

Cerebellum

Pons

Medulla

forming musician owes much to his or her cerebellum.) The cerebellum receives visual, auditory, vestibular, and somatosensory information, and it also receives information about individual muscular movements being directed by the brain. The cerebellum integrates this information and modifies the motor outflow, exerting a coordinating and smoothing effect on the movements. Cerebellar damage results in jerky, poorly coordinated, exaggerated movements; extensive cerebellar damage makes it impossible even to stand. As we will see in Chapter 14, recent studies have shown that the cerebellum is involved in learning.

Pons. The *pons,* a large bulge in the brain stem, lies between the mesencephalon and medulla oblongata, immediately ventral to the cerebellum. (*Pons* means "bridge," but it does not really look like one. Refer back to **Figure 4.22.**) The pons contains, in its core, a portion of the reticular formation, including some nuclei that appear to be important in sleep and arousal. It also contains nuclei that project to the cerebellum, as well as several cranial nerve nuclei that serve the head and facial region.

Myelencephalon: The Medulla
The main component of the *myelencephalon* is the *medulla oblongata* (literally, "oblong marrow"), usually just called the *medulla.* This structure is the most caudal portion of the brain stem; its lower border is the rostral end of the spinal cord. The medulla contains part of the reticular formation, including nuclei that control vital functions such as regulation of the cardiovascular system, respiration, and skeletal muscle tonus. It also contains nuclei that relay somatosensory information from the spinal cord to the thalamus. Several cranial nerve nuclei are located there, as well.

■ SPINAL CORD

The spinal cord is a roughly cylindrical structure, containing a bulge in its lower middle region and gradually tapering to a point in the lower back region. The place where the spinal cord bulges contains neurons that control movements of the arms and hands, which accounts for the increased size. The principal function of the spinal cord is to distribute motor fibers to the effector organs of the body (glands and muscles) and to collect somatosensory information to be passed on to the brain. The spinal cord also has a certain degree of autonomy from the brain; various reflexive control circuits (some of which are described in Chapter 8) are located there.

The spinal cord is protected by the vertebral column, which is composed of twenty-four individual vertebrae of the *cervical, thoracic,* and *lumbar* regions, and the fused vertebrae making up the *sacral* and *coccygeal* portions of the column. The spinal cord passes through a hole in each of the vertebrae (the *spinal foramens*). Figure 4.23 illustrates the divisions and structures of the spinal cord and vertebral column. Note that the spinal cord is only about two thirds as long as the vertebral column; the rest of the space is filled by a mass of *spinal roots* composing the *cauda equina* ("mare's tail"). (See **Figure 4.23.**)

Early in embryological development, the vertebral column and spinal cord are of the same length. As development progresses, the vertebral column grows faster than the spinal cord. This differential growth rate causes the spinal roots to be displaced downward; the most caudal roots travel the farthest before they emerge through openings between the vertebrae *(intervertebral foramens)* and thus compose the cauda equina. To produce the *caudal block* sometimes used in pelvic surgery or childbirth, a local anesthetic can be injected into the CSF contained

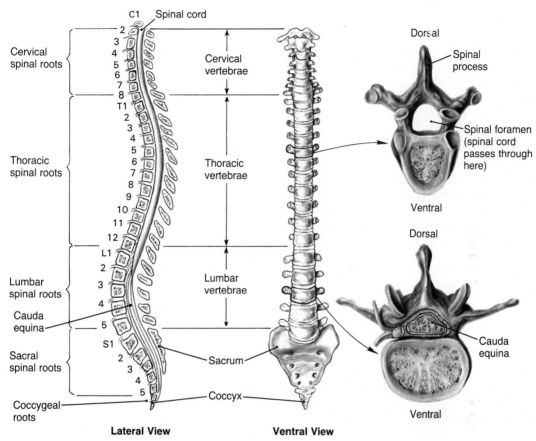

C1 Spinal cord

Cervical
spinal roots

Cervical
vertebrae

Thoracic
spinal roots

Thoracic
vertebrae

Lumbar
spinal roots

Lumbar
vertebrae

Cauda
equina

Sacral
spinal roots

Sacrum

Coccygeal
roots

Coccyx

Lateral View   **Ventral View**

Dorsal
Spinal
process

Spinal foramen
(spinal cord
passes through
here)

Ventral

Dorsal

Cauda
equina

Ventral

FIGURE 4.23

The human spinal column, with details showing the anatomy of the
vertebrae and the relation between the spinal cord and spinal column.

within the sac of dura mater surrounding the cauda equina. The drug blocks conduction in the axons of the cauda equina.

Small bundles of fibers (*fila,* or "threads") emerge from the spinal cord in two straight lines along its dorsolateral and ventrolateral surfaces. Groups of these fila fuse together and become the thirty-one paired sets of ***dorsal roots*** and ***ventral roots.*** As we will see, the dorsal roots contain axons that convey sensory information to the CNS, and the ventral roots contain axons that convey motor information to muscles and

glands. The dorsal and ventral roots join together as they pass through the intervertebral foramens and become spinal nerves. Figure 4.24 illustrates a cross section of the spinal column taken between two adjacent vertebrae, showing the junction of the dorsal and ventral roots in the intervertebral foramens. (See **Figure 4.24.**)

The spinal cord, like the brain, consists of white matter and gray matter. Unlike the brain, its white matter (consisting of ascending and descending bundles of myelinated axons) is on the outside; the gray matter

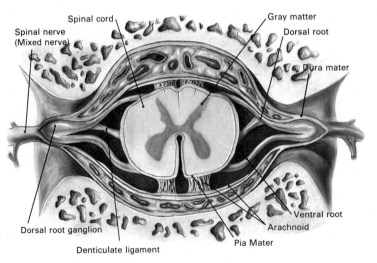

FIGURE 4.24
A cross section through a vertebra, showing the spinal cord, dorsal and ventral roots, and spinal nerves.

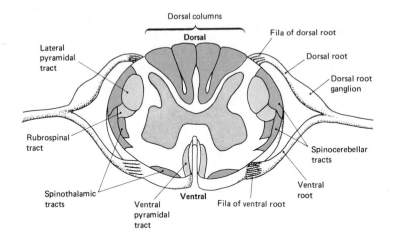

FIGURE 4.25
A cross section through the spinal cord, showing the principal ascending (somatosensory) tracts in dark blue and the principal descending (motor) tracts in light blue.

(mostly neural cell bodies and short, unmyelinated axons) is on the inside. Figure 4.25 shows a cross section through the spinal cord. Ascending tracts are shown in dark gray; descending tracts, in light gray. (See **Figure 4.25.**) The ascending (somatosensory) tracts are described in a section on somatosenses in Chapter 7. Similarly, the descending (motor) tracts will be described in Chapter 8.

■ PERIPHERAL NERVOUS SYSTEM

The brain and spinal cord communicate with the skeletal muscles and sensory systems of the rest of the body via the cranial nerves and spinal nerves. Smooth muscles, cardiac muscle, and many glands are regulated by the autonomic nervous system, a part of the peripheral nervous system consisting of offshoots of spinal and cranial nerves and the associated autonomic ganglia.

Spinal Nerves

The ***spinal nerves*** begin at the junction of the dorsal and ventral roots of the spinal cord. The nerves leave the vertebral column and travel, branching repeatedly as they go, to the muscles or sensory receptors they innervate. Branches of spinal nerves often follow blood vessels, especially those branches that innervate skeletal muscles. Figure 4.26 is a dorsal view of a human, showing a few branches of the spinal nerves. Note that the spinal nerves of the thoracic region follow spaces between the ribs. These *intercostal nerves* (*costa* means "rib") are paralleled by the intercostal arteries and veins. (See **Figure 4.26.**) Note also that some of the spinal nerves fuse together and then divide again; the fusions are referred to as ***plexuses*** ("braids").

Now let us consider the pathways by which sensory information enters the spinal cord and motor information leaves it. The cell bodies of all axons that bring sensory information into the brain and spinal cord are located outside the central nervous system. (The sole exception is the visual system; the retina of the eye is considered to be a part of the brain.) These incoming axons are referred to as *afferent* because they "bear toward" the CNS. The cell bodies that give rise to the axons that bring somatosensory information to the spinal cord reside in the ***dorsal root ganglia,*** rounded swellings of the dorsal root. These neurons are of the unipolar type (described in Chapter 2). The axonal stalk divides close to the cell body, sending one limb into the spinal cord and the other limb out to the sensory organ. Note that all of the axons in the dorsal root convey somatosensory information. (Refer back to **Figure 4.24.**)

Cell bodies that give rise to the ventral root

are located within the gray matter of the spinal cord. The axons of these multipolar neurons leave the spinal cord via a ventral root, which joins a dorsal root to make a spinal nerve (often referred to as a ***mixed nerve*** because it carries both sensory and motor fibers). The axons that leave the spinal cord through the ventral roots control muscles and glands. They are referred to as *efferent* because they "bear away from" the CNS.

Cranial Nerves

Twelve pairs of ***cranial nerves*** leave the ventral surface of the brain. Most of these nerves serve sensory and motor functions of the head and neck region. One of them, the *tenth,* or ***vagus nerve,*** regulates the functions of organs in the thoracic and abdominal cavities. It is called the *vagus* ("wandering") nerve because its branches wander throughout the thoracic and abdominal cavities. (The word *vagabond* has the same root.) Figure 4.27 presents a view of the base of the brain and illustrates the cranial nerves and the structures they serve. Note that efferent (motor) fibers are drawn as solid lines and that afferent (sensory) fibers are drawn as dashed lines. (See **Figure 4.27.**)

As I mentioned in the previous section, cell bodies of sensory nerve fibers that enter the brain and spinal cord (except for the visual system) are located outside the central nervous system. Somatosensory information (and also gustation, or taste) is received, via the cranial nerves, from unipolar neurons whose cell bodies reside in ***cranial nerve ganglia,*** which are similar to the dorsal root ganglia of the spinal cord. (See **Figure 4.27.**) Auditory, vestibular, and visual information is received via fibers of bipolar neurons (described in Chapter 2). Olfactory information is received via a complex system; the ***olfactory bulbs,*** which receive information from the olfactory receptors in the nose and transmit the infor-

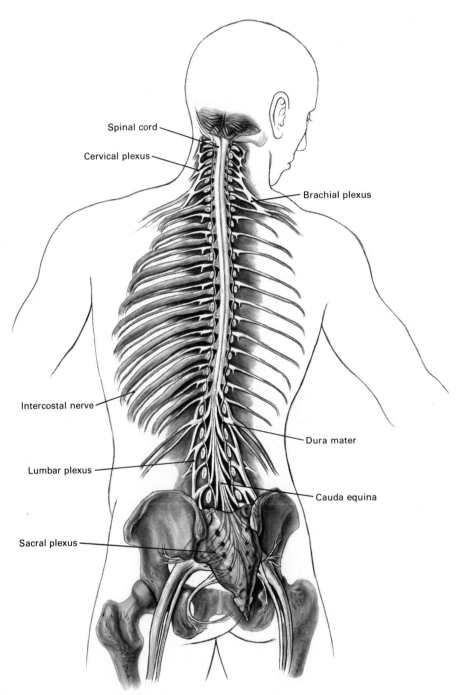

FIGURE 4.26
A dorsal view of the human spinal cord and some of the principal spinal nerves.

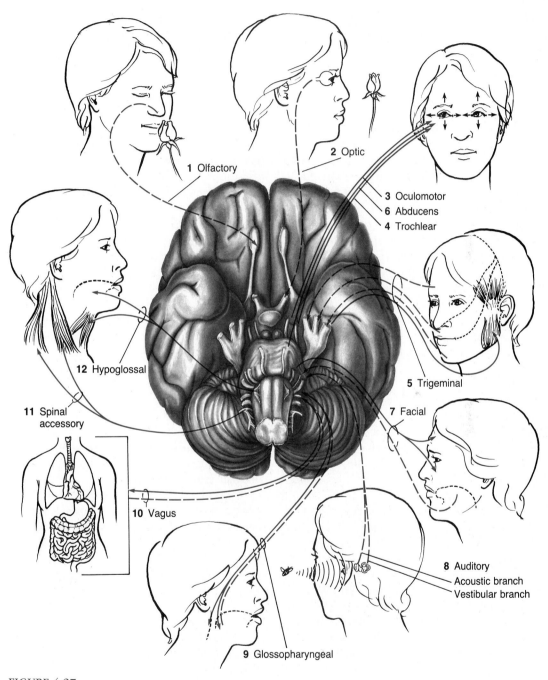

FIGURE 4.27

The names, numbers, locations, and functions of the twelve cranial nerves. Solid lines denote axons that control muscles or glands; broken lines denote sensory axons.

mation to the brain, contain a considerable amount of neural circuitry. Sensory mechanisms are described in more detail in Chapters 6 and 7.

Autonomic Nervous System

The **autonomic nervous system (ANS)** is concerned with regulation of smooth muscle, cardiac muscle, and glands (*autonomic* means "self-governing"). Smooth muscle is found in the skin (associated with hair follicles), in blood vessels, in the eyes (controlling pupil size and accommodation of the lens), and in the walls and sphincters of the gut, gallbladder, and urinary bladder. Merely describing the organs innervated by the autonomic nervous system suggests the function of this system: regulation of "vegetative processes" in the body. The ANS consists of two anatomically separate systems, the sympathetic division and the parasympathetic division.

Sympathetic Division of the ANS
The **sympathetic division** is most active when **catabolic** processes are required (that is, those involved with expenditure of energy from reserves that are stored in the body). For example, increased blood flow to skeletal muscles, secretion of epinephrine (resulting in increased heart rate and a rise in blood sugar level), and piloerection (erection of fur in mammals who have it and production of "goose bumps" in humans) are some effects that are mediated by the sympathetic nervous system during excitement. The cell bodies of sympathetic motor neurons are located in the gray matter of the thoracic and lumbar regions of the spinal cord (hence the sympathetic nervous system is also known as the **thoracolumbar system**). The fibers of these neurons exit via the ventral roots. After joining the spinal nerves, the fibers branch off and pass into **spinal sympathetic ganglia** (not to

be confused with the dorsal root ganglia). Figure 4.28 shows the relation of these ganglia to the spinal cord. Note that the various spinal sympathetic ganglia are connected to the neighboring ganglia above and below, thus forming the **sympathetic chain.** (See **Figure 4.28.**)

The axons that leave the spinal cord through the ventral root are part of the **preganglionic neurons.** All sympathetic preganglionic axons enter the ganglia of the sympathetic chain, but not all of them synapse there. Some leave and travel to one of the **sympathetic prevertebral ganglia,** located among the internal organs. All sympathetic preganglionic axons synapse on neurons located in one of the ganglia. The neurons upon which they synapse are called **postganglionic neurons.** In turn, the postganglionic neurons send axons to the target organs, such as the intestines, stomach, kidneys, or sweat glands. (See **Figure 4.29.**)

All synapses within the sympathetic ganglia are acetylcholinergic; the terminal buttons on the target organs, belonging to the postganglionic axons, are noradrenergic. The exception to this rule is provided by the sweat glands, which are innervated by acetylcholinergic terminal buttons. The medulla of the adrenal gland (described later in this chapter) is innervated directly by preganglionic sympathetic fibers, whose terminal buttons are acetylcholinergic. The secretory cells of the adrenal medulla may be thought of as the postganglionic cells; they are adrenergic, secreting epinephrine and norepinephrine. (See **Figure 4.29.**)

Parasympathetic Division of the ANS
The **parasympathetic division** of the autonomic nervous system supports **anabolic** activities, which are concerned with increases in the body's supply of stored energy. The anabolic and catabolic processes of the body together make up its **metabolism.** Such ef-

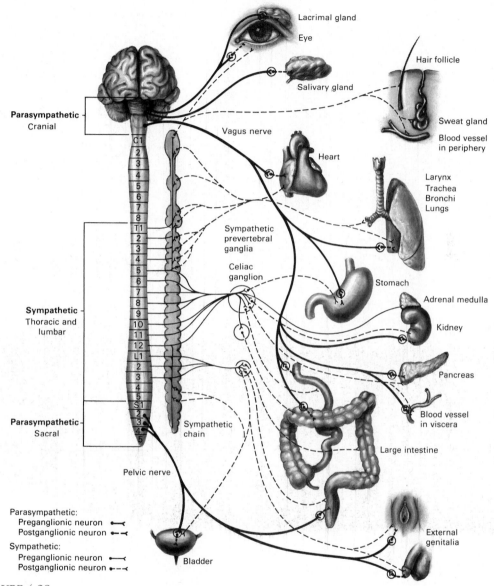

FIGURE 4.28

The autonomic nervous system and the target organs it serves.

fects as salivation, gastric and intestinal motility, secretion of digestive juices, and increased blood flow to the gastrointestinal system are mediated by the parasympathetic division of the ANS.

Cell bodies that give rise to preganglionic axons in the parasympathetic nervous system are located in two regions: the nuclei of some of the cranial nerves (especially the vagus nerve) and the intermediate horn of the gray matter in the sacral region of the spinal cord. Thus, the parasympathetic division of the ANS

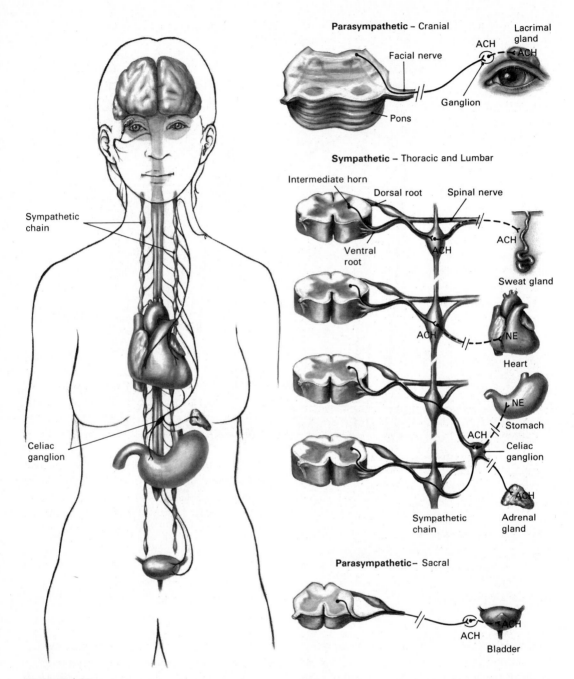

FIGURE 4.29
Preganglionic and postganglionic fibers of the two branches of the
autonomic nervous system. ACH = acetylcholinergic synapse; NE =
noradrenergic synapse.

has often been referred to as the ***craniosacral system.*** Parasympathetic ganglia are located in the immediate vicinity of the target organs; the postganglionic fibers are therefore relatively short. (See **Figure 4.29.**) The terminal buttons of both preganglionic and postganglionic neurons in the parasympathetic nervous system are acetylcholinergic.

■ CONTROL OF THE ENDOCRINE SYSTEM

Almost all glands are controlled by the brain. There are a few exceptions; for example, the parathyroid glands, which regulate calcium metabolism, respond directly to the calcium level of the blood. But most other glands either receive direct neural control or are controlled by a series of events initiated by hormones released by cells in the hypothalamus.

Exocrine Glands

Exocrine glands (literally, "outside-secreting") are those that have a duct through which the gland's products are secreted. For example, the lachrymal glands secrete tears through a duct to the inner surface of the eyelid; the liver and pancreas secrete digestive juices into the intestines; the seminal vesicles and prostate secrete fluids into the male genitourinary system; and the sweat glands and sebaceous glands secrete sweat and oil to the surface of the skin. All of the innervated exocrine glands are controlled by the autonomic nervous system. For example, the salivary glands receive postganglionic fibers of both the sympathetic and parasympathetic divisions. The parasympathetic division, which is active during such anabolic processes as digestion, produces a copious secretion of thin, watery saliva, useful in swallowing food. In contrast, activity of the sympathetic division causes secretion of a smaller quantity of thick, viscous saliva, which explains why the inside of your mouth feels sticky during periods of fright or excitement.

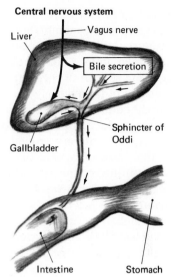

FIGURE 4.30
An example of neural control of an exocrine gland: neural control of bile secretion.

Some exocrine glands store their secretions and release them when stimulated to do so by the nervous system. For example, the liver produces bile, which is stored in the gallbladder and is retained there as long as the sphincter of Oddi is constricted. (A *sphincter* is a ring of smooth muscle that controls the passage of substances through a duct.) When stimulated by the vagus nerve, this sphincter relaxes and muscles in the wall of the gallbladder contract, causing it to deliver some of the stored bile to the digestive system. (See **Figure 4.30.**)

Endocrine Glands

Endocrine (or "inside-secreting") ***glands*** secrete their products into the extracellular fluid surrounding the capillaries; thus, the hormones they produce enter the bloodstream. These glands do not store hormones in containers like the gallbladder; instead, they store them in the way that neurons store transmitter substance: in vesicles in the cytoplasm. The release of hormones also resembles the release of transmitter substances: the vesicles migrate to the membrane, fuse with it, and rupture, spilling their contents into the extracellular fluid. Usually, the stimuli that trigger the release of the hormone also increase its rate of production.

Much of the endocrine system is controlled by hormones produced by cells in the hypothalamus. A small but very crucial vascular system (the *hypothalamic-hypophyseal portal system*) interconnects the hypothalamus and the *anterior pituitary gland,* or *adenohypophysis.* Arterioles of the hypothalamus branch into capillaries that drain into small veins. These veins travel to the anterior pituitary gland, where they branch into another set of capillaries. Therefore, substances that enter the hypothalamic capillaries of this system travel directly to the anterior pituitary gland before they are diluted in the large volume of blood in the vascular system. (See **Figure 4.31.**) The hypothalamic hormones are secreted by specialized neurons called *neurosecretory cells,* lo-

cated near the base of the pituitary stalk. These hormones are carried by the portal system to the anterior pituitary gland and stimulate it to secrete its hormones. For example, *gonadotropin releasing hormone* causes the anterior pituitary gland to secrete the *gonadotropic hormones.*

Most of the anterior pituitary hormones control the secretions of other endocrine glands. For example, adrenocorticotropic hormone (ACTH) stimulates the *adrenal cortex* (the outer layer of the adrenal gland) to secrete cortisone and related hormones. These hormones have effects on cells throughout the body, including some in the brain. Two other anterior pituitary hormones, prolactin and somatotropic hormone (growth hormone) do not control other glands but act as the final messenger. The behavioral effects of many of the anterior pituitary hormones are discussed in later chapters.

The hypothalamus also produces the hormones of the *posterior pituitary gland* (the *neurohypophysis*). These hormones in-

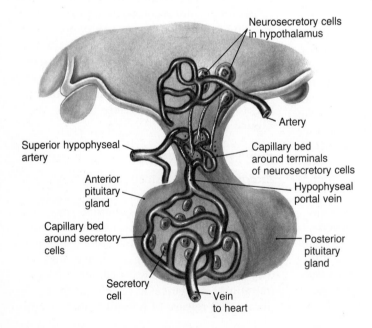

Neurosecretory cells in hypothalamus

Artery

Superior hypophyseal artery

Anterior pituitary gland

Capillary bed around secretory cells

Secretory cell

Vein to heart

Capillary bed around terminals of neurosecretory cells

Hypophyseal portal vein

Posterior pituitary gland

FIGURE 4.31

The anterior pituitary gland, showing the portal blood supply. Hormones released by neurosecretory cells in the hypothalamus enter capillaries and are conveyed to the anterior pituitary gland.

clude oxytocin, which stimulates ejection of milk and uterine contractions at the time of childbirth, and antidiuretic hormone, which regulates urine output by the kidneys. They are produced by neurons in the hypothalamus whose axons travel down the pituitary stalk and terminate in the posterior pituitary gland. The hormones are carried in vesicles through the axoplasm of these neurons and collect in the terminal buttons in the posterior pituitary gland. When these axons fire, the hormone contained within their terminal buttons is liberated and enters the circulatory system.

Endocrine glands produce two classes of hormones: polypeptides and steroids. For example, the pituitary hormones (of both the anterior and posterior lobes), insulin, and cortisone are polypeptides, consisting of chains of amino acids. They stimulate their target cells by interacting with receptors on the surface of these cells, in a manner very similar to the interaction between transmitter substance and receptor site. The acceptance of a hormone molecule by a receptor on the target cell initiates the appropriate changes in the cell. Most of these changes appear to be mediated by means of a second messenger such as cyclic AMP, which also mediates the postsynaptic effects of some neurotransmitters (see Chapter 3).

Steroid hormones, produced by the adrenal cortex, ovaries, and testes, consist of very small fat-soluble molecules that have no difficulty entering the target cells. (*Steroid* derives from *stereos,* "solid," and *oleum,* "oil." They are synthesized from cholesterol.) Steroid hormones pass easily through the cell membrane, attach to receptors in the cytoplasm, and are then transported to the nucleus, where they direct the machinery of the cell to alter its protein production. (See **Figure 4.32.**)

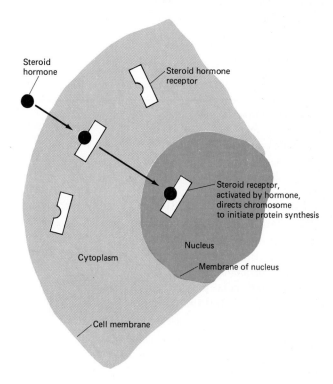

FIGURE 4.32
Steroid hormones affect their target cells by means of specialized receptors in the cytoplasm. Once a receptor binds with a molecule of a steroid hormone, it travels to the nucleus and causes genetic mechanisms to initiate protein synthesis.

Steroid hormone

Steroid hormone receptor

Steroid receptor, activated by hormone, directs chromosome to initiate protein synthesis

Nucleus

Cytoplasm

Membrane of nucleus

Cell membrane

The *adrenal medulla* consists of cells located in the center of the adrenal gland. It is controlled by the sympathetic nervous system and closely resembles a sympathetic ganglion. The adrenal medulla is innervated by preganglionic axons, and its secretory cells are analogous to postganglionic sympathetic neurons. These cells secrete epinephrine and norepinephrine when they are neurally stimulated. Secretions of the adrenal medulla function chiefly as an adjunct to the direct neural effects of sympathetic activity; for example, epinephrine increases heart rate and constricts peripheral blood vessels. The hormones that this gland secretes also stimulate a function that cannot be mediated neurally — an increase in the conversion of glycogen (animal starch) into glucose within skeletal muscle cells, which increases the energy available to them.

Table 4.2 lists the major endocrine glands, their hormones, the primary effects of these hormones, and the means by which the brain controls their secretion. (See **Table 4.2.**)

Concluding Remarks

Although this chapter describes only the most important features of the nervous system, I am sure that you now appreciate its immense complexity. This complexity should come as no surprise; after all, this organ is responsible for our perceptions, memories, thoughts, and feelings.

After having studied this chapter, you should be acquainted with the pathways by which information enters and leaves the central nervous system, its major structures and systems, and some of the functions they perform. You have also been introduced to the endocrine system and the means by which the brain controls it. I will have more to say about neuroanatomy in later chapters, when we deal with the physiology of particular classes of behaviors. Having learned the outline presented in this chapter, you are ready to master the details.

NEW TERMS

adenohypophysis p. 120
adrenal cortex p. 120
adrenal medulla p. 122
amygdala p. 101
amygdaloid complex p. 101
anabolic p. 116
anterior p. 86
anterior nuclei (of thalamus) p. 101
anterior pituitary gland p. 120
arachnoid granulations p. 93
arachnoid membrane p. 92
arachnoid trabeculae p. 92
association cortex p. 100
autonomic nervous system (ANS) p. 116
basal ganglia p. 101
brain stem p. 106
calcarine fissure p. 97

catabolic p. 116
cauda equina p. 110
caudal p. 86
caudal block p. 110
caudate nucleus p. 101
central canal p. 93
central nervous system (CNS) p. 86
central sulcus p. 97
cerebellar cortex p. 109
cerebellar peduncles p. 109
cerebellum p. 109
cerebral aqueduct p. 93
cerebral cortex p. 96
cerebrospinal fluid (CSF) p. 92
cervical p. 110
choroid plexus p. 93
cingulate gyrus p. 97

TABLE 4.2   The major endocrine glands, the hormones they secrete, and their principal functions

Gland	Hormone	Function
Adrenal Gland		
Cortex	Aldosterone	Excretion of sodium and potassium
	Androstenedione	Growth of pubic and underarm hair; sex drive (women)
	Cortisone	Metabolism; response to stress
Medulla	Epinephrine, norepinephrine	Metabolism; response to stress
Hypothalamus[a]	Releasing hormones	Control of anterior pituitary hormone secretion
Kidneys	Renin	Control of aldosterone secretion; blood pressure
Ovaries	Estradiol	Maturation of female reproductive system; secondary sex characteristics
	Progesterone	Maintenance of lining of uterus; promotion of pregnancy
Pancreas	Insulin, glucagon	Regulation of metabolism
Pituitary Gland		
Anterior	Adrenocorticotropic hormone	Control of adrenal cortex
	Gonadotropic hormones	Control of testes and ovaries
	Growth hormone	Growth; control of metabolism
	Prolactin	Milk production
	Thyroid-stimulating hormone	Control of thyroid gland
Posterior	Antidiuretic hormone[b]	Excretion of water
	Oxytocin[b]	Release of milk, contraction of uterus
Testes	Testosterone	Maturation of male reproductive system; sperm production; secondary sex characteristics; sex drive (men)
Thyroid Gland	Thyroxine	Energy metabolism; growth and development

[a] The hypothalamus, although it is part of the brain, secretes hormones; thus it can be considered to be an endocrine gland.
[b] These hormones are produced by the hypothalamus but are transported to and released from the posterior pituitary gland.

SUGGESTED READINGS

BARR, M.L., AND KIERNAN, J.A. *The Human Nervous System: An Anatomical Viewpoint,* fourth edition. Philadelphia: Harper & Row, 1983.

BRODAL, A. *Neurological Anatomy in Relation to Clinical Medicine.* Oxford: Oxford University Press, 1981.

DEARMOND, S.J., FUSCO, M.M., AND DEWEY, M.M. *Structure of the Human Brain: A Photographic Atlas.* New York: Oxford University Press, 1976.

GLUHBEGOVIC, N., AND WILLIAMS, T.H. *The Human Brain: A Photographic Guide.* New York: Harper & Row, 1980.

MOYER, K.E. *Neuroanatomy.* New York: Harper & Row, 1980.

NETTER, F.H. *The Ciba Collection of Medical Illustrations. Vol. 1, Nervous System.* Summit, N.J.: Ciba Pharmaceutical Products Co., 1953.

Research Methods of Physiological Psychology

5

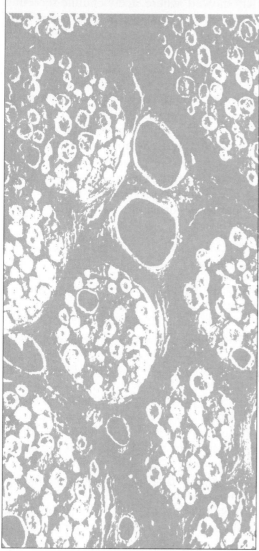

Study of the physiology of behavior involves the efforts of scientists in many disciplines, including physiology, neuroanatomy, biochemistry, psychology, endocrinology, and histology. To pursue a research project in physiological psychology requires competence in many experimental techniques. Because different procedures often produce contradictory results, investigators must be familiar with the advantages and limitations of the methods they employ. Scientific investigation entails a process of asking questions of nature. The method that is used frames the question. Often, we receive a puzzling answer, only to realize later that we were not asking the question we thought we were. As we will see, the best conclusions about the physiology of behavior are made by comparing the results of studies that approach the problem with different methods. (The use of two or more different methods to study a particular problem is called *converging operations.* I will have more to say about this topic later in this chapter.)

Physiological psychology is a biological science. Thus, most research in this area involves living organisms. Investigators must be certain that their subjects are housed in a comfortable and healthful environment and that any surgical procedures be carried out with the use of the appropriate anesthetics. Professional organizations such as the American Psychological Association and the Society for Neuroscience have established rules for the housing and treatment of laboratory animals.

The brain is so important that one hardly need explain the value of research designed to help us understand it. Along with the fascination of studying the organ that makes us what we are is the hope that we will discover principles of brain function that can be applied to the treatment of neurological disorders. For example, investigators have recently discovered that Alzheimer's disease,

a fatal degenerative brain disease, involves the destruction of acetylcholine-secreting neurons in a particular nucleus of the forebrain. This knowledge offers the hope that further research will determine the exact properties of these neurons that make them the target of the degenerative process. The discovery was possible because other investigators had developed the necessary research methods, including special stains that showed where acetylcholine-secreting neurons were concentrated. Of course, the developers of these research methods had no idea what problems others would attack with their techniques.

The experimental methods used by physiological psychologists include neuroanatomical techniques, destruction or removal of brain tissue, electrical recording, electrical stimulation, and chemical techniques. The boundaries of these categories are not distinct; for example, electrical stimulation and recording techniques can be used to obtain anatomical information.

■ NEUROANATOMICAL TECHNIQUES
Histological Procedures

The gross anatomy of the brain was described long ago, and everything that could be identified was given a name. Early anatomists named most brain structures according to their similarity to commonplace objects: amygdala, or "almond-shaped object"; hippocampus, or "sea horse"; genu, or "knee"; cortex, or "bark"; pons, or "bridge"; uncus, or "hook," to give a few examples. More recent names tend to be duller, such as the *nucleus ventralis medialis thalami, pars magnocellularis.* (This clever name means "large-celled part of the ventral medial nucleus of the thalamus.")

Detailed anatomical information about the brain has been obtained through use of various histological, or tissue-preparing, techniques. As we have seen, the brain consists of many billions of neurons and glial cells, the nerve cells forming distinct nuclei and fiber bundles. We cannot possibly see cellular detail by gross examination of the brain. And even a microscope is useless without *fixation* and *staining* of the neural tissue.

Fixation

If we hope to study the tissue in the form it had at the time of the organism's death, we must destroy the **autolytic enzymes** (*autolytic* means "self-dissolving"), which will otherwise turn the tissue into amorphous mush. The tissue must also be preserved, to prevent its decomposition by bacteria or molds. To achieve both of these objectives, the neural tissue is placed in a *fixative.* The most commonly used fixative is *formalin,* an aqueous solution of formaldehyde, a gas. Formalin halts autolysis, hardens the very soft and fragile brain, and kills any microorganisms that might destroy it.

Before the brain is fixed, it is usually perfused. **Perfusion** of tissue entails removal of the blood and its replacement with another fluid. The animal's brain is perfused because better histological results are obtained when there is no blood present in the tissue. The animal whose brain is to be studied is killed with an overdose of a general anesthetic (usually ether or sodium pentobarbital). The thoracic cavity is opened, and the *right atrium* (one of the chambers of the heart) is cut open. A needle is inserted into the heart, or a metal *cannula* (small tube) is inserted into the *aorta,* the large artery leaving the heart, and the animal's blood is replaced with a salt solution; the blood leaves via the cut in the atrium. Often the vascular system is then perfused with formalin, in order to speed up the process of fixation. The head is removed, the skull is opened, and the brain is removed and placed in a jar containing the fixative.

Once the brain has been fixed, the investigator must slice it into thin sections and stain various cellular structures in order to see anatomical details. Some procedures require that the tissue be stained before being sliced, but the techniques that physiological psychologists most commonly use call for sectioning first, and then staining. Therefore, I will describe the procedures in that order.

Sectioning

A **microtome** is used to slice neural tissue. This device (literally, "that which slices small") is an instrument capable of slicing tissue into very thin sections. Sections prepared for examination under a light microscope are typically 10 μm to 80 μm in thickness; those prepared for the electron microscope are generally cut at less than 1 μm. (A **micrometer,** abbreviated μm, is 1/1000 of a millimeter.) Electron microscopy will be discussed later in this chapter.

A microtome contains three parts: a knife, a platform on which to mount the tissue, and a mechanism that advances the knife (or the platform) the correct amount after each slice, so that another section can be cut. Figure 5.1 shows two commonly used microtomes. The one on the left is a sliding microtome. The knife holder slides forward on an oiled rail and takes a section off the top of the tissue mounted on the platform. The platform automatically rises by a predetermined amount as the knife and holder are pushed back. (See **Figure 5.1, top.**) To operate the rotary microtome shown on the right, you simply turn the wheel. The tissue platform moves up and down relative to the vertically mounted knife. The tissue is cut as it descends, and the platform is automatically advanced on the upstroke, moving the tissue into position for the next slice. (See **Figure 5.1, bottom.**)

Slicing brain tissue is not quite as simple as it might at first appear. As I mentioned, raw neural tissue is very soft. Fixation in formalin will harden the brain (to the texture of soft

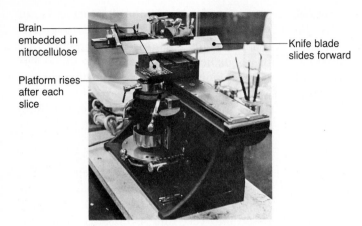

Brain embedded in nitrocellulose

Knife blade slides forward

Platform rises after each slice

Brain mounts on face of platform

Turning this handle operates mechanism

Knife blade

Platform travels up and down, slicing brain against knife blade; after each slice, platform moves forward

FIGURE 5.1
Top: Sliding microtome.
Bottom: Rotary microtome.

cheese), but it is still too soft to cut. Either of two techniques can be used to make the tissue hard enough to cut thinly: *freezing* or *embedding.*

Freezing is simplest. The tissue is chilled with a refrigeration device. Often the brain is first soaked in a sucrose (table sugar) solution, which minimizes tissue damage by preventing the formation of large ice crystals as the brain freezes. The temperature of the brain must be carefully regulated; if the block of brain tissue is too cold, the tissue will shatter into little fragments. If it is too warm, a layer of tissue will be torn off rather than sliced off. Frozen sections can be cut with either sliding or rotary microtomes.

The brain can also be embedded in materials that are of sliceable consistency at room temperature, such as paraffin or nitrocellulose. Paraffin comes in various grades, according to the room temperature at which it can best be sliced. The brain is first soaked in a solvent for paraffin (such as xylene) and is then soaked in successively stronger solutions of paraffin that are kept melted in an oven. The brain is then placed in a small container of liquid paraffin, which is allowed to cool and harden. The entire block is sliced, the paraffin providing the physical support for the tissue. A rotary microtome is used to cut these sections; as the knife passes through the block, it warms it slightly, so that the sections get glued together, end to end. (See **Figure 5.2.**) It is immensely gratifying, after having spent a lot of time preparing the tissue, to see the sections emerge in a beautiful ribbon.

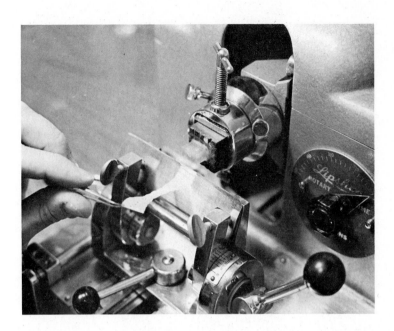

FIGURE 5.2
A "ribbon" being formed as a paraffin-embedded brain is sliced on a rotary microtome.

After the tissue is cut, the slices are usually mounted on glass microscope slides with an agent such as albumin (protein extracted from egg whites). The slides are dried and heated, which makes the albumin become insoluble and cements the tissue sections to the glass. The tissue can then be stained by putting the entire slide into various chemical solutions. The stained and mounted sections are covered with a mounting medium, and a very thin glass coverslip is placed over the sections. The mounting medium (which is thick and resinous) gradually dries out, keeping the coverslip in position.

Staining

If you looked at an unstained section of brain tissue under a microscope, you would be able to see the outlines of some large cellular masses and the more prominent fiber bundles, especially if the tissue were kept wet. However, no fine details would be revealed. For this reason, the study of microscopic neuroanatomy requires special histological stains. Three basic types of stains are used for

neural tissue: those that reveal cell bodies by interacting with the contents of the cytoplasm, those that selectively color myelin sheaths, and those that stain the cell membrane (of the entire cell, or just the axons).

Cell-Body Stains. In the late nineteenth century, Franz Nissl, a German neurologist, discovered that methylene blue, a dye derived from the distillation of coal tar, would stain the cell bodies of brain tissue. The material that takes up the dye, known as the *Nissl substance,* consists of RNA, DNA, and associated proteins located in the nucleus and scattered, in the form of granules, in the cytoplasm. Many dyes can be used to stain cell bodies, but the most frequently used is *cresyl violet.* Incidentally, the dyes were not developed for histological purposes but were originally manufactured for use in dyeing cloth.

The discovery of cell-body stains (also called *Nissl stains*) made it possible to identify nuclear masses in the brain. Figure 5.3 shows a frontal section of a cat brain stained with cresyl violet. Note that it is possible to

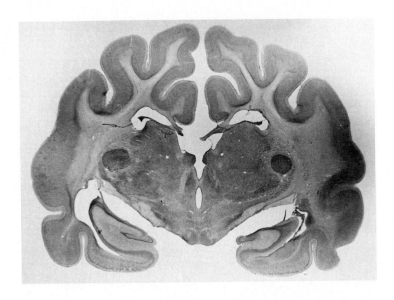

FIGURE 5.3
A frontal section of a cat brain, stained with cresyl violet, a Nissl stain. (Histological material courtesy of Mary Carlson.)

observe fiber bundles by their lighter appearance; they do not take up the stain. (See **Figure 5.3.**) The stain is not selective for *neural* cell bodies. All cells are stained, neurons and glia alike. It is up to the investigators to determine which is which—by size, shape, and location.

Myelin Stains. Myelin stains color myelin sheaths. These stains make it possible to identify fiber bundles. (What is light in Figure 5.3 is dark in Figure 5.4) However, pathways of single fibers cannot be traced. There is simply too much intermingling of the individual fibers. (See **Figure 5.4.**)

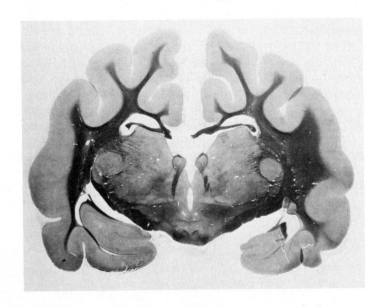

FIGURE 5.4
A frontal section of a cat brain, stained with a myelin stain. (Histological material courtesy of Mary Carlson.)

Membrane Stains. Membrane stains contain salts of various heavy metals, such as silver, uranium, or osmium, that interact with the somatic, dendritic, and axonal membranes. The ***Golgi-Cox stain*** (which uses silver) is highly selective, staining only a fraction of the neurons in a given region. Why this happens is not known, and the selectivity undoubtedly gives a biased view of the neurons that populate the region. But the selective staining makes it possible to observe the axonal and dendritic branches of individual neurons and to trace details of synaptic interconnections. Figure 5.5 shows the appearance of individual neurons of the cerebral cortex stained by a new modification of the Golgi-Cox stain. Note the individual neurons and their interconnecting processes. The large cells in the center are oligodendroglia, providing myelin sheaths for the bundles of fibers running horizontally. (See **Figure 5.5.**)

Degenerating-Axon Stains. A special variant of the cell-membrane stain was devised by Walle Nauta and Paul Gygax in the middle of this century. The Nauta-Gygax stain (which uses silver) identifies axons that are dying and are in the process of being destroyed by phagocytes. This stain might seem too esoteric to be of any practical use, but as we will see, it has contributed to our knowledge of the interconnection of various neural struc-

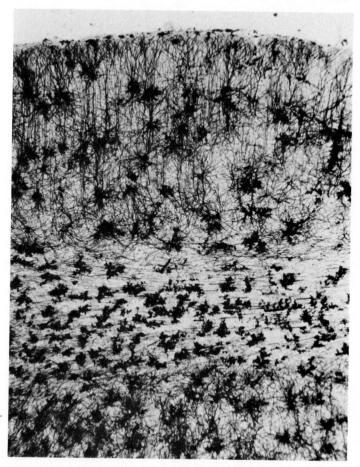

FIGURE 5.5

A section of cortex of a cat brain, stained by a modified Golgi-Cox method. (Histological material courtesy of D.N. Spinelli and J.K Lane.)

tures. However, we will also see that new techniques are replacing the Nauta-Gygax method.

Tracing Neural Pathways

The central nervous system contains many billions of neurons, most of which are gathered together in thousands of discrete nuclei. These nuclei are interconnected by incredibly complex systems of axons. The problem of the neuroanatomist is to trace these connections and find out which nuclei are connected to which others and what route is taken by the interconnecting fibers. The problem cannot be resolved by means of histological procedures that stain all neurons, such as cell-body, membrane, or myelin stains. Close observation of a brain that has been prepared by these means reveals a tangled mass of neurons. Special techniques must be used to make the connections that are being investigated stand out from all of the others.

Degeneration Studies
The first good method to identify individual neural connections used the Nauta-Gygax degenerating-axon stain. If a cell body is destroyed, or if the axon is cut, the distal portion of the axon quickly dies and disintegrates. This process is called ***anterograde degeneration***. (See **Figure 5.6.**) A degenerating-axon

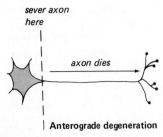

sever axon here

axon dies

Anterograde degeneration

FIGURE 5.6
Anterograde degeneration.

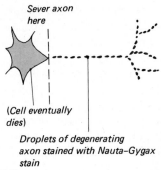

Sever axon here

(Cell eventually dies)

Droplets of degenerating axon stained with Nauta–Gygax stain

FIGURE 5.7
The Nauta-Gygax stain reveals degenerating axons as dark droplets.

stain will identify these dying axons as trails of black droplets. (See **Figure 5.7.**)

Because only degenerating axons are stained, the Nauta-Gygax technique can be used to label one specific set of axons. The procedure works like this: A specific region of the brain (for example, a particular nucleus) is destroyed by means of stereotaxic surgery (which will be described later in this chapter). The animal is permitted to live for a few days, so that the axons of the neurons in the destroyed area will have time to begin degenerating. The animal is then killed, the brain is removed and sliced, and the sections are prepared with the Nauta-Gygax stain. Only the degenerating axons will absorb the silver and thus be stained, which means that the neuroanatomist can trace the fibers that leave the area that was surgically destroyed.

This technique has been very useful and has supplied much of what we know about the circuitry of the brain. When it was developed, it revitalized the field of neuroanatomical research, which had reached the limits of the techniques that were then available. Now a new set of techniques has again revolutionized neuroanatomical investigations.

Amino Acid Autoradiography
Amino acids are used by neurons for the construction of proteins. These substances enter

the cell from the extracellular fluid by means of special uptake mechanisms in the membrane. Once they are within the cell, the amino acids are incorporated into proteins, which are then transported to where they are needed, including the terminal buttons. As we saw in Chapter 3, there is a special means of transportation, axoplasmic flow, that delivers substances — including proteins — through the axon to the terminal buttons. Thus, some of the amino acids that are present in the extracellular fluid that surrounds the cell body of a neuron will find their way to the terminal buttons of the neuron.

The technique of ***amino acid autoradiography*** takes advantage of the axoplasmic transport of proteins. The investigator injects radioactive amino acids into a particular region of the brain and permits the animal to live for a day or two. During this time, the cell bodies take up the radioactive amino acids and incorporate them into proteins, some of which are transported through the axons to the terminal buttons. The animal is then killed, its brain is removed and sliced, and the sections are placed on microscope slides. The slides are taken into a darkroom, where they are coated with a photographic emulsion (the substance found on photographic film). After a wait of several weeks, the slides, with their coatings of emulsion, are developed, just like photographic film. The radioactive proteins show themselves as black spots in the developed emulsion because the radioactivity exposes the emulsion, just as X-rays or light will do. The term ***autoradiography*** can roughly be translated as "writing with one's own radiation." (See **Figure 5.8**.)

Figure 5.9 illustrates the actual appearance of the grains of exposed silver in the photographic emulsion. A solution containing radioactive amino acids (proline and leucine) was injected into a rabbit's prefrontal cortex, where it was taken up by neural cell bodies, incorporated into protein, and transported through axons to their terminal but-

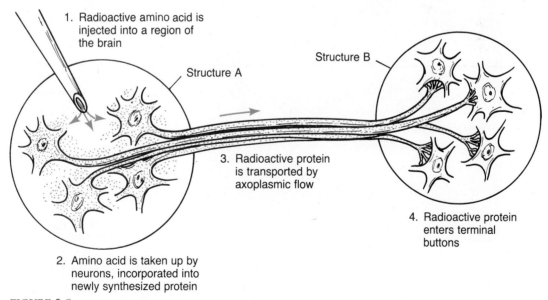

1. Radioactive amino acid is injected into a region of the brain

Structure A

Structure B

3. Radioactive protein is transported by axoplasmic flow

4. Radioactive protein enters terminal buttons

2. Amino acid is taken up by neurons, incorporated into newly synthesized protein

FIGURE 5.8
The procedure for the use of amino acid autoradiography to reveal the efferent axons of a brain region.

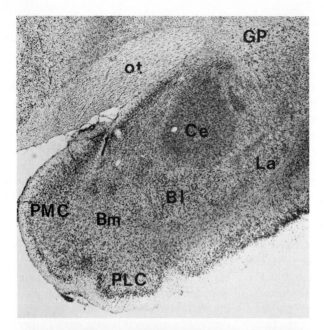

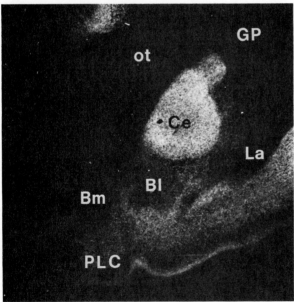

FIGURE 5.9
Amino acid autoradiography. A solution of radioactive proline and leucine was injected into the frontal cortex and was carried by axoplasmic flow to the central nucleus of the amygdala (Ce). The top photomicrograph is a standard exposure, and the bottom photomicrograph was taken under darkfield illumination, which shows the exposed grains of emulsion as spots of white against a dark background. Ot = optic tract. Other abbreviations label various nuclei of the amygdala. (From Kapp, B.S., Schwaber, J.S., and Driscoll, P.A., *Neuroscience,* 1985, in press.)

tons. The upper photomicrograph shows a Nissl-stained section through the anterior temporal lobe. The lower photomicrograph shows the section viewed under *dark-field illumination,* which makes the silver grains scatter a beam of light, and thus look white. You can clearly see the silver grains in the nucleus labeled *Ce* (the central nucleus of the amygdala). (See **Figure 5.9.**) The technique has revealed here that neurons in the prefrontal cortex of the rabbit have axons that form synapses with neurons in the central nucleus of the amygdala.

Horseradish Peroxidase Studies

Horseradish peroxidase is a rather unlikely name for a substance that is used in neuroanatomical research. (Believe it or not, there is also a turnip peroxidase.) Horseradish peroxidase (usually called *HRP*) is an enzyme — a protein that is capable of splitting certain peroxide molecules, turning them into insoluble salts. We already saw its use (in Chapter 3) as a tracer that demonstrated the recycling of the membrane of terminal buttons during the release of transmitter substances.

When HRP is injected into the brain, it is taken up, by means of active transport mechanisms, into axons and terminal buttons. (Why it is taken up is not known.) It is subsequently transported by retrograde axoplasmic flow — that is, flow directed back toward the cell soma. Thus, the HRP eventually reaches the cell bodies of neurons that send axons into the region of the brain that had received the injection.

The technique works like this: Some HRP is injected into the part of the brain that is under investigation. Axons and terminal buttons in that region take up the chemical and transport it back to the cell bodies. A recent refinement on the technique uses horseradish combined with a substance derived from wheat germ that prevents axons from taking up the compound. In this case, only terminal buttons take up the HRP, so that axons that pass through the region being studied but do not terminate there will not take it up. (See **Figure 5.10.**) After a survival time of a day or two, the animal is killed, the brain is sliced,

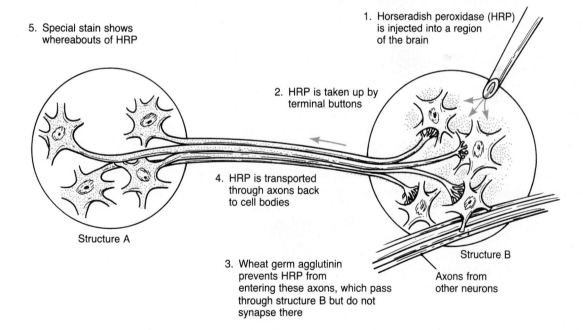

FIGURE 5.10
The procedure for the use of horseradish peroxidase to reveal the afferent neurons that send axons to a brain region.

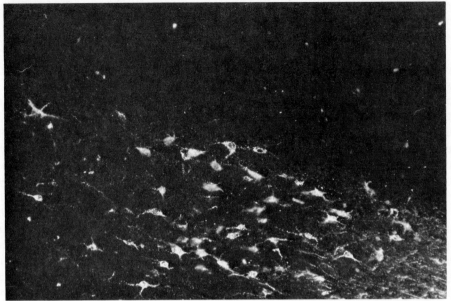

FIGURE 5.11

The horseradish peroxidase method. HRP was injected into the central
nucleus of the amygdala of a rabbit, taken into terminal buttons, and
carried back to the cell bodies located in the substantia nigra. The
photomicrograph was prepared under darkfield illumination, which
shows the HRP as spots of white against a dark background. Notice that
both axons and cell bodies are labeled. (Photograph courtesy of Bruce S.
Kapp.)

and the sections are soaked in a sequence of
chemical baths that visibly mark the location
of the HRP, which has been carried back to
the cell bodies. Thus, the HRP technique permits identification of neurons that project
axons *to* a particular region.

Figure 5.11 illustrates the appearance of
cells that have been labeled with HRP. The
chemical was injected into the central nucleus of the amygdala of a rabbit, where it was
taken up by terminal buttons. The HRP was
carried back, by retrograde axoplasmic flow,
to cell bodies located in the substantia nigra,
shown in the photomicrograph. The results
indicate that neurons in the substantia nigra
send axons to the central nucleus of the
amygdala. (See **Figure 5.11.**)

Together, the HRP technique and the radioactive amino acid technique permit investigators to discover the source of the inputs
into a particular part of the brain and the locations to which that region sends axons. Thus,
the specific interconnections of the brain can
be studied with a high degree of accuracy and
sensitivity.

Study of the Living Brain

Advances in X-ray techniques and computers
have led to the development of methods for
studying the anatomy of the living brain. G.N.
Hounsfeld and a British electronics company,
EMI, developed a technique called ***computerized axial tomography.*** This procedure,

usually referred to as a ***CAT scan,*** works as follows: The patient's head is placed in a large doughnut-shaped ring. The ring contains an X-ray tube, and directly opposite it (on the other side of the patient's head), an X-ray detector. The X-ray beam passes through the patient's head, and the amount of radioactivity that gets through it is measured by the detector. The X-ray emitter and detector scan the head from front to back. They are then moved around the ring by a few degrees, and the transmission of radioactivity is measured again. The process is repeated until the brain has been scanned from all angles. (See **Figure 5.12.**)

The computer takes the information and plots a two-dimensional picture of a horizontal section of the brain. The patient's head is then moved up or down through the ring, and a scan is taken of another section of the brain. Figure 5.13 shows a series of these scans taken through the head of a patient who sustained a stroke that damaged portions of the right parietal and occipital lobes. (See **Figure 5.13.**)

Computerized axial tomography has been used extensively in the diagnosis of various pathological conditions of the brain, including tumors, blood clots, hydrocephalus, and degenerative diseases such as multiple sclero-

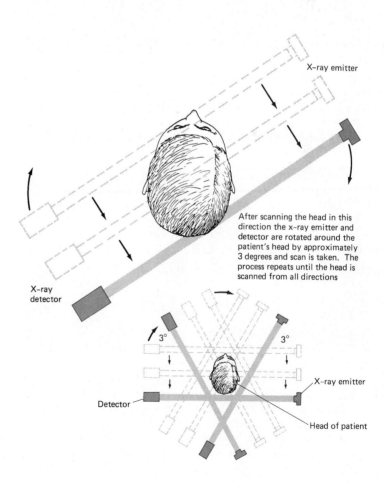

X–ray emitter

After scanning the head in this direction the x-ray emitter and detector are rotated around the patient's head by approximately 3 degrees and scan is taken. The process repeats until the head is scanned from all directions

X–ray detector

3°   3°

Detector

X–ray emitter

Head of patient

FIGURE 5.12
A computerized axial tomography (CAT) scanner.

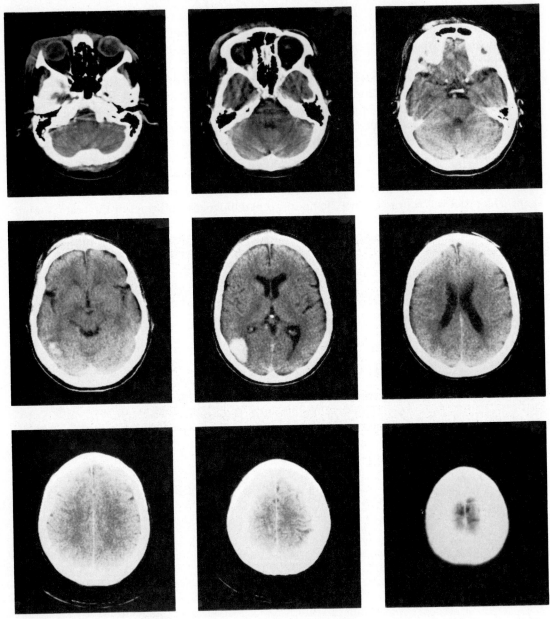

FIGURE 5.13
A series of CAT scans from a patient with a lesion in the right occipital-
parietal area (center scan). The lesion appears white because it was
accompanied by bleeding; blood absorbs more radiation than the
surrounding brain tissue. Rostral is up, caudal is down; left and right are
reversed. The upper left drawing shows a section through the eyes and the
base of the brain. (Courtesy of J.McA. Jones, Good Samaritan Hospital,
Portland, Oregon.)

sis. The benefits to the patient are obvious; a CAT scan can often tell the physician whether brain surgery is necessary. The technique is also of considerable importance to neuropsychologists, who try to infer brain functions by studying the behavioral capacities of people who have sustained brain damage by disease or physical injury. The CAT scan makes it possible for them to determine the approximate location of the lesion.

Another technique, ***positron emission tomography,*** or ***PET,*** permits investigators to assess the amount of metabolic activity in various parts of the brain. First, the patient receives an injection of radioactive ***2-deoxy-glucose (2-DG).*** Because this chemical resembles glucose, it is taken into cells, especially those that are metabolically active.

However, unlike glucose, 2-DG cannot be metabolized, so it accumulates within the cells. (Eventually, the chemical is broken down and leaves the cells.) The person's head is placed in a machine similar to a CAT scanner. When a beam of X-rays passes through the head, the radioactive molecules of 2-DG emit a particle called a positron, which is detected by the scanner. The computer determines which regions of the brain have taken up the radioactive substance, and it produces a picture of a slice of the brain, showing different amounts of metabolic activity. (See **Figure 5.14.**)

The most recently developed tool for seeing what is inside a person's head without opening it is called ***nuclear magnetic resonance*** scanning, or ***NMR.*** The NMR scanner

FIGURE 5.14
PET scans of a human brain. The top row shows three scans from a person at rest. The bottom row shows three scans from the same person while clenching and unclenching his right fist. The scans show increased uptake of [11C]-labeled 2-deoxyglucose in the cerebellum and left frontal lobe (the region of the primary motor cortex), indicating increased metabolic rate in these areas. The original scan is in color, with regions of highest activity shown in red. Arrows point to these regions. (Photo courtesy of the Brookhaven National Laboratory and the State University of New York, Stony Brook.)

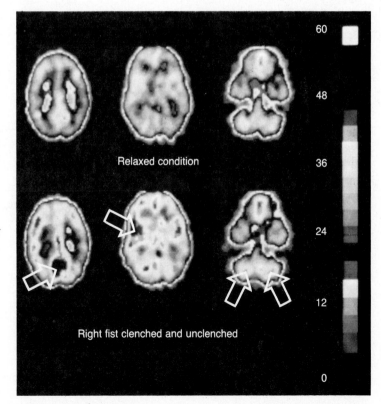

Relaxed condition

Right fist clenched and unclenched

60
48
36
24
12
0

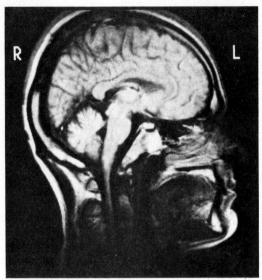

FIGURE 5.15
A midsagittal NMR scan of a human brain. (Photo courtesy of Philips Medical Systems.)

anatomical structures as synaptic vesicles and details of cell organelles, it is necessary to use an electron microscope. A beam of electrons is passed through the tissue to be examined. (The tissue must first be coated with a substance that produces detailed variations in the resistance to the passage of electrons, much like staining for light microscopy, causing various portions of the tissue to absorb light.) A shadow of tissue is then cast upon a sheet of photographic film, which is exposed by the electrons. Electron photomicrographs produced in this way can provide information about structural details on the order of a few Ångström units. (See **Figure 5.16.**)

A *scanning electron microscope* provides less magnification than a standard one,

resembles a CAT scanner, but it does not use radiation. Instead, it passes an extremely strong magnetic field through the patient's head. When a person's body is placed in a strong magnetic field, the nuclei of some molecules in the body spin with a particular orientation. If a radio-frequency wave is then passed through the body, these nuclei emit radio waves of their own. Different molecules emit energy at different frequencies. The NMR scanner is tuned to detect the radiation from hydrogen molecules. Because these molecules are present in different concentrations in different tissues, the scanner can use the information to prepare pictures of slices of the brain. (See **Figure 5.15.**)

Electron Microscopy

The light microscope is limited in its ability to resolve extremely small details. Because of the nature of light itself, magnification of more than approximately 1500 times does not add any detail. In order to see such small

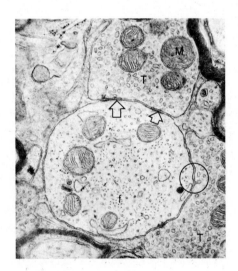

FIGURE 5.16
An electron photomicrograph of a section through an axodendritic synapse. Two synaptic regions are indicated by arrows, and a circle points out a region of pinocytosis in an adjacent terminal button, presumably representing recycling of vesicular membrane. T = terminal button; f = microfilaments; M = mitochondrion. (From Rockel, A.J., and Jones, E.G. *Journal of Comparative Neurology,* 1973, *147,* 61–92.)

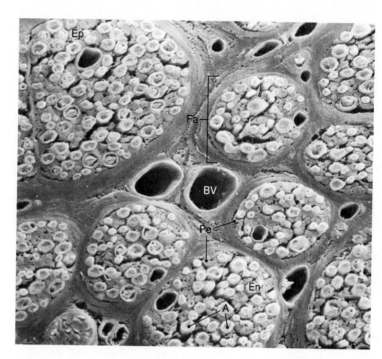

FIGURE 5.17
A scanning electron photomicrograph of the cut end of a peripheral nerve. Ep = epineurium (the connective tissue surrounding the nerve); Fa = fascicle (bundle of axons); Pe = perineurium (the connective tissue surrounding individual fascicles); En = endoneurium (the connective tissue surrounding single axons); A = axons; BV = blood vessel. (From Kessel, R.G., and Kardon, R.H. *Tissues and Organs: A Text-atlas of Scanning Electron Microscopy.* W.H. Freeman and Co. Copyright © 1979.)

which transmits the electron beam through the tissue. However, it shows objects in three dimensions. The microscope scans the tissue with a moving beam of electrons. The information received from the reflection of the beam is used to produce a remarkably detailed three-dimensional view. (See **Figure 5.17.**)

Stereotaxic Surgery

Many procedures used in neuroscience research require the investigator to place an object such as a wire or the tip of a metal cannula in a particular part of the brain. For example, the investigator might want to inject a chemical into the brain, which requires the insertion of a cannula, or to destroy a particular region of the brain, which requires the insertion of a metal electrode, through which destructive electrical current may be passed. If the investigator simply sliced the brain open to get to the appropriate part, great damage

would be done. Stereotaxic surgery permits the insertion of an object into the depths of the brain without serious damage to the overlying tissue.

Stereotaxis literally means "solid arrangement"; more specifically, it refers to the ability to locate objects in space. A stereotaxic apparatus permits the investigator to locate brain structures that are hidden from view. This device contains a holder that fixes the animal's head in a standard position and a carrier that moves an electrode or a cannula through measured distances in all three axes of space. However, in order to perform stereotaxic surgery one must first study a stereotaxic atlas, so I will describe the atlas first.

The Stereotaxic Atlas

No two brains of animals of a given species are completely identical, but there is enough similarity among individuals to predict the location of a particular brain structure, relative to external features of the head. For in-

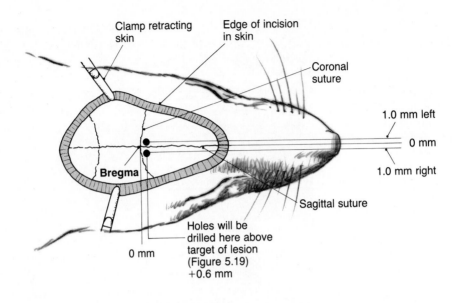

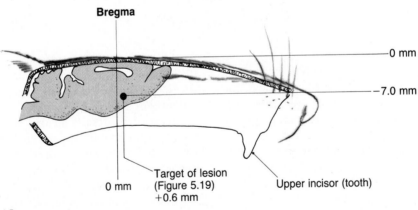

FIGURE 5.18

Relation of the skull sutures to a rat's brain, and the stereotaxic coordinates
for an electrode placement.

stance, a particular thalamic nucleus of a rat
might be so many millimeters ventral, anterior, and lateral to a point formed by the junction of several bones of the skull. Figure 5.18
shows two views of a rat skull: a drawing of
the dorsal surface and, beneath it, a midsagittal view. (See **Figure 5.18.**) The junction of
the coronal and sagittal *sutures* (seams between adjacent bones of the skull) is labeled

bregma. If the animal's skull is oriented as
shown in the illustration, a particular region
of the brain occupies a fairly constant location in space, relative to bregma. Not all atlases use bregma as the reference point, but
this reference is the easiest to describe.

A *stereotaxic atlas* contains pages that
correspond to frontal sections taken at various distances anterior and posterior to

bregma (or another reference point). For example, the page shown in Figure 5.19 contains a drawing of a slice of the brain located 0.6 mm anterior to bregma. If we wanted to place the tip of a wire in the structure labeled *F* (the fornix), we would have to drill a hole

through the skull 0.6 mm anterior to bregma (because the structure shows up on the 0.6-mm page) and 1.0 mm lateral to the midline. (See **Figures 5.18 and 5.19.**) The electrode would be lowered through the hole until the tip was 7.0 mm lower than the skull height at

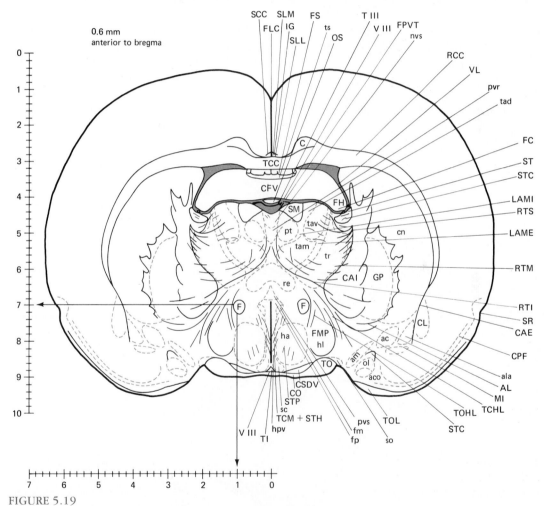

FIGURE 5.19

A page from a stereotaxic atlas of the rat brain. The scale on the side and bottom of the figure has been modified to be consistent with my description of bregma as a reference point. (From König, J.F.R., and Klippel, R.A., *The Rat Brain: A Stereotaxic Atlas of the Forebrain and Lower Parts of the Brain Stem.* Copyright 1963 by the Williams & Wilkins Co., Baltimore.)

bregma. (See **Figure 5.19.**) Thus, by finding a neural structure (which we cannot see in our animal) on one of the pages of a stereotaxic atlas, we can determine the structure's location relative to bregma (which we can see). I should note that, because of variations in different strains and ages of animals, the atlas gives only an approximate location. It is always necessary to try out a new set of coordinates, slice and stain the animal's brain, see where the lesion was made, correct the numbers, and try again.

There are human stereotaxic atlases, by the way. Sometimes a neurosurgeon produces subcortical lesions (for example, to reduce severe tremors caused by Parkinson's disease). Usually the surgeon uses multiple landmarks, and verifies the location of the wire (or other device) inserted into the brain by taking X-rays before producing a brain lesion.

The Stereotaxic Apparatus

A **stereotaxic apparatus** operates on simple principles. The device includes a head holder, which holds the animal's skull in the proper orientation, a holder for the electrode, and a calibrated mechanism that moves the electrode holder in measured distances along the three axes: anterior-posterior, dorsal-ventral, and lateral-medial. Figure 5.20 illustrates a stereotaxic apparatus designed for

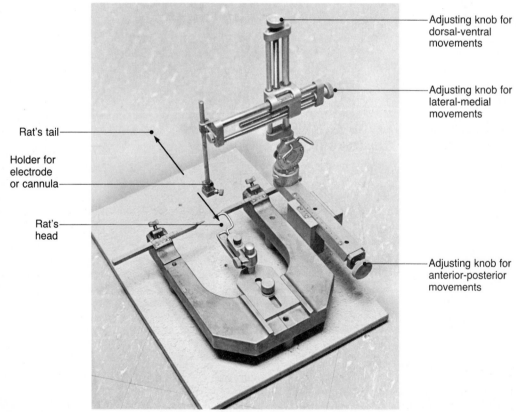

FIGURE 5.20
A stereotaxic apparatus for performing brain surgery on rats.

small animals; various head holders can be used to outfit this device for such diverse species as rats, mice, hamsters, pigeons, and turtles. (See **Figure 5.20.**)

Once the investigator has obtained the stereotaxic coordinates, he or she anesthetizes the animal, places it in the apparatus, and cuts the scalp open. This cut exposes the skull, so that the cannula or electrode can be placed with its tip on bregma. The investigator measures the location of bregma along each of the axes and moves the cannula or electrode the proper distance along the anterior-posterior and lateral-medial axes to a point just above the target. He or she then drills a hole through the skull just below the cannula or electrode, and lowers the device into the brain by the proper amount. Now, the tip of the cannula or electrode is in the correct position in the brain.

The next step depends upon what the investigator intends to accomplish by the surgery. In some cases, the cannula or electrode is permanently implanted with acrylic plastic, a procedure that will be described later in this chapter. In other cases, a chemical is infused into the brain through the cannula or an electrical current is passed through the electrode in order to stimulate or destroy brain tissue. In either of these situations, the device is subsequently removed from the brain. With any of these techniques, once surgery is complete the wound is sewed together, and the animal is taken out of the stereotaxic apparatus and allowed to recover from the anesthetic.

■ LESION PRODUCTION/BEHAVIORAL EVALUATION

One of the most important research methods used to investigate brain functions involves destroying part of the brain and evaluating the animal's subsequent behavior. This technique is not as glamorous as many of the more recently devised techniques, but it often serves as the final test that confirms or disproves conclusions made by means of other methods. For example, an investigator may find that neurons in a particular part of the brain become active when the animal performs a particular behavior. This finding suggests that the structure may be at least partly responsible for that behavior. If the animal no longer performs the behavior after the structure is destroyed, we become more confident of our conclusion about the structure's responsibility for the behavior. If the animal still performs the behavior, though, we know that the structure is not necessary for its performance. It may still play a role, but not an essential one. In this situation, then, the principle of converging operations (studying a problem by two or more different methods) can be put to use.

Evaluating the Behavioral Effects of Brain Damage

A *lesion* literally refers to a wound or injury, and when a physiological psychologist destroys part of the brain, he or she usually refers to the damage as a brain lesion. The rationale for lesion studies is that the function of an area of the brain can be inferred from the behavioral capacity that is missing from the animal's repertoire after the area is destroyed. For example, if an animal can no longer see after part of the brain is destroyed, we can conclude that the destroyed area plays some role in vision.

However, we must be very careful in interpreting the effects of brain lesions. For example, how do we ascertain that the lesioned animal is blind? Does it bump into objects, or fail to run through a maze toward the light that signals the location of food, or no longer constrict its pupils to light? An animal could bump into objects because of deficits in motor coordination, it could have lost its memory for the maze problem, or it could see quite well but could have lost its visual reflexes. The experimenter must be clever enough to ask the right question, especially when studying complex processes such as hunger, attention, or memory. Even when studying simpler processes, people can be fooled. For years people thought that the albino rat was blind. (It isn't.) Think about it: how would you test to see whether a rat can see? Remember, they have vibrissae (whiskers) that can be used to detect a wall before bumping into it or the edge of a table before walking off it. The animal can also follow odor trails around the room.

The interpretation of lesion studies is also complicated by the fact that all regions of the brain are interconnected, and no single part is wholly responsible for any one function. When a nucleus is destroyed, the lesion may also sever axons passing through the area. If a structure normally inhibits another, the observed changes in behavior might really be a function of disinhibition of that second structure. Also, we very often see a partial recovery of function some time after part of a brain is damaged. It is impossible to say whether this recovery results from a "taking over" of the function of the damaged structure by some other brain region or from repair of temporarily injured synapses. In later chapters, we will see many examples of the difficulty that occurs when trying to infer the role of a brain region from the behavior of an animal lacking that region.

I should also note that histological evaluation must be made of each animal's brain lesion. Brain lesions often miss the mark, and it is necessary to verify the precise location of the brain damage after testing the animals behaviorally. The investigator may have intended to destroy structure X but may have occasionally missed, destroying nearby structure Y in some animals instead. After the behavioral observations are completed, the ani-

mals are killed, and the investigator slices and stains the animals' brains to see where the damage is. Only the data collected from the animals in which structure X was destroyed are included in the final analysis. (Sometimes, interesting results are obtained accidentally; the investigator may find that structure Y is even more important than structure X to the function being studied.)

Producing Brain Lesions

It is easy to destroy parts of the dorsal surface of the cerebral or cerebellar cortex; the animal is anesthetized, the scalp is cut, part of the skull is removed, and the cortex is brought into view. Almost always, a suction device is used to aspirate the brain tissue. To accomplish this tissue removal, the dura mater is cut away, and a glass pipette is placed on the surface of the brain. A vacuum pump attached to the pipette is used to suck up the brain as if it were jelly. With practice, it is quite easy to aspirate away the cortical gray matter, stopping at the underlying layer of white matter, which has a much tougher consistency. A *cautery* (instrument with a heated point) can also be used to destroy regions of cortex, but the extent of the damage is more difficult to control.

Subcortical brain lesions are usually produced by passing electrical current through a stainless steel wire that is electrically insulated with paint or varnish except for a portion of the tip. The investigator guides the wire stereotaxically, so that its end reaches the appropriate location, and then turns on the lesion-making device. Two kinds of electrical current can be used. Direct-current (DC) devices create lesions by initiating chemical reactions whose products destroy the cells in the vicinity of the electrode tip. Radio-frequency (RF) lesion-making devices produce alternating current of a very high frequency. This current does not stimulate neural tissue, nor does it cause chemical reactions. Instead, it destroys nearby cells with the heat produced by the passage of the current through the tissue, which offers electrical resistance. Radio-frequency lesions have a distinct advantage: no metal ions are left in the damaged tissue. In contrast, when DC lesions are produced, some of the electrode is left behind in the brain, because ions of metal are carried away by the electrical current.

Lesions produced by means of radio frequency or direct current destroy everything in the vicinity of the electrode tip, including neuron cell bodies and the axons of neurons that pass through the region. A more selective method of producing brain lesions employs **kainic acid.** When this chemical is injected through a cannula into a region of the brain, it destroys cell bodies in the vicinity but spares axons that are passing nearby. This selectivity permits the investigator to determine whether the behavioral effects of destroying a particular brain structure occur because the cells there are killed or because the axons that pass nearby are severed. For example, as we will see in Chapter 9, radio-frequency lesions of a region of the pons abolish a particular form of sleep. But when kainic acid is used to destroy the neurons located there, the animals' sleep is *not* affected. Thus, the sleep-altering effects of radio-frequency lesions must be caused by destroying the axons that pass through the area, not the cell bodies that reside there.

Even more specific methods of lesion production are available. For example, the drug **6-hydroxydopamine (6-HD)** resembles the catecholamines norepinephrine and dopamine. You will recall that the postsynaptic effects of most neurotransmitters are terminated by re-uptake; the terminal button releases the neurotransmitter, then retrieves it. Because 6-HD resembles the catecholamines it is taken up by the axons of neurons that secrete dopamine or norepinephrine. Once

inside, the chemical poisons and kills the neurons. Thus, 6-HD can be injected directly into particular regions of the brain to kill specific populations of neurons that use one of these transmitter substances. If the investigator uses the proper concentration of 6-HD, only catecholamine-secreting neurons will be damaged.

■ RECORDING THE BRAIN'S ELECTRICAL ACTIVITY

Rationale

Axons produce action potentials, and terminal buttons elicit postsynaptic potentials in the membrane of the cells with which they form synapses. These electrical events can be recorded (as we have already seen), and changes in the electrical activity of a particular region can be used to determine whether that region plays a role in various behaviors. For example, recordings can be made during stimulus presentations, decision making, or motor activities. The rationale is sound, but, as we will see, electrical recordings of neural activity, especially of those electrical events that might be correlated with complex behaviors, are very difficult to interpret.

Recordings can be made chronically, over an extended period of time after the animal recovers from surgery, or acutely, for a relatively short period of time during which the animal is kept anesthetized. Acute recordings, made while the animal is anesthetized, are usually restricted to studies of sensory pathways or (in conjunction with electrical stimulation of the brain) investigations of anatomical pathways in the brain (to be described in a later section of this chapter). Acute recordings seldom involve behavioral observations, since the behavioral capacity of an anesthetized animal is limited, to say the least.

Chronic electrodes can be implanted in the brain with the aid of a stereotaxic appa-

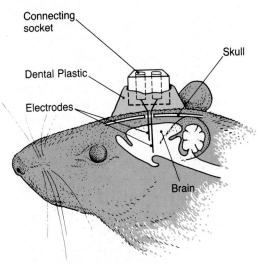

FIGURE 5.21
A permanently attached set of electrodes, with a connecting socket cemented to the skull.

ratus, and an electrical socket attached to the electrodes can be cemented to the animal's skull by means of an acrylic plastic that is normally used for making dental plates. Then, after recovery from surgery, the animal can be "plugged in" to the recording system. (See **Figure 5.21.**)

Electrical recordings can be taken through very small electrodes that detect the activity of one (or just a few) neurons or through large electrodes that respond to the electrical activity of large populations of neurons. In either case, the electrical signal detected by the electrode is quite small and must be amplified. A biological amplifier works just like the amplifiers in a stereo system, converting the weak signals recorded at the brain (about as weak as those produced by a phonograph cartridge) into stronger ones, large enough to be displayed on the appropriate device. (The analogy with the sound system even applies here, because recordings of the activity of single neurons are often played through loudspeakers, as we will see.) Output devices vary considerably. Their basic purpose is to convert the raw data (amplified electrical signals

from the brain) into a form we can perceive — usually a visual display.

Electrodes

Depending on the type of electrical signal he or she wishes to detect, the investigator constructs or purchases special electrodes. Although these electrodes come in many forms, they can be classified into two basic types.

Microelectrodes

Microelectrodes have a very fine tip, small enough to record the electrical activity of individual neurons. This technique is usually called **single-unit recording** (a unit refers to an individual neuron). Microelectrodes can be constructed of fine metal wires or glass tubes. Metal electrodes are sharpened by etching them in an acid solution. Current is passed through a fine wire as it is moved in and out of the solution. The tip erodes away, leaving a very fine, sharp point. The wire (usually of tungsten or stainless steel) is then insulated with a special varnish. The very end of the tip is so sharp that it does not retain insulation and thus can record electrical signals.

Electrodes can also be constructed of fine glass tubes. Glass tubes have an interesting property. If they are heated until soft, and if the ends are pulled apart, the softened glass will stretch into a very fine filament. However, no matter how thin the filament becomes, it will still have a hole running through it. To construct glass microelectrodes, the investigator heats the middle of a length of capillary tubing (glass with an outside diameter of approximately 1 mm) and then pulls the ends sharply apart. The glass tube is drawn out finer and finer, until the tube snaps apart. The result is two **micropipettes,** as shown in **Figure 5.22.** (These devices are usually produced with the aid of a special machine, called a micropipette

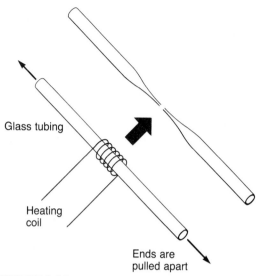

FIGURE 5.22
Micropipettes are produced by heating the center portion of a length of glass capillary tubing and pulling the ends apart.

Glass tubing

Heating coil

Ends are pulled apart

puller.) Glass will not conduct electricity, so the micropipette is filled with a conducting liquid, such as a solution of potassium chloride. Glass micropipettes were used to provide the data concerning axonal conduction and synaptic transmission described in Chapters 2 and 3.

Macroelectrodes

Macroelectrodes, which record the activity of a very large number of neurons, are not nearly so difficult to make or to use. They can be constructed from a variety of materials: Stainless steel or platinum wires, insulated except for the tip, can be inserted into the brain or placed on top of it. Small balls of metal can be placed on the surface of the brain. Wires can be attached to screws that are driven into holes in the skull. Flat disks of silver or gold can be attached to the scalp with an electrically conductive paste. (The last type of electrode is used for recordings of the electroencephalographic activity from the

human head, discussed in a subsequent section of this chapter.)

Macroelectrodes do not detect the activity of individual neurons; rather, the records obtained with these devices represent the postsynaptic potentials of many thousands — or millions — of cells in the area of the electrode. Recordings taken from the scalp, especially, represent the electrical activity of an enormous number of neurons.

Output Devices

After being amplified, electrical signals from the nervous system must be displayed so that we can see them and measure them. Obviously, we cannot directly observe the electrical activity from an amplifier; just as a sound system is useless without speakers or headphones, so a biological amplifier is useless without an output device.

Oscilloscope

In Chapter 2, I described the basic principle of an **oscilloscope**— the plotting of electrical potentials as a function of time. Figure 5.23 shows the display unit of an oscilloscope, the cathode-ray tube. This device contains an electron gun, which emits a focused stream of electrons toward the face of the tube. A special surface on the inside of the glass converts some of the energy of the electrons into a visible spot of light. Electrons are negatively charged and are thus attracted to positively charged objects and repelled by negatively charged ones. The plates arranged above and below the electron beam, and on each side, can be electrically charged, thus deflecting the beam and directing it to various places on the face of the tube. The dot can thus be moved independently by the horizontal and vertical deflection plates. (See **Figure 5.23.**)

The deflection plates that move the beam horizontally are usually attached to a timing circuit that sweeps the beam from left to right

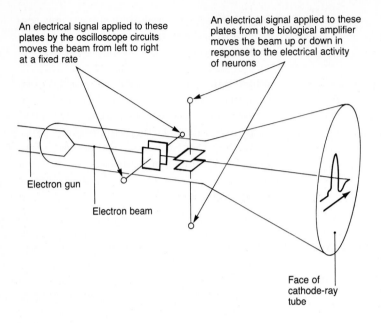

An electrical signal applied to these plates by the oscilloscope circuits moves the beam from left to right at a fixed rate

An electrical signal applied to these plates from the biological amplifier moves the beam up or down in response to the electrical activity of neurons

Electron gun

Electron beam

Face of cathode-ray tube

FIGURE 5.23
A simplified drawing of the cathode-ray tube from an oscilloscope.

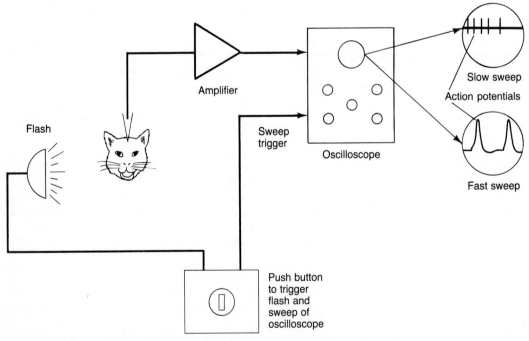

Amplifier

Flash

Sweep trigger

Oscilloscope

Slow sweep

Action potentials

Fast sweep

Push button to trigger flash and sweep of oscilloscope

FIGURE 5.24
The means by which the responses of single units to a flash of light can be recorded.

at a constant speed. Simultaneously, the output of the biological amplifier moves the beam up and down. We thus obtain a graph of electrical activity as a function of time.

To illustrate the use of an oscilloscope for the recording of single-unit activity, consider the procedure shown in Figure 5.24. A light is flashed in front of the cat, and, at the same time, the dot on the oscilloscope is started across the screen, moving from left to right. Thus, the vertical axis represents the electrical signal from a neuron and the horizontal axis represents time. Suppose we record from a cell in the visual cortex that responds to a light flash by giving a burst of action potentials. If we move the beam slowly, we will see the record of this event on the face of the oscilloscope as vertical lines superimposed on a horizontal one. If we move the beam rapidly, we will see the shapes of the individual action potentials. (See **Figure 5.24.**) You might wonder how the illustrated display can be seen; after all, the display consists of a moving dot, and I have shown a continuous line. The explanation is that most oscilloscope screens exhibit *persistence;* as the dot moves, it leaves a trace of its pathway behind, which slowly fades away.

When recording single-unit activity, the investigator usually also attaches the output of the amplifier to a loudspeaker. When an investigator lowers a microelectrode through the brain, he or she must stop before the optimal recording point, to allow the brain tissue, which has been pushed down by the progress

of the electrode, to spring back up. If the electrode goes down too far, the cell will probably be injured or killed by the electrode when the tissue moves up. Therefore, the investigator must detect the firing of a cell as soon as possible, so that he or she can stop moving the electrode before damage is done. Our ears are much more efficient than our eyes in extracting the faint signal of a firing neuron from the random background noise. We can hear the ticking, snapping sound of single-unit activity from the loudspeaker long before we can see the action potentials on the face of the oscilloscope. Our auditory system does an excellent job of extracting signal from noise.

Oscilloscopes are also ideal for the display of ***evoked potentials.*** Evoked potentials are electrical changes in the brain that are *evoked* by a stimulus, such as a sound or a flash of light. They are recordings made through macroelectrodes, and should not be confused with *action* potentials, which occur in single axons. When a stimulus is presented to an organism, a series of electrical events is initiated at the receptor organ. This activity is conducted into the brain, where it propagates through sensory pathways. If a macroelectrode is placed in or near one of these pathways, it will detect the electrical activity evoked by the stimulus. For example, we might place a scalp electrode on the back of a person's head and present a flash of light, while simultaneously triggering the sweep of an oscilloscope. Figure 5.25 shows such an

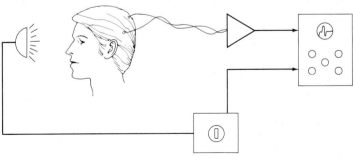

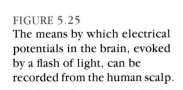

FIGURE 5.25
The means by which electrical potentials in the brain, evoked by a flash of light, can be recorded from the human scalp.

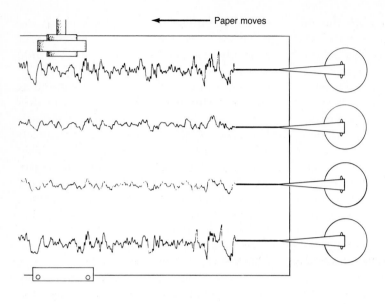

FIGURE 5.26
A record from an ink-writing oscillograph.

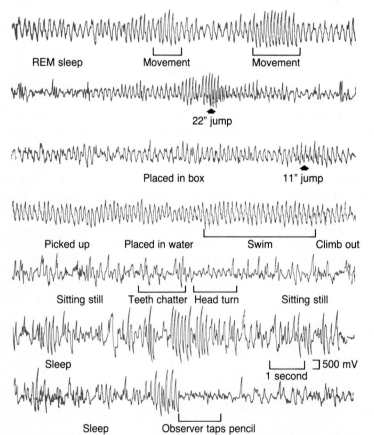

FIGURE 5.27
EEG activity from the rat hippocampus, recorded during various behaviors. (From Whishaw, I.Q., and Vanderwolf, C.H., *Behavioral Biology,* 1973, *8,* 461–484.)

experiment, along with the evoked potential from the visual cortex, recorded through the skull and scalp. (See **Figure 5.25.**)

Ink-Writing Oscillograph

Oscilloscopes are most useful in the display of phasic activity, such as an evoked potential, that occurs during a relatively brief period of time. If neural activity is continuously recorded and displayed on an oscilloscope screen, it will be seen as a series of successive sweeps of the beam, presenting a rather confusing picture. A much better device for such a purpose is the ink-writing oscillograph (often called a *polygraph*).

The time base of the polygraph is provided by a mechanism that moves a very long strip of paper past a series of pens. Essentially, the pens are the pointers of large voltmeters, moving up and down in response to the electrical signal sent to them by the biological amplifiers. Figure 5.26 illustrates a record of electrical activity recorded from macroelectrodes attached to various locations on a person's scalp. (See **Figure 5.26.**) Such records are called **electroencephalograms (EEGs),** or "writings of electricity from the head." They can be used to diagnose epilepsy or brain tumors, or to study the stages of sleep and wakefulness, which are associated with characteristic patterns of electrical activity. I should note that many modern polygraphs do not use ink; they print electrostatically, or with heated pens on specially treated paper. Nevertheless, their principle of operation is the same.

Figure 5.27 shows the EEG recorded from the hippocampus of a rat during sleep and during the performance of various behaviors while awake. You will see that the pattern of activity changes drastically during different behaviors. (See **Figure 5.27.**)

Computers

Electrophysiological data are often stored in computers, which can also be used to display the data. A computer can convert the analog signal (one that can continuously vary, like the EEG) received from the biological amplifier into a series of numbers (digital values). Figure 5.28 illustrates how an evoked potential can be represented by a series of digital values. Each point represents the voltage of the analog signal at successive millisecond intervals. The values were obtained from a rat's brain through screws attached to the skull, were stored in a computer, and were then displayed on the screen of an oscilloscope. (See **Figure 5.28.**)

A computer can do more than display the data; it can perform many kinds of analyses as well. For example, it can compute the delay between the presentation of a stimulus and the occurrence of an evoked potential, or it can count the number of action potentials that a stimulus produces in a single unit. One of the most common functions of a computer is the averaging of a series of individual evoked potentials.

Figure 5.29 shows a series of evoked potentials recorded from a rat's visual cortex in response to a flash of light. Notice that these

FIGURE 5.28

An evoked potential as represented by a display of points digitized by and stored in a computer.

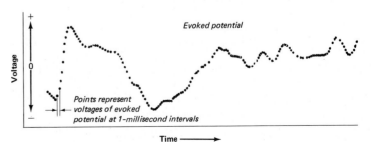

evoked potentials generally resemble one another but do not look identical. (See **Figure 5.29.**) The individual waves were converted to series of numbers by a computer, the numbers were added together, and the total was divided by the number of individual presentations (four, in this case). The resulting numbers describe the average wave, shown at the bottom. The individual variations of the single sweeps, which represent brain activity not related to the light flash, are "averaged out" by this process. Usually, many more than four waves are averaged together, and the result is even smoother than is shown in this example. (See **Figure 5.29.**)

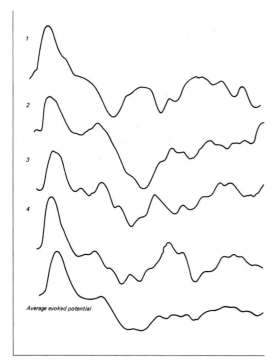

Average evoked potential

FIGURE 5.29
Evoked potentials that occurred in response to a flash of light, recorded from a rat's visual cortex. The top curves are individual evoked potentials; the bottom curve is the average of the individual curves.

The Use of Recording in Behavioral Studies

The usefulness of electrical recordings in the study of sensory pathways should be obvious. In these studies, we know when the electrical signals are elicited at the receptors, and we look for subsequent neural events. We can study motor systems in a similar manner. The recorded electrical activity is stored (on magnetic tape or in a computer memory), and when a movement is made the records are averaged *backward in time* from the beginning of the movement, to look for potentials that were present before the movement. Presumably, the potentials represent neural events that were instrumental in producing the movement.

Other studies might involve the correlation of continuously recorded electrical activity in various brain structures with the ongoing behavior of the animal. In fact, we saw an example of this correlation in Figure 5.27. (Look back at **Figure 5.27.**) Besides correlating the electrical activity of the brain with "spontaneous behaviors," we can also expose animals to various situations in order to observe the response of different parts of the brain. If we find that a brain region becomes more active after an animal is deprived of access to water, perhaps that region has something to do with thirst. The problems associated with the use of electrical recordings will be discussed in later chapters dealing with particular physiological and behavioral processes.

■ ELECTRICAL STIMULATION OF THE BRAIN

Neural activity can be elicited by electrical stimulation. In Chapter 2, I described the way in which action potentials could be produced by delivering electrical pulses to an axon. Various neural structures can also be stimulated through electrodes inserted into the brain.

Identifying Neural Connections

Perhaps the most straightforward use of electrical stimulation is demonstrated in neuroanatomical studies. If stimulation delivered through an electrode in structure A produces an evoked potential or increased single-unit activity in structure B, then the structures must be connected. Details of their interconnections, such as the directness of the pathway or the diffuseness of the connections, can also be inferred from the record obtained. (See **Figure 5.30**.)

Electrical Stimulation During Neurosurgery

One of the more interesting uses of electrical stimulation of the brain was developed by the late Wilder Penfield (see Penfield and Jasper, 1954) to treat *focal epilepsy.* This disease is characterized by a localized region of neural tissue that periodically irritates the surrounding areas, triggering an epileptic seizure (wild, sustained firing of cerebral neurons, resulting in some behavioral disruption). If severe cases of focal epilepsy do not respond

to medication, surgical excision of the focus is necessary. The focus is identified by means of EEG recordings before surgery and is confirmed by EEG recordings during surgery, after the brain is exposed.

Patients undergoing open-head surgery first have their heads shaved. Then a local anesthetic is administered to the scalp along the line that will be followed by the incision. A general anesthetic is not used, because the method requires that the patient be awake and conscious during surgery. The surgeon cuts the scalp and saws through the skull under the cut, so that a piece of skull can then be removed. Next, the surgeon cuts and folds back the dura mater, exposing the brain itself.

When removing an epileptic focus, the surgeon wants to cut away all the abnormal tissue, while sparing neural tissue that performs important functions, such as the comprehension and production of speech. For this reason, Penfield first stimulated parts of the brain to determine which regions he could safely remove, before removing the seizure focus. Penfield touched the tip of a metal electrode to various parts of the brain and observed the effects of stimulation on the patient's behavior. For example, stimulation of the primary motor cortex produced movement, and stimulation of the primary auditory

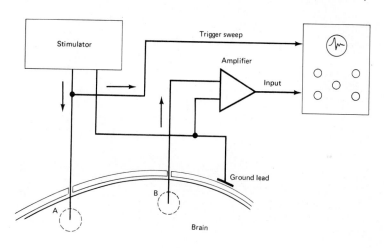

FIGURE 5.30

The means by which one area of the brain (A) can be stimulated while recording in another area (B). This procedure provides information about the nature of the neural connections between the areas.

cortex elicited reports of the presence of buzzing noises. Stimulation of portions of the temporal lobe and frontal lobe stopped the patient's ongoing speech and disrupted the ability to understand what the surgeon and his associates were saying.

After the surgeon removes the region of the brain that contains the seizure focus, the dura mater is sewn back together and the piece of skull is replaced.

Besides giving patients relief from their epileptic attacks, the procedure provided Penfield with interesting data. As he stimulated various parts of the brain, he noted the effect and placed a sterile piece of paper, on which a number was written, on the point stimulated. When various points had been stimulated, Penfield photographed the exposed brain with its numbered locations before removing the slips of paper and proceeding with the surgery. After the operation, he could then compare the recorded notes with the photograph of the patient's brain, showing the location of the points of stimulation. (See **Figure 5.31.**)

The Use of Electrical Stimulation in Behavioral Studies

Stimulation of the brain of an unanesthetized, freely moving animal often produces behavioral changes. For example, hypothalamic stimulation can elicit behaviors such as feeding, drinking, grooming, attack, or escape, which suggests that the hypothalamus is involved in their control. Stimulation of the caudate nucleus often halts ongoing behavior, which suggests that this structure is involved in motor inhibition. Brain stimulation can serve as a signal for a learned task or can even serve as a rewarding or punishing event, as we will see in Chapter 13.

There are problems in interpreting the significance of the effects of electrical brain stimulation. An electrical stimulus (usually a series of pulses) can never duplicate the natural neural processes that go on in the brain. The normal interplay of spatial and temporal patterns of excitation and inhibition is destroyed by the artificial stimulation of an area. Electrical brain stimulation is probably as nat-

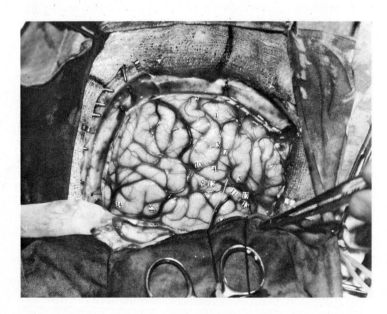

FIGURE 5.31
The appearance of the cortical surface of a conscious patient whose brain has been stimulated. The points of stimulation are indicated by the numbered tags placed there by the surgeon. (From Case, M.M., in Penfield, W., *The Mystery of the Mind: A Critical Study of Consciousness and the Human Brain.* Copyright 1975 by Princeton University Press; Princeton Paperback, 1978. Reprinted by permission of Princeton University Press.)

ural as attaching ropes to the arms of the members of an orchestra and then shaking all the ropes simultaneously to see what they can play. In fact, local stimulation is sometimes used to produce a "temporary lesion," by which the region is put out of commission by the meaningless artificial stimulation. The surprising finding is that stimulation so often *does* produce orderly changes in behavior.

■ CHEMICAL TECHNIQUES

A growing number of investigations into the physiological bases of behavior use various chemical techniques. The importance of these techniques will be made obvious to you as you read the rest of this book. In this section, I will only mention some of the basic procedures.

Microiontophoresis

The principal method for identifying receptors that respond to particular transmitter substances involves electrical recording along with a chemical technique called ***microiontophoresis.***

When postsynaptic receptors are exposed to the appropriate transmitter substance, they change the permeability of the membrane to various ions, resulting in excitatory or inhibitory postsynaptic potentials. These potentials increase or decrease the cell's firing rate. To determine which transmitter substances a particular neuron responds to, an investigator uses a ***double-barreled micropipette.*** This device consists of two micropipettes, one inside the other. The outer micropipette is filled with an ionized form of the neurotransmitter to be tested. When electrical current is passed through the outer micropipette, it carries some of the transmitter substance with it. Thus, extremely small quantities of the chemical can be injected. *Iontophoresis* means "ion carrying," from *pherein,* "to bear or carry." (See **Figure 5.32.**)

The inner micropipette is used to record the neural activity of the cell that is being exposed to the transmitter substance. It can be inserted through the membrane, to record postsynaptic potentials, or it can remain outside the cell, where it is still able to record the occurrence of action potentials. If the neuron

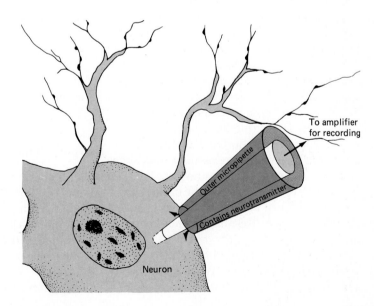

FIGURE 5.32
Microiontophoresis. Molecules of a neurotransmitter are carried out of the outer micropipette by an electrical current. Intracellular recordings from the inner micropipette determine whether the neuron responds to the neurotransmitter.

responds with postsynaptic potentials or with a change in its firing rate when some transmitter substance is ejected from the outer micropipette, we can conclude that it contains the appropriate receptors.

Immunological Techniques

The body's immune system has the ability to produce antibodies in response to antigens. *Antigens* are proteins (or peptides), such as those found on the surface of viruses. *Antibodies,* which are also proteins, are produced by white blood cells to destroy invading microorganisms. Antibodies are located on the surface of white blood cells, in the way in which neurotransmitter receptors are located on the surface of neurons. When the antigens present on the surface of a virus come into contact with the antibodies that recognize them, the antibodies trigger an attack on the virus by the white blood cells.

Special techniques developed by cell biologists permit them to produce antibodies to a wide variety of molecules. For example, they can produce antibodies to choline acetyltransferase, the enzyme that produces acetylcholine. These antibody molecules can be attached to molecules of special dyes that emit light when they are exposed to ultraviolet light. To determine where choline acetyltransferase is located in the brain, the investigator places fresh slices of brain tissue in a solution that contains the antibody/dye molecules. The antibodies attach themselves to their antigen — choline acetyltransferase. Then the investigator examines the slices with a microscope under ultraviolet light, he or she can see which parts of the brain — even which individual neurons — contain choline acetyltransferase. Presumably, these neurons are acetylcholinergic.

The technique I just described is an *immunohistochemical procedure. (Immuno-* refers to the antigen-antibody interaction of the immune system, and *histo-* refers to tissue.) As investigators develop ways to produce antibodies to more and more substances, including peptide neurotransmitters, neuromodulators, and hormones, immunohistochemical techniques are becoming increasingly important in neuroscience research.

Behavioral Effects of Drugs

In Chapter 3, I described various chemicals that mimic a particular transmitter substance, that inhibit or facilitate its production, or that prevent its destruction or re-uptake. Investigators often use these substances to determine the behavioral consequences of stimulating or inhibiting the effects of a particular neurotransmitter. For example, parachlorophenylalanine (PCPA) prevents the synthesis of serotonin and produces insomnia (at least temporarily), which suggests the involvement of this transmitter substance in sleep.

Particular kinds of synapses can be inhibited or stimulated by injecting various pharmacological agents directly into parts of the brain. This injection can even be done chronically: A metal cannula is placed in an animal's brain, and a fitting, attached to the cannula, is cemented to the skull. At a later date, a flexible tube is connected to the fitting, and a chemical is injected into the brain while the animal moves about freely. (See **Figure 5.33.**)

Radioactive Tracers

Radioactive tracers are radioactive chemicals that become incorporated into chemical processes within cells. They provide the investigator with a labeled substance whose location can be followed by various means. We saw one of the most important uses of radioactive tracers in amino acid autoradiography, which uses anterograde axoplasmic flow to trace the

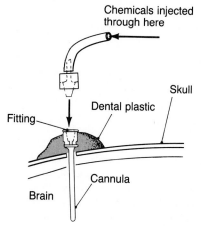

Chemicals injected
through here

Skull

Dental plastic

Fitting

Brain

Cannula

FIGURE 5.33

A chronic intracranial cannula. Chemicals can be infused into the brain through this device.

pathways followed by axons of neurons that reside in some particular region of the brain. I will describe some basic techniques here, with particular procedures to follow in later chapters.

Determining the Rate of Chemical Reactions

Radioactive chemicals can be used to determine the rate of incorporation of a given substance in various chemical reactions. For example, if we want to determine the relative rates of protein synthesis in various neural structures, we could inject an animal with a measured amount of radioactive amino acids, the building blocks of proteins. After waiting for a few days we would kill the animal, dissect the brain, and extract the protein. The amount of radioactivity in the protein extracted from a particular portion of brain tissue would tell us how much of that protein had been constructed since the radioactive amino acid had been administered. "Old" protein would not be radioactive; only "new" protein would be radioactive. The amount of radioactivity in a given amount of protein would tell us how much of that protein was "new."

Special Autoradiographic Techniques

Many hormones and neuromodulators have behavioral effects. Presumably, these chemicals produce their behavioral effects by affecting the activity of groups of neurons in the brain. A special autoradiographic technique can be used to locate these neurons. Suppose we were interested in finding out which neurons are stimulated by estradiol, a female sex hormone. We could inject an animal with radioactive estradiol, wait a while, then kill the animal, remove and slice the brain, place the sections on microscope slides, and prepare autoradiographs by coating the sections with a photographic emulsion. (I already described the technique of autoradiography in the section on amino acid autoradiography.) If some neurons selectively take up the estradiol they will have become radioactive, and these neurons will be covered by black spots in the developed photographic emulsion.

As we saw earlier in this chapter, the PET scanner uses radioactive 2-deoxyglucose (2-DG), in conjunction with a beam of radiation. A simpler technique uses 2-DG, along with autoradiography, to assess the metabolism of various regions of the brain. The experimenter injects radioactive 2-DG into the animal and permits the radioactive compound to be taken into cells. Because 2-DG resembles glucose, the most active cells take up the largest amounts. The experimenter then kills the animal, removes the brain, slices it, and prepares it for autoradiography. Those regions of the brain that were most active contain the most radioactivity; they show this radioactivity in the form of dark spots in the developed emulsion. Figure 5.34 shows an autoradiograph of a slice of a rat brain; the dark spots at the bottom (indicated by the arrow) are nuclei with an especially high

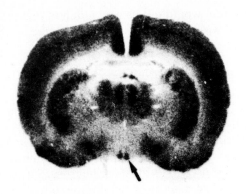

FIGURE 5.34
A 2-DG autoradiograph, showing especially high regions of activity in the pair of nuclei in the hypothalamus, at the base of the brain. (From Schwartz, W.J., and Gainer, H. *Science,* 1977, *197,* 1089–1091.)

metabolic rate. Chapter 9 describes these nuclei and their function. (See **Figure 5.34.**)

Concluding Remarks

In this chapter I referred to the strategy of converging operations. The results of any single research method are not definitive; each method has its limitations and ambiguities. Yet when several methods all yield the same conclusion—when their results *converge*—we can be much more confident that the conclusion is correct.

Let me give an example. Investigators have determined that the sexual behavior of female rats is stimulated by estradiol. Suppose we wanted to know about the location of the estradiol-sensitive neurons in the brain. I already described the use of autoradiography to determine which neurons selectively take up this hormone. These neurons are located in several parts of the brain, but particularly in the ventromedial nucleus of the hypothalamus. Consider what other methods, already described in this chapter, could be used to confirm these results. We might use stereotaxic surgery to destroy the ventromedial nucleus, predicting that the lesion would abolish the behavioral effects of estradiol on female sexual behavior. We might record the activity of these neurons while we infused estradiol into the region with a micropipette, expecting that their activity would change. We might administer a small amount of estradiol directly into the ventromedial nucleus with a small cannula, predicting that the hormone would stimulate sexual behavior. If these experiments produced consistent results, we might decide to investigate the connections of the neurons in the ventromedial hypothalamus with neurons elsewhere in the brain. To investigate, we would use amino acid autoradiography to see where their axons terminated and would then make lesions in *those* regions to see whether they affected sexual behavior. And so on.

As we will see in Chapter 10, these studies *have* been performed, and the results were as predicted. The rest of this book describes the efforts that have been made to understand the physiology of behavior. The quest involves many different methods, all devoted to a common goal. This chapter has introduced you to the most important methods used in neuroscience research, so you should have no trouble understanding the experiments that I describe in later chapters of the book. I hope that you have also learned enough so that you will be able to understand the rationale behind most experimental procedures you might read about in scientific journals or other books.

NEW TERMS

amino acid autoradiography p. 135
anterograde degeneration p. 134
autolytic enzyme p. 129
autoradiography p. 135

bregma p. 144
CAT scan p. 139
cautery p. 148
computerized axial tomography p. 138

cresyl violet p. 131

2-deoxyglucose (2-DG) p. 141

double-barreled micropipette p. 159

electroencephalogram (EEG) p. 155

evoked potential p. 153

fixation p. 129

fixative p. 129

focal epilepsy p. 157

formalin p. 129

Golgi-Cox stain p. 133

horseradish peroxidase p. 137

6-hydroxydopamine (6-HD) p. 149

immunohistochemical procedure p. 160

kainic acid p. 149

macroelectrode p. 151

membrane stain p. 133

microelectrode p. 150

microiontophoresis p. 159

micrometer p. 129

micropipette p. 150

microtome p. 129

myelin stain p. 132

Nissl substance p. 131

nuclear magnetic resonance (NMR) p. 141

oscilloscope p. 151

perfusion p. 129

positron emission tomography (PET) p. 141

scanning electron microscope p. 142

single-unit recording p. 150

staining p. 129

stereotaxic apparatus p. 146

stereotaxic atlas p. 144

SUGGESTED READINGS

Laboratory Manuals:

SKINNER, J.E. *Neuroscience: A Laboratory Manual.* Philadelphia: Saunders, 1971.

WEBSTER, W.G. *Principles of Research Methodology in Physiological Psychology.* New York: Harper & Row, 1975.

WELLMAN, P.J. *Laboratory Exercises in Physiological Psychology.* Boston: Allyn and Bacon, 1986.

Stereotaxic Atlases:

KOENIG, J.F.R., AND KLIPPEL, R.A. *The Rat Brain: A Stereotaxic Atlas of the Forebrain and Lower Parts of the Brain Stem.* Baltimore: Williams & Wilkins, 1963.

PELLIGRINO, L.J., AND CUSHMAN, A.J. *A Stereotaxic Atlas of the Rat Brain.* New York: Appleton-Century-Crofts, 1967.

SLOTNICK, B.M., AND LEONARD, C.M. *A Stereotaxic Atlas of the Albino Mouse Forebrain.* Rockville, Md.: Public Health Service, 1975. (U.S. Government Printing Office Stock Number 017-024-00491-0.)

SNIDER, R.S., AND NIEMER, W.T. *A Stereotaxic Atlas of the Cat Brain.* Chicago: University of Chicago Press, 1961.

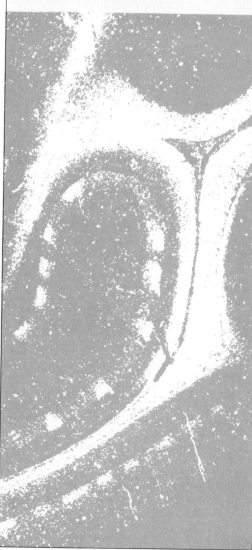

Vision

People often say that we have five senses: sight, hearing, smell, taste, and touch. Actually, we have more than five, but even experts disagree about how the lines between the various categories should be drawn. Certainly, we should add the vestibular senses; as well as providing us with auditory information, the inner ear supplies information about head orientation and movement. The sense of "touch" (or, more accurately, *somatosensation*) detects changes in pressure, warmth, cold, vibration, limb position, and events that damage tissue (that is, produce pain). Everyone agrees that we can detect these stimuli; the issue is whether or not they are detected by separate senses.

This chapter and the next are devoted to a discussion of the ways in which sensory organs detect changes in the environment and the ways in which the brain interprets neural signals from these organs. I need not stress the importance of these organs and the brain mechanisms that interpret them. Obviously, an organism deprived of information from its environment ceases to function.

This chapter considers vision, the sensory modality that receives the most attention from psychologists, anatomists, and physiologists. One reason for this attention derives from the fascinating complexity of the sensory organs of vision and the relatively large proportion of the brain that is devoted to the analysis of visual information. Another reason, I am sure, is that vision is so important to us as individuals. A natural fascination with such a rich source of information about the world leads to curiosity about how this sensory modality works. Chapter 7 deals with the

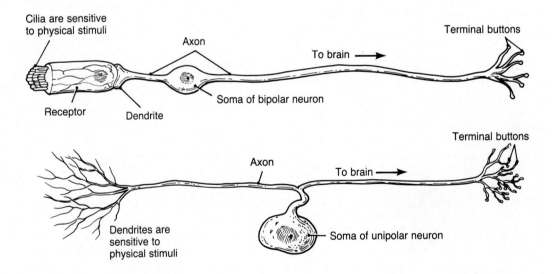

FIGURE 6.1
Bipolar (top) and unipolar (bottom) sensory neurons. Bipolar sensory neurons receive sensory information from receptors that lack axons; the dendrites of unipolar sensory neurons are themselves sensitive to physical stimuli.

other sensory modalities: audition, the somatosenses, the vestibular senses, gustation, and olfaction.

■ TRANSDUCTION AND SENSORY CODING

Before studying the particulars of vision, it is important to understand some general properties of sensory systems. This section considers the means by which neurons detect environmental changes, and the ways in which these changes are encoded in the nervous system.

We receive information about the environment from sensory receptors, specialized neurons that detect a variety of physical events. Stimuli impinge on the receptors and, through various processes, alter their membrane potentials. This process is known as *sensory transduction* because sensory events are *transduced* ("transferred") into changes in the cells' membrane potential. These electrical changes are called *receptor potentials.* Most receptors lack axons; a portion of their somatic membrane forms synapses with the dendrites of other neurons. Receptor potentials alter the rate at which these receptors release transmitter substances and hence modify the pattern of firing in neurons with which these cells form synapses. Ultimately, the information reaches the brain. (See **Figure 6.1, top.**) The exception to this scheme is provided by the receptors for the somatosenses (including the muscle and joint senses), which are sensitive to pressure, stretch, temperature, vibration, and stimuli that damage tissue. These receptors consist of unipolar neurons with specialized dendrites whose membrane potentials are depolarized by the stimuli they detect. The depolarizations increase the rate of firing of the cells' axons. The axons convey sensory information to the central nervous system. (See **Figure 6.1, bottom.**)

The transduction of sensory information into receptor potentials, and then into changes in neural firing, entails a form of code. The concept of *sensory coding* deserves some discussion. A code consists of a set of rules whereby information may be transformed from one set of symbols into another. For example, a written message might be given to the first of several people standing in a line. That person could read the message in Spanish to the second, who would say it in English to the third, who would convey it via semaphore signals to the fourth, who might tell the fifth person, "The message is Hamlet's soliloquy." Up to the fourth person, the representation of the message was transformed in reasonably simple ways. Transmission between the fourth and fifth persons did not resemble previous transmissions; the coding used here relied on the fact that the fourth and fifth persons were each familiar with Hamlet's soliloquy. As we will see, it appears that some elements of the sensory system "learn" frequently perceived stimuli; the subsequent presence of these stimuli can then be represented more simply by the activity of these elements.

Sensory information is coded in the nervous system by two basic means: spatial coding and temporal coding. *Spatial coding* is used by all sensory modalities, with the possible exception of olfaction. The principle is quite simple: different stimuli alter the activity of different neurons. For example, different receptors detect pressure applied to different parts of the body; thus, different sets of axons entering the spinal cord become active when a particular part of the skin is touched. The anatomical specificity is maintained up to the somatosensory cortex; neurons there receive information from receptors located in limited parts of the skin. Similarly, photoreceptors in different parts of the retina are stimulated by light reflected from different parts of the scene and send information to neurons in particular parts of the brain.

But we can perceive more than the location of a stimulus; we can determine its characteristics, such as its intensity. At the level of the receptor, sensory events can be represented in a graded manner. For example, cochlear microphonics (described in Chapter 7) encode auditory information perfectly, with all its nuances. But the information is transmitted to the brain by means of single axons, each of which has a one-letter alphabet available to it. An axon can either transmit an action potential or remain silent. In order to transmit information more complicated than the presence or absence of a particular stimulus, the axon must use the only dimension available to it—time. For instance, intensity of stimulation can be encoded by the rate of neural firing; the more intense the stimulus is, the faster the axon fires. This method of specifying information is called ***temporal coding.***

Temporal codes can be much more complicated than rate. For example, any complex message capable of being put into words can be transmitted via Morse code. And most computers communicate with remote instruments such as video terminals, printers, and even other computers by means of temporal-pulse codes transmitted on a single line. These devices use patterns of pulses, rather than mere rate, to represent information. The pulses represent successive *bits* (*b*inary dig*its*) of information, which in turn represent numbers or letters. For example, if the letter *B* is represented by the bit pattern 00110001, we could just as well signal the zeros and ones with the absence and presence of electrical pulses at the appropriate times. The pattern 00110001 would be transmitted as a short pause (two units long), two pulses, a longer pause (three units long), and another pulse. Of course, the receiving device would

have to know when the message started, and it would need some kind of clock to measure the interval between pulses to determine how many missing pulses (zeros) there were.

The nervous system might use temporal codes of similar complexity to represent sensory information. And spatial codes could be much more complex than "which neuron is firing?" Instead, the stimulus could be represented by the *pattern* of activity of many thousands of neurons. Perkel and Bullock (1968) list several ways in which the nervous system could code sensory information. They call these ways *candidate neural codes.* The modifier *candidate* is used to remind us that if we find that some complex pattern of neuronal firing is related to a certain stimulus dimension, we have not necessarily identified a neural code. The only way to find out whether a candidate code is actually one used by the nervous system is to see whether it conveys information that ultimately affects the behavior of the organism. The following analogy should make this point clear. Investigators have observed that porpoises and other marine mammals can produce a huge repertoire of complex sounds. Are these sounds used for communication? Do they encode information? Studies performed with a single porpoise could not answer these questions; they could do no more than establish candidate codes. We might find that particular sounds were associated with feeding, or play, or frustration. But unless we established that these sounds affect the behavior of other porpoises, we would not have shown them to be a means of communication. Similarly, what a given neuron does in response to stimulus changes does not provide enough information to establish a neural code. We must also show that other neurons are "listening" to that message. As you might imagine, very few neural codes have been established in such a way.

Another problem we encounter when we

consider sensory coding is the identification of the ultimate destination of the information. Where does the message go? We must be careful not to seek a decoder that looks at the neural representation of sensory information and interprets the pattern. If we do so, we commit the error of looking for a ***homunculus,*** a "little person" who resides in our heads, looking at and interpreting the activity of cortical neurons, in the way in which we might look at a display panel of some piece of complex machinery. The problem with the homunculus approach is that we must then explain how the homunculus works, which reintroduces the original problem. As we will see later in this chapter, observations of humans with brain damage have provided some answers about the nature of our ability to perceive and to be conscious of our perceptions. To a certain extent, these processes involve neural circuits in different parts of the brain.

With this introduction to the general characteristics of sensory processing, we will now turn to a specific channel — vision.

■ VISION: THE STIMULUS

As we all know, our eyes detect the presence of light. For humans, light is a narrow band of the electromagnetic spectrum. Electromag-

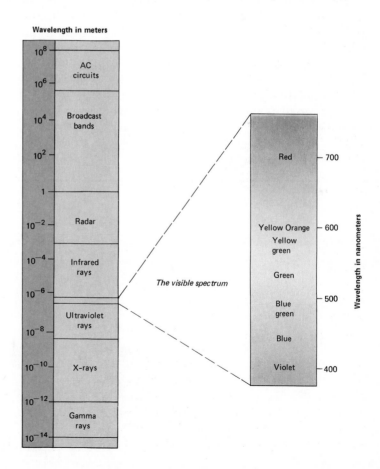

FIGURE 6.2
The electromagnetic spectrum.

netic radiation with a wavelength of between 380 and 760 nm (a nanometer is one billionth of a meter) is visible to us. (See **Figure 6.2.**) Other animals can detect different ranges of electromagnetic radiation. For example, a rattlesnake can detect its prey by means of infrared radiation; thus, it can locate warm-blooded animals in the dark. The range of wavelengths we call *light* is not qualitatively different from the rest of the electromagnetic spectrum; it is simply the part of the continuum that we humans can see.

Light has two properties. It acts as a continuous wave, with a particular frequency (and wavelength), and it also acts as if it were composed of packages of energy, called ***photons.*** First, let us consider light as a continuous wave of radiant energy. Light travels at a constant speed of approximately 300,000 km (186,000 miles) per second. Thus, if the frequency of oscillation of the wave is varied, the distance between the peaks of the waves will similarly vary, but in inverse fashion. Slower oscillations lead to longer wavelengths, and faster ones to shorter wavelengths. Wavelength determines one of the perceptual dimensions of light: its ***hue.*** The visible spectrum displays the range of hues that our eyes can detect.

Light can also vary in intensity. If the intensity of the electromagnetic signal is increased, the stimulus appears to increase in ***brightness,*** the second of the perceptual dimensions of light. The third dimension, ***saturation,*** refers to the relative purity of the light that is being perceived. If all the radiation is of one wavelength, the perceived color is pure, or fully saturated. Conversely, if the radiation contains all wavelengths, it produces no sensation of hue — it appears white. Colors with intermediate amounts of saturation consist of different mixtures. For example, if two beams of light, one blue and one white, intersect on a piece of white paper, their intersection will appear light blue in color. Thus, light blue is a desaturated version of blue. (See **Figure 6.3.**)

As I said, light also acts as if it consists of particles. These particles, called *photons,* have no mass and no electrical charge. If light

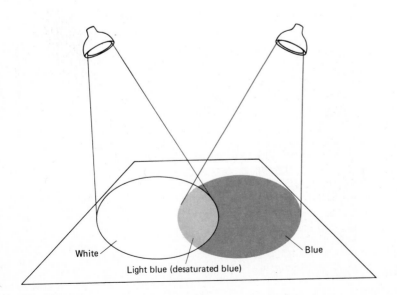

White

Light blue (desaturated blue)

Blue

FIGURE 6.3
A desaturated color such as light blue consists of a saturated color (blue) mixed with white light.

consists of particles, how, then, can we also refer to it as an electromagnetic radiation with a specific wavelength? We will have to live with this paradox, just as physicists do.

When investigators study the transduction of visual stimuli, they refer to the photons, or discrete particles of light energy, that are absorbed by the photopigment in the rods and cones in the retina. (I will discuss these receptor cells shortly.) Differences in intensity of the stimulus consist of different numbers of photons being absorbed in a given amount of time. On the other hand, when investigators study color perception, they refer to the absorption of light of various wavelengths. Both approaches are correct, but obviously they each reveal only part of the actual nature of light.

■ THE RECEPTIVE ORGAN

The eyes are suspended in the ***orbits,*** bony pockets in the front of the skull. They are moved by six extraocular muscles attached to the tough, fibrous outer coat of the eye (the ***sclera***). (See **Figure 6.4.**) Normally, we can-

not look behind our eyeballs and see these muscles because their attachments to the eyes are hidden by the ***conjunctiva.*** These mucous membranes line the eyelid and fold back to attach to the eye (thus preventing a contact lens that has slipped off the cornea from "falling behind the eye"). Figure 6.5 illustrates the external and internal anatomy of the eye. (See **Figure 6.5.**)

The outer layer of most of the eye, the sclera, is opaque, not permitting entry of light. However, the ***cornea,*** the outer layer at the front of the eye, is transparent and admits light. The amount of light that enters is regulated by the size of the ***pupil,*** formed by the opening in the ***iris,*** which consists of a ring of muscles situated behind the cornea. The iris contains two bands of muscles, the dilator (whose contraction enlarges the pupil) and the sphincter (whose contraction reduces it). The sphincter is innervated by acetylcholinergic fibers of the parasympathetic nervous system; acetylcholinergic blockers (for example, belladonna alkaloids such as atropine) thus produce pupillary dilation by relaxing the sphincter of the iris. In fact,

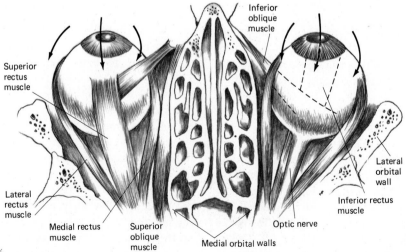

FIGURE 6.4
The extraocular muscles, which move the eyes.

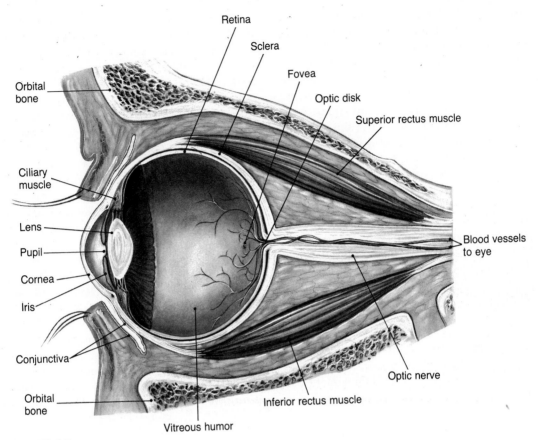

FIGURE 6.5
The human eye.

belladonna received its name from this effect. *Belladonna* means "beautiful lady" and was used in ancient times to enhance a woman's sex appeal by producing large, dilated pupils. (Dilated pupils often indicate interest, and most men are attracted to a woman who appears to find them interesting.)

The *lens* is situated immediately behind the iris. It consists of a series of transparent, onionlike layers. Its shape can be altered by contraction of the *ciliary muscles.* Because of the tension of elastic fibers that suspend it, the lens is normally relatively flat. In its flat state, the lens focuses the image of distant objects on the *retina,* the light-sensitive tissue layer that lines the inner portion of the

eye. When the ciliary muscles contract, tension is taken off these fibers, and the lens springs back to its normally rounded shape. Therefore, movements of the ciliary muscles determine whether the lens focuses images of near or distant objects on the retina, a process called *accommodation.*

Accommodation is normally integrated with *convergence* ("turning together") of the eyes. When we look at a near object, the eyes turn inward, so that the two images of the object fall on corresponding portions of the retinas. As we will see later, the images on the retinas lead to stimulation of neurons in the visual cortex that receive information from both retinas, yielding a fused image of the object. Convergence and accommodation normally occur together, so that the object on which the eyes are focused is also the object on which the eyes converge. If you hold a pencil in front of you and focus on a distant object, you will see two blurry pencils. If you then focus on the pencil, you will get two blurry views of the background. Control of eye movement is a very complicated process; as we study the process, we realize that it takes a sophisticated computer to accomplish what our brain does in moving the eyes.

After passing through the lens, light traverses the main part of the eye, which contains the **vitreous humor.** Vitreous humor ("glassy liquid") is a clear, gelatinous substance that gives the eye its bulk. After passing through the vitreous humor, light falls on the retina. In the retina are located the receptor cells, the **rods** and **cones** (named for their shapes), collectively known as **photoreceptors.** The human retina contains approximately 120 million rods and 6 million cones. Cones provide us with daytime vision. They are able to detect small features in the environment and thus provide vision of the highest sharpness, or *acuity* (from *acus,* meaning "needle"). The **fovea,** or central region of the retina, which mediates our most acute vision, contains only cones. Cones are also responsible for our ability to discriminate light of different wavelengths. Rods, which do not detect different colors, provide vision of poor acuity, but they are more sensitive to light. In a very dimly lighted environment, we use our rod vision; therefore, in dim light we are color-blind and lack foveal vision. You have probably noticed, while out on a dark night, that looking directly at a dim, distant light (that is, placing the image of the light on the fovea) causes it to disappear.

Another feature of the retina is the **optic disk,** where the axons conveying visual information gather together and leave the eye through the optic nerve. The optic disk produces a *blind spot,* because no receptors are located there. We do not normally perceive our blind spots, but their presence can be demonstrated. You can find yours by trying the exercise described in **Figure 6.6.**

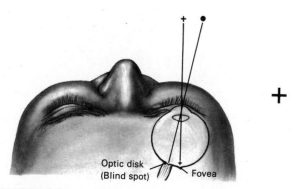

FIGURE 6.6

A test for the blind spot. With your left eye closed, look at the + with your right eye and move the page nearer and farther from you. When the page is about 20 cm from your face, the black circle disappears, because its image falls on the blind spot of your right eye.

Close examination of the retina shows that it consists of several layers of neuron cell bodies, their axons and dendrites, and the photoreceptors. Figure 6.7 illustrates a cross section through the primate retina, which is usually divided into three main layers: the photoreceptive layer, the bipolar cell layer, and the ganglion cell layer. Note that the photoreceptors are at the *back* of the retina; light must pass through the overlying layers to get to them. Fortunately, these layers are transparent. (See **Figure 6.7**.)

The photoreceptors form synapses with *bipolar cells.* In turn, these neurons form syn-

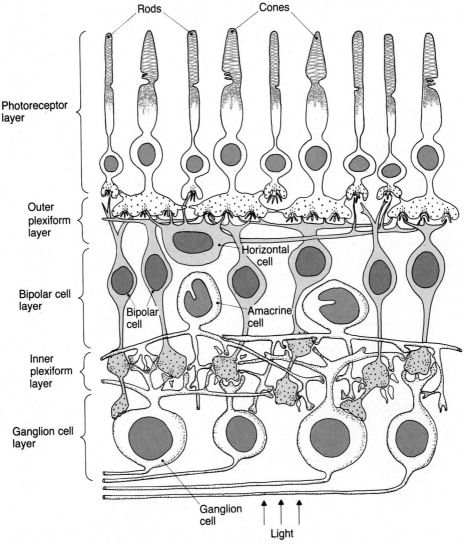

FIGURE 6.7

Details of retinal circuitry. (Redrawn from Dowling, J.E., and Boycott, B.B. *Proceedings of the Royal Society of London, B.*, 1966, *166*, 80 – 111.)

apses with the ***ganglion cells,*** whose axons travel through the optic nerves (the second cranial nerves) to the brain. In addition, the ***outer plexiform layer*** of the retina contains ***horizontal cells,*** and the ***inner plexiform layer*** contains ***amacrine cells,*** both of which transmit information in a direction parallel to the surface of the retina and thus combine messages from adjacent photoreceptors. The functions of these connections will be described later in this chapter. (See **Figure 6.7.**)

Photoreceptors

Figure 6.8 shows a drawing of a rod and a cone. Note that each photoreceptor consists of an outer segment connected by a cilium to the inner segment, which contains the nucleus. (See **Figure 6.8.**) The outer segment contains several hundred ***lamellae,*** thin plates of membrane. (*Lamella* and *omelet* derive from the same root word.) Although the outer segments of both types of receptors are layered, there is a basic difference. Rods con-

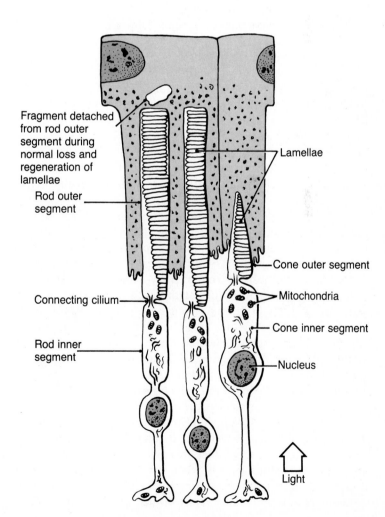

FIGURE 6.8
Photoreceptors. (Redrawn from Young, R.W., "Visual Cells." Copyright 1970 by Scientific American, Inc. All rights reserved.)

Fragment detached from rod outer segment during normal loss and regeneration of lamellae

Rod outer segment

Connecting cilium

Rod inner segment

Lamellae

Cone outer segment

Mitochondria

Cone inner segment

Nucleus

Light

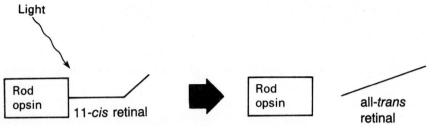

FIGURE 6.9
When light strikes rhodopsin, the 11-*cis* retinal straightens, becoming all-*trans* retinal, and detaches from the rod opsin. This event liberates energy, which initiates the steps that produce a receptor potential.

tain free-floating disks, whereas the lamellae of the cones consist of one continuous, folded membrane.

The first step in the process of transduction of light involves a special chemical called a ***photopigment.*** Photopigments consist of two parts, an ***opsin*** (a protein) and ***retinal*** (a lipid). There are several forms of opsin; for example, the photopigment of human rods, ***rhodopsin,*** consists of *rod opsin* plus retinal. (*Rhod-* actually refers to the Greek *rhodon,* "rose," and not to *rod.* Before it is bleached by the action of light, rhodopsin has a pinkish hue.) Molecules of photopigments are embedded in the membrane of the lamellae; a single human rod contains approximately 10 million rhodopsin molecules.

Retinal is synthesized from ***retinol*** (vitamin A), which explains why carrots, rich in retinol, are said to be good for your eyesight. Retinal is a molecule with a long chain that is capable of bending at a specific point. The straight-chained form of retinal is called ***all-trans retinal;*** the form with a bend is called ***11-cis retinal.*** The bent form, 11-*cis* retinal, is the only form of retinal capable of attaching to rod opsin to form rhodopsin. However, the 11-*cis* form of retinal is unstable; it can exist only in the dark. When a molecule of rhodopsin is exposed to light (that is, when it absorbs a photon), the bend in the retinal chain straightens out, and the retinal assumes the

all-*trans* form. Because rod opsin cannot remain attached to all-*trans* retinal, the rhodopsin breaks into its two constituents. When it does so, it changes from its rosy color to a pale yellow; hence, we say that the light *bleaches* the photopigment. (See **Figure 6.9.**)

The splitting of the photopigment causes a sudden decrease in the sodium permeability of the outer membrane of the photoreceptor, which hyperpolarizes the membrane. This change in the membrane potential constitutes the receptor potential. The fact that the absorption of a single photon by a single molecule of photopigment can produce a detectable receptor potential suggests that an intermediate messenger transmits information from the bleaching of a molecule of photopigment to the membrane of the cell.

Indeed, investigators have found that the bleaching of one rhodopsin molecule causes 50,000 molecules of cyclic GMP to disappear (Woodruff, Bownds, Green, Morrisey, and Shedlovsky, 1977; Woodruff and Bownds, 1979). You will recall from Chapter 3 that cyclic AMP and cyclic GMP serve as second messengers in some neurons, mediating the postsynaptic effects of transmitter substances. One hypothesis suggests that the fission of a molecule of photopigment activates molecules of phosphodiesterase, which, in turn, destroy molecules of cyclic GMP. The cyclic GMP normally holds open sodium channels in the membrane, so when cyclic GMP is destroyed, the sodium channels close. Thus the sodium conductivity of the membrane falls, and it becomes hyperpolarized. This *closing* of sodium channels contrasts with the *opening* of sodium channels that produces excitatory postsynaptic potentials in most neurons. (See **Figure 6.10.**)

The details of the process have not been worked out yet. In addition to alterations in cyclic GMP levels, the concentration of Ca^{2+} also changes, and some models give this ion a central role. (See Hubbell and Bownds, 1979, for a review.) The relationship between changes in cyclic GMP and Ca^{2+} is not known.

In most higher primates, photoreceptors contain four different opsins (rod opsin and three kinds of cone opsins), which bind with retinal to produce four different photopigments. Each of these compounds most readily absorbs light of a particular wavelength. A particular type of cone contains only one of the three cone photopigments; the three cones are thus maximally sensitive to light of long, medium, or short wavelength. The visual system uses information from these three types of cones to produce color vision.

Coding of Intensity in the Retina

The eye is a remarkably sensitive organ, responding to an incredible range of stimulus intensity. The smallest stimulus that can be detected is much less than one-millionth the intensity of the brightest light to which the eye can be exposed without damage. Obviously, then, this range of brightness cannot be faithfully represented by neural firing rate alone; a neuron cannot possibly vary its firing rate by a factor of more than a million. In fact, the upper limit of most neurons is less than a thousand impulses per second. One-millionth that rate would be one action potential every one and two-thirds minutes — a rate so slow as to be meaningless. How, then, does the visual system encode this tremendous range of intensity?

It does so in several ways. First, photic intensity is represented in a *nonlinear* fashion by the firing rate of neurons in the retina. Figure 6.11 illustrates the relationship between light intensity and the amplitude of the receptor potential produced by the photoreceptive cells in the eye of *Limulus* (the horseshoe crab). You can see that the curve in this figure is not at all linear: changes in intensity

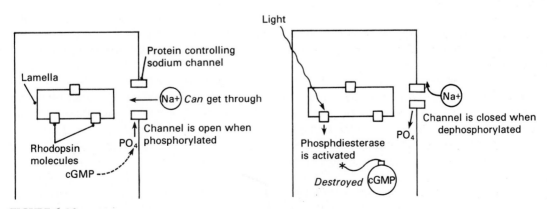

FIGURE 6.10
A hypothetical explanation for the production of receptor potentials in photoreceptors.

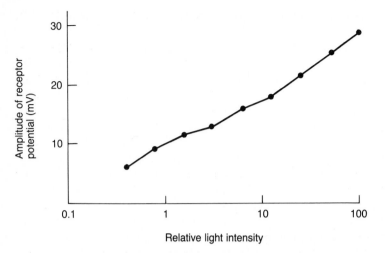

FIGURE 6.11
The relation between light
intensity and a receptor
potential in a photoreceptor in
the eye of a horseshoe crab.
(Adapted from Fuortes, M.G.F.
*American Journal of
Ophthalmology,* 1958, *46,*
210–223.) By permission.

of the light stimulus at the upper end of the scale produce hardly any alterations in the amplitude of the receptor potential. The receptors are much more sensitive to changes at the lower end of the brightness scale. (Note that the horizontal axis is logarithmic, not linear.) (See **Figure 6.11.**) This nonlinear responsiveness represents a compression of information. A large range of stimulus intensity is represented by a smaller range in the amplitude of the receptor potential.

A second method for extending the range of intensity that can be represented by the primate eye (and by the eye of most other mammals) is provided by the existence of two types of receptors. The ganglion cells that receive information from rods respond to light at levels of brightness too low to produce a response in the ganglion cells that receive information from cones. Intensity is thus represented by the firing rate of two populations of ganglion cells. For the visual system, then, spatial (line-specific) coding, as well as temporal coding (rate), is used to represent intensity.

Finally, some of the information about the range of intensity is just not needed. It is much more important for an animal to detect *changes* in brightness (which represent po-

tentially important changes in the world) or *differences* in the brightness of various portions of the visual field (which provide the basis of form perception). Most ganglion cells respond to regions of contrast between light and dark. Only a small percentage respond in a simple fashion to overall brightness (De-Valois, 1965). Psychologically, absolute brightness (except at the extremes of the range) is not an important variable. We tend to adapt to the overall level of illumination and judge various portions of the visual field in relation to the level of ambient (surrounding) illumination. A piece of white paper seen in dim light appears to us to be brighter than a piece of gray paper seen in brighter light, even though the intensity of light reflected from the gray paper might be greater. Therefore, we should not be surprised that most cells of our visual system exhibit a similar disregard for overall brightness.

INTERIM   SUMMARY

Freely moving animals such as ourselves require information about the environment in order to survive. Energy or molecules of particular chemicals cause receptor potentials in the neurons in our sensory organs. The receptor potentials alter the rate of firing of axons that communicate sensory information to the brain. The nervous system employs two basic schemes of sensory coding: spatial coding and temporal coding. The photoreceptors in the eyes are the rods and cones. The extraocular muscles move the eyes so that images of the environment fall on corresponding parts of each retina. Accommodation is accomplished by the ciliary muscles, which change the shape of the lens. Photoreceptors communicate synaptically with bipolar cells, which communicate synaptically with ganglion cells. In addition, horizontal cells (located in the outer plexiform layer) and amacrine cells (located in the inner plexiform layer) combine messages from adjacent photoreceptors.

When light strikes a molecule of photopigment in a photoreceptor, the 11-*cis* retinal molecule straightens out, becoming all-*trans* retinal, which detaches from the opsin molecule. This detachment initiates a series of chemical reactions that result in the destruction of cyclic GMP, closing sodium channels that are normally in the open state. The decreased influx of Na^+ causes the receptor potential by producing hyperpolarization of the photoreceptor membrane. The receptor potential decreases the release of transmitter substance by the photoreceptor. Intensity in the retina is coded temporally, by the rate of firing of the ganglion cell axons. However, because the eye responds to such a tremendous range of intensities, the code is not linear, and the visual system is better at detecting changes in illumination than at determining its absolute level.

■ CONNECTIONS BETWEEN EYE AND BRAIN

The Retinal Mosaic

The best word to describe the first level of analysis of the retinal image would be *mosaic*. Literally, a *mosaic* is a picture consisting of a large number of discrete elements — for example, bits of glass or ceramic. The lens of the eye casts an image of the environment

on the retinal photoreceptors, each of which responds to the intensity of the light that falls on it. The connection of photoreceptors to ganglion cells (whose axons transmit visual information over the optic nerves) does not occur on a one-to-one basis. At the periphery of the retina, many individual receptors converge on a single ganglion cell. Foveal vision is more direct, with approximately equal numbers of ganglion cells and cones. These receptor-to-axon relationships accord very well with the fact that our foveal (central) vision is most acute, while our peripheral vision is much less precise. In a sense, the pieces constituting the mosaic get larger as one goes from fovea to periphery, and the image transmitted to the brain becomes correspondingly cruder. (See **Figure 6.12.**)

The retina also contains neural circuitry that encodes the visual information in a more complex way. Ganglion cells do not simply respond in proportion to the amount of light that falls on the photoreceptors from which they receive information. However, before we examine the nature of this level of coding we should become acquainted with the anatomy of the ascending visual system.

The axons of the retinal ganglion cells ascend to the brain through the optic nerves and eventually reach the ***dorsal lateral geniculate nucleus*** of the thalamus. The terminal buttons of these axons synapse on cells in this nucleus, which in turn send their axons via the ***optic radiations*** to the primary visual cortex — the region surrounding the ***calcarine fissure*** (*calcarine* means "spur-shaped") at the most posterior region of the cerebrum. This area is often called the ***striate cortex*** because of the dark layer (*striation*) of cells it contains. (See **Figure 6.13.**)

Ignoring for a moment the complexities of coding that take place in the retina, we find that the visual system maintains the spatial code seen on the retinal mosaic all the way up

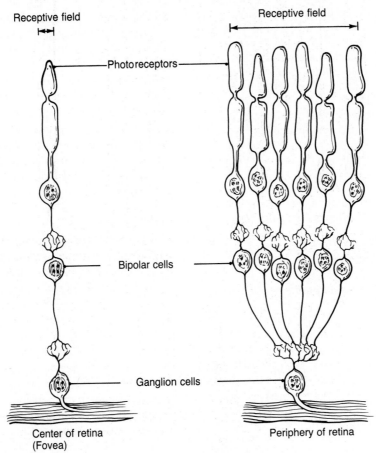

FIGURE 6.12
Ganglion cells in the fovea receive input from a smaller number of
photoreceptors than those in the periphery and hence provide more acute
visual information.

to the visual cortex. There is a **_retinotopic representation_** on the cortex. That is, stimulation of a particular region of the retina excites neurons in a particular region of the primary visual cortex, and adjacent retinal regions excite adjacent cortical areas. This topographical representation appears to be a real sensory code, not simply a candidate code. If a two-dimensional array of electrodes is placed over the human visual cortex, the person will report "seeing" geometrical shapes that correspond to the pattern of electrodes stimulated (Dobelle, Mladejovksy, and Girvin, 1974). This study was carried out on peripherally blinded people to ascertain the feasibility of providing visual prostheses. (A **_prosthesis,_** literally an "addition," is an artificial device made to take the place of a missing or damaged part of the body.) Unfortunately, long-term electrical stimulation causes tissue damage, thus ruling out the use of such synthetic replacement parts in the im-

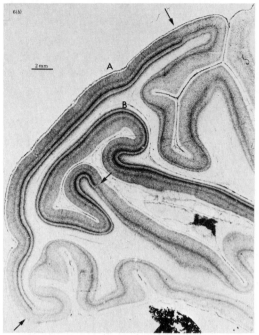

FIGURE 6.13
A photomicrograph of a cross section through the striate cortex of a rhesus macaque monkey. The ends of the striate cortex are shown by arrows. (From Hubel, D.H., and Wiesel, T.N. *Proceedings of the Royal Society of London, B.,* 1977, *198,* 1–59.)

mediate future, so some other way will have to be found to stimulate cortical neurons. Further evidence for the reality of the spatial code on the surface of the cortex comes from the finding that damage to restricted regions of the visual cortex produces localized areas of blindness *(scotomas).*

The retinal surface is not represented on the visual cortex in a linear fashion, though; the picture is much distorted. It is as if a picture were printed on a sheet of rubber that was then stretched in various directions. The center of the sheet is stretched the most; foveal vision, with its great acuity, takes up approximately 25 percent of the visual cortex.

The Ascending Visual Pathway

Let us now examine the ascending visual pathway in more detail. Figure 6.14 shows a diagrammatical view of the human brain as observed from below. The optic nerves join together at the base of the brain to form the *optic chiasm (khiasma* means "cross"). There, axons from ganglion cells serving the inner halves of the retina (the nasal sides) cross through the chiasm and ascend to the dorsal lateral geniculate nucleus of the opposite side of the brain. (See **Figure 6.14.**) The lens inverts the image of the world projected on the retina (and similarly reverses left and right). Therefore, because the axons from the nasal halves of the retinas cross to the other side of the brain, each hemisphere receives information from the contralateral half (opposite side) of the visual scene. That is, if a person looks straight ahead, the right hemisphere receives information from the left half of the visual field, and the left hemisphere receives information from the right. (See **Figure 6.14.**)

Each dorsal lateral geniculate nucleus then projects to the ipsilateral (same-side) visual cortex; as a matter of fact, the lateral geniculate nuclei provide the only subcortical input to the primary visual cortex of primates. Because there is a considerable amount of overlap in the visual fields of the two eyes, many cortical regions receive information about the same point in the visual field from both eyes.

Figure 6.15 shows the actual appearance of the base of the brain, with neural tissue dissected away so that the optic radiations can be seen. Note the heavy projection to the upper lip of the calcarine fissure. (See **Figure 6.15.**)

Besides the primary retino-geniculo-striate pathway, there are five other pathways taken by fibers from the retina:

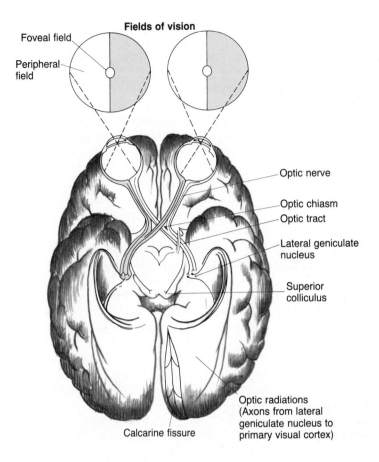

Fields of vision

Foveal field

Peripheral field

Optic nerve

Optic chiasm

Optic tract

Lateral geniculate nucleus

Superior colliculus

Optic radiations (Axons from lateral geniculate nucleus to primary visual cortex)

Calcarine fissure

FIGURE 6.14

The primary visual pathway. (Adapted with permission from McGraw-Hill Book Co. from *The Human Nervous System,* 2nd edition, by Noback and Demarest. Copyright 1975, by McGraw-Hill, Inc.)

1. **Suprachiasmatic nucleus.** This region of the hypothalamus controls behaviors and physiological processes that vary across the day/night cycle. Input from the retina synchronizes its activity. (This structure will be discussed in Chapter 9.)

2. **Accessory optic nuclei.** These nuclei, located in the brain stem, play a role in coordinating eye movements that compensate for head movements, thus keeping the eyes "on track" (Ito, 1977). This system also involves the floccular region of the cerebellum, discussed in Chapter 8.

3. **Pretectum.** This pathway terminates near the superior colliculus and plays a role in the control of pupillary size (Sprague, Berlucchi, and Rizzolatti, 1973).

4. **Superior colliculus.** The superior colliculus plays a role in attention to visual stimuli and control of eye movements. This structure sends fibers to various areas of the visual cortex, but not to the primary visual cortex. The superior colliculus also receives information from most areas of the visual cortex.

5. **Ventral lateral geniculate nucleus.** The dorsal lateral geniculate nucleus is the principal relay station between retina and striate cortex. The ventral lateral geniculate nucleus also receives direct visual input but relays it only to subcortical structures: the pretectum, superior colliculus, pontine nuclei, and suprachiasmatic nucleus. Its function is not known.

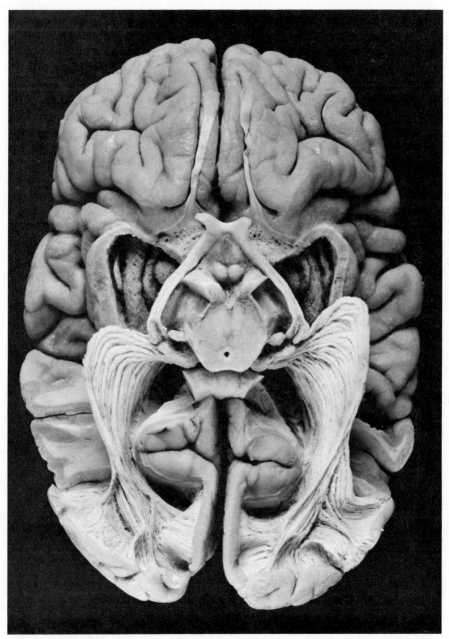

FIGURE 6.15
The base of the brain, with tissue dissected away so that the projections
(optic radiations) between the dorsal lateral geniculate nucleus and the
primary visual cortex are visible. (From Gluhbegovic, N., and Williams,
T.H. *The Human Brain: A Photographic Atlas.* Hagerstown, Md.: Harper
& Row, 1980.)

■ DETECTION OF FEATURES BY THE VISUAL SYSTEM

Receptive Fields and Feature Detection

The portion of the visual field to which a single neuron responds is called its **receptive field.** Obviously, the receptive field of a photoreceptor is determined by its location on the retinal mosaic. The receptive fields of neurons in subsequent levels of the visual pathways are determined by the details of their anatomical connections with the photoreceptors. As we have seen, a retinotopic representation is maintained up to the level of the visual cortex. Thus, the receptive fields of neurons in adjacent parts of the visual cortex are themselves adjacent; in other words, neighboring neurons respond to stimuli in adjacent parts of the visual field. However, from the ganglion cells onward, the receptive fields of neurons of the visual system are considerably more complex than those of the photoreceptors. For example, cells that respond to foveal stimulation have small receptive fields, whereas those that respond to stimulation of the peripheral retina have much larger ones. But an even more important characteristic of neurons in the visual system is that they respond most vigorously to stimuli of particular shapes. That is, they do not simply respond to the level of illumination in their receptive field; rather, they respond to a particular pattern of light and dark, such as a line segment of a given orientation and length. The neurons respond best to particular visual *features;* hence they are referred to as *feature detectors.*

The identification of a cell's receptive field and the type of stimulus to which it responds best is accomplished by a procedure called *mapping.* The animal is anesthetized and placed in front of a projection screen or, sometimes, a display terminal attached to a computer. A contact lens is usually placed on its eye to compensate for the paralysis of the ciliary muscle (which controls the lens) and thus to focus images properly on the retina. Recordings of action potentials are taken from single neurons while a visual stimulus moves around on the screen. The receptive field is defined as the area of the visual field in which the stimulus elicits a response from the cell. The "best" stimulus is determined by the shape of the visual stimulus that produces the largest response. In this case, *response* means a change in the rate of firing; the change can be either an increase or a decrease, because information is coded just as well by a decreased rate of firing as it is by an increased rate. Obviously, because the experimenter can never try out all possible visual stimuli, all that he or she can say is that the stimulus that produces the largest response is the best of the ones that were tried.

Ganglion Cells

Description of Receptive Fields

Kuffler (1952, 1953), recording from ganglion cells in the retina of the cat, discovered that their receptive field consists of a roughly circular center, surrounded by a ring. In his experiments, cells responded in opposite manner to light in the two regions of each receptive field. A spot of light presented to the central field *(center)* produced a burst of unit activity. However, when the spot was moved to the surrounding field *(surround),* the cell ceased firing, but it began firing vigorously for a while when the spot of light was turned off. The cell thus responded in a center-on, surround-off manner. Kuffler also identified cells that give a contrary, center-off, surround-on response. Simultaneous presentation of a stimulus to both center and surround produced little or no response. Therefore, these ganglion cells compare the brightness of the center spot with its surround, giving the greatest response when the contrast is maximal. (See **Figure 6.16.**)

Enroth-Cugell and Robson (1966) found that not all retinal ganglion cells show this cancellation effect. Those that do show a null position (i.e., center + surround stimulation counterbalancing each other) they called **X cells;** those that do not they called **Y cells.** X cells and Y cells differ in several ways. The axons of X cells conduct relatively slowly and

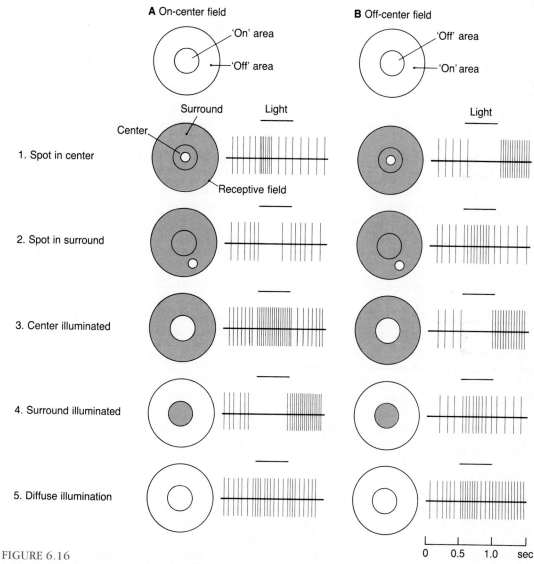

FIGURE 6.16

Responses of retinal ganglion cells with center-on *(left)* and center-off *(right)* receptive fields to various stimuli. (Adapted from Kandel, E.R., and Schwartz, J.H. *Principles of Neural Science.* New York: Elsevier Science Publishing Co., 1982, after Kuffler, S.W. *Cold Spring Harbor Symposium for Quantitative Biology,* 1952, *17,* 281–292.)

display a sustained response *(tonic response)* to a continuous stimulus in their receptive field, which tends to be small. These cells do not respond well to rapidly moving stimuli. In contrast, the axons of Y cells conduct relatively rapidly, and the cells show a brisk response to the onset of the stimulus but quickly cease responding to a continuous stimulus *(phasic response)*. The Y cells' receptive fields are larger than those of X cells, and they respond best to rapidly moving stimuli. In addition, they do not respond differentially to stimuli of different hues, whereas many X cells do.

Another class of ganglion cells was also discovered: *W cells* (Stone and Fukuda, 1974). These cells fire *weakly* (at a slow rate) in response to stimuli in their receptive fields, which are very large. Some W cells respond tonically, some phasically. Like Y cells, they respond best to moving stimuli. Many of the receptive fields of W cells are homogeneous, lacking the typical center/surround antagonism.

Anatomical studies have shown that X, Y, and W ganglion cells differ in shape and size, and that their axons terminate in different regions of the brain (see Rodieck, 1979, for a review). X cells are medium sized and have small dendritic fields (that is, their dendritic trees occupy a small area of the retina). The cells receive information from photoreceptors in a limited region of the retina; that is, they have small receptive fields. The axons of X cells, which compose approximately 55 percent of the total population of ganglion cells, terminate almost exclusively in the dorsal lateral geniculate nucleus. Y cells, which compose approximately 40 percent of the population, are large; their large dendritic fields account for their large receptive fields. Like X cells, their axons project to the dorsal lateral geniculate nucleus, but about half of these cells send branches to the superior colliculus as well. W cells constitute approxi-

mately 5 percent of all ganglion cells. They are the smallest of all ganglion cells but have thin dendrites that branch extensively, accounting for their large receptive fields. They project exclusively to the superior colliculus.

The response characteristics of X, Y, and W cells suggest that X cells supply information for perception of fine detail, while Y cells supply information about moving stimuli. Because both Y cells and W cells respond to movement and send axons to the superior colliculus, these cell types probably play a role in controlling eye movements and in directing the organism's attention to moving stimuli in the periphery of the visual field.

Retinal Circuitry of Center/Surround Receptive Fields

Investigators have made considerable progress in relating the circuitry of retinal photoreceptors and neurons to their functional characteristics. So many investigators have contributed to this story that I will simply refer you to Dowling (1979) for specific references. In the vertebrate retina, photoreceptors provide input to both bipolar cells and horizontal cells. They form two types of synapses with the dendrites of bipolar cells: *ribbon synapses* and *flat synapses.* (See **Figure 6.17.**) Two types of bipolar cells can be distinguished on the basis of their synaptic connections with photoreceptors: *invaginating bipolar cells* receive input from ribbon synapses, and *flat bipolar cells* receive input from flat synapses. In mammals, only cones form flat synapses. Horizontal cells receive synaptic input from photoreceptors by means of ribbon synapses and themselves form conventional synapses with the dendrites of both invaginating and flat bipolar cells. (See **Figure 6.18.**)

Amacrine cells connect with the axons of bipolar cells and the dendrites of ganglion cells. Most of the terminal buttons of bipolar cells form synapses with processes of two

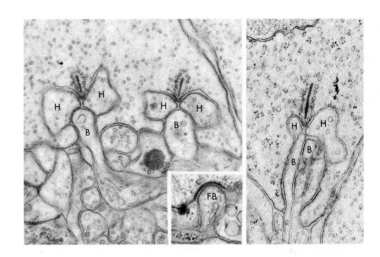

FIGURE 6.17

Electron photomicrographs of ribbon synapses and a flat synapse (insert) in the retina. H = dendrite of horizontal cell; B = dendrite of invaginating bipolar cell; FB = dendrite of flat bipolar cell. (From Dowling, J.E. *Investigative Ophthalmology,* 1970, *9,* 655–680.)

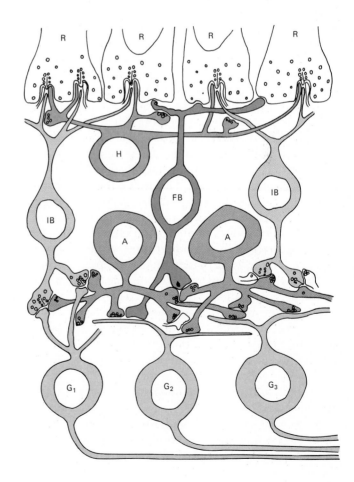

FIGURE 6.18

Three principal types of circuits connect photoreceptors with ganglion cells in the vertebrate retina. R = photoreceptor; H = horizontal cell; FB = flat bipolar cell; IB = invaginating bipolar cell; A = amacrine cell; G_1, G_2, and G_3 = ganglion cells. (From Dowling, J.E., in *The Neurosciences, Fourth Study Program,* edited by F.O. Schmitt and F.G. Worden. Cambridge, Mass.: MIT Press, 1979.)

other neurons: one ganglion cell and one amacrine cell, two amacrine cells, or two ganglion cells. Some ganglion cells (labeled G_1) receive most of their input from bipolar cells, others (labeled G_2) receive input from both bipolar and amacrine cells, and still others (labeled G_3) receive input from amacrine cells alone. (See **Figure 6.18.**) In primate retinas, the bipolar cells form many synapses directly with the dendrites of ganglion cells; thus, the cell labeled G_1 dominates in our eyes. The retinas of animals such as frogs and pigeons, whose ganglion cells respond best to moving stimuli, are dominated by G_3 ganglion cells. This relation suggests that the amacrine cells contribute to the movement sensitivity of Y and W ganglion cells.

Now let us see how the retinal circuitry produces the types of responses in ganglion cells that I have discussed so far. Figure 6.19 shows the neural circuitry that produces a ganglion cell of the typical center/surround type, showing excitation to a spot of light in the center, and inhibition to a spot of light in the surround. (A similar figure could be drawn for center-off, surround-on ganglion cells.) The circuitry is much simplified and omits the amacrine cells. The outer three types of cells, photoreceptors *(R)*, invaginating bipolar cells *(IB)*, and horizontal cells *(H)*, do not produce action potentials. Instead, their release of transmitter substance is regulated by the value of their membrane potential; depolarizations increase the release, and hyperpolarizations decrease it. The circles to the left indicate what would be seen on an oscilloscope screen recording changes in the cells' membrane potentials in response to a spot of light shone on the photoreceptor in the middle, which is located in the center of the receptive field. The stimulated neurons are shown in color.

As we have seen, the membranes of photoreceptors become hyperpolarized when they are stimulated by light; this is shown in the top left graph. The hyperpolarization reduces the release of transmitter substance by the photoreceptor. Because this transmitter substance hyperpolarizes the dendrites of the bipolar cell, a *reduction* in its release causes the membrane of the bipolar cell to *depolarize*. Thus, light hyperpolarizes the photoreceptor and depolarizes the bipolar cell. (See **Figure 6.19, left.**) The depolarization causes the bipolar cell to release more transmitter substance, which depolarizes the membrane of the ganglion cell *(G)*, causing it to increase its rate of firing. The result is a *center-on response.* (See **Figure 6.19, left.**)

The response of this same ganglion cell to light shining on photoreceptors in the outer ring of the receptive field is mediated by horizontal cells, as shown in the right half of Figure 6.19. When light falls on these photoreceptors, they hyperpolarize and release less transmitter substance. As a result, the membrane of the horizontal cell *hyperpolarizes.* The horizontal cell consequently releases less transmitter substance, and the level of excitation in the bipolar cell, and the ganglion cell with which it communicates, falls. Thus, light that shines on the outer ring of the receptive field decreases the rate of firing of the ganglion cell. The result is a *surround-off response.* (See **Figure 6.19, right.**)

I must emphasize that my description is a much simplified one. First, although I showed only five photoreceptors arranged in a line, the receptive field is actually a central circle surrounded by a ring, both of which contain several photoreceptors. (The number of photoreceptors depends on the location of the receptive field; those closer to the fovea are much smaller than those located in the periphery of the retina.) More important, the neural circuitry is more complex than I have shown, as you can see if you consult the references I mentioned previously. I have omitted the circuitry involving the amacrine cells, which produces the brief on-and-off responses seen in Y cells and some W cells, because these circuits are even more speculative than the ones I have included. In the future, investigators will doubtless learn more about the functions of the microcircuitry of the retina, and the circuits I have drawn here will be superseded with more accurate (and more complex) ones.

Lateral Geniculate Nucleus

The dorsal lateral geniculate nucleus receives inputs from the retinal ganglion cells — primarily X cells, but Y cells as well. This thalamic nucleus receives its name from its kneelike shape (*genu* means "knee"). The nucleus on each side of the brain contains six

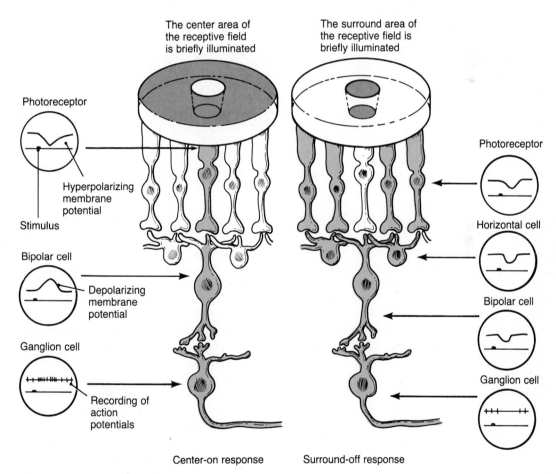

FIGURE 6.19
The retinal circuitry that produces cells with center-on, surround-off receptive fields. *Left:* Response to illumination of the center of the receptive field. *Right:* Response to illumination of the surround. (Adapted from Dowling, 1979.)

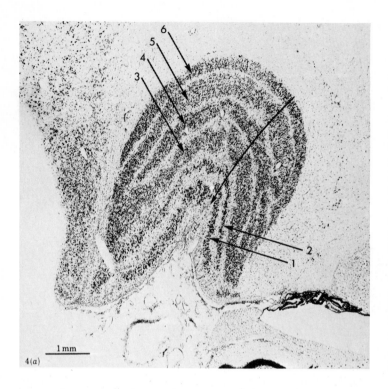

1 mm

4(a)

FIGURE 6.20
A photomicrograph of a
section through the right
lateral geniculate nucleus of a
rhesus monkey (cresyl violet
stain). Layers 1, 4, and 6
receive input from the
contralateral (left) eye, and
layers 2, 3, and 5 receive input
from the ipsilateral (right) eye.
The receptive fields of all
six layers are in almost
perfect registration; cells
located along the line of the
unlabeled arrow have
receptive fields centered on
the same point. (From
Hubel, D.H., Wiesel, T.N., and
Le Vay, S. *Philosophical
Transactions of the Royal
Society of London, B.,*
1977, *278,* 131–163.)

layers of neurons; each layer receives input from only one eye. (See **Figure 6.20.**)

The topographical arrangement of receptive fields of the retinal ganglion cells is maintained by the neurons in the lateral geniculate nucleus. These neurons also have the same response characteristics of the retinal X cells and Y cells, responding to spots of light with excitation or inhibition, and responding to stimulation of the surrounding ring with inhibition or excitation, respectively. X cells respond continuously, and Y cells respond transiently.

Primary Visual Cortex

Much of what we know about the response characteristics of single neurons in the visual cortex derives from the pioneering work of David Hubel and Torsten Wiesel of Harvard University, which began in the 1960s (see Hubel and Wiesel, 1977, 1979). Of course, their efforts were soon joined by those of other investigators.

Hierarchy of Feature Detectors

The primary visual cortex consists of six principal layers (and several sublayers), arranged in bands parallel to the surface. These layers contain the nuclei of cell bodies and dendritic arborizations that show up as bands of light or dark in sections of tissue that have been dyed with Nissl stain. (See **Figure 6.21.**)

In primates, axons from the dorsal lateral geniculate nucleus terminate on cortical neurons in layer IVc. All of these axons belong to X-type cells, and hence the cortical neurons in this layer show either sustained excitatory or sustained inhibitory responses to light in a circular region of the visual field, with the opposite response from light presented to the surrounding ring.

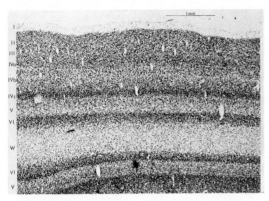

FIGURE 6.21

A photomicrograph of a small section of striate cortex, showing the six principal layers. The letter *W* refers to the white matter that underlies the visual cortex; beneath the white matter is layer VI of the striate cortex on the opposite side of the gyrus. (From Hubel, D.H., and Wiesel, T.N. *Proceedings of the Royal Society of London, B.,* 1977, *198,* 1–59.)

Neurons in layer IVc project to the layers just above (Lund, 1973). Neurons in layer IVb have somewhat larger receptive fields, longer than those of layer IVc neurons, but just as narrow. They respond best to a line with a particular *orientation.* That is, some neurons respond best to a vertical line, some to a horizontal line, and some to a line oriented somewhere in between. The selectivity of different neurons varies, but in general their response falls off when the line tilts by more than 10 degrees. (For comparison's sake, the angle between the hands of a clock at one o'clock is 30 degrees.)

Hubel and Wiesel speculate that these cells, which they call **simple cells,** receive input from a number of individual layer-IVc cells whose receptive fields are arranged in a straight line. If the stimulus is a line that excites the centers of the receptive fields of all

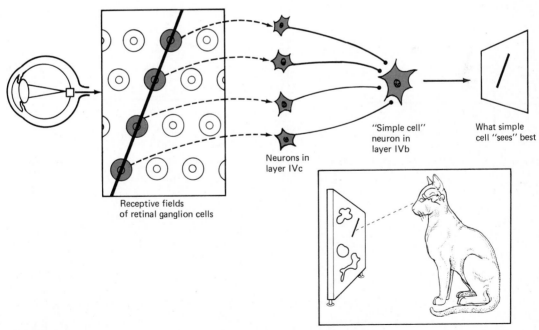

FIGURE 6.22

Hubel and Wiesel's model of the neural circuitry that determines what a simple cell "sees."

of the layer-IVc cells that project to a given simple cell, that cell will be maximally stimulated. (See **Figure 6.22.**)

Complex cells are found both above and below layer IV, in layers II, III, V, and VI. These cells, like simple cells, respond to segments of lines with a particular orientation. However, the receptive field is larger, and within it the line can be moved around and still continue to stimulate the cell. (By *stimulation* I refer to either excitation or inhibition.) For example, suppose that a particular complex cell is stimulated best by a 45-degree line, slanted from lower left to upper right. A simple cell that is stimulated by a 45-degree line will respond to it only if the line is placed in one particular location. In contrast, a complex cell will respond to a 45-degree line anywhere in its much larger receptive field. Moreover, it will respond even more if the line is moved perpendicular to its

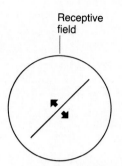

Response increases when line is moved in direction of either arrow

FIGURE 6.23
The most effective stimulus for a complex cell is a line of a particular orientation, moving perpendicular to its length.

orientation. (See **Figure 6.23.**) Hubel and Wiesel suggest that a complex cell receives input from a number of simple cells, all of which respond to line segments with the

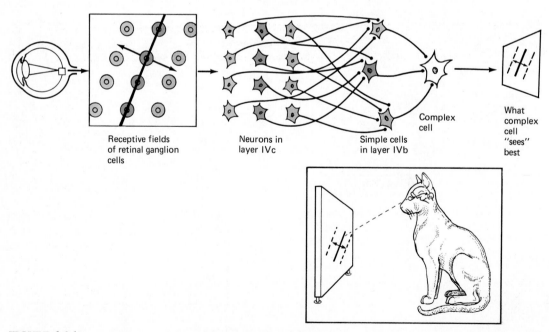

Receptive fields of retinal ganglion cells

Neurons in layer IVc

Simple cells in layer IVb

Complex cell

What complex cell "sees" best

FIGURE 6.24
Hubel and Wiesel's model of the neural circuitry that determines what a complex cell "sees."

same orientation, but within different regions of the visual field. (See **Figure 6.24.**)

Striate cortex also contains what Hubel and Wiesel refer to as ***hypercomplex cells.*** These cells, like complex cells, respond to lines of a particular orientation located anywhere within their receptive field. They are located in the same layers of cortex. However, unlike complex cells, their response diminishes and may disappear altogether if the line is too long and extends outside the receptive field. (See **Figure 6.25.**)

An important characteristic of the primary visual cortex is that it is arranged in *columns*. That is, if an investigator lowers a microelectrode perpendicular to the surface of the cortex, he or she will encounter several different types of cells: complex, hypercomplex, simple, and (in layer IVc) those with circular center/surround characteristics. However, the centers of the receptive fields of all of these cells will be approximately the same. In addition, the simple, complex, and hypercomplex cells in a particular column will all respond best to lines of the same orientation. Finally, they will all respond best to stimulation from the same eye. Although most neurons in the primate striate cortex are binocular (that is, they respond to stimulation of either eye), they respond more vigorously to stimulation of one eye or the other. (The ex-

ception are the center/surround neurons of layer IVc. Because they receive input solely from the lateral geniculate nucleus, these neurons are exclusively monocular.) Thus, a column of neurons in the visual cortex analyzes common features of a common portion of the visual scene.

Distribution of Orientation Columns

Hubel and Wiesel stress that the anatomy and response patterns of neurons show that information processing in the striate cortex is strictly a local matter. A particular region of cortex receives information from a fairly restricted area of the retina. For example, no neuron in the striate cortex receives information from both the center and the periphery of the visual field. Thus, although the primary visual cortex analyzes the visual scene into line segments of various orientations, a composite picture cannot be "put together" there. It is as if each column of cells in the striate cortex is attached to a few dots on a television screen. Because the columns do not exchange information with each other, no one of them can perceive what is happening. As we will see, this function appears to take place in the visual association cortex.

Hubel and Wiesel found that adjacent columns of cells in the striate cortex respond to lines of slightly different orientation. When

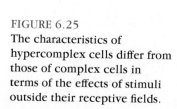

FIGURE 6.25
The characteristics of hypercomplex cells differ from those of complex cells in terms of the effects of stimuli outside their receptive fields.

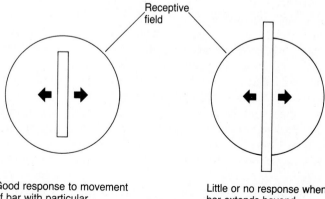

Good response to movement of bar with particular orientation

Little or no response when bar extends beyond receptive field

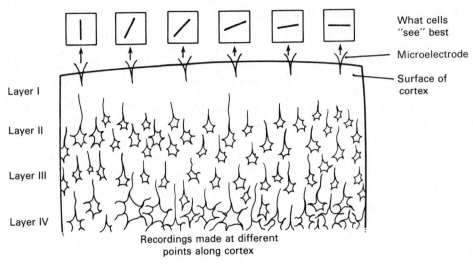

FIGURE 6.26
As the recording electrode moves across the surface of the visual cortex,
the orientation of the most effective stimulus for cortical neurons rotates.

they moved an electrode through the cortex obliquely to its surface, so that it passed through successive columns, they found that the preferred orientation of the lines rotated in a clockwise or counterclockwise direction; each 25 μm of lateral movement produced a corresponding rotation of 10 degrees in the preferred stimulus. (See **Figure 6.26.**)

A study by Hubel, Wiesel, and Stryker (1978) demonstrated the pattern of preference for lines of a particular orientation throughout the primary visual cortex. The investigators injected a monkey with radioactive 2-deoxyglucose (2-DG) and then presented a pattern of vertical stripes, moving back and forth from left to right. The injected chemical resembles normal glucose and hence is taken up in greatest quantities by neurons that have the highest metabolic rate. However, unlike glucose, 2-DG cannot be metabolized and, in addition, cannot leave the cell once it enters. Thus, the procedure labels metabolically active cells with radioactivity.

Because the retina was stimulated with a pattern of vertical lines in this experiment, those cortical neurons that respond best to lines of this orientation should have fired at the highest rate and hence should have been the most active metabolically. Therefore, they should also be the most radioactive. Those cells that respond best to lines of other orientations should contain relatively small amounts of radioactivity. The monkey was killed, its brain was sliced, and the sections were examined by means of autoradiography.

Figure 6.27 shows a slice through the striate cortex taken perpendicular to the surface. Note that columns of neurons, approximately 0.5 mm apart, were labeled with radiography, indicating that they responded best to vertically oriented lines. In contrast, neurons in layer IVc were uniformly dark, because they responded to any stimulus that passed through the center of their receptive field. (See **Figure 6.27.**)

Ocular Dominance
We have two eyes, and much of their visual fields overlap. As we saw earlier (Figure

FIGURE 6.27

An autoradiograph of a cross section through the striate cortex of a rhesus monkey that had been given an injection of [³H]-2-deoxyglucose and had been exposed to a moving pattern of vertical stripes. (From Hubel, D.H., Wiesel, T.N., and Stryker, M.P. *Journal of Comparative Neurology,* 1978, *177,* 361–380.)

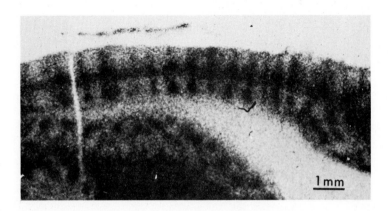

6.14), the right halves of the retinas (which see the left half of the visual field) project to the right hemisphere, and the left halves (which see the right visual field) project to the left hemisphere. How is the information from each eye combined within the primary visual cortex?

Hubel and Wiesel found that all neurons in layer IVc responded exclusively to stimuli presented to one eye or the other. Most neurons in other layers responded binocularly, but they responded more vigorously to stimuli presented to one eye. They found that eye preference, like preference for lines of a particular orientation, was consistent within a vertical column of neurons but varied as the electrode moved laterally along the surface of the cortex. That is, if recording started in a region of cortex containing neurons that responded exclusively to stimuli presented to the left eye, more and more responsiveness to the right eye would be recorded as the electrode was moved away from the starting point. Eventually, a region of exclusively "right eye" cells would be encountered. As it continued moving laterally, the electrode would then encounter some more neurons that responded to the left eye, and the cycle would begin again. Thus, striate cortex contains ocular dominance columns as well as orientation columns; in these columns, the responses of neurons are dominated by one eye.

To map the location of ocular dominance columns in the primary visual cortex, Hubel, Wiesel, and Stryker (1978) injected the left eye of a monkey with a radioactive amino acid. Anterograde axoplasmic flow carried the amino acid to the dorsal lateral geniculate nucleus. There, a small amount was released by the terminal buttons and was transported into cell bodies whose axons project to the striate cortex. The investigators used a very sensitive autoradiographic technique to determine the location of ocular dominance columns — that is, the cortical regions that received input from the left eye.

Figure 6.28 shows the results in a slice through the striate cortex, taken perpendicular to the surface. Dark and light stripes confirm the results of recording studies: alternating columns in the cortex are dominated by input from one eye or the other. (See **Figure 6.28.**)

"Blobs" in Cortical Columns

The research of Hubel and Wiesel and their colleagues has shown that the visual cortex consists of columns. The neurons within each column have approximately the same receptive field, respond best to lines of a particular orientation, and have similar ocular domi-

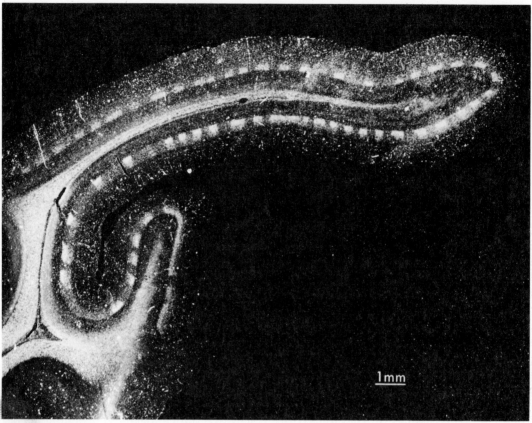

1mm

FIGURE 6.28

A dark-field autoradiograph (radioactivity is shown by light areas) of a
cross section through the striate cortex of a rhesus macaque monkey that
had received an injection of radioactive amino acid in one eye. (From
Hubel, D.H., and Wiesel, T.N. *Proceedings of the Royal Society of
London, B.,* 1977, *198,* 1–59.)

nance characteristics. An unusual characteristic of the primate striate cortex was discovered by Wong-Riley (1978). She found that a stain for the mitochondrial enzyme cytochrome oxidase showed a patchy distribution. Subsequent research with the stain (Horton and Hubel, 1980; Humphrey and Hendrickson, 1980) revealed the presence of a polka-dot pattern of "blobs" (the authors' term) approximately 200 μm in diameter and spaced at 0.5-mm intervals.

You may recall from a previous section that orientation columns progress in 10-degree steps approximately 25 μm apart. From these findings, we can deduce that the distance between columns that respond to the same line orientation (that is, those that are 180 degrees apart) is approximately 0.5 mm. Indeed, the spacing of an array of orientation columns and "blobs" is identical. Hubel and Livingstone (1983) presented an idealized model of the columnar arrangement of the primate visual cortex, showing the relation of these "blobs" to orientation and ocular dominance columns. (See **Figure 6.29.**)

Livingstone and Hubel (1982), using horseradish peroxidase and amino acid autoradiographic techniques, found that neurons in the "blobs" receive input directly from the dorsal lateral geniculate nucleus. Elsewhere in the visual cortex, only neurons in layer IVc receive thalamic input. The receptive characteristics of neurons in the "blobs" also differ from those of neurons located elsewhere. Most of them have concentric center/surround fields and thus respond to lines of any orientation. In addition, a high proportion of these cells respond maximally to specific wavelengths of light; thus, they may play a role in color vision (Hubel and Livingstone, 1983).

Perception of Depth: Disparity Detectors
The visual cortex of animals with good binocular vision, such as that of the rhesus monkey, contains cells whose response patterns appear to contribute to the perception of depth. These neurons exist in the striate cortex and also in level I of the visual association cortex. (See Poggio and Poggio, 1984, for a review.)

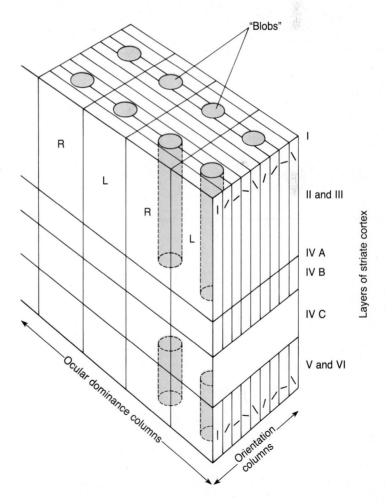

FIGURE 6.29
Hubel and Livingstone's model of orientation and ocular dominance columns in the primate visual cortex, with their "blobs" of hue-sensitive neurons. (From Hubel, D.H., and Livingstone, M.S., *Canadian Journal of Physiology and Pharmacology,* 1983, *61,* 1433–1441.)

Some of them will respond only when both eyes are simultaneously stimulated and will not respond to stimulation of one eye alone (Poggio and Fischer, 1977; Clarke and Whitteridge, 1978). In some cases, cells in corresponding locations on both retinas have identical receptive fields, but in most cases the cells respond most vigorously when each eye sees a stimulus in a slightly *different* location. That is, the neurons respond to **retinal disparity,** or a stimulus whose image falls on slightly different parts of each eye.

We perceive depth by many means, most of which involve cues that can be detected monocularly, by one eye alone. For example, perspective, relative retinal size, loss of detail

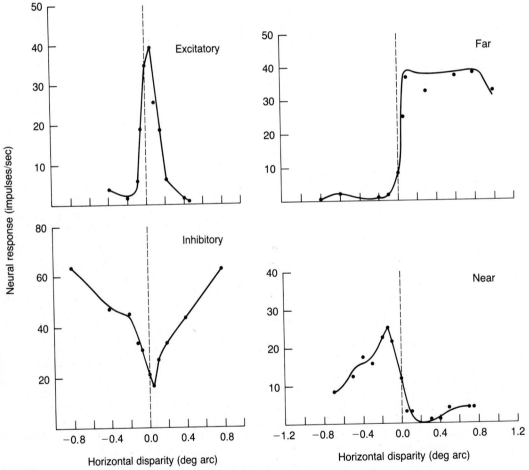

FIGURE 6.30
Responses of neurons in the visual cortex to horizontal disparity in stimuli presented to both eyes. *Left:* Maximal excitatory *(top)* or inhibitory *(bottom)* response to a particular amount of disparity. *Right:* Specific response to far *(top)* or near *(bottom)* stimulus. (Reproduced, with permission, from Poggio, G.F., and Poggio, T. *Annual Review of Neuroscience,* Volume 7, © 1984 by Annual Reviews Inc.)

through the effects of atmospheric haze, and relative apparent movement of retinal images as we move our heads all contribute to depth perception and do not require binocular vision. However, binocular vision provides a vivid perception of depth through the process of ***stereopsis.*** If you have used a stereoscope (such as a View Master) or seen a three-dimensional movie, you know what I mean.

Stereopsis (literally, "solid appearance") requires binocular retinal disparity of some elements of a visual stimulus. When you fix your gaze on an object in the middle distance, the convergence of your eyes causes that point, and other points an equal distance away from you, to fall on identical portions of each retina. These points fall on the *fixation plane.* (Actually, because the equidistant points fall on a portion of a sphere, the term *plane* is a misnomer.) This phenomenon is easy to demonstrate. Hold your hands in front of you, one at arm's length and the other at half that distance from your face. Extend a finger from each hand and focus on the farther one. You will see two images of the nearer one. Now slowly move the nearer finger away from you until it lies alongside the other. As you do so, you will see the two images of the moving finger merge. The cues for stereopsis are provided by stimuli located just off the fixation plane, which stimulate slightly different parts of the retina of each eye. As we saw, some neurons respond selectively to just this occurrence.

Investigators have found that the visual cortex contains two classes of neurons that are sensitive to retinal disparity. The first class responds with an increase or decrease in firing rate to a limited range of retinal disparity (± 0.2 degrees for the excitatory cells and ± 0.4 degrees for the inhibitory cells). The response of these neurons is shown in the left portion of Figure 6.30. (See **Figure 6.30, left.**) The second class of neurons selectively responds to stimuli nearer than or farther than the fixation plane. (See **Figure 6.30, right.**)

What do "nearer" and "farther" mean in terms of retinal disparity? This question can best be answered by repeating the earlier demonstration. Again put your arms in front of you so that one finger is extended at arm's length and the other is half that distance. Focus on the farther finger but pay attention to the double image you receive from the

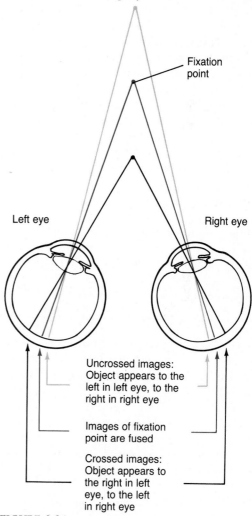

FIGURE 6.31

Stimuli nearer than the fixation plane produce "crossed" images on the retinas; those farther than the fixation plane produce "uncrossed" images. The lens reverses left and right on the retina.

nearer one. Now close your left eye. You will see that the right-hand image of the nearer finger disappears. Now open both eyes and focus on the nearer finger but pay attention to the double image of the farther one. When you again close your left eye you will see that the *left-hand* image of the farther finger disappears. Thus, the images of points farther than the fixation plane are *uncrossed,* but the images of nearer points are *crossed.* Some disparity-detecting neurons in the visual cortex respond best when a point occupies a part of the retina of one eye that is to the right of that of the other eye, and some respond best to the reverse situation. Thus, some neurons detect relative "nearness," and others detect relative "farness." (See **Figure 6.31.**)

The biological significance of these cells receives unusual support from the finding that there are two classes of people who have difficulty in judging the distance of objects by means of binocular cues: some of them misjudge objects in front of the fixation plane (closer to them), while others have difficulty with objects that are behind it (Richards, 1977). It seems likely that people with this affliction lack either "near-detecting" or "far-detecting" neurons. Another category of people can easily judge which of two objects is farther from them when both objects are almost the same distance but, surprisingly, have trouble judging which is closer when one object is much closer to them than the other (Jones, 1977). Presumably, these people are able to respond to small disparities by means of the finely tuned disparity detectors whose response was shown in the left half of Figure 6.30.

Feature Detection: Edges or Spatial Frequencies?

Hubel and Wiesel's research suggests that the retina, the dorsal lateral geniculate nucleus, and layer IVc of the primary visual cortex see the world in terms of spots. This information

Actual appearance of sine-wave grating

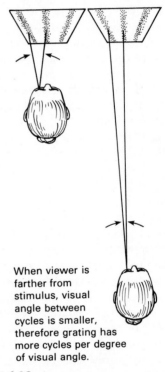

When viewer is farther from stimulus, visual angle between cycles is smaller, therefore grating has more cycles per degree of visual angle.

FIGURE 6.32

Sine-wave gratings and visual angle. The actual appearance of a sine-wave grating is shown at the top. A schematic explanation of the concepts of visual angle and spatial frequency is shown below. Angles are drawn between the sine waves, with the apex at the viewer's eye. The *visual angle* between adjacent sine waves is smaller when the observer is farther from the stimulus. (Photograph courtesy of S. Murray Sherman.)

is relayed to neurons in other layers of the primary visual cortex, where it is combined into information about lines or edges of a particular orientation. However, other research suggests that the best stimulus for most neurons in the visual cortex is not an edge or a sharp line; it is a ***sine-wave grating*** (De Valois, Albrecht, and Thorell, 1978). A sine-wave grating looks rather like a series of fuzzy, unfocused parallel bars. Figure 6.32 illustrates one. A sine-wave grating is designated by its ***spatial frequency.*** We are accustomed to frequencies (for example, of sound waves or radio waves) being expressed in terms of distance (such as cycles per meter). Because the image of a stimulus varies in size according to how close it is to the eye, ***visual angle*** is generally used instead of the physical distance between adjacent cycles. Thus, the spatial frequency of a visual stimulus is measured in cycles per degree of visual angle. (See **Figure 6.32.**)

Figure 6.33 shows the response of several different simple cells (top) and complex cells (bottom) to sine-wave gratings of different spatial frequencies. Note that each neuron (especially simple cells) responds best to a limited range of frequencies. (See **Figure 6.33.**)

You will recall that Hubel, Wiesel, and Stryker (1978) used 2-DG autoradiography to demonstrate the regular pattern of orientation columns in the visual cortex. In a similar study, Tootell, Silverman, and De Valois (1981) injected cats with radioactive 2-DG and presented each with a sine-wave grating pattern of a particular spatial frequency, ranging from 0.25 to 2.0 cycles per degree. Control animals saw patterns containing all of these frequencies. The investigators presented the patterns in all orientations and moved them in all directions, so that no subset of orientation-sensitive neurons would be selectively stimulated. They then killed the animals, treated slices of the visual cortex with a photographic emulsion, and later developed these exposures. Figure 6.34 shows examples of their results. In the experimental

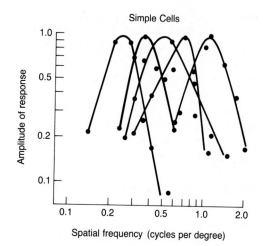

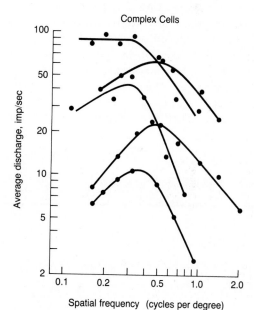

FIGURE 6.33
Responses of simple cells and complex cells to sine-wave gratings of various spatial frequencies. (From Maffei, L., and Fiorentini, A. *Vision Research,* 1973, *13,* 1255–1267. Copyright 1973 by Pergamon Press, Ltd.)

animals, they found evidence of radioactivity in discrete bands approximately 1.0 mm apart (top). In contrast, they observed uniform labeling in the cortex of the control cats, who saw all freqencies (bottom). (See **Figure 6.34.**) Thus, neurons in the striate cortex appear to be arranged in columns according to sensitivity to particular spatial frequencies, as well as to orientation and ocular dominance.

Hubel and Wiesel's feature-detection model has the advantage of simplicity; it is easy to conceive that the visual system uses information about edges—areas of sharp contrast in brightness—to construct a comprehensive image of the visual world. How can information about spatial frequencies be used to analyze visual information? Unfortunately, although we have good experimental evidence suggesting that the visual system does analyze information in terms of spatial frequency, we do not have adequate, comprehensive models to explain how it might do so. The best I can do is to give you some pieces of the picture. (The pun was not planned, but I like it.)

Consider the photograph shown in Figure 6.35. If we take a thin horizontal slice through it, we get a line that varies in brightness, much like one of the lines that constitute a television picture. (See **Figure 6.35.**) If we measure the brightness of all points on this line, we can draw a graph of changes in brightness along the length of it. (See **Figure 6.35.**)

The waveform that is shown in Figure 6.35 is a complex one. However, mathematicians have a technique called ***Fourier analysis*** that permits complex functions like these to be described in terms of simple sine waves. It is possible to calculate a series of pure sine waves of different frequencies that can be added together to produce the complex one that is shown in the figure. Perhaps the visual system performs a Fourier analysis. If there are different classes of neurons in the visual system that respond best to stimuli of particular spatial frequencies, then a slice of a visual scene (such as you see in Figure 6.35) might be analyzed in terms of different amounts of

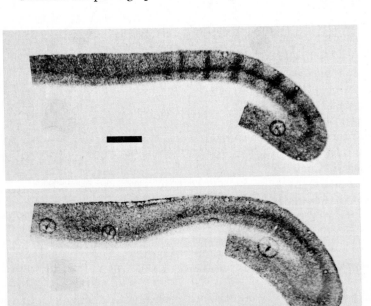

FIGURE 6.34
2-DG autoradiographs of cat visual cortex. *Top:* Experimental cat presented with a sine-wave grating of 2.0 cycles per degree. *Bottom:* Control cat presented with a sine-wave grating containing many different spatial frequencies. (From Tootell, R.B., Silverman, M.S., and De Valois, R.L. *Science,* 1981, *214,* 813–815. Copyright 1981 by the American Association for the Advancement of Science.)

FIGURE 6.35
A graph of the variation in brightness of a slice of a photograph. The
waveform shown could be analyzed for its content of various pure
sine-wave frequencies by Fourier analysis. Presumably, the visual system
performs a similar analysis.

activity in sets of neurons that respond to different spatial frequencies.

Of course, the process gets much more complicated when you consider a complete two-dimensional scene. Presumably, different neurons respond to different slices of the scene, sliced in many directions. In addition, you will remember that Hubel and Wiesel demonstrated that the information received by individual cortical neurons comes from a limited portion of the visual field; therefore, individual neurons do not respond to the spatial frequency of an entire slice but only to a limited length of it. If a Fourier analysis is performed by the brain, it must add together all of these small pieces of information.

Many investigators (see De Valois and De Valois, 1980, for a review) have shown that

neurons in the visual cortex respond best to stimuli of a particular spatial frequency at a particular orientation. Therefore, the visual system contains the raw information for a Fourier analysis — information about a wide range of spatial frequencies. In addition, nonphysiological perceptual studies strongly suggest that the brain uses information about spatial frequency to analyze the visual world. These studies (pioneered by Blakemore and Campbell, 1969) make use of the phenomenon of ***adaptation.***

When a particular stimulus is presented for a prolonged time, the sensory system becomes less sensitive to the stimulus; weak values of this stimulus, which were previously detectable, cannot be perceived any longer. When people stare at sine-wave gratings of particular frequencies at a particular orientation, they undergo a temporary loss of sensitivity to that frequency and orientation, but not to others. This adaptation is not a matter of fatigue in particular photoreceptors; the subjects do not have to stare at one point, but can let their eyes roam around the display, which means that a moving stimulus is presented to the retina. For example, if the subjects stare at a pattern of vertically oriented gratings and are then tested with a pattern of horizontally oriented gratings of the same spatial frequency, no loss in sensitivity is seen. This finding implies that different elements of the visual system look at different "slices" of the visual scene. These elements seem to be located in the cortex, because exposure of one eye to a particular spatial frequency causes a loss of sensitivity to patterns with the same frequency (and same orientation) presented to the opposite eye. If the analysis were performed within the retina itself, then adaptation of one eye should not affect the other. (See Sekuler, 1974, for a review of these studies.)

Consider the types of information provided by high and low spatial frequencies. Small objects and objects with sharp edges provide a signal rich in high frequencies (a high number of cycles per degree), whereas

large areas of light and dark are represented by low frequencies. An image that is deficient in high-frequency information looks fuzzy and out of focus, like that which is seen by a nearsighted person who is not wearing corrective lenses. This image still provides much information about forms and objects in the environment. However, when low-frequency information is removed the shapes of images are very difficult to perceive.

The importance of low-frequency information was illustrated very nicely by Harmon and Julesz (1973). Figure 6.36 (left) shows a picture that has been chopped into a series of squares. Hold the book close to your face and look at it. (See **Figure 6.36, left.**) Although the picture contains low-frequency information, it is difficult to recognize the image because the edges of the composite squares provide a considerable amount of high-frequency "noise." (Fourier analysis shows that abrupt edges contain much high-frequency information; in this case, the information is meaningless, because it is not related to the content of the figure.) The same figure, with the extraneous high-frequency information removed, is shown on the right. As you can see, this figure is much clearer, even though the low-frequency information is exactly the same in each case. (See **Figure 6.36,**

FIGURE 6.36
Both pictures contain the same amount of low-frequency information, but extraneous high-frequency information has been filtered from the picture on the right. If you look at the pictures from across the room, they look identical. (From Harmon, L.D., and Julesz, B. *Science,* 1973, *180,* 1191–1197. Copyright 1973 by the American Association for the Advancement of Science.)

right.) You can see the phenomenon even more dramatically if you put the book down and look at the figures from across the room. The distance "erases" the high frequencies, because they exceed the resolving power of the eye, and the two pictures look identical.

The physiological evidence for neurons that respond selectively to particular spatial frequencies is very good; so is the behavioral evidence concerning the importance of spatial frequencies in perception. What we do not know is how the information from individual frequency-sensitive and orientation-sensitive neurons is pooled to form images of the visual world. Understanding this process will not be a simple task, as you can surely appreciate.

Circumstriate Cortex

Neurons in the striate cortex send axons to other regions of the cortex, primarily the surrounding *circumstriate cortex.* (Some investigators refer to this area as the *prestriate cortex.*) Zeki and his colleagues have studied this region of visual cortex in some detail.

The striate cortex is sometimes referred to as *area V1,* because it is the sole projection area of the dorsal lateral geniculate nucleus. Neurons in V1 send axons to three regions of the circumstriate cortex, which have been designated as *areas V2, V3,* and *V4.* They also send axons to the cortex on the posterior bank of the *superior temporal sulcus.* In addition, another region of the circumstriate cortex, *area V3A,* receives projections from neurons in V3 but not directly from V1. Neurons in those regions of V1 that receive information from the fovea and those in regions that receive information from other portions of the retina (the *extrafoveal* regions) project differentially to the circumstriate cortex. Presumably, the regions that receive foveal projections analyze fine visual detail. Neurons in both the foveal and extrafoveal regions of V1 project to V2 and V3.

Only the foveal region of V1 projects to V4 and to the superior temporal sulcus, but V4 receives additional information from V2 about stimuli presented to the extrafoveal regions of the retina (Van Essen and Zeki, 1978; Zeki, 1978a, 1978b, 1978c). (See **Figure 6.37.**)

Each of these five areas, V2, V3, V3A, V4, and the superior temporal sulcus, contains one or more independent representations of the visual field. The interesting thing about these areas is that their neurons respond to different visual features (Zeki, 1978c). Most V2 neurons, like those in V1, are sensitive to stimulus orientation. In addition, a majority respond to binocular disparity and hence appear to participate in the perception of depth. A few are responsive to color, but these neurons are limited to the region of cells that respond to the central 5 degrees of vision. Although V3 and V3A are anatomically distinct, Zeki (1978b) reports that he has not been able to discover any obvious functional differences. Cells in these areas respond to orientation but not at all to color. Their receptive fields are larger than those of neurons in V2. Few neurons in V4 respond to orientation. However, more than half of them respond in an opponent fashion to color; their firing rate is increased by one wavelength of light and is inhibited by another. Obviously, this area is important for color vision, a topic that will be discussed later in this chapter. The special role of the posterior bank of the superior temporal sulcus appears to involve the analysis of movement at or near the point of fixation. Cells there respond selectively to movements in particular directions.

Inferior Temporal Cortex

In primates, the circumstriate cortex represents an intermediate level of visual analysis. The highest level of analysis, analysis of visual patterns and identification of particular objects, requires a region of the brain called the *inferior temporal cortex,* located on the ventral half of the temporal lobe. (See **Figure 6.37.**) This area of association cortex receives inputs from the circumstriate cortex and from various thalamic nuclei, especially the pul-

vinar. In many ways, it is the most interesting region of all, because neural circuits here "learn" to detect stimuli with particular shapes, regardless of their size or location.

An example of this role is illustrated in an

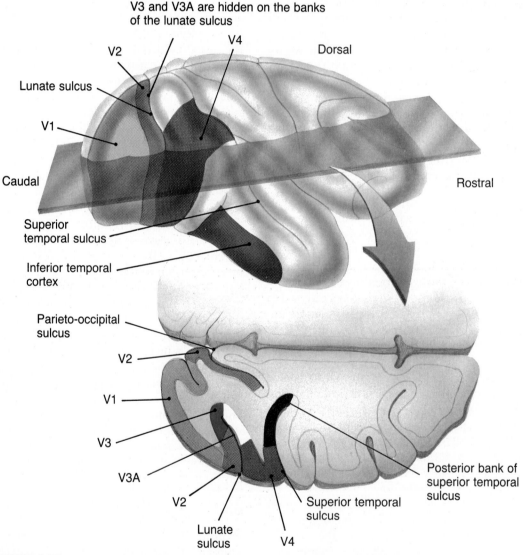

FIGURE 6.37
Areas of visual association cortex of the rhesus monkey brain. (Adapted from Zeki, 1978a.)

experiment by Iwai and Mishkin (1969). These investigators trained rhesus monkeys to discriminate between a plus sign and a square. (Correct responses were reinforced with a small piece of food.) Then they removed the inferior temporal cortex bilaterally and found that the monkeys required several hundred trials to relearn the task. Iwai, Osawa, and Umitsu (1979) found that slight differences in the stimuli disrupted the performance of monkeys with lesions of the inferior temporal cortex. Although the animals could be retrained to discriminate between the original stimuli, they failed to discriminate between the same patterns when they were superimposed on a different background. (See **Figure 6.38.**)

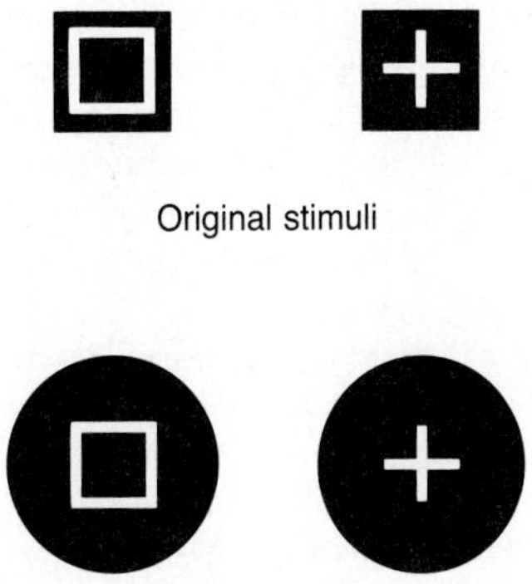

Many studies have investigated the functions of the primate inferior temporal cortex. Because these studies involve learned behaviors rather than simple response characteristics, I will discuss them in some detail in Chapter 14, which deals with the anatomy of learning. Destruction of visual association cortex in the temporal lobes of humans results in deficits in visual perception; these deficits will be discussed in the last section of this chapter.

Original stimuli

Same stimuli on
new background

FIGURE 6.38

After bilateral removal of the inferior temporal cortex, monkeys who had learned to discriminate between the top pair of stimuli failed to discriminate between the bottom pair.

INTERIM SUMMARY

Visual information from the retina reaches the primary visual cortex surrounding the calcarine fissure by means of the dorsal lateral geniculate nuclei. Several other regions of the brain, including the suprachiasmatic nucleus of the hypothalamus, the accessory optic nuclei of the brain stem, the pretectum, the superior colliculus, and the ventral lateral geniculate nucleus, also receive visual information. These latter regions help regulate activity during the day/night cycle, coordinate eye and head movements, control attention to visual stimuli, and regulate the size of the pupils.

Most ganglion cells respond in an opposing center/surround fashion, with excitation to light in one region and inhibition to light in the other. Ganglion cells have been classified into three basic types: X cells, Y cells, and W cells. If both the center and surround of the receptive field of an X cell are illuminated, the neuron will not respond; a Y cell will. Y cells have brief, brisk, phasic responses, whereas the response of an X cell is more sustained (tonic response). In addition, Y cells respond best to moving stimuli and have larger receptive fields. W cells respond weakly to visual stimuli: some phasically, and some tonically. Their receptive fields are very large, and most are not of the center/surround type. Apparently, X cells supply information about fine details, Y cells supply information about moving stimuli, and W cells (along with Y cells) direct eye movements toward moving stimuli in the periphery of the visual field.

The center-on response of a ganglion cell occurs when hyperpolarization of the photoreceptors in the center of the receptive field causes a depolarization in the bipolar cells, which causes them to release more transmitter substance, exciting the ganglion cell. The surround-off response is mediated through horizontal cells that connect the photoreceptors in the periphery of the receptive field with the bipolar cells that form synapses with the ganglion cell. Amacrine cells also contribute to the responses of ganglion cells, primarily (so far as we know) controlling their tonic or phasic nature.

The dorsal lateral geniculate nucleus consists of six layers of neurons, each containing a map of half of the retina of one eye; three layers are devoted to each eye. The neurons send axons to the primary visual cortex.

All projections from the dorsal lateral geniculate nucleus to the primary visual cortex are received from X-type cells, and they arrive in layer IVc. Neurons in layer IVc project to layer IVb, just above. Layer IVb neurons are simple cells, responding to line segments with a particular orientation. Complex cells, found in layers II, III, V, and VI, respond best to line segments of a particular orientation that move perpendicular to the orientation. Their receptive fields are larger. Hypercomplex cells, located in the same layers, have similar response characteristics but the response declines if the line segment extends outside their receptive field.

Neurons in the primary visual cortex are arranged in columns. As a microelectrode is moved from place to place parallel to the surface of the visual cortex, the response characteristics gradually change: the orientation sensitivity rotates and the proportion of "left-eye" and "right-eye" cells gradually shifts. The visual cortex also contains regions of color-sensitive neurons called "blobs," which receive direct input from the dorsal lateral geniculate nucleus and respond to lines of any orientation.

The visual cortex also contains neurons that serve as disparity detectors, which respond maximally when a visual stimulus falls on not-quite-corresponding portions of the two retinas. Some of these neurons detect objects closer to the observer than the fixation plane, others detect objects farther away, and others detect very small disparities in either direction.

Although Hubel and Wiesel have used lines in their research, other investigators suggest that neurons in the visual cortex respond best to sine-wave gratings. Different neurons respond to different spatial frequencies. Precisely how the visual system uses such information is not known.

The circumstriate cortex receives information from the primary visual cortex directly. It is divided into distinct regions in which reside neurons

with special functions. V1 and V2 neurons are sensitive to orientation and to binocular disparity. V3 neurons also respond to orientation, but have larger receptive fields. V4 neurons respond to color, in an opponent fashion. Presumably, they receive inputs from the "blobs" in the primary visual cortex. Neurons in the superior temporal sulcus respond to movement. The inferior temporal cortex receives information from the circumstriate cortex. It appears to play a crucial role in perception of objects.

■ COLOR VISION

Various theories of color vision have been proposed for many years — long before it was possible to disprove or validate them by physiological means. In 1802, Thomas Young, a British physicist and physician, proposed that the eye detected different colors because it contained three types of receptors, each sensitive to a single hue. His theory was suggested by the fact that, for a human observer, any color can be reproduced by mixing various quantities of three colors judiciously selected from different points along the spectrum. (Actually, if you accept some restrictions, you can choose any three colors, so long as any one cannot be produced by mixing the other two. We may ignore this detail because, as we will see, nature chose three colors judiciously.)

I want to emphasize that color mixing is different from pigment mixing. If we combine yellow and blue pigments (as when we mix paints), the resulting mixture is green. Color mixing refers to the addition of two or more light sources. If we shine a beam of red light and a beam of bluish green light together on a white screen, we will see yellow light. If we mix yellow and blue light, we get white light. When white appears on a color television screen, it actually consists of tiny dots of red, blue, and green light.

The concept of primary colors has been with us for a long time, and it appears to have some psychological validity. Humans have long regarded yellow, blue, red, and green as primary colors. (Black and white are primary, too, but we perceive them as colorless.) All other colors can be described as mixtures of these primary colors. One can speak of a bluish green or a yellowish green, and orange appears to have both red and yellow qualities. Purple resembles both red and blue. However, we would never describe yellow as anything but yellow; a slightly longer wavelength starts looking reddish, while a slightly shorter wavelength starts looking greenish. Similarly, we see green, blue, and red light as primary. The psychological reality of these four colors has suggested that their representation in the visual system provides the primary information for the perception of color.

Color Coding in the Retina

Physiological investigations of retinal photoreceptors in higher primates have found that Young was right: three different types of photoreceptors (three different types of cones) are responsible for color vision. Investigators

have studied the absorption characteristics of individual photoreceptors, determining the amount of light of different wavelengths that is absorbed by the photopigments. These characteristics are controlled by the particular opsin a photoreceptor contains; different opsins absorb particular wavelengths more readily. Figure 6.39 shows the absorption characteristics of the four types of photoreceptors in the human retina: rods and the three types of cones. (See **Figure 6.39.**) Recordings of receptor potentials provide similar results. Figure 6.40 shows receptor potentials from single cones in the retina of the carp (a fish) in response to brief pulses of light of varying wavelengths. (See **Figure 6.40.**)

The peak sensitivities of the three types of cones are approximately 420 nm (blue-violet), 530 nm (green), and 560 nm (yellow-green). The peak sensitivity of the short-wavelength cone is actually 440 nm in the intact eye, because the lens absorbs some short-wavelength light. For convenience, the short-, medium-, and long-wavelength cones are traditionally called "blue," "green," and "red" cones. The retina contains approxi-

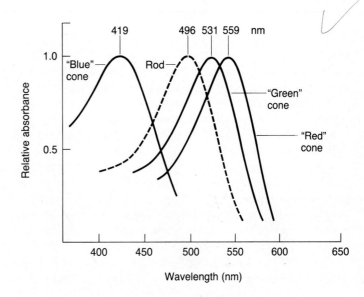

FIGURE 6.39
Relative absorbance of light of various wavelengths by rods and the three types of cones in the human retina. (From Dartnall, H.J.A., Bowmaker, J.K., and Mollon, J.D. Human visual pigments: Microspectrophotometric results from the eyes of seven persons. *Proceedings of the Royal Society (London), Series B,* 1983, *220,* 115–130.)

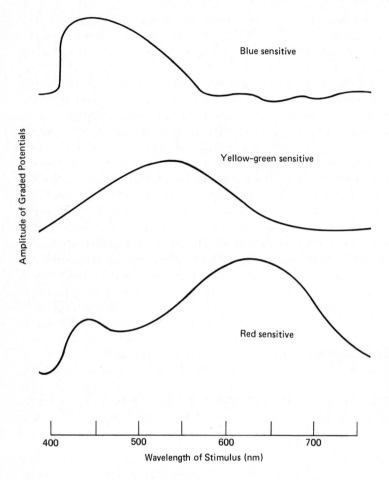

FIGURE 6.40
Receptor potentials from
single color-sensitive cones in
the carp retina. (Redrawn from
Tomita, T., Kaneko, A.,
Murakami, M., and Pautler, E.
Vision Research, 1967, 7,
519–537.)

mately equal numbers of "red" and "green" cones but a much smaller number of "blue" cones (approximately 8 percent of the total).

At the level of the retinal ganglion cell, the three-color code gets translated into an opponent-color system. Daw (1968) and Gouras (1968) found that these neurons respond specifically to pairs of primary colors, with red opposing green and blue opposing yellow. Most receptive fields of color-sensitive ganglion cells are arranged in a center/surround fashion. For example, a cell might be excited by red and inhibited by green in the center, while showing the opposite response in the surrounding ring. Other ganglion cells that receive input from cones do not respond differentially to different wavelengths but simply encode relative brightness in the center and surround.

The response characteristics of retinal ganglion cells to light of different wavelengths is obviously determined by the retinal circuitry. Figure 6.41 shows a schematic representation of the relation between the three types of cones and the two major types of color-coding ganglion cells. A third type of ganglion cells responds to light of any wavelength; these cells provide high-acuity monochromatic (black and white) information. No attempt is made to show the actual circuitry; the arrows refer merely to the effects of the photic stimulation. (See **Figure 6.41.**)

Genetic defects in color vision appear to result from anomalies in one or more of the three types of cones (Boynton, 1979). The first two kinds of defective color vision described here involve genes on the X chromosome; thus, because males have only one X chromosome, they are much more likely to have this disorder. People with **protanopia** ("first-color defect") confuse red and green. They see the world in shades of yellow and blue; both red and green look yellowish to them. Their visual acuity is normal, which suggests that their retinas do not lack "red" or "green" cones. This fact, and their sensitivity to lights of different wavelengths, suggests

that their "red" cones are filled with "green" cone opsin. People with **deuteranopia** ("second-color defect") also confuse red and green. Their "green" cones appear to be filled with "red" cone opsin.

Tritanopia ("third-color defect") is rare, affecting fewer than 1 in 10,000 people. This disorder involves a faulty gene that is not located on an X chromosome; thus, it is equally prevalent in males and females. People with tritanopia have difficulty with hues of short wavelengths and see the world in greens and reds. To them, a clear blue sky is a bright green, and yellow looks pink. Their retinas appear to lack "blue" cones. Because the retina contains so few of these cones, their absence does not noticeably affect visual acuity.

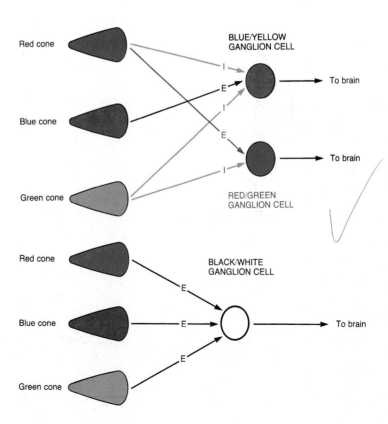

FIGURE 6.41

Opponent process: hypothetical connections between cones and yellow/blue, red/green, and black/white ganglion cells. Ganglion cells that are inhibited by blue and excited by yellow, inhibited by red and excited by green, and inhibited by light and excited by dark also exist. E = excitation; I = inhibition.

Color Coding in the Lateral Geniculate Nucleus

Neurons in the primate dorsal lateral geniculate nucleus encode color in the same way that retinal ganglion cells do, in opponent fashion to complementary colors. De Valois, Abramov, and Jacobs (1966), recording action potentials from neurons in the lateral geniculate nucleus, found two major types of opponent cells: red-green detectors and blue-yellow detectors. Each type of detector re-

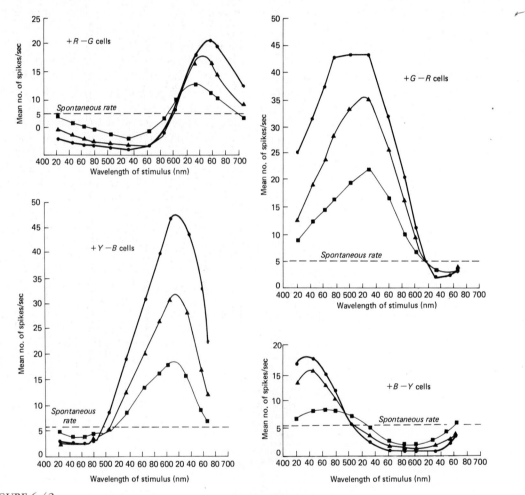

FIGURE 6.42

Responses recorded from single neurons in the lateral geniculate nucleus to light of various wavelengths. These neurons appear to encode color in an opponent-process fashion. *Spontaneous rate* refers to the baseline rate of neural firing in the absence of stimulation. R = red; G = green; Y = yellow; B = blue; + = excitation, − = inhibition. (From DeValois, R.L., Abramov, I., and Jacobs, G.H. *Journal of the Optical Society of America,* 1966, *56*, 966–977. By permission.)

sponded in excitatory or inhibitory fashion to one of the pair of colors in the center, and in the opposite manner to that color in the surround. Figure 6.42 shows the rate of firing of these types of cells as a function of the wavelength of a spot of light presented to the center of their receptive fields. (See **Figure 6.42.**)

Color Coding in the Cortex

As we saw earlier, neurons within the "blobs" in the primary visual cortex respond to colors. Like the ganglion cells in the retina and the neurons in the dorsal lateral geniculate nucleus, they respond in opponent fashion. Neurons in the "blobs" send axons to the circumstriate cortex, especially to V4. Zeki (1980) found that these neurons respond selectively to colors, often in opponent fashion, but their response characteristics are much

more complex. Unlike the neurons we have encountered so far, these neurons respond to a variety of wavelengths, not just those that correspond to red, green, yellow, and blue. Some neurons respond very selectively, their response rate dropping by a factor of two when the stimulus is as little as 10 nm away from their peak sensitivity. Figure 6.43 shows the sensitivity of several neurons in V4 in response to light of different wavelengths. Excitation is indicated by black lines, and inhibition by colored lines. (See **Figure 6.43.**)

Figure 6.44 shows a distribution of the peak sensitivities that Zeki recorded from sixty-two different cells in V4. Note that most of the visible spectrum is covered, with the exception of the range of 560 to 570 nm, which represents the peak sensitivity of the "red" cones. Perhaps, Zeki speculates, they actually exist, and he just happened to miss them. Also note that many neurons responded

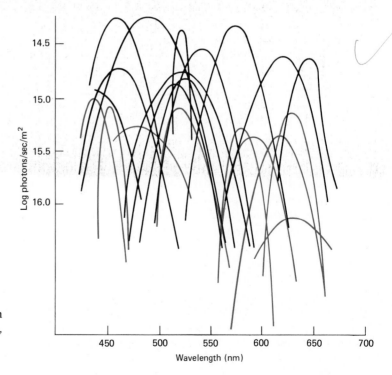

FIGURE 6.43
Response characteristics of individual neurons in area V4 of the rhesus monkey visual cortex after presentation of light of various wavelengths. (Reprinted by permission from Zeki, S.M., *Nature,* 1980, *284,* 412–418. Copyright © 1980 Macmillan Journals Limited.)

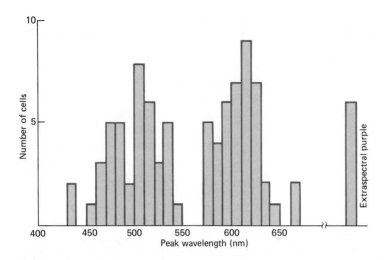

FIGURE 6.44
Distribution of peak
sensitivities of individual
neurons in area V4 of the
rhesus monkey visual cortex.
(Reprinted by permission from
Zeki, S.M., *Nature,* 1980, *284,*
412–418. Copyright © 1980
Macmillan Journals Limited.)

selectively to purple light, which is an *extra-spectral* color that consists of a mixture of light of short and long wavelengths. (See **Figure 6.44.**)

We learned that most neurons in the visual system respond best to brightness *contrast* rather than absolute levels of brightness. Thus, the perceived brightness of a particular stimulus depends on the relative amounts of light received from it and from other parts of the scene. The perceived color of a stimulus is similarly influenced by the surrounding scene. Using a procedure devised by Land (1977), Zeki (1980) demonstrated this fact dramatically. After locating a neuron in V4 that responded to red light, he placed a special display panel in front of the monkey. The display contained rectangular patches of paper of different colors. (The display is referred to as a *Mondrian,* because it resembles the style of paintings made by this artist.) He adjusted the position of the display so that a patch of red paper fell in the neuron's receptive field. The neuron responded. Then he illuminated the display panel with red light. Under these conditions, the red patch loses its vivid red appearance to a human observer. Even though its receptive field was flooded with red light, the neuron did *not* respond.

Similarly, the neuron failed to respond when he illuminated the display panel with green or blue light. Only when he shone all three lights on the panel (simulating white light) did the neuron respond. Under these conditions the red patch appears a vivid red to an observer; thus, the response of the neuron in V4 was in accordance with perception of the color red, which is influenced by the color of the surrounding area, not simply by the wavelength of the light shining on a particular part of the retina. (See **Figure 6.45.**)

Zeki found that the receptive fields of color-sensitive neurons in V4 did not show an orderly topographical relation. This finding contrasts the orderliness seen in the topographical representation of neurons in the striate cortex and in all other regions of the circumstriate cortex. However, because this region receives its primary input from the foveal area of the striate cortex, most cells respond to stimuli presented near the point of fixation. In addition, these cells do not show orientation sensitivity (which comes as no surprise, because the cells in the striate cortex "blobs" also lack orientation sensitivity). How the visual system puts topographical information together with information about color has yet to be determined.

INTERIM SUMMARY

Color vision occurs as a result of information provided by three types of cones, each of which is sensitive to light of a certain wavelength: long, medium, or short. Color-sensitive ganglion cells respond in an opposing center/surround fashion to the pairs of primary colors: red and green, and blue and yellow.

The absorption characteristics of the cones are determined by the particular opsin that their photopigment contains. Most forms of defective color vision appear to be caused by alterations in cone opsins. The "red" cones of people with protanopia appear to be filled with "green" cone opsin, and the "green" cones of people with deuteranopia appear to be filled with "red" cone opsin. The retinas of people with tritanopia appear to lack "blue" cones.

The color-sensitive cells of the dorsal lateral geniculate nucleus respond to red/green or yellow/blue in an opposing center/surround fashion. These neurons send information about color to the "blobs" in the primary visual cortex, which send information to area V4 of the circumstriate cortex. Neurons in V4 respond selectively to a wide range of wavelengths, and are not particularly responsive to spatial features of visual stimuli, such as orientation. The "Mondrian" experiment tells us that the responses of neurons in V4 closely correspond to some of the more complex phenomena of color perception.

■ EFFECTS OF EARLY EXPERIENCE ON DEVELOPMENT OF THE VISUAL SYSTEM

Normal development of the mammalian visual system depends on visual stimulation early in an organism's life. When this stimulation is prevented by temporarily sewing a young kitten's eyelid, the visual acuity of the occluded eye is severely reduced. In fact, if the occlusion starts early enough and lasts long enough, the animal will no longer see visual stimuli presented to this eye. As we will see, the changes responsible for this blind-

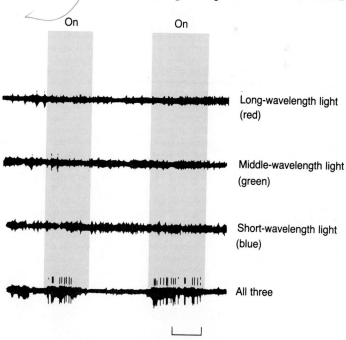

FIGURE 6.45

Response of a single neuron in area V4 of the rhesus monkey visual cortex whose receptive field included a red-colored patch on a multi-hued "Mondrian" when the entire display was illuminated with red, green, or blue light or with all three. (From Zeki, S.M., in *Brain Mechanisms of Sensation,* edited by Y. Katsuki, R. Norgren, and M. Sato. New York: John Wiley & Sons, 1981.)

ness occur in the circuitry of the visual cortex, not in the retina. The pioneering studies in this field were performed by Hubel and Wiesel, and it is this work that earned them a Nobel Prize in 1981. Specific references for the work I cite in this section can be found in the lecture Wiesel delivered at the Nobel Prize ceremony (Wiesel, 1982).

The earlier the visual deprivation, the more severe the deficit in adulthood. Before six weeks of age, a few days of eyelid closure produces detectable effects. However, by one year of age, even prolonged monocular deprivation has little effect on visual function later in life or on the response characteristics of cortical neurons. Thus, visual deprivation appears to affect the growth and development of neurons in the visual system, and not the response characteristics of already mature neurons.

The most striking effect of monocular deprivation is seen in the ocular dominance col-

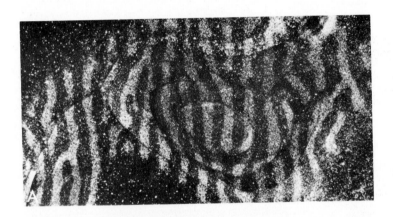

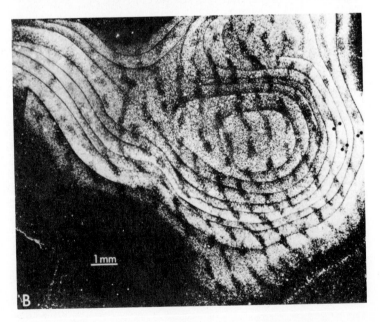

FIGURE 6.46

Dark-field autoradiographs of slices of monkey striate cortex prepared two weeks after injecting [3H]proline in the left eye. Increased radioactivity is shown by light areas. *Top:* Monkey deprived during the second year of life. Light and dark stripes are approximately equal. *Bottom:* Monkey whose right eye was closed for eighteen months early in life. Information from the normal eye is received by almost all regions of the striate cortex. (From Wiesel, T.N., *Nature,* 1982, *299,* 583–592. Copyright © 1982 Macmillan Journals Limited.)

umns of the visual cortex. After experiencing a period of monocular deprivation, monkeys received an injection of radioactive amino acid into the nonoccluded eye, and subsequent autoradiographs were prepared of their visual cortex. Figure 6.46 shows autoradiographs of slices of striate cortex of two rhesus monkeys: one whose right eye was sutured shut for fourteen months, starting at age fourteen months (top), and one whose right eye was closed for eighteen months, starting at two weeks of age (bottom). The radioactive labeling shows up as white areas. The monkey who was monocularly deprived later in life (top) shows nearly equal areas of left-eye and right-eye dominance; presumably, its visual system had developed enough so that no major changes occurred. However, the early visual deprivation greatly increased the number of cells that received input from the normal eye (white areas, bottom). (See **Figure 6.46.**)

As we saw earlier, different layers of the lateral geniculate nucleus contain cells that receive input from one eye or the other, not both. Neurons in these layers innervate alternating strips of visual cortex. The results of the previous experiment suggest that during development the terminal buttons that represent the two eyes compete for dendritic space on neurons in layer IVc. When one set of inputs fails to be activated by visual stimulation the terminal buttons grow more slowly, and the terminal buttons that represent the other eye form synapses with a larger number of cortical cells. This conclusion is supported by the finding that when *both* eyes are sutured shut early in life, equal numbers of neurons are dominated by the left and right eye.

Experiences other than total visual deprivation can affect the response characteristics of neurons in the visual system. Hirsch and Spinelli (1971) raised kittens in the dark from birth. At three weeks of age they fitted the animals with a special pair of goggles that presented a separate visual pattern to each eye. They presented one eye with a view of three horizontal bars; the other eye saw three vertical bars. Figure 6.47 shows a photograph of one of these kittens. (The kittens spent only a part of each day wearing the goggles; most of

FIGURE 6.47
A kitten wearing the training goggles from one of Spinelli's experiments. The horizontal and vertical stripes on the outside of the goggles are for identification purposes only; the actual stimuli are contained within the goggles and are illuminated by transparent openings at the sides (out of which the kitten cannot see). The cardboard cone prevents the kitten from dislodging the goggles.

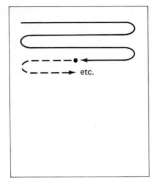 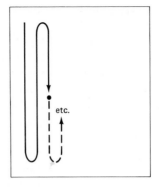

FIGURE 6.48
The horizontal and vertical
scanning procedure used by
Spinelli and his coworkers.

their time was spent — goggle-less — in the dark. See **Figure 6.47.**) When the cats were ten to twelve weeks of age, the investigators determined the receptive fields of cortical neurons by a computerized procedure.

The investigators placed a round black spot on a white screen and moved the spot by means of a magnet attached to a computer-driven device behind the screen. The spot could be moved throughout the entire area of the screen by means of a series of fifty sequential horizontal or vertical sweeps. (See **Figure 6.48.**) The stimulus spot was moved in a series of small discrete steps (fifty per line), and the computer recorded the number of action potentials produced by cortical neurons while the stimulus was in each of the 2500 positions. The receptive field of the neuron was displayed by the computer on the face of an oscilloscope. Each of the stimulus positions was presented by a corresponding location on the oscilloscope screen; if the number of action potentials recorded from the cell exceeded some criterion number while the stimulus was in a given position, a dot was displayed in the corresponding position on the oscilloscope.

Figure 6.49 presents some plots of two receptive fields, one vertically oriented and one horizontally oriented. (See **Figure 6.49.**) It is interesting that the specifically oriented receptive fields were produced by stimulation

of the eye that had been exposed to bars of the appropriate orientation. That is, receptive fields of neurons responding to the horizontally stimulated eye were found to be horizontal in their orientation; similarly, the vertically stimulated eye produced vertical receptive fields. Also, contrary to what is seen in normally reared kittens, the authors found no cells with binocular receptive fields. (The training procedure prevented stimuli from ever being binocularly perceived.)

These results suggest that experience can modify the response characteristics of neurons in the visual cortex. Although detec-

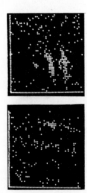

FIGURE 6.49
The receptive fields of single cortical neurons recorded from a cat that had worn goggles such as those shown in Figure 6.47. (From Hirsch, H.V.B., and Spinelli, D.N. *Experimental Brain Research,* 1971, *12,* 509–527.)

tion of the location, orientation, and spatial frequencies of visual stimuli appears to be a standard feature of cortical neurons, these response characteristics are not immutable. Obviously, the adult visual system is the product of interactions between experience and neural development.

■ EFFECTS OF BRAIN DAMAGE ON HUMAN VISUAL PERCEPTION

Damage to the eyes, optic nerves, optic tracts, lateral geniculate nucleus, optic radiations, or primary visual cortex results in loss of vision in particular portions of the visual field, or in complete blindness if the damage is total. These deficits confirm what we know about the anatomy of the visual system and its retinotopic representation, but they tell us nothing about perceptual analysis. However, the effects of lesions of the visual association cortex or its connections with the rest of the brain are much more interesting and informative.

Depending on the location of the lesion, damage to various parts of the human brain impairs people's ability to use visual information. Some deficits deal specifically with reading; these deficits will be discussed in Chapter 16. This chapter deals with the *visual agnosias.*

There are two major categories of disorders caused by brain damage that are related to visual perception: apperceptive agnosias and associative agnosias. *Agnosia* ("failure to know") refers to an inability to identify or perceive a stimulus by means of a particular sensory modality, even though its details can be detected by means of that modality and the person retains relatively normal intellectual capacity. Apperceptive agnosias are failures in high-level perception, whereas associative agnosias are disconnections between these perceptions and verbal systems. The distinction will be described in more detail shortly.

People with visual agnosia cannot identify or perceive common objects by sight, even though they have relatively normal visual acuity. In some cases, they can read small print but fail to recognize an object as common as a wrist watch. However, if they are permitted to hold the object (say, the wrist watch), they can immediately say what it is. You will note that I said inability to "identify or perceive." Normally we think of these words as being almost synonymous; it seems that if we can perceive something, we can also identify it. However, we will see that some forms of visual agnosia involve relatively normal perception but impaired ability to identify what is perceived.

Apperceptive Visual Agnosia

Apperceptive visual agnosia is a perceptual problem caused by brain damage. Although the person may have normal visual acuity, he or she cannot successfully recognize objects visually by their shape. For example, a patient studied by Benson and Greenberg (1969) was initially believed to be blind but was subsequently observed to navigate his wheelchair around the halls of the hospital. Testing revealed that his visual fields were full (there were no scotomas) and that he could pick up threads placed on a sheet of white paper. He could discriminate among stimuli that differed in size, brightness, or hue but could not distinguish those that differed only in shape.

Patients with apperceptive visual agnosia can display several different types of symptoms. Some have *achromatopsia* ("visual defect without color"). As the name suggests, they cannot distinguish colors; they see the world in shades of gray. Some patients with achromatopsia have relatively good form perception; we could speculate that their brain damage includes the human equivalent of V4, which contains color-sensitive cells. Autopsy studies have shown that the damage must include the inferior visual association cortex of the occipital lobe (Alexander and Albert, 1983). Unilateral damage to this area produces achromatopsia in the contralateral visual field.

Another symptom of visual agnosia is ***prosopagnosia,*** an inability to recognize faces (*prosopon* means "face"). Prosopagnosia is a subtle deficit that can occur even when a person has no apparent difficulty recognizing objects visually. Some patients who cannot recognize members of their own family by sight can nevertheless match photographs of profiles with full-face views of people they have never seen, which certainly requires good visual perception. Some investigators have speculated that facial recognition is mediated by special circuits in the brain. However, several observations suggest that the distinction between prosopagnosia and agnosia for common objects is quantitative, not qualitative; that is, visual agnosia for common objects is simply a more severe deficit, caused by more severe damage to the relevant parts of the visual association cortex. Alexander and Albert (1983) note that although prosopagnosia can be seen without visual object agnosia, all patients with visual object agnosia also have prosopagnosia.

Damasio, Damasio, and Van Hoesen (1982) describe three patients with prosopagnosia who could recognize familiar objects but had difficulty discriminating between particular objects of the same class. For example, none of them could recognize their own car, although they could tell a car from other types of motorized vehicles. One of them could find her own car in a parking lot only by reading all the license plates until she found her own. Another patient, a farmer, could no longer recognize his cows (Bornstein, Stroka, and Munitz, 1969). Although it is conceivable that the evolutionary process could have selected for neural mechanisms to recognize the faces of members of our own species, it is unlikely that it could have done so for the shapes of cars and cows. We can probably conclude that prosopagnosia is a relatively mild form of visual object agnosia.

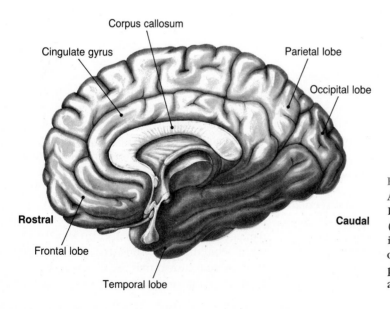

FIGURE 6.50
According to Damasio, Damasio, and Van Hoesen (1982), bilateral lesions of the inferior medial surface of the occipital and temporal lobes produce apperceptive visual agnosia.

The evidence for apperceptive visual agnosia being a deficit of form perception is strong. Perhaps the most striking piece of evidence is that many patients with visual object agnosia, who cannot identify simple objects like chairs and lamps, can still read. (As we will see in Chapter 16, some patients have the opposite kind of deficit: they can recognize objects but cannot read.)

Based on their own patients and on a review of the literature, Damasio, Damasio, and Van Hoesen conclude that apperceptive visual agnosias are most commonly caused by bilateral damage to the medial portion of the occipital and posterior temporal cortex, which includes regions of circumstriate cortex. (See **Figure 6.50.**) The syndrome is relatively rare, because bilateral damage to the same relatively small portion of the brain is uncommon. If the lesion is too large, it will invade the optic radiations that lie immediately beneath the cortex and thus produce blindness. Based on experiments with monkeys, we might predict that bilateral lesions of the inferior temporal cortex (on the lateral surface of the brain) would also produce deficits in visual perception.

Although the data are limited, the results of studies on humans with apperceptive visual agnosia are consistent with experimental studies on laboratory animals. The visual system of the human brain is undoubtedly quite similar to that of the rhesus monkey and other higher primates.

Associative Visual Agnosia

A person with apperceptive agnosia who cannot recognize common objects also cannot draw them or copy other people's drawings; thus we properly speak of a deficit in perception. However, people with an ***associative visual agnosia*** appear to be able to perceive relatively normally but fail to name what they have seen. For example, a patient studied by

Ratcliff and Newcombe (1982) could copy a drawing of an anchor (much better than I could have done). Thus, he could perceive the shape of the anchor. However, he could not recognize what he had just drawn. When asked on another occasion to draw (not copy) a picture of an anchor, he could not do so. (See **Figure 6.51.**) When asked (on yet an-

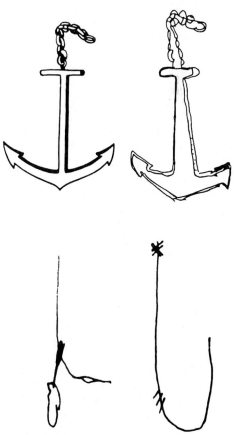

FIGURE 6.51

Associative visual agnosia. The patient successfully copied an anchor *(top)* but failed on two attempts to comply with a request to "draw an anchor" *(bottom)*. (From Ratcliff, G., and Newcombe, F., in *Normality and Pathology in Cognitive Functions,* edited by A.W. Ellis. London: Academic Press, 1982.)

other occasion) to define *anchor,* he said "a brake for ships," so we can conclude that he knew what the word meant.

One must carefully distinguish between associative visual agnosia and another deficit, called *anomia* (discussed in Chapter 16).

Anomia is a form of language disorder; people with anomia have difficulty thinking of words. They may see an object, recognize it for what it is, but fail to remember what it is called. For example, if shown a picture of a bicycle, they may say, "It is a thing that you

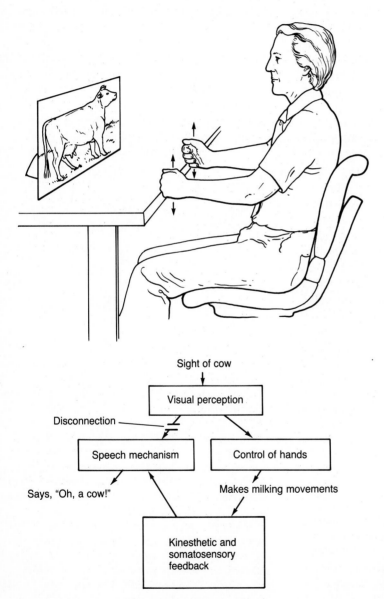

FIGURE 6.52
A patient with visual agnosia was able to identify a picture of a cow by observing himself make milking movements.

ride by pushing on the pedals," but not remember its name. If the experimenter says, "Is it a bicycle?" they will immediately say "yes." In contrast, people with apperceptive visual agnosia only fail to name items they *see*. For example, a patient may not be able to say what a pair of scissors is by looking at them but immediately says "scissors!" when he or she is permitted to pick them up and feel them.

Associative visual agnosia appears to involve difficulty in transferring visual information to verbal mechanisms. That is, the person perceives the object well enough to draw it, but his or her verbal mechanisms do not receive the necessary information to produce the appropriate word. (If this concept seems puzzling or difficult to believe, do not despair. I will describe similar phenomena in more detail in Chapter 16.) David Margolin and I studied a man who had sustained brain damage from an inflammatory disease that affected his cerebral blood vessels. (The damage was diffuse, so we could not make any conclusions about the anatomy of his disorder.) He suffered from an apparent visual agnosia, failing to identify most pictures of objects. However, he sometimes made unintentional gestures when he was studying a picture that gave him enough of a clue that he could identify it. For example, on one occasion while he was puzzling over a picture of a cow, he started making movements with both hands that were unmistakably ones he would make if he were milking a cow. He looked at his hands and said, "Oh, a cow!" (He was a farmer, by the way.)

We might speculate that his perceptual mechanisms, in the visual association cortex, were relatively normal, but that connections between these mechanisms and the speech mechanisms of the left hemisphere were disrupted. However, the connections between the perceptual mechanisms and the motor mechanisms of the frontal lobe were spared, permitting him to make appropriate movements when looking at some pictures. (See **Figure 6.52.**) In fact, a particularly observant and conscientious speech therapist helped the patient learn how to read by these means. She taught him the manual alphabet used by deaf people, in which letters are represented by particular hand and finger movements. (This system is commonly called *finger spelling*.) He could then look at individual letters of words he could not read, make the appropriate movements, observe the sequence of letters that he spelled, and decode the word.

The anatomical basis of associative visual agnosia has not been clearly established. Many investigators believe that the syndrome is caused by damage to white matter underlying the occipital and temporal lobes. The disruption of these axons disconnects regions of the brain that mediate visual perception from those that are needed for verbalization.

INTERIM SUMMARY

The visual system is affected by experience, both during development and later in life. When one eye of an infant animal is temporarily closed, the projections from the normal eye to the lateral geniculate nucleus become more extensive than they normally would, which suggests that during development, the projections from the retinas compete for space and eventually occupy equal areas because they are equally active. More subtle effects can also be seen: if a kitten sees only certain patterns during infancy, the response characteristics of many neurons in the visual cortex correspond to those patterns.

Visual perception consists largely of learning to recognize objects and shapes in our environment; thus, this learning continues to alter the visual system throughout life. Studies with humans who have sustained damage to the visual association cortex have discovered two basic forms of visual agnosia. Apperceptive visual agnosia involves difficulty in perceiving the shapes of objects, even though the fine details can often be detected. Achromatopsia, lack of color vision, often accompanies this disorder and probably results from damage to the human equivalent of V4. Prosopagnosia, failure to recognize faces, has traditionally been regarded as a separate disorder, but probably represents a mild form of apperceptive visual agnosia. The second basic form of visual agnosia, associative visual agnosia, is characterized by relatively good object perception but the inability to name what has been perceived. This disorder is probably caused by damage to axons that connect the visual association cortex with regions of the brain that are important for verbalization.

Concluding Remarks

Vision has long fascinated people, and research on this topic has occupied the efforts of many investigators and undoubtedly will continue to do so for many years. As you have seen in this chapter, biochemists are studying the process of sensory transduction, neuroanatomists are studying the details of neural connections in the retina, thalamus, midbrain, and neocortex, and other neuroscientists are studying the response characteristics of neurons in these structures. The functions of various regions of the visual association cortex are beginning to be mapped out, and neurologists and neuropsychologists are beginning to be able to characterize the nature of visual deficits in people with brain damage and to relate these deficits to research with laboratory animals.

NEW TERMS

accessory optic nuclei p. 182
accommodation p. 172
achromatopsia p. 219
adaptation p. 203
all-*trans* retinal p. 176
amacrine cell p. 175
apperceptive visual agnosia p. 219
associative visual agnosia p. 221
bipolar cell p. 174
brightness p. 170
calcarine fissure p. 179
ciliary muscles p. 172
circumstriate cortex p. 205
11-*cis* retinal p. 176
complex cell p. 192
cone p. 173
conjunctiva p. 171
convergence p. 172
cornea p. 171
deuteranopia p. 211
dorsal lateral geniculate nucleus p. 179
feature detector p. 182

flat bipolar cell p. 186
flat synapse p. 186
Fourier analysis p. 202
fovea p. 173
ganglion cell p. 175
homunculus p. 169
horizontal cell p. 175
hue p. 170
hypercomplex cell p. 193
inferior temporal cortex p. 206
inner plexiform layer p. 175
invaginating bipolar cell p. 186
iris p. 171
lamella p. 175
lens p. 172
opsin p. 176
optic chiasm p. 181
optic disk p. 173
optic radiation p. 179
orbit p. 171
outer plexiform layer p. 175
photon p. 170

SUGGESTED READINGS

BOYNTON, R.M. *Human Color Vision.* New York: Holt, Rinehart and Winston, 1979.

GREGORY, R.L. *Eye and Brain.* New York: McGraw-Hill, 1978.

KATSUKI, Y., NORGREN, R., AND SATO, M. *Brain Mechanisms of Sensation.* New York: John Wiley & Sons, 1981.

MOLLON, J.D. Color vision. *Annual Review of Psychology,* 1982, *33,* 41–86.

MOVSHON, J.A., AND VAN SLUYTERS, R.C. Visual neural development. *Annual Review of Neuroscience,* 1984, *7,* 477–522.

POGGIO, G.F., AND POGGIO, T. The analysis of stereopsis. *Annual Review of Neuroscience,* 1984, *7,* 379–412.

WEALE, R.A. *Focus on Vision.* Cambridge, Mass.: Harvard University Press, 1982.

Audition, Vestibular Senses, Somatosenses, Gustation, and Olfaction

One chapter was devoted to vision, but the rest of the sensory modalities must share a chapter. This unequal allocation of space reflects the relative importance of vision to our species and the relative amount of research that has been devoted to it. This chapter considers audition, the vestibular senses, the somatosenses (including kinesthesia), pain perception, gustation, and olfaction.

■ AUDITION

For most people, audition is the second most important sense. The value of verbal communication makes it even more important than vision in some respects; for example, a blind person can join others in conversation far more easily than a deaf person can. Acoustic stimuli also provide information about things that are hidden from view, and our ears work just as well in the dark.

The Stimulus

We hear sounds, which are produced by objects that vibrate and set the molecules of the air into motion. When an object vibrates, its movements cause the air surrounding it alternately to condense and rarefy (pull apart), producing waves that travel away from the object at approximately 700 miles per hour. If the vibration ranges between approximately 30 and 20,000 times per second,

these waves will stimulate receptive cells in our ears and will be perceived as sounds. We can also stimulate these receptors by placing a vibrating object against the bones of the head, bypassing air conduction altogether.

In Chapter 6 we saw that light has three perceptual dimensions — hue, brightness, and saturation — which correspond to three physical dimensions. Similarly, sounds vary in their pitch, loudness, and timbre. The perceived *pitch* of an auditory stimulus is determined by the frequency of vibration, which is measured in *hertz (Hz),* or cycles per second. (The term honors Heinrich Hertz, a nineteenth-century German physicist.) *Loudness* is a function of intensity — the degree to which the condensations and rarefactions of air differ from each other. More vigorous vibrations of an object produce more intense sound waves, and hence louder ones. *Timbre* provides information about the nature of the particular sound — for example, the sound of an oboe or a train whistle. Most natural acoustic stimuli are complex, consisting of several different frequencies of vibration. The particular mixture determines the sound's timbre. (See **Figure 7.1.**)

The eye is a *synthetic* organ (literally, "a putting together"). When two different wavelengths of light are mixed, we perceive a single color. In contrast, the ear is an *analytical* organ (from *analuein,* "to undo"). When

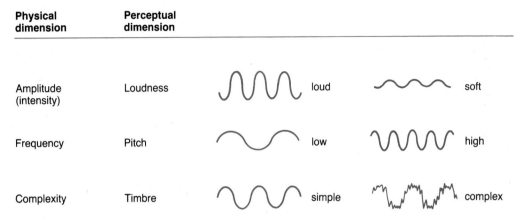

Physical dimension	Perceptual dimension		
Amplitude (intensity)	Loudness	loud	soft
Frequency	Pitch	low	high
Complexity	Timbre	simple	complex

FIGURE 7.1

The physical and perceptual dimensions of sound waves.

two different frequencies of sound waves are mixed, we do not perceive an intermediate tone. Instead, we hear both original tones. As we will see, the ability of our auditory system to detect the individual component frequencies of a complex tone gives us the capacity to identify the nature of particular sounds, such as different musical instruments.

Anatomy of the Ear

Figure 7.2 shows a section through the ear and auditory canal and illustrates the apparatus of the middle and inner ear. (See **Figure 7.2.**) Sound is funneled via the *pinna* (external ear) through the *external auditory canal* to the *tympanic membrane* (eardrum), which vibrates with the sound. We are not very good at moving our ears, but by orienting our heads, we can modify the sound that finally reaches the receptors. A muscle in the tympanic membrane (the *tensor tympani*) can alter the membrane's tension and thus control the amount of sound that is permitted to pass through to the middle ear.

The *ossicles,* the bones of the middle ear, are set into vibration by the tympanic membrane. The *malleus* (hammer) connects with the tympanic membrane and transmits vibra-

tions via the *incus* (anvil) and *stapes* (stirrup) to the *cochlea,* the inner ear structure containing the receptors. The baseplate of the stapes presses against the membrane behind the *oval window,* the opening in the bony process surrounding the cochlea. (See **Figure 7.2.**) The *stapedius muscle,* when contracted, directs the baseplate of the stapes away from its normal point of attachment to the oval window, hence dampening the vibration passed on to the receptive cells.

The cochlea is filled with fluid; therefore, sounds transmitted through the air must be transferred into a liquid medium. This process is normally very inefficient — 99.9 percent of the energy of airborne sound would be reflected away if the air impinged directly against the oval window of the cochlea. (If you have ever swum underwater, you have probably noted how quiet it is there; most of the sound arising in the air is reflected off the surface of the water.) The chain of ossicles serves as an extremely efficient means of energy transmission. The bones provide a mechanical advantage, with the baseplate of the stapes making smaller but more forceful excursions against the oval window than the tympanic membrane makes against the malleus.

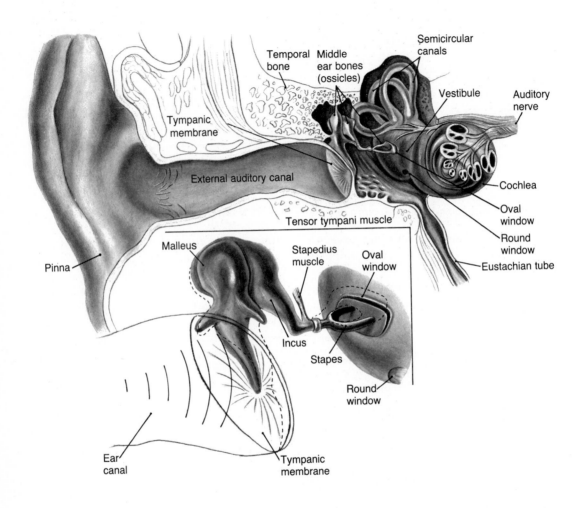

FIGURE 7.2
The auditory apparatus.

The name *cochlea* comes from the Greek word *kokhlos,* or "land snail." It is indeed snail-shaped, consisting of two and three-quarters turns of a gradually tapering cylinder. The cochlea is divided longitudinally into three sections, as shown in **Figure 7.3.** The auditory receptors are called **hair cells,** and they are anchored, via rodlike **Deiters's cells,** to the **basilar membrane.** The cilia of the hair cells pass through the **reticular membrane,** and their ends attach to the fairly rigid **tectorial membrane,** which projects overhead like a shelf. (The entire structure, including the basilar membrane, hair cells, and tectorial membrane, is referred to as the ***organ of Corti***). (See **Figure 7.3.**) Sound waves cause the basilar membrane to move relative to the tectorial membrane, which displaces the cilia of the hair cells. This displacement produces receptor potentials.

If the cochlea were a closed system, no vibration would be transmitted through the oval window, because liquids are essentially incompressible. However, there is a membrane-covered opening, the ***round window,*** which allows the fluid contents of the cochlea to move back and forth. The baseplate of the stapes presses against the membrane be-

hind the oval window, thus increasing the hydrostatic pressure within the *vestibule,* a chamber to which the cochlea is attached. The ***scala vestibuli*** (literally, the stairway of the vestibule) connects with the vestibule and conducts the pressure around the turns of the cochlea.

Although the process by which the organ of Corti converts mechanical energy into neural activity has received intense study, we still do not understand the details of this process. Georg von Békésy, in a lifetime of brilliant studies on the cochleas of various animals, from human cadavers to elephants, found that

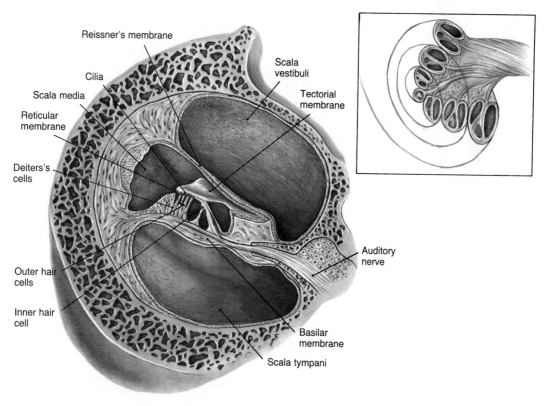

FIGURE 7.3
A cross section through the cochlea, showing the organ of Corti.

the vibratory energy exerted on the oval window results in deformations in the shape of the basilar membrane, called *traveling waves*. These deformations occur at different portions of the membrane, depending upon the frequency of the stimulus. The physics of the production of these waves is too complicated to be presented here (anyway, I take it on faith, myself). It suffices to say that because of the physical properties of the basilar membrane and the surrounding fluids, high-frequency sounds cause the end nearest the oval window to bend.

Figure 7.4 shows this process in a cochlea that has been partially straightened out. The baseplate of the stapes vibrates against the membrane behind the oval window and in-troduces sound waves of high or low frequency into the scala vestibuli. The vibrations cause part of the basilar membrane to flex back and forth, transmitting the pressure waves into the *scala tympani,* which lies beneath. Pressure changes in the scala tympani are transmitted to the membrane of the round window, which moves in and out in a manner opposite to the movements of the oval window. (See **Figure 7.4.**)

Auditory Hair Cells and the Transduction of Auditory Information

Two types of auditory receptors, *inner* and *outer* auditory hair cells, lie on the inside and outside of the cochlear coils, respectively.

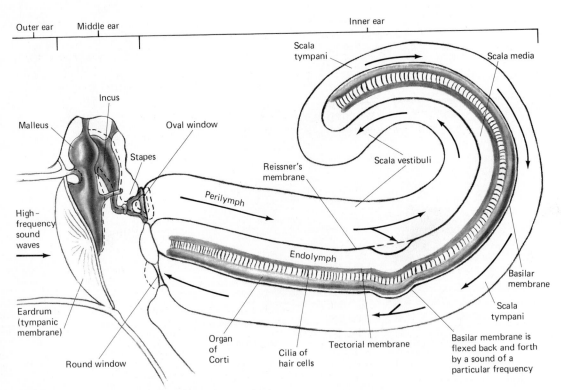

FIGURE 7.4
Sound waves transmitted through the oval window deform a portion of the basilar membrane.

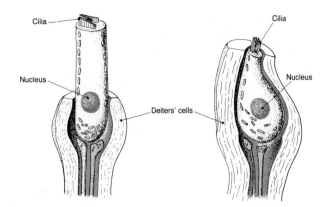

FIGURE 7.5
The auditory hair cells.
(Adapted from Gulick, W.L.
*Hearing: Physiology and
Psychophysics.* New York:
Oxford University Press, 1971.)

Hair cells contain *cilia* ("eyelashes"), fine hairlike appendages. The human cochlea contains 3400 inner hair cells and 12,000 outer hair cells. Figure 7.5 illustrates these cells and their supporting Deiters's cells. (See **Figure 7.5.**) The hair cells form synapses with dendrites of neurons that give rise to the auditory nerve axons. Figure 7.6 shows the actual appearance of the inner and outer hair cells and the reticular membrane in a photograph taken by means of a scanning electron microscope, which shows excellent three-di-

mensional detail. Note the three rows of outer hair cells on the right and the single row of inner hair cells on the left. (See **Figure 7.6.**)

As the basilar membrane bends, it moves relative to the tectorial membrane. Because the ends of the cilia of the hair cells are attached to the overlying tectorial membrane, this movement is transmitted to them. Adjacent cilia, which are stiff and rigid, are attached to each other near their tips. Thus, the relative movement of the basilar and tectorial membranes exerts a shearing force on the

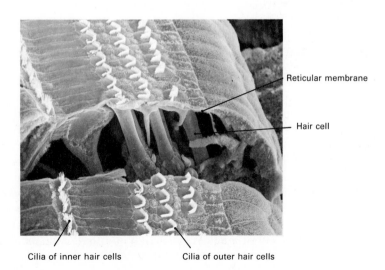

FIGURE 7.6
A scanning electron
photomicrograph of a portion
of the organ of Corti, showing
the cilia of the inner and outer
hair cells. (Photomicrograph
courtesy of I. Hunter-Duvar,
The Hospital for Sick Children,
Toronto, Ontario.)

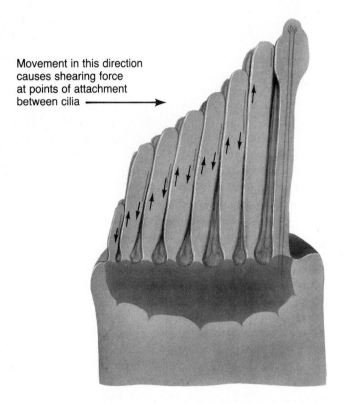

Movement in this direction
causes shearing force
at points of attachment
between cilia ⟶

FIGURE 7.7
Because adjacent cilia are
attached near their tips, force
exerted against the bundle of
cilia causes a shearing force in
each one at its point of
attachment. Reproduced with
permission, from *The Annual
Review of Neuroscience,* Vol.
7, ©1984 by Annual Reviews,
Inc.

cilia. The force is also transmitted to the *cuticular plate* to which the cilia are attached. (See **Figure 7.7.**)

This shearing force produces a receptor potential. How and where it does so is not yet understood, but the process, like other forms of transduction, involves the selective opening of ion channels. (See Dallos, 1981, and Hudspeth, 1983, for reviews.) The cochlea contains two types of liquid: the scala vestibuli and the scala tympani contain *perilymph* (which is similar to the interstitial fluid that bathes most cells of the body), and the *scala media* ("middle stairway") contains *endolymph.* As we saw in Chapter 2, interstitial fluid is rich in sodium (Na^+) but low in potassium (K^+). In contrast, endolymph is rich in K^+ but low in Na^+. In addition, the endolymph contains an 80-mV positive charge with respect to the perilymph. This additional charge means that the membrane potential of the cilia is approximately -150 mV (inside negative, outside positive). Thus, electrostatic and osmotic gradients tend to force K^+ into the hair cells. (See **Figure 7.8.**)

Mechanical stimulation of the cilia of hair cells apparently opens membrane channels that admit K^+; Valli, Zucca, and Casella (1979) found that removal of K^+ from the endolymph abolishes the hair cell receptor potential. Entry of the positive ion depolarizes the membrane, producing the receptor potential. The ion channels may be located near the ends of the cilia, where adjacent ones are attached, or they may be located in the cuticular plate to which the cilia are attached.

In 1930, Wever and Bray recorded signals from a cat's cochlear nerve and found that when these signals were amplified and sent to a loudspeaker, a listener could understand what was being said into the cat's ear. Because the ear served as a microphone, the electrical potentials were called ***cochlear microphonics.*** It turns out that cochlear microphonics are not caused by action potentials but are actually summed receptor potentials, transmitted passively by cable properties. When the blood supply to the inner ear is cut off, the action potentials in the cochlear nerve soon disappear. However, the cochlear microphonics remain for a few hours more, indicating that they do not consist of action potentials.

The Auditory Pathway

Connections with the Cochlear Nerve

The organ of Corti sends auditory information to the brain by means of the ***cochlear nerve,*** a branch of the auditory nerve (eighth cranial nerve). The neurons that give rise to the afferent axons that travel through this nerve are of the bipolar type. Their cell bodies reside in the ***cochlear nerve ganglion.*** These neurons have axonal processes, capable of sustaining action potentials, that protrude from both ends of the soma. The end of one process acts like a dendrite, responding with excitatory postsynaptic potentials when the transmitter substance is released by the auditory hair cells. The excitatory postsynaptic potentials

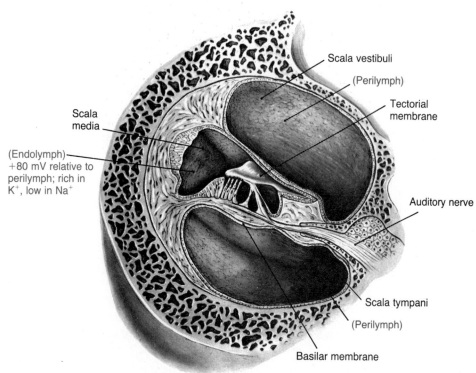

Scala vestibuli

(Perilymph)

Tectorial membrane

Scala media

(Endolymph) +80 mV relative to perilymph; rich in K$^+$, low in Na$^+$

Auditory nerve

Scala tympani

(Perilymph)

Basilar membrane

FIGURE 7.8

The electrical charge in the cochlea.

trigger action potentials in the auditory nerve axons, which forms synapses with neurons in the medulla. (See **Figure 7.9.**)

Figure 7.10 shows a diagram of the synaptic connections of inner and outer hair cells. Note that hair cells receive both afferent and efferent connections; the cochlear nerve contains both incoming and outgoing axons. (See **Figure 7.10.**) The transmitter substance at the afferent synapses appears to be an excitatory amino acid such as glutamate or aspartate. The hair cells also receive efferent connections from neurons located in the medulla. These terminal buttons secrete acetylcholine, which appears to have an inhibitory effect on the hair cells. The functional significance of these connections is not known; destruction of the efferent axons does not affect a cat's ability to perform tasks that

require intensity or frequency discrimination (Igarashi, Cranford, Allen, and Alford, 1979; Igarashi, Cranford, Nakai, and Alford, 1979).

The dendrites of approximately 95 percent of the afferent cochlear nerve fibers form synapses with the inner hair cells, on a one receptor/one neuron basis (Spoendlin, 1973). The other 5 percent of the sensory fibers form synapses with the much more numerous outer hair cells, on a ten receptors/one neuron basis. Thus, although the inner hair cells represent only 22 percent of the total number of receptive cells, they appear to be of primary importance in the transmission of auditory information to the central nervous system.

Physiological and behavioral studies confirm the inferences made from the synaptic connections of the two types of hair cells: The

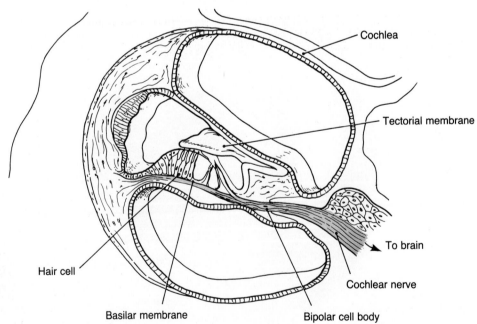

FIGURE 7.9
The axons of bipolar neurons constitute the cochlear nerve.

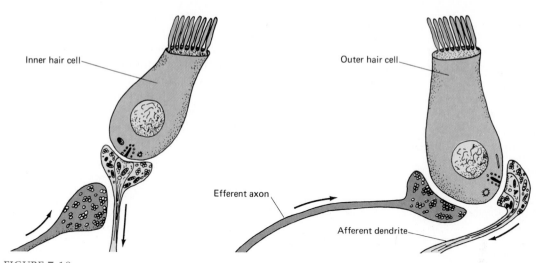

FIGURE 7.10

Details of the synaptic connections of the auditory hair cells. (Adapted from Spoendlin, H. In *Basic Mechanisms in Hearing,* edited by A.R. Møeller. New York: Academic Press, 1973.)

inner hair cells are necessary for normal hearing; however, no experiments have yet discovered the function of the more numerous outer hair cells. In fact, Deol and Glueck-sohn-Waelsch (1979) found that a mutant strain of mice whose cochleas contain *only* outer hair cells apparently cannot hear at all. Surprisingly, loss of inner hair cells has little effect on cochlear microphonics (Dallos and Cheatham, 1976); this finding suggests that receptor potentials in the outer hair cells are the largest contributor to this signal. Even more puzzling, investigators have not been able to distinguish by means of electrical recording between axons that receive information from inner and outer hair cells (Dallos, 1981). One would expect that 5 percent of the axons should exhibit different response characteristics.

The Central Auditory System

The anatomy of the auditory system is more complicated than that of the visual system. Rather than give a detailed verbal description

of the pathways, I will refer you to **Figure 7.11.** Note that axons enter the ***cochlear nuclei*** of the medulla and synapse there. Most of the neurons in the cochlear nuclei send axons to the ***superior olivary complex,*** also located in the medulla. Neurons there project axons through the ***lateral lemniscus*** (a large bundle of axons) to the inferior colliculus, located in the dorsal midbrain. Neurons there project to the medial geniculate nucleus, which sends axons to the auditory cortex of the temporal lobe. As you can see, there are many synapses along the way to complicate the story. Each hemisphere receives information from both ears but primarily from the contralateral one. And auditory information is relayed to the cerebellum and reticular formation as well. (See **Figure 7.11.**)

If we unrolled the basilar membrane into a flat strip and followed afferent axons serving successive points along its length, we would reach successive points in the nuclei of the auditory system and ultimately successive points along the surface of the primary auditory cortex. The *basal* end of the basilar membrane (the end toward the oval window) is represented most medially in the auditory cortex, and the *apical* end is represented most laterally there. Because, as we will see, different parts of the basilar membrane respond best to different frequencies of sound, this relationship between cortex and basilar membrane is referred to as ***tonotopic repre-***

sentation (*tonos* means "tone" and *topos* means "place").

Neurons in the primary auditory cortex send axons to the auditory association cortex. In Chapter 4, we saw that the primary auditory cortex lies hidden on the inside of the lateral fissure, and that the auditory association cortex lies on the superior part of the temporal lobe.

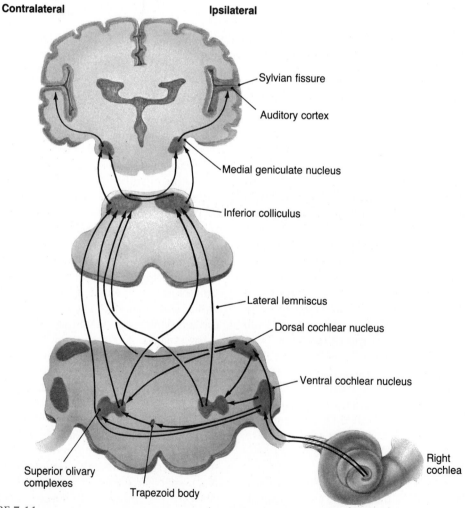

FIGURE 7.11
The pathway of the auditory system.

Detection of Pitch

As we have seen, the perceptual dimension of pitch corresponds to the physical dimension of frequency. The cochlea detects frequency by two means: high frequencies are coded anatomically (spatially), and low frequencies are coded temporally, by the rate of axonal firing.

Anatomical Coding of Pitch

The work of von Békésy has shown us that, because of the mechanical construction of the cochlea and basilar membrane, acoustic stimuli of different frequencies cause different parts of the basilar membrane to flex back and forth. Figure 7.12 illustrates the amount of deformation along the length of the basilar membrane produced by stimulation with tones of various frequencies. Note that higher frequencies produce more displacement at the basal end of the membrane (the end closest to the stapes). (See **Figure 7.12.**)

This spatial coding of frequency on the basilar membrane is more than just a candidate code. High doses of the antibiotic drugs kanamycin and neomycin produce degeneration of the auditory hair cells (and also, incidentally, of the vestibular hair cells). Damage to auditory hair cells begins at the basal end of the cochlea and progresses toward the apical end; this pattern can be verified by killing experimental animals after dosing them with the antibiotic for varying amounts of time. Longer exposures to the drug are associated with increased progress of hair cell damage down the basilar membrane. Stebbins, Miller, Johnsson, and Hawkins (1969) found that the progressive death of hair cells induced by an antibiotic closely parallels a progressive hearing loss: the highest frequencies are the first to go, and the lowest are the last.

Evidence from a variety of experiments has shown that although the basilar membrane codes for frequency along its length, the cod-

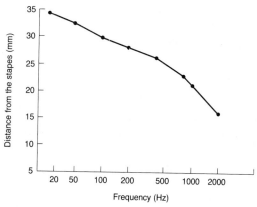

FIGURE 7.12

Stimuli of different frequencies maximally deform different regions of the basilar membrane. (From von Békésy, G., *Journal of the Acoustical Society of America,* 1949, *21,* 233–245.)

ing is not very specific. A given frequency causes a large region of the basilar membrane to be deformed. Even so, people can detect changes in frequency of only 2 or 3 Hz. Investigators have still not explained how such a broad bending of the basilar membrane produces such fine discrimination.

Recordings made from single axons in the cochlear nerve and single neurons in various parts of the auditory system show a very precise degree of frequency tuning. Figure 7.13 shows some V-shaped **auditory tuning curves.** The data were collected as follows: The investigator located an axon with a microelectrode and presented tones of various frequencies and intensities. For each cell, he plotted points that corresponded to the least intense tone that gave a response at a given frequency. The V shapes indicate that at higher intensities (the top of the V-shaped curves) a given axon responds to a wider range of frequencies. At low intensities (the bottom of the V-shaped curves), a given axon responds to a very limited range of frequencies. (See **Figure 7.13.**)

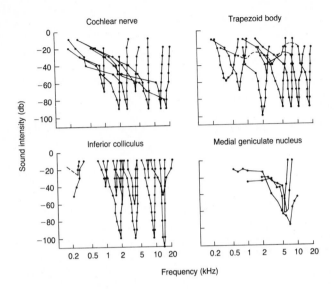

FIGURE 7.13
"Tuning curves" of single units in various portions of the auditory system. db = decibel; kHz = kilohertz (1000 Hz). (From Katsuki, Y. In *Sensory Communication,* edited by W.A. Rosenblith. Copyright 1961 by MIT Press.

Temporal Coding of Pitch

We have seen that frequency is nicely coded for in a spatial manner on the basilar membrane. However, the lowest frequencies do not appear to be accounted for in this manner. Kiang (1965) was unable to find any cells that responded best to frequencies of less than 200 Hz. How, then, can animals distinguish low frequencies? It appears that lower frequencies are encoded by neural firing that is synchronized to the movements of the apical end of the basilar membrane. The neurons fire in time with the sonic vibrations.

Miller and Taylor (1948) provided good evidence that pitch can be encoded by synchronized firing of the auditory hair cells. These investigators presented **white noise** (sound containing all frequencies, similar to the hissing sound you hear between FM radio stations) to human observers. When the investigators rapidly switched the white noise on and off, the observers reported that they heard a tone corresponding to the frequency of pulsation. The white noise, containing all frequencies, stimulated the entire length of the basilar membrane, so the frequency that was detected could not be coded for by place.

The only frequency-specific information the auditory system could have had was the firing rate of cochlear nerve axons.

Detection of Loudness

In Chapter 6 I noted that the visual system compresses the intensity range of light. This compression also occurs in the auditory system. Wilska (1935) used an ingenious procedure to estimate the smallest vibration to produce a perceptible sound. He glued a small wooden rod to a volunteer's tympanic membrane (temporarily, of course) and made the rod vibrate longitudinally by means of an electromagnetic coil that could be energized with alternating current. He could vary the frequency and intensity of the current, which consequently changed the perceived pitch and loudness of the stimulus. Wilska observed the rod under a microscope and measured the distance it moved in vibration. This movement was related to the amount of electrical current used, so that he could calculate the extremely minute vibrations of the eardrum that were too small to detect under the microscope. The astonishing result was that, in order for the subject to detect a sound, the eardrum need be vibrated a distance of less than the diameter of a hydrogen atom. Thus, in very quiet environments, a young, healthy ear is limited in its ability to detect sounds in the air by the masking noise of blood rushing through the cranial blood vessels, rather than by the sensitivity of the auditory system itself. More recent studies using modern instruments (reviewed by Hudspeth, 1983) have essentially confirmed Wilska's measurements. The softest sounds that can be detected appear to move the tip of the hair cells by between 1 and 100 picometers (trillionths of a meter). The softest sound we can detect is (I hesitate to say it) on the order of one 100-trillionth of the loudest sound that will not damage the inner ear (Uttal, 1973).

The axons of the cochlear nerve appear to encode loudness by rate. More intense vibrations produce a more intense shearing force on the cilia of the auditory hair cells, presumably causing them to release more transmitter substance, resulting in a higher rate of firing by the cochlear nerve axons. This explanation seems simple for the axons that encode pitch anatomically; in this case, pitch is encoded by which neurons fire, and loudness is encoded by their rate of firing. However, the neurons that encode lower frequencies do so by their rate of firing. If they fire more frequently, they would signal a higher pitch. Therefore, most investigators believe that the loudness of low-frequency sounds is encoded by the *number* of axons that are active at a given time.

I noted earlier that frequency is spatially coded on the surface of the auditory cortex. Tunturi (1952) found that intensity is also spatially coded along the cortical surface, at right angles to frequency. Tunturi placed electrodes at various locations on a dog's auditory cortex and recorded evoked potentials to sound. He then stimulated the animal's ear with various frequencies and intensities. His plot of the most effective stimuli is shown in Figure 7.14. The highest numbers (20–80 db) represent the loudest stimuli. (See **Figure 7.14.**) Low-frequency tones (below 100 Hz) are not represented; detection of these frequencies is presumably mediated by subcortical regions of the brain.

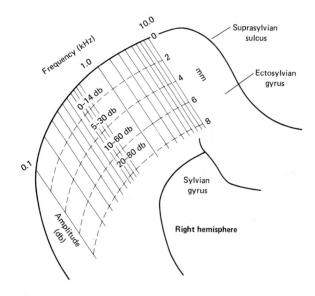

FIGURE 7.14

Coding of intensity and frequency of auditory stimuli by location along the surface of the primary auditory cortex of a dog. db = decibel; kHz = kilohertz (1000 Hz). (From Tunturi, A.R. *American Journal of Physiology*, 1952, *168*, 712–727.)

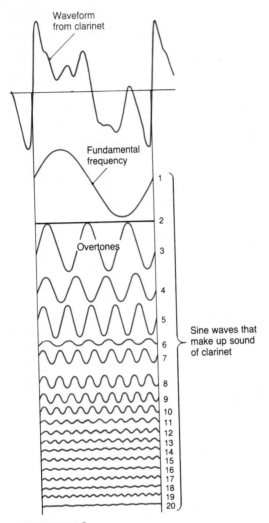

FIGURE 7.15

The shape of a sound wave from a clarinet *(top)* and the individual frequencies into which it can be analyzed. Reprinted from STEREO REVIEW, copyright ©1977, by Ziff-Davis Publishing Co.

Detection of Timbre

Although laboratory investigations of the auditory system often employ pure sine waves as stimuli, these waves are seldom encountered outside the laboratory. Instead, we hear sounds with a rich mixture of frequencies—

sounds of complex timbre. For example, consider the sound of a clarinet playing a particular note. If we hear it, we can easily say that it is a clarinet and not a flute or a violin. The reason we can do so is that these three instruments produce sounds of different timbre, which our auditory system can distinguish.

Figure 7.15 shows the waveform from a clarinet playing a steady note *(top)*. The shape of the waveform repeats itself regularly at the ***fundamental frequency,*** which corresponds to the perceived pitch of the note. Mathematical analyses of the waveform show that it actually consists of a series of sine waves that includes the fundamental frequency and many **overtones,** multiples of the fundamental frequency. Different instruments produce overtones with different intensities. (See **Figure 7.15.**) Electronic synthesizers simulate the sounds of real instruments by producing a series of overtones of the proper intensities, mixing them, and passing them through a loudspeaker.

When the basilar membrane is stimulated by the sound of a clarinet, different portions respond to each of the overtones. This response produces a unique anatomically coded pattern of activity in the cochlear nerve, which is subsequently identified by the auditory system of the brain. Just how this analysis is done is not known and probably will not be known for many years. When you consider that we can listen to an orchestra playing and identify several instruments that are playing simultaneously, you can appreciate the complexity of the analysis performed by the auditory system.

Feature Detection in the Auditory System

So far I have discussed coding of only pitch, loudness, and timbre (the last of which is actually a complex frequency analysis). The auditory system also responds to other qualities of acoustic stimuli. For example, our ears are very good at determining whether the source of a sound is to the right or left of us. (To discriminate front from back, we merely turn our heads, transforming the discrimination into a left-right decision.) Two separate physiological mechanisms detect the location of sound sources: we use phase differences for low frequencies (less than approximately 3000 Hz) and intensity differences for higher frequencies. Stevens and Newman (1936) found that localization is worst at approximately 3000 Hz, presumably because both mechanisms are rather inefficient at that frequency.

Localization by Means of Arrival Time and Phase Differences

If we are blindfolded, we can still determine the location of a stimulus that emits a click with rather good accuracy. We do so because neurons respond selectively to different *arrival times* of the sound waves at the left and right ears. If the source of the click is to the right or left of the midline, the sound pressure wave will reach one ear sooner and initiate action potentials there first. Only if the stimulus is straight ahead will the ears be stimulated simultaneously. Many neurons in the auditory system are **binaural,** responding to sounds presented to either ear. (Their counterparts in the visual system are the *binocular* neurons.) Some of these neurons, especially those in the superior olivary complex of the medulla, respond according to the difference in arrival times of sound waves produced by clicks presented to both ears. Their response rates reflect differences as small as a fraction of a millisecond. For example, Figure 7.16 shows the graph of a cell that responded most vigorously when the first of a pair of binaural clicks is presented first to the left ear. (See **Figure 7.16.**)

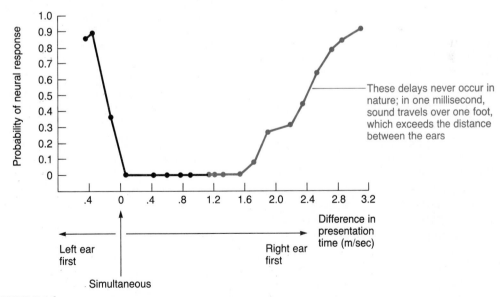

FIGURE 7.16
Neural responses to binaural pairs of clicks presented at slightly different times to the two ears. (From Moushegian, G., Rupert, A., and Langford, T.L. *Journal of Neurophysiology,* 1967, *30,* 1239–1261.)

Source of 1000-Hz
tone is to the right

Source of tone
is in front

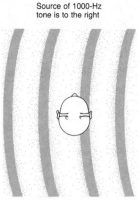

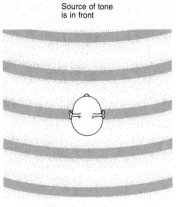

Right eardrum is in,
left eardrum is out

Both eardrums are in

FIGURE 7.17
Left: When a 1000-Hz tone is located to one side of the head, the eardrums vibrate out of phase. *Right:* When a 1000-Hz tone is located to the front or back of the head, the eardrums vibrate in phase.

We detect the source of continuous low-pitched sounds by means of ***phase differences.*** Phase differences refer to the simultaneous arrival, at each ear, of different portions (phases) of the oscillating sound wave. For example, if we assume that sound travels at 700 miles per hour through the air (the actual value depends on temperature, barometric pressure, and humidity), adjacent cycles of a 1000-Hz tone are 12.3 inches apart. Thus, if the source of the sound is located to one side of the head, one eardrum is pulled out while the other is pushed in. (See **Figure 7.17.**) If some auditory neurons respond only during a particular phase of a sound wave, a tone presented by a sound source closer to one ear than the other would produce firing patterns of axons from the two ears that are slightly out of synchrony.

Indeed, some auditory neurons do fire only during a particular phase of a sound wave (that is, during a particular portion of the cycle). Figure 7.18 illustrates this phenomenon, called ***phase locking.*** The sine wave at the top of the diagram represents the vibration of the basilar membrane produced by a pure tone. Line B shows the response of a cell that responds to every wave. Lines C and D show responses of cells that do not respond to every wave; however, when they fire, they do

so only during the same portion of the cycle. (See **Figure 7.18.**)

Rose, Brugge, Anderson, and Hind (1967) found evidence of phase locking in axons of the cochlear nerve. The graphs shown in Figure 7.19 are called *frequency histograms.* Note the regular peaks. (See **Figure 7.19.**) The horizontal axes represent the time between two successive action potentials. To construct such plots, we find an active axon and turn on the stimulus. We start a clock as soon as an action potential is recorded and stop it when we detect another one. We then

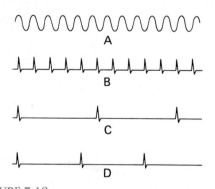

FIGURE 7.18
Phase locking. *A* represents the stimulus; *B*, *C*, and *D* represent the responses of different neurons.

note the time, reset the clock, and see how long it takes for another action potential to occur. (Of course, being poor mortals, we engage the services of a computer to do the timing and recording for us.) After we have recorded and timed for a while, we will have a series of numbers — inter-spike intervals. We see that the numbers are clustered: For a cell stimulated with a 1000-Hz tone, the inter-spike intervals tend to be 1, 2, 3, 4 (etc.) milliseconds. We find very few at 1.5, 2.5, 3.5 (etc.) milliseconds. The number of times each interval was seen is plotted in Figure 7.19. Note, especially, the graph for the 1000-Hz tone, with its regular clusters at even 1-millisecond intervals. (See **Figure**

7.19.) The cells clearly "lock on" to a portion of the wave of vibration, even if they do not always fire at the same rate.

The auditory system uses the differences in firing times of phase-locked neurons to localize the source of a continuous sound, just as it localizes the source of a single click. Figure 7.20 shows the response of two different neurons in the superior olivary complex to a 650-Hz tone as a function of binaural lead time. The phrase *ipsilateral leads* means that each wave of the stimulus reaches the ipsilateral ear first, by the amount of time shown on the horizontal axis. The phrase *contralateral leads* means that the contralateral ear receives each wave first. (See **Figure 7.20.**)

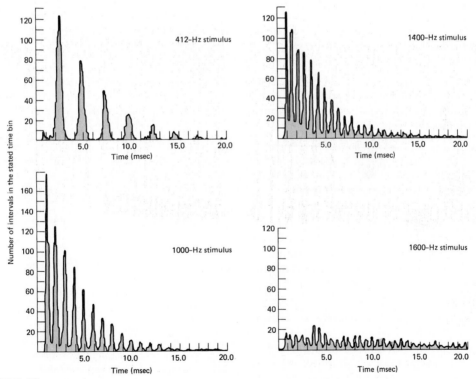

FIGURE 7.19

Evidence that individual auditory nerve axons show phase locking to pure tones. (From Rose, J.E., Brugge, J.F., Anderson, D.J., and Hind, J.E. *Journal of Neurophysiology,* 1967, *30,* 769–793.)

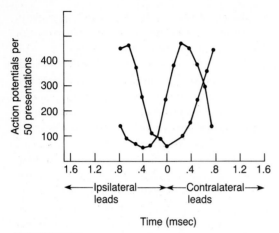

FIGURE 7.20
Responses of two neurons in the superior olivary complex to sine-wave stimuli presented binaurally with different phase relations. (From Moushegian, G., and Rupert, A.L. *Proceedings of the Society for Experimental Biology and Medicine,* 1974, *33,* 1924.)

Localization by Means of Intensity Differences

The auditory system cannot readily detect binaural phase differences of high-frequency stimuli. However, high-frequency stimuli occurring to the right or left of the midline stimulate the ears unequally. The head absorbs high frequencies, producing a "sonic shadow," so the ear opposite the source of the sound receives less intense stimulation. Some neurons in the auditory system respond differentially to binaural stimuli of different intensity in each ear. Figure 7.21 shows the response of two neurons to binaural stimuli of different frequencies, presented at different intensities to the ipsilateral and contralateral ear. Note that the response rate changes according to the relative intensity. (See **Figure 7.21.**)

The neurons that detect binaural differences in loudness are located in the superior olivary complex. But whereas those that detect binaural differences in phase or arrival time are located in the *medial* superior oli-

vary complex, these neurons are located in the *lateral* superior olivary complex. Information from both sets of neurons is sent to other levels of the auditory system.

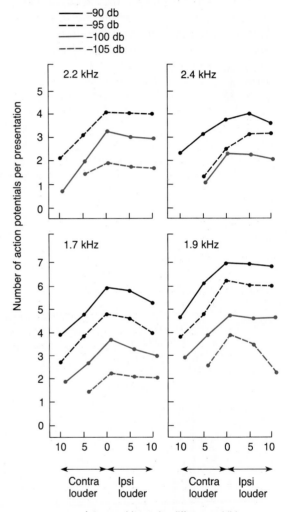

FIGURE 7.21
Responses of two neurons in the superior olivary complex to sine-wave stimuli presented binaurally with different intensities. db = decibel; kHz = kilohertz (1000 Hz). (From Moushegian, G., *et al.* In *Physiology of the Auditory System,* edited by M.B. Sachs. Baltimore: National Educational Consultants, 1971.

Detection of Other Features

The auditory system also detects other features, but the mechanisms are not nearly so well defined. Various studies (Whitfield and Evans, 1965; Saitoh, Maruyama, and Kudoh, 1981) have found cells that respond only to the onset or cessation of a sound (or to both), to changes in pitch or intensity (sometimes only to changes in one direction), or to complex stimuli that contain a variety of frequencies. These results accord with the observation that changing stimuli attract our attention better than do steady ones. Because data are scanty so far, we have no real conception of the coding mechanism that the brain uses for these changes, or even of precisely what features are coded.

Behavioral Functions of the Auditory System

Destruction of the primary visual cortex leads to blindness. In contrast, destruction of the auditory cortex — even in humans — does not impair simple intensity or frequency discriminations.

Neff (1977) reviewed a large number of studies that he and his colleagues performed with cats and monkeys to investigate the role of various levels of the auditory system in auditory discrimination, localization, and lateralization (the ability to discriminate to which ear a monaural stimulus is presented). To measure the animals' ability to discriminate between different acoustic stimuli, they placed them in a *shuttle box,* an apparatus with two chambers separated by a doorway. When the experimenters presented one stimulus (S⁺), the animals had several seconds to cross to the other side; otherwise, they would receive a foot shock through the floor that would continue until they escaped to the other chamber. When the experimenters presented the other stimulus (S⁻), the animals were required to do nothing; this stimulus was not followed by a foot shock. If the animals were able to discriminate between S⁺ and S⁻, they soon learned to enter the opposite chamber during the former and stay put during the latter.

In other studies, Neff and his colleagues evaluated the animals' ability to localize the sources of sounds by placing them in a wire cage, briefly presenting a sound through one of two loudspeakers in front of them, and then letting them leave the cage. If they approached the speaker that had just made a sound they would find some food. (See **Figure 7.22.**) In yet another set of studies, in-

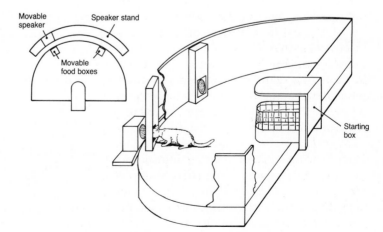

FIGURE 7.22
The experimental apparatus used by Neff and his colleagues to investigate localization of sound sources. (From Neff, W.D. *Annals of Otology, Rhinology and Laryngology,* 1977, *86,* 500–506.)

tended to test the animals' ability to determine which ear receives an acoustic stimulus, they fitted the animals with earphones and placed them in a shuttle box. Stimuli presented to one ear served as S$^+$, and those presented to the other ear served as S$^-$.

Their results were as follows: Bilateral removal of all areas of the auditory cortex (both primary auditory cortex and auditory association cortex) did not prevent the animals from learning to detect tones of different frequencies or intensities. However, they could not discriminate between different "tunes" or temporal patterns of acoustic stimuli, they could not detect changes in the duration of tones, they could not localize the source of sounds, they could not detect changes in complex sounds, and they could not determine which ear was stimulated. *Unilateral* removal of the auditory cortex abolished only the ability to localize sounds and to determine which ear was stimulated.

Bilateral destruction of the brachium of the inferior colliculus (which abolishes all auditory input to the medial geniculate nuclei but leaves the brain stem structures intact) does not affect the animals' ability to detect sounds (even very soft ones), but it impairs the ability to detect *differences* in the intensity of sounds and abolishes frequency discrimination. Thus, these two functions must require the thalamus (but not the cortex). Neff and his colleagues also destroyed the lateral lemniscus, which abolishes auditory input to the inferior colliculi. These animals appeared to be deaf. They could learn to respond to very loud tones, but these tones might be detected by nonauditory means; perhaps the animals *felt* vibrations taking place in their ears.

As we saw in the previous chapter, lesions of the visual association cortex in humans can produce visual agnosias. Similarly, lesions of the auditory association cortex can produce auditory agnosias, the inability to comprehend the meaning of sounds. If the lesion

occurs in the left hemisphere, the person will sustain a particular form of language disorder. If it occurs in the right hemisphere, the person will be unable to recognize the nature or location of nonspeech sounds. Because of the importance of audition to language, these topics are discussed in much more detail in Chapter 16.

INTERIM SUMMARY

The receptive organ for audition is the organ of Corti, located on the basilar membrane. When sound strikes the tympanic membrane, it sets the ossicles into motion, and the baseplate of the stapes pushes against the membrane behind the oval window. Pressure changes thus applied to the fluid within the cochlea cause a portion of the basilar membrane to flex. This flexion causes the basilar membrane to move laterally with respect to the tectorial membrane that overhangs it and exerts a shearing force on the cilia. This mechanical force opens ion channels in the hair cells and thus produces receptor potentials.

The hair cells form synapses with the dendrites of the bipolar neurons whose axons give rise to the cochlear branch of the eighth cranial nerve. The central auditory system involves several brain stem nuclei, including the cochlear nuclei, superior olivary complexes, and inferior colliculi. The medial geniculate nucleus relays auditory information to the primary auditory cortex on the medial surface of the temporal lobe.

Pitch is encoded by two means. High-frequency sounds cause the base of the basilar membrane (near the oval window) to flex, while lower-frequency sounds cause the apex (opposite end) to flex. Because high and low frequencies thus stimulate different groups of auditory hair cells, frequency is encoded anatomically. The lowest frequencies cause the apex of the basilar membrane to flex back and forth in time with the acoustic vibrations.

The auditory system is analytical in its operation. That is, it can discriminate between sounds with different timbres by detecting the individual overtones that constitute the sounds and by producing unique patterns of neural firing in the auditory system.

Left-right localization is performed by analyzing binaural differences in arrival time and in phase relations and binaural differences in intensity. The location of sources of brief sounds (such as clicks) and sounds of frequencies below approximately 3000 Hz is detected by neurons in the superior olivary complex that respond most vigorously when one ear receives the click first, or when the phase of a sine wave received by one ear leads that received by the other. The location of sources of high-frequency sounds is detected by neurons in the superior olivary complex that respond most vigorously when one organ of Corti is stimulated more intensely than the other. Removal of both the primary auditory cortex and the auditory association cortex does not affect the ability to detect differences in frequency or intensity; thus, this analysis must be performed by subcortical components of the auditory system. However, the cortical removal does impair localization of the source of sounds and discrimination between different "tunes," changes in the duration of sounds, and changes in complex sounds.

■ **THE VESTIBULAR SYSTEM**

The Stimuli

The vestibular system has two components: the *vestibular sacs* and the *semicircular canals.* They represent the second and third

components of the *bony labyrinths.* (We just studied the first component, the cochlea.) The vestibular sacs respond to the force of gravity and inform the brain about the head's orientation. The semicircular canals respond to angular acceleration — changes in the rotation of the head — but not to steady rotation. They also respond (but rather weakly) to changes in position or to linear acceleration.

The functions of the vestibular system include balance, maintenance of the head in an upright position, and adjustment of eye movement to compensate for head movements. Vestibular stimulation does not produce any readily definable sensation; certain low-frequency stimulation of the vestibular sacs can produce nausea, and stimulation of the semicircular canals can produce dizziness and rhythmic eye movements *(nystagmus).* However, we receive no primary sensation from these organs, unlike the organs of audition and vision, for example.

Anatomy of the Vestibular Apparatus

Figure 7.23 shows the bony labyrinths: the cochlea, the semicircular canals, and the two vestibular sacs: the *utricle* ("little pouch") and the *saccule* ("little sack"). (See **Figure 7.23.**) The semicircular canals approximate

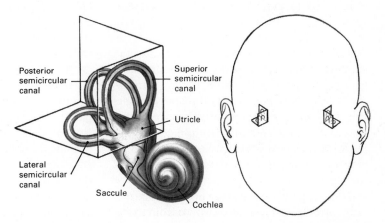

FIGURE 7.23
The bony labyrinths of the inner ear.

Posterior semicircular canal
Superior semicircular canal
Utricle
Lateral semicircular canal
Saccule
Cochlea

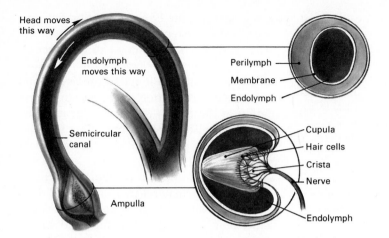

FIGURE 7.24
Cross sections through one semicircular canal.

the three major planes of the head: sagittal, transverse, and horizontal. Receptors in each canal respond maximally to angular acceleration in one plane. Figure 7.24 shows cross sections through one semicircular canal. The semicircular canal consists of a membranous canal floating within a bony one; the membranous canal contains endolymph and floats within perilymph. An enlargement called the *ampulla* contains the *crista,* the organ in which the sensory receptors reside. The sensory receptors are hair cells similar to those found in the cochlea. Their cilia are embedded in a gelatinous mass called the *cupula,* which blocks part of the ampulla. (See **Figure 7.24.**)

In order to explain the effects of angular acceleration on the semicircular canals, I will first describe an ''experiment.'' If we place a glass of water on the exact center of a turntable and then start the turntable spinning, the water in the glass will, at first, remain stationary (the glass will move with respect to the water it contains). Eventually, however, the water will begin rotating with the container. If we then stop the turntable the water will continue spinning for a while, because of its inertia.

The semicircular canals operate on the same principle. The endolymph within these canals, like the water in the glass, resists movement when the head begins to rotate. This inertial resistance pushes the endolymph against the cupula, causing it to bend, until the fluid begins to move at the same speed as the head. If the head rotation is then stopped, the endolymph, still circulating through the canal, pushes the cupula the other way. Angular acceleration is thus translated into bending of the crista, which exerts a shearing force on the cilia of the hair cells. This process was directly observed by Steinhausen (1931), who injected a drop of oil in the partially dissected semicircular canal of a pike, a fish with a large and easily accessible vestibular apparatus. Figure 7.25 shows the effects of rotation of the semicircular canal in a clockwise direction; the endolymph resists the rotation and pushes the cupula to the right. (See **Figure 7.25.**)

The vestibular sacs (the utricle and saccule) work very differently. These organs are roughly circular in shape, and each contains a patch of receptive tissue. The receptive tissue is located on the ''floor'' of the utricle and on the ''wall'' of the saccule, when the head is in an upright position. The receptive tissue, like that of the semicircular canals and cochlea, contains hair cells. The cilia of these receptors are embedded in an overlying gelatinous

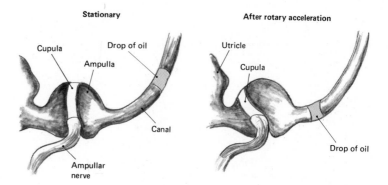

FIGURE 7.25
A diagram of Steinhausen's demonstration that movement of the endolymph causes displacement of the cupula. (Adapted from Dohlman, G. *Proceedings of the Royal Society of Medicine,* 1935, *28,* 1371–1380.)

mass, which contains something rather unusual: *otoconia,* which are small crystals of calcium carbonate. (See **Figure 7.26.**) The weight of the crystals causes the gelatinous mass to shift in position as the orientation of the head changes. Thus, movement produces a shearing force on the cilia of the receptive hair cells.

Anatomy of the Receptor Cells

The hair cells of the semicircular canal and vestibular sacs have similar structures. Two types of cells appear in both organs. The type I hair cell is embedded in a dendritic process (called a *calyx*) similar in shape to an egg-cup. Transmission appears to be chemically

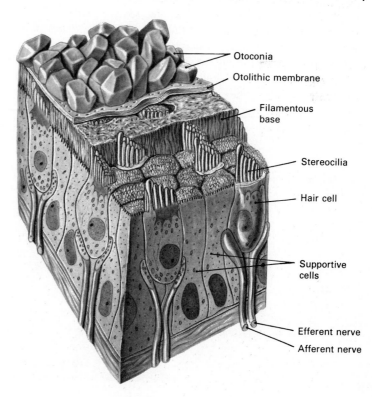

FIGURE 7.26
The receptive tissue of the utricle and saccule.

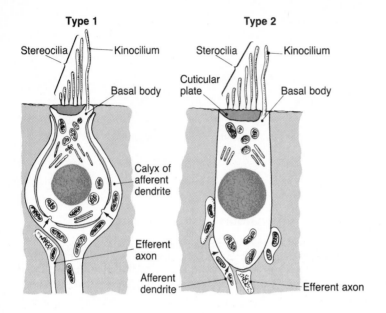

FIGURE 7.27

The two types of vestibular hair cells. (Adapted from Ades, H.W., and Engström, H. In *The Role of the Vestibular Organs in the Exploration of Space,* edited by A. Graybill. U.S. Naval School of Medicine: NASA SP-77, 1965.)

mediated across slight indentations, indicated by the small arrows in the drawing. (See **Figure 7.27.**) Efferent terminal buttons (apparently acetylcholinergic) synapse on the outside of the calyx but not on the type I hair cell itself. Type II hair cells are not surrounded by a calyx; they synapse with both afferent dendrites and efferent terminal buttons. Hair cells of both types may synapse with branches of the same dendrite. (See **Figure 7.27.**)

Each hair cell contains one long *kinocilium* and several *stereocilia,* which decrease in size away from the kinocilium. These cilia are rooted in a cuticular plate. A basal body underlies the kinocilium. Flock (1965) and Wersäll, Flock, and Lundquist (1965) have shown that the orientation of the cilia gives

FIGURE 7.28

Left: Oblique view of a normal bundle of vestibular hair cells, with an intact kinocilium. *Right:* Top view of a bundle of hair cells from which the kinocilium has been detached. (From Hudspeth, A.J., and Jacobs, R. *Proceedings of the National Academy of Sciences, USA,* 1979, 76, 1506–1509.)

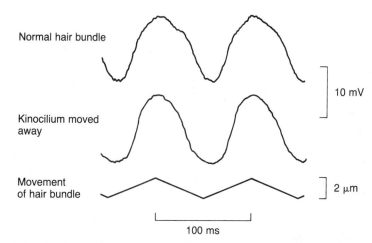

Normal hair bundle

Kinocilium moved away

Movement of hair bundle

10 mV

2 μm

100 ms

FIGURE 7.29
Normal receptor potentials from a bundle of vestibular hair cells from which the kinocilium has been detached. (From Hudspeth, A.J., and Jacobs, R. *Proceedings of the National Academy of Sciences, USA,* 1979, *76,* 1506–1509.)

the receptor maximal sensitivity to shearing force in one direction—namely, across the stereocilia, toward the kinocilium. (See **Figure 7.27.**)

Hudspeth and Jacobs (1979) used microscopic techniques to determine the function of the kinocilium. Figure 7.28 shows the appearance of a normal hair cell of a bullfrog saccule *(left)* and one in which they pulled the kinocilium away from the stereocilia *(right).* (See **Figure 7.28.**) They found that removing the kinocilium or bending it away had no effect on the receptor potentials. Figure 7.29 shows identical receptor potentials triggered by bending the cilia of a normal hair cell *(top)* and one whose kinocilium was bent away *(bottom).* (See **Figure 7.29.**) Their results suggest that the kinocilium does not play a direct role in transduction but probably serves as a mechanical link between the stereocilia and the rest of the receptive organ.

The hair cells of the crista in a semicircular canal are all oriented in one direction, and they are thus sensitive to movement of the cupula in one direction. When head rotation causes the cupula to bend toward the utricle, the hair cells are stimulated, which produces an increased firing rate of the associated afferent neurons in the ***vestibular nerve.*** Bending

of the cupula in the opposite direction produces a slight decrease in firing rate. Thus, the semicircular canals of the right and left ear together provide information about the magnitude and direction of angular rotation of the head. (See **Figure 7.30.**)

The hair cells of the utricle and saccule are oriented in various directions; thus, different

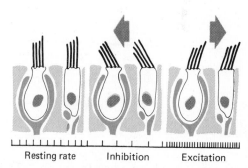

Resting rate   Inhibition   Excitation

Action potentials of vestibular axons

FIGURE 7.30
The rate of firing of axons of the vestibular nerve is increased or decreased, depending on the direction of displacement of the cilia of the vestibular hair cells. (Adapted from Ades, H.W., and Engström, H. In *The Role of the Vestibular Organs in the Exploration of Space,* edited by A. Graybill. U.S. Naval School of Medicine: NASA SP-77, 1965.)

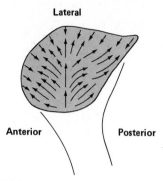

FIGURE 7.31
Hair cells in different regions of the utricle are sensitive to shearing forces in different directions. (Adapted from Flock, A. *Journal of Cell Biology,* 1964, *22,* 413–431.)

groups of hair cells signal different angles of head tilt. (See **Figure 7.31.**)

Transduction of Vestibular Information

As we saw in previous sections, the hair cells of the vestibular apparatus apparently produce a receptor potential in response to a shearing force across the cilia, and they pass this information on to the afferent neurons by means of chemical transmission. It is not known how the shearing force produces a receptor potential; it seems likely that the transduction mechanisms of vestibular and auditory hair cells are similar.

The Vestibular Pathway

Connections with the Vestibular Nerve

The vestibular and cochlear nerves constitute the two branches of the eighth cranial nerve (auditory nerve). The bipolar cell bodies that give rise to the afferent axons of the vestibular nerve are located in the ***vestibular ganglion,*** which appears as a nodule on the vestibular nerve. Efferent axons arise from cell bodies in the cerebellum and medulla and inhibit the activity of the vestibular hair cells. The firing rate of these axons changes during tactile stimulation, somatic movement, and eye movements (Goldberg and Fernandez, 1975), but their function is not known.

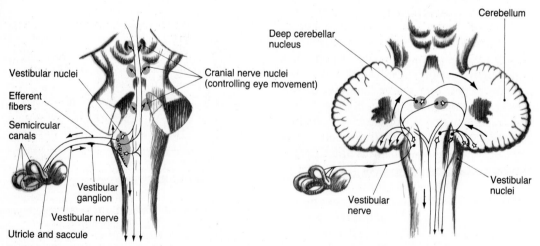

FIGURE 7.32
The pathways followed by neurons in the vestibular system. (Adapted with permission from McGraw-Hill Book Co. from *The Human Nervous System,* 2nd edition, by Noback and Demarest. Copyright 1975, by McGraw-Hill, Inc.)

The Central Vestibular System

Figure 7.32 illustrates the afferent and efferent axons of the vestibular system. (See **Figure 7.32.**) Most of the afferent axons of the vestibular nerve synapse within the four vestibular nuclei, but some axons travel to the cerebellum. Neurons of the vestibular nuclei send their axons to the cerebellum, spinal cord, medulla, and pons. (See **Figure 7.32.**) There also appear to be vestibular projections to the temporal cortex, but the precise pathways have not been determined. Most investigators believe that the cortical projections are responsible for feelings of dizziness, while the activity of projections to the lower brain stem can produce the nausea and vomiting that accompanies motion sickness. Projections to brain stem nuclei controlling neck muscles are clearly involved in maintaining an upright position of the head.

Perhaps the most interesting connections are those to the cranial nerve nuclei (third, fourth, and sixth) that control the eye muscles. As we walk or (especially) run, the head is jarred quite a bit. The vestibular system exerts direct control on eye movement, to compensate for the sudden head movements. This process, called the ***vestibulo-ocular reflex,*** maintains a fairly steady retinal image. Test this reflex yourself: Look at a distant object and hit yourself (gently) on the side of the head. Note that your image of the world jumps a bit, but not too much. People who have suffered vestibular damage, and who lack the vestibulo-ocular reflex, have difficulty seeing anything while walking or running. Everything becomes a blur of movement.

INTERIM SUMMARY

The semicircular canals are filled with fluid. When the head begins rotating or comes to rest after rotation, inertia causes the fluid to push the cupula to one side or the other. This movement exerts a shearing force on the crista, the organ containing the vestibular hair cells. The vestibular sacs contain a patch of receptive tissue that contains hair cells whose cilia are embedded in a gelatinous mass. The weight of the otoconia in the gelatinous mass shifts when the head tilts, causing a shearing force on some of the cilia of the hair cells.

Each hair cell contains one long kinocilium and several stereocilia. Transduction appears to involve only the stereocilia, because removal of the kinocilium has no apparent effect on receptor potentials of vestibular hair cells.

The vestibular hair cells form synapses with dendrites of bipolar neurons whose axons travel through the vestibular nerve. The receptors also receive efferent terminal buttons from neurons located in the cerebellum and medulla, but the function of these connections is not known. Vestibular information is received by the vestibular nuclei in the medulla, which relays it on to the cerebellum, spinal cord, medulla, pons, and temporal cortex. These pathways are responsible for control of posture, head movements, eye movements, and the puzzling phenomenon of motion sickness.

■ SOMATOSENSES

The somatosenses provide information about what is happening on the surface of our body and inside it. The ***cutaneous senses*** (skin senses) include several submodalities commonly referred to as *touch*. **Kinesthesia** provides information about body position and movement and arises from receptors in joints, tendons, and muscles. The muscle receptors are discussed in this section and in Chapter 8. The ***organic senses*** arise from receptors in and around the internal organs, providing us with unpleasant stimuli such as stomachaches or gallbladder attacks, or pleasurable ones such as the feeling of a warm drink in our stomach on a cold winter day. Because the cutaneous senses are the most studied of the somatosenses, both perceptually and physiologically, I will devote most of my discussion to them.

The Stimuli

The cutaneous senses respond to several different types of stimuli: pressure, vibration, heating, cooling, and events that cause tissue damage (and hence, pain). Feelings of pressure are caused by mechanical deformation of the skin. Vibration is produced in the laboratory or clinic by tuning forks or mechanical devices, but it more commonly occurs when we move our fingers across a rough surface. Thus we use vibration sensitivity to judge an object's roughness. Obviously, sensations of warmth and coolness are produced by objects that change skin temperature away from normal. Sensations of pain can be caused by many different types of stimuli, but it appears that most cause at least some tissue damage.

Kinesthesia is provided by stretch receptors in skeletal muscles that report changes in muscle length to the central nervous system and by stretch receptors in tendons that measure the force being exerted by the muscles. Receptors within joints between adjacent bones respond to the magnitude and direction of limb movement. The muscle length detectors (sensory endings on the ***intrafusal muscle fibers***) do not give rise to conscious sensations; their information is used to control movement. These receptors will be discussed separately in Chapter 8.

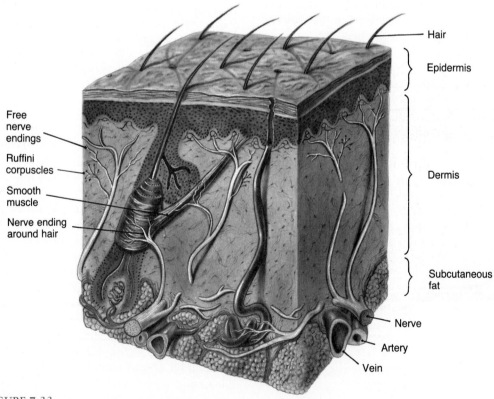

FIGURE 7.33

A cross section through hairy skin, showing the cutaneous receptors located there.

Organic sensitivity is provided by receptors in the linings of muscles, outer layers of the gastrointestinal system and other internal organs, and linings of the abdominal and thoracic cavities. Many of these tissues are sensitive only to stretch and do not report sensations when cut, burned, or crushed. In addition, the stomach and esophagus are responsive to heat and cold and to some chemicals.

Anatomy of the Skin and Its Receptive Organs

The skin is a complex and vital organ of the body — one that we tend to take for granted. We cannot survive without it; extensive skin burns are fatal. Our cells, which must be bathed by a warm fluid, are protected from the hostile environment by the skin's outer layers. The skin participates in thermoregulation by producing sweat, thus cooling the body, or by restricting its circulation of blood, thus conserving heat. Its appearance varies widely across the body, from mucous membrane to hairy skin to the smooth, hairless skin of the palms and on the soles of the feet.

Skin consists of subcutaneous tissue, dermis, and epidermis and contains various receptors scattered throughout these layers. Figures 7.33 and 7.34 show cross sections through hairy and ***glabrous skin*** (hairless skin, such as we have on our fingertips and

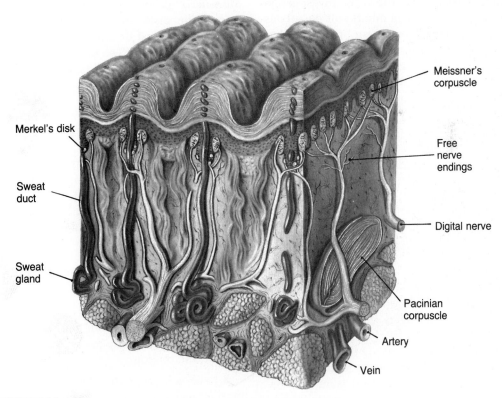

FIGURE 7.34

A cross section through glabrous (hairless) skin, showing the cutaneous receptors located there.

palms). Hairy skin contains unencapsulated (free) nerve endings and Ruffini corpuscles (described below). Free nerve endings are found just below the surface of the skin, in a basketwork around the base of hair follicles and around the emergence of hair shafts from the skin. (See **Figure 7.33.**)

Glabrous skin contains a more complex mixture of free nerve endings and axons that terminate within specialized end organs. The increased complexity probably reflects the fact that we use the palms of our hands and the inside surfaces of our fingers to explore the environment actively: We use them to hold and touch objects. In contrast, the rest of our body most often contacts the environment passively; that is, other things come in contact with it. Over the years, investigators have described a large number of cutaneous receptors, but subsequent research has shown many of them to be artifacts of the staining process used to reveal the microscopic structure of the skin. (*Artifact* means "made by art"—hence artificially introduced, not normally existing in the tissue.) Other specialized end organs have been shown to be variants of a single form, changing shape as a function of age. Iggo and Andres (1982) describe five major types of organized endings.

Pacinian corpuscles are the largest sensory end organs in the body. Their size, approximately 0.5 mm $\times$ 1.0 mm, makes them visible to the naked eye. They are found in the dermis of glabrous skin and in the external genitalia, mammary glands, and various internal organs. These receptors consist of up to seventy onionlike layers wrapped around the terminal button of a single myelinated axon. (See **Figure 7.34.**) They are especially sensitive to touch, with each axon giving a burst of responses when the corpuscle is moved relative to it. The inside of the corpuscle is filled with a viscous substance that offers some resistance to the movement of the nerve ending

inside. This construction gives the Pacinian corpuscle its special response characteristics: Pacinian corpuscles respond to vibration.

Ruffini corpuscles, found primarily in hairy skin, look rather like Pacinian corpuscles, but they are smaller and are covered by only three or four layers. They respond to low-frequency vibration, or "flutter." (See **Figure 7.33.**)

Meissner's corpuscles are found in *papillae* ("nipples"), small elevations of the dermis that project up into the epidermis. These end organs are innervated by between two and six axons. They respond to mechanical stimuli. (See **Figure 7.34.**)

Merkel's disks are found at the base of the epidermis, in the same general locations as Meissner's corpuscles, adjacent to sweat ducts. The disks are single, flattened dendritic endings that lie adjacent to specialized epithelial cells called *Merkel's cells*. Merkel's disks are probably found in hairy skin as well as glabrous skin. They respond to mechanical stimuli. (See **Figure 7.34.**)

Krause end bulbs are found in **mucocutaneous zones**—the junctions between mucous membrane and dry skin, such as the edge of the lips, eyelids, glans penis, and clitoris. They consist of loops of unmyelinated axons similar in appearance to balls of yarn. Each end bulb contains the endings of two to six axons. They probably respond to mechanical stimuli.

Anatomy of Kinesthetic Receptive Organs

A schematic view of a skeletal muscle is shown in **Figure 7.35.** Four kinds of information are received by afferent axons of the muscle and tendon:

1. The sensory endings on the intrafusal muscle fibers signal muscle length.

2. The sensory endings within the **Golgi tendon organ** at the muscle-tendon junction

respond to tension exerted by the muscle on the tendon.

3. The membranous covering of the muscle *(fascia)* contains Pacinian corpuscles. These receptors apparently signal deep pressure exerted upon muscles, which can be felt even if the overlying cutaneous receptors are anesthetized or denervated.

4. Throughout the muscle and its overlying fascia are distributed free nerve endings, which generally follow the blood supply.

These receptors presumably signal pain that accompanies prolonged exertion or muscle cramps.

The tissue that lines the joints contains free nerve endings and encapsulated receptors, such as Pacinian corpuscles. The encapsulated endings presumably mediate sensitivity to joint movement and position, while stimulation of the free nerve endings produces pain (such as that which accompanies arthritis). Pacinian corpuscles and free nerve endings

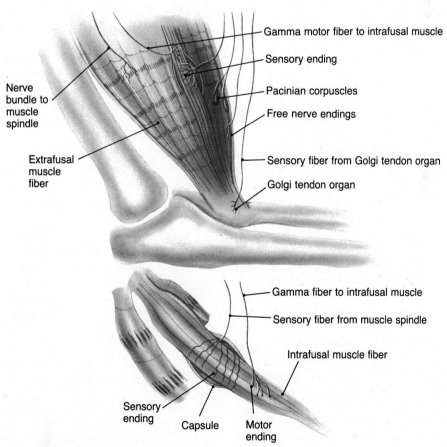

FIGURE 7.35
A skeletal muscle and its sense receptors.

are also found in the outer layers of various internal organs and give rise to organic sensations.

Transduction of Cutaneous Stimulation

Originally, investigators believed that different submodalities of the somatosenses were mediated by different types of receptors (Von Frey, 1906). This belief was challenged by other investigators, who asserted that the different categories of receptors were *not* specialized functionally, and that different submodalities were represented by the pattern of axonal firing (Sinclair, 1967). As we will see, the most recent evidence suggests that receptors *are* specialized functionally, and that the anatomical projections of different classes of receptors are segregated up to the level of the somatosensory cortex.

Mechanical Stimulation

Sensitivity to pressure and vibration are caused by movement of the skin. The skin is sensitive only to deformation, or bending, and not to pressure exerted evenly across its surface. For example, if you dipped your finger into a pool of mercury, pressure would be exerted on all portions of your skin below the surface of the liquid. Nevertheless, you would feel only a ring of sensation, at the air/mercury junction. This is the only part of the skin that is bent, and it is here that skin receptors are stimulated. (Because mercury is poisonous if it enters a break in the skin, please do not try this demonstration — just imagine it.)

Mechanical stimuli appear to be transduced by a variety of receptors, both encapsulated and unencapsulated. The best-studied one is the Pacinian corpuscle, which is primarily a detector of vibration. This organ responds to bending, relative to the axon that enters it. If the onionlike layers are dissected away, this receptor still responds to bending of the naked axon; thus, the transducer is the

terminal itself (Loewenstein and Rathkamp, 1958). The receptor potential is proportional to the degree of bending. If the threshold of excitation is exceeded, an action potential is produced at the first node of Ranvier. Loewenstein and Mendelson (1965) have shown that the layers of the corpuscle alter the mechanical characteristics of the organ, so that the axon responds briefly when the intact organ is bent and again when it is released. Thus, it is sensitive to vibration but not to steady pressure.

We do not know how bending of the tip of the nerve ending in a Pacinian corpuscle produces a receptor potential. Presumably, the bending changes the membrane permeability, and the resulting flow of the ions across the membrane alters its potential. Most likely, ion channels are opened by the bending, just as they are in the cilia of auditory and vestibular hair cells. Most investigators believe that the encapsulated endings serve only to modify the physical stimulus transduced by the axons that enter them.

Adaptation. Investigators have known for a long time that a moderate, constant stimulus applied to the skin fails to produce any sensation after it has been present for a while. We not only ignore the pressure of a wrist watch, but we cannot feel it at all if we keep our arm still (assuming that the band is not painfully tight). Physiological studies have shown that the reason for the lack of sensation is the absence of receptor firing; the receptors adapt to a constant stimulus.

This adaptation is not a result of any "fatigue" of physical or chemical processes within the receptor. Adaptation can be explained as a function of the mechanical construction of the receptors and their relationship to skin and (in some cases) end organs. As we saw earlier, the axons of Pacinian corpuscles respond once when the receptor is bent and again when it is released, because of the way the nerve ending "floats" within the viscous interior of the corpuscle. Therefore, these receptors adapt almost immediately to a constant stimulus. Most other axons adapt more slowly. Nafe and Wagoner (1941) recorded the sensations reported by human subjects as a stimulus weight gradually moved downward, deforming the skin. Pressure was reported until the weight finally stopped moving. When the weight was increased, pressure was reported until downward movement stopped again. Pressure sensations were also briefly recorded when the weight was removed, while the surface of the skin regained its normal shape.

Responsiveness to Moving Stimuli. A moderate, constant, nondamaging stimulus is rarely of any importance to an organism, so this adaptation mechanism is useful. Our cutaneous senses are used much more often to analyze shapes and textures of stimulus objects moving with respect to the surface of the skin. Sometimes the object itself moves, but more often we do the moving ourselves. If I placed an object in your palm and asked you to keep your hand still, you would have a great deal of difficulty recognizing the object by touch alone. If I said you could now move your hand, you would manipulate the object, letting its surface slide across your palm and the pads of your fingers. You would be able to describe its three-dimensional shape, hardness, texture, slipperiness, and so on. (Obviously, your motor system must cooperate, and you need kinesthetic sensation from your muscles and joints, besides the cutaneous information.) If you squeeze the object and feel a lot of well-localized pressure in return, it is hard. If you feel a less intense, more diffuse pressure in return, it is soft. If it produces vibrations as it moves over the ridges on your fingers, it is rough. If very little effort is needed to move the object while pressing it against your skin, it is slippery. If it does not produce vibrations as it moves across your skin, but moves in a jerky fashion, and if it takes effort to remove your fingers from its surface, it is sticky.

Temperature

Feelings of warmth and coolness are relative, not absolute (except at the extremes). There is a temperature level that, for a particular region of skin, will produce a sensation of temperature neutrality — neither warmth nor coolness. This neutral point is not an absolute value but depends on the prior history of thermal stimulation of that area. If the temperature of a region of skin is raised by a few degrees, the initial feeling of warmth is replaced by one of neutrality. If the skin temperature is lowered to its initial value, it now feels cool. Thus, increases in temperature lower the sensitivity of warmth receptors and raise the sensitivity of cold receptors. The converse holds for decreases in skin temperature. This adaptation to ambient temperature can be easily demonstrated by placing one hand in a bucket of warm water and the other in a bucket of cool water until some adaptation has taken place. If you then simultaneously immerse both hands in water at room temperature, it will feel warm to one hand and cool to the other.

Thermal receptors are difficult to study, because changes in temperature alter the metabolic activity, and also the rate of axonal firing, of a variety of cells. For example, a receptor that responds to pressure might produce varying amounts of activity in response to the same mechanical stimulus, depending upon the temperature. Nevertheless, most investigators agree that changes in temperature are detected by free nerve endings, and that warmth and coolness are detected by different populations of receptors (Sinclair, 1981). The transduction of temperature changes into the rate of axonal firing has not yet been explained.

An ingenious experiment by Bazett, McGlone, Williams, and Lufkin (1932) showed long ago that receptors for warmth and cold lie at different depths in the skin. The investigators lifted the prepuce (foreskin) of uncircumcised males with dull fishhooks. They applied thermal stimuli on one side of the folded skin and recorded the rate at which the temperature changes were transmitted through the skin by placing small temperature sensors on the opposite side. They then correlated these observations with verbal reports of warmth and coolness. The investigators concluded that cold receptors were close to the skin and that warmth receptors were located deeper in the tissue. (This experiment shows the extremities to which scientists will go to obtain information — pun intended.)

Pain

The story of pain is quite different from that of temperature and pressure; the analysis of this sensation is extremely difficult. It is obvious that our awareness of pain and our emotional reaction to it depend on central factors. For example, we can have a tooth removed painlessly while under hypnosis, which has no effect on the stimulation of pain receptors. Stimuli that produce pain also tend to trigger species-typical escape and withdrawal responses. Subjectively, these stimuli *hurt,* and we try hard to avoid them. However, sometimes we are better off ignoring pain and getting on with other tasks. In fact, our brains possess mechanisms that can reduce pain, largely through the activity of special opiate-like peptides. These mechanisms are described in more detail in a later section of this chapter.

Most investigators identify pain reception with the networks of free nerve endings in the skin. Pain appears to be produced by a variety of procedures. Intense mechanical stimulation activates a class of high-threshold

receptors that produce a sensation of pain. However, most painful stimuli cause tissue damage, which suggests that pain is also caused by the release of a chemical by injured cells. Many substances can be injected into the skin to produce pain, and several have been proposed as candidates for the role of the chemical mediator of pain. (The usual procedure for testing chemically mediated pain nowadays is to produce a blister with *cantharides*—Spanish fly—and then to pick off the top of the blister and treat the raw skin with the chemical to be tested.) Keele (1966) observed a good relationship between the intensity of pain and the concentration of the potassium ion. This relationship is of significance because tissue damage produces an extracellular increase in K^+ concentration. Other investigators have noted that pain is also produced by a low pH level (an acidic solution) and by histamine, acetylcholine, and serotonin (Sinclair, 1967). The chemical mediator has not yet been identified; the nature of the substance, when identified, should suggest the means of sensory transduction. (Of course, there could be more than one mediator.)

The Somatosensory Pathways

Somatosensory axons enter the central nervous system via spinal nerves and cranial nerves, principally the trigeminal nerve (fifth cranial nerve). The cell bodies of the unipolar neurons are located in the dorsal root ganglia and cranial nerve ganglia. Two anatomically distinct systems begin at this point: the lemniscal system, which conveys precisely localized information from mechanical receptors, and the spinothalamic system, which carries less precisely localized information from pain and temperature receptors.

Lemniscal System

Figure 7.36 shows the **lemniscal system.** The first-order neuron has a very long axon. In the

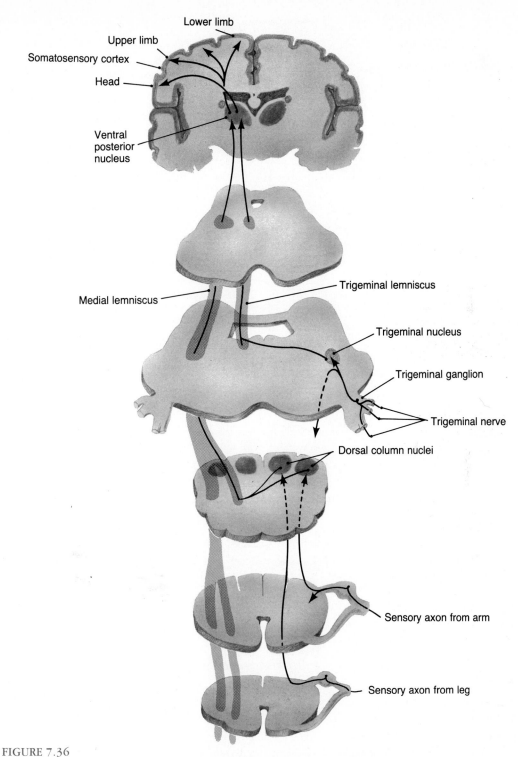

Lower limb

Upper limb

Somatosensory cortex

Head

Ventral posterior nucleus

Medial lemniscus

Trigeminal lemniscus

Trigeminal nucleus

Trigeminal ganglion

Trigeminal nerve

Dorsal column nuclei

Sensory axon from arm

Sensory axon from leg

FIGURE 7.36

The lemniscal system: pathways that mediate fine touch and pressure and kinesthetic feedback from the muscle and joint receptors.

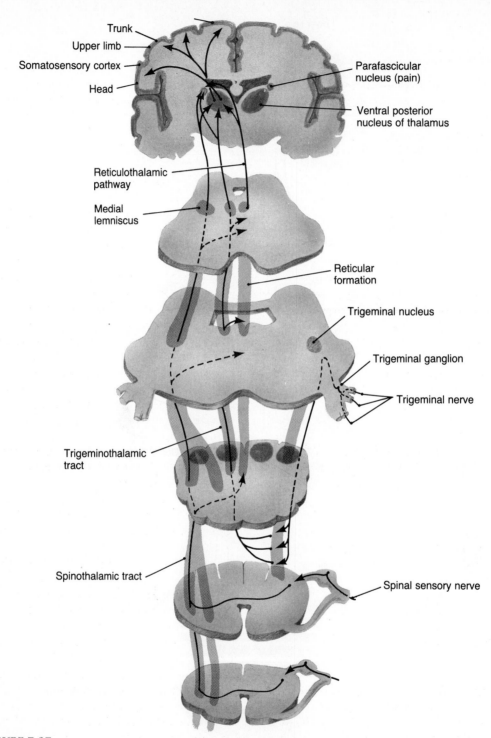

Trunk

Upper limb

Somatosensory cortex

Head

Parafascicular
nucleus (pain)

Ventral posterior
nucleus of thalamus

Reticulothalamic
pathway

Medial
lemniscus

Reticular
formation

Trigeminal nucleus

Trigeminal ganglion

Trigeminal nerve

Trigeminothalamic
tract

Spinothalamic tract

Spinal sensory nerve

FIGURE 7.37

The spinothalamic and reticulothalamic systems: pathways that mediate
temperature sensitivity and pain.

case of spinal afferent neurons, the axon ascends through the ***dorsal columns*** to the ***dorsal column nuclei*** of the medulla. (See **Figure 7.36.**) These axons are the longest nerve axons of the body; a touch receptor in the big toe is on one end of a single axon that stretches all the way to the medulla. Fibers of the second-order neurons decussate (cross to the opposite side of the brain) and travel through the ***medial lemniscus*** (a large bundle of axons) to the ventral posterior nuclei of the thalamus. The neurons synapse there, and third-order neurons project to the somatosensory cortex, located on the postcentral gyrus of the parietal lobe. (See **Figure 7.36.**)

Most touch receptors rostral to the ears send information via the trigeminal, facial, and vagus nerves. Let us consider the major pathway, from the trigeminal nerve. This pathway is almost a replica of the dorsal column pathway. Most second-order neurons decussate and travel via the *trigeminal lemniscus* (parallel to the medial lemniscus) to the ventral posterior nuclei. The third-order axons project to the somatosensory cortex. (See **Figure 7.36.**)

Spinothalamic and Reticulothalamic Pathways

Figure 7.37 illustrates the **spinothalamic system** and its offshoot, the **reticulothalamic system,** which carry information about temperature and pain. (See **Figure 7.37.**) The afferent axons synapse as soon as they enter the central nervous system, either in the dorsal horn of the spinal cord or in the ***trigeminal nucleus.***

Second-order neurons decussate immediately; some ascend via the spinothalamic (or trigeminothalamic) tracts directly to the ventral posterior and parafascicular nuclei of the thalamus. Others follow a diffuse, polysynaptic pathway through the reticular formation. Note that axons of the spinothalamic tract also give off branches to the reticular forma-

tion as they pass by. (See **Figure 7.37.**) The somatosensory cortex does not appear to receive direct, third-order input from pain receptors as it does from the other somatosensory receptors.

Kinesthetic and Organic Input

The cell bodies of kinesthetic receptors, like those of cutaneous receptors, reside within the dorsal root ganglia or cranial nerve ganglia. Kinesthetic axons are carried in the same nerves that convey motor fibers to the skeletal muscles. Organic sensitivity is conveyed over axons that travel with efferent axons of the autonomic nervous system and thus pass (without synapsing) through the autonomic ganglia on their way to the central nervous system. In general, organic pain is conveyed along with efferent sympathetic fibers, whereas nonpainful stimuli arising from the internal organs are transmitted via nerves that contain parasympathetic efferent axons.

Somatosensory Cortex

Figure 7.38 shows a lateral view of a monkey brain, with a drawing vaguely resembling two monkeys. These drawings roughly indicate which parts of the body project to which areas of primary and secondary somatosensory cortex (part of the somatosensory association cortex) of the parietal lobe. The mapping of the body on the surface of the cortex is called ***somatotopic representation.*** (You are already familiar with the retinotopic representation of the visual system and the tonotopic representation of the auditory system.) Note that a relatively large amount of cortical tissue is given to representation of fingers and lips, corresponding to the greater tactile sensitivity of these regions. (See **Figure 7.38.**) Although drawings like these have been accepted as definitive, more recent studies show that they are far too simple.

You will recall from Chapter 6 that the primary visual cortex contains columns of

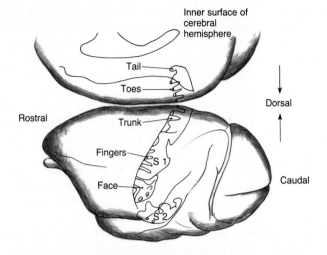

FIGURE 7.38
Sensory animunculi on the monkey brain, indicating the regions of the body that send cutaneous information to particular areas of the somatosensory cortex. (Adapted from Woolsey, C.N. In *Biological and Biochemical Bases of Behavior,* edited by H.F. Harlow and C.N. Woolsey. Madison: University of Wisconsin Press, 1958.)

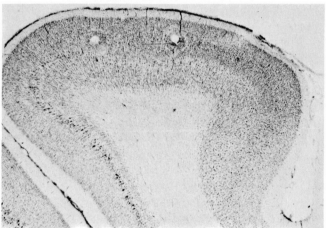

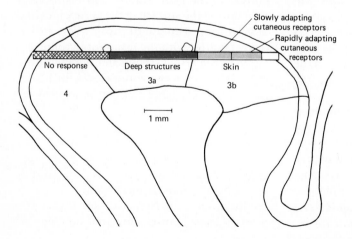

FIGURE 7.39
Different regions of somatosensory cortex contain neurons that receive information from different classes of receptors. The white spots in the photomicrograph are lesions the experimenters made to permit them to reconstruct the path of the microelectrode. The regions marked 3a, 3b, and 4 are histologically distinct areas of somatosensory cortex. (From Dykes, R.W., Rasmusson, D.D., and Hoeltzell, P.B. *Journal of Neurophysiology,* 1980, *43,* 1527–1545.)

cells, each of which responds to particular features, such as orientation, ocular dominance, or spatial frequency. Within these columns are "blobs" that contain cells that respond to particular colors. The somatosensory cortex also has a columnar arrangement; in fact, cortical columns were discovered there by Mountcastle (1957) before they were found in the visual and auditory cortex. Within a column, neurons respond to a particular type of stimulus (for example, temperature or pressure) applied to a particular part of the body.

Dykes (1983) has reviewed research that indicates that the primary and secondary somatosensory cortical areas are divided into at least five (and perhaps as many as ten) different maps of the body surface. Within each map, cells respond to a particular submodality of somatosensory receptors. So far, separate areas have been identified that respond to slowly adapting cutaneous receptors, rapidly adapting cutaneous receptors, receptors that detect changes in muscle length, receptors located in the joints, and Pacinian corpuscles.

Figure 7.39 shows an example of the precise boundary between cortical neurons that respond to muscle receptors and those that respond to cutaneous receptors (Dykes, Rasmusson, and Hoeltzell, 1980). The photograph shows a Nissl-stained slice perpendicular to the surface of the primary somatosensory cortex. (The two white spots are lesions that the investigators made to enable them to localize the cells from which they recorded.) The diagram shows the path of the microelectrode as it passed through successive columns. The open bar indicates no response, the black bar indicates responses from deep structures (elicited by massaging a muscle or moving a joint), and the colored bar indicates responses from cutaneous stimulation (elicited by touching and stroking the skin). Note the sharp boundaries. (See **Figure 7.39.**) Figure 7.40 shows a diagram of the

surface of the somatosensory cortex. Here, open circles indicate no response, gray and black circles indicate responses from cutaneous receptors, and colored circles indicate responses from deep structures. You can see that the response characteristics closely follow the borders of cortical areas 3a and 3b, which are defined by anatomical differences in the structure of the layers of the cortex. (See **Figure 7.40.**)

As you learned in Chapter 6, Zeki and his colleagues have shown that the circumstriate cortex consists of several subareas, each of which contains an independent representation of the visual field. They found that one

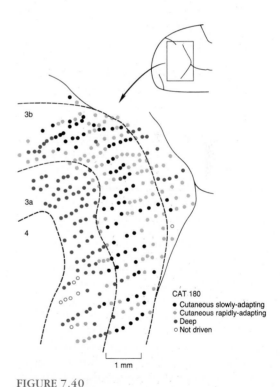

FIGURE 7.40
Neurons in anatomically distinct regions of the somatosensory cortex respond to different classes of receptors. (From Dykes, R.W., Rasmusson, D.D., and Hoeltzell, P.B. *Journal of Neurophysiology,* 1980, *43,* 1527–1545.)

area responds specifically to color, another to movement, and two others to orientation. The somatosensory cortex appears to follow a similar scheme: each cortical map of the body contains neurons that respond to a specific submodality of stimulation. Undoubtedly, further investigations will provide more accurate functional maps of the cortical subareas of both of these sensory systems.

Perception of Pain

Pain is a curious phenomenon. It is more than a mere sensation; it can be defined only by some sort of withdrawal reaction or, in humans, by verbal report. Pain can be modified by opiates, by hypnosis, by the administration of pharmacologically inert sugar pills, by emotions, and even by other forms of stimulation, such as acupuncture. Recent research efforts have made remarkable progress in discovering the physiological bases of these phenomena.

The importance of emotional and other "psychological" factors in the perception of pain (documented by Sternbach, 1968) suggests that there must be neural mechanisms that modify either the transmission of pain or the translation of central pain messages into unpleasant feelings. As we will see, there is excellent evidence for both types of interactions.

We might reasonably ask *why* we experience pain. In most cases, pain serves a constructive role. For example, people who have congenital insensitivity to pain suffer an abnormally large number of injuries, such as cuts and burns. One woman eventually died because she did not make the shifts in posture that we normally do when our joints start to ache. As a consequence, she suffered damage to the spine that ultimately resulted in death. Other people have died from ruptured appendixes and ensuing abdominal infections that they did not feel (Sternbach, 1968). I am sure that a person who is passing a kidney stone would not find much comfort in the fact that pain does more good than ill, but it is, nevertheless, very important to our existence.

Some environmental events diminish the perception of pain. For example, Beecher (1959) noted that wounded American soldiers back from the battle at Anzio, Italy, during World War II reported that they felt no pain from their wounds — they did not even want medication. It would appear that their perception of pain was diminished by the relief they felt from surviving such an ordeal. There are other instances in which people still report the perception of pain but are not bothered by it. Some tranquilizers have this effect.

Physiological evidence provides a clear distinction between the perception and tolerance of pain. Mark, Ervin, and Yakovlev (1962) made stereotaxically placed lesions in the thalamus in an attempt to relieve the pain of patients suffering from the advanced stages of cancer. Damage to the sensory relay nuclei (the ventral posteromedial and ventral posterolateral thalamic nuclei) produced a loss of cutaneous senses: touch, temperature, and superficial cutaneous pain. Lesions in the parafascicular nucleus and in the intralaminar nucleus were more successful; they abolished deep pain, but not cutaneous sensitivity. Finally, destruction of the dorsomedial and anterior thalamic nuclei left both cutaneous sensitivity and the perception of pain intact. However, patients with these lesions were not bothered by the pain — the emotional component was diminished. It is noteworthy that these nuclei are intimately involved with the limbic system, and that the dorsomedial nuclei project to the prefrontal cortex, the most anterior region of the frontal association cortex. Removal of this region **(prefrontal lobotomy)** also reduces the emotional aspects of pain perception.

It seems clear that pain perception and pain tolerance are separate phenomena. It appears that the intralaminar and parafascicular nuclei are necessary for the perception of pain, and that the dorsomedial and anterior thalamic nuclei, limbic system, and prefrontal cortex mediate its emotional component.

The study by Mark and his colleagues confirms the long-standing supposition that there are two types of pain: a rapidly felt "sharp" pain and a more gradual, but more unpleasant, "dull" pain. If you have ever stubbed your toe you know what I mean. The first flash of pain subsides fairly quickly, to be replaced by another that is longer-lived and more poorly localized. Because lesions of the ventral posteromedial and ventral posterolateral thalamic nuclei abolished pain felt from pinpricks, but not deep-seated pain, we might infer that the "bright pain" component but not the "dull pain" component is mediated by these nuclei.

The Endogenous Opiates

For many years investigators have known that perception of pain can be modified by environmental stimuli. Recent work, beginning in the 1970s, has revealed the existence of neural circuits whose activity can produce **analgesia,** a decreased sensitivity to pain (from *an,* "not," and *algos,* "pain"). A variety of environmental stimuli can activate these analgesia-producing circuits. An important component of these mechanisms is a class of neuromodulators called the **endogenous opiates.**

The Action of Opiates. As you know, opiates such as morphine produce analgesia. Several years ago it became clear that they did so by means of direct effects on the brain. In particular, microinjections of morphine into the periaqueductal gray matter of the midbrain produce analgesia, whereas injections into many other regions are ineffective (Tsou and

Jang, 1964; Herz, Albus, Metys, Schubert, and Teschemacher, 1970). Pert, Snowman, and Snyder (1974) discovered that neurons in the brain contain specialized receptors that respond to opiates. They homogenized the brains of rats and extracted portions of cell membranes. They incubated the membranes with radioactive naloxone and dihydromorphine, rinsed them, and found that the membranes became radioactive. (**Naloxone** is a drug that reverses the effects of opiates, and dihydromorphine is a synthetic opiate.) The finding that these two drugs both bind with molecules in fragments of postsynaptic neural membrane is strong evidence for the existence of specific opiate receptors. Naloxone blocks the effects of opiates by binding with, but not activating, the receptors.

Classes of Opiatelike Peptides. Of course, nature did not put opiate receptors in the brain for the amusement of neuroscientists. If there are receptors in the brain, then the brain must produce its own chemicals to occupy these receptors. And, in fact, it does. Terenius and Wahlström (1975) reported the existence of a substance in human cerebrospinal fluid that had a specific affinity for opiate receptors that had been extracted from rat brain. They called this chemical *morphine-like factor.*

Hughes, Smith, Kosterlitz, Fothergill, Morgan, and Morris (1975) found that the brain produces two morphinelike factors, which they identified as very small peptide chains, each containing five amino acids. They synthesized these substances and found that the artificial **enkephalins** (the authors' name for the substances) acted as potent opiates. The two enkephalins (labeled *leu*-enkephalin and *met*-enkephalin) were found to bind with opiate receptors even more effectively than morphine.

We now know that Leu- and Met-enkephalin, which contain the amino acid leucine or methionine, respectively, are only two members of a family of endogenous opiate peptides, all of which are synthesized from one of three large peptides that serve as precursors. (*Endogenous* means "produced from within.") Cells that produce one of the endogenous opiates synthesize them and also synthesize specialized enzymes that cut the precursor apart at specific locations. The active fragments are stored in vesicles, and the unneeded ones are destroyed. The three precursor peptides, along with their active fragments, are shown in Figure 7.41. The first, ***pro-opiomelanocortin*** gives rise to several hormones found in the pituitary gland, only one of which serves an opiatelike function (***β-endorphin***). The second, ***pro-enkepha-***

Pro-opiomelanocortin

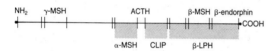

Pro-enkephalin

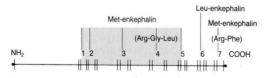

Pro-dynorphin

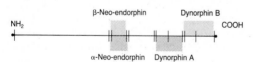

FIGURE 7.41

The three major precursors of endogenous opiates, and their products. MSH = melanocyte-stimulating hormone; ACTH = adrenocorticotropic hormone; CLIP = corticotropin-like intermediate lobe peptide; LPH = lipotropin. (Adapted from Akil, H., Watson, S.J., Young, E., Lewis, M.E., Khachaturian, H., and Walker, J.M. *Annual Review of Neuroscience,* 1984, *7,* 223–255.)

lin, gives rise only to enkephalins, of which there are several types. The third, ***pro-dynorphin,*** gives rise to several different kinds of ***dynorphins,*** another class of opiates that are active in the brain. (See **Figure 7.41.**)

Besides producing a large variety of opiates, the brain contains several different types of opiate receptors (Akil, Watson, Young, Lewis, Khachaturian, and Walker, 1984). However, investigators have not yet shown that different classes of receptors have different physiological or behavioral functions; therefore, I will not discuss them further. In addition, little is known about the specific functions of the various endogenous opiates.

The Anatomy of Opiate-Induced Analgesia
Electrical stimulation of particular locations within the brain can cause analgesia, which can even be profound enough to serve as an anesthetic for surgery in rats (Reynolds, 1969). The most effective locations appear to be within the periaqueductal gray matter and in the rostroventral medulla. For example, Mayer and Liebeskind (1974) reported that electrical stimulation of the periaqueductal gray matter produced analgesia in rats equivalent to that produced by at least 10 milligrams of morphine per kilogram of body weight, which is a large dose. The rats did not react to pain of any kind; the authors pinched their tails and paws, applied electrical shocks to their feet, and applied heat to their tails.

Analgesic brain stimulation apparently triggers the neural mechanisms that reduce pain. These mechanisms are normally stimulated through more natural means, which will be discussed later in this section. We now know that the periaqueductal gray matter and the rostroventral medulla are two components of a pain-attenuating circuit. Activity of this circuit inhibits the firing of neurons in the dorsal horn of the spinal cord gray matter, whose axons give rise to the spinothalamic the "gate"?

tract. Thus, this activity directly diminishes the signal that gives rise to sensations of pain. Basbaum and Fields (1978) summarized their work and that of others and proposed a neural circuit that mediates opiate-induced analgesia. A more recent review (Basbaum and Fields, 1984) elaborated (and complicated) their original model. Basically, they propose the following: Endogenous opiates (released by environmental stimuli or administered as a drug) stimulate opiate receptors on neurons in the periaqueductal gray matter. As we have already seen, electrical stimulation of this region or microinjection of opiates into it produces analgesia. In addition, microinjection of naloxone into the periaqueductal gray matter blocks the analgesic effect of the systemic injection of opiates (Yeung and Rudy, 1978), and administration of morphine increases the neural activity in this region (Criswell and Rogers, 1978; Urca and Nahin, 1978). Because the effect of opiates appears to be inhibitory (Nicoll, Alger, and Nicoll, 1980), Basbaum and Fields propose that the neurons that contain

opiate receptors are themselves inhibitory interneurons. Thus, the administration of opiates activates the neurons on which these interneurons synapse. (See **Figure 7.42.**)

Neurons in the periaqueductal gray matter send axons to the rostroventral medulla, especially to the ***nucleus raphe magnus.*** The terminal buttons of these neurons appear to release an excitatory peptide transmitter substance called ***neurotensin*** (Beitz, 1982b). In fact, Kalivas, Jennes, Nemeroff, and Prange (1982) found that infusion of neurotensin into the cerebral ventricles reduces animals' sensitivity to pain, presumably because it activates the neurons in the nucleus raphe magnus. (See **Figure 7.42.**)

The neurons in the nucleus raphe magnus send axons through the ***dorsolateral columns*** to the dorsal horn of the spinal cord gray matter. Destruction of these tracts abolishes morphine-produced analgesia. The raphe neurons secrete serotonin; thus, administration of PCPA (which prevents the biosynthesis of serotonin) also abolishes morphine-produced analgesia.

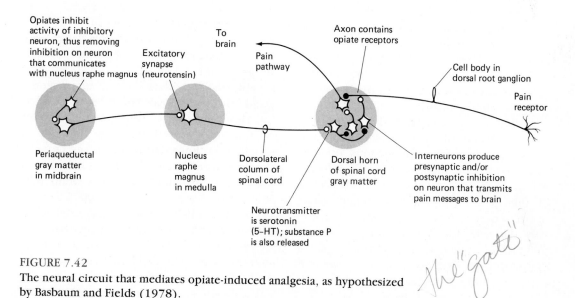

FIGURE 7.42
The neural circuit that mediates opiate-induced analgesia, as hypothesized by Basbaum and Fields (1978).

The neural circuitry within the dorsal gray matter of the spinal cord is not well understood. Basbaum and Fields (1984) review evidence that suggests that the inhibitory effects of the descending serotonergic neurons may be mediated by means of either presynaptic or postsynaptic inhibition, probably involving one or two interneurons that use various neurotransmitters. To further complicate matters, the raphe neurons that project to the spinal cord appear to release a peptide (substance P) along with serotonin, and the incoming pain-receptive axons in this area contain opiate receptors. Thus, endogenous opiates may mediate presynaptic inhibition there. (See **Figure 7.42.**)

Presumably, an important input to this system is mediated chemically by endogenous opiates that are released by neurosecretory cells. These chemicals are carried through the blood supply to the periaqueductal gray matter, where they stimulate opiate receptors. The periaqueductal gray matter receives inputs from the frontal cortex, amygdala, and hypothalamus (Beitz, 1982a; Mantyh, 1983). These inputs permit learning and emotional reactions to affect an animal's responsiveness to pain. In addition, pain-responsive regions of the brain stem and spinal cord also send axons to the periaqueductal gray matter, which may account for the fact that painful stimulation can itself diminish further sensitivity to pain (Gebhardt, 1982).

Analgesia that is produced by electrical stimulation of the brain is partly, but not completely, mediated by endogenous opiates. Akil, Mayer, and Liebeskind (1976) found that naloxone reduces the analgesic effect of stimulation of the periaqueductal gray matter but does not completely eliminate it. Presumably, there are at least two brain mechanisms for analgesia: one that involves the release of endogenous opiates and one that does not. (This possibility will be discussed later in this section.)

Biological Significance of Analgesia

It appears that a considerable amount of neural circuitry is devoted to reducing the intensity of pain. What functions do these circuits perform? When an animal encounters a noxious stimulus, it usually stops what it is doing and engages in withdrawal or escape behaviors. Obviously, these responses are quite appropriate. However, they are sometimes counterproductive. For example, if an animal sustains a wound that causes chronic pain, a tendency to engage in withdrawal responses will interfere with its performance of everyday activities, such as obtaining food. Thus, chronic, unavoidable pain would best be diminished.

Another useful function of analgesia is the suppression of pain during important behaviors such as fighting or mating. For example, males fighting for access to females during mating season will fail to pass on their genes if pain elicits withdrawal responses that interfere with fighting. As we will see, these conditions *do* diminish pain.

First, let us consider the effects of unavoidable pain. Several experiments have shown that analgesia can be produced by the application of painful stimuli, or even by the presence of nonpainful stimuli that have been paired with painful ones. For example, Maier, Drugan, and Grau (1982) administered inescapable shocks to rats' tails or administered shocks that the animals could learn to escape by making a response. Although both groups of animals received the same amount of shock, only those that received *inescapable* shocks showed analgesia. That is, when their pain sensitivity was tested, it was found to be lower than that of control subjects. The analgesia was abolished by administration of naloxone, which indicates that it was mediated by the release of endogenous opiates. (You will recall that naloxone blocks opiate receptors.) The results make good sense, biologically. If pain is escapable, it serves to motivate the animal to make appropriate responses. If it occurs whatever the animal does, then a reduction in pain sensitivity is in the animal's best interest.

Not all instances of analgesia produced by inescapable pain involve the secretion of endogenous opiates. For example, Lewis, Cannon, and Liebeskind (1980) found that intermittent, inescapable foot shock reduced an animal's sensitivity to painful stimuli whether the shock was given during a short session (three minutes) or a long one (twenty minutes). However, only the analgesia produced by long-term exposure could be reversed by naloxone; it had no effect on the analgesia produced by the three-minute exposure. Thus, the authors concluded that the treatments produced two types of analgesia, only one of which involved endogenous opiates. The reason for these two mechanisms is not yet known.

Fanselow (1979) found that a well-known behavioral phenomenon is related to pain-induced analgesia. Normally, animals prefer signaled foot shock to nonsignaled foot shock. That is, a shock that is preceded by the sound of a buzzer is preferred to a sudden foot shock that comes right out of the blue. The preference for signaled foot shock is eliminated by naloxone injections; then the rats do not care whether the shocks come with a warning. Presumably, the warning stimulus causes endogenous opiates to be secreted, which makes signaled shock less painful than nonsignaled shock. This physiological explanation is a lot simpler than the ones that had previously been advanced to account for this phenomenon.

Pain can be reduced by stimulating regions other than those that hurt. For example, people often rub or scratch the area around a wound, in an apparent attempt to diminish the severity of the pain. And, as you know, acupuncturists insert needles into various parts of the body in order to reduce pain. The needle is usually then rotated, thus stimulating axons and nerve endings in the vicinity. Often, the region that is stimulated is far removed from the region that becomes less sensitive to pain.

Several experimental studies have shown acupuncture to produce analgesia (Gaw, Chang, and Shaw, 1975; Mann, Bowsher, Mumford, Lipton, and Miles, 1973). Mayer, Price, Rafii, and Barber (1976) reported that the analgesic effects of acupuncture could be blocked by naloxone. However, when pain was reduced by hypnotic suggestion, naloxone had no effect. Thus, acupuncture, but not hypnosis, appears to cause analgesia through the release of endogenous opiates.

There is evidence that engaging in behaviors that are important to survival also reduces sensitivity to pain. For example, Komisaruk (1974) demonstrated a nice relationship between genital stimulation and analgesia. He gently probed the cervix of female rats with a glass rod and found that the procedure diminished the animals' sensitivity to pain. It also increased the activity of neurons in the periaqueductal gray matter. Presumably, copulation (and/or the birth process) stimulates the cervical region, activates neural mechanisms in the periaqueductal gray matter, and produces analgesia. Many studies have shown that electrical stimulation of the periaqueductal gray matter elicits various species-typical behaviors, including attack or sexual activity. Thus, the circuits that mediate these behaviors are tied to those that produce analgesia.

Pain can also be reduced, at least in some people, by administering a **placebo,** or pharmacologically inert substance. (The term *placebo* comes from *placere,* which means "to please." The physician pleases an anxious patient by giving him or her an innocuous substance.) The pain reduction seems to be mediated by endogenous opiates, because it is blocked by naloxone (Levine, Gordon, and

Fields, 1979). Somehow, when some patients take a medication that they think will reduce pain, it does so *pharmacologically,* by triggering the release of endogenous opiates. This pharmacological effect is eliminated by the opiate receptor–blocker naloxone. Thus, for some people, a placebo is not pharmacologically "inert." The placebo effect is probably mediated through the connections of the frontal cortex with the periaqueductal gray matter.

Other Effects of Endogenous Opiates
Endogenous opiates are found in several regions of the brain that do not appear to play a primary role in the perception of pain. Undoubtedly, they take part in many other functions. The investigation of the endogenous opiates is still very new, but already some hints of their additional roles are emerging. Endogenous opiates may play a role in thermoregulation; local injection into the hypothalamus produces changes in body temperature (Martin and Bacino, 1978), and the administration of naloxone disrupts thermoregulatory responses (Holaday, Wei, Loh, and Li, 1978). In addition, endogenous opiates are involved in the control of blood pressure (Holaday, 1983). As we will see in subsequent chapters, the endogenous opiates may even be involved in learning, especially in mechanisms of reinforcement. This connection should not come as a complete surprise, because many people have found injections of opiates like morphine or heroin to be extremely pleasurable. Belluzzi and Stein (1977) found that rats will perform a response in order to receive injections of Met- or Leu-enkephalin into the lateral ventricles.

The endogenous opiates were first discovered by scientists who were investigating the perception of pain; thus, many of the studies using these peptides have been devoted to their role in mechanisms of analgesia. However, it is possible that their role in other

functions is even more important. The answers await more research.

INTERIM SUMMARY

Cutaneous sensory information is provided by specialized receptors in the skin. Pacinian corpuscles provide information about vibration. Ruffini corpuscles, similar to Pacinian corpuscles but considerably smaller, respond to low-frequency vibration, usually referred to as "flutter." Meissner's corpuscles, found in papillae and innervated by several axons, respond to mechanical stimuli. Merkel's disks, also found in papillae, consist of single flattened dendritic endings next to specialized epithelial cells. They respond to mechanical stimulation. Krause end bulbs, found in the junction between mucous membrane and dry skin (mucocutaneous zones), consist of loops of unmyelinated axons. They probably respond to mechanical stimuli. Painful stimuli are detected primarily by free nerve endings.

Sensory endings in the Golgi tendon organs detect muscular tension, and sensory endings in the intrafusal muscle fibers detect changes in muscle length. Free nerve endings and Pacinian corpuscles are found in the fascia covering the muscles and in the tissue lining the joints, and the body of the muscles contains free nerve endings.

Our somatosensory system is most sensitive to changes in mechanical stimuli. Unless the skin is moving, we do not detect nonpainful stimuli, because the receptors adapt to constant mechanical pressure. Temperature receptors also adapt; moderate changes in skin temperature are soon perceived as "neutral," and deviations above or below this temperature are perceived as warmth or coolness.

Precise, well-localized somatosensory information is conveyed by the lemniscal system, which includes the pathway through the dorsal columns and their nuclei and the medial lemniscus, connecting the dorsal column nuclei with the ventral posterior nuclei of the thalamus. A similar pathway connects the sensory axons of the trigeminal nerve with the trigeminal nuclei and connects these nuclei with the thalamus. Information about pain and temperature ascends the spinal cord through the spinothalamic system, which sends offshoots through the reticulothalamic system. Organic sensibility reaches the central nervous system by means of axons that travel through nerves of the autonomic nervous systems.

The neurons in the primary somatosensory cortex are topographically arranged, according to the part of the body from which they receive sensory information (somatotopic representation). Columns within the somatosensory cortex respond to a particular type of stimulus from a particular region of the body. Recent studies have shown that different types of somatosensory receptors send their information to separate areas of the somatosensory cortex.

Pain perception is not a simple function of stimulation of pain receptors; it is a complex phenomenon that can be modified by experience and the immediate environment. Lesion studies have shown that pain perception involves the parafascicular and intralaminar nuclei of the thalamus, and that a person's emotional response to pain involves the limbic system and the prefrontal cortex, which receives projections from the dorsomedial thalamus.

Just as we have mechanisms to perceive pain, we have mechanisms to reduce it—to produce analgesia. Under the appropriate circumstances, neurons in the periaqueductal gray matter are stimulated through synaptic connections with the frontal cortex, amygdala, and hypothalamus. In addition, some neurosecretory cells in the brain release enkephalins, a class of endogenous opiates. These neuromodulators activate receptors on neurons in the periaqueductal gray matter and provide additional stimulation of neurons in this region. Connections from the periaqueductal gray matter to the nucleus raphe magnus of the medulla activate serotonergic neurons located there. These neurons send axons through the dorsolateral columns to the dorsal horn of the spinal cord gray matter, where they cause either presynaptic or postsynaptic inhibition of neurons whose axons transmit pain information to the brain.

Analgesia occurs when it is important for an animal to continue a behavior that would tend to be inhibited by pain—for example, mating or fighting. In addition, inescapable pain activates brain mechanisms that produce analgesia but escapable pain does not. This distinction makes sense: if the pain is escapable, its sensation should not be blunted but should serve to motivate the animal's efforts to escape. Because the endogenous opiates are found in several regions of the brain that are apparently not involved in pain perception, these neuromodulators undoubtedly serve functions besides analgesia, such as thermoregulation, control of blood pressure, and learning. The fact that many people have chosen to self-administer opiates extracted from the opium poppy attests to its potency as a reinforcer of behavior.

■ GUSTATION

The stimuli we have encountered so far produce receptor potentials by imparting physical energy: thermal, photic, or kinetic. However, the stimuli received by the last two senses to be studied, gustation and olfaction, interact with their receptors chemically.

The Stimuli

For a substance to be tasted, molecules of it must dissolve in the saliva and stimulate the taste receptors on the tongue. Tastes of different substances vary, but much less than we generally realize. There are only four qualities of taste: *bitterness, sourness, sweetness, and saltiness.* Flavor, as opposed to taste, is a composite of olfaction and gustation. Much of the flavor of a steak depends on its odor; to an *anosmic* person (lacking the sense of smell) or to a person whose nostrils are stopped up, an onion tastes like an apple, and a steak tastes like salty cardboard.

Most vertebrates possess gustatory systems that respond to all four taste qualities. (An exception is the cat, which does not detect sweetness.) In addition, some animals appear to have receptors that respond specifically to the taste of plain water. Most investigators believe that sweetness receptors are food detectors. Most sweet-tasting foods, such as fruits and some vegetables, are safe to eat. Saltiness receptors detect the presence of sodium chloride. In some environments, inadequate amounts of this mineral are obtained from the usual source of food, so sodium chloride detectors help the animal detect its presence. Injuries that cause bleeding rapidly deplete an organism of its supply of sodium, so the ability to find it quickly can be critical.

Most species of animals will readily ingest substances that taste sweet or somewhat salty. However, they will tend to avoid substances that taste sour or bitter. Because of bacterial activity, many foods become acidic when they spoil. The acidity tastes sour and causes an avoidance reaction. (Of course, we have learned to make highly preferred mixtures of sweet and sour, such as lemonade.) Bitterness is almost universally avoided and cannot easily be improved by adding some sweetness. Many plants produce poisonous alkaloids, which protect them from being eaten by animals. The bitterness receptor undoubtedly serves to warn animals away from these chemicals.

Anatomy of the Taste Buds and Gustatory Cells

The tongue, palate, pharynx, and larynx contain approximately ten thousand taste buds. Most of these receptive organs are arranged around *papillae,* small protuberances of the tongue. Papillae are surrounded by moat-like trenches that serve to trap saliva. The taste buds (approximately two hundred of them, for the larger papillae) surround the trenches, and their pores open into them. Figure 7.43 shows the appearance of papillae and a cross section through a trench that contains a taste bud. (See **Figure 7.43.**)

Taste buds that respond to the different taste qualities have different distributions on the tongue. The tip of the tongue is most sensitive to sweetness and saltiness, the sides are most sensitive to sourness, and the back of the tongue, throat, and soft palate are most sensitive to bitterness. (See **Figure 7.44.**) This distribution explains why saccharin, an artificial sweetener that tastes both sweet and bitter to some people, produces a sensation of sweetness on the front of the tongue when it is first tasted, and then a sensation of bitterness in the back of the mouth when it is swallowed.

Von Békésy (1964) was the first to study individual taste buds electrophysiologically. He placed a small glass tube over them and applied gentle suction, turning them inside out. He found that electrical or chemical stimulation produced only a single sensation, and he concluded that each papilla is specific

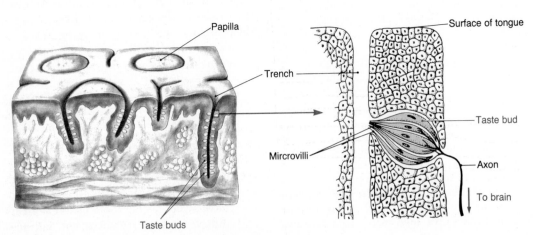

FIGURE 7.43
Left: Papillae on the surface of the tongue. *Right:* A taste bud.

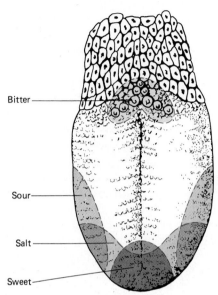

Bitter

Sour

Salt

Sweet

FIGURE 7.44

Different regions of the tongue are especially sensitive to different tastes.

for one of the four taste qualities. However, Bealer and Smith (1975) later found that one third of the papillae they tested produced responses to stimuli of all four taste qualities.

Taste receptors possess hairlike processes *(microvilli)* that project through the pores of the taste bud into the trench adjacent to the papilla. They form synapses with dendrites of sensory neurons that convey gustatory information to the brain. The receptors have a life span of only ten days. They quickly wear out, being directly exposed to a rather hostile environment. As they degenerate, they are replaced by newly developed cells; the afferent dendrite is passed on to the new cell (Beidler, 1970). The presence of vesicles within the cytoplasm of the receptor cell around the synaptic region suggests that transmission at this synapse is chemical.

Transduction of Gustatory Information

It seems most likely that transduction of taste is similar to the chemical transmission that

takes place at synapses: the tasted molecule binds with the receptor and produces changes in membrane permeability that cause receptor potentials. Different substances bind with different types of receptors, producing different taste sensations.

To taste salty, a substance must ionize. Although the best stimulus for saltiness receptors is sodium chloride (NaCl), a variety of salts containing metallic cations (such as Na^+, K^+, and Li^+) with a halogen or other small anion (such as Cl^-, Br^-, SO_4^{2-}, or NO_3^-) taste salty. Sourness receptors probably respond to the hydrogen ions present in acidic solutions. However, because the sourness of a particular acid is not simply a function of the concentration of hydrogen ions, the anions must have an effect, as well. Bitter and sweet substances are more difficult to characterize. The typical stimulus for bitterness is a plant alkaloid such as quinine, while for sweetness it is a sugar such as fructose. Because some molecules elicit both sensations, bitterness and sweetness receptors must be similar. For example, the Seville orange rind contains a glycoside (complex sugar) that tastes extremely bitter. However, Horowitz and Gentili (1974) discovered that the addition of hydrogen to the molecule makes it intensely sweet. Some amino acids taste sweet. Indeed, the commercial sweetener aspartame consists simply of two amino acids, aspartate and phenylalanine.

The Gustatory Pathway

Gustatory information is transmitted through three cranial nerves. Information from the anterior part of the tongue travels through the *chorda tympani,* a branch of the seventh cranial nerve (facial nerve). Taste receptors in the posterior part of the tongue send information through the lingual (tongue) branch of the ninth cranial nerve (glossopharyngeal nerve), while the tenth cranial nerve (vagus nerve) carries information from receptors of the palate and epiglottis. The chorda tympani gets its name because it passes through the middle ear just beneath the tympanic membrane. Because of its convenient location, it is accessible to a recording or stimulating electrode. Investigators have even recorded from this nerve during the course of human ear operations.

The first relay station for taste is the *nucleus of the solitary tract,* located in the medulla. (As we will see in Chapter 9, this region also plays a role in sleep.) The taste-sensitive neurons of this nucleus send their axons a short distance forward, to the *parabrachial nucleus* of the pons. The details of this second relay station have been determined only for the rat, but it is believed that a similar area can be found in primates (Pfaffmann, Frank, and Norgren, 1979). The pontine neurons then project to the *thalamic taste area,* situated at the most medial part of the ventral posterior group of thalamic nuclei (those that relay somatosensory information to the neocortex). Projections are also sent to the sub-

thalamus (a part of the motor system located beneath the thalamus), lateral hypothalamus, and various parts of the limbic system. Many investigators believe that the hypothalamic pathway plays a role in mediating the reinforcing effects of sweet and salty tastes. (Chapter 13 discusses the role of the lateral hypothalamus in reinforcement.)

The thalamic taste area projects to three areas in the primate brain: two regions at the base of the primary somatosensory cortex, and a region of the *anterior insular cortex,* a part of frontal cortex that is normally hidden under the anterior end of the temporal lobe. Unlike most other sense modalities, taste is ipsilaterally represented in the brain. (See **Figure 7.45.**)

Neural Coding of Taste

Almost all fibers in the chorda tympani respond to more than one taste quality, and many respond to changes in temperature, as well. However, most show a preference for

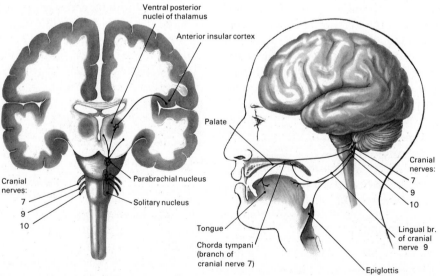

FIGURE 7.45
Neural pathways of the gustatory system.

one of the four qualities (sweet, salty, sour, or bitter). Figure 7.46 shows the average responses of fibers in the rat chorda tympani and glossopharyngeal nerve to sucrose (S), NaCl (N), HCl (H), quinine (Q), and water (W), as recorded by Nowlis and Frank (1977). These investigators stimulated three different kinds of taste buds (circumvallate, foliate, and fungiform) and found the same general types of responses from each of them. (See **Figure 7.46.**)

Similar kinds of response patterns are found in the nucleus of the solitary tract (Doetsch and Erickson, 1970). If anything, these neurons respond to even more qualities of taste. Funakoshi and Ninomiya (1977) reported data from cortical taste neurons in dogs and rats. Of sixty neurons from which they recorded, more than one third responded to only one of the five taste stimuli that were used, while another third responded to only two of them. Ten of the neurons tested were excited by one stimulus and inhibited by another. Thus, the response of the cortical neurons appears to be more sharply tuned than that of neurons in the periphery.

Yamamoto, Yuyama, and Kawamura (1981) attempted to determine whether the taste qualities were represented in different parts of the cortex. In general, they were. Dilute hydrochloric acid and quinine tended to stimulate neurons in adjacent regions at one end of the cortical taste area, while sucrose stimulated neurons located at the opposite end. Neurons that were sensitive to sodium chloride were spread throughout the area.

INTERIM SUMMARY

Taste receptors detect only four sensory qualities: bitterness, sourness, sweetness, and saltiness. Bitter foods often contain plant alkaloids, many of which are poisonous. Sour foods have usually undergone bacterial fermentation, which can produce toxins. On the other hand, sweet foods (such as fruits) are usually nutritious and safe to eat, and salty foods contain an essential cation, sodium. The fact that people in affluent cultures today tend to ingest excessive amounts of sweet and salty foods suggests that stimulation of these neurons is naturally reinforcing. The means of transduction of gustatory information is not known. Presumably, the mechanism utilizes receptors similar to those that detect hormones and transmitter substances.

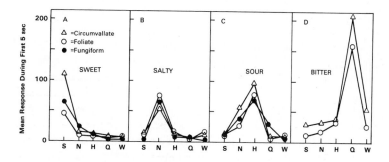

FIGURE 7.46
Mean number of responses recorded from axons in the chorda tympani and glossopharyngeal nerve during the first five seconds after the application of sweet, salty, sour, and bitter stimuli. The response characteristics of the axons are categorized as sweet, salty, sour, or bitter. (From Nowlis, G.H., and Frank, M. In *Olfaction and Taste 6,* edited by J. LeMagnen and P. MacLeod. Washington, D.C.: Information Retrieval, 1977.)

Gustatory information from the anterior part of the tongue travels through the chorda tympani, a branch of the facial nerve that passes beneath the eardrum on its way to the brain. The posterior part of the tongue sends gustatory information through the glossopharyngeal nerve, and the palate and epiglottis send gustatory information through the vagus nerve. Gustatory information is received by the nucleus of the solitary tract, located in the medulla. The information is relayed to the parabrachial nucleus of the pons, then to the thalamic taste area, and finally to the base of the somatosensory cortex, anterior insular cortex of the frontal lobe, subthalamus, lateral hypothalamus, and limbic system.

■ OLFACTION

Olfaction, the second chemical sense, helps us identify food and avoid food that has spoiled and is unfit to eat. It helps the members of many species identify receptive mates. For humans, olfaction is the most enigmatic of all sensory modalities. Odors have a peculiar ability to evoke memories, often vague ones that seem to have occurred in the distant past. Although people can discriminate among many thousands of different odors, we lack a good vocabulary to describe them. It is relatively easy to describe sights we have seen or sounds we have heard, but the description of an odor is difficult. At best, we can say it smells like something else. As we will see, the search for odor primaries, like those of taste, vision, and audition, has not yet progressed very far.

The Stimulus

The stimulus for odor consists of volatile substances having a molecular weight in the range of approximately 15 to 300. Almost all odorous compounds are organic in nature. However, many substances that meet these criteria have no odor at all, and we do not yet know why.

Anatomy of the Olfactory Apparatus

Our olfactory receptors reside within two patches of mucous membrane *(olfactory epithelium)*, each having an area of about one square inch. The olfactory epithelium is located at the top of the nasal cavity, as shown in **Figure 7.47.** Air that enters the nostrils is swept upward (especially when we sniff) by the action of the *turbinate bones* that project into the nasal cavity, until it reaches the olfactory receptors.

The inset in Figure 7.47 illustrates a group of olfactory receptor cells, along with their supporting cells. (See **inset, Figure 7.47.**) Olfactory receptors are bipolar neurons whose cell bodies lie within the olfactory mucosa that lines the *cribriform plate,* a bone at the base of the rostral part of the brain. The receptors send one process toward the surface of the mucosa, which divides into several cilia that penetrate the layer of mucus. Presumably, odorous molecules dissolve in the mucus and stimulate receptor molecules on the olfactory cilia. The olfactory receptors possess axons, which enter the skull through small holes in the cribriform ("perforated") plate. The olfactory mucosa also contains free nerve endings of trigeminal nerve axons; these nerve endings presumably mediate sensations of pain that can be produced by sniffing some irritating chemicals, such as ammonia.

The *olfactory bulbs* lie at the base of the brain on the ends of the stalklike olfactory tracts. Axons of the olfactory receptors terminate in one of the two olfactory bulbs, where they synapse with dendrites of *mitral cells.* These synapses take place in the complex axonal and dendritic arborizations called *olfactory glomeruli* (from *glomus,* "ball"). The axons of the mitral cells travel to the rest of the brain through the olfactory tracts. Some of these axons synapse in the brain, whereas others cross the brain, enter the other olfactory nerve, and synapse in the contralateral olfactory bulb.

Olfactory tract axons project to various parts of the limbic system — principally, the amygdala. They also project to the ventral frontal neocortex and to the limbic cortex. Unlike all other sense modalities, olfactory information is not relayed from thalamus to cortex. Indeed, the reverse occurs; neurons in the olfactory cortex project to the thalamic taste area. The fact that flavor is a composite of taste and smell may be related to this convergence of information. The hypothalamus also receives a considerable amount of olfac-

tory information, which is probably important for the acceptance or rejection of food and for the olfactory control of reproductive processes seen in many species of mammals.

Most mammals (but probably not adult humans) have another organ that responds to olfactory stimuli: the *vomeronasal organ*. Because it plays an important role in animals' responses to odors that affect sexual physiology and behavior, its structure and function are described in Chapter 10.

Efferent fibers from several locations in the brain enter the olfactory bulbs. The synapses of these fibers appear to be inhibitory, but

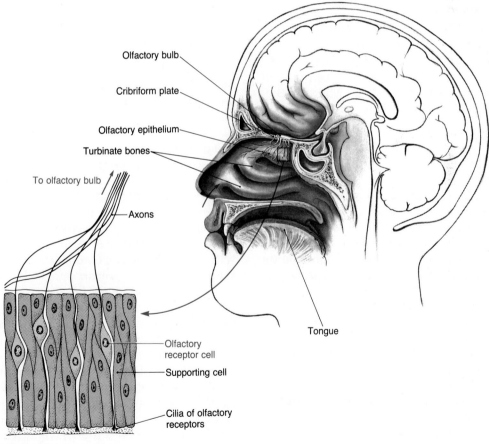

FIGURE 7.47
The olfactory system.

their role in the processing of olfactory information is a mystery. However, the brain controls the effects of olfactory stimuli in a more obvious way: we can sniff the air, maximizing the exposure of our olfactory epithelium to the odor molecules, or we can pinch our nostrils and breathe through the mouth, thus producing minimal olfactory stimulation.

Transduction of Olfactory Information

The means by which odor molecules produce receptor potentials is not known. Investigators assume that olfactory cilia contain receptor molecules (like those found on taste receptors and synaptic membranes) that are stimulated by odor molecules. The resting potential of olfactory neurons is approximately -45 mV, which is relatively weak. Stimulation with odorous molecules opens one or more ion channels, causing the neurons to depolarize slowly and increasing the firing rate of their axons (Lancet, 1984).

Coding of Odor Quality

Although investigators have made many attempts to identify odor primaries corresponding to the sweet, sour, bitter, and salty qualities of taste, we still cannot say with any assurance how odor quality is encoded. This lack of knowledge about coding at the peripheral level certainly hampers research on the central coding of olfactory information.

The concept of primary olfactory qualities has been prevalent for quite some time — partly because it is easier to conceive of coding the overwhelming number of discriminable odors by a few primary dimensions than by a myriad of different types of receptors. After all, new substances with new odors are synthesized every year, and it would be unreasonable to expect that we have already evolved specific receptors for all of the odors yet to be experienced.

Two other pieces of information suggest that odors may be sorted out according to some classification scheme. First, some people have very specific anosmias; they cannot detect certain odors. This occurrence would suggest that there are various receptor types, and that these people lack one or more kinds of specific receptors. Second, we humans seem to be able to reach some agreements about the similarities of odors. Classifications such as fruity, pinelike, and musky make sense to most of us, and we are willing to say that there is more similarity between the odors of pine oil and cedar oil than between skunk and the smell of limes. However, no coherent, testable theory exists that organizes olfactory qualities and explains differences among them (Cain, 1978).

Amoore's Stereospecific Theory

Although no investigators today (including Amoore) believe that the details of his theory are correct, Amoore's attempt to construct one is interesting and instructive. Amoore (1962, 1964) studied the chemical literature and decided that the terms used by chemists to describe the odor of a compound could be divided into seven categories: camphoraceous, ethereal, floral, musky, pepperminty, pungent, and putrid. He went on to examine the three-dimensional structures of the various molecules, to see if there could be any way to classify them according to shape. He suggested that the "primary odors" are characterized by seven different molecular configurations, recognized by receptive sites of similar shapes, two of which are shown in Figure 7.48. (See **Figure 7.48.**)

Amoore constructed plastic models of the molecules and receptors. Then he attempted, by several means, to correlate the "goodness of fit" of the molecular models and receptor models with observers' judgments of the similarities among odors each model represented. In other words, did the observers judge that odors whose molecules fit the receptor model well were more similar than odors

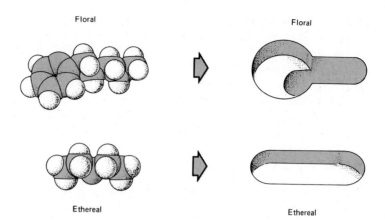

FIGURE 7.48
Examples of the molecular
shape of two odorous
substances, along with their
hypothesized receptors.
(Adapted from Amoore, J.E.,
Johnston, J.W., and Rubin, M.
Scientific American, 1964,
210 (2), 42–49.)

whose molecules fit the receptor model poorly? Unfortunately, the relationship was not good. In fact, Amoore (1970) abandoned his model of the hypothesized receptor sites and suggested that future research should concentrate on the configurations of the molecules themselves.

The Amoore theory did not identify the nature of the olfactory receptors; nor, for that matter, has any other theory. Various investigators have stressed other characteristics of odorous molecules besides their shape. For example, Wright (1974) has noted some correspondence between the odors of molecules and their patterns of absorption of infrared radiation. How this correlation may ultimately relate to the transduction of olfactory information is still a mystery.

Recordings of Neural Responses to Olfactory Stimuli

Unfortunately, recordings taken from single olfactory receptors have not helped to identify "odor primaries." Mathews (1972) recorded from nineteen olfactory receptors of the tortoise, stimulating them with twenty-seven different odors. Two of the receptors responded to only one odor, one responded to two odors, and sixteen responded to three or more odors. He found similar response characteristics in neurons in the olfactory

bulb. Gesteland (1978) found that no two olfactory receptors responded alike. He reported that although two similar odors might produce similar responses in different cells, a brief search would invariably find another cell that made a sharp distinction between the odors, and the original cells would respond differently to another pair of odors.

Recordings in more central levels of the olfactory system show that neural responses tend to be more finely tuned to particular odors. For example, Tanabe, Iino, Ooshima, and Takagi (1974) and Tanabe, Iino, and Takagi (1975) found that neurons in the olfactory area of the orbitofrontal cortex of monkeys were more selective. Of the forty cells from which they recorded, half responded to only one odor, and decreasing numbers responded to two, three, or four different odors. None responded to more than five odors. The results suggest that cortical neurons respond selectively to particular patterns of activity in neurons in more peripheral parts of the olfactory system. The nature of the coding system is unknown.

Stewart, Kauer, and Shepherd (1979) used the 2-deoxyglucose (2-DG) autoradiographic technique (described in Chapter 5) to investigate the responses of neurons in the olfactory bulb. Their results suggest that specific odors may produce responses of neurons in particular regions. They injected rats with radioactive 2-DG and exposed them to a particular odor. Then they killed the rats, removed and sliced their olfactory bulbs, and used a photographic emulsion to find the radioactivity. The results indicated that different odors increased the metabolic activity (and presumably, the synaptic activity) of different specific regions of the olfactory bulbs. The distribution of radioactivity in the olfactory bulbs of twenty-seven rats is shown in Figure 7.49. Six were exposed to the odor of camphor (colored areas), and twenty-one

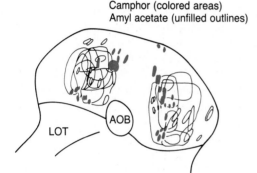

Camphor (colored areas)
Amyl acetate (unfilled outlines)

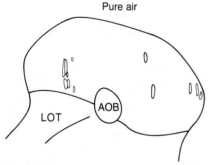

Pure air

FIGURE 7.49

Composite drawings prepared from 2-DG autoradiographs of rat olfactory bulbs after the animals were exposed to camphor (*top,* colored areas), amyl acetate (*top,* unfilled outlines), or pure air (*bottom,* unfilled outlines). LOT = lateral olfactory tract; AOB = accessory olfactory bulb. (From Stewart, W.B., Kauer, J.S., and Shepherd, G.M. *Journal of Comparative Neurology,* 1979, *185,* 715–734.)

were exposed to amyl acetate (unfilled outlines). (See **Figure 7.49.**)

The results suggest that odor quality is represented spatially by neurons in the olfactory system. Only further research will reveal whether this procedure can be used to identify categories of olfactory qualities.

INTERIM SUMMARY

The olfactory receptors consist of bipolar neurons located in the olfactory epithelium that lines the roof of the nasal sinuses, on the bone that underlies the frontal lobes. The receptors send processes toward the surface of the mucosa, which divide into cilia. The membranes of these cilia appear to contain receptors that detect aromatic molecules dissolved in the air that sweeps past the olfactory mucosa. The axons of the olfactory receptors pass through the perforations of the cribriform plate and form synapses with the dendrites of the mitral cells of the olfactory bulbs. These neurons send axons through the olfactory tracts to the brain, principally to the amygdala, ventral frontal neocortex, and the limbic cortex. Some axons travel to the thalamic taste area and may be responsible for at least some of the convergence of olfactory and gustatory information into the perception of flavor.

We do not know how aromatic molecules produce membrane potentials. Attempts to analyze odor primaries similar to the four primary tastes have met with failure. Amoore's stereospecific theory attempted to categorize odors by means of their molecular shape, but the theory has received little empirical support. Studies using 2-DG autoradiography have suggested that different odors excite neurons in particular regions of the olfactory bulbs, but we do not yet know whether these results imply the existence of a spatial code, or what its rules are.

Concluding Remarks

This chapter and Chapter 6 have summarized our knowledge about the physiology of sensation and perception. Obviously, far more is known than what I have been able to summarize here, but you now are familiar with the basic anatomy and physiology of the sensory modalities and the types of research issues that investigators are currently studying. The rest of the book deals with organisms' behaviors. Chapter 8 introduces the motor system, and the chapters that follow discuss particular classes of behavior. Some of the mechanisms and neural connections that you learned about here will be discussed again, as we see how various stimuli control organisms' behaviors.

NEW TERMS

ampulla p. 250
analgesia p. 269
anterior insular cortex p. 278
auditory tuning curve p. 239
basilar membrane p. 230
binaural p. 243
chorda tympani p. 277
cilia p. 233
cochlea p. 229
cochlear microphonics p. 235
cochlear nerve p. 235
cochlear nerve ganglion p. 235
cochlear nuclei p. 237
cribriform plate p. 280
crista p. 250
cupula p. 250
cutaneous senses p. 255
cuticular plate p. 234
Deiters's cells p. 230
dorsal column nuclei p. 265
dorsal columns p. 265
dorsolateral columns p. 271
dynorphin p. 270
endogenous opiate p. 269
endolymph p. 234
β-endorphin p. 270
enkephalin p. 269
external auditory canal p. 229
fundamental frequency p. 242
glabrous skin p. 257
Golgi tendon organ p. 258
hair cell p. 230
hertz (Hz) p. 228
incus p. 229
intrafusal muscle fiber p. 256

kinesthesia p. 255
kinocilium p. 252
Krause end bulb p. 258
lateral lemniscus p. 237
lemniscal system p. 262
loudness p. 228
malleus p. 229
medial lemniscus p. 265
Meissner's corpuscle p. 258
Merkel's disk p. 258
mitral cells p. 280
mucocutaneous zone p. 258
naloxone p. 269
neurotensin p. 271
nucleus of the solitary tract p. 278
nucleus raphe magnus p. 271
olfactory bulb p. 280
olfactory epithelium p. 280
olfactory glomerulus p. 280
organic senses p. 255
organ of Corti p. 231
ossicles p. 229
oval window p. 229
overtone p. 242
Pacinian corpuscle p. 258
parabrachial nucleus p. 278
perilymph p. 234
phase difference p. 244
phase locking p. 244
pinna p. 229
pitch p. 228
placebo p. 273
prefrontal lobotomy p. 268
pro-dynorphin p. 270
pro-enkephalin p. 270

pro-opiomelanocortin p. 270
reticular membrane p. 230
round window p. 231
Ruffini corpuscle p. 258
saccule p. 249
scala media p. 234
scala tympani p. 232
scala vestibuli p. 231
semicircular canals p. 249
somatotopic representation p. 265
spinothalamic system p. 265
stapedius muscle p. 229
stapes p. 229
stereocilia p. 252
superior olivary complex p. 237

tectorial membrane p. 230
tensor tympani p. 229
thalamic taste area p. 278
timbre p. 228
tonotopic representation p. 238
trigeminal lemniscus p. 265
trigeminal nucleus p. 265
tympanic membrane p. 229
utricle p. 249
vestibular ganglion p. 254
vestibular nerve p. 253
vestibular sac p. 249
vestibulo-ocular reflex p. 255
white noise p. 240

SUGGESTED READINGS

Audition

DALLOS, P. Cochlear physiology. *Annual Review of Psychology,* 1981, *32,* 153–190.

HUDSPETH, A.J. Mechanoelectrical transduction by hair cells in the acousticolateralis sensory system. *Annual Review of Neuroscience,* 1983, *6,* 187–216.

KATSUKI, Y. *Receptive Mechanisms of Sound in the Ear.* Cambridge: Cambridge University Press, 1982.

MØLLER, A.R. *Auditory Physiology.* New York: Academic Press, 1983.

YOST, W.A., AND NIELSEN, D.W. *Fundamentals of Hearing: An Introduction.* New York: Holt, Rinehart and Winston, 1977.

Somatosenses

AKIL, H., WATSON, S.J., YOUNG, E., LEWIS, M.E., KHACHATURIAN, H., AND WALKER, J.M. Endogenous opioids: Biology and function. *Annual Review of Neuroscience,* 1984, *7,* 223–256.

BASBAUM, A.I., AND FIELDS, H.L. Endogenous pain control systems: Brainstem spinal pathways and endorphin circuitry. *Annual Review of Neuroscience,* 1984, *7,* 309–338.

BOLLES, R.C., AND FANSELOW, M.S. Endorphins and behavior. *Annual Review of Psychology,* 1982, *33,* 87–102.

BURGESS, P.R., WEI, J.Y., CLARK, F.J., AND SIMON, J. Signaling of kinesthetic information by peripheral sensory receptors. *Annual Review of Neuroscience,* 1982, *5,* 171–188.

DARIAN-SMITH, I. Touch in primates. *Annual Review of Psychology,* 1982, *33,* 155–194.

DUBNER, R., AND BENNETT, G.J. Spinal and trigeminal mechanisms of nociception. *Annual Review of Neuroscience,* 1983, *6,* 381–418.

IGGO, A., AND ANDRES, K.H. Morphology of cutaneous receptors. *Annual Review of Neuroscience,* 1982, *5,* 1–32.

SINCLAIR, D. *Mechanisms of Cutaneous Sensation.* Oxford: Oxford University Press, 1981.

Olfaction and Gustation

LEMAGNEN, J., AND MACLEOD, P. *Olfaction and Taste 6.* London, Washington, D.C.: Information Retrieval, 1977.

All Senses

KATSUKI, Y., NORGREN, R., AND SATO, M. *Brain Mechanisms of Sensation.* New York: John Wiley & Sons, 1981.

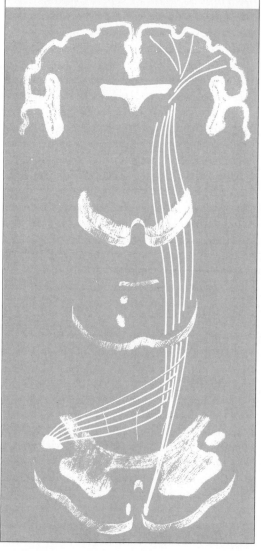

8

Control of Movement

So far, I have described the nature of neural communication, the basic structure of the nervous system, and the physiology of sensation. Now it is time to consider the ultimate function of the nervous system: control of behavior. The brain is the organ that moves the muscles. It does many other things, but all of them are secondary to making our bodies move. This chapter describes the principles of muscular contraction, some reflex circuitry within the spinal cord, and the means by which the brain initiates behaviors. The rest of the book describes the physiology of particular categories of behaviors and the ways in which our behaviors can be modified by experience.

■ MUSCLES

Mammals have three types of muscles: skeletal muscle, smooth muscle, and cardiac muscle.

Skeletal Muscle

Skeletal muscles are the ones that move us (our skeletons) around and thus are responsible for our behavior. Most of them are attached to bones at each end and move the bones when they contract. (Exceptions include eye muscles and some abdominal muscles, which are attached to bone at one end only.) Muscles are fastened to bones via *tendons,* strong bands of connective tissue. Several different classes of movement can be accomplished by the skeletal muscles, but I will refer principally to two of them: flexion and extension. Contraction of a flexor muscle produces *flexion,* the drawing in of a limb. *Extension,* which is the opposite movement, is produced by contraction of extensor muscles. These are the so-called *antigravity muscles* — the ones we use to stand up. When a four-legged animal lifts a paw, the movement is one of flexion. Putting it back down is one of extension. Sometimes people say they "flex" their muscles. This is an incorrect use of the term. Muscles *contract;* limbs *flex.* Body builders show off their arm muscles by simultaneously contracting the flexor and extensor muscles of that limb.

Anatomy

The detailed structure of a skeletal muscle is shown in **Figure 8.1.** As you can see, it consists of two types of muscle fibers. The *extrafusal muscle fibers* are served by axons of the *alpha motor neurons.* Contraction of these fibers provides the muscle's motive force. The *intrafusal muscle fibers* are specialized sensory organs that are served by two axons, one sensory and one motor. (These organs are also called *muscle spindles* because of their shape. In fact, the Latin word *fusus* means "spindle"; hence, *intrafusal* muscle fibers are found within the spindles, while *extrafusal* muscle fibers are found outside them.)

The central region *(capsule)* of the intrafusal muscle fiber contains sensory endings that are sensitive to stretch applied to the muscle fiber. Actually, there are two types of intrafusal muscle fibers, but for simplicity's sake only one kind is shown here. The efferent axon of the *gamma motor neuron* causes the intrafusal muscle fiber to contract; however, this contraction contributes an insubstantial amount of force. As we will see, the function of this contraction is to modify the sensitivity of the fiber's afferent ending to stretch.

A single myelinated axon of an alpha motor neuron serves several extrafusal muscle fibers. In primates, the number of muscle fibers served by a single axon varies considerably, depending on the precision with which the muscle can be controlled. In muscles that move the fingers or eyes the ratio can be less than one to ten; in muscles that move the leg it can be one to several hundred. An alpha motor neuron, its axon, and associated extrafusal muscle fibers constitute a *motor unit.*

288

A single muscle fiber consists of a bundle of *myofibrils,* each of which consists of overlapping strands of *actin* and *myosin.* Note the small protrusions on the myosin filaments; these structures *(myosin cross-bridges)* are the motile elements that interact with the actin filaments and produce muscular contractions. (See **Figure 8.1.**) The regions in which the actin and myosin filaments overlap produce dark stripes, or *striations;* hence, skeletal muscle is often referred to as *striated muscle.*

The Physical Basis of Muscular Contraction
The synapse between the terminal button of an efferent neuron terminal and the membrane of a muscle fiber is called a *neuromuscular junction.* The terminal buttons of the neurons synapse on *motor endplates,* located in grooves along the surface of the muscle fibers. When an axon fires, acetylcholine is liberated by the terminal buttons and produces a depolarization of the postsynaptic membrane *(endplate potential).* The endplate potential is much larger than an excita-

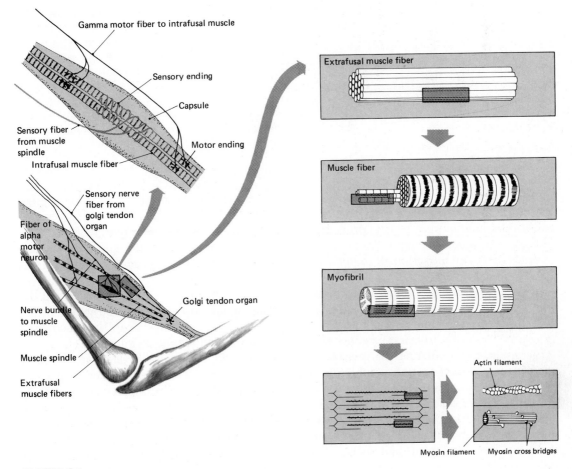

FIGURE 8.1
Anatomy of skeletal muscle. (Adapted from Bloom and Faucett, *A Textbook of Histology.* Philadelphia: W.B. Saunders, 1968.)

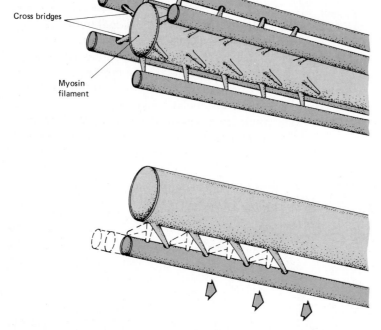

Actin
filaments

Cross bridges

Myosin
filament

FIGURE 8.2
The mechanism by which
muscles contract. The myosin
cross-bridges perform
"rowing" movements that
cause the actin and myosin
filaments to move relative to
each other. (Adapted from
Anthony, C.P., and Kolthoff,
N.J. *Textbook of Anatomy and
Physiology,* 8th edition. St.
Louis: C.V. Mosby, 1971.)

tory postsynaptic potential in synapses between neurons; an endplate potential *always*
causes the muscle fiber to fire, propagating
the potential along its length. This action potential induces a contraction, or *twitch,* of the
muscle fiber.

The depolarization of a muscle fiber opens
the gates of voltage-dependent calcium channels, permitting calcium ions to enter the cytoplasm. This event triggers the contraction.
Calcium acts as a cofactor that permits the
myofibrils to extract energy from the ATP that
is present in the cytoplasm. The myosin cross-
bridges alternately attach to the actin strands,
bend in one direction, detach themselves,
bend back, reattach to the actin at a point
farther down the strand, and so on. Thus,
the cross-bridges "row" along the actin filaments. Figure 8.2 illustrates this rowing sequence and shows how this sequence results

in shortening the muscle fiber. (See **Figure
8.2.**)

A single impulse of a motor neuron produces a single twitch of a muscle fiber. The
physical effects of the twitch last considerably longer than will the action potential, because of the elasticity of the muscle and the
time required to rid the cell of calcium. (Like
sodium, calcium is actively extruded by a
pump situated in the membrane.) Figure 8.3
shows how the physical effects of a series of
action potentials can overlap, causing a sustained contraction by the muscle fiber. A single motor unit in a leg muscle of a cat can raise
a 100-gram weight, which attests to the remarkable strength of the contractile mechanism. (See **Figure 8.3.**)

As you know from your own experience,
muscular contraction is not an all-or-nothing
phenomenon, as are the twitches of the con-

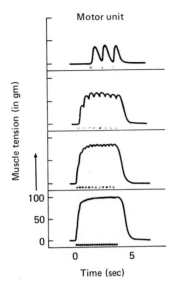

FIGURE 8.3

A rapid succession of action potentials can cause a muscle fiber to produce a sustained contraction. Each dot represents an individual action potential. (Adapted from Devanandan, M.S., Eccles, R.M., and Westerman, R.A. *Journal of Physiology (London)*, 1965, *178*, 359–367.)

stituent muscle fibers. Obviously, strength of muscular contraction is determined by the average rate of firing of the various motor units. If, at a given moment, many units are firing, the contraction will be forceful. If few are firing, the contraction will be weak.

Sensory Feedback from Muscles
As we saw, the intrafusal muscle fibers contain sensory endings that are sensitive to stretch. The intrafusal muscle fibers are arranged in parallel with the extrafusal muscle fibers. Therefore, they are stretched when the muscle lengthens and are relaxed when it shortens. Thus, even though these afferent neurons are *stretch receptors,* they serve as *muscle-length detectors.* This distinction is important. Stretch receptors are also located within the tendons, in the **Golgi tendon**

organ. These receptors detect the total amount of stretch exerted by the muscle, through its tendons, on the bones to which the muscle is attached. The stretch receptors of the Golgi tendon organ encode the degree of stretch by the rate of firing. They respond not to a muscle's length but to how hard it is pulling. In contrast, the receptors on intrafusal muscle fibers detect muscle length, not tension.

Figure 8.4 shows the response of afferent axons of the muscle spindles and Golgi tendon organ to various types of movements. Figure 8.4A shows the effects of passive lengthening of muscles, the kind of movement that would be seen if your forearm, held in a completely relaxed fashion, were slowly lowered by someone who was supporting it. The rate of firing of one type of muscle spindle afferent neuron (MS_1) increases, while the activity of the afferent of the Golgi tendon organ (GTO) remains unchanged. (See **Figure 8.4A.**) Figure 8.4B shows the same results if the arm were dropped quickly; note that this time the second type of muscle spindle afferent neuron (MS_2) fires a rapid burst of impulses. This fiber, then, signals rapid changes in muscle length. (See **Figure 8.4B.**) Figure 8.4C shows what would happen if a weight were suddenly dropped into your hand while your forearm was held parallel to the ground. MS_1 and MS_2 (especially MS_2, which responds to rapid changes in muscle length) briefly fire, because your arm lowers briefly and then comes back to the original position. The Golgi tendon organ, monitoring strength of contraction, fires in proportion to the stress on the muscle, so it increases its rate of firing as soon as the weight is added. (See **Figure 8.4C.**) I might note that, because of Archimedes's principle, which describes how force can be increased or decreased by means of levers, your biceps muscle must exert a force of 280 lb to support a weight of 40 lb carried in your hand. (See **Figure 8.5.**)

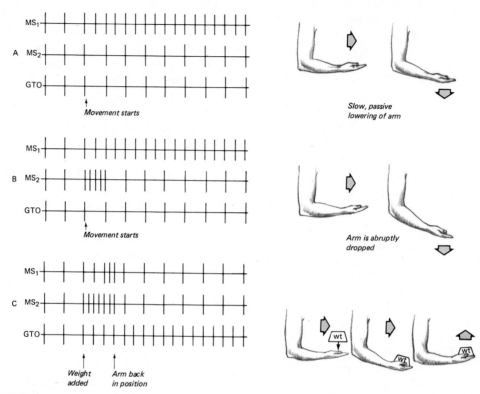

FIGURE 8.4

Effects of arm movements on the firing of muscle and tendon afferent axons. (A) Slow passive extension of the arm. (B) Rapid extension of the arm. (C) Addition of a weight to an arm held in a horizontal position. MS_1 and MS_2 are two types of muscle spindles; GTO is an afferent fiber from the Golgi tendon organ.

Smooth Muscle

Our bodies contain two types of *smooth muscle,* both of which are controlled by the autonomic nervous system. *Multiunit smooth muscles* are found in large arteries, around hair follicles (where they produce *piloerection,* or fluffing of fur), and in the eye (controlling lens adjustment and pupillary dilation). This type of smooth muscle is normally inactive, but it will contract in response to neural stimulation or to certain hormones. In contrast, *single-unit smooth muscles* nor-

mally contract in a rhythmical fashion. Some of these cells spontaneously produce *pacemaker potentials,* which we can regard as self-initiated excitatory postsynaptic potentials. These slow potentials elicit action potentials, which are propagated by adjacent smooth muscle fibers, causing a wave of muscular contraction. The efferent nerve supply (and various hormones) can modulate the rhythmical rate, increasing or decreasing it. Single-unit smooth muscles are found chiefly in the gastrointestinal system, uterus, and small blood vessels.

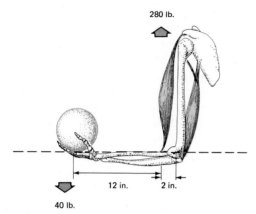

280 lb.

12 in.   2 in.

40 lb.

FIGURE 8.5
The force exerted by most muscles is considerably greater than the weight supported by the limb.

Cardiac Muscle

As its name implies, ***cardiac muscle*** is found in the heart. This type of muscle looks somewhat like striated muscle but acts like single-unit smooth muscle. The heart beats regularly, even if it is denervated. Neural activity and certain hormones (especially the catecholamines) serve to modulate the heart rate. A group of cells in the *pacemaker* of the heart are rhythmically active and initiate the contractions of cardiac muscle that constitute the heart beat.

INTERIM SUMMARY

Our bodies possess skeletal muscle, smooth muscle, and cardiac muscle. Skeletal muscles contain extrafusal muscle fibers, which provide the force of contraction. The alpha motor neurons form synapses with the extrafusal muscle fibers and control their contraction. Skeletal muscles also contain intrafusal muscle fibers, which detect changes in muscle length. The length of the intrafusal muscle fiber, and hence its sensitivity to increases in muscle length, is controlled by the gamma motor neuron. Besides the intrafusal muscle fibers, the

muscles contain stretch receptors in the Golgi tendon organs, located at the ends of the muscles.

The force of muscular contraction is provided by long protein molecules called actin and myosin, arranged in overlapping parallel arrays. When an action potential, initiated by the synapse at the motor endplate, causes Ca^{2+} to enter the muscle fiber, the myofibrils extract energy from ATP and cause a twitch of the muscle fiber, producing a ratchetlike "rowing" movement of the myosin cross-bridges.

Smooth muscle is controlled by the autonomic nervous system, through direct neural connections and indirectly through the endocrine system. Multiunit smooth muscles contract only in response to neural or hormonal stimulation. In contrast, single-unit smooth muscles normally contract rhythmically, but their rate is controlled by the autonomic nervous system. Cardiac muscle also contracts spontaneously, and its rate of contraction, too, is influenced by the autonomic nervous system.

■ REFLEX CONTROL OF MOVEMENT

Although behaviors are controlled by the brain, the spinal cord possesses a certain degree of autonomy. Particular kinds of somatosensory stimuli can elicit rapid responses through neural connections located within the spinal cord. These reflexes constitute the simplest level of motor integration.

The Monosynaptic Stretch Reflex

The activity of the simplest functional neural pathway in the body is easy to demonstrate. Sit on a surface high enough to allow your legs to dangle freely and have someone lightly tap your patellar tendon, just below the kneecap. This stimulus briefly stretches your quadriceps muscle, on the top of your thigh. The stretch causes the muscle to contract, which makes your leg kick forward. (I am sure few of you will bother with this demonstration, because you are already familiar with it; most physical examinations include a test of this reflex.) The time interval between the tendon tap and the start of the leg extension is about 50 msec. That interval is too short for the involvement of the brain; it would take considerably longer for sensory information to be relayed to the brain and for motor information to be relayed back. For example, suppose a person is asked to move his or her leg as quickly as possible after being *touched* on the knee. This response would not be reflexive but would involve sensory and motor mechanisms of the brain. In this case, the interval between the stimulus and the start of the response would be several times greater than the time required for the patellar reflex.

Obviously, the patellar reflex as such has no utility; no selective advantage is bestowed upon animals that kick a limb when a tendon is tapped. However, if a more natural stimulus is applied, the utility of this mechanism becomes apparent. Figure 8.6 reproduces part of Figure 8.4, showing the effects of placing a weight in a person's hand. However,

this time I have included a piece of the spinal cord, with its roots, to show the neural circuit that composes the ***monosynaptic stretch reflex.*** First follow the circuit: starting at the muscle spindle, afferent impulses are conducted to terminal buttons in the gray matter of the spinal cord. These terminal buttons synapse on an alpha motor neuron that innervates the extrafusal muscle fibers of the same muscle. Only one synapse is encountered along the route from receptor to effector — hence the term *monosynaptic*. (See **Figure 8.6.**)

Now consider a useful function this reflex performs. If the weight the person is holding is increased, the forearm begins to move down. This movement lengthens the muscle and increases the firing rate of the muscle spindle afferent neurons, whose terminal buttons then stimulate the alpha motor neurons, increasing their rate of firing. Consequently, the strength of the muscular con-

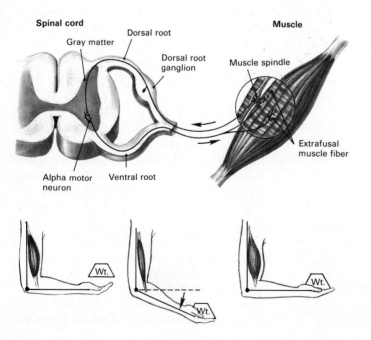

FIGURE 8.6
The monosynaptic stretch reflex.

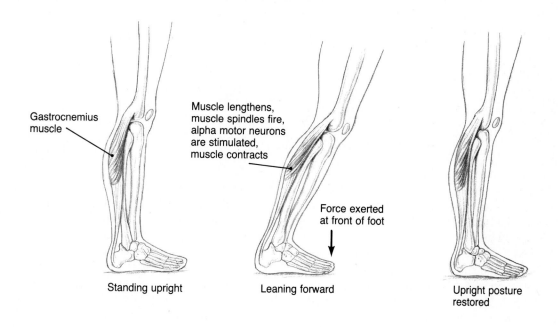

Gastrocnemius
muscle

Muscle lengthens,
muscle spindles fire,
alpha motor neurons
are stimulated,
muscle contracts

Force exerted
at front of foot

Standing upright   Leaning forward   Upright posture
                                                                       restored

FIGURE 8.7
The role of the monosynaptic stretch reflex in postural control.

traction increases, and the arm pulls the weight up. (See **Figure 8.6.**)

Another important role played by the monosynaptic stretch reflex is control of posture. In order to stand, we must keep our center of gravity above our feet, or we will fall. As we stand, we tend to oscillate back and forth, and from side to side. Our vestibular sacs and our visual system play an important role in the maintenance of posture. However, these systems are aided by the activity of the monosynaptic stretch reflex. For example, consider what happens when a person begins to lean forward. The large calf muscle (gastrocnemius) is stretched, and this stretching elicits compensatory muscular contraction that pushes the toes down, thus restoring upright posture. (See **Figure 8.7.**)

The Gamma Motor System

The muscle spindles are very sensitive to changes in muscle length; they will increase their rate of firing when the muscle is lengthened by a very small amount. The interesting thing is that this detection mechanism is adjustable. Remember that the ends of the intrafusal muscle fibers can be contracted by activity of the associated efferent axons of the gamma motor neurons; their rate of firing determines the degree of contraction. When the muscle spindles are relaxed, they are relatively insensitive to stretch. However, when the gamma motor neurons are active, they become shorter and hence become much more sensitive to changes in muscle length. This property of adjustable sensitivity simplifies

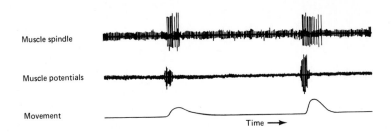

FIGURE 8.8

Evidence that the muscle begins moving before action potentials occur in the sensory endings of the muscle spindle proves that the alpha motor neurons directly initiate the movement. (From Vallbo, Å.B. *Journal of Physiology (London)*, 1971, *218*, 405–431.)

the role of the brain in controlling movement. The more control that can occur in the spinal cord, the fewer messages must be sent to and from the brain.

We already saw that the afferent axons of the muscle spindle help maintain limb position even when the load carried by the limb is altered. Efferent control of the muscle spindles permits these muscle-length detectors to assist in changes in limb position, as well. Consider a single muscle spindle. When its efferent axon is completely silent, the spindle is completely relaxed and extended. As the firing rate of the efferent axon increases, the spindle gets shorter and shorter. If, simultaneously, the rest of the entire muscle also gets shorter, there will be no stretch on the central region that contains the sensory endings, and the afferent axon will not respond. However, if the muscle spindle contracts faster than does the muscle as a whole, there will be a considerable amount of afferent activity.

The motor system makes use of this phenomenon in the following way: When commands from the brain are issued to move a limb, both the alpha motor neurons and the gamma motor neurons are activated. The alpha motor neurons start the muscle contracting. If there is little resistance, both the extrafusal and the intrafusal muscle fibers will contract at approximately the same rate, and little activity will be seen from the affer-

ent axons of the muscle spindle. However, if the limb meets with resistance, the intrafusal muscle fibers will shorten more than the extrafusal muscle fibers, and hence sensory axons will begin to fire and cause the monosynaptic stretch reflex to strengthen the contraction. Thus, the brain makes use of the gamma motor system in moving the limbs. By establishing a rate of firing in the *gamma motor system,* the brain controls the length of the muscle spindles and, indirectly, the length of the entire muscle.

Physiologists formerly thought that only the gamma motor neurons were activated to initiate movements, and that the alpha motor neurons were stimulated solely by the afferent axons of the muscle spindles. However, Vallbo (1971) put small electrodes into his own peripheral nerves and found that when he contracted the muscle that was innervated by the nerve, the contraction always preceded the activity of the afferent axon of the muscle spindle. Thus, the alpha motor neurons must have been activated directly by the brain, because the movement started before the afferent impulses were observed. (See **Figure 8.8.**)

Polysynaptic Reflexes

The monosynaptic stretch reflex is the only spinal reflex that we know of that involves

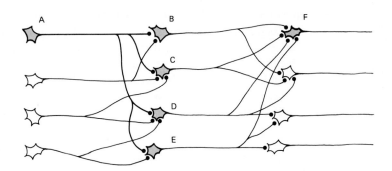

FIGURE 8.9
Examples of divergence
(neuron A synapses with
neurons B, C, D, and E) and
convergence (neurons B, C, D,
and E synapse with neuron F).

only one synapse. All others are *polysynaptic*. Examples include relatively simple ones, like limb withdrawal in response to pain, and relatively complex ones, like the ejaculation of semen. Spinal reflexes do not exist in isolation; they are normally controlled by the brain. For example, in Chapter 2 I described how inhibition from the brain can prevent a person from dropping a bunch of roses with thorns, even though the painful stimuli received by the fingers serve to cause reflexive extension of the fingers. In this section I will describe some general principles by which polysynaptic spinal reflexes operate.

Before I begin my discussion, I should mention that the simple circuit diagrams used here (including the one you just looked at in Figure 8.6) are much too simple. Reflex circuits are typically shown as a single chain of neurons, but in reality most reflexes involve thousands of neurons. Each axon usually synapses on many neurons, and each neuron re-

ceives synapses from many different axons. The multiple branching of axons is called *divergence*, and the multiple input on a single neuron is called *convergence*. (See **Figure 8.9.**)

As we previously saw, the afferent axons from the Golgi tendon organ serve as detectors of muscle stretch. There are two populations of afferent axons from the Golgi tendon organ, with different sensitivities to stretch. The more sensitive afferent axons tell the brain how hard the muscle is pulling. The less sensitive ones have an additional function. Their terminal buttons synapse on spinal cord *interneurons*, neurons that reside entirely within the gray matter of the spinal cord and serve to interconnect other spinal neurons. These interneurons synapse on the alpha motor neurons serving the same muscle. The terminal buttons liberate glycine and hence produce inhibitory postsynaptic potentials on the motor neurons. (See **Figure 8.10.**) The

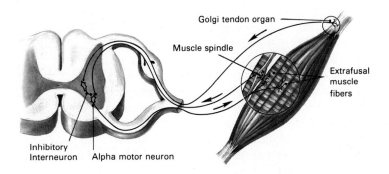

FIGURE 8.10
Input from the Golgi tendon
organ can cause inhibitory
postsynaptic potentials to
occur on the alpha motor
neuron.

function of this reflex pathway is to decrease the strength of muscular contraction when there is danger of damage to the tendons or bones to which the muscles are attached. Weight lifters can lift heavier weights if their Golgi tendon organs are deactivated with injections of a local anesthetic, but they run the risk of pulling the tendon away from the bone, or even breaking the bone.

The discovery of the inhibitory Golgi tendon organ reflex provided the first real evidence of neural inhibition, long before the synaptic mechanisms were understood. A *decerebrate* cat, whose brain stem has been cut through, exhibits a phenomenon known as *decerebrate rigidity.* The animal's back is arched, and its legs are extended stiffly from its body. This rigidity results from excitation originating in the caudal reticular formation, which greatly facilitates all stretch reflexes, especially of extensor muscles, by increasing the activity of the gamma motor system. Rostral to the brain stem transection is an inhibitory region of the reticular formation, which normally counterbalances the excitatory one. The transection removes the inhibitory influence, leaving only the excitatory one. If you attempt to flex the outstretched leg of a decerebrate cat, you will meet with increasing resistance, which suddenly melts away, allowing the limb to flex. It almost feels as though you were closing the blade of a pocketknife — hence the term *clasp-knife reflex.* The sudden release is, of course, mediated by activation of the Golgi tendon organ reflex.

Even the monosynaptic stretch reflex serves as the basis of polysynaptic reflexes. Muscles are arranged in opposing pairs. The *agonist* moves the limb in the direction being studied, and, because muscles cannot push back, the *antagonist* muscle must move the limb back in the opposite direction. Consider this finding: When a stretch reflex is elicited in the agonist, it contracts quickly, thus causing the antagonist to lengthen. It would appear, then, that the antagonist is presented with a stimulus that should elicit *its* stretch reflex. And yet the antagonist relaxes instead. Let us see why.

Afferent axons of the muscle spindles, besides sending terminal buttons to the alpha motor neuron and to the brain, also synapse on inhibitory interneurons. The terminal buttons of these interneurons synapse on the alpha motor neurons that innervate the antagonistic muscle. (See **Figure 8.11.**) Thus, a stretch reflex excites the agonist and *inhibits the antagonist,* so that the limb can move in the direction controlled by the stimulated muscle.

INTERIM SUMMARY

Reflexes are simple circuits of sensory neurons, interneurons (usually), and efferent neurons that control simple responses to particular stimuli. In the monosynaptic stretch reflex, the terminal buttons of axons that receive sensory information from the intrafusal muscle fibers synapse with alpha motor neurons that innervate the same muscle. Thus, a sudden lengthening of the muscle causes the muscle to contract. By setting the length of the intrafusal muscle fibers, and hence their sensitivity to increases in muscle length, the motor system of the brain can control limb position. Changes in weight that cause the limb to move will be quickly compensated for by means of the monosynaptic stretch reflex.

Polysynaptic reflexes contain at least one interneuron between the sensory neuron and the motor neuron. For example, when a strong muscular contraction threatens to damage muscles or limbs, the increased rate of firing of the afferent axons of Golgi tendon organs stimulates inhibitory interneurons, which inhibit the alpha motor neurons of those muscles. And when the afferent axons of intrafusal muscle fibers fire, they excite inhibitory interneurons that slow the rate of firing of the alpha motor neurons that serve the antagonistic muscles, which causes the antagonist to relax, permitting the agonist to contract.

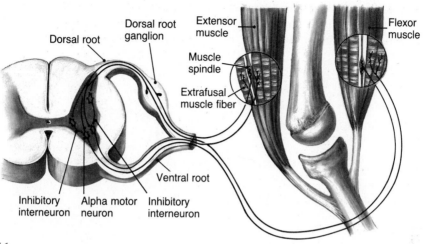

FIGURE 8.11
Firing of the muscle spindle causes excitation on the alpha motor neuron
of the agonist and inhibition on the antagonist.

■ CONTROL OF MOVEMENT BY THE BRAIN

Movements can be initiated by several means. For example, rapid stretch of a muscle triggers the monosynaptic stretch reflex, a stumble triggers righting reflexes, and the rapid approach of an object toward the face causes a startle response, a complex reflex consisting of movements of several muscle groups. Other stimuli initiate sequences of movements that we have previously learned. For example, the presence of food causes eating, and the sight of a loved one evokes a hug and a kiss. Because there is no single cause of behavior, we cannot find a single starting point in our search for the neural mechanisms that control movement.

The brain and spinal cord include several different motor systems, each of which can simultaneously control particular kinds of movements. For example, a person can walk and talk with a friend simultaneously. While doing so, he or she can make gestures with the hands to emphasize a point, scratch an itch, brush away a fly, wipe sweat off his or her forehead, and so on. Walking, postural adjustments, talking, movement of the arms, and movements of the fingers all involve different specialized motor systems.

Organization of Motor Cortex

The primary motor cortex lies on the precentral gyrus, just rostral to the central sulcus. Stimulation studies (including those in awake humans) have shown that the activity of particular parts of the primary motor cortex causes movements of particular parts of the body. Figure 8.12 shows a *motor homunculus* based on the observations of Penfield and Rasmussen (1950). Note that a disproportionate amount of cortical area is devoted to movements of the fingers and muscles used for speech. (See **Figure 8.12.**)

The principal cortical input to the primary motor cortex is the frontal association cortex, located rostral to it. Lesion studies (some of which I will describe later in this chapter) indicate that the planning of most complex behaviors takes place here. These plans are executed by the primary motor cortex, which directly controls particular movements. In turn, the frontal association cortex receives axons from association areas of the occipital, temporal, and parietal cortex. As we saw, the

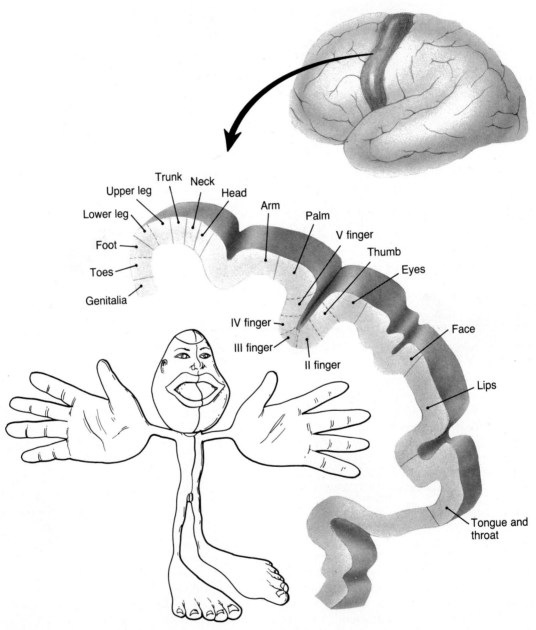

FIGURE 8.12

A motor homunculus. Stimulation of various regions of the primary motor cortex causes movement in muscles of various parts of the body.

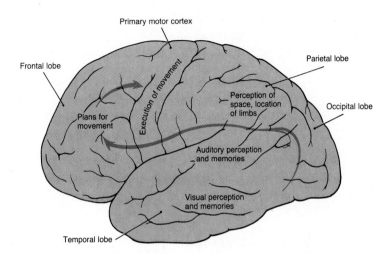

FIGURE 8.13

The posterior association cortex is involved with perceptions and memories, and the frontal association cortex is involved with plans for movement.

occipital and temporal lobes contain the visual association cortex, and the temporal lobe also contains the auditory association cortex. And as we will see later, the association cortex of the parietal lobes is responsible for a person's perception of space. Thus, the frontal association cortex receives information about the environment (including memories previously acquired by means of vision, audition, and somatosensation) from the posterior lobes and uses this information to plan movements. Because the parietal lobes contain spatial information, the pathway from them to the frontal lobes is especially important in controlling both locomotion and arm and hand movements. After all, meaningful locomotion requires us to know where we are, and meaningful movements of our arms and hands require us to know where objects are located in space. (See **Figure 8.13.**)

The primary motor cortex also receives projections from the adjacent primary somatosensory cortex, located just across the central sulcus. The connections between these two areas are quite specific: neurons in the primary somatosensory cortex that respond to stimuli applied to a particular part of the body send axons to neurons in the primary motor cortex that move muscles in the same part of the body. For example, Asanuma and Rosén

(1972) and Rosén and Asanuma (1972) found that somatosensory neurons that respond to a touch on the back of the thumb send axons to motor neurons that cause thumb extension, and somatosensory neurons that respond to a touch on the ball of the thumb send axons to motor neurons that cause thumb flexion. (See **Figure 8.14.**) This organization appears to provide rapid feedback to the motor system during manipulation of objects.

Evidence that supports this suggestion was obtained by Evarts (1974), who recorded the activity of single neurons in the precentral gyrus of monkeys. He trained his subjects to move a lever back and forth by means of wrist flexions and extensions. When the monkeys made the movements in the correct amount of time, they received a squirt of grape juice, a drink they appeared to enjoy. Figure 8.15 shows the experimental preparation as well as the relationship between lever movement and the firing of a cortical neuron. Note that the firing of this neuron is nicely related to the movement, with the rate increasing during flexion. (See **Figure 8.15.**) Evarts trained monkeys to produce a hand movement in response to a flash of a light or to a tactile stimulus delivered through the handle. He found that neurons in the motor cortex began firing

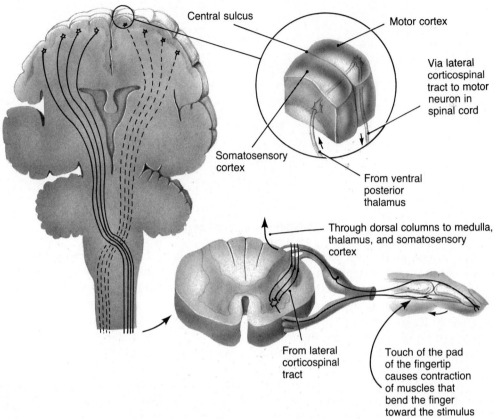

FIGURE 8.14
Connections between the primary somatosensory cortex and the primary
motor cortex are important for control of the fingers in grasping and
manipulating objects.

100 msec after a visual stimulus but responded as soon as 25 msec after a tactile
stimulus. These results confirm the conclusion that hand and finger movements are controlled by somatosensory feedback received
by neurons in the postcentral gyrus.

Cortical Control of Movement

Neurons in the primary motor cortex control
movements by four different pathways. They
directly control the corticospinal and corticobulbar pathways and indirectly control two
sets of pathways that originate in the brain

stem, which will be described later in this
section.

The ***corticospinal pathway*** consists of
axons of cortical neurons that terminate in the
gray matter of the spinal cord. The largest
concentration of cell bodies of these neurons
is located in the primary motor cortex, but the
parietal and temporal lobes also send fibers
through the corticospinal pathway. The
axons leave the cortex and travel through
subcortical white matter to the ventral midbrain, where they enter the cerebral peduncles. They leave the peduncles in the medulla
and join the ***pyramidal tracts,*** so-called be-

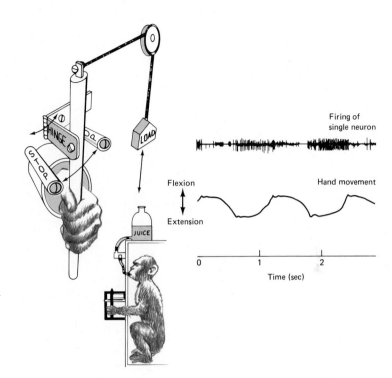

FIGURE 8.15
The relation between firing of single neurons in the motor cortex and hand movements. The single-unit records are redrawn from the original data and are therefore only approximate representations. (Redrawn from Evarts, E.V. *Journal of Neurophysiology,* 1968, *31,* 14–27.)

cause of their shape. At the level of the caudal medulla, most of the fibers decussate and descend through the contralateral spinal cord, forming the ***lateral corticospinal tract.*** The rest of the fibers descend through the ipsilateral spinal cord, forming the ***ventral corticospinal tract.*** (See black portion of **Figure 8.16.**)

The axons in the lateral corticospinal tract originate in the arm and hand region of the primary motor cortex. Most of them synapse directly on motor neurons in the dorsolateral part of the ventral horn. These motor neurons control the distal limb muscles, such as those that control the arms, hands, and fingers. Other axons synapse on interneurons located in the lateral intermediate zone of the spinal cord gray matter. These interneurons themselves send axons to the dorsolateral ventral horn. Thus, both projection regions control the extremities. Animals such as humans and

apes, who have excellent control of the hands and fingers, have a larger proportion of corticospinal neurons that form synapses directly with motor neurons, and not through interneurons. (See **Figure 8.16.**)

The axons in the ventral corticospinal tract originate in the trunk region of the primary motor cortex. They descend to the appropriate region of the spinal cord and divide, sending terminal buttons into both sides of the gray matter. They terminate on motor neurons in the ventromedial part of the ventral horn or on interneurons in the medial intermediate zone, which themselves terminate in the ventromedial zone. (See **Figure 8.16.**)

Lawrence and Kuypers (1968a) cut both pyramidal tracts in monkeys in order to assess their motor functions. Within six to ten hours after recovery from the anesthesia, the animals were able to sit upright, but their arms hung loosely from their shoulders. Within a day they could stand, hold the cage bars with their hands, and even climb a little. By six weeks the monkeys could walk and climb rapidly. Thus, posture and locomotion were not disturbed. However, the animals' manual dexterity was poor. They could reach for objects and grasp them, but they used their fingers together as if they were wearing mit-

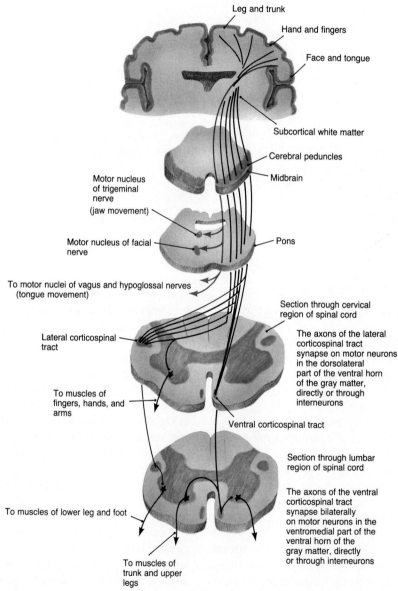

FIGURE 8.16

The corticospinal pathways (black) and corticobulbar pathway (color).

tens; they could not manipulate their fingers independently to pick up small pieces of food. And once they had grasped food with their hand, they had difficulty releasing their grip. They usually had to use their mouth to pry their hand open. In contrast, they had no difficulty releasing their grip when they were climbing the bars of their cage.

The results confirm what we would predict from the anatomical connections: The corticospinal pathway controls hand and finger movements and is indispensable for moving the fingers independently when reaching and manipulating. Postural adjustments of the trunk and use of the limbs for reaching and locomotion are unaffected; therefore, these types of movements are controlled by other systems. Because the monkeys had difficulty releasing their grasp when they picked up objects but did not have trouble doing so when climbing the walls of the cage, we may conclude that the same behavior (opening the hand) is controlled by different brain mechanisms in different contexts.

The *corticobulbar pathway* is similar to the corticospinal pathway, except that it terminates in the motor nuclei of the fifth, seventh, tenth, and twelfth cranial nerves (the trigeminal, facial, vagus, and hypoglossal nerves). (In this context, *bulb* refers to the medulla.) These nerves control movements of the face and tongue. (See colored portion of **Figure 8.16.**) Most of the terminations of the corticobulbar pathway are bilateral, sending axons to cranial nerve nuclei on both sides of the brain. However, the axons that control the muscles of the lower face are almost entirely contralateral. Thus, damage to the face region of the motor cortex on one side of the brain causes drooping of the contralateral lower face. Because the muscles of the contralateral upper face still receive inputs from the undamaged ipsilateral motor cortex, their movements remain relatively normal.

Two sets of pathways originate in the brain stem and terminate in the spinal cord gray matter: the ventromedial and dorsolateral pathways. Through indirect connections, the primary motor cortex can affect the activity of both sets of pathways. The first set, the ***ventromedial pathways***, includes the ***vestibulospinal tracts***, the ***tectospinal tracts***, and the ***reticulospinal tracts***. Neurons of all three of these tracts terminate on interneurons in the medial intermediate zone of the gray matter. Thus they primarily control movements of the trunk and proximal limb muscles. The cell bodies of neurons of the vestibulospinal tracts are located in the vestibular nuclei. As you might expect, this system plays a role in the control of posture. The cell bodies of neurons in the tectospinal tracts are located in the superior colliculus and are involved in coordinating head and trunk movements with eye movements. The cell bodies of neurons of the reticulospinal tracts are located in many nuclei in the brain stem and midbrain reticular formation. These neurons control several automatic functions, such as muscle tonus, respiration, coughing, and sneezing, but they are also involved in behaviors under direct neocortical control, such as walking. The most important components of the reticulospinal tracts are the lateral and medial tracts, which originate in the medullary and pontine reticular formation, respectively. Neurons of the lateral tracts facilitate flexor muscles, and those of the medial tracts facilitate extensor muscles. (See **Figure 8.17.**)

You will recall that the axons of the ventral corticospinal tract terminate in the medial intermediate zone of the spinal cord, on interneurons that synapse on motor neurons serving the trunk muscles. In their first study, Lawrence and Kuypers (1968a) found no deficits in postural movements after bilateral destruction of the pyramidal tracts, which cuts the axons of both the lateral and ventral corticospinal tracts. Presumably, the intact ventromedial pathways could compensate for the loss of the pyramidal control of the trunk muscles. The second study confirmed this speculation. Lawrence and Kuypers (1968b) cut the ventromedial fibers of some of the animals that had previously received bilateral pyramidal tract lesions. These animals

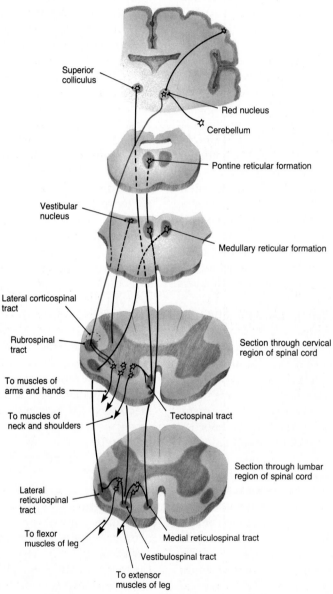

Superior colliculus

Red nucleus

Cerebellum

Pontine reticular formation

Vestibular nucleus

Medullary reticular formation

Lateral corticospinal tract

Section through cervical region of spinal cord

Rubrospinal tract

To muscles of arms and hands

To muscles of neck and shoulders

Tectospinal tract

Section through lumbar region of spinal cord

Lateral reticulospinal tract

To flexor muscles of leg

Medial reticulospinal tract

Vestibulospinal tract

To extensor muscles of leg

FIGURE 8.17

The ventromedial pathways (black) and the dorsolateral pathway (color).

showed severe impairments in posture. In fact, they could not sit upright until ten to forty days had elapsed after the second operation. They could eventually stand with great difficulty but could not take more than a few steps without falling. When they reached for food, their upper arms hung at their sides. They showed good control of elbow and wrist movements, but their finger movements were clumsy. Thus, we can conclude that the ventromedial pathways control the muscles of the trunk and proximal limbs, with supplementary control of the trunk muscles coming from the ventral corticospinal tract.

The second major pathway from the brain stem to the spinal cord gray matter is the ***dorsolateral pathway.*** The primary constituents of this pathway are the ***rubrospinal tracts,*** whose cell bodies are located in the red nucleus *(nucleus ruber)* of the midbrain. The red nucleus receives its most important inputs from the motor cortex and cerebellum. Axons of the rubrospinal tracts terminate on interneurons in the lateral intermediate zone of the spinal cord; these interneurons, in turn, synapse with motor neurons that control forelimb and hindlimb muscles (but not muscles that move the fingers). (See **Figure 8.17.**)

Lawrence and Kuypers (1968b) destroyed the rubrospinal tract *unilaterally* in some of the animals that had previously received bilateral lesions of the pyramidal tract. The rubrospinal tract lesion severely affected the animals' use of the ipsilateral arm. The arm tended to hang straight from the shoulder, with hand and fingers extended. If they could reach food only with the affected arm, they made a raking movement with the arm as a whole, bending their elbow and wrist as the food approached their mouth. The arm movement was accompanied by movements of the trunk. The monkeys did not hold the food with their hand, even with the "mittenlike" grasp that is produced by pyramidal tract le-

sions. The animals managed to hold onto cage bars with their affected hand, but the grip was weaker.

Lawrence and Kuypers concluded that the rubrospinal system controls independent movements of the forearms and hands — that is, movements that are independent of trunk movements. This control overlaps with that of the pyramidal system but does not include independent movements of the fingers. The finding that movements of the affected limb were clumsy and were accompanied by trunk movements suggests that the ventromedial system exerts limited control over distal limb muscles as well as proximal limb and trunk muscles. Presumably, postural movements initiated by the ventromedial system include movements of the arms.

Table 8.1 summarizes the names of these pathways, their locations, and the muscle groups they control. (See **Table 8.1.**)

Deficits of Verbally Controlled Movements: The Apraxias

Damage to the corpus callosum, frontal lobe, or parietal lobe of the human brain produces a category of deficits called ***apraxia.*** Literally, the term means "without action," but apraxia is different from paralysis or weakness that occurs when motor structures such as the precentral gyrus, basal ganglia, brain stem, or spinal cord are damaged. Apraxia is the "inability to properly execute a learned skilled movement" (Heilman, Rothi, and Kertesz, 1983, p. 381). Neuropsychological studies of the apraxias have provided information about the way in which skilled behaviors are organized and initiated.

There are four major types of apraxia, two of which I will discuss in this chapter. *Limb apraxia* refers to problems with movements of the arms, hands, and fingers. *Oral apraxia* refers to problems with movements of the muscles used in speech. *Apraxic agraphia*

T A B L E 8.1   Major motor pathways

	Origin	*Termination*	*Muscle Groups*
Corticospinal Pathways			
Lateral corticospinal tract	Finger, hand, and arm region of motor cortex	Spinal cord, ventral horn	Fingers, hands, and arms
Ventral corticospinal tract	Trunk and upper leg region of motor cortex	Spinal cord, ventral horn	Trunk and upper legs
Corticobulbar Pathway	Face region of motor cortex	Cranial nerve nuclei: V, VII, X, and XII	Face and tongue
Ventromedial Pathways			
Vestibulospinal tract	Vestibular nuclei	Spinal cord, ventral horn	Trunk and legs
Tectospinal tract	Superior colliculi	Spinal cord, ventral horn	Neck and trunk
Lateral reticulospinal tract	Medullary reticular formation	Spinal cord, ventral horn	Flexor muscles of legs
Medial reticulospinal tract	Pontine reticular formation	Spinal cord, ventral horn	Extensor muscles of legs
Dorsolateral Pathway			
Rubrospinal tract	Red nucleus	Spinal cord, ventral horn	Hands (not fingers), lower arms, feet, and lower legs

refers to a particular type of writing deficit. *Constructional apraxia* refers to difficulty in drawing or constructing objects. Because of their relation to language, I will describe oral apraxia and the agraphias in Chapter 16.

Limb Apraxia

Limb apraxia is characterized by movement of the wrong part of the limb, incorrect movement of the correct part, or correct movements but in the incorrect sequence. It is assessed by asking patients to perform movements. The most difficult ones involve pantomiming particular acts. For example, the examiner may ask the patient to "Pretend you have a key in your hand and open a door with it." In response, a patient with limb apraxia may wave his wrist back and forth rather than rotate it, or rotate his wrist first and then pretend to insert the key. Or, if asked to pretend

she is brushing her teeth, a patient may use her finger as if it were a toothbrush, rather than pretend to hold a toothbrush in her hand.

Performing behaviors on verbal command without having a real object to manipulate requires comprehension of the command and the ability to imagine the missing article as well as to make the proper movements; therefore, these requests are the most difficult to carry out. Somewhat easier are tasks that involve imitating behaviors performed by the experimenter. Sometimes a patient who cannot mime the use of a key can copy the examiner's hand movements. The easiest tasks involve the actual use of objects. For example, the examiner may give the patient a door key and ask him or her to demonstrate its use. If the brain lesion makes it impossible for the patient to understand speech, then the examiner cannot assess the ability to perform behaviors upon verbal command. In this case, the examiner can only measure the patient's ability to imitate movements or use actual objects. (See Heilman, Rothi, and Kertesz, 1983, for a review.)

Limb apraxia can be caused by three types of lesions. ***Callosal apraxia*** is apraxia of the left limb that is caused by damage to the anterior corpus callosum. The explanation for the deficit is the following: When a person hears a verbal request to perform a movement, the meaning of the speech is analyzed by circuits in the posterior left hemisphere (in *Wernicke's area,* discussed in Chapter 16). A neural command to make the movement is conveyed through long transcortical axons to the prefrontal area. There, the command activates neural circuits that contain the memory of the movements that constitute the behavior. This information is transmitted through the corpus callosum to the right prefrontal cortex, and from there to the right precentral gyrus. Neurons in this area control the individual movements. Damage to the anterior corpus callosum prevents communication between the left and right premotor areas, regions of the motor association cortex just rostral to the precentral gyrus. Thus, the right arm can perform the requested movement, but the left arm cannot. (See lesion A in **Figure 8.18.**)

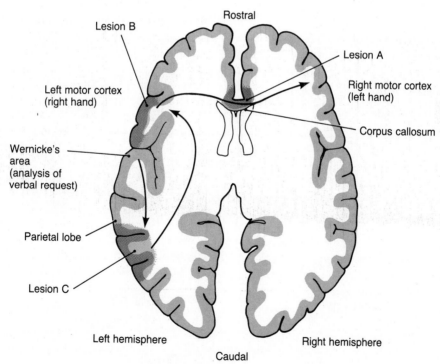

FIGURE 8.18

Lesion A causes callosal apraxia of the left limb, lesion B causes sympathetic apraxia of the right limb, and lesion C causes left parietal apraxia of both limbs.

310 CHAPTER 8/CONTROL OF MOVEMENT

A similar form of limb apraxia is caused by damage to the anterior left hemisphere, sometimes called *sympathetic apraxia.* Damage to the left premotor and motor cortex causes a primary motor impairment of the right arm and hand: full or partial paralysis. Like anterior callosal lesions, the damage also causes apraxia of the left arm. The term *sympathetic* was originally adopted because the clumsiness of the left hand looks as if the hand "sympathizes" with the paralyzed right one. (See lesion B in **Figure 8.18.**)

The third form of limb apraxia is *left parietal apraxia,* caused by lesions of the posterior left hemisphere. These lesions involve both limbs. The posterior parietal lobe contains areas of association cortex that receive information from the surrounding sensory association cortex of the occipital, temporal, and anterior parietal lobes. (See lesion C in **Figure 8.18.**)

Based on the effects of parietal lobe lesions in humans and monkeys, Mountcastle, Lynch, Georgopoulos, Sakata, and Acuna (1975) suggest that this region contains a sensory representation of the surrounding environment

and keeps track of the location of objects in the environment and the location of the organism's body parts in relation to them. Because the right parietal lobe is especially important for perception of three-dimensional space, information about location of objects external to the person is probably supplied from this region. According to Mountcastle and his colleagues, the left parietal region serves as a "command apparatus for the operation of the limbs, hands, and eyes within immediate extrapersonal space." For example, when a person hears a command to reach for a particular object, the meaning of the request is decoded by the left auditory association cortex and is passed on to the left parietal association cortex. Using information received from the right parietal association cortex about the spatial location of the pencil, neural circuits in the left parietal association cortex assess the relative location of the person's hand and the object and send information about the starting and ending coordinates to the left premotor cortex. There, the sequence of muscular contractions necessary to perform the movement is organized, and this sequence is

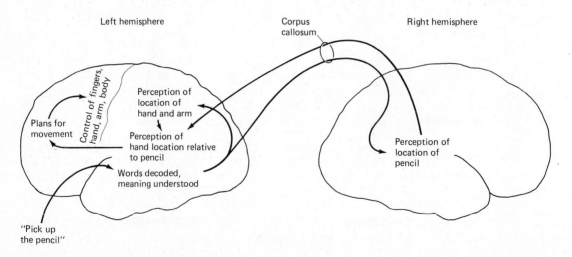

FIGURE 8.19
The "command apparatus" of the left parietal lobe.

executed through the primary motor cortex and its connections with the spinal cord and subcortical motor systems. (See **Figure 8.19.**)

Constructional Apraxia

Constructional apraxia is caused by lesions of the right hemisphere, particularly the right parietal lobe. People with this disorder do not have difficulty making most types of skilled movements with their arms and hands. They have no trouble using objects properly, imitating their use, or pretending to use them. However, they have trouble drawing pictures or assembling objects from elements such as toy building blocks.

The primary deficit in constructional apraxia appears to involve the ability to perceive and imagine geometrical relations. Because of this deficit, a person cannot draw a picture, say, of a cube, because he or she cannot imagine what the lines and angles of a cube look like, not because of difficulty controlling the movements of his or her arm and hand. (See **Figure 8.20.**) Besides being unable to draw accurately, a person with constructional apraxia invariably has trouble with other tasks involving spatial perception, such as following a map.

The Basal Ganglia

The basal ganglia constitute an important component of the motor system. We know they are important because their destruction by disease or injury causes severe motor deficits. The motor nuclei of the basal ganglia include the caudate nucleus, putamen, and globus pallidus. The basal ganglia receive inputs from the neocortex and cerebellum. They also communicate with the ventrolateral, ventral anterior, and midline nuclei of the thalamus, the subthalamic nucleus (located beneath the thalamus), the red nucleus, the substantia nigra, and parts of the brain

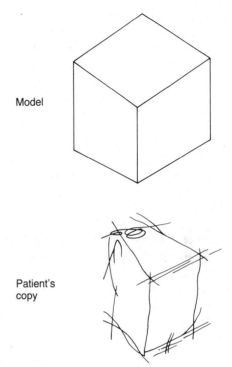

FIGURE 8.20

Attempt to copy a cube by a patient with constructional apraxia caused by a lesion of the right parietal lobe. (From *Fundamentals of Human Neuropsychology,* by B. Kolb and I.Q. Whishaw. W.H. Freeman and Company. Copyright © 1980.)

stem reticular formation. Through these connections they influence the activity of the corticospinal, rubrospinal, and ventromedial systems. (See **Figure 8.21.**)

We already saw in Chapter 3 that degeneration of the nigrostriatal bundle, the dopaminergic pathway from the substantia nigra of the midbrain to the caudate nucleus and putamen (the *neostriatum*) causes Parkinson's disease. The primary disorder is slowness of movement and difficulty in stopping one behavior and starting another. These deficits are seen in all muscle groups — those controlling fingers, hands, arms, and trunk. For example, once a person with Parkinson's disease is

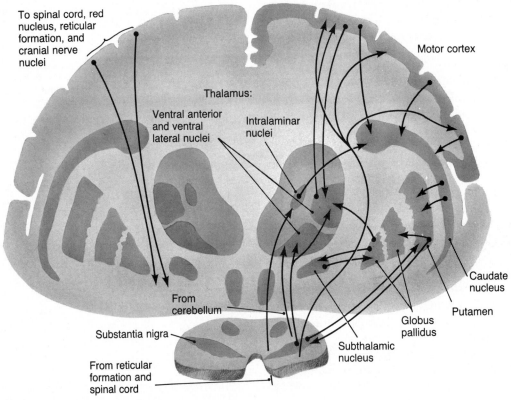

To spinal cord, red
nucleus, reticular
formation, and
cranial nerve
nuclei

Motor cortex

Thalamus:

Ventral anterior
and ventral
lateral nuclei

Intralaminar
nuclei

From
cerebellum

Caudate
nucleus

Putamen

Globus
pallidus

Substantia nigra

Subthalamic
nucleus

From reticular
formation and
spinal cord

FIGURE 8.21
Some important interconnections of the basal ganglia.

seated, he or she finds it difficult to arise. Once the person begins walking, he or she has difficulty stopping. Thus, a person with Parkinson's disease cannot easily pace back and forth across a room. Reaching for an object can be accurate, but the movement usually begins only after a considerable delay. Writing is slow and labored, and as it progresses the letters get smaller and smaller. Postural movements are impaired. If someone bumps into a normal person who is standing, he or she will quickly move to restore balance — for example, by taking a step in the direction of the impending fall or by reaching out with the arms to grasp onto a piece of furniture. However, a person with Parkinson's disease

fails to do so and simply falls. A person with this disorder is even unlikely to put out his or her arms to break the fall.

Parkinson's disease also produces a resting tremor — vibratory movements of the arms and hands that diminish somewhat when the individual makes purposeful movements. The tremor is accompanied by rigidity; the joints appear stiff. However, the tremor and rigidity are not the cause of the slow movements. Although the slowness appears to be caused by degeneration of the nigrostriatal bundle, the rigidity and tremor probably occur because of damage to neurons in other pathways. Indeed, experimental studies with laboratory animals have found that damage to the substantia nigra produces hypoactivity but not tremors. The tremors probably originate in a feedback circuit consisting of a loop of neurons from the ventral thalamus to the motor cortex and back again. Neurons in the ventral thalamus fire in synchrony with the vibratory movements of the tremor, and stereotaxic lesions of this area can eliminate or reduce the tremor and rigidity (Dray, 1980). However, the lesions do not affect the slowness of movement.

Another basal ganglia disease, *Huntington's chorea,* is caused by degeneration of the caudate nucleus and putamen, especially of GABAergic and acetylcholinergic neurons. Whereas Parkinson's disease causes a poverty of movements, Huntington's chorea causes uncontrollable ones, especially jerky limb movements. (*Chorea* derives from the Greek *khoros,* meaning "dance.") The movements of Huntington's chorea look like fragments of purposeful movements but occur involuntarily. The disease is progressive and eventually causes death.

A complete description of these two syndromes is much more complicated than my brief outline, but we can easily see that the basal ganglia can either inhibit or facilitate movements. Mainly on the basis of clinical observations of patients with motor disorders, Kornhuber (1974) suggests that the basal ganglia may play a special role in the control of slow, smooth movements. DeLong (1974) obtained some electrophysiological evidence that supports Kornhuber's hypothesis. He found that a majority of the neurons in the putamen fire before and during slow movements but not before and during rapid ones.

Damage to the caudate nucleus or putamen generally causes symptoms of *release;* the patients exhibit rigidity (excessive muscular contraction) or uncontrollable movements of the limbs or facial muscles. Damage to the globus pallidus or ventral thalamus generally cause symptoms of *deficiency,* such as *akinesia* (lack of movement) or mutism (failure to talk). Thus, the caudate nucleus and putamen appear to be inhibitory in function, and the globus pallidus and ventral thalamus appear to be excitatory. In Parkinson's disease, the slowness of movement probably occurs because degeneration of the nigrostriatal bundle disrupts an inhibitory input to the caudate nucleus (you will recall that dopamine is an inhibitory transmitter substance). Loss of inhibition increases the inhibitory function of the caudate nucleus, and movements become slower.

Besides having general excitatory and inhibitory functions, the basal ganglia appear to control specific behaviors, some of which will be discussed in later chapters. For example, as we will see in Chapter 13, portions of the basal ganglia may be critical in the performance of some classes of learned responses.

The Cerebellum

The cerebellum is an important part of the motor system. It receives inputs from the sensory systems and from the primary motor cortex. Its outputs influence the activity of the primary motor cortex, red nucleus, vestibular nuclei, and reticular formation.

The cerebellum consists of two hemispheres that contain several deep nuclei situated beneath the wrinkled and folded cerebellar cortex. Thus, the cerebellum resembles the cerebrum in miniature. The *flocculonodular lobe,* located at the caudal end of the cerebellum, receives input from the vestibular system and projects axons to the vestibular nucleus. You will not be surprised to learn that this system is involved in postural reflexes. The *vermis* ("worm"), located on the midline, receives cutaneous and kinesthetic information from the spinal cord and sends its outputs to the *fastigial nucleus* (one of the set of deep cerebellar nuclei). Neurons in the fastigial nucleus send axons to the vestibular nucleus and to motor nuclei in the reticular formation. Thus, they influence behavior through the vestibulospinal and reticulospinal tracts, two of the three ventromedial pathways. The rest of the cerebellar cortex receives inputs (relayed through nuclei in the pons) from the cerebral cortex, including the primary motor cortex and all regions of association cortex. The intermediate zone of the cerebellar cortex projects to the *interpositus nucleus,* which in turn projects to the red nucleus. The lateral zone projects to the *dentate nucleus,* which sends axons to the red nucleus and to the ventrolateral thalamus, the primary source of subcorti-

cal projections to the primary motor cortex. Figure 8.22 shows the major areas of the cerebellum, and Figure 8.23 shows the major connections of the cerebellum with other components of the motor system. (See **Figures 8.22 and 8.23.**)

In humans, lesions of different regions of the cerebellum produce different symptoms. Damage to the flocculonodular lobe or vermis causes disturbances in posture and balance. Damage to the intermediate zone produces deficits in movements controlled by the rubrospinal system. The principal symptom is limb rigidity. Damage to the lateral zone causes weakness and *decomposition of movement.* For example, if a person attempts to bring the hand to the mouth, he or

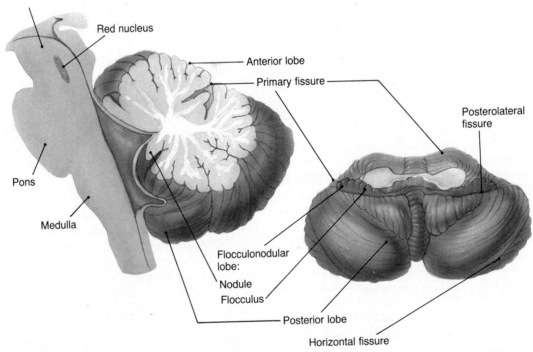

FIGURE 8.22
The cerebellar cortex. (Adapted with permission from McGraw-Hill Book Co. from *The Human Nervous System,* 2nd edition, by Noback and Demarest. Copyright 1975 by McGraw-Hill, Inc.)

she will make separate movements of the joints of the shoulder, elbow, and wrist instead of performing simultaneous smooth movements.

Lesions of the lateral zone of the cerebellar cortex also appear to impair the timing of rapid *ballistic* movements. Ballistic (literally, "throwing") movements occur too fast

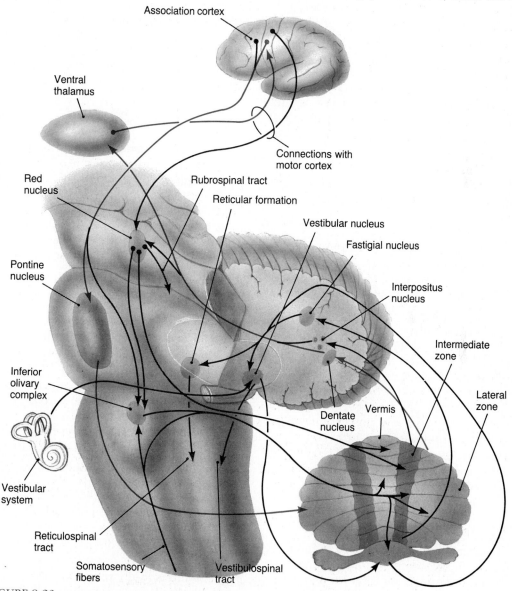

FIGURE 8.23

Connections between the cerebellum and other components of the motor system. The pathway shaded in color is particularly important in the control of rapid, skilled arm and hand movements.

to be modified by feedback. The sequence of muscular movements must then be programmed in advance, and the individual muscles must be activated at the proper times. You might like to try this common neurological test. Have a friend place his or her finger in front of your face, about three quarters of an arm's length away. While your friend slowly moves his or her finger around to serve as a moving target, alternately touch your nose and your friend's finger as rapidly as you can. If your cerebellum is normal, you can successfully hit your nose and your friend's finger without too much trouble. People with lateral cerebellar damage have great difficulty; they tend to miss the examiner's hand and poke themselves in the eye. (I have often wondered why neurologists do not adopt a less traumatic test.)

When we make rapid, aimed movements, we cannot rely on feedback to stop the movement when we reach the target. By the time we perceive that our finger has reached the proper place, it is too late to stop the movement, and we will overshoot the target if we try to stop it then. Instead of relying on feedback, the movement appears to be timed. We estimate the distance between our hand and the target, and our cerebellum calculates the amount of time that the muscles will have to be turned on. After the proper amount of time, the cerebellum briefly turns on antagonistic muscles to stop the movement. In fact, Kornhuber (1974) suggests that one of the primary functions of the cerebellum is timing the duration of rapid movements. Obviously, learning must play a role in controlling such movements.

The cerebellum also appears to integrate successive *sequences* of movements that must be performed one after the other. For example, Holmes (1939) reported that one of his patients said, "The movements of my left arm are done subconsciously, but I have to think out each movement of the right [affected] arm. I come to a dead stop in turning

and have to think before I start again." Thach (1978) obtained experimental evidence that corroborates this role. He found that many neurons in the dentate nuclei (which receive inputs from the lateral zone of the cerebellar cortex) showed response patterns that predicted the *next* movement in a sequence rather than the one that was currently taking place. Presumably, the cerebellum was planning these movements.

The Reticular Formation

The reticular formation consists of a large number of nuclei located in the core of the medulla, pons, and midbrain. The reticular formation controls the activity of the gamma motor system and hence regulates muscle tonus. In addition, the pons and medulla contain several nuclei with specific motor functions. For example, different locations in the medulla control automatic or semiautomatic responses such as respiration, sneezing, coughing, and vomiting. As we saw, the ventromedial pathways originate in the superior colliculi, vestibular nuclei, and reticular formation. Thus, the reticular formation plays a role in the control of posture.

The reticular formation also plays a role in locomotion. Stimulation of the **mesencephalic locomotor region,** located ventral to the inferior colliculus, causes even a decerebrate cat to make pacing movements (Shik and Orlovsky, 1976). The mesencephalic locomotor region does not send fibers directly to the spinal cord but apparently controls the activity of reticulospinal tract neurons.

Other motor functions of the reticular formation are also being discovered. Siegel and McGinty (1977) recorded from thirty-five single neurons in the reticular formation of unanesthetized, freely moving cats. Thirty-two of these neurons responded during *specific* movements of the head, tongue, facial muscles, ears, forepaw, or shoulder. The specific nature of the relations suggests that the neurons play some role in controlling the movements. For example, one neuron responded when the tongue moved out and to the left. The function of these neurons and the range of movements they control are not yet known.

INTERIM SUMMARY

The motor systems of the brain are complex. (Having read this section, you do not need me to tell you that.) A good way to review the systems is through an example. While following my description, you might want to look at Table 8.1 and Figures 8.16 and 8.17 again. Suppose you see, out of the corner of your eye, that something is moving. You quickly turn your head and eyes toward the source of the movement and discover that a vase of flowers on a table someone has just bumped is ready to fall. You quickly reach forward, grab it, and restore it to a stable upright position. (For simplicity's sake I will assume that you are right-handed.)

The rapid movement of your head and eyes is controlled by mechanisms that involve the superior colliculi and nearby nuclei. The head movement and corresponding movement of the trunk are mediated by the tectospinal tract. You perceive the tipping vase because of the activity of neurons in your visual association cortex. Your visual association cortex also contributes information about depth to your right parietal lobe, whose association cortex determines the exact spatial location of the vase. Your left parietal lobe uses the spatial information, together with its own record of the location of your hand, to compute the path your hand must travel to intercept the vase. The information is relayed to your left frontal lobe, where the motor association cortex starts the movement. Because the movement will have to be a ballistic one, the cerebellum controls its timing, based on information it receives from the association cortex of the frontal and parietal lobes. Your hand stops just as it touches the vase, and connections between the somatosensory cortex and the primary motor cortex initiate a reflex that closes your hand around the vase.

The movement of your hand is controlled through a cooperation between the corticospinal, dorsolateral, and ventromedial pathways. Even before your hand moves, the ventral corticospinal tract and the ventromedial pathways (vestibulospinal and reticulospinal system, largely under the influence of the basal ganglia) begin adjusting your posture so that you will not fall forward when you suddenly reach in front of you. Depending on how far forward you will have to reach, the reticulospinal tract may even cause one leg to step forward in order to take your weight. The dorsolateral pathway (rubrospinal tract) controls the muscles of your upper arm, and the lateral corticospinal tract controls your finger and hand movements. Perhaps you say, triumphantly, "I got it!" The corticobulbar pathway, under the control of speech mechanisms in the left hemisphere, cause the muscles of your vocal apparatus to say these words.

A person with apraxia will have difficulty making controlled movements of the limb in response to a verbal request. Most cases of apraxia are produced by lesions of the left parietal lobe, which sends information about the requested movement to the left frontal association cortex. This region directly controls movement of the right limb by activating neurons in the left primary motor cortex and indirectly controls movement of the left limb by sending information to the right frontal association cortex. Damage to the left frontal association cortex or its connections with the right hemisphere also produce apraxia.

Concluding Remarks

We have studied the basic physiology and pharmacology of cells of the nervous system, neuroanatomy, research methods, the physiology of sensation and perception, and the control of movements. Now, in the remainder of the book, we can concern ourselves with particular classes of behaviors: sleep cycles, sexual behavior, ingestive behavior, aggressive behavior, the acquisition of learned behaviors, communicative behaviors, and the abnormal behaviors that constitute mental disorders.

NEW TERMS

actin p. 289

agonist p. 298

akinesia p. 313

alpha motor neuron p. 288

antagonist p. 298

apraxia p. 307

callosal apraxia p. 309

cardiac muscle p. 293

chorea p. 313

clasp-knife reflex p. 298

constructional apraxia p. 311

convergence p. 297

corticobulbar pathway p. 305

corticospinal pathway p. 302

decerebrate p. 298

decerebrate rigidity p. 298

dentate nucleus p. 314

divergence p. 297

dorsolateral pathway p. 307

endplate potential p. 289

extension p. 288

extrafusal muscle fiber p. 288

fastigial nucleus p. 313

flexion p. 288

flocculonodular lobe p. 313

gamma motor neuron p. 288

Golgi tendon organ p. 291

Huntington's chorea p. 313

interneuron p. 297

interpositus nucleus p. 314

intrafusal muscle fiber p. 288

lateral corticospinal tract p. 302

left parietal apraxia p. 310

mesencephalic locomotor region p. 316

monosynaptic stretch reflex p. 294

motor endplate p. 289

motor unit p. 288

multiunit smooth muscle p. 292

myofibril p. 289

myosin p. 289

neuromuscular junction p. 289

pacemaker potential p. 292

pyramidal tract p. 302

reticulospinal tract p. 305

rubrospinal tract p. 307

single-unit smooth muscle p. 292

skeletal muscle p. 288

smooth muscle p. 292

striated muscle p. 289

sympathetic apraxia p. 310

tectospinal tract p. 305

ventral corticospinal tract p. 302

ventromedial pathways p. 305

vermis p. 313

vestibulospinal tract p. 305

SUGGESTED READINGS

KANDEL, E.R., AND SCHWARTZ, J.H. *Principles of Neural Science.* Amsterdam: Elsevier/North Holland, 1981.

LUCIANO, S.D., VANDER, A.J., AND SHERMAN, J.H. *Human Function and Structure.* New York: McGraw-Hill, 1978.

PENNEY, J.B., AND YOUNG, A.B. Speculations on the functional anatomy of basal ganglia disorders. *Annual Review of Neuroscience,* 1983, *6,* 73–94.

STELMACH, G.E., AND REQUIN, J. *Tutorials in Motor Behavior.* Amsterdam: North-Holland.

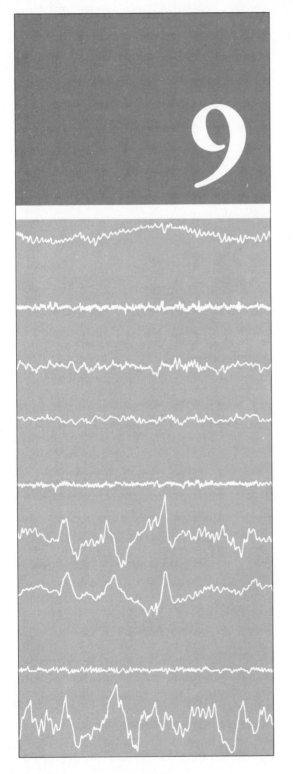

9

Sleep and Waking

Why do we sleep? Why do we spend at least one third of our lives doing something that provides most of us with only a few fleeting memories? I will attempt to answer this question in several ways. In the first part of this chapter, I will describe what is known about the phenomenon of sleep: How much do we sleep? What do we do while asleep? What happens if we do not get enough sleep? What factors affect the duration and quality of sleep? How effective are sleeping medications? Does sleep perform a restorative function? What do we know about sleepwalking and other sleep-related disorders? In the second part of the chapter, I will summarize the answers we have to slightly different questions: What makes us get sleepy at the end of a day — are there chemicals in our bloodstream that make us sleep? What brain mechanisms cause sleep and its counterpart, arousal?

■ SLEEP: A PHYSIOLOGICAL AND BEHAVIORAL DESCRIPTION

Sleep is a behavior. That statement may seem peculiar, because we usually think of behaviors as activities that involve movements, such as walking or talking. Movements do occur during sleep, but except for the rapid eye movements that accompany a particular stage, sleep is not distinguished by movement. What characterizes sleep is that the insistent urge of sleepiness forces us to seek out a quiet, comfortable place, lie down, and remain there for several hours. Because we remember very little about what happens while we sleep, we tend to think of sleep more as a state of consciousness than as a behavior. The change in consciousness is undeniable, but it should not prevent us from noticing the behavioral changes.

The Sleep Laboratory

The best research on human sleep is conducted in a sleep laboratory. A sleep laboratory, which is usually located at a university, consists of one or several small bedrooms adjacent to an observation room, where the experimenter spends the night (trying to stay awake). The experimenter prepares the sleeper for electrophysiological measurements by pasting electrodes to the scalp to monitor the electroencephalogram (EEG) and to the chin to monitor muscle activity, recorded as the ***electromyogram (EMG).*** Electrodes pasted around the eyes monitor eye movements, recorded as the ***electro-oculogram (EOG).*** In addition, other electrodes and transducing devices can be used to monitor autonomic measures such as heart rate, respiration, and skin conductance. Wires from the electrodes are bundled together in a "ponytail," which is then plugged into a junction box at the head of the bed. (See **Figure 9.1.**)

As you might imagine, a subject often has difficulty sleeping during the first night. Dreams then typically involve the laboratory situation. Careful investigators always take account of the "first-night phenomenon" and do not use data collected during this time unless there is a special reason to do so.

During wakefulness, the EEG of a normal person shows two basic patterns of activity:

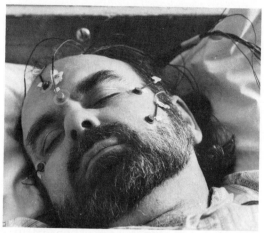

FIGURE 9.1

A subject prepared for a night's sleep in a sleep laboratory. (Photo credit: Woodfin Camp Associates)

alpha activity and *beta activity*. Alpha activity occurs when a person is resting quietly, not particularly aroused or excited and not engaged in strenuous mental activity (such as problem solving). Although alpha waves sometimes occur when a person's eyes are open, they are much more prevalent when the eyes are closed. The other type of waking EEG pattern, beta activity, occurs when a person is alert and aroused. If a person is asked to solve an arithmetic problem or hears a sudden loud noise, alpha activity is replaced by beta activity.

Figure 9.2 illustrates these two forms of the waking EEG. Note that beta activity consists of low-voltage, irregular, high-frequency waves (13–30 Hz). In contrast, alpha activity is much more regular. A lower-frequency wave (8–12 Hz) of higher voltage predominates. (See **Figure 9.2.**)

The Significance of Synchrony

As we saw in the Chapter **5** discussion of research methods, the EEG is a recording of the summed postsynaptic activity of neurons in the brain. Therefore, a low-frequency, high-voltage EEG (alpha activity, as opposed to beta activity) reflects neural **synchrony.** These waves are produced by a regular, synchronized pattern of activity in a large number of neurons. The activity of the individual neurons is analogous to a large number of people chanting the same words together (speaking synchronously). Similarly, beta activity is referred to as **desynchrony;** it is like a large number of people broken into many small groups, each carrying on an individual conversation.

The analogy helps explain why desynchrony is generally assumed to represent activation, whereas synchrony reflects a resting or depressed state. (As we will soon see, the EEG of a deeply sleeping person is even more synchronous than alpha activity.) A group of people who are all chanting the same message will process very little information; only one message is being produced. On the other hand, a desynchronized group will process and transmit many different messages. The alert, waking state of the brain is

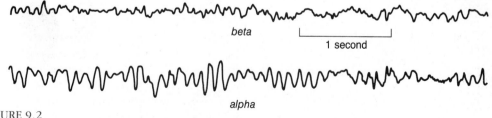

beta

1 second

alpha

FIGURE 9.2

EEG alpha activity (relaxed) and beta activity (aroused, alert).

more like the desynchronized group of people, with much information processing going on. During synchrony, the neurons of the resting brain (especially the cortex) quietly murmur the same message in unison.

Description of a Night's Sleep

Slow-Wave Sleep

During the transition from waking to sleep, the EEG record contains mostly irregular, low-voltage waves, but as sleep becomes deeper, more and more slow, regular, high-voltage **delta activity** (1 – 4 Hz) is seen. Sleep has been divided into stages 1 through 4, according to the type of EEG activity that is present, but because the boundaries between most of the stages are not distinct, the precise definitions of each stage are not important to

us here. What is important is to note that deeper stages of sleep (stages 3 and 4) are accompanied by increasing amounts of delta activity. Collectively, these stages are called **slow-wave sleep.**

Let us follow the progress of a volunteer — a male college student — in a sleep laboratory. Our subject has already slept there, so his sleep patterns are not unduly influenced by a new, unfamiliar environment. The experimenter attaches the electrodes, turns the lights off, and closes the door. Our subject becomes drowsy and enters stage 1 sleep, in which alpha activity and irregular fast activity alternate. (See **Figure 9.3A.**) About 10 minutes later he enters stage 2 sleep. The EEG looks much like that of stage 1, except that the alpha activity is gone, and occasionally a waveform called a **K complex** intrudes into

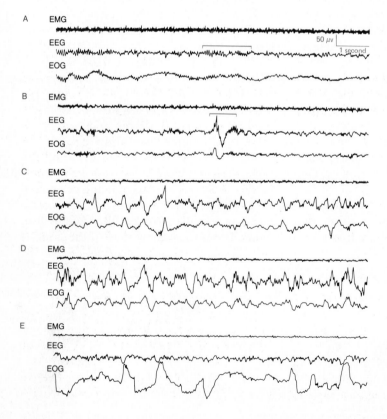

FIGURE 9.3
An EEG recording of the stages of sleep. (A) Stage 1. The bracket indicates alpha activity. (B) Stage 2. The bracket indicates a K complex. (C) Stage 3. (D) Stage 4. Note the predominance of delta activity: high-amplitude, low-frequency waves. (E) REM sleep. Note the low-amplitude, high-frequency activity that normally accompanies alertness and arousal, the relative lack of activity in the EMG, and the prominent eye movements indicated by the EOG. (From Cohen, D.B. *Sleep & Dreaming: Origins, Nature and Functions.* New York: Pergamon Press, 1979. Copyright 1979, Pergamon Press, Ltd.)

the record. (See **Figure 9.3B.**) The subject is sleeping soundly now, but if awakened he might report that he has not been asleep. This phenomenon is often reported by nurses who awaken loudly snoring patients early in the night (probably to give them a sleeping pill) and find that the patients insist they were lying there awake all the time. About 15 minutes later, the subject enters stage 3 sleep, signaled by the occurrence of a few delta waves. (See **Figure 9.3C.**) Gradually, over a 15-minute period, delta waves predominate, indicating that the subject has entered stage 4 sleep. (See **Figure 9.3D.**) Stage 4 is generally regarded as the deepest stage of sleep, because it is most difficult to awaken a person then.

REM Sleep

About 90 minutes after the beginning of sleep, we notice an abrupt change in a number of physiological measures recorded from our subject. The EEG suddenly becomes desynchronized; if we did not see our subject lying there, asleep, we would assume he was awake. We also note that his eyes are rapidly darting back and forth beneath his closed eyelids. We can see this activity in the EOG, recorded from electrodes pasted to the skin around his eyes, or we can observe the eye movements directly. The cornea produces a bulge in the closed eyelids that can be seen to move about. We also see that the EMG (an electrical recording of muscular activity) becomes silent; there is a profound loss of muscle tonus. (See **Figure 9.3E.**) If we try to elicit a stretch reflex by tapping our subject on a tendon with a rubber hammer, we find that he is completely unresponsive. However, we occasionally see brief twitching movements of the hands and feet, and our subject probably has an erection.

This peculiar stage of sleep is quite distinct from the quiet, slow-wave sleep we saw earlier. It is usually referred to as ***REM sleep*** (for the *r*apid *e*ye *m*ovements that characterize it). It has also been called ***paradoxical sleep,*** because of the presence of an aroused, "waking" EEG during sleep. The term *paradoxical* merely reflects people's surprise at observing an unexpected phenomenon, but the years since its first discovery (reported by Aserinsky and Kleitman in 1955) have blunted the surprise value.

If we arouse our volunteer during REM sleep and ask him what was going on, he will almost certainly report that he had been dreaming. The dreams of REM sleep tend to be narrative in form; there is a storylike progression of events. If we wake him during slow-wave sleep and ask "Were you dreaming?" he will most likely say "No." However, if we question him more carefully, he might report the presence of a thought, or an image, or some emotion. I will return to this issue later.

During the rest of the night, our subject's sleep alternates between periods of REM and slow-wave sleep. Each cycle is approximately 90 minutes long, containing a 20- to 30-minute bout of REM sleep. Thus, an 8-hour sleep will contain four or five periods of REM sleep. Hartmann (1967) has drawn a graph of a typical night's sleep, shown in Figure 9.4. Note that most stage 4 sleep occurs early in the night, and that subsequent bouts of slow-wave sleep become lighter and lighter. REM sleep is represented by the colored horizontal bars. (See **Figure 9.4.**)

The regular 90-minute cycles of REM sleep suggest a brain mechanism that alternately causes REM and slow-wave sleep. Dement and his colleagues (reported by Dement, 1974) tabulated the intervals between successive periods of one hundred cases of REM sleep. They found that once a period of REM sleep was over, there was a 95 to 98 percent probability that REM sleep would not occur again for at least 30 minutes. By 80 minutes after a period of REM sleep, the probability of another period of REM sleep was almost 100

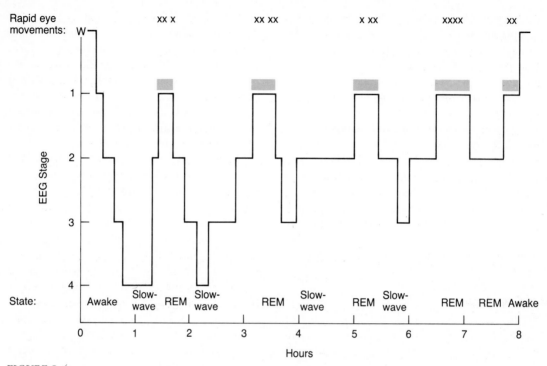

FIGURE 9.4

A typical pattern of the stages of sleep during a single night. (From
Hartmann, E. *The Biology of Dreaming,* 1967. Courtesy of Charles C
Thomas, Publisher, Springfield, Illinois.)

percent (unless the subject awakened). REM
sleep, then, occurs only at particular times.
There seems to be a refractory period after
each occurrence, during which time REM
sleep cannot again take place, and a period of
slow-wave sleep must precede the REM sleep.
(As we will see later, the sleep of people with
a particular form of sleep disorder does not
obey these rules.)

The cyclical nature of REM sleep appears
to be controlled by a "clock" in the brain that
also controls an activity cycle that continues
through waking. The first suggestion that a
90-minute activity cycle occurs throughout
the day came from the observation that infants
who are fed on demand show regular feeding patterns (Kleitman, 1961). Later studies
found 90-minute cycles of rest and activity,

including such activities as eating, drinking,
smoking, heart rate, oxygen consumption,
stomach motility, urine production, and performance on various tasks that make demands
upon a person's ability to pay attention. Kleitman termed this phenomenon the ***basic rest-
activity cycle (BRAC).*** (See Kleitman, 1982,
for a review.) As we will see later in this chapter, an internal "clock" in the medulla causes
regular changes in activity and alertness during the day and controls periods of slow-wave
and REM sleep at night.

More research has been devoted to REM
sleep than to slow-wave sleep, partly because
many investigators find it more interesting.
During REM sleep, we become paralyzed;
most of our spinal and cranial motor neurons
are strongly inhibited. (Obviously, the ones

that control respiration are spared.) At the same time, the brain is very active. Cerebral blood flow and oxygen consumption are accelerated. In addition, a male's penis will become at least partially erect, and a female's vaginal secretions will increase. However, Fisher, Gross, and Zuch (1965) found that in males, genital changes do not signify that the person is experiencing a dream with sexual content. Of course, people can have dreams with frank sexual content. In males, some of them culminate in ejaculation—the so-called nocturnal emissions, or "wet dreams." Females, too, sometimes experience orgasm during sleep.

The fact that penile erections occur during REM sleep, independent of sexual arousal, has been used clinically to assess the causes of impotence (Karacan, Salis, and Williams, 1978). A subject sleeps in the laboratory with a device attached to his penis that measures its circumference. If penile enlargement occurs during REM sleep, then his failure to obtain an erection during attempts at intercourse is not caused by physiological problems such as nerve damage or a circulatory disorder. Often, once a man finds out that he is physiologically capable of achieving an erection, the knowledge is therapeutic in itself. (A neurologist told me that there is a less expensive way to gather the same data. The patient obtains a strip of postage stamps, moistens them, and applies them around his penis before going to bed. In the morning he checks to see whether the perforations are broken.)

The important differences between REM and slow-wave sleep are listed in **Table 9.1.**

Mental Activity During Sleep

Although sleep is a period during which we do not respond very much to the environment, it is incorrect to refer to sleep as a state of unconsciousness. During sleep, our consciousness is certainly different from that

T A B L E   9.1   Principal characteristics of REM and slow-wave sleep

REM Sleep	Slow-Wave Sleep
EEG desynchrony	EEG synchrony
Lack of muscle tonus	Moderate muscle tonus
Rapid eye movements	Slow or absent eye movements
Penile erection or vaginal secretion	Lack of genital activity
PGO waves	Lack of PGO waves
Narrative-type dreams	Static dreams

which occurs during waking, but we *are* conscious. In the morning we usually forget what we experienced while asleep, and in retrospect we recall a period of "unconsciousness." However, when experimenters wake sleeping subjects, the reports that the subjects give make it clear that they were conscious.

Mental Activity During REM Sleep

Some people insist that they never dream. They are wrong: everyone dreams. What does happen, however, is that most dreams are subsequently forgotten. Unless a person awakens during or immediately after a dream, the dream will not be remembered. Many people who thought they had not had a dream for years have been startled by the vivid narrations they were able to supply when roused during REM sleep in the laboratory. Even the most vivid experiences can be completely erased from consciousness. I am sure that many of you have had the experience of waking during a particularly vivid dream. You decide to tell your friends about it, and you start to review what you will say. As you do so, the memory just slips away. You can't remember the slightest detail of the dream, which was so vivid and real just a few seconds ago. You may feel that if you could remember just one thing about it, everything would come back. Understanding this phenomenon would probably help us understand the more general issue of learning and forgetting.

Primitive people thought (and many modern people still think) that dreams provide magical insights. For example, prophetic dreams have altered military campaigns and changed the course of history. However, we need not conclude that dreams provide a magical kind of insight into the future. Freemon (1972) classifies prophetic dreams into three categories: (1) *after-the-fact dreams,* which can be culled out of a large store of dreams to suit the occasion (if the facts had been otherwise, a different prophetic dream would have been selected); (2) *statistical dreams,* which are remembered if the predicted event comes true and are conveniently forgotten (or at least not advertised) if it does not; and (3) *inner knowledge dreams,* which help us recognize something about ourselves that we were ignoring, perhaps actively. The latter category often includes dreams that are useful to a person or to his or her therapist, because they sometimes reveal thoughts or feelings that are suppressed during waking hours. Dement (1979) gave an example of another useful function of dreaming: a glimpse into a possible future. Here are his own words:

. . . [A] dream . . . may have saved my life. Some years ago I was smoking three packs of cigarettes a day. I coughed up blood. I had an X-ray, my lungs were full of cancer. I felt poignantly the intense reality of the premature termination of my life, and then *I woke up.* Given the opportunity to experience this alternative, the choice was obvious. I have not smoked a cigarette in the intervening 13 years. (p. 289)

Mental Activity During Slow-Wave Sleep
Although narrative, storylike dreaming occurs during REM sleep, mental activity also accompanies slow-wave sleep. Some of the most terrifying nightmares occur during slow-wave sleep, especially in stage 4 sleep (Fisher, Byrne, Edwards, and Kahn, 1970). If people are awakened from slow-wave sleep, they are unlikely to report a storylike dream. Instead they are likely to report a situation, such as being crushed or suffocated, or simply a feeling of fear or dread. This common sensation is reflected in the terms that some languages use for describing what we call a *nightmare.* For example, in French the word is *cauchemar,* or "pressing devil." Figure 9.5 shows a victim of a nightmare (undoubtedly in the throes of stage 4 slow-wave sleep) being squashed by an *incubus* (from the Latin *incubare,* "to lie upon"). (See **Figure 9.5.**)

The Evolution of Sleep

Sleep is an almost universal phenomenon among vertebrates. So far as we know, all mammals and birds sleep (Durie, 1981). Reptiles also sleep, and fish and amphibians enter periods of quiescence that can probably be called sleep. However, only warm-blooded vertebrates (mammals and birds) exhibit unequivocal REM sleep, with EEG signs of desynchrony along with rapid eye movements. (Obviously, birds such as flamingos, which sleep while perched on one leg, do not lose tone in the muscles they use to remain standing.) Because some species show periodic movements of eyes or other body parts during their quiescent period, we cannot be sure that REM sleep does not exist in animals other than birds and mammals. However, REM sleep as we know it appears to be of recent phylogenetic origin.

Although REM sleep occurred relatively recently in evolutionary history, it occurs quite early in an individual animal's development—early in its ontogeny. Prematurely born human infants appear to spend all their time in a stage that resembles REM sleep (Dreyfus-Brisac, 1968). The sleep of newborn full-term infants (of humans and other

FIGURE 9.5
The Nightmare, 1781, by
Henry Fuseli, Swiss, 1741–
1825. (Gift of Mr. and Mrs.
Bert L. Smokler and Mr. and
Mrs. Lawrence A. Fleischman,
Acc. No. 55.5. Courtesy of The
Detroit Institute of Arts.)

mammals) contains a very high proportion of REM sleep. The proportion decreases as the central nervous system matures. Infant guinea pigs, which are born with an almost fully mature nervous system, exhibit a lower percentage of REM sleep than other mammals (Jouvet-Mounier, Astic, and Lacote, 1970). Perhaps, as Roffwarg, Muzio, and Dement (1966) suggested, REM sleep facilitates neural growth in young animals. As we will see, experiments have shown that the rate of synthesis of brain proteins is highest during REM sleep, a finding that supports this hypothesis.

INTERIM SUMMARY

Sleep is generally regarded as a state, but it is, nevertheless, a behavior. As we will see later in this chapter, we do not sleep because our brains "run down"; instead, active brain mechanisms cause us to engage in the behavior of sleep. The stages of slow-wave sleep, stages 1 through 4, are defined by EEG activity. Alertness consists of desynchronous beta waves (13–30 Hz); relaxation and drowsiness consist of alpha waves (8–12 Hz);

stage 1 sleep consists of alternating periods of alpha activity and irregular fast activity; the EEG of stage 2 sleep is similar, but it contains no periods of alpha activity and contains occasional K complexes; stage 3 sleep consists of a few delta waves (1–4 Hz); and stage 4 sleep consists of a large proportion of delta activity. About 90 minutes after the beginning of sleep, people enter REM sleep. Cycles of REM and slow-wave sleep alternate, with a period of approximately 90 minutes.

Sleeping occurs in most vertebrates, but only birds and mammals show definite signs of REM sleep. Thus, REM sleep occurs later in evolutionary history. Animals of those species that exhibit REM sleep spend relatively more time in REM than in slow-wave sleep early in their development. As they mature, the ratio reverses; thus, REM sleep may be causally related to the rate of neural growth.

■ WHY DO WE SLEEP?

We all know how insistent the urge to sleep can be, and how uncomfortable we feel when we have to resist it and stay awake. With the exception of the effects of severe pain and the need to breathe, sleepiness is probably the most insistent drive. People can commit suicide by refusing to eat or drink, but even the most stoical person cannot indefinitely defy the urge to sleep. Sleep will come, sooner or later, no matter how hard a person tries to stay awake. The insistent nature of sleepiness suggests that sleep is a necessity of life. If this is true, then it should be possible to deprive people of sleep and (following the same logic that underlies brain lesion studies) see what capacities are disrupted. We should then be able to infer the role that sleep plays. However, the results of sleep-deprivation studies have not revealed as much as investigators had hoped.

Effects of Total Sleep Deprivation

There is a distinct difference between sleepiness and tiredness. We might want to rest after playing tennis or after having a vigorous swim, but that feeling is quite different from the sleepiness we feel at the end of a day — a sleepiness that occurs even if we have been relatively inactive. What we should do, therefore, to study the role of sleep (as opposed to the restorative function of rest) is to have our subjects rest without sleeping. Unfortunately, that is not possible. When Kleitman first began studying sleep in the early 1920s, he hoped to have subjects undress and lie quietly in bed. They would remain awake so that he could observe the effects of "pure" sleep deprivation. It did not work. People cannot stay awake without engaging in physical activity, no matter how hard they try. So Kleitman had to accept that because his subjects could stay awake only by being active, they were rest deprived as well as sleep deprived.

Kleitman (1963) observed that his subjects did not show a steady progression of sleepiness throughout the deprivation period. They were sleepiest at night but recovered considerably during the day. After two

sleepless days, the subjects did not report significant increases in sleepiness; their cycle of sleepiness continued, with the peak occurring at night, but Kleitman noted that after 62 to 65 hours, a person "was as sleepy as he was likely to be."

The amazing fact about these sleep-deprived subjects was how well they could perform, so long as the tasks were short. They had difficulty with prolonged, boring tasks, but if they were properly motivated, their performance on short tasks was as good as that of rested subjects. Thus, the major effect of sleep deprivation appeared to be intense feelings of sleepiness, but no serious deterioration in mental or physical capacities was seen.

Anecdotes about the effects of sleep deprivation suggest that it does serious harm to people's physical and emotional condition. For example, sleep deprivation was an important component of the "brainwashing" techniques used to persuade captured American servicemen to change their political beliefs during the Korean War. A famous case that occurred in 1959 lent further support to the belief that sleep deprivation would produce psychotic reactions. Peter Tripp, a New York disc jockey, stayed awake for 200 hours as a publicity stunt to raise money for charity. He made radio broadcasts from a glass booth in view of the public and was attended at all times to prevent surreptitious sleep. He developed a severe paranoid psychosis, with the delusion that he was being poisoned. His suspicion became so marked that he could not even be tested during the later stages of sleep deprivation (Dement, 1974).

However, a subsequent case (reported by Gulevich, Dement, and Johnson, 1966) showed that sleep deprivation does not necessarily produce personality changes. Randy Gardner, a 17-year-old boy, stayed awake for 264 hours, so that he could obtain a place in the *Guinness Book of World Records*. He had difficulty staying awake and consequently had to engage in physical activity. During the final night of sleeplessness, he beat Dr. Dement at one hundred straight games on a baseball machine in a penny arcade, which suggests that his motor coordination was not severely impaired. (I have no idea how well Dr. Dement plays this game.) After the ordeal, Randy Gardner slept for a little less than 15 hours and awoke feeling fine. He slept a normal 8 hours the following night. At no time did he exhibit any psychotic symptoms.

The results of this observation suggest that the psychotic symptoms sometimes seen during sleep deprivation are produced by the stress associated with staying awake rather than by a lack of some basic physiological function performed during sleep. Presumably, the general mental and physical health of the subject (and the conditions under which the sleep deprivation occurs) determines whether the stress will produce psychotic reactions. The servicemen in prisoner-of-war camps in Korea were certainly in an environment different from that of Randy Gardner.

The insistent, unyielding nature of sleepiness seems to be a convincing argument that we *need* to sleep. This may be true, but the effects of sleep deprivation on human performance have not pointed to any obvious function performed during sleep. The changes in performance after sleep deprivation do not prove that some neural mechanisms are "fatigued." Instead, the effort that a person must spend just trying to keep awake may simply detract from the attention that he or she can devote to a performance task.

Let me suggest a rough analogy. Suppose you hold your breath as long as you can. While doing so you try to solve a series of arithmetic problems. Eventually you find yourself fighting not to breathe. This struggle will undoubtedly impair your performance on the arithmetic task. Soon you lose the struggle and begin to breathe. The performance deficit is not caused by oxygen deprivation (you will be forced to breathe before that would occur) but by your having to fight a tendency to take a breath. Similarly, the performance deficits produced by sleep deprivation may be caused by the struggle against sleep.

Until recently, sleep-deprivation studies with animals have provided us with little insight into the role of sleep. Because animals cannot be "persuaded" to stay awake, it is especially difficult to separate the effects of sleep deprivation from those caused by the method used to keep the animals awake. We can ask a human volunteer to try to stay awake and can expect some cooperation. He or she will say, "I'm getting sleepy—help me to stay awake." However, animals are interested only in getting to sleep and must constantly be stimulated—and hence, stressed. A study by Rechtschaffen, Gilliland, Bergmann, and Winter (1983) attempted to control for the effects of forced exercise that are necessary to keep an animal from sleeping. They constructed a circular platform on which two rats lived, each restrained in a plastic cage. When the platform was rotated by an electrical motor, the rats were forced to walk to avoid falling into a pool of water. (See **Figure 9.6.**)

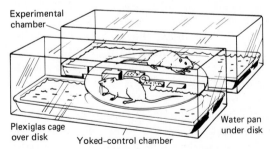

FIGURE 9.6
The apparatus used to deprive rats of sleep. Whenever one of the pair of rats in the experimental chambers fell asleep, the turntable was rotated until the animal was awake for 6 seconds. (Redrawn from Rechtschaffen, A., Gilliland, M.A., Bergmann, B.M., and Winter, J.B. *Science,* 1983, *221,* 182–184.)

Rechtschaffen and his colleagues employed a "yoked control" procedure to deprive one rat of sleep but force both members of the pair to exercise an equal amount of time. They used a computer to record both rats' EEGs and EMGs, so that they could detect both slow-wave and REM sleep. One rat served as the experimental (sleep-deprived) animal, and the other served as the yoked control. As soon as the EEG record indicated that the experimental animal was falling asleep, the computer turned on the motor that rotated the disk, forcing both animals to exercise. Because the platform rotated whenever the experimental animal started to sleep, the procedure reduced the experimental animal's total sleep time by 87 percent. However, the sleep time of the yoked control rat was reduced by only 31 percent. Eight pairs of rats were placed in the apparatus for a period of 5 to 33 days.

The effects of sleep deprivation were severe. The experimental animals looked sick and apparently stopped grooming their fur. They became weak and uncoordinated and often fell off the disk. Three animals died and four others were killed because death appeared imminent. On autopsy, several of the experimental animals were found to have had enlarged adrenal glands, stomach ulcers, fluid in the lungs and trachea, or internal hemorrhage. Because no signs of infection were detected, these findings suggest that the pathological conditions were induced by stress.

This experiment suggests that forced exercise that occurs just after an animal falls asleep produces severe stress that eventually is fatal. Thus, we must seriously consider the possibility that sleep performs a vital physiological function. However, it could be that the stressful event is forced exercise that occurs immediately after the onset of sleep, not the loss of sleep that this exercise causes. Being forced to begin walking just after falling asleep is undoubtedly more stressful than being forced to walk while awake, or after having been asleep for some time. The experiment provides important evidence, but further investigation is needed to determine the nature of the physiological role that sleep plays.

Investigators have suggested many hypotheses about the functions of sleep, but most of them are variations on two themes: (1) *Sleep is a period of restoration,* during which certain anabolic physiological processes occur. The wear-and-tear caused by activity during waking is repaired during sleep. This hypothesis conceives of sleep as a physiologically necessary function, just as vital as eating and drinking. (2) *Sleep is an adaptive response* — a behavior that serves a useful purpose. For example, sleep prevents an animal from wasting energy during a time of day that food is not available. This function is important but not physiologically necessary. In the rest of this section, I will consider these two general hypotheses: sleep as construction or repair, and sleep as an adaptive response. Although the evidence is not conclusive, sleep probably accomplishes *both* functions.

Sleep As Construction or Repair

A person who misses a meal will probably get hungry, even though his or her body has enough reserves to sustain many days of fasting. Similarly, when we attempt to hold our breath, we are forced to breathe before our brain is damaged by lack of oxygen. Perhaps, then, sleep deprivation produces sleepiness long before any serious physical symptoms can be detected. With this possibility in mind, we must acknowledge that although sleep-deprivation studies have failed to identify important functions of sleep, this failure does not prove that sleep lacks important physiological functions. Even though a person cannot hold his or her breath long enough to cause serious damage, other evidence tells us that this activity is absolutely vital.

Effects of Exercise on Sleep

If the function of sleep is to repair the effects of activity during waking hours, then we should expect that sleep and exercise are related. That is, we should sleep more after a day of vigorous exercise than after a day spent quietly at an office desk.

The relation between sleep and exercise is not very compelling. First, let me give you an example of a study with positive results. Shapiro, Bortz, Mitchell, Bartel, and Jooste (1981) carefully examined the sleep of trained athletes who competed in a 92-km (approximately 57-mile) marathon. Obviously, participation in the race required a drastic increase in energy expenditure. During the next two nights, the participants slept more than they did before the race: increases of 18 and 27 percent, respectively, for the two nights. However, when slow-wave sleep is considered separately, the increase is much more impressive: 40 and 45 percent. The participants actually spent *less* time in REM sleep during the two nights after the race. These results suggest that slow-wave sleep, in particular, is important for recuperation after vigorous activity.

However, several studies have shown that decreased activity does not substantially reduce the amount of time a person sleeps. For example, Ryback and Lewis (1971) found no changes in slow-wave or REM sleep of healthy subjects who spent six weeks resting in bed. If sleep repairs wear-and-tear, we would expect these people to sleep less. Adey, Bors, and Porter (1968) studied the sleep of *completely* immobile quadriplegics and paraplegics and found only a small decrease in slow-wave sleep as compared to normal people.

Selective Deprivation of Slow-Wave Sleep

It is impossible to deprive people of just slow-wave sleep without depriving them of REM sleep as well. Because REM sleep occurs only after a period of slow-wave sleep, waking people during slow-wave sleep would deprive them of REM sleep, too. However, it *is* possible to deprive people of stage 4 sleep, the deepest stage of slow-wave sleep. A buzzer (loud enough to lighten sleep, but not loud enough to awaken) can be sounded whenever the EEG record becomes dominated by synchronous delta waves. The procedure seems effective; people deprived of stage 4 sleep show a *rebound phenomenon:* they engage in more stage 4 sleep when they are permitted to sleep normally (Agnew, Webb, and Williams, 1964). The rebound suggests a need for a certain amount of slow-wave sleep.

Selective deprivation of stage 4 sleep does not produce severe deficits; at the most, it produces some physical lethargy and depression (Agnew, Webb, and Williams, 1967). Moldofsky and Scarisbrick (1976) found that subjects who had been deprived of stage 4 sleep complained of muscle and joint pains and reported a general increase in sensitivity to pain. As we saw earlier, vigorous, sustained exercise causes an increase in slow-wave sleep. Taken together, the results suggest that slow-wave sleep might indeed serve a restorative effect on the wear and tear that occurs during waking.

Products Synthesized During Sleep

Another way to investigate the possible restorative functions of sleep is to compare physiological processes that occur during sleep and waking. If some processes occur only during sleep (or occur at a much greater rate during sleep), then perhaps a function of sleep is to provide the condition under which these processes can occur.

Oswald (1980), one of the proponents of the hypothesis that sleep serves a restorative purpose, notes that sleep is a time of increased anabolism, including growth of bone length in children and increased rate of cell division in both children and adults. These effects are probably controlled by the secretion of **growth hormone (GH),** which increases the rate of cell division and facilitates the entry of amino acids into cells, thus promoting protein synthesis.

Growth hormone is secreted shortly after the first occurrence of delta activity in slow-wave sleep. Figure 9.7 shows the sleep cycles and secretion of GH in two subjects during a 24-hour period (Takahashi, 1979). Subject T.F., whose data are shown in the lower part of the figure, slept continuously, with only a few brief awakenings, and showed a single phase of GH secretion. (See **Figure 9.7.**) The sleep of subject B.B. *(above)* was interrupted

for several hours; his GH secretion was biphasic, occurring principally during stages 3 and 4 of slow-wave sleep. (See **Figure 9.7.**)

The production of GH during sleep provides excellent evidence for the sleep-as-repair hypothesis. However, life is seldom simple; nature often provides contradictory evidence. Children younger than 4 years of age, and many older people, do not secrete GH only during sleep (Finklestein, Roffwarg, Boyar, Kream, and Hellman, 1972; Carlson, Gillin, Gorden, and Snyder, 1972). Furthermore, the correlation between sleep and GH secretion breaks down during many pathological conditions, including various pituitary disorders, dwarfism, narcolepsy (a sleep disorder that will be discussed later in this chapter), schizophrenia, and depression (Takahashi, 1979). Finally, the secretion of GH in some mammals does not appear to be tied to slow-wave sleep (Quabbe, 1977).

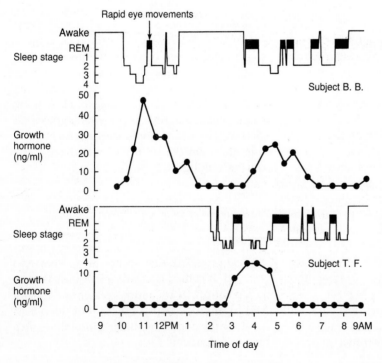

FIGURE 9.7
Plasma levels of growth hormone as a function of the stages of sleep and waking in two subjects. Note that the hormone is secreted during the deepest stages of slow-wave sleep. (From Takahashi, Y. In *The Functions of Sleep,* edited by R. Drucker-Colín, M. Shkurovich, and M.B. Sterman. New York: Academic Press, 1979.)

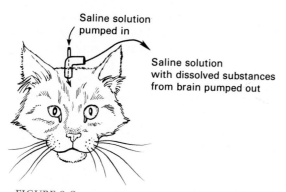

FIGURE 9.8

The push-pull cannula technique.

Evidence suggests that protein synthesis within the brain itself increases during REM sleep. A special technique developed by Myers (1970) permits the extraction of substances from the brain of a freely moving animal. A ***push-pull cannula*** is implanted into the animal's brain. This device consists of a small metal tube placed inside a slightly larger one. ***Ringer's solution*** (a solution of salts that closely duplicates those found in normal interstitial fluid) is slowly pumped through the smaller tube and is recovered from the larger one. As the Ringer's solution flows from one tube to the other, it picks up substances that are present in the interstitial fluid of the brain. (See **Figure 9.8.**)

Drucker-Colín and Spanis (1976) used the push-pull cannula technique to measure the rate of protein synthesis in the brain during stages of sleep and waking. These studies (using cats as subjects) have shown that much more protein synthesis occurs during sleep than during wakefulness. Specifically, the highest rate occurs during REM sleep. (See **Figure 9.9.**)

In conclusion, sleep is probably related to anabolic processes. The first bout of slow-wave sleep is usually (but not invariably) associated with secretion of GH, which facilitates cell division and protein synthesis. Protein synthesis in the brain increases during REM sleep. This correlation may be related to

FIGURE 9.9

Amounts of protein obtained from the brains of cats by means of the push-pull cannula technique during stages of sleep and waking. (From Drucker-Colín, R.R., and Spanis, C.W. *Progress in Neurobiology,* 1976, *6,* 1–12.)

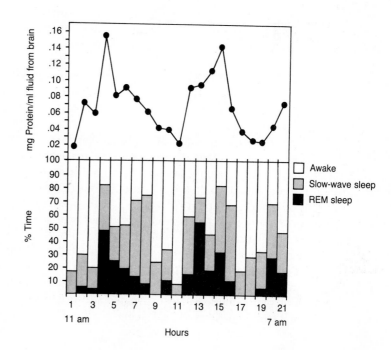

the possible role of REM sleep in memory consolidation, which is considered next.

Sleep As Construction: A Special Role for REM Sleep?

Because REM sleep occurs only after a period of slow-wave sleep, it is possible to deprive an animal selectively of REM sleep by awakening it only during REM sleep. Control subjects are awakened the same number of times, at random intervals, and thus engage in both REM and slow-wave sleep. The results of selective deprivation of REM sleep suggest that this stage of sleep has some special functions.

The Rebound Phenomenon. An early report on the effects of REM sleep deprivation (Dement, 1960) observed that as the deprivation progressed, subjects had to be awakened more frequently; the "pressure" to enter REM sleep built up. Furthermore, after several days of REM sleep deprivation, subjects would show a rebound phenomenon when permitted to sleep normally; they spent a much greater-than-normal percentage of the recovery night in REM sleep. This rebound suggests that there is a need for a certain amount of REM sleep—that REM sleep is controlled by a regulatory mechanism. If selective deprivation causes a deficiency in REM sleep, the deficiency is made up later, when uninterrupted sleep is permitted.

Fisher (1966) observed that when animals are selectively deprived of REM sleep, some of the phenomena that normally occur only during REM sleep begin to "escape" and occur during slow-wave sleep. For example, the REM sleep of many animals (particularly cats) contains brief, phasic bursts of electrical activity that occur in the pons, lateral geniculate nucleus, and visual (occipital) cortex (Brooks and Bizzi, 1963). These **PGO waves** (for *p*ons, *g*eniculate, and *o*ccipital) are often the first manifestations of REM sleep in cats. We do not know whether humans also have PGO waves, because their measurement would require the introduction of depth electrodes into the brain—and curiosity is not a good enough reason for such a procedure. Dement, Ferguson, Cohen, and Barchas (1969) deprived cats of REM sleep and found that PGO waves, which normally occur only during REM sleep, began to occur during slow-wave sleep and waking. The results indicate that at least some aspects of REM sleep can occur at other times when REM sleep is prevented. This finding suggests that some of the functions of REM sleep might be carried out even when animals are deprived of REM sleep.

Emotional Changes. Early studies suggested that REM sleep deprivation produces emotional changes, including anxiety, irritability, and an impaired ability to concentrate. However, later studies found no such changes in either humans or laboratory animals. Cats have been deprived of REM sleep for 70 days, and humans for 16 days, without any major impairment in psychological functions (Dement, 1974). But some subtle and interesting effects do occur. REM sleep deprivation does not impair people's performance on simple verbal tasks with no emotional content. (See McGrath and Cohen, 1978, for a review.) However, Greiser, Greenberg, and Harrison (1972) found that REM sleep deprivation impaired the recall of emotionally toned words. Cartwright, Gore, and Weiner (1973) asked subjects to sort a group of adjectives according to how accurately the words described themselves. REM sleep deprivation produced a lower recall for these words.

Another study examined the effects of REM sleep deprivation on the assimilation of anxiety-producing events. The subjects viewed a film that generally produces anxiety in the observers (a particularly gruesome circumcision rite performed with stone knives by members of a remote South Sea Island tribe).

Normally, people who see the film twice show less anxiety during the second viewing. Greenberg, Pillard, and Pearlman (1972) found that subjects who were permitted to engage in REM sleep between the first and second viewings of the film showed less anxiety the second time than subjects who were deprived of REM sleep. In addition, Breger, Hunter, and Lane (1971) found that the dream content of subjects viewing the film was affected by the anxiety-producing material. Taken together, the studies suggest that REM sleep (and perhaps the dreaming that occurs then) somehow assists people to come to grips with newly learned information that has emotional consequences. As we all know, things generally seem less disturbing after a good night's sleep.

The calming effect of REM sleep appears to be contradicted by a puzzling phenomenon. The symptoms of people with severe, psychotic depression are *reduced* when they are deprived of REM sleep (Vogel, Vogel, McAbee, and Thurmond, 1980). In addition, treatments that reduce the symptoms of depression, such as antidepressant drugs and electroconvulsive therapy, also suppress REM sleep (Scherschlicht, Polc, Schneeberger, Steiner, and Haefely, 1982; Zarcone, Gulevich, and Dement, 1967). (These results will be discussed in more detail in Chapter 17.) If REM sleep helps people assimilate emotionally relevant information, why should REM sleep deprivation relieve the symptoms of people who are suffering from a serious emotional disorder?

Learning. REM sleep appears to perform functions that facilitate learning. Experiments have shown that REM sleep deprivation retards memory formation, and that learning a new task causes an increase in REM sleep.

A special procedure has been developed to deprive laboratory animals of REM sleep. The subjects are placed in water-filled cages, on small platforms that are just large enough to hold them. (Often, inverted flowerpots are used—hence the term ***flowerpot technique.***) During slow-wave sleep, the animal snoozes quietly, its head held above the pool of water. But as you will recall, one of the components of REM sleep is a loss of muscle tonus. When the animal enters REM sleep, its head slumps downward, splashing into the water. The animal wakes up and soon resumes slow-wave sleep. (See **Figure 9.10.**) Once the subject is adapted to the apparatus, it learns to awaken as soon as its head begins to nod; it no longer gets its face wet.

Many studies have used this technique, with varied results. Although some experiments reported no effects of REM sleep deprivation on learning, others reported that deprived animals learned tasks more slowly. (See Fishbein and Gutwein, 1977, for a review.) The most consistent findings have been obtained with mice, which appear to adapt to life on a small island much better than rats do. Mice periodically jump up to the wire mesh lid of the cage just above them and obtain exercise by crawling upside down. Rats do not do this; thus, a REM sleep-deprived rat is also an exercise-deprived rat (at least, when the flowerpot technique is

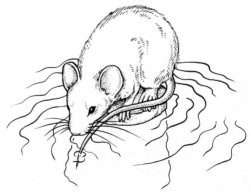

FIGURE 9.10
The flowerpot technique.

used). For this reason, mice are better subjects for these experiments.

Studies have also shown that when animals learn new tasks, they engage in more REM sleep. For example, Bloch, Hennevin, and Leconte (1977) gave rats daily training trials in a complex maze. They found that the experience enhanced subsequent REM sleep. Moreover, daily performance was related to subsequent REM sleep. The lower curve in Figure 9.11 shows REM sleep as a percentage of total sleep. The upper curve illustrates the animals' performance in the maze. You can see that the largest increase in running speed (possibly representing the largest increase in learning) was accompanied by the largest amount of REM sleep. Also note that once the task was well learned (after day 6), REM sleep declined back to baseline levels. (See **Figure 9.11.**)

The role of REM sleep in memory formation is certainly not an all-or-none relationship. In experimental animals, REM sleep deprivation retards memory formation but does not prevent its occurrence. In humans, REM sleep seems to be related to learning experiences that involve emotionally relevant material. Perhaps the relation between protein synthesis and REM sleep is important in this regard. As we will see in Chapter 15, learning almost certainly involves increased protein synthesis. REM sleep might thus provide a favorable condition for memory formation, or perhaps for a more subtle integration of new memories with old ones.

Sleep As an Adaptive Response

As we just saw, there is some evidence that sleep serves a restorative function. This section reviews evidence related to the hypothesis that sleep is an adaptive response — a behavior that serves useful purposes. One of the most active proponents of this hypothesis is Webb (1975, 1982). He suggests that sleep might not have special restorative properties but might simply be a behavior that keeps an animal out of harm's way when there is nothing important to do. We can imagine that our primitive ancestors benefited from irresistible periods of sleep that kept them from stumbling around in the dark, when predators were harder to see and injuries were more likely to occur.

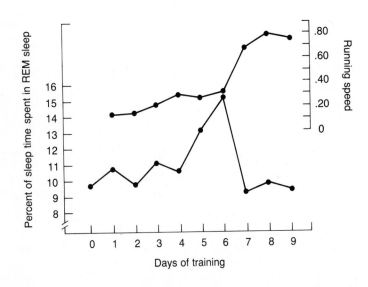

FIGURE 9.11
Percentage of sleep time spent in REM sleep *(lower curve)* as a function of maze-learning performance *(upper curve)*. (From Block, V., Hennevin, E., and Leconte, P., in *Neurobiology of Sleep and Memory,* edited by R.R. Drucker-Colín and J.L. McGaugh. New York: Academic Press, 1978.)

Many animals obtain food during only part of the day/night cycle. These animals profit from a period of inactivity, during which less energy is expended. In fact, animals who have safe hiding places (for example, rabbits) sleep a lot, unless they are very small and need to eat much of the time (for example, shrews). Large predators such as lions can safely sleep wherever and whenever they choose, and, indeed, they sleep many hours of the day. In contrast, large animals who are preyed upon and have no place to hide (for example, cattle) sleep very little. Presumably, they must remain awake to be alert for predators. In a study of the relation of sleep to various characteristics of species, Allison and Chichetti (1976) found that body weight and danger of being attacked accounted for 58 percent of the variability in length of sleep among species.

The hypothesis that sleep serves as an adaptive response has led Meddis (1977) to suggest that we could (theoretically, at least) dispense with sleep altogether, now that we have artificial lighting and are not endangered by predators (nonhuman ones, anyway). However, most sleep researchers disagree and doubt that we will ever be able to eliminate sleep by chemical or surgical means. After all, even if sleep originally evolved for one reason, it is still likely that it came to serve other functions once the mechanisms that produce it became established. The evidence for specific functions performed by sleep is still modest, but the insistence of the urge to sleep remains a convincing argument for most people that sleep must somehow be very important.

INTERIM SUMMARY

The insistent nature of sleepiness makes most of us conclude that sleep is essential to our well-being. However, unequivocal evidence that sleep performs a necessary physiological function has proved difficult to obtain. However, some deleterious effects of sleep deprivation have been obtained recently. Rechtschaffen and colleagues found that sleep-deprived rats became very sick after a week or more of sleep deprivation, whereas yoked-control subjects did not.

Studies have attempted to relate the expenditure of energy to the amount of sleep in which an organism subsequently engages. One study found that after participating in an extremely demanding running race, athletes did indeed sleep more during the next few nights. However, other studies have shown that remaining in bed does not cause a decrease in sleep.

Evidence from studies of selective deprivation of particular sleep stages is more positive than that from studies of total sleep deprivation. For example, selective deprivation of stage 4 sleep or REM sleep produces a rebound phenomenon when the person is permitted to sleep normally. Selective deprivation of REM sleep in humans retards adjustment to emotionally stressful events, and in laboratory animals produces moderate deficits in learning.

During REM sleep, the brain triggers the release of growth hormone, and studies with push-pull cannulas have found that the rate of protein synthesis in the brain increases during REM sleep; these phenomena suggest that REM sleep may perform special physiological functions. Indeed, a study found that the amount of REM sleep an animal receives each night is related to the amount of learning that occurred on that day.

The hypotheses that sleep serves as a time for construction or repair and that sleep serves as an adaptive response need not be mutually exclusive; both could be correct. I suspect that sleep originally evolved as a behavior that saved energy and, for some species, kept them out of danger as well. Then, once a regular period of inactivity was established, other functions began to be performed during this time, including restorative functions and functions related to memory. Perhaps the emergence of REM sleep relatively late in phylogeny is related to the fact that the behavior of mammals and birds is the most flexible and the most capable of modification through learning.

Kleitman (1982) suggests a useful analogy. In order to talk we force air out of our lungs and set our vocal cords into motion. We shape this sound into words by moving our tongue, palate, and lips. Thus, it is perfectly accurate to say that a function of breathing is communication, because breathing provides the necessary movement of air. However, no one would be so foolish as to say that we breathe in order to communicate. But because we know less about sleep, various investigators are tempted to conclude that any functions related to sleep define the purpose of sleep. Perhaps we do best to remain skeptical and, lacking definitive evidence, think of sleep as a behavior with many functions.

■ DISORDERS OF SLEEP

Insomnia

Insomnia is a problem that affects at least 20 percent of the population at some time (Raybin and Detre, 1969), but unfortunately, little is known about its causes. At the onset, I must emphasize that there is no single definition of insomnia that can apply to all people. The amount of sleep that individuals require is quite variable. A short sleeper may feel fine with 5 hours, while a long sleeper may still feel unrefreshed after 10 hours of sleep. Insomnia must be defined in relation to a person's particular sleep needs. Some short sleepers have sought medical assistance because they thought that they were supposed to get more sleep, even though they felt fine. These people should be reassured that whatever amount of sleep seems to be enough *is* enough. Meddis, Pearson, and Langford (1973) reported the case of a 70-year-old woman who slept approximately one hour each day (documented by sessions in a sleep laboratory). She felt fine and was of the opinion that most people "wasted much time" in bed.

Probably the most important cause of insomnia is sleeping medication. Insomnia is not a disease that can be corrected with a medicine, in the way in which diabetes can be treated with insulin. Insomnia is a symptom.

If it is caused by pain or discomfort, the physical ailment that leads to the sleeplessness should be treated. If it is secondary to personal problems or psychological disorders, these problems should be dealt with directly. Dement says that one of the things he hopes his students will remember, if they remember nothing else from his course, is that "sleeping pills cause insomnia" (Dement, 1974). Unfortunately, this fact is not appreciated by a very large number of people (or by their physicians, either). According to Freemon (1972), "the promiscuous prescribing of sleep medications is the most common error in medicine." Solomon (1956) classes it as "perhaps the commonest of iatrogenic disorders" (*iatrogenic* means "physician-produced").

I cite these authorities to emphasize that patients who receive a sleeping medication develop a tolerance to the drug and suffer rebound symptoms if it is withdrawn (Weitzman, 1981). That is, the drug loses its effectiveness, so the patient requests larger doses from the physician. If the patient attempts to sleep without the accustomed medication, or even takes a smaller dose one night, he or she is likely to experience a withdrawal effect: a severe disturbance of sleep. The patient becomes convinced that the insomnia is even worse than before and turns to more medication for relief. This common syndrome is referred to as ***drug-dependency insomnia.*** Kales, Scharf, Kales, and Soldatos (1979) found that withdrawal of some sleeping medications produced a rebound insomnia after the drugs were used for as few as 3 nights.

Most patients who receive a prescription for a sleeping medication are given one on the basis of their own description of their symptoms. That is, they tell their physician that they sleep very little at night, and the drug is prescribed on the basis of this testimony. Very few patients are observed during a night's sleep in a sleep laboratory; thus, insomnia is one of the few medical problems that physicians treat without having direct clinical evidence for its existence. But studies on the sleep of people who complain of insomnia show that most of them grossly underestimate the amount of time they actually sleep. Many patients with chronic insomnia report in the morning that they slept very little, or not at all, even though the EEG record shows that they slept for 6 or 7 hours (Weitzman, 1981). These people suffer from pseudoinsomnia rather than true sleeplessness.

Some people suffer from an interesting, but unfortunate, form of pseudoinsomnia: They dream that they are awake. They do not dream that they are running around in some Alice-in-Wonderland fantasy but that they are lying in bed, trying unsuccessfully to fall asleep. In the morning, their memories are of a night of insomnia, and they feel as unrefreshed as if they had really been awake.

Another form of insomnia—a true one, not a pseudoinsomnia—is caused by the inability to sleep and breathe at the same time. Patients with this disorder, called **sleep apnea,** fall asleep and then cease to breathe. (Nearly all people have occasional episodes of sleep apnea—especially people who snore—but not to the extent that it interferes with sleep.) During a period of sleep apnea, the level of carbon dioxide in the blood stimulates chemoreceptors, and the person wakes up, gasping for air. The oxygen level of the blood returns to normal, the person falls asleep, and the whole cycle begins again. Fortunately, many cases of sleep apnea are caused by an obstruction of the airway that can be corrected surgically.

Occasionally, infants are found dead in their cribs without any apparent signs of illness, victims of the *sudden infant death syndrome (SIDS)*. Many investigators believe that one of the principal causes for SIDS is sleep apnea; in these cases, however, the infants are *not* awakened by a high level of carbon dioxide in the blood. Baker and McGinty (1977) obtained evidence that supports this suggestion. They maintained kittens for 8 hours per day in a chamber that contained an atmosphere deficient in oxygen. Most kittens did well, increasing their rate of respiration to compensate for the lowered oxygen level. Their episodes of sleep apnea (which occur in cats as well as humans) decreased. However, some kittens did *not* compensate during sleep. Their periods of sleep apnea continued, and in a few cases led to death.

Evidence suggests that a susceptibility to SIDS is inherited; parents and siblings of some infants who have died of SIDS do not respond normally to increases in carbon dioxide (Kelly, Walker, Cahen, and Shannon, 1980; Schiffman, Westlake, Santiago, and Edelman, 1980). Perhaps a low-grade illness, which depresses respiratory mechanisms and increases the tissue need for oxygen, causes susceptible human infants to succumb, just as some kittens did in Baker and McGinty's experiment. Many infants' lives have been saved by monitoring devices that sound an alarm when a susceptible infant stops breathing during sleep, thus waking the parents in time for them to revive the child.

Narcolepsy

Narcolepsy is a serious disorder characterized by sleep (or some of its components) at inappropriate times. Although the physiological causes for this disorder have not yet been explained, the symptoms can be described in terms of what we know about the phenomena of sleep. The primary symptom of narcolepsy is the **sleep attack** (*narke* means "numbness," and *lepsis* means "seizure"). The narcoleptic sleep attack is an overwhelming urge to sleep that can happen at any time but occurs most often under monotonous, boring conditions. Sleep (which appears to be entirely normal) usually lasts for 2 to 5 minutes. The person usually wakes up feeling refreshed.

Another symptom of narcolepsy—in fact, the most striking one—is *cataplexy* (from *kata,* "down," and *plexis,* "stroke"). During a cataplectic attack, a person will suddenly wilt and fall like a sack of flour. The person will lie there, conscious, for a few seconds to several minutes. What apparently happens is that one of the phenomena of REM sleep— muscular paralysis—occurs at an inappropriate time. You will recall that the EMG indicates a loss of muscle tonus during REM sleep. As we will see later, this loss of tonus is caused by massive inhibition of motor neurons. (The flowerpot technique of REM sleep deprivation takes advantage of this phenomenon.) When muscular paralysis occurs during waking, the victim of a cataplectic attack falls as suddenly as if a switch had been thrown.

Cataplexy is quite different from a narcoleptic sleep attack; it is usually precipitated by strong emotion, or by sudden physical effort, especially if the patient is caught unawares. Laughter, anger, or trying to catch a suddenly thrown object can trigger a cataplectic attack. Common situations that bring on cataplexy are attempting to discipline one's children or making love (which, you must admit, is an awkward time to become paralyzed). Completely spontaneous attacks are rare.

REM sleep paralysis sometimes intrudes into waking, but at a time that does not present any physical danger—just before or just after normal sleep, when a person is already lying down. This symptom is referred to as *sleep paralysis,* an inability to move just before the onset of sleep, or upon waking in the morning. A person can be snapped out of sleep paralysis by being touched, or by hearing someone call his or her name. Sometimes, the mental components of REM sleep intrude into sleep paralysis; that is, the person dreams while lying awake, paralyzed. These epi-

sodes, called *hypnagogic hallucinations,* are often alarming or even terrifying.

It is almost certain that narcolepsy is produced by a brain abnormality that causes the neural mechanisms responsible for various aspects of REM sleep to become active at inappropriate times. Indeed, Rechtschaffen, Wolpert, Dement, Mitchell, and Fisher (1963) found that narcoleptic patients generally skip the slow-wave sleep that normally begins a night's sleep; instead they go directly into REM sleep from waking. This finding suggests a deficiency in control over the brain mechanisms that produce REM sleep. Narcolepsy appears to be a genetic disorder. Kessler, Guilleminault, and Dement (1974) found that relatives of narcoleptic patients are sixty times more likely to have this disorder themselves, as compared with people from the general population. In fact, researchers have even successfully bred dogs (Labrador retrievers and Doberman pinschers) that are afflicted with narcolepsy (Foutz, Mitler, Cavalli-Sforza, and Dement, 1979).

Narcolepsy may result from abnormalities in neurotransmitter synthesis, release, or reuptake. The symptoms of narcolepsy can be successfully treated with drugs. Sleep attacks are diminished by stimulants such as amphetamine, a catecholamine agonist, and the REM sleep phenomena (cataplexy, sleep paralysis, and hypnagogic hallucinations) can be alleviated by imipramine, which facilitates both serotonergic and catecholaminergic activity. Most often, the drugs are given together. Although specific abnormalities have not yet been detected in the brains of narcoleptic humans, Mefford, Baker, Boehme, Foutz, Ciaranello, Barchas, and Dement (1983) analyzed the brains of narcoleptic Labrador retrievers and Doberman pinschers and found evidence for decreased utilization of dopamine. Further study of these animals will undoubtedly increase our understanding of the disorder.

Problems Associated with Slow-Wave Sleep

Some maladaptive behaviors occur during slow-wave sleep, especially during its deepest phase, stage 4. These behaviors include bed-wetting *(nocturnal enuresis),* sleepwalking *(somnambulism),* and night terrors *(pavor nocturnus).* All three events occur most frequently in children. Bed-wetting can often be cured by training methods, such as having a bell ring when the first few drops of urine are detected in the bed sheet by a special electronic circuit (a few drops usually precede the ensuing flood). Night terrors consist of anguished screams, trembling, and a rapid pulse and usually no memory for what caused the terror. Night terrors and somnambulism usually cure themselves as the child gets older. Neither of these phenomena is related to REM sleep; a sleepwalking person is *not* acting out a dream. Most authorities firmly advise that the best treatment for these two disorders is no treatment at all. There is no evidence that they are associated (at least in childhood) with mental disorders or personality variables.

INTERIM SUMMARY

Although many people believe that they do not obtain as much sleep as they would like, insomnia is a symptom, not a disease. Insomnia can be caused by depression, pain, illness, or even excited anticipation of a pleasurable event. Far too many people receive sleeping medications, which often lead to a condition called drug-dependency insomnia. Sometimes insomnia is caused by sleep apnea, which can often be corrected surgically. When sleep apnea occurs in infants, it can lead to sudden infant death; hence, the respiration rate of susceptible infants should be monitored electronically until they are old enough to be past danger.

Narcolepsy is characterized by four symptoms.

Sleep attacks consist of overwhelming urges to sleep for a few minutes. Cataplexy is sudden paralysis, during which the person remains conscious. Sleep paralysis is similar to cataplexy, but it occurs just before sleep or upon waking. Hypnagogic hallucinations are dreams that occur during periods of sleep paralysis. Sleep attacks are treated with stimulants such as amphetamine, and the other symptoms are treated with drugs such as imipramine. Studies with narcoleptic dogs suggest that the disorder may involve biochemical abnormalities in the brain.

During slow-wave sleep, especially during stage 4, some people are afflicted by bed-wetting (nocturnal enuresis), sleepwalking (somnambulism), or night terrors (parvor nocturnus). These problems are most common in children, who usually outgrow them. Only if they occur in adults do they suggest the existence of a physical or psychological disorder.

■ CHEMICAL CONTROL OF SLEEP

Because sleep and wakefulness last for extended periods of time, it is possible that these states are regulated by neuromodulators that affect the activity of a large number of neurons. Several investigators have attempted to find chemicals that might be responsible for sleep and waking. In general, they have taken two approaches. The first assumes that waking activity produces a *hypnogenic chemical* (*hypnos* means "sleep"), which eventually accumulates in sufficient quantities to trigger sleep. Perhaps increased physical activity causes more of the hypnogenic chemical to be produced, resulting in longer and deeper sleep. The other approach suggests that neuromodulators are produced during sleep. When the neural mechanisms that control sleep become active, perhaps they cause the secretion of neuromodulators that alter the activity of neurons throughout the brain, causing them to enter the sleeping state.

Hypnogenic Chemicals Produced During Wakefulness

The search for chemicals that control sleep began many years ago. Piéron and Legrende (Piéron, 1913; Legrende and Piéron, 1913) kept dogs awake for several days, which they expected would increase the level of hypnogenic chemicals that might accumulate during wakefulness. They removed cerebrospinal fluid from these animals and injected it into the ventricular system of recipient dogs, who subsequently went to sleep for 2 to 6 hours. Schnedorf and Ivy (1939) replicated the phenomenon, but they noted that the injections of cerebrospinal fluid increased the intracerebral pressure, causing hyperthermia, so the notion of a central sleep-producing substance fell into disrepute.

More recently, Fencl, Koski, and Pappenheimer (1971) have discovered a sleep-promoting factor that they extracted by selective filtration from the cerebrospinal fluid of sleep-deprived goats. This chemical (which they named *factor S*) increased the duration of sleep and decreased locomotor activity in recipient subjects. The investigators also discovered an excitatory factor *(factor E),* which produced hyperactivity in the recipient that lasted for several days.

Pappenheimer and his colleagues subsequently found factor S in human urine; they extracted 30 micrograms from 4.5 tons of urine (Krueger, Pappenheimer, and Karnovski, 1982). An unusual feature of this chemical is that it contains two amino acids, muramic acid and diaminopimelic acid, that are usually found in bacteria, not in mammalian cells. This finding suggests that the factor is synthesized by bacteria in the intestines and is absorbed into the general circulation.

Until more study is done, we must be cautious in accepting factor S as a sleep-promoting factor. The body (and the bacteria that live in the intestinal tract) produces thousands of different substances. With so many to choose from, it is not surprising that some of them are found to have effects on sleep and wakefulness. If we wish to conclude that a naturally occurring substance serves a hypnogenic function, the following criteria must be met: the substance must be shown to be effective at doses comparable to the levels in which it is found in the body, and its concentration must be shown to vary with the sleep and waking cycles that it supposedly controls. Most investigators do not believe that our sleep cycles are regulated by secretions of bacteria in the intestinal tract.

Neuromodulators Produced During Sleep

The second approach to the chemical control of sleep is to look for neuromodulators that may be produced by active sleep mechanisms. These substances would be expected to be in highest concentrations during sleep, and in lowest concentrations during waking. This approach has been taken by Monnier and his colleagues. Low-frequency electrical stimulation of the midline nuclei of the thalamus produces cortical synchrony, one of the manifestations of sleep. Several studies (e.g., Monnier, Koller, and Graber, 1963) have shown that when the blood supplies of two rabbits are connected, thalamic stimulation of one animal will increase the occurrence of cortical synchrony in the other. Monnier and Hösli (1964, 1965) successfully extracted a substance from the cerebral blood of a thalamically stimulated rabbit that would produce this synchronizing effect in a recipient animal. Later studies (Monnier, Dudler, Gächter, Maier, Tobler, and Schoenenberger, 1977) identified the sleep-promoting substance as a simple peptide consisting of nine amino acids. This peptide was given the name of *delta sleep-inducing peptide.* Synthetic delta sleep-inducing peptide was found to produce EEG signs of slow-wave sleep in recipient rabbits.

The role of this chemical is uncertain. Ringle and Herndon (1968) were unable to find a sleep-promoting substance in the blood of rabbits that had been deprived of sleep; thus, the substance appears to be secreted (at least, in substantial amounts) only during electrical stimulation of the thalamus. Moreover, other laboratories have failed to obtain a sleep-inducing effect of delta sleep-inducing peptide (Drucker-Colín, 1981).

Evidence from Siamese twins suggests that chemicals in the blood probably do not play an important role in regulating sleep and arousal. Lenard and Schulte (1972) reported that Siamese twins who share a common cerebral blood supply have independent sleep cycles. If sleep and wakefulness were controlled by factors present in the blood, one would expect that the sleep cycles of these twins would be synchronized.

Perhaps sleep-regulating neuromodulators do not cross the blood-brain barrier and hence are found only in the brain. (In the case of Siamese twins whose sleep cycles are not synchronized, the neuromodulator would be found in one brain but not the other.) To test this hypothesis, Drucker-Colín and Spanis (1976) implanted push-pull cannulas in cats.

They perfused Ringer's solution through the midbrain reticular formation of donor cats and then injected it into the brains of recipient cats. This procedure would presumably transfer substances present in the brains of donor animals to the brains of the recipients. The investigators found that Ringer's solution perfused through a sleeping donor would cause the recipient to go to sleep faster than control injections of plain Ringer's solution. Conversely, Ringer's solution perfused through an awake donor would cause a sleeping recipient to wake up. Thus, the brain appears to produce different chemicals during sleep and waking. (See **Figure 9.12**.)

One more line of research suggests the presence of a hypnogenic neuromodulator. The most commonly used sleeping medications come from a class of drugs called benzodiazepines, including diazepam (Valium) and flurazepam (Dalmane). As we saw in Chapter 3, these drugs stimulate benzodiazepine receptors, thereby increasing the sensitivity of GABA receptors. (As you will recall, GABA is an inhibitory neurotransmitter.) Mendelson, Cain, Cook, Paul, and Skolnick (1983) found that a drug that blocks benzodiazepine receptors (3-hydroxymethyl-β-carboline) prevents the sleep-promoting effects of flurazepam. Even more interesting is the

FIGURE 9.12

Effects of transfusion of perfusate obtained by use of the push-pull cannula technique. (From Drucker-Colín, R.R., and Spanis, C.W. *Progress in Neurobiology*, 1976, 6, 1–12.)

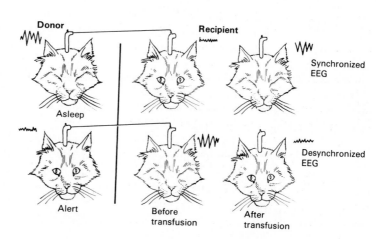

finding that when given by itself, this drug delayed the onset of normal sleep. Rats who were given a placebo fell asleep in 18 minutes, while those who received the drug stayed awake for 54 minutes. The drug did not simply appear to cause arousal; in contrast to activating drugs like amphetamine, it did not cause an increase in locomotor activity.

These results suggest that the brain produces a neuromodulator that activates benzodiazepine receptors. Although attempts to find an endogenous neuromodulator that fits these receptors have so far been unsuccessful, perhaps when one is found it will turn out to be a natural sleep producer, playing a role in the control of sleep.

INTERIM SUMMARY

Attempts to find neuromodulators or other naturally occurring chemicals that produce sleep have produced only modest results so far. The cerebrospinal fluid of sleep-deprived goats appears to contain a peptide that increases the duration of sleep in recipient animals. This substance (factor S) is also present in trace amounts in human urine. Because the chemical is apparently produced by bacteria in the intestines, it appears unlikely that factor S plays a critical role in regulating sleep. The fact that Siamese twins, even those with a common cerebral blood supply, have independent sleep cycles suggests that the search for blood-borne hypnogenic chemicals is doomed to failure.

It is possible that neuromodulators that control sleep are present within the brain itself and do not escape into the general circulation. Indeed, fluid perfused through the brain of a sleeping animal will induce drowsiness when it is infused into the brain of a recipient. Also, the fact that benzodiazepines promote sleep by stimulating a special class of receptors suggests that the brain produces a neuromodulator that normally stimulates the receptors. When these receptors are blocked by a drug, animals fall asleep less readily, which suggests that the drug is interfering with the action of a naturally occurring hypnogenic substance.

■ BIOLOGICAL CLOCKS

Much of our behavior follows regular rhythms. For example, we saw that the stages of sleep are organized around a 90-minute cycle of REM and slow-wave sleep. The same rhythm continues during the day as the basic rest-activity cycle (BRAC). And, of course, our daily pattern of sleep and waking follows a 24-hour cycle. In recent years, investigators have learned much about the neural mechanisms responsible for these rhythms.

Circadian Rhythms and Zeitgebers

Daily rhythms in behavior and physiological processes are found throughout the plant and animal world. These cycles are generally called *circadian rhythms.* (*Circa* means "about," and *dies* means "day"; therefore, a circadian rhythm is one that varies on a 24-hour cycle.) Some circadian rhythms, such as the rate of plant growth, are a direct consequence of variations in the level of illumination, and have no relevance to the study of sleep. However, other rhythms are controlled by mechanisms within the organism. For example, Figure 9.13 shows the activity of a rat during various conditions of illumination. Each horizontal line represents 24 hours. Vertical tick marks represent the animal's activity in a running wheel. The upper portion of the figure shows the activity of the rat during a normal day/night cycle, with alternating 12-hour periods of light and dark. Note that the animal is active during the night, which is normal for a rat. (See **Figure 9.13.**)

Next, the day was moved forward by 6 hours; the animal's activity cycle quickly followed the change. (See **Figure 9.13.**) Finally, dim lights were left on continuously. The cyclical pattern in the rat's activity remained. Because there were no cycles in the rat's environment, the source of rhythmicity must be

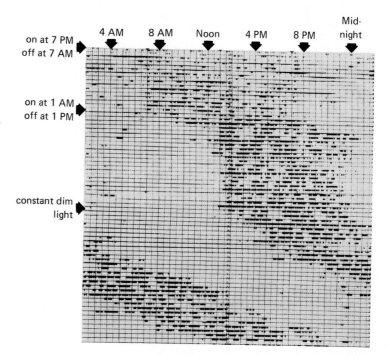

FIGURE 9.13

Wheel-running activity of a rat. Note that the animal's activity occurs at "night" (that is, during the 12 hours the light is off) and that the active period is reset when the light period is changed. When the animal is maintained in constant dim illumination, it displays a free-running activity cycle of approximately 25 hours. (From Groblewski, T.A., Nuñez, A., and Gold, R.M. Paper presented at the meeting of the Eastern Psychological Association, April 1980.)

located within the animal; that is, the animal must contain an internal, biological clock. You can see that the rat's clock was not set precisely to 24 hours; when the illumination was held constant, the clock ran a bit slow. The animal began its bout of activity about one hour later each day. (See **Figure 9.13**.)

The phenomenon illustrated in Figure 9.13 is typical of the circadian rhythms shown by many species. A free-running clock, with a cycle a little longer than 24 hours, controls some biological functions — in this case, motor activity. Regular daily variation in the level of illumination (that is, sunlight and darkness) normally keeps the clock adjusted to 24 hours. In the parlance of scientists who study circadian rhythms, light serves as a ***zeitgeber*** (German for "time giver"); it synchronizes the endogenous rhythm. Studies with many species of animals have shown that if they are maintained in constant darkness, a brief flash of light will reset their internal

clock, advancing or retarding it, depending upon when the light flash occurs (Aschoff, 1979). In the absence of light cycles, other environmental stimuli (such as fluctuations in temperature) can serve as zeitgebers, synchronizing the animal's rhythms.

Like other animals, humans exhibit circadian rhythms. Our normal period of inactivity begins several hours after the start of the dark portion of the day/night cycle and persists for a variable amount of time into the light portion. Without the benefits of modern civilization, we would probably go to sleep earlier and get up earlier than we do; we use artificial lights to delay our bedtime, and window shades to extend our time for sleep. Under constant illumination, our biological clocks will run free, gaining or losing time like a not-too-accurate watch. Different people have different cycle lengths, but most people in that situation will begin to live a "day" that is approximately 25 hours long.

The Neural Basis of Biological Clocks

It has been suspected for some time that the biological clocks of mammals are neural mechanisms, and that light is the primary zeitgeber. If rats are blinded, their activity cycles become free running (Browman, 1937; Richter, 1965). The observation that medial hypothalamic lesions abolished a rat's activity cycles (Richter, 1965, 1967) suggested that the clock may be located there.

Researchers working independently in two laboratories (Moore and Eichler, 1972; Stephan and Zucker, 1972) later discovered that the primary biological clock of the rat is located in the *suprachiasmatic nucleus (SCN)* of the hypothalamus. Figure 9.14 shows the suprachiasmatic nuclei in a transverse section through the hypothalamus of a mouse; they appear as two clusters of dark-staining neurons at the base of the brain, just above the optic chiasm. (See **Figure 9.14.**)

Because light is the primary zeitgeber for most mammals' activity cycles, one would expect that the SCN receives fibers from the visual system. Indeed, autoradiographic techniques have revealed a direct projection of fibers from the retina to the SCN (Hendrickson, Wagoner, and Cowan, 1972). If you look carefully at Figure 9.14, you can see small dark spots within the optic chiasm, just ventral and medial to the base of the SCN; these are cell bodies of oligodendroglia that serve axons that enter the SCN and provide information from the retina. (See **Figure 9.14.**)

The suprachiasmatic nuclei of the rat consist of approximately ten thousand small neurons, tightly packed into a volume of 0.05 cubic millimeters. The dendrites of these neurons synapse with each other—a phenomenon that is found only in this part of the hypothalamus and that undoubtedly relates to the special function of these nuclei (Güldner and Wolff, 1974; Güldner, 1976). A group of neurons is found clustered around the capillaries that serve the SCN. These neurons contain a large amount of rough endoplasmic reticulum, which suggests that they may be neurosecretory cells (Moore, Card, and Riley, 1980; Card, Riley, and Moore, 1980). Thus, it is possible that some of the control that the SCN exerts over other parts of the brain is accomplished by the secretion of neuromodulators.

Besides the fibers from the retina, the SCN also receives input from the various regions of

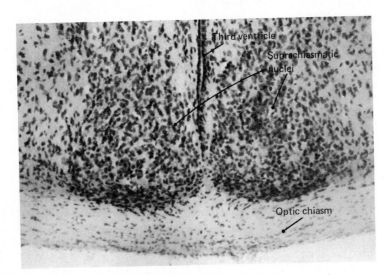

FIGURE 9.14
A transverse section through a mouse brain, showing the location and appearance of the suprachiasmatic nuclei. Cresyl violet stain.

the diencephalon and brain stem (Aghajanian, Bloom, and Sheard, 1969; Riback and Peters, 1975). The biological clock can function without these inputs; circadian rhythms are still seen after they are interrupted (Coindet, Chovet, and Mouret, 1975; Block and Zucker, 1976). Neurons of the SCN project caudally to the midbrain and to other hypothalamic nuclei, dorsally to other diencephalic regions, and rostrally to other hypothalamic nuclei and to the septum (Swanson and Cowan, 1975; Sofroniew and Weindl, 1978; Moore-Ede, Sulzman, and Fuller, 1982). Knife cuts that interrupt the caudal efferent axons of the SCN abolish hormonal rhythms, including those that control estrous cycles in female rats (Moore and Eichler, 1972), but they do not affect cycles of feeding, drinking, and activity (Nuñez and Casati, 1979). Presumably, the dorsal projections convey this control.

Effects of Lesions of the SCN on Sleep/ Waking Cycles

The suprachiasmatic nuclei appear to provide the primary control over the timing of sleep and waking cycles. Rats are nocturnal animals; they sleep during the day and forage and feed at night. Lesions of the SCN abolish this pattern; sleep occurs in bouts randomly dispersed throughout both day and night (Ibuka and Kawamura, 1975; Stephan and Nuñez, 1977). However, rats with SCN lesions still obtain the same amount of sleep that normal animals do. The lesions disrupt the circadian pattern but do not affect the total amount of sleep.

For two reasons, this finding is important. First, the fact that SCN lesions do not alter total sleep time per day means that an animal's quantity of sleep is *regulated*. This finding implies that some mechanism monitors the amount of sleep that an animal receives and controls the neural mechanisms responsible for this behavior. Clearly, the SCN does not perform these functions; rather, it exerts an influence that determines when sleep can occur. Second, the fact that such a discrete region of the brain is able to control sleep and waking means that we should be able to learn much about the neural mechanisms that regulate sleep by studying the efferent pathways of the SCN. Of course, the control may be chemical, in which case it would be profitable to find out what chemicals are secreted by the SCN and which neurons in other parts of the brain possess receptors for these chemicals.

Evidence for Intrinsic Rhythms in the SCN

A study by Schwartz and Gainer (1977) nicely demonstrates day/night fluctuations in the activity of the SCN. These investigators injected rats with radioactive 2-deoxyglucose (2-DG). As you will recall, this chemical is structurally similar to ordinary glucose; thus, it is taken up by cells that are metabolically active. However, it cannot be utilized, nor can it leave the cell. Therefore, metabolically active cells will accumulate radioactivity. (This technique was also used in a study on the visual mechanisms of the cerebral cortex, reported in Chapter 6.)

The investigators injected some rats with radioactive 2-DG during the day and injected others at night. The animals were then killed, and autoradiographs of cross sections through the brain were prepared. Figure 9.15 shows photographs of two of these cross sections. Note the evidence of radioactivity (and hence, a high metabolic rate) in the SCN of the brain that was injected during the day *(left)*. (See **Figure 9.15**.)

Recordings of electrical activity support the conclusions made from other approaches. Inouye and Kawamura (1979) recorded the activity of neurons in the hypothalamus and in other parts of the brain, such as the caudate nucleus. Neurons in both regions showed a regular fluctuation in firing rate across day/

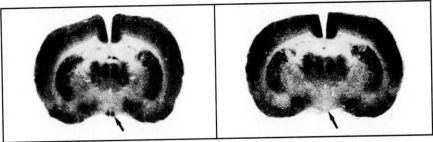

FIGURE 9.15
Autoradiographs of transverse sections through the brains of rats that had
been injected with carbon-14-labeled 2-deoxyglucose during the day
(left) or the night *(right)*. The dark region at the base of the brain
(arrows) indicates increased metabolic activity of the suprachiasmatic
nuclei. (From Schwartz, W.J., and Gainer, H. *Science,* 1977, *197,*
1089–1091.)

night cycles. Presumably, these fluctuations were controlled by the SCN. However, when knife cuts completely separated the hypothalamus from the rest of the brain, the firing rate of neurons in the caudate nucleus became constant, while those of hypothalamic neurons remained cyclical. (See **Figure 9.16.**)

Excellent evidence indicates that the effect of light as a zeitgeber is exerted through the direct connections between the retina and the SCN. Ibuka, Inouye, and Kawamura (1977) made lesions in the optic tract, caudal to the SCN. Although the animals were blind, their activity cycles were still entrained to the 24-hour light/dark cycle. (See **Figure 9.17.**) Also, Rusak and Groos (1982) found that electrical stimulation of the SCN had the same effect as brief pulses of light. Depending on the time of day, the stimulation would advance or retard the biological clock. That is, a pulse of electrical stimulation early in the animals' active period would delay the clock; the animals would remain active even longer. In contrast, electrical stimulation late in the animals' active period would stop their activity early and begin the period of sleep.

Although experimental studies have obviously not been done, it appears likely that the primary biological clock that controls human sleep and waking cycles is also located in the SCN. Anatomical studies clearly show that humans have suprachiasmatic nuclei (Lydic, Schoene, Czeisler, and Moore-Ede, 1980). In addition, brain tumors that damage the region of the SCN have been reported to produce disorders in sleep/waking cycles (Fulton and Bailey, 1929).

The Physiological Basis of Circadian Rhythms

All clocks must have a time base. Mechanical clocks use flywheels or pendulums; electronic clocks use quartz crystals. The SCN, too, must contain a physiological mechanism that parses time into units. So far, we do not know what this mechanism is. One hypothesis suggests that a time base may be provided by the synthesis of proteins (Jacklet, 1978). Perhaps cells begin to synthesize protein, and, as the level of this product rises, negative feedback shuts down the synthetic process. The protein is then degraded or dispersed over time, and the low level of protein permits the cycle to begin again. The presence of the protein could affect some property of neurons in the region (for example, their

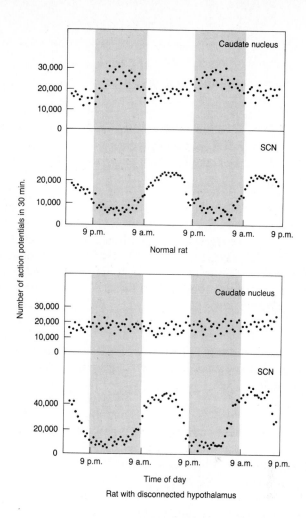

FIGURE 9.16
Activity of single units in the caudate nucleus and suprachiasmatic nucleus in an intact rat *(top)* and in a rat whose hypothalamus had been surgically disconnected *(bottom)*. (Previously unpublished graph courtesy of S.T. Inouye.)

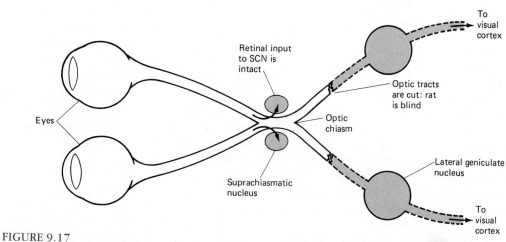

FIGURE 9.17
A summary of the experiment by Ibuka, Inouye, and Kawamura (1977).

membrane permeability) and alter their rate of firing.

This hypothesis remains speculative, but Jacklet (1977) has shown that a drug that inhibits protein synthesis (anisomycin) stops the biological clock contained in the isolated eye of *Aplysia* (a marine invertebrate). Furthermore, even brief exposure to anisomycin, which causes a brief drop in the rate of protein synthesis, resets the clock to a new time. This observation suggests that the intrinsic activity of the *Aplysia* eye might use the process of protein synthesis for its time base. Whether the same mechanism operates in the SCN is still not known.

Evidence for Other Biological Clocks

Quite clearly, the SCN is not the only biological clock in the mammalian nervous system. For example, Fuller, Lydic, Sulzman, Albers, Tepper, and Moore-Ede (1981) found that destruction of the SCN in squirrel monkeys abolished circadian rhythms in sleep/activity patterns but did not affect daily rhythms in body temperature. Thus, the biological clock that controls body temperature must be located outside the SCN. Evidence suggests that the SCN normally coordinates the activity of other biological clocks, some of which have shorter periods. For example, Rusak (1977, 1979) found that after SCN lesions, the wheel-running activity of hamsters maintained in constant dim illumination consisted of two or three peaks each day, instead of the single peak that normally occurs.

Animals who are fed on a regular daily schedule will soon become active just before the feeding time. This anticipation obviously depends upon some internal clock, because it occurs in the absence of environmental cues. Boulos, Rosenwasser, and Terman (1980) found that rats showed this anticipation even after their SCN was destroyed; therefore, another clock must be able to perform this function. (See **Figure 9.18.**)

It appears that the SCN normally dominates this other clock. If food is presented every 18 hours or every 30 hours, rats do not show anticipatory activity; presumably these times are too different from the 24-hour rhythm of the SCN for that clock to be useful. However, Boulos and associates found that after they destroyed the rats' SCN, the animals *could* learn to anticipate short or long feeding cycles. Once the influence of the SCN was gone, the remaining clock could become synchronized to a new rhythm.

Although the SCN has an intrinsic rhythm of approximately 24 hours, it plays a role in much longer rhythms. Male hamsters show annual rhythms of testosterone secretion, which appear to be based upon the amount of light that occurs each day. Their breeding season begins as the day length increases and ends when it decreases. Lesions of the SCN abolish these annual breeding cycles; the animals' testes then secrete testosterone all year (Rusak and Morin, 1976). It is possible that the lesions disrupt these annual cycles because they destroy the 24-hour clock against which the daily light period is measured to determine the season. That is, if the light period is considerably shorter than 12 hours, the season is winter; if it is considerably longer than 12 hours, the season is summer.

Much progress has been made in the investigation of the neural mechanisms of biological rhythms during the last few years. The unanswered questions concern the nature of the physiological processes that provide the underlying rhythm, the location of biological clocks other than the SCN, and the means by which these clocks influence cyclic behaviors such as sleep and waking.

INTERIM   SUMMARY

Our daily lives are characterized by cycles in physical activity, sleep, body temperature, secretion of hormones, and many other physiological changes.

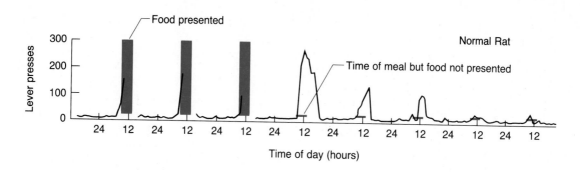

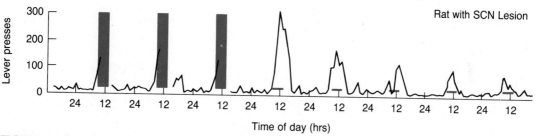

FIGURE 9.18

After being fed at the same time each day, both a normal rat *(top)* and a rat with bilateral SCN lesions *(bottom)* increase their lever-pressing activity at the customary time for feeding. (From Boulos, Z., Rosenwasser, A.M., and Terman, M. *Behavioral Brain Research,* 1980, *1,* 39–65.)

Circadian rhythms, those with a period of approximately one day, are controlled by biological clocks in the brain. The principal biological clock appears to be located in the suprachiasmatic nuclei of the hypothalamus; lesions of these nuclei disrupt most circadian rhythms, and the metabolic activity of neurons located there correlates with the day/night cycle. We do not know how biological clocks keep time, although some investigators suggest that the rate of protein synthesis times the individual "ticks."

Light serves as a zeitgeber for most circadian rhythms. That is, the biological clocks tend to run a bit slow, with a period of approximately 25 hours. Studies that have cut the optic tracts caudal to the SCN or have administered pulses of electrical stimulation to the SCN support the hypothesis that the sight of sunlight in the morning is conveyed from the retina to the SCN, resetting the clock to the start of a new cycle.

■ **NEURAL MECHANISMS OF SLEEP AND WAKING**

What neural mechanisms control waking and the two major stages of sleep? Clearly, sleep does not occur simply because neurons get tired and begin to fire more slowly. Indeed, Moruzzi (1972) reviewed electrophysiological evidence that neurons in the neocortex, lateral geniculate nucleus, reticular formation, and hypothalamus generally decrease their rate of firing during slow-wave sleep, but during REM sleep they fire as fast as (or faster than) during wakefulness. For example, neurons in the motor cortex fire more often during sleep than during inactive wakefulness (Evarts, 1965). Other units (such as those of the hippocampus) fire slowly during

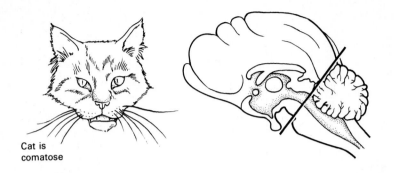

Cat is
comatose

FIGURE 9.19
Cerveau isolé. (From Bremer,
F. *Bulletin de l'Academie
Royale de Belgique,* 1937, *4,*
68–86.)

REM sleep. The point to be made is that there is not a *universal* decline in firing rate during sleep.

Brain Stem Mechanisms of Sleep and Arousal: Evidence from Early Studies

Bremer (1937), in an investigation of neural sleep and arousal mechanisms, showed that brain mechanisms that were important for arousal were located in the brain stem. He severed the brain stem of a cat between the superior and inferior colliculi. The cat survived for only a few days and showed a permanently synchronized EEG and pupillary constriction, indicating that the animal was comatose (unconscious). The effects of this *midcollicular transection,* which Bremer called *cerveau isolé,* or "isolated brain," are shown in **Figure 9.19.** Bremer also made a transection at the caudal end of the medulla, just above the spinal cord (producing *encéphale isolé,* or "isolated head contents"). The result was a cat that demonstrated normal sleep and waking cycles. The animal was paralyzed, of course, because the brain and spinal cord were disconnected, so waking could not be evaluated in the normal fashion. However, the EEG showed periodic episodes of desynchronized and synchronized activity. During desynchrony, the cat's pupils were dilated, and the eyes followed a moving object. During synchrony, the pupils were constricted, and the eyes showed no reaction to visual stimuli. Therefore, the animal alternately slept and woke. Figure 9.20 shows the

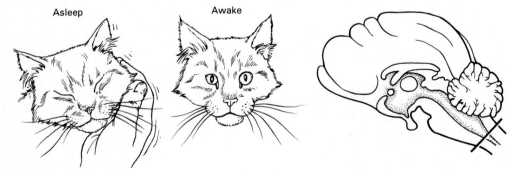

Asleep   Awake

FIGURE 9.20
Encéphale isolé. (From Bremer, F. *Bulletin de l'Academie Royale de Belgique,* 1937, *4,* 68–86.)

location of the brain stem transection and the arousing effects of the experimenter handling the cat's head. (Because somatosensory information is received from the head region by means of the trigeminal nerve, this input is not disconnected in encéphale isolé.) (See **Figure 9.20.**)

Subsequent studies showed that sleep is not a passive process; it is an active one. Batini, Moruzzi, Palestini, Rossi, and Zanchetti (1958, 1959) cut through the midbrain of a cat, a few millimeters caudal to the midcollicular transection of Bremer. This operation, which the authors called a ***midpontine pretrigeminal transection,*** produced insomnia; the EEG and other signs indicated wakefulness 70 to 90 percent of the time. In contrast, a normal cat is awake approximately 30 to 40 percent of the time.

Let us examine further evidence that the brain stem contains mechanisms that are important for producing sleep and arousal. Magni, Moruzzi, Rossi, and Zanchetti (1959) tied off some cerebral blood vessels, so that the arterial blood supply to the medulla and lower pons was separated from the blood supply to the upper pons and cerebrum. (See **Figure 9.21.**) When they injected an anes-

thetic (thiopental) into the blood supply of the rostral pons and cerebrum of a waking cat, the cat became unconscious. (Obviously, this is not a surprising result.) However, when they injected the anesthetic into the caudal brain stem of a sleeping cat, the cat would wake up. How can anesthetizing part of the brain awaken a sleeping animal?

The answer seems to be this: The activity of some region in the caudal brain stem must be necessary to put an animal to sleep. Remember, sleep is a *behavior.* When the activity of this region is temporarily suppressed by an injection of thiopental, the sleeping brain awakens — the behavior of sleep ceases. Like the midpontine pretrigeminal transection, this observation provides further evidence that sleep is an active process. Two conclusions can be based on these studies:

1. A brain region between the midcollicular transection of Bremer and the midpontine transection of Batini and colleagues is important in producing wakefulness. The rostral transection disconnects the cerebrum from this region, whereas the midpontine transection does not.

2. A sleep-producing region lies somewhere between the midpontine transection

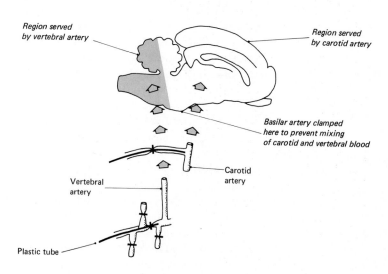

FIGURE 9.21
The procedure of Magni and colleagues, which allowed the injection of an anesthetic (thiopental) into different regions of the brain. (Adapted from Magni, F., Moruzzi, G., Rossi, G.N., and Zanchetti, A. *Archives Italiennes de Biologie,* 1959, *97,* 33–46.)

Region served by vertebral artery

Region served by carotid artery

Basilar artery clamped here to prevent mixing of carotid and vertebral blood

Carotid artery

Vertebral artery

Plastic tube

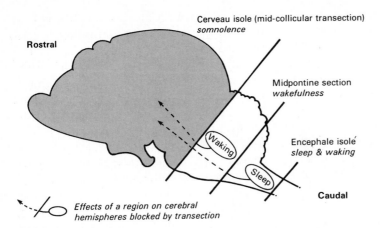

Effects of a region on cerebral
hemispheres blocked by transection

FIGURE 9.22
A summary of the results of the
three brain stem transections.

and the caudal part of the medulla—the encéphale isolé transection of Bremer. Animals with the midpontine transection show very little sleep, whereas those with the caudal transection show normal sleep/waking cycles.

These results are summarized in **Figure 9.22.**

It appears, then, that a mechanism in the rostral pons plays a role in wakefulness, and another mechanism in the caudal pons (and/or medulla) is important for sleep.

Brain Stem Arousal Mechanisms

The Reticular Formation
The somnolence of cerveau isolé, but not the midpontine pretrigeminal transection, suggests that the rostral pons is important for arousal. There is much evidence that supports this suggestion. In 1949, Moruzzi and Magoun found that electrical stimulation of the brain stem reticular formation produced arousal. The reticular formation, which occupies the central core of the brain stem, receives collateral axons from ascending sensory pathways. Presumably, sensory stimulation, the primary instigator of arousal, activates the reticular formation by means of these collateral axons. The activated reticular formation then arouses the cerebral cortex by

means of direct axonal connections and by connections relayed through various nuclei of the thalamus.

Lindsley, Schreiner, Knowles, and Magoun (1950) obtained evidence that the arousing effect of sensory stimulation is indeed mediated through the reticular formation. They made lesions that disrupted the direct sensory pathways that run through the pons and midbrain. They found that tactile stimulation of these animals aroused them. Because the lesions destroyed the direct sensory pathways (which go to the thalamus, and from there to the somatosensory cortex), the arousal was obviously mediated by the indirect projections through the reticular formation. Although the animals presumably could not "feel" the stimulation, they nevertheless were aroused by it. In contrast, when the investigators made lesions that destroyed the reticular formation, sensory stimulation produced only a very brief period of arousal. (See **Figure 9.23.**)

Recording studies soon provided evidence that supported the stimulation and lesion studies. Multiple-unit activity (the action potentials of a large population of neurons located near the tip of the recording electrode) showed a relation between arousal and the firing rate of neurons in the midbrain reticular formation. Machne, Calma, and Magoun

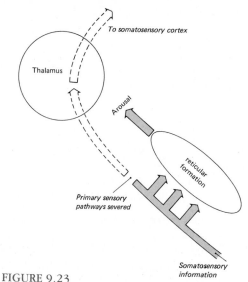

FIGURE 9.23

A summary of the results of the experiment by Lindsley and colleagues (1950).

(1955) found that neurons in the reticular formation increased their firing rate when cats were aroused by stimulating a peripheral nerve. Bambridge and Gijsbers (1977) found a correlation between behavioral arousal and multiple-unit activity of the reticular formation in unrestrained cats. In addition, two events that produce arousal also increased the firing rate of reticular formation neurons: anticipation of food (Olds, Mink, and Best, 1969) and anticipation of painful shock (Unemoto, Murai, Kodama, and Kido, 1970). In contrast, when cats are relaxed by petting, feeding, or grooming them, multiple-unit activity in the reticular formation decreases (Beyer, Almanza, de la Torre, and Guzman-Flores, 1971).

The reticular formation is an extensive and complex brain structure, and once its role in arousal was well accepted, investigators attempted to find out the specific location of the arousal mechanisms. They began to study single-unit activity in freely moving cats, which allows for maximum specificity. Unfortunately, careful study of the activity patterns of individual neurons failed to support the hypothesis that the reticular formation performs a general arousal function. Investigators found that the activity of individual neurons was closely related to specific movements of the eyes, ears, face, head, body, and limbs (Siegel, 1979; 1983). In general, their response rate was not related to general levels of arousal or to sleep/waking cycles.

Siegel suggests two reasons for the discrepancy. First, relations between movements and single-unit activity obviously cannot be observed in anesthetized or physically restrained cats. Many studies have used such cats and consequently have failed to observe the animals' behavior. Second, multiple-unit recording averages the activity of many neurons. If different groups of neurons are active during different types of movements, then the population *as a whole* may respond nonspecifically, which may lead the investigator to conclude erroneously that *all* of them are responding nonspecifically. Siegel explains the increased activity of neurons in the reticular formation in terms of their relation to movement. For example, suppose that an investigator finds that multiple-unit activity increases when a cat anticipates painful foot shock or receiving some food. Because both events can be thought of as "arousing," the investigator may conclude that the units mediate nonspecific arousal. However, the results could actually have been produced by two different groups of neurons: one group that fires during ear flattening (a response that cats commonly make when they are fearful) and another group that fires during the postural adjustments the cat makes in anticipation of obtaining food.

The Noradrenergic System of the Locus Coeruleus

Investigators have long known that catecholamine agonists such as amphetamine produce arousal and sleeplessness. Several studies

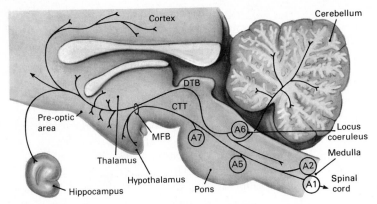

FIGURE 9.24
The principal noradrenergic pathways. CTT = central tegmental tract; DTB = dorsal tegmental bundle; MFB = medial forebrain bundle.

have suggested that these effects are mediated by the noradrenergic system of the *locus coeruleus,* which also plays a more general role in arousal. Neurons of the locus coeruleus, located in the dorsal pons, send axons that branch widely, terminating in the neocortex, hippocampus, thalamus, cerebellar cortex, and medulla; thus, they potentially affect widespread and important regions of the brain. (See **Figure 9.24.**) Jones, Bobillier, and Jouvet (1969) made a lesion that interrupted the ascending axons from the neurons of the rostral locus coeruleus. They found that the animals became hypersomniac; their REM sleep and slow-wave sleep increased dramatically. Thus, there is evidence that the ascending noradrenergic system is involved in arousal (or, at least, in the suppression of sleep).

Although the noradrenergic system of the locus coeruleus may play a role in arousal, the activating effects of electrical stimulation of the reticular formation do not appear to be caused by excitation of this system. Robinson, Vanderwolf, and Pappas (1977) found that electrical stimulation of the locus coeruleus was not very effective in producing EEG or behavioral arousal. In contrast, stimulation of the pontine reticular formation was much more effective.

More recent studies have clarified the role that the locus coeruleus appears to play in arousal. Aston-Jones and Bloom (1981) recorded from noradrenergic neurons of the locus coeruleus across the sleep/waking cycle in unrestrained rats. As Figure 9.25 shows, these neurons exhibited an excellent relation to behavioral arousal. Note the decline in firing rate before and during sleep, and the abrupt increase when the animal wakes. (See **Figure 9.25.**)

Aston-Jones and Bloom found that when they aroused the animals by sudden environmental stimuli during sleep or quiet wakefulness, the noradrenergic neurons suddenly increased their activity. In addition, they increased their rate of firing approximately 3 seconds before waking (as defined by changes in the EMG record). Thus, these neurons may well be involved in arousal. The authors suggest that the specific function of these neurons is to increase the animal's sensitivity to environmental stimuli. This function was demonstrated by earlier studies (Segal and Bloom, 1976a, 1976b) that found that electrical stimulation of the locus coeruleus or application of norepinephrine by means of microiontophoresis made neurons that receive noradrenergic projections become more responsive to external stimuli. If their conclusion is true, amphetamine may cause arousal and increase sleeplessness by increasing the animal's sensitivity to stimuli in its environment.

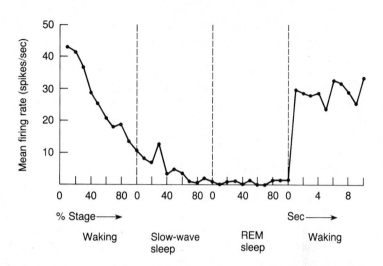

FIGURE 9.25
Activity of noradrenergic neurons in the locus coeruleus of freely moving cats during various stages of sleep and waking. (From Aston-Jones, G., and Bloom, F.E. *The Journal of Neuroscience,* 1981, *1,* 876–886. Copyright 1981, The Society for Neuroscience.)

Some investigators have suggested that the locus coeruleus plays a role in REM sleep as well as arousal; this suggestion will be discussed in a later section of this chapter.

Brain Stem Mechanisms of Slow-Wave Sleep

The effects of brain stem transections and the activating effects of an anesthetic injected into the blood supply of the brain stem suggest the presence of neural mechanisms whose activity is important for sleep. The precise location of the brain stem sleep mechanisms is not known for certain, but investigators have proposed two candidates: the raphe and the nucleus of the solitary tract.

The Raphe

The **raphe** (say "ra-FAY") consists of a group of nuclei running through the core of the brain stem from the medulla to the back of the midbrain. Figure 9.26 shows the location of the raphe in a midsagittal section through the

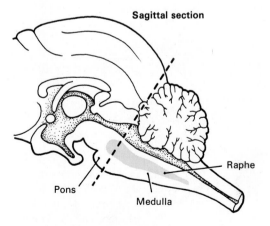

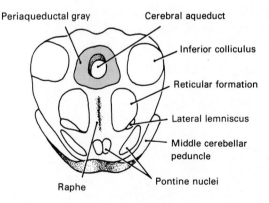

FIGURE 9.26
Location of the raphe nuclei.

brain stem; you can see how the midpontine pretrigeminal transection separates much of the raphe from the cerebrum. Perhaps, then, the transection produces sleeplessness by disconnecting the raphe from the cerebrum. (See **Figure 9.26.**) The transverse section in the same figure shows how this structure got its name: *rhaphe* means "crease" or "seam."

Jouvet and Renault (1966) produced large lesions that destroyed 80 to 90 percent of the raphe in cats. The cats showed complete insomnia for 3 to 4 days. Slow-wave sleep (but not REM sleep) gradually returned but never exceeded approximately 2½ hours per day. Smaller lesions resulted in more recovery, but REM sleep did not reappear until slow-wave sleep totaled approximately 3½ hours per day. Several investigators have attempted to produce sleep by electrically stimulating the raphe, but the results have been mixed; some investigators (e.g., Gumulka, Samanin, Val-

zelli, and Consolos, 1971) report success, while others (e.g., Polc and Monnier, 1966) produced *arousal* with raphe stimulation.

Histofluorescence studies have shown that the neurons of the raphe nuclei are rich in serotonin (5-HT). Jouvet (1968) found that raphe lesions depressed cerebral levels of 5-HT, and that the amount of time the animals spent sleeping correlated with the amount of 5-HT still present in the brain. This observation suggested that sleep might be produced by the activity of serotonergic neurons, whose cell bodies are located in the raphe nuclei. In support of this hypothesis, Jouvet reported that when he administered a single dose of parachlorophenylalanine (PCPA), which inhibits the biosynthesis of 5-HT, the cats did not sleep. Figure 9.27 shows the effects of PCPA on the brain levels of 5-HT and on sleep. Note that the percentage of sleep *(top curve)* and the percentage of 5-HT *(bottom curve)* both begin to drop at ap-

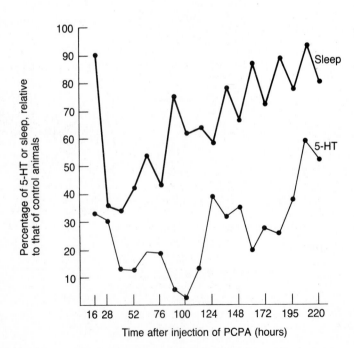

FIGURE 9.27
Effects of a single injection of PCPA on sleep and on the amount of 5-HT in the brain. (From Mouret, J.R., Bobillier, P., and Jouvet, M. *European Journal of Pharmacology,* 1968, *5,* 17–22.)

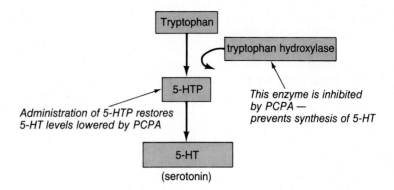

FIGURE 9.28
Biosynthesis of 5-HT, and the effects of administering PCPA and 5-HTP.

proximately 16 hours after the injection and show a parallel recovery course. (See **Figure 9.27.**)

Brain levels of 5-HT can be restored after treatment with PCPA by injecting 5-hydroxy-tryptophan (5-HTP), the precursor of 5-HT. Figure 9.28 illustrates the biosynthetic pathway for 5-HT and shows how PCPA blocks the production of 5-HT and how 5-HTP restores it. (See **Figure 9.28.**) It would be much more straightforward, of course, to inject 5-HT itself, but this substance does not cross the blood-brain barrier, whereas 5-HTP does. Insomnia produced by an injection of PCPA can be quickly reversed (that is, sleep can be restored) by an injection of 5-HTP (Pujol, Buguet, Froment, Jones, and Jouvet, 1971).

Unfortunately, the story becomes complicated when PCPA is administered chronically. Dement, Mitler, and Henriksen (1972) found that when a cat is given daily injections of PCPA, the insomnia eventually disappears; both REM sleep and slow-wave sleep return to approximately 80 percent of their normal levels. This recovery occurs even though 5-HT levels remain depressed by 90 percent. (See **Figure 9.29.**) The results suggest that the activity of serotonergic neurons of the raphe is not essential for sleep.

Why does treatment with PCPA cause temporary insomnia? Henriksen, Dement, and Barchas (1974) suggested that serotonergic

neurons play a role in controlling some components of REM sleep. They also suggested that inhibition of serotonin synthesis disrupts this control, thus interfering with sleep. They found that when a cat that receives injections of PCPA every day begins

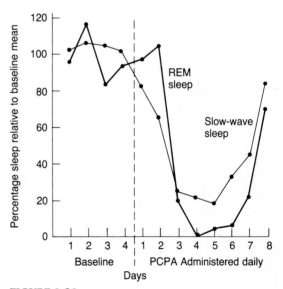

FIGURE 9.29
Effects of daily administration of PCPA on sleep. (From Dement, W., Mitler, M., and Henriksen, S. *Revue Canadienne de Biologie,* 1972, *31,* 239–246.)

sleeping again, the phasic effects of REM sleep (PGO waves, muscular twitches, and rapid eye movements) "escape" and begin to intrude during slow-wave sleep and even during waking. The cats have sudden attacks of emotional behavior, such as snarling and hissing. These episodes probably disturb the animal and tend to keep it awake. However, after a few days the cats become habituated to the attacks and manage to sleep.

Recording studies support the suggestion that the dorsal raphe nuclei normally suppress components of REM sleep. Trulson and Jacobs (1979) recorded the activity of neurons in these nuclei during sleep and waking. As you can see in Figure 9.30, these

neurons were most active during waking. Their firing rate declined during slow-wave sleep and became virtually zero during REM sleep. However, once the period of REM sleep ended, the neurons temporarily became very active again. (See **Figure 9.30.**)

When these results are considered along with the effects of PCPA, a good case can be made that the dorsal raphe nuclei inhibit the phasic components of REM sleep and thus prevent them from occurring at inappropriate times. The activity of serotonergic neurons is low during REM sleep and is higher at other times. However, the dorsal raphe nuclei must have other functions, as well. Lesions of the raphe or administration of 5,6-di-

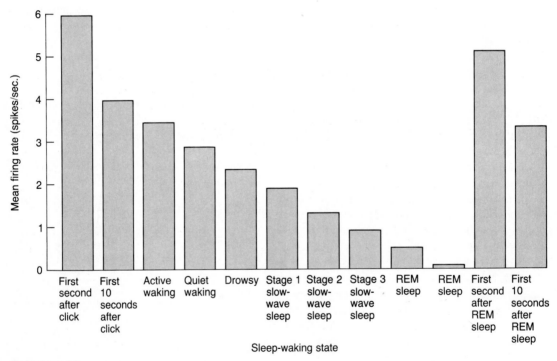

FIGURE 9.30

Activity of serotonergic (5-HT-secreting) neurons in the dorsal raphe nuclei of freely moving cats during various stages of sleep and waking. (From Trulson, M.E., and Jacobs, B.L. *Brain Research,* 1979, *163,* 135–150.)

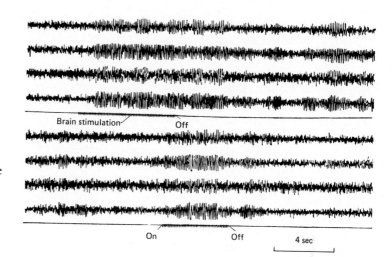

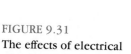

FIGURE 9.31

The effects of electrical stimulation in the region of the nucleus of the solitary tract. (From Magnes, J., Moruzzi, G., and Pompeiano, O. *Archives Italiennes de Biologie,* 1961, *99*, 33–67.)

hydroxytryptamine (which kills serotonergic neurons) increase a variety of behaviors, including eating, locomotion, sexual behavior, aggression, and reaction to environmental stimuli, while administration of 5-HTP (which raises brain levels of serotonin) decreases these behaviors (Trulson and Jacobs, 1979). These results suggest that the function of intact serotonergic neurons is to suppress reactions to stimuli. In fact, Trulson, Jacobs, and Morrison (1981) hypothesize that the inhibiting role that the dorsal raphe plays in REM sleep is secondary to a more general role in inhibiting behavior. Obviously, we need further evidence before we can make any definitive statements about the behavioral functions of the dorsal raphe.

The Nucleus of the Solitary Tract

The **nucleus of the solitary tract** is a structure located in the medulla that receives taste information and visceral sensation. Evidence suggests that it plays a role in sleep. Berlucchi, Maffei, Moruzzi, and Strata (1964) cooled the medulla by placing a metal plate on the floor of the fourth ventricle, through which a cold liquid could be circulated. The cooling, which produces a temporary lesion,

resulted in behavioral and EEG arousal, even if the cat was previously asleep. This study suggests that the activity of some region of the medulla is necessary for sleep.

Magnes, Moruzzi, and Pompeiano (1961) stimulated the region of the nucleus of the solitary tract with low-frequency electrical current. The stimulation had a synchronizing effect on the cat's EEG, which is usually synonymous with sleepiness. Figure 9.31 shows the effects of such stimulation on the EEG. The tick marks on the lower line represent the stimulation; note that the cortical synchrony continues even after the stimulation is turned off. (See **Figure 9.31**.)

The nucleus of the solitary tract receives sensory information from the tongue and from various internal organs. Bonvallet and Sigg (1958) found that stimulation of the vagus nerve (which sends fibers to this region) produces EEG synchrony. Pompeiano and Swett (1962) stimulated cutaneous nerves in unanesthetized, freely moving cats and found that repetitive, low-frequency stimulation produced EEG synchrony when the cat was in a relatively quiet state. They subsequently found that neurons in the medulla fired in response to this nerve stimulation (Pompeiano and Swett, 1963). However, they found that high-intensity nerve stimulation, which produces arousal, activated neurons in the pontine and midbrain reticular formation. Kukorelli and Juhasz (1977) found that electrical stimulation of the intestines, which send information to the nucleus of the solitary tract, increased sleep. This increase occurred even in cats who were deprived of food and would normally be alert and active.

It seems likely that the calming effects of gentle rocking (which usually soothes a baby) are mediated by neurons in the nucleus of the solitary tract. Perhaps we can also thus account for the fact that a large meal makes us sleepy, because the nucleus of the solitary tract receives sensory inputs from the digestive tract. So far, this region of the medulla seems to be the most likely candidate in the search for brain stem mechanisms of sleep.

Forebrain Mechanisms of Slow-Wave Sleep

The *preoptic–basal forebrain region*— an area of the forebrain just rostral to the hypothalamus — also appears to play a role in sleep. Nauta (1946) found that destruction of this area produced total insomnia in rats. The animals subsequently fell into a coma and died; the average survival time was only 3 days. McGinty and Sterman (1968) found that cats reacted somewhat differently; the animals did not become sleepless until several days after the lesion was made. Two of the cats, whose sleep was totally suppressed, died within 10 days. Figure 9.32 illustrates this effect. (See **Figure 9.32.**)

The effects of basal forebrain stimulation are consistent with the lesion experiments. Sterman and Clemente (1962a, 1962b) found that electrical stimulation of this region produced cortical synchrony and drowsiness in unanesthetized, freely moving cats. The average latency period between stimulation and EEG synchrony was 30 seconds; often, the effect was immediate. Behavioral sleep frequently followed. (See **Figure 9.33.**)

Another study provides further support. Roberts and Robinson (1969) warmed the preoptic area, thereby stimulating thermoreceptors that are located there, and observed drowsiness and EEG synchrony. Thus, a more ''natural'' stimulation mimics the effects of electrical stimulation. The excessive sleepiness that accompanies a fever may be pro-

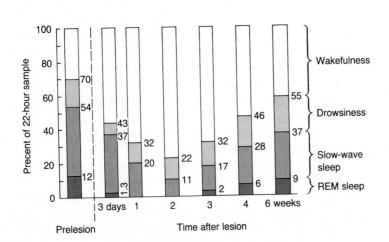

FIGURE 9.32

Effects of lesions of the preoptic area on sleep. (From McGinty, D.J., and Sterman, M.B. *Science,* 1968, *160,* 1253–1255. Copyright 1968 by the American Association for the Advancement of Science.)

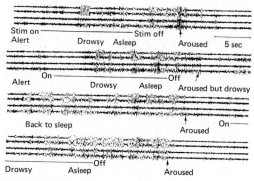

Stim on ———————— Stim off

Alert   Drowsy   Asleep   Aroused   5 sec

On ————————————— Off

Alert   Drowsy   Asleep   Aroused but drowsy

                                              On ———

Back to sleep   Aroused

                        ———Off

Drowsy   Asleep   Aroused

FIGURE 9.33

Sleep produced by prolonged electrical stimulation of the basal forebrain region. (From Sterman, M.B., and Clemente, C.D. *Experimental Neurology,* 1962, *6,* 103–117.)

duced by this mechanism. Thermoreceptors in the skin also relay information to the preoptic area; perhaps preoptic stimulation accounts for the drowsiness and lassitude we feel on a hot day. Pavlov (1923) noted that when thermal stimulation of the skin was used as a stimulus in studies of classical conditioning, the dogs he was training often fell asleep.

Bremer (1970) provided electrophysiological evidence for an inhibitory influence on behavioral arousal. When the preoptic stimulation was presented simultaneously with sensory stimulation or electrical stimulation of the reticular formation, the arousing effects of the latter two procedures were diminished. The opposite effect was also seen: stimulation of the reticular formation inhibited the preoptic sleep-producing area (Bremer, 1975). Moreover, transection of the brain stem just rostral to the midbrain reticular formation caused an immediate increase in the activity of neurons in the preoptic area, which suggests that the transection removed an inhibitory influence on the preoptic sleep-producing area. Bremer also found that activity of preoptic neurons was related to the animal's sleep cycles, with the activity being

highest during slow-wave sleep. This relation was therefore disrupted by the brain stem transections placed just rostral to the midbrain reticular formation.

Neural Mechanisms of REM Sleep

As we have seen, evidence suggests that the dorsal raphe nuclei play a role in suppressing components of REM sleep. Investigators have also studied neural mechanisms that might *produce* REM sleep.

Pharmacological Studies

Pharmacological data suggest that noradrenergic, serotonergic, and acetylcholinergic neurons all play some role in the control of REM sleep.

Norepinephrine. As you will recall from the earlier discussion of narcolepsy, noradrenergic antagonists increase REM sleep, and noradrenergic agonists decrease it. In addition, the study by Aston-Jones and Bloom (1981) found that the rate of firing of noradrenergic neurons is at its lowest point during REM sleep. These facts suggest that REM sleep is inhibited by noradrenergic neurons, most of which are located in the locus coeruleus. α-Methyl-p-tyrosine (AMPT), which blocks the synthesis of the catecholamines, causes a temporary increase in REM sleep in humans (Vaughan, Wyatt, and Green, 1972). Reserpine, which prevents the storage of the catecholamines (and also serotonin) also increases REM sleep in humans (Coulter, Lester, and Williams, 1971). In contrast, the tricyclic antidepressant drugs, which act as catecholamine agonists, cause temporary decreases in REM sleep (Baekeland, 1967; Dunleavy, Brezinová, Oswald, MacLean, and Tinker, 1972). Thus, substantial evidence suggests that noradrenergic neurons play an inhibitory role in REM sleep.

Serotonin. As we saw earlier, PCPA, which blocks the synthesis of serotonin, permits elements of REM sleep to occur at inappropriate times. This effect occurs in humans as well as cats. Some cancer patients with tumors (outside the nervous system) that secreted high levels of serotonin were given PCPA. The drug produced hallucinations (Engelman, Lovenberg, and Sjoerdsma, 1967). Perhaps the hallucinations were actually a REM sleep phenomenon — dreaming — that occurred during waking. In addition, various hallucinogens, such as lysergic acid diethylamide (LSD) and mescaline, are also potent serotonin antagonists.

Consistent with these findings, certain monoamine oxidase inhibitors, which serve as serotonin agonists, cause decreases in REM sleep (Wyatt, 1972). And as we saw earlier, imipramine (a monoamine agonist) has been successfully used to treat cataplexy, sleep paralysis, and hypnagogic hallucinations, all manifestations of REM sleep. Amphetamine, a potent catecholamine agonist that has little effect on serotonergic neurons, is not very effective in treating these symptoms. Thus, the pharmacological data support the suggestion that serotonergic neurons exert an inhibitory effect on brain mechanisms that are active during REM sleep.

Acetylcholine. Drugs that excite acetylcholinergic synapses facilitate REM sleep. Stoyva and Metcalf (1968) found that people who have been exposed to organophosphate insecticides, which inhibit acetylcholinesterase (AChE) and therefore increase the postsynaptic effects of acetylcholine, spend an increased time in REM sleep. In a controlled experiment, Sitaram, Wyatt, Dawson, and Gillin (1976) administered intravenous injections of an AChE inhibitor (physostigmine) to human subjects during sleep. If the subjects were in slow-wave sleep, the injections induced REM sleep. Sitaram, Moore, and Gillin (1978) compared the effects of an

AChE inhibitor (arecoline), a muscarinic blocker (scopolamine) and a placebo on REM sleep. Relative to the placebo, the acetylcholinergic agonist (arecoline) shortened the interval between periods of REM sleep, and the cholinergic antagonist (scopolamine) lengthened it.

Jasper and Tessier (1969) analyzed the levels of acetylcholine that had been released by terminal buttons in the cat cerebral cortex. The levels were highest during waking and REM sleep and were lowest during slow-wave sleep. This finding suggests that the activity of acetylcholinergic neurons is related to the desynchrony seen in these two states.

Acetylcholine appears to exert its effects in the pons; local stimulation of this region by injection of a drug that provides long-lasting stimulation of acetylcholinergic synapses (carbachol) produces muscular flaccidity, cortical desynchrony, and rapid eye movements in cats (Amatruda, Black, McKenna, McCarley, and Hobson, 1975).

Brain Transection Studies

REM sleep is almost certainly produced by a mechanism that resides within the brain stem, somewhere between the upper border of the spinal cord and the anterior pons. Jouvet (1962) made a transection through the rostral pons and found that the cats engaged in periods of REM sleep, characterized by loss of neck muscle tonus and rapid eye movements. Because the nerves that control the eye and neck muscles leave the central nervous system caudal to the location of the transection, the results imply that the neural mechanisms that trigger REM sleep must also be located caudal to the transection. If the REM sleep mechanisms were located rostral to the transection, they would not be able to control the eye muscles. (See **Figure 9.34.**)

Siegel and his colleagues (reported by Siegel, 1983) made a caudal pontine transection and carefully observed the electrophysiological and behavioral signs of sleep and waking

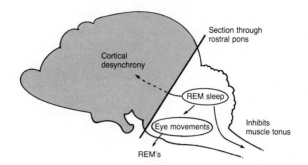

FIGURE 9.34

Effects of a transection through the rostral pons on EEG desynchrony, rapid eye movements, and muscle atonia.

in the parts of the brain rostral and caudal to the transection. They observed some elements of REM sleep in the rostral portion of the brain (cortical desynchrony and PGO waves), but these events never occurred together. They observed periods of phasic activation of responses controlled by mechanisms caudal to the transection, including increases in heart rate, respiration, and muscle tone. These states occurred every 24 minutes, which is the period of the REM sleep cycle in cats.

Siegel concluded that neither the rostral nor the caudal portion of the brain stem could produce REM sleep by itself but that each part of the brain generates some of its aspects. The rostral portion of the pons contains mechanisms responsible for PGO waves and cortical desynchronization, while the caudal portion (undoubtedly, the medulla) contains circuits that can produce muscular, cardiovascular, and respiratory activation. In addition, the caudal part of the brain stem (probably the caudal pons) contains the biological clock responsible for the basic rest-activity cycle, which causes cycles of REM and slow-wave sleep. These results suggest that a large region of the brain stem, including the medulla and pons, participates in the generation of REM sleep.

A human case study supports the conclusion that a neural mechanism in the pons is particularly important for REM sleep. Lavie, Pratt, Scharf, Peled, and Brown (1984) reported that a 33-year-old man whose head was

injured by shrapnel at age 20 engaged in almost no REM sleep. In the sleep laboratory, the man slept an average of $4\frac{1}{2}$ hours. On 3 of 8 nights, he engaged in no REM sleep, while the average on the other 5 nights was approximately 6 minutes. The pieces of metal damaged the pons, left temporal lobe, and left thalamus. Previous research with animals has shown that lesions of the pons, but not unilateral lesions of the temporal lobe or thalamus, can affect sleep cycles. Therefore, the authors concluded that the lack of REM sleep was produced by the pontine damage. Incidentally, the almost complete lack of REM sleep did not appear to cause serious side effects. After receiving his injury, the man completed high school, attended law school, and began practicing law. Unless 6 minutes of REM sleep is all that is necessary, it appears that the functions served by REM sleep are not essential ones.

Control of Motor Inhibition During REM Sleep

Jouvet (1962) reported that small lesions in the pons abolished the profound motor inhibition that normally accompanies REM sleep. During REM sleep, cats with these lesions became active and looked as though they were "acting out their dreams."

. . . to a naive observer, the cat, which is standing, looks awake since it may attack unknown enemies, play with an absent mouse, or display flight behavior. There are orienting movements of the head or eyes toward imaginary stimuli, although the animal does not respond to visual or auditory stimuli. These extraordinary episodes . . . are a good argument that "dreaming" occurs during [REM sleep] in the cat. . . . (Jouvet, 1972, pp. 236–237)

We now know that Jouvet's lesions interrupted the caudally projecting axons of neurons located in and around the locus coeruleus (Jones, Harper, and Halaris, 1977). These neurons send fibers to the **nucleus reticularis magnocellularis** in the medulla. Kanamori, Sakai, and Jouvet (1980) recorded from single neurons in this medullary nucleus in unrestrained cats and found that they became active during REM sleep, showing intense increases during PGO waves and bursts of rapid eye movements. The axons of these neurons project to the spinal cord, where they form inhibitory synapses with motor neurons (Jankowska, Lund, Lundberg, and Pompeiano, 1968). Thus, the loss of muscle tone during REM sleep appears to be mediated by this circuit.

It is important to note that the neurons in and around the locus coeruleus that are involved in the loss of muscle tone are *not* noradrenergic. They must not be confused with the noradrenergic neurons of the locus coeruleus that appear to have an inhibitory effect on REM sleep. Unlike the noradrenergic neurons, which cease firing during REM sleep, the non-noradrenergic neurons in and around the locus coeruleus become *active* during REM sleep (Sakai, 1980) and excite the inhibitory neurons in the medulla. These neurons apparently receive input from acetylcholinergic neurons that stimulate REM sleep; Van Dongen, Broekkamp, and Cools (1978) found that injections of carbachol, an acetylcholinergic agonist, into the locus coeruleus produced a loss of muscle tone. (See **Figure 9.35**.)

Why are the motor systems of the brain so active during REM sleep? So far, we can only speculate. Perhaps the motor components of dreams are as important as the sensory components; perhaps the practice our motor system gets during sleep helps us perform behaviors we have learned that day. The inhibition of the motor neurons prevents the practiced movements from actually occurring, with the exception of a few twitches of the hands and feet.

INTERIM SUMMARY

The behavior we call sleep is caused by the activity of neural mechanisms in the brain stem (perhaps in the nucleus of the solitary tract) and forebrain (probably in the preoptic area). The effects of brain transections suggested that a region of the rostral pons was important for arousal and that a region of the caudal pons or medulla was important for sleep. The conclusion about the location of the brain stem sleep mechanism was supported by the experiments that awakened sleeping cats by administering an anesthetic to the caudal brain stem or by cooling the floor of the fourth ventricle.

The noradrenergic neurons of the locus coeruleus have been implicated in arousal: Drugs that serve as noradrenergic agonists (such as amphetamine) cause arousal and wakefulness; lesions that interrupt the ascending axons of neurons in the locus coeruleus produce hypersomnia; and single units in the locus coeruleus respond at their highest rate during alert wakefulness and at their slowest rate during sleep, especially during REM sleep.

Some studies suggested that slow-wave sleep occurs through activation of 5-HT neurons of the raphe nuclei. However, animals quickly resume sleeping after daily administration of PCPA. Indeed, serotonergic neurons in the raphe nuclei fire at their lowest rate during sleep, just like the noradrenergic neurons of the locus coeruleus. If the activity of these neurons produced sleep, one would expect them to be more active then.

The solitary tract nucleus may be a better candidate for a crucial role in the initiation of sleep. Electrical stimulation of this region produces drowsiness and synchronous EEG rhythms. This nucleus receives sensory information from the

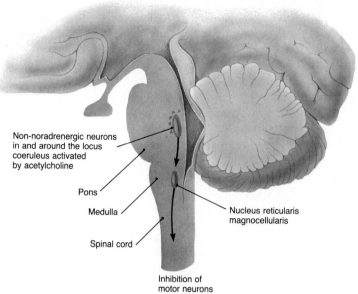

FIGURE 9.35

The neural circuit through which muscular atonia is produced during REM sleep.

tongue and internal organs, and may be responsible for the soothing effects of gentle, rhythmical rocking.

The preoptic-basal forebrain region appears to contain neurons that participate in sleep. Damage to this region causes insomnia, and its stimulation with electricity or heat causes drowsiness and EEG synchrony.

Pharmacological studies suggested that both noradrenergic and serotonergic neurons normally inhibit REM sleep mechanisms; agonists for these transmitter substances inhibit the components of REM sleep. In addition, noradrenergic antagonists increase REM sleep and serotonin antagonists produce hallucinations, characteristic of dreaming. Acetylcholinergic neurons in the pons appear to facilitate REM sleep; infusion of acetylcholinergic agonists there evokes some of the behavioral components of REM sleep. Transection studies suggested that the neural circuits responsible for the components of REM sleep are distributed throughout the brain stem, with the pacemaker that controls the basic rest-activity cycle located in the caudal brain stem.

The motor inhibition that accompanies REM sleep is accomplished by non-noradrenergic neurons in the vicinity of the locus coeruleus, which are activated by acetylcholine. These neurons synapse with neurons in the nucleus reticularis magnocellularis in the medulla, which in turn inhibit motor neurons in the spinal cord. Presumably, untimely activation of the neurons near the locus coeruleus is responsible for cataplexy.

Concluding Remarks

So far, the search for chemicals that produce sleep has identified some possible candidates, but a specific role has not been established for any of them. There is good evidence that the suprachiasmatic nucleus controls the distribution of sleep and waking in animals that display circadian rhythms of these states. There is also good evidence for brain stem sleep and waking mechanisms and for a forebrain sleep mechanism. The clock that controls the cycles of REM sleep appears to be located in the caudal brain stem, but we still do not know precisely where. Although it seems that the total amount of sleep that an animal obtains is regulated, we have no idea what mechanisms monitor total sleep time. The past few years have provided us with much information about the physiology of sleep and waking, but the basic process still remains a mystery.

NEW TERMS

alpha activity p. 321
basic rest-activity cycle (BRAC) p. 324
beta activity p. 321
cataplexy p. 340
cerveau isolé p. 352
circadian rhythm p. 344
delta activity p. 322
delta sleep–inducing peptide p. 342
desynchrony p. 321
drug-dependency insomnia p. 338
electromyogram (EMG) p. 320
electro-oculogram (EOG) p. 320
encéphale isolé p. 352
factor E p. 342
factor S p. 342
flowerpot technique p. 335
growth hormone (GH) p. 332
hypnagogic hallucination p. 340
hypnogenic chemical p. 341
K complex p. 322
locus coeruleus p. 356
midcollicular transection p. 352

midpontine pretrigeminal transection p. 353
narcolepsy p. 339
nocturnal enuresis p. 341
nucleus of the solitary tract p. 361
nucleus reticularis magnocellularis p. 366
paradoxical sleep p. 323
pavor nocturnus p. 341
PGO wave p. 334
preoptic–basal forebrain region p. 362
push-pull cannula p. 333
raphe p. 357
REM sleep p. 323
Ringer's solution p. 333
sleep apnea p. 339
sleep attack p. 339
sleep paralysis p. 340
slow-wave sleep p. 322
somnambulism p. 341
suprachiasmatic nucleus (SCN) p. 346
synchrony p. 321
zeitgeber p. 345

SUGGESTED READINGS

COHEN, D.B. *Sleep and Dreaming: Origins, Nature and Functions.* Oxford: Pergamon Press, 1979.

DEMENT, W.C. *Some Must Watch While Some Must Sleep.* San Francisco: W.H. Freeman, 1974.

DRUCKER-COLÍN, R., SHKUROVICH, M., AND STERMAN, M.B. *The Functions of Sleep.* New York: Academic Press, 1979.

MOORE-EDE, M.C., SULZMAN, F.M., AND FULLER, C.A. *The Clocks That Time Us.* Cambridge, Mass.: Harvard University Press, 1982.

WEBB, W.B. *Sleep: The Gentle Tyrant.* Englewood Cliffs, N.J.: Prentice-Hall, 1975.

WHEATLEY, D. *Psychopharmacology of Sleep.* New York: Raven Press, 1981.

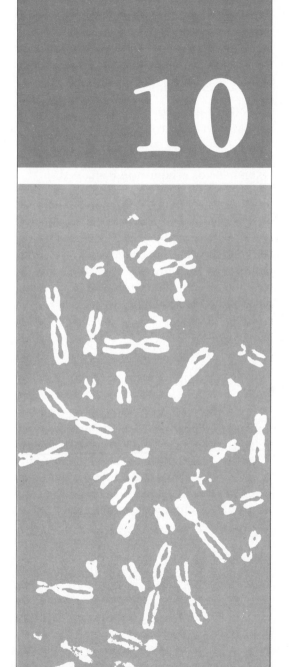

10

Reproductive Behavior

The subject of this chapter is important to almost all of us. The topics of other chapters might (I hope) be interesting, but discussion of them does not evoke the kinds of reactions that may accompany discussions of sexual development and sexual behavior. We all have our individual beliefs about what constitutes appropriate and inappropriate sexual behavior and what behaviors and interests should or should not be associated with a person's gender. However, the discussion of reproductive behavior in this chapter is related to its biology, not its ethics.

Sex hormones, produced by the pituitary gland, ovaries, and testes, affect sexual behavior in two ways. First, they have an *organizational effect,* shaping the development of a person's sex organs and brain. Exposure to certain sex hormones before birth will *organize* the development of male or female sex organs. (If the exposure is abnormal, the cells may develop into something between the male and female forms.) Furthermore, exposure to hormones before birth affects the developing brain; the brains of males and females are not precisely the same. The second role of sex hormones is their *activational effect.* For example, hormones activate the production of sperms, make erection and ejaculation possible, and induce ovulation. Because the bodies of males and females are organized differently, sex hormones have different activational effects in the two sexes.

In this chapter I begin by discussing sexual development, the organizational control exerted by hormones, and their activational effects in adults. Next I discuss evidence concerning the neural bases of sexual behavior, and the way in which hormones interact with these neural circuits. Finally, I discuss the physiology of a reproductive behavior made necessary by sexual activity: care of offspring.

■ SEXUAL DEVELOPMENT

A person's chromosomal sex is determined at the time of fertilization. However, this event is merely the first in a series of steps that culminate in the development of a male or female. This section considers the major features of sexual development.

Production of Gametes

All cells of the body (other than sperms or ova) contain twenty-three pairs of chromosomes, including a pair of sex chromosomes. The genetic information that programs the development of a human is contained in the DNA that constitutes these chromosomes. (Our ability to miniaturize computer circuits on silicon chips looks primitive when we consider that the blueprint for a human being is too small to be seen by the naked eye.) The nature of the sex chromosomes determines an individual's sex. There are two types of these chromosomes: X and Y chromosomes. The cells of females contain two of one type, making them XX cells. The cells of males contain one of each, making them XY cells. Thus it is the possession of a Y chromosome that distinguishes the cells of a male from those of a female.

We can observe the twenty-three pairs of human chromosomes by scraping epithelial cells from the mucous membrane of the inside of the cheek and placing them in a culture medium that supports their growth and division. During cell division, which is called *mitosis,* the chromosomes duplicate themselves, thus giving each of the two daughter cells the entire complement of genetic material. (When cells divide, the products of the division are called *daughter cells,* regardless of the sex of the donor.) Figure 10.1 shows this process. For simplicity's sake, the cells contain only two pairs of chromosomes, rather than twenty-three. (See **Figure 10.1.**) Once cellular division has begun, the culture is treated with colchicine, a drug that dissolves the spindle fibers that pull the chromosomes apart and thus halts the process in the phase shown in part C. (See **Figure 10.1C.**)

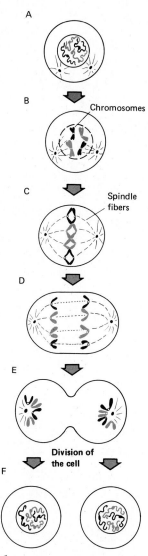

A

B

Chromosomes

C

Spindle
fibers

D

E

**Division of
the cell**

F

FIGURE 10.1

Mitosis, the process by which a somatic cell
replicates itself. (From Orians, G.H. *The Study
of Life.* Boston: Allyn and Bacon, 1973.)

The dividing cells now contain a double
set of twenty-three pairs of chromosomes in
the nucleus, straightened out and easy to see.
The cells are then squashed, so as to flatten
the chromosomes, and the genetic material is
stained. Then many cells are searched until
one is found in which all the chromosomes

can readily be seen. A photograph is taken,
and pictures of the individual chromosomes
are cut out and rearranged according to size.
Figure 10.2 illustrates a set of human chromosomes prepared in this way, before and
after rearrangement. Remember, we can see
twice as many chromosomes as the cell normally contains, since the process of cell division was arrested just before the members of a
duplicated chromosome, joined near the
center, would normally separate and travel to
each of the daughter cells. (See **Figure 10.2.**)
We know that the **karyotype** (literally, "nucleus mark") shown in this figure is that of a
male, because we can see a Y chromosome.

The production of **gametes** (ova and
sperms — *gamein* means "to marry") entails
a different form of cell division. **Meiosis** produces cells that contain only one member of
each of the twenty-three pairs of chromosomes. The development of a human begins
when a single sperm and ovum join, sharing
their twenty-three single chromosomes to re-
constitute the twenty-three pairs. So far as we
know, the particular member of each chromosome pair that goes to a particular gamete
is determined randomly. If we toss a coin
twenty-three times, we will obtain one of
8,388,608 different sequences of heads and
tails. Because the segregation of the chromosome pairs appears to be as random as the coin
toss, a person can produce 8,388,608 different kinds of gametes. Because it takes the
combination of two gametes to produce another human, a single couple could produce
8,388,608 × 8,388,608, or something like
70,368,774,177,664 genetically different
types of children. A couple *could* conceive
genetically identical siblings at different
times, but the probability is rather low.

Fertilization

Fertilization is the union of a single sperm
with a single ovum, thus combining their genetic material. Because women have XX cells,

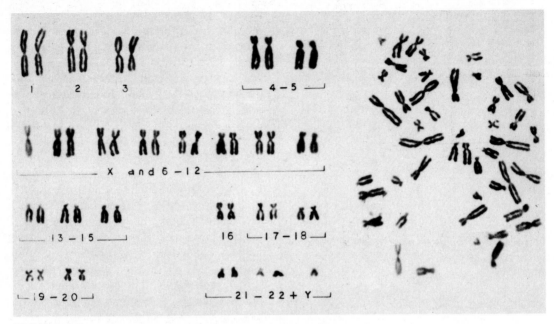

FIGURE 10.2
A karyotype of a cell whose division was arrested in metaphase (phase C of Figure 10.1). (From Money, J., and Ehrhardt, A. *Man & Woman, Boy & Girl.* Copyright 1973 by The Johns Hopkins University Press, Baltimore, Maryland. By permission.)

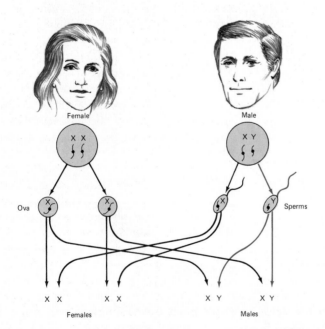

FIGURE 10.3
The gender of the offspring depends on whether the sperm cell that fertilizes the ovum carries an X or a Y chromosome.

all of their ova contain a single X chromosome (along with twenty-two other single chromosomes, of course). Because men have XY cells, half of their sperms are X bearing and half are Y bearing. Thus, the gender of the offspring is determined by the type of sex chromosome contained in the sperm that fertilizes the ovum. If it is X bearing, the offspring will be female. If it is Y bearing, it will be male. (See **Figure 10.3.**)

Development of the Gonads

The first sex organs to differentiate are the **gonads** (from the Greek *gonos,* meaning "procreation"), which become ovaries or testes. At first, male and female embryos are identical. Their gonads, which begin developing during the fifth and sixth week after the mother's last menstrual cycle, are undifferentiated. In this state, they are referred to as **primordial gonads.** (*Primordial* means "first begun.") But during the seventh and eighth weeks, the gonads differentiate; either the cells of the cortex (the outer layers) develop into ovaries, or the cells of the medulla (the inner layers) develop into testes. (See **Figure 10.4.**)

The differentiation of the primordial gonads is controlled by the presence or absence of a protein called the **H-Y antigen** (Haseltine and Ohno, 1981). This protein was discovered by researchers investigating the factors that control the compatibility of different tissues with respect to transplantation. They discovered that female mice would reject grafts of skin from males because an antigen (a type of protein) was present on the surface of male cells. Further studies found that the important function of the H-Y antigen is an organizational effect on cells of the primordial gonads. When it stimulates receptors on the surface of these cells, it causes the gonads to develop as testes. If the protein is not present, or if an experimenter administers

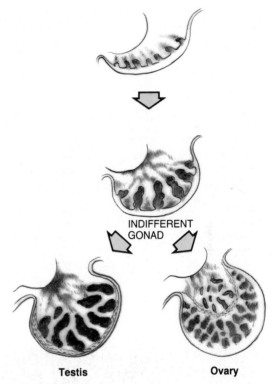

INDIFFERENT GONAD

Testis   **Ovary**

FIGURE 10.4
Development of the gonads (testes and ovaries). (Adapted from Burns, R.K. In *Analysis of Development,* edited by B.H. Willier, P.A. Weiss, and V. Hamberger. Philadelphia: Saunders, 1955.)

an antibody to the H-Y antigen, the primordial gonads develop into ovaries. As you may have expected, production of the H-Y antigen is controlled by a gene on the Y chromosome.

Development of the Internal Sex Organs

As we just saw, prior to the seventh week the embryonic gonads are unisexual. In contrast, the other internal sex organs are *bisexual;* that is, all embryos contain precursors for both female and male sex organs. However, during the third month of gestation, only one of these precursors develops. The precursor of the internal female sex organs is called the

Müllerian system, which develops into the fimbriae and Fallopian tubes, the uterus, and the inner two thirds of the vagina. (See **Figure 10.5.**) The precursor of the internal male sex organs is called the *Wolffian system,* which develops into the epididymis, vas deferens, seminal vesicles, and prostate. (See **Figure 10.5.**)

The gender of the fetal internal sex organs is determined by the presence or absence of testes. That is, if testes are present, the Wolffian system develops. If they are not, the Müllerian system develops. The Müllerian (female) system needs no special stimulus from the gonads to develop; it just normally does so. In contrast, the cells of the Wolffian (male) system require hormonal stimulation. Thus, testes secrete two classes of hormones. *Müllerian-inhibiting substance* does ex-

actly that: it prevents the Müllerian system from developing. It therefore has a *defeminizing* effect. *Androgens* (primarily testosterone and dihydrotestosterone) stimulate the development of the Wolffian system. (This class of hormone is also aptly named: *andros* means "man," and *gennan* means "to produce.") Androgens have a *masculinizing* effect.

Experiments with laboratory animals have shown that ovaries are not necessary for the development of the Müllerian system. This finding has led to the dictum "Nature's impulse is to create a female." A genetic anomaly demonstrates the validity of this statement in humans. People with *Turner's syndrome* have only one sex chromosome: an X chromosome. (Thus their sex karyotype is XO.) Apparently, the ovum that gives rise to such

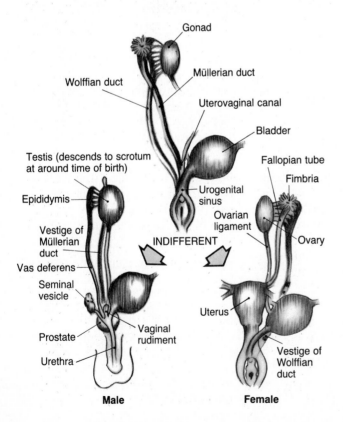

FIGURE 10.5
Development of the internal sex organs. (Adapted from Corning, H.K. *Lehrbuch der Entwicklungsgeschichte des Menschen.* Munich: J.F. Bergman, 1921.)

an individual is fertilized by a sperm that lost its sex chromosome during meiosis. Because a Y chromosome is not present, H-Y antigen is not produced, and testes do not develop. In addition, because only one X chromosome is present, ovaries are not produced, either. (For some reason, two X chromosomes are needed to produce ovaries.) Even though they have no gonads at all, people with Turner's syndrome develop into females, with normal female internal sex organs.

Development of the External Genitalia

The external genitalia are the visible sex organs, including the penis and scrotum in males and the labia, clitoris, and outer part of the vagina in females. Whereas male and female internal sex organs develop from different sets of precursors, the external genitalia, like the gonads, develop from bipotential primordia, which are capable of assuming either male or female form. Figure 10.6 illustrates

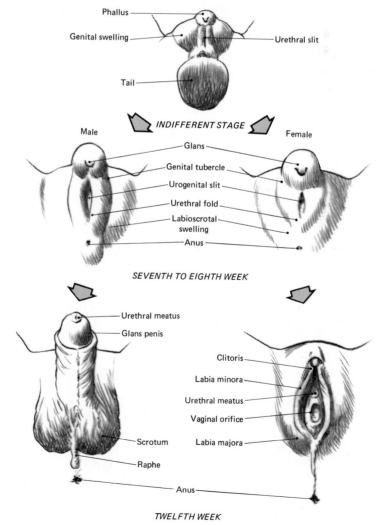

FIGURE 10.6
Development of the external genitalia. (Adapted from Spaulding, M.H. In *Contributions to Embryology,* Vol. 13. Washington, D.C.: Carnegie Institute of Washington, 1921.)

the development of male and female external genitalia from the bipotential genital primordia. Note that the primordial phallus gives rise to the glans penis or to the clitoris; the genital swelling gives rise to the scrotum or to the labia majora; and the genital tubercle gives rise to the shaft of the penis or to the labia minora and outer third of the vagina. (See **Figure 10.6.**)

Without hormonal stimulation, the external genitalia will become female, regardless of the organism's chromosomal sex. However, the presence of androgens causes masculine development. Thus, the presence or absence of testes determines whether a person's external genitalia are male or female. As you might predict, therefore, people with Turner's syndrome have female external genitalia even though they lack ovaries.

Sexual Maturation

Secondary sex characteristics, such as enlarged breasts and widened hips or a beard and deep voice, do not appear until puberty. Without seeing genitals, we must guess the sex of a prepubescent child from his or her haircut and clothing; the bodies of young boys and girls are rather similar. However, at puberty the gonads are stimulated to produce their hormones, and these hormones cause the person to mature sexually. The onset of puberty occurs when cells in the hypothalamus secrete **gonadotropin releasing hormones (GnRH),** which stimulate the production and release of two **gonadotropic hormones** by the anterior pituitary gland. The gonadotropic ("gonad-turning") hormones stimulate the gonads to produce *their* hormones, which are ultimately responsible for sexual maturation. (See **Figure 10.7.**)

The two gonadotropic hormones are *follicle-stimulating hormone (FSH),* and *luteinizing hormone (LH),* named for the effects they produce in the female (*follicle* production and its subsequent *luteinization,* to be described in the next section of this chapter). However, the same hormones are produced in the male, where they stimulate the testes to produce sperms and to secrete testosterone. If male and female pituitary glands are exchanged in rats, the ovaries and testes respond perfectly to the hormones secreted by the new glands (Harris and Jacobsohn, 1951–1952).

In response to the gonadotropic hormones (usually called *gonadotropins*), the gonads secrete sex steroid hormones. The ovaries produce *estradiol,* one of a class of hormones

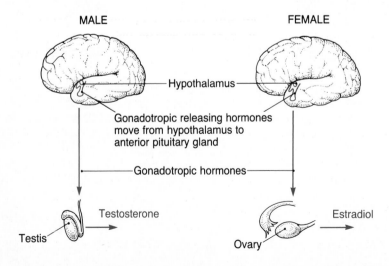

FIGURE 10.7
Puberty is initiated when the hypothalamus secretes gonadotropin releasing hormones.

T A B L E 10.1   Classification of sex steroid hormones

Class	Principal Hormone in Humans (Where Produced)	Examples of Effects
Androgens	Testosterone (testes)	Maturation of male genitalia; production of sperms, growth of facial, pubic, and axillary hair; muscular development; enlargement of larynx; inhibition of bone growth
	Androstenedione (adrenal glands)	In females, growth of pubic and axillary hair; less important than testosterone in males
Estrogens	Estradiol (ovaries)	Maturation of female genitalia; growth of breasts; alterations in fat deposits; growth of uterine lining; inhibition of bone growth
Gestagens	Progesterone (ovaries)	Maintenance of uterine lining

known as **estrogens.** The testes chiefly produce **testosterone** (an androgen). Both glands also produce a small amount of the hormones of the opposite sex. The gonadal hormones have effects on many parts of the body. Both estradiol and testosterone initiate closure of the *epiphyses* (growing portions of the bones) and thus halt skeletal growth. Estradiol also causes breast development, growth of the lining of the uterus, changes in the deposition of body fat, and maturation of the female genitalia. Testosterone stimulates growth of facial, axillary (underarm), and pubic hair, lowers the voice, alters the hairline on the head (sometimes causing baldness later in life), stimulates muscular development, and causes genital growth. This description leaves out two of the female secondary characteristics: axillary and pubic hair. These characteristics are produced not by estrogens but rather by **androstenedione,** an androgen secreted by the cortex of the adrenal glands. Even a male who is castrated before puberty (a *eunuch*) will grow axillary and pubic hair, in response to his own androstenedione. (See **Table 10.1.**)

The bipotentiality of many of the secondary sex characteristics remains throughout life. If a man is treated with an estrogen (for example, to control an androgen-dependent tumor), he will grow breasts, and his facial hair will become finer and softer. However, his voice will remain low, because the enlargement of the larynx is permanent. Conversely, a woman who receives high levels of an androgen (usually from a tumor that secretes androstenedione) will grow a beard, and her voice will become lower.

Several pathological conditions can prevent normal development of an individual into a male or female. Such people (or animals) are called **hermaphrodites,** after the mythical bisexual offspring of Hermes and Aphrodite. Originally, hermaphroditism referred to the ability to function reproductively as both a male and a female (seen in some nonmammalian species), but the term has been extended to individuals with ambiguous genital structure, internally or externally (Money and Ehrhardt, 1972). Nature's experiments in the production of such individuals have added much to our knowledge of the biological bases of differences in the behavior of human males and females.

INTERIM SUMMARY

Gender is determined by the sex chromosomes: XX produces a female, and XY produces a male. Males are produced by the action of a gene on the Y chromosome that contains the code for the production of a protein, the H-Y antigen, that causes the primordial gonads to become testes. In the absence of testicular hormones, the Müllerian system will develop into the female internal sex organs and the Wolffian system will fail to develop. We know that this is true because a person with Turner's syndrome (XO) fails to develop gonads but nevertheless develops female internal sex organs. However, the testes secrete two kinds of hormones that cause a male to develop. Androgens stimulate the development of the Wolffian system, and Müllerian-inhibiting substance suppresses the development of the Müllerian system. The external genitalia develop from common precursors. In the absence of gonadal hormones the precursors develop the female form; in the presence of androgens they develop the male form.

Sexual maturity occurs when the hypothalamus begins secreting gonadotropin releasing hormone, which stimulates the secretion of follicle-stimulating hormone and luteinizing hormone by the anterior pituitary gland. These hormones stimulate the gonads to secrete their hormones, which cause the genitals to mature and cause the body to develop the secondary sex characteristics.

■ HORMONAL CONTROL OF SEX-RELATED BEHAVIOR

We have seen that hormones are responsible for *sexual dimorphism* (male-female differences) in the structure of the body and its

organs. Hormones have organizational and activational effects on the internal sex organs, genitals, and secondary sex characteristics. Naturally, all of these effects influence a person's behavior. Hormones also affect behavior by interacting directly with the nervous system. Androgens present during prenatal development affect the development of the nervous system of laboratory animals, and probably that of humans, too. In addition, sex hormones have activational effects on the adult nervous system, influencing physiological processes and behavior. This section considers some of these effects.

Hormonal Control of Female Reproductive Cycles

Menstrual and Estrous Cycles
The reproductive cycle of female primates is called a **menstrual cycle** (from *mēnsis,* meaning "month"). Females of other species of mammals also have reproductive cycles, called **estrous cycles.** *Estrus* means "gadfly"; when a female rat is in estrus, her hormonal condition goads her to act differently than she does at other times. (For that matter, it affects the behavior of male rats, too.) The primary feature that distinguishes menstrual cycles from estrous cycles is the monthly growth and loss of the lining of the uterus. The other features are approximately the same.

Menstrual cycles and estrous cycles consist of a sequence of events that are controlled by hormonal secretions of the pituitary gland and ovaries. These glands interact, the secretions of one affecting those of the other. A cycle begins with the secretion of gonadotropins by the anterior pituitary gland. These hormones (especially FSH) stimulate the growth of **ovarian follicles,** small spheres of epithelial cells surrounding each ovum. Women normally produce one ovarian follicle each month; if two are produced and ferti-

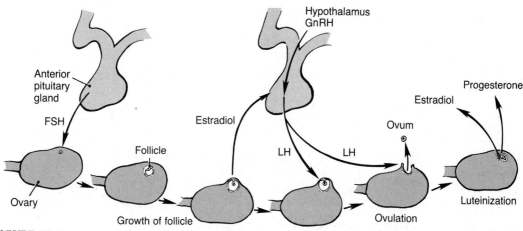

FIGURE 10.8
Neuroendocrine control of the menstrual cycle.

lized, dizygotic (fraternal) twins will develop. As ovarian follicles mature, they secrete estradiol, which causes the growth of the lining of the uterus in preparation for implantation of the ovum, should it be fertilized by a sperm. Feedback from the increasing level of estradiol eventually triggers the release of a surge of LH by the anterior pituitary gland. (See **Figure 10.8.**)

The LH surge causes *ovulation:* the ovarian follicle ruptures, releasing the ovum. Under the continued influence of LH, the ruptured ovarian follicle becomes a ***corpus luteum*** ("yellow body"), which produces estradiol and ***progesterone.*** (See **Figure 10.8.**) The latter hormone is a ***gestagen,*** or pregnancy-promoting hormone. It maintains the lining of the uterus. Meanwhile, the ovum, which is released into the abdominal cavity, enters one of the Fallopian tubes and begins its progress toward the uterus. The ovum is directed into the Fallopian tube by the "rowing" action of the ciliated cells of the fimbria, which form a fringe around the opening. This process works remarkably well; women who have lost an ovary on one side and a Fallopian tube on the other have

nevertheless become pregnant. Obviously their ova had to find their way across the abdominal cavity and into the Fallopian tube on the other side. If an ovum meets sperm cells during its travel down the Fallopian tube and becomes fertilized, it begins to divide, and several days later it attaches itself to the uterine wall.

If the ovum is not fertilized, if it is fertilized too late for it to develop sufficiently by the time it gets to the uterus, or if implantation is prevented by the presence of an intrauterine device (IUD), the corpus luteum will cease producing estradiol and progesterone, and the lining of the walls of the uterus will slough off. Menstruation will commence. (See **Figure 10.9.**)

Control of Gonadotropin Secretion by the Ovaries

As we have just seen, ovulation occurs when the blood level of estradiol, secreted by an ovarian follicle, reaches a critical level. In primates, this effect of estradiol takes place in the hypothalamus and anterior pituitary gland. The anterior pituitary gland is controlled by the hypothalamus, which secretes

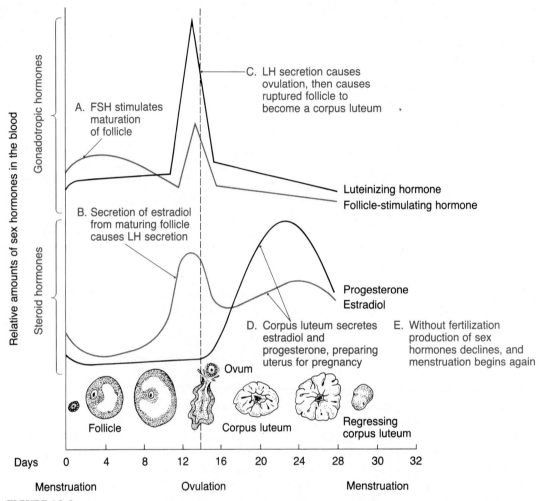

FIGURE 10.9
The hormonal and physical elements of the menstrual cycle.

releasing hormones into the portal blood supply. Gonadotropin releasing hormone (GnRH), which controls the secretion of gonadotropins, is produced by neurons located in the *arcuate nucleus* of the hypothalamus. These neurons secrete a pulse of GnRH every 1 to 2 hours, causing the anterior pituitary gland to release similar pulses of gonadotropins (Pohl and Knobil, 1982). During the early part of the menstrual cycle, the gonadotropins stimulate the development of an ovar-

ian follicle. The ripening ovarian follicle secretes estradiol; when the blood level of estradiol reaches a critical level of 200 pg/ml for two days, it stimulates a surge of gonadotropins, which causes ovulation. (A picogram, abbreviated pg, is one trillionth of a gram.) The estradiol acts directly on the pituitary gland, stimulating it to produce the preovulatory LH surge. Hess, Wilkins, Moossy, Chang, Plant, McCormack, Nakai, and Knobil (1977) found that estradiol would stimulate a gonadotropin surge even after they had removed all of the rhesus monkey brain anterior and dorsal to the medial basal hypothalamus. In fact, estradiol stimulates gonadotropin release even after the arcuate nucleus is surgically destroyed (Wildt, Hausler, Hutchison, Marshall, and Knobil, 1981).

The arcuate nucleus continues to secrete pulses of GnRH even after ovulation has occurred. However, the progesterone secreted by the corpus luteum inhibits the effects of the gonadotropins on the ovaries and prevents another ovarian follicle from developing. If fertilization does not occur, the corpus luteum dies in approximately 14 days, and the level of progesterone falls. As we saw, this fall causes the lining of the uterus to slough off. It also removes the inhibiting effect of progesterone on the ovaries, which permits the development of a new ovarian follicle.

Thus, the length of a menstrual cycle is controlled by the ovaries; it takes 14 days for a new ovarian follicle to develop and produce a critical amount of estradiol, and a corpus luteum lives and produces progesterone for 14 days more. (See **Figure 10.10**.)

Hormonal Control of Sexual Behavior of Laboratory Animals

The interactions between sex hormones and development of the human brain are difficult to study. We must turn to three sources of information: experiments with animals; various developmental disorders in humans, which serve as Nature's own "experiments"; and unexpected fetal side effects of medical treatments of pregnant women. Let us first consider the evidence gathered from research with laboratory animals.

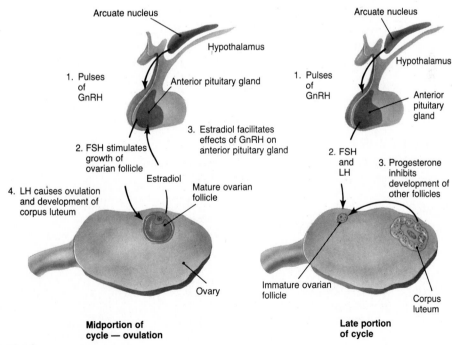

Midportion of cycle — ovulation

Late portion of cycle

FIGURE 10.10
Control of ovulation in primates.

The metabolic pathways for the sex steroid hormones are shown in Figure 10.11. As you can see, the precursor for all of them is cholesterol. (See **Figure 10.11.**) All of these hormones are produced in both males and females, but they are produced in different amounts. The adrenal glands mainly produce such nonsex steroid hormones as corticosterone and aldosterone, but they also produce sex hormones. For example, you will recall that androstenedione, produced by the adrenal glands, stimulates growth of a woman's pubic and axillary hair. The testes produce androgens (mainly testosterone), but they also make a little estradiol. Note that the ovaries are obliged to produce testosterone in making estradiol; some of this testosterone escapes into the general circulation. (See **Figure 10.11.**) The blood testosterone level of women is approximately one-tenth that of men.

Male Sexual Behavior

For fertilization to occur, a male mammal must emit sperm-containing semen into the female's vagina. Some male mammals are ready and willing to do so any season of the year, depending only on the receptivity of the female. Others, such as deer, are seasonal breeders, becoming sexually active only at certain times of the year. In fact, during the off-season their testes regress and produce almost no testosterone.

Male sexual behavior is quite varied, although the essential features of *intromission* (entry of the penis into the female's vagina), *pelvic thrusting* (rhythmic movement of the hindquarters, causing genital friction), and *ejaculation* (discharge of semen) are characteristic of all male mammals. Humans, of course, have invented all kinds of copulatory and noncopulatory sexual behavior. For example, the pelvic movements leading to ejaculation may be performed by the woman, and sex play can lead to orgasm without intromission.

Of all laboratory animals, the sexual behavior of rats has been studied the most. When a male rat encounters a receptive female, he will spend some time nuzzling her and sniffing and licking her genitals, mount her, and engage in pelvic thrusting. He will mount her

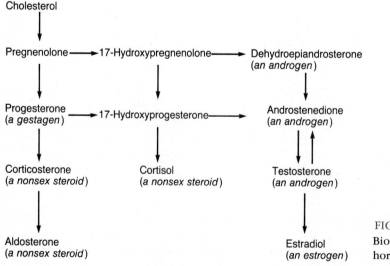

FIGURE 10.11

Biosynthesis of sex steroid hormones.

several times, achieving intromission on most of the mountings. After eight to fifteen intromissions approximately one minute apart (each lasting only about one quarter of a second) the male will ejaculate. At the time of ejaculation, he shows a deep pelvic thrust and arches backward. The copulatory behavior of a mouse is similar, and even more dramatic. During the final intromission the male takes all four feet off the floor, climbing completely on top of the female. When he ejaculates, he quivers and falls sideways to the ground. (Sometimes the female falls with him.)

The male rat (along with many other male mammals) is most responsive to females who are in estrus ("in heat"). Males will ignore a female whose ovaries have been removed, but an injection of estradiol will restore her sex appeal (and also change her behavior toward the male). The stimuli that arouse a male rat's sexual interest include her odor and her behavior. In some species, visible changes, such as the swollen sex skin in the genital region of a female monkey, also affect sex appeal.

After ejaculating, the male refrains from sexual activity for a period of time (minutes, in the rat). Most mammals will return to copulate again, and again, showing a longer pause *(refractory period)* after each ejaculation. An interesting phenomenon occurs in some mammals. If a male, after finally becoming "exhausted" by repeated copulation with the same female, is presented with a new female, he begins to respond quickly — often as fast as he did in his initial contact with the first female. Successive introductions of new females can keep up his performance for prolonged periods of time. (This phenomenon, also seen in roosters, has been called the *Coolidge effect.* The following story is reputed to be true, but I cannot vouch for that fact. If it is not true, it ought to be. The late former U.S. president Calvin Coolidge and his wife were touring a farm, when Mrs. Coolidge asked the farmer whether the continuous and vigorous sexual activity among the flock of hens was the work of just one rooster. The reply was yes. "You might point that out to Mr. Coolidge," she said. Calvin Coolidge then asked the farmer whether a different hen was involved each time. The answer, again, was yes. "You might point that out to Mrs. Coolidge.")

The Coolidge effect is especially strong in the ram (male sheep). Beamer, Bermant, and Clegg (1969) gave a ram a new female after each ejaculation and found that he kept up his performance (ejaculations in less than 2 minutes) with at least twelve different ewes. The experimenters, rather than the ram, got tired of shuffling sheep around. Figure 10.12 shows the striking difference in latency to ejaculate after reintroduction of the same female *(upper curve)* as opposed to introduction of new females *(lower curve)*. (See **Figure 10.12.**) The experimenters tried to

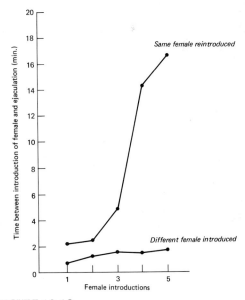

FIGURE 10.12

An example of the Coolidge effect. (From Beamer, W., Bermant, G., and Clegg, M. *Animal Behaviour,* 1969, *17,* 706–711.)

disguise a female by putting a series of different coats and Halloween face masks on her. The males were not fooled. They apparently smelled the same ewe, despite her varied disguise. (Yes, the ewes, dressed in coats and masks, looked just as ridiculous as you might imagine.)

These phenomena — a renewal of interest in sexual behavior with a new female and a good memory for females already copulated with — are undoubtedly useful for species in which a single male inseminates all the members of his harem. Other mammalian species with approximately equal numbers of reproductively active males and females are less likely to show these phenomena, at least as strongly.

The fact that the sexual behavior of male rodents depends on testosterone has long been recognized (Bermant and Davidson, 1974). If a male rat is castrated (that is, if his testes are removed), his sexual activity eventually ceases. However, the behavior can be reinstated by injections of testosterone. I will describe the neural basis of this activational effect later in this chapter.

Female Sexual Behavior

The mammalian female is generally described as being the passive participant in copulation. It is true that in many species, the female's role during mounting and intromission is merely to assume a posture that exposes her genitals to the male (the *lordosis* response, from the Greek *lordos,* meaning "bent backward"). She will also move her tail away (if she has one) and stand rigidly enough to support the weight of the male.

The behavior of a female laboratory animal in initiating copulation is often very active, however. Certainly, if copulation with a nonestrous rodent is attempted, she will either actively flee or rebuff the male. But when she is in a receptive state, she will often approach the male, nuzzle him, sniff his geni-

tals, and show behaviors characteristic of her species. For example, a female rat will exhibit quick, short, hopping movements and rapid ear wiggling, which male rats find irresistible (McClintock and Adler, 1978).

Sexual behavior of female rodents depends on the gonadal hormones present during estrus: estradiol and progesterone. In rats and guinea pigs, estradiol increases about 40 hours before the female becomes receptive, and just before receptivity occurs the corpus luteum begins secreting large quantities of progesterone (Feder, 1981). Although sexual receptivity can be produced in ovariectomized rodents by administering large doses of estradiol alone, the most effective treatment duplicates the normal sequence of hormones: a small amount of estradiol, followed by progesterone. Progesterone alone is ineffective; thus, the estradiol "primes" its effectiveness. Priming with estradiol takes about 16 to 24 hours, after which an injection of progesterone produces receptive behaviors within an hour (Lisk, 1978). The neural mechanisms that mediate these effects will be described later in this chapter.

Organizational Effects of Androgens on Behavior: Masculinization and Defeminization

The dictum "Nature's impulse is to create a female" applies to sexual behavior as well as to sex organs. That is, if a rodent brain is *not* exposed to androgens during a critical period around the time of birth, the animal will engage in female sexual behavior as an adult if it receives estradiol and progesterone then. Thus, if a male rodent is castrated immediately after birth, permitted to grow to adulthood, and then given injections of estradiol and progesterone, it will respond to another male by arching its back and presenting its hindquarters. In contrast, if a rodent brain is exposed to androgens during development, two phenomena occur: behavioral defeminization and behavioral masculinization. *Behavioral defeminization* refers to the organizational effect of androgens that prevents the animal from displaying female sexual behavior in adulthood. For example, if a female rodent is ovariectomized and given an injection of testosterone immediately after birth, she will *not* respond to a male rat when, as an adult, she is given injections of estradiol and progesterone. *Behavioral masculinization* refers to the organizational effect of androgens that enables animals to engage in male sexual behavior in adulthood. For example, if the female rodent in my previous example is given testosterone in adulthood, rather than estradiol and progesterone, she will mount and attempt to copulate with a receptive female. (See Feder, 1984, for references to specific studies.) (See **Figure 10.13.**)

The organizational effects of androgens on sexual behavior occur in the brain. Defeminization suppresses the development of neural circuits that are sensitive to estradiol and progesterone and that initiate female sexual behavior. Masculinization stimulates the development of neural circuits that are sensitive to testosterone and that initiate male sexual behavior. The location of these circuits is discussed later in this chapter.

Androgens have organizational effects on behaviors other than copulatory activity. For example, Bridges, Zarrow, and Dennenberg (1973) found that young females or neonatally castrated male rats are more likely than normally androgenized males to exhibit maternal behavior (care of young pups). Aggressive behavior of mice (a characteristic of males) can be stimulated by testosterone administration only if the animals have been an-

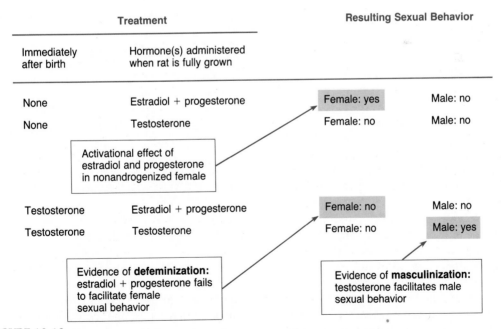

FIGURE 10.13

Organizational effects of testosterone around the time of birth masculinize and defeminize rodents' sexual behavior.

drogenized immediately after birth (Bronson and Desjardins, 1969, 1970; Barkley, 1974). Normal male rats, and females who have been androgenized soon after birth, show more timidity in leaving their home cage to explore a new environment than normal, nonandrogenized females do (Pfaff and Zigmond, 1971). The sexually dimorphic posture shown by an adult dog when urinating is also controlled by exposure of the developing brain to androgens. A female dog that receives androgens at the time of birth will lift a leg and urinate like a male once she reaches adulthood (Beach, 1970). Finally, the social behavior of juvenile rhesus monkeys is affected by prenatal androgenization (Goy and Goldfoot, 1973). Thus, a variety of sex differences in behavior are determined by the organizational effects of androgens. The weight of this evidence suggests that we must seriously consider the possibility that human behaviors, too, might be influenced by the action of androgens on the developing brain.

Effects of Pheromones

Hormones transmit messages from one part of the body (the secreting gland) to another (the target tissue). Another class of chemicals, called *pheromones,* carry messages from one animal to another. These chemicals, like hormones, affect reproductive behavior. Karlson and Luscher (1959) coined the term, from *pherein,* "to carry," and *horman,* "to excite." Pheromones are released by one animal and directly affect the physiology or behavior of another. Most pheromones are detected by means of olfaction, but some are ingested or absorbed through the skin.

Several phenomena related to sex pheromones in mammals influence preferences for sex partners, pregnancy, and estrous or menstrual cycles. For example, Mainardi (cited by Bruce, 1960a) reported that female mice prefer males of other genetic strains than their

own as sex partners. This preference appears to be controlled by the male's odor. Its selective value is probably to increase the likelihood of outbreeding (the opposite of inbreeding), which is genetically healthier.

Two other effects demonstrate that females can influence each other's estrous cycles. In the *Lee-Boot effect* (van der Lee and Boot, 1955), female mice housed together in groups of four or more tend to become *pseudopregnant;* that is, although they are virgins, they develop longlived progesterone-secreting corpora lutea as if they were pregnant. The *Whitten effect* (Whitten, 1959) occurs when mice are housed in larger groups. Their estrous cycles become longer and longer and eventually stop. Both of these effects are controlled by pheromones in urine; they can be stimulated in mice housed individually if the experimenter puts urine from other female mice into their cages.

The Lee-Boot and Whitten effects occur only when females are housed apart from males. If a normal male mouse is present, an odor in his urine causes their cycles to resume and to become synchronized (Bronson and Whitten, 1968). The urine of a castrated male mouse has no effect.

The *Bruce effect* (Bruce, 1960a, 1960b) is a particularly interesting phenomenon: when a recently impregnated female mouse encounters a normal male mouse other than the one with which she mated, the pregnancy is very likely to fail. This effect, too, is caused by a substance secreted in the urine of intact males, but not of males that have been castrated. Thus, a male mouse is able to kill the genetic material of another male and subsequently impregnate the female himself.

Many of the effects of pheromones on behavior appear to be mediated by the *vomeronasal organ,* which consists of a small group of sensory receptors arranged around a pouch connected to the nasal passage. The vomeronasal organ, which is present in all orders of mammals except for cetaceans (whales and dolphins), projects to the ***accessory olfactory bulb,*** immediately behind the olfactory bulb (Wysocki, 1979). (See **Figure 10.14.**)

Removal of the accessory olfactory bulb disrupts the Lee-Boot and Bruce effects in female mice (Reynolds and Keverne, 1979; Bellringer, Pratt, and Keverne, 1980). In male hamsters, although mating continues after deafferentation of either the primary or accessory olfactory systems, deafferentation of both systems abolishes male sexual behavior (Powers and Winans, 1975; Winans and Powers, 1977). Deafferentation of the primary olfactory system is accomplished by irrigating the olfactory epithelium with zinc sulfate; deafferentation of the accessory olfactory system is accomplished by cutting the vomeronasal nerve.

Both the primary and accessory olfactory systems send fibers to the medial nucleus of the amygdala. Lehman and Winans (1982) used autoradiography to identify the precise projection regions of these systems. They injected radioactive amino acids into the primary and accessory olfactory bulbs and examined sections of the amygdala. Next they made lesions of the amygdala that destroyed both sets of projection areas and found that the lesions abolished sexual behavior of males. Olfaction is especially important for the mating behavior of male hamsters. Males are attracted to female secretions, and they sniff and lick the female's genitals before copulating. The effectiveness of these odors depend on androgens; Gregory, Engle, and Pfaff (1975) found that castration decreased males' interest in the odor of females. Significantly, cells in the medial nucleus of the amygdala contain androgen receptors (Sheridan, 1979). Thus, if the results of all these

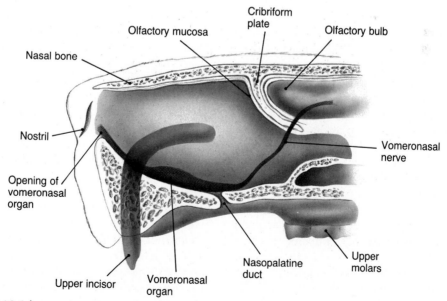

FIGURE 10.14

The rodent accessory olfactory system. (Adapted from Wysocki, C.J. *Neuroscience & Biobehavioral Reviews,* 1979, *3,* 301–341.)

studies are taken together, a coherent picture emerges: androgens activate neural circuits in the medial nucleus of the amygdala, so that they respond to the odor of vaginal secretions, obtained by means of the olfactory bulbs and vomeronasal organs.

It appears that at least some pheromone-related phenomena occur in humans. For example, Collet, Wertenberger, and Fiske (1954) observed a rather high percentage of unusually long menstrual cycles in female college students. The investigators hypothesized that these long cycles reflected normal developmental changes in young women. However, McClintock (1971) noticed that most of the women in this study had attended all-female colleges. To determine whether this phenomenon resembled the Whitten effect in female mice, she studied the menstrual cycles of women attending an all-female college. She found that women who spent a large amount of time together tended to have synchronized cycles—their menstrual periods began within a day or two of each other. In addition, women who regularly spent some time in the presence of men tended to have shorter cycles than those who rarely spent time with (smelled?) men.

Russell, Switz, and Thompson (1977) obtained evidence that olfactory stimuli can synchronize women's menstrual cycles, suggesting the presence of pheromones. The investigators collected daily samples of a woman's underarm sweat. They dissolved the samples in alcohol and swabbed them on the upper lips of a group of women three times each week, in the order in which they were originally taken. The cycles of the women who received the extract (but not those of control subjects whose lips were swabbed with pure alcohol) began to synchronize with the cycle of the odor donor.

Because studies have shown that the accessory olfactory system appears to mediate the Lee-Boot and Bruce effects in mice, the question arises as to whether the effects of olfactory stimuli on human reproductive cycles are also mediated by this system. However, anatomical studies are equivocal. Most investigators agree that vomeronasal organs can be found in all human fetuses, in most infants, but only in some adults (Wysocki, 1979). Thus, we do not yet know whether the accessory olfactory system plays a role in the pheromonal control of human reproductive cycles.

What about human sexual attractants? Some investigators obtained evidence that olfactory stimuli affect sexual attraction in laboratory primates, suggesting the possibility of a similar phenomenon in humans. Keverne and Michael (1971) reported that a mixture of short-chain fatty acids was secreted by a female monkey's vagina around the time of ovulation. When they swabbed these compounds on the genital regions of ovariectomized females, males became more sexually interested in them. These results suggested that the chemicals served as sexual-attractant pheromones. This phenomenon would encourage sexual intercourse during the time the female is most likely to become pregnant.

However, Goldfoot, Krevetz, Goy, and Freeman (1976) tested the hypothesized sexual attractant but found that it had no effect on the females' attractiveness to males. They did find that when they rinsed females' vaginas with a saline solution and applied it to the genital areas of ovariectomized females, males became interested in the test animals if the fluid contained semen that had previously been ejaculated into the donor animals. This result led them to suggest that the odor of the semen, not the short-chain fatty acids, may have influenced the males' behavior. In addition, they found that the fatty acids were actually secreted in greatest quantity during the luteal (postovulatory) phase of the menstrual cycle, when copulatory activity is at a low point. Thus, the evidence that pheromones influence sexual attraction in higher primates is not at all conclusive.

Goldfoot and his colleagues (reported by Goldfoot, 1981) also found that many male monkeys responded positively to *changes* in odor, even when these changes were not related to natural vaginal secretions. For example, they found that a mixture of the plant extracts grisalva and galbazene (which together smell something like green peppers) increased copulatory activity when painted on the females' genital areas. (See **Figure 10.15.**) Thus, the substances that Keverne and Michael swabbed on the ovariectomized females may have stimulated the males' interest simply because of the novelty. In addition, Goldfoot and his colleagues presented male monkeys with blocks of wood that had been swabbed with various substances. They found that sexually inexperienced males did not pay special attention to blocks of wood that contained the vaginal secretions from a female monkey at midcycle. However, sexually ex-

perienced males did sniff them more than blocks of wood containing other odors. These results suggest that the experienced males had learned to recognize the odor of a pre-ovulatory female, not that the secretions produced then act as an automatic sexual attractant. The role of olfactory stimuli as discriminative cues is different from—and much more complex than—pheromonal control of male sexual interest by chemicals secreted by the female.

Some investigators have studied the possibility that odors produced by vaginal secretions may affect a woman's sexual attractiveness. Doty, Ford, Preti, and Huggins (1975) found that both males and females rated these odors as unpleasant, although secretions obtained around the time of ovulation were rated as less unpleasant. Thus, a woman's menstrual cycle appears to affect the odor of her vaginal secretions, but there is no direct evidence that these changes increase her sexual attractiveness.

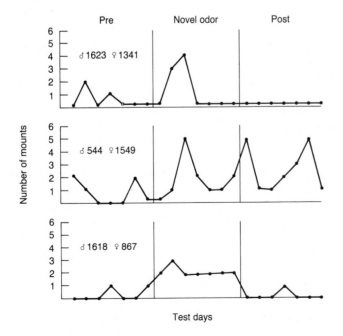

FIGURE 10.15

Response of male monkeys to odors swabbed on the the genitals of ovariectomized female monkeys. (From Goldfoot, D.A., *American Zoologist*, 1981, *21*, 153–164.)

While there is currently no evidence that pheromones play a role in sexual attraction in higher primates, the familiar odor of a sex partner may have a positive effect on sexual arousal. Although we are not generally conscious of the fact, we can identify other people on the basis of olfactory cues. For example, a study by Russell (1976) found that people were able to distinguish by odor between T-shirts that they had worn and those previously worn by other people. They could also tell whether the unknown owner of a T-shirt was male or female. Thus, it is likely that men and women can learn to be attracted by their partners' characteristic odors. However, this is a different phenomenon from the responses produced by pheromones, which apparently need not be learned.

Human Sexual Behavior

Human sexual behavior, like that of other mammals, is influenced by the activational effects of gonadal hormones. However, as we will see, the effects are different.

Effects of Androgenization

A myth that should be dispelled immediately is that men and women would exchange their behavioral roles if their hormonal balances were reversed (subject, of course, to anatomical differences). Nothing of the sort would happen. A loss of testosterone and its replacement with estradiol and progesterone would alter a normal man's body, but he would not begin to act like a woman. He would regret his loss of potency, but the hormonal change would not cause him to become interested in assuming the female role in sexual activity. Homosexuality cannot be produced in a heterosexual adult male by castrating him and administering female gonadal hormones. Similarly, testosterone treatment will not cause a heterosexual woman to lose her sexual interest in men or to want to engage in sexual activity with other women. Nor will she lose her sex drive (even though men might be turned off by her beard and husky voice). In fact, she may become even more interested in sex than she was before.

So far, there is no conclusive evidence that exposure to prenatal androgens affects a person's sexual behavior during adulthood. It is possible that androgens do have defeminizing and masculinizing effects on the human brain that influence subsequent sexual behavior, just as they do in other mammals, but the data do not permit absolute conclusions to be made. Even if prenatal androgenization does influence human sexual behavior, the effect is different from that which occurs in laboratory animals. The most important reason for this difference is that, unlike rodents, human males and females do not exhibit rigidly different sexual behaviors. Male rats mount, intromit, and perform pelvic thrusts. Female rats arch their backs, move their tails, and stand still. The sexual behavior of humans shares an important element with other species, namely, the movement of the penis in the vagina. However, this movement can be accomplished by the man, the woman, or both. Human sexual activity comes in a variety of forms. Except for the obvious effects of anatomical differences, we cannot characterize particular sets of movements as "male" or "female."

What does distinguish between heterosexual men and women is the gender of their preferred sex partner. Heterosexual men prefer women, and heterosexual women prefer men (which is convenient for all concerned). If the brain of a human fetus is affected by exposure to testosterone, we might expect the hormone to bias the choice of a person's preferred sex partner. This possibility will be explored later in this chapter, when I discuss sexual preferences.

Prenatal Androgenization of Human Females. Evidence suggests that prenatal androgenization affects human social behavior, as well as anatomy. If a female human fetus is exposed to androgens, she will be born with some degree of clitoral hypertrophy (enlargement in size), and perhaps her labia will be partly fused. (Remember, the scrotum and labia majora develop from the same primordia.) Such effects were seen in the cases of ten girls whose mothers received a synthetic gestagen in order to prevent miscarriage (Money and Ehrhardt, 1972). Unfortunately, it was subsequently discovered that this gestagen (which is no longer used) sometimes had androgenizing effects. The clitoral enlargement and labial fusion were surgically corrected after birth. A similar syndrome is seen in girls whose adrenal glands secrete abnormal amounts of androgens, producing ***adrenogenital syndrome.*** (Note that the word is *adreno*genital, because of the involvement of the adrenal glands, not *andro*genital.)

Money and Ehrhardt studied the prenatally androgenized girls, all of whom were raised and dressed as girls. Their gender identity was female. However, they described themselves as "tomboys." They preferred playing with toy trucks and guns rather than dolls. They tended to choose boys, rather than other girls, as playmates. The girls did not dislike wearing dresses on special occasions, but they mostly preferred slacks and shorts. (If this study were conducted now, such a finding would cause no surprise. Most North American girls prefer slacks and shorts.) The investigators observed no special differences in their childhood sex play, but because such behavior — in both males and females — is suppressed in our society, one could hardly expect otherwise. (See **Table 10.2.**)

I must hasten to note that the behavior of none of the androgenized girls was "abnormal." Many girls prefer toy trucks and cars to dolls and like to play baseball. However, in a group of normal girls, one would expect to find a *range* of interests, from "masculine" to "feminine." The fact that the group of prena-

T A B L E 10.2   Sex-role – related behavior in fetally androgenized girls and in girls with adrenogenital syndrome*

Behavioral Signs	*Androgenized*	*Adrenogenital*
Known to self and mother as tomboy	More	More
Satisfaction with female sex role	Same	Less
Athletic interests and skills	More	More
Preference for male versus female playmates	Prefer male	Prefer male
Childhood fights	Same	Same
Preference for slacks versus dresses	Prefer slacks	Prefer slacks
Interest in jewelry, perfume, and hair styling	Same	Same

Source: Adapted from Money, J., and Ehrhardt, A. *Man & Woman, Boy & Girl.* Baltimore: The Johns Hopkins University Press, 1972.
* All comparisons are made with a matched group of control subjects.

tally androgenized girls differed statistically from the matched control subjects suggests that prenatal androgens do indeed affect human social behavior. It is possible that the primary effect is on the child's activity level. If prenatal androgenization makes children become more active, the preference for active rather than quiet games might lead the girls to prefer the company of boys and their more active play.

The case of the androgenized girls does not provide *conclusive* evidence that prenatal androgens have organizational effects on human behavior. The girls' parents knew that they had been affected by the drug (or by their own adrenal glands), because their genitals had been somewhat masculinized. It is possible that this knowledge led them to treat their daughters somewhat differently, and that this treatment affected their behavior. (I must confess that I would expect a parent to treat them *more,* rather than *less,* like girls, to compensate for their masculinization. However, we must still consider the issue as unproved.)

A follow-up study of the ten girls who were androgenized with the synthetic gestagen (and two others who were not included in the original study) found no evidence of homosexuality (Money and Mathews, 1982). Indeed, those who were willing to report about their sexual activity indicated normal heterosexual relations. However, although the data are not conclusive, there is a suggestion that adrenogenital syndrome may increase the incidence of bisexuality in females (Ehrhardt and Meyer-Bahlburg, 1981).

Goy and his colleagues (Goy and Phoenix, 1972; Goy and Kemnitz, 1983) assessed the effects of prenatal androgenization on the social behavior of young female monkeys. They administered testosterone to pregnant monkeys, so that their female offspring would be androgenized. The behavior of young male and female monkeys is very different — much

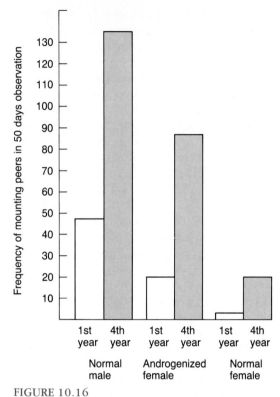

FIGURE 10.16

Malelike mounting behavior of normal male, androgenized female, or normal female monkeys. (From Goy, R.W., and Kemnitz, J.W. In *Application of Behavioral Pharmacology in Toxicology,* edited by G. Zbinden. New York: Raven Press, 1983.)

more so than boys and girls. Compared with females, infant male monkeys are much more likely to initiate periods of play, to engage in rough-and-tumble play, and to make playful threat gestures. The androgenized females acted like males. They were more likely to mount other monkeys (male sexual behavior) than to present their hindquarters (female sexual behavior), just as males typically do. In fact, 90 percent of the androgenized females mounted their peers, compared to 15 percent of the control animals. (See **Figure 10.16.**) A high level of mounting behavior and rough-and-tumble play was seen even in females whose genitals were only slightly masculinized; thus, it appears unlikely that the changes in behavior were caused by alterations in sensory feedback from the genitals.

Failure of Androgenization in Human Males. Nature has performed the equivalent of the prenatal castration experiment in humans (Money and Ehrhardt, 1972). Some people are insensitive to androgens; they have ***androgen insensitivity syndrome,*** one of the more aptly named disorders. The cause of androgen insensitivity syndrome is a genetic mutation that prevents the formation of functioning androgen receptors. The primordial gonads of a genetic male with androgen insensitivity syndrome become testes and secrete Müllerian-inhibiting substance and androgens. However, only the Müllerian-inhibiting substance has an effect on development. Because the cells cannot respond to the androgens, the person develops female external genitalia. The Müllerian-inhibiting substance prevents the female internal sex organs from developing, though; the uterus is atrophic (underdeveloped), and the vagina is shallow.

If an individual with this syndrome is raised as a girl, all is well. At puberty the body will become feminized by the small amounts of estradiol produced by the testes. (In normal males, the estradiol is counteracted by the far greater amounts of testosterone.) At adulthood the individual will function sexually as a woman, although surgical lengthening of the vagina may be necessary. Women with this syndrome report average sex drives, including normal frequency of orgasm in intercourse. Most marry and lead normal sex lives. Of course, lacking a uterus and ovaries, they cannot have children.

The success of testicular estradiol in producing a female body is attested to in Figure 10.17. (See **Figure 10.17.**) I think this photograph illustrates why it would be a tragedy to

raise such an individual as a boy, even though the person has the XY sex karyotype. Testosterone treatment at puberty would be ineffec-

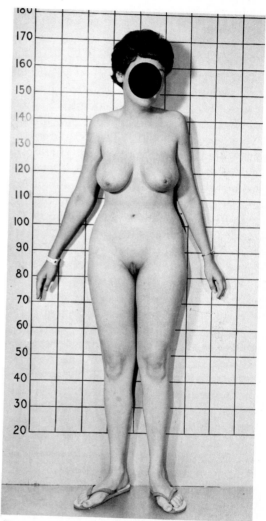

FIGURE 10.17

An XY female displaying androgen insensitivity syndrome. The absence of pubic hair can be explained by the person's insensitivity to androstenedione. (From Money, J., and Ehrhardt, A.A. *Man & Woman, Boy & Girl.* Copyright 1973 by The Johns Hopkins University Press, Baltimore, Maryland. By permission.)

tive; all that could be done would be to prevent development of the breasts. The voice would remain high, and no beard would grow. The woman in this figure lacks pubic hair and axillary hair because of an insensitivity to androstenedione, the androgen that normally stimulates its growth.

Are the Effects of Androgenization Permanent? Money and Ehrhardt (1972) reported a case that apparently showed that socialization could reverse the effects of complete, natural prenatal androgenization. Identical twin boys were born to a couple and were raised normally until 7 months of age, at which time one of them suffered accidental removal of his penis during an attempted circumcision. The surgeon was using a cautery, a device that cuts tissue by means of electrical current. Unfortunately, the current was adjusted too high, so instead of removing the foreskin, the current burned off the entire penis. After a period of agonized indecision and consultation with experts, the parents decided to raise the boy (then 17 months old) as a girl. Surgeons performed the first stage of plastic surgery to create a vagina, and the parents began treating the child as a girl. The child responded almost immediately to this treatment, manifesting many behaviors typical of girls. According to her mother, she became neat and tidy, as opposed to her rather messy twin brother, and modeled her behavior on that of her mother. Because the two children are genetically identical, the difference in behavior was attributed to the powerful effects of differential treatment of children who are perceived as boys and girls.

This case appeared to demonstrate that in humans, at least, prenatal androgenization could be reversed by socialization. However, Diamond (1982) provides evidence that the girl's development during adolescence was not as smooth as it had apparently been dur-

ing childhood. She was teased by other adolescents, who called her "cavewoman," apparently because of her masculine gait. She had trouble making friends and found it difficult to accept her role as a female. When a psychiatrist asked her to draw a picture of a woman, she refused, saying that it was much easier to draw pictures of men.

Of course, this child is not the only one who had a difficult adolescence, or who was not happy with her role as a female. We certainly cannot conclude that her unhappiness was a direct result of her prenatal androgenization. However, the reevaluation of the case eliminates the one documented instance in which the effects of normal prenatal androgenization were successfully reversed. As Diamond notes, this case should be considered when parents and physicians must decide how to raise children whose penises have been accidentally amputated. (Unfortunately, this does occasionally occur.)

Activational Effects of Sex Hormones on Women's Sexual Behavior

As we saw, the sexual behavior of female mammals other than higher primates is controlled by gonadal hormones. However, this is not the case for women. Although estradiol and progesterone may influence sexual activity, they do not *control* it. Most women do not exhibit large changes in receptivity during their menstrual cycle, as laboratory rodents do. As we saw, a female rat will copulate only during estrus, when her estradiol and progesterone levels are high. However, women can become sexually aroused at any time of their menstrual cycle. This is not to say that gonadal hormones have *no* effects in women. Adams, Gold, and Burt (1978) found that women were more likely to engage in autosexual activity (masturbation, sexual fantasies, and arousal from books and films) or to initiate sexual activity with their partners at the time of ovulation. This peak did not occur in women who were taking birth control pills, presumably because the pills prevent ovulation and the accompanying hormonal fluctuations.

The relatively minor effects of female gonadal hormones are exemplified by the effects of ovariectomy on women's sexual activity. Ovariectomy, sometimes carried out when a hysterectomy is performed, does not abolish a woman's interest in sexual activity, nor does menopause, Nature's own "ovariectomy." Loss of estradiol may produce vaginal dryness, which can make intercourse painful, but this effect on sexual behavior is obviously an indirect one. (It can be alleviated by the use of a lubricating jelly or eliminated by the administration of estradiol pills.)

Another difference between women and animals with estrous cycles is indicated by their contrasting reactions to androgens. Testosterone usually produces a small increase in malelike mounting behavior in female rats, even if they were not androgenized early in life. However, androgens do not stimulate *male* sexual behavior in women. On the contrary, in heterosexual women these hormones appear to increase heterosexual desire. Removal of the adrenal glands (which secrete an androgen — androstenedione) appears to decrease sexual desire in women, even though ovariectomy does not (Waxenberg, Drellich, and Sutherland, 1959). However, the adrenalectomies in this study were performed for treatment of cancer, so it is difficult to draw definitive conclusions.

More compelling evidence for an activational effect of androgens on women's sexual behavior comes from a study by Persky, Lief, Strauss, Miller, and O'Brien (1978). These investigators studied the sexual activity and blood levels of gonadal hormones in married couples over a period of three menstrual cycles. They rated the husbands' and wives' responsivity (willingness to engage in sexual activity) and initiation (instigation of sexual activity). The husband's testosterone level was correlated with mutual interest in sexual activity, whether initiated by the husband or the wife. Frequency of intercourse over the entire cycle was related to the wife's peak testosterone level during ovulation. In addition, the wives reported more sexual gratification when their testosterone levels were high, and women with high baseline levels of testosterone tended to report greater satisfaction with sexual activity.

Although experiments with humans are not possible, research on the effects of hormones on female sexual behavior has been performed with rhesus macaques, a common species of laboratory monkey. In general, results have confirmed a role for androgens in the sexual behavior of this species. Everitt, Herbert, and Hamer (1972) found that removal of the adrenal glands decreased the sexual interest of female rhesus macaques who had previously been ovariectomized. The effect was seen most strikingly in the animals' soliciting behavior — what researchers have called *proceptivity*. Removal of the adrenal glands had a much smaller effect on *receptivity* — the animal's willingness to engage in sexual activity with a male who initiates the behavior. Administration of testosterone reinstituted these behaviors to normal levels. A subsequent study (Everitt and Herbert, 1975) showed that the effective site of action of the testosterone was in the anterior hypothalamus. Intracerebral implants of the hormone were effective when they were placed in this region, but these implants did not affect the behavior of adrenalectomized and ovariectomized monkeys when they were placed in the posterior hypothalamus, thalamus, or midbrain. Thus, the brains of female monkeys appear to contain androgen-sensitive neurons that stimulate female sexual activity.

Activational Effects of Sex Hormones in Men

Although women and female rodents are very different in their behavioral responsiveness to sex hormones, men and male rodents (and other mammals, for that matter) resemble each other in their behavioral responsiveness to testosterone. With normal levels, they can be potent and fertile; without testosterone, sperm production ceases, and the animals eventually become unable to achieve penile erections. Some investigators have said that the sexual activity of humans is "emancipated" from the effects of hormones. In one sense this is true. Men who have been castrated for medical reasons do report a continuing interest in sexual activity with their wives, even after their penis can no longer become erect. Obviously, sexual activity can no longer take the form of intercourse, but other types of sexual contact can occur. However, a man's ability to copulate ultimately depends on an adequate level of testosterone in the blood.

Davidson, Camargo, and Smith (1979) performed a double-blind study that demonstrates the activational effects of testosterone on men's sexual activity. Their subjects were married men whose testes failed to produce adequate amounts of testosterone. The investigators administered injections of testosterone (high or low doses) or a placebo and asked the subjects to keep a written log of various sexual activities. Figure 10.18 shows the men's sexual activity during a 4-week interval after each injection; note the increase caused by the testosterone, especially the higher dose. (See **Figure 10.18**.)

The decline in copulatory ability after castration varies considerably among individ-

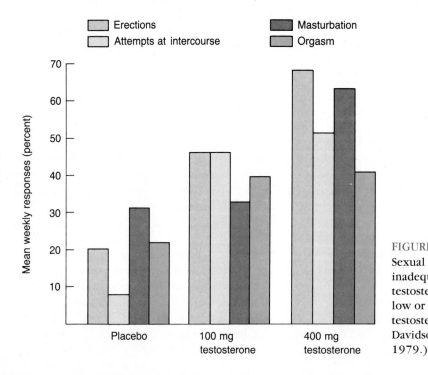

FIGURE 10.18
Sexual responses of males with inadequate levels of testosterone given a placebo or low or high levels of testosterone. (Data from Davidson, Camargo, and Smith, 1979.)

uals, even of the same species. Most rats cease to copulate within a few weeks, but some retain this ability for up to 5 months (Davidson, 1966). Because the average lifespan of a rat is a little over 2 years, this performance compares favorably with that of castrated humans, taking the different lifespans into account. As reported by Money and Ehrhardt (1972), some men lose potency immediately, whereas others show a slow, gradual decline over several years. Prior experience has an effect on the decline, at least in some mammals; Rosenblatt and Aronson (1958a, 1958b) found that high levels of sexual activity before castration substantially prolonged subsequent potency in cats.

A scientist stationed on a remote island demonstrated that testosterone level can be affected by environmental factors (Anonymous, 1970). He removed his beard with an electrical shaver each day and weighed the clippings. Just before he left for visits to the mainland (and to female company), his beard began growing faster. Because rate of beard growth is related to androgen levels, the effect indicates that his anticipation of sexual activity stimulated testosterone production. Conversely, stress (during wartime) can lower testosterone levels (Rose, Bourne, Poe, Mougey, Collins, and Mason, 1969).

Sexual Orientation

What controls a person's sexual orientation, the gender of the preferred sex partner? Some people are exclusively homosexual, choosing only partners of the same sex; some are bisexual, choosing members of both sexes; and some are heterosexual, choosing only partners of the opposite sex. Many humans (especially males) who are essentially heterosexual engage in homosexual episodes sometime during their lives. In some societies, homosexual behavior is the norm during adolescence, followed by marriage and a normal heterosexual relationship (Money and Ehr-

hardt, 1972). Although many animals occasionally engage in sexual activity with a member of the same sex, *exclusive* homosexuality appears to occur only in humans (Ehrhardt and Meyer-Bahlburg, 1981).

Some investigators believe that homosexuality is a result of childhood experiences, especially interactions between the child and parents. A large-scale study of several hundred male and female homosexuals reported by Bell, Weinberg, and Hammersmith (1981) attempted to assess the effects of these factors. The researchers found no evidence that homosexuals had been raised by domineering mothers or submissive fathers, as some clinicians had suggested. The best predictor of adult homosexuality was a self-report of homosexual feelings, which usually preceded homosexual activity by 3 years. The investigators concluded that their data did not support social explanations for homosexuality but were consistent with the possibility that homosexuality is at least partly biologically determined.

Suspecting that male homosexuality might be caused by differences in levels of gonadal hormones, investigators have measured them in homosexuals and heterosexuals. Some early studies reported differences, but most investigators now believe that the results were biased by the stress experienced by homosexual people who felt harassed by society. This stress lowered the subjects' androgen levels. It appears that well-adjusted male homosexuals have normal levels of gonadal hormones (Tourney, 1980).

Given what we now know about the effects of gonadal hormones, we would not predict that their activational effects are responsible for a person's homosexuality. After all, androgens appear to be important for the sexual desire and activity of both men and women. Therefore, the activational effects of sex hormones are probably the same in homosexuals and heterosexuals. However, we saw earlier that the organizational effects of androgens bias the later sexual proclivities of many species of animals. Therefore, if homosexuality does have a physiological cause, it is more likely to be a more subtle difference in brain structure caused by the presence or absence of prenatal androgenization.

As we saw, men and women do not differ from one another so much in their sexual *behavior* as they do in their choice of partner. The same comparison is true for heterosexual and homosexual people; their choice of partner, not the kind of sexual activity they engage in, distinguishes them. Therefore, if prenatal androgenization influences human brain development, the effects are likely to be seen in a person's choice of sex partner, not in the form of his or her sexual behavior. You will recall that exposure of a developing rodent brain to androgens causes masculinization or defeminization, depending on the time during which the exposure occurs. By analogy, we might predict that androgenization would defeminize a human female's choice of partner, making her less likely to choose a male, and then masculinize her choice, making her more likely to choose a female. If this is true, then perhaps the brains of male homosexuals are neither masculinized nor defeminized, those of female homosexuals are masculinized and defeminized, and those of bisexuals are masculinized but not defeminized. Of course, these are speculations that so far cannot be supported by human data.

A study by Gladue, Green, and Hellman (1984) examined the response of the anterior pituitary gland to estradiol. As you learned, when the concentration of estradiol reaches a critical level, it triggers the release of LH. Gladue and his colleagues injected adult male homosexuals, male heterosexuals, and female heterosexuals with an estrogen. The blood levels of LH in the women showed a dramatic rise; those of the heterosexual men did not. The change in blood levels of LH in the homosexual men was intermediate; they showed a statistically significant increase, but one smaller than that of the women. Certainly, we cannot conclude that the men's homosexuality was caused by differences in the response of their pituitary glands to estrogens. However, the results suggest that the homosexual men's pituitary glands (and hence, their brains) may have received less exposure to androgens during some critical stage of prenatal development. This decreased exposure may have increased the likelihood of their developing a preference for male sex partners later.

There is also some empirical support from twin studies for the hypothesis that male homosexuality may have biological causes. Almost always, if one male monozygotic (identical) twin is homosexual, the other is, too. In fact, Zuger (1976) found only nine cases of discordance (that is, one member heterosexual and the other homosexual) reported in the scientific literature. Heston and Shields (1968) studied a remarkable family of fourteen children that contained three pairs of male monozygotic twins. Two pairs were homosexual and the third pair was heterosexual. They could find no obvious differences in the children's environment that could account for the development of their sexual orientations. Because monozygotic twins are genetically identical and develop together in the uterus, the high correlation could be caused by heredity or by prenatal environmental factors.

A study performed with laboratory animals suggests that prenatal stress can alter adult sexual behavior. Ward (1972) kept pregnant rats under a bright light, which causes stress. This treatment increased the amount of stress-related steroid hormones secreted by the mothers' adrenal cortex. A later study (Ward and Weisz, 1980) confirmed that this treatment suppresses androgen production in male fetuses. The male rats born to the stressed mothers had smaller external genitalia as adults. Compared with normal control subjects, the animals were less likely to display male sexual behavior and were more likely to display female sexual behavior when they were given injections of estradiol and progesterone. Although we cannot generalize these results to humans, the study is consistent with the hypothesis that male homosexuality may be related to inadequate androgenization.

Several studies have shown that prenatal events can increase the incidence of male sexual behavior in female rats. For example, Clemens (1971) found that the probability of malelike mounting behavior was highest in female rats that shared their mother's uterus with several brothers; fewer brothers resulted in less male sexual behavior. Presumably, the females were partially androgenized by their brothers' testosterone. Because most humans do not have any company in the uterus, this factor apparently is not of much importance in human female homosexuality.

As we saw earlier, there is a suggestion of an increased incidence of bisexuality in women who are affected with adrenogenital syndrome. These women received an increased dose of androgens from their own adrenal glands before birth, which may have caused some androgenization of the brain that manifested itself in bisexuality. But I must emphasize again that the data are not conclusive.

For some people, homosexuality is immoral; others regard it as a mental disorder. However, both of these characterizations have been denounced by professional mental health organizations. It is clear that homosexuals can be as happy and as well adjusted as heterosexuals (Bell and Weinberg, 1978). If the hypotheses I have outlined here are correct, then homosexuals are no more responsible for their sexual orientation than heterosexuals are. The question "Why does someone become homosexual?" will probably be answered when we find out why someone becomes *heterosexual*.

INTERIM SUMMARY

The female reproductive cycle (menstrual cycle or estrous cycle) begins with the maturation of one or more ovarian follicles, which occurs in response to the secretion of FSH by the anterior pituitary gland. As the ovarian follicle matures, it secretes estradiol, which causes the lining of the uterus to develop. When estradiol reaches a critical level, it causes the pituitary gland to secrete a surge of LH, triggering ovulation. The empty ovarian follicle becomes a corpus luteum, under the continued influence of LH, and secretes estradiol and progesterone. If pregnancy does not occur, the corpus luteum dies and stops producing hormones, and menstruation begins.

In most mammals, female sexual behavior is the norm, just as the female body and female sex organs are the norm. That is, unless prenatal androgens masculinize and defeminize the animal's brain, its sexual behavior will be feminine. Behavioral masculinization refers to the androgen-stimulated development of neural circuits that respond to testosterone in adulthood, producing male sexual behavior. Behavioral defeminization refers to the inhibitory effects of androgens on the development of neural circuits that respond to estradiol and progesterone in adulthood, producing female sexual behavior.

The sexual behavior of males of all mammalian species appears to depend on the presence of androgens. Female mammals other than primates depend primarily on estradiol and progesterone and will copulate only during the period of estrus when the levels of these hormones are high.

Pheromones can affect sexual physiology and behavior. Odorants present in the urine of female mice affect their estrous cycles, either lengthening and eventually stopping them (Whitten effect) or causing pseudopregnancy (Lee-Boot effect). Odorants present in the urine of male mice abolish these effects and cause the females' cycles to become synchronized. In addition, the odor of the urine from a male other than one that impregnated the female mouse will cause her to abort (Bruce effect). In the hamster, the attractiveness of an estrous female to the male derives in part from the odor of her vaginal secretions, detected by the vomeronasal organ. Connections between the olfactory system and the amygdala appear to be important in stimulating male sexual behavior. Although some studies have shown that odors can play a role in the sexual attractiveness of female monkeys, it does not appear that the effect is caused by pheromones, which involve automatic responses to particular chemicals.

The behavioral effects of prenatal androgenization in humans, if any, are not well understood. Studies of prenatally androgenized girls suggest only modest effects on social behavior, perhaps as a result of an increased tendency to be more active. Differences in sexual preference have not been clearly demonstrated. Men, like other male mammals, require testosterone in order to be able to have an erection and to ejaculate. Women do not require estradiol or progesterone in order to experience sexual interest and engage in sexual behavior, although these hormones may affect the quality and intensity of their sex drive. Instead, the most important activational effect on women's sex drives seems to be provided by androgens.

Sexual orientation (that is, heterosexuality or homosexuality) may be influenced by prenatal androgenization, but conclusive evidence is lacking. Evidence from twin studies suggests that genetics or common environmental influences during prenatal development play a role in the development of homosexuality or heterosexuality. In addition, one study found that the LH response of homosexual men was intermediate to that of heterosexual males and females, which suggests a lesser degree of prenatal androgenization.

■ NEURAL CONTROL OF SEXUAL BEHAVIOR

Spinal Mechanisms

Genital stimulation can elicit sexual movements and postures in female cats and rats even after their spinal cord is transected

below the brain (Beach, 1967; Hart, 1969). Thus, at least some elements of sexual behavior are organized at the level of the spinal cord.

The reflex mechanisms responsible for the control of penile erection and ejaculation are located in the spinal cord of the male animal. Hart (1967) severed the spinal cords of dogs and observed not only erection and ejaculation but also the characteristic pelvic thrusting, leg kicking, and arching back. A refractory period of 5 to 30 minutes followed ejaculations, during which time the animal was unresponsive. This contrasts with sexual behavior in the intact dog, which typically shows a pause of more than 30 minutes before sexual activity is resumed. Thus, the spinal cord is ready for more sexual activity before the brain is.

Hart obtained evidence that the brain inhibits spinal sexual reflexes. He found that intense ejaculatory reactions, which can easily be obtained by means of mechanical stimulation of the penis of a dog with a spinal transection, cannot be produced in a normal intact dog unless a receptive bitch is present. The odor and sight of a receptive female apparently disinhibit the cerebral mechanisms that normally prevent the expression of the intense ejaculatory response. (See **Figure 10.19.**)

Emission of semen, as we have seen, is produced by a spinal reflex. Humans with spinal damage occasionally produce an erection and ejaculate. They have even become fathers, when their wives have been artificially inseminated with semen obtained by mechanical stimulation (Hart, 1978). Because the spinal damage prevents sensory information from reaching the brain, they do not experience an orgasm as a result, and thus they are unaware of the erection and ejaculation unless they see it happening. However, they do occasionally experience a "phantom erection" along with an orgasm, despite penile

Dog with severed spinal cord

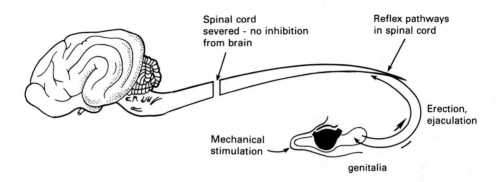

Spinal cord
severed - no inhibition
from brain

Reflex pathways
in spinal cord

Erection,
ejaculation

Mechanical
stimulation

genitalia

Normal dog

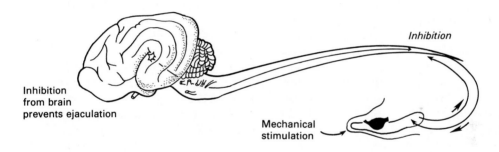

Inhibition

Inhibition
from brain
prevents ejaculation

Mechanical
stimulation

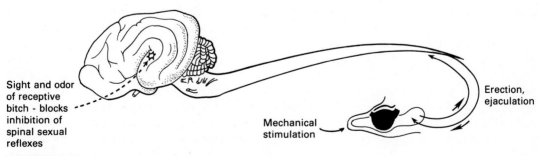

Sight and odor
of receptive
bitch - blocks
inhibition of
spinal sexual
reflexes

Mechanical
stimulation

Erection,
ejaculation

FIGURE 10.19

A schematic explanation of the experiment by Hart (1967).

quiescence (Money, 1960; Comarr, 1970). Nothing happens to their genitals or internal sex organs, but the spontaneous activity of various brain mechanisms gives rise to feelings of arousal and orgasm.

Breedlove and his colleagues have studied (in rats) a nucleus in the ventral horn of the lumbar region of the spinal cord called the *spinal nucleus of the bulbocavernosus.* This nucleus contains motor neurons whose axons innervate the bulbocavernosus muscle, which is attached to the base of the penis and is involved in sexual activity. Although the muscle is not present in female rats, it is present in both sexes in humans. (It is usually called the *sphincter vaginae* in women.)

Breedlove and Arnold (1980, 1983) discovered that the spinal nucleus of the bulbocavernosus is present only in male rats, and they showed that its neurons selectively accumulate androgens. They injected the animals with radioactive testosterone, dihydrotestosterone, or estradiol and used autoradiography (described in Chapter 5) to detect cells that took up the hormone. Only the androgens accumulated in the spinal nucleus.

Breedlove, Jacobson, Gorski, and Arnold (1982) found that if female rats were injected with testosterone on the second day after birth, the spinal nucleus of the bulbocavernosus would develop. Conversely, if male rats were treated prenatally by injecting the pregnant females with drugs that inhibit the effects of androgens and were then castrated postnatally, the spinal nucleus would not develop. Figure 10.20 shows photographs of sections of the rat spinal cord. The nuclei *(arrows)* are present in normal males *(top left)* and androgenized females *(bottom right)* but not in normal females *(top right)* or nonandrogenized males *(bottom left).* (See **Figure 10.20.**)

Although there is no evidence for a nucleus in the spinal cord that exists in females only, estradiol has direct effects on neurons in the spinal cord, facilitating sexual reflexes when implanted there (Hart, 1978). In addition, autoradiographic studies have shown that neurons of the spinal cord take up estradiol directly (Stumpf and Sar, 1976).

Brain Mechanisms

Males

The *medial preoptic area,* located just rostral to the hypothalamus, is the forebrain region that is most critical for male sexual behavior. Stimulation of this region elicits male copulatory behavior (Malsbury, 1971). Conversely, its destruction permanently abolishes it (Heimer and Larsson, 1966/1967), and so does a lesion that cuts axons that leave it and travel caudally (Conrad and Pfaff, 1976). This latter result suggests that the medial preoptic area exerts its effect by controlling motor mechanisms in the midbrain and brain stem; however, little is known about these mechanisms. Female lordosis is facilitated, not abolished, by preoptic area lesions. However, the occasional mounting behavior seen in normal females disappears after lesions of the preoptic region (Singer, 1968). Thus, the region is part of a mechanism controlling male sexual behavior in *both* sexes.

Androgens have organizational and activational effects on neurons in the medial preoptic area. First let us consider the activational effects. If a normally androgenized male rat is castrated in adulthood, its sexual behavior will cease, but the behavior will be reinstated by the implantation of a small amount of testosterone directly into the medial preoptic area (Davidson, 1980). However, the behavior will not be as vigorous, probably because testosterone also has important activational effects on cells in the spinal cord (as we just saw) and on cells in the penis itself (Beach and Westbrook, 1968). Autoradiographic studies with radioactive androgens

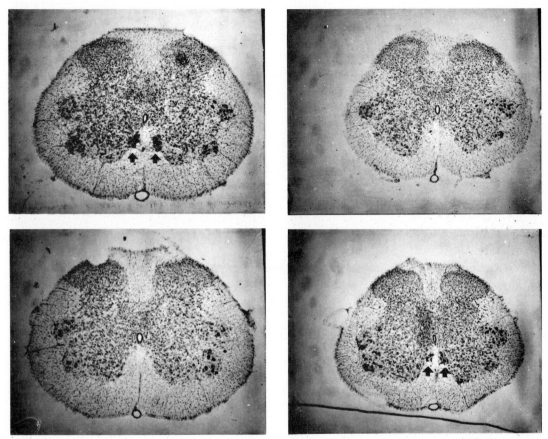

FIGURE 10.20

Photomicrographs of sections of the rat spinal cord through the region of the spinal nucleus of the bulbocavernosus. *Top left:* Normal male. *Top right:* Normal female. *Bottom left:* Castrated male treated with an antiandrogen prenatally. *Bottom right:* Androgenized female. (From Breedlove, S.M., and Arnold, A. *Journal of Neuroscience,* 1983, *3,* 417–423; 424–432.)

have confirmed that cells in the medial preoptic area contain androgen receptors (Morrell and Pfaff, 1978).

What about the organizational effects of androgens on brain development? Gorski, Gordon, Shryne, and Southam (1978) discovered a nucleus within the preoptic area of the rat brain that is three to seven times larger in males. This area is called (appropriately enough) the ***sexually dimorphic nucleus*** of the preoptic area. (See **Figure 10.21.**)

Gorski and his colleagues found that the sex-related size difference in the sexually dimorphic nucleus was the result of an organizational effect of androgens; the nucleus was 50 percent smaller in rats that had been castrated immediately after birth. Jacobson, Csernus, Shryne, and Gorski (1981) found

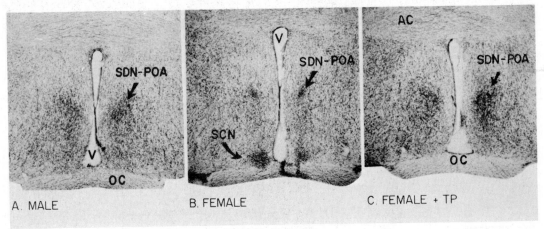

FIGURE 10.21

Photomicrographs of sections through the preoptic area of the rat brain. *Left:* Normal male. *Center:* Normal female. *Right:* Androgenized female. SDN-POA = sexually dimorphic nucleus of the preoptic area; OC = optic chiasm; V = third ventricle; SCN = suprachiasmatic nucleus; AC = anterior commissure. (From Gorski, R.A., *Neuroendocrine Perspectives*, Vol. 2, edited by E.E. Müller and R.M. MacLeod. Amsterdam: Elsevier-North Holland, 1983.)

that the effect of castration on the size of the nucleus could be reversed by giving the rats injections of testosterone. The function of the sexually dimorphic nucleus is not yet known. Arendash and Gorski (1983) found that small lesions in the nucleus did not block male sexual behavior, but small lesions just dorsal to it did. Thus, although we know that the medial preoptic area is critical for male sexual behavior, that the size of a specific region of this area is controlled by the organizational effects of androgens, and that the major activational effect of androgens is exerted on neurons of the preoptic region, we do not know which neurons are involved, or precisely what they do.

The temporal lobes of the brain appear to play a role in the modulation of sexual arousal, and in its direction toward an appropriate goal object, especially in higher mammals. We have already seen (in Chapter 6) that the temporal cortex plays a role in the visual recognition of objects. Monkeys with temporal lobe damage can "see" objects; they can orient in space quite normally and can pick up small objects. However, they cannot visually discriminate nuts and bolts from raisins and other small pieces of food. They must put everything into their mouth first, rejecting inedible objects and chewing and swallowing the edible ones. Temporal lobe damage also appears to impair an animal's ability to choose an appropriate sex object; male cats with these brain lesions have been reported to attempt copulation with everything in sight—the experimenter, a teddy bear, furniture—everything that is remotely mountable (Schreiner and Kling, 1956; Green, Clemente, and DeGroot, 1957).

In humans, temporal lobe dysfunctions are often correlated with decreased sex drives. For example, focal epilepsy (brain seizures that originate from localized, irritative lesions) of the temporal lobes is sometimes associated with lack of interest in sexual activity (Blumer, 1975; Blumer and Walker, 1975). Usually, if the seizures are successfully treated by medication or by surgical removal of the affected tissue, the person attains normal sexual interest.

Temporal lobe abnormalities are occasionally associated with unusual sexual activities. For example, Mitchell, Falconer, and Hill (1954) reported the case of a man with a safety pin fetish, who had a compulsion to gaze at a safety pin. The staring would then trigger a seizure, after which he would often dress in his wife's clothing. His seizures were eliminated by temporal lobe surgery, and along with them went his sexual aberrations.

Kolářský, Freund, Machek, and Polák (1967) examined the cases of men with sexual disorders and found a strong correlation between the disorders and actual or presumptive temporal lobe damage, especially if the damage occurred early in life. It is interesting to note that unusual sexual activities, such as fetishes, pedophilias (sexual interest in children), and transvestism are much more common in men than in women (Masters, Johnson, and Kolodny, 1982). We do not know whether the cause for this discrepancy is biological or cultural (or both).

Females

The one part of the brain that is most critical for performance of female sexual behavior is the ***ventromedial nucleus*** of the hypothalamus. Female rats with bilateral lesions of the ventromedial nuclei will not display lordosis behavior, even if they are treated with estradiol and progesterone. In fact, when trapped in a corner by a male rat, they will attack him. Conversely, electrical stimulation of the ventromedial nucleus facilitates female sexual behavior (Pfaff and Sakuma, 1979).

As we saw earlier, androgenization has two organizational effects on behavior: masculinization and defeminization. At least part of the

defeminizing effects of androgens on behavior take place in the ventromedial nucleus. Although exposure of the developing brain to androgens does not grossly affect the structure of the ventromedial nucleus, it does cause subtle changes in receptors, which I will describe shortly.

Estradiol and progesterone have activational effects on female sexual behavior in rats. As we saw earlier, estradiol "primes" the brain so that it is ready to respond to progesterone. Evidence indicates that the activational effects of both of these hormones occur in the ventromedial nucleus. Rubin and Barfield (1980) implanted minute quantities of estradiol bilaterally into the ventromedial nuclei of ovariectomized female rats. Next, they administered an injection of progesterone. The rats exhibited proceptive and receptive sexual behaviors when males were present: darting, hopping, ear wiggling, and lordosis. The effects were seen only if the estradiol implants were within 0.25 mm of the ventromedial nucleus. In a subsequent study, Davis, Krieger, Barfield, McEwen, and Pfaff (1983) confirmed that the relevant location was the ventromedial nucleus. They implanted minute quantities of *radioactive* estradiol and then injected the rats with progesterone. After confirming that the treatment produced female sexual behavior, the investigators killed the animals, removed the brains, and localized the radioactivity with autoradiography. They found that the estradiol did not diffuse more than 0.5 mm away from the tip of the cannulas; thus, the effect of the estradiol definitely occurred within the ventromedial nuclei.

The effects of progesterone also occur in the ventromedial nuclei. Barfield, Rubin, Glaser, and Davis (1983) found that a small priming dose of estradiol followed by an implant of progesterone in the ventromedial nucleus stimulated receptive and proceptive sexual behaviors. Because relatively large

amounts of progesterone are needed to induce female sexual activity, the authors could
not perform an autoradiographic study similar to the one done with estradiol. However,
after implanting radioactive progesterone in
the ventromedial nuclei, they cut the brains
into pieces and analyzed the radioactivity of
these pieces. The analysis confirmed that little progesterone escaped the vicinity of the
ventromedial nuclei.

Autoradiographic studies have found that
estrogen receptors are located in the medial
preoptic area, medial hypothalamus, amygdala, and lateral septum in all animals that
have been examined so far (Pfaff and Mc-
Ewen, 1983). The brains of both males and
females contain these receptors; however,
Rainbow, Parsons, and McEwen (1982)
found that compared with female rat brains,
male rat brains contained 58 percent fewer
estrogen receptors in the medial preoptic
area, and 61 percent fewer progesterone receptors in the ventromedial nucleus of the
hypothalamus. Presumably, these differences
are among the defeminizing effects that androgens have on the developing brain.

The priming effect of estradiol on the
activating effect of progesterone appears to
involve increased production of progesterone receptors. Blaustein and Feder (1979)
administered estradiol to ovariectomized
guinea pigs and found a 150-percent increase
in the number of progesterone receptors in
the hypothalamus, with smaller increases
elsewhere in the brain. In a subsequent study,
Blaustein and Feder (1980) administered a
priming dose of estradiol and then followed it
40 hours later with an injection of progesterone. They killed animals at varying times after
the progesterone injection and examined the
number of progesterone receptors in the cytoplasm and nucleus of cells of the basal
forebrain. They observed a rapid fall in the
number of progesterone receptors in the cytoplasm and a rapid increase in the number in

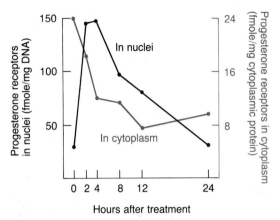

FIGURE 10.22
Quantity of progesterone receptors in the nuclei
and cytoplasm of female guinea pigs after
receiving an injection of progesterone 40 hours
subsequent to a priming dose of estradiol.
fmol = femtomole, or one quadrillionth (10^{-15})
of a mole, a basic unit of molecular weight.
(From Blaustein, J.D., and Feder, H.H.
Endocrinology, 1980, *106*, 1061–1069.)

the nuclei. The results suggest that the progesterone bound with the cytoplasmic receptors and caused them to be carried into the
nucleus, where the behavioral effects were
triggered. (See **Figure 10.22.**)

Once hormones stimulate estradiol and
progesterone receptors in neurons in the ventromedial nucleus, what happens next?
Cohen and Pfaff (1981) used an electron microscope to examine neurons in the ventromedial nucleus of the hypothalamus to see
whether estradiol treatment affected the
cells' structure. They found that compared
with ovariectomized females, the endoplasmic reticulum in neurons of the estradiol-
treated rats was stacked in parallel arrays
rather than in discrete sacs. In addition, the
neurons of estradiol-treated rats contained
vesicles with dense cores in the vicinity of the
Golgi apparatus; this finding suggests that the
cells were producing a substance — perhaps
a neurotransmitter or a neuromodulator —

destined to be transported down the axons. (See **Figure 10.23.**)

A subsequent study by Harlan, Shivers, Kow, and Pfaff (1982) supported the implications of the electron microscope experiment. The investigators infused colchicine

FIGURE 10.23

Electron photomicrographs of neurons in the ventromedial nucleus of female rats. The nucleus (Nu) of this type of cell is large, and the cells contain an aggregation of granular material *(arrows)* near the nucleoli (N). The nuclear membranes are strongly invaginated *(arrowheads)*. A. Ovariectomized rat (control). B. Ovariectomized rat treated with estradiol. The endoplasmic reticulum (er) of the estradiol-treated rat is stacked in parallel arrays, in contrast to the discrete sacs seen in the control animal. C. A closer view of the Golgi apparatus from an estradiol-treated rat, showing the dense-cored vesicles *(arrowheads)* that presumably are destined for transport out of the cell. Significantly more of these vesicles are found in estradiol-treated rats. (From Cohen, R., and Pfaff, D.W. *Cell and Tissue Research,* 1981, *217,* 451–470.)

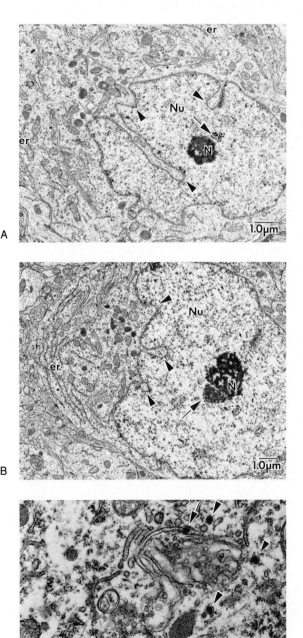

into the ventromedial nuclei of ovariecto-mized rats 24 hours before giving them an injection of estradiol. As we saw at the beginning of this chapter, colchicine blocks cell division by dissolving the spindle fibers that pull the chromosomes apart. In addition, colchicine disrupts the microtubules that are necessary for fast axoplasmic flow. These fibers run the length of the axon and transport substances (including synaptic vesicles) toward the terminal buttons. Harlan and colleagues found that the colchicine delayed the stimulating effects of estradiol on lordosis by 2 days. Presumably, the effects of the colchicine wore off in this amount of time. (See **Figure 10.24.**)

The neurons of the ventromedial nucleus send axons to the ***periaqueductal gray matter*** of the midbrain, surrounding the cerebral aqueduct (Krieger, Conrad, and Pfaff, 1979). This region, too, has been implicated in female sexual behavior; Sakuma and Pfaff

(1979a, 1979b) found that electrical stimulation of this region facilitates lordosis in female rats, and that lesions there disrupt it. In addition, Sakuma and Pfaff (1980a, 1980b) found that estradiol treatment or electrical stimulation of the ventromedial nuclei increased the firing rate of neurons in the periaqueductal gray matter.

The neurons of the periaqueductal gray matter send axons to the reticular formation of the medulla (Krieger and Pfaff, 1980). Cells there send axons to the spinal cord. Thus, a pathway from the ventromedial nucleus to the spinal cord exists that may very well control the lordosis response in female rats.

INTERIM SUMMARY

Some sexual reflexes, such as erection, ejaculation, and lordosis, are organized by neural circuits in the spinal cord. Studies with male dogs showed that the ejaculatory response is normally inhibited by neurons in the brain: only when the spinal cord was severed, or when a receptive bitch was present, would ejaculation occur in response to mechanical stimulation. In addition, the refractory period was shorter after the spinal cord was severed.

Two nuclei in the nervous system develop only if a rodent is exposed to androgens early in life: the spinal nucleus of the bulbocavernosus, located in the spinal cord, and the sexually dimorphic nucleus, located in the preoptic area of the forebrain.

The medial preoptic area is the forebrain region most critical for male sexual behavior. Stimulation of this area produces copulatory behavior; lesioning abolishes it. Implantation of testosterone directly into this area reinstates copulatory behavior that was previously abolished by castration in adulthood. Autoradiographic studies showed that neurons in the medial preoptic area contain testosterone receptors.

The temporal lobe, which plays a role in visual recognition, also plays a role in recognition of appropriate sex objects. Laboratory animals with

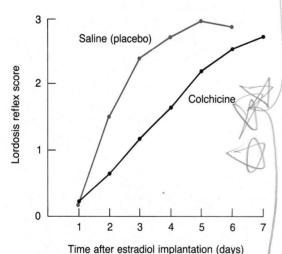

FIGURE 10.24
Amount of lordosis behavior after receiving implants of estradiol in rats treated with colchicine or a placebo. (From Harlan, R.E., Shivers, B.D., Kow, L.-M., and Pfaff, D.W. *Brain Research,* 1982, *238,* 153–157.)

temporal lobectomies, and humans with temporal lobe abnormalities, are more likely than normal individuals to exhibit abnormal sexual behavior.

The most important forebrain region for female sexual behavior is the ventromedial nucleus of the hypothalamus. Its destruction abolishes copulatory behavior, and its stimulation facilitates the behavior. Both estradiol and progesterone exert their facilitating effects on female sexual behavior in this region; implantation of these hormones in the ventromedial nucleus of ovariectomized animals reinstates both receptive and proceptive sexual behavior. Autoradiographic studies confirm the existence of progesterone and estrogen receptors there. Estradiol injections facilitate the activating effects of progesterone on female sexual behavior. These priming effects are caused by the ability of estradiol to increase production of progesterone receptors in the hypothalamus.

The neurons of the ventromedial nucleus send axons to the periaqueductal gray matter of the midbrain; presumably, neurons in the midbrain, through their connections with the medullary reticular formation and spinal cord, control the particular responses that constitute female sexual behavior.

■ MATERNAL BEHAVIOR

In most mammalian species, reproductive behavior takes place after the offspring are born, as well as at the time they are conceived. This section examines the role of hormones in the initiation and maintenance of maternal behavior and the role of the neural circuits that are responsible for their expression. Most of the research has involved rodents; less is known about the neural and endocrine bases of maternal behavior in primates.

In focusing on maternal behavior, I do not deny the existence of paternal behavior, but male parental behavior is most prominent in higher primates such as humans—and we know little about the neurological basis of human parental behavior. Male rodents do not show parental behavior except under special circumstances. There are, of course, other classes of animals (for example, many

species of fish) in which the male takes care of the young, and in many species of birds the task of caring for the offspring is shared equally. However, neural mechanisms of parental behavior have not received much study in these species.

Maternal Behavior in Rodents

The final test of the fitness of a given animal's genes is the number of offspring that survive to a reproductive age. Just as the process of natural selection favors reproductively competent animals, it favors those that care adequately for their young (if their young in fact require any care). Rat and mouse pups certainly do require care; they cannot survive without a mother who attends to their needs.

At birth, rats and mice resemble fetuses. The infants are blind (their eyes are still shut), and they can only helplessly wriggle. They are poikilothermous ("cold-blooded"); their brain is not yet developed enough to regulate body temperature. They even lack the ability to release their own urine and feces spontaneously and must be helped to do so by their mother. As we will see shortly, this phenomenon actually serves a useful function.

Why are most rodent neonates born in such an immature state? We might speculate as follows: In the case of rodents, natural selection has undoubtedly favored organisms that produce a large number of young. The result is large litters, spaced closely together. A mouse can carry a litter of twelve (or even more) pups. A pregnant mouse looks like she swallowed a golf ball; one cannot imagine the animal carrying any more weight than she does. Therefore, if mice (or rats) gave birth to young that were larger and more mature, they would have to carry a smaller number of them. Also, the sooner the uterus is cleared out, the sooner the mouse can become pregnant again. As a matter of fact, some mice can become pregnant on top of a current pregnancy. This phenomenon, called *superfeta-*

tion, is supposedly rare, but I observed it often in a breeding colony I ran in my laboratory. If I left a male with a female for around 15 days, one litter of pups would be born (approximately 20 days after insemination), and approximately 15 days after that, a second litter would be born.

During gestation, female rats and mice build nests. The form this structure takes depends on the material available for its construction. In the laboratory, the animals are usually given strips of paper or lengths of rope or twine. A good *brood nest,* as it is called, is shown in Figure 10.25. This nest is made of hemp rope, a piece of which is shown below. The mouse laboriously shredded the rope and then wove an enclosed nest, with a small hole for access to the interior. (See **Figure 10.25.**)

At the time of *parturition* (delivery of off-spring), the female begins to groom and lick the area around the vagina. As a pup begins to emerge, she assists the uterine contractions by pulling the pup out with her teeth. She then eats the placenta and umbilical cord and cleans off the fetal membranes — a quite delicate operation. (A newborn pup looks like it is sealed in very thin plastic wrap.) After all the pups are born and cleaned up, the mother will probably nurse them. Milk is usually present very near the time of birth.

Periodically, the mother licks the pups' anogenital region, stimulating reflexive urination and defecation. Friedman and Bruno (1976) have shown the utility of this mechanism. They noted that a lactating female rat produces approximately 48 gm of milk (containing approximately 35 ml of water) on the tenth day of lactation. They injected some of the pups with tritiated (radioactive) water

FIGURE 10.25
A mouse's brood nest. Beside it is a length of the kind of rope the mouse used to construct it.

and later found radioactivity in the mother and in the litter mates. Friedman and Bruno calculated that a lactating rat normally consumes 21 ml of water in the urine of her young, thus recycling approximately two thirds of the water she gives to the pups in the form of milk. The water, traded back and forth between mother and young, serves as a vehicle for the nutrients — fats, protein, and sugar — contained in milk. Because the milk production of a lactating rat each day is approximately 14 percent of her body weight (for a human weighing 120 pounds, that would be around 2 gallons), the recycling is extremely useful, especially when the availability of water is a problem.

Besides cleaning, nursing, and purging her offspring, a female rodent will retrieve pups if they leave or are removed from the nest. The mother will even construct another nest in a new location and move her litter there, should the conditions at the old site become unfavorable (for example, when an inconsiderate experimenter puts a heat lamp over it). The way a female rodent picks up her pup is quite consistent: she gingerly grasps the animal by the back, managing not to injure it with her very sharp teeth. (I can personally attest to the ease with which these teeth can penetrate skin.) She then carries the pup with a characteristic prancing walk, her head held high. (See **Figure 10.26.**) The pup is brought back to the nest and is left there. The female then leaves the nest again to search for another pup. She continues to retrieve pups until she finds no more; she does not count her pups and stop retrieving when they are all back. A mouse or rat will usually accept all the pups she is offered, if they are young enough. I once observed two lactating female mice with nests in corners of the same cage, diagonally opposite each other. I disturbed their nests, which triggered a long bout of retrieving, during which each mother stole youngsters from the other's nest. The mothers kept up their exchange for a long time, passing each other in the middle of the cage.

Maternal behavior begins to wane as the pups become more active and begin to look more like adult mice. At around 16 to 18 days of age, they are able to get about easily by themselves, and they begin to obtain their own food. The mother ceases to retrieve them when they leave the nest and will eventually run away from them if they attempt to nurse.

Stimuli That Elicit and Maintain Maternal Behavior

Most virgin female rats will begin to retrieve and care for young pups after having infants placed with them for several days — a process called sensitization or ***concaveation*** (Wiesner and Sheard, 1933). The same phenomenon can be observed in mice, but a

FIGURE 10.26
A female mouse carrying one of her pups.

higher percentage of these animals are spontaneously "maternal" anyway. Olfaction and audition appear to be the primary senses involved in sensitization, but they act in different ways. Noirot (1972) exposed virgin female mice to the sound of the distress calls of an isolated pup; these mice engaged in more nest-building behavior than did controls. On the other hand, she found that exposure to the odor but not the sound of pups (the presence of a nest that had previously held a litter of mice) enhanced subsequent handling and licking of pups, but not nest building.

Mouse, rat, and hamster pups emit at least two different kinds of ultrasonic calls (Noirot, 1972). These sounds cannot be heard by humans; they have to be translated into lower frequencies by a special device (a "bat detector") in order to be perceived by the experimenter. Of course, the mother can hear these calls. When a pup gets cold (as it would if it were removed from the nest), it emits a characteristic call that brings the mother out of her nest. The sound is so effective that female mice have been observed to chew the cover off a loudspeaker that is transmitting a recording of this call. Once out of the nest, the female uses olfactory cues as well as auditory ones to find the pups; she can find a buried, anesthetized baby mouse that is unable to make any noise. The second call is made in response to rough handling. When a mother hears this sound, she stops what she is doing. Typically, it is she who is administering the rough handling, and the distress call makes her stop. The mechanism undoubtedly plays an important role in training mother mice to handle pups properly.

Olfaction plays an important role in controlling maternal behavior. Removal of the olfactory bulbs causes pup killing and cannibalism in female rats (Fleming and Rosenblatt, 1974a) and mice (Gandelman, Zarrow, Denenberg, and Myers, 1971). However, Fleming and Rosenblatt (1974b) found that

eliminating olfactory sensitivity by applying zinc sulfate to the olfactory mucosa facilitated sensitization of virgin female rats to pups. These rats showed less of the ambivalence normally shown by naive rats toward pups; instead of approaching them gingerly, sniffing them, and then suddenly jumping back, the animals approached them more boldly. Apparently some aspect of the odor of the pups had an inhibitory effect. The difference between the effects of removing the olfactory bulbs and deafferentating the olfactory system implies that the olfactory bulbs do more than mediate olfactory sensitivity; their presence somehow inhibits adult females from killing and eating infant pups.

Fleming, Vaccarino, Tambosso, and Chee (1979) found that cutting the vomeronasal nerve, thus deafferentating the accessory olfactory system, also facilitated the responsiveness of virgin females to pups. Thus, the accessory olfactory system also plays a role in olfactory control of maternal behavior. You will recall that both the primary and accessory olfactory systems project to the medial amygdala. Fleming, Vaccarino, and Luebke (1980) found that lesions there also facilitated responsiveness, as did lesions of the *stria terminalis,* a fiber bundle that connects the medial amygdala with various forebrain regions, including the medial preoptic area. (As we will see, the latter structure is essential for maternal behavior.)

Another aspect of rodent pups, besides their odor, appears to identify them as juveniles. A lactating mouse will often exhibit maternal aggression, attacking other mice that venture near her nest. However, she will almost never attack a baby mouse, even if it belongs to a litter other than her own. Svare and Gandelman (1973) showed that the most important distinguishing characteristic that controlled a mouse's attack was the presence or absence of hair; a strange 14-day-old (adolescent) mouse will be attacked unless its hair has been shaved off. The absence of hair appears to identify a mouse as an infant, thus protecting it from attack.

Hormonal Control of Maternal Behavior

Nest-building behavior appears to be primarily dependent on progesterone, the principal hormone of pregnancy. Lisk, Pretlow, and Friedman (1969) found that nonpregnant female mice built brood nests after a pellet of progesterone was implanted under the skin. The pellet slowly dissolved, maintaining a continuously high level of progesterone. The enhanced nest building was suppressed by the administration of estradiol. After parturition, mothers continue to maintain their nests, and they construct new nests if necessary, even though their blood level of progesterone is very low then. Voci and Carlson (1973) found that hypothalamic implants of *prolactin* (an anterior pituitary hormone that is responsible for milk production) as well as progesterone facilitated nest building

in mice. Presumably, nest building can be facilitated by either hormone: progesterone during pregnancy and prolactin after parturition.

Although pregnant female rats will not immediately care for foster pups that are given to them during pregnancy, they will do so as soon as their pups are born (Rosenblatt, 1969). However, the experience of parturition itself is not necessary for the onset of maternal behavior; Moltz, Robbins, and Parks (1966) found that even if the offspring are removed by caesarian section, female rats will care for them soon after they recover from the anesthetic. These observations suggest that hormonal changes around the time of parturition sensitize neural circuits that are responsible for maternal behavior.

Figure 10.27 shows the levels of the three hormones that have been implicated in maternal behavior: estradiol, progesterone, and prolactin. Note that just before parturition the level of estradiol begins rising, then the level of progesterone falls dramatically, fol-

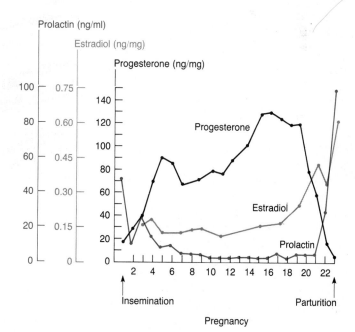

FIGURE 10.27

Blood levels of progesterone, estradiol, and prolactin in pregnant rats. (From Rosenblatt, J.S., Siegel, H.I., and Mayer, A.D. *Advances in the Study of Behavior,* 1979, *10,* 225–311.)

lowed by a sharp increase in prolactin. (See **Figure 10.27.**) Moltz, Lubin, Leon, and Numan (1970) simulated this sequence of hormones in virgin female rats by administering estradiol for 11 days, progesterone on days 6 through 9, and prolactin on days 9 and 10. Rats who received this treatment began caring for foster pups within 1 to 2 days. In contrast, rats that received placebo injections required 7 days of exposure to pups. The behavior of one group that received estradiol and progesterone, but not prolactin, was also somewhat facilitated. However, Amenomori, Chen, and Meites (1970) showed that the administration of this sequence of hormones will itself stimulate prolactin secretion.

Subsequent research suggests that estradiol is more important than prolactin in the facilitation of maternal behavior. Rosenblatt and Siegel terminated rats' pregnancies by removing the uterus and found that the rats began caring for pups within a day or two (Rosenblatt and Siegel, 1975; Siegel and Rosenblatt, 1975). In contrast, still pregnant females were not responsive. Thus, the hormonal effects of hysterectomy appear to sensitize the neural circuits that are responsible for maternal behavior. Hysterectomy of a pregnant rat causes the progesterone level to fall, primarily because the influence of the placenta on the corpora lutea is removed. (The placenta is an endocrine organ that pro-

duces a hormone similar to the gonadotropins.) In addition, estradiol levels increase (Rosenblatt, Siegel, and Mayer, 1979). However, prolactin levels do *not* increase. Rosenblatt and Siegel (1975) found that if pregnant rats are ovariectomized when they are hysterectomized, facilitation of maternal behavior does not occur, but if estradiol is administered as well, maternal behavior *is* facilitated. Rodriguez-Sierra and Rosenblatt (1977) found that administration of estradiol facilitates maternal behavior even when the secretion of prolactin is inhibited with apomorphine; thus, the experimental evidence suggests that estradiol can facilitate maternal behavior without causing the secretion of prolactin. (See **Figure 10.28.**)

So far, investigators have not devoted much attention to the role of hormones in facilitating maternal behavior in primates. What little evidence we have suggests that a monkey's experience is more important than its endocrine levels. Holman and Goy (1980) tested adult female rhesus monkeys, some of whom were ovariectomized, and some of whom were intact. They found that 90 percent of the females who had previously raised their own offspring immediately cared for foster infants, regardless of their hormonal status. In fact, the experimenters had to restrain the monkeys and forcibly remove the foster infants at the end of the testing sessions.

Treatment	Effect on hormones	Effect on maternal Behavior
Remove uterus	Progesterone ↓ Estradiol ↑	Facilitation
Remove uterus and ovaries	Progesterone ↓ Estradiol ↓	No facilitation
Administer estradiol and apomorphine	Estradiol ↑ Prolactin ↓	Facilitation

FIGURE 10.28

Effects of removal of uterus, removal of uterus and ovaries, or administration of estradiol and apomorphine on maternal behavior in the experiments by Rosenblatt and his colleagues.

In contrast, females who had never had infants of their own did not exhibit maternal behavior. Although it is possible that hormones are involved in instituting maternal behavior around the time of parturition, once rhesus monkeys have taken care of infants their tendency to do so endures.

Neural Control of Maternal Behavior

The most critical brain region responsible for maternal behavior appears to be the medial preoptic area. Numan (1974) found that medial preoptic lesions, or knife cuts that isolated this region from the medial forebrain bundle, disrupted both nest building and pup care. The mothers simply ignored their offspring. However, female sexual behavior was unaffected by these lesions. You will recall that male sexual behavior, but not female sexual behavior, is also disrupted by lesions of the medial preoptic area.

Numan and Callahan (1980) found that bilateral knife cuts just lateral to the medial preoptic area abolished maternal behavior. The authors concluded that the behavioral effects of the knife cuts were caused by cutting axons that leave this region and travel to motor nuclei in the midbrain and brain stem.

Subsequent research revealed the particulars of these connections. The medial preoptic area sends axons to the ***ventral tegmental area*** of the midbrain. (As we will see in later chapters, this brain region, which contains dopaminergic neurons, plays a role in several species-typical behaviors such as drinking and aggressive behavior, and in reinforcement.) Numan and Smith (1984) found that bilateral lesions of the ventral tegmental area severely disrupted female rats' maternal behavior. They also made unilateral knife cuts lateral to the medial preoptic area and unilateral lesions of the ventral tegmental area. When the forebrain and midbrain lesions were both on the same side of the brain, the

animal's maternal behavior was temporarily impaired, but returned to normal. However, when the two lesions were on opposite sides of the brain, the impairment was severe and long-lasting. The authors concluded that an important component of the neural circuitry responsible for maternal behavior involves an ipsilateral connection between the medial preoptic nucleus and the ventral tegmental area. When both lesions are on the same side of the brain, one pathway is still intact, but when the two lesions are on opposite sides of the brain, both pathways are interrupted.

The medial preoptic area contains estrogen receptors (Pfaff and Keiner, 1973). It appears that the stimulating effect of estradiol on maternal behavior occurs in this region. Numan, Rosenblatt, and Komisaruk (1977) found that direct implants of estradiol in the medial preoptic area facilitate maternal behavior in ovariectomized and hysterectomized rats. As we just saw, olfactory deafferentation, lesions of the medial amygdala, or lesions of the stria terminalis (which connects the medial amygdala with the medial preoptic area) all facilitate maternal behavior in virgin female rats. This effect apparently occurs because the animals no longer avoid contact with the pups. Perhaps the stimulating effect of estradiol on the medial preoptic area works in a similar fashion, removing the inhibitory influence of the amygdala. (See **Figure 10.29.**)

Various lesions of the limbic system will disrupt the sequence, but not the elements, of maternal behavior. Slotnick (1967) found that lesions of the cingulate cortex in rats scrambled the normal sequence of pup retrieval. The mother would pick up a pup, enter the nest, walk out again still carrying the pup, drop it, try to nurse one pup outside the nest, remove pups from the nest, and, in general, act confused. The component behavioral acts that make up pup care (e.g., picking up the pup and licking its anogenital region)

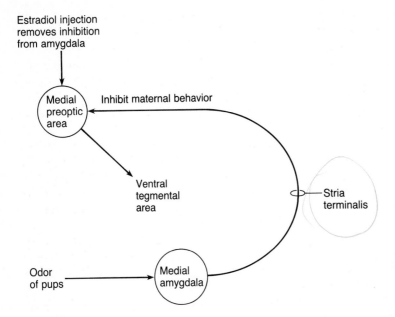

FIGURE 10.29

A possible explanation of the facilitating effects of estradiol on maternal behavior.

were still present, but the behaviors appeared to occur at random. Carlson and Thomas (1968) observed an even more severe deficit after lesions of the septum in mice. Besides exhibiting a disordered sequence of pup retrieval, the mice failed to build nests. The deficit in nest building was not restricted to behavior that was stimulated hormonally. Normal mice, both males and females, will build nests to conserve body heat if the ambient temperature falls. I have found that when mice with septal lesions are placed in a refrigerator, they fail to build nests. (I should note that the refrigerated mice did not appear to suffer any ill effects from their ordeal.)

The septum and medial preoptic area are interconnected; these connections probably explain the lack of nest building and disorganized pup retrieval seen in rodents with septal lesions. Another possible reason for the disrupting effects of septal lesions is the role of this structure in controlling the neural activity of another part of the limbic system, the hippocampus. As we will see in Chapter 14, the hippocampus plays a role in spatial perception; animals with hippocampal lesions or lesions that disconnect the septum and hippocampus have difficulty finding their way around their environment. This effect may explain why rats and mice with septal lesions do not build nests and have trouble retrieving: they do not recognize a "home" site in their cage. Perhaps the hippocampal-septal system communicates with the medial preoptic area, controlling the species-typical maternal behaviors according to the animal's location in its environment.

Human Maternal Behavior

Certainly, the behavior of human parents (both maternal and paternal) is not controlled by innate factors, as it is in some other species. Thus, I have little to say about the physiology of human maternal behavior. However, some investigators have suggested that even humans possess an innate tendency to care for their offspring, which is triggered by a specific experience soon after birth. In some mammalian species, mothers will accept and care for their infants only if they are able to see and smell their offspring during the first day of life. For example, Klopfer, Adams, and Klopfer (1964) reported that if a lamb is removed from its mother immediately after birth and is brought back a day later, the mother will reject it. However, if she is in contact with her lamb for just a few minutes after birth, she will accept it and care for it when it is given back to her the next day. This phenomenon is called ***bonding.***

Klaus, Jerauld, Krieger, McAlpine, Steffa, and Kennell (1972) reported that bonding also occurs in humans when an infant is placed naked against its mother's skin soon after it is born. The experimenters tested mothers who were having their first child. Women in the control group experienced what was then the usual hospital procedure, seeing their babies for a short time at birth and feeding them (by bottle) five times a day. Mothers in the extended-contact group received their babies for an hour soon after birth and for 5 hours each afternoon on the next 3 days. Thus, these mothers were in contact with their babies for 16 hours more than the mothers in the control group. A month later, the mothers were interviewed during their infant's one-month checkup. The mothers in the extended-contact group acted more concerned about their babies, holding and fondling them slightly more than the mothers in the control group. Small differences in the behavior of the 2 groups of mothers were still present as long as two years later. As a result of studies like this one, many hospitals have changed their procedures to ensure that a mother becomes "bonded" to her infant; the baby is placed against its mother's abdomen, so that skin-to-skin contact occurs.

Although the study by Klaus and colleagues is interesting, the conditions were not controlled well enough to prove that a maternal bond develops this early. The mothers in the experimental group were aware that they were being treated differently, because they had their babies with them longer than other mothers who shared the rooms. In addition, nurses may have inadvertently communicated to them that it was important to spend more time with their infants. Either of these variables may have accounted for the fact that they were observed to interact with their babies slightly more a few months later. In fact, recent research conducted under more carefully controlled conditions has failed to confirm the results of the earlier studies. For example, Svejda, Campos, and Emde (1980) first made sure that the mothers in their study who received extended contact with their babies did not perceive themselves as "special." These investigators found that extended contact had no effect on interactions between mothers and their infants. Therefore, although a mother's first contact with her child can undoubtedly be a pleasurable and memorable experience, there is no conclusive evidence that this event instigates a physiological reaction that increases her attentiveness to her child.

INTERIM SUMMARY

Many species must care for their offspring. Among rodents, this duty falls to the mother, who must build a nest, deliver her own pups, clean them, keep them warm, nurse them, and retrieve them if they are moved out of the nest. They must even induce their pups' urination and defecation, and their ingestion of the urine recycles water, which is often a scarce commodity.

Exposure to young pups (concaveation) stimulates maternal behavior within a few days. Apparently, the odor of pups elicits handling and licking, whereas the sound of their distress calls elicits nest building. Removal of the olfactory bulbs causes rats to kill and eat pups, but deafferentation of the olfactory system without destruction of the olfactory bulbs actually causes the animals to begin caring for pups more quickly. The inhibitory

effect of the odor of pups may be mediated by the accessory olfactory system; cutting the vomeronasal nerve facilitates maternal behavior. Both components of the olfactory system project to the medial amygdala. Lesions of the medial amygdala or the stria terminalis also facilitate maternal responsiveness. Therefore, the effects of olfaction on maternal behavior may be mediated by the pathway from the olfactory system to the medial amygdala to the medial preoptic area (via the stria terminalis).

Nest building appears to be facilitated by progesterone during pregnancy and by prolactin during the lactation period. Both estradiol and prolactin have been implicated in the induction of maternal behavior. Because maternal behavior occurs in response to estradiol even when the secretion of prolactin is inhibited by apomorphine, the effectiveness of estradiol does not depend on its ability to stimulate the secretion of prolactin.

The medial preoptic area is the most important forebrain structure for maternal behavior, and the ventral tegmental area of the midbrain is the most important brain stem structure. Neurons in the medial preoptic area send axons laterally and then caudally to the ventral tegmental area; if these connections are interrupted bilaterally, rats cease pro-

viding maternal care of offspring. Lesions of the cingulate cortex or septum disrupt the sequence of maternal behavior without affecting the animal's willingness to emit appropriate component behavioral acts. The effects of septal lesions may occur because the medial septum plays an important role in controlling the activity of the hippocampus, which is necessary for spatial perception.

The one aspect of human maternal behavior that appeared to be innately determined was a phenomenon called bonding, which occurs in other female mammals, such as sheep. However, more recent studies suggest that women need not experience direct skin contact with their babies soon after birth in order to form close attachments with them.

Concluding Remarks

Fortunately for the survival of our species, sexual behavior continues to interest most of us. The hormonal and neural interactions that influence and control sexual development and behavior are indeed complex, but research efforts have made great progress in unfolding a fascinating story.

NEW TERMS

accessory olfactory bulb p. 387
activational effect (of hormone) p. 370
adrenogenital syndrome p. 391
androgen p. 374
androgen insensitivity syndrome p. 393
androstenedione p. 377
arcuate nucleus p. 380
bonding p. 417
Bruce effect p. 386
concaveation p. 411
Coolidge effect p. 383
corpus luteum p. 379
estradiol p. 376
estrogen p. 377
estrous cycle p. 378

follicle-stimulating hormone (FSH) p. 376
gamete p. 371
gestagen p. 379
gonad p. 373
gonadotropic hormone p. 376
gonadotropin releasing hormone (GnRH) p. 376
hermaphrodite p. 377
H-Y antigen p. 373
karyotype p. 371
Lee-Boot effect p. 386
lordosis p. 384
luteinizing hormone (LH) p. 376
medial preoptic area p. 402
meiosis p. 371
menstrual cycle p. 378

mitosis p. 370

Müllerian system p. 374

Müllerian-inhibiting substance p. 374

organizational effect (of hormone) p. 370

ovarian follicle p. 378

periaqueductal gray matter p. 408

pheromone p. 386

primordial gonad p. 373

progesterone p. 379

prolactin p. 413

pseudopregnancy p. 386

sexually dimorphic nucleus p. 403

spinal nucleus of the bulbocavernosus p. 402

stria terminalis p. 412

superfetation p. 409

testosterone p. 377

Turner's syndrome p. 374

ventral tegmental area p. 415

ventromedial nucleus (of hypothalamus) p. 405

vomeronasal organ p. 386

Whitten effect p. 386

Wolffian system p. 374

SUGGESTED READINGS

ARNOLD, A.O., AND GORSKI, R.A. Gonadal steroid induction of structural sex differences in the central nervous system. *Annual Review of Neuroscience,* 1984, *7,* 413–442.

BERMANT, G., AND DAVIDSON, J.M. *Biological Bases of Sexual Behavior.* New York: Harper & Row, 1974.

FEDER, H.H. Hormones and sexual behavior. *Annual Review of Psychology,* 1984, *35,* 165–200.

MONEY, J., AND EHRHARDT, A.A. *Man & Woman, Boy & Girl.* Baltimore: Johns Hopkins University Press, 1972.

PFAFF, D.W. *Estrogens and Brain Function: Neural Analysis of a Hormone-Controlled Mammalian Reproductive Behavior.* New York: Springer-Verlag, 1980.

PFAFF, D.W. *The Physiological Mechanisms of Motivation.* New York: Springer-Verlag, 1982.

ROSENBLUM, L.A., AND MOLTZ, H. *Symbiosis in Parent-Offspring Interactions.* New York: Plenum Press, 1983.

The 20 March 1981 issue of *Science* (vol. 211, no. 4488) is devoted to the topic of sexual dimorphism.

11

Ingestive Behavior

As the French physiologist Claude Bernard (1813–1878) said, "The constancy of the internal milieu is a necessary condition for a free life." This famous quote succinctly states what organisms must do to be able to exist in environments hostile to the living cells that compose them (i.e., to live a "free life"): they must regulate various characteristics of the internal fluid that bathes their cells.

The evolutionary process has not produced "hardier" cells. Instead, when our ancestors left the sea millions of years ago, they took with them the ability to regulate the constituents of the "seawater" that bathed their cells. Cells must be surrounded by water that contains the proper concentration of solutes, or osmosis will cause them to lose water and shrink or to gain water and swell. The fluid surrounding the cells must also contain nutrients and oxygen, and waste products from the cells must not accumulate there. Temperature must remain constant.

Single-celled organisms living in the ocean are obviously not able to regulate characteristics of their extracellular fluid, the sea itself. At best, they can swim a limited distance if local conditions become unfavorable. More complex, multicellular organisms require regulatory mechanisms. Cells in the interior of their bodies require special means to bring them nutrients from the environment and to remove waste products: digestive, respiratory, circulatory, and excretory systems. Land-dwelling animals must locate sources of water and must periodically ingest it to prevent dehydration. And, unlike the cold-blooded *poikilothermous* ("varied-heat") animals, mammals possess mechanisms for generating heat or for dissipating it into the environment as required. These *homoiothermous* ("constant heat," from *homoios*, "similar") animals can therefore venture into regions far removed in temperature from their 37° to 38° C interiors.

Regulation of the fluid that bathes our cells is part of a process called *homeostasis* ("similar standing"). This chapter discusses the means by which we mammals achieve homeostatic control of the vital characteristics of our extracellular fluid through our *ingestive behavior:* intake of food, water, and minerals such as sodium. First we will examine the general nature of regulatory mechanisms.

■ THE NATURE OF PHYSIOLOGICAL REGULATORY MECHANISMS

A physiological regulatory mechanism is one that maintains the constancy of some internal characteristic of the organism in the face of external variability—for example, maintenance of a constant body temperature despite changes in the ambient temperature. A regulatory mechanism contains four essential features: the *system variable* (the characteristic to be regulated), a *set point* (the optimal value of the system variable), a *detector* that monitors the value of the system variable, and a *correctional mechanism* that restores the system variable to the set point.

An example of a regulatory system is a room whose temperature is regulated by a thermostatically controlled heater. The system variable is the air temperature of the room, and the detector for this variable is a thermostat. This device can be adjusted so that contacts of a switch will be closed when the temperature falls below a preset value (the set point). Closure of the contacts turns on the correctional mechanism — the coils of the heater. (See **Figure 11.1.**)

If the room cools below the set point of the thermostat, the thermostat turns the heater on, which warms the room. The rise in room temperature causes the thermostat to turn the heater off. Because the activity of the correctional mechanism (heat production) feeds back to the thermostat and causes it to turn the heater off, this process is called *negative*

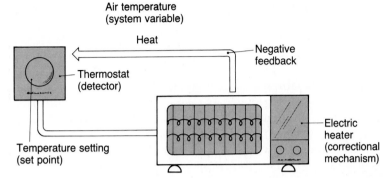

FIGURE 11.1

An example of a regulatory system.

feedback. Negative feedback is an essential characteristic of all regulatory systems.

This chapter considers regulatory systems that involve ingestive behaviors: drinking and eating. These behaviors are correctional mechanisms that replenish the body's depleted stores of water or nutrients. Because of the delay between ingestion and replenishment of the depleted stores, ingestive behaviors are controlled by *satiety mechanisms* as well as by detectors that monitor the system variables. Satiety mechanisms are required because of the physiology of our digestive system. For example, suppose you exercise in a hot, dry environment and lose body water. The loss of water causes internal detectors to initiate the correctional mechanism — drinking. You quickly drink a glass or two of water and then stop. What stops your ingestive behavior? The water is still in your diges-

tive system, not yet in the fluid surrounding your cells, where it is needed. Therefore, although drinking was initiated by detectors that measure your body's need for water, it was stopped by other means. There must be a satiety mechanism that says, in effect, "Stop — this water, when absorbed by the digestive system into the blood, will eventually replenish the body's need." Satiety mechanisms monitor the activity of the correctional mechanism (in this case, drinking) and stop it *in anticipation* of the replenishment that will occur later. (See **Figure 11.2.**)

■ **WATER BALANCE**

The two major ingestive behaviors, eating and drinking, are obviously related and often occur together. Drinking is considered first because we know more about the nature of

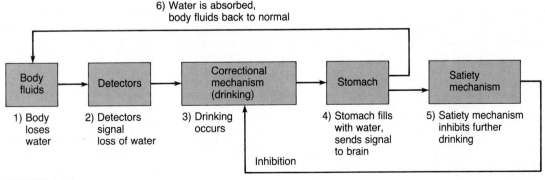

FIGURE 11.2

An outline of the system that controls drinking.

the relevant system variables, the detectors, and the satiety mechanisms.

Fluid Compartments of the Body

The body contains four major fluid compartments: one compartment of intracellular fluid and three compartments of extracellular fluid. Approximately two thirds of the body's water is contained in the *intracellular fluid* — the fluid portion of the cytoplasm of cells. The rest is *extracellular fluid,* including the blood plasma, the cerebrospinal fluid, and the *interstitial fluid. Interstitial* means "standing between"; indeed, the interstitial fluid stands between our cells — it is the "seawater" that bathes our cells. (See **Figure 11.3.**)

Normally, the interstitial fluid is *isotonic* (from *isos,* "same" and *tonos,* "tension") with the intracellular fluid. That is, the concentration of solutes in the interstitial fluid is such that water does not tend to move into or out of the cells. If the interstitial fluid loses

water it becomes **hypertonic** and consequently water moves out of the cells, down its concentration gradient. If the interstitial fluid gains water it becomes **hypotonic,** and as a result water moves into the cells. Either condition endangers cells; a loss of water deprives them of the ability to perform many chemical reactions, and a gain of water can cause their membrane to rupture. Thus, the osmotic pressure of the interstitial fluid must be closely regulated.

Another extracellular fluid compartment, the blood plasma, must also be closely regulated. First, changes in the osmotic pressure of the blood plasma will affect the interstitial fluid. For example, if the blood plasma becomes more concentrated (say, after an organism ingests a salty meal), the interstitial fluid, too, becomes more concentrated, and water is drawn from the cells. Second, the volume of the blood plasma must remain within close limits. Too much volume causes dangerously high blood pressure, and too little volume prevents the heart from pumping efficiently. Extremes in either direction can cause heart failure.

The fluid compartments are coupled to each other, being separated by means of semipermeable barriers. The walls of the capillaries lie between the blood plasma and the interstitial fluid, and the cell membranes lie between the interstitial fluid and the intracellular fluid. Therefore, if one compartment loses water and its osmotic pressure consequently increases, water is drawn from the other compartments by osmosis. For example, consider the loss of water through evaporation. (This evaporation occurs continuously and is not the same as the loss of water and salt through sweat, which is actively secreted by the sweat glands.) The water evaporates from the interstitial fluid, which causes its solute concentration to increase. This increase draws water from the cells and from the capillaries by osmosis. (See **Figure 11.4.**)

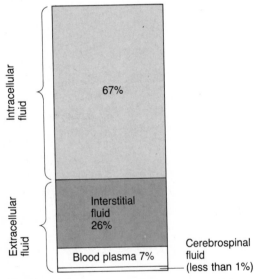

FIGURE 11.3
The relative size of the body's fluid compartments.

Loss of water through evaporation

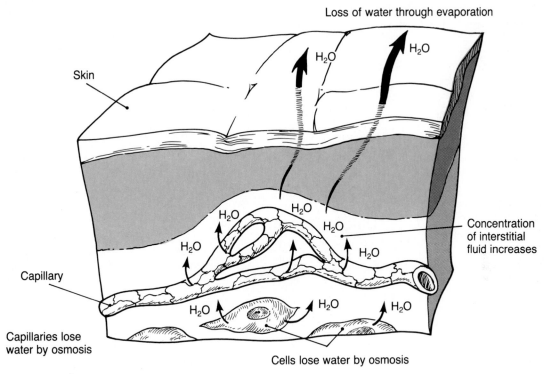

FIGURE 11.4
The loss of water through evaporation.

Physiological Control of Water and Sodium Balance

Fluid regulation is achieved principally by controlling the intake and excretion of two substances: water and the sodium ion. Usually, we drink more water than our body needs, and the excess is excreted by the kidneys. Similarly, we ingest more sodium than we need, and the kidneys get rid of the surplus. Thus, to understand the means of controlling our water and sodium balance, we must understand the way in which the kidneys handle these regulatory processes.

The Kidneys

Figure 11.5 shows the anatomy of a human kidney. This organ consists of approxi-

mately one million functional units called ***nephrons.*** Each nephron extracts fluid from the blood and carries it, through collecting ducts, to the ***ureter.*** The ureter, in turn, connects the kidney to the urinary bladder. (See **Figures 11.5 and 11.6.**) During urination, the ***urethra*** passes the urine to the outside of the body. For our purposes, urine is outside the body once it reaches the bladder. Our society has developed customs pertaining to the release of urine from the bladder, but these customs have nothing to do with water regulation.

The kidneys control the amount of water that the body excretes. If the organism has drunk plenty of water and must get rid of the excess, the kidneys pass a large quantity of dilute urine on to the bladder. However, if the organism has lost water through evaporation,

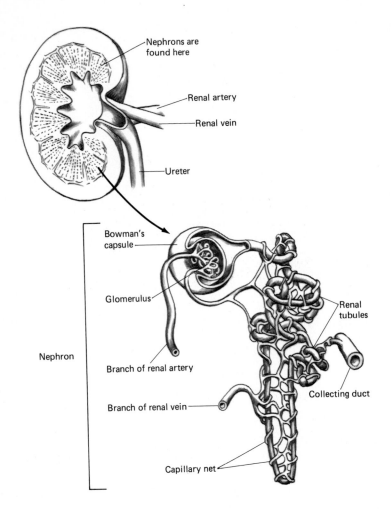

FIGURE 11.5
Anatomy of the kidney and an
individual nephron. (From
Orians, G.H. *The Study of Life.*
Boston: Allyn and Bacon,
1973.)

the kidneys conserve water, producing a small quantity of concentrated urine. In addition, by controlling the excretion of sodium, the kidneys control the amount of salt that the body retains.

Production of urine begins in the **glomerulus.** Protein-free plasma is filtered from the capillaries and enters **Bowman's capsule.** (See **Figure 11.5.**) If this fluid were then passed to the bladder unaltered, we would urinate ourselves to death in short order. Each day approximately 47 gallons of water (180 liters) is filtered into the Bowman's capsules,

so obviously most of the fluid reenters the capillaries somewhere.

Approximately 99 percent of the water filtered by the glomeruli is subsequently reabsorbed through the walls of the **renal tubules** and **collecting ducts.** (*Renal* means ''of the kidney.'') Sodium pumps in the walls of the renal tubules actively pump sodium (Na^+) back into the surrounding interstitial fluid. The negatively charged chloride ion (Cl^-) follows. This pumping causes the interstitial fluid to become hypertonic, drawing water out of the renal tubules and collecting ducts.

The sodium chloride (NaCl) and water then reenter the capillaries. (See **Figure 11.7.**)

The amounts of sodium and water that the kidneys excrete are controlled by two hormones: aldosterone and antidiuretic hormone. Sodium excretion is controlled by *aldosterone,* a steroid hormone secreted by the adrenal cortex. The hormone directly stimulates the sodium pumps in the walls of the renal tubules. Thus, if the body contains too much salt, a low aldosterone level causes it to be excreted in the urine. If too little salt is present, a high aldosterone level causes it to be conserved. (See **Figure 11.8.**)

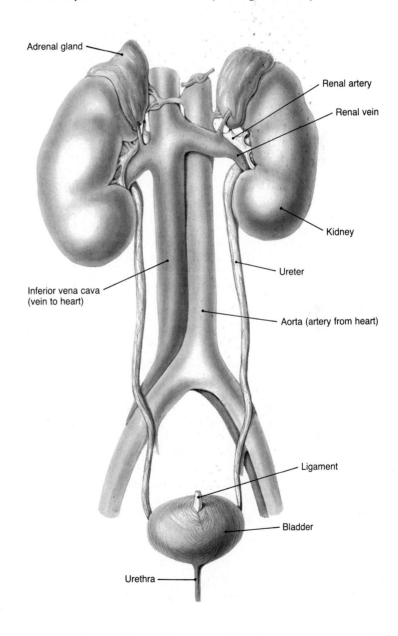

FIGURE 11.6
The urinary system.

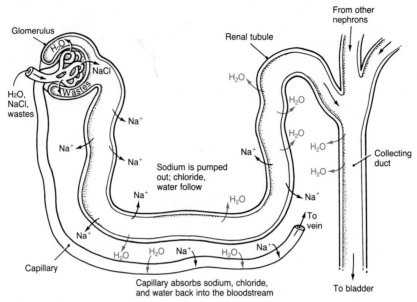

FIGURE 11.7
The glomerulus absorbs water, sodium chloride (NaCl), and wastes. A
sodium pump in the renal tubule returns sodium to the interstitial fluid;
chloride and water follow. From there, they reenter the nearby capillary.
Note that movement of the chloride ion is omitted from this diagram.

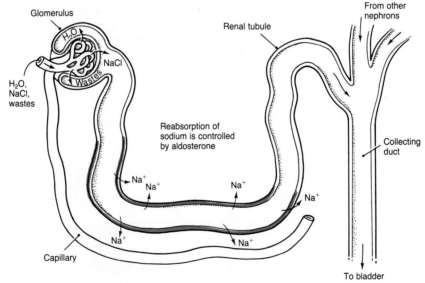

FIGURE 11.8
The rate at which sodium is pumped from the renal tubule back to the
interstitial fluid is controlled by aldosterone, an adrenocortical hormone.

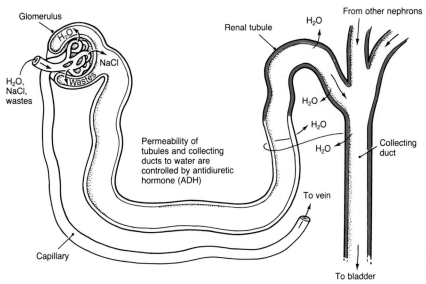

FIGURE 11.9

Reabsorption of water from the renal tubule and collecting duct is
controlled by antidiuretic hormone (ADH), a posterior pituitary hormone.

Excretion of water is controlled by ***antidiuretic hormone (ADH),*** a peptide hormone
secreted by the posterior pituitary gland. You
will recall that water is reabsorbed through
the walls of the renal tubules and collecting
ducts into the interstitial fluid. Antidiuretic
hormone increases the permeability of the
renal tubules and collecting ducts to water;
thus, the amount of ADH that is present determines how much water is reabsorbed. If we
drink more water than our body needs, the
posterior pituitary gland stops secreting ADH,
and the kidneys excrete the excess water. If
we become dehydrated, the posterior pituitary gland increases ADH secretion, and the
kidneys excrete a minimum amount of water.
(See **Figure 11.9.**)

I have told you that the excretion of salt
and water is controlled by aldosterone and
ADH, but what factors control *their* release?
Two factors stimulate the secretion of aldosterone: increased activity of the sympathetic
axons to the kidneys and a fall in blood flow
through the kidneys. These events cause the
juxtaglomerular cells of the kidneys to secrete an enzyme called ***renin*** (from Latin
rēnēs, "kidneys"). Renin enters the blood,
where it catalyzes the conversion of a substance called ***angiotensinogen*** into ***angiotensin I,*** which quickly becomes ***angiotensin II.*** Angiotensin II has several effects, one
of which is to stimulate the adrenal cortex to
produce aldosterone. Therefore, a reduction
in blood flow or increased activity of the sympathetic efferent axons to the kidneys causes
sodium to be retained by the body. (See **Figure 11.10.**) I will explain how this system
operates in the next section.

The secretion of ADH by the posterior pituitary gland is controlled by the activity of
neurons in two nuclei of the hypothalamus:
the ***supraoptic nucleus*** and the ***paraventricular nucleus.*** Antidiuretic hormone is actually produced by neurons in these nuclei
and transported, in vesicles, through axons to
the terminal buttons, which are located in the
posterior pituitary gland. When the neurons
in the supraoptic and paraventricular nuclei

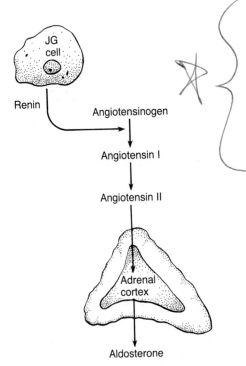

FIGURE 11.10
Aldosterone secretion is controlled by the
juxtaglomerular cells of the kidney, which
secrete renin.

become active, their terminal buttons release
ADH, which enters the blood supply.

   Figure 11.11 summarizes the role of the
kidneys in controlling the water and sodium
balance. (See **Figure 11.11.**)

INTERIM   SUMMARY

The glomeruli absorb water, minerals, and waste
products. Under the influence of aldosterone, a
pump in the walls of the renal tubules transports
sodium back into the interstitial fluid, and from
there to the capillaries. Thus, aldosterone controls
the excretion of sodium chloride. Antidiuretic
hormone renders the walls of the renal tubules and
collecting ducts permeable to water, which leaves
and reenters the capillaries, because of the concentration gradient caused by the reabsorption of
sodium. Thus, ADH controls the excretion of

water. These two hormones provide physiological
regulation of the osmotic pressure of the body's
fluids and the volume of the blood plasma. Aldosterone secretion is stimulated by angiotensin II,
which is produced when the kidneys secrete renin
in response to neural stimulation or to decreased
blood flow. The secretion of antidiuretic hormone
is under the control of the activity of neurons in
the supraoptic and paraventricular nuclei of the
hypothalamus.

System Variables and Detectors

We just saw how aldosterone and ADH control
the excretion of sodium chloride and water.
Now it is time to examine the system variables
and detectors that cause these hormones to be
released in response to changes in the body's
fluid compartments. A water deficit may be
incurred by three means: *loss of isotonic
fluid* through bleeding, sweating, vomiting,
or diarrhea; *loss of water* through evaporation from cells of the skin and the lining of the
lungs; and *ingestion of salt,* which causes
water to be lost through the kidneys. Losses of
water, salt, or both substances have different
consequences on the composition of the fluid
compartments of the body.

   Loss of isotonic fluid through bleeding,
sweating, vomiting, or diarrhea depletes the
volume of the extracellular fluid compartments — the blood plasma, the interstitial
fluid, or both. The clearest example is bleeding. Because the fluid that is lost from the
blood vessels is isotonic, the osmotic pressure of the interstitial fluid does not change.
Consequently, the volume of the intracellular
fluid is not affected. Any such loss of fluid
from the extracellular fluid compartments is
called **hypovolemia.**

   Loss of blood plasma can have serious consequences. To operate normally, the heart
must have an adequate return of venous
blood. Hypovolemia causes the output of the
heart to drop, which causes a further reduction in blood pressure. Blood from the venous
system is received into the right atrium of the
heart. The walls of this chamber contain re-

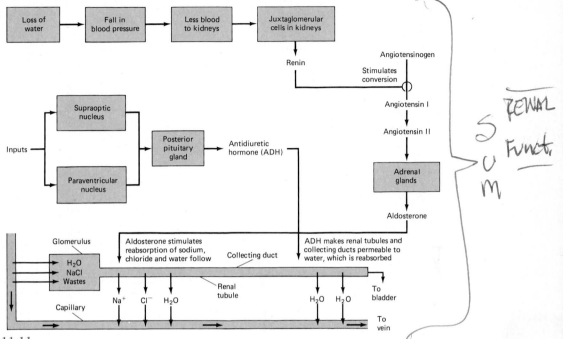

FIGURE 11.11
Control of the kidney.

ceptors that are stimulated by pressure; these ***baroreceptors*** detect changes in the venous blood pressure. When their firing rate falls, reflex mechanisms in the brain trigger ADH secretion and the release of renin by the kidneys. The ADH secretion causes the kidneys to conserve water, and the renin secretion (and subsequent secretion of aldosterone) causes the kidneys to conserve sodium. Blood vessels also contract, partially compensating for the loss in blood volume. In addition to this mechanism, decreased blood flow through the kidneys themselves causes renin secretion by stimulating receptors within the kidneys. (See **Figure 11.12.**)

We have just seen that loss of extracellular fluid activates mechanisms that conserve the body's supply of sodium and water. These mechanisms obviously cannot *restore* the volume of fluid lost; they can only prevent further loss. Restoration requires ingestive

behavior, which will be discussed shortly. As we will see, some of the same mechanisms that cause the kidneys to conserve fluid also stimulate drinking.

Two events, loss of water (primarily through evaporation from the skin and the lining of the lungs) and ingestion of salt, can increase the solute concentration of the extracellular fluid, thus drawing water out of the cells. Loss of intracellular water initiates secretion of ADH, which minimizes further loss through the urine. Presumably, the detectors that stimulate ADH secretion are neurons, each firing at a rate that is proportional to its own volume. Because cell volume is determined by the osmotic pressure of the interstitial fluid, the neurons are referred to as ***osmoreceptors.*** Verney (1947) obtained evidence for their existence by infusing hypertonic sodium chloride into dogs' carotid arteries, thus depleting the intracellular

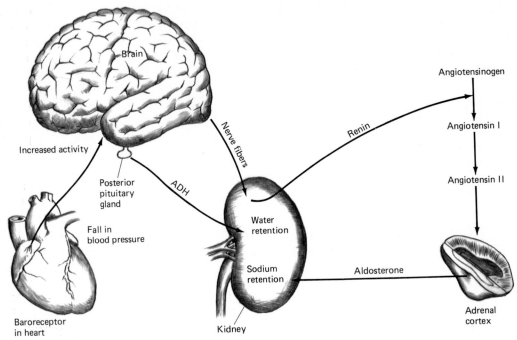

FIGURE 11.12

Control of ADH and aldosterone secretion by baroreceptors in the right atrium of the heart.

volume of cells in the brain. As Figure 11.13 shows, the infusion stimulated the secretion of ADH and the consequent retention of urine. (See **Figure 11.13.**) Later, Jewell and Verney (1957) suggested that the receptors were located in the hypothalamus.

More recently, Hatton (1976) has obtained evidence for the existence of a pair of specific sensory organs in the hypothalamus, very near the walls of the third ventricle, that

FIGURE 11.13

Effects of an injection of hypertonic saline solution into a dog's carotid artery. The solution removed water from cells in the brain and caused the posterior pituitary gland to secrete ADH. The hormone caused water to be retained by the kidneys, reducing the flow of urine. (From Verney, E.G. *Proceedings of the Royal Society (London) Series B*, 1947, *135*, 25 – 106.)

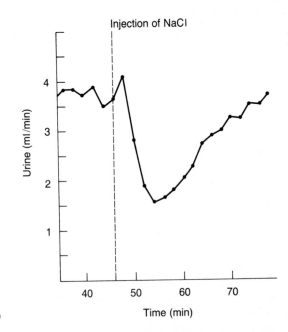

regulate the secretion of ADH. The organ is called the ***nucleus circularis.*** This nucleus is very small, consisting of approximately 275 cells in the rat. It is football shaped, with its long axis running in a rostral-caudal direction, and it appears ringlike in cross section, with a hollow interior. The neurons in this nucleus lie within a capillary bed and are surrounded by heavily myelinated fibers. These fibers appear to enclose the cells, along with the capillary bed and surrounding interstitial fluid, in a watertight compartment. (See **Figure 11.14.**) The nucleus circularis sends fibers to the supraoptic nucleus (which contains neurons that produce ADH) and also toward the posterior pituitary gland itself.

Hatton found that electrical stimulation of the nucleus circularis, but not of adjacent regions, caused water to be retained, presumably because of ADH secretion. Furthermore, water deprivation led to an increase in the number of nucleoli in the cells of the nucleus. You will recall from Chapter 2 that the ribosomes (the sites of protein synthesis) are produced by the nucleoli; hence, increases in the number of nucleoli suggest increased protein synthesis, perhaps as a result of stimulation caused by increased osmotic pressure. In addition, destruction of the region that includes the nucleus circularis produces deficits in the release of ADH in response to increased osmotic pressure of the extracellular fluid. Thus, the nucleus circularis appears to contain osmoreceptors that control the secretion of ADH.

Osmoreceptors outside the brain may also control ADH release. For example, when a thirsty animal drinks, ADH secretion is inhibited even before substantial amounts of water leave the digestive system (Nicolaidis, 1969). The location of the receptors appears to be in the tongue (Vincent, Arnauld, and Bioulac, 1972) and in the liver (Haeberich, 1968; Rogers and Novin, 1983). The role of osmoreceptors in the tongue is obvious: this place is the first to contact water that is being drunk. The role of the osmoreceptors in the liver is less obvious. Water in the intestines

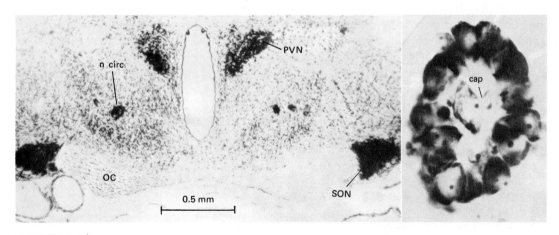

FIGURE 11.14
Photomicrograph of a cross section through the rat hypothalamus, showing the location and appearance of the nucleus circularis (n circ). OC = optic chiasm; PVN = paraventricular nucleus; SON = supraoptic nucleus; cap = capillary. (From Hatton, G.I., *Brain Research Bulletin,* 1976, *1,* 123–131.)

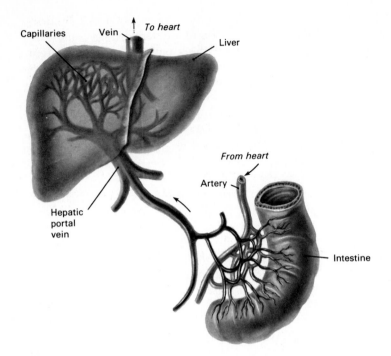

FIGURE 11.15
The liver receives water,
minerals, and nutrients from
the digestive system through
the hepatic portal blood supply.

enters capillaries that drain into a set of veins called the ***hepatic portal system.*** These veins travel directly to the liver, where they branch into another set of capillaries; thus, the liver is the first internal organ to be "informed" about water absorbed from the digestive system. (See **Figure 11.15.**)

INTERIM SUMMARY

Hypovolemia, caused by loss of isotonic fluid, stimulates the release of ADH and renin (and hence aldosterone). The ADH and aldosterone cause the kidneys to conserve water and sodium. The detectors for this effect are baroreceptors located in the walls of the atria of the heart and in the kidneys themselves. Loss of intracellular volume, caused by increased solute concentration of the extracellular fluid, also causes ADH release. In this case, the detectors are osmoreceptors located in the hypothalamus, probably in the nucleus circularis. In addition, osmoreceptors in the tongue and liver inhibit ADH secretion after a drink of water, in anticipation of the replenishing effects.

■ DRINKING

As we saw, the kidney excretes waste products, and if the organism ingests more water and salt than is needed (which is usually the case), it can rid the body of excessive amounts of these substances. However, if the body suffers a shortage of water and sodium, the best the kidneys can do (under the influence of high levels of aldosterone and ADH) is to conserve what remains. Deficits must be made up by ingestive behavior.

We saw that the secretion of renin/aldosterone and ADH are controlled by two system variables: the volume of the blood plasma and its effects on blood pressure, and the concentration of the interstitial fluid and its effects on cell volume. Detectors that respond to these two system variables also control ingestive behavior. Thus, we have two types of thirst: volumetric thirst and osmometric thirst.

Volumetric Thirst

When we lose water through evaporation, we usually lose it from both fluid compartments, extracellular and intracellular. Thus, normal dehydration produces both volumetric thirst and osmometric thirst. Only under special circumstances is just one of the two fluid compartments depleted. For example, bleeding causes hypovolemia without loss of intracellular fluid, and the ingestion of a salty meal causes loss of intracellular fluid without hypovolemia. Because drinking is stimulated by two different systems, I will describe volumetric thirst and osmometric thirst separately.

System Variables and Detectors for Volumetric Thirst

Thirst initiated by hypovolemia is called ***volumetric thirst*** ("volume-measuring" thirst). The easiest way to produce hypovolemia in experimental animals would be to bleed them. A less drastic procedure is to inject a ***colloid*** into the peritoneal (abdominal) cavity (Fitzsimons, 1961). Colloids are gluelike substances made of large molecules that cannot cross cell membranes. Thus, they stay in the peritoneal cavity. Because these molecules exert osmotic pressure, they draw extracellular fluid into the abdomen. The fluid that leaves the blood plasma is isotonic, so no water is drawn from the intracellular fluid compartment. Within an hour, the baroreceptors trigger the release of ADH, and urine volume drops. At the same time, the animal begins to drink, and it continues to do so until most of the volume of fluid stolen from the extracellular fluid has been replaced.

Fitzsimons injected a colloid called ***polyethylene glycol*** into the peritoneal cavity of rats and then drained the fluid that accumulated, ridding the body of the colloid, along with the water and sodium it had drawn from the extracellular fluid. The loss of water caused a considerable thirst; the animals drank water copiously. One or two days later, he presented the rats with both water and a hypertonic 1.8-percent saline solution, which rats normally refuse to drink. Now, the rats avidly consumed the saline solution to replace the sodium that had been withdrawn from their blood. The animals showed a strong ***sodium appetite.*** Once the sodium was ingested, the rats' blood plasma volume was restored to normal, and drinking and urine production returned to their usual levels.

What detectors are responsible for initiating volumetric thirst and a sodium appetite? We already know that the detectors that cause ADH and renin/aldosterone to be secreted in response to hypovolemia are located in the atria of the heart (measuring venous blood pressure) and in the kidneys themselves (measuring blood flow). Perhaps one or both of these detectors might also be involved in volumetric thirst.

Indeed, both receptors do stimulate volumetric thirst. Stricker (1973) injected polyethylene glycol into the peritoneal cavity of rats whose kidneys had been removed. The colloid drew fluid from the extracellular compartments, but not from the cells. Because the kidneys were gone, the reduced volume of the extracellular fluid and the corresponding fall in venous blood pressure could stimulate the baroreceptors in the heart but could not initiate release of renin/angiotensin. Nevertheless, the rats drank. Thus, the baroreceptors in the heart can stimulate thirst. (See **Figure 11.16.**)

Fitzsimons (1972) obtained evidence that receptors in the kidneys can also initiate drinking. He restricted the blood flow to the kidneys by partially constricting the abdomi-

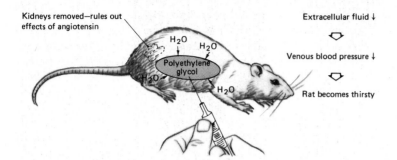

Kidneys removed—rules out effects of angiotensin

H₂O H₂O

Polyethylene glycol

H₂O

H₂O

Extracellular fluid ↓

⬇

Venous blood pressure ↓

⬇

Rat becomes thirsty

FIGURE 11.16
The experiment by Stricker (1973).

nal aorta (a major artery) above the renal arteries, or by partially constricting the renal arteries themselves. (Neither of these procedures lowered venous blood pressure.) The animals drank. However, when the constriction of the abdominal aorta was made *below* the renal arteries, thus not affecting renal blood flow, the rats did not drink. Similarly, constriction of the aorta had no effect on drinking in rats whose kidneys had been removed. (See **Figure 11.17.**) The experiments by Stricker and Fitzsimons confirm that the baroreceptors and renal blood flow detectors can both stimulate drinking. Thus, hypovolemic thirst has two different causes.

The Role of Angiotensin
As we just saw, hypovolemia is detected by baroreceptors on the venous side of the blood supply, and also by receptors in the kidneys that monitor blood flow. Both of these mecha-

nisms cause the kidneys to release renin; the baroreceptors do so through a reflex circuit that increases sympathetic activity in the kidneys, and the decreased renal blood flow does so directly. Perhaps, then, renin (or angiotensin II) acts on some cells in the brain and initiates thirst.

Early studies (for example, Asscher and Anson, 1963) showed that injections of kidney extracts caused drinking. Later, Fitzsimons and Simons (1969) showed that angiotensin II produces drinking in rats that would not otherwise be thirsty. Another study (Malvin, Mouw, and Vander, 1977) showed that the administration of **saralasin,** a drug that blocks angiotensin receptors, decreased the amount of water drunk by thirsty rats. The investigators injected the saralasin into the ventricular system of the brain; presumably, it blocked the receptors in the brain that normally respond to angiotensin.

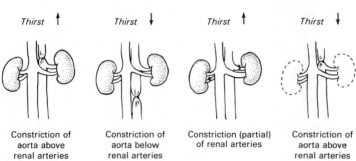

Thirst ↑   Thirst ↓   Thirst ↑   Thirst ↓

Constriction of aorta above renal arteries

Constriction of aorta below renal arteries

Constriction (partial) of renal arteries

Constriction of aorta above renal arteries in a nephrectomized rat

FIGURE 11.17
The experiments by Fitzsimons (1972).

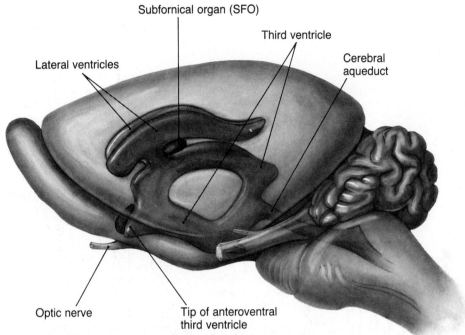

Subfornical organ (SFO)

Third ventricle

Cerebral aqueduct

Lateral ventricles

Optic nerve

Tip of anteroventral third ventricle

FIGURE 11.18

Location of the subfornical organ (SFO) and the anteroventral tip of the third ventricle in the rat brain.

Angiotensin is a peptide composed of eight amino acids, and, as far as we know, all peptides that directly affect behavior do so by interacting with specific receptors in neural membranes. Therefore, researchers hypothesized that the brain contains neurons that initiate thirst when they detect the presence of angiotensin. Because angiotensin does not cross the blood-brain barrier (Volicer and Loew, 1971), a likely site of action would be one of the regions of the brain where this barrier is low. Angiotensin could leave the capillaries in one of these regions, enter the interstitial fluid, and stimulate angiotensin receptors. Indeed, studies have shown that the neurons with angiotensin receptors do lie within one of these regions, the ***subfornical organ (SFO).*** This structure lies just below the commissure of the ventral fornix, where it protrudes into the junction of the lateral ventricles. (See **Figure 11.18.**)

For several years, researchers argued about the location of the angiotensin-sensitive neurons. Simpson, Epstein, and Camardo (1978) found that very low doses of angiotensin injected into the SFO caused drinking. Phillips and Felix (1976) found that microiontophoretic injections of angiotensin there increased the firing rate of neurons; presumably, these neurons contained angiotensin receptors. However, Johnson and Buggy (1977) found injections of angiotensin into another region of the brain also produced drinking: the area surrounding the ***anteroventral tip of the third ventricle.*** This region includes the border between the anterior hypothalamus and the preoptic area. Near it lies another organ with a low blood-brain barrier, which Johnson and Buggy thought contained the angiotensin-sensitive neurons. (See **Figure 11.18.**)

The issue was resolved when investigators

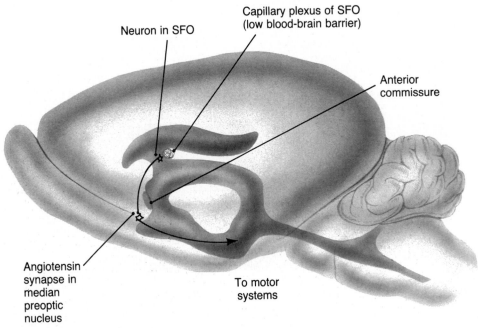

Neuron in SFO

Capillary plexus of SFO
(low blood-brain barrier)

Anterior
commissure

Angiotensin
synapse in
median
preoptic
nucleus

To motor
systems

FIGURE 11.19

Sagittal section through the rat brain, showing the location of angiotensin-sensitive neurons in the SFO and their angiotensin-secreting synapses with neurons in the median preoptic nucleus.

discovered that angiotensin in the blood does stimulate neurons in the SFO, but that these neurons send axons to a nucleus located near the anteroventral tip of the third ventricle: the *median preoptic nucleus* (not to be confused with the medial preoptic area). (See **Figure 11.19.**) The terminal buttons of these axons release angiotensin as a *neurotransmitter;* hence, the neurons in the median preoptic nucleus contain postsynaptic angiotensin receptors. Thus, when Johnson and Buggy infused angiotensin in the region of the anteroventral tip of the third ventricle, they directly stimulated these postsynaptic receptors and caused drinking.

Here is some of the evidence. As we saw, electrophysiological evidence established that the SFO contains neurons that respond to angiotensin, and behavioral evidence showed that infusions of angiotensin in the SFO cause

drinking. However, Simpson, Epstein, and Camardo (1978) found that angiotensin does not cause drinking when saralasin, the angiotensin receptor blocker, is first injected directly into the SFO or when the SFO is surgically destroyed. Thus, the SFO appears to mediate drinking caused by blood-borne angiotensin.

Miselis, Shapiro, and Hand (1979) and Miselis (1980) injected radioactive amino acids into the SFO and used autoradiographic techniques to trace the efferent axons. They found projections to the supraoptic nucleus and to two regions near the anteroventral tip of the third ventricle, including the median preoptic nucleus. Shrager and Johnson (1980) found that of these three regions, only lesions of the median preoptic nucleus abolished drinking stimulated by angiotensin. In addition, Lind and Johnson (1982) made knife cuts that interrupted the axons that travel from the SFO to the median preoptic nucleus. These cuts also abolished the animals' drinking in response to angiotensin. Thus, angiotensin in the blood causes drinking by stimulating neurons in the SFO whose angiotensin-secreting terminal buttons synapse with neurons in the median preoptic nucleus.

INTERIM SUMMARY

Volumetric thirst occurs when an animal loses extracellular fluid volume. Pure hypovolemia occurs when an animal loses blood, but when an animal is unable to drink for an extended period both major fluid compartments — intracellular as well as extracellular — lose volume. Hypovolemia causes both thirst and a sodium appetite; the animal needs sodium because the missing extracellular fluid cannot simply be replaced with pure water.

Hypovolemia is detected by two means: by baroreceptors in the atrium of the heart and by receptors in the kidneys that monitor blood flow. Both detection mechanisms cause the kidneys to secrete renin; the receptors in the kidneys do so directly, and the baroreceptors in the heart stimulate reflex brain mechanisms that increase the activity of sympathetic axons to the kidneys. Renin converts angiotensinogen in the blood to the active form, angiotensin.

Angiotensin in the blood penetrates the low blood-brain barrier of the subfornical organ and stimulates angiotensin receptors on neurons located there. These neurons send axons to the median preoptic nucleus. Their terminal buttons secrete angiotensin as a neurotransmitter, activating the efferent neurons of the median preoptic nucleus to stimulate drinking.

Because rats whose kidneys were removed become thirsty when hypovolemia is experimentally induced, we must conclude that the baroreceptors in the heart can directly stimulate brain mechanisms that instigate drinking, even in the absence of angiotensin.

Osmometric Thirst

As everyone knows, a salty meal produces thirst. In experimental animals, drinking can be stimulated by an injection of hypertonic saline, which draws fluid out of the cells but does not reduce the volume of the extracellular fluid. (In fact, it increases it temporarily, at the expense of the intracellular fluid, until the kidneys rid the body of the excess salt.) Therefore, some mechanism must detect either the increased osmotic pressure of the interstitial fluid (caused by the injection) or the ensuing loss of intracellular fluid. The craving for water that follows is called ***osmometric thirst.***

Fitzsimons (1972) nephrectomized a group of rats to prevent the kidneys from eliminating salt or water. Next, he injected the animals with hypertonic solutions of substances that can enter cells (such as glucose and methyl glucose) or substances that cannot (such as sodium chloride, sodium sulfate, and sucrose — table sugar).

His results confirmed earlier studies showing that cellular dehydration produces thirst; the only animals that drank excessively were those that received substances such as sodium chloride, sodium sulfate, and sucrose, which cannot enter the cells and hence draw water from them. Glucose and methyl glucose (which can enter the cells) did not produce thirst.

As we saw earlier, Verney (1947) and Jewell and Verney (1957) found that injections of hypertonic saline solution into the blood supply of the diencephalon triggered ADH secretion, which caused the kidneys to retain water. Their results suggested that the brain contained osmoreceptors, perhaps in the hypothalamus. Indeed, Andersson (1953) found that injections of hypertonic saline solution into the rostrolateral hypothalamus produced drinking but not ADH release, whereas injections into caudal hypothalamic regions stimulated ADH secretion but not thirst. Thus, different sets of receptors appeared to mediate drinking and ADH release in response to hypertonicity. We already saw that Hatton has implicated the nucleus circularis in the control of ADH secretion.

An extensive mapping study by Peck and Blass (1975) suggested that the osmoreceptors that stimulate thirst in rats are located near the junction of the *lateral preoptic area* and the *lateral hypothalamus,* in the medial portion of these regions. Injections of hypertonic sucrose there produced drinking. (See **Figure 11.20.**) In addition, Blass and Epstein (1971) found that injections of water into the lateral preoptic area suppressed drinking caused by subcutaneous injections of hypertonic saline; presumably, the water turned off the signal for thirst at the detectors. Injections of water had no effect on drinking

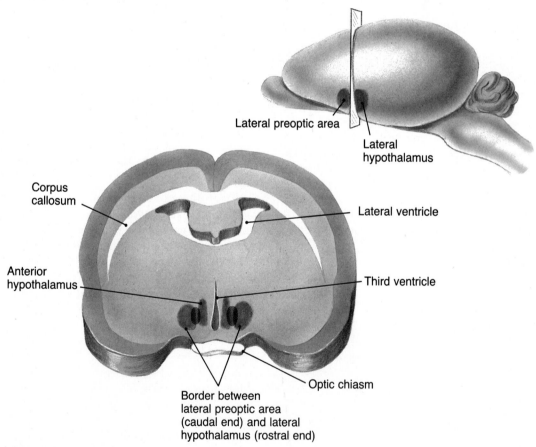

FIGURE 11.20
Injection of hypertonic sucrose near the junction of the lateral preoptic area and the lateral hypothalamus produces drinking, presumably by stimulating osmoreceptors located there. (Adapted from Peck, J.W., and Blass, E.M. *American Journal of Physiology,* 1975, *4,* 1501–1509.)

stimulated by angiotensin, so the suppression of drinking behavior was specific to osmometric thirst.

Many electrophysiological studies have found evidence of neurons whose firing rate is altered by infusions of hypertonic solutions. Water deprivation or systemic injections of hypertonic saline produce responses of neurons in the lateral preoptic area (Arnauld, Dufy, and Vincent, 1975; Blank and Wayner, 1975). However, these studies do not prove that these neurons are osmoreceptors; Rolls and Rolls (1982) suggest that some may simply receive synaptic input from osmoreceptors.

As we saw earlier, osmoreceptors in the tongue and liver play a role in controlling the release of ADH. Perhaps these detectors also control drinking. As we will see, behavioral evidence suggests that receptors in the tongue and liver (and in the stomach and intestines, as well) do play a role in satiety.

INTERIM SUMMARY

Osmometric thirst occurs when cells lose water because of an increase in the solute concentration of the extracellular fluid. This event can occur after eating a salty meal or after losing water through evaporation. But whereas a salty meal produces only osmometric thirst, the loss of water through evaporation reduces the volume of both the intracellular and extracellular fluid compartments.

Injections of hypertonic solutions into the border of the lateral preoptic area and the lateral hypothalamus produce drinking, and injections of water there suppress drinking caused by an injection of hypertonic saline into the blood. In addition, electrical recordings have shown that neurons in this region increase their firing rate during osmometric thirst. Most investigators believe that the region contains neurons whose firing rate is controlled by their degree of hydration; thus they are osmoreceptors.

Satiety

When permitted to drink after having been deprived of the opportunity to do so for a period of time, most animals rapidly drink enough water to restore their loss and then stop. In most cases, satiety occurs before substantial amounts of water are absorbed from the digestive system. For example, a dog consumes the water it needs within 2 to 3 minutes (Adolph, 1939). However, replenishment of the water previously lost from the blood plasma does not begin for 10 to 12 minutes and is not completed until 40 to 45 minutes (Ramsay, Rolls, and Wood, 1977). Perhaps satiety is produced by anticipatory mechanisms that are controlled by receptors in the mouth or digestive tract.

Receptors in the mouth and throat do influence the amount of water an organism drinks, but their effects are secondary to those of receptors in the stomach, small intestine, and liver. Miller, Sampliner, and Woodrow (1957) allowed thirsty rats to drink 14 ml of water or administered it directly into the stomach through a tube that had previously been placed there. At various times after the preload, the rats were permitted to drink. As Figure 11.21 shows, rats who received the 14-ml preload by mouth drank less than those that received it directly into the stomach. Thus, stimulation of receptors in the mouth and throat plays a role in satiety. (See **Figure 11.21.**) However, many studies, dating from Bernard (1856), have shown that *sham drinking* is not satiating. To produce sham drinking, the esophagus is diverted to the outside of the body, so that ingested water spills to the ground. (See **Figure 11.22.**) Under these conditions a thirsty animal of most species will drink until it becomes exhausted; satiety does not occur.

Because the blood supply from the small intestine goes directly to the liver, and because receptors there appear to play a role in

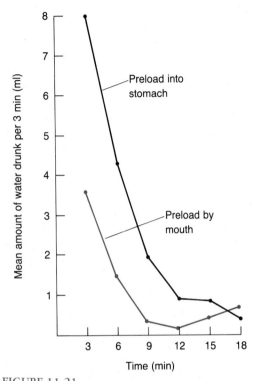

FIGURE 11.21

Effects of receiving 14 ml of water by mouth or through a tube inserted into the stomach on subsequent drinking of thirsty rats. (From Miller, N.E., Sampliner, R.I., and Woodrow, P. *Journal of Comparative and Physiological Psychology,* 1957, *50,* 1–5.)

controlling ADH secretion, many investigators believe that they may also play a role in satiety produced by the absorption of water from the digestive system. Indeed, Kozlowski and Drzewiecki (1973) obtained evidence supporting this hypothesis. They infused water into the hepatic portal vein, which conveys blood from the intestine to the liver. The infusions inhibited osmometric drinking initiated by injections of hypertonic saline.

Hall (1973) and Hall and Blass (1977) prepared a noose out of fine fishing line, passed it around the *pylorus,* the junction of the small intestine with the stomach, and threaded the line through a plastic tube. They brought the end of the tube through the rat's skin and fastened it to the top of the rat's head. The experimenters could tighten and loosen the noose without disturbing the rats. (See **Figure 11.23.**) When the experimenters tightened the noose, the pylorus closed, and contents of the stomach could not enter the intestine. When water could not leave the stomach, thirsty rats drank *more* water than when the noose was open. These results suggest that signals from the small intestine or liver are important in satiety; the noose prevented water from reaching them, thus preventing these signals from being sent.

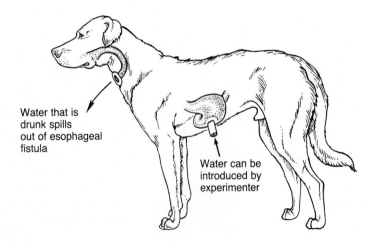

FIGURE 11.22
Esophagotomy.

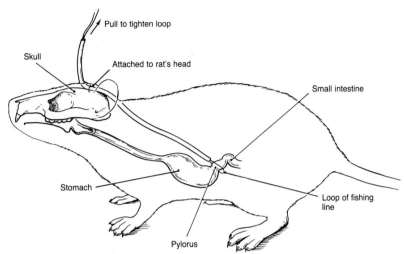

FIGURE 11.23
The procedure used by Hall and Blass (1977) to prevent water from leaving the stomach.

Other studies suggest that gastric factors are important as well. (The word *gastric* refers to the stomach; it derives from the Greek *gastēr,* "stomach.") Maddison, Rolls, Rolls, and Wood (1980) implanted a tube in monkeys' stomachs so that water could be drained from them. They prevented the monkeys from drinking for a while, thus making them thirsty. Then the experimenters permitted the monkeys to drink their fill. Once they stopped drinking, the drain tube was opened. As soon as the stomach began emptying, the monkeys began drinking again — often within seconds. Thus, gastric receptors appear to be able to inhibit drinking. We cannot be sure that this inhibition is actually *satiety;* it is possible that the monkeys stopped drinking not because they were no longer thirsty but because their stomachs were uncomfortably full.

Anticipation of Future Needs

As we all know, a meal without a beverage is thirst provoking. In acknowledgment of this fact, we almost always drink water (in one form or another) with each meal. So does a rat. Fitzsimons and LeMagnen (1969) showed that rats appear to ingest as much water as they will *subsequently* need to counteract the dehydrating effects of their meal.

All meals produce a certain degree of hypovolemia. Secretion of digestive juices into the digestive tract entails a temporary loss of water from the extracellular fluid. This hypovolemia leads to thirst. A meal rich in protein is particularly dehydrating. The presence of amino acids in the digestive tract exerts considerable osmotic pressure, withdrawing fluid from the extracellular space. If you eat a large steak without taking any beverage, you will later become thirsty. (Here is an experiment you might want to try for yourself.)

LeMagnen and Tallen (1966) observed that rats ingest an amount of water that is closely related to the osmotic demand placed upon them by their meal. However, Oakley and Toates (1969) found that they drank the water *before* the body fluid entered the intestines, so the drinking was not initiated by hypovolemia. Fitzsimons and LeMagnen (1969) showed that this matching of water intake to water need appears to be learned. They maintained rats on a carbohydrate diet and found that the rats ingested almost equal amounts of water and food. They then fed the rats a diet rich in protein (which causes more hypovolemia), and the animals responded by ingesting 1.47 times more water than food. At first, they drank most of the water *after* the meal, when the osmotic demands were being felt. However, within a few days the animals began drinking more water with the meals. They apparently learned the association of the new diet with subsequent thirst and drank in anticipation of that thirst.

INTERIM   SUMMARY

Control of fluid volume requires anticipation: thirsty animals stop drinking before their extracellular fluid is completely restored, and they drink water that anticipates the hypovolemia that will be produced by the meal they are eating. Water that is tasted is more satiating than water simply injected into the stomach; therefore, osmoreceptors in the tongue apparently provide a satiety signal to the brain. However, because sham drinking does not produce satiety, we must conclude that the contribution of these receptors is relatively minor. The finding that a full stomach can inhibit further drinking suggests that gastric receptors may play a role in satiety. Even more important are receptors in the small intestine or liver. When water is confined to the stomach by means of a noose of fishing line, rats drink more than when it is allowed to escape into the small intestine (and from there through the blood to the liver). In addition, infusions of water into the hepatic portal vein cause satiety.

When animals eat meals that cause a temporary hypovolemia, they drink enough water to match the loss of extracellular fluid. They do so in anticipation of the loss, not in response to the hypovolemia itself. This anticipation requires learning, and the animals adjust their drinking to the taste of foods that produce different amounts of hypovolemia.

Neural Control of Drinking

So far we have considered the location of neurons that respond to angiotensin or to increased osmotic pressure of the extracellular fluid. Now we will consider the brain mechanisms that more directly control the behavior of drinking. Teitelbaum and Stellar (1954) found that lesions of the lateral hypothalamus produce a temporary lack of eating and drinking, followed by gradual recovery. However, when drinking behavior recovers, it occurs only during meals, when the rats are eating dry food. Injection of hypertonic saline solution no longer causes drinking (Epstein and Teitelbaum, 1964). Nor does hypovolemia produced by injections of polyethylene glycol into the peritoneal cavity (Stricker and Wolf, 1967). Neither of the normal signals, then, produces drinking.

Swanson, Kucharczyk, and Mogenson (1978) used amino acid autoradiography to trace the route taken by the axons of the angiotensin-sensitive neurons. They found two efferent pathways that ended in the midbrain. The first pathway passed through the lateral hypothalamus, terminating in the ventral tegmental area. Presumably, this pathway mediates the effects of angiotensin on drinking. The second pathway terminated in the periaqueductal gray matter. This pathway appears to mediate the effects of angiotensin on blood pressure. (See **Figure 11.24.**)

It appears likely that lateral hypothalamic lesions interrupt a system that modulates the activity of motor mechanisms in the brain stem that control drinking behavior. Kucharczyk and Mogenson (1975, 1976) found that lesions of the midlateral hypothalamus disrupted drinking stimulated by angiotensin but did not disrupt osmometric thirst. In contrast, far lateral lesions did the opposite: they disrupted osmometric drinking but not drinking that was elicited by angiotensin. More caudal lesions that included the ventral

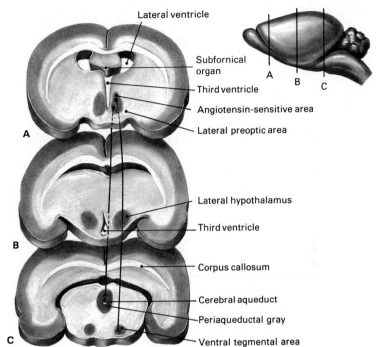

Lateral ventricle

Subfornical organ

Third ventricle

Angiotensin-sensitive area

Lateral preoptic area

A

Lateral hypothalamus

Third ventricle

B

Corpus callosum

Cerebral aqueduct

Periaqueductal gray

Ventral tegmental area

C

FIGURE 11.24
Efferent pathways from the angiotensin-sensitive area near the anteroventral tip of the third ventricle to the ventral tegmental area and periaqueductal gray matter. (Adapted from Swanson, L.W., Kucharczyk, J., and Mogenson, G.J. *Journal of Comparative Neurology,* 1978, *178,* 645–660.)

tegmental area disrupted drinking produced by angiotensin but did not affect the osmometric drinking that follows the injection of hypertonic saline (Kucharczyk and Mogenson, 1977).

INTERIM SUMMARY

At least two pathways that control drinking appear to reside in (or pass through) the lateral hypothalamus. A medial system, which originates in the median preoptic nucleus, terminates in the ventral tegmental area, and controls angiotensin-stimulated drinking. A more lateral system, which perhaps originates in the osmosensitive region of the lateral hypothalamus/lateral preoptic area, terminates in brain stem motor nuclei and mediates osmometric thirst.

We have seen that in order to understand the neural control of drinking we must understand the essentials of water balance: the nature of the fluid compartments of the body and their interrelations; the operations of the kidneys and the effects of aldosterone and ADH on these operations; the nature and location of receptors in the kidneys, heart, and brain; and the neural circuits that these receptors control. Dehydration normally depletes both intracellular and extracellular fluid compartments, but some events, such as bleeding or ingestion of salty food, can deplete only one of them. Thus, the body contains mechanisms that monitor each of these compartments.

We saw that some of the mechanisms that control physiological processes also control behavior. For example, hypovolemia triggers renin release, which produces angiotensin. Angiotensin contracts blood vessels, which helps correct the fall in blood pressure, and stimulates aldosterone secretion, which causes the kidneys to conserve sodium. Angiotensin also stimulates drinking, so that the animal regains the water it has lost. In addition, aldosterone stimulates a sodium appetite, which helps the animal regain the lost sodium. Thus, internal physiological mechanisms and behavioral mechanisms work in parallel.

■ EATING

Ingestion of food is affected by many factors: characteristics of the available food, including its appearance, taste, odor, and texture; characteristics of the environment, including the presence of others who are themselves eating; and characteristics of the organism, including eating habits, the presence or absence of food in the digestive system, and the quantity of nutrients stored in the cells of the body. The study of the variables that control food intake is one of the oldest problems in physiological psychology. For many years, physiological psychologists assumed that hunger was caused by detectors located within the brain and that hunger and satiety were produced by activity of the lateral hypothalamus and ventromedial hypothalamus, respectively. However, recent evidence indicates that these beliefs are too simple. Although there are nutrient detectors in the brain, their role in the day-to-day control of eating appears to be minor compared with detectors located elsewhere in the body. And the lateral and ventromedial hypothalamus do not appear to contain "hunger" or "satiety" mechanisms.

As we will see, hunger is produced by metabolic signals associated with depletion of stored nutrients. The detectors for these signals appear to be located primarily in the liver (or its blood vessels), but some are also located in the brain. Satiety is produced by a number of anticipatory signals, some learned and some apparently innate. When the food is familiar, the organism eats what it has learned to be a proper amount, based on the amount swallowed and on feedback from the digestive system. The presence of food in the digestive system sends signals to the brain by means of neural and hormonal routes.

Control of body weight entails more than a single correctional mechanism, the ingestion of food. Recent studies have shown that metabolic rate is not a constant factor; instead, it can vary according to the amount of nutrients that are consumed. If an organism begins to starve, its metabolic rate declines, thus conserving energy. If it overeats and begins to gain weight, its metabolic rate increases and "burns off" some of the unneeded calories. Indeed, there are large individual differences in metabolic rate among people, and these differences contribute substantially to their ability to maintain a healthful body weight.

Before I describe the evidence, it is necessary to present some basic facts about digestion and metabolism.

The Digestive Process

Digestion begins in the mouth. We use our teeth to break down the food into pieces small enough to swallow safely, and, in so doing, we mix the food with saliva, which serves several functions. It lubricates dry food and adds a digestive enzyme that begins the process of breaking down starches into sugars; it also dissolves molecules of the food, permitting the taste buds to be stimulated. Of course, besides stimulating taste receptors, the food stimulates olfactory receptors. In fact, odor molecules enter the nose even before we begin to eat. The odor and taste of food play an important role in recognition of nutrients. Because we can learn to eat different amounts of food with different nutritional values, this recognition is important.

Once food is swallowed and enters the stomach, this organ begins to secrete hydrochloric acid and the enzyme *pepsin* (one of the few enzymes that does not end in -*ase*). Hydrochloric acid breaks the food into small particles, and pepsin breaks proteins in the food into their constituent amino acids. The muscles in the wall of the stomach become active, churning the food so that it becomes well mixed with the digestive juices. (See **Figure 11.25.**)

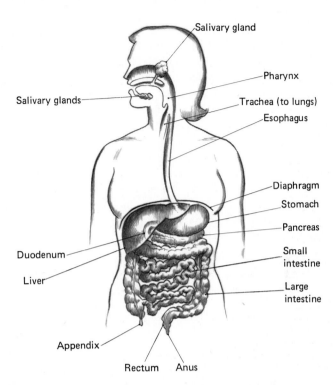

Salivary gland

Pharynx

Trachea (to lungs)

Esophagus

Salivary glands

Diaphragm

Stomach

Pancreas

Small intestine

Large intestine

Duodenum

Liver

Appendix

Rectum   Anus

FIGURE 11.25
The digestive system.

The wall of the stomach contains stretch receptors and chemoreceptors. These receptors respond to the bulk and chemical nature of the contents of the stomach, and their activity plays a role in the control of the digestive processes. The receptors in the wall of the stomach also provide feedback to the brain and control food intake.

The stomach empties into the ***duodenum,*** the upper portion of the small intestine. (*Duodecim* means "twelve"; the duodenum is approximately twelve fingerwidths long.) The rate of gastric emptying is controlled by the composition of nutrients received by the duodenum. The walls of the duodenum contain chemoreceptors that regulate gastric activity by means of neural reflexes, and by the release of various hormones. For example, if the duodenum receives large concentrations of fat from the stomach, it inhibits gastric emptying, because it takes much longer to digest this nutrient. Proteins and carbohy-

drates are much more readily digested, so the duodenum permits the stomach to empty more quickly when it contains a meal low in fats. The duodenal receptors also stimulate secretion of the peptide hormone ***cholecystokinin (CCK),*** which causes the gallbladder (the *cholecyst*) to contract, releasing bile (described later) into the duodenum. As we will see, researchers have suggested that this hormone and others released by the digestive system convey signals to the brain that play a role in satiety.

The pancreas, which is located below the stomach, communicates with the duodenum by means of the pancreatic duct. As we will see, the pancreas also produces two hormones, insulin and glucagon, and thus qualifies as an endocrine gland as well as an exocrine gland. Pancreatic enzymes break down proteins, lipids, starch, and nucleic acids, thus continuing the digestive process. The pancreas also secretes bicarbonate, which neutralizes stomach acid. As the products of digestion begin to be absorbed into the bloodstream, and as the acid is neutralized by the bicarbonate, the stomach empties more of its contents into the duodenum.

In the digestive system, carbohydrates are broken down into simple sugars, and proteins are broken down into amino acids. These water-soluble nutrients enter the capillaries of the intestinal *villi* (singular: villus), fingerlike structures that protrude into the interior of the intestine. (See **Figure 11.26.**) These capillaries drain into the hepatic portal system and reach the liver before reaching any other portion of the body.

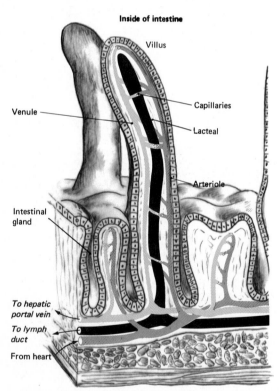

FIGURE 11.26
Intestinal villi. (Adapted from Vander, A.J., Sherman, J.H., and Luciano, D.S., *Human Physiology: The Mechanisms of Body Function,* 2nd edition. New York: McGraw-Hill, 1975.)

Fats are not soluble in water and must be emulsified before they can be absorbed. **Emulsification** refers to the breakdown of fat globules into tiny particles. For example, milk is an emulsion, containing very fine particles of butterfat suspended in water. In fact, the word *emulsion* comes from the Latin word *mulgere,* which means "to milk." In the digestive system, emulsification is accomplished by **bile,** a substance produced by the liver and stored in the gallbladder. When chemoreceptors in the duodenum detect the presence of fats, they initiate the secretion of CCK, which causes bile to be released into the intestine. Emulsified fats are absorbed into the *lacteals* located within the villi; the lacteals communicate with the lymphatic system, which then brings the fats to a lymph duct that empties into veins in the neck.

The meal passes through the small intestine, where most of the available nutrients are absorbed; the residue enters the large intestine. Hardly any nutrients are absorbed in the large intestine, but water and electrolytes are reabsorbed there. Bacteria in the large intestine live mainly on undigested cellulose. They produce some vitamins (especially vitamin K, important in the clotting of blood) that are absorbed into the body. Note that I said "into the body." Strictly speaking, the contents of the digestive tract are not within the body. If we are reduced to our simplest form, topologically, we find that we are doughnut shaped. The gastrointestinal tract is the hole in the doughnut.

Storage and Utilization of Nutrients

The metabolic processes of the body are beautifully interrelated. At different times, the processes cooperate to produce the **absorptive phase,** which occurs while a meal is being absorbed from the intestine, and the **fasting phase,** which occurs after the nutrients have been absorbed and usually leads to hunger and ingestion of the next meal. As we will see, the factors that cause metabolism to enter the fasting phase are also the ones that induce hunger.

Absorptive Phase

Description. If a well-balanced meal is eaten, the body receives three types of nutrients from the intestines during the absorptive phase of metabolism: glucose (derived from carbohydrates), amino acids (derived from proteins), and fats. During the absorptive phase, more nutrients are received from the digestive system than the body needs right then, so excess amounts are converted to fats and **glycogen** (an insoluble carbohydrate often referred to as *animal starch*). The fats and glycogen are stored and can be broken down and metabolized later, when they are needed.

Figure 11.27 illustrates the most important metabolic pathways of the absorptive phase. The numbers in the following list correspond to the numbers (in color) in the figure. Ignore the gray letters for now; they will be referred to later. (See **Figure 11.27.**)

1. The principal source of energy for all tissue is glucose.

2. Excess glucose is converted to glycogen in the liver (2a) and muscles (2b). Excess glucose can also be converted to fats in the liver (2c) or in *adipose tissue* (fat tissue) (2d). The liver does not store fats but sends them through the blood to adipose tissue for storage.

3. Amino acids are used to construct proteins and other peptides wherever they are needed (for example, in muscle tissue).

4. Excess amino acids, like excess glucose, are converted to fats in the liver and are sent to adipose tissue for storage.

5. Fats received from the digestive system are stored in adipose tissue.

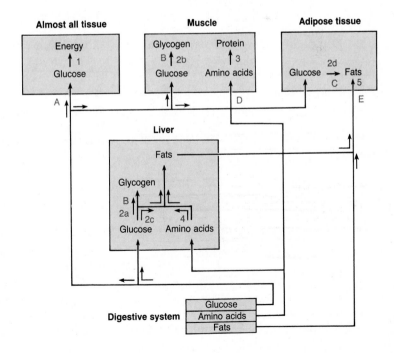

FIGURE 11.27
The absorptive phase of metabolism.

To summarize: During the absorptive phase, glucose is the primary fuel. Excess glucose is stored as glycogen and fat. Amino acids are used for protein synthesis as needed, and excess amounts are stored as fat. Fats are not used as a fuel but are put into storage in adipose tissue.

Control. The absorptive phase of metabolism is produced primarily by the effects of insulin, one of the hormones secreted by the *islet cells* of the pancreas in its role as an endocrine gland. Insulin is a vital hormone; the disease *diabetes mellitus* occurs when the pancreas loses the ability to produce insulin. If it is not treated with injections of insulin, severe diabetes can result in death.

The primary effect of insulin is to permit the entry of glucose into cells. Without the presence of insulin in the interstitial fluid, cells cannot take in glucose. Thus, lack of insulin causes a very high blood level of glucose, because the glucose cannot enter cells and be metabolized or be stored as glycogen or fat. Deprived of glucose, the cells of a diabetic rely principally on fats for energy. The unabsorbed glucose is passed through the kidneys and, in the process, causes a loss of sodium. If the loss is severe enough, the low blood pressure it produces can be fatal. Diabetes mellitus literally means "passing through of honey," because the urine of an untreated diabetic tastes sweet. (Fortunately, the diagnosis of this disease can now be accomplished by chemical procedures and no longer requires the sense of taste.) The presence of sugar in the urine led an observant physician to note, several hundred years ago, that diabetes could be diagnosed by seeing whether a person's shoes attracted flies.

Insulin has several metabolic effects, all of which promote the storage of nutrients during the absorptive phase. These effects are shown in Figure 11.27 in gray letters, corresponding to the letters in the following list.

A. Insulin facilitates the entry of glucose into the cell. Without insulin, body tissue cannot readily utilize glucose in metabolic processes. The nervous system is an exception; it can use glucose independently of insulin.

B. Insulin increases the conversion of glucose to glycogen in the liver and muscles.

C. Insulin increases the conversion of glucose into fats; thus, the buildup of stored fat is facilitated.

D. Insulin facilitates the transport of amino acids into cells, thus permitting protein synthesis to occur.

E. Insulin facilitates the transport of fats into adipose cells, promoting fat storage.

All these effects facilitate the metabolic pathways of the absorptive phase of metabolism: storage of nutrients and utilization of glucose.

Two principal factors stimulate insulin secretion. First, the islet cells in the pancreas respond directly to the presence of glucose and amino acids in the blood. During the absorptive phase of metabolism, glucose and amino acids are received from the intestines, so the blood level of these substances consequently rises. In response, the islet cells in the pancreas release insulin. During the fasting phase, when the gut is empty of nutrients, the levels of these nutrients fall, and the secretion of insulin decreases. Second, insulin secretion is stimulated by the activity of parasympathetic axons that innervate the pancreas. When an organism begins to eat a meal, conditioned reflexes cause the secretion of saliva, gastric juices, and insulin. The secretion of insulin starts to prepare the animal for the absorptive phase that will soon follow. Under the influence of insulin, cells begin to take up glucose. Of course, this action causes the blood level of glucose to fall temporarily, which at least partly accounts for the stimulating effect that a small portion of tasty food (like a potato chip or two) has on hunger. The food causes the reflexive release of insulin, which lowers the blood glucose level and increases hunger.

Fasting Phase

Description. After a meal has been absorbed from the digestive system, glucose is no longer abundant, so the body organs must use other fuels. During the fasting phase, most cells live on stored fats. Fats are stored in adipose tissue in the form of **triglycerides,** molecules consisting of *glycerol* (a soluble carbohydrate, also called *glycerine*) combined with three **fatty acids** (stearic acid, oleic acid, and palmitic acid). The cells of the body cannot directly metabolize triglycerides. Instead, these molecules break down into glycerol and fatty acids, which are then released by adipose cells into the bloodstream. All tissues *except the brain* can use fatty acids. The brain continues to use glucose.

Figure 11.28 illustrates the most important metabolic pathways of the fasting phase. As in the previous figure, the numbers in the following list correspond to numbers (in color) in the illustration. (See **Figure 11.28.**)

1. Most body organs (including the liver but excluding the brain) use fatty acids, released from adipose tissue.

2. The brain metabolizes glucose, which comes from three primary sources. Glycerol (derived from triglycerides) is released by adipose tissue and is converted to glucose in the liver (2a). Liver glycogen is converted into glucose (2b). During periods of prolonged fasting, muscle protein is broken down to amino acids, which the liver converts to glucose (2c).

3. If fasting is prolonged, the liver oxidizes some of the fatty acids it receives and converts them into **ketones.** The liver cannot metabolize ketones, but the rest of the body can, including the brain. It is sometimes said

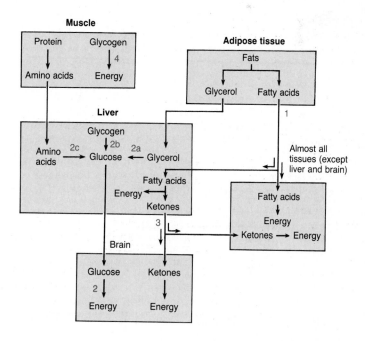

FIGURE 11.28

The fasting phase of metabolism.

that the brain can use only glucose as a fuel, but this statement is not true; it can use ketones as well.

4. Muscle tissue can use its own stored glycogen as a source of energy. This metabolic pathway is more complicated than I have indicated, but the intricacies are not important for our purposes.

To summarize: During the fasting phase, most of the body uses fatty acids as fuel. Glycerol, amino acids, and glycogen can be converted to glucose by the liver, for use by the brain. The liver can also convert fatty acids to ketones, which it cannot metabolize but which can be used by the rest of the body (including the brain).

Control. The most important control factor in the fasting phase of metabolism is a low level of insulin and a high level of glucagon (described shortly). Without insulin, only cells of the nervous system can utilize glucose; thus, all the blood glucose is spared for their use during this phase. Also, the lack of insulin permits fats to be broken down to fatty acids and glycerol. As we saw, fatty acids are used by most tissues for fuel, and glycerol is converted to glucose by the liver. Of course, the brain gets this glucose.

The islet cells of the pancreas produce another hormone, **glucagon.** This hormone is secreted when the blood glucose level falls, as it begins to do when all the food is absorbed from the digestive system. It causes liver glycogen to be broken down to glucose, which the brain uses. It also promotes the breakdown of fats, so that fatty acids are available for other tissues of the body. (It is easy to confuse the words *glycogen* and *glucagon;* because they occur several more times in this chapter, it is worthwhile making sure you have them straight.)

In times of increased need, such as during vigorous exercise or stress, the brain causes the adrenal medulla to release epinephrine and the adrenal cortex to release glucocorticoids. These hormones promote the breakdown and utilization of muscle glycogen.

INTERIM SUMMARY

Unless you have already taken a nutrition course, you have been introduced to several new concepts. Rather than repeat the summaries of the absorptive and fasting phases of metabolism that I provided in Figures 11.27 and 11.28, I suggest that you look at them again and reread the accompanying descriptions.

The controlling influence in the absorptive phase is the high level of insulin, which permits nutrients to enter cells and promotes their storage as glycogen and triglycerides. Because insulin is present during this phase, all cells of the body can readily utilize glucose as their primary fuel. The controlling influence during the fasting phase is the low level of insulin, which prevents most organs from using the available glucose. However, because the cells of the nervous system do not require insulin to utilize glucose, they do so. Other hormones, especially glucagon, promote the conversion of triglycerides to fatty acids and glycerol and the conversion of glycogen to glucose.

What Starts a Meal?

The physiological signals we have studied so far deal with the metabolism of food that has already been ingested. But what controls ingestive behavior itself? Hunger can be produced by a variety of stimuli, including the presence of appetizing food, the company of people who are eating, or the words "It's time to eat!" Even in the absence of a need for food, people will eat sweets or munch on snacks when there is nothing else to do. Considering that our ancestors often confronted times of famine, this eating may have had some survival value in the past. In that context it was *anticipatory* in nature — anticipating future times when food might not be available, and when a good supply of body fat could mean the difference between starvation and survival. However, this section considers eating caused by need: the physiological variables related to the body's supply of nutrients that stimulate hunger.

The Role of Glucose

A low level of glucose in the blood may be the most important physiological stimulus for hunger. During the absorptive phase of metabolism, the body receives glucose from the digestive system. Even after the gut is empty, plenty of glucose is still available for the nervous system (from liver glycogen and from glycerol) and plenty of fatty acids are available for the rest of the body. However, once the liver glycogen becomes depleted (which occurs in sedentary humans within a few hours), the blood level of glucose begins to fall, and the organism becomes hungry. Of course, plasma glucose does not fall drastically; people can fast for many days, living off their stored fat and eventually consuming their muscle protein. But they will become very hungry.

System Variables. Mayer (1955) proposed the **glucostatic hypothesis** of hunger. The suffix *-static* means "standing in place," in the sense of a stabilizer; a *glucostat* is a hypothetical detector of blood glucose, just as a thermostat is a detector of temperature. Mayer suggested that the rate of firing of a set of specialized neurons (glucostats) was inversely related to the level of glucose in the interstitial fluid. Low levels of glucose would produce high rates of firing, which would result in hunger.

Actually, the glucostatic hypothesis is a bit more complicated than that. People with untreated diabetes have high levels of plasma glucose, but because their insulin level is low they are chronically hungry. Because insulin is necessary for the utilization of glucose, this hyperglycemia is useless to cells; they starve in the midst of plenty. (**Hyperglycemia** and **hypoglycemia** refer, respectively, to abnormally high or unusually low levels of plasma glucose.) Mayer suggested that the glucostats actually respond to the *availability* of glucose, not its mere presence. The system variable, then, is the ability of cells to obtain and utilize glucose, which depends on two factors: glucose and insulin. If this situation is true, then glucostats are different from other neurons, which can take in and utilize glucose in the absence of insulin.

Good evidence suggests that hunger is closely related to glucose availability. In fact, the only way that we know to produce immediate hunger in experimental animals is to cause a drastic reduction in glucose availability. If an animal is given a large injection of insulin, it becomes hypoglycemic and very hungry. The insulin causes cells to take up and store glucose, and soon there is none available for utilization. In contrast, a small amount of insulin combined with a high blood glucose level is satiating. Nicolaidis and Rowland (1976) injected glucose intravenously into rats through permanently attached cannulas. The glucose had modest effects on eating; each calorie of glucose reduced voluntary intake by only 0.4 calorie. However, when insulin was infused along with the glucose, the glucose reduced food intake on a one-to-one basis. Presumably, the insulin increased the ability of the rats' cells to utilize the injected glucose and increased its satiating effect.

Detectors. For years psychologists and physiologists sought glucose receptors in the brain. Indeed, they succeeded in finding them there but had difficulty confirming their importance in the control of feeding. For example, Blass and Kraly (1974) destroyed the lateral hypothalamus, which contains many of the brain's glucose receptors.

Even after recovering from the short-term effects of the surgery, the rats no longer ate in response to hypoglycemia produced by large injections of insulin. However, their eating continued to be controlled by nutritional factors. For example, they ate more when given a diluted liquid diet and ate less of a concentrated diet. They ate more when the room temperature was lowered (hence increasing their metabolic rate) and ate less when it was warmed. Thus, although the lateral hypothalamus contains glucose receptors, they do not appear to play a crucial role in the regulation of food intake. Perhaps the glucose receptors are part of an emergency system that stimulates eating when the blood glucose level becomes dangerously low.

The brain is not the only organ that contains glucose receptors; evidence suggests that glucose receptors in the liver play an important role in the control of food intake. Russek (1971) noted that although intravenous (IV) injections of glucose had little effect on food intake, *intraperitoneal (IP)* injections (that is, into the abdominal cavity) suppressed eating. This observation certainly does not favor the hypothesis that glucose receptors in the brain are important in food regulation. An IV injection of glucose raises the blood sugar level, but an IP injection has little effect. Conversely, most of the glucose injected into the abdominal cavity is taken up by the liver and stored as glycogen. The finding that the glucose injected intraperitoneally probably got no farther than the liver but nevertheless inhibited eating suggested to Russek that the liver might contain receptors that were sensitive to glucose. Perhaps these receptors send signals to the brain that activate mechanisms that control eating.

To test this hypothesis Russek attached two chronic cannulas in a dog, one in the hepatic portal vein (the system that carries blood from the intestine to the liver) and another in the jugular vein, located in the neck. Injec-

tion in the jugular vein introduces a substance into the general circulation. By the time the substance reaches the liver it is already diluted by the blood. In contrast, injection in the hepatic portal vein introduces a substance directly into the liver. An injection of glucose into the hepatic portal vein produced long-lasting satiety, whereas a similar injection into the jugular vein had no effect on food intake. Several other studies (for example, Novin, Robinson, Culbreth, and Tordoff, 1983) confirmed these results.

A study by Novin, VanderWeele, and Rezek (1973) suggested that receptors in the liver can stimulate hunger as well as produce satiety; when these cells are deprived of nutrients they cause eating. The investigators infused 2-deoxyglucose (2-DG) into the hepatic portal vein. This form of glucose cannot be metabolized, and by binding with enzymes that break glucose down, it blocks the metabolic processes of the cell. Thus, 2-DG causes cells to starve. (You will recall from Chapter 5 that small amounts of radioactive 2-DG can be used with PET scans or autoradiography to identify neurons with high rates of metabolism.) Novin and his colleagues found that the intraportal infusions of 2-DG caused immediate eating. The effect appeared to be mediated by the neural connections between the liver and the brain, because it was largely eliminated by cutting the vagus nerve.

Electrophysiological studies have found glucose-sensitive receptors in the liver that send information through afferent fibers in the vagus nerve (Niijima, 1969, 1982). These receptors appear to provide "hunger" signals; they fire at a high rate when the level of glucose in the hepatic portal blood is low and fire at a low rate when the glucose level is high.

If an important hunger signal is received by the brain from the liver via the vagus nerve, then cutting this nerve should abolish these signals and decrease eating. However, several experiments have shown that hepatic denervation does not prevent hunger. For example, Tordoff, Hopfenbeck, and Novin (1982) found that cutting the hepatic branch of the vagus nerve had little effect on eating. Therefore, we must conclude that even if the liver does play a role in hunger, it is not the *sole* source of hunger signals.

There is good evidence for interactions between hepatic and hypothalamic glucose receptors. Shimizu, Oomura, Novin, Grijalva, and Cooper (1983) used multibarreled glass micropipettes for recording and for microiontophoretic injection of glucose to identify glucose receptors in the brain. When they located a neuron that responded to glucose (with a decrease in response rate) they injected glucose into the hepatic portal vein. Sixty-seven percent of the hypothalamic glucose receptors also decreased their firing rate in response to hepatic portal glucose. In contrast, the hepatic portal injections inhibited the firing of only 7 percent of hypothalamic neurons that did not themselves respond to locally applied glucose. This convergence of information suggests that in the absence of either brain or liver glucose receptors, hunger can be evoked by activity of the other system.

The Role of Lipids

Calories that are ingested in excess of tissue need will be converted to fat *(lipids)*, regardless of whether the calories are ingested in the form of fats, carbohydrates, or protein. During fasting, the body's reserves of fat are broken down to glycerol and fatty acids and used as a source of energy. Hence, it is possible that fat deposits might play a role in the long-term control of food intake. There is good evidence that they do; fat deposits appear to be regulated. There is even some preliminary evidence that lipids (or other metabolites that are derived from them) may serve as system variables for the control of food intake.

System Variables. The principal fuel for diabetic animals is lipids, because these are the only nutrients that can easily enter cells without the presence of insulin. Glucose and amino acids are largely excluded. Friedman (1978) made rats diabetic by injecting them with *alloxan,* a derivative of uric acid that destroys the insulin-producing islet cells of the pancreas. These animals ate more than normal, primarily because large amounts of sugar were lost in the urine. He fed them diets that contained various concentrations of nutrients. Normal rats will respond to changes in the caloric value of their food; they will eat less of a concentrated diet, and more of a dilute diet. This pattern is true whether the calories are available as fats or carbohydrates. However, Friedman found that diabetic rats did not respond to a reduction in the amount of carbohydrates in their diet, but they greatly increased their intake if the amount of fats was reduced.

The rats were given a basal diet of fat, cornstarch, and casein (a protein found in milk). Diabetic rats ate relatively normal amounts of this diet, presumably because the fat content was high. When most of the fat content was replaced with nonnutrient petroleum jelly (Vaseline) or most of the carbohydrate content was replaced with powdered cellulose (which contains no substantial caloric value), normal rats ate more food, thus keeping their daily caloric intake relatively constant. (See **Figure 11.29.**) However, diabetic rats ate only slightly more food when the carbohydrate content of their diet was reduced. Because their blood already contained excessive amounts of unusable glucose, a reduction in dietary carbohydrates was not of any consequence. But when the fat content was reduced, they ate much more food. (See **Figure 11.29.**)

This experiment shows that food intake is modulated by available calories, whether they are in the form of carbohydrates or

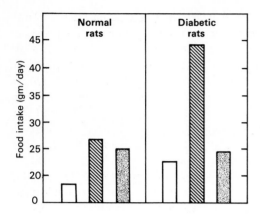

FIGURE 11.29
Effects of dilution of fats or carbohydrates in the diet on food intake of normal and diabetic rats. (From Friedman, M.I. *Journal of Comparative and Physiological Psychology,* 1978, *92,* 109–117. Copyright 1978 by the American Psychological Association. Reprinted by permission of the author.)

lipids. The experiment suggests the possible existence of "lipostats" as well as glucostats, or perhaps of receptors that respond to some intermediate product of metabolism.

Long-Term Regulation. There is good evidence that the amount of body fat is regulated. Liebelt, Bordelon, and Liebelt (1973) described a number of studies they performed to investigate the regulation of adipose tissue. They found that the body's total amount of fat appears to be regulated. When a piece of adipose tissue is transplanted from one mouse into another, the transplanted tissue normally withers away. However, when the experimenters first removed some of the adipose tissue belonging to the recipient animals, the transplants "took." In other words, when the total amount of fat tissue in the recipient mouse was surgically reduced, an implant grew—presumably in response to mechanisms encouraging growth of such tissue. Furthermore, when mice were given a brain lesion that causes overeating and subsequent obesity (more about this phenomenon later), their bodies accepted a graft of adipose tissue while they were gaining weight, as though the lesion had raised the "adipose tissue set point."

Another piece of evidence for regulation of body fat is that animals that are force-fed through a gastric tube—and hence become fat—will reduce their food intake until their weight returns to normal levels (Hoebel and Teitelbaum, 1966; Steffens, 1975). Because excess weight is carried mainly as body fat, perhaps adipose tissue produces a satiety signal when the amount of tissue exceeds some set point. The evidence for mechanisms that regulate the storage of fat seems quite convincing.

INTERIM SUMMARY

Although we often eat by habit, when we are not really hungry, the physiological event that is probably most important in starting a meal is a low level of glucose in the blood (or, in the case of diabetics, low glucose availability to the cells). Investigators have discovered glucose receptors in the brain, but when these receptors are damaged rats still regulate their food intake in response to changes in diet or metabolic requirements. Thus, these receptors cannot be the sole detectors of metabolic need.

Another set of glucose receptors is located in the liver. The liver receives blood directly from the digestive system and hence is in a location to detect when food is being absorbed. When glucose is injected into the hepatic portal vein a hungry animal stops eating, and when an infusion of 2-DG starves liver cells a satiated animal starts eating. Of course, the liver does not directly control the jaw muscles; the hepatic receptors communicate with the brain through axons that travel in the vagus nerve.

Fats also play a role in both short-term and long-term regulation. Diabetic rats, which rely principally on fats for their nutrition, eat more food when the fat content of their diet is reduced. Thus, their behavior responds to short-term signals related to lipid intake. In addition, transplants of fat tissue survive and grow only if the animal has already lost some of its body fat. Thus, mechanisms also control long-term fat storage.

What Stops a Meal?

The single most important physiological factor that *initiates* eating appears to be low glucose availability. But what signal causes the animal to *stop* eating? As we saw in the discussion of regulation at the beginning of the chapter, satiety must be anticipatory; that is, ingestive behaviors must cease even before the system variables are restored to the set point. If we ate until our supplies of nutrients were replenished, we would burst our stomachs. Evidence suggests that many factors produce satiety.

Head Factors

The head contains several sets of receptors that play a role in the control of ingestive behavior. We respond to the sight, odor, taste, and texture of food, and we can monitor the amount of food that is swallowed. Thus, head factors include vision, olfaction, gustation, and the somatosensory and kinesthetic feedback from chewing and swallowing food.

Satiety can be produced by head factors, but this effect is weak compared to the satiety that arises from the digestive system and liver. In the section on drinking we saw that a thirsty esophagotomized animal will drink until it is exhausted; thus, little or no satiety for water is produced by head factors. In contrast, when an esophagotomized animal **sham**

eats the first time, it does not eat indefinitely. Instead, it swallows a somewhat larger-than-normal meal, then stops eating (Janowitz and Grossman, 1949). However, an animal that sham eats soon returns to eat again, which indicates that the satiety produced by head factors is short-lived and normally must be superseded by satiety factors caused by the presence of food in the gastrointestinal system.

Perhaps the most important role of head factors in satiety is their provision of discriminative stimuli, which permit organisms to learn about the metabolic consequences of eating different kinds of food. Booth (1981) stressed that learning is an important component of satiety — how much we eat of a particular food depends heavily on experience. He noted that satiety is determined by the menu eaten, time of day, status of the digestive system, and boredom with the food that has just been ingested. Satiety is expressed as a slower rate of eating and a decreased reinforcing value of food. That is, at the beginning of a meal food is pleasant, and we are willing to work for it. However, at the end of a meal, food becomes unpleasant. Being forced to eat when satiated is an aversive event.

Several studies have shown that people can regulate their caloric intake but do so best when eating a familiar food. This finding suggests that we do not respond automatically to physiological signals but learn from previous consequences of eating particular foods. Booth, Mather, and Fuller (1982) fed people a three-course meal. The first course was a hot soup; the second was a plate of small sandwiches, from which the subjects could eat all they wanted; and the third was a fixed amount of gelatin dessert. The nutritional value of the soup could be altered by adding starch, which itself could not be detected by taste. Different flavorings were added to the soups, providing discriminative stimuli as to caloric content. On the first day

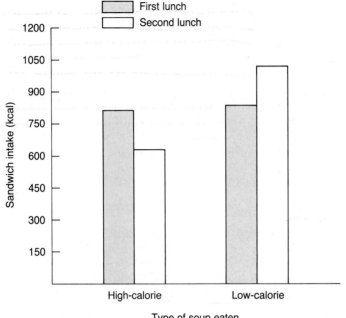

FIGURE 11.30
Sandwich intake after eating
high-calorie or low-calorie
soup. kcal = kilocalorie (often
called Calorie), the customary
measure of energy content of
food. (Data from Booth, D.A.,
Mather, P., and Fuller, J.
Appetite, 1982, *3*, 163–184.)

the subjects ate the same number of sandwiches after eating the high-calorie or low-
calorie soups — the extra calories in the soup
had no immediate effect. However, after experience with the nutritional effects of the
two kinds of lunches, their behavior began to
differentiate between the two diets; they ate
fewer sandwiches after being served the
high-calorie soup and more sandwiches after
the low-calorie soup. (See **Figure 11.30.**)
Presumably, the meal with the enriched soup
led to feelings of overfullness later, whereas
the meal with the low-calorie soup led to
later feelings of hunger. The experience
caused the subjects to adjust their subsequent
intake accordingly.

Gastric Factors
Although most people associate feelings of
hunger with "hunger pangs" in the stomach
and feelings of satiety with an impression of
gastric fullness, the stomach is not necessary
for feelings of hunger. Humans whose stom-

achs have been removed because of cancer or
the presence of large ulcers still periodically
get hungry (Ingelfinger, 1944). Of necessity,
these people eat frequent, small meals; in
fact, a large meal causes nausea and discomfort, apparently because the duodenum
quickly fills up. However, although the stomach may not be especially important in producing hunger, it does appear to play an important role in satiety.

Evidence for a Role in Satiety. It has been
known for a long time that a hungry animal
will eat less if nutrients are injected directly
into its stomach just before it is given access
to food (Berkun, Kessen, and Miller, 1952).
A much smaller effect is seen if a nonnutritive
saline solution is loaded into the stomach,
which suggests that there are receptors that
respond specifically to the presence of nutrients. There also appear to be stretch receptors whose activity will suppress food intake,
but these receptors are probably not impor-

tant when the animal eats meals of normal size. Janowitz and Hollander (1953) were able to suppress food intake by inflating a balloon that had been placed in a dog's stomach, but the stomach had to be distended more than it would be by a normal meal. Presumably, stomach distention is monitored by stretch receptors in the walls of the stomach. The two sets of receptors play different roles: the nutrient receptors mediate satiety, and the stretch receptors prevent organisms from injuring themselves by overfilling their stomachs.

Let us consider the effects of nutrients. Davis and Campbell (1973) allowed rats to eat their fill, and shortly thereafter they removed food from the rats' stomachs through an implanted tube. When the rats were permitted to eat again, they ate almost exactly the same amount of food that had been taken out. This finding suggests that animals are able to monitor the amount of food in their stomachs.

Deutsch and Gonzalez (1980) operated on rats and attached an inflatable cuff around the pylorus. When they pumped water into the cuff it would inflate and compress the pylorus, preventing the stomach from emptying. As we saw earlier, Hall and Blass used a similar device, in which a noose of fishing line could be tightened to prevent water from leaving the stomach. With their device, Deutsch and Gonzalez could confine food to the stomach, eliminating the possible influence of receptors in the intestine or liver. After observations were made, the cuff could be deflated so that the stomach would empty normally.

Each day the investigators inflated the pyloric cuff and gave the rats a 30-minute opportunity to drink a commercial high-calorie liquid diet. Because the rats had not eaten for 15 hours, they readily consumed the liquid diet. After the meal the investigators removed 5 ml of the stomach's contents through an implanted tube. On some days they replaced the contents with a saline solution, and on others they let the rats eat without intervention. The rats adjusted their food intake perfectly, compensating for the calories that were removed but ignoring the added nonnutritive saline solution. The results indicate that animals can monitor the total amount of nutrients received by the stomach. The finding that they compensated for the food that had been removed indicates that they were not simply monitoring the amount of food that they consumed. The finding that the injection of moderate amounts of a saline solution did not affect their intake indicates that they were not simply responding to the total volume of stomach contents. Finally, the use of the pyloric cuff to prevent the stomach from emptying indicates that intestinal or liver factors did not play a role.

Nature of the Gastric Receptors. How can the receptors in the stomach measure the calories present in its contents? Deutsch (1978) suggested a possible mechanism. He hypothesized that the stomach walls contain nutrient receptors whose activity is proportional to the concentration of nutrients in the stomach. Their activity produces satiety. Many of these receptors are buried deep in pits or fold of the mucous membrane that lines the stomach. As the stomach fills and expands, more and more of these receptors are exposed to the gastric contents. Thus, the concentration and quantity of nutrients can compensate for each other. A small volume of rich nutrients stimulates a high rate of firing in a small number of receptors, whereas a large volume of dilute nutrients stimulates a low rate of firing in a large number of receptors, and a large volume of rich nutrients stimulates a high rate of firing in a large number of receptors. Thus, the stomach can monitor nutrient content without using stretch receptors. (See **Figure 11.31.**)

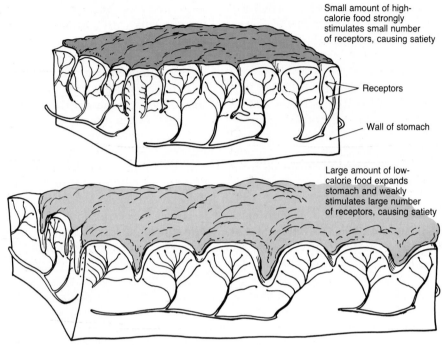

Small amount of high-calorie food strongly stimulates small number of receptors, causing satiety

Receptors

Wall of stomach

Large amount of low-calorie food expands stomach and weakly stimulates large number of receptors, causing satiety

FIGURE 11.31

Deutsch's proposed explanation for the means by which receptors in the stomach wall detect the quality and quantity of nutrients (Deutsch, 1978).

Deutsch and his colleagues have obtained evidence that the gastric receptors respond to the presence of breakdown products as food is digested. Young and Deutsch (1981) allowed hungry rats to eat a mixture of starch and water for 30 minutes. Next, they injected **phaseolamin,** an extract of white beans that inactivates **amylase,** an enzyme that breaks down starch. (Amylase is secreted in saliva and carried to the stomach when food is swallowed.) The phaseolamin injection increased the rats' starch intake by 84 percent, from 4.3 gm to 7.9 gm. In a second study, the investigators found that rats did not decrease their food intake when they injected fresh corn oil into the rats' stomachs—they acted as if no extra nutrients had been received. However, when the experimenters injected corn oil removed from the stomachs of other rats, the animals ate substantially less. Presumably,

the partially digested corn oil contained breakdown products that stimulated the receptors in the recipient rats' stomachs, whereas the raw corn oil did not.

Connections Between Stomach and Brain.
How are the signals transmitted from the stomach to the brain? The most likely route would be the gastric branch of the vagus nerve. Indeed, the signals from stretch receptors in the walls of the stomach are conveyed this way. Gonzalez and Deutsch (1981) equipped rats with pyloric cuffs and found that the animals would stop eating when they injected large amounts of saline into their stomach. Almost certainly, this inhibitory effect is not satiety but simply discomfort. The rats' stomachs were too full to accept any food. If the animals' vagus nerves were sev-

ered, though, an injection of saline into the stomach would *not* inhibit eating.

Although the signal from the stomach's stretch receptors is conveyed neurally, the signal from the stomach's nutrient receptors to the brain appears to be conveyed hormonally. Gonzalez and Deutsch found that even after the rats' vagus nerves were severed, the animals would increase their food intake to compensate for food that the experimenters had removed from their stomachs. Thus, information about nutrients in the stomach is not conveyed to the brain through the vagus nerve.

It is possible that afferent fibers through the sympathetic nerves that connect the stomach to the spinal cord may convey nutritional information to the brain, but an experiment by Koopmans (1981) suggests that the route is hormonal, not neural. He transplanted a large section of the gastrointestinal system from one rat to another: stomach, duodenum, and jejunum (the middle part of the small intestine), with the pancreas attached. (The rats were genetically identical members of an inbred strain, so there was no problem with tissue rejection.) He did *not* remove any organs from the recipient rat. He attached the end of the transplanted jejunum to the side of the recipient's own jejunum and prepared an opening into the extra stomach so that he could insert food into it. (See **Figure 11.32.**)

Koopmans found that when he infused various foods into the extra stomach, the animal

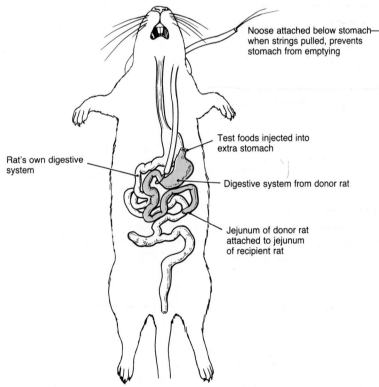

FIGURE 11.32

Implantation of an extra stomach and small intestine in a rat, performed by Koopmans (1981).

ate less than it normally would; saline injections did not have this effect. Rats whose extra stomachs received 8 ml of a commercial liquid diet ate only half as much as those whose extra stomachs received 8 ml of saline. The effect occurred even when a pyloric noose prevented food from leaving the stomach, which rules out the effects of intestinal receptors or the absorption of nutrients into the blood. Because the transplanted gastrointestinal system had no neural connection with the recipient animal, the effect must have been chemically (probably hormonally) mediated. What hormone could this be? The stomach is known to produce two peptide hormones, *gastrin* and *somatostatin.* However, Lorenz, Kreielsheimer, and Smith (1979) found that gastrin does not affect food intake, even at high doses, and the structure of somatostatin-secreting neurons in the stomach suggests that this peptide serves local functions and is not released into the general circulation (Larsson, Goltermann, Magistris, Rehfield, and Schwartz, 1979). There are four other types of cells in the stomach wall that appear to secrete hormones, but the chemicals secreted have not been identified yet (Solcia, Polak, Larsson, Buchan, and Capella, 1980). Perhaps one of them is the responsible agent.

Gut Peptides

Three peptide hormones produced by the gut have been implicated in satiety: glucagon, cholecystokinin (CCK), and bombesin. Although the status of glucagon appears to be well established, some controversy still exists about whether CCK and bombesin produce true satiety or merely suppress eating because their effects are aversive. Because the same argument has been raised against CCK and bombesin, I will discuss only CCK.

Glucagon. Glucagon is produced by the islet cells of the pancreas, but also by the gut.

Animals that receive injections of this hormone eat smaller meals (Geary and Smith, 1982). There is good evidence that the satiating effect of glucagon is mediated through the liver. Glucagon causes the conversion of liver glycogen into glucose; perhaps this glucose then stimulates hepatic glucose receptors and decreases their hunger signals. Langhans, Geary, and Scharrer (1982) measured blood glucose in the hepatic portal vein (which goes *to* the liver) and in the hepatic vein (which goes *from* the liver) in a 50-minute period before, during, and after a meal. Although the amount of glucose in the hepatic portal vein increased only slightly, the amount of glucose in the vein coming *from* the liver increased dramatically. We can infer that the source of the glucose was liver glycogen, being broken down by the action of glucagon. (See **Figure 11.33.**)

Martin, Novin, and VanderWeele (1978) observed that glucagon produced satiety only when the liver contained sufficient amounts of glycogen. In addition, cutting the vagus nerve abolished the satiating effect, which suggests that the signals are carried to the brain by means of afferent fibers in the vagus nerve. In addition, Langhans, Zieger, Scharrer, and Geary (1982) found that injection of an antibody to glucagon increased the size and duration of meals of hungry rats. Presumably, the glucagon antibody destroyed glucagon, and hence its satiating effect. The investigators also measured blood glucose in the hepatic portal vein and hepatic vein and confirmed that the antibody blocked the conversion of liver glycogen to glucose. Thus, we can conclude that glucagon produces satiety by breaking down liver glycogen to glucose.

Cholecystokinin. As we saw earlier, cholecystokinin (CCK), a hormone, is released by the duodenum when food is received from the stomach. This hormone causes the gallbladder to contract and inhibits gastric emp-

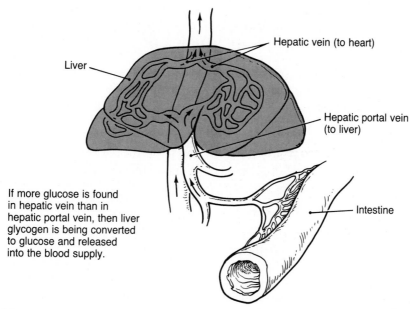

Liver

Hepatic vein (to heart)

Hepatic portal vein
(to liver)

Intestine

If more glucose is found
in hepatic vein than in
hepatic portal vein, then liver
glycogen is being converted
to glucose and released
into the blood supply.

FIGURE 11.33
The method used by Langhans, Geary, and Scharrer (1982) for measuring
the conversion of liver glycogen into glucose.

tying. Because blood levels of CCK might be expected to be related to the amount of nutrients that the duodenum receives from the stomach, perhaps CCK is monitored by the brain as a satiety signal. In fact, many studies have indeed found that injections of CCK suppress eating (Gibbs, Young, and Smith, 1973a, 1973b; Smith, Gibbs, and Kulkosky, 1982).

The suppressive effect of CCK on eating is well established. However, Deutsch and his colleagues suggest that the suppression is caused by an aversive effect, which is different from natural satiety. For example, Deutsch and Hardy (1977) gave thirsty rats drinks of flavored water. Flavors A and B were received on alternate days. Experimental rats received injections of CCK after drinking flavor A, while control rats received injections of a saline solution. No injections were paired with flavor B for either group. On the test day that followed, the rats were allowed to

choose between both flavors. Control rats drank similar amounts of both flavors: 8.6 ml of flavor A (previously paired with saline) and 8.9 ml of the unpaired flavor B. In contrast, experimental rats drank 3.3 ml of flavor A (previously paired with CCK) and 9.4 ml of flavor B. The results provide good evidence that CCK has an aversive effect. Pain or nausea are certainly different from satiety.

In response, Smith, Gibbs, and Kulkosky (1982) acknowledge that CCK can produce a conditioned aversion, but they point out that rats who have received just enough CCK to suppress their intake of food do not show the postures typically exhibited by sick animals, and that CCK does not affect the animal's rate of eating at the beginning of a meal but instead causes the meal to end earlier than it otherwise would. They note that the suppressive effects of CCK on eating are abolished by cutting the gastric branch of the vagus nerve but not by cutting the branches to the liver and pancreas. They suggest that the apparent satiety is produced when CCK stimulates receptors on smooth muscles in the stomach, causing them to contract. This contraction might then increase the rate of firing of stretch receptors in the stomach walls and send a satiety message to the brain.

The question of whether a particular physiological manipulation produces satiety or simply inhibits eating by indirect aversive effects is difficult to answer. Even after much experimental investigation, careful and conscientious researchers still disagree about why CCK suppresses eating. The issue is further complicated by the fact that even *food* can be aversive under some conditions, which has led some investigators to conclude that any manipulation that causes satiety can produce aversive effects. For example, Booth (1981) found that early in a meal rats preferred a flavor that was associated in the past with a 40-percent starch solution, but later in the meal the animals avoided the flavor. In contrast, preference remained high for a flavor that was previously associated with a more dilute 10-percent starch solution. Thus, even stimuli that are eagerly approached by a hungry animal can produce aversion when the animal is partly satiated. The controversy about the role of CCK in satiety will probably continue until investigators find a way to rule out extraneous factors and obtain unequivocal evidence.

Liver

Satiety produced by head factors and gastrointestinal factors is anticipatory in nature; that is, these factors predict the eventual restoration of the system variables that cause hunger. Food in the mouth or stomach does not restore the body's store of nutrients. Not until nutrients are absorbed from the gut are the internal system variables that cause hunger returned to normal. As we saw earlier, hunger is probably produced by low glucose availability, detected by receptors in the liver and brain. The final stage of satiety occurs here also; receipt of nutrients through the hepatic portal blood supply turns off the activity of the glucose receptors that originally signaled hunger.

A study by Stricker, Rowland, Saller, and Friedman (1977) provides evidence that hunger produced by hypoglycemia can effectively be turned off by liver receptors. The investigators injected rats with a large dose of insulin, which produces hunger. Along with the insulin they also injected the sugar glucose, fructose, or mannose or a control solution of saline. All of the sugar injections produced satiety. The crucial factor is that fructose cannot cross the blood-brain barrier; thus, this sugar does not satisfy the glucose receptors in the brain, which presumably continue to signal a lack of available nutrients. The liver *can* metabolize fructose, so apparently its influence dominates that of the brain. (See **Figure 11.34**.) In a follow-up study, Granneman and Friedman (1978) cut the vagus nerves of rats and then injected them with insulin and fructose. These animals ate; in the absence of information from the liver, glucose receptors in the brain are able to cause hunger.

As Novin, Robinson, Culbreth, and Tordoff (1983) suggest, the receptors in the liver participate in anticipatory satiety, as well as responding to nutrients in the hepatic portal blood supply. As we saw in the section on glucagon, this hormone is released early in a meal, even before nutrients are being absorbed from the intestine. If the animal's previous meal was eaten not too long ago, the liver will still contain reasonable amounts of glycogen, which the glucagon will cause to be broken down to glucose; the glucose will then turn off the hunger signals originating from the hepatic glucose receptors. However, if the previous meal was eaten some time ago, so that liver glycogen had been de-

Animal does *not eat*,
despite "hungry brain"

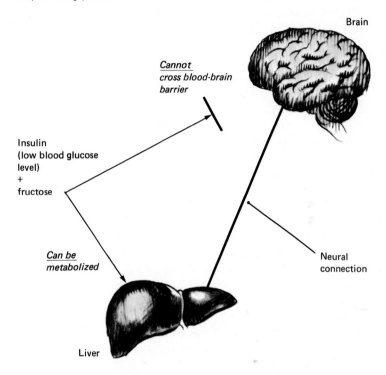

Cannot
cross blood-brain
barrier

Brain

Insulin
(low blood glucose
level)
+
fructose

Can be
metabolized

Neural
connection

Liver

FIGURE 11.34
Summary of the experiment by
Stricker and his colleagues
(1976).

pleted, the glucagon will have no effect
there, and the glucose receptors will continue to signal hunger. Thus, the liver's anticipatory satiety mechanism can be adjusted by
the animal's degree of need.

INTERIM SUMMARY

What stops a meal? Apparently, detectors in the
head, stomach, and liver. The effects of some of
these detectors are mediated both neurally and
hormonally. Head factors—sight, taste, smell,
and texture—are most important for learning the
consequences of eating a particular food. When a
particular flavor is regularly associated with a
high-calorie meal, people (and other animals)
will learn to eat less of it.

Two types of receptors in the stomach can sup-

press eating, but it appears that only one type
causes true satiety. When the stomach is overfull
(even with a nonnutritive substance), stretch receptors signal the brain, through the vagus nerve,
not to eat any more. This response is a protective
one that should not be confused with satiety. When
an animal is hungry, it eats a meal of a particular
size. If some of the food is removed from the stomach, the animal eats again to replace what has been
lost. This phenomenon occurs even when the pylorus is compressed, so we can be sure that gastric
receptors are responsible. Cutting the vagus nerve
does not abolish this response, so it appears to be
hormonal, not neural. Indeed, food placed in an
extra stomach transplanted into a recipient animal
inhibits eating. Because there is no neural connection between the extra stomach and the recipient
animal, the effect *must* be mediated chemically.

The gut secretes several peptide hormones.
One of them, glucagon, clearly plays a role in sa-

tiety. When it is released in response to a meal, it causes liver glycogen to be broken down to glucose. The glucose presumably causes satiety by stimulating receptors in the liver that send axons to the brain through the vagus nerve; the response is abolished by cutting this nerve. If the liver's supply of glycogen is low, glucagon does *not* produce satiety. Cholecystokinin, produced by the duodenum, suppresses eating. However, investigators disagree about whether it produces *satiety* or simply makes the animal feel unwell.

We already saw that the satiating effect of glucagon is mediated by the liver. In addition, receptors in the liver monitor nutrients present in the blood. A hungry rat is satiated by an injection of fructose, which can be used by the liver but not by the brain.

Neural Mechanisms

Ingestive behaviors are phylogenetically ancient; obviously, all our ancestors ate and drank or died. Thus, we should expect that the basic ingestive behaviors of chewing and swallowing are programmed by phylogenetically ancient brain circuits. Indeed, studies have shown that these behaviors can be performed by decerebrate rats, whose brains were transected between the diencephalon and the midbrain (Norgren and Grill, 1982). The decerebrate animals could even distinguish between different tastes; they drank and swallowed sweet or slightly salty liquids and spat out bitter ones. However, the brain stem mechanisms that program ingestive behavior are themselves controlled by more rostrally located mechanisms that respond to the animal's internal and external environment. Although we are far from understanding these mechanisms, some progress has been made.

Control of Eating by the Hypothalamus

Not too many years ago, textbooks proclaimed the "dual-centers" theory of eating and satiety. The lateral hypothalamus was conceived of as a "hunger center," the ventromedial hypothalamus as a "satiety center."

It is true that large lesions that include these brain regions produce undereating and overeating, respectively. However, we have learned enough about the neurological basis of feeding to know that these statements are inaccurate. The truth is simpler in some respects, and more complex in others. I will review the current status of hypothalamic involvement in hunger and satiety. As you will see, some of the mechanisms do not control feeding directly but do so indirectly, by altering the activity of the endocrine system.

The Lateral Hypothalamus. Destruction of the lateral hypothalamus affects ingestive behavior. It causes **adipsia** (absence of drinking), **aphagia** (absence of eating), and weight loss (Anand and Brobeck, 1951). Electrical stimulation of the same region elicits eating, drinking, or both. These findings led investigators to refer to this area as the "hunger center." However, investigators soon reported that rats with lateral hypothalamic lesions, if they were carefully nursed with intragastric injections of food, would gradually recover (Teitelbaum and Stellar, 1954). The recovery was characterized by several stages. First, the animals began to accept wet, very palatable food, such as water-soaked chocolate-chip cookies. Later, they would accept their normal diet, although they still would not drink. Consequently, the food had to be moist. Finally, the animals began to drink and to eat dry food. However, all the water was consumed with meals, suggesting that they only drank in order to eat (Teitelbaum and Epstein, 1962).

Although early investigators focused on changes in animals' ingestive behaviors, lateral hypothalamic lesions impair many other functions; animals with these lesions exhibit severe motor deficits. This finding led some investigators to suggest that the lack of eating and drinking was part of a general loss of behavioral functions. Not only did the animals fail to eat and drink, but they failed to groom themselves, did not right themselves when they were turned on their sides, and slid off a tilted platform onto which a normal animal could easily cling.

It now appears that the behavioral deficits result from destruction of the **nigrostriatal bundle**, a collection of dopaminergic fibers that passes through the far lateral hypothalamic area on its way from the substantia nigra to the caudate nucleus, a part of the motor system. (You will recall that degeneration of these neurons is the cause of Parkinson's disease.) Electrolytic lesions of the substantia nigra or chemical destruction of the nigrostriatal fibers with 6-hydroxydopamine (6-HD) results in aphagia, adipsia, and a decrease in movement (Ungerstedt, 1971). Other investigators have shown that these lesions also eliminate sexual, thermoregulatory, and avoidance behaviors (see Stricker, 1982, for a review). Furthermore, other lesions (such as those of the globus pallidus, another part of the motor system) produce adipsia and aphagia (Morgane, 1961) and lower the concentration of dopamine in the caudate nucleus (Anden, Fuxe, Hamberger, and Hökfelt, 1966). The nigrostriatal dopaminergic system thus appears to be important in a variety of species-typical behaviors, and not simply in ingestive behavior.

The behavior of animals that have recovered from the effects of lateral hypothalamic lesions appears to depend on the presence of remaining undamaged dopaminergic fibers. The administration of dopamine antagonists such as α-methyl-p-tyrosine(AMPT), which inhibits the synthesis of the catecholamines, or spiroperidol, which blocks dopamine receptors, reinstates the animals' adipsia, aphagia, and other motor deficits (Heffner, Zigmond, and Stricker, 1977; Marshall, 1979). On the other hand, dopamine agonists facilitate recovery (Ljungberg and Ungerstedt, 1976).

An interesting procedure also facilitates recovery of animals with lateral hypothalamic lesions: gentle tail pinching. Antelman, Szechtman, Chin, and Fisher (1975) discovered that a gentle pinch of a rat's tail with padded forceps caused the animal to begin eating immediately. There is nothing special about the tail; it merely provides a convenient place to stimulate the animal and produce mild arousal. This arousal elicits eating if food is present, drinking if water is present, fighting if another male is present, and copulation if a receptive female is present. Thus, the effects are not peculiar to eating but affect species-typical behaviors in general. Antelman, Rowland, and Fisher (1976) found that such tail pinching can reverse the effects of lesions of the lateral hypothalamus or the nigrostriatal dopaminergic system on eating. When their tails were gently pinched, the aphagic animals would begin to eat. If they were stimulated often enough, a large proportion of these animals would eat sufficient amounts of food to "nurse themselves" to recovery.

Antelman, Szechtman, Chin, and Fisher (1975) demonstrated that eating induced by tail pinching is apparently caused by stimulation of dopaminergic fibers. Drug studies showed that the effect could be blocked by dopamine antagonists but not by norepinephrine antagonists. These results confirm the general facilitative role played by dopaminergic neurons of the nigrostriatal bundle with respect to a variety of behaviors, including ingestion.

Saller and Chiodo (1980) provided evidence for a direct link between hunger signals and activity of dopaminergic neurons of the substantia nigra. These investigators found that intravenous infusions of glucose decreased the activity of these neurons. Presumably, this effect is related to the decrease in hunger that accompanies an increased blood sugar level.

These studies provide strong evidence for the participation of dopaminergic fibers passing through the far lateral hypothalamic area in a variety of behaviors, including eating and drinking. Most investigators believe that the aphagia and adipsia produced by lateral hypothalamic lesions is caused by the interruption of ascending dopaminergic fibers that pass through this area. The earlier suggestion that the lateral hypothalamus served as a "feeding center" is certainly too simple.

The Periformical Region of the Hypothalamus. Several studies have shown that infusion of very small amounts of either dopamine or epinephrine into the region of the hypothalamus in the vicinity of the fornix inhibits eating. (See **Figure 11.35.**) This phenomenon appears to be related to the ability of amphetamine to reduce appetite.

It has long been known that amphetamine is an *anorectic,* or appetite-suppressing,

drug (from *an-,* "without" and *orexis,* "appetite"). The observation that infusion of dopamine or epinephrine into the ***periformical region*** of the hypothalamus suppresses eating suggested that amphetamine may exert its anorectic effect by stimulating catecholamine receptors there (Hoebel and Leibowitz, 1981). In fact, Leibowitz (1982) found that chronic infusion of dopamine or amphetamine into the periformical region reduces rats' food intake and weight gain. In contrast, infusion of drugs that block dopamine receptors causes eating in satiated rats (Leibowitz, 1980).

Lesions of the periformical region block the anorectic effects of systemically administered amphetamine (McCabe and Leibowitz, 1980). In addition, midbrain lesions that interrupt catecholamine axons that project to this region disrupt the anorectic effect of systemic amphetamine (Ahlskog, 1974). Thus, midbrain catecholaminergic neurons appar-

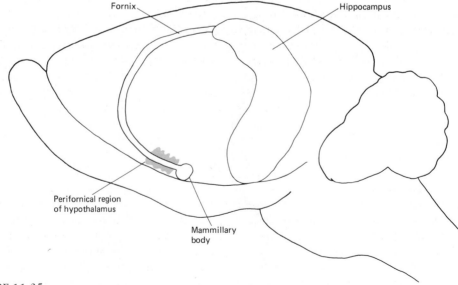

FIGURE 11.35
Infusion of dopamine or epinephrine into the periformical region of the hypothalamus inhibits eating.

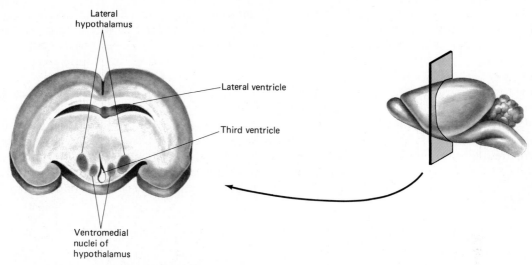

FIGURE 11.36

A frontal section through the rat brain, showing the location of the
ventromedial nucleus of the hypothalamus (VMH).

ently inhibit eating. We do not yet know
whether the inhibitory neurons secrete dopamine or epinephrine, or whether there are
some of both types of neurons. Neither do we
know the function performed by this inhibition. It will be interesting to determine the
anatomical details that underlie the mechanism by which dopamine and epinephrine inhibit eating; perhaps these investigations will
tell us something about the neural basis of
satiety.

   *The Paraventricular Nucleus of the Hypo-
thalamus.* Tumors in the hypothalamic–pituitary stalk region were long ago shown to
be associated with extreme obesity and,
often, with genital atrophy. It was later
shown that the genital atrophy resulted from
interference with gonadotropin secretion,
but the obesity was found to be an independent phenomenon. The overeating and weight
gain could be produced by lesions in the region of the ***ventromedial nucleus*** of the
hypothalamus—the VMH (Hetherington and
Ranson, 1939). (See **Figure 11.36.**)

   Many investigators concluded that the effects of VMH lesions implicated a medial
hypothalamic ''satiety center'' that comple-
mented a lateral hypothalamic ''hunger center.'' However, more recent evidence shows
that the VMH is not the critical region,
and that the effects of lesions there do not
remove satiety—they alter the animal's
metabolism.

   Gold and his colleagues (Gold, 1973;
Gold, Jones, Sawchenko, and Kapatos, 1977)
have shown that obesity is not produced by
damage to cells of the VMH but by disruption
of fibers connecting cells of the paraventricular nucleus with brain stem regions. As we saw
earlier in this chapter, the paraventricular
nucleus contains cells that produce peptide
hormones secreted by the posterior pituitary
gland, including ADH. Recent anatomical
studies have shown that the paraventricular
nucleus is subdivided into several discrete
regions, many of which have specific inputs
and outputs (Swanson and Sawchenko,
1983). The cells that control the posterior

pituitary gland are distinct from those that are involved in "VMH" obesity.

It now appears that VMH lesions produce obesity by interrupting axons that travel from the paraventricular nucleus to nuclei in the brain stem that control the activity of parasympathetic fibers of the vagus nerve: the ***dorsal motor nuclei of the vagus.*** The paraventricular nucleus also sends axons to the area around the pituitary stalk, where they apparently affect the release of hypothalamic hormones that control the secretions of the anterior pituitary gland; disruption of these fibers may also play a role. Lesions of the VMH cause a variety of hormonal effects, including an increase in insulin secretion (through the activity of the dorsal motor nuclei of the vagus) and a decrease in glucagon secretion (perhaps through indirect mechanisms involving the secretion of adrenocorticotropic hormones by the anterior pituitary gland). An animal with a high insulin and low glucagon level in its blood will overeat; this condition causes glucose and amino acids to

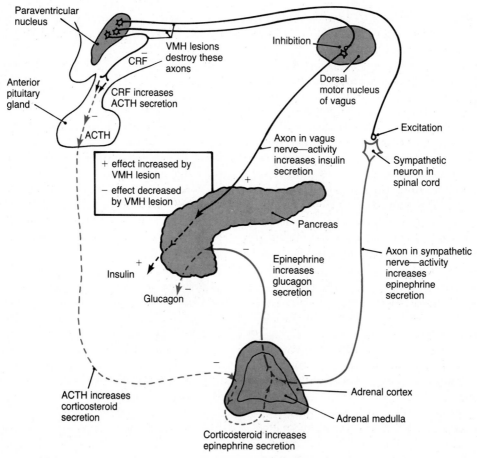

FIGURE 11.37

Effects of interruption of some efferent axons of the paraventricular nucleus on metabolism. ACTH = adrenocorticotropic hormone.

be stored away as glycogen and fats and prevents them from being used as fuel. The animal remains chronically stuck in the absorptive phase of metabolism. As a consequence, it must eat almost continuously. Because it cannot use its stored nutrients, it must exist on food being absorbed from the digestive system. (See **Figure 11.37.**)

Here is some of the relevant evidence. The details of the anatomy have been established by careful studies with horseradish peroxidase and dyes bonded to antibodies to specific peptide neurotransmitters (Swanson and Sawchenko, 1983). Infusion of small amounts of norepinephrine into the paraventricular nucleus inhibits the firing of neurons there (Moss, Urban, and Cross, 1972) and induces eating (Leibowitz, 1978). As we already saw, damage to the fibers that project to the dorsal motor nuclei of the vagus produces overeating, increases the level of insulin, and decreases the level of glucagon (Gold and Simson, 1982). As you would expect, destruction of the paraventricular nucleus itself also causes overeating (Leibowitz, Hammer, and Chang, 1981). Eating induced by injections of norepinephrine into the paraventricular nucleus is reduced by cutting the branch of the vagus nerve that innervates the pancreas. Thus, the effects could indeed be caused by changes in the secretion of insulin. It appears that the paraventricular nucleus, through its control of the secretion of insulin (and, indirectly, glucagon), normally mediates the switch from the fasting phase to the absorptive phase of metabolism. Because removal of this influence by brain lesions increases insulin secretion, the influence appears to be inhibitory.

Destruction of the noradrenergic input to the paraventricular nucleus removes this source of inhibition and results in anorexia and weight loss (Leibowitz and Brown, 1980). Food deprivation increases the release of norepinephrine in the medial hypo-thalamus (Stachowiak, Bialowas, and Jurkowski, 1978), and, conversely, injection of food into the stomach decreases its release (Myers and McCaleb, 1980). According to Novin, Robinson, Culbreth, and Tordoff (1983), the neural pathway that mediates this linkage may be the following: Receptors on the tongue and in the liver both send information to the nucleus of the solitary tract, which in turn sends fibers to the parabrachial nucleus of the pons. Both of these nuclei send axons to the paraventricular nuclei. In addition, neurons in the nucleus of the solitary tract that receive information from the liver glucose receptors also send axons directly to the dorsal motor nucleus of the vagus. (See **Figure 11.38.**) Thus, both the taste of food and the activity of glucose receptors in the liver can potentially influence the paraventricular nucleus and hence its control of insulin secretion.

INTERIM SUMMARY

Basic ingestive behaviors appear to be programmed by neural circuits in the brain stem, but these circuits are subject to controlling influences from circuits in the forebrain.

The hypothalamus appears to play some important roles in controlling ingestive behavior. Several years ago, many investigators thought that hunger was controlled by the lateral hypothalamus and satiety by the ventromedial hypothalamus, but these beliefs have been challenged by more recent evidence. Lateral hypothalamic lesions do produce aphagia and adipsia, but they also impair performance of a variety of behaviors. Most investigators believe that these lesions abolish ingestive behaviors by interrupting dopaminergic fibers that pass through the hypothalamus on their way to forebrain motor systems.

Infusion of two catecholamines, dopamine and epinephrine, into the perifornical region of the hypothalamus inhibits eating. This phenomenon appears to be the cause of the well-known anorectic effect of amphetamine. Whether the inhibition

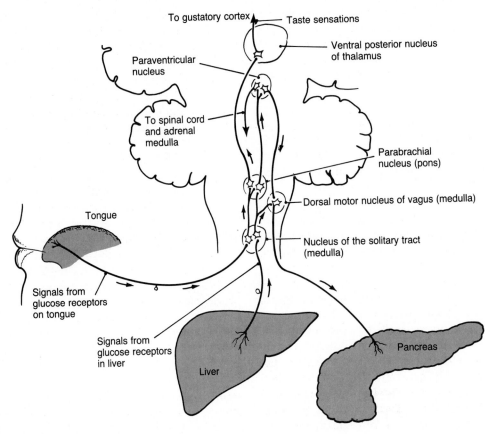

FIGURE 11.38
Interaction of sensory receptors in the tongue and liver that respond to
the presence of glucose, according to Novin, Robinson, Culbreth, and
Tordoff (1983).

of eating means that the system plays a role in satiety is not yet known.

Lesions of the region of the ventromedial nuclei
of the hypothalamus cause overeating and obesity.
Recent evidence has shown that the relevant region is actually not the VMH. Instead, the lesions
interrupt axons from the paraventricular nuclei of
the hypothalamus that synapse near the pituitary
gland and in the dorsal motor nuclei of the vagus.
The effect of these lesions is a high level of insulin
and a low level of glucagon, which causes nutrients to be stored as fat and glycogen and prevents
their utilization as sources of fuel. Thus, animals
with lesions of the paraventricular or ventromedial
nuclei must eat continuously to survive. An impor-

tant input into the paraventricular nucleus is noradrenergic, and its destruction causes anorexia and
weight loss. This system appears to be influenced
by glucose receptors in the tongue and liver.

Eating Disorders

We humans are susceptible to eating disorders. Some of us grow obese, even though
our society regards this condition as unattrac-
tive, and in spite of the higher mortality associated with being overweight. Others (especially young women) become obsessed with
leanness, eating little and increasing their ac-

tivity level until their body weight becomes extremely low — often fatally so. Has what we have learned about the physiology of appetite helped us understand these conditions?

Obesity

There are undoubtedly many causes of obesity, including learning, environmental stress, and innate or acquired differences in metabolism. The behavior of eating, like most other behaviors, is subject to modification through learning. As children, we learn to eat what is put on our plates; indeed, many children are praised for eating all that they have been given and punished for failing to do so. As we get older, our metabolic requirements decrease, and if habit causes us to continue to eat as we did when we were younger, we tend to accumulate fat. The inhibitory signals associated with food consumption are certainly not absolute; they can be overridden by habit or by the simple pleasure of ingesting good-tasting food. In fact, the typical arrangement of meals into courses followed by a dessert overcomes the influence of head factors, whose inhibitory effect tends to be specific for a particular flavor.

Weingarten (1983) demonstrated that eating can be classically conditioned in rats. He turned on a buzzer and a light (CS+) for 4½ minutes and then delivered a liquid diet during the last 30 seconds of the stimulus. The animals received six of these meals per day. Another stimulus, a tone (CS−), was turned on intermittently between meals. The conditioning procedure lasted for 11 days.

During test days following the training, food was always available. The experimenter periodically turned on CS+ and CS− and observed the animals' eating behavior. He found that the rats began eating within 5 seconds after CS+ was presented, even when they were satiated, but responded very slowly to CS−. It is possible that people's eating behav-

ior can also be classically conditioned to stimuli like the sight, sounds, and odors of preparing and serving food. Have you ever sat down to (or started cooking) a meal and found yourself suddenly getting hungry?

Mild stress may also increase food intake. As we saw earlier, gentle tail pinching causes rats to eat by increasing the activity of dopaminergic neurons. In fact, Rowland and Antelman (1976) found that rats whose tails were pinched during two daily sessions increased their caloric intake by up to 129 percent. Perhaps physical or psychological stress (even that associated with the negative aspects of obesity itself) may induce some people to overeat.

People's early experience may affect their subsequent behavior. One obvious way for early experience to cause obesity later in life is through learning to eat large meals of high-calorie food. In this way, learned overeating and consequent obesity could be passed on through subsequent generations. Evidence also suggests that some early experiences affect people's food intake by means other than learning. For example, some studies suggest that obesity early in life causes obesity later, perhaps by increasing the number of adipose cells (Knittle and Hirsch, 1968; Hirsch and Knittle, 1970). A different phenomenon was discovered by Ravelli, Stein, and Susser (1976), who examined the records of draftees in the Dutch armed forces whose mothers had been malnourished during the *Hungerwinter* of 1944–1945, caused by the German occupation. Men whose mothers had received little food during the first two trimesters of pregnancy were twice as likely as others to be obese. Jones and Friedman (1982) confirmed this phenomenon in rats by starving pregnant females during the first 2 weeks of gestation. Surprisingly, they found that only male offspring were affected and that the overeating occurred after puberty, which suggests the involvement of male sex hormones. The mechanism by which this phenomenon operates is not known.

It is now apparent that people's metabolic rates differ widely. People matched for other variables such as weight, height, age, and activity level can differ by a factor of two in their intake of food (Rose and Williams, 1961). Obviously, some people convert calories into body tissue very efficiently, whereas others "waste" their calories, presumably by losing more heat to the environment. (If activity levels are equivalent, heat production is the only other way to lose calories.) Efficient converters have great difficulty keeping slim; they have to eat a meagre diet to do so.

Sims and Horton (1968) enlisted the participation of some prison inmates in an experiment to determine the effects of overeating on body weight. The subjects, men of normal weight, were fed varied and tasty meals several times a day and were asked to eat all they could. (I doubt whether the ethics review board had too much trouble permitting this study.) Some participants ate up to 8000 calories per day, an enormous quantity for relatively sedentary people. Weight gains were modest, and at the end of the experiment the subjects had no difficulty reducing their weights to normal. In contrast, obese people usually have great difficulty losing weight. Thus, people of normal weight respond differently from obese people to increased food intake.

Griffiths and Payne (1976) obtained evidence that suggests that differences in metabolic activity are hereditary. They found that the children of obese parents weighed more than other children, even though they ate less. In an environment in which food is difficult to obtain, metabolic efficiency is clearly advantageous. For example, Whitehead, Rowland, Hutton, Prentice, Müller, and Paul (1978) reported that physically active lactating Gambian women managed to maintain a normal body weight on as little as 1500 calories per day. Obviously, in an environment where high-calorie food is cheap and plentiful, such efficiency would easily promote obesity.

Body heat is produced by metabolizing nutrients. Some of the energy is converted to heat by muscular activity, either through exercise or shivering. In addition, many animals possess specialized adipose cells that convert calories of food directly into heat. These cells are especially important for hibernating animals, who periodically increase their body temperature while remaining inactive in a cold environment and must warm up before they can wake in the spring. These specialized fat cells are rich in mitochondria, which serve as sites of fuel breakdown and heat production (Nichols, 1979). The mitochondria give the fat a brown appearance, which gives this tissue the name **brown adipose tissue.** Differences in the amount and activity of brown adipose tissue may account for some of the observed differences in people's metabolic efficiency.

Rothwell and Stock (1979) fed rats a very palatable diet consisting of supermarket "junk" foods such as potato chips and cookies, which caused them to increase their daily caloric intake greatly. Despite an average caloric increase of 80 percent, weight gain was only 27 percent higher than that of control animals. For this effect to occur, the animals would have had to increase their energy expenditure by approximately 100 percent. Indeed, their resting oxygen consumption was consistently higher than that of control animals. However, the increase was probably not caused by an increase in physical activity, because the animals were housed in pairs in small cages, and they would have had to walk 6 km per day to expend this much energy.

In rats, brown adipose tissue is located just beneath the skin of the back, between the shoulder blades. These bones are called the *scapulae;* hence the tissue is referred to as the *interscapular brown adipose tissue.* The metabolism of these cells is controlled by β-noradrenergic receptors on their membranes (Bukowiecki, Folléa, Vallières, and Leblanc, 1978); thus β-noradrenergic agonists such as norepinephrine or isoproterenol activate nonshivering thermogenesis (heat production), and β-noradrenergic antagonists such as propranolol inhibit it. Rothwell and Stock (1979) found that injections of propranolol reduced the resting oxygen consumption of the rats eating the supermarket diet, but not that of the normally fed rats. In addition, injection of norepinephrine, which activates brown adipose tissue, caused more of a temperature rise in the skin of these rats.

The study by Rothwell and Stock suggests that normal rats are protected at least partially from the effects of overeating by a compensatory increase in nonshivering thermogenesis, mediated by the activity of the brown adipose tissue. Indeed, Glick, Teague, and Bray (1981) found that a single meal increased the metabolism of brown adipose tissue by up to 200 percent. Studies have shown that genetically obese mice differ from normal mice in the thermogenic ability of their brown adipose tissue (Trayhurn, Thurlby, Woodward, and James, 1979). This finding suggests that people's differences in metabolic activity may also be a function of their brown adipose tissue. Humans do possess this tissue, but investigators still disagree about its role in obesity (Blaza, 1983; Himms-Hagen, 1980). Clearly, metabolic differences are an important cause of human obesity, but the sources of these differences are not yet known.

Anorexia Nervosa

Most people, if they have an eating problem, tend to overeat. However, some people, especially young postpubescent women, have the opposite problem: they suffer from *anorexia nervosa,* characterized by a severe decrease in eating. The word *anorexia* suggests a loss of appetite, but this is not generally true. Their limited intake of food occurs despite intense preoccupation with food and its preparation. They may enjoy preparing meals for others to consume, collect recipes, and even hoard food that they do not eat. They have an intense fear of becoming obese, and this fear continues even if they become dangerously thin. Many exercise by cycling or running, or by almost constant walking and pacing. Sometimes their control of food intake fails and they gorge themselves with food, a phenomenon known as *bulimia* (from *bous,* "ox," and *limos,* "hunger"). These episodes are usually followed by self-induced vomiting or use of laxatives, along with feelings of depression and guilt (Mawson, 1974; Halmi, 1978).

The fact that anorexia nervosa is seen primarily in young women has prompted both biological and social explanations. Because the subject matter of this book is the physiology of behavior, I will consider only the biological explanations here. It is possible that changes in a young woman's endocrine status alter her metabolism or the neural mechanisms involved in feeding. Indeed, progesterone and estradiol affect the food intake and body weight of laboratory animals through their interactions with steroid receptors in various organs, including the brain and adipose tissue (Wade and Gray, 1979). But there is no evidence yet that anorexia nervosa in humans is related to this phenomenon.

Many studies have found evidence of metabolic differences between anorexics and people of normal weight, but because prolonged fasting and the use of laxatives themselves have many effects, it is difficult to interpret these differences (Halmi, 1978). Leibowitz (1983) has suggested that one cause of anorexia nervosa may be derangement of the normal activity of the brain mechanisms that control feeding and metabolism. In particular, she suggests that the symptoms may be caused by a decrease in the activity of noradrenergic neurons in the hypothalamus. As we saw, destruction of the noradrenergic fibers that project to the paraventricular nuclei caused a chronic decrease in food intake. There is no direct evidence linking the human disorder to specific brain abnormalities, but we can hope that an understanding of the control of feeding and metabolism in experimental animals will help us understand this puzzling and dangerous disorder.

INTERIM SUMMARY

Obesity has many causes. Eating at a particular time of day, whether you are hungry or not, can become a habit. Mild stress, which increases the activity of dopaminergic neurons, may also contribute to overeating. The primary physiological cause of obesity appears to be an especially efficient metabolism, which converts calories to body fat. Differences in metabolism are probably largely inherited, but early experiences may also have an effect.

One of the ways in which calories are converted into heat is through brown adipose tissue, which contains cells rich in mitochondria. When rats are fed very palatable high-calorie diets, the overeating causes an increase in the thermogenic activity of the brown adipose tissue and hence

prevents much of the weight gain that would otherwise occur. The relevance of brown adipose tissue to obesity is suggested by the fact that its thermogenic ability in genetically obese mice differs from that found in normal mice. Whether brown adipose tissue plays a role in human obesity is still not known.

The causes of anorexia nervosa are still not known, but it is possible that the disorder may have some physiological bases. Leibowitz suggests that one cause may be underactivity of noradrenergic neurons in the hypothalamus.

Concluding Remarks

The control of ingestion is complex, primarily because so many characteristics of our interstitial fluid and the contents of our cells must be controlled: quantity of water, concentration of various solutes, amounts of nutrients stored as glycogen and triglycerides, amounts of nutrients available in the interstitial fluid, and many others. Most of the control mechanisms are hidden from us, involving detection of system variables, secretion of hormones, changes in neural activity, and consequent changes in metabolic pathways, of which we are not aware. But some of the control mechanisms involve eating and drinking, and we certainly notice their effects. To understand the causes of the overt ingestive behaviors, we must understand what is taking place inside, and research efforts have made much progress on this task in the past few decades.

NEW TERMS

absorptive phase p. 448

adipose tissue p. 449

adipsia p. 466

aldosterone p. 427

alloxan p. 455

amylase p. 460

angiotensin I p. 429

angiotensin II p. 429

angiotensinogen p. 429

anorectic p. 468

anorexia nervosa p. 475

anteroventral tip of the third ventricle p. 437

antidiuretic hormone (ADH) p. 429

aphagia p. 466

baroreceptor p. 431

bile p. 448

Bowman's capsule p. 426

brown adipose tissue p. 474

SUGGESTED READINGS

Thirst

FITZSIMONS, J.T. *The Physiology of Thirst and Sodium Appetite*. Cambridge: Cambridge University Press, 1979.

PFAFF, D.W. *The Physiological Mechanisms of Motivation*. New York: Springer-Verlag, 1982.

ROLLS, B.J., AND ROLLS, E.T. *Thirst*. Cambridge, England: Cambridge University Press, 1982.

Hunger

DARBY, P.L., GARFINKEL, P.E., GARNER, D.M., AND
COSCINA, D.V. *Anorexia Nervosa: Recent Developments in Research*. New York: A.R. Liss,
1983.

HOEBEL, B.G., AND NOVIN, D. *The Neural Basis of
Feeding and Reward*. Brunswick, Maine: The
Haer Institute for Electrophysiological Research, 1982.

PFAFF, D.W. *The Physiological Mechanisms of
Motivation*. New York: Springer-Verlag,
1982.

12

Aggressive Behavior

Almost all species of animals engage in aggressive behaviors, which involve threatening gestures or actual attack directed toward another animal. Members of each species display similar kinds of aggressive behavior, which qualifies them as species-typical behaviors. This chapter considers the neural and hormonal control of aggression and the attempts to control human violence by means of psychosurgery.

■ NATURE AND FUNCTIONS OF AGGRESSIVE BEHAVIORS

It is clear that aggression can take different forms. Several classification schemes (for example, Moyer, 1976; Brain, 1979) have been devised to categorize different types of aggression. Some of the more important types are listed below.

1. **Social aggression** is the attack of an individual animal on another member of the same species and can be stimulated by several means. The most commonly studied form of social aggression is the **intermale aggression** of rodents, which occurs when two strangers meet on neutral territory. In addition, many mammals, both male and female, exhibit **territorial aggression** when an intruder of the same sex invades the resident's territory. **Irritable aggression** can be elicited by thwarting an animal's goal-directed behavior or by pain. If a pair of normally docile animals are given a painful foot shock, they will often attack each other. This category also includes attack upon an inanimate object (for example, angry tennis players breaking their rackets). **Sex-related aggression** occurs in laboratory animals when an inexperienced male attempts to copulate with a nonestrous female, is rebuffed, and then attacks her. Human sexual behavior is usually not violent, but men have been known to attack brutally the victims of their sexual assaults. Whether human sex-related aggression should be classified with that of other animals is still an unanswered question.

2. **Self-defense** occurs when an animal is attacked by another and fights back. If an opportunity for escape exists, the animal will usually turn and flee rather than fight. Thus, self-defense is typically not the dominant behavior, but one that emerges when flight is thwarted.

3. **Maternal aggression** is displayed by a lactating mammal when disturbed near her nesting site or near her young.

4. **Infanticide** refers to the killing of very young animals by adults. As we will see, the reasons for infanticide vary.

5. **Predatory aggression** is different from all others, and some investigators do not consider it to be a form of aggression. When a lion attacks a zebra, or a fox attacks a rabbit, the predator does not appear to be angry at its prey. Even though the behavior may not be "aggressive" in this sense, it will be discussed in this chapter.

In the rest of this chapter I will discuss research on the neural and hormonal control of aggression. As you will see, not all of the behaviors that have been studied fall neatly into one of the categories listed above.

■ NEURAL CONTROL OF AGGRESSION

One of the surest signs of a species-typical behavior is the ability to produce it by means of localized brain stimulation. Indeed, three forms of attack can be elicited by such stimulation. As we will see, these behaviors are organized and controlled by different neural pathways.

Species-Typical Nature of Attack

The target of an animal's attack can certainly be modified by experience, and the method an animal uses to kill its prey or subdue another member of its own species is improved with practice, but the basic patterns of behavior do not appear to have to be learned. That is to say, the behavior patterns are species typical. A cat kills a rat with an efficient bite to the back of the neck but attacks another cat with its claws. A male deer attacks a rival with his horns but defends himself against a predator with his hooves. A mouse chases a cockroach and kills it by biting its head off.

Predatory attack is the means by which some animals obtain food. Thus, it is obviously closely related to feeding behavior, but the behaviors of eating and predatory attack are clearly controlled by different neural systems. Although Paul, Miley, and Baenninger (1971) found that food deprivation increases the probability of spontaneous mouse killing in rats, Karli (1956) found that some rats never became killers but would starve to death in the presence of live mice — even if they had previously learned to eat dead ones.

Moyer and his colleagues attempted to teach rats to attack mice. They chose a group of rats that did not spontaneously kill mice and rewarded them for attacking a mouse. (Some rats do spontaneously kill mice and therefore do not have to be taught.) As Moyer (1976) reported, "It is relatively easy to induce the rat to chase, harass, and nip at the mouse. However, although we have tried repeatedly we have been unable to induce mouse killing by this procedure" (p. 15). Although Moyer and his colleagues failed to teach rats to kill mice, evidence that will soon be presented here suggests that the neural circuitry that controls attack is present even in the brains of rats that do not normally kill mice. Many studies have shown that animals that do not spontaneously attack others will immediately do so if the appropriate region of their brain is electrically stimulated. Presumably, some individual animals do not attack

because their neural mechanisms are not easily aroused by the sight of a mouse.

Another piece of evidence that supports the contention that some forms of attack are inborn, species-typical behaviors is the observation that frog killing is not observed in rats until they reach the age of 50 days, and that prior experience with frogs does not alter the time at which the behavior emerges. Johnson, DeSisto, and Koenig (1972) raised rats and frogs in a bathtub. The rats lived on a raft floating in the water. Young rats did not molest the frogs when they climbed onto the platform. However, once they reached 50 days of age, they began killing the frogs. As the authors put it: "Rats began to patrol the edge of the platform in an effort to snare passing frogs, and they became so skillful that replacement frogs were quickly captured and devoured" (Johnson et al., 1972, p. 239). The age at which the attacks began was the same when the rats were not raised with frogs. Thus, it appears that the emergence of this behavior is controlled by maturational factors, such as development of the nervous system, or by the activational effects of a hormone secreted in adulthood.

Attack Elicited by Electrical Brain Stimulation

Electrical stimulation of localized regions of the brain can elicit at least three types of aggressive behavior: *affective attack,* predatory attack, and fear-induced aggression. Although electrical stimulation occasionally produces only elements of attack or a half-hearted display of aggression, full-blown attack, when it occurs, appears identical to that which is elicited naturally.

Affect (as a noun) refers to positive or negative feelings. Affective attack is dramatic and certainly indicates strong feelings. Cats who display this behavior adopt a "Halloween-cat" posture, with arched back, erect fur on the back and neck, dilated pupils, and bared teeth. If another cat is nearby, it will be attacked. However, rather than have one cat attack another, experimenters use rats to serve as subjects of the aggression. When the current is passed through the electrode the cat will viciously attack a nearby rat with its claws, sometimes screaming as it does so. If the stimulation continues, the cat will often begin biting the rat. We cannot know how the cat feels, but it acts as if it were extremely angry. Affective attack probably constitutes the behavior seen during social and maternal aggression.

Predatory attack is quite different from affective attack. Predation is not accompanied by a strong display of rage. The cat stalks the rat and suddenly pounces on it, directing powerful bites to the head and neck region. The cat does not growl or scream, and it stops attacking once the rat ceases to move. This type of attack appears more cold-blooded and ruthless than affective attack. (It is more likely to kill the rat, too.) It may seem surprising that a cat should need any special treatment to induce it to attack a rat, but most laboratory cats do *not* spontaneously attack rats.

As I mentioned earlier, predation obtains food, but it is not exactly synonymous with feeding. Hutchinson and Renfrew (1966) found that brain stimulation that elicited eating in cats would also produce predatory attack on rats if the intensity of the stimulating current was increased. However, the animals did *not* eat the rats they killed. Roberts and Kiess (1964) implanted stimulating electrodes in the brains of cats in a location that produced predatory attack. The cats learned to run through a maze in order to obtain a rat to attack, but they would do so only while the brain stimulation was turned on. When it was off, they would not seek out the rat. When stimulation was turned on, a hungry cat would even leave a dish of food to run

through the maze and attack the rat, which it would not subsequently eat. Therefore, predatory attack is not synonymous with feeding. It provides a means for carnivores to obtain food, but the neural mechanisms for attack and eating are different.

If you have ever watched a cat stalk and pounce on a bird or rodent you will agree that the animal acts as if the behavior were enjoyable. In contrast, animals who are fighting do not act as if they were ''happy.'' Panksepp (1971a) observed a significant difference in rats' preference for receiving electrical brain stimulation that elicits predatory attack or affective attack. If he turned on the stimulation that produced affective attack but permitted the rats to press a lever to turn it off, they quickly learned to do so. Thus, brain stimulation that elicits affective attack appears to be aversive. In contrast, rats quickly learned to press a lever that turned *on* stimulation that elicited predatory attack. Thus, brain stimulation that elicits predatory attack appears to be reinforcing. Furthermore, injections of amphetamine accentuated affective attack but diminished predatory attack (Panksepp, 1971b). These physiological data only reinforce the behavioral differences between these two forms of electrically elicited attack.

Self-defense is seen when an animal is frightened and is prevented from escaping. Electrical brain stimulation can elicit vigorous attempts to run and hide, and an experimenter who is so foolish as to get between the animal and its means of escape will get clawed or bitten. However, the primary effect of the stimulation is to induce flight, not attack.

Neural Control of Aggression

As we will see, the neural control of aggression is hierarchical. That is, the particular muscular movements are programmed by neural circuits in the midbrain and brain stem but are controlled by other circuits. Whether an animal attacks depends on many factors, including the nature of the eliciting stimuli in the environment and the animal's previous experience. The activity of the midbrain and brain stem circuits appears to be controlled by the hypothalamus, which also influences many other species-typical behaviors. The limbic system also modulates aggressive behaviors, partly through its influence on the hypothalamus. And, of course, the activity of the limbic system is controlled by perceptual systems that detect the status of the environment, including the presence of other animals.

Hypothalamus and Midbrain

Attack can most readily be elicited by electrical stimulation of the hypothalamus and mid-brain. In general, stimulation of the medial hypothalamus produces affective attack, and stimulation of the lateral hypothalamus produces predation. These effects appear to be true for cats (Flynn, Vanegas, Foote, and Edwards, 1970), opossums (Roberts, Steinberg, and Means, 1967), monkeys (Delgado, 1969), and rats (Panksepp, 1971a). Furthermore, stimulation of the dorsal hypothalamus often produces flight: the animal breathes rapidly, its pupils dilate, it might urinate or defecate, and it exhibits frantic attempts to escape the chamber in which it is confined (Clemente and Chase, 1973). If restrained, the animal will frequently attack in an attempt to flee.

Hypothalamic stimulation appears to produce attack by increasing the activity of axons that project caudally. (See **Figure 12.1.**) Af-

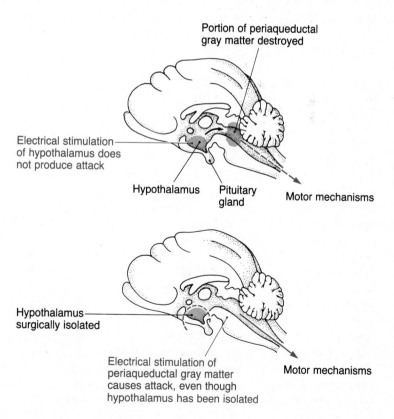

FIGURE 12.1
The effects of electrical stimulation of the hypothalamus on aggressive behavior are mediated by circuits in the midbrain and brain stem.

Portion of periaqueductal gray matter destroyed

Electrical stimulation of hypothalamus does not produce attack

Hypothalamus   Pituitary gland

Motor mechanisms

Hypothalamus surgically isolated

Electrical stimulation of periaqueductal gray matter causes attack, even though hypothalamus has been isolated

Motor mechanisms

fective attack appears to be produced by a circuit from the medial hypothalamus to the periaqueductal gray matter of the midbrain. Like medial hypothalamic stimulation, stimulation of the ventrolateral periaqueductal gray matter elicits affective attack (Skultety, 1963; Edwards and Flynn, 1972). As we saw, predatory attack can be elicited by stimulation of the lateral hypothalamus. The next step in the pathway that mediates this behavior appears to involve the ventral tegmental area. Neurons in the lateral hypothalamus send axons to the ventral tegmental area (Fuchs, Dalsass, Siegel, and Siegel, 1981), and stimulation there produces predatory attack (Bandler, Chi, and Flynn, 1972). Lesions that disconnect the hypothalamus from the midbrain abolish both the affective attack and the predation elicited by hypothalamic stimulation. However, animals with hypothalamic lesions will continue to attack prey or react aggressively in response to electrical stimulation of the periaqueductal gray matter or to a tail pinch, although their behavior will not be as vigorous (Ellison and Flynn, 1968; Berntson and Micco, 1976). Thus, the effects of hypothalamic stimulation are transmitted "downstream" to the periaqueductal gray matter and the ventral tegmentum. As we saw, flight is elicited by stimulation of the dorsal hypothalamus. This behavior, too, is undoubtedly mediated by motor systems caudal to the hypothalamus, but their location is not known.

MacDonnell and Flynn (1966) demonstrated the facilitative effect of hypothalamic stimulation on a reflex that appears to be a component of predatory attack. They observed that a cat normally turns its head away when a stick is touched to the side of its cheek. However, when they simultaneously stimulated the cat's hypothalamus through an electrode that normally elicited a predatory attack, the animal instead turned toward the stick so that the object met its lips. When this

contact occurred, the cat's mouth opened. (See **Figure 12.2.**) At low levels of stimulation, a rather small region of the cat's face produced this set of responses when touched, but as the intensity increased, the sequence could be elicited by touching the cat farther and farther from the front of its mouth.

Bandler and Flynn (1972) observed a similar interaction in a reflex component of affective attack. They found that when a cat's lateral hypothalamus was electrically stim-

Most extensive region from which head-orienting response could be elicited during brain stimulation

Region from which jaw-opening response could be elicited during brain stimulation

FIGURE 12.2
Tactile stimuli applied to the cat's face cause head turning or mouth opening during electrical stimulation of the hypothalamus. (From MacDonnell, M.F., and Flynn, J.P. *Science,* 1966, *152,* 1406–1408. Copyright 1966 by the American Association for the Advancement of Science.)

ulated, it showed a reflexive striking movement when a specific region of its front leg was touched. When they increased the intensity of the hypothalamic stimulation, the reflex could be elicited by touching more widespread areas of the cat's leg. The reflex could be triggered by touching either leg, but a more vigorous reaction was produced by touching the leg contralateral to the hypothalamic stimulation.

The effects of midbrain stimulation appear to be mediated directly by brain stem motor mechanisms, and not by the motor cortex. When electrical stimulation of a cat's midbrain causes it to attack a rat with its claws, it strikes out with the forepaw contralateral to the stimulating electrode. Flynn, Vanegas, Foote, and Edwards (1970) reported that even after a cat's pyramidal tract was cut on

the same side of the brain as the stimulating electrode, the animal continued to use the contralateral forepaw, not the ipsilateral one. Because the ipsilateral pyramidal tract was cut, the movement could not have been mediated by the motor cortex. (See **Figure 12.3**.)

Amygdala

The amygdaloid complex is located in the rostromedial temporal lobe in humans, and in analogous locations in other mammals. It contains several nuclei, divided into two principal groups: the ***corticomedial group*** (phylogenetically older) and the ***basolateral group*** (evolved more recently). Neurons in the corticomedial group send axons through the ***stria terminalis*** to the hypothalamus and other forebrain structures,

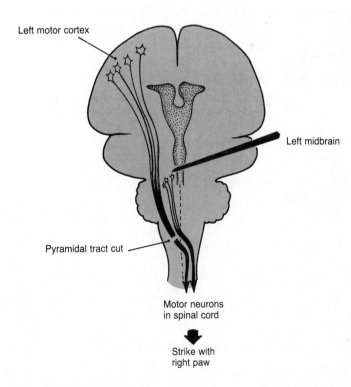

FIGURE 12.3
Even after the pyramidal tract is cut on one side of the brain, electrical stimulation of the midbrain causes the cat to strike with its contralateral paw; thus, the "aggression circuits" of the midbrain connect directly with lower motor systems.

while neurons in the basolateral group send axons through the more diffuse ***ventral amygdalofugal pathway*** (*amygdalofugal* means "amygdala-fleeing"). The ventral amygdalofugal pathway reaches the hypothalamus, preoptic region, and septal nuclei, and also sends fibers to the midbrain tegmentum and periaqueductal gray matter. The amygdala receives inputs from the olfactory system, temporal neocortex, thalamus, midbrain, and hypothalamus. Electrical recordings have shown that the amygdala is responsive to a variety of sensory stimuli. The anatomy of the amygdala thus provides a basis for its role in modulating hypothalamic-midbrain mechanisms in aggressive and defensive behavior. (See **Figure 12.4.**)

The corticomedial amygdala appears to play a role in the control of predatory attack. Its influence is inhibitory. Vergnes (1975) found that 88 percent of her rats with lesions of this region began attacking mice after being deprived of food for 3 days. In contrast, only 16 percent of the hungry control rats did

so. Thus, the lesions appear to have removed inhibitory control. In a subsequent study, Vergnes (1976) found that lesions of the stria terminalis, which conveys the efferent axons of the corticomedial amygdala, also facilitated predatory attack. However, affective attack was not altered.

A study by Bolhuis, Fitzgerald, Dijk, and Koolhaas (1984) obtained evidence that the corticomedial amygdala plays a special role in affective attack. When an animal suffers a defeat from an opponent, the next time it confronts that animal or another dominant male, it is less likely to fight and more likely to act submissively. The investigators arranged fights between males and bilaterally destroyed the corticomedial amygdala of the animal that was defeated. They found that the next time the animal met the opponent, it fought just as much as it did previously; it did *not* show submissive behavior. Thus, the corticomedial amygdala appears to be necessary for learning to be submissive after losing a fight.

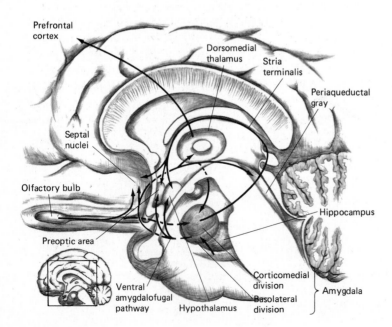

FIGURE 12.4

The amygdaloid complex and some of its important afferent and efferent connections.

The principal role of the basolateral amygdala in aggressive behavior appears to be an excitatory influence on affective attack. Stimulation of the basolateral amygdala produces affective attack, and lesions of the lateral nucleus (a part of the basolateral group) decrease the affective attack elicited by footshock but do not affect predatory attack (Hilton and Zbrozyna, 1963; Vergnes, 1976). Hilton and Zbrozyna found that electrical stimulation of the amygdala produced affective attack even after the stria terminalis had been cut. Thus, the excitatory influence of the basolateral amygdala must be conveyed by the ventral amygdalofugal pathway. The influence could be mediated by connections with the hypothalamus, the periaqueductal gray matter, or both.

As we saw in Chapter 10, the amygdala contains estrogen and androgen receptors and receives input from the primary and accessory olfactory systems. Lesions of the amygdala reduce a male hamster's attraction to the odor of the urine of receptive females and remove the inhibitory effects of the odor of rat pups on the behavior of virgin female rats. As we will see in Chapters 13 and 14, the amygdala plays a role in learning about dangerous or reinforcing stimuli. With the evidence presented in this chapter, we can conclude that the amygdala is at least partly responsible for the expression of species-typical and learned responses that have emotional significance to the animal. Future studies will have to focus on specific nuclei, which have specific inputs and outputs, and undoubtedly have specific roles.

Septum

In some species, the septum appears to exert an inhibitory influence on aggressive behaviors. Electrical stimulation of the septum inhibits attack elicited by hypothalamic stimulation in cats, which suggests that it plays an inhibitory role (Siegal and Skog, 1970).

Brady and Nauta (1953) found that septal lesions produce a profound lowering of a rat's "rage threshold." Animals with these lesions show signs of extreme emotional arousal if someone approaches their cage, and they will usually scream and jump wildly around the cage if the experimenter pokes at them with a stick or disturbs them with a puff of air. If someone is so foolhardy as to put a hand into their cage, the rats will launch a vicious, bloody attack on it. (One of my most memorable experiences as an undergraduate student was to watch an escaped rat with bilateral lesions of the septum chase two laboratory instructors around the animal room.) However, this increased emotionality subsides within a couple of weeks. Gotsick and Marshall (1972) found that the speed with which the syndrome disappears seems to be a function of environmental variables; for example, handling promotes its disappearance. (As you might expect, an investigator wears thick gloves while handling rats with septal lesions.)

Other rodents, such as mice (Slotnick, McMullen, and Fleischer, 1974), show increases in flight behavior rather than affective aggression when the septum is destroyed. A mouse with bilateral septal lesions will jump wildly around in its cage if it is disturbed, which means that the mouse is difficult to catch if (perhaps I should say *when*) it escapes. These animals will not attack a human, although they will attempt to bite if they are held. In contrast with rats, these animals remain hyperemotional indefinitely; in fact, they get better at escaping if they are handled repeatedly. If a battle is staged between a normal mouse and one with bilateral septal lesions, the brain-damaged animal will invariably lose (Slotnick and McMullen, 1972). Thus, these animals cannot be called "aggressive."

The hyperemotionality (increased aggressiveness or fearfulness) seen in rodents with lesions of the septum is not seen in most other animals; some investigators report slightly increased rage in cats with septal lesions (Moore, 1964), whereas others find that some of these cats act more affectionate (Glendenning, 1972). Monkeys apparently show no change in emotionality after septal lesions (Buddington, King, and Roberts, 1967). The effects of these lesions appear to depend upon the species involved; therefore, no general statement can be made about the role of the septum in emotional behavior.

INTERIM SUMMARY

Aggressive behaviors are species typical and serve useful functions most of the time. Social aggression involves intraspecific attack; it includes intermale aggression on neutral territory, territorial aggression in defense of one's own turf, irritable aggression induced by pain or frustration, and sex-related aggression directed by a male toward a reluctant female. Other forms of aggression include self-defense, maternal aggression, infanticide, and predatory aggression.

Electrical stimulation of the brain can produce three types of aggression: affective attack (similar to that seen in social aggression), predatory attack, and fear-induced aggression (similar to self-defense). Predatory attack elicited by electrical brain stimulation is not simply an adjunct of eating; hungry cats who receive such stimulation will leave a dish of food to attack a rat.

Attack can be elicited by electrical stimulation of the hypothalamus, amygdala, or midbrain. Stimulation of the lateral hypothalamus usually produces predation, stimulation of the medial hypothalamus usually produces affective attack, and stimulation of the dorsal hypothalamus usually produces flight (and fear-induced aggression, if the animal's escape is thwarted). The effects of hypothalamic stimulation appear to be mediated by axons that travel to the midbrain: from the medial hypothalamus to the ventrolateral periaqueductal gray matter, and from the lateral hypothalamus to the ventral tegmental area. The projections

of the dorsal hypothalamus that are responsible for flight are not yet known.

The amygdala is also involved in aggression. The corticomedial amygdala inhibits predatory attack through the connections of the stria terminalis with the basal forebrain, and it also appears to be involved in learning submissive behavior. The basolateral amygdala appears to facilitate affective attack through the connections of the ventral amygdalofugal pathway with the hypothalamus and midbrain. Estrogen and androgen receptors in the amygdala undoubtedly mediate the influences of these classes of hormones on species-typical behaviors, including aggression. The septum, too, plays some role in aggression, but exactly what this role is has not been determined.

■ HORMONAL CONTROL OF AGGRESSION

With the exception of self-defense and predatory aggression, most instances of aggression are in some way related to reproduction. Thus, we might expect that most forms of aggression, like mating, are affected by hormones.

Intermale Aggression

Androgens
Adult males of many species fight for territory or access to females. In laboratory rodents, androgen secretion occurs prenatally, decreases, and then increases again at the time of puberty. Intermale aggressiveness also begins around the time of puberty, which suggests that the behavior is controlled by neural circuits that are stimulated by androgens. Indeed, many years ago Beeman (1947) found that castration reduced aggressiveness and that injections of testosterone reinstated it. However, animals do not *require* androgens to engage in aggressive behavior. Maruniak, Desjardins, and Bronson (1977) found that dominant male mice that had already won fights with other males continued to display

aggressiveness and maintain their dominance after they were castrated.

We saw in Chapter 10 that early androgenization has an *organizational effect*. The secretion of androgens early in development modifies the developing brain, making neural circuits that underlie male sexual behavior more responsive to testosterone. Similarly, early androgenization has an organizational effect that stimulates the development of testosterone-sensitive neural circuits that facilitate intermale aggression. Conner and Levine (1969) compared intermale aggression in rats that had been castrated immediately after birth with that of rats that were not castrated until after puberty. Injections of testosterone produced aggression only in the rats that had been castrated later in life; the injections were ineffective in those that had been castrated neonatally. Thus, the testosterone had an *activational effect* only in those animals in which an organizational effect had occurred. Edwards (1968) found that androgen-sensitive neural circuits could be masculinized in females. He found that injections of testosterone during adulthood increased the aggressiveness of female mice that had received an injection of testosterone immediately after birth. However, females that had received placebo injections immediately after birth did *not* respond to injections of testosterone as adults. (See **Figure 12.5.**)

More recent evidence has shown that prolonged administration of testosterone will eventually induce intermale aggression even in rodents that were castrated immediately after birth. Data reviewed by vom Saal (1983) show that exposure to androgens early in life decreases the amount of exposure that is necessary to activate aggression later in life. Early androgenization *sensitizes* the neural circuits, and the earlier the androgenization, the more effective the sensitization. Thus, the organizational effect of androgens on intermale aggressiveness is not an all-or-none phenomenon.

As we saw in Chapter 10, androgens stimulate male sexual behavior by interacting with androgen receptors in neurons located in the medial preoptic area. This region appears also to be important in mediating the effects of androgens on intermale aggression. Bean

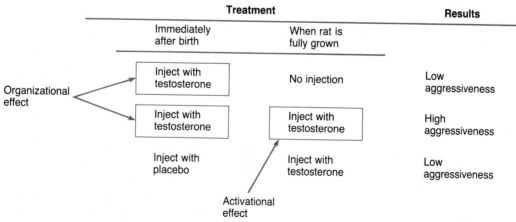

FIGURE 12.5

Organizational and activational effects of testosterone on social aggression demonstrated by Conner and Levine (1969).

and Conner (1978) found that implanting testosterone in the medial preoptic area reinstated intermale aggression in castrated male rats. Presumably, the testosterone directly activated the behavior by stimulating the androgen-sensitive neurons located there.

Androgens do not appear to have direct effects on self-defense. Adams (1983) found that male and female rats respond similarly to opponents that attack them. In addition, Korn and Moyer (1968) reported that males and females do not differ in their response to handling by an experimenter.

Males usually do not attack females. The inhibition appears to be caused by a female's odor; Dixon and Mackintosh (1971) found that the application of urine of female mice prevented intermale aggression. Dixon (1973) found that the urine had to be painted on the male mice; the airborne odor of female urine had no effect on fighting. Evans, Mackintosh, Kennedy, and Robertson (1978) attempted to extract and analyze the compound responsible for the inhibitory effect. They were not able to identify the substance, but they did establish that it was not very volatile. This finding confirms Dixon's observation that it was effective only at close range. As we saw in Chapter 10, the accessory olfactory system, which mediates some effects of pheromones, sends axons to the medial nucleus of the amygdala. It would be interesting to determine whether damage to the accessory olfactory system or medial nucleus would abolish the antiaggression effect of female urine.

Adrenal Corticosteroids and ACTH

Hormones other than testosterone appear to affect intermale aggression. Harding and Leshner (1972) found that adrenalectomy decreased the aggressiveness of male mice. Walker and Leshner (1972) found that administration of *corticosterone,* an important hormone secreted by the adrenal cortex, restored the aggressiveness of adrenalecto-

mized mice. We cannot conclude that the decreased aggression of adrenalectomized mice was a result of decreased corticosterone levels, though, because the procedure causes changes in the levels of at least two other hormones besides those produced by the adrenal glands: (1) A fall in adrenal glucocorticoids such as corticosterone leads to a compensatory increase in *adrenocorticotropic hormone (ACTH),* the pituitary hormone that stimulates the adrenal glands to produce corticosteroids. Normally, the adrenal glands respond to the ACTH, and the rise in glucocorticoid level in the blood inhibits the further secretion of ACTH. However, adrenalectomy prevents the production of glucocorticoids, so the level of ACTH remains high. (2) High levels of ACTH suppress production of testosterone (Bullock and New, 1971). Because testosterone is involved in intermale aggression, a fall in this hormone could be responsible for the inhibitory effects of adrenalectomy on aggressiveness. (See **Figure 12.6.**)

Leshner, Walker, Johnson, Kelling, Kreisler, and Svare (1973) performed a series of experiments to determine whether ACTH directly decreased intermale aggressiveness. They adrenalectomized and castrated a group of mice and gave the animals controlled amounts of corticosterone and testosterone. Because the investigators controlled the amounts of corticosterone and testosterone the subjects received, variations in the levels of these hormones could not affect the results. When, in addition to corticosterone and testosterone, the investigators also administered ACTH, the animals' aggressiveness declined; thus, we must conclude that ACTH itself has an inhibitory effect on aggression.

Subsequent studies suggest that both ACTH and corticosterone play specific roles in regulating an animal's aggressiveness. Leshner (1975) noted that Bronson and Eleftheriou (1964, 1965a, 1965b) had found that when a male mouse was defeated in a fight with an-

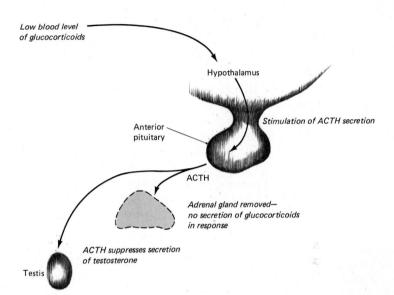

Low blood level
of glucocorticoids

Hypothalamus

Anterior
pituitary

Stimulation of ACTH secretion

ACTH

Adrenal gland removed—
no secretion of glucocorticoids
in response

ACTH suppresses secretion
of testosterone

Testis

FIGURE 12.6
Adrenalectomy indirectly
suppresses testosterone
secretion.

other male, its levels of ACTH and cortico-sterone increased. Thus, he hypothesized that these hormones may be at least partly responsible for the decreased aggressiveness and increased submissiveness shown by defeated animals. To test this hypothesis, Nock and Leshner (1976) performed several experiments to control each of the relevant hormones so that their effects on aggression and submission could be assessed. They found that the two hormones had different but complementary effects: ACTH decreased aggressiveness, and corticosterone increased submissiveness.

Social Aggression by Females

Many researchers have asserted that in most species, females are less aggressive than males. Indeed, when two adult female rodents meet in a neutral territory, they are unlikely to fight, whereas adult males are very likely to do so. However, when a female mouse meets an *immature* mouse in a neutral territory, it is just as likely as a male to attack it, and if a lactating mouse enters a cage of females who have been reared together, they will attack her and drive her away (Floody, 1983). Presumably, aggression by females has evolutionary consequences just as aggression by males does: in times of competition for territory and resources, only the fittest animals successfully reproduce. Indeed, studies have shown that low-status females are generally less fertile, and fewer of their offspring survive (Zimen, 1976; Drickamer, 1974). Now that more research effort is being devoted to aggression by females, investigators are abandoning the belief that females are invariably less aggressive than males.

The females of some species of mammals are more aggressive than males. For example, female hamsters are aggressive at all times except during estrus. Their aggressiveness is apparently not hormone dependent. Indeed, the only effect that hormones have on this behavior is inhibitory. Floody and Pfaff (1977) found that after being ovariectomized, female hamsters were continuously aggressive. Because the operation eliminated their period of estrus, it also eliminated their period of nonaggressiveness. When the experimenters administered estradiol and progesterone (the hormones that produce estrus), the animals became both sexually receptive and nonaggressive. Injections of estradiol, progesterone, or testosterone alone had no effect. The investigators suggested that the inhibitory effects of estradiol and progesterone on aggression are indirect—the hormones stimulate sexual behavior, which competes with aggressiveness.

Females of some primate species (for example, rhesus monkeys and baboons) are more likely to engage in fights around the time of ovulation (Carpenter, 1942; Saayman, 1971). This phenomenon is probably caused by their increased sexual interest and consequent proximity to males. As Carpenter noted, "She actively approaches males and must overcome their usual resistance to close association, hence she becomes an object of attacks by them" (p. 136). Another period of fighting occurs just before menstruation (Sassenrath, Powell, and Hendrickx, 1973; Mallow, 1979). During this time, females tend to attack other females. The story in chimpanzees is different; around the time of ovulation, sexually receptive females are *less* likely to be attacked by dominant animals (Crawford, 1940).

Researchers have studied the possibility that irritability and aggressiveness may increase in women just before the time of menstruation, as it does in some other primate species. Floody (1983) reviewed the literature on the so-called *premenstrual syndrome (PMS)*. Almost all studies that observed actual aggressiveness, primarily of women in institutions, found decreases around the time of ovulation and increases just before menstruation. Clearly, the changes in irritability are not universal; some women experience little or no mood shift before menstruation. And even if changes in mood occur, most women do not actually become aggressive. Whereas women with a history of criminal behavior (such as those in prison) may indeed exhibit premenstrual aggressiveness, emotionally stable women may fail to show even a small increase in aggressiveness (Persky, 1974). Depending on their history and temperament, different people respond differently to similar physiological changes.

I mentioned previously that female rodents are just as likely as males to attack juveniles. This behavior appears to be under the control of androgens. Gray, Whitsett, and Ziesenis (1978) found that ovariectomy abolished attacks of female mice on juveniles. Injections of estradiol or progesterone did not reinstate the behavior, but injections of testosterone did. Therefore, the small amount of testosterone produced by the ovaries appears to stimulate the attack of female mice on juveniles.

When groups of male and female rats are housed together, males will attack strange adult males that enter their home cage, and females will attack strange adult females. As we have seen, intermale aggression is stimulated by testosterone. However, the aggressive attack of a female rat on another female is not stimulated by testosterone unless the female's brain was masculinized by an injection of testosterone immediately after birth (vom Saal, 1979).

DeBold and Miczek (1984) attempted to determine whether ovarian hormones played a role in interfemale aggression. They raised rats in groups of four: two males and two females. They tested their aggressiveness by removing the less aggressive male and the less aggressive female and introducing either a male or a female intruder. The male attacked only the male, and the female attacked only the female. In addition, females (but not males) attacked castrated males that had been given injections of estradiol and progesterone; presumably this treatment made them resemble females.

The investigators then removed the experimental animals' gonads to determine whether gonadal hormones affected their tendency to attack. As expected, castration decreased males' tendency to attack male intruders but did not increase their tendency to attack females. Ovariectomy had no effect; the females continued to attack female intruders but did not attack males. (See **Figure 12.7.**) The results of this study indicate that unlike intermale aggression, interfemale aggression is not stimulated by gonadal hormones. Whether other hormones affect this behavior remains to be determined.

So far I have been discussing the *activational* effects of hormones on aggression by females. Do hormones normally have an *organizational* effect on this behavior? As we saw

in the previous section, injections of testosterone immediately after birth will organize malelike aggressiveness in females, but of course this is not a *normal* effect of hormones. However, prenatal androgenization can occur naturally and can have effects on subsequent aggressiveness in adulthood.

Most rodent fetuses share their mother's uterus with brothers and sisters, arranged in a row like peas in a pod. A female mouse may have zero, one, or two brothers adjacent to her. Researchers refer to these females as 0M, 1M, or 2M, respectively. (See **Figure 12.8.**) Being next to a male fetus has an effect on a female's blood levels of androgens prenatally. Vom Saal and Bronson (1980b) found that females located between two males had significantly higher levels of testosterone in

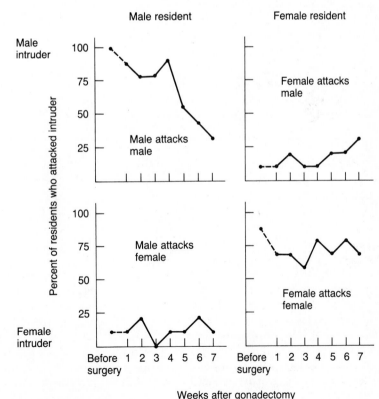

FIGURE 12.7

Effects of gonadectomy on attacks against intruders of the same or opposite sex. (From DeBold, J.E., and Miczek, K.A. *Hormones and Behavior,* 1984, *18,* 177–190.)

their blood than females located between two females (or between a female and the end of the uterus).

When they are tested as adults, 2M females are more likely to exhibit interfemale aggressiveness, and they are more likely to respond to an injection of testosterone with an attack on either male or estrous female intruders. (See **Figure 12.9.**) Vom Saal (1983) suggests that this phenomenon may have ecological significance. When the environment becomes crowded, the more aggressive 2M females are more likely to defend their territory against other females and successfully reproduce. Vom Saal and Bronson (1980a) found that the small amount of androgenization the 2M rats receive as fetuses has no deleterious effect on their fertility or maternal behavior.

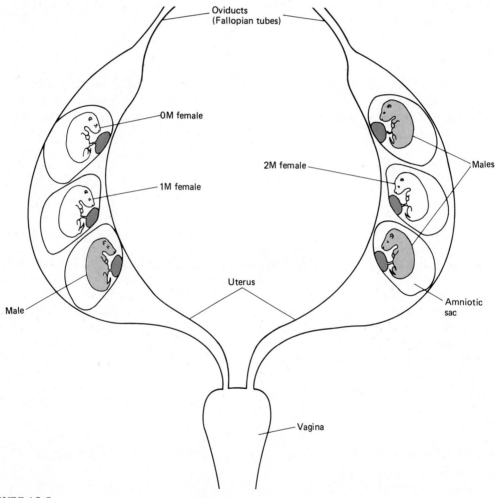

FIGURE 12.8

0M, 1M, and 2M female mouse fetuses. (Adapted from vom Saal, F.S. In *Hormones and Aggressive Behavior,* edited by B.B. Svare. New York: Plenum Press, 1983.)

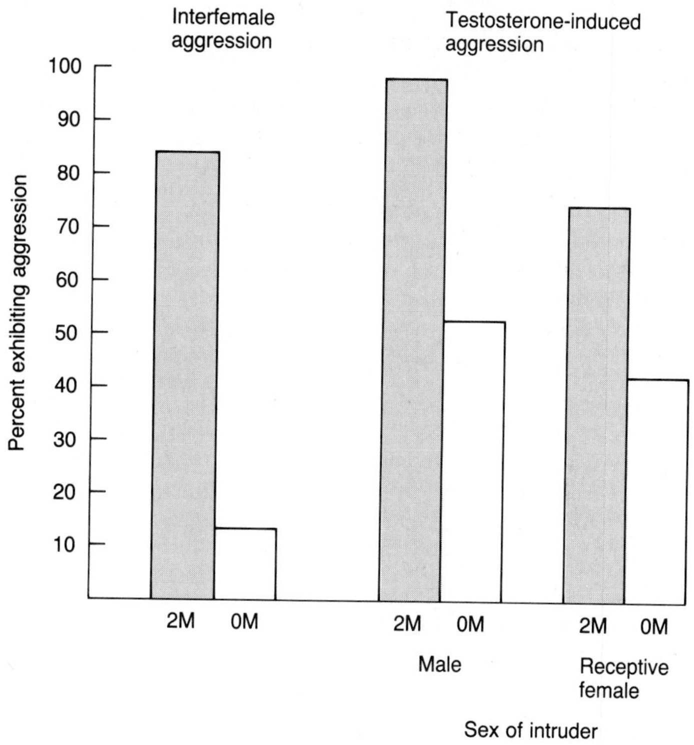

Interfemale aggression

Testosterone-induced aggression

FIGURE 12.9
Interfemale aggression and
testosterone-induced
aggression of 0M and 2M
female mice. (From vom Saal,
F.S. In *Hormones and
Aggressive Behavior,* edited by
B.B. Svare. New York: Plenum
Press, 1983.)

Maternal Aggression

Most parents who actively raise their offspring will vigorously defend them against
intruders. In the case of laboratory rodents
the responsible parent is the female, so the
most commonly studied form of parental defense is maternal aggression. Female mice
very effectively defend their young, driving
away intruding adults of either sex. Counter-
attacks by the intruder are rare (Svare, Betteridge, Katz, and Samuels, 1981). Whereas
strange males who encounter each other engage in mutual investigation for a minute or
two before fighting begins, the attack of a lactating female on an intruder is immediate
(Svare, 1983).

Lactating female mice do not attack infants, but they vigorously attack juveniles or

adults. The presence of hair appears to be an
important distinguishing feature. As we saw
in Chapter 10, Svare and Gandelman (1973)
found that a lactating female will not attack a
14-day-old juvenile whose hair has been
shaved off, but it will attack one with hair.
Females are also more likely to attack unfamiliar intruders than familiar ones. Svare and
Gandelman housed male mice for several
days behind a wire mesh partition in the cage
of a lactating female. When these mice were
introduced into the female's cage they were
not attacked, whereas unfamiliar males were.
The most important stimulus by which familiar males are recognized appears to be olfactory; Lynds (1976) found that when familiar
intruders were coated with the urine of
strangers, lactating females vigorously attacked them.

The tendency for a lactating female mouse to attack a stranger is induced by her offspring. If the newborn mice are removed, the mother fails to become aggressive. The activating stimulus appears to be produced by suckling. If the mother's nipples are surgically removed, she does not become aggressive, even if pups are present (Svare and Gandelman, 1976; Gandelman and Simon, 1980). Although virgin female mice will begin exhibiting maternal behavior when they are housed with pups, they fail to show maternal aggression. However, the studies I just mentioned found that if virgin females are given daily injections of estrogen and progesterone, which causes their nipples to develop, the stimulation of suckling by foster pups *will* produce maternal aggression. The process takes approximately 48 hours.

Prenatal exposure to androgens facilitates the later development of maternal aggression. As we saw in the previous section, female mice who were located between two males in the uterus (2M females) are more likely to attack other females and are more responsive to the activating effects of androgens in adulthood. Vom Saal and Bronson (1980a) also found that 2M females are more maternally aggressive than 0M females. (See **Figure 12.10**.)

Maternal aggressiveness does not appear to require an activational effect of hormones during adulthood. Svare and Gandelman (1976) found that removal of the ovaries and adrenal glands did not affect maternal aggression, and Mann, Broida, Michael, and Svare (1980) found that removal of the pituitary glands also had no effect. Thus, although the neural circuits that promote maternal aggression can be sensitized by prenatal androgens, they appear to be activated by environmental stimuli (primarily tactile stimulation provided by suckling).

Infanticide

Although the evolutionary process has selected parents who nurture and defend their young, adults—both male and female—sometimes kill infants, including their own. Although this behavior may appear to be aberrant and maladaptive, under some circumstances it has survival value for the species.

Hrdy (1977), in a report of infanticide among langurs (a primate species), suggested that the killing of infants by a male who was not the father "is a reproductive strategy whereby the usurping male increases his own reproductive success at the expense of the former leader (presumably the father of the infant killed) . . ." (p. 48). Because lactation suppresses a female's fertility, she is unlikely to become pregnant by the new male. However, when the male kills her offspring, she soon becomes fertile and thus capable of becoming pregnant by him. (The male tends *not* to kill his own offspring.)

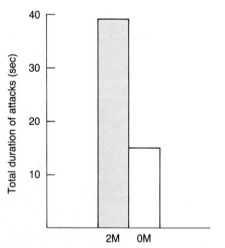

FIGURE 12.10
Maternal aggression toward a female intruder of lactating 0M and 2M female mice. (From vom Saal, F.S. In *Hormones and Aggressive Behavior,* edited by B.B. Svare. New York: Plenum Press, 1983.)

You will recall a related phenomenon that I mentioned in Chapter 10: the Bruce effect (Bruce, 1960a, 1960b). When a newly pregnant mouse encounters the odor of a strange male, she tends to abort spontaneously. Thus, the male unintentionally kills her yet-unborn offspring, making it possible for him to impregnate her and propagate his own genes.

Androgens have an effect on infanticide by male rodents. Rosenberg, Denenberg, Zarrow, and Frank (1971) found that only 10 percent of male rats that were castrated before puberty killed infants, whereas 58 percent of normal rats did so. Rats who were castrated after puberty did kill infants. Thus, the maturational effects of testosterone are important for the development of the behavior, but testosterone need not be present for the behavior to be expressed. Presumably, sexual maturation brings with it development of neural circuits that facilitate infanticide, but, once developed, these circuits do not require testosterone for their activation.

The effect of androgens early in development appears to be paradoxical: increased exposure of male rodents to androgens before or immediately after birth *inhibits* infanticide in adulthood. Gandelman and vom Saal (1977) injected male mice with testosterone immediately after birth and observed an increase in intermale aggression and a decrease in infanticide once the animals became adults. In addition, vom Saal (1983) compared the behavior of adult 2M male mice (those that were located between two brothers prenatally) with 0M male mice. The 2M mice, which presumably received a larger dose of prenatal androgens, were more likely to care for pups than kill them, whereas the 0M mice were more likely to kill them than care for them. Just why early androgenization should decrease the tendency for infanticide by males has not yet been explained.

When female rodents kill pups, they usually kill their own; thus, infanticide by males and females must occur for different reasons. Indeed, female infanticide appears to achieve at least two advantages: it decreases crowding, and it helps attain an optimal litter size. The first hypothetical advantage was supported by Calhoun (1962), who reported that severe crowding greatly increased the incidence of female infanticide in rats. Presumably, this behavior helped prevent the crowding from increasing still further. Gandelman and Simon (1978) obtained data that supported the second hypothetical advantage. They adjusted the size of litters of newborn mice to either twelve or sixteen pups by adding foster pups or removing them. In both groups, the mean number of surviving offspring was nine. The mothers with sixteen pups tended to kill more than those with twelve pups. The smallest pups were most likely to be killed. Because these pups were probably the least fit, the behavior tends to select for an optimally sized litter that consists of the healthiest pups. (Mice have ten nipples, which suggests that the optimal size is ten or less.)

Effects of Androgens on Human Aggressive Behavior

Boys are generally more aggressive than girls. This is as true of 3- to 6-year-old children as it is of 7- to 10-year-old children (D'Andrade, 1966). Clearly, Western society tolerates assertiveness and aggression from boys more than girls. However, if socialization were the *sole* cause of the sex difference in aggression, we would expect that the difference between older (more socialized) boys and girls would be larger than that between younger boys and girls. Because this is not the case, D'Andrade's finding suggests that biological differences such as those produced by prenatal androgenization may be at least partly responsible for the increased aggression in males.

I have already reviewed some of the evidence concerning intermale aggression in laboratory animals, and we saw that androgens have strong organizational and activational effects. Prenatal androgenization increases aggressive behavior in all species that have been studied, including primates. Therefore, if androgens did not affect aggression in humans, our species would be exceptional. Boys' testosterone levels begin to increase during the early teens, at which time aggression and intermale fighting also increase (Mazur, 1983). Of course, boys' social status changes during puberty, and their testosterone affects their muscles as well as their brains, so we cannot be sure that the effect is hormonally produced, or, if it is, that it is mediated neurally.

Males of many species can be gentled by castration. This observation has led authorities to castrate convicted male sex offenders. Investigators have reported that both heterosexual and homosexual aggressive attacks disappear, along with the offender's sex drive (Hawke, 1951; Sturup, 1961; Laschet, 1973). However, the studies typically lack appropriate control groups and do not always measure aggression directly. Hawke (1951) reported the following:

Many of these individuals so treated were . . . very brutal in attacks on small children. They were very unstable and would create a disturbance at every opportunity. After castration, they became stabilized, and those who cannot be paroled are good useful citizens in the institution.

In our experimental work, we have administered Testosterone, the male hormone [to some castrates]. . . . In a number of cases, after we had treated them for a period of two or three weeks, the floor supervisor would call me up and ask if I would not be willing to stop administering Testosterone to certain individuals who had reverted to all of their anti-social tendencies, were attacking small children, starting fights, breaking windows and destroying furniture. We would stop the ad-

ministration of Testosterone in these individuals, and within a few days they would be restabilized and cause no further ward disturbances. We have felt that this proves the male hormone is the exciting factor in these cases. (p. 222)

Because the studies with castrated males were not performed with the appropriate double-blind controls, we cannot be sure whether the androgen was the responsible agent for the increase in aggression. Certainly, the conclusion that it was is a reasonable one, but it must be determined scientifically. However, ethical standards that have been adopted by the panels that review human biomedical research will probably prevent studies that could provide a definitive answer. First, we must decide whether castration is justified in cases of brutal aggression. Second, even if a violent man is castrated and his violence ceases, can we ethically subject other people to possible harm by administering replacement doses of testosterone?

Another way to approach the problem is to examine the testosterone levels of people who exhibit varying levels of aggression. However, even though this approach poses fewer ethical problems, it presents methodological ones. First let me review the evidence. Kreuz and Rose (1972) measured the testosterone levels of twenty-one male prisoners with a history of violent crime and found that the androgen levels were not related to their level of violence in prison. However, the hormone *was* related to their history of aggression during adolescence. Another study (Ehrenkranz, Bliss, and Sheard, 1974) compared three groups of prisoners: (1) socially dominant but unaggressive men, who had been convicted of nonviolent crimes; (2) chronically aggressive men, who had been convicted of violent crimes; and (3) nonaggressive, nondominant men. The testosterone levels of groups 1 and 2 were both high, compared with that of the third group. Thus, this study suggests that testosterone may promote dominance that is achieved by behaviors other than aggressive ones (leadership without bullying) as well as aggression. On the other hand, perhaps testosterone simply promotes dominance in men. Those who are able to achieve dominance nonviolently do so, but those who are not intelligent or socially adept enough resort to cruder means.

The methodological problem with all correlational studies like the ones I just cited is that a man's environment can affect his testosterone level. For example, Mazur and Lamb (1980) found that men who decisively lost a tennis match had significantly lower blood levels of testosterone an hour later, and men who won had significantly higher levels. Similar effects were found in college wrestlers who won or lost competitive matches (Elias, 1981). Thus, we cannot be sure that high testosterone levels *caused* some prisoners to become dominant or violent; perhaps their success increased their testosterone levels relative to those of the prisoners they dominated.

INTERIM SUMMARY

Aggressive behaviors, like reproductive behaviors, are influenced by hormones, especially sex steroid hormones. Androgens have organizational and activational effects on male aggressive behavior, just as they have on male sexual behavior. However, prolonged exposure to androgens during adulthood eventually produces aggressiveness even in nonandrogenized animals. The effects of androgens on intermale aggression appear to be mediated by the medial preoptic area. The inhibition of an attack by a male on a female mouse is mediated by her odor, perhaps through the connections of the accessory olfactory system with the medial nucleus of the amygdala.

Both ACTH and corticosterone affect aggression: ACTH inhibits intermale aggressiveness, and corticosterone increases the likelihood of submissiveness following a defeat.

Female aggressiveness is more common than was previously believed. For example, female hamsters are normally aggressive, but become less so when high levels of progesterone and estradiol promote estrus. In contrast, female primates are most likely to fight around the time of ovulation, perhaps because their increased sexual interest brings them closer to males. Although some women report irritability just before menstruation, the phenomenon is not universal.

The attack of female rodents on juveniles is apparently controlled by androgens secreted by their ovaries. However, their tendency to attack strange females is not affected by ovariectomy. The higher level of blood testosterone in female mice who were located between two brothers in the uterus increases their tendency to attack male or estrous female intruders. The tendency for a mother mouse to attack an intruder is facilitated by suckling; the mere presence of pups is not sufficient to induce this behavior. In addition, prenatal androgenization facilitates this behavior: 2M females are more likely than 0M females to display maternal aggression. The behavior does not require the activational effects of ovarian, pituitary, or adrenal hormones.

Infanticide by male rodents is promoted by androgens early in life, but it continues to occur even after castration in adulthood. However, large doses of androgens around the time of birth inhibit infanticide; thus the nature of the development of this form of aggression is not well understood. Female infanticide appears to promote optimal litter size and tends to weed out less healthy offspring.

Androgens apparently promote aggression in humans, but this topic is more difficult to study in our species than in laboratory animals. Differences in testosterone levels have been observed in criminals with a history of violence, but we cannot be sure whether higher androgen levels promote violence or whether successful aggression increases androgen levels.

■ PSYCHOSURGERY AND THE SUPPRESSION OF HUMAN VIOLENCE

No reasonable person would deny that there is too much violence in the world. Wars and individual acts of aggression are responsible for much human misery. Can the neuroscientist contribute to the solution of this problem? Perhaps we can modify human violence by means of medication or surgery.

Clearly, laboratory studies on the physiology of aggression cannot affect social variables such as poverty that increase the incidence of violence. Nor are neuroscientists likely to learn how to prevent wars. More people are killed by wars than by individual acts of violence, but the factors that cause wars are probably very different from those that are responsible for the attack of one organism upon another. Fear-induced aggression certainly occurs in battle, but individual soldiers do not start wars; politicians do. I doubt that we will understand why they do so by studying their amygdala, hypothalamus, or midbrain.

The one possible contribution that physiological research on aggression may have to the reduction of human violence is to help us understand the causes of individual acts of irrational violence that might be produced by neuropathological conditions. For example, Charles Whitman, who killed fourteen people and then himself from a tower at the University of Texas, was found to have a malignant tumor in the vicinity of the amygdala. The obvious inference is that the tumor caused the violence by stimulating neural circuits involved in aggressive behavior, and that prompt diagnosis and surgery could have prevented the tragic results of this violence. It is to issues like these that the following discussion is addressed.

Most brain surgery is performed for reasons that are not at all controversial: removal of brain tumors, repair of aneurysms (balloon-shaped enlargements of blood vessels caused by weakness in their walls), removal of scar tissue that triggers seizures, reduction of intractable pain by destruction of brain circuits conveying this sensation, and alleviation of motor disturbances by producing localized brain lesions. *Psychosurgery* is different. It involves intentional damage to brain tissue in an attempt to alter people's behavior, even though there is no direct evidence of any brain damage or disease. Psychosurgery has been severely criticized.

Elliot Valenstein has written excellent reviews and critiques of attempts to correct human aggressive behavior by means of brain stimulation and ablation procedures (Valenstein, 1973, 1980). His conclusions are rather pessimistic: investigators have failed to establish a good relation between malfunctioning brain mechanisms and violent behavior, and most of the clinical reports that purport to show improvement after psychosurgical correction of this behavior do not contain adequate, impartial descriptions of preoperative and postoperative behavior. Valenstein also served as one of the investigators and authors of a report for the United States government on the use of psychosurgery (National Commission, 1977). This report concluded that some forms of psychosurgery appeared to produce good therapeutic results in cases of severe depression or compulsive disorders. In this section, I refer not to these forms of psychosurgery but only to its use in the treatment of aggressive behavior.

The Case for Psychosurgery: The "Dyscontrol Syndrome"

Mark and Ervin (1970) are among the most prominent supporters of the use of psychosurgery to treat violent and aggressive behavior. They believe that a substantial number of people who suffer from what they call the "dyscontrol syndrome" have localized brain abnormalities that trigger neural circuits responsible for aggressive behavior.

There is no doubt that some people engage

in periodic outbursts of uncontrollable rage and violence. For example, Ervin (1973) reported the following case:

We had a patient whom we had in fact operated on. We had done the diagnostic procedure and had wires in his brain. A guy who had a very dramatic "flip-flop" in his personality state, he was either aggressive, paranoid, litigious, difficult to deal with or he was a very sweet, reasonable, passive, dependent kind of neurotic. These were his two modes of existence. Long before he had also happened to have epilepsy which is why he had come to us. In fact, there were two patients. I had a choice as to which one to deal with. These two patients were a great stress on the wife of the single body in whom they were contained. On this occasion she broke down and wept and said, "Who are you, honey? I don't know who you are." He had gotten extremely upset on the ward. We could not hold him against his will in the hospital since our hospital is a voluntary hospital and he could only be there by his own choice. He threatened to leave and was, in fact, in the process of leaving, ostensibly to kill his wife. At least that is what he said he was going to do, and I rather believed him. In the course of the day, we managed to get him into the laboratory and stimulate [his amygdala]. . . . In about a minute he visibly relaxed. He took a deep breath and said, "You know you nearly let me get out of here?" . . . I said, "Yes, I couldn't have held you." He said, "You've got to do something to keep me from getting out of here. I think if you had the nurse hide my pants, I wouldn't have left." I thought that was a good suggestion and followed it. We had a very reasonable discussion and he was very grateful for my having stopped him. I said, "Well, I guess we won't have to go through this very much longer because tomorrow morning we have planned to make the definitive lesion and I wanted to talk to you about that. What we are going to do is burn out this little part of the brain that causes all the trouble." He said, "Yeah, that's great." Well, the next morning about 9:00 he was brought down and he said, "You're going to burn what out of my brain? Not on your bloody life you're not!" He would easily at the earlier point have signed anything I asked for. He was guilty; he

was sweet; perhaps he was reasonable. But which of those two states I should deal with posed a real problem for me. So informed consent isn't all it's cracked up to be. Voluntary understanding has its problems. (pp. 177–178)

Mark and Ervin appear to be careful and conservative in their choice of candidates for surgery, but even their results do not appear to be uniformly good. Mark, Sweet, and Ervin (1972) reported on patients exhibiting violent or fearful behavior who were treated by lesions of the amygdala. Most of the patients showed some improvement, but in some cases the surgery produced side effects such as hyperphagia or impotence. Some people were not helped or showed only a temporary reduction in violent behavior. The most successful case was that of a woman who fell and injured her head. She subsequently had seizures and assaulted people violently. Her seizures were reduced by amygdalectomy, and her attacks of rage were eliminated. However, her history of head injury and seizure activity provided clear evidence of brain injury, which makes her case different from most.

Even some clear cases of pathological conditions of the brain might not necessarily be related to violent behavior. Charles Whitman, who killed fourteen people, did indeed have a rapidly growing temporal lobe tumor. However, his diary showed that he had been carefully planning the shooting episode and provided evidence of severely disordered thought processes. Valenstein (1973) points out that we cannot even determine what triggered Whitman's behavior, but it certainly does not appear that he was in the throes of a sudden, episodic attack of violence. The history of careful planning stands in contrast with the spasms of rage we might expect to see if the developing brain tumor were stimulating neural circuits that underlie aggressive behavior.

Rationale for Psychosurgery: Animal Studies

Neurosurgeons generally base their psychosurgical procedures on data from experiments performed with animals. As you might predict from what you learned in the first part of this chapter, they have destroyed parts of the amygdala, hypothalamus, and periaqueductal gray matter. However, Valenstein (1973) points out that many of the surgeons displayed "tunnel vision" when they looked at the experimental evidence. They tended to see only the potentially beneficial aspects of the procedure and to ignore its harmful aspects. For example, some neurosurgeons have produced lesions in the region of the anterior cingulate gyrus (a portion of the limbic cortex) based on studies with monkeys that reported "taming" effects from these lesions. However, Ward (1948) notes that "tameness" is a poor word to use in describing the postoperative behavior of one of these monkeys.

. . . the most marked change was in social behavior. The monkey's mimetic activity decreased and it lost its preoperative shyness and fear of man. It would approach me and curiously examine my finger instead of cowering in the far corner of the cage. It was more inquisitive than the normal monkey of the same age. In a large cage with other monkeys of the same size it showed no grooming or acts of affection toward its companions. In fact, it behaved as though they were inanimate. It would walk over them, walk on them if they happened to be in the way, and would even sit on them. It would openly take food from its companions and appeared surprised when they retaliated. . . . (p. 15)

The monkey did not attack the handler, but it would obviously be a mistake to focus on this "tameness" while ignoring the severe disruption in the animal's social behavior.

The rationale for amygdalectomy in humans is, of course, that it suppresses violent behavior. As we saw, lesions of the basolateral amygdala tend to suppress affective intermale aggression. However, amygdalectomies have some serious effects on the lives of monkeys who subsequently live in the wild. Kling, Lancaster, and Benitone (1970) captured some wild rhesus monkeys and removed parts of their amygdalas. They found that the monkeys did appear less aggressive and more friendly toward humans. However, their interactions with their peers in the wild was another matter. After they had been released, they acted confused and fearful. They sometimes responded to dominance gestures from higher-ranked monkeys in an inappropriate way and consequently got thrashed. In general, they appeared to have trouble interpreting the signs by which monkeys communicate with each other, and they eventually became outcasts. They all subsequently died. Although humans with lesions of the amygdala do not show these severe defects, it would be illogical to attend solely to the interaction of the brain-damaged monkeys with humans in the laboratory, ignoring their fate in the wild, and thereby conclude that amygdalectomy has a taming effect on monkeys.

Although stimulation of the amygdala can produce aggressive or flight reactions in laboratory animals, such stimulation does not appear to do so in normal humans—only in those who show regular episodes of violent behavior (Kim and Umbach, 1972). These results suggest that the stimulation does not directly trigger neural circuits responsible for aggression. Instead, it may produce an aversive effect that indirectly stimulates aggression in a person who is already prone to this type of behavior.

Alternatives to Psychosurgery

An example of the beneficial effects that can be achieved with drugs is given in the following case, in which an anticonvulsant drug was used to treat a child who exhibited violent behavior, apparently caused by a seizure-producing focus in the temporal lobe:

A good example is Jimmy, whom we saw at age 9 because of serious rage reactions and aggressiveness leading to threatened expulsion from school. He was one of nine children, and the only one who had any behavior problem. In fact, the other children were considered outstanding in the community and at school. Jimmy had an identical twin, Johnny, who was considered a "model child." Jimmy's EEG showed left temporal spikes, Johnny's was negative. On methsuximide [an anticonvulsant drug], Jimmy became an entirely different boy, a "model child" like his twin. When medication was omitted for a short time, he reverted to his old self by the third day. . . . (Gross, 1971, p. 89)

Not many cases are so clear-cut as this; we have evidence that the home environment of the nine children was such that they did not all become violent. In fact, the contrary was seen. The violent boy even had a normal identical twin, so we cannot blame any genetic factors. Furthermore, his EEG was abnormal, indicating that there very probably had been some degree of brain damage. I think that everyone would agree that this child is much better off with the drug treatment, and that this means of therapy should be explored thoroughly before resorting to surgery.

INTERIM SUMMARY

Although psychosurgery might ameliorate some instances of violent behavior, it appears to be most effective when there are definite signs of some form of neuropathological disorders, above and beyond the behavioral manifestations of violence. Although neurosurgeons have based their procedures on animal studies, research with animals has not yet provided us with a clear enough picture of the neural mechanisms underlying aggressive behavior to justify removal of healthy parts of the brain. Control of violent outbursts from people who hurt or kill others is an honorable goal, but the evidence suggests that psychosurgery is not the answer to the problem.

Concluding Remarks

Aggression is an important class of behaviors. For example, it serves to disperse members of a species, to provide mating opportunities for the most vigorous males, to provide nesting space for the most vigorous females, and to reduce litters to their optimal size. Our understanding of the different types of aggression, the conditions under which they occur, and their neural and hormonal basis complements our knowledge of the physiology of other species-typical behaviors. Perhaps someday we will be able to use this knowledge to reduce the incidence of human violence, but at present the application of data obtained from animals to humans seems premature.

NEW TERMS

adrenocorticotropic hormone (ACTH) p. 490
affective attack p. 481
basolateral group p. 485
corticomedial group p. 485
corticosterone p. 490
infanticide p. 480

intermale aggression p. 480
irritable aggression p. 480
maternal aggression p. 480
predatory aggression p. 480
psychosurgery p. 500
self-defense p. 480

sex-related aggression p. 480
social aggression p. 480
stria terminalis p. 485

territorial aggression p. 480
ventral amygdalofugal pathway p. 486

SUGGESTED READINGS

SIMMEL, E.C., HAHN, M.E., AND WALTERS, J.K. *Aggressive Behavior: Genetic and Neural Approaches.* Hillsdale, N.J.: Lawrence Erlbaum Associates, 1983.

SVARE, B.B. *Hormones and Aggressive Behavior.* New York: Plenum Press, 1983.

VALENSTEIN, E.S. *The Psychosurgery Debate: Scientific, Legal, and Ethical Perspectives.* San Francisco: W.H. Freeman, 1980.

VALZELLI, L. *Psychobiology of Aggression and Violence.* New York: Raven Press, 1981.

13

Reinforcement

■ THE NATURE OF LEARNING

Most species of animals can profit from experience. Although some behaviors of complex organisms can be described as species typical, the precise form of these behaviors and the conditions under which they occur depend on an individual's interactions with its environment. In addition, organisms can learn to perform altogether new responses. This chapter considers the physiology of reinforcement, the means by which organisms learn to perform behaviors that have beneficial consequences.

Psychologists have discovered two major classes of learning. The first, called *classical conditioning,* involves learning to perform a behavior in response to a stimulus that did not previously cause the behavior to occur. For example, we flinch when we see a balloon being overinflated. The flinch is a species-typical defensive reaction that serves to protect our eyes. Normally, this reaction occurs when we hear a loud noise, when something rapidly approaches our face, or when our eyes or the skin around them is touched. We respond to the sight of an overinflated balloon because of our prior experience with bursting balloons. Sometime in the past, probably when we were children, an overinflated balloon burst near our face, and the blast of air elicited a defensive flinch. Through classical conditioning, the stimulus that preceded the blast of air — the sight of an overinflated balloon — became an elicitor of flinching.

The names that have been assigned to the stimuli and responses that constitute classical conditioning are shown in Figure 13.1. The blast of air, the original eliciting stimulus, is called the *unconditional stimulus (US):* it unconditionally elicits the species-typical response. The response of flinching is itself

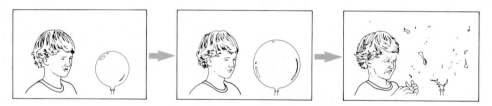

The child watches the balloon grow large
(neutral stimulus) until it bursts (US),
which causes a defensive startle reaction (UR).

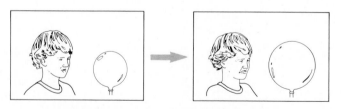

After the child's first experience with a bursting
balloon, the mere sight of an inflating balloon
(CS) elicits a defensive reaction (CR).

FIGURE 13.1
A model of classical conditioning.

called the *unconditional response (UR).* After a few experiences with bursting balloons, the sight of the balloon — the *conditional stimulus (CS)* — comes to elicit flinching, which is now called the *conditional response (CR):* the response is conditional on the pairing of the conditional and unconditional stimuli. (See **Figure 13.1.**)

Classical conditioning occurs when a neutral stimulus is followed by one that automatically elicits a response. By these means, organisms learn to make species-typical responses under new conditions. Thus, classical conditioning serves to prepare an organism for a forthcoming event. For example, a warning signal can permit the organism to defend itself against harm, stimuli associated with a potential mate can cause it to emit a response that serves as a sexual display, and stimuli associated with food can cause secretion of saliva, digestive juices, and insulin. Hollis (1982) demonstrated the utility of classical conditioning under natural conditions. She classically conditioned an attack response in male fish by presenting experimental subjects with a flashing red light immediately followed by the sight of a rival behind a glass partition. She presented control subjects with a rival but no flashing light. In test conditions when the partition was removed and the fish were permitted to fight, a trained fish was more likely to attack the rival with biting and tail beating and drive it away when it was warned of the impending contest by the red light. The warning caused the trained animal to begin its attack sooner, which caught the rival off guard when they actually encountered each other. (See **Figure 13.2.**) In the wild, the conditional stimulus will certainly not be a red light, but it might be a shadow or flash of color caused by movement of an intruder into the fish's territory.

Classical conditioning serves another role, which is probably even more important: the establishment of previously neutral stimuli as conditioned reinforcers. Because this func-

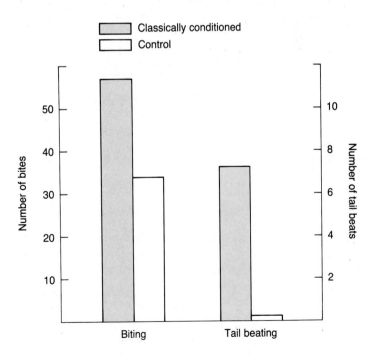

FIGURE 13.2
Effects of classical conditioning on attack behavior of male fish. (From Hollis, K.L. *Advances in the Study of Behavior,* 1982, *12,* 1–64.)

tion serves the process of instrumental conditioning, I will discuss it a little later.

The second major class of learning is **instrumental conditioning,** or **operant conditioning.** Many responses that an organism makes have important consequences for the organism. Some consequences lead to an increase in the likelihood of making the response again; others lead to a decrease. The consequences that increase the frequency of the response are called **reinforcing stimuli,** or simply **reinforcers.** Those that decrease the frequency of the response are called **punishing stimuli,** or **punishers.** For example, a response that enables a hungry organism to find food will be reinforced, and a response that causes pain will be punished.

It is important to note that reinforcement and punishment refer to the *effect* of the reinforcing and punishing stimuli, not to the *intent* of someone who may administer them. Psychologists have adopted the term *reinforcement* in preference to the more common term *reward* because the latter implies that the organism has done something praiseworthy. However, the process of reinforcement is a neutral one. Suppose, in its clumsy exuberance, a large friendly dog accidentally knocks a small child to the ground. The child drops a candy bar, which the dog finds and eats. This experience causes the dog to begin knocking children down. By dropping the candy the child inadvertently reinforced the dog's behavior. We would not want to say the child *rewarded* it.

Unfortunately, psychologists have not replaced the term *punishment* with a neutral one. If we ask a father why he is scolding his son, he is likely to say, "I am punishing him for his bad behavior." But punishment refers to an effect, not an intent. Perhaps the child misbehaves because he has learned that doing so gets attention from his father that he would not otherwise receive. In this case, the scolding serves to reinforce the boy's behavior, not

punish it. When a psychologist uses the term *punishment,* it means that a stimulus (the punisher) makes the response occur less often in a particular situation.

In order for a response to be reinforced by its consequences, it must first occur. Therefore, most reinforced responses are those that are at least somewhat likely in a given situation. For example, if a cat is confined in a small cage, it will pace around, push its body against the walls, claw at them, and perhaps bite parts of the cage. When Thorndike (1905) placed hungry cats in cages with doors that could be opened by manipulating a latch, the cats behaved in this way. Eventually, their responses accidentally caused the latch to operate, and the door opened. The cats left the cage and ate some food in a dish outside. Through this process, which Thorndike called "learning by trial and accidental success," the cats eventually learned to escape the cages efficiently; only the responses that operated the latch were followed by opening of the door, and hence only these responses were reinforced.

The number of intrinsically reinforcing stimuli is probably very small: food to a hungry organism, water to a thirsty one, warmth to a cold one, a receptive partner to a sexually aroused one, and a few others. However, the process of classical conditioning makes it possible for almost any stimulus to become a reinforcer. As we saw, if a neutral stimulus (such as a buzzer) is regularly followed by an unconditional stimulus (such as food), the neutral stimulus becomes able to evoke responses (such as salivation) caused by the eliciting stimulus. In addition, the neutral stimulus assumes the ability of the eliciting stimulus to reinforce or punish behaviors. That is, just as food itself can reinforce the behavior of a hungry organism, so can the sound of a buzzer that has been followed by the presentation of food. Similarly, just as the sting of a wasp can punish behaviors such as approaching a wasp nest, so can the buzzing noise that a wasp makes, once you have experienced its sting. These phenomena, called *conditioned reinforcement* and *conditioned punishment,* greatly increase the adaptability of an organism's behavior to its environment. Most human behavior is shaped by encounters with conditioned reinforcers (such as money, social approval, or good grades) and with conditioned punishers (such as traffic tickets, social disapproval, or bad grades). These reinforcers and punishers gained their potency because they previously occurred in association with reinforcers or punishers, including previously established conditioned reinforcers or punishers. For example, money is desirable because it can provide reinforcers, and traffic tickets are undesirable because they cause trips to court and the loss of money.

Although instrumental conditioning is usually described as a relation between a response and a reinforcer or punisher, it is clearly more complex than that. Reinforcement and punishment do not simply change the likelihood of a response's occurring; they alter the likelihood of the response *in a particular situation*. Once a rat learns to operate a lever that causes food to be dispensed, it does not begin to wave its paws against the walls of its home cage when it gets hungry; it does so only against the lever in the experimental apparatus. And if the lever "works" only when the light in the chamber is turned on, the rat will not press the lever when it is dark. The sight of the lever and the light serve as *discriminative stimuli,* by which the rat discriminates between conditions under which lever pressing is reinforced and those under which it is not. Thus, instrumental conditioning does not simply make a response more likely; it makes the stimuli in a particular situation become capable of eliciting a behavior. The stimuli associated with the experimental chamber, including the sight of the

lever and the overhead light, elicit lever-pressing behavior from the hungry rat. To understand the process of reinforcement, we must understand the neural mechanisms that (1) detect the reinforcing event and, as a consequence, (2) establish or strengthen connections between the neurons that detect the discriminative stimuli and those that control the behavior, so that in the future, activity of the former neurons brings about activity in the latter neurons. A possible mechanism is shown in **Figure 13.3.**

The detection of a reinforcing event is complex: a stimulus that serves as a reinforcer on one occasion may fail to do so on another. For example, food will reinforce the behavior of a hungry organism but not one that has just eaten. In fact, being forced to eat when one is not hungry can be an aversive event. Thus, a particular stimulus can be appetitive or aversive, depending on the organism's physiological state. Another way to describe this phenomenon is to say that motivational variables can alter the *hedonic value* of a stimulus. (*Hedonic* derives from the Greek *hēdonē,* meaning "pleasure.") The study of factors that change the hedonic value of a stimulus is an important topic in the field of motivation.

Many psychologists prefer to define reinforcers as those that provide an opportunity to perform a behavior rather than as stimuli with a particular hedonic value (Premack, 1965). In this view, *eating,* and not the presence of food, is the reinforcing event. Eating occurs only when the organism is hungry; therefore, the presence of food does not reinforce the behavior of a satiated organism, because the organism does not eat. In fact, it is a general principle that *reinforcing stimuli are elicitors of behavior* (Donahoe, Crowley, Millard, and Stickney, 1982). If this characterization is correct, then the neurons that cause reinforcement may not be part of the perceptual mechanisms that detect reinforcing stimuli; instead, they may be part of the system responsible for the production of the appetitive behaviors. Feedback from making a response such as eating causes reinforcement, strengthening the link between the discrimi-native stimulus and the previous response (the instrumental response). Figure 13.4 presents a revision of the model shown in Figure 13.3 that utilizes this feedback, rather

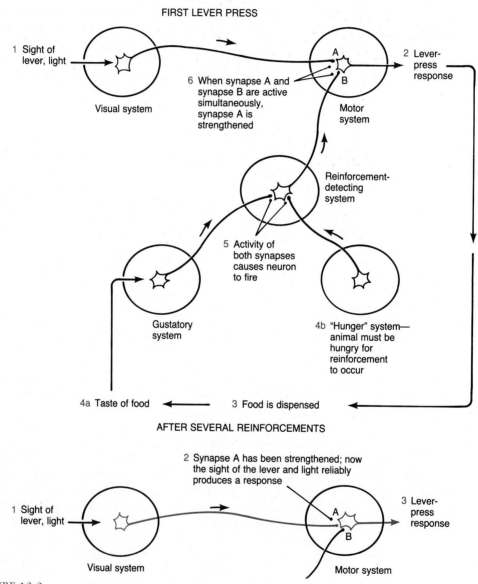

FIGURE 13.3

A hypothetical neural model of instrumental conditioning by means of reinforcement.

than the detection of a reinforcing stimulus, as the event that causes reinforcement. (See **Figure 13.4.**)

The effects of aversive stimuli can be analyzed in a similar manner. Aversive stimuli elicit species-typical defensive responses such as flinching, limb withdrawal, crouching, huddling down as if hiding, or fleeing. Many psychologists believe that aversive stimuli punish behaviors by strengthening a link between discriminative stimuli and species-typical defensive responses (Bolles, 1970).

These responses then compete with other responses, including the one that was just emitted (the punished response). For example, a dog approaches a porcupine and gets a faceful of quills. The pain causes defensive reactions, including fleeing. Later, when the dog encounters a porcupine again, the sight of the animal elicits a withdrawal reaction, which competes with approach. (Sometimes we can see approach and withdrawal reactions to the same stimulus, as when a dog approaches a porcupine, then retreats when it gets very

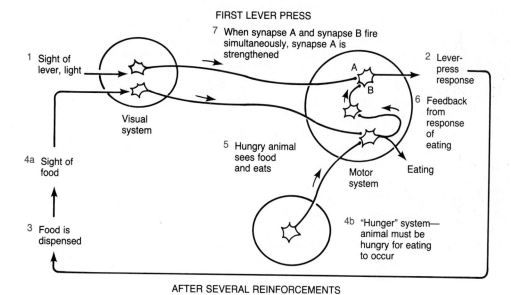

FIGURE 13.4

A revised hypothetical neural model of instrumental conditioning by means of reinforcement that utilizes feedback from making an appetitive response.

close, then approaches again, and so on.) When we view the punishing effects of aversive stimuli in this way, the process looks very much like classical conditioning: perception of the porcupine is followed by a faceful of quills (unconditional stimulus) that elicits a defensive reaction (unconditional response). This pairing causes the appearance of a porcupine to serve as a conditional stimulus, eliciting a conditional withdrawal response. The withdrawal competes, with approach, which leads us to observe that approach has been punished. (See **Figure 13.5.**)

The model of reinforcement presented here has replaced an older one called the ***drive-reduction hypothesis.*** This hypothesis stated that a variety of physiological factors could produce aversive states called *drives.* The most usual cause of a drive would be deprivation of contact with a reinforcing stimulus such as food. Food deprivation eventually causes a homeostatic need for food and results in a drive we call *hunger.* This unpleasant state arouses an animal and causes its activity to increase. Eventually, if this increased activity brings the animal in contact with food, it eats. Eating reduces hunger, and this reduction of an unpleasant stimulus reinforces the behaviors that brought the animal in contact with the food.

Although the drive-reduction hypothesis is plausible, it eventually encountered difficulty. A large variety of stimuli can serve as reinforcers, thus implying the existence of a large variety of drives. For example, many animals will learn to press a lever for the opportunity to look out a window. The drive-reduction hypothesis suggests they do so because of a "curiosity drive," possibly aroused when the animal has not recently had an opportunity to explore new environments. To test experimentally whether the opportunity to look out a window reinforces behavior because it reduces a curiosity drive, we must be able to measure this drive. However, there is no direct way to do so; the only indication of a curiosity drive is the fact that an animal will work in order to look out the window. The logical dilemma is this: We have hypothesized that reduction of state A (drive) produces phenomenon B (reinforcement). If the only way we can determine whether state A is present is to see whether state B occurs, then we cannot prove that A causes B. Doing so would be logically equivalent to saying that earthquakes occur when a subterranean dragon is angry. We know this is true because whenever he is angry, an earthquake occurs. How do we tell that he is angry? Why, we notice whether the ground is trembling.

To prove that the dragon's anger causes earthquakes (that is, that drive reduction causes reinforcement) we have to find the dragon. If we do find him in his lair, then we can see whether his behavior causes earthquakes. Similarly, to prove the drive-reduction hypothesis we would have to find physiological evidence for the existence of a drive — say, activity of a particular group of neurons — that increases during deprivation and decreases when a reinforcing stimulus is presented. So far, we have not found such a dragon.

The drive-reduction hypothesis has empirical difficulties as well as logical ones. For example, the hypothesis predicts that as a hungry organism eats, it gets less and less hungry with each bite of food. After all, it is the reduction of drive that causes the reinforcement to occur. However, as an animal begins its meal, its eating gets more and more vigorous, which implies that its hunger increases. Only after several mouthfuls are swallowed does an accumulation of food in the stomach begin to produce satiety. A hungry animal that has just eaten a small piece of food is not *less* hungry than it was before; it is *more* hungry. (Do you feel less hungry after you eat one peanut or one potato chip?)

This chapter considers the neural basis of

reinforcement. The anatomical basis of learning is discussed in Chapter 14, and the physiological and biochemical basis of learning is discussed in Chapter 15. As we will see in this chapter, good evidence relates the activity of neurons in particular parts of the brain with

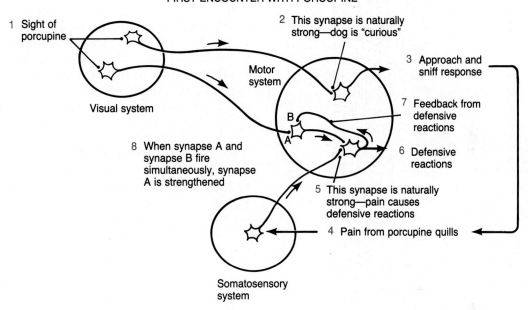

FIRST ENCOUNTER WITH PORCUPINE

1 Sight of porcupine

Visual system

2 This synapse is naturally strong—dog is "curious"

Motor system

3 Approach and sniff response

7 Feedback from defensive reactions

B

A

8 When synapse A and synapse B fire simultaneously, synapse A is strengthened

6 Defensive reactions

5 This synapse is naturally strong—pain causes defensive reactions

4 Pain from porcupine quills

Somatosensory system

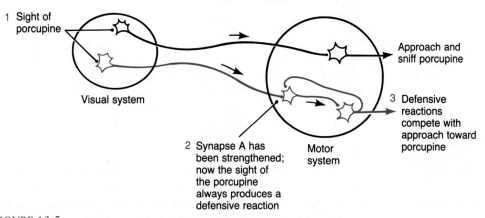

AFTER FIRST ENCOUNTER (PUNISHMENT)

1 Sight of porcupine

Visual system

Approach and sniff porcupine

3 Defensive reactions compete with approach toward porcupine

2 Synapse A has been strengthened; now the sight of the porcupine always produces a defensive reaction

Motor system

FIGURE 13.5

A hypothetical neural model of instrumental conditioning by means of punishment.

the phenomenon of reinforcement, and some important neurotransmitters have been identified in this process. Evidence also suggests that the elicitation of species-typical responses is associated with reinforcement, which is predicted by the model of reinforcement that I just outlined.

INTERIM SUMMARY

Through classical conditioning, an organism learns to emit a behavior in response to a stimulus that previously had no effect. Through instrumental conditioning, an organism learns to repeat or avoid making a response in the presence of a discriminative stimulus. By these means, an organism's behavior adapts to its environment.

Classical conditioning occurs when a response is elicited by an unconditional stimulus. This event strengthens the connection between neurons that detect the stimulus and neurons that control the elicited response. Reinforcement occurs when a response such as eating, drinking, or sexual behavior is performed. This event increases the strength of connections between neurons that detect the discriminative stimulus and those that evoke the instrumental response. Punishment occurs when a defensive reaction is elicited by an aversive stimulus. This event strengthens the connection between neurons that detect the discriminative stimulus and those that evoke the defensive reaction. When the defensive response occurs, it competes with other responses, including the one that is punished.

The drive-reduction hypothesis of reinforcement suggested that drives provided the motivation for an organism to become aroused and active. If increased activity led the organism to emit a response that produced a stimulus that reduced the drive, the animal's response was reinforced. However, logical and empirical arguments refuted the drive-reduction hypothesis. As we will see in the next section, data from studies of reinforcing brain stimulation further contradict this hypothesis.

■ REINFORCING BRAIN STIMULATION

Its Discovery

The discovery of the ability of electrical brain stimulation to reinforce behavior was made by accident. James Olds was trying to determine whether electrical stimulation of the reticular formation might increase arousal and thus facilitate learning. He was assisted in this project by Peter Milner, who was a graduate student at the time. Olds had heard a talk by Neal Miller that described the aversive effects of electrical stimulation of the brain. Therefore, he decided to make sure that stimulation of the reticular formation was not aversive — if it were, the effects of this stimulation on the speed of learning would be difficult to assess. Fortunately for the investigators, one of the electrodes missed its target; the tip wound up some millimeters away, probably in the hypothalamus. (Unfortunately, the brain of the animal was lost, so histological verification could not be obtained.) If all of the electrodes had reached their intended target, Olds and Milner would not have discovered what they did.

Here is Olds's description of what happened when he tested this animal to see if the brain stimulation was aversive:

I applied a brief train of 60-cycle sine-wave electrical current whenever the animal entered one corner of the enclosure. The animal did not stay away from the corner, but rather came back quickly after a brief sortie which followed the first stimulation and came back even more quickly after a briefer sortie which followed the second stimulation. By the time the third electrical stimulus had been applied the animal seemed indubitably to be "coming back for more." (Olds, 1973, p. 81)

Olds and Milner were intrigued and excited by this result. They implanted electrodes in the brains of a group of rats and allowed the animals to administer their own stimulation by pressing a lever-operated

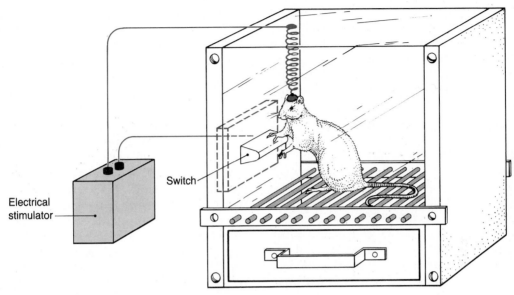

FIGURE 13.6
An operant chamber with a lever, used in studies of the effects of
reinforcing brain stimulation.

switch in an operant chamber. (See **Figure 13.6.**) The animals readily pressed the lever; in their initial study, Olds and Milner (1954) reported response rates of over seven hundred per hour. In subsequent studies, rates of many thousands of responses per hour have been obtained. Clearly, electrical stimulation of the brain can be a very potent reinforcer.

The anatomy of reinforcement will be discussed in a later section of this chapter. Here, it suffices to say that electrical stimulation of many parts of the brain can reinforce behavior. In general, stimulation of parts of the limbic system and motor system are effective, but the best and most reliable location is the **medial forebrain bundle (MFB),** a bundle of axons that travel in a rostral-caudal axis from the midbrain to the rostral basal forebrain. The MFB passes through the lateral hypothalamus, and it is in this region that most investigators place the tips of their electrodes. The MFB contains long ascending and descending axons that interconnect forebrain and midbrain structures, and short axons that connect adjacent regions. It also contains ascending catecholaminergic and serotonergic axons on their way from the brain stem to their diencephalic and telencephalic projection areas. As we will see later in this chapter, recent studies suggest that a particular subset of these fibers is responsible for the reinforcing effects of stimulation of the MFB.

How Does Brain Stimulation Reinforce Behavior?

Response-Eliciting Effects of Reinforcing Brain Stimulation

As we saw earlier in this chapter, the event that reinforces a behavior is the elicitation of a response — usually, an **appetitive response.** (*Appetitive* responses include such behaviors as eating, drinking, nest building, copulating, or exploring a new environment.) For example, feedback from the responses associated with eating (including salivation, chewing, swallowing, and various internal reflexes) reinforces the ability of the currently present stimuli to cause the animal to emit whatever behavior just occurred, such as lever pressing. Therefore, we might expect that reinforcing brain stimulation would in some way be related to the elicitation of responses. Indeed, this is the case: reinforcing brain stimulation almost always elicits responses. For example, if the tip of an electrode is placed in a rat's MFB, electrical stimulation will elicit a variety of species-typical behaviors. Depending on the location of the electrode and the objects present in the rat's environment, the stimulation will evoke eating, drinking, fighting, copulation, gnawing on wooden blocks, carrying of objects, or shredding of nesting material. When no objects are present, the rat will engage in sniffing and frantic exploratory behavior. If the rat is placed in an operant chamber that contains a lever but no other objects, it will learn to press the lever if doing so turns on the stimulator.

Proponents of the drive-reduction hypothesis of reinforcement could not explain why stimulation that causes eating or drinking can also reinforce behavior. The drive-reduction hypothesis stated that drives like hunger and thirst were aversive, and that reinforcers like food and water derived their reinforcing status from the fact that they reduced these aversive drives. Because stimulation of the MFB apparently increases drive, it should be aversive. However, the hypothesis that reinforcement is produced by the feedback from an organism's own responding (for example, its eating or drinking) is consistent with the response-eliciting effects of electrical brain stimulation. We can hypothesize that the artificial brain stimulation in some way mimics the feedback from making an appetitive re-

sponse. Even in the absence of food, water, or other objects, electrical stimulation of the MFB simulates natural reinforcers, strengthening the connection between neurons that are activated by the stimuli in the environment and those that produce the behavior that just occurred (for example, pressing the lever). (See **Figure 13.7.**)

Electrical stimulation of some parts of the brain causes aversive effects, not reinforcing ones. If an animal presses a lever that delivers electrical stimulation that has these effects, it will avoid pressing it again — in other words, the lever pressing is punished. An animal will also learn to make a response that turns off such stimulation or prevents it from happening. In general, aversive brain stimulation, like reinforcing brain stimulation, elicits species-typical behaviors, but these behaviors tend to be defensive in nature. As you recall, the most important effect of a punishing stimulus is that it elicits species-typical defensive responses. These responses become classically conditioned to the stimuli that are present at the time. When these stimuli are encountered later, they evoke the defensive responses, which interfere with other responses, including the one that is being punished. The dog's tendency to withdraw from the porcupine interferes with its approaching the animal.

Examples of species-typical defensive responses produced by brain stimulation are flight reactions produced by stimulation of the dorsal hypothalamus (Clemente and Chase, 1973) and irritable aggression produced by stimulation of the medial hypothalamus (Flynn, Vanegas, Foote, and Edwards, 1970; Panksepp, 1971a). Stimulation that produces these reactions is aversive. In contrast, stimulation that produces predatory aggression (such as that normally displayed by a carnivorous animal) is reinforcing. Apparently, aversive brain stimulation punishes a response by strengthening the connection be-

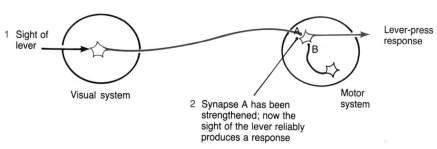

FIRST LEVER PRESS

AFTER SEVERAL REINFORCEMENTS

FIGURE 13.7
A hypothetical neural model of instrumental conditioning (reinforcement)
by means of electrical brain stimulation.

tween neurons that are activated by the stimuli in the present environment and the neurons that control the defensive reaction. For example, if a rat presses a lever that turns on stimulation that elicits flight, the sight of the lever itself comes to elicit running away, just as the sight of a porcupine comes to elicit withdrawal for a dog that has had experience with the effects of its quills. (See **Figure 13.8.**)

Interactions with Conditions of Deprivation and Satiety
Variables related to motivation can interact with the effects of reinforcing brain stimula-

tion. Conditions that alter the probability or strength of naturally elicited responses (such as eating or drinking) also affect responding for reinforcing brain stimulation. For example, when a rat is pressing a lever that produces electrical stimulation of the MFB, its rate of responding will vary with alterations in hunger, no matter how these alterations are produced. In several studies, investigators increased hunger by depriving rats of food or injecting them with insulin and observed corresponding increases in the animals' rate of responding for MFB stimulation. They decreased hunger by feeding the rats, placing food directly into their stomach through an

FIRST LEVER PRESS

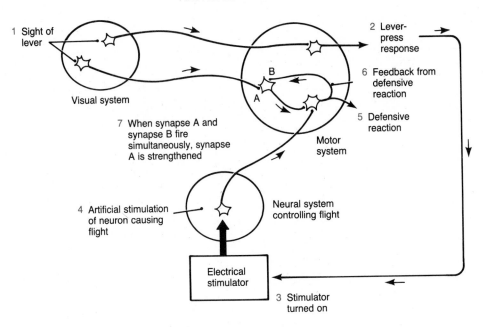

AFTER SEVERAL PUNISHMENTS

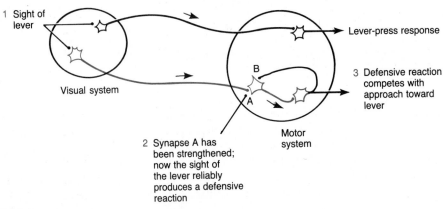

FIGURE 13.8
A hypothetical neural model of instrumental conditioning (punishment)
by means of aversive electrical brain stimulation.

implanted tube, or injecting them with glucagon; these manipulations decreased response
rates (Balagura and Hoebel, 1967; Mount and
Hoebel, 1967; Hoebel, 1968). Thus, the potency of reinforcing brain stimulation ap-

pears to be increased when deprivation conditions increase the likelihood or strength of
an elicited response and to be decreased
when satiety decreases its strength or likelihood. Presumably, this interaction occurs be-

cause reinforcing brain stimulation mimics the effects of the performance of an appetitive response; just as deprivation or satiation alters the strength of an appetitive response, it alters the effectiveness of the brain stimulation.

There is some evidence that specific motivational conditions affect the potency of reinforcing stimulation of different parts of the brain. Caggiula (1970) found that treatments that increased or decreased the probability of specific behaviors interacted with different forms of reinforcing brain stimulation. He trained male rats to respond for lateral hypothalamic or posterior hypothalamic stimulation. When water or receptive females were present, lateral hypothalamic stimulation produced drinking and posterior hypothalamic stimulation produced copulation. Castration, which reduces male sexual behavior, reduced the rate of responding for self-administered posterior hypothalamic stimulation; replacement therapy with testosterone increased the response rates once more. However, these manipulations had no effect on responding for lateral hypothalamic stimulation, which is affected by changes in thirst. Thus, there is evidence for at least some response-specific separation in the effects of reinforcing brain stimulation.

There is also evidence that reinforcing brain stimulation is a nonspecific elicitor of behaviors. Valenstein, Cox, and Kakolewski (1970) found that a rat that ate food in response to electrical stimulation of the MFB could be induced to drink if the food was removed and water was presented instead. Thus, although stimulation of some locations is more likely to produce a particular kind of behavior than another, stimulation of many locations facilitates a *range* of behaviors. The particular behavior that the animal performs depends upon the environment. This phenomenon may be related to the one discussed in the next section.

Aftereffects of Reinforcing Stimuli

So far, my discussion of elicited behaviors has concerned their effects on responses that preceded them and hence were reinforced. But elicited behaviors have an effect on responses that *follow* them, as well. Experiments suggest that these aftereffects are at least somewhat nonspecific. When a response is elicited, it temporarily increases the potency of many stimuli to elicit their associated responses. Put in more familiar terms, the occurrence of a vigorous response causes temporary *arousal*. Some psychologists have described arousal in terms of increased attention to stimuli, but it is clear that the important effect of arousal is the increased likelihood that the animal will emit a response. Attention, like a drive or an unseen dragon, reveals its presence only through its effects on behavior.

An example of the aftereffects of an appetitive response was provided by Panksepp and Trowill (1967), who took advantage of the fact that rats, like humans, enjoy sweets even when they are not hungry. The investigators attached plastic tubes to the rats' heads so that a small amount of sweetened chocolate milk was injected directly into their mouths whenever the rats pressed a lever. The investigators made the rats hungry and trained them to press the lever. During later sessions, when these rats were not hungry, they would usually not bother to press the lever when they were placed in the apparatus. However, when the investigators manually operated the apparatus so that the rats received a taste of the chocolate milk, the rats would immediately run to the lever and begin pressing. The aftereffect of tasting and swallowing the milk strengthened the ability of the lever to elicit pressing. (This phenomenon resembles the excitatory effect that occurs when we eat a peanut or potato chip—the "appetizer effect.")

Falk (1972) discovered how dramatic the

excitatory aftereffects of reinforcing stimuli can be. He found that when a very hungry rat receives small pieces of food at infrequent intervals — say, every 2 minutes — the animal becomes very active, engaging in a variety of species-typical behaviors. If water is present the animal will drink copiously, sometimes consuming an amount equal to 30 percent of its body weight during a 3-hour session. The behaviors are not limited to ingestive ones; if a block of wood is present the rat will gnaw on it, if another male is present the rat will attack it, and so on. Behaviors elicited by these means are called *adjunctive behaviors,* because they occur as an adjunct to intermittent reinforcement. Clearly, reinforcing stimuli have an excitatory effect on an organism's subsequent behavior.

As we have seen, reinforcing brain stimulation appears to mimic the effects of feedback from making an appetitive response. Thus, we would predict that electrical brain stimulation should also have aftereffects. We might expect that eliciting stimuli that occurred during these aftereffects would produce more vigorous responses. As we will see, this is indeed the case.

Even the earliest studies of reinforcing brain stimulation discovered that some animals that had responded at high rates on one

day ignored the lever the next day when put into the testing chamber. However, if the experimenters gave the animals one or two free *priming* shots of electrical brain stimulation, they ran to the lever and began responding again. (The term *priming* comes from the fact that a pump that has not been used for a while often needs to be "primed" with some water to get it working again.) These phenomena — overnight decrements and priming — have been observed in a large number of studies (e.g., Olds and Milner, 1954; Wetzel, 1963). Because Panksepp and Trowill (1967) observed the same effects from their nonhungry rats that received oral injections of chocolate milk, these phenomena do not appear to be peculiar to electrical brain stimulation, as most investigators had previously believed.

Gallistel (1969) investigated the decay of the aftereffects of reinforcing brain stimulation. He reinforced running with "trains" of brief pulses of current to the brain. (The term *train* refers to the appearance of a graph of these pulses, which come one after the other like a string of boxcars.) The rats were taught to run through an alley to a goal box, at which point they received a train of pulses. First, the rats received a variable number (one to twenty) of priming pulse trains (sixty-four

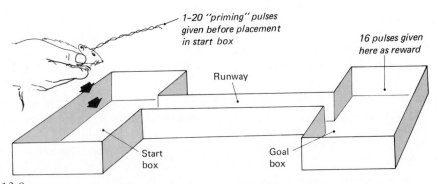

FIGURE 13.9
The procedure used by Gallistel (1969) to test the effects of priming on reinforcement by electrical brain stimulation.

pulses in each train) just before they were placed in the starting box. Then, once they reached the goal box at the end of the alley, they received a fixed number of pulses (sixteen) to reinforce their running. This procedure is outlined in **Figure 13.9.**

Gallistel found that the speed of running depended on two factors: the number of priming pulses the subject received, and the amount of time that had elapsed since the pulses were administered. Figure 13.10 shows data obtained from one rat; note how one priming pulse train facilitated running only slightly, whereas twenty priming pulse trains produced a much more striking increase in running speed. (See **Figure 13.10.**) The data appear to show that reinforcing brain stimulation has an aftereffect that can influence subsequent responding.

Evidence suggests that the aftereffects of reinforcement are largely nonspecific; that is, they facilitate the elicitation of a variety of responses, not just the one that is elicited by the reinforcing stimulus. This process is probably the one that produces adjunctive behaviors. It is probably also the same one that I described in another context in Chapter 11. As we saw there, a rat can be induced to eat or drink (depending on whether food or water is present) merely by pinching its tail. Other behaviors can also be elicited, including the gnawing of blocks of wood or sexual activity (Antelman, Rowland, and Fisher, 1976). Again, the behavior that is observed depends upon the objects that are present at the time of testing.

The arousal produced by this form of mild stress appears to be mediated by a system of

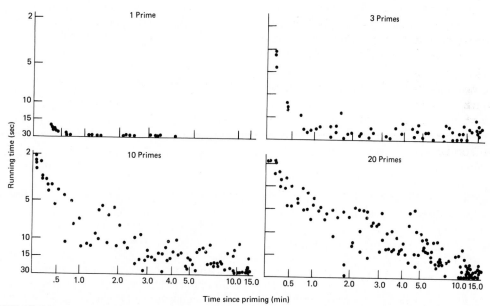

FIGURE 13.10

Data from the procedure shown in Figure 13.9. Running time as a function of delay after varying amounts of priming stimulation. (From Gallistel, C.R., *Journal of Comparative and Physiological Psychology,* 1969, *69,* 713–721. Copyright 1969 by the American Psychological Association. Reprinted by permission of the author.)

dopamine-secreting neurons. Antelman and his colleagues found that dopamine antagonists, but not norepinephrine antagonists, blocked the behavior-eliciting effects of tail pinching. As we will see, dopaminergic mechanisms have been implicated in the reinforcing effects of electrical brain stimulation, which suggests that reinforcement and elicitation of behaviors are related physiologically.

Koob, Fray, and Iversen (1976) and Fray, Koob, and Iversen (1978) attached paper clips to rats' tails and found that this source of stimulation induced them to run through a maze in order to find a block of wood, which they would then proceed to gnaw on. Subjects without the paper clips did not do so. Presumably, the arousal caused by the stimulation of the tail facilitated the effectiveness of the presence of a block of wood to elicit gnawing. The act of gnawing reinforced the rats' running through the maze. More specifically, it increased the ability of the stimuli associated with the maze to produce running.

The studies I just cited underscore the relation between reinforcement and elicitation: the aftereffects of reinforcing stimuli (or, indeed, of any eliciting stimulus) cause arousal that increases the eliciting properties of other stimuli in the environment. Thus, the "priming effect" of reinforcing brain stimulation or small amounts of tasty substances like chocolate milk, the adjunctive behaviors, and the behaviors induced by tail pinching are probably all mediated by a common neural mechanism, which appears to involve dopaminergic neurons.

INTERIM SUMMARY

Olds and Milner discovered that rats would perform a response that caused electrical current to be delivered through an electrode placed in their brain. Subsequent studies found that stimulation

of many locations had reinforcing effects, but that the medial forebrain bundle produced the strongest and most reliable ones.

Reinforcing brain stimulation appears also to elicit behaviors, or at least to increase the ability of environmental stimuli to elicit behaviors. Although there is some anatomical specificity (for example, MFB stimulation tends to produce ingestive behaviors, and posterior hypothalamic stimulation tends to produce sexual behaviors), the effects of reinforcing brain stimulation are to a certain extent general. In an environment containing food, MFB stimulation elicits eating; in one containing water, it elicits drinking; and so on. These effects can be explained by the model of reinforcement I presented in the first section of this chapter: the stimulation mimics the feedback from having made an appetitive response, which is the normal condition for reinforcement. This artificial feedback strengthens the connection between neurons that detect stimuli and neurons whose activity produces behaviors. For example, if an animal receives MFB stimulation when it presses a lever, the sight of the lever becomes an eliciting stimulus that produces pressing.

As we saw, conditions such as deprivation or satiety, which increase or decrease the strength of naturally elicited responses, interact with the effects of reinforcing brain stimulation in a predictable way: a hungry animal presses more vigorously for electrical stimulation that elicits eating, and a satiated animal presses less. Because the effects of the electrical stimulation in some way resemble the feedback from making an appetitive response, these effects are increased by conditions that facilitate such responses and are decreased by conditions that inhibit them.

Natural reinforcers have nonspecific aftereffects: stimuli that elicit vigorous behaviors activate behavior in general, making all eliciting stimuli become more potent. The "appetizer effect" and adjunctive behaviors are clear-cut examples of this phenomenon. In a similar manner, reinforcing brain stimulation has an excitatory aftereffect that can be seen in the priming phenomenon. Nonspecific arousal produced by tail pinching can facilitate the effectiveness of an otherwise neutral stimulus enough to make it become a reinforcer: when wearing a paper clip on its tail, a rat gnaws a block of wood, and this elicited behavior strengthens the animal's tendency to approach the wood.

■ ANATOMY OF REINFORCEMENT

An animal's behavior can be reinforced by electrical stimulation of many parts of the brain, including the olfactory bulb, prefrontal cortex, nucleus accumbens, caudate nucleus, putamen, various thalamic nuclei, reticular formation, amygdala, ventral tegmental area, substantia nigra, locus coeruleus, and, of course, the MFB (Olds and Fobes, 1981). The finding that stimulation of so many structures is reinforcing suggests that more than one system is involved in reinforcement. During the 1960s, investigators attempted to determine whether any one part of the brain played a critical role in reinforcement by producing brain lesions and observing whether electrical brain stimulation in any of the remaining areas was still reinforcing. In a review of these studies, Valenstein (1966) concluded that no one structure appeared to be of singular importance. A few years later, Olds and Olds (1969) found that large brain lesions caudal to stimulating electrodes in the MFB did abolish their reinforcing effect, suggesting that these electrodes stimulated descending axons that produced effects in the midbrain or brain stem. As we will see, this finding has been supported by recent evidence.

In the past several years, investigators have made considerable progress in identifying the neural systems that mediate reinforcement. We now know that catecholamine-secreting neurons (particularly dopaminergic ones) play a critical role, and that the axons that are activated by stimulation of the MFB descend to brain stem structures, including a nucleus that contains dopaminergic neurons. We also know that other systems of neurons, which do not involve fibers of the MFB, mediate reinforcing effects, too. Furthermore, the endogenous opiates have been shown to play a role in reinforcement, perhaps by modulating the effectiveness or activity of catecholamine-secreting neurons.

Anatomy of Catecholaminergic Pathways

The development of the histofluorescence techniques permitted investigators to trace the pathways of monoaminergic neurons. They soon discovered that the distribution of reinforcing electrode sites nicely coincided with the distribution of catecholaminergic neurons — those that secrete norepinephrine and dopamine. That is, brain stimulation through electrodes whose tips were placed in fiber bundles that contained catecholaminergic axons or in structures that received catecholaminergic projections generally had reinforcing effects. Furthermore, the administration of amphetamine, a potent catecholamine agonist, greatly increased the rate at which animals would respond for reinforcing brain stimulation (Stein, 1964). These findings suggested that catecholaminergic neurons participate in the process of reinforcement.

There are several systems of neurons whose terminal buttons secrete dopamine or norepinephrine. First, let us consider the two principal noradrenergic pathways, the *central tegmental tract* and the *dorsal tegmental bundle* (Moore and Bloom, 1979). The central tegmental tract arises in the medulla, from groups of cell bodies labeled by Ungerstedt (1971) as A1 and A2, and in the pons, from cell bodies in group A5 and in the subcoeruleus cell group, located just ventral to the locus coeruleus. The axons of almost all of these neurons terminate in the hypothalamus. (See **Figure 13.11.**) The cell bodies of the second major noradrenergic system, the dorsal tegmental bundle, are contained in the locus coeruleus. Their axons project to the

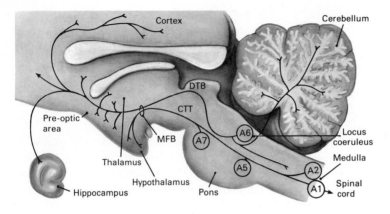

FIGURE 13.11
The principal noradrenergic pathways. CTT = central tegmental tract; DTB = dorsal tegmental bundle; MFB = medial forebrain bundle.

neocortex, hippocampus, thalamus, cerebellar cortex, and medulla. (See **Figure 13.11.**)

The major pathways of dopaminergic neurons begin in the substantia nigra and the ventral tegmental area (Moore and Bloom, 1978; Lindvall, 1979). The *nigrostriatal system* starts in the *pars compacta* of the substantia nigra (usually abbreviated as *SNC,* for "substantia nigra compacta") and projects to the *neostriatum*—the caudate nucleus and putamen. As we saw earlier, this system is important in the control of movement; its degeneration results in Parkinson's disease. (See **Figure 13.12.**) The *tegmentostriatal system* begins in the ventral tegmental area *(VTA)* and projects to the **nucleus accumbens,** a region of the basal forebrain rostral to the preoptic area and immediately

adjacent to the septum. (The nucleus accumbens, which is closely associated with the limbic system, is part of the *paleostriatum.*) As we will see, this system appears to play the most important role in reinforcement. Many investigators believe that excessive activity of this system in humans can result in schizophrenia, a hypothesis I will discuss in detail in Chapter 17. (See **Figure 13.12.**) The *mesolimbic/mesocortical system* begins in both brain stem areas, SNC and VTA, and projects to several forebrain regions of the cortex and limbic system, including the olfactory tubercle, septum, amygdala, lateral and medial prefrontal cortex, and entorhinal (limbic) cortex. (See **Figure 13.12.**) You should note that the major catecholaminergic pathways pass through the MFB on their way

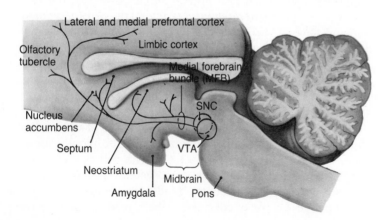

FIGURE 13.12
The principal dopaminergic pathways. SNC = pars compacta of the substantia nigra; VTA = ventral tegmental area.

forward. Thus, stimulation of the MFB could potentially activate axons of all of these systems.

There are five other dopaminergic pathways: one in the retina; one in the olfactory bulb; one that projects from the zona incerta to the medial preoptic area, hypothalamus, and septum; one that projects from the periaqueductal gray matter to the medial thalamus and hypothalamus; and one that projects from the hypothalamus to the pituitary stalk. So far, none of these pathways has been implicated in reinforcement.

Neurochemistry of Reinforcement

Norepinephrine

The noradrenergic system whose cell bodies are located in the locus coeruleus was the first specific system to be implicated in reinforcement (Stein, 1964, 1968). Animals will work for stimulation delivered there (Crow, Spear, and Arbuthnott, 1972). Furthermore, after one hour of electrical stimulation delivered to the locus coeruleus, increased production of norepinephrine is observed in the cortex, which suggests that the reinforcing effect may be related to the release of norepinephrine (Anlezark, Arbuthnott, Crow, Eccleston, and Walter, 1973). In addition, a rat whose lever pressing is reinforced by electrical stimulation of the locus coeruleus will respond faster after receiving an injection of amphetamine, a catecholamine agonist (Ritter and Stein, 1973).

Subsequent research contradicted the noradrenergic hypothesis of reinforcement. Although electrical stimulation of the region of the locus coeruleus is reinforcing, a number of studies suggest that the effect is not mediated by noradrenergic neurons. Routtenberg and Malsbury (1969) found that electrical stimulation of the **superior cerebellar peduncle** was reinforcing. Because this bundle of fibers contains noradrenergic axons from the locus coeruleus that project to the cerebellum, this finding suggested that activation of these neurons may have been responsible for this effect. However, Amaral and Routtenberg (1975) used low-intensity electrical current, delivered through thin electrodes, to minimize the likelihood that adjacent regions would be stimulated. (See **Figure 13.13.**) They found that electrical stimulation of the locus coeruleus was *not* reinforcing, but that stimulation near the superior cerebellar peduncle was. In addition, Clavier and Routtenberg (1975) found that

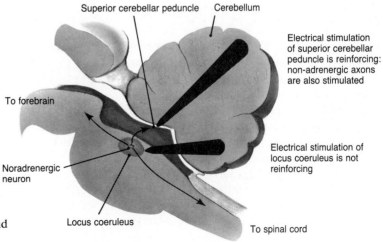

Superior cerebellar peduncle   Cerebellum

Electrical stimulation of superior cerebellar peduncle is reinforcing: non-adrenergic axons are also stimulated

To forebrain

Electrical stimulation of locus coeruleus is not reinforcing

Noradrenergic neuron

Locus coeruleus

To spinal cord

FIGURE 13.13
The experiment by Amaral and Routtenberg (1975).

lesions of the locus coeruleus, which killed the noradrenergic axons that travel through the superior cerebellar peduncle, had little or no effect on reinforcement produced by stimulation of the superior cerebellar peduncle. Thus, although some axons that travel through the superior cerebellar peduncle are involved in reinforcement, they do not appear to be noradrenergic. As we will see in Chapter 14, recent studies have found that cells of the cerebellum whose axons pass through the superior cerebellar peduncle play an important, perhaps crucial, role in some forms of classical conditioning. It is possible that these axons also play a role in reinforcement and are responsible for the reinforcing effect of stimulation of the superior cerebellar peduncle.

Pharmacological evidence also contradicts the hypothesis that noradrenergic neurons mediate the reinforcing effects of electrical stimulation elsewhere in the brain. Lippa, Antelman, Fisher, and Canfield (1973) injected rats with FLA-63, a specific inhibitor of dopamine β-hydroxylase, the enzyme that converts dopamine to norepinephrine. Even though this drug reduced brain levels of norepinephrine by 70 percent, the animals' rate of responding for brain stimulation was unchanged.

Although evidence suggests that noradrenergic neurons are not essential for the reinforcing effects of MFB stimulation, they may play a role in other forms of reinforcement. Martin and Myers (1975) measured the release of norepinephrine in the medial hypothalamus and observed an increase just after the onset of a spontaneous meal. (You will recall from Chapter 11 that infusion of norepinephrine into the paraventricular nucleus, located in this region, elicits eating.) Cytawa, Jurkowlaniec, and Bialowas (1980) found that injections of norepinephrine could reinforce behavior. They successfully trained rats to run to one arm of a T-maze, where they received injections of norepinephrine through cannulas whose tips were located in the region of the paraventricular nuclei. They did not observe reinforcing effects when they injected dopamine, serotonin, or acetylcholine. The reinforcing effect did not appear to be related directly to feeding; infusions in some locations reinforced the rat's behavior in the maze but did not increase eating. In another study, Jurkowlaniec and Bialowas (1981) found that infusions of norepinephrine into the dorsomedial amygdala had reinforcing effects, but only if the rats had been deprived of food. Therefore, noradrenergic neurons do appear to be involved in some forms of reinforcement, but their precise role is still uncertain.

Dopamine

Many studies have implicated dopaminergic systems in brain mechanisms of reinforcement. Electrical stimulation of areas of the brain that contain the cell bodies of the principal dopaminergic systems — the pars compacta of the substantia nigra (SNC) or the ventral tegmental area (VTA) — is reinforcing (Routtenberg and Malsbury, 1969; Crow, 1972). Furthermore, stimulation of many of the regions in which these neurons terminate (e.g., the caudate nucleus, nucleus accumbens, septum, and prefrontal cortex) is also reinforcing (Olds and Fobes, 1981). And the MFB, the stimulation of which is consistently and reliably reinforcing, is rich in dopaminergic axons (along with many other kinds, of course).

Several studies have suggested that the tegmentostriatal dopaminergic system may play a role in reinforcement caused by electrical stimulation of the MFB. Mora, Sanguinetti, Rolls, and Shaw (1975) placed stimulating electrodes in the MFB. They observed that injections of spiroperidol, a potent blocker of dopamine (DA) receptors, into the nucleus

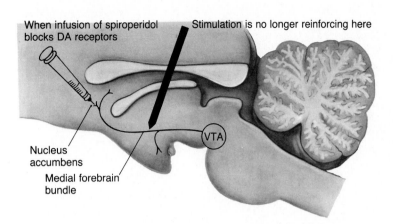

When infusion of spiroperidol blocks DA receptors

Stimulation is no longer reinforcing here

Nucleus accumbens

Medial forebrain bundle

VTA

FIGURE 13.14
The experiment by Mora, Sanguinetti, Rolls, and Shaw (1975).

accumbens abolished responding for MFB stimulation. (See **Figure 13.14.**) These results suggested that the reinforcing effect was transmitted by means of ascending dopaminergic fibers that pass through the MFB and synapse in the nucleus accumbens. In a related study, Roberts, Corcoran, and Fibiger (1977) infused 6-hydroxydopamine, a drug that destroys dopaminergic axons and terminal buttons, into the nucleus accumbens. The destruction of the dopaminergic axons abolished the reinforcing effects of cocaine; rats with these lesions would no longer make a response in order to inject themselves with this drug. (Cocaine, like amphetamine, is a potent dopamine agonist.)

Injections of a variety of drugs that block dopamine receptors, including pimozide, spiroperidol, and haloperidol, suppress responding for previously reinforcing brain stimulation (Fibiger, 1978). The question is this: is the suppression caused by inhibition of reinforcement mechanisms, or do the drugs simply prevent the animals from responding? As we will see, the results favor the reinforcement hypothesis.

Rolls, Rolls, Kelly, Shaw, Wood, and Dale (1974) evaluated the effects of spiroperidol on responding for food and water and for electrical stimulation of the ventral tegmental area, hippocampus, hypothalamus, sep-

tum, and nucleus accumbens. The drug (a blocker of dopamine receptors) suppressed responding for *all* kinds of reinforcers. The question was whether the animals stopped responding because the food, water, or electrical stimulation was no longer reinforcing, or whether they stopped because the drug interfered with motor systems that controlled their behavior. We just cannot decide from their data.

A study by Fouriezos and Wise (1976) suggested that drugs that block dopamine receptors impair reinforcement, not simply motor performance. If an animal's behavior is reinforced, and if the reinforcement is then terminated (for example, by disconnecting the food-dispensing mechanism), the animal will respond for a while and then gradually cease to respond. In other words, the behavior *extinguishes,* but not immediately. (*Extinction* refers to the decline of nonreinforced responses.) Fouriezos and Wise reasoned that if a drug suppresses neural systems that mediate reinforcement, then a drugged animal should act like one that has been placed on an extinction schedule — it should respond normally for a while, and then gradually stop. On the other hand, if the drug simply interferes with motor performance, then the animal's rate of responding should be low right from the time it is placed in the chamber.

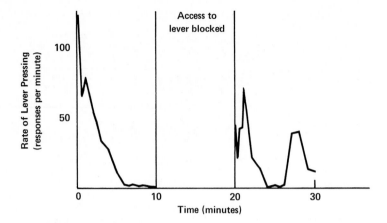

FIGURE 13.15
Lever-pressing responses made by a rat that had received an injection of pimozide, a blocker of dopamine receptors. Note that the rate of responding is high early in the session. (From Fouriezos, G., and Wise, R.A. *Brain Research,* 1976, *103,* 377–380.)

Fouriezos and Wise trained rats to press a lever for electrical brain stimulation. Next, they gave the animals injections of pimozide (a drug that blocks dopamine receptors). When the rats were placed in the operant chamber, they began pressing at a normal rate but soon slowed down; their behavior resembled that of rats placed on an extinction schedule. (See **Figure 13.15.**) Another study confirmed this one and ruled out the possibility that pimozide simply made the animals become fatigued more rapidly. Gallistel, Boytim, Gomita, and Klebanoff (1982) reinforced two different behaviors by MFB stimulation: pressing a lever and running through a maze. Next, they injected the rats with pimozide and permitted them to perform one task until they had "extinguished." Finally, they placed the rats in the other apparatus. The animals immediately began responding. Because the experience on the first task did not interfere with performance on the second, the rats were obviously not simply fatigued. Thus, pimozide does indeed mimic the effects of extinction, presumably because it blocks the reinforcing effect of brain stimulation.

Several studies by Spyraki, Fibiger, and Phillips (1982a, 1982b, 1983) suggest that the stimulation of dopamine receptors is necessary for the reinforcing effects of several kinds of stimuli. They used a special apparatus to establish a conditioned place preference. They placed rats in a small chamber that permitted access to two other chambers, one painted black and the other painted white, so that they could easily be discriminated. After testing the rats' initial preference for entering the white or the black room, the experimenters administered reinforcers on 8 successive days. On days 1, 3, 5, and 7, they injected the rats with haloperidol 45 minutes before placing them in the *nonpreferred* chamber, where they received the reinforcer. On days 2, 4, 6, and 8, they injected them with a placebo and later placed them in the *preferred* chamber, where they received nothing. The rationale was this: if the dopamine receptor blocker had no effect on reinforcement, then the rats should learn to prefer the nonpreferred side, where reinforcers were delivered. However, if the drug abolished the effectiveness of the reinforcer, then the animals should not learn a new preference. (Control experiments determined that the haloperidol itself did not produce a conditioned place aversion. See **Figure 13.16.**)

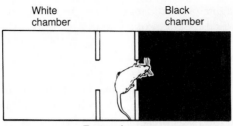

White chamber   Black chamber

Test preference
(For simplicity's sake, assume
all rats prefer black chamber)

CONTROL GROUP   EXPERIMENTAL GROUP

Food is available, rat eats it   Food is available, rat eats it

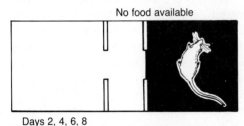
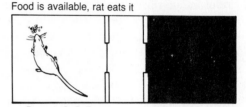

Days 1, 3, 5, 7   Days 1, 3, 5, 7
Inject with placebo, 45 min. later place in white chamber   Inject with haloperidol, 45 min. later place in white chamber

No food available   No food available

Days 2, 4, 6, 8   Days 2, 4, 6, 8
Inject with placebo, 45 min. later place in black chamber   Inject with placebo, 45 min. later place in black chamber

TRAINING
- -
TEST

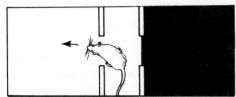

Day 9: Test preference
Rat has learned to prefer white chamber

Day 9: Test preference
Rat still prefers black chamber: has not learned

FIGURE 13.16
A diagram of one of the experiments by Spyraki and her colleagues.

Spyraki and her colleagues found that haloperidol prevented the establishment of a conditioned place preference reinforced by food, amphetamine, or heroin; thus, the reinforcing effects of food, a catecholamine agonist, and an opiate all appear to depend on the stimulation of dopamine receptors. The investigators noted that when food was present in the chamber on odd-numbered training days the rats *did* eat. Thus, haloperidol did not simply block the response normally elicited by the reinforcing stimulus; it blocked the reinforcing consequences of this response. Because the animals were tested in a drug-free condition, the effects cannot readily be attributed to changes in motor performance.

Opiates

Opiate receptors, as well as dopamine receptors, may play a role in reinforcement. This suggestion was first prompted by the observation that opiates such as morphine and heroin have reinforcing effects that cause some people to become addicted to the drugs. When opiate receptors and the endogenous opiates were discovered, it became apparent that these reinforcing effects were caused by activation of opiate receptors in the brain. This finding suggested that the release of opiates by natural causes might play a role in reinforcing behavior.

Neurons that contain opiate receptors are found in several regions of the brain in which electrical stimulation has reinforcing effects: the hypothalamus, nucleus accumbens, periaqueductal gray matter, and locus coeruleus. Rats will press a lever that causes opiates to be injected into their brains, thus activating these receptors. In addition, morphine and other opiates increase the rate of responding for reinforcing brain stimulation, and naloxone, an opiate receptor blocker, decreases the response rate (Olds and Fobes, 1981).

The reinforcing effect of opiates appears to involve dopaminergic neurons. As we saw in the previous section, Spyraki and her colleagues found that haloperidol blocked the ability of heroin to reinforce a conditioned place preference. In addition, two studies (Phillips and LePiane, 1980; Bozarth and Wise, 1981) found that a conditioned place preference could be reinforced by injections of morphine into the ventral tegmental area, but not by injections 2 mm ventral or 1 mm caudal to this structure. These results suggest that the morphine activates receptors directly on dopaminergic neurons, or perhaps on neurons that stimulate them.

Other studies suggest that opiates can reinforce behavior indirectly, by reducing species-typical defensive responses. Kapp, Gallagher, Applegate, and Frysinger (1982) found that the infusions of a synthetic opiate into the central nucleus of the amygdala blocked the development of classically conditioned changes in heart rate in response to a tone followed by an electrical shock. Conversely, infusions of naloxone, which blocks opiate receptors, facilitated the conditioning. These results suggest that stimulation of opiate receptors in the amygdala inhibits learned responses that have been classically conditioned to aversive stimuli. It is possible that under some conditions this effect prevents species-typical defensive responses from competing with other, appetitive responses. Here is a hypothetical example: Suppose a male rat learns to avoid a particular location where he was previously hurt or frightened. Later he encounters a sexually receptive female near that location. He follows her into the place he has learned to avoid. His sexual arousal causes the release of endogenous opiates, which inhibit conditioned defensive responses that would otherwise cause him to leave, and he copulates with the female. I admit that this example goes beyond the available data, but it provides a plausible account of the adaptive value of the experimental findings.

Neural Pathways That Mediate the Reinforcing Effects of Electrical Brain Stimulation

The Medial Forebrain Bundle

For many years the strong evidence implicating dopaminergic neurons (especially those that synapse in the nucleus accumbens) in mechanisms of reinforcement led most investigators to conclude that stimulation of the MFB reinforced behavior by triggering action potentials in ascending dopaminergic axons. However, recent studies indicate that the relevant axons are descending, not ascending, and that the release of dopamine in the forebrain is a secondary effect of this activation.

I already mentioned that Olds and Olds (1969) found that lesions caudal to an electrode placed in the MFB eliminated the reinforcing effect of stimulation delivered through it. In addition, Huang and Routtenberg (1971) made lesions through electrodes in the MFB that they had previously used to provide reinforcing brain stimulation. They used a degenerating axon stain to determine which parts of the brain received projections from the axons passing through the vicinity of the electrodes. Significantly, they traced degenerating fibers back to the ventral tegmental area.

Two techniques, 2-deoxyglucose (2-DG) autoradiography and classical electrophysiological methods, have revealed that the implication of the studies by Olds and Olds and Huang and Routtenberg is correct: electrical stimulation of the MFB initiates action potentials in descending axons that synapse in the ventral tegmental area. The stimulation then apparently activates dopaminergic neurons there that send fibers through the MFB to the nucleus accumbens and other forebrain structures.

You will recall from Chapter 5 that radioactive 2-DG can be used to determine the relative metabolic activity of the various regions of the brain. Yadin, Guarini, and Gallistel (1983) inserted stimulation electrodes in the MFB of rats. While the animals were actively pressing a lever for brain stimulation, the investigators injected them with radioactive 2-DG and let them continue responding for 45 minutes. During this time, the labeled 2-DG accumulated in highest concentrations in metabolically active cells. Because the chemical resembles glucose in its molecular structure, it enters cells, along with glucose. However, because it cannot be metabolized, it remains within the cells. Thus, a cell's radioactivity is proportional to its metabolic activity.

The rats were killed and their brains were sliced and placed on pieces of X-ray film. After allowing time for the radioactivity in the brain slices to expose the film, the investigators developed the film and analyzed the images with a computerized density-measuring system. They found evidence of increased activity at both ends of the MFB, in the ***nucleus of the diagonal band*** and the medial part of the lateral preoptic area, and in the ventromedial tegmentum (including the ventral tegmental area and the substantia nigra). (See **Figure 13.17.**)

Electrophysiological techniques confirm the 2-DG autoradiographic study. Stimulation of the MFB appears to produce reinforcing effects by activating long, myelinated axons with a diameter of 0.5 to 2.0 μm that descend to the ventromedial tegmentum. The cell bodies of these axons probably lie in the nucleus of the diagonal band and the lateral preoptic area, regions that were implicated by the autoradiographic study. Indeed, Phillipson (1979) injected horseradish peroxidase in the ventral tegmental area and found retrograde labeling of cell bodies in these two telencephalic structures. The size and direction of travel of these axons do not correspond with those of any known monoaminergic axons. Although dopaminergic and noradrenergic axons do travel through the MFB, they are thin and unmyelinated and are therefore difficult to stimulate electrically.

The evidence for these conclusions about the nature of the stimulated axons comes from several different types of electrophysio-

Rostral

— Nucleus of the diagonal band

— Medial forebrain bundle

— Path of stimulating electrode

— Periaqueductal gray matter

— Ventral tegmentum

Caudal

logical studies, two of which I will describe. The first method used pairs of pulses of electrical current delivered to the MFB to determine the refractory period of the stimulated axons. Yeomans (1975) measured the effectiveness of trains of twenty pulses (ten pairs) as reinforcers of lever pressing. When the pulses were evenly spaced, they produced their maximum effect. However, when the pairs were closely spaced, they were no more effective than ten single pulses. The reason for this result is that once an axon is stimulated, it becomes refractory to further stimulation and cannot respond again until it has recovered. Yeomans found that when the pulse pairs were separated by at least 1.2 msec, the reinforcing effect was as strong as that produced by twenty individual pulses; hence, the refractory period for the MFB axons was under 1.2 msec. (See **Figure 13.18.**)

From these results and the results of another (more complicated) electrophysiological experiment, Bielajew and Shizgal (1982) calculated that the velocity of action potentials in axons that mediate the reinforcing effect of MFB stimulation is between 2 and 8 meters per second, which implies that they are myelinated and have a diameter between 0.5 and 2.0 μm. Thus, they are not monoaminergic neurons, which are thinner and nonmyelinated.

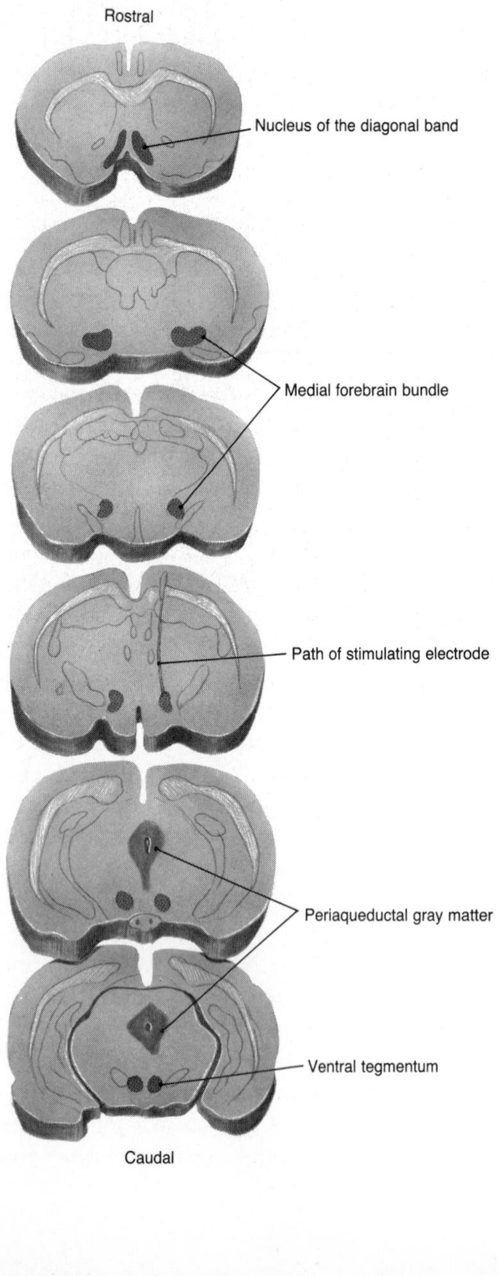

FIGURE 13.17
Drawings of 2-DG autoradiographs of a rat that had been receiving reinforcing stimulation of the medial forebrain bundle. The individual drawings are frontal sections, arranged from rostral to caudal. The colored regions were the most metabolically active. (Adapted from Gallistel, C.R. In *The Physiological Basis of Memory,* 2nd edition, edited by J.A. Deutsch. New York: Academic Press, 1983.)

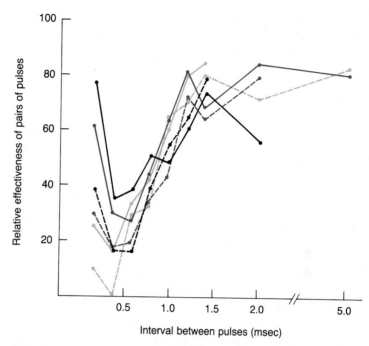

FIGURE 13.18
Effects of the interval between pairs of pulses delivered to the medial forebrain bundle on the strength of reinforcement. (From Yeomans, J.S. *Physiology & Behavior,* 1975, *15,* 593–602.)

Shizgal, Bielajew, and Kiss (1980) obtained evidence that the axons responsible for the reinforcing effects of electrical stimulation of the MFB are descending, having their origin in the forebrain and terminating in the midbrain. (In contrast, catecholaminergic axons in the MFB are ascending.) The investigators placed electrodes in the rostral and caudal ends of the MFB and passed negative (depolarizing) pulses of current through one electrode and positive (hyperpolarizing) pulses through the other. When the depolarizing stimulation was passed through the electrode in the caudal (midbrain) end, the rats pressed the lever rapidly. When the current was reversed, they pressed more slowly. Thus, the stimulation was most effective when the caudal stimulation was depolarizing. These results indicate that the cell bodies of the axons that mediate reinforcement are located rostrally, and the terminal buttons are located caudally. (See **Figure 13.19.**)

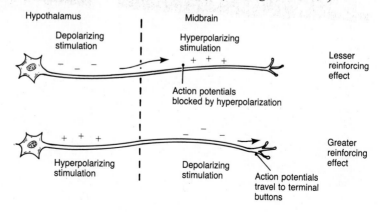

FIGURE 13.19
Effects of hyperpolarizing and depolarizing electrical stimulation on the effectiveness of reinforcing electrical brain stimulation, observed by Shizgal, Bielajew, and Kiss (1980).

In summary, the axons that produce the reinforcing effects of MFB stimulation are not ascending dopaminergic fibers. However, these axons terminate in the ventral tegmental area, where they activate dopaminergic neurons that ascend to the forebrain. Therefore, let us turn our attention to the forebrain.

Role of the Nucleus Accumbens
Pharmacological studies that I reviewed earlier suggest that dopamine receptors on neurons in the nucleus accumbens play an important role in the reinforcing effects of MFB stimulation. Although investigators previously believed that MFB stimulation directly activated ascending dopaminergic axons that synapse in the nucleus accumbens, the evidence I just reviewed suggests that their activation is indirect. Stimulation of the MFB appears to trigger action potentials in descending axons whose cell bodies lie in the nucleus of the diagonal band and the lateral

preoptic area and whose terminal buttons synapse with neurons in the ventromedial tegmentum, including the dopaminergic neurons of the ventral tegmental area. These neurons become active and cause dopamine (DA) to be released in the nucleus accumbens. (See **Figure 13.20.**) The obvious questions are, then, "When natural reinforcers occur, what stimulates the neurons in the diagonal band and lateral preoptic area?" and "What are the behavioral consequences of dopamine release in the nucleus accumbens?"

I will describe research that attempts to answer the first question in Chapter 14. As we will see there, some evidence indicates that neurons in the amygdala respond when reinforcing stimuli have been perceived, and their influence, along with the influence of neurons that signal hunger, activates neurons in the diagonal band and lateral preoptic area.

Several studies have provided a tentative

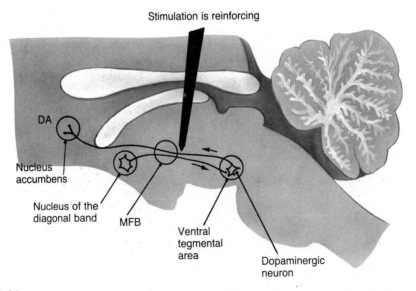

FIGURE 13.20
When the medial forebrain bundle is electrically stimulated, axons of dopaminergic neurons are indirectly stimulated by way of the ventral tegmental area.

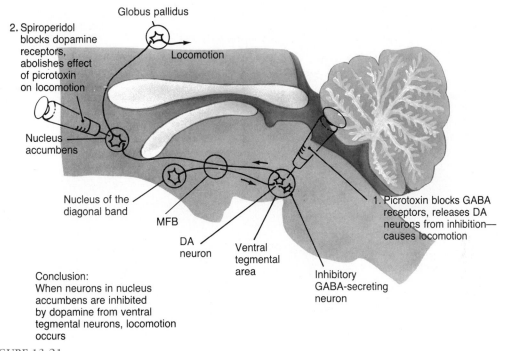

FIGURE 13.21

Locomotion occurs when neurons in the nucleus accumbens are inhibited
by dopamine-secreting synapses.

answer to the second question. The nucleus accumbens sends efferent axons to the globus pallidus, an important component of the motor system. Some investigators believe that these connections enable cells of the nucleus accumbens to modulate the activity of the globus pallidus, and hence an organism's behavior. Mogenson and Yim (1981) describe a series of electrophysiological studies that demonstrate a functional pathway from the ventral tegmental area to the nucleus accumbens to the globus pallidus. Pijnenburg and Van Rossum (1973) found that injection of dopamine into the nucleus accumbens elicited a behavior — locomotor activity — in rats. Mogenson and his colleagues (see Mogenson and Yim, 1981) found that injection of picrotoxin into the ventral tegmental area also produced locomotion. Because this

drug blocks inhibitory GABA receptors, the authors suggested that the effect was caused by removing inhibition from dopaminergic neurons there, and hence increasing their rate of firing. They confirmed this hypothesis by showing that injections of spiroperidol (a dopamine receptor blocker) into the nucleus accumbens blocked the behavioral effectiveness of picrotoxin in the ventral tegmental area. (See **Figure 13.21.**)

The cells of the nucleus accumbens that send fibers to the globus pallidus appear to be GABAergic (Pycock and Horton, 1976). Mogenson and his colleagues found that injections of picrotoxin into the globus pallidus increased the locomotor activity produced by injections of dopamine into the nucleus accumbens. Conversely, injections of GABA into the globus pallidus reduced locomotion

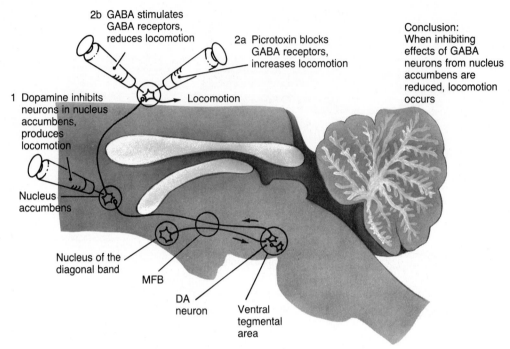

FIGURE 13.22
Locomotion occurs when inhibitory GABA-secreting synapses on neurons
in the globus pallidus decrease their activity.

produced by picrotoxin injections into the ventral tegmental area. Presumably, the GABAergic cells of the nucleus accumbens inhibit cells in the globus pallidus that stimulate behavior; dopamine secretion within the nucleus accumbens inhibits the GABAergic neurons and removes their inhibitory effects on behavior. Note that *inhibition* in the nucleus accumbens elicits a behavior by *removing inhibition* in the globus pallidus. (See **Figure 13.22.**)

The studies reviewed in this section provide a possible means by which dopamine secretion can affect behavior—the connection of the nucleus accumbens with the globus pallidus. Other experiments will have to determine whether this connection plays a role in a variety of reinforced behaviors.

Prefrontal Cortex: Part of Another System of Reinforcement?

Routtenberg and Sloan (1972) discovered that lever pressing can be reinforced with electrical stimulation of two regions of the prefrontal cortex of rats: the ***sulcal prefrontal cortex*** and the ***medial prefrontal cortex.*** The sulcal prefrontal cortex forms the dorsal bank of the *rhinal sulcus,* a groove that runs along the lateral side of the cerebrum, dividing the frontal neocortex from a region of basal frontal limbic cortex. The medial prefrontal cortex is located medial to the sulcal prefrontal cortex, along the interhemispheric fissure. (See **Figure 13.23.**)

Both regions of prefrontal cortex receive terminal buttons from dopaminergic axons of neurons of the ventral tegmental area; hence many investigators hypothesized that stimulation of these areas was reinforcing because it activated dopaminergic axons and terminal buttons. Indeed, injections of spiroperidol into the medial prefrontal cortex reduce the rate of responding reinforced by electrical stimulation of this region (Robertson and Mogenson, 1978). However, several studies that attempted to destroy dopaminergic axons that travel to the prefrontal cortex produced conflicting results (Clavier and Gerfen, 1979; Simon, Stinus, Tassin, Lavielle, Blanc, Thierry, Glowinski, LeMoal, 1979).

Gerfen and Clavier (1981) implanted thin, electrically insulated stainless-steel hypodermic needles into the sulcal prefrontal cortex and trained rats to press a lever for electrical stimulation delivered through the cannula (which served as an electrode). Next they injected either 6-hydroxydopamine or kainic acid through the cannula into the region surrounding its tip. The 6-hydroxydopamine lesions destroyed dopaminergic and noradrenergic axons and terminal buttons in the area, an effect the experimenters confirmed by means of histofluorescence techniques. The kainic acid destroyed cell bodies, which effect was confirmed with a cell-body stain. The destruction of dopaminergic and noradrenergic axons and terminal buttons did

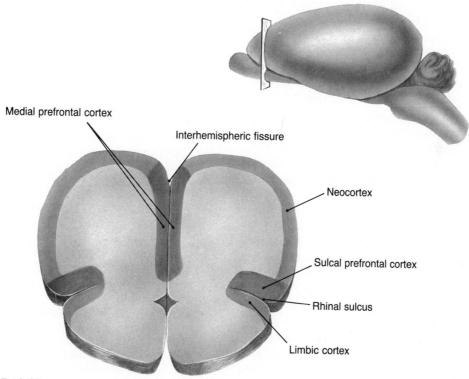

FIGURE 13.23

The location of the sulcal prefrontal cortex and the medial prefrontal cortex in the rat brain.

not diminish the reinforcing effect of stimulation of the sulcal prefrontal cortex; hence the release of these neurotransmitters is not necessary for the effect. However, the investigators found that destruction of cell bodies with kainic acid abolished responding for stimulation of the sulcal prefrontal cortex, which suggested to them that the reinforcing effects of such stimulation are mediated by axons that leave the sulcal prefrontal cortex and project caudally.

Gerfen and Clavier used the Fink-Heimer method to stain degenerating axons of sulcal prefrontal neurons that had been killed by the kainic acid lesions. They found that most of these axons projected to the basal ganglia, substantia nigra, midbrain reticular formation, and periaqueductal gray matter. Other regions, including the medial thalamus, lateral hypothalamus, and ventral tegmental area, received a few terminal buttons. The investigators noted that electrical stimulation of all of these regions has been shown to be reinforcing, but they also noted that lesions of the medial thalamus or the ventral tegmental area do not diminish the reinforcing effect of stimulation of the sulcal prefrontal cortex. Therefore, one or more of the other projection regions must mediate the reinforcing effect.

You will recall from the previous section that Yadin, Guarini, and Gallistel (1983) used 2-DG autoradiography to determine the location of neurons that were activated by stimulation of the MFB. These investigators also studied the effects of reinforcing stimulation of the medial prefrontal cortex. They found evidence for activation of the rhinal cortex, the *claustrum* (part of the paleostriatum), the basolateral amygdala, the dorsolateral septum, and the anterior part of the medial thalamus. However, they saw no activation of the nucleus of the diagonal band or the ventromedial tegmentum, the two regions they found to be activated by reinforcing MFB stimulation.

The significance of the areas implicated by Yadin and colleagues awaits further study; we cannot say whether the reinforcing effects of stimulation of the lateral (sulcal) and medial prefrontal cortex are mediated by the same or by different circuits. However, the studies by Gerfen and Clavier and by Yadin and colleagues both suggest that prefrontal stimulation and MFB stimulation reinforce behavior by different means. In addition, Corbett, Laferriere, and Milner (1980) obtained reinforcing effects by stimulating the medial prefrontal cortex even after they cut the connections between this area and the MFB.

INTERIM SUMMARY

For several years, investigators have believed that the catecholamines—norepinephrine and dopamine—play a role in reinforcement. This belief was suggested by the observation that amphetamine and cocaine, potent catecholamine agonists, have strong reinforcing effects. It appears that noradrenergic neurons play a role in food-related reinforcement. The role of dopaminergic neurons is probably more general. Infusions of dopamine antagonists into the nucleus accumbens, a forebrain nucleus that receives many dopaminergic terminal buttons, blocks the reinforcing effects of MFB stimulation and many natural reinforcers. Several studies have shown that the effect is specific to reinforcement and does not seem to be caused by interference with motor mechanisms.

The opiates appear to play two different roles in reinforcement. Infusion of opiates into the ventral tegmental area is reinforcing and perhaps partly accounts for the addicting potential for this class of drug. When injected into the amygdala, opiates also inhibit species-typical defensive responses, thus preventing these responses from competing with others.

The reinforcing effects of MFB stimulation are blocked by lesions caudal to the electrode, which suggests that the axons that mediate the effects travel caudally. Electrophysiological studies have shown that the axons directly activated by the stimulation are myelinated, have a diameter between 0.5 and 2.0 μm, and travel caudally, terminating in the ventral midbrain. There, they activate dopaminergic neurons, which send their axons rostrally, especially to the nucleus accumbens. Studies using 2-DG autoradiography confirm that electrical stimulation of the MFB increases the metabolic activity of the ventral tegmentum and the basal forebrain.

Pharmacological studies have suggested that an important projection region of the nucleus accumbens is the globus pallidus, a part of the motor system. (By definition, reinforcement mechanisms must affect behavior.) When neurons in the ventral tegmental area are activated, they release dopamine in the nucleus accumbens, which inhibits neurons there. The fall in the activity of these neurons reduces their inhibitory effect (mediated by GABA) on neurons of the globus pallidus. The activity of *these* neurons increases, and behavior occurs.

Two regions of prefrontal cortex are involved in a separate system capable of reinforcing animals' behavior. Because lesions produced by 6-hydroxydopamine in these regions do not reduce the reinforcing effect of electrical stimulation there, the system does not involve catecholaminergic neurons. The role that this system plays in behavior is not yet known.

Concluding Remarks

This chapter has described the nature of classical conditioning and instrumental conditioning and has discussed research on the physiology of reinforcement. As we have seen, events that reinforce behaviors also tend to elicit them; thus, brain mechanisms that reinforce behaviors are closely allied with the motor systems that produce them. In the next two chapters we will further investigate the topic of learning: its anatomy, and its physiology.

NEW TERMS

adjunctive behavior p. 520
appetitive response p. 515
central tegmental tract p. 523
classical conditioning p. 506
conditional response (CR) p. 507
conditional stimulus (CS) p. 507
conditioned punishment p. 509
conditioned reinforcement p. 509
discriminative stimulus p. 509
dorsal tegmental bundle p. 523
drive-reduction hypothesis p. 512
hedonic value p. 509
instrumental conditioning p. 508

medial forebrain bundle (MFB) p. 515
medial prefrontal cortex p. 536
nucleus accumbens p. 524
nucleus of the diagonal band p. 531
operant conditioning p. 508
priming p. 520
punishing stimulus (punisher) p. 508
reinforcing stimulus (reinforcer) p. 508
sulcal prefrontal cortex p. 536
superior cerebellar peduncle p. 525
unconditional response (UR) p. 507
unconditional stimulus (US) p. 506
ventral tegmental area p. 524

SUGGESTED READINGS

PFAFF, D.W. *The Physiological Mechanisms of Motivation.* New York: Springer-Verlag, 1982.

HOEBEL, B.G., AND NOVIN, D. *The Neural Basis of Feeding and Reward.* Brunswick, Maine: The Haer Institute for Electrophysiological Research, 1982.

OLDS, J. *Drives and Reinforcements: Behavioral Studies of Hypothalamic Functions.* New York: Raven Press, 1977.

OLDS, M.E., AND FOBES, J.L. The central basis of motivation: Intracranial self-stimulation studies. *Annual Review of Psychology,* 1981, *32,* 523–574.

14

Anatomy of Learning

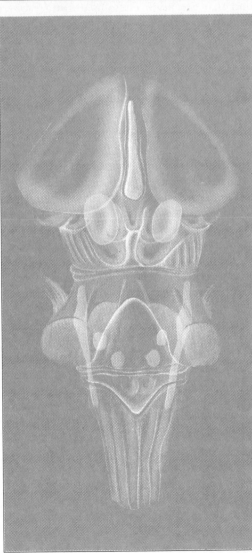

Experiences change us; encounters with our environment alter our behavior by modifying our nervous system. This belief has long been an article of faith among natural scientists. Given that our behavior is controlled by our physiology, changes in the ways in which we respond to a particular stimulus must reflect changes in our physiology. For many years, neuroscientists have sought ways to locate and identify these changes.

Until recently, the search for the neural basis of memory has seemed disappointingly slow. The brain is complex, and so is learning. Although the individual changes that occur within the cells of the brain may be relatively simple, the brain consists of billions of neurons. Therefore, isolating and identifying the particular changes responsible for a particular memory is difficult. Similarly, although the elements of a particular learning task may be simple, its implications for an organism may be complex. The behavior that the investigator observes and measures may be only one of many that change as a result of an experience. However, despite the difficulties, the long years of work finally seem to be paying off. New approaches and new methods have evolved from old ones, and real progress has been made in understanding the anatomy and physiology of learning and remembering.

This chapter discusses research on the anatomy of learning: it describes investigations that have attempted to determine which parts of the brain are involved in learning. Obviously, this topic overlaps with that of the previous chapter, which discussed an important aspect of learning, reinforcement. The next chapter discusses what we have learned about the structural and biochemical changes that occur in the nervous system when learning takes place.

■ MEMORY

We use the word *memory* as if it described a tangible object—a note we make to our-selves and put away for future reference. However, when we say we *store* memories and later *retrieve* them, we are speaking metaphorically. Although it is convenient to describe memories as if they were notes placed in filing cabinets, this is certainly not the way in which experiences are reflected within the brain. Experiences are not "stored"; they change the way we perceive, perform, think, and plan. Therefore, we should not expect to find that the brain contains a filing cabinet with memories whose contents are examined when needed; we should expect learning to be expressed by changes in the neurons that participate in perceiving, performing, thinking, and planning. Thus, *learning probably changes neurons throughout the brain.*

Karl Lashley (1890–1958) was one of the first scientists to try to discover where memories are located. After many years of research, he concluded that memories were not localized—that they appeared to be interwoven in the network of neural connections throughout the brain. In some studies, he trained hungry rats to run through a complex maze to a goal box that contained food. If he removed a large portion of a trained animal's cerebral cortex, the rat might make errors for a while, but it usually learned to perform well again within a relatively small number of trials. For example, the original learning might take one hundred trials, but the relearning might take only thirty trials. Because the animal relearned the task faster than it originally did, the operation certainly did not remove all of the memory. Therefore, the memory was not all located in one place in the brain. Lashley (1950) found that the deficit caused by the surgery was proportional to the amount of cerebral cortex he removed: the more tissue gone, the worse the performance. In addition, the location of the damage was less important than the amount of tissue destroyed. He suggested that this result reflected the fact that the cerebral cortex acted as a whole to store memories, and that individual memories were not localized.

Lashley's conclusion appears to be wrong. In the rest of this chapter, I present evidence that supports a contrary conclusion—that different experiences cause different changes in localized regions of the brain. What, then, accounts for Lashley's results? The answer is probably the following: When an animal learns to run through a maze, its brain is changed in many ways. As it travels, it learns by means of visual, olfactory, auditory, kinesthetic, and proprioceptive stimuli. Thus, although its memories may be individually localized, so much is learned from the situation that changes in the brain are widespread. Damage to one part of the cerebral cortex may disrupt some of the changes, but others are likely to remain, and the animal can use them as a basis for relearning the maze more quickly the second time.

Some psychologists believe that all instances of learning can be analyzed in terms of classical and instrumental conditioning. Others disagree, asserting that different principles apply to some forms of learning, especially complex ones that are accompanied by thinking. We do not have enough evidence to determine who is correct, but in some ways it does not matter. Some investigators have studied the physiology of simple classically conditioned responses in laboratory animals, while others have studied the effects of localized brain injury on various kinds of learning in humans. These two types of studies ask very different questions: the former asks about the physical changes in neurons that cause conditional stimuli to elicit conditional responses, and the latter asks about the location of brain regions that are necessary for various aspects of learning and performance. Eventually, we will discover the fundamental principles that underlie complex human learning; classical conditioning, reinforcement, punishment, and cognitive processes will ultimately be ex-

plained in terms of the physiological and environmental events that produce them. Until that time, we must be content with realizing that the physiology of learning can be studied on more than one level.

This chapter is devoted to the anatomy of learning. As we will see, many parts of the brain have been shown to be important for one or more types of learning. The simplest forms of learning—learning to make a simple response to a simple stimulus by means of classical conditioning—are mediated by neural circuits in the hindbrain. This fact was appreciated several years ago, but only recently have the details of the necessary neural circuitry been discovered. More elaborate and more complex forms of learning, such as learning to detect a complex stimulus, learning to respond in different ways in different contexts, or learning complex motor responses, require cortical association areas. Learning is not the exclusive province of any one part of the brain; in fact, it is possible that the ability to undergo change is a general property of most neural circuits. Different neurons, in different parts of the brain, are changed in ways that contribute to the many components of learning.

■ LEARNING TO PERCEIVE

This section describes research on perceptual learning—in particular, learning to respond to visual stimuli. Because more is known about visual memories than those acquired through the other senses, I will restrict my discussion to this modality.

The simplest kind of learning to perceive is learning to recognize stimuli we have encountered before. For example, let us consider how we learn to recognize a particular visual stimulus. Information about elements of the stimulus is conveyed to the primary visual cortex, where an analysis is made in terms of simple characteristics. (As we saw in

Chapter 6, this process may entail the distribution of spatial frequencies across the visual scene.) The results of this analysis are sent to surrounding areas of visual association cortex in the occipital lobe, and then to other areas in the temporal lobe. Somehow, the particular patterns of neural activity that result are recognized as resembling patterns that were produced on earlier occasions.

But what do we mean by the word *recognize?* Where does recognition occur? We have already rejected the naive model of the homunculus sitting in the brain, looking at the pattern of neural activity as if it were a television screen. This model is useless, because it only postpones the problem — if we try to explain how the homunculus works, we encounter the same difficulty again. The answer, I think, is that recognition is more than a perceptual phenomenon, narrowly defined. Perception is best conceived as an instigator of behavior. Seeing a familiar object makes it possible for us to respond in a particular way. The neural systems that control behaviors recognize the familiar stimulus when they receive signals from the visual system that are similar to signals that were received before. What they do in consequence depends on prior experience with that particular perception and on what is happening at that time. In some cases, the only behaviors elicited by a stimulus are looking at it and thinking about what it is.

Memory of a Particular Visual Stimulus: Role of Inferior Temporal Cortex

A large part of the mammalian brain is devoted to the analysis of sensory stimuli. In order for an animal to learn to perform a particular behavior in response to a particular stimulus, connections between the perceptual system and the motor system must be strengthened. It is apparent that these connections can be made among a variety of neural systems. For example, Lashley (1950) found that rats could learn to perform a brightness discrimination task after he had removed all their visual cortex; that is, they could learn to jump from a platform toward the brighter of two stimuli. Because the only part of the visual system that was left was the optic tectum (the superior colliculi and related nuclei), this structure is obviously able to detect the relevant stimulus and to control the animal's movements by means of connections with the motor system. But a rat with an intact visual cortex does not appear to learn the brightness discrimination task by means of the optic tectum. If it is trained and then its visual cortex is removed, the rat does not perform correctly (although it can learn to do so), whereas if it is trained and then its optic tectum is removed, it continues to perform without error. Thus, rats learn the brightness discrimination task by means of the optic tectum only if the visual cortex is removed; otherwise, they learn it by means of the visual cortex. (See **Figure 14.1.**)

Although the optic tectum can perform a sensory analysis that will permit a rat to learn a simple brightness discrimination task, the neocortex is needed for an animal to learn to respond differentially to more complex visual stimuli. In mammals with larger brains, visual stimuli are analyzed by neurons in the visual association cortex. As we saw in Chapter 6, each neuron in the primary visual cortex receives information from photoreceptors in a restricted region of the retina, and hence each neuron can analyze only a small part of the visual scene. Therefore, perception of forms and shapes must take place in neurons that can integrate the information received by neurons located throughout the primary visual cortex. These neurons are located in the visual association cortex.

The role of the regions of visual association cortex in the monkey brain has been the subject of many investigations. Although at least a dozen different regions have been discovered, most investigators use the terminology of von Bonin and Bailey (1947) to subdivide the visual cortical areas. (See **Figure 14.2.**) Area *OC* is the primary visual cortex (also called the *striate cortex*), which receives direct projections from the lateral geniculate nucleus of the thalamus. This area sends axons to areas *OA* and *OB*, which together constitute what has been called the *circum-*

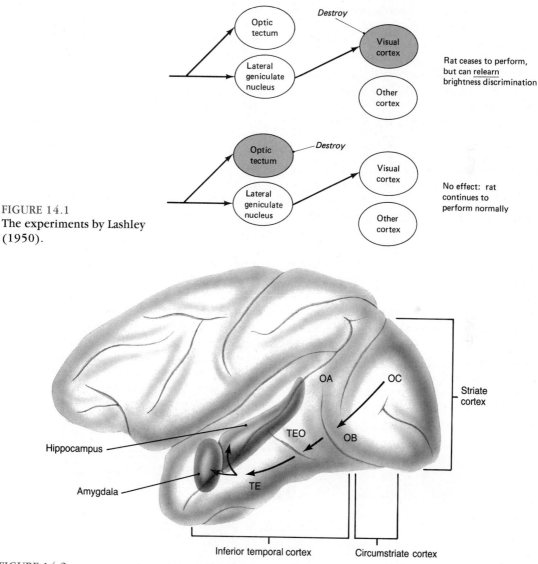

FIGURE 14.1
The experiments by Lashley (1950).

FIGURE 14.2
The major divisions of the visual cortex, according to von Bonin and Bailey (1947). (From Mishkin, M. *Philosophical Transactions of the Royal Society of London, Series B,* 1982, *298,* 85–95.)

striate cortex. Areas OA and OB send axons to area **TEO,** which, in turn, sends axons to area **TE.** Areas TEO and TE are located in the inferior temporal lobe; area TE, the farthest away from the primary visual cortex, performs the highest level of perceptual analysis. (See **Figure 14.2.**) Of course, in order for visual stimuli to control behaviors, there must be outputs from the inferior temporal lobe that connect the visual system with other parts of the brain. Indeed there are, and the functions of these connections will be discussed later in this section.

Several experiments have shown that neurons in successive regions of the visual association cortex (proceeding from areas OA and OB toward area TE) respond to successively more complex aspects of visual stimuli. The receptive fields of neurons in the inferior temporal cortex tend to be large, indicating that these neurons receive input from neurons throughout the primary visual cortex. They respond to complex, three-dimensional stimuli better than they do to two-dimensional ones, and they continue to respond even as the object is moved around in the visual field. For example, Gross, Rocha-Miranda, and Bender (1972) found one neuron in the inferior temporal cortex that responded most vigorously to the sight of a bottle brush, and another that responded to a monkey's hand. Presumably, the receptive

characteristics of these neurons have been acquired by experience; they represent visual memories. Figure 14.3 shows a set of shapes arranged in order of their effectiveness in eliciting a response from one of these neurons; note that the stimuli look more and more like a monkey's hand. (See **Figure 14.3.**) Of course, it is possible that the neuron would have responded even better to another stimulus, so we cannot be certain that the "best" stimulus is a monkey's hand, only that it was the best of the stimuli the experimenters presented.

Lesion studies confirm the recording studies. Long ago, Klüver and Bucy (1939) discovered that monkeys with bilateral lesions of the temporal lobes (including subcortical structures as well as neocortex) had difficulty perceiving visual stimuli. They referred to the phenomenon as "psychic blindness." The animals could move around in their environment and could see well enough to pick up small objects. However, they had great difficulty recognizing what they saw. They would pick up items from a tray containing small edible and inedible objects, bring them to their mouth, and then eat the pieces of food and drop the pieces of hardware. They showed no signs of fear to visual stimuli that normal monkeys avoid, such as snakes.

Mishkin (1966) showed that the inferior temporal cortex, through its connection with

Ineffective   Most effective

*Relative effectiveness of various stimuli
in changing activity of unit*

FIGURE 14.3
A rank-ordering of the effectiveness of various stimuli in producing a response in a single neuron located in the inferior temporal cortex. (From Gross, C.P., Rocha-Miranda, C.E., and Bender, D.B. *Journal of Neurophysiology,* 1972, *35,* 96–111.)

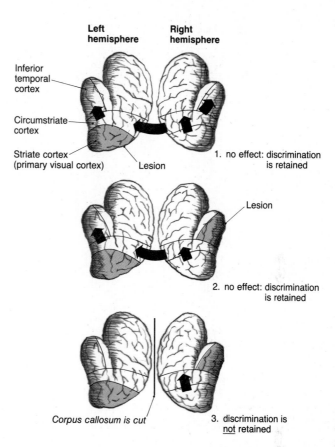

FIGURE 14.4

The procedure used by
Mishkin (1966). Not all of the
control groups used in the
experiment are shown here.
(Adapted from Mishkin, M. In
*Frontiers in Physiological
Psychology,* edited by R.W.
Russell. New York: Academic
Press, 1966.)

the primary visual cortex, is necessary for recognition of complex visual stimuli. First, he
removed the striate cortex on one side of the
brain and tested the monkeys' ability to discriminate between visual patterns. The monkeys performed well. Next, he removed the
contralateral inferior temporal cortex: no deficit. Finally, he cut the corpus callosum,
which isolated the remaining inferior temporal cortex from the remaining primary visual cortex. The animals could no longer
perform the visual discrimination task. Therefore, we can conclude that the inferior temporal cortex is necessary for visual pattern
discrimination, and that it must receive information from the primary visual cortex. (See
Figure 14.4.)

Subsequent studies have shown that the
two major regions of the inferior temporal
cortex, TEO and TE, perform different functions. Area TEO, closer to the primary visual
cortex, is necessary for perception of shape;
its removal impairs monkeys' ability to discriminate among different two-dimensional
patterns (Blake, Jarvis, and Mishkin, 1977).
In contrast, removal of area TE impairs monkeys' ability to discriminate among different
three-dimensional objects. Mishkin and his
colleagues (reported by Mishkin, 1982)
trained monkeys on a *delayed nonmatching-
to-sample task.* They showed monkeys a
small three-dimensional object (the *sample*)
from a large collection of "junk" assembled
for that purpose. The monkeys moved the ob-

Movable shutter

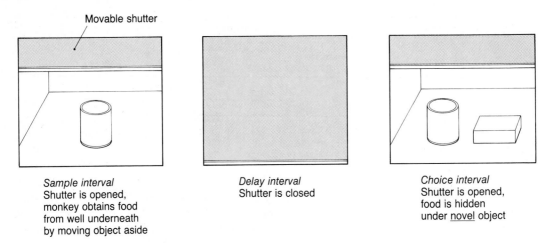

Sample interval
Shutter is opened,
monkey obtains food
from well underneath
by moving object aside

Delay interval
Shutter is closed

Choice interval
Shutter is opened,
food is hidden
under <u>novel</u> object

FIGURE 14.5
The delayed nonmatching-to-sample procedure used by Mishkin and his
colleagues (reported by Mishkin, 1982).

ject aside to uncover and eat a peanut placed in a small well underneath. After a 10-second delay, the experimenters showed the monkeys two objects: the one they had just seen and a new one. If the monkeys moved the *new* object they found another peanut, but none was to be found under the old one. A different stimulus was used on each trial. This task is easy for monkeys to perform; they learn it within a few days. (See **Figure 14.5.**)

After the preliminary training, Mishkin and his colleagues removed area TEO or TE bilaterally. After surgery, animals with TEO lesions required 73 trials to relearn the task, whereas those with TE lesions required 1500 trials and even then did not quite attain the criterion of 90 percent correct. After administering these retraining trials, the experimenters tested the monkeys with delays longer than 10 seconds. The monkeys with TE lesions performed poorly when the delay was lengthened, while those with TEO lesions performed well on delays up to 120 seconds. Thus, area TE plays an important role in a monkey's ability to remember a particular three-dimensional object. (See **Figure 14.6.**)

Several investigators have studied the role of the inferior temporal cortex in visual memory by means of electrical stimulation. For example, Kovner and Stamm (1972) trained monkeys to perform a visual *delayed matching-to-sample task.* They presented a visual pattern (the sample), which was then turned off for several seconds. At the end of the delay interval, they presented two patterns (the *matching stimuli*): the one just shown and a different one. If the monkey pressed the correct panel, it received a piece of food.

Kovner and Stamm electrically stimulated the animals' inferior temporal cortex through electrodes they had previously placed there. When they administered the stimulation during the delay interval, just before they showed the monkeys the matching stimuli, the animals performed poorly on that trial. Stimulation of the circumstriate cortex did not impair their performance. In addition, stimulation of the inferior temporal cortex during a *simultaneous* matching-to-sample task had no effect. In this task, all three stimuli were present at the same time; the monkeys had to select which of two lower stimuli matched

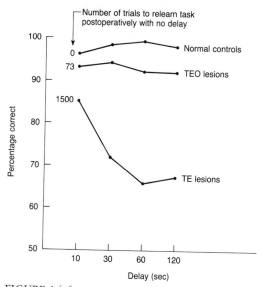

FIGURE 14.6

Effects of TE and TEO lesions on performance of a delayed nonmatching-to-sample task. (From Mishkin, M. *Philosophical Transactions of the Royal Society of London, Series B,* 1982, *298,* 85–95.)

the upper stimulus. Thus, it was only when the animals had to make a choice based on a visual memory of a stimulus they had just seen that the electrical stimulation disrupted performance. It was as if the stimulation "erased" the memory of the sample.

Kovner and Stamm's findings are supported by an electrophysiological study by Fuster and Jervey (1981), who obtained evidence that neurons in the inferior temporal cortex retain information about a just-perceived stimulus. They turned on a colored light (yellow, green, red, or blue) behind a translucent disk (the sample stimulus), turned it off, and, after a delay interval, turned on yellow, green, red, and blue lights behind four other disks (the matching stimuli). (See **Figure 14.7.**) If the monkey pressed the disk whose color matched the one it had just seen, it received a reinforcer. The experimenters

recorded the activity of single neurons in the inferior temporal cortex. Some neurons responded selectively to color, maintaining a high response rate during the delay interval. For example, Figure 14.8 shows data from a neuron that responded to red light, but not to green light, during a 16-second delay interval. The horizontal lines above each graph represent individual trials; vertical tick marks represent action potentials. The graphs beneath the horizontal lines are sums of the individual trials, showing the total responses during successive intervals. (See **Figure 14.8.**) Under normal conditions, a stimulus causes a neuron to respond briefly. Thus, the sustained response during the delay interval suggests that the neuron is participating in remembering a just-perceived stimulus.

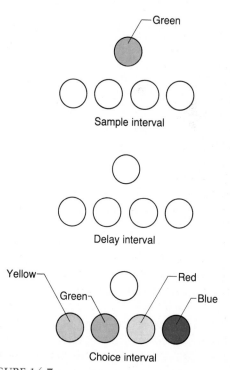

FIGURE 14.7

The delayed matching-to-sample procedure used by Fuster and Jervey (1981).

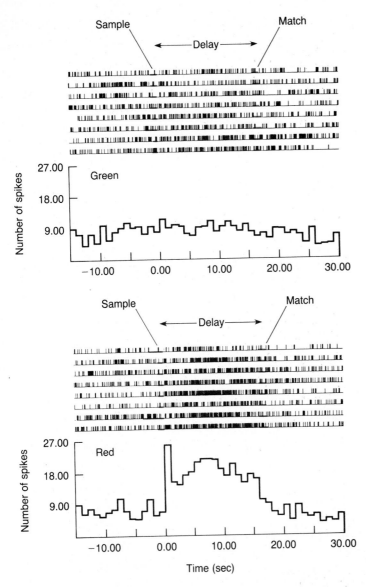

FIGURE 14.8
Responses of a single unit
during the presentation of the
sample stimulus, the delay
interval, and the presentation
of matching stimuli in the
experiment outlined in Figure
14.7. (From Fuster, J.M. In
*Conditioning: Representation
of Involved Neural Functions,*
edited by C.D. Woody. New
York: Plenum Press, 1982.)

Connections of Inferior Temporal Cortex with Other Structures

As we have just seen, neurons of the visual association cortex on the inferior temporal lobes appear to participate in learning about visual stimuli; animals learn to recognize objects by means of circuits of neurons located there. Thus, this region of neocortex is necessary for the formation of visual memories of objects. But memories do not exist in isolation; for perceptions to affect behavior, there must be connections with motor systems. Investigators have studied several of the connections of the inferior temporal cortex with other parts of the brain and have found that different connections serve different functions.

Connections with the Amygdala and Hippocampus

As we will see later in this chapter, bilateral damage to the medial temporal lobe produces a dramatic memory impairment in humans. This finding has focused research attention on two important components of the limbic system that are located in the medial temporal lobe: the amygdala and the hippocampus. Because I discuss them separately in later sections, I will not describe their anatomical connections in detail here. It suffices to say that both of these structures receive visual information from the inferior temporal cortex. The amygdala receives this information directly, and the hippocampus receives it indirectly, via the **entorhinal cortex,** a region of limbic cortex near the base of the cerebral hemispheres. The amygdala and hippocampus both send information to the diencephalon and mesencephalon. (See **Figure 14.9.**)

The reason I discuss the amygdala and hippocampus together is that Mishkin and his colleagues have shown that damage to either structure does not significantly affect monkeys' ability to recognize stimuli they have just seen, but damage to both structures does. In addition, lesions that disconnect the amygdala and hippocampus from the inferior temporal cortex also impair visual recognition.

Here is the evidence: Mishkin (1978) trained monkeys on a visual object recognition task like the one I just described: the

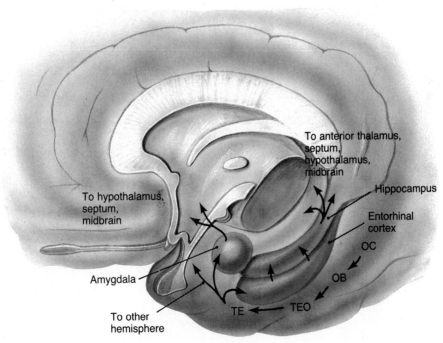

FIGURE 14.9
Principal afferent and efferent connections of the hippocampus and amygdala.

animals had to choose the novel object, not the one they had just seen (a delayed non-matching-to-sample task). Bilateral lesions of the hippocampus or amygdala alone had no effect on the animals' performance, but combined lesions produced a profound impairment. In a subsequent study, Mishkin (1982) demonstrated that the connection between the inferior temporal cortex and the amygdala/hippocampus was critical for performance on this task. He destroyed the amygdala and hippocampus on one side of the brain and destroyed areas TE and TEO on the other. The operation produced only a small impairment. Next, he cut the ***anterior commissure,*** a bundle of axons that contains fibers that connect the left and right anterior temporal cortex. This operation caused a further impairment; in fact, the monkeys performed as poorly as those with bilateral lesions of area TE or bilateral lesions of the amygdala and hippocampus. (See **Figure 14.10.**) The second operation did not further damage the amygdala or hippocampus; it simply isolated the intact amygdala and hippocampus from information provided by the contralateral temporal lobe.

The role of the amygdala and hippocampus in learning does not appear to be restricted to visual learning; Murray and Mishkin (1983) found that bilateral lesions that damaged both structures produced a severe deficit in tactual memory—the ability to recognize objects by means of touch. This finding suggests that

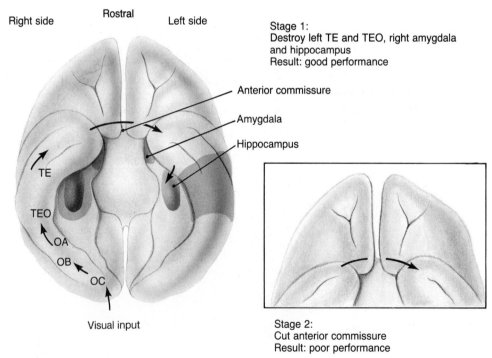

FIGURE 14.10
The procedure used by Mishkin (1982). (Adapted from Mishkin, M. *Philosophical Transactions of the Royal Society of London,* 1982, *298,* 85-95.)

other regions of sensory association cortex may also communicate with motor systems through the amygdala and hippocampus.

One might expect that if a monkey cannot remember for even a few seconds which of two objects it has just seen, then it would have great difficulty learning to respond differentially to visual stimuli. And yet Malamut, Saunders, and Mishkin (1980) observed quite the contrary. They trained monkeys on a simple long-term visual discrimination task. They presented the animals with a set of twenty pairs of objects, one pair at a time. One member of each pair was *always* associated with a piece of food. If the monkey pushed this object aside, it would find a peanut; if it pushed the other one aside, it found nothing. The monkeys saw each of the twenty pairs once a day. Lesions of the amygdala/hippocampus had no effect on acquisition of this task; the brain-damaged monkeys learned to choose the appropriate member of each pair just as fast as normal monkeys did. Thus, the ability to remember a stimulus that was just perceived is different from the ability to learn, on a long-term basis, to make a particular response to a particular stimulus. As we will see in the next section, another pathway

is necessary for long-term, but not short-term, remembering.

Connections Through the Temporal Stem
Zola-Morgan, Squire, and Mishkin (1982) obtained evidence that complements that obtained by Malamut, Saunders, and Mishkin. They found that the ability to learn a long-term visual discrimination task, but not the ability to recognize objects that were just seen, was impaired by destruction of the ***temporal stem.*** The temporal stem consists of a bundle of axons that connect the cortex of the temporal lobe with other parts of the brain, including the medial thalamus and the basal ganglia. Confirming Mishkin's earlier results, lesions of the amygdala/hippocampus impaired delayed recognition performance; the animals required more than five times the normal number of trials to learn the nonmatching-to-sample task, and once they relearned it they performed poorly at longer delay intervals. The temporal stem lesions had no effect on learning this task. (See **Figure 14.11.**) In contrast, lesions of the temporal stem severely impaired the animals' ability to learn a simple long-term discrimination task requiring them to choose between a

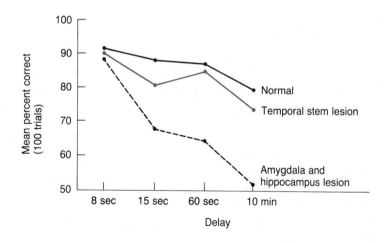

FIGURE 14.11
Combined lesions of the amygdala and hippocampus, but not lesions of the temporal stem, impair performance on a delayed nonmatching-to-sample task. (From Zola-Morgan, S., Squire, L.R., and Mishkin, M. *Science,* 1982, *218,* 1337–1339. Copyright 1982 by the American Association for the Advancement of Science.)

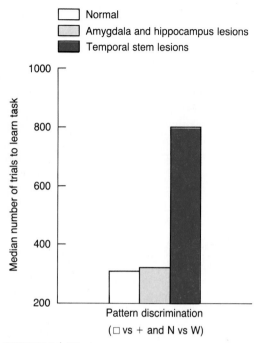

FIGURE 14.12

Lesions of the temporal stem, but not combined lesions of the amygdala and hippocampus, impair performance on a simple long-term visual discrimination task. (From Zola-Morgan, S., Squire, L.R., and Mishkin, M., *Science,* 1982, *218,* 1337–1339. Copyright 1982 by the American Association for the Advancement of Science.)

square and a plus or between the letters *N* and *W*. Lesions of the amygdala and hippocampus had no effect on this task. (See **Figure 14.12.**)

It is possible that long-term visual discriminations are learned by way of the connections of the inferior temporal cortex, through the temporal stem, with the caudate nucleus and pulvinar. These nuclei are important components of the basal ganglia, which are involved in the control and organization of movements. Two studies have shown that bilateral damage to the portions of the caudate nucleus and pulvinar that receive visual input

from the temporal lobe impairs the acquisition of a simple long-term visual discrimination task (Divac, Rosvold, and Szwarcbart, 1967; Buerger, Gross, and Rocha-Miranda, 1974).

These contrasting effects of lesions of the amygdala/hippocampus and temporal stem force us to conclude that remembering an object that has just been seen and learning to make a particular response to a particular visual pattern on a long-term basis involve different neural systems. Although the distinction between these two forms of learning may seem obscure, we will encounter it later, when we consider the nature of amnesia caused by brain damage in humans.

INTERIM SUMMARY

What we call memory consists of changes in connections between neurons in the brain that cause us to respond in particular ways to particular stimuli. Lashley concluded from his research that memories were diffusely located in the brain. However, more recent studies suggest that although no one part of the brain serves as a repository for all memories, particular kinds of memories are located in particular places.

Learning to perceive particular stimuli entails changes in neurons in sensory systems, particularly in areas of sensory association cortex. The most important region for visual recognition of three-dimensional objects is the inferior temporal cortex, the third level of visual cortex (after the striate and circumstriate cortex). Neurons in the inferior temporal cortex respond best to particular complex, three-dimensional objects, which suggests that they are part of circuits of neurons that have been modified by experience so that they recognize the stimuli. Lesions of the inferior temporal cortex impair visual perception, as do lesions that deprive this region of visual information from the striate and circumstriate cortex. In particular, lesions of area TE produce poor performance in visual discrimination tasks that require monkeys to remember an object for more than a few seconds.

Neurons in the inferior temporal cortex appear to hold a temporary "image" of a stimulus. Electrical stimulation of this region appears to "erase" a monkey's memory of a simple stimulus that it has just seen, probably because the current disrupts ongoing patterns of activity that represent the stimulus. In addition, the firing of single units that respond to particular colors in a delayed matching-to-sample task continues during the delay interval, perhaps because the neurons are holding the information until the monkey gets an opportunity to respond.

The inferior temporal cortex sends information to several brain regions, including the hippocampus and amygdala. Mishkin and his colleagues found that damage to both of these structures, but not to either one alone, severely disrupted monkeys' ability to recognize objects they had just seen a few seconds ago. However, the lesions did not impair the monkeys' ability to learn to respond to a *particular* set of objects. In contrast, damage to the temporal stem, which connects the temporal neocortex with the thalamus and basal ganglia, impairs long-term learning to respond to particular sets of objects but does not impair the ability to recognize objects seen a few seconds ago. This distinction will be explored in more detail later in this chapter.

■ RECOGNIZING BIOLOGICALLY RELEVANT STIMULI

As we saw, Klüver and Bucy found that temporal lobectomy in monkeys causes several deficits, including the inability to recognize food, dangerous stimuli, or appropriate sex partners. These deficits can partly be explained as effects of destruction of the inferior temporal cortex, the region of the visual association cortex that is most involved in object recognition. However, destruction of the amygdala also accounts for some of the behavioral effects of temporal lobectomy. A study by Downer (1962) provides a good example of the special role of the amygdala in recognizing biologically relevant stimuli. Downer destroyed the amygdala on one side of the brain and cut the corpus callosum, anterior

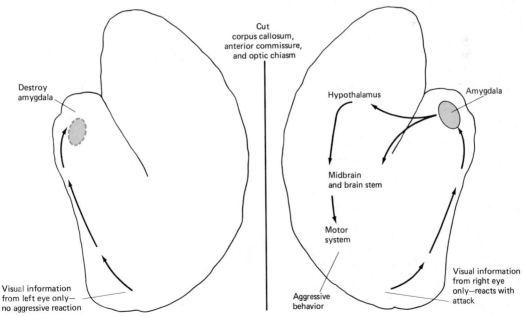

FIGURE 14.13
The results of the experiment by Downer (1962).

commissure, and optic chiasm. These lesions ensured that visual information to each eye reached only the ipsilateral side of the brain. Thus, only one eye sent visual information to the intact amygdala. After surgery, the monkey, who was wild and aggressive, would attack stimuli presented to the eye ipsilateral to the intact amygdala but would not attack stimuli presented to the other side of the brain. The results suggest that visual information must reach the amygdala for a stimulus to be recognized as one with biological relevance. (See **Figure 14.13.**)

Anatomy and Connections of the Amygdaloid Nuclei

The amygdala consists of several nuclei located in the anterior portion of the medial temporal lobe, just in front of the hippocampus. (See **Figure 14.14.**) As we saw in the previous section, the amygdaloid nuclei receive information from the visual association cortex in the inferior temporal lobe. They also receive information from the auditory as-

sociation cortex of the superior temporal lobe. In addition, the amygdaloid nuclei receive olfactory information directly from the olfactory bulb, and gustatory and visceral information from the nucleus of the solitary tract. Finally, various thalamic and hypothalamic nuclei project axons to the amygdala.

The amygdaloid nuclei send fibers to many parts of the brain, including the preoptic-basal forebrain region, the hypothalamus, the dorsomedial thalamus, the periaqueductal gray matter, and various midbrain and brain stem nuclei. Through these connections, the amygdala has the opportunity to control a variety of species-typical appetitive, aggressive, and defensive behaviors. In addition, the connections with the basal forebrain region and lateral hypothalamus may affect the activity of neurons involved in reinforcement, which I discussed in Chapter 13.

Recognition of Food

Many studies suggest that the amygdala plays an important role in the recognition of items that are suitable foods, and of those that are to

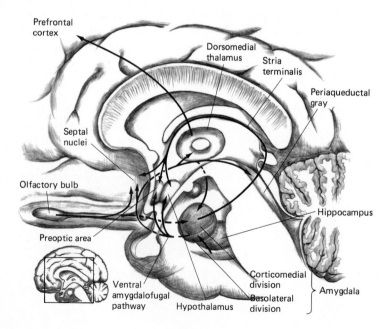

FIGURE 14.14
The amygdala and its principal afferent and efferent connections.

be avoided because they contain poisons. As we saw earlier, Klüver and Bucy found that monkeys with bilateral temporal lobectomies could detect small items visually but could not determine whether the items were pieces of food or bits of metal hardware until they put them into their mouths. A series of experiments by Rolls and his colleagues (summarized in Rolls, 1982) have recorded the electrical activity of neurons in the visual association cortex, amygdala, and basal forebrain in response to visual stimuli that had been associated with food.

Rolls and his colleagues found that individual neurons in the visual association cortex of the inferior temporal lobe responded to particular objects, but that the patterns of response did not discriminate between those that had been associated with food and those that had been associated with an unpleasant-tasting hypertonic solution of sodium chloride. In addition, the response characteristics of these neurons were not affected by the motivational state of the monkeys; the neurons responded the same way when the animal was hungry or satiated.

The investigators recorded from 1754 neurons in the amygdala. Of these, 113 (6.4 percent) responded to visual stimuli. The majority were located in the *dorsolateral* amygdala, which receives input from neurons in the visual association cortex of the inferior temporal lobe. Some of these neurons responded primarily to food, while others responded primarily to aversive stimuli. However, none of them responded exclusively to either class of stimuli. Rolls suggests that the amygdala constitutes the first level of analysis of information related to the significance of stimuli as reinforcers and punishers, and that it sends the information elsewhere for further analysis.

The amygdaloid nuclei send axons to the hypothalamus and basal forebrain, including the preoptic area and the nucleus of the diagonal band. As we saw in Chapter 13, neurons in the basal forebrain send axons to the ventral tegmental area and may mediate the reinforcing effects of electrical stimulation of the medial forebrain bundle. Rolls and his colleagues recorded the activity of neurons in the lateral hypothalamus and basal forebrain and found that 14.6 percent of the 764 neurons whose activity they recorded made responses that were related to feeding. Some responded to the taste of food, but not to mouth movements made during eating. Others responded to the sight of food but not to inedible objects. Still others responded both to the sight and taste of food. A particularly interesting class of neurons responded to stimuli that the monkeys had learned to be associated with food. For example, these neurons might respond when the monkey was shown a blue syringe that the experimenters had used to inject some food into their mouth, but not to a red one that had not been used to deliver food. If the experimenters then switched the syringes, using the red one but not the blue one to feed the monkeys, the neurons began responding to the red syringe instead of the blue one. In addition, these neurons responded to the sight of stimuli associated with food only when the monkey was hungry; thus, they must receive information about the motivational status of the animal as well as what the animal sees.

Rolls and his colleagues stimulated various regions of the brain while recording from the food-related neurons in the lateral hypothalamus and basal forebrain to determine where the axons of these neurons go. When they electrically stimulated the prefrontal association cortex and the supplementary motor cortex anterior to the precentral gyrus, they recorded short-latency action potentials in these neurons. These results indicate that the current stimulated the ends of the axons, causing action potentials to been sent backward toward the cell bodies. Thus, the neurons in the lateral hypothalamus and basal forebrain send axons to the prefrontal cortex, where they may influence movements and programming of response strategies.

Recognition of Poisons

Nature is full of poisons; both plants and animals produce them to protect themselves against being eaten. Animals that consume a wide variety of foods must learn how to avoid poisonous plants and animals if they are to survive. When animals encounter harmful objects, they learn thereafter to avoid them. For example, a dog that obtains a faceful of quills from a porcupine avoids future encounters with porcupines, and a blue jay that eats a poisonous monarch butterfly gets sick and thereafter leaves other monarch butterflies alone. In both of these examples, an aversive stimulus punishes a behavior, presumably because species-typical defensive responses become classically conditioned to the stimuli that were present before the responses occurred—the sight of the porcupine or the sight of the butterfly. The defensive responses prevent the animal from approaching the object that provides the conditional stimuli. (I described the logic of this phenomenon more fully in Chapter 13.)

Avoidance behaviors caused by pain or by sickness appear to be learned by different means. The consequences of getting a faceful of porcupine quills are immediate; the pain that this event causes occurs almost instantaneously, and the species-typical defensive responses that the pain produces also have a short latency. However, when an animal ingests a food that contains a poison, the effects are usually delayed by many minutes, or even an hour or two. Therefore, learning to avoid poisons—that is, developing a **conditioned food aversion**—entails a very long delay between a stimulus and the response it produces. For a conditioned food aversion to

occur, neurons in the animal's brain must retain information relating to the stimulus for a long interval. Although the location of these neurons is not yet known, the amygdala plays an essential role in the acquisition and retention of conditioned food aversions.

Some animals consume a very limited number of foods—sometimes, only a single item. For example, the koala bear eats only eucalyptus leaves, and the yucca moth feeds only on yucca blossoms. These animals rely on genetically controlled mechanisms to recognize nutrients. This method of recognizing food requires a minimum of neural complexity, but it leaves the species subject to extinction if the source of food should disappear from their habitat. Animals that consume a wide variety of foods can adapt more easily to changing environments, but they run the risk of encountering foods that contain poisons. Therefore, they must be able to learn to avoid those that do. Most omnivorous animals exhibit *neophobia*—fear of novelty. Specifically, if they encounter a food they have not eaten before, they treat it cautiously, eating only a small portion. This tendency assures that if the food is poisonous, they are unlikely to receive a lethal dose. If they do not become ill, they will thereafter eat the food readily. However, if they do become ill—and if they survive the illness—they will thereafter shun the food.

A study by Garcia and Koelling (1966) established that rats could learn a conditioned food aversion over a long delay interval, and that gustatory, not visual or auditory stimuli, were responsible for this learning. They presented thirsty rats with water associated with one of two kinds of discriminative stimuli and followed this presentation with one of two kinds of punishing stimuli. The discriminative stimuli comprised a taste or a noise and a flashing light. In the *taste* condition, the water was flavored with saccharin. In the *bright & noisy* condition, each time the rat's

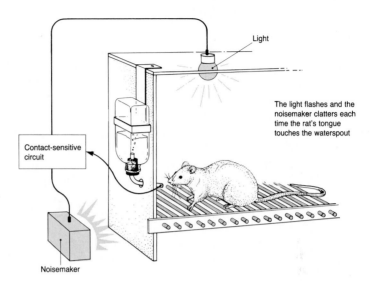

FIGURE 14.15
Conditioned aversion: a rat
drinks "bright & noisy" water
in the experiment by Garcia
and Koelling (1966).

tongue touched the waterspout it caused a contact-sensitive circuit to flash a light and make a noise. (See **Figure 14.15.**) The punishing stimuli consisted of foot shock, delivered through the floor of the chamber right after the animals drank the water, or an injection of lithium chloride, a chemical that made the animals become ill a few hours later. (Humans who ingest too much lithium chloride become nauseated, so presumably rats have a similar experience.) Four groups of rats were tested using each combination of discriminative stimulus with punishing stimulus. As Figure 14.16 shows, only two groups learned to avoid drinking at the waterspout: rats that received a painful foot shock immediately after drinking the "bright & noisy" water, and those that got sick after drinking saccharin-flavored water. (See **Figure 14.16.**)

The behavior of the animals in the group that received a painful foot shock immediately after drinking the "bright & noisy" water was expected; this is simply another example of a punished behavior established in the presence of visual and auditory discriminative stimuli. Visual or auditory stimuli

usually have immediate consequences, or they have none at all. Thus, it makes sense for the "bright & noisy"/shock group, but not the "bright & noisy"/illness group, to learn to avoid the waterspout. In addition, it makes sense for the rats to learn to avoid the saccharin-flavored water, but only if it was followed many minutes later by illness. Thus, taste plays a special role for rats in developing conditioned aversions to particular foods. This connection is probably related to rats' natural habit of smelling and nibbling novel foods, often in the dark. In contrast, quail, which recognize their food by sight, and which often eat seeds encased in a tasteless husk, form conditioned food aversions by

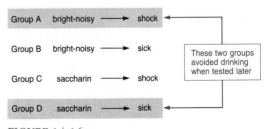

FIGURE 14.16
Results of the experiment by Garcia and Koelling (1966).

means of vision, not taste (Wilcoxon, Dragoin, and Kral, 1971).

As you know, flavors consist of mixtures of odor and taste. For rats, the discriminative stimuli involved in most natural conditioned aversions can be odors, but only if they are accompanied by tastes. Rusiniak, Hankins, Garcia, and Brett (1979) found that if a particular odor is paired with water and is then followed by illness, rats will *not* avoid that odor; presumably, many different odors are encountered during the delay interval, and the animals have no reason to learn to avoid any one of them. However, if the odor is paired with water that contains a distinctive flavor such as saccharin and is then followed by illness, rats learn an aversion to the odor. The gustatory stimulus appears to make the novel odor become special, so that it is remembered for a long interval of time.

Conditioned aversions require a rat to detect two classes of stimuli: the taste and odor of the discriminative stimuli, and the nausea or other aspects of illness produced by the punishing stimulus. Different brain mechanisms are responsible for the detection of different stimuli. Pure taste aversions are disrupted by lesions of the gustatory cortex, located at the base of the primary somatosensory cortex of the postcentral gyrus (Braun, Slick, and Lorden, 1972). However, Kiefer and Rusiniak (1979) found that these lesions do not disrupt conditioned aversions developed to a compound olfactory-gustatory stimulus; the gustatory stimulus still makes the novel odor become special. Thus, subcortical mechanisms mediate the interaction between gustatory and olfactory stimuli in the formation of conditioned food aversions.

The amygdala plays a critical role in learning conditioned food aversions. Kemble and Nagel (1973) found that rats with lesions of the amygdala failed to develop an aversion to saccharin after being made sick by injec-

tions of lithium chloride. Nachman and Ashe (1974) found that the critical region appears to be the *basolateral* amygdala; after lesions of this area rats do not learn a conditioned aversion, and those who learned one preoperatively do not show the aversion after such a lesion is produced.

We do not yet have enough evidence to conclude that the "memory" of the discriminative stimuli or the punishing stimuli entails changes in neurons in the amygdala. However, the basolateral amygdala does appear to play a critical role in learning and retaining a conditioned food aversion, and identification of a critical component of a behavior narrows the search for the specific mechanism.

Recognition of Other Dangerous Stimuli

The amygdala appears to play a role in controlling species-typical defensive responses, a task that may be related to its role in recognition of foods and poisons. For example, Roldan, Alvarez-Pelaez, and Fernandez deMolina (1974) found that electrical stimulation of the amygdala elicited defensive reactions, including "initial attention, retraction and lowering of the head, flattening of ears, crouching, dilation of pupils, piloerection [erection of hairs in the animal's fur], and growling or hissing" (p. 780).

The effects of lesions of the central nucleus of the amygdala are consistent with the effects of electrical stimulation. Lesions of this structure impair the acquisition of a passive avoidance task. Grossman, Grossman, and Walsh (1975) trained thirsty rats to drink water from a drinking tube. Then they delivered electrical shocks through the tube directly to the rats' mouths. Normal rats stopped drinking from the tube after receiving an average of nine and one-half shocks; rats with lesions of the central nucleus of the amygdala persisted

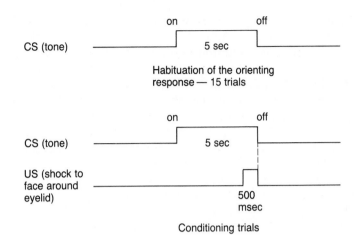

FIGURE 14.17

The procedure used by Kapp and colleagues (1979) to produce classically conditioned bradycardia in rabbits.

longer, requiring an average of twenty shocks before they stopped. Presumably, the punishing stimulus was less effective because the animals were less likely to develop species-typical defensive responses that compete with drinking.

The central nucleus of the amygdala sends efferent axons to various regions of the midbrain, pons, and medulla (Hopkins and Holstege, 1978). Kapp, Gallagher, Applegate, and Frysinger (1982) note that stimulation of these brain stem regions produces elements of the behavioral and autonomic responses seen during species-typical defensive reactions. As we have already seen, the amygdala receives sensory information and plays a role in controlling the animal's responses to foods and poisons. Therefore, it is reasonable to conclude that it might play a role in controlling defensive behaviors, as well.

Kapp, Frysinger, Gallagher, and Haselton (1979) studied an autonomic response in rabbits — *bradycardia,* a decrease in heart rate — classically conditioned to a threatening stimulus. The response is an appropriate one, because rabbits exhibit a dramatic bradycardia in the presence of a predator (von Frisch, 1966). Kapp and his colleagues presented a 5-second tone by itself for fifteen

trials. At first, the rabbits showed bradycardia in response to the novel stimulus, but this response soon habituated. (When a novel stimulus occurs, animals usually exhibit a short-lived *orienting response:* they turn toward the stimulus, their pupils dilate, and their heart rate slows.) Next the experimenters began classical conditioning trials. They turned on the tone (CS) for 5 seconds, and then delivered a 500-msec shock (US) to the rabbit's eyelid just as the tone was turned off. (See **Figure 14.17.**) Lesions of the central nucleus of the amygdala interfered with classical conditioning but did *not* affect the bradycardia response to the novel stimulus or the habituation of this response. That is, rabbits who received these lesions showed a normal slowing of the heart rate when the tone was presented by itself, and the response soon habituated. However, when the tone was paired with the shock, the lesioned rabbits did not learn to make conditional responses to the conditional stimulus. In contrast, normal rabbits acquired the conditional response quickly. The results suggest that the amygdala may play a role in *learning* to make the bradycardia response to a neutral stimulus, not simply in the ability to produce the responses. (See **Figure 14.18.**)

Electrical Activity of Neurons in the Central Nucleus

Electrical recording studies support the suggestion that the central nucleus of the amygdala mediates the classical conditioning of autonomic responses to an aversive stimulus. Applegate, Frysinger, Kapp, and Gallagher (1981) recorded multiple-unit activity of neurons in the central nucleus during habitu-

ation of the orienting response and during classical conditioning of bradycardia. Neurons in some locations (twelve out of thirty-four) showed a short-latency response to the tone (CS) during conditioning. Figure 14.19 shows the response of neurons at one such location; the height of the vertical lines indicates the number of action potentials recorded during time intervals before and af-

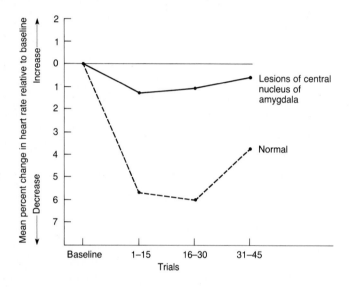

FIGURE 14.18
Effects of lesions of the central nucleus of the amygdala on conditioned bradycardia. (From Kapp, B.S., Frysinger, R.C., Gallagher, M., and Haselton, J. *Physiology and Behavior,* 1979, *23,* 1109–1117.)

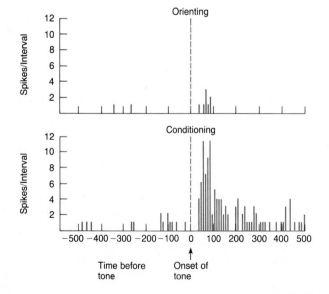

FIGURE 14.19
Multiple-unit activity in the central nucleus of the amygdala during habituation of the orienting response and during conditioning and extinction of the bradycardia response. (From Kapp, B.S., Gallagher, M., Applegate, C.D., and Frysinger, R.C. In *Conditioning: Representation of Involved Neural Functions,* edited by C.D. Woody. New York: Plenum Press, 1982.)

ter the conditional stimulus. (See **Figure 14.19.**)

Effects of Opiates

The central nucleus of the amygdala contains a rich concentration of opiate receptors. Because opiates generally inhibit an animal's species-typical defensive responses, Gallagher, Kapp, McNall, and Pascoe (1981) examined the effects on classically conditioned bradycardia of injecting an opiate agonist (levorphanol) or an opiate antagonist (naloxone) into the central nucleus of the amygdala. They found that the opiate antagonist facilitated classical conditioning, whereas the opiate agonist retarded it. (See **Figure 14.20.**) Neither drug affected the orienting response to the tone during habituation trials. In addition, other studies showed that systemic injection of naloxone (Goldstein, Pryor, Otis, and Larsen, 1976) and injection of

levorphanol into the amygdala (Rodgers, 1978) have no effect on an animal's sensitivity to pain; thus these drugs do not appear simply to have decreased the effectiveness of the shock (US). The results of the study by Gallagher and colleagues imply that opiates inhibit the acquisition of a classically conditioned species-typical defensive response.

As we saw in Chapter 13, the principal way in which an animal's response can be punished is through the classical conditioning of competing species-typical defensive responses. For example, conditioned defensive responses caused by a faceful of quills compete with a dog's approach to a porcupine. Because the amygdala appears to play a role in classically conditioned defensive responses, it therefore appears to play a role in mediating the punishing effects of aversive stimuli. The endogenous opiates are released while an animal is engaging in behaviors with important

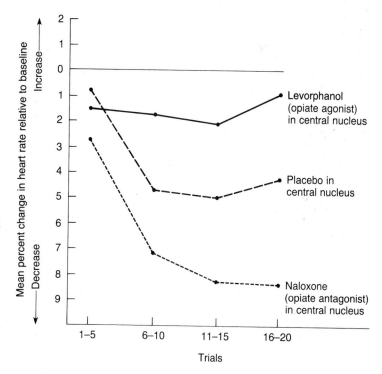

FIGURE 14.20

Effects of an opiate agonist and antagonist on conditioning of the bradycardia response. (From Kapp, B.S., Gallagher, M., Applegate, C.D., and Frysinger, R.C. In *Conditioning: Representation of Involved Neural Functions,* edited by C.D. Woody. New York: Plenum Press, 1982.)

survival value, such as mating. Because the opiates suppress the acquisition of defensive responses, their release during sexual activity makes it more likely that an animal will continue the mating sequence and not be frightened away. This phenomenon may be especially important in preventing the females of many species from fleeing a larger male.

Efferent Connections with Motor Systems
The bradycardia response is produced by preganglionic neurons whose cell bodies are located in the dorsal motor nucleus of the vagus nerve, the nerve that innervates the heart. Schwaber, Kapp, and Higgins (1980) and Schwaber, Kapp, Higgins, and Rapp (1980) used injections of horseradish peroxidase and radioactive amino acids to determine that the central amygdaloid nucleus sends axons that synapse in this region. In addition, Kapp, Gallagher, Underwood, McNall, and Whitehorn (1981) found that stimulation of the central nucleus caused an immediate bradycardia and behavioral arrest (a species-typical defensive response in rabbits). These findings support the conclusion that the central nucleus is able to control classically conditioned bradycardia.

Sensory Inputs
So far, I have described research that implicates the central nucleus of the amygdala and its efferent connections to the dorsal motor nucleus of the vagus nerve in classically conditioned bradycardia to an aversive stimulus. What about the inputs to the central nucleus? Sakaguchi, LeDoux, and Reis (1983) obtained evidence that a component of the medial geniculate nucleus, and not the auditory cortex, is critical for establishing a classically conditioned autonomic response to an auditory conditional stimulus. These investigators presented rats with a 10-second tone (CS), followed by a 0.5-second foot shock (US), and looked at changes in blood pressure,

heart rate, and a species-typical defensive response, freezing. Lesions of the medial geniculate nucleus, but not the lateral geniculate nucleus or auditory cortex, impaired acquisition of all three conditional responses. However, because lesions of the medial geniculate nucleus had no effect on unconditional responses to the shock itself, the results suggest that the sensory analysis of the tone, but not the shock, was disrupted.

LeDoux, Sakaguchi, and Reis (1983) injected horseradish peroxidase in the medial geniculate nucleus of rats and studied its anterograde transport from the cell bodies to the terminal buttons. The researchers found that besides projecting to the auditory cortex, the medial geniculate nucleus sends axons to several subcortical nuclei, including the central nucleus of the amygdala. Thus, it is possible that the connection between the medial geniculate nucleus and the central nucleus is an essential component of classical conditioning of autonomic responses to auditory stimuli.

Weinberger and his colleagues (reported by Weinberger, 1982) have obtained evidence that neurons in a particular part of the medial geniculate nucleus, the ***magnocellular medial geniculate nucleus*** alter their response characteristics during classical conditioning. They presented a tone followed by a shock and found that neurons in the *ventral* medial geniculate nucleus, which projects to the auditory cortex, responded in a constant, unchanging fashion throughout conditioning. However, the responses of neurons in the magnocellular medial geniculate nucleus changed. Figure 14.21 shows the responses of a single neuron in this nucleus during ten trials of a control procedure and ten trials of conditioning (two trials per graph). During the control procedure, the tone (CS) and the shock (US) were presented at random intervals and were not paired. During conditioning, the tone was followed by the shock. The data show that during the control procedure, the neuron initially responded to the tone (indicated by the colored horizontal line), but that this response soon habituated. However, once conditioning trials began, the neuron quickly began responding during the tone. (See **Figure 14.21**.)

The results of this study suggest that the magnocellular medial geniculate nucleus plays a role in classical conditioning. It is possible that its destruction caused the deficits in autonomic conditioning in the study by Sakaguchi and colleagues. Whether this area specifically projects to the central nucleus of the amygdala has yet to be determined.

INTERIM SUMMARY

The amygdaloid nuclei play an especially important role in the recognition of biologically relevant stimuli. For example, when a lesion prevents an aggressive monkey's amygdala from receiving visual information, the animal will remain quiet when it sees a target it would normally attack. The amygdaloid nuclei receive information from the visual association cortex of the inferior temporal lobe, from the auditory association cortex of the superior temporal lobe, from the olfactory bulb, from the nucleus of the solitary tract, and from various thalamic and hypothalamic nuclei. They send fibers to the basal forebrain, hypothalamus, dorsomedial thalamus, periaqueductal gray matter, and various midbrain and brain stem nuclei, permitting them to influence species-typical behavior and reinforcement mechanisms.

Neurons in the dorsolateral amygdala respond to food or aversive stimuli and send information to the hypothalamus and basal forebrain, including regions involved in reinforcement. Neurons in the basal forebrain selectively respond to particular classes of stimuli associated with feeding. Some even respond to the sight of food only when the animal is hungry. These neurons send axons to the prefrontal association cortex and the supplementary motor cortex, where they presumably influence movements and response strategies.

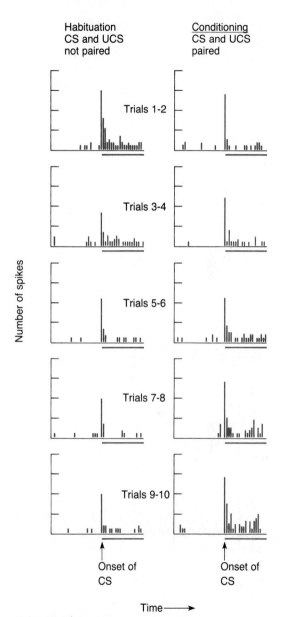

FIGURE 14.21

Responses of a single neuron in the magnocellular medial geniculate nucleus during aversive classical conditioning. (From Weinberger, N.M. In *Conditioning: Representation of Involved Neural Functions,* edited by C.D. Woody. New York: Plenum Press, 1982.)

The recognition of poisons appears to involve the basolateral nucleus of the amygdala; lesions there prevent the acquisition of a conditioned food aversion and disrupt the performance of animals who acquired an aversion before the surgery.

The central nucleus of the amygdala sends efferent axons to regions of the brain stem that appear to be involved in the performance of species-typical defensive responses. Stimulation of these neurons elicits species-typical defensive responses. Lesions impair avoidance behaviors and also impair classical conditioning of bradycardia elicited by electrical shock. Neurons in the central nucleus increase their response rate to the tone (CS) during classical conditioning. Conditioning appears to be inhibited by opiate receptors, which play a role in inhibiting species-typical defensive responses.

The medial geniculate nucleus sends axons to the central nucleus of the amygdala. Destruction of the medial geniculate nucleus, but not the primary auditory cortex, impairs acquisition of classically conditioned defensive responses using a tone as a conditional stimulus. The responses of neurons in the magnocellular medial geniculate nucleus increase during classical conditioning; perhaps these neurons send the critical auditory information to the central nucleus of the amygdala.

■ HUMAN ANTEROGRADE AMNESIA

Several forms of brain damage produce a permanent, dramatic *anterograde amnesia* in humans — an inability to learn new information. Early studies suggested that the deficit, and its anatomical basis, were simple and straightforward: destruction of the hippocampus, mammillary bodies, or other components of a circuit of interconnected structures of the limbic system prevented the acquisition of new memories. However, more recent evidence has forced investigators to revise their conclusions about the nature of the deficit and its anatomical basis. Although the story is still incomplete and the details are complex, study of the nature and causes of

human anterograde amnesia has provided some very interesting evidence about the way in which we learn and remember.

Korsakoff's Syndrome

In 1889, Sergei Korsakoff, a Russian physician, first described a severe memory impairment caused by brain damage, and the disorder was given his name. The most profound symptom of *Korsakoff's syndrome* is a severe anterograde amnesia; the patients appear to be unable to form new memories, although they can still remember old ones. They can converse normally and can remember events that happened long before their brain damage occurred, but they cannot remember events that occur afterward.

Korsakoff's syndrome occurs most often in chronic alcoholics. The disorder results from a thiamine deficiency caused by the alcoholism (Adams, 1969). Because alcoholics receive a substantial number of calories from the alcohol they ingest, they usually eat a poor diet, so their vitamin intake is consequently low. Furthermore, alcohol appears to interfere with intestinal absorption of thiamine (vitamin B_1), and the ensuing deficiency produces brain damage. Thiamine is essential for a step in metabolism: the carboxylation of pyruvate, an intermediate product in the metabolism of carbohydrates, fats, and amino acids. Brain damage sometimes occurs in people who have been severely malnourished and have then received intravenous infusions of glucose; the sudden availability of glucose to the cells of the brain without adequate thiamine with which to metabolize it damages them, perhaps because the cells accumulate pyruvate. Hence, standard medical practice is to administer thiamine along with intravenous glucose to severely malnourished patients. I will discuss the location of the brain damage that causes Korsakoff's syndrome later in this section.

Temporal Lobectomy

Scoville and Milner (1957) reported that bilateral removal of the medial temporal lobe produced a memory impairment in humans that was apparently identical to that seen in Korsakoff's syndrome. Thirty operations had been performed on psychotic patients in an attempt to alleviate their mental disorder, but it was not until this operation was performed on patient H.M. that the anterograde amnesia was discovered. The psychotic patients' behavior was already so disturbed that amnesia was not detected. However, patient H.M. was reasonably intelligent and was not psychotic; therefore, his postoperative deficit was discovered immediately.

Patient H.M. had very severe epilepsy before the operation. Even though he received medication at what was described as near-toxic levels, he suffered major convulsions approximately once a week and had dozens of minor attacks each day. After bilateral removal of the medial temporal lobes, he showed considerable recovery. He received moderate doses of anticonvulsant medication, and had only one or two minor seizures each day. Major convulsions occurred very rarely—one every two or three years. The surgery successfully treated his seizure disorder.

However, it became apparent after surgery that H.M. suffered a memory impairment. Subsequently, Scoville and Milner (1957) tested eight of the psychotic patients who were able to cooperate with them. They found that some of these patients also had anterograde amnesia; the deficit appeared to occur when the hippocampus was removed, but not when the amygdala and overlying temporal cortex were removed, sparing the hippocampus. Thus, they concluded that the hippocampus was the critical structure destroyed by the surgery. As we will see, subsequent research suggests that other structures, especially the amygdala, are also involved.

Penfield and Milner (1958) reported similar findings with patient P.B. Parts of this patient's left temporal lobe were removed in two stages, on separate occasions. No memory disorder was seen after the first operation. During the second operation the surgeon removed the amygdala and hippocampus, which caused a severe anterograde amnesia. Because unilateral temporal lobe damage had never been shown to cause a severe memory impairment, this effect was unexpected. Patient P.B. died 12 years later (of unrelated causes), and Penfield and Mathieson (1974) examined his brain. They found that the right hippocampus had been damaged, probably at the time of birth. Thus, the left temporal lobectomy removed the only functioning hippocampus. The authors concluded that removal of the hippocampus had produced the amnesia.

Anatomy of Anterograde Amnesia

For many years, researchers believed that bilateral medial temporal lobectomy produced anterograde amnesia because the hippocampus was destroyed. This conclusion appeared to be confirmed by postmortem examination of the brains of patients with Korsakoff's syndrome (Barbizet, 1963). Korsakoff's syndrome is almost always associated with degeneration of the mammillary bodies, situated at the posterior end of the hypothalamus. Many years previously, Papez (1937) had reported the existence of a closed circuit of interconnected diencephalic and telencephalic structures that included both the mammillary bodies and the hippocampus. (See **Figure 14.22.**) Perhaps this circuit was necessary for the formation of long-term memories, and thus bilateral damage anywhere in the circuit would produce anterograde amnesia.

Other evidence suggests that this conclusion may not be true. Although people with

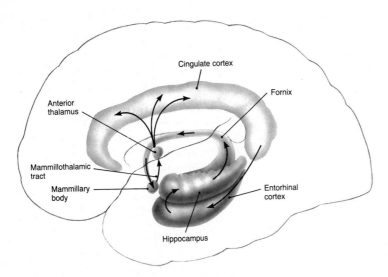

FIGURE 14.22
Papez's circuit.

Korsakoff's syndrome usually incur damage to the mammillary bodies, the association is not inevitable. Victor, Adams, and Collins (1971) studied the autopsies of patients with Korsakoff's syndrome. They concluded that amnesia was more reliably associated with damage to the dorsomedial thalamic nuclei than with damage to the mammillary bodies. They found five cases of severe damage to the mammillary bodies without a corresponding memory loss, whereas all thirty-eight patients with amnesia also had damage to the dorsomedial thalamus. In addition, Squire and Moore (1979) performed a CAT scan of a patient who exhibited severe anterograde amnesia after receiving a wound from a fencing foil that entered his nostril and penetrated the brain through the base of the skull. The stab wound apparently missed the fornix (part of Papez's circuit) but damaged the dorsomedial thalamus. Most investigators believe that we can safely conclude that damage to the dorsomedial thalamus produces anterograde amnesia, but a possible role for the mammillary bodies cannot yet be ruled out with certainty.

Horel (1978) provided an alternative to the hypothesis that bilateral temporal lobec-

tomies produced anterograde amnesia because they destroyed the hippocampus. He suggested that the temporal stem, not the hippocampus, is the critical brain region. He noted that the approach that Scoville used in performing his temporal lobectomies (including that of patient H.M.) necessarily invaded the temporal stem. Therefore, patient H.M. must have suffered damage to the temporal stem. As we saw earlier, the temporal stem connects the amygdala and temporal neocortex with several structures, including the basal ganglia and medial thalamus. Because damage to the medial thalamus appears to be associated with anterograde amnesia, Horel suggested that the temporal stem hypothesis united the evidence from temporal lobe amnesia and Korsakoff's amnesia.

Horel's hypothesis did not receive support from subsequent research with primates. As we saw in an earlier section, damage to the temporal stem did not impair monkeys' ability to recognize a group of stimuli they had just seen (delayed nonmatching-to-sample task) but the lesions did disrupt performance on a simple long-term visual discrimination task. In contrast, monkeys with combined lesions of the hippocampus and amygdala performed poorly on the visual recognition task but readily learned the simple long-term visual discrimination task (Zola-Morgan, Squire, and Mishkin, 1982). As we will see, the performance of humans with anterograde amnesia is more similar to that of the monkeys with the combined lesions of the hippocampus and amygdala than to that of the monkeys with lesions of the temporal stem.

The anatomy of human anterograde amnesia is far from being understood. At present, most investigators believe that although a role for the mammillary bodies has not been ruled out, the medial thalamus appears to be more important. Primarily because of research with laboratory animals (which I will review later in this chapter) many investigators do not believe that the amnesia produced by temporal lobe lesions is solely a result of bilateral hippocampal damage; they tentatively accept the hypothesis that the deficit is caused by damage to both the amygdala and hippocampus.

The Nature of Anterograde Amnesia

In order for you to understand more fully the nature of anterograde amnesia, I will discuss the case of patient H.M. in more detail (Milner, Corkin, and Teuber, 1968; Milner, 1970; Corkin, Sullivan, Twitchell, and Grove, 1981). Patient H.M. has been extensively studied because his amnesia is relatively pure. His intellectual ability and his immediate verbal memory appear to be normal. He can repeat seven numbers forward and five numbers backward, and he can carry on conversations, rephrase sentences, and perform mental arithmetic. He has a partial amnesia for events of the two years preceding the operation, but he can recall older memories very well. He showed no personality change after the operation, and he appears to be a polite and well-mannered person.

However, since the operation H.M. has, with rare exceptions, been unable to learn anything new. He cannot identify by name people he met since the operation (performed in 1953, when he was 27 years old) nor can he find his way back home if he leaves his house. (His family moved to a new house after his operation, and he has been unable to learn how to get around the new neighborhood.) He is aware of his disorder and often says something like this:

> Every day is alone in itself, whatever enjoyment I've had, and whatever sorrow I've had. . . . Right now, I'm wondering. Have I done or said anything amiss? You see, at this moment everything looks clear to me, but what happened just before? That's what worries me. It's like waking from a dream; I just don't remember. (Milner, 1970, p. 37)

H.M. is capable of remembering a small amount of verbal information as long as he is not distracted; constant rehearsal can keep an item in his immediate memory for a long time. However, rehearsal does not appear to have any long-term effects; if he is distracted for a moment, he will completely forget whatever he had been rehearsing. He works very well at repetitive tasks. Indeed, because he so quickly forgets what previously happened, he does not become bored easily. He can endlessly reread the same magazine or laugh at the same jokes, finding them fresh and new each time. His time is typically spent solving crossword puzzles and watching television.

H.M. also shows a few symptoms that do not appear to be related to his memory impairment. He has no interest in sexual behavior; he does not express feelings of hunger or satiety, although he will eat when food is in front of him; and he shows almost no reaction to painful stimuli. As a matter of fact, an attempt was made to ascertain whether H.M. could be classically conditioned to produce an autonomic response to a stimulus paired with a painful shock. The attempt was abandoned when the experimenters found that

H.M. did not react to shock levels that normal people would find quite painful. He said that he could feel the shock, but it did not appear to bother him.

Because H.M. is able to remember events that occurred before his operation, Milner and her colleagues concluded that the structures that had been removed did not themselves contain long-term memories; if they had, old as well as new memories would have been destroyed. Nor were these structures necessary for immediate verbal memories; the fact that H.M. could carry on a conversation indicated that his ability to establish these memories had not been destroyed. The investigators concluded that what had been damaged was the ability to convert immediate memories into long-term ones.

Spared Learning Abilities

H.M.'s memory deficit is striking and dramatic. However, when he and other patients with anterograde amnesia are more carefully studied, it becomes apparent that the amnesia does not represent a total failure in learning ability; when they are appropriately trained and tested, patients with anterograde amnesia can learn many different kinds of tasks. For example, Milner (1965) presented H.M. with a mirror-drawing task. This procedure re-

FIGURE 14.23
The mirror-drawing task.

quires the subject to trace the outline of a figure (in this case, a star) with a pencil while looking at the figure in a mirror. (See **Figure 14.23.**) The task may seem simple, but it is actually rather difficult and requires some practice to perform well. With practice, H.M. became proficient at mirror drawing. Figure

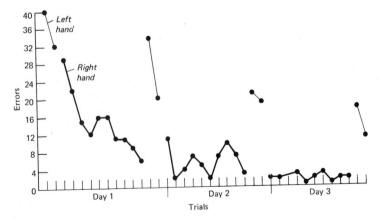

FIGURE 14.24
Data obtained from patient H.M. on the mirror-drawing task. (From *Cognitive Processes in the Brain,* edited by P.M. Milner and S. Glickman. © 1965 by Litton Educational Publishing, Inc. Reprinted by permission of D. Van Nostrand Company.)

14.24 illustrates his improvement; his errors were reduced considerably during the first session, and his improvement was retained on subsequent days of testing. (See **Figure 14.24.**) However, when Milner questioned H.M., he insisted that he did not remember having performed the task. He expressed no sense of familiarity with it.

H.M.'s learning ability is not restricted to a motor skill; he shows the ability to form perceptual memories, as well. Figure 14.25 shows two sample items from a test of the ability to recognize broken drawings; note

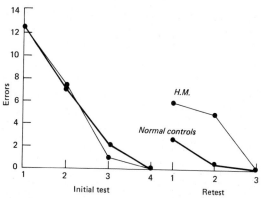

FIGURE 14.26

Learning and long-term retention demonstrated by patient H.M. on the broken-drawing task. (From Milner, B., in *Biology of Memory,* edited by K.H. Pribram and D.E. Broadbent. New York: Academic Press, 1970.)

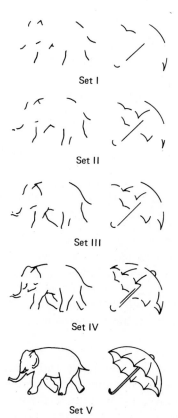

FIGURE 14.25

Examples of broken drawings. (Reprinted by permission of author and publisher from Gollin, E.S. *Perceptual and Motor Skills,* 1960, *11,* 289–298.)

how the drawings are successively more complete. (See **Figure 14.25.**) Subjects are first shown the least-complete version (set I) of each of twenty different drawings. If they do not recognize a figure, they are shown more complete versions until they identify it. One hour later the subjects are tested again for retention, starting with set I. H.M. was given this test and, when retested an hour later, showed considerable improvement (Milner, 1970). When he was retested 4 months later, he still showed this improvement. His performance was poorer than that of normal control subjects, but he showed unmistakable evidence of long-term retention. (See **Figure 14.26.**)

H.M. even shows evidence of learning rather complex behavioral strategies. Cohen and Corkin (1981) attempted to teach him a puzzle called the Tower of Hanoi. This puzzle consists of three wooden spindles, one of which contains five disks arranged according to size, the smallest on top. The task is to place the disks, still arranged according to size, on another spindle, moving one disk at a time. There is one restriction: a disk can be

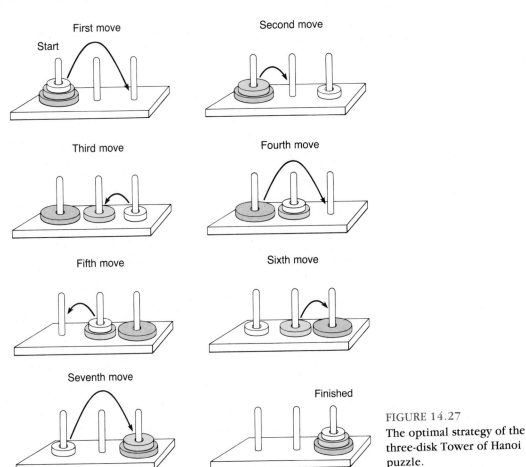

FIGURE 14.27
The optimal strategy of the
three-disk Tower of Hanoi
puzzle.

placed on an empty position or on top of a larger disk, but never on top of a smaller one. The strategy for this task is not immediately obvious but must be learned through trial and error. Figure 14.27 shows the optimal strategy for a three-disk puzzle, which takes a minimum of seven moves. The five-disk puzzle is much more difficult, taking a minimum of thirty-one moves. (See **Figure 14.27**.)

Cohen and Corkin showed the Tower of Hanoi puzzle to H.M. and asked him to try to solve it. H.M. worked on the puzzle four times a day for 4 days, then for 4 more days after a week's interval. His performance gradually improved until he finally learned the correct sequence almost perfectly, taking an average

of thirty-two moves. Obviously, he learned and remembered a rather complex behavior. However, he did not remember having tried solving the puzzle before and expressed surprise at being able to do so well.

Disrupted Short-Term Memories

Although the immediate verbal memory of amnesic patients appears to be relatively normal, most tests of their immediate *nonverbal* memory show it to be severely impaired. For example, Prisko (1963) presented H.M. with pairs of tones, colored lights, or auditory patterns of clicks and found that he had great difficulty judging whether the two stimuli were identical or different. The poor performance appeared to be caused by difficulty remembering the first stimulus long enough to compare it with the second.

An experiment by Sidman, Stoddard, and Mohr (1968) nicely contrasts H.M.'s performance on verbal and nonverbal delayed matching-to-sample tasks, which provide good tests of immediate memory. They presented visual stimuli with a slide projector located behind a display panel that contained an array of nine frosted Plexiglas squares, arranged in a 3 × 3 grid. First they presented a stimulus (the sample) on the middle square. H.M. would press the square, and the stimulus would disappear. Immediately or after a variable delay interval, the experimenters presented eight different stimuli in the surrounding squares. One of these stimuli would be the same as the sample stimulus, and if H.M. pressed the proper square, a penny would fall into a dish. Figure 14.28 illustrates the apparatus, along with the two types of items that were used: verbal stimuli (three consonants) and nonverbal stimuli (ellipses of various shapes). (See **Figure 14.28.**)

Figure 14.29 shows H.M.'s performance on the matching-to-sample problem for the nonverbal stimuli (ellipses), along with data from two normal preadolescent children (shown below), for comparison. The numbers on the horizontal axis to the right and left of the 0 (correct choice) refer to responses made to ellipses "fatter" or "thinner" than the sample. Note that H.M. performed fairly well when there was no delay, but that his performance quickly deteriorated as a delay was introduced. In contrast, the children had no trouble remembering the sample stimulus. (See **Figure 14.29.**)

When Sidman and his colleagues presented H.M. with verbal stimuli (three consonants), he had no trouble selecting the matching stimulus, even after a 40-second delay. Why should his verbal immediate memory be so much better than his nonverbal immediate memory? As the experimenters note, H.M. can easily rehearse verbal information. In fact, they saw him form the letters of the stimulus with his lips. For example, if the sample was *cqv,* he repeatedly said "c-q-v" to himself and thus retained the information. Verbal information can be rehearsed through overt or pri-

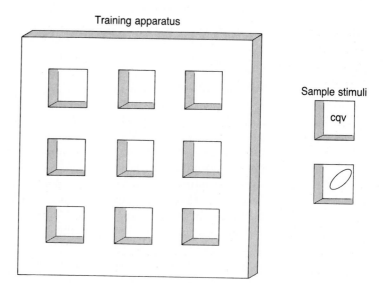

Training apparatus

Sample stimuli

cqv

FIGURE 14.28
The apparatus used by Sidman, **Stoddard,** and Mohr (1968).

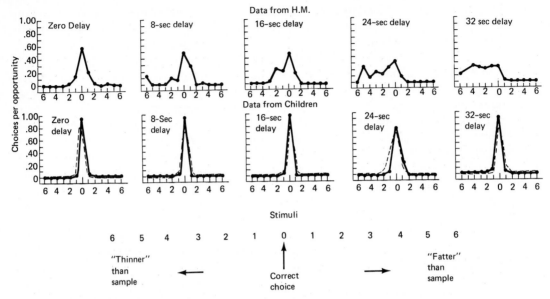

FIGURE 14.29

Data from the ellipse matching-to-sample task. (From Sidman, M.,
Stoddard, L.T., and Mohr, J.P. *Neuropsychologia,* 1968, *6,* 245–254.)

vate repetition of a motor sequence that is normally used to articulate the words (or in this case, the letters) that are being remembered. H.M. already knows the names of letters and has no trouble repeating them to himself. However, he never learned names for different shapes of ellipses, so he could not remember them by repeating words to himself. When the task required him to maintain an *image* of a nonverbal visual stimulus in immediate memory, he failed to do so.

Perhaps you have noticed that this study is similar to the delayed nonmatching-to-sample task employed by Mishkin and his colleagues in their studies with monkeys. You will recall that Zola-Morgan, Squire, and Mishkin (1982) found that monkeys with bilateral lesions of the hippocampus and amygdala had difficulty remembering which of two stimuli they had just seen, but that they could learn a simple long-term visual discrimination task. In contrast, bilateral lesions of the temporal stem impaired learning of the

simple long-term visual discrimination task but not the delayed nonmatching-to-sample task. H.M., too, can learn nonverbal long-term visual discrimination tasks but has difficulty with *immediate* nonverbal memory. Because of these similar results, Zola-Morgan and his colleagues concluded that medial temporal lobectomy produces amnesia because it damages both the amygdala and the hippocampus.

Failure to Remember Contextual Stimuli
Warrington and Weiskrantz (1974, 1978) presented data that suggest that although patients with anterograde amnesia can learn to recognize a stimulus, they have difficulty remembering the context in which the stimulus was presented. They prepared two lists of words. Each list consisted of one member of a pair of words that started with the same three letters; for example, *puddle* and *soft* appeared on one list, *pudding* and *sofa* on the other. The experimenters had their subjects

—control subjects and people with anterograde amnesia—read the first list aloud. Then they presented the first three letters of the words and asked the subjects to try to remember the entire word. Both groups did well. Next, they presented the second list four times, testing with the three-letter prompts each time. After the four trials the control subjects were performing well, but the amnesic patients did poorly; they kept saying words from the first list. In another experiment, Warrington and Weiskrantz presented control subjects and amnesic subjects with a list of words that were uniquely specified by the first three letters. For example, *juice* is the only common word that begins with *jui-, ankle* with *ank-,* and *aisle* with *ais-.* The performance of the amnesic patients was as good as that of control subjects when tested one hour later. When tested 24 hours later they actually performed somewhat *better* than the controls.

The results suggest that people with anterograde amnesia are capable of good long-term perceptual and perceptual-response learning. However, they learn little or nothing about the context in which the learning takes place—in this case, whether a word occurred on the first or second list. The subjects in Warrington and Weiskrantz's first experiment did not learn to distinguish between the responses they made while reading the first list and the responses they made while reading the second list.

Tentative Conclusions

We have seen that humans with anterograde amnesia can, under some conditions, learn new tasks, including rather complicated ones, but that they cannot recall doing so. Most of them learn to recognize the faces of people they see each day, but they rarely learn their names or recall the occasions on which they met them. In addition, although their immediate verbal memory is good (if it were not, they would not be able to carry on a conversation) their immediate nonverbal memory is poor. How can all these facts be reconciled?

First, let us consider the kinds of long-term memory tasks that can be learned by patients with anterograde amnesia. The one factor that all these tasks appear to have in common is that the subjects are trained with a particular set of stimuli, and then their performance is tested with the same set of stimuli. In addition, their *performance* is tested, not their ability to recall the stimuli verbally. Indeed, they cannot do the latter task. Remember, amnesic patients can perform a mirror-drawing task, recognize broken drawings, or solve the Tower of Hanoi puzzle. What they cannot do is say that they remember seeing the stimuli or performing the task before.

What is the difference between learning to perform a particular response to a particular stimulus and being able to remember that an experience occurred? In the first case, learning would seem to consist of strengthened connections between neurons that perceive a stimulus and neurons that control a behavior. This basic capacity is not damaged in people with anterograde amnesia. In addition, they can learn even complex behavioral sequences, such as the moves that must be made to solve the Tower of Hanoi puzzle. But to talk about an event, one must make novel responses—responses different from the ones made while learning the task. Solving a mirror-drawing task is very different from describing the apparatus and the occasion on which one worked with it. When a normal person learns to perform a task, he or she learns much more than a particular behavior. The person learns about associated stimuli: the time the training occurred, who else was present, what the room looked like, how he or she felt at the time, and so on. When the person sees the apparatus later, the perception can evoke many responses. The person can say when he or she previously encountered the apparatus, who else was present at the time, and so on.

In contrast, the memories of a person with anterograde amnesia are restricted to the particular task they learned. When they see the apparatus they do not automatically remember when they saw it, who else was present, and so on. For some reason, they cannot remember the context in which they learned the task. Squire (1982) has referred to the two kinds of memory as *procedural knowledge* and *declarative knowledge:* learning to perform a task (a procedure) as opposed to being able to describe an experience verbally (declare its details). We cannot yet determine whether amnesic patients fail to recognize different contexts (a problem related to perception) and thus fail to learn events associated with them, or whether they fail to establish the links between the memories of various sensory components of a particular situation.

You will readily perceive that my conclusion is not very specific and does not go too much beyond a restatement that people with anterograde amnesia can learn some things but cannot tell you they learned them. The reason for the lack of precision is that we still have much to discover about how we learn and remember things, particularly how we learn about associations and relationships between the multitude of perceptions that constitute an event's context. When I go to work I park my car in the same lot each day, but when I leave I usually remember where it is and do not confuse the most recent experience with the hundreds of other times I parked there. How do I do so? And why does seeing a painting on my wall remind me of a friend who painted it, and of the time I chose it from a group of other pictures she painted? I recall the place, the other people present, and the other pictures I chose not to buy. I can recall the entire episode, from walking into

her studio to watching her husband wrap the picture I had selected. Thus, even the sequence of events is preserved. Why does temporal lobectomy or damage to the medial thalamus (and perhaps the mammillary bodies) disrupt a person's ability to recall episodes that happened after the time of their brain injury? Because these people can remember *earlier* episodes, the structures that contain these memories, and the mechanisms needed for remembering them, must still remain. What seems to be missing is the ability to integrate new experiences into a cohesive whole that they can remember and describe.

INTERIM SUMMARY

Brain damage caused by thiamine deficiency (usually as a result of long-term alcoholism) or bilateral removal of the temporal lobes causes anterograde amnesia — the inability to learn some classes of new information. If you want to review the evidence presented in this section, reread my tentative conclusions, above.

■ THE ROLE OF THE HIPPOCAMPUS IN LEARNING

The discovery that bilateral temporal lobectomy produced anterograde amnesia, and the indication that the hippocampus was the critical structure, stimulated interest in the possible role of the hippocampus in learning. It now appears that hippocampal lesions alone are not responsible for human amnesia, and that amnesia is not simply a failure to learn new information. However, the many studies that investigated the hippocampus showed it to be an interesting, if perplexing, structure.

I should like first to tell you what the hippocampus does and then summarize the research that led to the conclusion. However, I cannot do so; hippocampal lesions or lesions that damage pathways into and out of the hippocampus produce a variety of deficits that defy simple characterization. The hippocampus may participate in spatial perception, temporal perception, conditional discrimination, memory of recent events, and modulation of certain categories of species-typical and learned behaviors. These may be independent functions, or they may represent different aspects of a common function that we have not yet been able to identify.

Anatomy

As you already know, the hippocampal formation is situated in the medial temporal lobe. It consists of several allied structures: the hippocampus proper (also called ***Ammon's horn***), the ***dentate gyrus,*** and the ***subiculum,*** which lie alongside the inferior horns of the lateral ventricles. The hippocampus proper and dentate gyrus consist of *archicortex,* the evolutionarily oldest form of cortex. The subiculum consists of a transitional form of cortex, intermediate in form between archicortex and neocortex. (See **Figure 14.30.**) Afferent and efferent fibers pass through two major fiber systems: the fimbria/fornix and the perforant path. Axons that travel through the fimbria/fornix system funnel through the ***fimbria,*** located on the lateral border of the hippocampus proper. As

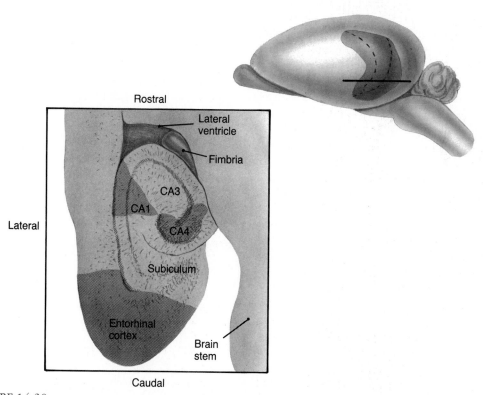

FIGURE 14.30

Location of the hippocampal formation in the human brain. CA1-CA4 = fields of *Cornu Ammonis,* or Ammon's horn.

these bundles leave the hippocampus rostrally, they become part of two long, arching fiber tracts called the *fornix columns.* (*Fornix* means "arch"; in fact, the term *fornicate* derives from the fact that prostitutes and other poor people in early Roman times lived in underground dwellings with arched ceilings.) As the two fornix columns arch forward they sweep downward and finally backward, ending in the mammillary bodies in the posterior hypothalamus. In addition, some fibers branch off and travel to the anterior thalamic nuclei. Other fibers leave the fimbria and travel forward through the *precommissural fornix* to the septum, located between the superior horns of the lateral ventricles. The fornix columns carry hippocampal efferent axons, whereas the precommissural fornix carries both efferent and afferent axons; the efferent axons go to the lateral septal nuclei, and the afferent axons come from the medial septal nuclei. In addition, the precommissural fornix also conveys serotonergic and noradrenergic axons to the hippocampus from neurons in the brain stem. (See **Figure 14.31.**)

Most of the sensory information received by the hippocampal formation comes via the entorhinal cortex, which receives projections from the amygdala, limbic cortex, and all areas of neocortex. Neurons in the entorhinal cortex send axons to the hippocampus directly, and through the **perforant path** to the dentate gyrus, which projects to the hippocampus. Most of the efferent axons leave via the subiculum, which, besides sending axons through the fornix columns, also projects to the posterior cingulate cortex. Thus, the hippocampus receives sensory information and information about the animal's motor activity. (See **Figure 14.31.**)

Theta Activity and Motor Performance

Green and Arduini (1954) discovered that the hippocampus produces a regular rhythmical pattern of electrical activity called **theta activity**—medium-amplitude, medium-frequency (5–8 Hz) waves. Theta activity can be produced by sensory stimulation or electrical stimulation of the reticular formation; therefore, some investigators have concluded that theta activity is related to arousal (see Vanderwolf and Robinson, 1981).

Vanderwolf and his colleagues (Vanderwolf, 1969; Vanderwolf, Kramis, Gillespie, and Bland, 1975) observed that hippocampal

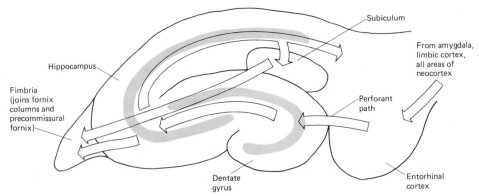

FIGURE 14.31
Connections of the components of the hippocampal formation.

theta activity shows a better relation to the type of behavior an animal is performing than it does to the animal's state of "arousal," an inferred process that cannot be observed directly. In rats, *theta behaviors* include walking, running, rearing up on the hindlegs, jumping, swimming, manipulating food with the forepaws, and changing posture. *Nontheta behaviors* include alert immobility ("freezing"); self-directed licking, scratching, or grooming; chewing; chattering of the teeth; and shivering.

Theta rhythms are controlled by pacemaker cells in the medial septum (Mayer and Stumpf, 1958; Rawlins, Feldon, and Gray, 1979). These cells send acetylcholinergic terminal buttons to the hippocampus (Lynch, Rose, and Gall, 1978); thus, drugs that block acetylcholine receptors abolish theta rhythms. We cannot be sure whether theta waves control the types of behaviors an animal engages in or whether they are simply a consequence of engaging in different types of behaviors. As we will see, drugs that block acetylcholine receptors or lesions of the medial septum or fimbria/fornix, both of which abolish theta rhythms, disrupt the animal's performance on some learning tasks. Therefore, these rhythms reflect an important aspect of hippocampal functioning. Just what that function is we do not yet know.

Spatial Perception and Learning

With the rise of the hippocampal hypothesis to explain temporal lobe amnesia, experimenters began making lesions of the hippocampal formation to see what role it played in learning. They quickly found that the animals remained capable of learning most tasks. However, consistent deficits were seen in tasks with an important spatial component; hippocampal lesions impaired animals' ability to learn complex mazes. The lesions also impaired reversal of a simple spatial discrimi-

nation task; once having learned to go one place but not the other, animals with hippocampal lesions had difficulty doing the opposite when the experimenter suddenly changed the rules. (See Isaacson, 1974, for a review.)

Remembering Places Visited

Olton and Samuelson (1976) devised a task that requires rats to remember where they have just been and discovered that hippocampal lesions impaired performance even more than they do on a standard maze task. The investigators placed the rats on a circular platform located at the junction of eight arms, which radiated away like the spokes of a wheel. (See **Figure 14.32.**) The entire maze was elevated above the ground high enough so that the rats would not jump to the floor. Before placing the rats on the center platform, the experimenters put a piece of food at the end of each of the arms. The rats (who were hungry, of course) were permitted to explore the maze and eat the food. The animals soon learned to retrieve the food efficiently, entering each arm once. After twenty trials most animals did not enter an arm from which they had already obtained food during that session. A later study (Olton, Collison, and Werz,

FIGURE 14.32
A radial maze. This one contains twelve arms, not eight. (Photograph courtesy of D.S. Olton.)

1977) showed that rats could perform well even when they were prevented from following a fixed sequence of visits to the arms; thus, they had to remember where they had been, not simply follow the same pattern of responses each time. Control procedures in several studies ruled out the possibility that rats simply smelled their own odor in arms they had previously visited.

The radial-arm maze is symmetrical, and few cues are present to distinguish one part of the apparatus from another. It is clear that if a rat can see objects in the environment around the maze, it uses these objects for navigation. For example, if a set of doors is used to confine a rat to the central platform between trials and then the maze is rotated, the rat will visit the arms that point to the environmental locations that were not previously visited. If the rat already visited the arm that pointed toward the north wall, it will avoid whatever arm points north even after the experimenters rotate the maze between trials. A rat's choice will also be displaced if external stimuli, rather than the maze, are moved between trials. O'Keefe and Conway (1980) attached stimuli to the inside of a black curtain that surrounded a maze. When they moved the stimuli as a group, maintaining their relative positions, the animals reoriented their responses accordingly. However, when they interchanged the stimuli so that they were arranged in a new order, the animals' performance was disrupted. (Imagine how disoriented you might be if you entered a familiar room and found that the windows, doors, and furniture were in new positions.)

The radial-arm maze task uses a behavioral capacity that is well developed in rats. Rats are scavengers and often find food in different locations each day. Thus, they must be able to find their way around the environment efficiently, not getting lost and not revisiting too soon a place where they found food. Of course, they must also learn which places in the environment are likely to contain food and visit them occasionally. Although these two abilities might appear to require the same brain functions, they do not. First, let us consider the ability to avoid revisiting a place where food was just found. Olton and his colleagues (reviewed by Olton, 1983) found that lesions of the hippocampus, fimbria/fornix, or entorhinal cortex severely disrupted the ability of rats to visit the arms of a radial maze efficiently. In fact, their postoperative performance reached chance levels; they acted as if they had no memory of which arms they had previously entered. They eventually obtained all the food, but only after entering many of the arms repeatedly.

Thus, hippocampal lesions disrupt animals' ability to remember the places they have just visited. However, this deficit does not impair the second type of learning—learning to visit locations that sometimes contain food and to avoid visiting locations that never do. Olton and Papas (1979) trained rats in a seventeen-arm maze. Before each session, eight of the arms were baited with food; the other nine *never* were. Although rats with lesions of the fimbria/fornix visited the baited arms randomly, failing to avoid visiting the ones in which they had just eaten, they learned to stay away from the nine arms that never contained food. They apparently could not remember where they had just been, but they could learn which locations regularly contained food.

Spatial Memory or Working Memory?
Olton (1983) suggests that the deficit produced by hippocampal lesions is not caused by a failure to incorporate spatial information; rather, it stems from a memory deficit that includes other kinds of information as well. Olton and Feustle (1981) trained rats in a four-arm maze, the arms of which were covered with tunnels; thus, the animals could not see environmental cues outside the maze. The

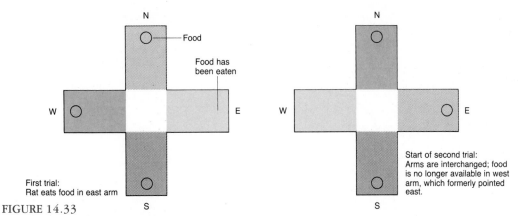

FIGURE 14.33
The experiment by Olton and Feustle (1981).

experimenters painted distinctively different patterns on each of the arms and covered the floors with materials of different textures, so that they could easily be discriminated. After a rat had visited an arm, the experimenters confined the rat in the central chamber by closing a set of doors. During this time the experimenters detached the arms, moved them to new positions, and opened the doors again. The rats learned to visit each arm only once, and because the position of the arms was changed after each visit, the choice could not have been made on the basis of spatial location. (See **Figure 14.33.**) Nevertheless, lesions of the fimbria/fornix severely disrupted performance; the animals performed at chance levels. (See **Figure 14.34.**)

Olton (1983) suggests that lesions of the hippocampus or its connections impair *working memory* but leave *reference memory* relatively intact. Working memory consists of information about things that have just happened, which are useful in the immediate future, but which change from day to day. Thus, it is "erasable" memory that is replaced on a regular basis. Reference memory is more permanent memory, produced by consistent conditions. For example, my remembering where I parked my car in lot number 40 *today* is working memory. Tomorrow I will park in a

new place and remember that. However, my remembering how to get from home to lot number 40 is reference memory, which is unchanging. As you may have noted, there is some similarity between this distinction and the one Squire has made between *declarative knowledge* and *procedural knowledge*. Of course, a rat cannot "declare" that it knows how to perform a particular task.

Whether or not the deficit caused by lesions of the hippocampal formation is one of working memory, the hippocampal formation does certainly play a special role in spatial perception. Morris, Garrud, Rawlins, and O'Keefe (1982) trained rats to perform a task that required them to find a particular location in space solely by means of visual cues external to the apparatus. The "maze" consisted of a circular pool, 1.3 meters in diameter, filled with a mixture of water and milk. The milk hid the location of a small platform, situated just beneath the surface of the liquid. The experimenters put the rats into the milky water and let them swim until they encountered the hidden platform and climbed onto it. They released the rats from a new position on each trial. After a few trials, normal rats learned to swim directly to the hidden platform from wherever they were released. However, rats with hippocampal lesions swam in

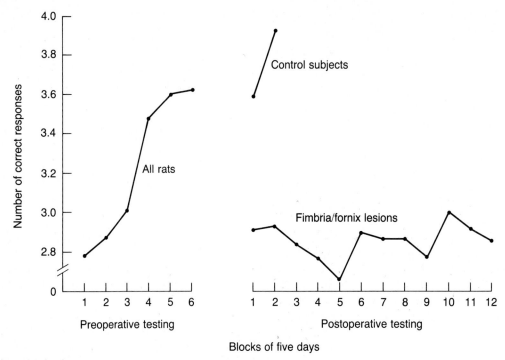

FIGURE 14.34

Preoperative acquisition by and postoperative testing of control rats and
rats with fimbria/fornix lesions in the experiment shown in Figure 14.33.
(From Olton, D.S., and Feustle, W. *Experimental Brain Research,* 1981,
41, 380–389.)

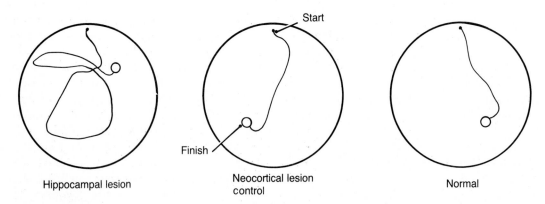

FIGURE 14.35

Effects of hippocampal lesions and neocortical control lesions on
performance in the circular "milk maze." Reprinted by permission from
Nature, 297, 681. Copyright ©, Macmillan Journals Limited.

what appeared to be an aimless fashion until they encountered the platform. Figure 14.35 shows the performance of three rats: a normal rat, one with a neocortical lesion (to control for the fact that removal of the hippocampus entails damage to the overlying neocortex), and one with a hippocampal lesion. The results speak for themselves. (See **Figure 14.35.**)

The experiment by Morris and his colleagues provides evidence that the hippocampus is involved in long-term ("reference") memory for spatial locations as well as in a temporary, immediate ("working") memory for places just visited. This evidence contrasts with Olton and Papas's finding that rats with hippocampal lesions learned to avoid visits to the nine arms of a seventeen-arm maze that were never baited with food. Perhaps the rats in this study learned to avoid the nine empty arms by means of subtle differences in the construction of the individual arms, and not by means of their spatial location.

Recording Studies: Neurons That Respond to Particular Places

Other data support the suggestion that the hippocampal formation participates in spatial perception. O'Keefe and Dostrovsky (1971) recorded the activity of individual neurons in the hippocampus as an animal moved around the environment and discovered that some neurons fired at a high rate only when the rat was in a particular location. Different neurons had different **spatial receptive fields;** that is, they responded in different locations. When a rat is in a radial-arm maze, its hippocampal neurons respond to places defined in relation to objects in the environment outside the maze (for example, lighting fixtures, cabinets, and racks of cages). If a particular neuron is active when the rat is at the end of the arm that points north, the neuron will continue to fire in the end of the northern arm, even after the maze is

rotated so that a different arm points north. Figure 14.36 shows the activity of a neuron as a rat explores an eight-arm radial maze (Miller and Best, 1980). Note that the cell responds when the rat enters arm 1 of an eight-arm maze. After the maze is rotated 90 degrees, arm 3 now occupies the former location of arm 1, and the neuron now fires when the rat enters this arm. (See **Figure 14.36.**) Hippocampal place neurons respond differently when an animal is placed in an enclosed chamber. In this case, the neurons define location relative to the walls of the apparatus; their spatial receptive fields move with the rotation of the chamber (Kubie and Ranck, 1982).

Because different hippocampal neurons respond while the animal is located in different places, it appears that the hippocampus contains a record of where an animal is at any moment. This finding helps explain why animals with lesions of the hippocampus or its connections perform poorly on tasks that involve perceptions of space, such as the radial-arm maze or the circular "swimming pool." However, you will recall that Olton and Feustle observed poor performance in brain-damaged rats when they interchanged distinctively different arms of a four-arm maze between trials. This experiment indicates that the role of the hippocampus is not limited to spatial memories.

Participation in Classical Conditioning

Several studies by Berger and his colleagues (reviewed by Berger, 1984b) have shown that cells in the hippocampus respond not only to an animal's location in the environment. They also respond when the animal makes a learned response, but not an unlearned one. The experimenters used a procedure developed by Gormezano (1972) to classically condition a *nictitating membrane response* in rabbits. Because so much progress has been made in understanding the

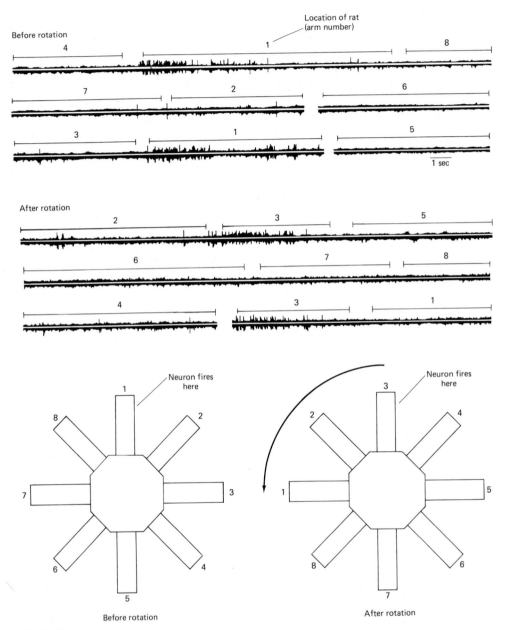

FIGURE 14.36

Response of a single unit in the hippocampus of a freely moving rat as the animal explores an eight-arm radial maze, before and after a 90-degree rotation of the arms of the maze. Note that the unit responds most rapidly when the animal is in the arm facing a particular direction. (From Best, P.J., and Hill, A.J. In *Conditioning: Representation of Involved Neural Functions,* edited by C.D. Woody. New York: Plenum Press, 1982.)

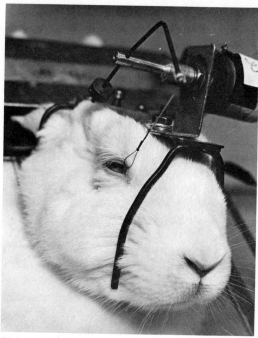

FIGURE 14.37

A rabbit prepared for measurement of the nictitating membrane response.

anatomy of the neural pathways that participate in this form of learning, I will describe the procedure in detail.

The **nictitating membrane** (from *nictitare,* "to wink") is a tough inner eyelid possessed by many mammals, birds, and fish. Each eye has one nictitating membrane, which moves laterally across the eye, from the nasal side to the temporal side. When a stimulus threatens the animal's eye, the nictitating membrane sweeps across the eye, covering it. In order to record movement of the membrane, the experimenter attaches a loop of nylon thread to its edge and then places the animal in a restraining cage. A lever mounted on a small movement transducer is attached to the loop of thread. When the membrane moves it causes the lever to move, which activates the transducer. (See **Figure 14.37.**) Most investigators send an electrical signal

from the transducer to a computer and use it to monitor the response.

Unconditional responses of the nictitating membrane are elicited either by directing a puff of air to the rabbit's eye or by administering a small, brief electrical shock through an electrode attached to the skin near the eyelids. In the studies I will describe, the conditional stimulus is always a tone. In most cases the experimenter turns on the tone (CS) and then 250 msec later turns on the unconditional stimulus—a puff of air or a shock (US). The CS and the US are then terminated simultaneously. At first, the animal makes only unconditional responses, but then it begins to move its nictitating membrane in anticipation of the shock or puff of air. These anticipatory responses are conditional responses, and they gradually occur earlier and earlier in the interval between the CS and the US. (See **Figure 14.38.**)

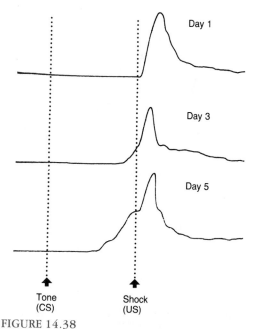

FIGURE 14.38

Acquisition of a classically conditioned nictitating membrane response. (Graphs courtesy of J.W. Moore.)

Berger and his colleagues (see Berger, 1984b) recorded from single neurons in the hippocampus while they trained the animals to make classically conditioned nictitating membrane responses. They discovered that the pattern of unit activity recorded from these neurons was closely correlated with the movement of the membrane during a conditional response, but *not* during an unconditional response elicited by the puff of air alone. Figure 14.39 shows the pattern of firing (series of vertical bars) of single hippocampal neurons, along with a graph of the movement of the nictitating membrane, recorded by the transducer. The top two records are from a rabbit that had learned to make a conditional response to the tone; the

fact that the membrane began to move before the puff of air indicates that the response was a learned one, and not a reflexively elicited one. Note the good correspondence between the firing pattern of the neuron and the movement of the nictitating membrane. The neural response precedes the movement by approximately 40 msec. (See **Figure 14.39, top.**) The bottom two records are from a rabbit that was presented with a puff of air (US) but no tone (CS). Note that the hippocampal neurons do not alter their rate of firing during the unconditional responses. (See **Figure 14.39, bottom.**)

Several investigators have recorded from neurons in various regions that send axons to the hippocampus in order to determine

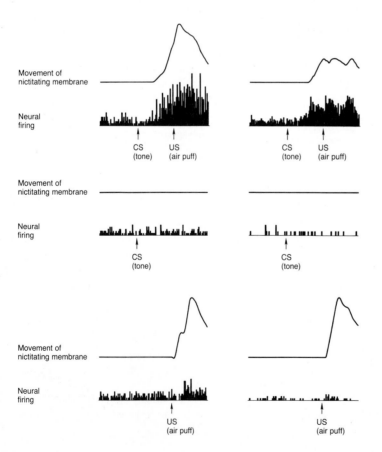

FIGURE 14.39
Pattern of firing of single units in the rabbit hippocampus (H) along with a record of the movement of the nictitating membrane (NM). *Top row:* Conditional responses of two trained rabbits. Note that the response and unit firing begin before the unconditional stimulus. *Middle row:* Lack of response from two rabbits presented with the tone alone. *Bottom row:* Unconditional responses of two rabbits presented with the puff of air alone. Note that the activity of the hippocampal units does not increase with the unconditional response. (From Berger, T.W., Rinaldi, P.C., Weisz, D.J., and Thompson, R.F. *Journal of Neurophysiology,* 1983, *50,* 1197–1219.)

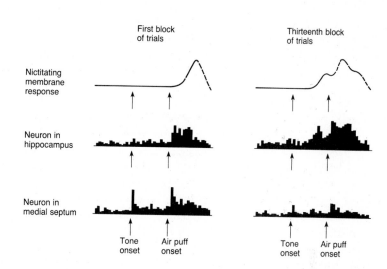

FIGURE 14.40

The pattern of firing of neurons in the hippocampus, but not in the medial septum, resembles the shape of the graph of the conditional nictitating membrane response. (From Berger, T.W., Clark, G.A., and Thompson, R.F. *Physiological Psychology,* 1980, *8,* 155–167.)

whether the pattern of activity that correlates with conditional responses develops in the hippocampus, or whether the pattern develops elsewhere and is passively transmitted there. The results suggest that the pattern develops elsewhere but is "magnified" in the hippocampus. Berger, Clark, and Thompson (1980) reported that neurons in the medial septum (which project to the hippocampus) responded briefly to the onset of the tone and puff of air, but this response soon habituated. These neurons also increased their rate of firing during the unconditional response, but *not* during the conditional response. (See **Figure 14.40.**) Although the authors did not include in their article histograms of the responses of single units in the entorhinal cortex, they reported that neurons in the entorhinal cortex (which project to both the dentate gyrus and the hippocampus proper) had a pattern of responding that resembled the conditional response. However, the activity of neurons in the hippocampus increased much more during conditioning trials than did that of neurons in the entorhinal cortex.

Berger (1984b) also reported that neurons in the lateral septum, which receive inputs from the hippocampus, showed a pattern of responding like that of hippocampal neurons; thus, the hippocampus sends the information predicting a conditional response to this region. Neurons in the mammillary bodies and the anterior thalamic nuclei, which receive inputs from the hippocampus via the fornix columns, did not show this pattern. What happens to the information after it reaches the lateral septum? So far we do not know.

The finding that the response pattern of hippocampal neurons resembled the shape of a conditional (learned) response and not that of an unconditional (unlearned) response suggests that the hippocampus may participate in learning the conditional response. However, research has shown that the role it plays is not an essential one; Solomon and Moore (1975) found that rabbits with bilateral hippocampal lesions learned a conditional nictitating membrane response as rapidly as nonlesioned animals. Why, then, does the hippocampus "know" that the animal is about to make a learned response? Subsequent research has suggested some tentative answers.

Weisz, Solomon, and Thompson (1980) established conditional nictitating mem-

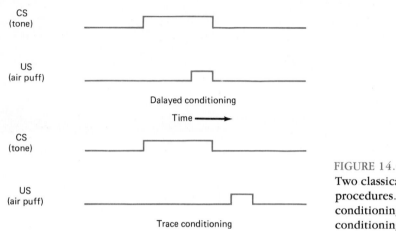

FIGURE 14.41
Two classical conditioning
procedures. *Top:* Delayed
conditioning. *Bottom:* Trace
conditioning.

brane responses with a procedure known as *trace conditioning.* In the usual procedure, called *delayed conditioning,* the experimenter turns on the conditional stimulus, then the unconditional stimulus, and then turns them both off together. (See **Figure 14.41, top.**) In trace conditioning the experimenter turns the conditional stimulus on and off and then after a delay turns the unconditional stimulus on and off. (See **Figure 14.41, bottom.**) The term *trace conditioning* derives from the fact that the unconditional stimulus is paired with a "memory trace" of the conditional stimulus rather than the actual conditional stimulus. Weisz and his colleagues found that hippocampal lesions prevented the animals from learning a conditional nictitating membrane response by means of trace conditioning. However, when the same animals were subsequently trained on the standard delayed conditioning procedure, they soon began making conditional responses.

This finding suggests that the hippocampus may play an essential role in remembering a stimulus that has just been perceived, so that it can come to control a response produced by an unconditional stimulus. Electrical recordings of hippocampal

neurons during trace conditioning support this conclusion. Figure 14.42 shows a graph of the pattern of neural firing (of many units, not a single one) during early and late trace conditioning. Note that the neurons began firing in response to the tone early in training, but that by the time the conditional response was well established, their firing pattern resembled the shape of the response. This pattern suggests that during learning, neurons in the hippocampus "remember" the conditional stimulus. (See **Figure 14.42.**)

A second possible role of the hippocampus in classical conditioning was suggested by an experiment by Berger and Orr (1983). These investigators trained normal rabbits and rabbits with hippocampal lesions or neocortical (control) lesions with a *differential classical conditioning procedure.* They presented tones of two different frequencies, only one of which (CS$^+$) was followed by the puff of air (US). The CS$^-$ was presented by itself, alone. The lesions had no effect on learning the discrimination; all groups learned to make a conditional response when the CS$^+$ was presented, but not when the CS$^-$ was presented. However, when the experimenters reversed the meaning of the tones, so the CS$^+$ became the CS$^-$ and vice versa, the animals with hippocampal lesions learned very slowly. (See **Figure 14.43.**) The results suggest that the hippocampus plays a role in *unlearning* to make a response to one stimulus and learning to make it to another instead.

Research by Deadwyler and his colleagues (reported by Deadwyler, 1982) provides electrophysiological evidence that supports this conclusion. They trained rats in an operant discrimination task and simultaneously recorded the electrical activity of the dentate

gyrus, which sends axons to the hippocampus. One stimulus (S⁺) signaled the availability of food; the other (S⁻) signaled that

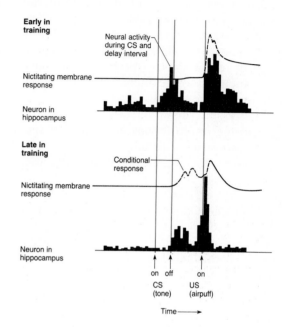

FIGURE 14.42

Response patterns of a group of neurons in the hippocampus trace during classical conditioning of the nictitating membrane response. (From Thompson, R.W., Berger, T.W., Berry, S.D., Clark, G.A., Kettner, R.N., Lavond, D.G., Mauk, M.D., McCormick, D.A., Solomon, P.R., and Weisz, D.J. In *Conditioning: Representation of Involved Neural Functions,* edited by C.D. Woody. New York: Plenum Press, 1982.)

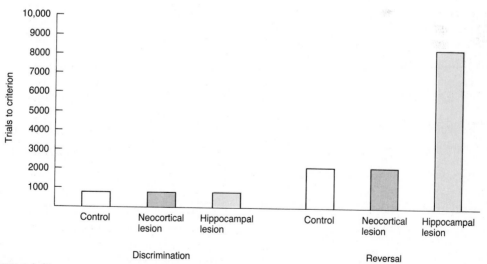

FIGURE 14.43

Effects of hippocampal lesions on acquisition of a differential classical conditioning procedure and its reversal. (From Berger, T.W., and Orr, W.B. *Behavioural Brain Research,* 1983, *8,* 49–68.)

responses would not be reinforced. The rats learned to respond during the S^+ but not during the S^-. Next, the experimenters reversed the meaning of the stimuli. As soon as they did so, they observed large changes in the electrical activity evoked in the dentate gyrus by the discriminative stimuli. Perhaps this change in activity reflects the fact that the animals must pay attention to the altered meaning of the discriminative stimuli.

Berry and Thompson (1979) reported a surprising result: lesions of the medial septum disrupted the acquisition of a classically conditioned nictitating membrane response, even though hippocampal lesions did not. Because medial septal lesions disrupt hippocampal theta rhythms, the effect may have been caused by this disruption. Other experimental manipulations that disrupt hippocampal theta rhythms also interfere with classical conditioning, including injections of scopolamine (Moore, Goodell, and Solomon, 1976). This drug, which blocks acetylcholine receptors, apparently disrupts hippocampal theta rhythms because the neurons of the medial septum that project to the hippocampus secrete acetylcholine. In fact, Solomon, Solomon, Vander Schaaf, and Perry (1983) found that scopolamine retarded classical conditioning only in normal rabbits; the drug had no effect on the rate of learning in animals with hippocampal lesions. This finding suggests that, at least with respect to classical conditioning, a malfunctioning hippocampus is worse than none at all. The results support the conclusion that the hippocampus modulates the activity of structures that participate in learning; when it is malfunctioning, it disrupts their activity and interferes with learning.

The evidence cited in this section strongly suggests that although the hippocampus is not essential for some types of classical conditioning, it does participate in the learning process. The finding that its removal prevents trace conditioning suggests that it contains a temporary record of the conditional stimulus that is used to establish the neural connections necessary for learning the task. The finding that its removal severely retards reversal learning of a classically conditioned task suggests that it plays an important role in modifying already-established learning. A more precise definition of its role in classical conditioning awaits further research.

INTERIM SUMMARY

The hippocampal formation, including Ammon's horn, the dentate gyrus, and the subiculum, receives inputs from the entorhinal cortex via the perforant path and from the medial septum via the precommissural fornix. Most of its efferent axons originate in the subiculum and proceed to the anterior thalamic nuclei and the mammillary bodies via the fornix columns, but some axons originate in Ammon's horn and travel to the septum via the precommissural fornix.

Although recent studies have discovered some very interesting information about the hippocampus, this structure remains an enigma. Neurons in the hippocampus respond when an animal is in a particular location, and lesions of the hippocampus or of its connections impair an animal's ability to remember where it has just been. In addition, lesions of the septum that disrupt hippocampal theta activity also disrupt normal hippocampal functioning. These findings led O'Keefe and Nadel (1978) to propose that the hippocampus contains a "cognitive map" of the environment. Olton, the developer of the radial-arm maze, disagrees, insisting that the hippocampus is necessary for working memory. He and Feustle found that hippocampal lesions impaired rats' ability to remember which arm of a four-arm maze they had previously entered, even when the arms could be distinguished on the basis of tactile and visual cues, but not spatial ones. However, the experiment using the milk-filled swimming pool demonstrates that even long-term spatial learning can be impaired by hippocampal lesions. Thus, although the hippocampus does appear to play a role in the temporary remembering of events that just occurred, it also has a special role in spatial perception.

Recording studies have shown that the pattern of firing of neurons in the hippocampus closely resembles the shape of the classically conditioned nictitating membrane response, but not the unconditional response. However, the role of these neurons is not a straightforward one; hippocampal lesions do not impair simple delayed classical conditioning. The lesions do impair trace conditioning or reversal of a differential classical conditioning task, which suggests that the neurons help the animal to remember the conditional stimulus during a delay interval and to pay attention to changes in the meaning of discriminative stimuli. Destruction of the medial septum, which controls hippocampal theta rhythms through its acetylcholinergic connection via the precommissural fornix, impairs classical conditioning. Presumably, abnormal activity of the hippocampus disrupts the functions of other brain structures, thus preventing learning from taking place.

■ CLASSICAL CONDITIONING

In the past few years, much progress has been made in identifying neural structures that participate in various forms of learning. I have described some of the research on the neural basis of perceptual learning, learning to recognize biologically relevant stimuli, and human anterograde amnesia and on the role of the hippocampus in learning. In the final section of this chapter, I describe the research devoted to understanding the neural pathways by which a rabbit acquires a classically conditioned nictitating membrane response. The anatomical basis of this learned behavior is better understood than any other in mammals. The work is important because it raises the possibility that studies in the near future will be able to identify the biochemical and structural changes in neurons responsible for memory. When the pathways necessary for a particular form of learning are understood, investigators know where to look for changes.

The earlier studies on the physiology of classical conditioning focused on the role of the hippocampus. These studies still continue, but as we saw in the last section, the role of this structure is not an essential one, except for trace conditioning, which requires a specific form of immediate memory. Several studies have shown that classical conditioning of a simple response to a simple conditional stimulus can be accomplished in the brain stem. For example, Norman, Buchwald, and Villablanca (1977) transected cats' brain stems at the level of the pons. Even after this disconnection of midbrain and forebrain structures from the hindbrain, animals could still acquire a classically conditioned eyeblink response to an auditory stimulus. Because the sensory input for the CS (audition) and US (somatosensation) and the motor control of the response (eye blink) are conveyed to the brain through cranial nerves located caudal to the transection, the learning must have taken place solely in hindbrain neurons.

Investigations carried out in several laboratories have discovered many elements of the circuit by which rabbits learn a classically conditioned nictitating membrane response. These studies have traced the efferent pathway that controls the nictitating membrane response, the afferent pathways that convey the somatosensory information of the US (air puff or shock), and the nuclei that are necessary for conditional, but not unconditional, responses.

Movement of the rabbit's nictitating membrane is controlled by a special muscle, which runs parallel to the optic nerve. Contraction of this muscle, called the *retractor bulbi* (*bulbus,* "onion," refers to the eye), pulls the eye back into its socket, and the natural elasticity of the nictitating membrane causes it to wipe across the eye. The sixth cranial nerve (abducens nerve) innervates the retractor bulbi, and the neurons that send axons to this muscle lie in the *accessory ab-*

ducens nucleus, just adjacent to the abducens nucleus in the caudal pons (Powell, Berthier, and Moore, 1979). Therefore, the pathways by which conditional or unconditional nictitating membrane responses are produced must terminate in this region.

Unconditional nictitating membrane responses are elicited by means of an electrical shock around the eyelid or a puff of air delivered to the eye. This somatosensory information is transmitted through the fifth cranial nerve (trigeminal nerve) to the rostral nuclei of the trigeminal nuclear complex (Berthier and Moore, 1983). Second-order neurons in these nuclei send axons to the accessory abducens nucleus, which contains the motor neurons that cause contraction of the retractor bulbi. (See **Figure 14.44.**)

Only recently has the attention of scientists

investigating the anatomy of learning been focused on the cerebellum. In the past, this structure was generally considered to be important only in motor control. People were surprised, therefore, to learn that lesions of the cerebellum permanently abolished conditional nictitating membrane responses, but not unconditional ones (Lincoln, McCormick, and Thompson, 1982; Yeo, Hardiman, Glickstein, and Steele-Russell, 1982). That is, although the rabbits would continue to make unconditional nictitating membrane responses when a puff of air was directed to their eye, they no longer made conditional responses to a tone that had been paired with the puff of air. A subsequent study revealed that unilateral lesions restricted to a particular deep nucleus of the cerebellum, the *interpositus nucleus,* also abolished condi-

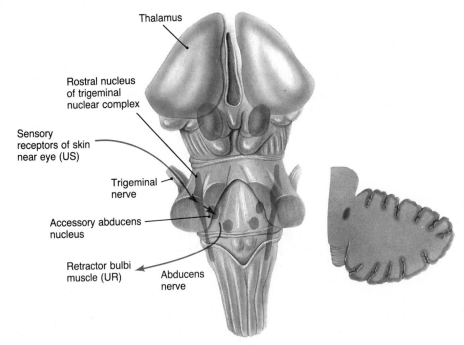

FIGURE 14.44
Proposed neural pathway that mediates the unconditional nictitating membrane response.

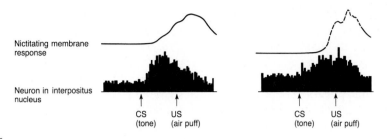

FIGURE 14.45

Responses of groups of neurons in two different locations of the interpositus nucleus of the rabbit cerebellum during classical conditioning. (From McCormick, D.A., and Thompson, R.F. *Science,* 1984, *223,* 296–299. Copyright 1984 by the American Association for the Advancement of Science.)

tional, but not unconditional, responses (McCormick and Thompson, 1984). The deficit was unilateral; the lesions did not disrupt classical conditioning in the contralateral eye. In addition, recordings of neurons in the interpositus nucleus and in the cerebellar cortex showed response patterns that were closely correlated with the shape of the nictitating membrane response. (See **Figure 14.45.**) Finally, electrical stimulation of the interpositus nucleus produced nictitating membrane responses.

The cerebellum receives input from all sensory modalities and also receives information about impending movements from the motor system. Thus, it receives both auditory information about the conditional stimulus and somatosensory information about the unconditional stimulus. Somatosensory information appears to be transmitted to the cerebellum through the rostromedial *inferior olive,* a group of nuclei in the medulla that serves as an important source of input to the cerebellum. This input appears to be important for classical conditioning; McCormick and Thompson (1983) found that lesions of the rostromedial inferior olive abolished conditional nictitating membrane responses.

The neurons of the interpositus nucleus send their axons to the brain stem by means of

the superior cerebellar peduncle. As you might expect, lesions of the superior cerebellar peduncle abolish conditional responses but not unconditional responses (McCormick, Guyer, and Thompson, 1982). Once they enter the brain stem, some of the efferent axons of the interpositus nucleus travel rostrally, cross the midline, and then travel to the contralateral red nucleus, located in the midbrain (Brodal, 1981). The red nucleus is an important relay station of the motor system, receiving axons from many regions of the brain, including the basal ganglia and motor cortex as well as the cerebellum. Like lesions of the interpositus nucleus of the cerebellum, lesions of the red nucleus abolish conditional nictitating membrane responses but not unconditional ones (Rosenfield and Moore, 1983). Therefore, the red nucleus appears to be the next link in the chain. In support of this conclusion, McCormick and Thompson (1983) found that the activity of neurons in the red nucleus is correlated with the shape of the conditional nictitating membrane response.

Desmond, Rosenfield, and Moore (1983) found that besides sending axons to the spinal cord, the red nucleus also sends axons to the contralateral accessory abducens nucleus, the location of the motor neurons responsible for the nictitating membrane response. Thus, much of the neural circuitry responsible for the classically conditioned nictitating membrane response has been traced. (See **Figure 14.46**.)

The cerebellum appears to be involved in more than one form of classical conditioning. Donegan, Lowery, and Thompson (1983) trained rabbits to perform a classically conditioned leg flexion response. They presented a 350-msec tone as a CS, the last 100 msec of which overlapped with the US, a shock to the left hindpaw that caused the animals to flex their hindleg. After the animals had learned to make a conditional leg flexion response to the tone, the experimenters destroyed the interpositus nucleus ipsilateral to the leg that received the shock. The lesions abolished conditional responses to the tone, but not unconditional responses to the shock.

The role of the cerebellar cortex in classical conditioning is uncertain. McCormick and Thompson (1984) reported that although the pattern of activity of single neurons in the cerebellar cortex mirrored the shape of a conditional nictitating membrane response, large lesions of the cerebellar cortex appeared not to prevent classical conditioning from occurring. Given the role of the cerebellar cortex in learning various skilled motor behaviors, this finding is surprising. In contrast to McCormick and Thompson's report, Yeo, Hardiman, and Glickstein (1984) reported that lesions of a particular region of cerebellar cortex, the **simplex lobe,** abolished conditional nictitating membrane responses but not unconditional ones. Future research will be needed to resolve this issue.

The studies that I have described tell us that the interpositus nucleus of the cerebel-

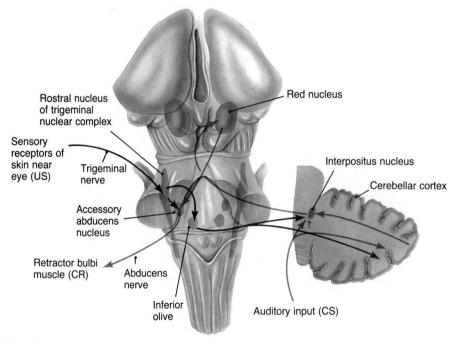

FIGURE 14.46
Proposed neural pathway that mediates the classically conditioned nictitating membrane response (colored arrows).

lum, the cerebellar cortex, the red nucleus of the midbrain, the inferior olive of the medulla, and the fibers that interconnect them are essential for the establishment and retention of a conditional nictitating membrane response. However, the studies do not tell us in which of these structures the physical changes produced by learning take place. It is possible that changes take place in more than one of them.

The goal of many neuroscientists is to discover the particular changes in neurons that occur when learning takes place. Some of the attempts to do so are described in the next chapter. The recent research on the neuroanatomy of simple classical conditioning is especially important, because it has identified structures that are essential for a particular form of learning. With the hundreds of millions of neurons in even the smallest mammalian brain, discovering the structural basis of learning is much more formidable than finding a needle in a haystack. However, the research described in this section has helped divide the haystack into more manageable pieces. Perhaps in the next few years investigators will begin to discover what kinds of changes occur in neurons in these parts of the brain during classical conditioning.

INTERIM SUMMARY

In the past few years, much progress has been made in tracing the neural circuits that are responsible for a rabbit's learning of a classically conditioned nictitating membrane response. A puff of air or shock to the face near the eye causes the unconditional response by means of the following circuit: The trigeminal nerve conveys the somatosensory information to the rostral nuclei of the trigeminal nuclear complex. Neurons there send axons to the accessory abducens nucleus. Finally, motor neurons there send axons to the retractor bulbi, the muscle that retracts the eye and permits the nictitating membrane to sweep across the eye.

The conditional response involves the participation of neurons in the cerebellum. Somatosensory information about the unconditional stimulus reaches the cerebellum through the inferior olive of the medulla. Axons leave the interpositus nucleus through the superior cerebellar peduncle and travel rostrally to the contralateral red nucleus of the midbrain. Neurons in the red nucleus send axons to the contralateral accessory abducens nucleus, where they presumably control the activity of the motor neurons that produce the nictitating membrane response. Investigators do not yet agree whether the cerebellar cortex or only the interpositus nucleus is involved in the circuit.

Concluding Remarks

Learning involves changes in neurons, and the location of the changes depends on the nature of what is being learned. Learning to perceive visual stimuli involves neurons in the visual association cortex, especially the inferior temporal cortex. Learning to respond to biologically relevant stimuli that control species-typical defensive behaviors or conditioned food aversions involves neurons in various nuclei of the amygdala. Learning a classically conditioned nictitating membrane response involves a circuit of neurons in the cerebellum and brain stem. The progress that has been made in recent years in finding these circuits of neurons will provide investigators with the opportunity to determine just what kinds of changes neurons undergo when the organism learns something.

The hippocampus plays an important role in spatial perception and memory and may also serve as a temporary repository for memories. In the next chapter, I describe some recent research devoted to discovering the changes in neural connections that may be responsible for storing memories of recent events. The reason that temporal lobe lesions or medial thalamic lesions impair the ability of humans to learn verbal material and to talk about nonverbal material they have learned is still not understood.

NEW TERMS

accessory abducens nucleus p. 591

Ammon's horn p. 577

anterior commissure p. 552

anterograde amnesia p. 566

bradycardia p. 561

conditioned food aversion p. 558

delayed conditioning p. 588

dentate gyrus p. 577

entorhinal cortex p. 551

fimbria p. 577

fornix columns p. 578

inferior olive p. 593

interpositus nucleus p. 593

Korsakoff's syndrome p. 566

magnocellular medial geniculate nucleus p. 564

nictitating membrane p. 585

OA p. 545

OB p. 545

OC p. 545

perforant path p. 578

precommissural fornix p. 578

reference memory p. 581

retractor bulbi p. 591

simplex lobe p. 594

spatial receptive field p. 583

subiculum p. 577

TE p. 546

temporal stem p. 553

TEO p. 546

theta activity p. 578

trace conditioning p. 588

working memory p. 581

SUGGESTED READINGS

BUTTERS, N., AND SQUIRE, L.R. *The Neuropsychology of Memory.* New York: Guilford Press, 1984.

DEUTSCH, J.A. *The Physiological Basis of Memory.* New York: Academic Press, 1983.

SQUIRE, L.R. The neuropsychology of human memory. *Annual Review of Neuroscience,* 1982, *5,* 241–274.

WOODY, C.D. *Conditioning: Representation of Involved Neural Functions.* New York: Plenum Press, 1982.

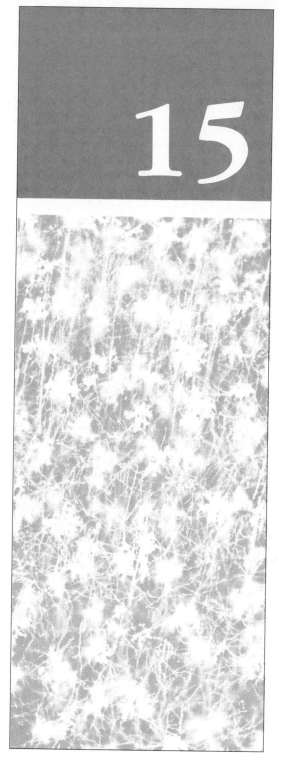

15

Physiology and Biochemistry of Learning

Having considered the physiology of reinforcement and the anatomy of memory in Chapters 13 and 14, it is time to review research devoted to discovering the nature of the physiological changes that experiences produce. Just *how* do experiences change us?

Most investigators believe that experiences cause at least two different kinds of changes in our brains: immediate ones that temporarily represent events we have just perceived, and slow-developing ones that serve as their permanent (or at least long-lasting) representation. The early form of storage appears to entail neural activity, and the second form appears to entail physical changes in the structure of neurons. In addition, there also appears to be a third form of "erasable" memory, corresponding to the working memory described in Chapter 14. This form of storage also entails physical changes in neural structure.

■ THE LEARNING PROCESS

The time course of learning can be subdivided into two behaviorally and physiologically distinct components: memory for events that just occurred, and memory for events that occurred in the more remote past.

We seem to remember recent and remote events differently. In fact, there is evidence that *short-term memory* and *long-term memory* are two different entities. Short-term memory, for humans, is loosely defined as our present awareness of what has just happened. As William James (1890) put it, an event in short-term memory "never was lost; its date was never cut off in consciousness from that of the immediately present moment. In fact it comes to us as belonging to the rearward portion of the present space of time, and not to the genuine past." In contrast, long-term memories are memories of events that occurred in the past and were dropped from consciousness for some time; James (1890) describes these memories as "the knowledge of an event, or fact, of which meantime we have not been thinking, with the additional consciousness that we have thought or experienced it before."

Suppose you look up a number in the telephone directory. You repeat the number to yourself and dial it. The number does not ring, so you dial it again; obviously, the information is still in your short-term memory. This time you hear the number ringing and you relax a little, because you need not keep rehearsing the number. Then you hear a voice saying, "The number you have reached is not in service. What number did you dial?" And you don't remember. Once you relaxed and stopped rehearsing, you were unable to remember the number.

We can, of course, memorize telephone numbers so that they will remain in memory without having to be rehearsed constantly. The process of rehearsal, carried out for a long enough period of time, renders us able to remember the information later. We can do our rehearsing all in one bout, or we can learn a telephone number by looking it up on repeated occasions. The more time a given piece of information spends in short-term memory, the more likely it becomes that it can be retrieved later from long-term memory.

Retrograde Amnesia

Even before scientists began making formal investigations of the physiology of memory, it was apparent to careful observers that short-term memory differed physiologically from long-term memory. A blow to a person's head can produce disturbances in memory. These disturbances are most likely to occur when there is diffuse, rather than localized, head injury, such as that produced by a blow to the head with a blunt object (Russell and Nathan, 1946). The following hypothetical example illustrates how a temporary disruption of normal brain functions produces effects that can best be understood in terms of a two-process model of memory:

Bill and John are walking down the street, engaged in conversation. They pass the drugstore, the hardware store, and the dress shop on the corner and start to cross the street. Suddenly John looks up and shouts, "Look out!" jumping back on the curb as he does so. Bill reacts too late and is struck by an oncoming car. He is thrown several feet, his head strikes the pavement, and he is knocked unconscious.

Fortunately, Bill is not seriously injured. He recovers consciousness in a few minutes, and an examination at the hospital reveals that he received no permanent injuries. He returns home a few hours later. The next time Bill sees John, he discusses the accident with him. He says, "For the life of me, I can't remember what happened. The last thing I can recall was passing the hardware store."

"Don't you remember watching that deliveryman rolling the rack of clothes into the dress shop? You were looking at them and said you'd have to remember to mention them to your wife. As a matter of fact, I think that's why you didn't notice the car — you were looking back at the dress shop."

"No, I don't remember that at all."

What does this incident tell us? Bill has forgotten events that occurred just before his head injury, but he remembers events that occurred earlier. This phenomenon is called ***retrograde amnesia***— amnesia going back in time, prior to this head injury. He remembers passing the drugstore and the hardware store, but he does not remember anything after that. Conveniently, we have a witness who can attest to the fact that there were events that Bill should have remembered later. (See **Figure 15.1**.)

A reasonable way to explain this phenomenon is to hypothesize that (1) we remember events that just occurred and those that occurred in the more remote past by different means, and (2) short-term memories can be converted into long-term memories, but the conversion takes time. The logic is as follows: While Bill was walking down the street, his experiences were retained in short-term memory, probably in the form of neural activity. In time, some of these experiences caused the structural changes in neurons that constitute long-term memory. However, these structural changes do not occur immediately. The head injury temporarily depressed neural activity in many parts of the brain, and in doing so it erased the short-term memories that were present at the time. When Bill recovered later, he could remember only those events that had caused structural changes in

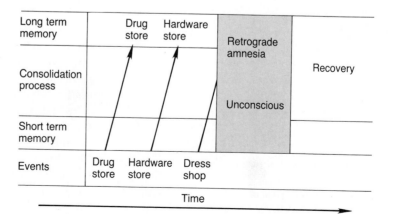

FIGURE 15.1
An explanation of the amnesia in the fictitious anecdote.

his brain. The events that occurred just before the accident had not yet caused structural changes; no long-term memories had yet been formed. The formation of long-term memories from short-term memories is called *consolidation*—the short-term memories are "made solid."

Experimental Amnesia

The evidence obtained from the effects of head injury in humans tells us something about the memory process, but further study with animals obviously requires a better method for producing amnesia. I suppose one *could* train some rats and then hit them on the head, but fortunately, better techniques are available.

During the 1930s Ugo Cerletti, an Italian psychiatrist, developed a technique called *electroconvulsive therapy (ECT)*. The procedure entails passing a brief shock of electricity through electrodes attached to a person's head. The effect of the current is to induce a seizure similar to that which occurs naturally in people with epilepsy. The original purpose of the procedure was to alleviate the symptoms of schizophrenia, but clinicians soon found that ECT had little effect on the hallucinations and delusions they hoped to reduce. However, they did discover that

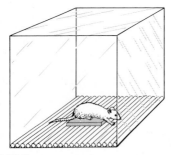

FIGURE 15.2
The step-down apparatus for testing retention of a passive avoidance response.

ECT improved the mood of people with severe depression. Because depression can be a fatal condition (a significant number of depressed people commit suicide), ECT is still used today to treat some patients. But that is another story, which I will discuss in Chapter 17.

The relevance of seizures produced by ECT for the topic of this chapter is that patients who receive it inevitably forget events that occurred shortly before the seizure. That is, they show a retrograde amnesia. Perhaps the seizure disrupts ongoing short-term memories, preventing their consolidation into long-term memory. Many studies with patients undergoing ECT have documented the amnestic (amnesia-producing) effect of the seizure. These studies also demonstrate a *temporal gradient* of retrograde amnesia. The shorter the interval of time between the learning experience and the seizure, the greater the likelihood that the material will be forgotten.

As you might expect, experimental seizures have been employed by many investigators to study the consolidation process in animals. (When it is used experimentally, the technique is more appropriately called *electroconvulsive shock,* or *ECS,* rather than *electroconvulsive therapy.*) The procedure most commonly used today to test for consolidation employs a *passive avoidance task.* For example, Chorover and Schiller (1965) used an apparatus consisting of a chamber with a grid floor, in the middle of which was a small wooden platform. (See **Figure 15.2.**) The experimenters placed rats on the platform and gave them a brief foot shock as soon as they left it and stepped onto the floor. They removed the animals from the chamber and put them back into their home cage. The next day they placed the rats on the platform again. This time the animals stayed put; they showed that they remembered receiving the painful shock after stepping down the previous day. The shock they received the first day had successfully punished the response of stepping off the platform.

Because the rats learned the task after a single trial, the experimenters knew precisely when the punishing stimulus (the foot shock) occurred. Chorover and Schiller trained several groups of rats in this way, following the foot shock with an artificially induced seizure. Several days before the experimental session, they pierced the rats' ears and fitted them with a set of earrings made from metal dress snaps. They attached wires to these earrings before placing the rats on the platform. After the rats stepped off the platform and received a foot shock, the experimenters passed a brief pulse of electricity through the wires. The current passed through the rats' brains and induced a seizure. Different groups of rats received seizures at different time intervals after the foot shock. Figure 15.3 shows the data. Animals that received ECS within a few seconds after the punishing foot shock stepped off the platform quickly the next day; they did not appear to remember the experience. However, as the interval between the foot shock and the seizure increased, more and more subjects remained on the platform when tested the next day. The results suggest that in rats, an electrically induced seizure disrupts consolidation of short-term memories if it occurs within a few seconds of an experience. (See **Figure 15.3.**)

Implications of Experimental Amnesia

The simplest explanation for the amnestic effects of a seizure is that short-term memories consist of neural activity and that the seizure — a bout of wild, uncontrolled neural firing — disrupts this activity the way a sudden storm disrupts the delicate pattern of ripples caused by a stone cast into a pond. Presumably, a stimulus that is incorporated into short-term memory causes a particular pattern of neural activity in the appropriate sensory region of the brain. In the case of the platform task, the most important sensory information relates to the act of stepping down and feeling something painful with the feet. The particular pattern of neural firing encodes the details of the experience. If a seizure disrupts this pattern before consolidation has taken place, the memory is irretrievably lost.

However, the simplest explanation, presented above, may not be the best explana-

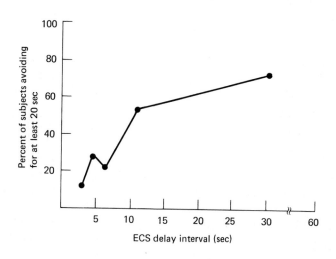

FIGURE 15.3
Effects of ECS delay interval on passive avoidance performance. (From Chorover, S.L., and Schiller, P.H. *Journal of Comparative and Physiological Psychology,* 1965, *59,* 73–78. Copyright 1965 by the American Psychological Association. Reprinted by permission of the author.)

tion. Although many experiments have employed ECS, not all investigators agree that the memory impairment is caused by erasure of short-term memories. We can say that ECS produces amnesia, but we cannot say whether the information was never stored, or whether it was stored in such a way that it cannot be retrieved. In fact, it is logically impossible to prove that a particular experience never produced a permanent alteration somewhere in the brain. If something is not found after a search, we cannot know for sure that it does not exist; perhaps we were looking in the wrong places.

It is possible that instead of erasing short-term memories, a seizure adds neural activity that itself initiates permanent changes in the brain. Because the neural activity that constitutes a seizure is incoherent and does not represent sensory information, it can be regarded as "noise." Perhaps the "noise" becomes consolidated along with the short-term memories; that is, the seizure causes meaningless physical changes in neurons in addition to the meaningful ones produced by the experience. Then, when it comes time to retrieve the information that has been stored, it cannot be found because it cannot be distinguished from the "noise."

One of the reasons the storage of "noise" might disrupt later recall is that it might interfere with a cataloging process (proposed by Miller and Springer, 1973). The authors do not explicitly define cataloging, but they present an analogy that explains what they mean. Consolidation is similar to the placement of a new book on the shelf of a library. It is there, but unless you know of its existence and where to find it, it will not be available. The cataloging process of memory provides a sort of index that makes it possible to locate the consolidated information.

Individual memories do not occur in isolation — linkages are established between ones that are related. This is true whether the individual experiences that give rise to these memories take place at the same or at different times. That is, new experiences do more than establish new memories — they also revise old ones. Let me give a concrete example. Suppose you are browsing through a store and see some attractive and interesting house plants on sale. You remember that a friend of yours loves house plants and would probably appreciate having one of these, so you decide to buy one of the plants for her. Right at the time, your short-term memory consists of images of the plant and of your friend, and you probably imagine yourself giving the plant to her. All of these memories become consolidated and linked to one another. You purchase the plant and bring it home. Later, you meet your friend on the street and suddenly think of the plant. The sight of your friend activates memories linked to her, including the one of your purchasing the house plant.

There is evidence that learning does indeed entail modification of old memories, and that ECS can disrupt this process. On three successive days, Robbins and Meyer (1970) trained several groups of rats in a series of three different discrimination tasks. The tasks could be appetitively or aversively motivated; that is, the experimenters could teach the animals to choose a particular stimulus by reinforcing their choice with a food pellet or with escape from a mild foot shock. The animals learned each of the three discrimination tasks, but with different reinforcers. For example, some rats first learned a shock-motivated task (S_1), then a second, food-motivated task (F_2), and finally a third, shock-motivated task (S_3). The sequence for these rats would then be $S_1F_2S_3$. Six groups of animals learned the three tasks under different orders of motivational conditions.

Immediately after the rats learned the third task, the experimenters gave them ECS. Later, they tested them on tasks 1 and 2. The interesting result was that the animals' performance was impaired on the tasks they learned earlier; normally, we would not expect ECS to affect performance on a task learned several days previously. Furthermore, the impairment was selective; if task 3 (the one followed by ECS) had been motivated by food, performance on the previous food-motivated (but *not* shock-motivated) task was impaired. Similarly, if task 3 had been motivated by shock, performance on the previous shock-motivated task was impaired. (See **Figure 15.4.**)

Robbins and Meyer found that a seizure affects not just the most recent memories but also memories for previously learned habits that were acquired under similar motivational conditions. The investigators suggested that the ECS did not erase long-term memories but impaired their accessibility. Consider the $S_1F_2S_3$ condition. When the rats learned the last task (S_3), their memory of the earlier shock-motivated task (S_1) was probably activated. Because the new and old experiences were related, linkages between them began to be established. However, the process was disrupted by ECS before it was complete. Perhaps the meaningless electrical activity produced by the seizure caused meaningless alterations to be made in the old information that was then being revised. In other words, "noise" was added to these particular long-term memories. These changes interfered with retrieval of the appropriate information when the experimenters later tested the rats' performance on task S_1.

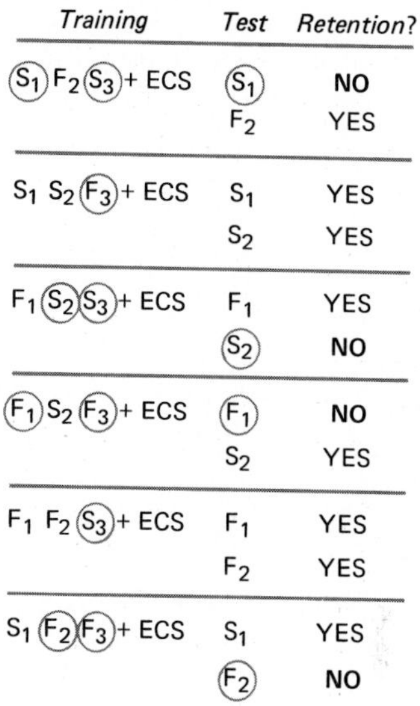

INTERIM SUMMARY

Most investigators believe that learning takes place in two stages: immediate short-term memories eventually become consolidated into long-term memories. Many investigators also believe that a third form of memory exists, the "erasable" work-

Training	Test	Retention?
(S_1) F_2 (S_3) + ECS	(S_1)	NO
	F_2	YES
S_1 S_2 (F_3) + ECS	S_1	YES
	S_2	YES
F_1 $(S_2)(S_3)$ + ECS	F_1	YES
	(S_2)	NO
(F_1) S_2 (F_3) + ECS	(F_1)	NO
	S_2	YES
F_1 F_2 (S_3) + ECS	F_1	YES
	F_2	YES
S_1 $(F_2)(F_3)$ + ECS	S_1	YES
	(F_2)	NO

FIGURE 15.4

A summary of the data from the experiment by Robbins and Meyer (1970).

ing memory described in Chapter 14. Because this form of memory can last many hours, we cannot regard it as short-term. However, its temporary nature also distinguishes it from long-term memory. The physiological basis of working memory is discussed later in this chapter.

As we have seen, short-term memory contains information about events that were just perceived. Because this phase of memory is an active, ongoing process, and because humans, at least, can prolong it indefinitely by rehearsing ("thinking about") it, we can probably conclude that short-term memories consist of neural activity. However, long-term memories must certainly consist of something more permanent, such as structural changes in the brain. If the neural activity that represents information in short-term memory persists long enough, perhaps it causes long-term physical changes in neurons—the ones that are representing the short-term memory, or others that receive inputs from them. These long-term changes alter the way in which the brain responds to a subsequent presentation of that stimulus, or to related stimuli.

The two major hypothetical explanations for the amnestic effects of ECS are both consistent with these conclusions. Seizures may disrupt short-term memories, preventing them from becoming consolidated, or they may add "noise," making the newly consolidated information inaccessible. Perhaps *both* of these events occur: partial erasure of short-term memories and the addition of meaningless patterns of activity.

■ THE PHYSIOLOGICAL BASIS OF SHORT-TERM AND LONG-TERM MEMORY

Short-Term Memory

Short-term memories appear to be disrupted by blunt head injury or ECS. This effect suggests that short-term memory involves coherent neural activity that can be disrupted by events that temporarily suppress neural activity or that induce incoherent, meaningless firing of neurons (as ECS does). Head injury and ECS are not the only events that disrupt short-term memory; anesthesia, cooling of the brain, temporary anoxia (lack of oxygen), and treatment with various drugs will also do so (Jarvik, 1972). However, long-term memories are not susceptible to damage from these events unless, as Robbins and Meyer's experiment showed, they are in the process of being updated with new information.

What kind of neural activity could possibly represent short-term memories? Hebb (1949) proposed that groups of neurons, arranged in interconnected loops, could maintain a representation of a stimulus by means of *reverberation.* Activity initiated in an intercon-

nected network of neurons is presumed to cause recurrent excitation that circulates around sets of loops. Figure 15.5 presents this concept more concretely. *Theoretically,* the initiation of an action potential in neuron A could cause incessant firing of the circuit: A excites B, which fires and then excites C, and so on, back to A, where the process begins again. (See **Figure 15.5.**)

Of course, we know that a circuit of four neurons would not continue to fire in this manner. An excitatory postsynaptic potential from a single terminal button does not provide enough excitation to trigger an action potential in a postsynaptic neuron. But consider Figure 15.6, a slightly more redundant version of the simpler circuit. Neural activity might continue in this circuit for a much longer time. (See **Figure 15.6.**)

Is there any evidence that reverberation actually takes place? Burns (1958) studied the properties of the *isolated cortical slab* and obtained data that suggest that it does. An isolated cortical slab is produced by undercutting a section of cortex so that it is not connected neurally to any other region of the brain. Care is taken to preserve the blood supply that runs along the top of the cortex. (See **Figure 15.7.**) Electrical recordings of isolated cortical slabs reveal that the neurons in them are normally quiet, but if the slab is stimulated with a train of electrical pulses,

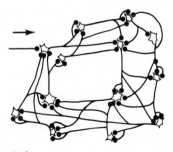

FIGURE 15.6
A reverberatory circuit that is slightly more realistic than that shown in Figure 15.5.

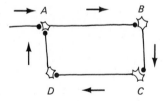

FIGURE 15.5
A reverberatory circuit.

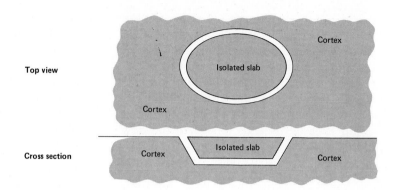

FIGURE 15.7
An isolated cortical slab.

bursts of activity are recorded. If the stimulus is intense enough, firing will continue for up to 30 minutes.

This prolonged neural activity suggests that reverberation can indeed occur in networks of neural tissue. Burns noted that if the activity is a result of recirculation of excitation in loops of neurons, then the researcher should be able to halt this activity by stimulating the neurons to discharge all at the same time. That way, the cells would simultaneously be in the refractory state, during which an action potential cannot be elicited. The neurons would all quickly recover, but none of them would be firing. Picture what would happen if all four neurons in Figure 15.5 fired simultaneously. Reverberation could not continue. (See **Figure 15.5.**) Burns's prediction was borne out; a single shock of sufficient intensity, delivered to the center of the slab, halted the neural activity of the slab.

Some experiments I discussed in Chapter 14 provide evidence that short-term memory involves neural activity. For example, you will recall that Fuster and Jervey (1981) found that neurons in the inferior temporal cortex of monkeys were excited by the sample stimulus in a visual delayed matching-to-sample task and continued to fire for the duration of the delay interval, even after the stimulus was turned off. In addition, different neurons responded to different colors of light. We can speculate that a particular sample stimulus activated a particular set of neural circuits, causing them to continue to fire while the excitation reverberated around the loops. Once the matching stimuli were presented and the animal made its choice, the activity was no longer needed.

Because the animals in Fuster and Jervey's experiment saw the same set of stimuli again and again, the short-term memory activated by a sample stimulus was not a novel one. Thus, the neural activity represents recognition of a familiar stimulus. Most stimuli we perceive are probably hybrids: partly familiar, partly novel. For example, the words you are reading now (except for the ones I put in boldface italics and perhaps a few others) are familiar, but their arrangement is novel. We can hypothesize that your past experience with these words has led to the establishment of neural circuits, so that seeing particular words activates particular circuits, and this activation constitutes your short-term memory for the words. Unfamiliar words do not automatically activate circuits; new circuits must be established. Perhaps they consist of collections of smaller circuits that represent the constituent letters or, more likely, groups of letters. I once showed the word *hippocampus* to a woman with a specific disability that made it very difficult for her to sound out new words. However, she had no trouble sounding out *hippocampus;* she saw in it the words *hippo* and *campus.* Apparently, neural circuits that recognize these constituents already existed in her brain. She put the neural circuit for *hippo* together with the neural circuit for *campus,* making a new circuit that could later be used to recognize the new word.

Although my discussion so far implies that all long-term memories are derived from repeated activity of neurons that contain short-term memories, it is possible that some forms of learning do not require this process. Much of the thinking and speculating that neuroscientists have engaged in about the nature of short-term memory is based on our own experience. And our most obvious experience of short-term memory is that of repeating verbal material such as words or telephone numbers to ourselves. We have seen that head injuries or seizures disrupt this activity, producing retrograde amnesia. Because seizures also produce retrograde amnesia in laboratory animals, we may infer that similar processes occur in other species (nonverbally, of course). But some experiences, especially those that cause learning to occur gradually over many trials, might initiate long-term changes directly, without a separate intervening stage of short-term memory.

For example, I suspect that classical conditioning of the nictitating membrane response in a rabbit need not involve a reverberatory phase of short-term memory. As we saw in Chapter 14, the circuitry for this learned behavior is rather simple, consisting of a handful of neurons in the brain stem and cerebellum. Each CS-US pairing could cause small changes in neurons in the relevant location; when a sufficient number of trials has occurred, the changes would be substantial enough so that presentation of the CS alone triggers the response. At least this pattern appears to occur in the case of delayed conditioning, in which the CS and US overlap in

time. However, in the case of trace conditioning, in which the CS and US are presented separately with a brief delay between them, some short-term mechanism must retain a memory of the CS. In fact, we saw that the likely circuitry for this temporary memory is in the hippocampus. Thus, although we have evidence for short-term memory and for long-term memory, we cannot assume that *all* instances of learning are acquired through a transition from one type to the other.

Long-Term Memory

I know of no neuroscientist who questions the assumption that long-term memory storage entails some physical changes in neurons. For example, in the case of classical conditioning, particular stimuli that previously elicited only an orienting response now cause the activation of motor neurons that produce the conditional response. A possible explanation for this phenomenon is shown in Figure 15.8. The conditional stimulus (a tone) and unconditional stimulus (a puff of air) both activate axons that form excitatory synapses with the same neuron. Before learning takes place, only the axon that is activated by the unconditional stimulus causes enough excitation to fire the neuron and produce a response. However, when the CS synapse is activated at the same time that the cell fires in response to the US, the CS synapse is strengthened, so that in the future it produces an excitatory postsynaptic potential strong enough to evoke a response by itself. (See **Figure 15.8.**)

This model is essentially what Hebb (1949) proposed as the elementary basis of long-term memory. The phenomenon it refers to is now called ***heterosynaptic facilitation,*** meaning that the activity of one synapse on a particular neuron strengthens the effectiveness of another. In this instance, the US synapses strengthen the effectiveness of the CS synapses. Hebb hypothesized that synaptic

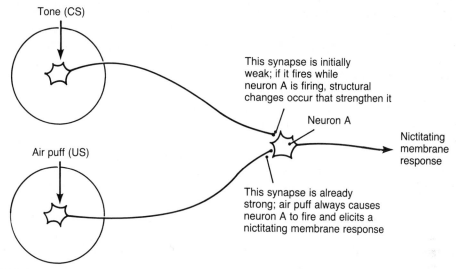

Tone (CS)

This synapse is initially weak; if it fires while neuron A is firing, structural changes occur that strengthen it

Neuron A

Air puff (US)

Nictitating membrane response

This synapse is already strong; air puff always causes neuron A to fire and elicits a nictitating membrane response

FIGURE 15.8

Heterosynaptic facilitation: the presumed basis of long-term memory.

strengthening occurred only when the postsynaptic neuron actually fired. As we will see, we finally have evidence that heterosynaptic facilitation exists, and we even have some good hints about its physiological basis.

How might heterosynaptic facilitation take place? Let us consider the possibilities before we examine the evidence. (1) Synapses could change in size — presynaptically, postsynaptically, or both. (2) The number of receptors for the neurotransmitter in the postsynaptic membrane could increase. (3) New terminal buttons could sprout from axons and establish entirely new synapses with other neurons. Any of these alterations would affect the way in which circuits of neurons would interact with each other and could serve as the basis of long-term memory.

How does one approach the problem of isolating the physical changes that constitute long-term memory? The problem is exceptionally complex. Only after many years of research are investigators finally beginning to find physical changes that appear to be related specifically to learning. The following discussion describes the two ways in which the problem has been attacked: 1) manipulate experience, observe physiology; 2) manipulate physiology, observe the effects on learning.

Manipulate Experience, Observe Physiology. We can train some animals and look for changes in the structure, physiology, or biochemistry of their neurons. If we find structural changes under the microscope, or observe that the electrical activity of a neural pathway is altered, or obtain evidence of new chemicals being produced by the brain, then perhaps we have found changes caused by learning. There are two problems with this approach. The first is a problem of "signal" versus "noise" (otherwise known as the "needle in the haystack" problem). If we look for the structural changes produced by the learning (the "signal"), how can we expect to detect them among the several billions of neurons in the brain (the "noise")? No two brains are exactly alike; therefore, we cannot begin to compare the brain of an animal that has learned a particular task with one that has not, unless we know where to look. Furthermore, the brains will look different even if both animals have received the *same* training. Thus, we will need to examine the details of a large number of brains, which becomes a formidable task.

Three types of approaches have been used to try to get around the problem of "signal" versus "noise." Some investigators have tried to teach some animals many things, comparing their brains with those of animals that have lived in a sterile environment in which there was little to learn. Others have taught animals a specific task very early in life, before the brain had attained its adult state, with the hope that the changes would be more widespread. Still others have investigated the nature of changes in restricted locations in the brain. The last approach depends on knowing something about the anatomical basis of various forms of learning. Fortunately, we are learning more about the anatomy of learning, so this general approach is becoming more feasible. As we saw in Chapter 14, most of the anatomy of the conditional nictitating membrane response appears to have been traced. As we will see in this chapter, all three approaches have been successful, and investigators using these approaches have indeed found structural, biochemical, or physiological changes in the brain after learning experiences.

The second problem with this general strategy is that it is impossible to design two experiences that are identical in all respects except that one causes learning but the other does not. We know that experiences produce many physiological effects besides learning. For example, if an animal is given a foot shock in an avoidance task, the stressful situation will cause the secretion of various hormones and neuromodulators, such as ACTH, corticosteroids, and endogenous opiates. In addition, unconditional responses to the shock may increase the animal's activity. All these responses will affect the animal's metabolism and will certainly produce many biochemical changes. They may even cause structural changes in the brain. The investigator, by presenting a discriminative stimulus just before the foot shock, is permitting the experimental group to learn to avoid the shock. In contrast, control subjects receive the foot shock without the opportunity to learn to avoid it. But can we assume that the control animals learn *nothing?* More likely, they learn something different. Comparisons between experimental and control animals then are not simply comparisons between trained and untrained animals. This problem, which is most acute in studies that look for biochemical changes throughout the brain, has not been solved. It is minimized in experiments that investigate specific pathways known to play a role in learning a particular task.

Manipulate Physiology, Observe the Effects on Learning. This approach is an extension of the lesion technique. If biochemical or structural changes are believed to be necessary for learning to occur, then treatments that prevent these changes from happening would be expected to interfere with learning. If the change is specific, and if the investigator knows where it must occur, then this would be an excellent technique. However, in the past the manipulations have been nonspecific. For example, investigators have administered drugs that prevent protein synthesis, in an attempt to determine whether the formation of long-term memories requires the production of proteins. Unfortunately, the inhibition of protein synthesis causes many effects; it interferes with a variety of normal physiological processes that are probably not directly related to memory. Therefore, when these drugs impair learning, we cannot be sure why they do so. The most successful attempts to determine the effects of physiological alterations have used specific treatments, such as drugs that block the synthesis of a particular substance or that stimulate a particular set of receptors. These studies, too, provide the most useful information when the manipulations are made in specific parts of the brain that are known to play a role in the particular learning task. Thus, understanding the anatomy of learning greatly facilitates our ability to study the physiology and biochemistry of learning.

INTERIM SUMMARY

Short-term memory appears to entail some kind of neural activity, perhaps maintained by means of reverberation. Studies with isolated cortical slabs suggest that reverberation can occur. The activity of neurons during the delay interval in the experiment on delayed matching-to-sample of colors described in Chapter 14 may have been maintained by reverberation. Long-term memories may be the result of synaptic changes in circuits of neurons, induced by their participation in reverberatory circuits. Some very simple forms of learning (such as delayed classical conditioning of the nictitating membrane response) may occur without a short-term reverberatory phase, but others (such as trace classical conditioning) do require short-term memory.

The basic element of long-term memory appears to be heterosynaptic facilitation, whereby the activity of one synapse on a particular neuron strengthens the effectiveness of another. Such a strengthening may entail changes in the presynaptic neuron, the postsynaptic neuron, or both. There are two basic approaches to the study of the physical basis of long-term memory. The first approach, manipulating experience and observing physiology, encounters the problems of isolating "signal" from "noise" and of designing control procedures that differ from the experimental procedure only in that they do not produce learning. The second approach, manipulating physiology and observing the effects on learning, works best when the investigator has some ideas about what

physiological processes are involved in memory. Manipulations with widespread effects, such as the administration of drugs that block protein synthesis, have not led to important discoveries.

■ EFFECTS OF EXPERIENCES ON THE STRUCTURE OF THE NERVOUS SYSTEM

Many studies have shown that experiences can alter the structure of the nervous system. These alterations probably represent memories, but we cannot yet say for certain that they do.

Effects of Enriched Environments

Because the brain is so exceedingly complex, we can hardly hope to train an animal to learn a particular task and then find the particular changes in its brain that this experience produces unless we know exactly which parts of the brain are essential for learning that task. More than 25 years ago, Rosenzweig and his colleagues began a research program designed to circumvent this problem by teaching animals *many* things and comparing their brains with those of animals that learned very little (Rosenzweig, 1984). That way they might be able to see the kinds of changes that learning produces, even though they would not be able to determine which changes were caused by which experiences. The experimenters divided litters of rats and placed the animals into two kinds of environments: enriched and impoverished. The enriched environment contained such things as running wheels, ladders, slides, and "toys" that the animals could explore and manipulate. The experimenters changed these objects every day to maximize the animals' experiences and thus ensure that they would learn as much as possible. The impoverished environments were plain cages in a dimly illuminated, quiet room.

Rosenzweig and his colleagues found many differences in the brains of animals raised in the two environments. The brains of rats raised in the enriched environment had a thicker cortex, a better capillary supply, more glial cells, more protein content, and more acetylcholinesterase (and, by inference, more acetylcholine-secreting terminal buttons). As we will see later in this chapter, acetylcholine has been implicated in memory; thus, this last finding may be especially noteworthy. The investigators found changes on a microanatomical level as well. Globus, Rosenzweig, Bennett, and Diamond (1973) observed increased numbers of dendritic spines on cortical neurons; Greenough and Volkmar (1973) observed increases in dendritic branching, and Diamond, Lindner, Johnson, Bennett, and Rosenzweig (1975) observed increases in the area of contact at synapses.

These studies provided evidence that learning produces changes in the nervous system that we can detect by present methods. Of course, it is possible that the particular changes that have been observed do not themselves represent memories but are simply a result of better health, or some other nonspecific effect of living in a more stimulating environment. In fact, the "enriched" laboratory environment is undoubtedly more normal than the impoverished one, compared with the environment in which wild rats live. Thus, it might be more fair to say that an impoverished environment leads to a thinner cortex, poorer capillary supply, and so on. However, there is no reason *not* to believe that at least some of the differences between the two groups of animals are a direct result of learning. The next step is to train animals to perform particular tasks and look for changes in those parts of the brain that receive the relevant stimuli and that control the relevant responses.

Training of Young Animals

Two experiments by Spinelli and his colleagues have identified changes in the functional properties and physical characteristics of neurons that appear to be related to learning. In the hopes that a meaningful experience would cause a larger change in a young animal than in an older one, they trained 4-week-old kittens. Spinelli and Jensen (1979) trained the animals to flex a foreleg in order to avoid a mild shock. They suspended the kittens in a cloth sling, their legs protruding downward through four holes. A rubber band held a shock electrode on a foreleg. The kittens wore goggles, through which visual stimuli could be presented. When a kitten held its foreleg down, it received electrical shocks and saw a pattern of horizontal lines with one eye. When the foreleg was flexed (pulled up), the shock was turned off, and a pattern of vertical lines was presented to the other eye. (For some kittens, the patterns were reversed.) Thus, one eye saw a "danger" pattern, while the other saw a "safety" pattern. The kittens learned the task very quickly, keeping their foreleg up over 95 percent of the time. The training sessions were very brief: 8 minutes per day.

After 10 weeks of training, the experimenters made single-unit recordings from neurons in the somatosensory cortex, primary visual cortex, and visual association cortex. They found the kinds of changes you might expect. They measured somatosensory representation by recording from individual neurons in the somatosensory cortex and then touching the animal's skin, to see which areas of the body surface produced a response in each cell. They found that tactile stimuli applied to the shocked region of skin produced a response in a much larger area of somatosensory cortex than stimuli applied to the same region of skin on the nonshocked foreleg. Thus, the training enlarged the area of somatosensory cortex that was connected to receptors in the skin of the shocked (trained) foreleg. In addition, 75 percent of the cells that responded to touch from the shocked areas also responded to visual stimuli, whereas only 30 percent of the corresponding cells on the other side of the brain did so. And most of the cells on the trained side responded selectively to the "danger" stimulus. As the authors noted, this finding is significant, because the "danger" stimulus was seen for approximately 10 minutes in total, compared with 250 minutes for the "safety" stimulus. In fact, the kittens who learned the fastest (and thus saw the "danger" stimulus the least) had the *largest* percentage of cells in the somatosensory cortex that responded to the "danger" stimulus. Similar results were found in the primary visual cortex and visual association cortex; cells tended to respond to lines oriented like the two stimuli, especially the "danger" stimulus.

In a follow-up study, Spinelli, Jensen, and DiPrisco (1980) trained kittens in a similar manner and examined the architecture of neurons in the animals' somatosensory cortex. They killed the animals and then stained the brains with the Golgi-Cox technique, which makes the entire membrane of the neuron visible, including the dendritic branches. The investigators found significant increases in the number and complexity of dendritic branches in the region of somatosensory cortex that had received information from the shocked foreleg. The effect was striking, as Figure 15.9 shows. The photomicrograph on the left is from "untrained" somatosensory cortex; the one on the right is from "trained" cortex. (See **Figure 15.9.**)

The results suggest that the method might profitably be used to investigate the physical basis of memory. However, we cannot be certain that the observed changes constitute "memory." The authors used immature animals in order to increase the likelihood of obtaining measurable changes. Indeed, they also trained an older kitten, beginning at 11

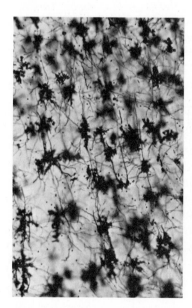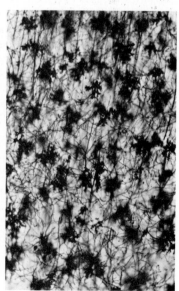

FIGURE 15.9
Dendrites of neurons from "untrained" somatosensory cortex *(left)* and "trained" somatosensory cortex *(right)*. Golgi-Cox stain. (From Spinelli, D.N., Jensen, F.E., and DiPrisco, G.V. *Experimental Neurology,* 1980, *62,* 1–11.)

weeks of age, but failed to detect any changes in the response characteristics of cortical neurons. Obviously, because the older cat learned the task, changes were there, but they were apparently too subtle to be detected. We can hope that the changes that occurred in the kittens' brains were simply "magnifications" of the changes that occur in the brains of older animals, but we cannot be sure that this is the case.

INTERIM SUMMARY

Experiences can affect the structure of the nervous system, especially if they occur in young animals. Rats raised in an enriched environment, full of objects and happenings, have larger brains with a thicker cortex, more dendritic spines, and a higher level of acetylcholinesterase. In addition, kittens trained in a simple avoidance task have a larger area of somatosensory cortex devoted to analysis of the unconditional stimulus (shock) and more neurons in the visual cortex devoted to analysis of the visual discriminative stimuli. Although we cannot be sure that the physiological effects of experience on brain development are identical to those that occur in the brains of mature animals, the results suggest that there is some hope of isolating the needle from the haystack.

■ EFFECTS OF ARTIFICIAL STIMULATION ON THE STRUCTURE OF THE NERVOUS SYSTEM

Although the search for physical changes in the structure of neurons caused by learning has had some success, much more impressive results have been obtained by using artificial stimulation. Learning requires sensory stimulation, which causes neural activity. The results of this activity are alterations in the characteristics of neurons, caused, no doubt, by structural changes. As we have seen, the changes are subtle and difficult to detect in an organ as complex as the brain. Therefore, re-

searchers have turned to electrical stimulation of neural systems, with the hope that these interventions will cause measurable physical changes. The stimulation causes more neural activity than natural sensory stimulation does, and it can be restricted to a particular location. Thus, the investigators know where to look, and they have a reasonable expectation of finding changes there.

Kindling

Many people who receive a head injury that results in brain damage begin to have seizures several months later. The seizures appear to be caused by irritation produced by scar tissue. The fact that they develop slowly suggests that the irritation produces a gradual increase in the excitability of neurons, which eventually becomes strong enough to cause a seizure. These seizures can develop in many parts of the brain, but the most seizure-prone location is the medial temporal lobe.

A similar phenomenon can be produced experimentally, in laboratory animals. Goddard (1967) implanted electrodes in the brains of rats and administered a weak electrical stimulus once a day. At first he observed no behavioral disruption, but after several days the stimulation began to trigger convulsions. The effects were gradual; by contrast, a large amount of stimulation delivered all at once had no effect. Goddard called the phenomenon *kindling,* because it resembled the way a small fire can be kindled to start a larger one. Figure 15.10 shows the gradual development of seizures in an animal that received a brief stimulation in the amygdala each day (Goddard and Morrell, cited by Morrell, 1969). The experimenters recorded the brain's electrical activity through the stimulating electrode and measured the duration of the *afterdischarge,* the abnormally slow and synchronous activity that is characteristic of seizures. Note that the plot looks very much

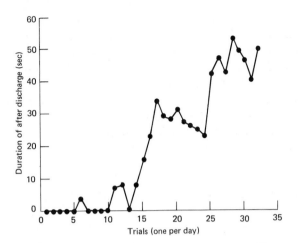

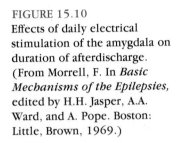

FIGURE 15.10
Effects of daily electrical stimulation of the amygdala on duration of afterdischarge. (From Morrell, F. In *Basic Mechanisms of the Epilepsies,* edited by H.H. Jasper, A.A. Ward, and A. Pope. Boston: Little, Brown, 1969.)

like a learning curve — a graph of an animal's performance while learning a task. (See **Figure 15.10.**)

Kindling appears to be analogous to learning, and it presumably involves changes in synaptic efficiency. Although the most common location for kindling is the amygdala, seizures can also be kindled through stimulation of the basal ganglia, limbic cortex, neocortex, septum, preoptic area, and olfactory bulb, but not the superior colliculus, reticular formation, or cerebellum (Goddard, McIntyre, and Leech, 1969). When one region is stimulated, changes occur throughout the brain. For example, Racine (1972) stimulated the amygdala with brief test pulses and recorded evoked potentials from the frontal cortex, ventromedial hypothalamus, preoptic area, and hippocampus. After he had kindled a seizure focus, he found that these evoked potentials were much larger in size.

Many investigators have tried to find changes in the structure of neurons after kindling an epileptic focus in the amygdala, without much success (McNamara, Byrne, Dasheiff, and Fitz, 1980). For example, Goddard and Douglas (1975) kindled seizures and then made a small lesion by passing enough current through the stimulating electrode to destroy some neural tissue. After letting the rats survive long enough for anterograde degeneration of axons to occur, they killed the rats, sliced the brains, and stained them with a degenerating axon stain. Presumably, the degenerating axons were those that were stimulated by the kindling procedure. They compared the degenerating terminal buttons and postsynaptic dendritic spines of experimental (kindled) and control (nonkindled) animals but found no differences.

More recent studies have investigated a similar phenomenon that occurs in the hippocampal complex and have had better luck finding structural changes. Therefore, let us examine this phenomenon.

Long-Term Potentiation

The Phenomenon
Stimulation of the efferent axons of the hippocampal formation can lead to changes in its physiological properties. Lømo (1966) discovered that intense electrical stimulation of the perforant path caused a long-term increase in the magnitude of excitatory postsynaptic potentials in the dentate gyrus; this increase has come to be called ***long-term potentiation.*** (You will recall from Chapter

14 that the entorhinal cortex sends axons through the perforant path to the dentate gyrus, part of the hippocampal complex.) A single electrical shock applied to the perforant path causes an evoked potential in the dentate gyrus that is called the *extracellular population spike.* The potential is referred to as a *spike* because it looks something like a nail. It is recorded through a macroelectrode inserted into the dentate gyrus, and hence it is *not* a single-unit action potential, which is also often called a *spike.* Long-term potentiation is initiated by bombarding the perforant path with approximately one hundred pulses of electrical stimulation, delivered within 1 to 10 seconds. Five to twenty minutes later, the size of the extracellular population spike (evoked by a single pulse) increases, usually by approximately 250 percent. Single-unit recordings have confirmed that the extracellular population spike represents the frequency of firing of many individual neurons (Lømo, 1971); thus, the change indicates increased synaptic strength: the synapses between the afferent axons and the neurons of the dentate gyrus become more effective. Figure 15.11 shows an extracellular population spike re-

corded in the dentate gyrus before and after long-term potentiation. (See **Figure 15.11.**)

Long-term potentiation can last for several months (Bliss and Lømo, 1973). Thus, its characteristics resemble those of learning: it is initiated by a brief burst of neural activity and causes persistent changes in particular neural circuits. Long-term potentiation may well be the means by which kindling occurs. Racine, Milgram, and Hafner (1983) found that after they kindled an epileptic focus, they could no longer obtain long-term potentiation by stimulating the perforant path. This finding suggests that the kindling had already increased synaptic strength in these neurons, and no further increase was possible. The fact that kindling develops much more slowly than long-term potentiation suggests that kindling requires increases in synaptic strength in many more neurons in many more circuits before the general level of excitability becomes high enough to cause seizures.

Long-term potentiation can be produced in isolated slices of hippocampus as well as in the brains of living animals. The brain is removed from the skull, the hippocampal complex is dissected, and slices are placed in a

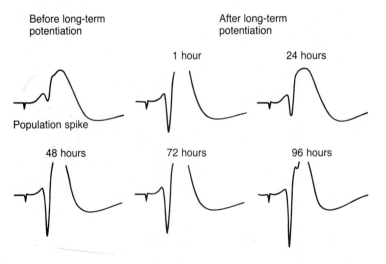

FIGURE 15.11
An extracellular population spike recorded from the dentate gyrus before and after electrical stimulation that led to long-term potentiation. (From Berger, T.W. *Science,* 1984, *224,* 627–630. Copyright 1984 by the American Association for the Advancement of Science.)

temperature-controlled chamber. This in vitro technique permits the investigator to alter the ionic and chemical content of the fluid that bathes the tissue. In addition, because the system is isolated from its connections with other parts of the brain, the investigator can be sure the observed effects take place in the cells of the hippocampal formation. Figure 15.12 shows a 400-μm slice of hippocampal formation being maintained in a tissue chamber. Under optimal conditions a slice remains alive for up to 40 hours. (See **Figure 15.12.**)

Relevant Anatomy

Figure 15.13 shows a diagram of the principal cells of the hippocampal formation and their connections (Swanson, 1982). The subiculum and its connections are not shown. The perforant path carries axons from cells in the entorhinal cortex to the dentate gyrus, where they synapse with the **granule cells.** These cells send their **mossy fibers** to area CA3, where they synapse on proximal dendrites of **pyramidal cells,** named for their shape. (*CA* stands for the alternative name for the hippocampus proper, *cornu ammonis,* or

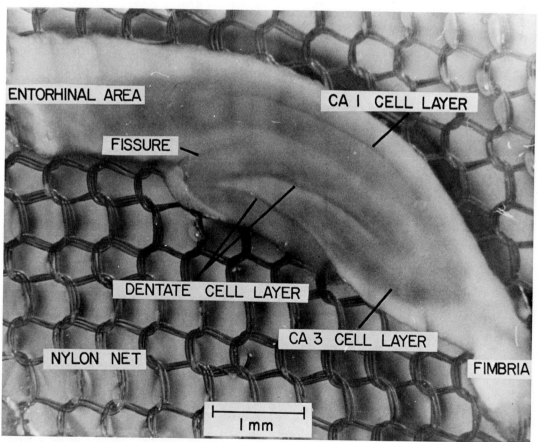

FIGURE 15.12

A photograph of a hippocampal slice in a tissue chamber. (From Teyler, T.J. *Brain Research Bulletin*, 1980, *5*, 391–403.)

"Ammon's horn.") The CA3 pyramidal cells send axons called *Schaffer collateral fibers* to CA1, where they synapse on the distal dendrites of CA1 pyramidal cells. Finally, the CA1 pyramidal cells send axons back to the entorhinal cortex, closing the loop that has been called the *trisynaptic circuit.* In addition, CA3 and CA1 pyramidal cells send axons to the lateral septum through the fimbria/fornix and receive acetylcholinergic inputs from the medial septum. Long-term potentiation can be produced in any component of the trisynaptic circuit. (See **Figure 15.13.**)

Physiology and Biochemistry of Long-Term Potentiation

Several studies have used the phenomenon of long-term potentiation to provide evidence of heterosynaptic facilitation, supporting the hypothetical cellular basis of long-term mem-

ory that Hebb proposed. For example, Levy and Steward (1983) stimulated rats' entorhinal cortex bilaterally and recorded excitatory postsynaptic potentials in the dentate gyrus on one side. The dentate gyrus on each side receives afferent axons from the entorhinal cortex on both sides of the brain, but the contralateral projections are very sparse. In fact, stimulation of the entorhinal cortex does not excite the contralateral dentate gyrus enough to produce long-term potentiation there. Levy and Steward stimulated the entorhinal cortex on both sides of the brain and found that if the ipsilateral stimulation occurred simultaneously with the contralateral stimulation, or if it followed it by 20 msec or less, heterosynaptic facilitation occurred. That is, the pairing increased the synaptic strength of the sparse contralateral projections. However, if the ipsilateral stimu-

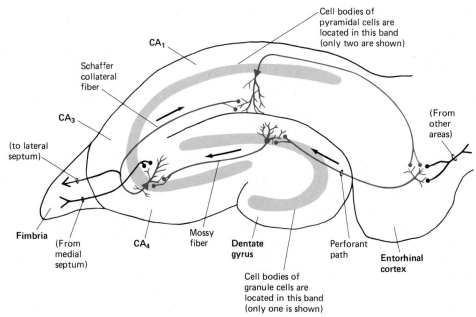

FIGURE 15.13

The trisynaptic circuit of the entorhinal cortex, dentate gyrus, and Ammon's horn (CA).

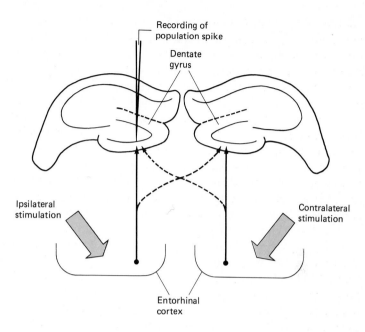

FIGURE 15.14

The procedure of Levy and Steward. (Adapted from Levy, W.B., and Steward, O. *Neuroscience,* 1983, *8,* 791–797.)

1. Repeated contralateral stimulation: no change in response

2. Repeated contralateral stimulation followed by ipsilateral stimulation: increased response to contralateral stimulation when presented alone

lation occurred first, or if it followed the contralateral stimulation by 200 msec, the experimenters observed *decreased* synaptic strength. The results show that activity of some synapses on a group of neurons can increase the strength of other synapses if the latter are active at the appropriate time. As you can see, these contingencies resemble what is presumed to occur during classical conditioning. (See **Figure 15.14.**)

The heterosynaptic facilitation that appears to underlie long-term potentiation could be caused by several different means. It could be produced presynaptically, through increased release of transmitter substance, or it could be produced postsynaptically, through an increased number of receptors, increased binding ability of receptors, or increased ability of the receptors to activate changes in the permeability of the postsynap-

tic membrane. Evidence suggests that the relevant changes are postsynaptic.

The principal excitatory transmitter substance in the hippocampal formation appears to be an amino acid, glutamate. Dunwiddie, Madison, and Lynch (1978) found that 2-amino-4-phosphonobutyric acid (APB), a drug that blocks glutamate (glutamic acid) receptors, prevented long-term potentiation in CA1 pyramidal cells in hippocampal slices. Because the drug blocks postsynaptic potentials without directly affecting presynaptic terminal buttons, these results suggest that long-term potentiation takes place postsynaptically and requires the activation of postsynaptic glutamate receptors. Supporting this suggestion, Wigström and Gustafsson (1983) found that drugs that block GABA receptors (bicuculline and picrotoxin) *facilitated* long-term potentiation. Because GABA is an inhibitory transmitter substance, drugs that block GABA receptors reduce inhibitory postsynaptic potentials and thus increase the responsiveness of postsynaptic neurons to excitatory postsynaptic potentials. Therefore, these results also favor the hypothesis that long-term potentiation is caused by postsynaptic changes.

The postsynaptic change responsible for long-term potentiation appears to be an increase in the number of glutamate receptors in the postsynaptic membrane. Lynch, Halpain, and Baudry (1982) prepared hippocampal slices and stimulated the fibers that synapse on CA1 pyramidal cells. They stimulated some slices with high-frequency pulses and others with low-frequency pulses. Because only high-frequency stimulation causes long-term potentiation, the second set of slices served as controls. After stimulating the slices, they homogenized each of them and extracted the synaptic membranes. They incubated the membranes for 15 minutes with radioactive glutamate, rinsed them, and measured their radioactivity. The rinsing washed away any radioactive glutamate that was not bound to postsynaptic receptors. Compared with the low-frequency control slices, the high-frequency experimental slices, which had exhibited robust long-term potentiation, displayed 30 percent more radioactivity. Hence, long-term potentiation was accompanied by a 30-percent increase in the number of glutamate receptors.

Long-term potentiation also includes postsynaptic structural changes in CA pyramidal cells and in granule cells of the dentate gyrus. Lee, Schottler, Oliver, and Lynch (1980) found that stimulation caused a decrease in variability in the size of the dendritic spines; they interpreted this decrease as reflecting fewer small spines. Desmond and Levy (1983) found that stimulation of the entorhinal cortex attached to isolated hippocampal slices caused an increase in the number of large dendritic spine synapses in the dentate gyrus. These postsynaptic structural changes may be correlated with the increased number of glutamate receptors that Lynch and his colleagues observed.

An essential step in the production of long-term potentiation is the entry of the calcium ion (Ca^{2+}) into the cytoplasm of the postsynaptic cell. When an excitatory postsynaptic potential is produced, calcium ions, as well as sodium ions, enter the postsynaptic neuron. Dunwiddie and Lynch (1979) bathed hippocampal slices in a liquid that was deficient in calcium, so that when the cells were stimulated, little Ca^{2+} could enter. This treatment inhibited the establishment of long-term potentiation; therefore, long-term potentiation appears to require the entry of Ca^{++} into the postsynaptic neurons. In addition, Lynch, Larson, Kelso, Barrionuevo, and Schottler (1984) injected EGTA directly into hippocampal pyramidal cells. This chemical binds with calcium and makes it insoluble, destroying its biological activity. The EGTA blocked the establishment of long-term potentiation in the injected cells; their excitability, unlike that of their neighbors, was not increased by high-frequency stimulation of their afferent fibers.

Calcium appears to act directly on molecules bound to the postsynaptic membrane. Baudry and Lynch (1980) homogenized tissue from various parts of the brain and extracted synaptic membranes. They added varying concentrations of calcium to the liquids in which the synaptic membranes were suspended and then assessed the number of glutamate receptors by incubating the membranes with radioactive glutamate. They found that calcium doubled glutamate binding in membranes extracted from the hippocampus, cortex, and corpus striatum. They obtained a moderate effect in membranes extracted from the hypothalamus, and a small one in membranes from the cerebellum. Fig-

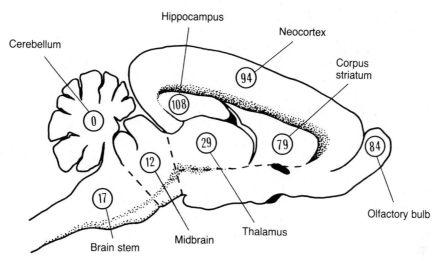

FIGURE 15.15

Percentage increase in active glutamate receptors caused by increased
Ca^{2+} concentration. (Adapted from Lynch, G., and Baudry, M. *Science,*
1984, *224,* 1057–1063. Figure courtesy of G. Lynch and M. Baudry.)

ure 15.15 shows the effect; even very low
concentrations caused a substantial increase
in binding in membranes extracted from the
telencephalon. (See **Figure 15.15.**)

Lynch and his colleagues hypothesized
that calcium increases the number of glutamate receptors by activating a particular kind
of enzyme, a calcium-activated proteinase.
Calcium-activated proteinases alter the structure of proteins by irreversibly breaking the
chain of amino acids. Baudry, Bundman,
Smith, and Lynch (1981) incubated synaptic
membranes with **leupeptin,** a chemical that
inhibits proteinases. The leupeptin blocked
the effects of calcium, preventing it from increasing the number of glutamate receptors.
This finding suggests that the increase in glutamate receptors does indeed involve a calcium-activated proteinase. Siman, Baudry,
and Lynch (1983) found a particular calcium-activated proteinase, **calpain,** in synaptic membranes extracted from the hippocampus, and they suggested that this is the

enzyme responsible for the increase in glutamate receptors.

How might the activation of calpain cause
an increase in the number of glutamate receptors? Calcium can increase the number of glutamate receptors in vitro, in a suspension of
isolated fragments of synaptic membrane; it is
obvious that the effect is not produced by
synthesis of new receptor molecules, because
protein synthesis can occur only in intact
neurons. Therefore, it appears that calpain
somehow activates receptors that are already
present but inactive. Lynch and Baudry
(1984) suggested that calcium-activated calpain breaks apart strands of a protein called
fodrin, which lines the inside of neural
membranes, especially in the postsynaptic region (Carlin, Bartelt, and Siekevitz, 1983).
The cleavage of the fodrin releases glutamate
receptors that were previously covered and
hence inactive. (See **Figure 15.16.**)

Lynch and Baudry (1984) suggest that this
mechanism may also account for the change

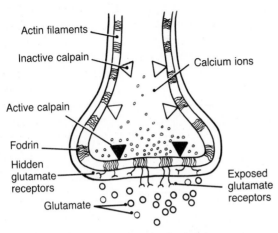

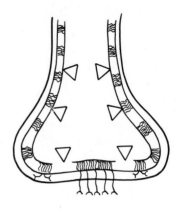

A. Molecules of glutamate activate
   exposed receptors, permitting
   calcium to enter dendritic spine;
   calcium activates calpain, which
   degrades fodrin, uncovering more
   glutamate receptors

B. Calcium is pumped out; note
   newly exposed glutamate
   receptors

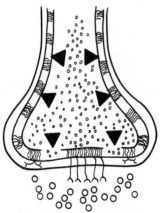

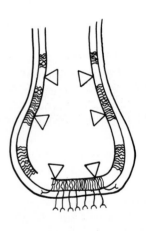

C. Molecules of glutamate activate
   exposed receptors; because there
   are more of them, more calcium
   enters the dendritic spine, causing
   calpain to degrade more fodrin

D. More glutamate receptors are
   exposed and shape of dendritic
   spine is altered by degradation
   of fodrin

FIGURE 15.16
Lynch and Baudry's hypothetical model of the cellular basis of long-term
potentiation. (From Lynch, G., and Baudry, M. *Science,* 1984, *224,*
1057–1063. Copyright 1984 by the American Association for the
Advancement of Science.)

in size of dendritic spines caused by long-term potentiation. Perhaps the cleavage of the fodrin acts like the release of a spring, permitting the membrane of the spine to expand.

Relation to Learning

If the mechanism proposed by Lynch and Baudry (1984) describes the physical basis of long-term potentiation, and if long-term potentiation is responsible for at least some forms of learning, then learning and long-term potentiation should interact with each other. Indeed, there is evidence that they do.

As we saw in Chapter 14, particular neurons in the hippocampal formation respond when the animal is present in particular locations. The sensory information reaches the dentate gyrus from the entorhinal cortex by means of the perforant path. If learning about complex environments produces changes in the hippocampal formation similar to those caused by high-frequency stimulation, then learning should alter the excitability of granule cells in the dentate gyrus. Sharp, McNaughton, and Barnes (1983) measured the extracellular population spike in the dentate gyrus in response to a single shock delivered to the perforant path. Next, they placed the rats in an enriched environment filled with boxes, ramps, and other objects. They found that this experience increased the extracellular population spike by 48 percent. Thus, an animal's experience can affect synaptic strength in the hippocampal formation. The effect was not permanent; after continued exposure to the enriched environment, the excitability of the granule cells returned to baseline levels.

Although the hippocampus is not necessary for simple delayed classical conditioning of a nictitating membrane response, you will recall from Chapter 14 that cells there "learn" to fire in a way that conforms to the shape of the conditional response. Thus, it is not surprising that classical conditioning training also affects synaptic strength in the hippocampal formation. Weisz, Clark, Yank, Thompson, and Solomon (1982) found that the amplitude of the extracellular population spike in the dentate gyrus doubled during the course of classical conditioning of the nictitating membrane response. (See **Figure 15.17**.) In addition, Thompson, Mamounas,

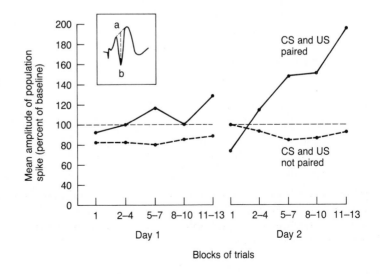

FIGURE 15.17

Amplitude of the extracellular population spike in the dentate gyrus of a rabbit during classical conditioning of the nictitating membrane response. The inset indicates the method of measuring the extracellular population spike. (From Weisz, D.J., Clark, G.A., Yank, B., Thompson, R.F., and Solomon, P.R. In *Conditioning: Representation of Involved Neural Functions,* edited by C.D. Woody. New York: Plenum Press, 1982.)

Lynch, and Baudry (1983) found increased glutamate binding in synaptic membranes extracted from the hippocampus of rabbits who received this training.

Berger (1984a) also found evidence for an interaction between long-term potentiation and classical conditioning. He stimulated the perforant path and produced long-term potentiation. Rabbits who received this treatment learned a classically conditioned nictitating membrane response faster than control animals who received low-frequency stimulation. He suggested that the increased synaptic strength in the dentate gyrus permitted more efficient entry of information into the hippocampus during training, and hence caused more rapid conditioning.

If learning a spatially guided task requires the kinds of neural changes seen in long-term potentiation, then treatments that interfere with long-term potentiation should also interfere with this type of learning. Lynch and Baudry (1984) trained rats to find food efficiently in an eight-arm radial maze. Next, they implanted devices in the animals that continuously infused low levels of leupeptin into their brain. To do this they used a miniature pump, connected by means of a plastic tube to a metal cannula inserted in the lateral ventricle. You will recall that leupeptin inactivates calpain and thus prevents intracellular calcium from releasing hidden glutamate receptors. The rats who received the leupeptin acted like animals with hippocampal lesions; they entered the arms randomly, often visiting locations where they had already received food. The behavior of rats that received control infusions of saline was normal. Leupeptin does not impair all kinds of learning; Lynch and Baudry found that the experimental animals performed normally on an active avoidance task, which is *not* disrupted by hippocampal lesions. These results, along with the others I just described, suggest that the participation of the hippocampal formation in

learning may indeed be mediated by Lynch and Baudry's hypothesized calpain-fodrin mechanism.

Lynch and Baudry noted that the calpain-fodrin mechanism appears to exist only in the telencephalon. In addition, in vitro experiments showed that the mechanism is very sensitive to temperature, so it could not work in animals with low brain temperatures, such as fish or amphibians that live in cool climates. These two observations suggest that the mechanism evolved in warm-blooded animals. The authors also note that classical conditioning of the nictitating membrane response, which may be learned through neural changes in the hindbrain and midbrain (most likely, the cerebellum and red nucleus), must be mediated by means other than the calpain-fodrin mechanism.

INTERIM SUMMARY

Artificial stimulation also affects brain structure. Repeated stimulation of many parts of the brain leads to the development of epileptic foci, a phenomenon called kindling. Presumably, the stimulation causes gradual increases in the strength of excitatory synapses. A similar phenomenon, long-term potentiation, occurs in the hippocampal formation. The trisynaptic circuit travels from the entorhinal cortex to the dentate gyrus to CA3 to CA1 and back to the entorhinal cortex. High-frequency stimulation of any element of this circuit leads to increases in the size of the extracellular population spike evoked by a brief test shock. This phenomenon has been used to demonstrate heterosynaptic facilitation. Simultaneous stimulation of the ipsilateral and contralateral entorhinal cortex results in long-term potentiation of the extracellular population spike produced by test shocks applied to the contralateral entorhinal cortex, but stimulation of the ipsilateral entorhinal cortex alone does not have this effect.

Lynch and Baudry believe that long-term potentiation is produced by increased sensitivity of postsynaptic glutamate receptors in neurons within the trisynaptic circuit, because APB, a drug that blocks glutamate receptors, also prevents long-term potentiation. They also observed increased binding of radioactive glutamate in synaptic membranes extracted from hippocampal slices that had been subjected to the long-term potentiation procedure. Lynch and Baudry believe that long-term potentiation occurs when calcium ions enter the cytoplasm of the postsynaptic cell and activate a proteinase called calpain, which destroys a special protein (fodrin). When the protein is broken, it releases formerly inactive glutamate receptors. They found that EGTA, which binds calcium, prevented long-term potentiation. In addition, leupeptin, a drug that inactivates calpain, prevented the increase in glutamate receptors.

Long-term potentiation appears to be related to learning. When rats are exposed to novel, complex environments, or when rabbits are trained with a classical conditioning procedure, the extracellular population spike in the dentate gyrus increases, just as it does when the entorhinal cortex is subjected to high-frequency stimulation. In addition, when rabbits are exposed to a long-term potentiation procedure, they acquire a conditional nictitating membrane response faster. Finally, leupeptin, which blocks the activity of calpain, impairs rats' performance of a radial-arm maze task.

■ LEARNING IN A SIMPLE ORGANISM

Pursuit of the physiology of learning has been most successful when experiments have focused on simple tasks that produce changes in specific regions of the brain. Another fruitful approach has been to study learning in organisms with relatively simple nervous systems. For several years, Kandel and his colleagues have been studying *Aplysia californica* (the sea hare), a shell-less marine mollusc. They have discovered much about the physiological basis of habituation and sensitization, and recently, about classical conditioning, as well. These changes appear to be presynaptic; thus, they are quite unlike the physiological changes that are responsible for long-term potentiation. We hope that what they have

learned will help other investigators discover more about the cellular basis of learning in more complex organisms.

Habituation and Sensitization of the Retraction Response

Behavioral studies of *Aplysia* have focused on the external organs of the mantle cavity: the gill, mantle shelf, and siphon. The gill exchanges gases with the seawater, thus obtaining oxygen and releasing carbon dioxide. The mantle shelf is a protective sheet that forms a funnel-like siphon at its posterior end. Normally, movements of the mantle cause water to be pumped into and out of the mantle cavity. (See **Figure 15.18.**)

When the siphon or mantle shelf is touched, all three external organs retract into the mantle cavity. This defensive response

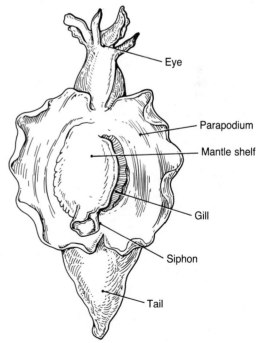

FIGURE 15.18
Aplysia californica.

presumably serves to protect these appendages from harm. When a weak stimulus is applied repeatedly to one location (say, the siphon), the response eventually habituates. This habituation is specific to a particular afferent pathway; if the experimenter now stimulates another location (say, the mantle shelf), the siphon, mantle shelf, and gill will all retract. In contrast to habituation, sensitization is a more general phenomenon. The presentation of a noxious stimulus, such as an electrical shock applied to the tail, will increase the amplitude of withdrawal responses elicited by gentle touch of any part of the mantle cavity area. Figure 15.19 shows habituation of the gill-withdrawal response after one, six, eleven, and thirteen gentle tactile stimuli applied to the siphon, followed by sensitization of this response produced by

an electrical shock to the tail (Kandel and Schwartz, 1982). (See **Figure 15.19.**)

Kandel and his colleagues (for specific references, see Kandel and Schwartz, 1982) have identified most of the neurons that participate in the withdrawal reflex. They have located five motor neurons that innervate the gill, seven that innervate the siphon, and one that innervates both. Two groups of twenty-four sensory neurons, one group serving the mantle shelf and one group serving the skin of the siphon, activate these motor neurons. In addition, several interneurons produce excitation or inhibition. Habituation is caused by a decrease in the release of transmitter substance by the sensory neurons; smaller excitatory postsynaptic potentials are produced when the afferent axons fire, even though the sensitivity of the postsynaptic receptors is unchanged. Sensitization is caused by a corresponding increase in the release of transmitter substance.

Sensitization is produced by facilitatory interneurons that are activated by noxious stimuli. L28, a single neuron, is activated by noxious stimuli delivered to the head of *Aplysia*. The L29 group of neurons is activated by noxious stimuli delivered to the tail. These neurons appear to secrete serotonin, because the effects of their activation can be produced by applying serotonin and can be abolished by applying drugs that block serotonin receptors. All of these cells form axoaxonic synapses with sensory neurons and produce presynaptic facilitation when they are activated. (See **Figure 15.20.**)

Presynaptic facilitation appears to depend on the synthesis of cyclic AMP and on the activation of a protein kinase in the sensory neurons. (The role of cyclic AMP in synaptic transmission was discussed in Chapter 3.) Brunelli, Castellucci, and Kandel (1976) found that injecting cyclic AMP directly into sensory neurons increased the amount of transmitter substance the cells' terminal but-

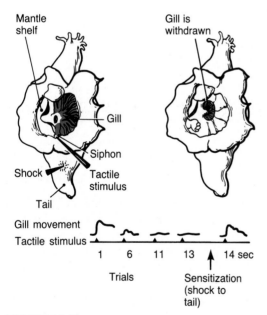

FIGURE 15.19

Habituation and sensitization of the gill-withdrawal response. (From Kandel, E.R., and Schwartz, J.H. *Science,* 1982, *218,* 433–443. Copyright 1982 by the American Association for the Advancement of Science.)

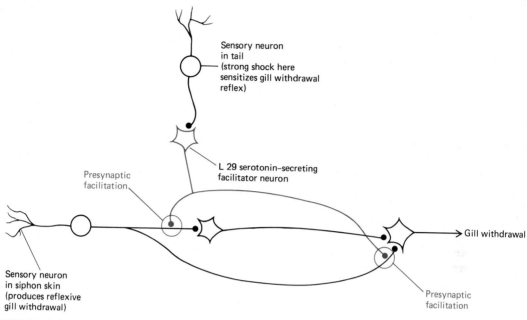

FIGURE 15.20

Serotonin-secreting neurons L28 and L29, which apparently produce the presynaptic facilitation that causes sensitization of the gill-withdrawal response. (Adapted from Kandel, E.R., and Schwartz, J.H., *Science*, 1982, *218*, 433–443.)

tons released. Castellucci, Kandel, Schwartz, Wilson, Nairn, and Greengard (1980) found that injecting an activated protein kinase produced the same effect, and Castellucci, Nairn, Greengard, Schwartz, and Kandel (1982) found that injecting a protein kinase inhibitor blocked presynaptic facilitation.

You will recall from Chapter 3 that release of the transmitter substance is triggered by the entry of calcium ions into the terminal buttons. The calcium apparently activates protein molecules that propel the synaptic vesicles to the presynaptic membrane, where they burst and spill their contents into the synaptic cleft. Klein and Kandel (1978) found that the presynaptic facilitation caused by the activation of L28 and L29 neurons is produced by an increased influx of Ca^{2+}. In a subsequent study, Klein and Kandel (1980)

found that this increased Ca^{2+} influx was a result of a *decrease* in the *efflux* of the potassium ion (K^+).

Let us see why this series of events occurs. You will recall that the depolarizing phase of the action potential is caused by the entry of the sodium ion (Na^+) into the cell. As soon as the voltage-dependent sodium channels open, Na^+ enters the cell down its electrostatic and osmotic gradients, and as it does so the membrane becomes further depolarized. Soon, however, the voltage-dependent sodium channels close. Meanwhile the voltage-dependent potassium channels have been opening. Because the inside of the membrane is now temporarily negative, K^+ flows out. The efflux of this cation brings the membrane potential back to normal. (See **Figure 15.21**.) But why should a *decrease* in potassium ef-

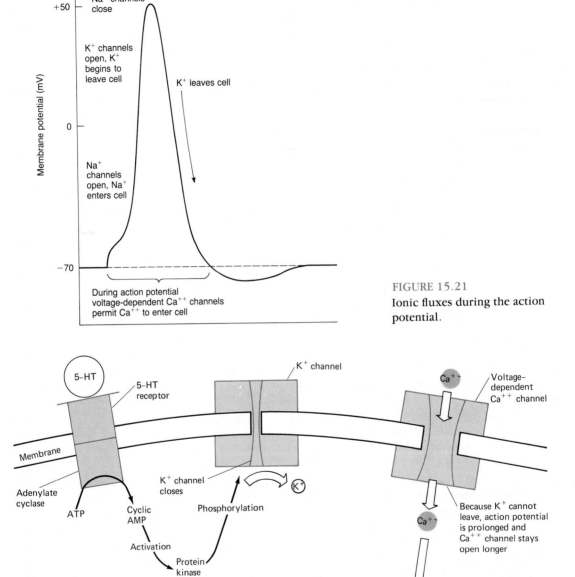

FIGURE 15.21

Ionic fluxes during the action potential.

FIGURE 15.22

If K+ channels close, the falling phase of the action potential is prolonged, and more Ca2+ enters the axon and terminal buttons.

flux cause an *increase* in the influx of calcium? If something prevents voltage-dependent potassium channels from opening, the membrane potential returns back to the baseline level much more slowly. Calcium is normally in excess outside the cell; thus, like sodium, osmotic and electrostatic pressure tend to force it in. However, the gates of the voltage-dependent calcium channels are closed at the normal resting potential. These gates open when the membrane is depolarized. Thus, during the long, slow return of the membrane potential back to the baseline level, a large quantity of calcium can enter the neuron.

Kandel and his colleagues hypothesized the following mechanism to explain sensitization: Noxious stimulation of the head or tail activates L28 or L29 neurons. The terminal buttons of these neurons release serotonin (5-HT), which activates receptors in the presynaptic terminal buttons of the sensory neurons with which the L28 and L29 neurons synapse. Activation of the serotonin receptors causes synthesis of cyclic AMP, activation of a protein kinase, and phosphorylation of membrane proteins that control the gates of potassium channels. In these neurons, the phosphorylated proteins keep the gates *closed,* which prevents the efflux of potassium and thus prolongs the falling phase of action potentials in these terminal buttons. As a result, more calcium enters the cell, and more transmitter substance is released. (See **Figure 15.22.**)

Classical Conditioning of the Withdrawal Response

Sensitization occurs in mammals, not just in *Aplysia,* but the reason I described the studies by Kandel and his colleagues in some detail is that the mechanism they discovered appears to apply to classical conditioning as well. Withdrawal of the siphon and gill can be clas-

sically conditioned by following a light touch applied to the siphon or mantle (CS) with a strong electrical shock to the tail (US). In fact, the response can be differentially conditioned. Carew, Hawkins, and Kandel (1983) applied gentle tactile stimuli to two different places, the siphon and mantle, but followed only one of these stimuli (CS$^+$) with a noxious shock; the other stimulus (CS$^-$) was never followed by shock. After fifteen training trials, the CS$^+$ was more likely than the CS$^-$ to produce a prolonged withdrawal reaction. (See **Figure 15.23.**)

Hawkins, Abrams, Carew, and Kandel (1983) isolated the *Aplysia* central nervous system from the rest of the animal, leaving it attached to the tail. They inserted stimulating electrodes into two sensory neurons serving the skin of the siphon and inserted a recording electrode into a motor neuron that innervates the siphon. (You can see the advantage of using an animal with such a simple nervous system.) They used the stimulating electrodes to present conditional stimuli, and they recorded the activity of the siphon motor neuron (the response). Stimulation of one neuron in the intact nervous system (CS$^+$) was paired with the unconditional stimulus, a shock to the tail. Stimulation of the other neuron (CS$^-$) was not. The procedure worked: within five trials, the CS$^+$ produced conditional responses (increased excitatory postsynaptic potentials), but the CS$^-$ did not. (See **Figure 15.24.**)

Hawkins and his colleagues then followed the same training procedure and measured the efflux of potassium caused by stimulating each of the sensory neurons. They found that stimulating the "paired" neuron (CS$^+$) produced a smaller outward flow of potassium than stimulating the "unpaired" neuron (CS$^-$). These effects are similar to those produced by sensitization. The investigators suggested that when a sensory neuron and a facilitator neuron (in this case, an L29 neuron) are

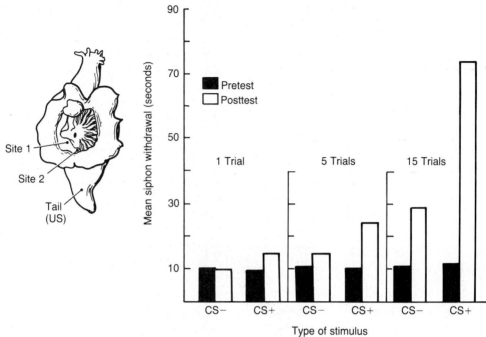

FIGURE 15.23

Differential classical conditioning of the siphon-withdrawal reflex. CS⁺ and CS⁻ are tactile stimuli applied to different portions of the siphon and mantle. The pretest occurred before training and the posttest occurred 24 hours after training. (From Carew, R.J., Hawkins, R.D., and Kandel, E.R. *Science,* 1983, *219,* 397–400. Copyright 1983 by the American Association for the Advancement of Science.)

activated at the same time, the potassium channels in the terminal buttons of the sensory neuron are closed, which prolongs calcium influx, release of transmitter substance, and excitation of the postsynaptic neuron. (Look back at **Figure 15.20.**)

Is this mechanism a good candidate for the cellular basis of classical conditioning in mammals, or is it an adaptation peculiar to some invertebrates? A decrease in potassium flow seems to be a good candidate for relatively short-term memory, but can it explain memories that last for years? Are some terminal buttons permanently facilitated? If so, then there would appear to be no further use

for the presynaptic terminal buttons that synapse on them. Even if the mechanism that Kandel and his colleagues are studying is not the basis of long-term memory in more complex organisms, it still may be an important component of short-term memory.

INTERIM SUMMARY

Some researchers have investigated the cellular mechanisms of learning in simple organisms with simple nervous systems in the hope that what they discover will help others understand such mechanisms in more complex organisms. The sensitization of the habituated retraction response in

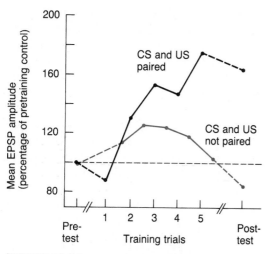

FIGURE 15.24

Classical conditioning of activity of a motor neuron that innervates the siphon. CS = stimulation of a sensory neuron serving the skin; US = shock to the tail. (From Hawkins, R.D., Abrams, T.W., Carew, T.J., and Kandel, E.R. *Science,* 1983, *219,* 400–405. Copyright 1983 by the American Association for the Advancement of Science.)

Aplysia appears to be caused by serotonergic facilitatory interneurons that are activated by noxious stimuli. When these neurons are stimulated, calcium enters their terminal buttons, thus activating protein kinases. These activated enzymes phosphorylate membrane proteins that control the gates of potassium channels, causing them to close. Their closure prolongs the action potential because potassium cannot easily leave the neuron, and consequently more serotonin is released.

The withdrawal response of *Aplysia* can also be classically conditioned. This form of learning, too, appears to involve closure of potassium channels — in this case, those in terminal buttons of sensory neurons that respond to the conditional stimuli. The closure of the potassium channels occurs when sensory neurons excited by the conditional stimulus and a facilitator neuron excited by the unconditional stimulus are activated at the same time. Only further research will determine whether these presynaptic events are related to the cellular changes that learning produces in the mammalian nervous system.

■ EFFECTS OF NEUROTRANSMITTERS AND NEUROMODULATORS

Researchers have suggested that several neurotransmitters and neuromodulators play a role in learning: the catecholamines, acetylcholine (ACh), the endogenous opiates, and antidiuretic hormone (also called vasopressin). As we saw in Chapter 13, dopamine appears to be important in reinforcement. Because I discussed it there, I will not say more about it in this chapter. We saw earlier in this chapter that glutamate plays a special role in long-term potentiation. And although there is evidence that epinephrine and norepinephrine may affect learning and performance, the data from different laboratories are still contradictory and inconclusive. The role of ACh seems to be more certain; drugs that affect acetylcholinergic synapses also affect memory. In addition, Alzheimer's disease, characterized by a progressive memory loss, entails the loss of ACh-secreting neurons. Peptide neuromodulators may also play a role in learning. The evidence for the role of the endogenous opiates is the strongest and least controversial. It is possible that the endogenous opiates may help control what is remembered or forgotten.

Acetylcholine

J.A. Deutsch has suggested that acetylcholinergic neurons may play an important role in the storage and retrieval of memory. He and his colleagues performed several studies during the 1960s and 1970s (reviewed by Deutsch, 1983) that support this suggestion. In particular, they found that drugs that affect transmission at ACh-secreting synapses impair or facilitate learning, depending on when these drugs are administered.

Interest in acetylcholinergic neurons has been rekindled in recent years by the discovery that the loss of ACh-secreting terminal buttons is related to human dementia. The term *dementia* derives from the Latin word for "madness." However, in current usage it refers to deterioration of intellectual abilities resulting from an organic brain disorder. The most common forms of dementia are *Alzheimer's disease* and the closely related *senile dementia of the Alzheimer's type* (SDAT). The essential difference between these disorders is the age of onset; if an elderly person becomes demented, he or she is diagnosed as having SDAT rather than Alzheimer's disease. Because the neuropathological changes and behavioral and cognitive deficits in both cases are similar, most investigators lump them together. I will use the term *Alzheimer's disease* to refer to them both.

Alzheimer's disease occurs in approximately 5 percent of the population above the age of 65. It is characterized by progressive loss of memory and other mental functions. At first, the person may have difficulty remembering appointments and sometimes fails to think of words or people's names. As time passes, he or she shows increasing confusion and increasing difficulty with tasks such as balancing a checkbook. The memory deficit most critically involves recent events, and it thus resembles the anterograde amnesia of Korsakoff's syndrome. If the person ventures outside alone, he or she is likely to get lost. Eventually, the person becomes bedridden and completely helpless and finally succumbs (Terry and Davies, 1980).

Alzheimer's disease produces severe degeneration of the hippocampus and neocortex, especially the frontal and temporal lobes. Figure 15.25 shows a CAT scan of the brain of a patient with Alzheimer's disease *(left)* and that of a nondemented person *(right)*. Note how much wider the sulci are, especially in the frontal and temporal lobes, indicating substantial loss of cortical tissue. (See **Figure 15.25.**) On autopsy, slices of hippocampus and neocortex show three characteristic signs of Alzheimer's disease: neuritic plaques, neurofibrillary tangles, and granulovacuolar degeneration. *Neuritic plaques* are abnormally shaped axon terminal buttons, associated with a core of *amyloid,* a protein-starch complex that is deposited in tissues during the course of several different degenerating diseases. *Neurofibrillary tangles* are found in the cell bodies of cortical neurons. They consist of tangles of abnormal protein

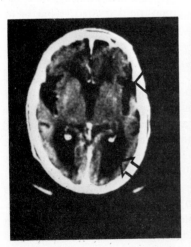 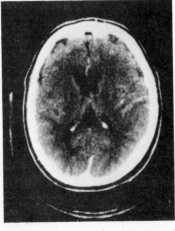

FIGURE 15.25
CAT scans. *Left:* Patient with Alzheimer's disease. Arrows point to one of the widened lateral fissures and to the enlarged lateral ventricles. *Right:* Nondemented person. (CAT scans courtesy of J.McA. Jones, Good Samaritan Hospital and Medical Center, Portland, Oregon.)

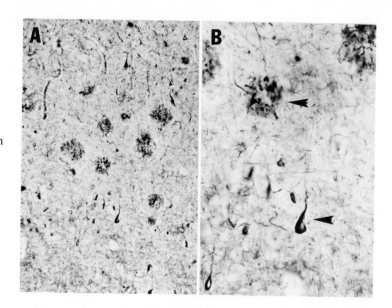

FIGURE 15.26
Low power (A) and high power (B) photomicrographs from the brain of a person with Alzheimer's disease, showing neuritic plaques (upper arrow) and neurofibrillary tangles (lower arrow). (From Coyle, J.T., Price, D.L., and DeLong, M.R. *Science,* 1983, *219,* 1184–1190. Copyright 1983 by the American Association for the Advancement of Science.)

fibers that normally serve as the cell's internal skeleton. (See **Figure 15.26.**) *Granulovacuolar degeneration* is seen in the hippocampus; pyramidal cells acquire empty spaces (vacuoles) in their cytoplasm as they degenerate.

As we have already seen, Parkinson's disease is caused by the death of a specific class of neurons — the dopamine-secreting neurons of the nigrostriatal bundle. Investigators have analyzed the brains of deceased patients who had Alzheimer's disease, with the hopes of finding specific degeneration in them, as well. Many studies found evidence for decreased ACh activity in the neocortex and hippocampus. These studies (reviewed by Coyle, Price, and DeLong, 1983) found that the activity of choline acetyltransferase (the enzyme that synthesizes ACh from choline and acetyl coenzyme A) was markedly reduced in these areas. This reduction indicates a loss of ACh-secreting terminal buttons, which contain the enzyme. In contrast, there was evidence of little or no loss of terminal buttons that secrete other neurotransmitters.

The cell bodies of ACh-secreting neurons reside in subcortical areas, not in the neocortex or hippocampus itself. The cell bodies of neurons that project to the neocortex are located in the *nucleus basalis of Meynert,* located in the basal forebrain near the preoptic area. Whitehouse, Price, Struble, Clark, Coyle, and DeLong (1982) examined slices of the basal forebrain of deceased patients with Alzheimer's disease. They found that the number of neurons in this nucleus was decreased by 79 percent in the brains of these patients, compared with age-matched normal controls. Figure 15.27 shows the microscopic appearance of tissue from normal and diseased brains. (See **Figure 15.27.**)

During the early stages of the disease, the cortical degeneration in Alzheimer's disease appears primarily to involve presynaptic terminal buttons, not postsynaptic neurons. (Eventually, much of the cortical gray matter degenerates.) Several studies (reviewed by Bartus, Dean, Beer, and Lippa, 1982) have assessed the number of postsynaptic ACh receptors in the brains of patients with Alzheimer's disease. Ten of the eleven studies found no significant decrease in receptor

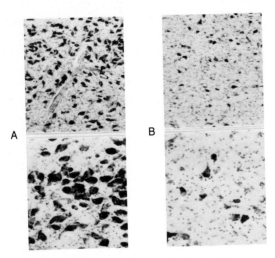

FIGURE 15.27

Photomicrographs from the midportion of the nucleus basalis of Meynert. (A) Age-matched normal person. *Top:* Low magnification. *Bottom:* High magnification. (B) Person with Alzheimer's disease. *Top:* Low magnification. *Bottom:* High magnification. (From Whitehouse, P.J., Price, D.L., Struble, R.G., Clark, A.W., Coyle, J.T., and DeLong, M.R. *Science,* 1982, *215,* 1237–1239. Copyright 1982 by the American Association for the Advancement of Science.)

density. If the neurons upon which the ACh-secreting terminal buttons synapse had died, the investigators should have found a decreased number of ACh receptors.

Several studies have shown that memory impairments can be produced in humans and laboratory animals by administering drugs that block muscarinic ACh receptors. For example, Drachman and Leavitt (1974) found that scopolamine, administered to normal young human subjects, selectively impaired recent memory without affecting recall of old memories. Sitaram, Weingartner, and Gillin (1978) had normal subjects learn lists of words. Subjects who received an injection of arecoline, a drug that stimulates muscarinic receptors, learned the words faster than those who received a placebo. In contrast, subjects who received an injection of scopolamine learned the list slower. Furthermore, this deficit could be reversed with a subsequent injection of arecoline. Thus, the level of ACh activity does indeed affect people's learning ability.

What is the function of the acetylcholinergic neurons of the basal forebrain? As we saw in Chapter 14, Rolls and his colleagues found that neurons in this area respond to the presence of food and other stimuli associated with reinforcement. We also saw that reinforcing electrical stimulation of the medial forebrain bundle increases the metabolic activity of neurons in the basal forebrain region (and also in the ventral tegmental area). The principal effects of such stimulation appear to be mediated by the activation of dopamine-secreting neurons located in the ventral tegmental area. However, it is also possible that events that reinforce behavior do so at least partly by activating acetylcholinergic neurons that project to the neocortex and hippocampus. Some investigators suggest that the acetylcholinergic neurons may convey specific stimulus-related information, in contrast to dopaminergic neurons, which appear to have a general modulatory function (Coyle, Price, and DeLong, 1983).

The inputs to the nucleus basalis of Meynert include the amygdala, hypothalamus, and various brain stem nuclei. The outputs, besides the neocortex, include the entorhinal cortex, amygdala, thalamus, hypothalamus, olfactory bulb, hippocampus, and brain stem nuclei. This pattern of anatomical connections is consistent with the possibility that the nucleus basalis of Meynert plays a role in controlling the formation of memories.

The discovery that Alzheimer's disease involves the degeneration of acetylcholinergic neurons in the nucleus basalis of Meynert will undoubtedly prompt investigators to determine the effects of lesions of this nucleus in experimental animals. In fact, some preliminary studies indicate that these lesions impair learning. Fibiger, Murray, and Phillips (1983) first destroyed the nucleus basalis of Meynert in rats and then trained them in a sixteen-arm radial maze. The lesions decreased neocortical choline acetyltransferase activity by 50 percent but did not affect the hippocampal levels of this enzyme; thus, the lesions damaged the acetylcholinergic input to the neocortex, but not to the hippocampus. At the beginning of each session, nine of the arms were baited with food; the other seven arms never were. The rats learned to avoid entering arms in which they had just obtained food (thus showing good "working memory"). However, their "reference memory" was poor; they did not learn to avoid entering arms that were never baited. The rats' performance could be improved to near-normal levels by injections of physostigmine, an ACh agonist. These intriguing results suggest that ACh may play complementary roles in the hippocampus and neocortex: in the hippocampus it may be involved in memory for recent events, whereas in the neocortex it may be involved in the formation of long-term memory.

The precursor of dopamine, L-DOPA, has been successfully used to treat the symptoms of Parkinson's disease, which is caused by degeneration of dopaminergic neurons. Thus, because Alzheimer's disease involves degeneration of ACh-secreting neurons, it occurred to investigators to try to improve patients' cognitive performance with choline, the precursor of acetylcholine, or with *its* precursor, lecithin. Unfortunately, these treatments have not been very successful in either healthy elderly people or patients with Alzheimer's disease; only one of seventeen studies reviewed by Bartus, Dean, Beer, and Lippa (1982) observed a substantial memory improvement. Some improvement in the memory ability of people with Alzheimer's disease has been obtained by administering arecoline, an ACh agonist (Christie, Shering, Ferguson, and Glen, 1979). However, the effects are short-lived, and the drug produces adverse side effects; hence, it would not be useful as a therapeutic medication.

An intriguing method for reversing the effects of aging on learning ability is the surgical implantation of grafts of brain tissue. Gage, Björklund, Stenevi, Dunnett, and Kelly (1984) trained aged rats (almost 2 years old) and young rats (3 months old) in the circular "milk maze" I described in Chapter 14. The experimenters divided the aged rats who performed poorly into two groups, one group of which received a graft of brain tissue. The new brain tissue was taken from the septal region of embryonic rats, an area rich in acetylcholinergic neurons, and was implanted bilaterally in the old rats' hippocampal formations. Because the fetal brain tissue was immature, the cells divided and sprouted axons that established synaptic connections with neurons in the old rats' brains. Histological examination revealed that these connections were rich in acetylcholinesterase, which implies that they were acetylcholinergic.

The experimenters tested the rats' maze performance approximately 3 months after the new brain tissue was implanted. They found that the performance of eight of the eleven experimental animals improved significantly, although their performance was still poorer than that of the young rats. The results provide further support to the suggestion that ACh plays an important role in learning. Whether implants of immature brain tissue (perhaps obtained by means of tissue-culture techniques) will ever ameliorate the memory loss of patients with Alzheimer's disease depends on the results of further research.

Endogenous Opiates

Opiates have important effects on behavior. In general, they decrease sensitivity to pain and inhibit species-typical defensive responses that interfere with the performance of other behaviors, such as fighting or mating. Opiates facilitate the learning of some tasks and inhibit others. As we saw in Chapter 14, Gallagher, Kapp, McNall, and Pascoe (1981) found that injection of an opiate agonist into the central nucleus of the amygdala impaired the acquisition of a classically conditioned decrease in heart rate, whereas naloxone, an opiate receptor blocker, facilitated it. In contrast, Belluzzi and Stein (1982) found that injection of morphine or Met-enkephalin immediately after a training trial facilitated the learning of a passive avoidance task.

Because opiates appear to affect different behaviors in different ways, and because they can have punishing effects on behavior as well as the more usual reinforcing effects (Jacquet, 1973), it has proved difficult to determine just what effect these substances have on learning. Before investigators can be certain that opiates directly influence the formation of memories, they must control for unconditional effects of these substances on the performance of various classes of behaviors and for possible reinforcing or punishing effects.

Collier and Routtenberg (1984) have obtained evidence for an interesting property of endogenous opiates: the editing of memory. They trained rats in a spatial matching-to-sample task in an eight-arm radial maze. On the first trial, one arm was baited with food (the sample arm), and the rats were placed on the center platform and permitted to find the food. Twenty minutes later, the same arm was baited again, and the rats were placed on the center platform again. A correct response would be to enter the arm that contained food on the first trial. Each day a different arm was

baited on the two trials. Within 15 to 25 days, the rats learned the task; on the second trial, they approached the correct arm.

Once the rats had learned the task, the experimenters implanted a stimulating electrode in the granule cell layer of the dentate gyrus. After the animals recovered from the surgery, the experimenters tested the effects of 10 seconds of low-intensity electrical stimulation through the electrodes immediately after the first trial. The stimulation appeared to "erase" the animals' memory of the location of the baited arm; they entered an average of four and one-half arms before finding the food, which is about what would be expected by chance. Granule cells of the dentate gyrus and their axons, the mossy fibers, appear to contain enkephalins (Gall, Brecha, Karten, and Chang, 1981). To test their hypothesis that the effects of the stimulation were mediated by the release of opiates, Collier and Routtenberg pretreated some animals with naloxone, which blocks opiate receptors. Indeed, the naloxone prevented the amnestic effect of the electrical stimulation; these animals performed almost perfectly.

As we have seen in this chapter and the last, the hippocampal system plays an important role in what Olton (1983) calls "working memory"—remembering information that can change from day to day, or from trial to trial. Quite possibly, this storage is mediated through the calpain-fodrin system outlined by Lynch and his colleagues. For this mechanism to work, there must be some means to erase old information when new information is presented. Collier and Routtenberg's finding suggests that the erasure may be produced by the release of enkephalin. Of course, this suggestion is speculative; further studies will have to be performed to confirm or refute it. In addition, the anatomy of the opiate-releasing neurons must be clarified. As we saw in the section on long-term potentiation, the trisynaptic circuit (from the entorhinal cortex to the dentate gyrus to CA3 to CA1 and back to the entorhinal cortex) appears to use glutamate as a transmitter substance. Where are the opiate-secreting terminal buttons? Are opiate-secreting granule cells a subpopulation of the neurons in the dentate gyrus? Further research must provide the answers.

INTERIM SUMMARY

As we saw in Chapter 13, dopaminergic neurons play an important role in reinforcement. Acetylcholinergic neurons also appear to participate in learning. An early symptom of Alzheimer's disease, which eventually produces degeneration of the hippocampus and cerebral cortex, is loss of memory. This loss is correlated with the death of ACh-secreting neurons of the nucleus basalis of Meynert, in the basal forebrain. Neurons in this nucleus send axons to the cerebral cortex. Drugs that block muscarinic ACh receptors produce symptoms that mimic the memory loss of Alzheimer's disease, and these symptoms can be reversed by administration of a muscarinic agonist. In animals, lesions of the nucleus basalis of Meynert do not impair "working memory" but do disrupt the acquisition of "reference memory" in a radial-arm maze. This deficit can be reversed by administration of an ACh agonist. The implantation of brain tissue removed from the septum of fetal rats into the brains of aged rats improves their performance in learning maze tasks, which provides some hope that therapeutic procedures may be discovered that will alleviate the symptoms of Alzheimer's disease in humans.

Learning is also affected by the endogenous opiates. As we saw in Chapter 14, an opiate agonist injected into the central nucleus of the amygdala impaired the acquisition of a classically conditioned decrease in heart rate, whereas an opiate antagonist injected there facilitated it. Many stud-

ies have shown that opiates can either facilitate or retard the rate of learning, but because opiates have reinforcing effects of their own, we cannot yet be sure what conclusions to draw from these experiments. Another study found that electrical stimulation of the dentate gyrus erased "working memory" in a radial-arm maze task. However, when the rats were pretreated with the opiate receptor blocker naloxone, the stimulation did not have an amnestic effect. The results suggest that opiates may perform some role in determining when information temporarily stored in the hippocampus gets erased.

Concluding Remarks

Investigators have employed many different approaches to study the physiology of learning. Finally, after many years of study, some of these approaches are beginning to pay off. We now have evidence that experience can produce physiological changes in the brain, and the details of some kinds of changes (for example, those that accompany long-term potentiation in mammals and learning in *Aplysia*) are being uncovered. Almost certainly, many neurotransmitters and neuromodulators are involved in learning. So far, investigators have obtained good evidence that dopamine, glutamate, acetylcholine, and the endogenous opiates are important, and epinephrine and norepinephrine are probably important as well. The physiology of learning is such an important (and interesting) topic that many laboratories are currently investigating different phenomena, making it difficult to keep informed about major new research. My hope is that this chapter has covered enough of the field to give you an appreciation for the problems encountered in such research and for the fruits of the investigators' efforts.

NEW TERMS

afterdischarge p. 612
Alzheimer's disease p. 630
amyloid p. 630

calpain p. 619
consolidation p. 600
dementia p. 630

electroconvulsive shock (ECS) p. 600
electroconvulsive therapy (ECT) p. 600
extracellular population spike p. 614
fodrin p. 619
granule cell p. 615
granulovacuolar degeneration p. 630
heterosynaptic facilitation p. 606
isolated cortical slab p. 604
kindling p. 612
leupeptin p. 619
long-term memory p. 598
long-term potentiation p. 613
mossy fiber p. 615

neuritic plaque p. 630
neurofibrillary tangle p. 630
nucleus basalis of Meynert p. 631
passive avoidance task p. 600
pyramidal cell p. 615
retrograde amnesia p. 599
reverberation p. 604
Schaffer collateral fiber p. 616
senile dementia of the Alzheimer's type p. 630
short-term memory p. 598
temporal gradient p. 600
trisynaptic circuit p. 616

SUGGESTED READINGS

BUTTERS, N., AND SQUIRE, L.R. *The Neuropsychology of Memory.* New York: Guilford Press, 1984.

DEUTSCH, J.A. *The Physiological Basis of Memory.* New York: Academic Press, 1983.

MCGAUGH, J.L. Hormonal influences on memory. *Annual Review of Psychology,* 1983, *34,* 297–324.

NRP Work Session on Long-Term Potentiation. *Neurosciences Research Program Bulletin,* 1981, *20,* 613–769.

THOMPSON, R.F., BERGER, T.W., AND MADDEN, J. Cellular processes of learning and memory in the mammalian CNS. *Annual Review of Neuroscience,* 1983, *6,* 447–492.

WOODY, C.D. *Conditioning: Representation of Involved Neural Functions.* New York: Plenum Press, 1982.

16

Human Communication

Verbal behaviors constitute one of the most important classes of human social behavior. Our cultural evolution has been possible because we can talk and listen, write and read. We share many behaviors with other species of organisms, and hence research with laboratory animals has contributed much to our understanding of the physiology of human behavior. However, if we want to understand the physiology of human communication, we must study ourselves.

■ SPEECH DISORDERS

Our knowledge of the physiology of language has been obtained primarily by observing the effects of brain lesions on people's verbal behavior. Although investigators have studied people who have undergone brain surgery or who have sustained head injuries, brain tumors, or infections, most of the observations have been made on people who have suffered strokes, or *cerebrovascular accidents.* The most common type of cerebrovascular accident is caused by obstruction of a blood vessel (almost always an artery, but sometimes a vein). The interruption in blood flow deprives a region of the brain of its blood supply, which causes cells in that region to die. Obstructive strokes can be caused by thrombi or emboli. A *thrombus* is a blood clot — an aggregation of insoluble material produced by a complex series of reactions that involve the *platelets,* small cell fragments found in the blood. Thrombi form in blood vessels, especially in areas where their walls are damaged. Platelets adhere to the walls and then to each other, until the clot becomes so large that blood cannot flow through the vessel. People susceptible to the formation of thrombi usually take drugs such as aspirin, which makes the platelets less "sticky" and hence helps prevent clot formation. An *embolus* (from the Greek *embolos,* "something inserted") is a plug that forms in one part of the vascular system, breaks off, and is carried through the bloodstream until it reaches an artery too small to pass through. It lodges there, damming the flow of blood through the rest of the vascular tree (the "branches" and "twigs" arising from the artery). Emboli can consist of a variety of materials, including bacterial debris from an infection in the lining of the heart or pieces broken off from a blood clot.

Most strokes that affect verbal behavior occur in the region of the brain served by the middle cerebral artery. This vessel branches off the internal carotid artery, follows the lateral fissure, and feeds most of the lateral surface of the brain. In addition, branches of the middle cerebral artery penetrate and feed subcortical regions such as the thalamus, basal ganglia, and white matter. The posterior cerebral artery supplies the posterior medial portion of the cerebrum, principally the occipital cortex and underlying white matter. Strokes in its territory sometimes produce reading deficits. Strokes of the anterior cerebral artery, which supplies most of the anterior and dorsal medial region of the cerebral hemispheres, seldom produce language disturbances. (See **Figure 16.1.**)

Study of human brain functions presents difficulties that are not encountered by investigators who use laboratory animals. The brain lesion occurs naturally and is not placed in a specific location by the investigator. In the past, scientists possessed only crude techniques to infer the location of a living patient's lesion. To be certain where the lesion was, they had to wait until the patient died so they could examine the brain. This situation meant that unless the patient died soon after being studied, the brain was usually not available to the investigator. Even if the patient did die soon, the family might not give permission for the brain to be removed and examined. Thus, the development of the CAT scanner (described in Chapter 5) revolutionized

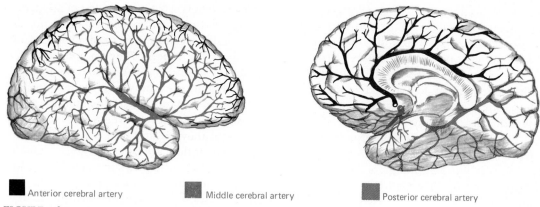

Anterior cerebral artery   Middle cerebral artery   Posterior cerebral artery

FIGURE 16.1

Regions of the human cerebral cortex served by the anterior (black), middle (color), and posterior (gray) cerebral arteries. (Adapted from Netter, F.H. *The Ciba Collection of Medical Illustrations. Vol. 1, Nervous System.* Summit, N.J.: Ciba Pharmaceutical Products Co., 1953.)

the study of the anatomy of verbal behavior. CAT scans provide remarkably good views of obstructive strokes, permitting the investigator to see which regions of the brain are damaged. In the past few years, CAT scans have resolved many controversies about the location of damage that produces specific deficits.

The most important category of speech disorders is *aphasia,* a primary disturbance in the comprehension or production of speech, which is caused by brain damage. Not all speech disturbances are aphasias. To be classified as aphasic, a patient must have difficulty comprehending, repeating, or producing meaningful speech, and this difficulty must not be caused by simple sensory or motor deficits or by lack of motivation. For example, deafness or paralysis of the speech muscles do not produce aphasia. The deficit must be relatively isolated; that is, the patient must appear to be aware of what is happening in his or her environment and to comprehend that others are attempting to communicate. Thus, a person suffering from dementia is not considered to be aphasic.

Verbal behavior is a lateralized function.

That is, most language disturbances occur after damage to one side of the brain — in most cases, the left side. In over 90 percent of the right-handed population, the left hemisphere is the dominant one for speech. In left-handed people, too, the left hemisphere is usually dominant for speech, but the percentage is much lower. Therefore, unless I say otherwise, you can assume that the lesions I describe in this chapter are in the left hemisphere.

Wernicke's Aphasia: Speech Comprehension

The primary characteristics of **Wernicke's aphasia** are poor speech comprehension and production of meaningless speech. These characteristics may be related: if one cannot understand what words mean, how can one possibly use them correctly in one's own speech? Wernicke's aphasia is fluent and unlabored; the person does not strain to articulate words and does not appear to be searching for them. The patient maintains a melodic line, with the voice rising and falling normally. When you listen to the speech of a person with Wernicke's aphasia, it appears to be grammatical. That is, the person uses grammatical connecting words like *and* and *but* and employs complex verb tenses and subordinate clauses. However, the words they string together just do not make much sense. They often make **paraphasic errors**— substitutions of incorrect words or sounds. For example, *table* might be pronounced as "trable" or "fable." In the extreme, speech deteriorates into a meaningless jumble called **jargon speech,** illustrated by the following quote:

Examiner: What kind of work did you do before you came into the hospital?

Patient: Never, now mista oyge I wanna tell you this happened when happened when he rent. His —his kell come down here and is—he got ren something. It happened. In thesse ropiers were with him for hi—is friend—like was. And it just happened so I don't know, he did not bring around anything. And he did not pay it. And he roden all o these arranjen from the pedis on from iss pescid. In these floors now and so. He hadn't had em round here. (Kertesz, 1981, p. 73)

Because of their speech deficit, the ability of people with Wernicke's aphasia to comprehend speech must be assessed by asking them to make nonverbal responses to verbal requests. That is, we cannot assume they do not understand what other people say to them just because they do not give the proper answer. A commonly used test of comprehension assesses their ability to respond to questions by pointing to objects on a table in front of them. For example, they are asked to "Point to the one with ink." If they point to an object other than the pen, they have not comprehended the request. When tested this way, people with severe Wernicke's aphasia show poor comprehension.

A remarkable fact about people with Wernicke's aphasia is that they are often unaware of their deficit. That is, they do not appear to recognize that their speech is faulty, nor do they recognize that they cannot understand the speech of others. They do not look puzzled when someone tells them something, even though they obviously cannot understand what they hear. Perhaps their comprehension deficit prevents them from realizing that what they say and hear makes no sense. They still follow social conventions, taking turns in conversation with the examiner, even though they do not understand what the examiner says. They remain sensitive to the other person's facial expression and tone of voice and begin talking when he or she asks a question and pauses for an answer. One patient with Wernicke's aphasia made the following responses when asked to name ten common objects:

toothbrush → "stoktery," *cigarette* → "cigarette," *pen* → "tankt," *knife* → "nike," *fork* → "fahk," *quarter* → "minkt," *pen* → "spentee," *matches* → "senktr," *key* → "seek," *comb* → "sahk."

He acted sure of himself and gave no indication that he recognized that most of his responses were meaningless.

Even when patients recognize that something is wrong, they appear unsure of what the problem is. The following quote (Kertesz, 1980) illustrates this puzzlement.

Examiner: Can you tell me a little bit about why you're here?

Patient: I don't know whata wasa down here for me, I just don't know why I wasn't with up here, at all you, it was neva, had it been walked me today ta died.

Examiner: Uh huh. Okay.

Patient: Sine just don't know why, what is really wrong, I don't know, cause I can eaten treffren eatly an everythin like that I'm all right at home.

The patient appears to recognize that she has a problem of some kind, but she is also saying (I think) that at home she can prepare her own meals and otherwise take care of herself.

Karl Wernicke (1874) reported that the aphasia that soon thereafter received his name is produced by damage to the posterior portion of the superior temporal gyrus, now called ***Wernicke's area.*** Subsequent studies, including recent ones using CAT scans, have proved him correct (Kertesz, 1979; Damasio, 1981). Because the superior temporal gyrus is a region of auditory association cortex, and because a comprehension deficit is so prominent in Wernicke's aphasia, this disorder has been characterized as a *receptive* aphasia. Some investigators have suggested that the primary function of Wernicke's area is to store memories of the sequences of sounds that constitute words, and to recognize these sequences when they are heard. Thus, the cortex of the superior temporal gyrus recognizes the sounds of words, just as the cortex of the inferior temporal gyrus recognizes the sight of objects. (See **Figure 16.2.**)

Of course, Wernicke's area must do more than perform auditory analyses. After all, people with Wernicke's aphasia have a speech production deficit as well as a speech comprehension deficit. Wernicke believed (and many modern investigators continue to believe) that the superior temporal gyrus is necessary for the formation of a particular class of memories: auditory "images" of words. For example, if a person is asked to say the name of an object, perception of the object evokes neural activity in Wernicke's area that corresponds to the sequence of sounds that constitutes the appropriate word. This neural pattern is transmitted to motor systems in the frontal lobe, which eventually cause movements of the muscles that produce speech. If Wernicke's area is damaged, people will be unable to comprehend words spoken to them, and when they try to produce their

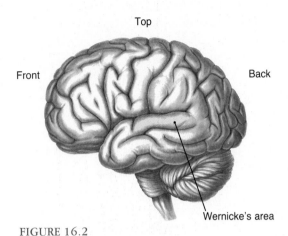

Top

Front

Back

Wernicke's area

FIGURE 16.2

The location of Wernicke's area in the left posterior superior temporal lobe.

own, the lack of adequate auditory patterns will prevent them from producing meaningful speech. (See **Figure 16.3.**)

Wernicke's area must do even more than this. As we saw in Chapter 6, damage to the inferior temporal lobe produces visual agnosia: people are not able to recognize common objects by sight, even though they can perceive fine visual details. But they are aware of their deficit; people with visual agnosia recognize that their visual perception is faulty. The fact that damage to the visual and auditory association areas of cortex produce such different effects suggests that Wernicke's area plays a special role in thinking as well as in listening and talking.

Pure Word Deafness: Auditory Disconnection of Wernicke's Area

The special role of Wernicke's area in the production of speech is demonstrated by another syndrome: ***pure word deafness.*** The term for this disorder is apt; people with pure word deafness have a pure disorder, uncontaminated by other problems. Although they are not deaf, they cannot understand speech. As

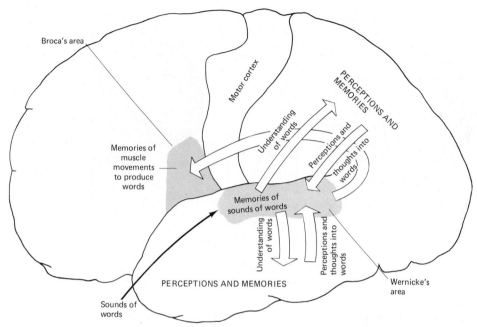

FIGURE 16.3
The role of Wernicke's area.

one patient put it, "I can hear you talking, I just can't understand what you're saying." They can detect sounds, and they respond appropriately to nonspeech sounds such as the barking of a dog, the sound of a doorbell, the chirping of a bird, and so on. More significantly, their own speech is excellent.

Pure word deafness is produced by *bilateral* destruction of the primary auditory cortex or by lesions deep in the left temporal lobe that destroy fibers that connect Wernicke's area with both the left and right primary auditory cortex (Coslett, Brashear, and Heilman, 1984). (See **Figure 16.4.**) Wernicke's area is not damaged, which accounts for the patients' ability to produce normal speech. In addition, they can read and write normally, and they often ask people to communicate with them by writing.

Although some people do not classify pure word deafness as one of the aphasias, this disorder illustrates the importance of Wer-

nicke's area in the acoustical analysis of words. It also provides an excellent example of a ***disconnection syndrome.*** Verbal behavior consists of many related skills: perceiving a word, understanding its meaning, thinking of a particular word to express a concept, pronouncing a word, and so on. Although no area of the brain stands in isolation, different regions perform different functions, receiving information from some areas, analyzing this information, and passing on the results of the analysis to other areas. If a particular input is destroyed, the area is said to be disconnected from the source of that input, and it obviously can no longer analyze the information normally received by this pathway. Brain damage that produces pure word deafness deprives Wernicke's area of auditory information and thus abolishes the patient's ability to understand spoken words. However, the person can still perform other verbal functions. For example, because the lesion does not disrupt

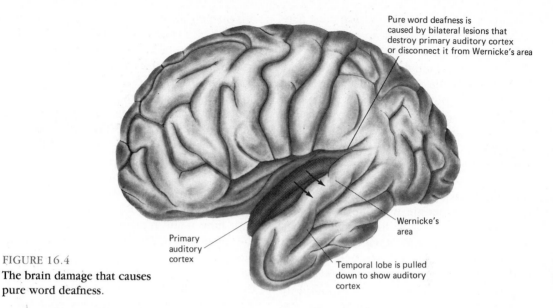

Pure word deafness is caused by bilateral lesions that destroy primary auditory cortex or disconnect it from Wernicke's area

Wernicke's area

Temporal lobe is pulled down to show auditory cortex

Primary auditory cortex

FIGURE 16.4

The brain damage that causes pure word deafness.

visual input to Wernicke's area or output from Wernicke's area to motor mechanisms in the frontal lobe, the person can read or can look at an object and say its name. (See **Figure 16.5.**)

Broca's Aphasia: Speech Production

Unlike Wernicke's aphasia, ***Broca's aphasia*** is characterized by slow, laborious, and nonfluent speech. When trying to converse with

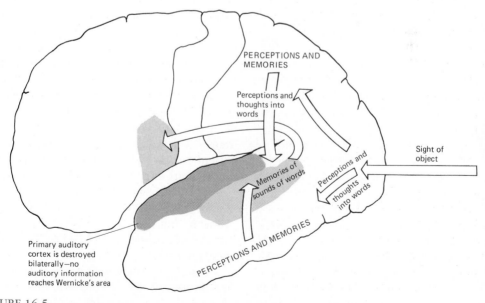

PERCEPTIONS AND MEMORIES

Perceptions and thoughts into words

Memories of sounds of words

Perceptions and thoughts into words

Sight of object

PERCEPTIONS AND MEMORIES

Primary auditory cortex is destroyed bilaterally—no auditory information reaches Wernicke's area

FIGURE 16.5

The basis of object naming by patients with pure word deafness.

patients who have Broca's aphasia, most people find it hard not to try to help them by supplying the words they are obviously groping for. But although they often mispronounce words, the ones they manage to come out with are meaningful. As we saw, the speech of people with Wernicke's aphasia is full of the little words with grammatical meaning, such as *a, the, some, in,* or *about.* These words — called *function words,* because they have an important grammatical function — are almost completely absent in the speech of people with Broca's aphasia. Conversely, the words that convey meaning — called *content words,* for obvious reasons — are sparse in the speech of people with Wernicke's aphasia but rich in the speech of Broca's aphasics. Here is a sample of speech from a man with Broca's aphasia, who is telling the examiner why he has come to the hospital. The dots indicate long pauses.

Ah . . . Monday . . . ah Dad and Paul [patient's name] . . . and Dad . . . hospital. Two . . . ah doctors . . . , and ah . . . thirty minutes . . . and yes . . . ah . . . hospital. And, er Wednesday . . . nine o'clock. And er Thursday, ten o' clock . . . doctors. Two doctors . . . and ah . . . teeth. Yeah, . . . , fine. (Goodglass, 1976, p. 278)

People with Broca's aphasia can comprehend speech much better than they can produce it. In fact, some observers have said that their comprehension is unimpaired, but, as we will see, this is not quite true. Broca (1861) suggested that this form of aphasia is produced by a lesion of the frontal cortex, just anterior to the face region of the primary motor cortex. Subsequent research proved him to be essentially correct, and we now call the region *Broca's area.* Lesions that produce Broca's aphasia are certainly centered in this location, although investigators disagree about how large the lesion must be, and whether a purely cortical lesion will produce

this speech disorder (Kertesz, 1979; Damasio, 1981). (Look back at **Figure 16.3.**)

Wernicke (1874) suggested (and many modern investigators concur) that Broca's area contains memories for the sequences of muscular movements that are needed to articulate words. For example, consider your ability to say the word *ball.* You take a breath, press your lips together, begin expelling air through your vocal cords, and simultaneously open your lips, letting out a small puff of air, forming the sound of the *b.* Your tongue begins in a relaxed position in the middle of your mouth and remains there as you make the vowel sound. Then the end of your tongue moves up and touches the roof of your mouth behind your teeth, remains for a while, and then falls back, forming the sound of the *l.* The word completed, you relax your vocal cords and stop exhaling. (Try saying the word as you read this description again.) Obviously, circuits of neurons somewhere in your brain represent this pattern and, when properly activated, will cause the sequence of movements to be executed. Because damage to the inferior caudal left frontal lobe (including Broca's area) disrupts the ability to articulate words, this region is the most likely candidate for the location of these "programs."

However, the story is not that simple. Most modern investigators believe that although damage limited to Broca's area may produce a transient deficit in speech production, a persistent disorder occurs only when surrounding regions of cortex, as well as subcortical areas beneath Broca's area, are also damaged (Mohr, Pessin, Finkelstein, Funkenstein, Duncan, and Davis, 1978). The location of the critical lesion is still controversial (Levine and Sweet, 1983).

In general, three major speech deficits are produced by lesions in and around Broca's area: agrammatism, anomia, and articulation difficulties. Although all patients with Broca's aphasia will have all of these deficits to some degree, their severity can vary considerably from person to person. Perhaps clinical/anatomical studies will eventually reveal the relation between brain damage and the appearance of each of these symptoms.

Agrammatism refers to a patient's difficulty using grammatical constructions. As we saw, people with Broca's aphasia rarely use function words. In addition, they rarely use grammatical markers such as *-ed* or auxiliaries such as *have* (as in *I have gone*). For some reason, they *do* often use *-ing,* perhaps because this ending converts a verb into a noun. A study by Saffran, Schwartz, and Marin (1980) illustrates this difficulty. The following quotations are from agrammatic patients attempting to describe pictures:

Picture of a boy being hit in the head by a baseball:

Boy is hurting to it.
The boy is catch . . . the boy is hitch . . . the boy is hit the ball. (p. 229)

Picture of a boy giving a valentine to a girl:

The boy and a valentine and a girl . . . boy . . . the boy put the valentine into this girl. (p. 235)

Picture of a girl giving flowers to her teacher:

Girl . . . wants to . . . flowers . . . flowers and wants to . . . . The woman . . . wants to . . . . The girl wants to . . . the flowers and the woman. (p. 234)

The second major speech deficit seen in Broca's aphasia is *anomia* ("without name"). Anomia refers to a word-finding difficulty, and because all aphasics omit words or use inappropriate ones, anomia is actually a primary symptom of *all* forms of aphasia.

However, because their speech lacks fluency, the anomia of Broca's aphasics is especially apparent; their facial expression and frequent use of sounds like "uh" make it obvious that they are groping for the correct words. In contrast, people with Wernicke's aphasia seldom pause in their speech and appear satisfied with their utterances; thus their anomia is less apparent. (As we will see, there is also a category of patients with a fluent anomic aphasia quite different from the Wernicke type.)

The third major characteristic of Broca's aphasia is *difficulty with articulation.* Patients mispronounce words, often altering the sequence of sounds. For example, *lipstick* might be pronounced "likstip." Unlike Wernicke's aphasics, people with Broca's aphasia recognize that their pronunciation is erroneous, and they usually try to correct it. Articulation difficulties are often accompanied by *oral apraxia.* As we saw in Chapter 8, apraxia ("without action") is an inability to perform purposive movements that is not caused by simple perceptual or motor disturbances. A person with oral apraxia has difficulty making specific movements with the lips and tongue on command or has difficulty imitating oral movements made by the examiner. For example, when asked to stick out the tongue, the person may open the mouth and make nodding movements with the head or make pursing movements with the lips. However, when eating sticky food, the same person sticks out the tongue to lick the lips; thus, the deficit is not simply in the motor neurons that control the muscles of the tongue.

As I said, these three deficits are seen in various combinations in different patients, depending on the exact location of the lesion, and, to a certain extent, on their stage of recovery. Although the anatomical correlates are not yet worked out, we can characterize these deficits hierarchically. On the lowest, most elementary level is control of the sequence of movements of the muscles of speech. The next higher level is selection of the particular ''programs'' for individual words. Finally, the highest level is selection of grammatical structure, including word order, use of function words, and word endings. Presumably, the control of articulation involves the face area of the primary motor cortex and portions of the basal ganglia, while the selection of words, word order, and grammatical markers involves Broca's area and other regions of the frontal association cortex. (See **Figure 16.6.**)

So far, I have described Broca's aphasia as a disorder in speech production. In an ordinary conversation, Broca's aphasics seem to understand everything that is said to them. They appear to be irritated and annoyed by their inability to express their thoughts well, and they often make gestures to supplement their scanty speech. The marked disparity between their speech and their comprehension often leads people to assume that their comprehension is normal. But it is not. Schwartz, Saffran, and Marin (1980) showed Broca's aphasics pairs of pictures in which agents and objects of the action were reversed: for example, a horse kicking a cow and a cow kicking a horse, a truck pulling a car and a car pulling a truck, and a dancer applauding a clown and a clown applauding a dancer. As they showed each pair of pictures, they read the subject a sentence: for example, *The horse kicks the cow*. The subject's task was to point to the appropriate picture, indicating whether they understood the grammatical construction of the sentence. On the average, they scored 62 percent correct, which is only slightly above chance.

The correct picture in the study by Schwartz and her colleagues was specified by a particular aspect of grammar: word order. In the active construction *(The horse kicks the cow)* the agent comes first, the object second. In the passive construction *(The cow is kicked by the horse)* the agent-object order is reversed. The agrammatism that accompanies Broca's aphasia appears to disrupt patients' ability to use grammatical information, including word order, to decode the meaning of a sentence. Thus, their deficit in comprehension parallels their deficit in production. Other experiments have shown that people with Broca's aphasia have difficulty carrying out a sequence of commands such as ''Pick up the red circle and touch the green square with it'' (Boller and Dennis, 1979). This finding, along with the other symptoms I have de-

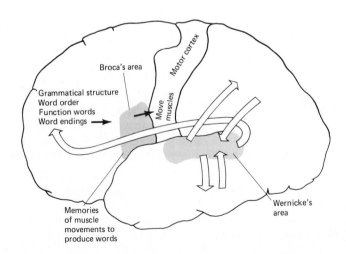

FIGURE 16.6
The hierarchical control of speech.

scribed in this section, suggests that an important function of the left frontal lobe is sequencing—of movements of the muscles of speech (producing words) and of words (comprehending and producing grammatical speech).

Conduction Aphasia: Another Disconnection Syndrome

Wernicke (1874) predicted that if a lesion in the inferior parietal lobe were to interrupt the flow of information from the auditory association cortex of the superior temporal gyrus to the speech production area in the inferior frontal lobe (that is, disconnect Wernicke's area from Broca's area), then the person should not be able to repeat speech. However, if the temporal lobe was intact he or she should be able to comprehend speech, and if the frontal lobe was intact he or she should be able to produce fluent spontaneous speech. Subsequent observations proved Wernicke to be correct; *conduction aphasia* is produced by damage to the inferior parietal lobe that disrupts subcortical white matter, including axons that connect Wernicke's area with Broca's area (Damasio and Damasio, 1980). (See **Figure 16.7**.)

Conduction aphasia is characterized by meaningful (but often paraphasic) fluent speech, relatively good comprehension, but very poor repetition. For example, patient L.B. (observed by Margolin and Walker, 1981) was able to answer the examiners' questions quite fluently, with occasional word-finding difficulties and paraphasias. For example, when asked about his employer, he said, "There was five boys owned a . . . start . . . er . . . had trucks." Apparently, he could not think of an appropriate phrase such as "trucking firm." But errors like this were not frequent; usually, he simply paused for a second or two, as if seeking the correct word, and then continued, having

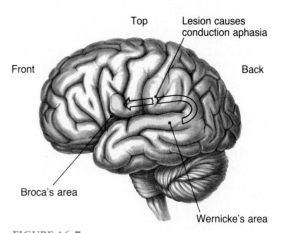

Top   Lesion causes conduction aphasia

Front   Back

Broca's area

Wernicke's area

FIGURE 16.7
A lesion that interrupts direct communication between Wernicke's area and Broca's area causes conduction aphasia.

successfully found it. If the conversation had been overheard by people not familiar with the speech of aphasics, they would be unlikely to notice anything amiss in either his comprehension or his production. At the most, they might suspect the man was slightly hard of hearing, because occasionally he asked the examiner to repeat a question.

But let us see how patient L.B. performed when he was asked to repeat words.

Examiner: bicycle

Patient: bicycle

Examiner: hippopotamus

Patient: hippopotamus

Examiner: blaynge

Patient: I didn't get it.

Examiner: Okay, some of these won't be real words, they'll just be sounds. Blaynge.

Patient: I'm not . . .

Examiner: blanch

Patient: blanch

Examiner: north

Patient: north

Examiner: rilld

Patient: Nope, I can't say.

You will notice that the patient can repeat individual words (all nouns, in this case) but utterly fails to repeat nonwords. Now let us see how he does when he is given three-word sequences.

Examiner: Up and down.

Patient: Up and down.

Examiner: look, car, house

Patient: I didn't get it.

Examiner: Save your money.

Patient: Save your money.

Examiner: yellow, big, south

Patient: yellen . . . Can't get it.

Examiner: They ran away.

Patient: They ran away.

Examiner: look, catch, sell

Patient: like . . . [shakes head, laughs] . . . That's the trouble!

So the patient could repeat single words but not nonwords and could repeat meaningful three-word phrases but not three unrelated words. The important distinction seems to be *meaning.* People with conduction aphasia can repeat speech sounds they hear only if these sounds have meaning. Geschwind (1965) suggests that when people with severe conduction aphasia repeat words, they do so by alternative routes. For example, when the examiner said "bicycle," patient L.B. presumably perceived and understood the word and pictured a bicycle. The information was sent through cortical association fibers from the visual association cortex to Broca's area, where it initiated the appropriate sequence of sounds. When the examiner said "blaynge," the patient could not picture anything, and hence meaningful information could not be sent to Broca's area. This roundabout route appears to be inefficient; it cannot accommodate three unrelated words, although it can accommodate three words that express meaning. (See **Figure 16.8**.)

Geschwind notes that some patients cannot even reliably repeat single words. They may correctly repeat a concrete noun, such as *chair,* but sometimes supply a synonym: for example, saying "car" when they hear "automobile." If the patient repeats the word by

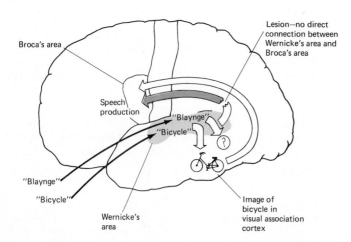

FIGURE 16.8

A patient with conduction aphasia could repeat *bicycle* but not *blaynge.*

describing the image evoked by the word *automobile,* the response "car" is obviously appropriate. Some data support this explanation. People with severe conduction aphasia have much more difficulty repeating abstract words, such as *apparently.* In contrast to concrete words, abstract words do not represent objects or actions that can easily be imagined, and thus they cannot easily be repeated. Geschwind further notes that patients with severe conduction aphasia can repeat numbers better than words. In this case, they may be imagining a somatosensory/kinesthetic "image," such as holding up four fingers when they hear the number *four.* (Children usually learn to count on their fingers.) The route in this case would be from Wernicke's area to somatosensory areas to Broca's area, leading to articulation.

Anomic Aphasia: Memory of Words

As I already noted, anomia, in one form or other, is a hallmark of aphasia. However, one category of aphasia consists of almost pure anomia, the other symptoms being inconsequential. Speech of patients with pure anomia is fluent and grammatical, and their comprehension is excellent, but they have difficulty finding the appropriate words. They often employ *circumlocutions* (literally, "to speak in a roundabout way") to get around missing words. For example, the following quote is from a patient that some colleagues and I studied (Margolin, Marcel, and Carlson, 1985). We asked her to describe the picture shown in **Figure 16.9.** Her pauses, which are marked with three dots, indicate word-finding difficulties. In some cases, when she could not find a word, she supplied a definition instead or went off on a new track. I have added the words in brackets that I think she intended to use.

Examiner: Tell us about that picture.

Patient: It's a woman who has two children, a son and a daughter, and her son is to get into the . . . cupboard in the kitchen to get out *[take]* some . . . cookies out of the *[cookie jar]* . . . that she possibly had made, and consequently he's slipping *[falling]* . . . the wrong direction *[backward]* . . . on the . . . what he's standing on *[stool]*, heading to the . . . the cupboard *[floor]* and if he falls backwards he could

FIGURE 16.9

The drawing of the kitchen story, part of the Boston Diagnostic Aphasia Test. (From Goodglass, H., and Kaplan, E. *The Assessment of Aphasia and Related Disorders.* Philadelphia: Lea & Febiger, 1972.)

have some problems *[get hurt]*, because that *[the stool]* is off balance.

The patient's anomia was most obvious when we asked her to name pictures of common objects. On one occasion, she correctly named only fourteen of a list of fifty of them. Here is her attempt to name a picture of a carpenter's saw. Note that she tried to remember the word by starting sentences that would use it. She almost, but not quite, got the word. Clearly, she knows what the object is, so her deficit is not one of perception or comprehension.

Patient: I know what it is. I can't tell you—maybe I can. If I was to carry the wood and cut it in half with that . . . you know, if I had to cut the wood down and bring it in . . .

Examiner: You'd use one of these?

Patient: It's called a . . . I have 'em in the garage. They are your . . . You cut the wood with them . . . it . . . sah! . . . ah . . . Ss . . . sahbing . . . sah . . . I can't say it. I know what it is and I can cut the wood with it and it's in my garage. . . .

Anomia has been characterized as a partial amnesia for words. It can be produced by both anterior and posterior lesions (that is, lesions that include Broca's area or Wernicke's area), but only posterior lesions produce a *fluent* anomia. Little is known about the location of lesions that produce anomia without the other symptoms of aphasia, such as comprehension deficits, agrammatism, or difficulties in articulation. Obviously, when we !earn more about the anatomy of pure anomia, we will know more about the anatomy of verbal memories.

Transcortical Sensory Aphasia: Speech without Comprehension

As we have seen, the superior temporal gyrus, the caudal inferior frontal lobe, and their interconnections through the inferior parietal lobe play a special role in language comprehension and production. They are necessary for recognition of spoken words, comprehension and production of grammatical structure, and articulation of words. But these regions cannot function in isolation. Recognition of words is one thing; comprehension is another. Similarly, articulation of words is one thing; having something to say is another. The functions of the verbal areas of the brain that I have described so far deal with perception and complex motor sequences, not with meaning.

Words refer to objects, actions, or relations in the world. Their meaning depends on the existence of memories other than knowing how they sound or how to say them. We know what the word *tree* means because we can imagine what trees look like, what the wind sounds like blowing through their leaves, what the bark feels like, and so on. We also have learned facts about them: for example, about their roots, buds, flowers, nuts, and the chlorophyll in their leaves. These memories are not stored in the primary speech areas but in other parts of the brain, especially regions of association cortex. Obviously, the ability of the sound of the word *tree* to evoke these memories depends on connections between circuits in the superior temporal lobe and circuits in other parts of the brain. Similarly, the ability of a thought to evoke an utterance also depends on these connections, but in reverse: the sight (or thought) of a tree activates the appropriate pattern of activity in the speech areas, resulting in articulation of the proper word.

A syndrome called **transcortical sensory aphasia** occurs when the speech areas are disconnected from the posterior association cortex (Kertesz, 1979). (Some investigators do not distinguish between this disorder and **isolation aphasia,** which includes disconnection of the speech areas from the prefrontal association cortex as well.) Patients with transcortical sensory aphasia (or isolation aphasia) cannot comprehend speech, do not answer questions, and produce no spontaneous speech of their own. However, they can repeat what they hear; thus, their disorder is the opposite of conduction aphasia. A classic case of this disorder was reported by Geschwind, Quadfasel, and Segarra (1968). A woman sustained brain damage after inhaling carbon monoxide from a faulty water heater. The lesion bordered the primary speech areas and their interconnections, isolating them from the surrounding cortex. (See **Figure 16.10.**)

The woman spent several years in the hospital before she died, without ever saying anything meaningful on her own. She did not follow verbal commands or otherwise give signs of understanding them. However, she often repeated what was said to her. The repetition was not parrotlike; she did not imitate accents different from her own, and she sometimes corrected ungrammatical constructions. Often she did not simply repeat words but continued a sequence they started. For example, when an examiner said "Roses are red, violets are blue," she continued with

"Sugar is sweet and so are you." She could sing and would do so when someone started singing a song she knew. She even learned new songs from the radio while in the hospital. Remember, she gave no signs of understanding anything she heard or said. Her case suggests that the brain mechanisms needed to perceive and recognize words, to learn and remember sequences of words, and to articulate them are different from the brain mechanisms needed to understand the meaning of words.

Obviously, the speech mechanisms of the brain are at the service of other regions, which contain neural circuits that analyze and organize sensory information and integrate this information with what has already been learned. This relation can be appreciated even more clearly by considering the effects of lesions that damage specific parts of the posterior association cortex. I met a patient who had recently had a stroke that damaged a part of her parietal lobe that played a role in spatial perception. She was alert and intelligent and showed no signs of aphasia. However, she was confused about directions and other spatial relations. When asked to,

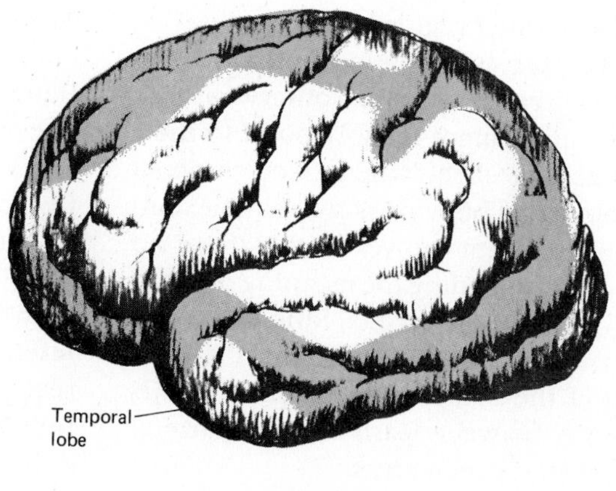

FIGURE 16.10
Brain damage (shaded area) produced by inhalation of carbon monoxide in the patient, reported by Geschwind, N., Quadfasel, F.A., and Segarra, J.M. *Neuropsychologia,* 1968, *13,* 229–235.

Dorsal

Rostral

Caudal

Temporal lobe

Ventral

she could point to the ceiling and the floor, but she could not say which was *over* the other. Her perception of other people appeared to be entirely normal, but she could not say whether a person's head was at the *top* or *bottom* of the body.

I wrote a set of multiple-choice questions to test her ability to use words denoting spatial relations. The results of the test indicated that she did not know the meaning of words such as *up, down,* or *under* when they referred to spatial relations, but she could use these words normally when they referred to nonspatial relations. For example, here are some of her incorrect responses when the words referred to spatial relations:

A tree's branches are *under* its roots.

The sky is *down.*

The ceiling is *under* the floor.

She made only ten correct responses on the sixteen-item test. In contrast, she got all eight items correct when the words referred to nonspatial relations like the following:

After exchanging pleasantries they got *down* to business.

He got sick and threw *up.*

Damage to other regions of the parietal association cortex can produce an inability to name body parts. People who otherwise converse normally cannot reliably point to their elbow, knee, or cheek when asked to do so and cannot name body parts when the examiner points to them. However, they have no difficulty understanding the meaning of other words. Given that the parietal lobes deal with somatosensation, it makes sense that the meaning of the names of body parts entails connections between parts of the parietal cortex and the speech areas.

The picture I have drawn so far suggests

that comprehension of speech includes a flow of information from Wernicke's area to the surrounding regions of association cortex, and that production of spontaneous speech includes the same connections, operating in reverse. This model is certainly an oversimplification, but it is a useful starting point in conceptualizing basic mental processes. For example, we can conceive of complex mental activity that includes "thinking in words" in terms of coordinated two-way communication between the speech areas and surrounding association cortex (and subcortical regions such as the hippocampus and amygdala, of course).

Transcortical Motor Aphasia: The Impetus for Speech

The final aphasic disorder, ***transcortical motor aphasia,*** is characterized by good comprehension, good repetition, but very little speech output. The patients just do not say much. They also exhibit anomia, doing poorly when asked to name common objects. The disorder is caused by frontal lesions that do not involve Broca's speech area but that damage the **supplementary motor area** in the superior frontal lobe or the connections between this region and Broca's area (Damasio, 1981; Freedman, Alexander, and Naeser, 1984). (See **Figure 16.11.**) To keep from confusing transcortical *sensory* aphasia with transcortical *motor* aphasia, remember that one involves a lesion in the posterior (sensory) cortex, and the other involves a lesion in the frontal (motor) cortex.

Little is known about the functions of the supplementary motor area. Because patients with transcortical motor aphasia appear indifferent and do not try to communicate the way that patients with Broca's aphasia do, some investigators have stressed its importance in *volition.* However, attributing a disorder to a deficit in "will power" certainly does not ex-

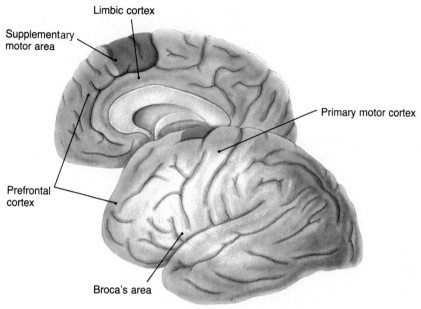

FIGURE 16.11

Damage to the left supplementary motor area in the superior frontal lobe causes transcortical motor aphasia.

plain it. In fact, we know less about the functions of the frontal lobes than we do about any other part of the brain. We know that the frontal lobes are involved in planning strategies as well as sequences of motor movement, but we cannot say much more than that.

Prosodic Disorders

When we speak, we do not merely utter words. Our speech has a regular rhythm and cadence, we give some words stress (that is, pronounce them louder), and we vary the pitch of our voice to indicate phrasing and to distinguish between assertions and questions. In addition, we can impart information about our emotional state through the rhythm, emphasis, and tone of our speech. These rhythmic, emphatic, and melodic aspects of speech are referred to as *prosody*. The importance of these aspects of speech is illustrated by our use of punctuation symbols to indicate some elements of prosody when we write. For example, a comma indicates a short pause, a period indicates a longer one with an accompanying fall in the pitch of the voice, a question mark indicates a pause and a rise in the pitch of the voice, an exclamation mark indicates that the words are articulated with special emphasis, and so on.

The prosody of people with fluent aphasias, caused by posterior lesions, sounds normal. Their speech is rhythmical, pausing after phrases and sentences, and has a melodic line. Even when the speech of a person with severe Wernicke's aphasia makes no sense, the prosody sounds normal. As Goodglass and Kaplan (1972) note, a person with Wernicke's aphasia may "sound like a normal speaker at a distance, because of his fluency and normal melodic contour of his speech." (Up close, of course, we hear the speech clearly enough to realize that it is meaningless.) In contrast, just as the lesions that produce Broca's aphasia destroy grammar, they also severely disrupt prosody. In patients with Broca's aphasia, articulation is so labored and words are uttered so slowly that there is little opportunity for the patient to demonstrate any rhythmic elements, and because of the relative lack of function words, there is little variation in stress or pitch of voice.

Evidence from studies of normal people and patients with brain lesions suggests that prosody is a special function of the right hemisphere. This function is undoubtedly related to the more general role of this hemisphere in musical skills and the expression and recognition of emotions; production of prosody is rather like singing, and prosody often serves as a vehicle for conveying emotion.

Weintraub, Mesulam, and Kramer (1981) tested the ability of patients with right-hemisphere damage to recognize and express prosodic elements of speech. In one experiment they showed their subjects two pictures, named one of them, and asked them to point to the appropriate one. For example, they showed them a picture of a greenhouse and a house that was painted green. In speech we distinguish between *greenhouse* and *green house* by stress: *GREEN house* means the former and *GREEN HOUSE* (syllables equally stressed) means the latter. In a second experiment Weintraub and her colleagues tested the subjects' ability simply to detect differences in prosody. They presented pairs of sentences and asked the subjects whether they were the same or different. The pairs of sentences either were identical or differed in terms of intonation (for example, *Margo plays the piano?* and *Margo plays the piano*) or location of stress (for example, *STEVE drives the car* and *Steve drives the CAR*). The patients with right-hemisphere lesions (but not control subjects) performed poorly on both of these tasks. Thus, they showed a deficit in prosodic comprehension.

To test production, the investigators presented two written sentences and asked a question about them. For example, they presented the following pair:

The man walked to the grocery store.

The woman rode to the shoe store.

The subjects were instructed to answer questions by reading one of the sentences. Try this one yourself. Read the question below and then read aloud the sentence (above) that answers it.

Who walked to the grocery store, the man or the woman?

The question asserts that someone walked to the grocery store but asks who that person was. When answering a question like this, people normally stress the requested item of information — in this case, *man*. However, Weintraub and her colleagues found that although patients with right-hemisphere brain damage chose the correct sentence, they either failed to stress a word or stressed the wrong one. Thus, the right hemisphere plays a role in production as well as perception of prosody.

Ross (1981) described several cases of ***aprosodias*** — disturbances in comprehension and production of prosody, caused by brain damage. He suggested that comprehension and production are posterior and frontal functions, respectively, and claimed that the disorders he saw were parallel to the speech disturbances caused by left-hemisphere damage. For example, he identified cases of *motor aprosodia, sensory aprosodia,* and *transcortical sensory aprosodia.* Because his testing used material with emotional content, I will describe his results in more detail when I describe expression and comprehension of emotion, in the last section of this chapter.

INTERIM SUMMARY

INTERIM SUMMARY

Two regions of the brain are especially important in understanding and producing speech. Wernicke's area, in the posterior superior temporal lobe, is involved with speech perception and is necessary for the production of meaningful speech. Broca's area, in the frontal lobe just rostral to the region of the primary motor cortex that controls the muscles of speech, is involved with speech production. Presumably, Wernicke's area contains memories of the sounds of words, each of which is connected with memories about the properties of the things the words denote, and Broca's area contains memories of the sequences of muscular movements that produce words, each of which is connected with its auditory counterparts in the posterior part of the brain. Disconnection syndromes, such as pure word deafness and conduction aphasia, can occur when connections between various components of the mechanisms devoted to language are damaged.

Prosody includes changes in intonation, rhythm, and stress that add meaning, especially emotional meaning, to the sentences that we speak. The neural mechanisms that control the prosodic elements of speech appear to be in the right hemisphere.

Because so many terms and symptoms were described in this section, I have provided a table that summarizes them. (See **Table 16.1.**)

■ READING AND WRITING DISORDERS

Relation to Aphasia

With few exceptions, the reading and writing skills of people with aphasia are similar to their speaking and comprehending abilities. For example, patients with Wernicke's aphasia have as much difficulty reading and writing as they do speaking and understanding speech. Patients with Broca's aphasia comprehend what they read about as well as they can understand speech, but their reading aloud is poor, of course. If their speech is agrammatical, so is their writing, and to the extent that they fail to comprehend grammar when listening to speech, they fail to do so when reading. Patients with conduction aphasia generally have some difficulty reading, and when they read aloud they often make semantic paraphasias (saying synonyms for some of the words they read), just as they do when attempting to repeat what they hear. Depending on the location of the lesion, some patients with transcortical sensory aphasia may read aloud accurately but fail to comprehend what they read.

Alexia with Agraphia

Some reading and writing difficulties are not accompanied by aphasia. For example, *alexia with agraphia* includes the inability to read (alexia) or write (agraphia). Most cases of alexia with agraphia are caused by damage to the left *angular gyrus,* a region of the parietal lobe behind the end of the lateral fissure (Dejerine, 1891; Benson and Geschwind, 1969). A fluent anomia is often associated with this syndrome. Some investigators believe that the angular gyrus, which receives visual, auditory, and somatosensory input, plays a special role in the integration of polysensory information, including that which is necessary to read and write. (See **Figure 16.12.**) Because I describe the varieties of reading disorders in the remainder of this section, I will say no more here.

Pure Alexia

Dejerine (1892) described a remarkable syndrome, which we now call *pure alexia* (or sometimes *pure word blindness* or *alexia without agraphia*). His patient had a lesion in the left occipital lobe and the posterior end of the corpus callosum. The patient lost the ability to read, but he could still write. In fact, if he was shown some of his own writing, he could not read it.

TABLE 16.1   Aphasia syndromes produced by strokes

	Area of Lesion	Spontaneous Speech	Comprehension	Repetition	Naming	Reading Comprehension	Writing
Wernicke's aphasia	Posterior portion of superior temporal gyrus (Wernicke's area)	Fluent	Poor	Poor	Poor	Poor	Poor
Pure word deafness	Both primary auditory cortices, or connection between them and Wernicke's area	Fluent	Poor	Poor	Good	Good	Good
Broca's aphasia	Frontal cortex rostral to base of primary motor cortex (Broca's area)	Nonfluent	Good	Poor[a]	Poor	Good	Poor
Global aphasia	Broca's area and Wernicke's area	Nonfluent	Poor	Poor	Poor	Poor	Poor
Conduction aphasia	Area of parietal lobe superior to lateral fissure	Fluent	Good	Poor	Good	Good to poor	Good
Anomic aphasia	Various parts of parietal or temporal lobes	Fluent	Good	Good	Poor	Good to poor	Good to poor
Transcortical sensory aphasia	Connections between speech areas and posterior association cortex	Nonfluent or even absent	Poor	Good	Poor	Poor[b]	Poor
Transcortical motor aphasia	Supplementary motor area	Nonfluent	Good	Good	Poor	Good	Poor

[a] May be better than spontaneous speech.
[b] Patient may be able to read words without comprehending them.

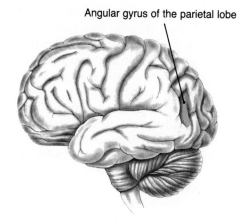

Angular gyrus of the parietal lobe

FIGURE 16.12

Damage to the left angular gyrus causes alexia with agraphia.

Although patients with pure alexia cannot read, they can recognize words that are spelled aloud to them. Pure alexia is obviously a perceptual disorder; you will no doubt recognize its similarity to pure word deafness. It is caused by lesions that disconnect the angular gyrus from all visual input (Damasio and Damasio, 1983). Figure 16.13 shows a diagram of the brain damage of Dejerine's original patient. Notice how the two lesions disrupt the path of visual information from both the right and the left visual cortex. The occipital lobe lesion produces blindness in the right visual field, and the callosal lesion prevents visual information from reaching the posterior left hemisphere. (See **Figure 16.13.**)

Patients with pure alexia can usually recognize objects and supply their names; thus,

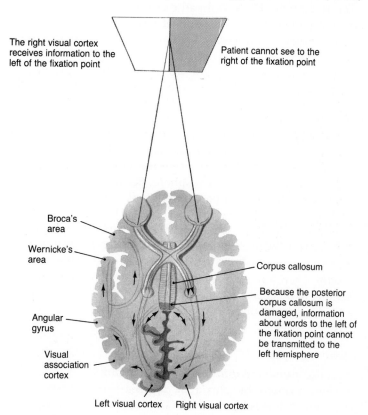

The right visual cortex receives information to the left of the fixation point

Patient cannot see to the right of the fixation point

Broca's area

Wernicke's area

Corpus callosum

Angular gyrus

Because the posterior corpus callosum is damaged, information about words to the left of the fixation point cannot be transmitted to the left hemisphere

Visual association cortex

Left visual cortex   Right visual cortex

FIGURE 16.13

The brain damage in Dejerine's original patient with pure alexia. (Adapted from Geschwind, N., *Scientific American*, 1972, *226*, 76–83.)

they do not have anomia or visual agnosia. You will recall that visual agnosia is caused by bilateral damage to the visual association cortex. (And do not confuse *agnosia* — failure to perceive objects — with *anomia* — failure to be able to name them.) If the damage spares the angular gyrus and does not prevent visual information from reaching there, the person will be able to read but will not be able to perceive common objects visually. Visual object perception appears to be accomplished by the inferior temporal cortex of both hemispheres, whereas reading requires the left angular gyrus.

The ability of patients with pure alexia to name objects that they see suggests that visual information concerning words and visual information concerning objects are transmitted across different parts of the corpus callosum. Let us see why this is so. In all cases of pure alexia, patients have some sort of visual defect in their right visual field, caused by the left occipital lesion. In some cases, the defect is a complete right **homonymous hemianopia** — half-blindness in the same (right) visual field of both eyes. These people cannot see anything presented to the portions of their retinas that send information to the left hemisphere; thus, when they name an object that they see, they are using the visual functions of their right hemisphere. Because naming is a left-hemisphere function, the visual information must cross the corpus callosum somewhere. As we already saw, visual information pertaining to reading is interrupted by a lesion of the posterior corpus callosum. Therefore, the visual information pertaining to objects must travel through a more anterior portion of the corpus callosum. (See **Figure 16.14.**)

Pure Agraphia

Because **pure agraphia** — that is, agraphia unaccompanied by alexia or aphasia — is rare, much less is known about the anatomical basis of writing than about the anatomical basis of reading. Writing depends on knowledge of the words that are to be used, along with the proper grammatical structure of the sentences they are to form. Thus, if a patient is unable to express himself or herself by speech, we should not be surprised to see a writing disturbance as well. Some forms of agraphia are caused by motor disturbances that prevent the person from forming letters well — or drawing pictures or performing other kinds of manual constructional skills. As we saw in Chapter 8, lesions of the left parietal lobe cause apraxia, difficulty in making movements — especially a series of movements — on command. You will not be surprised to learn that these lesions also impair writing skills. I think it would be inaccurate to characterize such a disorder as language related.

Most people first learn the sounds of words, then learn to say them, then learn to read, and then learn to write. Undoubtedly, reading and writing depend heavily on the skills that are learned earlier. For example, in order to write most words, we must be able to "sound them out in our heads," that is, to hear them and to articulate them subvocally. If you try the following experiment, you will appreciate the relation between writing and thinking about the sounds of words.

Try to write a long word that you know how to pronounce but do not write very often — for example, *antidisestablishmentarianism*. Pay attention to how you do it. If you are like me, you will probably find that you conjure up an "auditory image" of the sounds of the individual syllables and then write out the corresponding letters. Now try writing the word again (on a fresh sheet of paper), but this time sing "Happy Birthday" (or any other song you know) as you attempt to write the word. Unless you are much more talented than I am, you will find that you have to write during pauses in the words of the song. How-

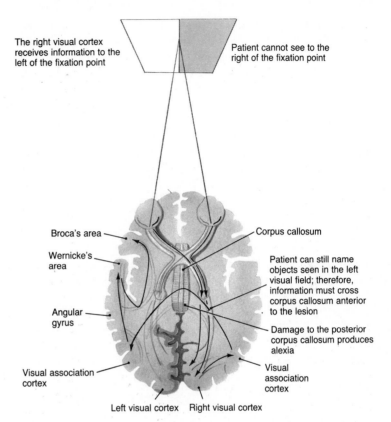

The right visual cortex receives information to the left of the fixation point

Patient cannot see to the right of the fixation point

Broca's area

Wernicke's area

Angular gyrus

Visual association cortex

Left visual cortex   Right visual cortex

Corpus callosum

Patient can still name objects seen in the left visual field; therefore, information must cross corpus callosum anterior to the lesion

Damage to the posterior corpus callosum produces alexia

Visual association cortex

FIGURE 16.14
Damage to the posterior corpus callosum impairs interhemispherical transfer of words being read but not of pictures being viewed.

ever, if you try to draw a picture instead of writing a long word, there should be no interference. So try that: draw a picture of a simple house, or anything else, while you sing your song. No problem, right?

I urge you to try these little experiments. They prove that talking and singing do not interfere substantially with complex hand and finger movements themselves; rather, these activities only interfere with hand and finger movements that are producing words different from the ones that are being sung or spoken. Thus, writing and speaking (or singing) appear to draw upon the resources of the same brain mechanisms, whereas picture-drawing and speaking (or singing) do not.

Now try a final experiment. *Copy* the word *antidisestablishmentarianism* (or whatever word you chose), writing it beneath your

first successful attempt. At the same time, sing your song. It was much easier, wasn't it? This experiment suggests that visual information (the sight of the written letters) has direct access to mechanisms that control writing movements, independent of the word's acoustical representation. These conclusions are summarized schematically in **Figure 16.15.**

If our ability to write most words depends upon a transfer of information between memories of sounds (presumably, in the left superior temporal gyrus) and motor movements that represent those sounds, then damage to the auditory association cortex should not impair written symbols that represent *visually* acquired memories. (Remember, you can draw a picture or copy a word while singing; therefore, drawing or copying is at least somewhat independent of acoustical memories.) This situation does indeed seem to be true. The Japanese language makes use of two kinds of written symbols. *Kanji* symbols are pictographs, like Chinese characters. Thus they represent concepts by means of

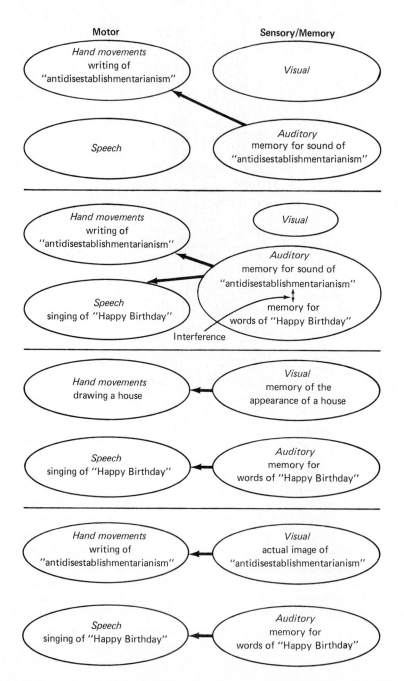

FIGURE 16.15
Conclusions of the "antidis-establishmentarianism"
experiment.

visual symbols but do not provide a guide to their pronunciation. *Kana* symbols are phonetic representations of syllables; thus, they encode acoustical information. Sasanuma (1975) found that lesions of the left temporal lobe in Japanese patients interfered with the writing of *kana* symbols (acoustical), but not *kanji* symbols (visual). In contrast, other brain damage (probably to visual association areas) impaired a patient's ability to write *kanji* symbols, but not *kana* symbols. Thus, Japanese people base their writing on different brain functions, depending on the kinds of symbols they use.

Actually, although I do not have neurological evidence to support my conclusions, I think that even English-speaking people write by more than one means. As we saw, we write most long words by spelling out the sequence of sounds. We probably also learn sequences of letters that spell some words the way we learn poems or the lyrics to a song. For example, many Americans learned to spell *Mississippi* with a singsong chant that goes like this: **M**-i-s-s-**I**-s-s-**I**-p-p-**I**, emphasizing the boldfaced letters. (Similarly, most speakers of English say the alphabet with the rhythm of a nursery song that is commonly used to teach it.) This method involves memorizing sequences of letter names, not translating sounds into the corresponding letters.

A third way of writing entails transcribing an image of what a particular word looks like. Have you ever looked off into the distance to imagine how you should spell a word? Many people find words difficult to spell orally; they have to write them down to see whether they look correct. This method involves visual memories, not acoustical ones. Finally, we probably memorize motor sequences for very familiar words, such as our own names. Most of us need not sound out our names to ourselves when we write our signature, nor need we say the sequence of letters to ourselves, nor need we imagine what our signature looks like.

The fact that at least four plausible means of writing (acoustical, letter sequence, visual, and motor) can reasonably be outlined suggests the difficulty involved in understanding the physiological basis of this behavior. But the effort is interesting and, I think, worthwhile.

Subcategories of Dyslexias: Toward an Understanding of Reading

As we have seen, reading involves the same regions of the brain that are required for comprehension of speech, along with an additional area, the angular gyrus. Of course, because speech comprehension requires other regions of the brain, particularly the association cortex, we would predict that the same is true for reading comprehension as well. Indeed, as we will see, some patients can read aloud but cannot understand what they are saying, just as those with transcortical sensory aphasia can repeat speech without comprehension.

Study of the deficits caused by brain damage has contributed much to our understanding of the ways in which we read. Just as there is no one model that completely accounts for writing, reading can be accomplished by several means. So far, I have used the word *alexia* in this chapter, but from now on I will use *dyslexia* instead. The prefix *a-* means "without," implying absolutely no ability to read, whereas *dys-* means "bad," or "faulty," which describes the deficits more accurately. As you will see, most of the interesting conclusions drawn from the study of dyslexic patients come from what they *can* do. The next several subsections describe some varieties of **acquired dyslexias.** The term *acquired* means that the reading disorders were caused by brain damage after the people had already learned to read. In contrast, **developmental dyslexias** refer to reading difficulties that become apparent when children are learning to read. Developmental dyslexias may indeed involve anomalies in brain circuitry, and they are discussed in a later section.

Spelling Dyslexia

A common form of acquired dyslexia has been called **spelling dyslexia** (Kinsbourne and Warrington, 1962) or **word-form dyslexia** (Warrington and Shallice, 1980). Most patients with pure alexia demonstrate the symptoms described here. Although patients with spelling dyslexia cannot immediately recognize words, they can read them if they are permitted to name the individual letters. Thus, they read slowly, taking more time with longer words. As you might expect, they can identify words that someone else spells aloud, just as they can recognize their own oral spelling.

Warrington and Shallice suggested the term *word-form dyslexia* because they concluded that these patients have a type of perceptual deficit: they are unable to recognize words as a whole. In fact, sometimes the deficit is so severe that patients have difficulty identifying individual letters, in which case they make mistakes in spelling that prevent them from reading test words. For example, a patient studied by Patterson and Kay (1980) was shown the word *men* and said "h, e, n, hen."

Speedie, Rothi, and Heilman (1982) suggest that the letter-by-letter reading exhibited by people with spelling dyslexia is not a normal form of reading, but that it represents a compensatory strategy. Normally, they say, people do not have to say letter names to themselves when they read, even when they read unfamiliar words they must sound out. For example, read the following pronounceable nonwords aloud:

trape   lidrig   slafmet

I doubt whether you have seen them before, but we would probably agree on how they should be pronounced. I suspect you were able to read them quickly, certainly faster than you could say the individual letters to yourself.

Speedie and her colleagues suggest that naming letters is similar to naming objects and other shapes and therefore can be accomplished by the intact right hemisphere. They characterize spelling dyslexia as a disconnection syndrome that is circumvented by an alternative strategy. That is, because the region of the left hemisphere that recognizes word forms (presumably, the angular gyrus) is disconnected from visual input, words cannot be read in the normal fashion. However, the intact right hemisphere recognizes the letters, and the results of the analysis are sent over the corpus callosum to the speech areas, resulting in the patient's saying the names of the letters. The patient then hears the sequence, recognizes the word, and says it. It should also be possible to accomplish this task subvocally, "thinking" rather than overtly articulating the letters. (See **Figure 16.16.**)

Phonological Dyslexia

Patients with **phonological dyslexia** can read most words rather well but have great difficulty reading nonwords such as the ones I just asked you to try to pronounce (Beauvois and Dérouesné, 1979; Dérouesné and Beauvois, 1979). *Phonology* (loosely translated as "laws of sound") refers to the relation between letters and the sounds they represent. Phonological dyslexia provides strong evidence for the existence of two different classes of reading: word-form reading and phonological reading. In word-form reading we apparently perceive the entire shape of the word and immediately recognize it. (In the case of long words, we might instead perceive segments of several letters each.) Phonological reading, which is required for reading nonwords or words we have not yet learned, entails some sort of letter-to-sound

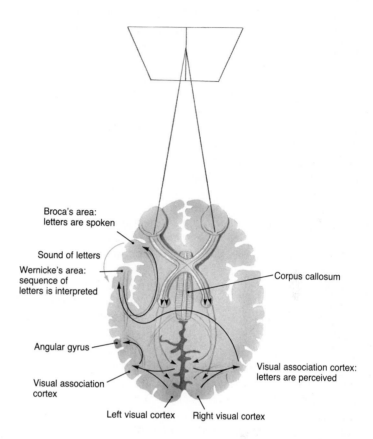

FIGURE 16.16
An explanation of spelling dyslexia.

Broca's area: letters are spoken

Sound of letters

Wernicke's area: sequence of letters is interpreted

Corpus callosum

Angular gyrus

Visual association cortex

Visual association cortex: letters are perceived

Left visual cortex

Right visual cortex

decoding. Obviously, phonological reading of English requires more than decoding of the sounds produced by single letters, because, for example, some sounds are transcribed as two-letter sequences (such as *th* or *sh*) and the addition of the letter *e* to the end of a word lengthens an internal vowel (*can* becomes *cane*).

Some patients with phonological dyslexia have trouble reading function words. They may make substitutions, even when the word they actually say has a quite different meaning—for example, saying "that" for *yet* and "you" for *those*. They also tend to have difficulty with what linguists call **bound morphemes**—inflections and derivational endings, such as *-ed* and *-tion*. However, they do not have trouble reading the root word.

(For example, a patient might read *walked* as "walking" or "walks.") This phenomenon suggests that meaningful content words and bound morphemes are represented by different neural systems. As we saw earlier, patients with Broca's aphasia also have trouble using grammatical features such as these, so the suggestion appears to be a reasonable one.

Because only a few cases of phonological dyslexia have been reported so far, little is known about the anatomical basis of this disorder.

Surface Dyslexia
A third form of reading disorder, **surface dyslexia,** also supports the distinction between phonological and word-form reading (Marshall and Newcombe, 1973; Shallice and

Warrington, 1980). The term *surface* reflects the fact that people with this disorder make errors related to the visual appearance of the words and to pronunciation rules, not to the meaning of the words, which is metaphorically "deeper" than the appearance. I will make this distinction clearer in the next section. In some ways, the reading ability of patients with surface dyslexia is opposite to that of patients with phonological dyslexia. That is, they have no trouble reading nonwords, and indeed they often act as if words are nonwords to them. Linguists classify words as "regularly" and "irregularly" spelled, according to whether they conform to phonological rules they have deduced (such as the "*e* on the end" rule). Regularly spelled words include *table, cane,* and *those,* while irregularly spelled ones include *choir, through,* and *enough.* We can "sound out" regularly spelled words (that is, read them phonologically), but we have to memorize the pronunciation of irregularly spelled words.

A patient with surface dyslexia may read *pint* as "pinnt" or *yacht* as "yatchet." These errors suggest that they have difficulty with word-form reading but not with phonological reading. However, the disorder cannot be explained this easily. Patients sometimes make visual errors—for example, saying "increase" for *incense,* "lift" for *life,* or "gorge" for *gauge.* Thus, it seems likely that surface dyslexia entails some sort of perceptual deficit. Whether a single perceptual deficit accounts for difficulty in recognizing words as a whole and the tendency to misperceive them will have to be resolved by further research.

There is one more interesting fact about surface dyslexia: this disorder closely resembles developmental dyslexias (Coltheart, 1981). Little is currently known about the location of lesions that produce surface dyslexia, but perhaps when more is learned the anatomical knowledge can be applied to the analysis of developmental dyslexias, as well.

As we will see, developmental dyslexia may be caused by abnormal development of parts of the brain that participate in language-related functions.

Deep Dyslexia

Deep dyslexia is caused by massive damage to the left hemisphere, so I will say at the outset that the anatomical basis of this disorder is not known. Most patients have Broca's aphasia as well as a reading deficit. Given the severity of the lesions that produce it, we are unlikely to be able to use the disorder to make specific inferences about the anatomy of language functions. However, deep dyslexia is interesting because its symptoms combine most of those we have encountered in the reading disorders and because of its similarity to conduction aphasia.

People with deep dyslexia are very poor readers. Those words they successfully read almost always represent concrete objects or actions; the patients almost never successfully read abstract words. In addition, when they attempt to read a concrete word they often make semantically related substitutions. For example, *dream* might become "sleep," *Eskimo* might become "iceman" (Coltheart, Patterson, and Marshall, 1980). The patients cannot read phonologically. If they attempt to read pronounceable nonwords they usually make no response, or if they do, they tend to say a visually related word. For example, one patient said "city" for *cit,* and "flute" for *frute* (Patterson and Marcel, 1977). Sometimes, their responses to nonwords obviously have a semantic origin; for example, *rud* was read as "naughty," and *glem* as "jewel." The nonword *glem* looks like *gem,* and presumably the word evoked an image of a gem. This information was transmitted to frontal speech mechanisms, and the word *jewel* was produced as a result. (See **Figure 16.17.**)

You will readily notice the similarity be-

Normal person

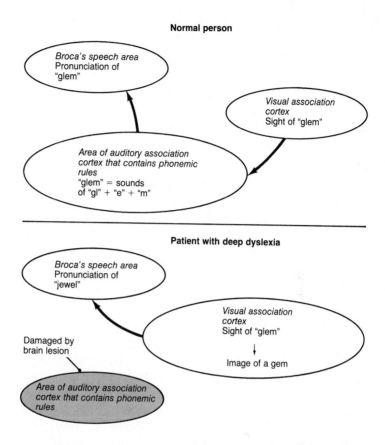

FIGURE 16.17

An explanation of the response "jewel" to the stimulus *glem* by a patient with deep dyslexia.

tween deep dyslexia and conduction aphasia. People with conduction aphasia find it almost impossible to repeat nonwords, have difficulty repeating abstract words, and when repeating concrete words sometimes say synonyms (that is, make semantically related errors). Presumably, their lesion disconnects speech perception mechanisms from speech production mechanisms, so the transfer of information must be accomplished indirectly, perhaps by means of visualization. We can hypothesize that deep dyslexia entails damage to phonological reading, so that words cannot be sounded out, and also a disconnection between mechanisms for perceiving word-forms and producing speech. The fact that deep dyslexics can sometimes read concrete words (or make semantically related re-

sponses) indicates that they retain some ability to recognize words visually. (See **Figure 16.18.**)

Earlier I promised to say more about the term *surface dyslexia*. The reason for the name *deep dyslexia* is that the reading errors the patients make tend to be semantically related to the word they are looking at. In contrast, the reading errors of patients with surface dyslexia are related to a more superficial aspect of words—their visual appearance and their pronunciation.

Reading without Comprehension
You will recall that patients with transcortical sensory aphasia (and isolation aphasia) can repeat what is said to them but show no signs of understanding what they hear or say. A

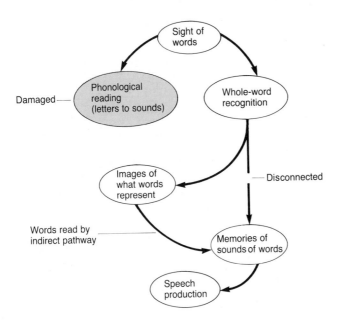

FIGURE 16.18
An explanation of deep dyslexia.

related reading disorder was reported by Schwartz, Marin, and Saffran (1979), who studied a woman (W.P.) with progressive dementia of the Alzheimer's type. As we saw in Chapter 15, this disease produces diffuse damage throughout most regions of the neocortex and also in the hippocampus; thus, we cannot use data from a case like this one to make neuroanatomical conclusions. However, the case does prove that perceiving and saying words can occur independently from understanding their meaning.

Patient W.P.'s spontaneous speech was fluent but devoid of content; however, it did not contain paraphasic errors like the speech of someone with Wernicke's aphasia. Here is a sample of her speech (from Marin, 1982):

I went up to the shoppin' center and I thought, oh well, and I think, oh lady, and she said, "oh, tea?" and I said, "uh-huh," (laughing) and I said (laughing) she says, uh, "all right, all right," I thought oh wow, and I thought, well she gimme tea, and she said, uh, well, she said, uh, oh like "this is shoppin' center," and then "this is yours." And she said "Oh, good!" (laughter).

Patient W.P. could read almost normally. She had no difficulty with irregularly spelled words, correctly reading aloud words such as *blow, one, post,* and *climb.* (Contrast their pronunciation with *cow, bone, cost,* and *limb,* which she also read correctly.) However, just as patients with transcortical sensory aphasia can repeat but not understand speech, she did not understand the words she read. She could not match pictures with written words that represented them.

The case of patient W.P. contrasts with another patient that some colleagues and I studied (Margolin, Marcel, and Carlson, 1985). Our patient, R.F., sustained a head injury in an automobile accident that destroyed much of her left temporal lobe and part of the anterior occipital lobe. (Despite the location of the lesion, she did *not* have Wernicke's aphasia.) She had a classic case of anomic aphasia — in fact, I quoted her in the earlier section on that topic. Although her speech was fluent and she was able to repeat whatever we said to her, she could not name most common objects, nor could she read most words. Nevertheless, she could match pictures of objects she could not name with words she could not read. For example, when we showed her the picture and words that appear in Figure 16.19, she immediately pointed to the correct word, *flag,* even though she could not name the object or read any of the words. (See **Figure 16.19.**)

These two cases illustrate the independence of reading a word aloud and understanding its meaning. Patient W.P. could read aloud with reasonable fluency but did not understand what she read. Our patient, R.F., failed to read even simple words but often appeared to understand words she could not read. She often made very similar responses when attempting to name objects or read the words that denote them. For example, on one occasion, when attempting to read the word *caboose,* she said "That's the back of the train, that's the very last one on the train." On another occasion, when attempting to name a picture of a caboose she said "that's the back of the train, the very last one on the train." It appears that the visual perception of words, the visual perception of objects, and memories concerning these objects could interact, but that the information specifying these objects could not successfully reach speech production mechanisms. (See **Figure 16.20.**)

Developmental Dyslexias

As I mentioned earlier, some children have great difficulty learning to read and never become fluent readers, even though they are otherwise intelligent. Specific language learning disorders, called *developmental dyslexias,* tend to occur in families, which suggests a genetic (and hence, biological) component. In addition, most people with developmental dyslexias are male, which suggests a possible link with the Y chromosome or with the presence of androgens during development (Rutter and Yule, 1975).

FIGURE 16.19

Patient R.F. chose the correct word to accompany the picture, even though she could not name the object shown in the picture or read the words.

Galaburda and Kemper (1979) obtained evidence that brain abnormalities may be responsible for at least some cases of developmental dyslexia. They obtained the brain of a young man with a history of developmental dyslexia who had died in an accident. They found abnormalities in the *planum temporale,* a part of Wernicke's area. The left planum temporale is normally much larger than the right one (Galaburda, Le May, Kemper, and Geschwind, 1978), but in this case it was the same size on both sides of the brain. Even more significantly, the microscopic appearance of this region was abnormal. Figure 16.21 shows a section through the left planum temporale of a normal person *(top)* and of the dyslexic accident victim *(bottom).* Notice the regular columnar arrangement of cells in the normal brain, but not in

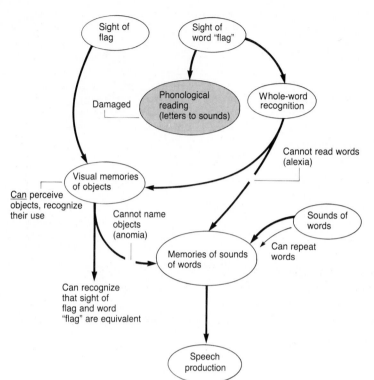

FIGURE 16.20
An explanation of patient R.F.'s language disorder.

the brain of the dyslexic accident victim. (See **Figure 16.21.**) Galaburda and Kemper (1979) observed that certain cells apparently failed to migrate during development and were left in the location they occupied during an earlier fetal stage. Cortical neurons develop in the central core of the brain before the twentieth week of gestation and then migrate to the position they are to occupy (Rakic, 1972). It appears that in this case something prevented normal migration of these cells.

Galaburda and Geschwind (1984) report that although studies that examined CAT scans of normal children and children with developmental dyslexias have produced contradictory results, several studies have found evidence of left-sided EEG abnormalities. These results corroborate Galaburda and

Kemper's observations, although definitive confirmation will occur only after more brains of dyslexics are studied histologically.

Geschwind and Behan (1982) noted that investigators have long recognized the fact that a disproportionate number of people with developmental dyslexias are also left-handed. Furthermore, clinical observations suggested a relation between left-handedness and various immune disorders. Therefore, Geschwind and Behan studied a group of left-handed and right-handed people to see whether the relations were statistically significant. They found that they were: the left-handed subjects were ten times more likely to have specific learning disorders (10 percent versus 1 percent) and two and one-half times more likely to have immune disorders (8 percent versus 3 percent). The immune dis-

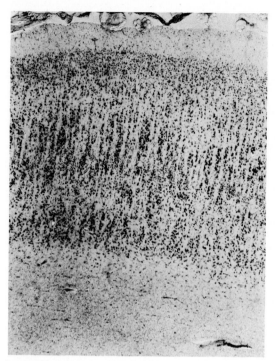 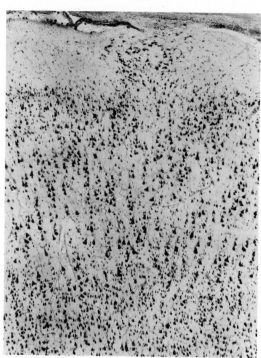

FIGURE 16.21

Photomicrographs of the left planum temporale (a portion of Wernicke's area) of a normal person *(left)* and a person with developmental dyslexia *(right)*. Nissl stain. (Photographs courtesy of A. Galaburda.)

orders included various thyroid and bowel diseases, diabetes, and rheumatoid arthritis. Of course, although the relation was statistically significant, it was not perfect. After all, the world is full of healthy left-handed people.

Geschwind and Behan suggested that left-handedness, developmental dyslexia, and immune disorders are causally related. They noted that although the superior temporal gyrus develops one to two weeks earlier on the right, the left superior temporal gyrus ultimately becomes larger (Chi, Dooling, and Gilles, 1977). In fact, retardation in the rate of development may be the mechanism that causes the left language areas to become larger than corresponding regions of the right

hemisphere; by growing more slowly, it ultimately achieves a larger size. Perhaps dyslexia occurs when the development of the left hemisphere is suppressed so much that it fails to develop normally. This suppression would cause left-handedness as well. Several studies reviewed by Galaburda and Geschwind (1982) suggested that testosterone slows brain development and suppresses development of the thymus, an important part of the immune system. This effect might account for the fact that males with a family history of specific learning disorders are much more likely than females to exhibit developmental dyslexias. The hypothesis is interesting, but much research has yet to be done to test it experimentally.

T A B L E 16.2   Types of dyslexias, their symptoms, and typical errors

Disorder	Primary Symptoms	Typical Errors
Spelling dyslexia (word-form dyslexia)	Cannot recognize words as a whole; less difficulty with individual letters	Must spell out letter by letter; may mistake letter: *men* → "h, e, n, hen"
Phonological dyslexia	Difficulty applying phonological principles (reading phonetically)	Good reading of familiar words; cannot read unfamiliar words or pronounceable nonwords
Surface dyslexia	1) Irregular words are often read phonetically 2) Visual errors	1) *yacht* → "yatchet" 2) *lift* → "life"
Deep dyslexia	Cannot read abstract words or pronounceable nonwords	Complete failure to read word is common; errors tend to be semantic substitutions: *Eskimo* → "iceman"
Reading without comprehension	Can read aloud, but no understanding of what is read	Reading is generally accurate

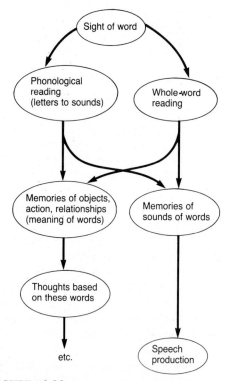

FIGURE 16.22

A hypothetical diagram of the major components of the reading process.

I N T E R I M   S U M M A R Y

Brain damage can produce reading and writing disorders. All cases of aphasia are accompanied by writing deficits that parallel the speech production deficits and by reading deficits that parallel the speech comprehension deficits. The reading and writing abilities of a person with pure word deafness, which is not an aphasic disorder, are generally good. The first reading and writing disorders to be identified that were not accompanied by aphasia were pure alexia and alexia with agraphia. Pure alexia is caused by lesions that produce blindness in the right visual field and that destroy fibers of the posterior corpus callosum. Alexia with agraphia is usually caused by lesions of the left angular gyrus. Pure agraphia is rare, and its anatomical basis is poorly understood.

Research in the past few decades has discovered that acquired reading disorders (dyslexias) can fall into one of several categories, and the study of these disorders has provided neuropsychologists and cognitive psychologists with thought-provoking information that has helped them understand how normal people read. Table 16.2 presents a summary of the categories of acquired dyslexia, and Figure 16.22 presents a simplified diagram of the major components of the reading process. (See **Table 16.2** and **Figure 16.22**.)

■ COMMUNICATION OF EMOTIONS

Not all human communication is conveyed by means of spoken or written words. We also communicate our feelings through tone of voice, facial expression, gestures, and body postures. Research by Ekman and his colleagues (Ekman and Friesen, 1971; Ekman, 1980) tends to confirm Darwin's hypothesis that facial expression of emotion uses an innate, species-typical repertoire of movements of facial muscles (Darwin, 1872/ 1965). For example, Ekman and Friesen (1971) studied the ability of members of an isolated tribe of people in New Guinea to recognize facial expressions of emotion produced by westerners. They had no trouble doing so and themselves produced facial expressions that westerners readily recognized. Because the same facial expressions were used by people who had not previously been exposed to each other, Ekman and Friesen concluded that the expressions were unlearned behavior patterns. In contrast, different cultures use different words to express particular concepts; production of these words does not involve innate responses but must be learned.

Investigators have not yet determined whether other means of communicating emotions, such as tone of voice or hand movements, are learned or whether they are at least partly innate. However, as we will see, some progress has been made in studying the anatomical basis of expressing and recognizing emotions.

Studies with Normal Subjects

Comprehension of Emotion

We recognize other people's feelings by means of vision and audition, seeing their facial expressions and hearing their tone of voice and choice of words. Several studies by Bryden, Ley, and colleagues have found that the right hemisphere plays a more important role than the left hemisphere in comprehension of emotion. The rationale for these studies is based on the fact that each hemisphere directly receives information from the contralateral part of the environment. For example, when a person looks directly ahead, visual stimuli to the left of the fixation point (seen with *both* eyes) are transmitted to the right hemisphere, and stimuli to the right are transmitted to the left hemisphere. Of course, the hemispheres exchange information by means of the corpus callosum, but it appears that this transcommissural information is not as precise and detailed as that which is directly received. Similarly, although each hemisphere receives auditory information from both ears, the contralateral projections are richer than the ipsilateral ones. Thus, when stimuli are presented to the left visual field or left ear, the right hemisphere receives more specific information than the left hemisphere does.

To study hemispherical differences in visual recognition, stimuli are usually presented with a ***tachistoscope*** (literally, "seen most swiftly"), which flashes an image in a specific part of the visual field so fast that the subject does not have time to move his or her eyes. Many studies (reviewed by Bryden and Ley, 1983) have shown that the left hemisphere is better than the right at recognizing words or letter strings. Knowing what you do about the verbal functions of the left hemisphere, this finding will come as no surprise to you. However, when a person is required to discriminate among different faces or detect differences in the tilt of lines presented to one side of the visual field, the right hemisphere performs better than the left.

Ley and Bryden (1979) prepared cartoon drawings of five different people, each displaying one of five facial expressions, ranging from negative to neutral to positive. (See **Figure 16.23.**) They showed these drawings

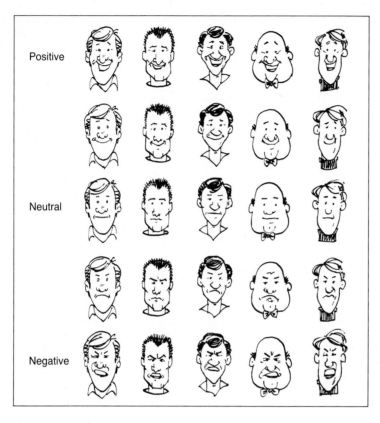

Positive

Neutral

Negative

FIGURE 16.23
The faces and expressions used as stimuli in the study by Ley and Bryden. (Redrawn from Ley, R.G., and Bryden, M.P., *Brain and Language,* 1979, 7, 127–138.)

briefly in the right or left visual field, one at a time. After each presentation they showed the same face or a different one in the center of the visual field (to both hemispheres) and asked the subjects to say whether the same emotion was presented. When the experimenters showed the subjects neutral or mild expressions, the hemispheres performed approximately the same. However, when the experimenters showed the subjects strong expressions, the right hemisphere judged them more accurately. (See **Figure 16.24.**)

When auditory stimuli are presented to one ear, most subjects recognize words better when the right ear (left hemisphere) hears them, but they recognize music or nonverbal environmental sounds better when the left ear (right hemisphere) hears them (Bryden and Ley, 1983). Bryden, Ley, and Sugarman

(1982) presented subjects with little melodies played in the major or minor mode. Most westerners perceive major tunes as happy, and minor ones as sad. The investigators simultaneously presented a different melody to each ear and asked the subjects to pay attention to only one of them and say whether it was happy or sad. When the modes of the melodies were different, subjects judged the one presented to the left ear (right hemisphere) more accurately than the one presented to the right ear (83 percent versus 62 percent correct). Again, the study suggests the superiority of the right hemisphere in judging emotional connotation.

Ley and Bryden (1982) also investigated perception of tone of voice by similar means. They simultaneously presented different verbal messages with a different (happy, neutral,

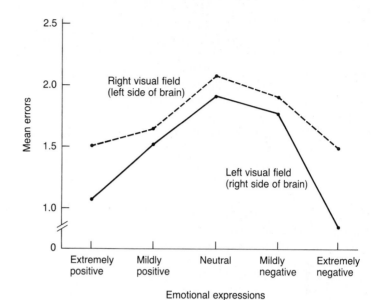

FIGURE 16.24
Mean errors in ratings of facial expressions of emotion in drawings presented to the right or left side of the brain. (Data from Ley, R.G., and Bryden, M.P., *Brain and Language,* 1979, *7,* 127–138.)

or sad) tone of voice to each ear and asked the subjects to attend to the message presented to one ear and report on its verbal content and emotion. Ninety percent of the subjects more accurately detected the verbal content of the message presented to the left hemisphere, whereas 77 percent of them more accurately detected the emotional tone of the voice presented to the right hemisphere. The results suggested that when a message is heard, the right hemisphere assesses the emotional expression of the voice, while the left hemisphere assesses the meaning of the words.

Expression of Emotion

When people show emotions with their facial muscles, the left side of the face usually makes a more intense expression. For example, Sackheim and Gur (1978) cut photographs of people who were posing emotions into right and left halves, prepared mirror images of each of them, and pasted them together. They found that the left halves were more expressive than the right ones. (See **Figure 16.25.**) Because motor control is contralateral, the results suggest that the right hemisphere is more expressive than the left.

FIGURE 16.25
An example of a stimulus used by Sackheim and Gur (1978). *(Left)* Composite of the left side. *(Middle)* Original photo. *(Right)* Composite of the right side. (From Sackheim, H.A., and Gur, R.C. *Neuropsychologia,* 1978, *16,* 473–482.)

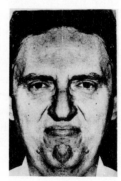

Moscovitch and Olds (1982) made more natural observations of people in restaurants and parks and found that the left side of their faces appeared to make stronger expressions of emotions. They confirmed these results in the laboratory by analyzing videotapes of people telling sad or humorous stories. In addition, they found that although people tended to use their right hands more than their left hands when making gestures that accompanied speech (which suggests left-hemisphere dominance in manual gestures), they did *not* do so when their facial expression was changing. This observation suggests that when a different emotional state is being expressed, the right hemisphere dominates the person's nonverbal gesturing.

Studies with Neurological Patients

Long ago, Babinski (1914) noted that people with right-hemisphere damage often acted indifferent or euphoric, which suggested that this hemisphere was involved in the normal expression of emotions. Later, Goldstein (1948) observed that people with left-hemisphere damage were more likely to exhibit what he called a **catastrophic reaction,** a strong display of sadness and despair caused by their neurological deficit. In contrast, damage to the right hemisphere, even when it resulted in paralysis of the left side of the body, was more likely to be met with indifference. These results suggest that when the left side of a person's brain is damaged, the intact right hemisphere recognizes the loss and consequently expresses grief. However, when the right side is damaged, the person may be able to acknowledge the deficit verbally but fails to react emotionally. For example, I once examined a man who had sustained a right-hemisphere stroke. Even though his left arm and leg were paralyzed, he was cheerful and indifferent to his disability. He even at-

tempted several times to walk down the stairs, although he did acknowledge, when asked why he was in a wheelchair, that he could not move the left side of his body. He was alert and intelligent and received superior scores on the verbal components of an intelligence test, so his failure to react emotionally to his deficit cannot be explained by a simple comprehension deficit.

Comprehension of Emotion

Damage to the right hemisphere (especially the area posterior to the central sulcus) appears to impair the recognition of emotions being expressed by other people. For example, Heilman, Scholes, and Watson (1975) presented patients who had right or left lesions of the temporal-parietal region with sentences with neutral content (such as *The boy went to the store*) said in a happy, sad, angry, or indifferent tone of voice. Patients with right-hemisphere damage judged the emotion being expressed less accurately. Tucker, Watson, and Heilman (1977) performed a similar experiment, this time requiring the subjects simply to say whether the tone of voice of two sentences was the same or different. Again, right-hemisphere damage impaired the subjects' ability to discriminate the tone of voice more than left-hemisphere damage.

Heilman, Watson, and Bowers (1983) presented an interesting case of a man with pure word deafness who could not comprehend the meaning of speech but who had no difficulty identifying the emotion being expressed by its intonation. This case demonstrates that comprehension of words and recognition of tone of voice are independent functions.

Visual recognition of emotions, as well as auditory recognition, also appears to be a right-hemisphere function more than a left-hemisphere function. DeKosky, Heilman, Bowers, and Valenstein (1980) found that right-hemisphere damage, more than left-hemisphere damage, disrupted patients' ability to discriminate among different facial expressions of emotion. In addition, Bowers and Heilman (1981) reported the case of a patient with a large tumor of the posterior right hemisphere who could accurately distinguish among faces of different people, but not among different emotional expressions. In contrast, he had no trouble recognizing the emotional content of voices. Thus, although recognition of different faces and different expressions are both primarily right-hemisphere tasks, their anatomical basis differs.

Expression of Emotion

Left-hemisphere lesions do not usually impair vocal expressions of emotion. For example, a person with Wernicke's aphasia usually modulates his or her voice according to mood. Even people with Broca's aphasia, who exhibit deficits in prosodic expression, can laugh and express emotions by tone of voice when uttering expletives. (When a Broca's aphasic says "Damn!" he sounds as if he means it.) However, right-hemisphere lesions do impair expression of emotion, both facially and by tone of voice.

Buck and Duffy (1980) showed slides that were designed to elicit expressions of emotions to patients with damage to the right or left hemisphere. For example, they showed a picture of a starving child and a crying woman. The investigators found that people with right-hemisphere damage showed fewer facial expressions of emotion. Heilman, Watson, and Bowers (1983) asked patients with unilateral brain lesions to *pose* expressions of emotions and found no differences between right and left lesions. However, they suggest a plausible explanation for this failure. As you know, people with Broca's aphasia often exhibit an oral and facial apraxia, having difficulty making particular movements on command. Thus, they have difficulty responding

to the suggestion to smile but nevertheless smile spontaneously when they are told a joke. (You have probably noticed how difficult it is to smile when someone asks you to do so while taking your picture. In contrast, a smile occurs automatically when we are amused. Sometimes, we even have to fight to suppress a smile when we do not want to offend someone who has said or done something foolish.) So far, no one has compared the effects of left and right brain lesions on posed expressions of emotions versus real ones, elicited by actual changes in mood.

Morrow, Urtunski, Kim, and Boller (1981) obtained evidence that the decreased tendency of patients with right-hemisphere lesions to respond emotionally is not restricted to facial expression. To assess the motor effects of emotional stimuli, they recorded changes in skin conductivity, which presumably correlate with alterations in sweat production and blood flow, and hence with autonomic arousal. When they presented emotionally loaded stimuli, they found that patients with right-hemisphere damage exhibited less intense changes than those with left-hemisphere damage.

Ross (1981) suggested that the comprehension and expression of emotions are performed by neural circuits in the right hemisphere similar to those in the left hemisphere that are necessary for the comprehension and expression of speech. For example, he found three patients with frontal lesions who could recognize emotions portrayed by facial expressions or tone of voice but who could not express their own emotions, and he found a patient with a posterior lesion who could express but not comprehend emotions. Obviously, these cases correspond to Broca's and Wernicke's aphasia. In addition, he found cases of what he called *transcortical sensory aprosodia* and *global aprosodia*. (See **Figure 16.26.**) Although more cases will have to be observed before we can evaluate the accu-

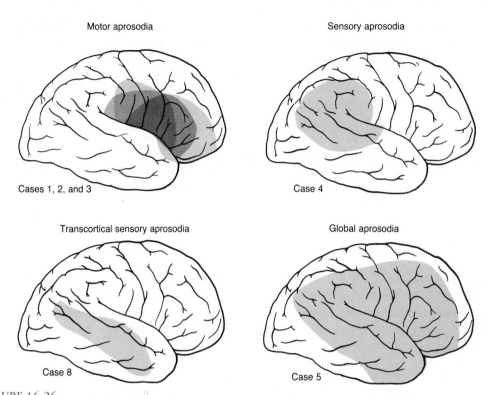

FIGURE 16.26
Brain damage that caused different forms of aprosodia. (From Ross, E.D.
Archives of Neurology, 1981, *38,* 561. Copyright 1981, American
Medical Association.

racy of Ross's conclusions, his results suggest
interesting similarities in the functions of the
hemispheres with respect to different types of
information.

INTERIM SUMMARY

An important form of nonverbal communication is
the use of facial expressions to show our feelings.
Expression and comprehension of emotions involves the right hemisphere more than the left.
Studies with normal people have shown that people can judge facial expressions, tone of voice, or
mode of music better when the information is presented to the right hemisphere than when it is pre-

sented to the left hemisphere. In addition, the left
halves of people's faces tend to be more expressive
than the right halves, and emotional hand gestures
are produced more often by the left hand. (As you
know, control of movement is contralateral.)

Damage to the right hemisphere is more likely
to produce deficits in expression and comprehension of emotions conveyed by tone of voice or by
facial expression than damage to the left hemisphere. In fact, people with right-hemisphere lesions sometimes do not even react emotionally to
their own neurological deficits. It is possible that
the right hemisphere contains mechanisms of
emotional comprehension and expression that are
parallel to the mechanisms of speech comprehension and expression in the left hemisphere, but
further research will be needed to confirm this
possibility.

Concluding Remarks

Many people have pointed out that our ability to communicate with each other by means of speech and writing is the most important distinguishing feature of the human species. Because such communication is so important, most people find the specific language disorders caused by brain damage to be very interesting. Verbal communication involves memories of the sounds of words and their visual appearance when written, of the movements of the muscles necessary to pronounce or write them, of the relation between the words and our knowledge of objects and events in the world (that is, the words' meanings), and of the grammatical relations among words that define sentence structure. Neuropsychological research is helping us understand how the brain accomplishes such verbal tasks.

Because the expression of emotions is less specific and is not as rule-governed as verbal communication, not as much is presently known about this topic. We will examine another aspect of emotion, affective disorders, in the next chapter.

NEW TERMS

acquired dyslexia p. 661
agrammatism p. 645
alexia with agraphia p. 655
angular gyrus p. 655
anomia p. 645
aphasia p. 639
aprosodia p. 654
bound morpheme p. 663
Broca's aphasia p. 643
Broca's area p. 644
catastrophic reaction p. 674
cerebrovascular accident p. 638
circumlocution p. 649
conduction aphasia p. 647
content word p. 644
deep dyslexia p. 664
developmental dyslexia p. 661
disconnection syndrome p. 642
dyslexia p. 661
embolus p. 638
function word p. 644
homonymous hemianopia p. 658

isolation aphasia p. 650
jargon speech p. 640
oral apraxia p. 645
paraphasic error p. 640
phonological dyslexia p. 662
planum temporale p. 667
platelet p. 638
prosody p. 653
pure agraphia p. 658
pure alexia p. 655
pure word deafness p. 641
spelling dyslexia p. 662
supplementary motor area p. 652
surface dyslexia p. 663
tachistoscope p. 671
thrombus p. 638
transcortical motor aphasia p. 652
transcortical sensory aphasia p. 650
Wernicke's aphasia p. 639
Wernicke's area p. 641
word-form dyslexia p. 662

SUGGESTED READINGS

COLTHEART, M., PATTERSON, K., AND MARSHALL, J.C. *Deep Dyslexia.* London: Routledge & Kegan Paul, 1980.

DAMASIO, A.R., AND GESCHWIND, N. The neural basis of language. *Annual Review of Neuroscience,* 1984, *7,* 127–148.

HEILMAN, K.M., AND SATZ, P. *Neuropsychology of Human Emotion.* New York: The Guilford Press, 1983.

KERTESZ, A. *Aphasia and Associated Disorders: Taxonomy, Localization, and Recovery.* New York: Grune & Stratton, 1979.

KERTESZ, A. *Localization in Neuropsychology.* New York: Academic Press, 1983.

KOLB, B., AND WHISHAW, I.Q. *Fundamentals of Human Neuropsychology,* second edition. San Francisco: W.H. Freeman, 1985.

SARNO, M.T. *Acquired Aphasia.* New York: Academic Press, 1981.

17

Physiology of Mental Disorders

- **SCHIZOPHRENIA**
  Description
  Heritability
  Pharmacology of Schizophrenia: The Dopamine Hypothesis
  Drugs That Alleviate Positive Symptoms of Schizophrenia
  The Pharmacological Effects of Antischizophrenic Drugs
  Drugs That Produce Positive Symptoms of Schizophrenia
  Biochemical Abnormalities in Schizophrenic Patients
  Tardive Dyskinesia
  The Relation of Dopamine to Symptoms of Schizophrenia
  Schizophrenia As a Neurological Disorder
  Evidence for Brain Damage
  Evidence for a Pathological Process
- **MAJOR AFFECTIVE DISORDERS**
  Description
  Heritability
  Physiological Treatments for the Affective Disorders
  The Monoamine Hypothesis
  Alternatives to the Monoamine Hypothesis
  The Histamine Hypothesis
  Long-Term Changes in Receptor Sensitivity
  REM Sleep Deprivation

Most of the discussion in this book has concentrated on the physiology of normal, adaptive behavior. But the behavior of some people —those who suffer from mental disorders— is often maladaptive. Their symptoms include deficient social behaviors, illogical and incoherent thoughts, inappropriate emotional responses, and delusions and hallucinations. Because normal behaviors, thoughts, emotions, and perceptions have a physiological basis, perhaps some mental disorders are actually physiological disorders—malfunctions of brain mechanisms.

The most serious mental disorders are called *psychoses.* The two most important psychoses, schizophrenia and the major affective disorders, can disrupt people's behavior so severely that they cannot survive without the care of others. In contrast, *neuroses* are generally less severe. People with neuroses are often unhappy, but they can generally reason normally and do not have hallucinations or delusions. They often have good insight into their problems and can articulate them very well. We can all sympathize with neurotics and perhaps understand them, for many of their problems seem like exaggerations of our own. However, the thoughts and behaviors of people with psychoses are quite abnormal. They sometimes seem to follow a different logic, which is probably why past generations blamed these disorders on inhuman devils.

■ SCHIZOPHRENIA

Description

Schizophrenia is the most common psychosis, afflicting approximately 1 percent of the population. The term *schizophrenia,* invented by Eugen Bleuler, a Swiss psychiatrist and neurologist, means "split mind," which leads some people to the erroneous conclusion that the word refers to multiple personality. In popular usage, a desire for two incompatible goals is often referred to as "schizophrenic." ("She felt herself pulled, schizophrenically, by the desire to be taken care of by someone stronger than she and the need to establish and assert her own personality.") But this usage is incorrect: Bleuler intended the term *schizophrenia* to refer to a break with reality. This break with reality consists of thought disorders, which include incoherence, illogical thinking, *delusions* (beliefs that are contrary to normally accepted evidence), and *hallucinations* (perceptions of imaginary events and objects).

The symptoms of schizophrenia vary enough for several subtypes to have been identified. *Paranoid schizophrenia* is characterized by delusions of grandeur, persecution, or control. For example, a paranoid schizophrenic might believe that he or she is God, is being spied upon by secret agents that have landed in flying saucers, or is being controlled by a miniature radio receiver that was secretly installed in his or her brain. *Disorganized schizophrenia* (previously called *hebephrenic schizophrenia* for Hebe, the cupbearer to the gods, who often got tipsy and silly from sampling the wine) represents a total break with reality. People with disorganized schizophrenia do not express coherent delusions; their speech deteriorates into meaningless jumbles of words. *Catatonic schizophrenia* refers to unusual motor symptoms: rigidity or (more rarely) wild excitement and hyperactivity. The most usual manifestation of catatonic schizophrenia is *waxy flexibility,* in which the limbs show some resistance to being moved, but remain in whatever position they are placed. This physical inactivity does not necessarily indicate that mental functions have ceased; these patients often reveal later that their thoughts were proceeding furiously while their bodies were motionless.

Not all people with schizophrenia can be placed into one of these discrete categories; many exhibit different symptoms at different times, and many show no distinct pattern of symptoms other than thought disturbances. A much more important distinction is the rate of onset of the symptoms. If an episode of schizophrenia comes on suddenly, with serious, full-blown symptoms, it is called *acute schizophrenia*. This disorder has a good prognosis; the patient will probably get better soon and may not suffer from another attack later. In contrast, *chronic schizophrenia* has a slow onset and a bad prognosis. At first, symptoms are sparse and not very severe. However, they gradually get worse, until the person needs to be put into an institution. Many patients suffer from this disorder, with periodic remissions and relapses, for the rest of their lives.

Recent research has revealed another important distinction, between the *positive* and *negative* symptoms of schizophrenia (Crow, 1980; Crow, Cross, Johnstone, and Owen, 1982). Positive symptoms include delusions, hallucinations, and thought disorders — symptoms that make themselves known by their presence. In contrast, negative symptoms are known by the absence of normal behaviors: flattened emotional response, poverty of speech, loss of drive, and social withdrawal. As we will see, there is good evidence that these two sets of symptoms result from different physiological disorders: positive symptoms appear to involve an imbalance in some neurotransmitters, possibly including dopamine, and negative symptoms appear to be caused by brain damage, perhaps of viral origin.

Heritability

One of the strongest pieces of evidence that schizophrenia is a biological disorder is that it appears to be heritable. Kety, Rosenthal, Wender, and Schulsinger (1968) performed one of the best-known studies. In Denmark, a record is kept of all citizens, which makes it possible to trace the family history of people with various disorders. Kety and his colleagues identified a group of schizophrenic people who had been adopted when they were children. Because of the Danish *folkeregister,* the investigators were able to identify the patients' biological families, as well as their adopted families. They found that the incidence of schizophrenia in the adopted families of the patients was exactly what would be expected in the general population. Thus, it did not appear that the patients became schizophrenic because they were raised in a family of schizophrenics. However, the investigators did find an unusually high incidence of schizophrenia in the patients' *biological* relatives (parents and siblings), even though they were not raised by and with them — and probably, in most cases, did not even know them. The results clearly favor the conclusion that a tendency to develop schizophrenia can be transmitted by means of heredity.

This study also found that chronic schizophrenia and acute schizophrenia appear to have different causes. People with chronic schizophrenia tended to have schizophrenic biological relatives, but people with acute schizophrenia did not; only chronic schizophrenia was heritable. Chronic schizophrenia appears to be the end of a continuum of disorders, which includes the less serious *latent schizophrenia* or *borderline schizophrenia* (now termed **schizotypal personality disorder**). Many studies have shown schizotypal personality disorder to be part of the genetic picture of schizophrenia (Crowe, 1982).

The study by Kety and his colleagues started with schizophrenic patients and looked at the incidence of schizophrenia in their relatives. Another study took the opposite approach. Heston (1966) identified schizophrenic mothers whose children had been given up for adoption within 2 weeks of birth. Thus, it would be unlikely that the mothers' behavior could have had a chance to affect their children. For comparison, he selected a group of nonschizophrenic mothers whose children had also been given up for adoption. The results, like those of Kety and his colleagues, supported the hypothesis that schizophrenia is heritable. Seventeen percent of the children of schizophrenic mothers later became schizophrenic, whereas *none* of the children of the nonschizophrenic mothers did. In addition, the children of the schizophrenic mothers tended to have an unusually high incidence of emotional disorders, even if they did not become schizophrenic. Many were arrested for antisocial crimes, and many became alcoholics or drug addicts.

Twin studies have also confirmed the heritability of schizophrenia. If one of two genetically identical monozygotic twins is diagnosed as schizophrenic, the likelihood that the other twin will also receive a diagnosis of schizophrenia is between 35 and 58 percent, whereas the concordance rate is between 9 and 26 percent for dizygotic twins, who have, on the average, 50 percent common chromosomes (Gottesman and Shields, 1976). So many studies have confirmed the heritability of a tendency toward schizophrenia that the matter is no longer in dispute among researchers in this area.

If schizophrenia were a simple trait produced by a single gene, we would expect to see this disorder in at least 50 percent of the children of two schizophrenic parents if the gene were dominant. If it were recessive, all children of two schizophrenic parents should become schizophrenic. However, the actual incidence is less than 50 percent, which has led investigators to suggest that the genetics of schizophrenia is complex, and that environmental factors probably play a role in its

development. What may be inherited is a biological susceptibility to develop schizophrenia. In certain kinds of environments, the susceptible individual develops schizophrenia or at least a schizotypal personality disorder. As we will see, evidence suggests that one of the inherited traits may include susceptibility to a viral disorder that causes brain damage.

Although many environmental factors, such as child-rearing practices and family dynamics, have been suggested as possible causes of schizophrenia, compelling evidence to support these claims has not yet been obtained. If a person's social environment during childhood is an important factor in the development of schizophrenia, we could reasonably suppose that having a schizophrenic parent would increase the likelihood of schizophrenia. However, Wender, Schulsinger, Rosenthal, Kety, and Welner (1974) found that the children of normal parents who are adopted and raised by families with a schizophrenic parent (or a parent with a diagnosis of what we would now call schizotypal personality disorder) were no more likely to become schizophrenic than children adopted and raised by nonschizophrenic parents.

Pharmacology of Schizophrenia: The Dopamine Hypothesis

Good evidence suggests that at least some of the symptoms of schizophrenia involve a biochemical disorder. The explanation that has accrued the most evidence is the *dopamine hypothesis,* which suggests that schizophrenia is caused by overactivity of the mesolimbic and mesocortical dopaminergic neurons, projecting from the ventral tegmental area to the basal forebrain, limbic cortex, and neocortex. (These circuits were described in Chapter 13.) Most investigators believe that this overactivity is caused by hypersensitivity of postsynaptic dopamine receptors, although some believe that the problem may lie in regulation of dopamine release. As we will see, recent evidence suggests that the dopamine hypothesis applies only to positive symptoms of schizophrenia. Negative symptoms appear to have other causes.

Drugs That Alleviate Positive Symptoms of Schizophrenia
The treatments for most physiological disorders are developed after we understand their causes. For example, once it was discovered that diabetes was caused by the lack of a hormone produced by the pancreas, researchers were able to extract a substance from pancreatic tissue (insulin) that would alleviate the symptoms of this disease. However, in some cases treatments are discovered before the causes of the disease. For example, natives of tropical regions discovered that tea made from the bark of the cinchona tree would prevent death from malaria many years before scientists discovered that this disease is caused by microscopic parasites that are transmitted in the saliva of a certain species of mosquito. (The bark of the cinchona tree contains quinine, now used to treat malaria.)

In the case of schizophrenia, a treatment was discovered before its causes were understood. (In fact, its causes are *still* not completely understood.) The discovery was accidental (Snyder, 1974). Antihistamine drugs were discovered in the early 1940s and were found to be useful in the treatment of allergic reactions. Because one of the effects of histamine release is a lowering of blood pressure, a French surgeon named Henri Laborit began to study the effects of antihistamine drugs on the sometimes-fatal low blood pressure that can be produced by surgical shock. He found that one of the drugs, promethazine, had an interesting effect: it reduced anxiety in his presurgical patients without causing mental confusion.

Laborit's findings spurred drug companies to examine other antihistamine drugs for sedative effects. Paul Charpentier, a chemist with a French drug company, developed *chlorpromazine,* which appeared to be promising, based on tests with animals. Laborit tried the drug in humans, and found that it had profound calming effects but did not seem to decrease the patient's alertness. This drug produced "not any loss in consciousness, nor any change in the patients' mentality but a slight tendency to sleep and above all 'disinterest' for all that goes on around him" (Laborit, 1950, quoted by Snyder, 1974). Chlorpromazine was tried on patients with a variety of mental disorders: mania, depression, anxiety, neuroses, and schizophrenia (Delay and Deniker, 1952a, 1952b). The drug was not very effective in treating neuroses or affective psychoses, but it had dramatic effects on schizophrenia.

The discovery of the antischizophrenic effects of chlorpromazine profoundly altered the way in which physicians treated schizophrenic patients and made prolonged hospital stays unnecessary for many of them (the patients, that is). Throughout this century the patient population of mental hospitals in the United States grew continuously until around 1955, when the antischizophrenic drugs became widely adopted. (See **Figure 17.1.**)

The efficacy of antischizophrenic drugs has been established in many double-blind studies (Baldessarini, 1977). They actually eliminate, or at least diminish, the patients' symptoms; they do not simply mask them by tranquilizing the patients. Although some antischizophrenic drugs do have tranquilizing effects, these effects are not related to the amount of relief the patients receive from their psychotic symptoms. And benzodiazepines, such as diazepam (Valium) and chlordiazepoxide (Librium), are very effective tranquilizers, but they do not reduce the symptoms of schizophrenia. Moreover, anti-

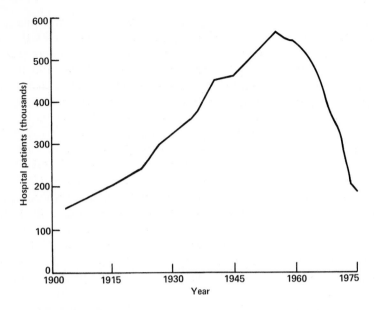

FIGURE 17.1
Number of patients in public
mental hospitals from 1900 to
1975. (Redrawn from Bassuk,
E.L., and Gerson, S. *Scientific
American,* 1978, *238,*
46–53.)

schizophrenic drugs can have either activating or calming effects, depending upon the patient's symptoms. An immobile patient with catatonic schizophrenia becomes more active, whereas a furiously active patient who is suffering from frightening hallucinations becomes more calm and placid. The results are not just a change in the patient's attitudes; the hallucinations and delusions go away, or at least become less severe.

The Pharmacological Effects of Antischizophrenic Drugs

If we can find out what antischizophrenic drugs do, pharmacologically, perhaps we can infer what sort of defect in brain structure or metabolism might be responsible for schizophrenia. The one pharmacological effect that these drugs appear to have in common is a blocking of dopamine receptors. In fact, a common side effect of the antischizophrenic drugs is the production of symptoms of Parkinson's disease. This disorder is known to be caused by degeneration of dopaminergic neurons of the nigrostriatal bundle, which connect the substantia nigra with the caudate

nucleus. Therefore, antischizophrenic drugs produce these symptoms by blocking dopamine receptors on neurons in the caudate nucleus.

Another piece of evidence that suggests that antischizophrenic drugs produce their therapeutic effect by blocking dopamine receptors is that the effectiveness of these drugs is increased if patients are also treated with α-methyl *p*-tyrosine (AMPT), which blocks the activity of tyrosine hydroxylase and thus interferes with the synthesis of dopamine and norepinephrine (Walinder, Skott, Carlsson, and Roos, 1976).

More direct evidence for an antidopamine effect of the antischizophrenic drugs comes from studies on dopamine receptors. Kebabian, Petzold, and Greengard (1972) extracted from the caudate nucleus of the rat brain an adenylate cyclase bound to dopamine receptors that converted ATP to cyclic AMP when it was exposed to dopamine. (See Figure 3.6, page 58, if your memory needs to be refreshed.) When antischizophrenic drugs were also administered, dopamine was less effective in stimulating the production of cyclic AMP; the drugs appeared to block the dopamine receptors. However, one class of antischizophrenic drugs (the ***butyrophenones***), which are clinically many times more potent than equal amounts of drugs like chlorpromazine, were *less* effective than chlorpromazine in inhibiting the production of cyclic AMP. What was the reason for this discrepancy? We now know that there are two different kinds of dopamine receptors, which have been labeled as D_1 and D_2 (Kebabian and Calne, 1979). D_1 receptors are bound to adenylate cyclase and are probably located postsynaptically, on cell bodies. D_2 receptors are not bound to adenylate cyclase and are probably autoreceptors, located on the mem-

brane of dopaminergic neurons. Butyrophenones, such as ***haloperidol,*** bind especially well with D_2 receptors.

Snyder, Burt, and Creese (1976) used a technique called ***competitive binding*** to assess the ability of various antischizophrenic drugs to bind with what are now called D_2 receptors. They exposed cell membranes extracted from caudate nuclei of calf brains to haloperidol that had been made radioactive by the addition of a tritium ion (^3H). (See **Figure 17.2.**) They then washed the membrane very quickly, to remove the labeled drug from every place but the receptors. Next, they measured the radioactivity of the sample, which provided an estimate of the

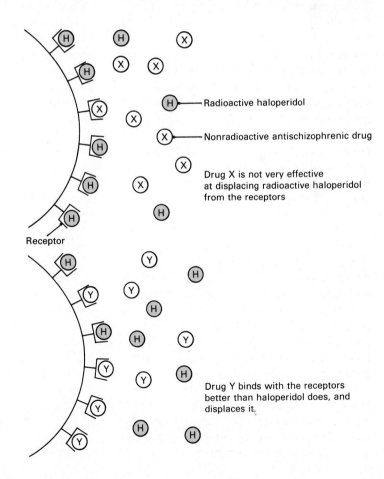

Radioactive haloperidol

Nonradioactive antischizophrenic drug

Drug X is not very effective
at displacing radioactive haloperidol
from the receptors

Receptor

Drug Y binds with the receptors
better than haloperidol does, and
displaces it.

FIGURE 17.2
The competitive binding study
by Snyder and colleagues
(1976).

amount of binding of the labeled substance with receptors. Then they mixed [³H]haloperidol with various concentrations of several other antischizophrenic drugs. The better a particular drug binds with the dopamine receptors, the more effectively it prevents the labeled haloperidol from occupying these receptors (that is, the more effectively the drug competes with it). Thus, the affinity of a particular antischizophrenic drug for D₂ dopamine receptors can be determined by measuring the radioactivity of the sample of cell membrane that had been exposed to the [³H]haloperidol along with the antischizophrenic drug—the *lower* the radioactivity, the *better* the drug binds with the receptor. (See **Figure 17.2.**)

Snyder and his colleagues found that the potency of a given drug in inhibiting the binding of [³H]haloperidol was closely related to its clinical effectiveness. That is, drugs that were effective in inhibiting the binding of [³H]haloperidol alleviated the symptoms of schizophrenia in low doses, whereas drugs

that were not very effective in displacing [³H]haloperidol from the receptors had to be administered in higher doses to be clinically useful. (See **Figure 17.3.**) These results suggest that the efficacy of an antischizophrenic drug is related to its ability to bind with D₂ dopamine receptors. The functional significance of this is not yet known; I will discuss some possibilities later in this section.

Drugs That Produce Positive Symptoms of Schizophrenia

We do not know how to produce schizophrenia by behavioral means. Although stressful situations can produce psychotic episodes in some people, once the stress-producing stimuli are removed the symptoms usually disappear. If long-lasting effects occur, they are not likely to resemble schizophrenia. In contrast, some drugs greatly intensify the positive symptoms of schizophrenia and can even *induce* them in an apparently normal volunteer.

The drugs that can produce these symptoms have one known pharmacological effect

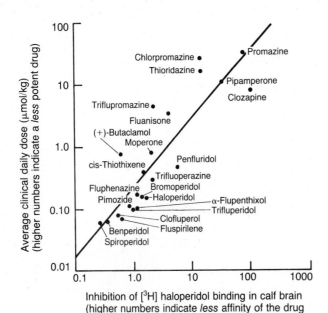

FIGURE 17.3
The relation between the ability of an antischizophrenic drug to inhibit binding of [³H]haloperidol with receptors on cell membranes extracted from calf caudate nucleus and the dose of the drug needed to achieve a therapeutic response. (From Snyder, S.H. *Journal of Continuing Education in Psychiatry,* 1978, *39,* 21–31.)

in common: they act as dopamine agonists. These drugs include amphetamine, cocaine, L-DOPA, and methylphenidate (Ritalin). Moreover, the symptoms that these drugs produce can be alleviated with antischizophrenic drugs, which further strengthens the argument that these drugs exert their therapeutic effects by blocking dopamine receptors.

Davis (1974) provided a dramatic illustration of the way in which symptoms of schizophrenia can be exacerbated by dopaminergic stimulation. He and his colleagues injected small doses of methylphenidate (a potent dopamine agonist) into the veins of schizophrenic patients who were in a fairly quiet state. Within a minute after the injection, each patient was transformed "from a mild schizophrenic into a wild and very florid schizophrenic." One of the patients began to make a clacking noise after the injection. He then took a pad of paper, which he pounded repeatedly and ultimately shredded with a pencil. He said he had been "sending and receiving messages from the ancient Egyptians." Catatonic patients became more catatonic, displaying their characteristic waxy flexibility. Thus, it cannot be said that the drug merely made the patients more active.

If large doses of amphetamine or cocaine are given to normal, nonpsychotic people, they will eventually develop symptoms like the positive symptoms of schizophrenia. Griffith, Cavanaugh, Held, and Oates (1972) recruited a group of people who had a history of amphetamine use and gave them large doses (10 mg) of dextroamphetamine every hour for up to 5 days. (Experimentally, it would have been better to study nonusers. Ethically, it was better not to introduce this drug to people who did not normally use it.) None of the subjects had prior histories of psychotic behavior. All seven volunteers became psychotic within 2 to 5 days. The first symptoms were sleeplessness and loss of ap-

petite. However, the drug-induced psychoses could not be attributed to these effects, because some subjects became psychotic in less than 48 hours; neither a 2-day fast nor a sleepless night will normally produce psychotic symptoms.

Biochemical Abnormalities in Schizophrenic Patients

What, physiologically, might be wrong with schizophrenic patients? The evidence that we just examined suggests that the disorder might be caused by hyperactivity in dopaminergic synapses. (As we will see, this hypothesis applies only to the positive symptoms of schizophrenia.) Some possibilities are that too much dopamine is synthesized, too much is released, too many dopamine receptors are located on postsynaptic neurons, or the autoreceptors on dopaminergic neurons do not function properly to regulate the release of the neurotransmitter. Or perhaps nothing is wrong with dopaminergic neurons or dopamine receptors; perhaps the abnormality is elsewhere. It is possible that normal brain functions require a balance between dopaminergic transmission and transmission in another system, and that damage to the second system disrupts the balance, resulting in the positive symptoms of schizophrenia. Treatment with dopamine receptor blockers suppresses the activity of the dopaminergic system, restoring the balance again.

Evidence in support of the simplest hypothesis — that more dopamine is secreted in the brains of patients with schizophrenia — is mixed. Bowers (1974) and Post, Fink, Carpenter, and Goodwin (1975) indirectly measured the amount of dopamine release in the brains of schizophrenic and nonschizophrenic people. First, they treated the subjects with probenecid, a drug that prevents the breakdown products of dopamine metabolism from being transported from the cerebrospinal fluid (CSF) to the blood, where they are normally destroyed. Thus, probenecid treatment causes the breakdown products to accumulate in the CSF. If more dopamine is released in the brains of schizophrenic patients, then more breakdown products should be found in the CSF. The investigators withdrew some CSF from schizophrenic patients and analyzed it. They found no evidence for increased amounts of homovanillic acid, a metabolite of dopamine; in fact, they found *less.* However, Mackay, Iversen, Rossor, Spokes, Bird, Arregui, Creese, and Snyder (1982) made direct measurements of dopamine in the brains of deceased schizophrenic patients and found small but significantly increased levels in the caudate nucleus and nucleus accumbens, relative to control subjects. The increase occurred whether or not the patients were given antischizophrenic medication. Thus, the data on the amount of dopamine released by neurons in the brains of schizophrenic patients are inconclusive.

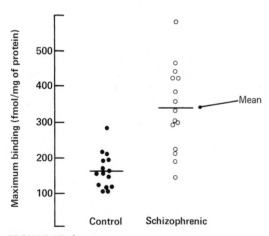

FIGURE 17.4

Amount of binding of [³H]spiroperidol in the cortex and caudate nucleus of brains of deceased schizophrenics and nonschizophrenic controls. (From Crow, T.J., Johnstone, E.C., Longden, A.J., and Owen, F. *Life Sciences,* 1978, *23,* 563–568. Copyright 1978, Pergamon Press, Ltd.)

In contrast to the inconclusive results on the release of dopamine, at least two studies have reported an increase in the numbers of dopamine receptors in the brains of deceased schizophrenics, as compared with nonschizophrenic controls (Owen, Cross, Crow, Longden, Poulter, and Riley, 1978; Lee and Seeman, 1980). Owen and his colleagues assessed dopamine receptors by competitive binding with [³H]spiroperidol, a butyrophenone similar to haloperidol. Five of the patients had not received antischizophrenic drugs for a year before they died, and two of them apparently had never received such medication, yet the rate of [³H]spiroperidol binding was significantly higher in extracts from their brains. Therefore, the results do not seem to have been produced by treatment with antischizophrenic drugs, which themselves can affect the binding of spiroperidol. (See **Figure 17.4.**)

This study suggests that there may be more dopamine receptors in the brains of patients with schizophrenia, which implies that schizophrenia may be caused by the increased postsynaptic effects of dopamine. However, Cross, Crow, and Owen (1981) assessed the numbers of D_1 (postsynaptic) and D_2 (autoreceptor) dopamine receptors in the brains of deceased schizophrenic patients. The number of D_1 receptors did not differ from that of control subjects, but significantly more D_2 receptors were found. (See **Figure 17.5.**) The functional significance of these findings is not at all clear. Most investigators believe that autoreceptors inhibit the production and release of neurotransmitter when they are activated; thus, one would expect that an increase in the number of D_2 receptors would cause *less* dopamine to be released. The most we can say at present is that there is evidence for differences in dopaminergic systems in the brains of schizophrenic patients. Future research will have to tell us precisely what these differences are and what they mean.

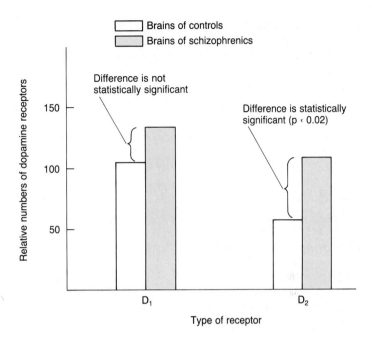

FIGURE 17.5
Relative amounts of D_1 and D_2 dopamine receptors from the brains of deceased schizophrenics and nonschizophrenic controls in the study by Cross, Crow, and Owen (1981).

Several studies have found that chronic schizophrenic patients have below-normal levels of monoamine oxidase (MAO) in blood platelets, white blood cells, and muscle (Wyatt, Potkin, and Murphy, 1979; Sullivan, Cavenar, Stanfield, and Hammett, 1978; Meltzer and Arora, 1980). Because a decreased level of MAO in the brain could cause hyperactivity of monoaminergic (including dopaminergic) synapses, these results were received with great interest. However, several studies have found no differences in the levels of MAO in the *brains* of deceased schizophrenic patients and normal control subjects. Figure 17.6 shows the results of a study by Reveley, Glover, Sandler, and Spokes (1981). The graph indicates activity levels of MAO extracted from the cortex and caudate nucleus, assessed by its ability to oxidize three monoamines: dopamine, phenylethylamine, and serotonin (5-HT). There is no consistent difference between values for schizophrenic and control brains. (See **Figure 17.6.**)

Tardive Dyskinesia

As we saw, a common side effect of antischizophrenic drugs is symptoms of Parkinson's disease, including loss of facial expression, muscular rigidity, and tremors. In addition, approximately 10 percent of the patients who receive these drugs suffer from a motor disorder called **tardive dyskinesia.** *Tardus* means "slow" and *dyskinesia* means "faulty movement"; thus, tardive dyskinesia is a late-developing movement disorder. This syndrome includes peculiar facial tics and gestures, including tongue protrusion, cheek puffing, and pursing of the lips. In some cases, speech is affected. Sometimes, writhing movements of the hands and trunk are also seen. Tardive dyskinesia appears to be the opposite of Parkinson's disease. Indeed, dyskinesia commonly occurs when patients with Parkinson's disease receive too much L-DOPA. In schizophrenic patients, tardive dyskinesia is made worse by withdrawal of the antischizophrenic drug but is improved by

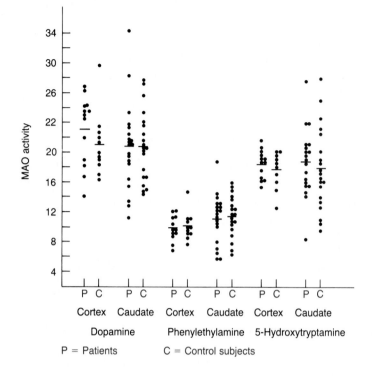

FIGURE 17.6
Monoamine oxidase (MAO) activity in the caudate nucleus of schizophrenic patients *(P)* and nonschizophrenic controls *(C)*, assessed by three different procedures. (From Reveley, M.A., Glover, V., Sandler, M., and Spokes, E.G. *Archives of General Psychiatry,* 1981, *38,* 663–665.)

increasing the dose. The symptoms are also intensified by dopamine agonists such as L-DOPA or amphetamine (Baldessarini and Tarsy, 1980). Therefore, the disorder appears to be produced by an overstimulation of dopamine receptors. If this is so, why should it be originally caused by antischizophrenic drugs, which are dopamine antagonists?

The answer seems to be provided by a phenomenon called ***denervation supersensitivity.*** Within a few days after the nerve to a muscle is cut, the muscle develops an increased sensitivity to acetylcholine. That is, a given amount of acetylcholine produces a larger effect than it previously did. This phenomenon is caused by an increase in the number of postsynaptic acetylcholinergic receptors on the muscle (Miledi, 1959). Presumably, decreased incoming traffic induces a regulatory mechanism to increase the muscle's sensitivity to acetylcholine. Investiga-

tors have found that neurons, as well as muscles, can develop denervation supersensitivity (Baldessarini and Tarsy, 1980). If a particular input ceases to be active, regulatory mechanisms increase the neuron's sensitivity to that input. Thus, in the case of tardive dyskinesia, blocking dopamine receptors in the caudate nucleus causes a compensatory supersensitivity to this transmitter substance. This supersensitivity results in dyskinesia when the drug is withdrawn. In cases in which the antischizophrenic medication continues for a long time, the supersensitivity becomes so great that it overcompensates for the effects of the drug, causing the tardive dyskinesia to occur even while the drug is still being administered.

So far, so good. But consider this question: why does a patient not develop "tardive schizophrenia"? If positive symptoms of schizophrenia are alleviated by drugs that block dopamine receptors, we might expect denervation supersensitivity to cause *schizophrenic* symptoms to recur. The fact that a rebound effect is not seen in the symptoms of schizophrenia even when the drug treatment is prolonged has puzzled investigators for several years. This apparent contradiction remains one of the principal objections to the dopamine hypothesis of schizophrenia.

Not all investigators believe that the primary cause of tardive dyskinesia is antischizophrenic medication. If it is not, then the absence of "tardive schizophrenia" does not contradict the dopamine hypothesis. Crow, Cross, Johnstone, Owen, Owens, and Waddington (1982) obtained data that suggest that the current explanation for tardive dyskinesia does not completely explain the phenomenon. First, they noted that dyskinesias had been reported in schizophrenic patients long before antischizophrenic drugs were discovered. They cited the following quotation from Kraepelin (1919):

The spasmodic phenomena in the musculature of the face and speech, which often appear, are extremely peculiar disorders. . . . Some of them resemble movements of expression, wrinkling of the forehead, distortion of the corners of the mouth, irregular movements of the tongue and lips. . . . Connected with these are further smacking and clicking of the tongue. . . . [and] tremors of the muscles of the mouth. . . . Several patients continually carried out peculiar sprawling, irregular [jerky] outspreading movements. . . . (p. 83)

Thus, tardive dyskinesia is not a new phenomenon, introduced with the advent of antischizophrenic medication. Crow and his colleagues also reported that dyskinesias were at least as prevalent in a group of schizophrenic patients who had never received drug treatment as in those who had. Furthermore, although rats who were given antischizophrenic drugs for 6 months developed oral/facial dyskinesias, no corresponding differences were seen in the sensitivity of dopamine receptors. Finally, they found no differences in either D_1 or D_2 receptors in the brains of deceased patients with or without a history of movement disorders. (See **Figure 17.7**.)

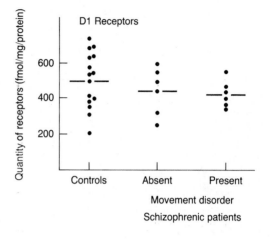

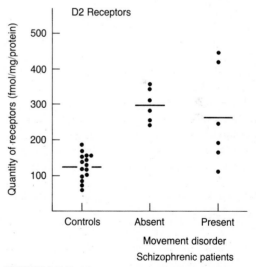

FIGURE 17.7

Quantity of D_1 and D_2 receptors in the brains of controls and schizophrenic patients with and without movement disorders. (From Crow, T.J., Cross, A.J., Johnstone, E.C., Owen, F., Owens, D.G.C., and Waddington, J.L. *Journal of Clinical Psychopharmacology,* 1982, *2,* 336–340.) © The Williams & Williams Co., Baltimore.

There is no doubt that dyskinesias are made worse by dopaminergic agonists and are alleviated by dopaminergic antagonists, but the study by Crow and his colleagues suggests that supersensitivity may not be the cause. Clearly, this issue merits further research, on both theoretical and practical grounds.

The Relation of Dopamine to Symptoms of Schizophrenia

If the positive symptoms of schizophrenia are caused by overactivity of a system of dopaminergic neurons, what do these neurons normally do, and why does their overactivity cause the symptoms? As we saw in earlier chapters, dopaminergic neurons play an important role in arousal and reinforcement. Is it possible that hyperarousal and "hyperreinforceability" (if I can call it that) might produce positive symptoms of schizophrenia?

Many investigators believe so. One of the dominant explanations for the positive symptoms of schizophrenia is the attentional hypothesis. According to the hypothesis, these symptoms are a result of deficiencies in selective attention.

If there is any creature who can be accused of not seeing the forest for the trees, it is the schizophrenic. If he is of the paranoid persuasion, he sticks even more closely than the normal person to the path through the forest, examining each tree along the path, sometimes even each tree's leaves with meticulous care. . . . If at the other extreme he follows the [disorganized schizophrenic] pattern, then he acts as if there were no paths, for he strays off the obvious path entirely; he is attracted not only visually but even [by smell and taste], by any and all trees and even the undergrowth and floor of the forest, in a superficial flirting, apparently forgetting in the meantime about the place he wants to get to. (Shakow, 1962, p. 30)

An articulate woman who suffered from schizophrenic episodes appears to agree with this description.

Each of us is capable of coping with a large number of stimuli, invading our being through any one of the senses. We could hear every sound within earshot and see every object, line, and color within the field of vision, and so on. It is obvious that we would be incapable of carrying on any of our daily activities if even one-hundredth of all these available stimuli invaded us at once. So the mind must have a filter which functions without our conscious thought, sorting stimuli, and allowing only those which are relevant to the situation in hand to disturb consciousness. And this filter must be working at maximum efficiency at all times, particularly when we require a high degree of concentration. What had happened to me . . . was a breakdown in the filter, and a hodge-podge of unrelated stimuli were distracting me from things which should have had my undivided attention. (McDonald, 1960, p. 218)

Drugs such as amphetamine and methylphenidate, which can cause positive symptoms of schizophrenia in normal people, are used to treat a disorder characterized as extreme distractibility and hyperactivity. This condition, the *attention deficit disorder,* is seen in children. Children with attention deficit disorder are always up and about; they have great difficulty remaining seated and are unable to concentrate on a single task. They are continually distracted, dashing from one activity to the next. As a result, they come into conflict with teachers who try to restrain them and make them settle down to work. Amphetamine and methylphenidate have remarkable effects on children with attention deficit disorder; their ability to concentrate increases dramatically, and they cease their restless activity. This disorder contrasts with schizophrenia, which can be regarded as a *surplus* of indiscriminate attention. Also in contrast to schizophrenia, attention deficit disorder is successfully treated with dopamine *agonists.*

It is possible that the attentional changes in schizophrenic patients are caused by changes in reinforcement systems. Consider what the effects of indiscriminate activity of these systems might be. If ongoing thoughts and behaviors were inappropriately reinforced, they would increase in frequency, and the person would perceive these thoughts and behaviors as important. Trivial ideas and fantasies would assume much greater importance than they deserved and might become the delusions and hallucinations that are so characteristic of schizophrenia. This hypothesis is supported by the following facts: (1) amphetamine is both a potent reinforcer and an inducer of positive symptoms of schizophrenia; (2) drugs that block dopamine receptors suppress both schizophrenic symptoms and the reinforcing effects of natural appetitive stimuli, amphetamine, or electrical brain stimulation; and (3) the onset of an episode of positive schizophrenic symptoms is often accompanied by feelings of elation and pleasure.

As we saw in Chapter 13, the dopaminergic pathway that travels from the ventral tegmental area to various forebrain regions (including the nucleus accumbens and frontal neocortex) plays an important role in reinforcement. Perhaps hyperactivity of this system causes the positive symptoms of schizophrenia. There is no evidence that the other major dopaminergic pathway, from the substantia nigra to the neostriatum, plays any role in schizophrenia; instead, its function appears to be restricted to movement.

Schizophrenia As a Neurological Disorder

So far, I have been discussing the physiology of the positive symptoms of schizophrenia — principally, hallucinations, delusions, and thought disorders. These symptoms are plausibly related to the known functions of dopaminergic neurons: attention and reinforcement. But the negative symptoms of schizophrenia — social withdrawal, flattened emotional reaction, and poverty of thought and speech — are very different. Whereas the positive symptoms are unique to schizophrenia (and amphetamine psychosis), the negative symptoms are similar to those produced by brain damage in a variety of locations. Many pieces of evidence suggest that the negative symptoms of schizophrenia are a result of brain damage.

Evidence for Brain Damage

Although schizophrenia has been labeled as a psychiatric disorder for many years, most patients with schizophrenia exhibit neurological symptoms that suggest the presence of brain damage. These symptoms include catatonia; facial dyskinesias; unusually high or low rates of blinking; staring and avoidance of eye contact; absent blink reflex in response to a tap on the forehead; episodes of deviation of the eyes (especially to the right), accompanied by speech arrest; paroxysmal bursts of jerky eye movements; very poor visual pursuit of a smoothly moving object; inability to move the eyes without moving the head; poor pupillary light reactions; and continuous elevation of the brows, causing characteristic horizontal creasing of the forehead (Stevens, 1982a). Although these symptoms can be caused by a variety of neuropathological conditions and are hence not unique to schizophrenia, their presence suggests that schizophrenia may be associated with brain damage of some kind.

Stevens (1982b) studied sections from the brains of deceased chronic schizophrenic patients and compared them with those of patients with nonschizophrenic psychiatric disorders who had been residents of the same hospital. She found significantly more signs of damage, including neural cell loss and gliosis, in the sections from the brains of the schizophrenic patients. (*Gliosis* refers to the presence of glial cells in the places formerly occupied by now-dead neurons.) There was some evidence of a relation between symptoms and location of damage: Assaultive behavior, flat affect, catatonia, and seclusiveness were associated with periventricular, limbic, and hypothalamic damage; disorders in speech articulation, poor prosody, and poverty of speech were associated with globus pallidus and limbic damage; and stereotyped behavior was associated with hypothalamic and hippocampal damage. The damage looked like that which is produced by a neuropathological process that was previously active and subsequently healed, or perhaps one that had been slowly progressing.

Several studies have found evidence of brain damage from CAT scans of schizophrenic

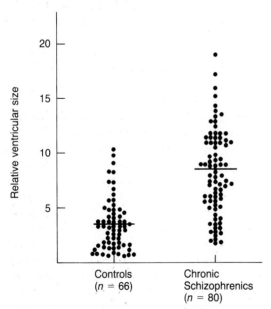

FIGURE 17.8
Relative ventricular size in chronic schizophrenics and controls. (From Weinberger, D.R., and Wyatt, R.J. In *Schizophrenia as a Brain Disease,* edited by F.A. Henn and H.A. Nasrallah. New York: Oxford University Press, 1982.)

patients. For example, Weinberger and Wyatt (1982) obtained CAT scans of eighty chronic schizophrenics and sixty-six normal controls of the same mean age (29 years). Without knowledge of the patients' diagnoses, they measured the area of the lateral ventricles in the scan that cut through them at their largest extent, and they expressed this area relative to the area of brain tissue in the same scan. The relative ventricle size of the schizophrenic patients was more than twice as great as that of normal control subjects. (See **Figure 17.8.**) Studies of the CSF dynamics of forty-three of the patients showed no evidence of increased pressure that might produce hydrocephalus. This finding indicates that the increased ventricular size was not caused by increased intraventricular pressure. The most likely cause of the enlarged ventricles is therefore loss of brain tissue. Thus, the CAT scans provide evidence that chronic schizophrenia is associated with brain damage.

To be certain that enlarged ventricle size was not simply an inherited trait that might be noncausally related to schizophrenia, Weinberger, DeLisi, Neophytides, and Wyatt (1981) compared the CAT scans of ten schizophrenic patients with their twelve nonschizophrenic brothers and sisters. In every family, the sibling with the largest ventricles was the one with schizophrenia; thus, enlarged ventricles and schizophrenia appear to be causally related.

It is possible, of course, that the brain damage could have been caused by the drug treatment that most schizophrenics receive. However, Johnstone, Crow, Frith, Husband, and Kreel (1976) found that four schizophrenic patients who had not received antischizophrenic drugs or electroconvulsive therapy had ventricles just as large as those of patients who had received one or both of these treatments.

Enlarged ventricles are related to the nega-

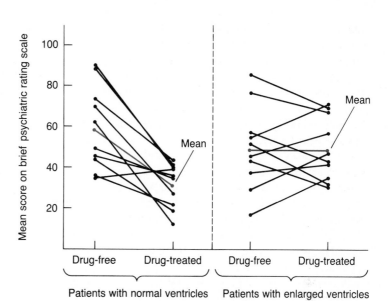

FIGURE 17.9

Response to drug treatment in schizophrenic patients with normal or enlarged ventricles. (From Weinberger, D.R., Bigelow, L.B., Kleinman, J.E., Klein, S.T., Rosenblatt, J.E., and Wyatt, R.J. *Archives of General Psychiatry,* 1980, *37,* 11–13.)

tive, and not the positive, symptoms of schizophrenia. For example, Johnstone, Crow, Frith, Stevens, Kreel, and Husband (1978) recorded a correlation between relative ventricle size and intellectual ability of −.70, which indicates that the brain damage is related to intellectual deterioration. In contrast, there was no correlation between relative ventricle size and the occurrence of hallucinations or delusions, both of which are positive symptoms. A retrospective study by Weinberger, Cannon-Spoor, Potkin, and Wyatt (1980) examined the medical records of schizophrenic patients and found that the twenty-one patients with enlarged ventricles had shown poorer school and social adjustment than the thirty patients with no appearance of brain atrophy. This finding suggests that the pathological process may have begun in childhood.

Two types of schizophrenia may be differentiated on the basis of response to drugs, and this distinction appears to be related to brain damage. Angrist, Rotrosen, and Gershon (1980) compared the effects of amphetamine and antischizophrenic medication on the positive and negative symptoms of schizophrenic patients. They found that amphetamine increased positive symptoms, and antipsychotic medication reduced them, whereas neither drug affected negative symptoms. Weinberger, Bigelow, Kleinman, Klein, Rosenblatt, and Wyatt (1980) studied the response of twenty schizophrenic patients to 8 weeks of antischizophrenic drug therapy. Ten of the patients had enlarged ventricles, and ten had ventricles of normal size. The patients without evidence of brain atrophy responded significantly better to the drug. (See **Figure 17.9.**) These studies indicate that negative symptoms and poor response to antischizophrenic drugs are related to brain damage (enlarged ventricles), and positive symptoms and good response to antischizophrenic drugs are related to absence of brain damage (normal ventricles).

Evidence for a Pathological Process

As we saw earlier, schizophrenia is a heritable disease, but its heritability is less than perfect. Why do fewer than half the children of parents with chronic schizophrenia become schizophrenic? A possible answer is that what is inherited is a susceptibility to the damaging effects of a viral disease. If a child with schizophrenic parents contracts the disease, he or she is likely to develop brain damage. If a person without a family history of schizophrenia contracts the same disease, brain damage is unlikely.

No direct evidence for virally induced schizophrenia exists, but evidence reveals similarities between schizophrenia and known viral disorders. Several epidemiological factors suggest that the causal factor in chronic schizophrenia is some kind of pathogen. Americans born between December and May, especially those born in March and April, are more likely to develop schizophrenia than those born in other months (Torrey, Torrey, and Peterson, 1977). The authors of this study suggested that the causal factor could be seasonal variations in nutritional factors or — more likely — variations in toxins or infectious agents in air, water, or food. The fact that known viruses such as rubeola (measles), rubella (German measles), and varicella (chickenpox) show similar seasonality suggests that the causal factor might be a virus. Many viruses can cause brain damage; for example, herpes zoster, which often infects nerves that serve the genital region, can also produce serious encephalopathy, destroying the hippocampus, amygdala, and much of the temporal neocortex. The virus that caused the 1918 influenza epidemic caused brain damage in many patients and produced illnesses that resembled schizophrenia (Menninger, 1926).

Torrey, Yolken, and Winfrey (1982) examined the CSF of 178 schizophrenic patients and found that 11 percent (20) contained an antibody for *cytomegalovirus (CMV),* a member of the herpes family. No antibody was found in the CSF of 41 normal controls. The presence of an antibody in the CSF indicates that the virus had been present (or was still present) in the brain. The authors found no differences between schizophrenic patients and normal controls in cytomegalovirus antibodies in the blood plasma, which indicates that the two groups had received equivalent exposure to the virus. A possible explanation is that equal numbers of both groups had been exposed to cytomegalovirus early in life, but that the heredity of the schizophrenics predisposed them to develop a brain infection.

Stevens (1982a) notes some interesting similarities between schizophrenia and a known neuropathological condition, multiple sclerosis. As we saw in Chapter 2, multiple sclerosis appears to be an autoimmune disease, in which the patient's own immune system attacks myelin, presumably because a virus causes damage to the blood-brain barrier, permitting myelin protein to leave the central nervous system. The natural histories of multiple sclerosis and schizophrenia are similar in several ways. Both diseases are more prevalent and more malignant in people who spent their childhood in latitudes far from the equator. Both diseases are more common in people with low socioeconomic status, who live in crowded, deprived conditions, and both show seasonal variations according to month of birth. Both diseases are characterized by one of three general courses: (1) attacks followed by remissions, many of which produce no residual deficits; (2) recurrent attacks with only partial remissions, causing an increasingly major deficit; or (3) an insidious onset with a steady and relentless progression, leading to permanent and severe deficits. These similarities suggest that schizophrenia, like multiple sclerosis, could be a virally induced autoimmune disease.

Although investigators have only recently come to realize that the positive and negative symptoms of schizophrenia are different in their nature, in their relation to brain damage, and in their response to drugs, it is still possible that they are part of the same process. Perhaps the positive symptoms are manifestations of an active disease process that alters dopaminergic transmission and may or may not cause residual damage. These positive symptoms respond to dopamine antagonists. Some patients have one or several attacks of positive symptoms without developing negative symptoms. In others, each attack produces more and more brain damage, which causes increasing amounts of negative symptoms. In still others, deterioration begins early in life, and very few positive symptoms ever occur. At first, the dopamine hypothesis promised a unified explanation for schizophrenia, but evidence gathered in the past few years suggests that we still do not understand all the causes of this disorder.

In the interest of clarity and brevity, I have been selective in my review of research on schizophrenia. This puzzling and serious disorder has stimulated many ingenious hypotheses and much research. Some hypotheses have been proved wrong, while others have not yet been adequately tested. It is possible that future research will find that all of these hypotheses (including the ones I have discussed) are incorrect, or that one that I have not mentioned is correct. However, I am impressed with recent research, and I believe that we have real hope of finding the causes of schizophrenia in the next few years. With the discovery of the causes, we can hope for the discovery of methods of prevention.

INTERIM SUMMARY

Researchers have made considerable progress in the past few years in their study of the physiology of mental disorders. Because schizophrenia is at least somewhat heritable, it appears to have a biological basis. The dopamine hypothesis, inspired by the findings that dopamine antagonists alleviate the positive symptoms of schizophrenia and that dopamine agonists potentiate or even produce them, still dominates. The hypothesis that tardive dyskinesia is produced by drug-induced supersensitivity of dopamine receptors is generally accepted, but some studies suggest that the disorder can occur even in patients who have not received antischizophrenic medication. Studies of the epidemiology of schizophrenia suggest that, like multiple sclerosis, it may be the result of an infectious process in people who are genetically vulnerable, and the finding of cytomegalovirus antibodies in the CSF of schizophrenic patients supports this suggestion. The development of the CAT scanner has made it possible to study brains in vivo, and several investigations have shown that chronic schizophrenia is associated with loss of brain tissue. The negative symptoms of social withdrawal, flat affect, and poverty of speech appear to be related to neurological damage, whereas the positive symptoms of delusions and hallucinations appear to be related to a biochemical imbalance that can be treated by the dopamine-blocking antischizophrenic drugs.

■ MAJOR AFFECTIVE DISORDERS

Affect, as a noun, refers to feelings or emotions. Just as the primary symptom of schizophrenia is disordered thoughts, the ***major affective disorders*** are characterized by disordered feelings. Of course, feelings and emotions are essential parts of human existence; they represent our evaluation of the events in our lives. In a very real sense, feelings and emotions are what human life is all about.

Description

The emotional state of most of us reflects what is happening to us: our feelings are tied to events in the real world, and they are usually the result of reasonable assessments of the importance these events have for our lives. But for some people, affect becomes divorced from reality. These people have feelings of extreme elation *(mania)* or despair *(depression)* that are not justified by events in their lives. For example, depression that accompanies the loss of a loved one is normal, but depression that becomes a way of life, and will not respond to the sympathetic effort of friends and relatives or even to psychotherapy, is pathological. Almost everyone experiences some depression from time to time, mostly caused by events that sadden us. Occasionally, these periods of depression become severe enough that the person can profit from professional assistance. The major affective disorders are quite different.

There are two principal types of major affective disorders. The first type is characterized by alternating periods of mania and depression—a condition called **bipolar affective disorder.** This disorder afflicts men and women in approximately equal numbers. Episodes of mania can last a few days or several months, but they usually take a few weeks to run their course. The episodes of depression that follow generally last three times as long as the mania. The second type is **unipolar depression,** or depression without mania. This depression may be continuous and unremitting or, more typically, may come in episodes. Unipolar depression strikes women two to three times more often than men. Mania without periods of depression sometimes occurs, but it is rare.

The affective disorders are serious, and they are classified as psychoses. They are also dangerous, because a person who suffers from depression runs a considerable risk of death by suicide. Psychotically depressed people usually feel extremely unworthy and have strong feelings of guilt. Often, they believe that their insides are rotting away in retribution for sins that they have committed. These beliefs can certainly be characterized as delusions, but the thoughts of people with psychotic depression are generally better organized than those of people with schizophrenia. Depressed people have very little

energy, and they move and talk slowly, sometimes becoming almost torpid. At other times, they may pace around restlessly and aimlessly. They may cry a lot. They lose their appetite for food and sex. They usually fall asleep readily but awaken early and find it impossible to get to sleep again. (In contrast, people with neurotic depression usually have trouble falling asleep and do not awaken early.) Even their body functions become depressed; they often become constipated, and secretion of saliva decreases.

The following interview illustrates a case of psychotic depression. Note that the patient is not simply sad; he also has delusions that his brain is disintegrating.

Th.: Good morning, Mr. H., how are you today?

Pt.: (Long pause—looks up and then head drops back down and stares at floor.)

Th.: I said good morning, Mr. H. Wouldn't you like to tell me how you feel today?

Pt.: (Pause—looks up again) . . . I feel . . . terrible . . . simply terrible.

Th.: What seems to be your trouble?

Pt.: . . . There's just no way out of it . . . nothing but blind alleys . . . I have no appetite . . . nothing matters anymore . . . it's hopeless . . . everything is hopeless.

Th.: Can you tell me how your trouble started?

Pt.: I don't know . . . it seems like I have a lead weight in my stomach . . . I feel different . . . I am not like other people . . . my health is ruined . . . I wish I were dead.

Th.: Your health is ruined?

Pt.: . . . Yes, my brain is being eaten away. I shouldn't have done it . . . If I had any willpower I would kill myself . . . I don't deserve to live . . . I have ruined everything . . . and it's all my fault.

Th.: It's all your fault?

Pt.: Yes . . . I have been unfaithful to my wife and now I am being punished . . . my health is ruined . . . there's no use going on . . . (sigh) . . . I have ruined everything . . . my family . . . and now myself . . . I bring misfortune to everyone . . . I am a moral leper . . . a serpent in the Garden of Eden . . . why don't I die . . . why don't you give me a pill and end it all before I bring catastrophe on everyone . . . No one can help me . . . It's hopeless . . . I know that . . . it's hopeless. (Coleman, 1976, p. 347)

Episodes of mania are characterized by a sense of euphoria that does not seem to be justified by circumstances. The diagnosis of mania is partly a matter of degree — one would not call exuberance and a zest for life pathological. People with mania usually exhibit nonstop speech and motor activity. They flit from topic to topic and usually have delusions, but they lack the severe disorganization that is seen in schizophrenia. They are usually full of their own importance and become angry or defensive if they are contradicted. Frequently, they go for long periods without sleep, working furiously on projects that are often unrealistic.

The following interview illustrates a case of mania:

Therapist: Well, you seem pretty happy today.

Client: Happy! Happy! You certainly are a master of understatement, you rogue! (Shouting, literally jumping out of seat.) Why, I'm ecstatic. I'm leaving for the West coast today, on my daughter's bicycle. Only 3100 miles. That's nothing, you know. I could probably walk, but I want to get there by next week. And along the way I plan to contact a lot of people about investing in my fishing equipment. I'll get to know more people that way — you know, doc, "know" in the biblical sense (leering at therapist seductively). Oh, god, how good it feels. It's almost like a nonstop orgasm. (Davison and Neale, 1982, p. 232)

The fact that mania is rarely seen without depression suggested to some clinicians that mania is a defense mechanism — an attempt to ward off a period of depression. They noted that there is often something brittle and unnatural about the happiness of the manic phase. This fact is illustrated in the following description:

He neglected his meals and rest hours, and was highly irregular, impulsive, and distractible in his adaptations to ward routine. Without apparent intent to be annoying or disturbing he sang, whistled, told pointless off-color stories, visited indiscriminately, and flirted crudely with the nurses and female patients. Superficially he appeared to be in high spirits, and yet one day when he was being gently chided over some particularly irresponsible act he suddenly slumped in a chair, covered his face with his hands, began sobbing, and cried, "For Pete's sake, doc, let me be. Can't you see that I've just got to act happy?" (Masserman, 1961, pp. 66–67)

Heritability

Like schizophrenia, a tendency to develop an affective disorder appears to be heritable. For example, Rosenthal (1971) found that close relatives of people who suffer from affective psychoses are ten times more likely to develop these disorders than people without afflicted relatives. Of course, this study does not prove that genetic mechanisms are operating; relatives have similar environments as well as similar genes. However, Gershon, Bunney, Leckman, Van Eerdewegh, and DeBauche (1976) found that if one member of a set of monozygotic twins was afflicted with an affective disorder, the likelihood that the other twin was similarly afflicted was 69 percent. In contrast, the concordance rate for dizygotic twins was only 13 percent. Furthermore, the concordance rate for monozygotic twins appears to be the same whether the twins were raised together or apart (Price, 1968). The heritability of the affective disorders suggests that they have a physiological basis.

Physiological Treatments for the Affective Disorders

There are three effective physiological treatments for unipolar depression: electroconvulsive therapy (ECT), monoamine oxidase (MAO) inhibitors, and the tricyclic antidepressant drugs. Bipolar affective disorders are effectively treated by lithium salts. The response of these disorders to medical treatment provides additional evidence that they have a physiological basis. Furthermore, the fact that lithium is very effective in treating bipolar affective disorders but not unipolar depression suggests that there is a fundamental difference between these illnesses.

A depressed patient does not immediately respond to treatment with MAO inhibitors or one of the tricyclic antidepressant drugs; improvement in symptoms is not usually seen before 2 to 3 weeks of drug treatment. In contrast, the effects of ECT are more rapid. A few seizures induced by ECT can often snap a person out of a deep depression within a few days. Although prolonged and excessive use of ECT causes long-lasting impairments in memory (Squire, 1974), the judicious use of ECT during the interim period before antidepressant drugs become effective has undoubtedly saved the lives of some suicidal patients (Baldessarini, 1977). In addition, some severely depressed people are not helped by drug therapy; for them, occasional ECT is the only effective treatment.

The drug treatment for affective disorders prior to the 1950s was limited to amphetamine (for depression) or the barbiturates (for agitation). Neither type of drug was satisfactory, and neither is used today to treat these conditions. In the late 1940s, clinicians noticed that some drugs used for treating tuberculosis seemed to elevate the patient's mood. Researchers subsequently found that a derivative of these drugs, iproniazid, reduced symptoms of psychotic depression (Crane,

1957). Iproniazid inhibits the activity of MAO, which destroys excess monoamine neurotransmitters within terminal buttons. Thus, the drug increases the release of the monoamine neurotransmitters: dopamine, norepinephrine, and serotonin. Other MAO inhibitors were soon discovered. Unfortunately, MAO inhibitors can have harmful side effects. The most common problem, and therefore the most serious one, is the *cheese effect*. Many foods (for example, cheese, yogurt, wine, yeast breads, chocolate, and various fruits and nuts) contain ***pressor amines***— substances similar to catecholamines. Normally, these amines are deactivated by MAO, which is present in the blood and in other tissues of the body. But a person who is being treated with an MAO inhibitor may suffer a serious sympathetic reaction after eating food containing pressor amines. The pressor amines simulate the effects of increased activity of the sympathetic nervous system, increasing blood pressure and heart rate. The reaction can raise blood pressure enough to produce intracranial bleeding or cardiovascular collapse.

Fortunately, another class of antidepressant drugs was soon discovered: the ***tricyclic antidepressants.*** Figure 17.10 illustrates the molecular structure of ***imipramine,*** the first of these drugs to be discovered; you can see why it is called *tricyclic*. (See **Figure 17.10.**) These drugs were found to inhibit re-uptake of neurotransmitter by the terminal buttons of monoaminergic neurons. By retarding re-uptake, the drugs keep the neurotransmitter in contact with the postsynaptic receptors, thus prolonging the postsynaptic potentials. Thus, both the MAO inhibitors and the tricyclic antidepressant drugs are monoaminergic agonists.

The therapeutic effect of ***lithium,*** the drug used to treat bipolar affective disorders, is very rapid. This drug, which is administered in the form of lithium carbonate, is most effective in treating the manic phase of a bipolar affective disorder; once the mania is eliminated, depression usually does not follow. This pattern suggests that the depression is a reaction to the mania, and not the reverse. A patient in the manic phase of a bipolar affective disorder usually responds as soon as the lithium ion in the blood reaches a therapeutic level (Gerbino, Oleshansky, and Gershon, 1978). Many clinicians and investigators have referred to lithium as psychiatry's wonder drug: it does not interfere with a person's sex drive, and it leaves patients able to feel and express joy and sadness to events in their lives. Similarly, it does not impair intellectual processes; many patients have received the drug continuously for years without any apparent ill effects (Fieve, 1979). Reifman and Wyatt (1980) calculated that during a 10-year period in the United States, lithium treatment saved at least $4 billion in treatment costs and lost productivity. Investigators have not yet discovered the pharmacological effects of lithium that are responsible for its ability to eliminate mania. Some suggest that the drug stabilizes the population of certain classes of neurotransmitter receptors in the brain, thus preventing wide shifts in neural sensitivity. In a later section I will describe research with other drugs that suggests

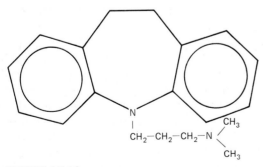

FIGURE 17.10
The molecular structure of a tricyclic antidepressant, imipramine.

the relevance of receptor sensitivity to the treatment of the affective disorders.

The Monoamine Hypothesis

The fact that depression can be treated effectively with tricyclic antidepressants and MAO inhibitors, both of which are monoamine agonists, suggested the monoamine hypothesis: depression is caused by insufficient activity of monoaminergic neurons. Because the symptoms of depression do not respond to potent dopamine agonists such as amphetamine or cocaine, most investigators have focused their research efforts on norepinephrine and serotonin.

As we saw, the dopamine hypothesis of schizophrenia receives support from the fact that dopamine agonists can produce the symptoms of schizophrenia. Similarly, the monoamine hypothesis of depression receives support from the fact that depression can be caused by monoamine antagonists. Many hundreds of years ago, an alkaloid extract from *Rauwolfia serpentina,* a shrub of Southeast Asia, was found to be useful for treating snakebite, circulatory disorders, and insanity. Modern research has confirmed that the alkaloid, now called reserpine, has both an antischizophrenic effect and a hypotensive effect (that is, it lowers blood pressure). The effect on blood pressure precludes its use in treating schizophrenia, but the drug is still occasionally used to treat patients with high blood pressure.

Reserpine has a serious side effect: it can cause depression. In fact, in the early years of its use as a hypotensive agent, up to 15 percent of the people who received it became depressed (Sachar and Baron, 1979). Reserpine acts on the membrane of synaptic vesicles in the terminal buttons of monoaminergic neurons, making the membranes "leaky," so that the neurotransmitters are lost from the vesicles and are destroyed by MAO. Thus, the drug serves as a potent norepinephrine, dopamine, and serotonin antagonist. The pharmacological and behavioral effects of reserpine complement the pharmacological and behavioral effects of the drugs used to treat depression—MAO inhibitors and most of the tricyclic antidepressants. That is, a monoamine antagonist produces depression, whereas monoamine agonists alleviate it.

One class of tricyclic antidepressant drugs (including imipramine) has a more pronounced effect on the re-uptake of serotonin than on that of norepinephrine. These drugs appear to have a sedating effect, whereas the other tricyclic antidepressants (including desipramine) have a more activating effect, presumably because they affect norepinephrine more than serotonin (Baldessarini, 1977). Thus, we might conclude that depression is caused by insufficient activity in monoaminergic synapses. Too little noradrenergic activity results in lethargic depression, and too little serotonergic activity results in agitated depression.

Several studies have found that suicidal depression is related to decreased CSF levels of *5-hydroxyindoleacetic acid (5-HIAA),* a metabolite of serotonin. A decreased level of 5-HIAA implies that less 5-HT (serotonin) is being produced and released in the brain. Träskmann, Åsberg, Bertilsson, and Sjöstrand (1981) found that CSF levels of 5-HIAA in people who had attempted suicide were significantly lower than those of controls. In a follow-up study of depressed and potentially suicidal patients, 20 percent of those with levels of 5-HIAA below the median subsequently killed themselves, while none of those with levels above the median committed suicide. Sedvall, Fyrö, Gullberg, Nybäck, Wiesel, and Wode-Helgodt (1980) analyzed the CSF of healthy, nondepressed volunteers. The families of subjects with unusually high or low levels of 5-HIAA were 2.7 times more likely to include people with psychiatric disorders: schizophrenia was associated with high levels, and depression with low levels. The results suggest that serotonin metabolism or release is genetically controlled, and that it is linked to psychotic disorders, including depression. Thus, these findings clearly support the monoamine hypothesis.

Alternatives to the Monoamine Hypothesis

Although the monoamine hypothesis dominated research on the physiology of depression for many years, recent research suggests that other approaches may also be fruitful.

The Histamine Hypothesis

Some recently discovered drugs cast doubt on the validity of the monoamine hypothesis of depression. These drugs, called **atypical antidepressants,** have little or no effect on the re-uptake of norepinephrine or serotonin. In fact, one of them (mianserin) has been shown to block serotonergic receptors. However, the drugs have potent antidepressant effects. If they are not noradrenergic or serotonergic agonists, how do they work?

Independent evidence from two laboratories (Green and Maayani, 1977; Kanof and Greengard, 1978) suggests that the clinically effective antidepressants are potent blockers of H_2 histamine receptors. There is good evidence that histamine is a neurotransmitter in the brain (Schwartz, 1977). In fact, a system of histaminergic neurons ascends through the medial forebrain bundle and projects diffusely to widespread regions of the forebrain. The anatomy at least supports the possibility that histaminergic neurons could have a modulating effect on mood. As Kanof and Greengard pointed out, the only known common site of biochemical activity of all of these drugs is on the histamine receptors.

Not all evidence supports the hypothesis that depression is caused by overactivity of histaminergic neurons and alleviated by blocking H_2 histamine receptors. For example, MAO inhibitors are effective in treating depression, but they do not affect histamine receptors (Kanof and Greengard, 1978). In addition, several drugs (such as cyproheptadine, LSD, 2-bromo-LSD, and many antischizophrenic drugs) block H_2 histamine receptors but do not produce antidepressant effects (Maayani, Hough, Weinstein, and Green, 1982). Thus, the histamine hypothesis remains unproved. As we will see in the next section, another explanation has been suggested for the effects of the atypical tricyclic antidepressant drugs.

Long-Term Changes in Receptor Sensitivity
Although researchers have known for a long time that depression does not respond immediately to antidepressant medication, they investigated the effects of these drugs by studying their acute, immediate pharmacological effects in animals. In recent years, the approach to the problem has changed. Perhaps the acute effects of the drugs, such as retardation of monoamine re-uptake and inhibition of MAO, are not the pharmacological effects that relieve the symptoms of depression. Instead, the relevant effects may take 2 to 3 weeks to develop, because the delay in symptom reduction takes this long.

Norepinephrine. Sulser (1982) reviewed research from his laboratory that suggests that the long-term effect of most, if not all, biological treatments for depression causes a *subsensitivity* of postsynaptic β noradrenergic receptors, which are coupled to adenylate cyclase (the enzyme that produces cyclic AMP, the second messenger). The subsensitivity, which is just the opposite of denervation supersensitivity, appears to represent decreased numbers of β receptors. Table 17.1 illustrates some of the drugs and other biological treatments that are effective in reducing the symptoms of depression and that also produce subsensitivity to the postsynaptic effects of iontophoretically applied norepinephrine or isoproterenol (a β receptor agonist) or actual reduction in the density of β receptors. To be

TABLE 17.1 Antidepressant treatments that produce subsensitivity of β noradrenergic receptors

Antidepressant drugs that block re-uptake of 5-HT and/or NE
Chlorimipramine
Imipramine
Amitriptyline

Antidepressant drugs that predominantly block re-uptake of NE
Desipramine
Nisoxetine

Antidepressant drugs that block MAO
Pargyline
Nialamide
Tranylcypromine

Electroconvulsive therapy

REM sleep deprivation

Source: Adapted from Sulser, F. in *Typical and Atypical Antidepressants: Molecular Mechanisms,* edited by E. Costa and G. Racagni. New York: Raven Press, 1982.

effective, these treatments must be applied chronically, over many days; subsensitivity is not produced by short-term treatment. (See **Table 17.1.**)

As you can see, tricyclic antidepressants (including the atypical ones), MAO inhibitors, serotonin re-uptake inhibitors, ECT, and REM sleep deprivation all affect the sensitivity of β noradrenergic receptors. (I will discuss the significance of REM sleep deprivation later.) This effect does not occur immediately but takes about as much time as the therapeutic response. The time course is not affected by dose; all doses of a given drug that are above a minimum therapeutic dose produce subsensitivity in the same amount of time. Electroconvulsive therapy, the treatment that produces the quickest therapeutic effects, also produces the fastest change in sensitivity of β receptors. (The mechanism by which ECT affects these receptors is not known.) In addition, reserpine, which can produce symptoms of depression, makes β receptors *super*sensitive (Leonard, 1982).

Studies have suggested that at least one of the ways that antidepressant treatments produce subsensitivity of β receptors is by first stimulating them. This finding implies that the subsensitivity is a regulatory response, just as supersensitivity is a response to drugs that block receptors or prevent the release of the neurotransmitter. Wolfe, Harden, Sporn, and Molinoff (1978) found that when β receptors were blocked with propranolol, chronic treatment with a tricyclic antidepressant (desipramine) failed to produce subsensitivity. An even more conclusive experiment was performed by Janowsky, Steranka, and Sulser (1981). They made unilateral lesions in the locus coeruleus, which contains noradrenergic neurons. They then administered long-term desipramine treatments and observed subsensitivity only on the nonlesioned side. Desipramine is a noradrenergic agonist by virtue of its ability to block the re-uptake of

norepinephrine. Thus, it could have no effect on the lesioned side, because the noradrenergic axons there had degenerated.

Little can be said about the physiological relevance of the subsensitivity of β receptors. For example, desipramine acts acutely as a noradrenergic agonist, but its chronic effect would appear to classify it as a noradrenergic antagonist. What, then, is the net effect of this drug on the noradrenergic synapses? Are antidepressant treatments correcting overactivity or underactivity of noradrenergic synapses? We have insufficient information to answer these questions.

Dopamine. Serra, Argiolas, Klimek, Fadda, and Gessa (1979) proposed an alternative to the hypothesis that depression is alleviated by treatments that produce subsensitivity to β noradrenergic receptors. They suggested that the relevant change is a subsensitivity in dopamine D_2 autoreceptors. Antelman, Chiodo, and DeGiovanni (1982) obtained data that support this suggestion. They reported that long-term treatment with imipramine, amitriptyline, iprindole, and ECS all caused subsensitivity of dopamine autoreceptors on neurons in the substantia nigra; in fact, the effect of these receptors on dopaminergic neurons was switched from inhibition to excitation by these treatments.

Figure 17.11 shows the effects of acute and chronic antidepressant treatments on the firing rate of dopaminergic neurons in the substantia nigra in response to apomorphine, a drug that directly stimulates dopamine autoreceptors. Normally, by stimulating the autoreceptors, an infusion of apomorphine inhibits firing of dopaminergic neurons. However, after the animal had received an antidepressant drug for several days, the neurons began to fire *faster* when apomorphine was infused. (See **Figure 17.11.**)

The authors suggest that the reversal of the

FIGURE 17.11
Response of a single dopaminergic neuron in the substantia nigra to microiontophoretic injection of apomorphine in rats pretreated with amitriptyline or a placebo for 10 days. (From Antelman, S.M., Chiodo, L.A., and DeGiovanni, L.A. In *Typical and Atypical Antidepressants: Molecular Mechanisms,* edited by E. Costa and G. Racagni. New York: Raven Press, 1982.)

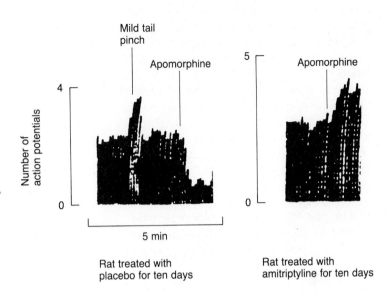

effects of dopamine autoreceptors might correspond to the delayed therapeutic effects of antidepressant drugs and perhaps also to the switch from depression to mania. As we saw in Chapter 13, dopaminergic neurons appear to play an important role in reinforcement. Thus, treatments that make dopaminergic neurons more active would probably stimulate reinforcement mechanisms. Depression might very well be caused by unresponsive reinforcement mechanisms; with little or no reinforcement, one's interest in living would certainly be expected to decline. Therefore, treatments that stimulate reinforcement mechanisms might be expected to alleviate the symptoms of depression: life becomes worth living again. In addition, mania could be caused by *hyperactive* reinforcement mechanisms; the switch of the effect of dopamine autoreceptor stimulation from inhibition to excitation might represent the change from hypoactivity to hyperactivity.

This hypothesis is not without problems. First, amphetamine causes dopamine autoreceptors to switch to the excitatory state, but amphetamine is not a good antidepressant drug. In addition, overactive dopamine neurons are presumed to be responsible for schizophrenia. Of course, it is possible that some other neurotransmitters also play a role in one or both of these disorders, and that changes in dopamine autoreceptors may be common to mania *and* schizophrenia. The fact that antischizophrenic drugs are at least somewhat effective in treating mania lends some support to this suggestion.

Serotonin. As we saw in an earlier section, CSF levels of the serotonin metabolite 5-HIAA are related to suicidal depression; thus, it is possible that serotonin receptors may also be affected by some long-term antidepressant treatments. Indeed, Savage, Mendels, and Frazer (1980a, 1980b) obtained evidence that supports this suggestion. The investigators chronically administered two antidepressant drugs to rats, an inhibitor of 5-HT (serotonin) re-uptake (amitriptyline) and an MAO inhibitor (nialamide). The MAO inhibitor significantly reduced binding of tritium-labeled serotonin ([³H]serotonin) in the cerebral cortex, hippocampus, brain stem, and

spinal cord. However, the re-uptake blocker
had no effect. (See **Figure 17.12**.) Fuxe,
Ögren, Agnati, Andersson, and Eneroth (1982)
found that long-term treatment with some
blockers of serotonin re-uptake decreased
the number of serotonin receptors, while
treatment with others increased it. Furthermore, the effect varied in different regions
of the brain. A third study showed that
mianserin, an atypical antidepressant, had no
effect on [³H]serotonin binding (Leonard,
1982). Therefore, although depression may
well be related to altered serotonergic mechanisms, the therapeutic effects of antidepres-

sant drugs do not appear to be consistently
related to changes in serotonin receptors.

REM Sleep Deprivation

Kupfer (1976) reported that compared with
nondepressed people, the latency to the first
period of REM sleep is shorter in patients with
depression, and REM sleep dominates the first
half of sleep rather than the second. As we
saw in Chapter 9, REM sleep deprivation is
an effective treatment for depression (Vogel,
Vogel, McAbee, and Thurmond, 1980). In addition, regardless of their pharmacological

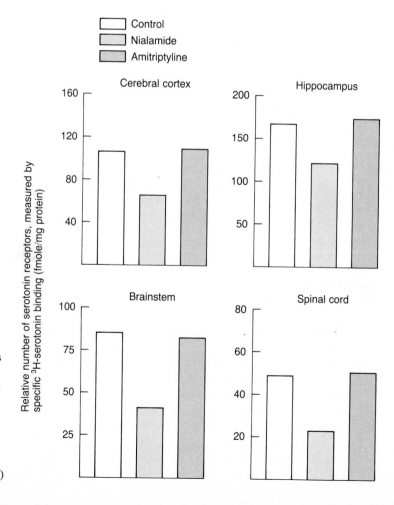

FIGURE 17.12
Effects of chronic
administration of nialamide
(an MAO inhibitor) and
amitryptyline (a 5-HT re-
uptake inhibitor) on the
number of serotonin receptors
in various parts of the rat
central nervous system. (From
Frazer, A., and Lucki, I. In
*Typical and Atypical
Antidepressants: Molecular
Mechanisms,* edited by
E. Costa and G. Racagni.
New York: Raven Press, 1982.)

effects, other treatments for depression affect sleep patterns, delaying the onset of REM sleep. Perhaps REM sleep and affect are somehow causally related.

The effects of twenty effective antidepressant drugs on the sleep cycles of cats were studied by Scherschlicht, Polc, Schneeberger, Steiner, and Haefely (1982). They found that all of them profoundly reduced REM sleep, slightly increased slow-wave sleep, and had mixed effects on total wakefulness. (See **Figure 17.13.**)

Goodwin, Wirz-Justice, and Wehr (1982) suggested that affective disorders are caused by a disturbance in circadian rhythms. They noted that affective disorders are cyclical in nature; even unipolar depression is not constant but usually waxes and wanes. As we saw in Chapter 9, the brain contains several biological clocks that are normally coupled to each other and entrained to environmental zeitgebers. Goodwin and his colleagues suggested that in patients with affective disorders, some of these clocks become free running, thus drifting into and out of phase with each other. As they do so, they produce the waxing and waning symptoms of depression or the alternate periods of mania and depression. These investigators proposed that, in particular, depression is caused by a phase advance of circadian mechanisms that control REM sleep.

As we saw in Chapter 9, several hormonal and biochemical systems are linked to various stages of sleep. Goodwin and his colleagues reviewed a large number of studies that measured physiological and biochemical rhythms in depressed subjects. As Figure 17.14 shows, almost all of the rhythms occurred earlier in depressed subjects than in normal subjects. The zero line indicates the mean value for control subjects; points to the left represent phase advances (earlier occurrences). (See **Figure 17.14.**)

Several studies have followed long-term circadian rhythms in body temperature in pa-

tients with bipolar affective disorder. There was some indication that the switch from mania to depression occurred when the rhythm reached its maximum phase advance (Goodwin, Wirz-Justice, and Wehr, 1982). Thus, depression may indeed be related to disorders in circadian rhythms.

INTERIM SUMMARY

The major affective disorders include bipolar affective disorder, with its cyclical episodes of mania and depression, and unipolar depression. Several lines of evidence suggest that depression is caused by abnormalities in monoamine metabolism, release, or transmission. Indeed, low levels of 5-HIAA (a serotonin metabolite) in the cerebrospinal fluid correlate with attempts at suicide. Early studies focused on the acute effects of tricyclic antidepressant drugs and MAO inhibitors, which are agonistic to noradrenergic and serotonergic synapses. However, because the effects of antidepressant treatment are delayed, more recent investigations have studied the chronic effects, which are quite different. The dominant hypothesis is currently that all effective treatments for depression work by reducing the number or sensitivity of postsynaptic β noradrenergic receptors, although there is some evidence that dopamine D_2 autoreceptors may also be involved. The histamine hypothesis, which was proposed a few years ago, has not received strong support. The relation between suicide and 5-HIAA levels is not yet understood. Because sleep disturbances are characteristic of affective disorders, and because REM sleep deprivation alleviates depression, some researchers have speculated that these disorders may be caused by abnormalities in circadian pacemakers, perhaps through their regulatory effects on neurotransmitter receptors.

Concluding Remarks

Schizophrenia and the major affective disorders are serious problems. Early in this century most psychiatrists believed that they were caused by brain abnormalities, but with the ascendancy of

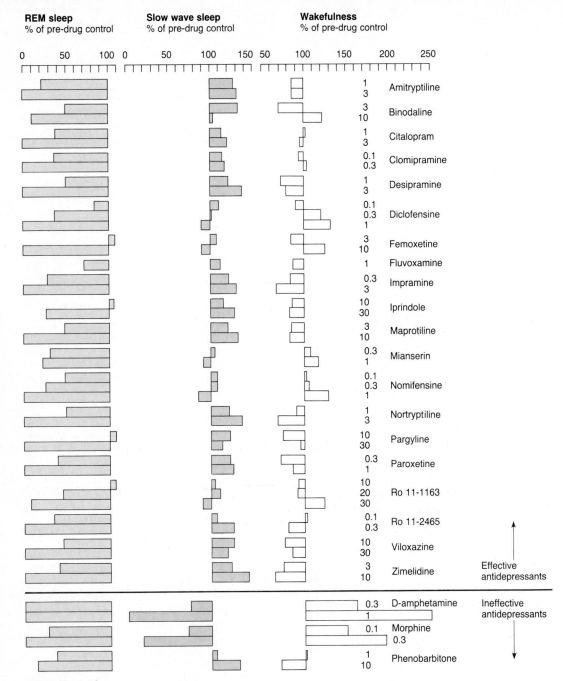

FIGURE 17.13

Effects of twenty effective antidepressant drugs and three ineffective drugs on the sleep/wakefulness cycle of cats. (From Scherschlicht, R., Polc, P., Schneeberger, J., Steiner, M., and Haefely, W. In *Typical and Atypical Antidepressants: Molecular Mechanisms,* edited by E. Costa and G. Racagni. New York: Raven Press, 1982.)

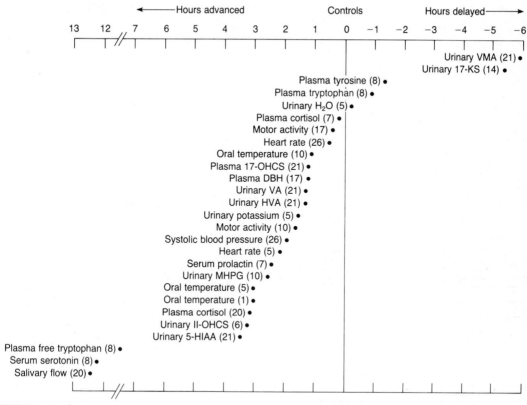

FIGURE 17.14

Summary of studies that found early occurrence of various physiological measures in depressed patients, relative to controls. (From Goodwin, F.K., Wirz-Justice, A., and Wehr, T.A. In *Typical and Atypical Antidepressants: Clinical Practice,* edited by E. Costa and G. Racagni. New York: Raven Press, 1982.)

psychotherapy, this belief fell into disrepute. More recently, with the discovery of the hereditary basis of these disorders and the efficacy of drug treatment, most researchers and clinicians again believe that the serious mental disorders reflect abnormalities in brain structure or biochemistry. We have seen some of the more important hypotheses being investigated by researchers today, and some of the progress that has been made in understanding and treating the disorders. The future offers hope to people who suffer from the major mental disorders, and to their families and friends.

NEW TERMS

affect p. 697
attention deficit disorder p. 692
atypical antidepressant p. 702

bipolar affective disorder p. 698
butyrophenone p. 685
catatonic schizophrenia p. 680

chlorpromazine p. 683
competitive binding p. 685
cytomegalovirus (CMV) p. 696
denervation supersensitivity p. 690
disorganized schizophrenia p. 680
haloperidol p. 685
5-hydroxyindoleacetic acid (5-HIAA) p. 702
imipramine p. 700
lithium p. 700
major affective disorder p. 697
neurosis p. 680

paranoid schizophrenia p. 680
pressor amine p. 700
psychosis p. 680
schizophrenia p. 680
schizotypal personality disorder p. 681
subsensitivity (of receptors) p. 703
tardive dyskinesia p. 689
tricyclic antidepressant p. 700
unipolar depression p. 698
waxy flexibility p. 680

SUGGESTED READINGS

BUCHSBAUM, M.W., AND HAIER, R.J. Psychopathology: Biological approaches. *Annual Review of Psychology,* 1983, *34,* 401–430.

COSTA, E., AND RACAGNI, G. *Typical and Atypical Antidepressants: Molecular Mechanisms.* New York: Raven Press, 1982.

COSTA, E., AND RACAGNI, G. *Typical and Atypical Antidepressants: Clinical Practice.* New York: Raven Press, 1982.

HENN, F.A., AND NASRALLAH, H.A. *Schizophrenia as a Brain Disease.* New York: Oxford University Press, 1982.

Glossary

Absorptive phase. The phase of metabolism during which nutrients are absorbed from the digestive system. Glucose and amino acids constitute the principal source of energy for cells during this phase. Stores of glycogen are increased, and excess nutrients are stored in adipose tissue in the form of triglycerides.

Acetylcholine (ACh). A neurotransmitter found in the brain, spinal cord, ganglia of the autonomic nervous system, and postganglionic terminal buttons of the parasympathetic division of the autonomic nervous system.

Acetylcholinesterase (AChE). The enzyme that destroys acetylcholine soon after it is liberated by the terminal buttons, thus terminating the postsynaptic potential.

Achromatopsia. Inability to discriminate among different hues; caused by damage to the visual association cortex.

Acquired dyslexia. Reading deficit in someone who could previously read; caused by brain damage.

ACTH. See *adrenocorticotropic hormone (ACTH)*.

Actin. Actin and myosin are the proteins that provide the physical basis for muscular contraction. See Figure 8.1.

Action potential. The brief electrical impulse that provides the basis for conduction of information along an axon. The action potential results from brief changes in membrane permeability to sodium and potassium ions. See Figure 2.28.

Activational effects. See under *hormone.*

Adaptation. Decreasing sensitivity to a stimulus that is applied continuously.

Adenine. One of the nucleotide bases of RNA and DNA.

Adenohypophysis. See under *pituitary gland.*

Adenosine triphosphate (ATP). A molecule of prime importance to cellular energy metabolism: the conversion of ATP to adenosine diphosphate (ADP) liberates energy. ATP can also be converted to cyclic AMP, which serves as an intermediate messenger in the production of postsynaptic potentials by some neurotransmitters and in the me-

diation of the effects of polypeptide hormones. See also *adenylate cyclase* and Figure 3.6.

Adenylate cyclase. An enzyme that converts ATP to cyclic AMP when the postsynaptic receptor to which it is bound is stimulated by the appropriate substance. Important in mediating the intracellular effects of many neurotransmitters and polypeptide hormones. See also *adenosine triphosphate (ATP)* and Figure 3.6.

ADH. See *antidiuretic hormone (ADH).*

Adipose tissue. Fat tissue, composed of cells that can absorb nutrients from the blood and store them in the form of lipids during the absorptive phase or release them in the form of fatty acids and ketones during the fasting phase.

Adipsia. Complete lack of drinking; can be produced by lesions of the lateral hypothalamus or the region around the anteroventral tip of the third ventricle.

Ad libitum. Literally, "to the desire." More generally, "as much as is wanted."

Adrenal gland. An endocrine gland located atop the kidney. The *adrenal cortex* produces steroid hormones such as corticosterone, androstenedione, and aldosterone. The *adrenal medulla,* controlled by sympathetic nerve fibers, secretes epinephrine and norepinephrine.

Adrenalin. See *epinephrine.*

Adrenocorticotropic hormone (ACTH). A hormone produced and liberated by the anterior pituitary gland in response to corticotropin releasing hormone, produced by the hypothalamus. ACTH stimulates the adrenal cortex to produce various steroid hormones. ACTH also inhibits testosterone-dependent intermale aggression.

Adrenogenital syndrome. A condition characterized by hypersecretion of androgens by the adrenal cortex. The result, in females, is masculinization of the external genitalia.

Affect. An emotional state of strong feelings, either positive or negative in nature.

Affective attack. A highly emotional attack of one animal upon another; can be elicited by electrical stimulation of certain regions of the brain.

Afferent. Toward a structure; all neurons afferent to the central nervous system convey sensory information.

Afterdischarge. Abnormally slow and synchronous electrical discharges recorded by the EEG; produced by electrical stimulation of the brain and characteristic of seizures.

Agonist. Literally, a contestant, or one who takes part in the contest. An agonistic drug facilitates the effects of a particular neurotransmitter on the postsynaptic cell. An agonistic muscle produces or facilitates a particular movement. Antonym: antagonist.

Agrammatism. One of the usual symptoms of Broca's aphasia; difficulty in comprehending or properly employing grammatical devices, such as verb endings and word order.

Agraphia. Inability to write, caused by brain damage.

Aldosterone. A hormone of the adrenal cortex that causes the retention of sodium by the kidneys.

Alexia. Inability to read, caused by brain damage.

All-or-none law. States that once an action potential is triggered in an axon, it is propagated, without decrement, to the end of the fiber.

Alloxan. An oxidative product of uric acid; used experimentally to destroy animals' pancreatic islet cells and thus produce diabetes mellitus.

Alpha activity. Smooth electrical activity of 8 to 12 Hz recorded from the brain. Alpha activity is generally associated with a state of relaxation.

Alpha motor neuron. A neuron whose cell body is located in the ventral horn of the spinal cord or in one of the motor nuclei of the cranial nerves. Stimulation of an alpha motor neuron results in contraction of the extrafusal muscle fibers upon which its terminal buttons synapse.

Alzheimer's disease. A degenerative brain disorder of unknown origin; causes progressive memory loss, motor deficits, and eventual death. Acetylcholine-secreting neurons are the first to be affected.

Amacrine cell. Neuron in the retina that interconnects adjacent ganglion cells and the inner arborizations of the bipolar cells.

Amino acid. A molecule that contains both an amino group and a carboxyl group. Amino acids are linked together by peptide bonds and serve as the constituents of proteins.

Amino acid autoradiography. A neuroanatomical technique that permits the tracing of efferent pathways from a region of the brain. A radioactive amino acid such as proline is injected into a region, where it is taken up by neurons and incorporated into proteins. These radioactive proteins are carried by axoplasmic transport to the terminal buttons. The location of the terminal buttons is determined by means of autoradiography.

Amino group. NH_2; two atoms of hydrogen attached to an atom of nitrogen.

Amitriptyline. A monoamine agonist: retards re-uptake by the terminal buttons.

Ammon's horn. The hippocampus proper; part of the hippocampal formation; consists of fields CA1–CA4 (for *cornu Ammonis*).

Amphetamine. A catecholamine agonist: facilitates neurotransmitter release, stimulates postsynaptic receptors (slightly), and retards re-uptake by the terminal buttons.

AMPT. See *α-methyl-p-tyrosine (AMPT).*

Amygdala. The term commonly used for the *amygdaloid complex,* a set of nuclei located in the base of the temporal lobe. The amygdala is a part of the limbic system.

Analgesia. Lack of sensitivity to pain.

Androgen. A male sex steroid hormone. Testosterone is the principal mammalian androgen.

Androgen insensitivity syndrome. A condition, also called *testicular feminization,* caused by a congenital lack of functioning androgen receptors. Because androgens cannot exert their effects, a person with XY sex chromosomes develops as a female, with female external genitalia. Because the fetal testes produce Müllerian-inhibiting substance neither the Wolffian nor the Müllerian systems develop into internal sex organs.

Androgenization. The process initiated by exposure of the cells of a developing animal to androgens. Exposure to androgens causes embryonic sex organs to develop as male and produces certain changes in the brain. See also *hormone.*

Androstenedione. An androgen secreted by the adrenal cortex of both males and females.

Angiotensin. See under *renin.*

Angiotensinogen. See under *renin.*

Angular gyrus. A gyrus in the parietal lobe; the left angular gyrus is important for verbal functions, especially reading.

Anion. See under *ion.*

Anomia. Difficulty in finding (remembering)

the appropriate word to describe an object, action, or attribute; one of the symptoms of aphasia.

Anorexia nervosa. A disorder that most frequently afflicts young women; exaggerated concern with overweight that leads to excessive dieting and often compulsive exercising; can lead to starvation.

ANS. See *autonomic nervous system (ANS)*.

Antagonist. An antagonistic muscle produces a movement contrary or opposite to the one being described. An antagonistic drug opposes or inhibits the effects of a particular neurotransmitter on the postsynaptic cell. Antonym: agonist.

Anterior. See Figure 4.1.

Anterior nuclei (of thalamus). A group of three nuclei of the thalamus (anterodorsal, anteromedial, and anteroventral); part of the limbic system; receive input from the hippocampus (via the fornix columns) and mammillary bodies of the hypothalamus; send axons to the cingulate gyrus.

Anterior pituitary gland. See under *pituitary gland.*

Anterograde amnesia. Amnesia for events that occur after some disturbance to the brain, such as head injury, electroconvulsive shock, or certain degenerative brain diseases.

Anterograde degeneration. Rapid degeneration of an axon distal to its point of damage. See Figure 5.6.

Antidiuretic hormone (ADH). A hormone secreted by the posterior pituitary gland that causes the kidneys to excrete a more concentrated urine, thus retaining water in the body.

Antipsychotic drug. A drug that reduces or eliminates the symptoms of psychosis. Antischizophrenic drugs appear to exert their effect by antagonizing dopaminergic synapses.

Aphagia. Complete lack of eating; can be produced by lesions of the lateral hypothalamus.

Aphasia. Difficulty in producing or comprehending speech; not produced by deafness or a simple motor deficit caused by brain damage.

Apperceptive visual agnosia. See under *visual agnosia.*

Apraxia. Difficulty in carrying out purposeful movements, in the absence of paralysis or muscular weakness.

Aprosodia. Difficulty in producing or comprehending those aspects of speech that are conveyed by changes in intonation or emphasis; apparently related to difficulties in the communication or perception of emotions.

Arachnoid membrane. The middle layer of the meninges, between the outer dura mater and inner pia mater. The subarachnoid space beneath the arachnoid membrane is filled with cerebrospinal fluid, which cushions the brain.

Arcuate nucleus. The hypothalamic nucleus that contains the cell bodies of the neurosecretory cells that produce the hypothalamic hormones.

Area postrema. A region of the medulla where the blood-brain barrier is weak. Systemic poisons can be detected there and can initiate vomiting.

Association cortex. Those regions of cortex that receive information from the sensory areas (sensory association cortex) or that project to the primary motor cortex (motor association cortex); plays an important role in perception, learning, and planning.

Associative visual agnosia. See under *visual agnosia.*

Astrocyte (astroglia). A glial cell that provides support for neurons of the central nervous system. Astrocytes also participate in the formation of scar tissue after injury to the brain or spinal cord.

ATP. See *adenosine triphosphate (ATP)*.

Auditory nerve. The auditory nerve has two principal branches. The *cochlear nerve* transmits auditory information, and the *vestibular nerve* transmits information related to balance.

Autonomic ganglion. See under *ganglion.*

Autonomic nervous system (ANS). The portion of the peripheral nervous system that controls the body's vegetative function. The *sympathetic division* mediates functions that accompany arousal, while the *parasympathetic division* mediates functions that occur during a relaxed state.

Autoradiography. A procedure that locates radioactive substances in body tissue, usually in the brain or spinal cord. The tissue is sliced, mounted on a microscope slide, and covered with a photographic emulsion or piece of film. The radiation exposes the emulsion, which is subsequently developed.

Autoreceptor. A receptor molecule located on a neuron that responds to the neurotransmitter or neuromodulator that the neuron itself secretes. Some autoreceptors are located on the presynaptic membrane; they participate in the regulation of the amount of neurotransmitter that is synthesized and released.

Axoaxonic synapse. The synapse of a terminal button upon the axon of another neuron, near its terminal buttons. These synapses mediate presynaptic inhibition.

Axodendritic synapse. The synapse of a terminal button of the axon of one neuron upon the dendrite of another neuron.

Axon. A thin, elongated process of a neuron that can transmit action potentials toward its terminal buttons, which synapse upon other neurons, gland cells, or muscle cells.

Axon hillock. The initial part of the axon, at the junction of the axon and soma. It is capable of producing an action potential and generally has a slightly lower threshold of excitation than the rest of the axon.

Axoplasmic transport. An active mechanism involving proteins similar to actin and myosin that propel substances down the axons from the soma to the terminal buttons. A slower form of axoplasmic transport carries substances in the opposite direction.

Axosomatic synapse. The synapse of a terminal button of the axon of one neuron upon the membrane of the soma of another neuron.

Baroreceptor. A special receptor that transduces changes in barometric pressure (chiefly within the heart or blood vessels) into neural activity.

Basal ganglia. Caudate nucleus, globus pallidus, putamen, and amygdala. The first three are important parts of the motor system.

Basic rest-activity cycle (BRAC). A 90-minute cycle (in humans) of waxing and waning alertness, controlled by a biological clock in the caudal brainstem; during sleep, it controls cycles of REM sleep and slow-wave sleep.

Basilar artery. An artery found at the base of the brain, connecting the blood supplies of the vertebral and carotid arteries.

Basilar membrane. A membrane in the cochlea of the inner ear; contains the organ of Corti, the receptor organ for hearing.

Basolateral group. The phylogenetically newer portion of the amygdaloid complex.

Benzodiazepine. A class of drug with anxiolytic ("tranquilizing") effects; works by activating benzodiazepine receptors coupled to GABA receptors on neurons, making the latter more sensitive to the neurotransmitter.

Beta activity. Irregular electrical activity of 13 to 30 Hz recorded from the brain. Beta activity is generally associated with a state of arousal.

Bilateral. On both sides of the midline of the body.

Bipolar affective disorder. A psychosis characterized by cyclical periods of mania and depression; effectively treated with lithium carbonate.

Bipolar neuron. A neuron with only two processes—a dendritic process at one end and an axonal process at the other end. (See Figure 2.8.) *Bipolar cells* constitute the middle layer of the retina, conveying information from the receptor cells to the ganglion cells, whose axons give rise to the optic nerves.

Blood-brain barrier. A barrier produced by the astrocytes and cells in the walls of the capillaries in the brain; this barrier permits passage of only certain substances.

Botulinum toxin. An acetylcholine antagonist: prevents release by terminal buttons.

BRAC. See *basic rest-activity cycle (BRAC).*

Brain stem. The "stem" of the brain, from the medulla to the midbrain, excluding the cerebellum.

Bregma. The junction of the sagittal and coronal sutures of the skull. It is often used as a reference point for stereotaxic brain surgery.

Broca's area. A region of frontal cortex, located just rostral to the base of the left primary motor cortex, that is necessary for normal speech production. Damage to this region results in *Broca's aphasia,* characterized by extreme difficulty in speech articulation.

Brown adipose tissue. Fat cells densely packed with mitochondria, which can generate heat; important in hibernating animals and thought to play an important role in converting excessive calories of nutrients into heat rather than increased size of fat deposits.

Bruce effect. Termination of pregnancy caused by the odor of a pheromone in the urine of a male other than the one that impregnated the female; first identified in mice.

Bulimia. Bouts of excessive hunger and eating; often seen in people with anorexia nervosa.

Butyrophenone. A class of drugs used to treat

the symptoms of schizophrenia (examples: haloperidol, spiroperidol, pimozide).

Cable properties. Passive conduction of electrical current, in a decremental fashion, down the length of an axon, similar to the way in which electrical current traverses a submarine cable.

Caffeine. An alkaloid drug found in coffee, chocolate, and other commonly ingested substances; blocks the activity of phosphodiesterase, an enzyme that destroys cyclic nucleotides, the second messengers in the response of many cells to neurotransmitters, neuromodulators, or peptide hormones.

Calcarine fissure. A horizontal fissure on the inner surface of the posterior cerebral cortex; the location of the primary visual cortex.

Calpain. A proteolytic (protein-cleaving) enzyme; thought to cause some of the cellular changes responsible for long-term potentiation by cleaving fodrin, a protein found immediately inside the neural membrane.

Cannula. A small tube that may be inserted into the body to permit introduction of chemicals or removal of fluid for analysis.

Carboxyl group. COOH; two atoms of oxygen and one atom of hydrogen bound to a single atom of carbon.

Carotid artery. An artery, the branches of which serve the rostral portions of the brain.

Cataplexy. A symptom of narcolepsy; complete paralysis that occurs during waking. Thought to be related to REM sleep mechanisms.

Catecholamine. A class of biologically active amines that includes the neurotransmitters dopamine, norepinephrine, and epinephrine.

Cation. See under *ion*.

CAT scanner. A device that uses a computer to analyze data obtained by a scanning beam of X-rays to produce a two-dimensional picture of a "slice" through the body.

Caudal. See Figure 4.1.

Caudate nucleus. A telencephalic nucleus, one of the basal ganglia. The caudate nucleus is principally involved with inhibitory control of movement.

CCK. See *cholecystokinin (CCK)*.

Central canal. The narrow tube, filled with cerebrospinal fluid, that runs through the length of the spinal cord.

Central nervous system (CNS). The brain and spinal cord.

Central sulcus. The sulcus that separates the frontal lobe from the parietal lobe.

Central tegmental tract. An alternative name for the ventral noradrenergic bundle, which carries fibers of noradrenergic neurons from regions of the medulla and from the locus coeruleus and the subcoerulear area of the pons to the hypothalamus.

Cerebral aqueduct. A narrow tube interconnecting the third and fourth ventricles of the brain.

Cerebral cortex. The outermost layer of gray matter of the cerebral hemispheres.

Cerebrospinal fluid (CSF). A clear fluid, similar to blood plasma, that fills the ventricular system of the brain and the subarachnoid space surrounding the brain and spinal cord.

Cerveau isolé. A brain stem transection at the level of the colliculi that results in a chronically comatose animal.

Chemoreceptor. A receptor that responds, by means of receptor potentials or neural impulses, to the presence of a particular chemical.

Chlorpromazine. A dopamine antagonist that blocks postsynaptic receptors. It is the most commonly prescribed antischizophrenic drug.

Cholecystokinin (CCK). A hormone secreted by the duodenum that regulates gastric motility and causes the gallbladder (cholecyst) to contract, expelling bile into the digestive system; also found in neurons in the brain, where it may serve as a neurotransmitter or neuromodulator.

Choline acetyltransferase. The enzyme that transfers the acetate ion from acetyl coenzyme A to choline, producing the neurotransmitter acetylcholine.

Chorda tympani. A branch of the facial nerve (seventh cranial nerve) that passes beneath the eardrum; conveys taste information from the anterior part of the tongue and controls the secretion of some salivary glands.

Chorea. A movement disorder characterized by uncontrollable jerky movements.

Choroid plexus. Highly vascular tissue that protrudes into the ventricles and produces cerebrospinal fluid.

Chromosome. Strand of DNA, with associated proteins, found in the nucleus; carries genetic information.

Ciliary muscles. Muscles arranged around the lens of the eye; control the shape of the eye to focus images of near or distant objects on the retina.

Cingulate gyrus. A strip of limbic cortex lying along the lateral walls of the groove separating the cerebral hemispheres, just above the corpus callosum. See also *Papez's circuit*.

Circadian rhythm. A daily rhythmical change in behavior or physiological process.

Circumstriate cortex. A region of visual association cortex; receives fibers from the striate cortex and from the superior colliculi and projects (in primates) to the inferior temporal cortex.

Citric acid cycle. See *Krebs cycle*.

Classical conditioning. A learning procedure. When a stimulus that initially produces no more than an orienting response is followed several times by an *unconditional stimulus* that produces a defensive or appetitive response (the *unconditional response*), the first stimulus (now called a *conditional stimulus*) itself evokes the response (now called a *conditional response*).

CNS. Central nervous system; the brain and spinal cord.

Cocaine. A drug that retards the re-uptake of the catecholamines, especially dopamine; a potent dopamine agonist.

Cochlea. The snail-shaped structure of the inner ear that contains the auditory transducing mechanisms.

Cochlear microphonics. Electrical activity recorded from the cochlear nerve that corresponds to the sound vibrations received at the oval window.

Cochlear nerve. See under *auditory nerve*.

Codon. The basic three-letter word of the genetic code. Each codon (represented by a sequence of three nucleotide bases on a strand of messenger RNA) specifies a particular amino acid that will be added to a polypeptide chain.

Commissure. A fiber bundle that interconnects corresponding regions on each side of the brain.

Computerized axial tomography. See *CAT scanner*.

Conditional response (CR). See under *classical conditioning*.

Conditional stimulus (CS). See under *classical conditioning*.

Conditioned food aversion. The avoidance of a relatively unfamiliar food that previously caused (or was followed by) illness.

Conduction aphasia. Damage to the connections between Wernicke's area and Broca's area; results in the inability to repeat words that are heard, although they can usually be understood and responded to appropriately.

Cone. See under *photoreceptor*.

Consolidation. The process by which short-term memories are converted into long-term memories.

Constructional apraxia. Difficulty in drawing pictures or diagrams or in making geometrical constructions of elements such as building blocks or sticks; caused by brain damage, especially to the right parietal lobe.

Contralateral. Residing in the side of the body opposite to the reference point.

Convergence. See Figure 8.9.

Coolidge effect. The restorative effect of introducing a new female sex partner to a male that has apparently become "exhausted" by sexual activity.

Cornea. The transparent outer surface of the eye, in front of the iris and pupil.

Coronal section. See Figure 4.2.

Corpus callosum. The largest commissure of the brain, interconnecting the areas of neocortex on each side of the brain.

Corpus luteum. After ovulation, the ovarian follicle develops into a corpus luteum and secretes estradiol and progesterone.

Correctional mechanism. In a regulatory process, the correctional mechanism is the one that is capable of changing the value of the system variable.

Corticobulbar pathway. A bundle of axons from the neocortex (principally the primary motor cortex) to the nuclei of the fifth, seventh, and twelfth cranial nerves in the medulla, which control movements of the face and tongue.

Corticomedial group. The phylogenetically older portion of the amygdaloid complex.

Corticospinal pathway. The system of axons that originates in the cortex (especially the primary motor cortex) and terminates in the ventral gray matter of the spinal cord. Axons of the *lateral corticospinal tract* cross the midline in the pyramids of the medulla and synapse on spinal motor neurons and interneurons that control the arms and hands. Axons of the *ventral corticospinal tract* cross the midline near their site of termination in the spinal cord and primarily control movements of the trunk muscles.

CR. Conditional response. See under *classical conditioning.*

Cranial nerve. One of a set of twelve pairs of nerves that exit from the base of the brain.

Cranial nerve ganglion. See under *ganglion.*

Cross section. See Figure 4.2.

CS. Conditional stimulus. See under *classical conditioning.*

CSF. See *cerebrospinal fluid (CSF).*

Cyclic adenosine monophosphate (cyclic AMP). Intermediate messenger in the production of postsynaptic potentials by some neurotransmitters and in the mediation of the effects of peptide hormones. See also *adenylate cyclase.*

Cyclic guanosine monophosphate (cyclic GMP). Similar in form and function to cyclic adenosine monophosphate, except that guanosine substitutes for adenosine. See also *cyclic adenosine* and *adenylate cyclase.*

Cyclic nucleotide. A compound such as cyclic AMP or cyclic GMP, important in mediating the intracellular effects of many neurotransmitters and peptide hormones. See also *adenylate cyclase.*

Cytoplasm. The viscous, semiliquid substance contained in the interior of a cell.

DA. See *dopamine (DA).*

Decerebrate. Describes an animal whose brain stem has been transected.

Decremental conduction. Conduction of a subthreshold stimulus along an axon, according to its cable properties.

Decussation. Crossing of a fiber to the other side of the brain.

Deep dyslexia. A language disorder caused by massive damage to the left hemisphere; characterized by Broca's aphasia (usually) and difficulty reading words other than concrete nouns.

Delayed conditioning. A classical conditioning procedure in which the unconditional stimulus is presented just before the conditional stimulus is turned off (both stimuli are turned off at the same time).

Delta activity. Regular, synchronous electrical activity of approximately 1 to 4 Hz recorded from the brain. Delta activity is generally associated with slow-wave sleep.

Dementia. Loss of cognitive abilities such as memory, perception, verbal ability, and judgment. Common causes are multiple strokes or Alzheimer's disease.

Dendrite. Treelike process attached to the soma of a neuron, which receives messages from the terminal buttons of other neurons.

Dendritic spine. Small buds on the surface of a dendrite, upon which terminal buttons from other neurons synapse.

Dendrodendritic synapse. Synaptic connections between dendrites of adjacent neurons.

Denervation supersensitivity. Increased sensitivity of neural postsynaptic membrane or motor end plate to the neurotransmitter: caused by damage to the afferent axons or long-term blockage of neurotransmitter release.

Dentate gyrus. Part of the hippocampal formation; receives inputs from the entorhinal cortex via the perforant path and projects to the CA3 field of the hippocampus proper (Ammon's horn).

2-Deoxyglucose (2-DG). A sugar that interferes with the metabolism of glucose.

Deoxyribonucleic acid (DNA). A long, complex macromolecule consisting of two interconnected helical strands. Strands of DNA, along with their associated proteins, constitute the chromosomes, which contain the genetic information of the animal.

Depolarization. Reduction (toward zero) of the membrane potential of a cell from its normal resting potential of approximately −70 mV.

Desynchrony. Irregular electrical activity recorded from the brain, generally associated with periods of arousal. See also *beta activity.*

Detector. In a regulatory process, a mechanism that signals when the system variable deviates from its set point.

Developmental dyslexia. Reading difficulty in a person of normal intelligence and perceptual ability; of genetic origin or caused by prenatal or perinatal factors.

2-DG. See *2-deoxyglucose (2-DG).*

Diabetes mellitus. A disease that results from insufficient production of insulin, thus causing, in an untreated state, a high level of blood glucose.

Diencephalon. See Table 4.1.

Diffusion. Movement of molecules from regions of high concentration to regions of low concentration.

L-Dihydroxyphenylalanine. See *L-DOPA*.

Discriminative stimulus. A stimulus that signifies that a particular response will be followed by a particular event; in an instrumental conditioning task, a discriminative stimulus indicates that a response will be reinforced.

Divergence. See Figure 8.9.

DNA. See *deoxyribonucleic acid (DNA)*.

L-DOPA. The levorotatory isomeric form of dihydroxyphenylalanine; the precursor of the catecholamines dopamine, norepinephrine, and epinephrine. Often used to treat Parkinson's disease because of its effect as a dopamine agonist.

DOPA decarboxylase. The enzyme that converts the L-DOPA to the neurotransmitter dopamine.

Dopamine (DA). A neurotransmitter; one of the catecholamines.

Dopamine β-hydroxylase. The enzyme that converts dopamine to the neurotransmitter norepinephrine; the conversion occurs within synaptic vesicles.

Dorsal. See Figure 4.1.

Dorsal columns. Vertically oriented bundles of axons in the dorsal spinal cord; convey somatosensory information to the brain.

Dorsal lateral geniculate nucleus. See under *lateral geniculate nucleus*.

Dorsal motor nuclei of the vagus. Nuclei of the tenth cranial nerve; control parasympathetic functions of the vagus nerve, such as the secretion of insulin.

Dorsal root. See under *spinal root*.

Dorsal root ganglion. See under *ganglion*.

Dorsal tegmental bundle. An alternative name for the dorsal noradrenergic bundle, which carries fibers of noradrenergic neurons from the locus coeruleus to various forebrain structures.

Dorsolateral column. A fiber bundle in the spinal cord that contains serotonergic axons that mediate opiate-induced analgesia.

Dorsolateral pathway. The system of axons that travel from the brain stem to the spinal cord, primarily those of the *rubrospinal tract,* which controls muscles that move the forelimbs.

Drive-reduction hypothesis. The hypothesis that reinforcement occurs when a drive (presumed to be aversive) is reduced; for example, when hunger is reduced by eating.

Duodenum. The portion of the small intestine immediately adjacent to the stomach.

Dura mater. The outermost layer of the three meninges.

Dynorphin. See under *endogenous opiate*.

Dyslexia. A term that refers to a variety of reading disorders.

EEG. See *electroencephalogram (EEG)*.

Efferent. Away from a structure; efferent axons of the central nervous system control the muscles and glands.

Electroconvulsive shock (ECS). A brief electrical shock, applied to the head, that results in electrical seizure and convulsions. Used therapeutically to alleviate severe depression, and experimentally (in animals) to study the consolidation process.

Electrode. A conductive medium (generally made of metal) that can be used to apply electrical stimulation or to record electrical potentials.

Electroencephalogram (EEG). Electrical brain potentials recorded by placing electrodes on or in the scalp or on the surface of the brain.

Electrolyte. An aqueous solution of a material that ionizes—namely, a soluble acid, base, or salt.

Electromyogram (EMG). Electrical potential recorded from an electrode placed on or in a muscle.

Electro-oculogram (EOG). Electrical potentials from the eyes, recorded by means of electrodes placed on the skin around them; detects eye movements.

Electrostatic pressure. The attractive force between atomic particles charged with opposite signs, or the repulsive force between atomic particles charged with the same sign.

Embolus. A piece of matter (such as a blood clot, fat, or bacterial debris) that dislodges from its site of origin and occludes an artery; in the brain, an embolus can lead to a stroke.

Encéphale isolé. An animal whose central nervous system has been severed transversely between the brain and spinal cord, resulting in paralysis but normal sleep and waking cycles.

Endocrine gland. A gland that liberates its secretions into the extracellular fluid around capillaries and hence into the bloodstream.

Endogenous opiate. A class of peptides secreted by the brain or pituitary gland that act as opiates. Includes the *endorphins, dynorphins,* and *enkephalins.*

Endorphin. See under *endogenous opiate.*

Endplate potential. The postsynaptic potential that occurs on the membranes of muscle fibers in response to release of acetylcholine by terminal buttons.

Enkephalin. See under *endogenous opiate.*

Entorhinal cortex. A region of the limbic cortex that provides the major source of input to the hippocampal formation.

Enzyme. A protein that facilitates a biochemical reaction without itself becoming part of the end product.

EOG. See *electro-oculogram (EOG).*

Ependyma. The layer of tissue around blood vessels and on the interior walls of the ventricular system of the brain.

Epinephrine. A hormone, secreted by the adrenal medulla, that produces physiological effects characteristic of the sympathetic division of the autonomic nervous system.

EPSP. See under *postsynaptic potential.*

Equilibrium. A balance of forces, during which the system is not changing.

Estradiol. The principal estrogen of many mammals, including humans.

Estrogen. A class of sex hormones that cause maturation of the female genitalia, growth of breast tissue, and development of other physical features characteristic of females. Estrogens are also necessary for normal sexual behavior of most mammals other than primates.

Estrous cycle. A cyclic change in the hormonal level and sexual receptivity of subprimate mammals.

Estrus. That portion of the estrous cycle during which a female is sexually receptive.

Evoked potential. A regular series of alterations in the slow electrical activity recorded from the central nervous system, produced by a sensory stimulus or an electrical shock to some part of the nervous system.

Excitatory postsynaptic potential (EPSP). See under *postsynaptic potential.*

Exocrine gland. A gland that liberates its secretions into a duct.

Extension. Movements of limbs that tend to straighten their joints; the opposite of flexion. The muscles that support the weight of a four-legged animal are those that produce extension.

Extracellular fluid. All body fluids outside cells: interstitial fluid, blood plasma, and cerebrospinal fluid.

Extracellular population spike. An evoked potential recorded from portions of the trisynaptic circuit of the hippocampal formation; long-term potentiation is detected by recording the extracellular population spike.

Extrafusal muscle fiber. One of the muscle fibers that are responsible for the force exerted by a muscular contraction.

Fasting phase. The phase of metabolism during which nutrients are not available from the digestive system. Glucose, amino acids, fatty acids, and ketones are derived from glycogen, protein, and adipose tissue during this phase.

Fatty acid. A substance of importance to metabolism during the fasting phase. Fats can be broken down to fatty acids and glycerol. Fatty acids can be metabolized by most cells of the body. Their basic structure is an alkyl group (CH) attached to a carboxyl group (COOH).

Feature detector. A neuron whose synaptic connections with afferent neurons causes it to respond when particular classes of stimuli, with characteristic features, are detected.

Fimbria. A fiber bundle that runs along the lateral surface of the hippocampal complex, connecting this structure with other regions of the forebrain. The fibers of the fimbria become the *fornix* as they course rostrally from the hippocampal formation. The *precommissural fornix* conveys axons from the medial septum to the hippocampus, and from the hippocampus to the lateral septum. The *fornix columns* convey axons from the *subiculum* to the anterior thalamic nuclei and to the mammillary bodies of the hypothalamus.

Fissure. A major groove in the surface of the brain. A smaller groove is called a sulcus.

Fixation. The chemical preparation and preservation of body tissue, usually with formalin.

Flexion. Movements of the limbs that tend to bend their joints; opposite of extension.

Focal epilepsy. A condition in which recurrent

seizures are produced by hyperirritability of a localized region of the brain, especially the medial temporal lobe or orbital frontal lobe.

Fodrin. A protein that lies just inside the neural membrane; thought to be involved in the structural changes that accompany long-term potentiation. See also *calpain.*

Follicle. A small secretory cavity. The *ovarian follicle* consists of epithelial cells surrounding an oocyte, which develops into an ovum.

Follicle-stimulating hormone (FSH). The hormone of the anterior pituitary gland that causes development of an ovarian follicle and the maturation of its oocyte into an ovum.

Foramen. A normal passage that allows communication between two cavities of the body. The *intervertebral foramen* permits passage of the spinal nerves through the vertebral column. The *foramens of Magendie and Luschka* permit the passage of cerebrospinal fluid out of the fourth ventricle and into the subarachnoid space. The *foramen of Monro* interconnects the lateral and third ventricles.

Forebrain. See Table 4.1.

Formalin. The aqueous solution of formaldehyde gas; the most commonly used tissue fixative.

Fornix. See under *fimbria.*

Fornix columns. See under *fimbria.*

Fourth ventricle. See under *ventricle.*

Fovea. The region of the retina that mediates the most acute vision of birds and higher mammals. Color-sensitive cones constitute the only type of photoreceptor found in the fovea.

Frontal section. See Figure 4.2.

FSH. See *follicle-stimulating hormone (FSH).*

GAD. See *glutamic acid decarboxylase (GAD).*

Gamete. A mature reproductive cell; a sperm or ovum.

Gamma-aminobutyric acid (GABA). An important inhibitory transmitter substance.

Gamma motor neuron. A lower motor neuron whose terminal buttons synapse upon intrafusal muscle fibers.

Ganglion. A collection of neural cell bodies, covered with connective tissue, located outside the central nervous system. *Autonomic ganglia* contain the cell bodies of postganglionic neurons of the sympathetic and parasympathetic branches of the autonomic nervous system. *Dorsal root ganglia (spinal nerve ganglia)* contain cell bodies of afferent spinal nerve neurons. *Cranial nerve ganglia* contain cell bodies of afferent cranial nerve neurons. The *basal ganglia* include the amygdala, caudate nucleus, globus pallidus, and putamen; in this case the term *ganglion* is a misnomer, since the basal ganglia are actually brain nuclei.

Ganglion cells. Neurons located in the retina; receive visual information from bipolar cells; their axons give rise to the optic nerve.

Gene. The functional unit of the chromosome, which directs synthesis of one or more proteins.

Gestagen. A group of hormones that promote and support pregnancy. Progesterone is the principal mammalian gestagen.

GH. See *growth hormone (GH).*

Glia (glial cells). The supportive cells of the central nervous system — the astroglia, oligodendroglia, and microglia.

Globus pallidus. One of the basal ganglia; an excitatory structure of the extrapyramidal motor system.

Glucagon. A pancreatic hormone that promotes the conversion of liver glycogen into glucose.

Glucocorticoid. One of a group of hormones of the adrenal cortex that are important in protein and carbohydrate metabolism, secreted especially in times of stress.

Glucose. A simple sugar, of great importance in metabolism. Glucose and ketones constitute the major sources of energy for the brain.

Glucostatic hypothesis. A hypothesis that states that the level or availability of glucose in the interstitial fluid determines whether an organism is hungry or satiated.

Glutamic acid (glutamate). An amino acid; an important excitatory transmitter substance.

Glutamic acid decarboxylase (GAD). The enzyme that converts glutamic acid into GABA, an important inhibitory transmitter substance.

Glycerol (glycerin). A trihydric alcohol; the breakdown of triglycerides (fats stored in adipose tissue) yields fatty acids and glycerol; can be converted by the liver into glucose.

Glycine. An amino acid; an important inhibitory transmitter substance.

Glycogen. A polysaccharide often referred to as

animal starch. The hormone glucagon causes conversion of liver glycogen into glucose.

Golgi apparatus. A complex of parallel membranes in the cytoplasm that wraps the products of a secretory cell.

Golgi tendon organ. The receptor organ at the junction of the tendon and muscle that is sensitive to stretch.

Gonadotropic hormone. A hormone of the anterior pituitary gland that has a stimulating effect on cells of the gonads. See *follicle-stimulating hormone (FSH)* and *luteinizing hormone (LH)*.

Granule cell. Small, granular cells. The granule cells of the dentate gyrus are part of the trisynaptic circuit; they send axons to the CA3 field of Ammon's horn.

Growth hormone (GH). A hormone that is necessary for the normal growth of the body before adulthood; also causes the conversion of glycogen to glucose and thus has an anti-insulin effect. Also called *somatotropic hormone (STH)*.

Guanine. One of the nucleotide bases of RNA and DNA.

Gyrus. A convolution of the cortex of the cerebral hemispheres, separated by sulci or fissures.

Hair cell. The receptive cell of the auditory or vestibular apparatus.

6-HD. See *6-hydroxydopamine (6-HD)*.

Hepatic portal system. The system of blood vessels that drain the capillaries of the digestive system, travel to the liver, and divide again into capillaries.

Hertz (Hz). Cycles per second; a measure of frequency of vibration.

Heterosynaptic facilitation. The ability of the activity of one synapse on a cell to increase the effectiveness of another synapse, belonging to another neuron, on the same cell; thought to be an essential feature of learning.

5-HIAA. See *5-hydroxyindoleacetic acid (5-HIAA)*.

Hindbrain. See Table 4.1.

Hippocampal formation. A forebrain structure of the temporal lobe, constituting an important part of the limbic system. Includes the hippocampus proper (Ammon's horn), dentate gyrus, and subiculum.

Histology. The microscopic study of tissues of the body.

Histone protein. A basic, water-soluble protein that is found in the nucleus, attached to chromosomes; acts as an inhibitor of transcription, or the production of mRNA.

Homeostasis. The process by which the body's substances and characteristics (such as temperature and glucose level) are maintained at their optimal level.

Homoiothermous. A "warm-blooded" animal, which regulates its body temperature by altering its metabolic activity.

Horizontal cell. Neuron in the retina that interconnects adjacent photoreceptors and the outer arborizations of the bipolar cells.

Horizontal section. See Figure 4.2.

Hormone. A chemical substance liberated by an endocrine gland that has effects on target cells in other organs. *Organizational effects* of a hormone affect tissue differentiation and development; for example, androgens cause prenatal development of male genitalia. *Activational effects* of a hormone are those that occur in the fully developed organism; many of them depend upon the organism's prior exposure to the organizational effects of hormones.

Horseradish peroxidase (HRP). An enzyme extracted from the horseradish root. Can be made visible by special histological techniques. Since it is taken up by terminal buttons or by severed axons and is carried by axoplasmic transport, it is useful in anatomical studies.

5-HTP decarboxylase. The enzyme that converts 5-hydroxytryptophan (5-HTP) to the neurotransmitter 5-hydroxytryptamine (5-HT, or serotonin).

H-Y antigen. A protein produced by a gene on the Y chromosome that appears to play an essential role in converting the primordial gonads of the embryo into testes.

Hydrocephalus. A condition in which all or some of the brain's ventricles are enlarged. *Obstructive hydrocephalus* occurs when the normal flow of cerebrospinal fluid is impeded, increasing the intraventricular pressure. *Hydrocephalus ex vacuo* occurs when brain tissue degenerates and the ventricles expand to take up the space the tissue formerly occupied.

6-Hydroxydopamine (6-HD). A chemical that is selectively taken up by axons and terminal buttons of noradrenergic or dopaminergic neurons and that acts as a poison, damaging or killing them.

5-Hydroxyindoleacetic acid (5-HIAA). A breakdown product of the neurotransmitter serotonin.

5-Hydroxytryptamine (5-HT). An indolamine transmitter substance; also called *serotonin*.

5-Hydroxytryptophan (5-HTP). Derived from the amino acid tryptophan; converted to the neurotransmitter 5-hydroxytryptamine (5-HT) by the enzyme 5-HTP decarboxylase.

Hyperpolarization. An increase in the membrane potential of a cell, relative to the normal resting potential. Inhibitory postsynaptic potentials (IPSPs) are hyperpolarizations.

Hypnagogic hallucinations. A symptom of narcolepsy; vivid dreams that occur just before a person falls asleep; accompanied by sleep paralysis.

Hypoglycemia. A low level of blood glucose.

Hypopolarization. See *depolarization*.

Hypothalamic hormone. A hormone produced by cells of the hypothalamus that affects the secretion and production of hormones of the anterior pituitary gland. The effects are excitatory in the case of releasing hormones and inhibitory in the case of inhibitory hormones.

Hypothalamic-hypophyseal portal system. A system of blood vessels that connect capillaries of the hypothalamus with capillaries of the anterior pituitary gland. Hypothalamic hormones travel to the anterior pituitary gland by means of this system.

Hypovolemia. See under *volumetric thirst*.

Hz. See *hertz (Hz)*.

Imipramine. A noradrenergic agonist: retards reuptake of norepinephrine by terminal buttons. One of the most commonly used tricyclic antidepressants.

Immune system. The system by which the body protects itself from foreign proteins. In response to an infection, the white blood cells produce antibodies that attack and destroy the foreign antigen.

Incus. One of the bones of the middle ear, shaped somewhat like an anvil. See Figure 7.2.

Inferior. See Figure 4.1.

Inferior colliculi. Protrusions on top of the midbrain that relay auditory information to the medial geniculate nucleus.

Inferior temporal cortex. In monkeys, the highest level of visual association cortex, located on the inferior surface of the temporal lobe.

Inhibitory postsynaptic potential (IPSP). See under *postsynaptic potential*.

Instrumental conditioning. A learning procedure whereby the effects of a particular behavior in a particular situation increase (reinforce) or decrease (punish) the probability of the behavior; also called *operant conditioning*.

Insulin. A pancreatic hormone that facilitates entry of glucose and amino acids into the cell, facilitates conversion of glucose into glycogen, and facilitates transport of fats into adipose tissue.

Interstitial fluid. The fluid that bathes the cells of the body, filling the space between the cells of the body (the "interstices").

Intervertebral foramen. See under *foramen*.

Intracellular fluid. The fluid contained within cells.

Intrafusal muscle fiber. A muscle fiber that functions as a stretch receptor, arranged parallel to the extrafusal muscle fibers, thus detecting muscle length. Also called *muscle spindle*.

Intraperitoneal (IP). Pertaining to the peritoneal cavity, the space surrounding the abdominal organs.

Intromission. Insertion of one part into another, especially of a penis into a vagina.

Ion. A charged molecule; *cations* are positively charged, and *anions* are negatively charged.

Ion channel. A specialized protein molecule that permits specific ions to enter or leave cells. *Voltage-dependent ion channels* open or close according to the value of the membrane potential. *Neurotransmitter-dependent ion channels* open when they detect molecules of the appropriate neurotransmitter or molecules of a cyclic nucleotide that serves as a second messenger.

IP. See *intraperitoneal (IP)*.

Iproniazid. A monoamine agonist: deactivates monoamine oxidase and thus prevents destruction of extravesicular monoamines in the terminal buttons.

Ipsilateral. Located on the same side of the body as the point of reference.

IPSP. See under *postsynaptic potential*.

Isolated cortical slab. A region of cortex surgically separated from the surrounding tissue but with a relatively intact blood supply.

Isotonic. Equal in osmotic pressure to the contents of a cell. A cell placed in an isotonic solution neither gains nor loses water.

Juxtaglomerular cell. A cell in the kidney located near the glomerulus that secretes renin in response to a low flow of blood through the kidney or in response to activity of the kidney's sympathetic innervation.

Kainic acid. A molecule similar to glutamic acid that destroys neurons with which it comes in contact, apparently by causing continuous excitation; used to produce brain lesions that spare axons that pass through the area containing the cells targeted for destruction.

Ketone. An organic acid consisting of two hydrocarbon radicals attached to a carbonyl group (CO). Ketones are produced from the breakdown of fats and can be utilized by the brain. Often called *ketone bodies.*

Kindling. The establishment of a seizure focus by daily administration of a small amount of localized electrical brain stimulation; used to produce animal models of focal epilepsy.

Kinesthesia. Perception of the body's own movements.

Korsakoff's syndrome. Permanent anterograde amnesia (inability to learn new information) caused by brain damage resulting from chronic alcoholism or malnutrition.

Krebs cycle (citric acid cycle, tricarboxylic acid cycle). A series of chemical reactions that involve oxidation of pyruvate. The Krebs cycle takes place on the cristae of the mitochondria and supplies the principal source of energy to the cell.

Lateral. See Figure 4.1.

Lateral corticospinal tract. See under *corticospinal pathway.*

Lateral fissure. The fissure that separates the temporal lobe from the overlying frontal and parietal lobes.

Lateral geniculate nucleus. A group of cell bodies within the lateral geniculate body of the thalamus. The *dorsal lateral geniculate nucleus* receives fibers from the retina and projects fibers to the primary visual cortex.

Lateral hypothalamus. A region of the hypothalamus that contains cell bodies and diffuse fiber systems. Destruction of the lateral hypothalamus produces a relative lack of spontaneous movement, adipsia, aphagia, and weight loss, from which the animal at least partially recovers.

Lateral lemniscus. A band of fibers running rostrally through the medulla and pons; carries fibers of the auditory system.

Lateral preoptic area. See under *preoptic area.*

Lateral ventricle. See under *ventricle.*

Lee-Boot effect. The increased incidence of false pregnancies seen in female animals that are housed together; caused by a pheromone in the animals' urine; first observed in mice.

Lemniscal system. The somatosensory fibers of the lateral or trigeminal lemniscus, as contrasted with the extralemniscal system, a polysynaptic pathway that ascends through the reticular formation.

Leupeptin. A drug that inactivates calpain, an enzyme that cleaves fodrin, a protein present just inside the neural membrane.

LH. See *luteinizing hormone (LH).*

Limbic cortex. Phylogenetically old cortex, located at the edge ("limbus") of the cerebral hemispheres; part of the limbic system.

Limbic system. A group of brain regions including the anterior thalamic nuclei, amygdala, hippocampus, limbic cortex, and parts of the hypothalamus, as well as their interconnecting fiber bundles.

Locus coeruleus. A dark-colored group of noradrenergic cell bodies located in the pons near the rostral end of the floor of the fourth ventricle.

Long-term memory. Relatively stable memory, as opposed to short-term memory.

Long-term potentiation. An increase in the excitability of neurons in the trisynaptic circuit of the entorhinal cortex and hippocampal formation, caused by repeated electrical stimulation; thought to be related to learning and to the phenomenon of kindling.

Lordosis. A spinal sexual reflex seen in many four-legged female mammals; arching of the back in response to approach of a male or to touching the flanks, which elevates the hindquarters.

Lower motor neuron. A neuron located in the intermediate horn or ventral horn of the gray matter of the spinal cord or in one of the motor nuclei of the cranial nerves, the axon of which synapses on muscle fibers.

Luteinizing hormone (LH). A hormone of the anterior pituitary gland that causes ovulation and development of the ovarian follicle into a corpus luteum.

Lysergic acid diethylamide (LSD). A serotonin antagonist: stimulates autoreceptors on serotonergic neurons, thus inhibiting neurotransmitter release. Acts as a hallucinogen.

Macroelectrode. A relatively large electrode (larger than a microelectrode) that is used to record action potentials or spontaneous EEG activity.

Malleus. One of the bones of the middle ear, shaped somewhat like a hammer. See Figure 7.2.

Mammillary body. A protrusion of the bottom of the brain at the posterior end of the hypothalamus, containing the medial and lateral mammillary nuclei.

MAO. See *monoamine oxidase (MAO)*.

Massa intermedia. A bridge of tissue across the third ventricle that connects the right and left portions of the thalamus.

Medial. See Figure 4.1.

Medial forebrain bundle (MFB). A fiber bundle that runs in a rostral-caudal direction through the basal forebrain and lateral hypothalamus.

Medial geniculate nucleus. A group of cell bodies within the medial geniculate body of the thalamus; part of the auditory system.

Medial lemniscus. A fiber bundle that ascends rostrally through the medulla and pons, carrying fibers of the somatosensory system.

Medial preoptic area. See *preoptic area*.

Medulla oblongata (usually medulla). The most caudal portion of the brain, immediately rostral to the spinal cord.

Meiosis. The process by which a cell divides to form gametes (sperms or ova).

Membrane. A structure consisting principally of lipid molecules that defines the outer boundaries of a cell and also constitutes many of the cell organelles, such as the Golgi apparatus.

Membrane potential. The electrical charge across a cell membrane; the difference in electrical potential inside and outside the cell; expressed as inside voltage relative to outside voltage (e.g., -70 mV signifies that the inside is 70 millivolts negative to the outside).

Meninges (singular: **meninx**). The three layers of tissue that encase the central nervous system: the dura mater, arachnoid membrane, and pia mater.

Mesencephalon. See Table 4.1.

Messenger ribonucleic acid (mRNA). See under *ribonucleic acid*.

Metabolism. The sum of all physical and chemical changes that take place in an organism, including all reactions that liberate energy. See also *absorptive phase* and *fasting phase*.

Metencephalon. See Table 4.1.

α-Methyl-*p*-tyrosine (AMPT). A substance that interferes with the activity of tyrosine hydroxylase and thus prevents the synthesis of dopamine and norepinephrine.

MFB. See *medial forebrain bundle (MFB)*.

Microelectrode. A very fine electrode, generally used to record activity of individual neurons.

Microglia. Small glial cells that serve as phagocytes.

Micrometer (μm). Unit of measurement; one millionth of a meter, or 1/1000 of a millimeter.

Midbrain. See Table 4.1.

Midcollicular transection. See *cerveau isolé*.

Midline nuclei (of thalamus). Thalamic nuclei that lie near the midline of the brain.

Midpontine pretrigeminal transection. A transection through the middle of the pons, which produces ocular and electroencephalographic signs of wakefulness that are present in the animal most of the time.

Midsagittal plane. The plane that divides the body in two symmetrical halves through the midline.

Mitochondrion. A cell organelle in which the chemical reactions of the Krebs cycle take place.

Mitosis. Duplication and division of a somatic cell into a pair of daughter cells.

Monoamine. A class of amines that includes indolamines (e.g., serotonin) and catecholamines (e.g., dopamine and norepinephrine).

Monoamine oxidase (MAO). A class of enzymes that destroy the monoamines: dopamine, norepinephrine, and serotonin.

Monosynaptic stretch reflex. A reflex consisting of the afferent axon of the intrafusal muscle fiber synapsing upon an alpha motor neuron, and the efferent axon of the alpha motor neuron synapsing on the extrafusal muscle fibers in the same muscle. When a muscle is quickly stretched, the monosynaptic stretch reflex causes it to contract.

Morphology. Physical shape and structure.

Motor end plate. Region of the membrane of a muscle fiber upon which the terminal buttons of the efferent axon synapse.

Motor neuron (motoneuron). A neuron, the stimulation of which results in contractions of muscle fibers.

Motor unit. A motor neuron and its associated muscle fibers.

mRNA. See under *ribonucleic acid (RNA)*.

Müllerian-inhibiting substance. A peptide secreted by the fetal testes that inhibits the development of the Müllerian system, which would otherwise become the female internal sex organs.

Müllerian system. The embryonic precursors of the female internal sex organs.

Multipolar neuron. A neuron with a single axon and numerous dendritic processes originating from the somatic membrane.

Muscle spindle. See *intrafusal muscle fiber*.

Myelencephalon. See Table 4.1.

Myelin. A complex fatlike substance produced by the oligodendroglia in the central nervous system and by the Schwann cells in the peripheral nervous system, which surrounds and insulates myelinated axons.

Myosin. Actin and myosin are the proteins that provide the physical basis for muscular contraction. See Figure 8.1.

Naloxone. A drug that blocks opiate receptors and thus blocks the effects of endogenous and exogenous opiates; used to treat opiate overdoses and in experimental investigations.

Narcolepsy. A sleep disorder characterized by periods of irresistible sleep, attacks of cataplexy, sleep paralysis, and hypnagogic hallucinations.

NE. See *norepinephrine (NE)*.

Negative feedback. A process whereby the effect produced by an action serves to diminish or terminate that action. Regulatory systems are characterized by negative feedback loops.

Neocortex. The phylogenetically newest cortex, including primary sensory cortex, primary motor cortex, and association cortex.

Neostriatum. The caudate nucleus and putamen.

Neural integration. The process by which inhibitory and excitatory postsynaptic potentials summate and control the rate of firing of a neuron.

Neuraxis. An imaginary line drawn through the center of the length of the central nervous system, from the bottom of the spinal cord to the front of the forebrain.

Neuroglia. The formal name for *glia*.

Neurohypophysis. See under *pituitary gland*.

Neuromodulator. A naturally secreted substance that acts like a neurotransmitter except that it is not restricted to the synaptic cleft but diffuses through the interstitial fluid. Presumably, it activates receptors on neurons that are not located at synapses.

Neuromuscular junction. The synapse between the terminal buttons of an axon and a muscle fiber.

Neurosecretory cell. A neuron that secretes a hormone or hormonelike substance into the interstitial fluid.

Neurotransmitter. See under *transmitter substance*.

Neurotransmitter-dependent ion channel. See under *ion channel*.

Nigrostriatal bundle. A bundle of axons originating in the substantia nigra and terminating in the neostriatum (caudate nucleus and putamen).

Nissl substance. Cytoplasmic material dyed by cell-body stains (Nissl stains).

Node of Ranvier. A naked portion of a myelinated axon, between adjacent oligodendroglia or Schwann cells.

Nonhistone protein. An acidic protein that is found in the nucleus, attached to chromosomes; acts as a disinhibitor of transcription, or the production of mRNA.

Noradrenalin. See *norepinephrine*.

Norepinephrine (NE). A neurotransmitter found in the brain and in the terminal buttons of postganglionic fibers of the sympathetic division of the autonomic nervous system.

Nucleolus. An organelle within the nucleus of a cell that produces the ribosomes.

Nucleotide base. One of several compounds that forms one of the elements of ribonucleic acid and deoxyribonucleic acid: adenine, guanine, cytosine, thymine, and uracil.

Nucleus. 1. The central portion of an atom. 2. A spherical structure, enclosed by a membrane, located in the cytoplasm of most cells and containing the chromosomes. 3. A histologically identifiable group of neural cell bodies in the central nervous system.

Nucleus accumbens. A nucleus of the basal forebrain near the septum; receives dopamine-secreting terminal buttons from neurons of the ventral tegmental area; thought to be involved in reinforcement and attention.

Nucleus basalis of Meynert. A nucleus of the basal forebrain that contains most of the acetylcholine-secreting neurons that send axons to the neocortex; degenerates in patients with Alzheimer's disease.

Nucleus circularis. A small, football-shaped nucleus in the hypothalamus; may contain receptors that induce secretion of antidiuretic hormone in response to increased osmotic pressure of the interstitial fluid.

Nucleus of the diagonal band. A nucleus of the basal forebrain located medial to the nucleus accumbens; contains neurons that send axons to the ventral tegmental area that may be involved in reinforcement.

Nucleus of the solitary tract. A nucleus of the medulla that receives information from visceral organs and from the gustatory system; appears to play a role in sleep.

Nucleus raphe magnus. One of the nuclei of the raphe; contains serotonin-secreting neurons that project to the dorsal gray matter of the spinal cord via the dorsolateral columns; involved in analgesia produced by opiates.

OA. See Figure 14.2.

OB. See Figure 14.2.

OC. See Figure 14.2.

Olfactory bulb. The protrusion at the end of the olfactory nerve; receives input from the olfactory receptors.

Oligodendroglia. A type of glial cell in the central nervous system that forms myelin sheaths.

Operant conditioning. See *instrumental conditioning.*

Opsin. A class of protein that, together with retinal, constitutes the photopigments that are responsible for the transduction of visual information in the eye.

Optic chiasm. A cross-shaped connection between the optic nerves, located below the base of the brain, just anterior to the pituitary gland.

Optic disk. See under *optic nerve.*

Optic nerve. The second cranial nerve, carrying visual information from the retina to the brain. The *optic disk* is formed at the exit point from the retina of the fibers of the ganglion cells that form the optic nerve.

Optic radiation. The band of axons that project from the dorsal lateral geniculate nuclei of the thalamus to the primary visual cortex.

Organizational effects. See under *hormone.*

Organ of Corti. The receptor organ situated on the basilar membrane of the inner ear.

Oscilloscope. A laboratory instrument capable of displaying a graph of voltage as a function of time on the face of a cathode-ray tube.

Osmometric thirst. Thirst produced by an increase in the osmotic pressure of the interstitial fluid relative to the intracellular fluid, thus producing cellular dehydration.

Osmosis. Movement of ions through a semipermeable membrane, down their concentration gradient.

Outer plexiform layer. The layer of the retina that contains synapses between the arborizations of bipolar cells, horizontal cells, and photoreceptors.

Oval window. An opening in the bone surrounding the cochlea. The baseplate of the stapes presses against a membrane exposed by the oval window and transmits sound vibrations into the fluid within the cochlea.

Ovarian follicle. See *follicle.*

Paleostriatum. The globus pallidus.

Papez's circuit. A neural circuit consisting of the mammillary bodies, anterior thalamic nuclei, cingulate cortex, entorhinal cortex, hippocampus, and their interconnecting fibers.

Parabrachial nucleus. A nucleus of the pons; relays gustatory information from the nucleus of the solitary tract of the medulla to the thalamic taste area.

Para-chlorophenylalanine (PCPA). A substance that blocks the action of the enzyme tryptophan hydroxylase and hence prevents synthesis of serotonin (5-HT).

Paradoxical sleep. See *REM sleep.*

Paraphasic error. A speech error characterized by unintended or transposed syllables, words, or phrases.

Parasympathetic division. See under *autonomic nervous system (ANS).*

Paraventricular nucleus. A hypothalamic nucleus that contains cell bodies of neurons that produce antidiuretic hormone and oxytocin, and transport it through their axons to the posterior pituitary gland.

Parkinson's disease. A neurological disease that is characterized by fine tremor, rigidity, and difficulty in movement. Caused by degeneration of the nigrostriatal bundle.

PCPA. See *para-chlorophenylalanine (PCPA)*.

Peptide. A chain of amino acids joined together by peptide bonds. Many peptides produced by cells of the brain serve as neurotransmitters, neuromodulators, or hormones. Proteins are long peptides.

Peptide bond. A bond between the amino group of one amino acid and the carboxyl group of its neighbor. Peptide bonds link amino acids to form polypeptides or proteins.

Perforant path. The system of axons that travel from cells in the entorhinal cortex to the dentate gyrus of the hippocampal formation.

Periaqueductal gray matter. The region of the midbrain that surrounds the cerebral aqueduct; contains neural circuits that control aggressive behavior and female sexual behavior and opiate-sensitive cells that mediate analgesia.

Peripheral nervous system (PNS). The cranial nerves, spinal nerves, and peripheral ganglia.

Permeability. The degree to which a membrane permits passage of a particular substance.

PGO waves. Bursts of phasic electrical activity originating in the pons, followed by activity in the lateral geniculate nucleus and visual cortex; a characteristic of REM sleep.

Phagocytosis. The process by which cells engulf and digest other cells or debris caused by cellular degeneration; the cells that perform this function are *phagocytes*.

Pheromone. A chemical released by one animal that affects the behavior or physiology of another animal; usually smelled or tasted.

Phosphodiesterase. A class of enzymes that deactivate cyclic nucleotides.

Phosphorylation. The addition of phosphate to a protein, thus altering its physical characteristics.

Photoreceptor. The receptor cell of the retina, which transduces photic energy into electrical potentials. *Cones* are maximally sensitive to one of three different wavelengths of light and hence encode color vision, whereas all *rods* are maximally sensitive to light of the same wavelength and hence do not encode color vision.

Physostigmine. An acetylcholine agonist: inactivates acetylcholinesterase.

Pia mater. The layer of the meninges adjacent to the surface of the brain.

Pinocytosis. Pinching off of a bud of cell membrane, which travels to the interior of the cell; used to incorporate substances present in the interstitial fluid and to recycle pieces of the membrane used for producing synaptic vesicles.

Pituitary gland. The "master endocrine gland" of the body, attached to the base of the brain. The *anterior pituitary gland* (adenohypophysis) secretes hormones in response to the hypothalamic hormones. The *posterior pituitary gland* (neurohypophysis) secretes oxytocin or antidiuretic hormone in response to stimulation from its neural input.

Placebo. An inert substance given to an organism in lieu of a physiologically active drug; used experimentally to control for the effects of mere administration of a drug.

Platelet. A cell fragment that is necessary for the formation of blood clots.

Plexus. A network formed by the junction of several adjacent nerves.

PNS. The peripheral nervous system; the cranial nerves, spinal nerves, and peripheral ganglia.

Poikilothermous. Not capable of regulating body temperature by producing heat endogenously. Most poikilothermous animals regulate their body temperature but must approach or avoid sources of heat to do so.

Pons. The region of the brain rostral to the medulla and caudal to the midbrain.

Posterior. See Figure 4.1.

Posterior pituitary gland. See under *pituitary gland*.

Postganglionic neurons. Neurons of the autonomic nervous system that synapse directly upon their target organ.

Postsynaptic membrane. The cell membrane opposite the terminal button in a synapse; the membrane of the cell that receives the message.

Postsynaptic potential. Alterations in the membrane potential of a postsynaptic neuron, produced by liberation of transmitter substance at the synapse. *Excitatory postsynaptic potentials (EPSPs)* are depolarizations and increase the probability of firing of the postsynaptic neuron. *Inhibitory postsynaptic potentials (IPSPs)* are hyperpolarizations and decrease the probability of neural firing.

Postsynaptic receptor. A receptor molecule in the postsynaptic membrane of a synapse that detects the presence of a neurotransmitter and controls neurotransmitter-dependent ion channels, thus producing excitatory or inhibitory postsynaptic potentials.

Precommissural fornix. See under *fimbria*.

Predatory aggression. Attack of one animal directed at an individual of another species, on which the attacking animal normally preys.

Preganglionic neuron. The efferent neuron of the autonomic nervous system whose cell body is located in a cranial nerve nucleus or in the intermediate horn of the spinal gray matter and whose terminal buttons synapse upon postganglionic neurons in the autonomic ganglia.

Preoptic area. An area of cell bodies (usually divided into the *lateral preoptic area* and *medial preoptic area*) just rostral to the hypothalamus. Some investigators refer to the preoptic area as a part of the hypothalamus, although embryologically they are derived from different tissue.

Presynaptic. Referring to a neuron that synapses upon another one. See also *postsynaptic*.

Presynaptic membrane. The membrane of a terminal button that lies parallel to the postsynaptic membrane.

Primary motor cortex. The precentral gyrus, which contains neurons that control movements of skeletal muscles.

Primary sensory cortex. Regions of cortex whose primary input is from one of the sensory systems.

Priming. A phenomenon often observed in studies that investigate the response of animals to rewarding brain stimulation. Priming refers to the fact that an animal that previously responded for brain stimulation will fail to do so until it is given a few "reminder shots" of brain stimulation. The analogy is to priming a pump that has run dry.

Primordial. In embryology, refers to the undeveloped early form of an organ.

Progesterone. A steroid hormone produced by the ovary; maintains the endometrial lining of the uterus during the later part of the menstrual cycle and during pregnancy; along with estradiol, promotes receptivity in female mammals with estrous cycles.

Projection. The efferent connection between neurons in one specific region of the brain and those in another region.

Prolactin. A hormone of the anterior pituitary gland, necessary for production of milk and (in some subprimate mammals) development of a corpus luteum. Occasionally called luteotropic hormone.

Propranolol. A noradrenergic antagonist: blocks postsynaptic β noradrenergic receptors.

Prosody. The use of changes in intonation and emphasis to convey meaning in speech besides that specified by the particular words; an important means of communication of emotion.

Prosopagnosia. The inability to recognize people by the sight of their faces.

Prosthesis. A device used to substitute for a missing or damaged part of the body.

Protein. A long peptide that can serve in a structural capacity or as an enzyme.

Protein kinase. An enzyme that attaches a phosphate (PO_4) to a protein and thereby causes it to change its shape. Protein kinases are activated by cyclic nucleotides and open ion channels by phosphorylating membrane proteins.

Psychosurgery. Destruction of brain tissue to treat behavioral disorders in the absence of verified brain damage.

Pure word deafness. The ability to hear, to speak, and (usually) to write, without being able to comprehend the meaning of speech; caused by bilateral temporal lobe damage.

Putamen. One of the nuclei that constitute the basal ganglia. The putamen and caudate nucleus compose the neostriatum.

Pylorus. The ring of smooth muscle at the junction of the stomach and duodenum that controls the release of the stomach contents.

Pyramidal cell. A category of large neurons with a pyramid shape; found in the cerebral cortex and Ammon's horn of the hippocampal formation.

Pyramidal tract. A fiber bundle that contains axons of the lateral and ventral corticospinal tracts.

Raphe. A group of nuclei located in the reticular formation of the medulla, pons, and midbrain, situated along the midline.

Receptive field. That portion of the visual field in which the presentation of visual stimuli will produce an alteration in the firing rate of a particular neuron.

Receptor blocker. A drug that blocks postsynaptic receptors without stimulating them, thus preventing the neurotransmitter from acting on them.

Receptor cell. A specialized type of cell that transduces physical stimuli into slow, graded receptor potentials.

Receptor molecule. A protein molecule situated in the membrane of a cell that is sensitive to a particular chemical, such as a neurotransmitter or hormone. When the appropriate chemical stimulates a receptor site, changes take place in the membrane or within the cell.

Receptor potential. A slow, graded electrical potential produced by a receptor cell in response to a physical stimulus. Receptor potentials alter the firing rate of neurons upon which the receptor cells synapse.

Red nucleus. A large nucleus of the midbrain that receives inputs from the cerebellum and motor cortex and sends axons to the spinal cord via the rubrospinal tract and to various subcortical motor nuclei.

Reflex. A stereotyped glandular secretion or movement produced as the direct result of a stimulus.

REM sleep. A period of desynchronized EEG activity during sleep, at which time dreaming, rapid eye movements, and muscular paralysis occur. Also called *paradoxical sleep.*

Renin. Sympathetic stimulation of the kidney, or reduction of its blood flow, results in the liberation of renin, a hormone that causes the conversion of *angiotensinogen* in the blood into *angiotensin.* Angiotensin produces thirst, constricts blood vessels (thus raising blood pressure), and stimulates the adrenal cortex to produce aldosterone, a hormone that stimulates the kidney to retain sodium.

Reserpine. A monoamine antagonist: makes synaptic vesicles leaky, so that the neurotransmitter (dopamine, norepinephrine, or serotonin) cannot be kept inside.

Resting potential. The membrane potential of a neuron when it is not being altered by excitatory or inhibitory postsynaptic potentials; approximately −70 mV.

Reticular formation. A large network of neural tissue located in the central region of the brain stem, from the medulla to the diencephalon.

Reticulospinal tract. A bundle of axons that travel from the reticular formation to the gray matter of the spinal cord; controls the muscles responsible for postural movements.

Retina. The neural tissue and photoreceptive cells located on the inner surface of the posterior portion of the eye.

Retrograde amnesia. Amnesia for events that preceded some disturbance to the brain, such as a head injury or electroconvulsive shock.

Re-uptake. The re-entry of a transmitter substance just liberated by a terminal button back through its membrane, thus terminating the postsynaptic potential that is induced in the postsynaptic neuron.

Reverberation. Circulating electrical activity maintained in a closed loop of neurons, which might constitute the physical basis for short-term memory.

Rhodopsin. A particular opsin found in rods.

Ribonucleic acid (RNA). A complex macromolecule composed of a sequence of nucleotide bases attached to a sugar-phosphate backbone. *Messenger RNA (mRNA)* delivers genetic information from a portion of a chromosome to a ribosome, where the appropriate amino acids are assembled to produce the polypeptide coded for by the active portion of the chromosome.

Ribosome. A cytoplasmic structure, made of protein, that serves as the site of production of proteins translated from mRNA.

Ringer's solution. An aqueous solution of electrolytes designed to duplicate interstitial fluid.

RNA. See *ribonucleic acid (RNA).*

Rod. See under *photoreceptor.*

Rostral. See Figure 4.1.

Round window. An opening in the bone surrounding the cochlea of the inner ear that permits vibrations to be transmitted, via the oval window, through the fluids and receptive tissue contained within the cochlea.

Rubrospinal tract. See under *dorsolateral pathway.*

Sagittal section. See Figure 4.2.

Saltatory conduction. Conduction of action potentials by myelinated axons; the action potential "jumps" from one node of Ranvier to the next.

Satellite cell. A cell that serves to support neurons of the peripheral nervous system, such as the Schwann cells that provide the myelin sheath.

Satiety. Cessation of hunger, produced by adequate and available supplies of nutrients.

Schwann cell. A cell in the peripheral nervous system that is wrapped around a myelinated axon, providing one segment of its myelin sheath.

SCN. See *suprachiasmatic nucleus (SCN)*.

Scotoma. A region of blindness within an otherwise-normal visual field, produced by localized damage somewhere in the visual system.

Semicircular canal. One of the three ringlike structures of the vestibular apparatus that transduce changes in head rotation into neural activity.

Sensory coding. Representation of sensory events in the form of neural activity.

Sensory modality. A particular form of sensory input, such as vision, audition, or olfaction.

Sensory transduction. The process by which sensory stimuli are transduced into slow, graded receptor potentials.

Septum. A portion of the limbic system, lying between the walls of the anterior portions of the lateral ventricles.

Serotonin. An alternative name for the neurotransmitter 5-hydroxytryptamine (5-HT); named because of its constricting effect on blood vessels.

Set point. The optimal value of the system variable in a regulatory mechanism. The set point for human body temperature, recorded orally, is approximately 37° C.

Sexually dimorphic nucleus. A nucleus in the preoptic area that is much larger in males than in females; first observed in rats.

SFO. See *subfornical organ (SFO)*.

Short-term memory. Immediate memory for sensory events that may or may not be consolidated into long-term memory.

Single unit. An individual neuron.

Sleep apnea. Failure to breathe while asleep; periods of sleep apnea occur in normal people, but when they are especially frequent they substan-

tially disturb sleep and pose a risk to life in infants and old or debilitated people.

Slow-wave sleep. Non-REM sleep, characterized by synchronized EEG activity during its deeper stages.

Smooth muscle. Nonstriated muscle innervated by the autonomic nervous system, found in the walls of blood vessels, in sphincters, within the eye, in the digestive system, and around hair follicles.

Sodium-potassium pump. A metabolically active process in the cellular membrane that extrudes sodium from and transports potassium into the cell.

Solitary nucleus. See *nucleus of the solitary tract*.

Soma. A cell body or, more generally, the body.

Somatosenses. Bodily sensation; sensitivity to such stimuli as touch, pain, and temperature.

Somatosensory cortex. The gyrus caudal to the central sulcus, which receives many projection fibers from the somatosensory system.

Somatotropic hormone (STH). See *growth hormone (GH)*.

Species-typical behavior. A behavior that is typical of all or most members of a species of animal, especially a behavior that does not appear to have to be learned.

Spelling dyslexia. A disorder in which a person can read a word only after spelling out the individual letters; caused by brain damage.

Spinal nucleus of the bulbocavernosus. A nucleus located in the lower spinal cord; in laboratory rodents the nucleus has been found to be sexually dimorphic, being present only in males.

Spinal root. A bundle of axons surrounded by connective tissue that occurs in pairs, which fuse and form a spinal nerve. The *dorsal root* contains afferent fibers, whereas the *ventral root* contains efferent fibers.

Stapes. One of the bones of the inner ear, shaped somewhat like a stirrup. See Figure 7.2.

Stereotaxic apparatus. A device that permits the experimenter to place an object such as an electrode or cannula into a specific part of the brain.

Steroid hormone. A hormone of low molecular weight, derived from cholesterol. Steroid hormones affect their target cells by attaching to receptors found within the cell.

STH. See *growth hormone (GH)*.

Striate cortex. Primary visual cortex.

Stria terminalis. A long fiber bundle that connects portions of the amygdala with the hypothalamus.

Subarachnoid space. The fluid-filled space between the arachnoid membrane and the pia mater.

Subcortical. Located within the brain, as opposed to being located on its cortical surface.

Subfornical organ (SFO). A small organ located in the confluence of the lateral ventricles, attached to the underside of the fornix; contains neurons that detect the presence of angiotensin in the blood and excite neural circuits that initiate drinking.

Subiculum. Part of the hippocampal formation. See under *fimbria*.

Substantia nigra. A darkly stained region of the tegmentum, which communicates with the neostriatum via the nigrostriatal bundle.

Sulcus. A groove in the surface of the cerebral hemisphere, smaller than a fissure.

Superior. See Figure 4.1.

Superior cerebellar peduncle. One of the three pairs of bands of white matter connecting the cerebellum and brain stem.

Superior colliculi. Protrusions on top of the midbrain; part of the visual system.

Suprachiasmatic nucleus (SCN). A nucleus situated atop the optic chiasm; contains a biological clock responsible for organizing many of the body's circadian rhythms.

Supraoptic nucleus. A hypothalamic nucleus that contains cell bodies of neurons that produce antidiuretic hormone and transport it through their axons to the posterior pituitary gland.

Sympathetic division. See under *autonomic nervous system (ANS)*.

Synapse. A junction between the terminal button of an axon and the membrane of another neuron.

Synaptic cleft. The space between the presynaptic membrane and the postsynaptic membrane.

Synaptic vesicle. A small, hollow, beadlike structure found in terminal buttons. Synaptic vesicles contain transmitter substance.

Synchrony. High-voltage, low-frequency electroencephalographic activity, characteristic of slow-wave sleep or coma. During synchrony, neurons are presumably firing together in a regular fashion.

System variable. That which is controlled by a regulatory mechanism; for example, temperature in a heating system.

Tardive dyskinesia. A movement disorder that occasionally occurs after prolonged treatment with antischizophrenic medication, characterized by involuntary movements of the face and neck, sometimes interfering with speech.

Target cell. The type of cell that is directly affected by a hormone or nerve fiber.

TE. See Figure 14.2.

Tectospinal tract. A bundle of axons that travel from the tectum to the spinal cord; coordinates head and trunk movements with eye movements.

Tectum. The roof of the midbrain, comprising the inferior and the superior colliculi.

Tegmentum. The portion of the midbrain beneath the tectum, containing the red nucleus and nuclei of various cranial nerves.

Telencephalon. See Table 4.1.

Temporal stem. A bundle of axons that communicate between the temporal cortex, diencephalon, and basal ganglia.

Tentorium. The tentlike fold of dura mater that separates the occipital lobe from the cerebellum.

TEO. See Figure 14.2.

Terminal button. The rounded swelling at the end of an axonal process that synapses upon another neuron, muscle fiber, or gland cell.

Testicular feminization. See *androgen insensitivity syndrome*.

Testosterone. The principle androgen found in males.

Theta activity. EEG activity of 5–8 Hz. Theta activity of the hippocampus is an important indication of its physiological state.

Third ventricle. See under *ventricle*.

Threshold of excitation. The value of the membrane potential that must be reached in order to produce an action potential.

Thrombus. A blood clot that forms within a blood vessel, which may occlude it.

Thymine. One of the nucleotide bases found in DNA. In RNA this base is replaced by uracil.

Trace conditioning. A classical conditioning procedure; the unconditional stimulus follows the conditional stimulus by a short interval of time.

Transmitter substance. A chemical that is liberated by the terminal buttons of an axon and produces an EPSP or an IPSP in the membrane of the postsynaptic cell. Also called *neurotransmitter.*

Transverse section. See Figure 4.2.

Tricarboxylic acid cycle. See *Krebs cycle.*

Tricyclic antidepressant. A class of drugs that are used to treat psychotic depression, named for their molecular structure.

Trigeminal lemniscus. A bundle of fibers running parallel to the medial lemniscus; conveys afferent fibers from the trigeminal nerve to the thalamus.

Triglyceride. The form of fat storage in adipose cells; consists of a molecule of glycerol joined with the three fatty acids: stearic acid, oleic acid, and palmitic acid.

Trisynaptic circuit. The recurrent circuit formed by connections between the entorhinal cortex, dentate gyrus, and CA1 and CA3 fields of Ammon's horn. Repeated stimulation of this circuit leads to long-term potentiation of the extracellular population spike.

Tryptophan. An amino acid; the precursor for 5-HT (serotonin).

Tryptophan hydroxylase. The enzyme that converts tryptophan to 5-hydroxytryptophan (5-HTP).

Tyrosine. An amino acid; the precursor of the catecholamines: dopamine, norepinephrine, and epinephrine.

Tyrosine hydroxylase. The enzyme that converts tyrosine to L-DOPA, the immediate precursor of dopamine.

Unconditional response (UR). See under *classical conditioning.*

Unconditional stimulus (US). See under *classical conditioning.*

Unipolar depression. A psychosis; unremitting depression, or periods of depression that do not alternate with periods of mania.

Unipolar neuron. A neuron with a long, continuous fiber that has dendritic processes on one end and axonal processes and terminal buttons on the other. The fiber connects with the soma of the neuron by means of a single, short process.

Uracil. One of the nucleotide bases of RNA. See also *thymine.*

Vagus nerve. The largest of the cranial nerves, conveying efferent fibers of the parasympathetic division of the autonomic nervous system to organs of the thoracic and abdominal cavities. The vagus nerve also carries nonpainful sensory fibers from these organs to the brain.

Ventral. See Figure 4.1.

Ventral amygdalofugal pathway. The diffuse system of fibers connecting portions of the amygdala with various forebrain structures.

Ventral corticospinal tract. See under *corticospinal pathway.*

Ventral horn (of gray matter of spinal cord). Location of the cell bodies of alpha and gamma motor neurons of the spinal cord.

Ventral posterior nucleus (of thalamus). The thalamic nucleus that projects to the primary somatosensory cortex.

Ventral root. See under *spinal root.*

Ventral tegmental area. A nucleus in the ventral tegmentum that contains dopamine-secreting neurons whose axons project to the forebrain, especially to the cortex and nucleus accumbens; thought to be important in arousal and reinforcement.

Ventricle. One of the hollow spaces within the brain, filled with cerebrospinal fluid, including the *lateral, third,* and *fourth ventricles.*

Ventrolateral nucleus (of thalamus). A nucleus that receives inputs from the cerebellum and sends axons to the primary motor cortex.

Ventromedial nucleus of the hypothalamus (VMH). A large nucleus of the hypothalamus located near the walls of the third ventricle; important in controlling female sexual behavior.

Ventromedial pathways. The vestibulospinal, tectospinal, and reticulospinal tracts.

Vertebral artery. An artery, the branches of which serve the posterior region of the brain.

Vestibular nerve. See under *auditory nerve.*

Vestibulospinal tract. A bundle of axons from the vestibular nuclei of the brain stem to the gray matter of the spinal cord; controls postural movements in response to information from the vestibular system.

Visual agnosia. Deficits in visual perception in the absence of blindness; caused by brain damage. *Apperceptive visual agnosia* is a failure to perceive objects, even though detection of individual components is relatively normal. *Associative visual agnosia* is the inability to name objects that are perceived visually, even though the form of the perceived object can be matched with similar objects.

VMH. See *ventromedial nucleus of the hypothalamus (VMH)*.

Voltage-dependent ion channel. See under *ion channel*.

Volumetric thirst. Thirst produced by *hypovolemia*, or reduction in the amount of extracellular fluid. Volumetric thirst is produced by baroreceptors in the right atrium of the heart, and by reduced blood flow from the kidneys.

Vomeronasal organ. A sensory organ in some species that detects the presence of certain chemicals, especially when a liquid is actively sniffed; mediates the effects of some pheromones.

W cell. A neuron of the visual system that responds weakly to visual stimuli, especially moving stimuli. The receptive field is very large and is usually not organized in an opponent center/surround fashion.

Wernicke's area. A region of auditory association cortex on the left temporal lobe of humans, which is important in the comprehension of words and the production of meaningful speech. *Wernicke's aphasia,* which occurs as a result of damage to this area, results in fluent but meaningless speech.

Whitten effect. The synchronization of the menstrual or estrous cycles of a group of females, which occurs only when a male (or his pheromone) is present.

Wolffian system. The embryonic precursors of the male internal sex organs.

X cells. Neurons of the visual system that respond in a sustained manner. The receptive field is organized in an opponent center/surround fashion. Many X cells respond differentially to stimuli with different hues. Stimuli that fill both the central and surrounding area of the receptive field can produce no change in the cells' firing rate.

Y cells. Neurons of the visual system that respond briskly but briefly, especially to moving stimuli. Receptive fields are larger than those of X cells. Cancellation cannot be produced by simultaneously stimulating the central and surrounding areas of the receptive field.

References

ADAMS, D.B. Hormone-brain interactions and their influence on agonistic behavior. In *Hormones and Aggressive Behavior,* edited by B.B. Svare. New York: Plenum Press, 1983.

ADAMS, D.B., GOLD, A.R., AND BURT, A.D. Rise in female-initiated sexual activity at ovulation and its suppression by oral contraceptives. *New England Journal of Medicine,* 1978, *299,* 1145–1150.

ADAMS, R.D. The anatomy of memory mechanisms in the human brain. In *The Pathology of Memory,* edited by G.A. Talland and N.C. Waugh. New York: Academic Press, 1969.

ADEY, W.R., BORS, E., AND PORTER, R.W. *Archives of Neurology,* 1968, *19,* 377–383.

ADOLPH, E.F. Measurements of water drinking in dogs. *American Journal of Physiology,* 1939, *125,* 75–86.

AGHAJANIAN, G.K., BLOOM, F.E., AND SHEARD, M.N. Electron microscopy of degeneration within the serotonin pathway of rat brain. *Brain Research,* 1969, *13,* 266–273.

AGNEW, H.W., JR., WEBB, W.B., AND WILLIAMS, R.L. The effects of stage four sleep deprivation. *Electroencephalography and Clinical Neurophysiology,* 1964, *17,* 68–70.

AHLSKOG, J.E. Food intake and amphetamine anorexia after selective forebrain norepinephrine loss. *Brain Research,* 1974, *82,* 211–240.

AKIL, H., MAYER, D., AND LIEBESKIND, J.C. Antagonism of stimulation-produced analgesia by Naloxone, a narcotic antagonist. *Science,* 1976, *191,* 961–962.

AKIL, H., WATSON, S.J., YOUNG, E., LEWIS, M.E., KHACHATURIAN, H., AND WALKER, J.M. Endogenous opioids: Biology and function. *Annual Review of Neuroscience,* 1984, *7,* 223–255.

ALEXANDER, M.P., AND ALBERT, M.L. The anatomical basis of visual agnosia. In *Localization in Neuropsychology,* edited by A. Kertesz. New York: Academic Press, 1983.

ALLISON, T., AND CHICHETTI, D. Sleep in mammals: Ecological and constitutional correlates. *Science,* 1976, *194,* 732–734.

AMARAL, D.G., AND ROUTTENBERG, A. Locus coeruleus and intracranial self-stimulation: A cautionary note. *Behavioral Biology,* 1975, *13,* 331–336.

AMATRUDA, T.T., BLACK, D.A., McKENNA, T.M., McCARLEY, R.W., AND HOBSON, J.A. Sleep control and cholinergic mechanisms: Differential effects of carbachol injections at pontine brain stem sites. *Brain Research,* 1975, *98,* 501–515.

AMENOMORI, Y., CHEN, C.L., AND MEITES, J. Serum prolactin levels in rats during different reproductive states. *Endocrinology,* 1970, *86,* 506–510.

AMOORE, J.E. The stereochemical theory of olfaction. 1. Identification of the seven primary odours. *Proceedings of the Scientific Section, Toilet Goods Association,* 1962, *suppl. 37,* 1–12.

AMOORE, J.E. Current status of the steric theory of odor. *Annals of the New York Academy of Sciences,* 1964, *116,* 457–476.

AMOORE, J.E. *Molecular Basis of Odor.* Springfield, Ill.: Charles C Thomas, 1970.

ANAND, B.K., AND BROBECK, J.R. Hypothalamic control of food intake in rats and cats. *Yale Journal of Biology and Medicine,* 1951, *24,* 123–140.

ANDEN, N.-E., FUXE, K., HAMBERGER, B., AND HÖKFELT, T. A quantitative study on the nigrostriatal dopamine neuron system in the rat. *Acta Physiologica Scandinavica,* 1966, *67,* 306–312.

ANDERSSON, B. The effect of injections of hypertonic NaCl solutions in different parts of the hypothalamus of goats. *Acta Physiologica Scandinavica,* 1953, *28,* 188–201.

ANGRIST, B.J., ROTROSEN, J., AND GERSHON, S. Positive and negative symptoms in schizophrenia — differential response to amphetamine and neuroleptics. *Psychopharmacology,* 1980, *72,* 17–19.

ANLEZARK, G.M., ARBUTHNOTT, G.W., CROW, T.S., ECCLESTON, D., AND WALTER, D.S. Intracranial self-stimulation and noradrenaline metabolism in the cortex. *British Journal of Pharmacology,* 1973, *47,* 645P.

ANONYMOUS. Effects of sexual activity on beard growth in man. *Nature,* 1970, *226,* 867–870.

ANTELMAN, S.M., CHIODO, L.A., AND DeGIOVANNI, L.A. Antidepressants and dopamine autoreceptors: Implications for both a novel means of treating depression and understanding bipolar illness. In *Typical and Atypical Antidepressants: Molecular Mechanisms,* edited by E. Costa and G. Racagni. New York: Raven Press, 1982.

ANTELMAN, S.M., ROWLAND, N.E., AND FISHER, A.E. Stress related recovery from lateral hypothalamic aphagia. *Brain Research,* 1976, *102,* 346–350.

ANTELMAN, S.M., SZECHTMAN, H., CHIN, P., AND FISHER, A.D. Tail pinch-induced eating, gnawing and licking behavior in rats: Dependence on the nigrostriatal dopamine system. *Brain Research,* 1975, *99,* 319–377.

APPLEGATE, C.D., FRYSINGER, R.C., KAPP, B.S., AND GALLAGHER, M. Neuronal activity recorded from the amygdala central nucleus during aversive Pavlovian heart rate conditioning in the rabbit. *Society for Neuroscience Abstracts,* 1981, *7,* 750.

ARENDASH, G.W., AND GORSKI, R.A. Effects of discrete lesions of the sexually dimorphic nucleus of the preoptic area or other medial preoptic regions on the sexual behavior of male rats. *Brain Research Bulletin,* 1983, *10,* 147–154.

ARNAULD, E., DUFY, B., AND VINCENT, J.D. Hypothalamic supraoptic neurons: Rates and patterns of action potential firing during water deprivation in the unanesthetized monkey. *Brain Research,* 1975, *100,* 315–325.

ASANUMA, H., AND ROSÉN, I. Topographical organization of cortical efferent zones projecting to distal forelimb muscles in monkey. *Experimental Brain Research,* 1972, *13,* 243–256.

ASCHOFF, J. Circadian rhythms: General features and endocrinological aspects. In *Endocrine Rhythms,* edited by D.T. Krieger. New York: Raven Press, 1979.

ASERINSKY, N.E., AND KLEITMAN, N. Regularly occurring periods of eye motility and concomitant phenomena during sleep. *Science,* 1955, *118,* 273–274.

ASSCHER, A.W., AND ANSON, S.G. A vascular permeability factor of renal origin. *Nature,* 1963, *198,* 1097–1099.

ASTON-JONES, G., AND BLOOM, F.E. Activity of norepinephrine-containing locus coeruleus neurons in behaving rats anticipates fluctuations in the sleep-waking cycle. *The Journal of Neuroscience,* 1981, *1,* 876–886.

BABINSKI, J. Contribution à l'étude des troubles mentaux dans l'hémiplégie organique cérébrale (anosognosia). *Revue Neurologique,* 1914, *27,* 845–848.

BAEKELAND, F. Pentobarbital and dextroamphetamine sulfate: Effects on the sleep cycle in man. *Psychopharmacologia,* 1967, *11,* 388–396.

BAKER, T.L., AND MCGINTY, D.J. Reversal of cardiopulmonary failure during active sleep in hypoxic kittens: Implications for sudden infant death. *Science,* 1977, *198,* 419–421.

BALAGURA, S., AND HOEBEL, B.G. Self-stimulation of the lateral hypothalamus modified by insulin and glucagon. *Physiology and Behavior,* 1967, *2,* 337–340.

BALDESSARINI, R.J. *Chemotherapy in Psychiatry.* Cambridge, Mass.: Harvard University Press, 1977.

BALDESSARINI, R.J., AND TARSY, D. Dopamine and the pathophysiology of dyskinesias induced by antipsychotic drugs. *Annual Review of Neuroscience,* 1980, *3,* 23–42.

BAMBRIDGE, B., AND GIJSBERS, K. The role of tonic neural activity in motivational processes. *Experimental Neurology,* 1977, *56,* 370–385.

BANDLER, R.J., CHI, C.C., AND FLYNN, J.P. Biting attack elicited by stimulation of the ventral midbrain tegmentum of cats. *Science,* 1972, *177,* 364–366.

BANDLER, R.J., AND FLYNN, J.P. Control of somatosensory fields for striking during hypothalamically elicited attack. *Brain Research,* 1972, *38,* 197–201.

BARBIZET, J. Defect of memorizing of hippocampal-mammillary origin: A review. *Journal of Neurology, Neurosurgery and Psychiatry,* 1963, *26,* 127–135.

BARFIELD, R.J., RUBIN, B.S., GLASER, J.H., AND DAVIS, P.G. Sites of action of ovarian hormones in the regulation of oestrous responsiveness in rats. In *Hormones and Behaviour in Higher Vertebrates,* edited by J. Balthazart, E. Pröve, and R. Gilles. Berlin: Springer-Verlag, 1983.

BARKLEY, M.S. Testosterone and the ontogeny of sexually dimorphic aggression in the mouse. Ph.D. Thesis, University of Connecticut, 1974.

BARTUS, R.T., DEAN, R.L., BEER, B., AND LIPPA, A.S. The cholinergic hypothesis of geriatric memory dysfunction. *Science,* 1982, *217,* 408–417.

BASBAUM, A.I., AND FIELDS, H.L. Endogenous pain control mechanisms: Review and hypothesis. *Annals of Neurology,* 1978, *4,* 451–462.

BASBAUM, A.I., AND FIELDS, H.L. Endogenous pain control systems: Brainstem spinal pathways and endorphin circuitry. *Annual Review of Neuroscience,* 1984, *7,* 309–338.

BATESON, P.P.G., HORN, G., AND ROSE, S.P.R. Effects of early experience on regional incorporation of precursors into RNA and protein in the chick brain. *Brain Research,* 1972, *39,* 449–465.

BATESON, P.P.G., ROSE, S.P.R., AND HORN, G. Imprinting: Lasting effects on uracil incorporation into chick brain. *Science,* 1973, *181,* 576–578.

BATINI, C., MORUZZI, G., PALESTINI, M., ROSSI, G.F., AND ZANCHETTI, A. Persistent patterns of wakefulness in the pretrigeminal midpontine preparation. *Science,* 1958, *128,* 30–32.

BATINI, C., MORUZZI, G., PALESTINI, M., ROSSI, G.F., AND ZANCHETTI, A. Effects of complete pontine transections on the sleep-wakefulness rhythm: The midpontine pretrigeminal preparation. *Archives Italiennes de Biologie,* 1959, *97,* 1–12.

BAUDRY, M., BUNDMAN, M., SMITH, E., AND LYNCH, G. Micromolar levels of calcium stimulate proteolytic activity and glutamate receptor binding in rat brain synaptic membranes. *Science,* 1981, *212,* 937–938.

BAUDRY, M., AND LYNCH, G. Regulation of hippocampal glutamate receptors: Evidence for the involvement of a calcium-activated protease. *Proceedings of the National Academy of Sciences (U.S.A.),* 1980, *77,* 2298–2302.

BAZETT, H.C., MCGLONE, B., WILLIAMS, R.G., AND LUFKIN, H.M. Sensation. I. Depth, distribution, and probable identification in the prepuce of sensory end-organs concerned in sensations of temperature and touch: Thermometric conductivity. *Archives of Neurology and Psychiatry (Chicago),* 1932, *27,* 489–517.

BEACH, F.A. Cerebral and hormonal control of reflexive mechanisms involved in copulatory behavior. *Physiological Review,* 1967, *47,* 289–316.

BEACH, F.A. Coital behavior in dogs. VI. Long-term effects of castration upon mating in the male. *Journal of Comparative and Physiological Psychology,* 1970, *70,* 1–32.

BEACH, F.A., AND WESTBROOK, W.H. Dissociation of androgen effects on sexual morphology and behavior in male rats. *Endocrinology,* 1968, *83,* 395–398.

BEALER, S.L., AND SMITH, D.V. Multiple sensitivity to

chemical stimuli in human taste papillae. *Physiology and Behavior*, 1975, *14*, 795–800.

BEAMER, W., BERMANT, G., AND CLEGG, M. Copulatory behavior of the ram, *Ovis aries*. II. Factors affecting copulatory satiety. *Animal Behavior*, 1969, *17*, 706–711.

BEAN, N.J., AND CONNER, R. Central hormonal replacement and home-cage dominance in castrated rats. *Hormones and Behavior*, 1978, *11*, 100–109.

BEAUVOIS, M.F., AND DÉROUESNÉ, J. Phonological alexia: Three dissociations. *Journal of Neurology, Neurosurgery and Psychiatry*, 1979, *42*, 1115–1124.

BEECHER, H.K. *Measurement of Subjective Responses: Quantitative Effects of Drugs*. New York: Oxford University Press, 1959.

BEEMAN, E.A. The effect of male hormone on aggressive behavior in mice. *Physiological Zoology*, 1947, *20*, 373–405.

BEIDLER, L.M. Physiological properties of mammalian taste receptors. In *Taste and Smell in Vertebrates*, edited by G.E.W. Wolstenholme. London: J.&A. Churchill, 1970.

BEITZ, A.J. The organization of afferent projections to the midbrain periaqueductal gray of the rat. *Neuroscience*, 1982a, *7*, 133–159.

BEITZ, A.J. The sites of origin of brain stem neurotensin and serotonin projections to the rodent nucleus raphe magnus. *Journal of Neuroscience*, 1982b, *7*, 829–842.

BELL, A.P., AND WEINBERG, M.S. *Homosexualities: A Study of Diversity among Men and Women*. New York: Simon & Schuster, 1978.

BELL, A.P., WEINBERG, M.S., AND HAMMERSMITH, S.K. *Sexual Preference: Its Development in Men and Women*. Bloomington: Indiana University Press, 1981.

BELLRINGER, J.F., PRATT, H.P.M., AND KEVERNE, E.B. Involvement of the vomeronasal organ and prolactin in pheromonal induction of delayed implantation in mice. *Journal of Reproduction and Fertility*, 1980, *59*, 223–228.

BELLUZZI, J.D., AND STEIN, L. Brain endorphins: Possible role in long-term memory. *Annals of the New York Academy of Sciences*, 1982, *398*, 221–229.

BENSON, D.F., AND GESCHWIND, N. The alexias. In *Handbook of Clinical Neurology, Vol. 4*, edited by P. Vinken and G. Bruyn. Amsterdam: North-Holland, 1969.

BENSON, D.F., AND GREENBERG, J. Visual form agnosia. *Archives of Neurology*, 1969, *20*, 82–89.

BERGER, T.W. Long-term potentiation of hippocampal synaptic transmission affects rate of behavioral learning. *Science*, 1984a, *224*, 627–630.

BERGER, T.W. Neural representation of associative learning in the hippocampus. In *The Neuropsychology of Memory*, edited by M. Butters and L.R. Squire. New York: Guilford Press, 1984b.

BERGER, T.W., CLARK, G.A., AND THOMPSON, R.F. Learning-dependent neuronal responses recorded from limbic system brain structures during classical con-

ditioning. *Physiological Psychology*, 1980, *8*, 155–167.

BERGER, T.W., AND ORR, W.B. Hippocampectomy selectively disrupts discrimination reversal conditioning of the rabbit nictitating membrane response. *Behavioural Brain Research*, 1983, *8*, 49–68.

BERKUN, M.A., KESSEN, M.L., AND MILLER, N.E. Hunger-reducing effects of food by stomach fistula versus food by mouth measured by a consummatory response. *Journal of Comparative and Physiological Psychology*, 1952, *45*, 550–554.

BERLUCCHI, G., MAFFEI, L., MORUZZI, G., AND STRATA, P. EEG and behavioral effects elicited by cooling of medulla and pons. *Archives Italiennes de Biologie*, 1964, *102*, 372–392.

BERMANT, G., AND DAVIDSON, J.M. *Biological Bases of Sexual Behavior*. New York: Harper & Row, 1974.

BERNARD, C. *Leçons de Physiologie Expérimentale Appliquée à la Médecine Faites au Collège de France, Vol. 2*. Paris: Baillière, 1856.

BERNTSON, G.G., AND MICCO, D.J. Organization of brainstem behavioral systems. *Brain Research Bulletin*, 1976, *1*, 471–483.

BERRY, S.D., AND THOMPSON, R.F. Medial septal lesions retard classical conditioning of the nictitating membrane response in rabbits. *Science*, 1979, *205*, 209–211.

BERTHIER, N.E., AND MOORE, J.W. The nictitating membrane response: An electrophysiological study of the abducens nerve and nucleus and the accessory abducens nucleus in rabbit. *Brain Research*, 1983, *258*, 201–210.

BEYER, C., ALMANZA, J., DE LA TORRE, L., AND GUZMAN-FLORES, C. Brain stem multi-unit activity during "relaxation" behavior in the female cat. *Brain Research*, 1971, *29*, 213–222.

BIELAJEW, C., AND SHIZGAL, P. Behaviorally derived measures of conduction velocity in the substrate for rewarding medial forebrain bundle stimulation. *Brain Research*, 1982, *237*, 107–119.

BLAKE, L., JARVIS, C.D., AND MISHKIN, M. Pattern discrimination thresholds after partial inferior temporal or lateral striate lesions in the monkey. *Brain Research*, 1977, *120*, 209–220.

BLAKEMORE, C., AND CAMPBELL, F.W. On the existence of neurones in the human visual system selectively sensitive to the orientation and size of retinal images. *Journal of Physiology (London)*, 1969, *203*, 237–260.

BLANK, D.L., AND WAYNER, M.J. Lateral preoptic single unit activity: Effects of various solutions. *Physiology and Behavior*, 1975, *15*, 723–730.

BLASS, E.M., AND EPSTEIN, A.N. A lateral preoptic osmosensitive zone for thirst. *Journal of Comparative and Physiological Psychology*, 1971, *76*, 378–394.

BLASS, E.M., AND KRALY, F.S. Medial forebrain bundle lesions: Specific loss of feeding to decreased glucose utilization in rats. *Journal of Comparative and Physiological Psychology*, 1974, *86*, 679–692.

BLAUSTEIN, J.D., AND FEDER, H.H. Cytoplasmic progestin receptors in guinea pig brain: Characteristics and relationship to the induction of sexual behavior. *Brain Research,* 1979, *169,* 481–497.

BLAUSTEIN, J.D., AND FEDER, H.H. Nuclear progestin receptors in guinea pig brain measured by an in vitro exchange assay after hormonal treatments that affect lordosis. *Endocrinology,* 1980, *106,* 1061–1069.

BLAZA, S. Brown adipose tissue in man: A review. *Journal of the Royal Society of Medicine,* 1983, *76,* 213–216.

BLISS, T.V.P., AND LØMO, T. Long-lasting potentiation of synaptic transmission in the dentate area of the anaesthetized rabbit following stimulation of the perforant path. *Journal of Physiology (London),* 1973, *232,* 331–356.

BLOCH, V., HENNEVIN, E., AND LECONTE, P. Interaction between post-trial reticular stimulation and subsequent paradoxical sleep in memory consolidation processes. In *Neurobiology of Sleep and Memory,* edited by R.R. Drucker-Colín, and J.L. McGaugh. New York: Academic Press, 1977.

BLOCK, M., AND ZUCKER, I. Circadian rhythms of rat locomotor activity after lesions of the midbrain raphe nuclei. *Journal of Comparative Physiology,* 1976, *109,* 235–247.

BLUMER, D. Temporal lobe epilepsy and its psychiatric significance. In *Psychiatric Aspects of Neurologic Disease,* edited by D.F. Benson and D. Blumer. New York: Grune & Stratton, 1975.

BLUMER, D., AND WALKER, A.E. The neural basis of sexual behavior. In *Psychiatric Aspects of Neurologic Disease,* edited by D.F. Benson and D. Blumer. New York: Grune & Stratton, 1975.

BOLHUIS, J.J., FITZGERALD, R.E., DIJK, D.J., AND KOOLHAAS, J.M. The corticomedial amygdala and learning in an agonistic situation in the rat. *Physiology and Behavior,* 1984, *32,* 575–579.

BOLLER, F., AND DENNIS, M. (EDS.) *Auditory Comprehension: Clinical and Experimental Studies with the Token Test.* New York: Academic Press, 1979.

BOLLES, R.C. Species-specific defense reactions and avoidance learning. *Psychological Review,* 1970, *77,* 32–48.

BONVALLET, M., AND SIGG, B. Etude électrophysiologique des afférences vagales au neveau de leur pénétration dans le bulbe. *Journal of Physiology (Paris),* 1958, *50,* 63–74.

BOOTH, D.A. The physiology of appetite. *British Medical Bulletin,* 1981, *37,* 135–140.

BOOTH, D.A., MATHER, P., AND FULLER, J. Starch content of ordinary foods associatively conditions human appetite and satiation, indexed by intake and eating pleasantness of starch-paired flavours. *Appetite,* 1982, *3,* 163–184.

BORNSTEIN, B., STROKA, H., AND MUNITZ, H. Prosopagnosia with animal face agnosia. *Cortex,* 1969, *5,* 164–169.

BOULOS, Z., ROSENWASSER, A.M., AND TERMAN, M. Feeding schedules and the circadian organization of behav-

ior in the rat. *Behavioural Brain Research,* 1980, *1,* 39–65.

BOWERS, D., AND HEILMAN, K.M. A dissociation between the processing of affective and nonaffective faces. Paper presented at the meeting of the International Neuropsychological Society, Atlanta, 1981.

BOWERS, M.B. Central dopamine turnover in schizophrenic syndromes. *Archives of General Psychiatry,* 1974, *31,* 50–54.

BOYNTON, R.M. *Human Color Vision.* New York: Holt, Rinehart and Winston, 1979.

BOZARTH, M.A., AND WISE, R.A. Dopaminergic mediation of opiate reward. *Neuroscience Abstracts,* 1981, *7,* 50.

BRADY, J.V., AND NAUTA, W.J.H. Subcortical mechanisms in emotional behavior: Affective changes following septal forebrain lesions in the albino rat. *Journal of Comparative and Physiological Psychology,* 1953, *46,* 339–346.

BRAIN, P.F. Dividing up aggression and considerations in studying the physiological substrates of these phenomena. *The Behavioral and Brain Sciences,* 1979, *2,* 216.

BRAUN, J.J., SLICK, T.B., AND LORDEN, J.F. Involvement of gustatory neocortex in the learning of taste aversions. *Physiology and Behavior,* 1972, *9,* 637–641.

BREEDLOVE, S.M., AND ARNOLD, A. Hormone accumulation in a sexually dimorphic motor nucleus of the rat spinal cord. *Science,* 1980, *210,* 564–566.

BREEDLOVE, S.M., AND ARNOLD, A. Sex differences in the pattern of steroid accumulation by motoneurons of the rat lumbar spinal cord. *Journal of Comparative Neurology,* 1983, *215,* 211–216.

BREEDLOVE, S.M., JACOBSON, C.D., GORSKI, R., AND ARNOLD, A.P. Masculinization of the female rat spinal cord following a single neonatal injection of testosterone propionate but not estradiol benzoate. *Brain Research,* 1982, *237,* 173–181.

BREGER, L., HUNTER, I., AND LANE, R.W. The effects of stress on dreams. *Physiological Issues Monograph Number 27.* New York: International University Press, 1971.

BREMER, F. L'activité cérébrale au cours du sommeil et de la narcose. Contribution à l'étude du mécanisme du sommeil. *Bulletin de l'Académie Royale de Belgique,* 1937, *4,* 68–86.

BREMER, F. Preoptic hypnogenic focus and mesencephalic reticular formation. *Brain Research,* 1970, *21,* 132–134.

BREMER, F. A further study of the inhibitory processes induced by the activation of the preoptic hypnogenic structure. *Archives Italiennes de Biologie,* 1975, *113,* 79–88.

BRIDGES, R.S., ZARROW, M.X., AND DENNENBERG, V.H. The role of neonatal androgen in the expression of hormonally induced maternal responsiveness in the adult rat. *Hormones and Behavior,* 1973, *4,* 315–322.

BROCA, P. Remarques sur le siège de la faculté du langage

articulé, suivies d'une observation d'aphemie (perte de la parole). *Bulletin de la Société Anatomique (Paris),* 1861, *36,* 330–357.

BRODAL, A. *Neurological anatomy in relation to clinical medicine.* Oxford, England: Oxford University Press, 1981.

BRONSON, F.H., AND DESJARDINS, C. Aggressive behavior and seminal vesicle function in mice: Differential sensitivity to androgen given neonatally. *Endocrinology,* 1969, *85,* 971–974.

BRONSON, F.H., AND DEJARDINS, C. Neonatal androgen administration and adult aggressiveness in female mice. *General and Comparative Endocrinology,* 1970, *15,* 320–325.

BRONSON, F.H., AND ELEFTHERIOU, B.E. Chronic physiological effects of fighting. *Genetic and Comparative Endocrinology,* 1964, *4,* 9–14.

BRONSON, F.H., AND ELEFTHERIOU, B.E. Adrenal response to fighting in mice: Separation of physical and psychological causes. *Science,* 1965a, *147,* 627–628.

BRONSON, F.H., AND ELEFTHERIOU, B.E. Relative effects of fighting on bound and unbound corticosterone in mice. *Proceedings of the Society for Experimental Biology and Medicine,* 1965b, *118,* 146–149.

BRONSON, F.H., AND WHITTEN, W. Estrus accelerating pheromone of mice: Assay, androgen-dependency, and presence in bladder urine. *Journal of Reproduction and Fertility,* 1968, *15,* 131–134.

BROOKS, D., AND BIZZI, E. Brain stem electrical activity during sleep. *Archives Italiennes de Biologie,* 1963, *101,* 648–665.

BROWMAN, L.G. Light in its relation to activity and estrous rhythms in the albino rat. *Journal of Experimental Zoology,* 1937, *75,* 375–388.

BRUCE, H.M. A block to pregnancy in the mouse caused by proximity of strange males. *Journal of Reproduction and Fertility,* 1960a, *1,* 96–103.

BRUCE, H.M. Further observations of pregnancy block in mice caused by proximity of strange males. *Journal of Reproduction and Fertility,* 1960b, *2,* 311–312.

BRUNELLI, M., CASTELLUCCI, V.F., AND KANDEL, E.R. Synaptic facilitation and behavioral sensitization in *Aplysia:* Possible role of serotonin and cyclic AMP. *Science,* 1976, *194,* 1178–1181.

BRYDEN, M.P., AND LEY, R.G. Right-hemispheric involvement in the perception and expression of emotion in normal humans. In *Neuropsychology of Human Emotion,* edited by K.M. Heilman and P. Satz. New York: Guilford Press, 1983.

BRYDEN, M.P., LEY, R.G., AND SUGARMAN, J.H. A left ear advantage for identifying the emotional quality of tonal sequences. *Neuropsychologia,* 1982, *20,* 83–87.

BUCK, R., AND DUFFY, R.J. Nonverbal communication of affect in brain damaged patients. *Cortex,* 1980, *16,* 351–362.

BUDDINGTON, R.W., KING, F.A., AND ROBERTS, L. Emotionality and conditioned avoidance responding in the squirrel monkey following septal injury. *Psychonomic Science,* 1967, *8,* 195–196.

BUERGER, A.A., GROSS, C.H., AND ROCHA-MIRANDA, C.E. Effects of ventral putamen lesions on discrimination learning by monkeys. *Journal of Comparative and Physiological Psychology,* 1974, *86,* 440–446.

BUKOWIECKI, L., FOLLÉA, N., VALLIÈRAS, J., AND LEBLANC, J. β-adrenergic receptors in brown-adipose tissue. Characterization and alterations during acclimation of rats to cold. *European Journal of Biochemistry,* 1978, *92,* 189–196.

BULLOCK, N.P., AND NEW, M.I. Testosterone and cortisol concentration in spermatic, adrenal and systemic venous blood in adult male guinea pigs. *Endocrinology,* 1971, *88,* 523–526.

BURNS, B.D. *The Mammalian Cerebral Cortex.* London: Arnold, 1958.

CAGGIULA, A.R. Analysis of the copulation-reward properties of posterior hypothalamic stimulation in male rats. *Journal of Comparative and Physiological Psychology,* 1970, *70,* 399–412.

CAIN, W.S. History of research on smell. In *Handbook of Perception, vol. VIA: Tasting and Smelling,* edited by E.C. Carterette and M.P. Friedman. New York: Academic Press, 1978.

CALHOUN, J. Population density and social pathology. *Scientific American,* 1962, *206,* 139–148.

CARD, J.P., RILEY, J.N., AND MOORE, R.Y. The suprachiasmatic hypothalamic nucleus: Ultrastructure of relations to optic chiasm. *Neuroscience Abstracts,* 1980, *6,* 758.

CAREW, T.J., HAWKINS, R.D., AND KANDEL, E.R. Differential classical conditioning of a defensive withdrawal reflex in *Aplysia californica. Science,* 1983, *219,* 397–400.

CARLIN, R.K., BARTELT, D.C., AND SIEKEVITZ, P. Identification of fodrin as a major calmodulin-binding protein in postsynaptic density preparations. *Journal of Cell Biology,* 1983, *96,* 443–448.

CARLSON, H.E., GILLIN, J.C., GORDEN, P., AND SNYDER, F. Absence of sleep-related growth hormone peaks in aged normal subjects and in acromegaly. *Journal of Clinical Endocrinology and Metabolism,* 1972, *34,* 1102–1105.

CARLSON, N.R., AND THOMAS G.J. Maternal behavior of mice with limbic lesions. *Journal of Comparative and Physiological Psychology,* 1968, *66,* 731–737.

CARPENTER, C.R. Sexual behavior of free ranging rhesus monkeys *(Macaca mulatta).* I. Specimens, procedures and behavioral characteristics of estrus. *Journal of Comparative Psychology,* 1942, *33,* 113–142.

CARTWRIGHT, R.D., GORE, S., AND WEINER, L. Paper presented at the meeting of the Association for the Psychophysiological Study of Sleep, San Diego, 1973.

CASTELLUCCI, V.F., KANDEL, E.R., SCHWARTZ, J.H., WILSON, F.D., NAIRN, A.C., AND GREENGARD, P. Intracellular injection of the catalytic subunit of cyclic AMP-dependent protein kinase simulates facilitation of transmitter release underlying behavioral sensitization in *Aplysia. Proceedings of the National Academy of Sciences (U.S.A.),* 1980, *77,* 7492–7496.

CASTELLUCCI, V.F., NAIRN, A., GREENGARD, P., SCHWARTZ, J.H., AND KANDEL, E.R. Inhibitor of adenosine 3′ : 5′-monophosphate–dependent protein kinase blocks presynaptic facilitation in *Aplysia*. *The Journal of Neuroscience*, 1982, *2*, 1673–1681.

CHI, J.G., DOOLING, E.C., AND GILLES, F.H. Gyral development of the human brain. *Annals of Neurology*, 1977, *1*, 86–93.

CHOROVER, S.L., AND SCHILLER, P.H. Short-term retrograde amnesia in rats. *Journal of Comparative and Physiological Psychology*, 1965, *59*, 73–78.

CHRISTIE, J.E., SHERING, A., FERGUSON, J., AND GLEN, A.I.M. *British Journal of Psychiatry*, 1979, *138*, 46–50.

CLARK, A.W., HURLBUT, W.P., AND MAURO, A. Changes in the fine structure of the neuromuscular junction of the frog caused by black widow spider venom. *Journal of Cell Biology*, 1972, *52*, 1–14.

CLARKE, P.G.H., AND WHITTERIDGE, D. A comparison of stereoscopic mechanisms in cortical visual areas V1 and V2 of the cat. *Journal of Physiology (London)*, 1978, *275*, 92–93.

CLAVIER, R.M., AND GERFEN, C.R. Neural inputs to the prefrontal agranular insular cortex in the rat—horseradish peroxidase study. *Brain Research Bulletin*, 1979, *4*, 347–353.

CLAVIER, R.M., AND ROUTTENBERG, A. Ascending monoamine-containing fiber pathways related to intracranial self-stimulation: Histochemical fluorescence study. *Brain Research*, 1975, *101*, 251–271.

CLEMENS, L.G. Influence of prenatal litter composition on mounting behavior of female rats. *American Zoologist*, 1971, *11*, 617–618.

CLEMENTE, C.D., AND CHASE, M.H. Neurological substrates of aggressive behavior. *Annual Review of Physiology*, 1973, *35*, 329–356.

COHEN, H.D., ERVIN, F., AND BARONDES, S.H. Puromycin and cyclohexamide: Differential effects on hippocampal electrical activity. *Science*, 1966, *154*, 1557–1558.

COHEN, N.J., AND CORKIN, S. The amnesic patient H.M.: learning and retention of a cognitive skill. *Society for Neuroscience Abstracts*, 1981, *7*, 235.

COHEN, R., AND PFAFF, D.W. Ultrastructure of neurons in the ventromedial nucleus of the hypothalamus in ovariectomized rats with or without estrogen treatment. *Cell Tissue Research*, 1981, *217*, 451–470.

COINDET, J., CHOVET, B., AND MOURET, J. Effects of lesions of the suprachiasmatic nuclei on paradoxical sleep and slow wave sleep circadian rhythms in the rat. *Neuroscience Letters*, 1975, *l*, 243–247.

COLEMAN, J.C. *Abnormal Psychology and Modern Life*. Glenview, Ill.: Scott, Foresman, 1976.

COLLET, M.E., WERTENBERGER, G.E., AND FISKE, V.M. The effect of age upon the pattern of the menstrual cycle. *Fertility and Sterility*, 1954, *5*, 437–448.

COLLIER, T.J., AND ROUTTENBERG, A. Editing the contents of memory: Participation of granule cell opioid peptides. Unpublished manuscript, 1984.

COLTHEART, M. Disorders of reading and their implications for models of normal reading. *Visible Language*, 1981, *15*, 245–286.

COLTHEART, M., PATTERSON, K., AND MARSHALL, J.C. *Deep Dyslexia*. London: Routledge & Kegan Paul, 1980.

COMARR, A.E. Sexual function among patients with spinal cord injury. *Urologia Internationalis*, 1970, *25*, 134–168.

CONNER, R.L., AND LEVINE, S. Hormonal influences on aggressive behaviour. In *Aggressive Behaviour*, edited by S. Garattini and E.B. Sigg. New York: John Wiley & Sons, 1969.

CONRAD, L.C.A., AND PFAFF, D.W. Efferents from medial basal forebrain and hypothalamus in the rat. I. An autoradiographic study of the medial preoptic area. *Journal of Comparative Neurology*, 1976, *169*, 185–200.

CORBETT, D.R., LAFERRIERE, A., AND MILNER, P. Self-stimulation of the medial frontal cortex does not involve the medial forebrain bundle. *Neuroscience Abstracts*, 1980, *6*, 725.

CORKIN, S., SULLIVAN, E.V., TWITCHELL, T.E., AND GROVE, E. The amnesic patient H.M.: Clinical observations and test performance 28 years after operation. *Society for Neuroscience Abstracts*, 1981, *7*, 235.

COSLETT, H.B., BRASHEAR, H.R., AND HEILMAN, K.M. Pure word deafness after bilateral primary auditory cortex infarcts. *Neurology*, 1984, *34*, 347–352.

COTMAN, C.W., AND NIETO-SAMPEDRO, M. Brain function, synapse renewal, and plasticity. *Annual Review of Psychology*, 1982, *33*, 371–402.

COULTER, J.D., LESTER, B.K., AND WILLIAMS, H.L. Reserpine and sleep. *Psychopharmacologia*, 1971, *19*, 134–147.

COYLE, J.T., PRICE, D.L., AND DeLONG, M.R. Alzheimer's disease: A disorder of cortical cholinergic innervation. *Science*, 1983, *219*, 1184–1190.

CRANE, G.E. Iproniazid (Marsilid) phosphate, a therapeutic agent for mental disorders and debilitating diseases. *Psychiatry Research Reports*, 1957, *8*, 142–152.

CRAWFORD, M.P. The relation between social dominance and the menstrual cycle in female chimpanzees. *Journal of Comparative Psychology*, 1940, *30*, 483–513.

CRISWELL, H.E., AND ROGERS, F.B. Narcotic analgesia: Changes in neural activity recorded from periaqueductal gray matter of rat brain. *Society for Neuroscience Abstracts*, 1978, *4*, 458.

CROSS, A.J., CROW, T.J., AND OWEN, F. ³H-flupenthixol binding in postmortem brains of schizophrenics: Evidence for a selective increase in dopamine D-2 receptors. *Psychopharmacology*, 1981, *74*, 122–124.

CROW, T.J. A map of the rat mesencephalon for electrical self-stimulation. *Brain Research*, 1972, *36*, 265–273.

CROW, T.J. Molecular pathology of schizophrenia: More than one disease process? *British Medical Journal*, 1980, *280*, 66–68.

CROW, T.J., CROSS, A.J., JOHNSTONE, E.C., AND OWEN, F. Two syndromes in schizophrenia and their pathogenesis. In *Schizophrenia As a Brain Disease*, edited by F.A. Henn and H.A. Nasrallah. New York: Oxford University Press, 1982.

CROW, T.J., CROSS, A.J., JOHNSTONE, E.C., OWEN, F., OWENS, D.G.C., AND WADDINGTON, J.L. Abnormal involuntary movements in schizophrenia: Are they related to the disease process or its treatment? Are they associated with changes in dopamine receptors? *Journal of Clinical Psychopharmacology,* 1982, *2,* 336–340.

CROW, T.J., SPEAR, P.J., AND ARBUTHNOTT, G.W. Intracranial self-stimulation with electrodes in the region of the locus coeruleus. *Brain Research,* 1972, *36,* 275–287.

CROWE, R.R. Recent genetic research in schizophrenia. In *Schizophrenia As a Brain Disease,* edited by F.A. Henn and H.A. Nasrallah. New York: Oxford University Press, 1982.

CYTAWA, J., JURKOWLANIEC, E., AND BIALOWAS, J. Positive reinforcement produced by noradrenergic stimulation of the hypothalamus of rats. *Physiology and Behavior,* 1980, *25,* 615–619.

DALLOS, P. Cochlear physiology. *Annual Review of Psychology,* 1981, *32,* 153–190.

DALLOS, P., AND CHEATHAM, M.A. Production of cochlear potentials by inner and outer hair cells. *Journal of the Acoustical Society of America,* 1976, *60,* 510–512.

DAMASIO, A.R., AND DAMASIO, H. The anatomic basis of pure alexia. *Neurology,* 1983, *33,* 1573–1583.

DAMASIO, A.R., DAMASIO, H., AND VAN HOESEN, G.W. Prosopagnosia: Anatomic basis and behavioral mechanisms. *Neurology,* 1982, *32,* 331–341.

DAMASIO, H. Cerebral localization of the aphasias. In *Acquired Aphasia,* edited by M.T. Sarno. New York: Academic Press, 1981.

DAMASIO, H., AND DAMASIO, A. The anatomical basis of conduction aphasia. *Brain,* 1980, *103,* 337–350.

D'ANDRADE, R. Sex differences and cultural institutions. In *The Development of Sex Differences,* edited by E. Maccoby. Stanford, Calif.: Stanford University Press, 1966.

DARWIN, C. *The Expression of the Emotions in Man and Animals.* Chicago: University of Chicago Press, 1872/1965.

DAVIDSON, J.M. Characteristics of sex behavior in male rats following castration. *Animal Behaviour,* 1966, *14,* 266–272.

DAVIDSON, J.M. Hormones and sexual behavior in the male. In *Neuroendocrinology,* edited by D.T. Krieger and J.C. Hughes. Sunderland, Mass.: Sinauer Associates, 1980.

DAVIDSON, J.M., CAMARGO, C.A., AND SMITH, E.R. Effects of androgen on sexual behavior in hypogonadal men. *Journal of Clinical Endocrinology and Metabolism,* 1979, *48,* 955–958.

DAVIS, J.D., AND CAMPBELL, C.S. Peripheral control of meal size in the rat: Effect of sham feeding on meal size and drinking rate. *Journal of Comparative and Physiological Psychology,* 1973, *83,* 379–387.

DAVIS, J.M. A two-factor theory of schizophrenia. *Journal of Psychiatric Research,* 1974, *11,* 25–30.

DAVIS, P.G., KRIEGER, M.S., BARFIELD, R.J., MCEWEN, B.S., AND PFAFF, D.W. The site of action of intrahypothalamic estrogen implants in feminine sexual behavior: An autoradiographic analysis. *Endocrinology,* 1983, *111,* 1581–1586.

DAVISON, G.C., AND NEALE, J.M. *Abnormal Psychology: An Experimental Clinical Approach,* third edition. New York: John Wiley & Sons, 1982.

DAW, N.W. Colour-coded ganglion cells in the goldfish retina: Extension of their receptive fields by means of new stimuli. *Journal of Physiology (London),* 1968, *197,* 567–592.

DEADWYLER, S.A. The functional basis of LTP in the behaving animal — Sensory evoked potentials in the dentate gyrus. *Neurosciences Research Progress Bulletin,* 1982, *20,* 696–705.

DEBOLD, J.E., AND MICZEK, K.A. Aggression persists after ovariectomy in female rats. *Hormones and Behavior,* 1984, *18,* 177–190.

DEJERINE, J. Contribution à l'étude anatomo-pathologique et clinique des différentes variétés de cécité verbale. *Comptes Rendus des Séances de la Société de Biologie et de Ses Filiales,* 1892, *4,* 61–90.

DEJERINE, J. Sur un cas de cécité verbale avec agraphia, suivi d'autopsie. *Comptes Rendus des Séances de la Société de Biologie et de Ses Filiales,* 1891, *3,* 197–201.

DEKOSKY, S., HEILMAN, K.M., BOWERS, D., AND VALENSTEIN, E. Recognition and discrimination of emotional faces and pictures. *Brain and Language,* 1980, *9,* 206–214.

DELAY, J., AND DENIKER, P. Le traitement des psychoses par une methode neurolytique derivée d'hibernothéraphie; le 4560 RP utilisée seul en cure prolongée et continuée. *Comptes Rendus Congrès des Médecins Aliénistes et Neurologistes de France et des Pays de Langue Française,* 1952a, *50,* 497–502.

DELAY, J., AND DENIKER, P. 38 cas des psychoses traitées par la cure prolongée et continuée de 4560 RP. *Comptes Rendus Congrès des Médecins Aliénistes et Neurologistes de France et des Pays de Langue Française,* 1952b, *50,* 503–513.

DELGADO, J.M.R. *Physical Control of the Mind.* New York: Harper & Row, 1969.

DELONG, M. Motor functions of the basal ganglia: Single-unit activity during movement. In *The Neurosciences: Third Study Program,* edited by F.O. Schmitt and F.G. Worden. Cambridge, Mass.: MIT Press, 1974.

DEMENT, W.C. The effect of dream deprivation. *Science,* 1960, *131,* 1705–1707.

DEMENT, W.C. *Some Must Watch While Some Must Sleep.* San Francisco: W. H. Freeman, 1974.

DEMENT, W.C. The relevance of sleep pathologies to the function of sleep. In *The Functions of Sleep,* edited by R. Drucker-Colín, M. Shkurovich, and M.B. Sterman. New York: Academic Press, 1979.

DEMENT, W.C., FERGUSON, F., COHEN, H., AND BARCHAS, J. Nonchemical methods and data using a biochemical model: The REM quanta. In *Psychochemical Research in Man,* edited by A.J. Mandell and M.P. Mandell. New York: Academic Press, 1969.

DEMENT, W.C., MITLER, M., AND HENRIKSEN, S. Sleep changes during chronic administration of parachlorophenylalanine. *Revue Canadienne de Biologie,* 1972, *31,* 239–246.

DEOL, M.S., AND GLUECKSOHN-WAELSCH, S. The role of inner hair cells in hearing. *Nature,* 1979, *278,* 250–252.

DÉROUESNÉ, J., AND BEAUVOIS, M.F. Phonological processing in reading: Data from alexia. *Journal of Neurology, Neurosurgery and Psychiatry,* 1979, *42,* 1125–1132.

DESMOND, J.E., ROSENFIELD, M.E., AND MOORE, J.W. An HRP study of the brainstem afferents to the accessory abducens region and dorsolateral pons in rabbit: Implications for the conditioned nictitating membrane response. *Brain Research Bulletin,* 1983, *10,* 747–763.

DESMOND, N.L., AND LEVY, W.B. Synaptic correlates of associative potentiation/depression: An ultrastructural study in the hippocampus. *Brain Research,* 1983, *265,* 21–30.

DEUTSCH, J.A. The stomach in food satiation and the regulation of appetite. *Progress in Neurobiology,* 1978, *10,* 135–153.

DEUTSCH, J.A. The cholinergic synapse and the site of memory. In *The Physiological Basis of Memory,* edited by J.A. Deutsch. New York: Academic Press, 1983.

DEUTSCH, J.A., AND GONZALEZ, M.F. Gastric nutrient content signals satiety. *Behavioral and Neural Biology,* 1980, *30,* 113–116.

DEUTSCH, J.A., AND HARDY, W.T. Cholecystokinin produces bait shyness in rats. *Nature,* 1977, *266,* 196.

DE VALOIS, R.L. Behavioral and electrophysiological studies of primate vision. In *Contributions to Sensory Physiology, Vol. l,* edited by W.D. Neff. New York: Academic Press, 1965.

DE VALOIS, R.L., ABRAMOV, I., AND JACOBS, G.H. Analysis of response patterns of LGN cells. *Journal of the Optical Society of America,* 1966, *56,* 966–977.

DE VALOIS, R.L., ALBRECHT, D.G., AND THORELL, L. Cortical cells: Bar detectors or spatial frequency filters? In *Frontiers in Visual Science,* edited by S.J. Cool and E.L. Smith. Berlin: Springer, 1978.

DE VALOIS, R.L., AND DE VALOIS, K.K. Spatial vision. *Annual Review of Psychology,* 1980, *31,* 309–341.

DIAMOND, M. Sexual identity, monozygotic twins reared in discordant sex roles and a BBC follow-up. *Archives of Sexual Behavior,* 1982, *11,* 181–186.

DIAMOND, M.C., LINDNER, B., JOHNSON, R., BENNETT, E.L., AND ROSENZWEIG, M.R. Differences in occipital cortical synapses from environmentally enriched, impoverished, and standard colony rats. *Journal of Neuroscience Research,* 1975, *1,* 109–119.

DIVAC, I., ROSVOLD, H.E., AND SZWARCBART, M.K. Behavioral effects of selective ablation of the caudate nucleus. *Journal of Comparative and Physiological Psychology,* 1967, *63,* 184–190.

DIXON, A.K. The effect of olfactory stimuli upon the social behaviour of laboratory mice *(Mus musculus L).* Ph.D. thesis, Birmingham University, Birmingham, England, 1973.

DIXON, A.K., AND MACKINTOSH, J.H. Effects of female urine upon the social behaviour of adult male mice. *Animal Behaviour,* 1971, *19,* 138–140.

DOBELLE, W.H., MLADEJOVSKY, M.G., AND GIRVIN, J.P. Artificial vision for the blind: Electrical stimulation of visual cortex offers hope for a functional prosthesis. *Science,* 1974, *183,* 440–444.

DOETSCH, G.S., AND ERICKSON, R.P. Synaptic processing of taste quality information in the nucleus tractus solitarius of the rat. *Journal of Neurophysiology,* 1970, *33,* 490–507.

DONAHOE, J.W., CROWLEY, M.A., MILLARD, W.J., AND STICKNEY, K.A. A unified principle of reinforcement: Some implications for matching. In *Quantitative Analyses of Behavior: Vol. 2. Matching and Maximizing Accounts,* edited by M.L. Commons, R.J. Herrnstein, and H. Rachlin. New York: Ballinger, 1982.

DONEGAN, N.H., LOWERY, R.W., AND THOMPSON, R.F. Effects of lesioning cerebellar nuclei on conditioned leg-flexion responses. *Society for Neurosciences Abstracts,* 1983, *9,* 331.

DOTY, R.L., FORD, M., PRETI, G., AND HUGGINS, G.R. Changes in the intensity and pleasantness of human vaginal odors during the menstrual cycle. *Science,* 1975, *190,* 1316.

DOWLING, J.E. Information processing by local circuits: The vertebrate retina as a model system. In *The Neurosciences: Fourth Study Program,* edited by F.O. Schmitt and F.G. Worden. Cambridge, Mass.: MIT Press, 1979.

DOWNER, J.L. DEC. Interhemispheric integration in the visual system. In *Interhemispheric Relations and Cerebral Dominance,* edited by V.B. Mountcastle. Baltimore: Johns Hopkins University Press, 1962.

DRACHMAN, D.A., AND LEAVITT, J. Human memory and the cholinergic receptor. *Archives of Neurology,* 1974, *30,* 113–121.

DRAY, A. The physiology and pharmacology of mammalian basal ganglia. *Progress in Neurobiology,* 1980, *14,* 221–335.

DREYFUS-BRISAC, C. Sleep ontogenesis in early human prematurity from 24 to 27 weeks of conceptual age. *Developmental Psychobiology,* 1968, *1,* 162–169.

DRICKAMER, L.C. A ten-year summary of reproductive data for free-ranging *Macaca mulatta. Folia Primatologica,* 1974, *21,* 61–80.

DRUCKER-COLÍN, R. Endogenous sleep peptides. In *Psychopharmacology of Sleep,* edited by D. Wheatley. New York: Raven Press, 1981.

DRUCKER-COLÍN, R.R., AND SPANIS, C.W. Is there a sleep transmitter? *Progress in Neurobiology,* 1976, *6,* 1–22.

DUNLEAVY, D.L., BREZINOVÁ, V., OSWALD, I., MACLEAN, A.W., AND TINKER, M. Changes during weeks in effects of tricycle drugs on the human sleeping brain. *British Journal of Psychiatry,* 1972, *120,* 663–672.

DUNN, A.J. Neurochemistry of learning and memory: An evaluation of recent data. *Annual Review of Psychology,* 1980, *31,* 343–390.

DUNN, A.J., REES, H.D., AND IUVONE, P.M. ACTH and the stress-induced changes of lysine incorporation into brain and liver protein. *Pharmacology, Biochemistry and Behavior,* 1978, *8,* 455–465.

DUNWIDDIE, T., AND LYNCH, G. The relationship between extracellular calcium concentrations and the induction of hippocampal long-term potentiation. *Brain Research,* 1979, *169,* 103–110.

DUNWIDDIE, T., MADISON, D., AND LYNCH, G. Synaptic transmission is required for initiation of long-term potentiation. *Brain Research,* 1978, *150,* 413–417.

DURIE, D.J. Sleep in animals. In *Psychopharmacology of Sleep,* edited by D. Wheatley. New York: Raven Press, 1981.

DYKES, R.W. Parallel processing of somatosensory information: A theory. *Brain Research Reviews,* 1983, *6,* 47–115.

DYKES, R.W., RASMUSSON, D.D., AND HOELTZELL, P.B. Organization of primary somatosensory cortex in the cat. *Journal of Neurophysiology,* 1980, *43,* 1527–1545.

EDWARDS, S.B., AND FLYNN, J.P. Corticospinal control of striking in centrally elicited attack behavior. *Brain Research,* 1972, *41,* 51–65.

EDWARDS, D.A. Mice: Fighting by neonatally androgenized females. *Science,* 1968, *161,* 1027–1028.

EHRENKRANZ, J., BLISS, E., AND SHEARD, M. Plasma testosterone: Correlation with aggressive behavior and social dominance in man. *Psychosomatic Medicine,* 1974, *36,* 469–475.

EHRHARDT, A.A., AND MEYER-BALBURG, H.F.L. Effects of prenatal sex hormones on gender-related behavior. *Science,* 1981, *211,* 1312–1318.

EICHENBAUM, H., QUENON, B.A., HEACOCK, A., AND AGRANOFF, B.W. Differential behavioral and biochemical effects of regional injections of cyclohexamide into mouse brain. *Brain Research,* 1976, *101,* 171–176.

EINSTEIN, E.R. Basic protein of myelin and its role in experimental allergic encephalomyelitis and multiple sclerosis. In *Handbook of Neurochemistry, Vol. 7,* edited by A. Lajtha. New York: Plenum Press, 1972.

EKMAN, P. *The Face of Man: Expressions of Universal Emotions in a New Guinea Village.* New York: Garland STPM Press, 1980.

EKMAN, P., AND FRIESEN, W.V. Constants across cultures in the face and emotion. *Journal of Personality and Social Psychology,* 1971, *17,* 124–129.

ELIAS, M. Serum cortisol, testosterone and testosterone binding globulin responses to competitive fighting in human males. *Aggressive Behavior,* 1981, *7,* 215–224.

ELLISON, G.D., AND FLYNN, J.P. Organized aggressive be-

havior in cats after surgical isolation of the hypothalamus. *Archives Italiennes de Biologie,* 1968, *106,* 1–20.

ENGELMAN, K., LOVENBERG, W., AND SJOERDSMA, A. Inhibition of serotonin synthesis by parachlorophenylalanine in patients with the carcinoid syndrome. *New England Journal of Medicine,* 1967, *277,* 1103–1108.

ENROTH-CUGELL, C., AND ROBSON, J.G. The contrast sensitivity of retinal ganglion cells of the cat. *Journal of Physiology (London),* 1966, *187,* 517–552.

EPSTEIN, A.N., AND TEITELBAUM, P. Severe and persistent deficits in thirst produced by lateral hypothalamic damage. In *Thirst: Proceedings of the First International Symposium on Thirst in the Regulation of Body Water,* edited by M.J. Wayner. Oxford, England: Pergamon Press, 1964.

ERVIN, F.R. Discussion in workshop on regulation of behavior. In *Ethical Issues in Biology and Medicine,* edited by P.N. Williams. Cambridge, Mass.: Schenkman, 1973.

EVANS, C.M., MACKINTOSH, J.H., KENNEDY, J.F., AND ROBERTSON, S.M. Attempts to characterise and isolate aggression reducing olfactory signals from the urine of female mice *Mus musculus L. Physiology and Behavior,* 1978, *20,* 129–134.

EVARTS, E.V. Relation of discharge frequency to conduction velocity in pyramidal tract neurons. *Journal of Neurophysiology,* 1965, *28,* 215–228.

EVARTS, E.V. Sensorimotor cortex activity associated with movements triggered by visual as compared to somesthetic inputs. In *The Neurosciences: Third Study Program,* edited by F.O. Schmitt and F.G. Worden. Cambridge: MIT Press, 1974.

EVERITT, B.J., AND HERBERT, J. The effects of implanting testosterone propionate into the central nervous system on the sexual behavior of adrenalectomized female rhesus monkeys. *Brain Research,* 1975, *86,* 109–120.

EVERITT, B.J., HERBERT, J., AND HAMER, J.D. Sexual receptivity of bilaterally adrenalectomised female rhesus monkeys. *Physiology and Behavior,* 1972, *8,* 409–415.

FALCK, B., HILLARP, N.-Å. THIEME, G., AND TORP, A. Fluorescence of catechol amines and related compounds condensed with formaldehyde. *Journal of Histochemistry and Cytochemistry,* 1962, *10,* 348–364.

FALK, J.L. The nature and determinants of adjunctive behavior. In *Schedule Effects: Drugs, Drinking, and Aggression,* edited by R.M. Gilbert and J.D. Keehn. Toronto: University of Toronto Press, 1972.

FALLON, J.H., KOZIELL, D.A., AND MOORE, R.Y. Catecholamine innervation of the basal forebrain. II. Amygdala, suprarhinal cortex and entorhinal cortex. *Journal of Comparative Neurology,* 1978, *180,* 509–532.

FANSELOW, M.S. Naloxone attenuates rat's preference for signaled shock. *Physiological Psychology,* 1979, 7, 70–74.

FEDER, H.H. Estrous cyclicity in mammals. In *Neuroendocrinology of Reproduction,* edited by N.T. Adler. New York: Plenum Press, 1981.

FEDER, H.H. Hormones and sexual behavior. *Annual Review of Psychology,* 1984, *35,* 165–200.

FENCL, V., KOSKI, G., AND PAPPENHEIMER, J.R. Factors in cerebrospinal fluid from goats that affect sleep and activity in rats. *Journal of Physiology (London),* 1971, *216,* 565–589.

FIBIGER, H.C. Drugs and reinforcement mechanisms: A critical review of the catecholamine theory. *Annual Review of Pharmacology and Toxicology,* 1978, *18,* 37–56.

FIBIGER, H.C., MURRAY, C.L., AND PHILLIPS, A.G. Lesions of the nucleus basalis magnocellularis impair long-term memory in rats. *Society for Neuroscience Abstracts,* 1983, *9,* 332.

FIEVE, R.R. The clinical effects of lithium treatment. *Trends in Neurosciences,* 1979, *2,* 66–68.

FINKELSTEIN, J.W., ROFFWARG, H.P., BOYAR, R.M., KREAM, J., AND HELLMAN, L. Age-related change in the twenty-four-hour spontaneous secretion of growth hormone. *Journal of Clinical Endocrinology and Metabolism,* 1972, *35,* 665–670.

FISHBEIN, W., AND GUTWEIN, B.M. Paradoxical sleep and memory storage processes. *Behavioral Biology,* 1977, *19,* 425–464.

FISHER, C. Dreaming and sexuality. In *Psychoanalysis: A General Psychology,* edited by L. Lowenstein, M. Newman, M.M. Schur, and A. Solnit. New York: International University Press, 1966.

FISHER, C., BYRNE, J., EDWARDS, A., AND KAHN, E. A psychophysiological study of nightmares. *Journal of the American Psychoanalytic Association,* 1970, *18,* 747–782.

FISHER, C., GROSS, J., AND ZUCH, J. Cycle of penile erection synchronous with dreaming (REM) sleep. Preliminary report. *Archives of General Psychiatry,* 1965, *12,* 29–45.

FITZSIMONS, J.T. Drinking by rats depleted of body fluid without increase in osmotic pressure. *Journal of Physiology (London),* 1961, *159,* 297–309.

FITZSIMONS, J.T. Thirst. *Physiological Reviews,* 1972, *52,* 468–561.

FITZSIMONS, J.T., AND LEMAGNEN, J. Eating as a regulatory control of drinking in the rat. *Journal of Comparative and Physiological Psychology,* 1969, *67,* 273–283.

FITZSIMONS, J.T., AND SIMONS, B.J. The effect on drinking in the rat of intravenous infusion of angiotensin, given alone or in combination with other stimuli of thirst. *Journal of Physiology (London),* 1969, *203,* 45–57.

FLEMING, A., AND ROSENBLATT, J.S. Olfactory regulation of maternal behavior in rats. I. Olfactory bulbectomy in experienced and inexperienced females. *Journal of Comparative and Physiological Psychology,* 1974a, *86,* 221–232.

FLEMING, A., AND ROSENBLATT, J.S. Olfactory regulation of maternal behavior in rats. II. Effects of peripherally induced anosmia and lesions of the lateral olfactory tract in pup-induced virgins. *Journal of Comparative and Physiological Psychology,* 1974b, *86,* 233–246.

FLEMING, A., VACCARINO, F., AND LUEBKE, C. Amygdaloid inhibition of maternal behavior in the nulliparous female rat. *Physiology and Behavior,* 1980, *25,* 731–745.

FLEMING, A., VACCARINO, F., TAMBOSSO, L., AND CHEE, P. Vomeronasal and olfactory system modulation of maternal behavior in the rat. *Science,* 1979, *203,* 372–374.

FLOCK, A. Transducing mechanisms in the lateral line canal organ receptors. *Cold Spring Harbor Symposia on Quantitative Biology,* 1965, *30,* 133–146.

FLOODY, O.R. Hormones and aggression in female mammals. In *Hormones and Aggressive Behavior,* edited by B.B. Svare. New York: Plenum Press, 1983.

FLOODY, O.R., AND PFAFF, D.W. Aggressive behavior in female hamsters: The hormonal basis for fluctuations in female aggressiveness correlated with estrous state. *Journal of Comparative and Physiological Psychology,* 1977, *91,* 443–464.

FLYNN, J., VANEGAS, H., FOOTE, W., AND EDWARDS, S. Neural mechanisms involved in a cat's attack on a rat. In *The Neural Control of Behavior,* edited by R.F. Whalen, M. Thompson, M. Verzeano, and N. Weinberger. New York: Academic Press, 1970.

FOURIEZOS, G., AND WISE, R.A. Pimozide-induced extinction of intracranial self-stimulation: Response patterns rule out motor or performance deficits. *Brain Research,* 1976, *103,* 377–380.

FOUTZ, A.S., MITLER, M.M., CAVALLI-SFORZA, L.L., AND DEMENT, W.C. Genetic factors in canine narcolepsy. *Sleep,* 1979, *1,* 413–421.

FRAY, P.J., KOOB, G.F., AND IVERSEN, S.D. Tail pinch versus brain stimulation: Problems of comparison. Reply to letters by Perochio and Hendon, and Katz. *Science,* 1978, *201,* 841–842.

FREEDMAN, M., ALEXANDER, M.P., AND NAESER, M.A. Anatomic basis of transcortical motor aphasia. *Neurology,* 1984, *34,* 409–417.

FREEMON, F.R. *Sleep Research: A Critical Review.* Springfield, Ill.: Charles C Thomas, 1972.

FRIEDMAN, M.I. Hyperphagia in rats with experimental diabetes mellitus: A response to a decreased supply of utilizable fuels. *Journal of Comparative and Physiological Psychology,* 1978, *92,* 109–117.

FRIEDMAN, M.I., AND BRUNO, J.P. Exchange of water during lactation. *Science,* 1976, *191,* 409–410.

FRISCH, O.V. Herzfrequenzänderung bei Drückreaktion junger Nestflücher. *Zeitschrift für Tierpsychologie,* 1966, *23,* 497–501.

FUCHS, S.A.G., DALSASS, M., SIEGEL, H.E., AND SIEGEL, A. The neural pathways mediating quiet-biting attack behavior from the hypothalamus in the cat: A functional autoradiographic study. *Aggressive Behavior,* 1981, *7,* 51–67.

FULLER, C.A., LYDIC, R., SULZMAN, F.M., ALBERS, H.E., TEPPER, B., AND MOORE-EDE, M.C. Circadian rhythm of body temperature persists after suprachiasmatic lesions in the squirrel monkey. *American Journal of Physiology,* 1981, *241,* R385–R391.

FULTON, J.F., AND BAILEY, P. Tumors in the region of the third ventricle: Their diagnosis and relation to pathological sleep. *Journal of Nervous and Mental Disorders,* 1929, *69,* 1–25, 145–164, 261–277.

FUNAKOSHI, M., AND NINOMIYA, Y. Neural code for taste quality in the thalamus of the dog. In *Food Intake and Chemical Senses,* edited by Y. Katsuki, M. Sateo, S.F. Takagi, and Y. Oomura. Tokyo: University of Tokyo Press, 1977.

FUSTER, J.M., AND JERVEY, J.P. Inferotemporal neurons distinguish and retain behaviorally relevant features of visual stimuli. *Science,* 1981, *212,* 952–955.

FUXE, K., ÖGREN, S.-O., AGNATI, L.F., ANDERSSON, K., AND ENEROTH, P. Effects of subchronic antidepressant drug treatment on central serotonergic mechanisms in the male rat. In *Typical and Atypical Antidepressants: Molecular Mechanisms,* edited by E. Costa and G. Racagni. New York: Raven Press, 1982.

GAGE, F.H., BJÖRKLUND, A., STENEVI, U., DUNNETT, S.B., AND KELLY, P.A.T. Intrahippocampal septal grafts ameliorate learning impairments in aged rats. *Science,* 1984, *225,* 533–536.

GALABURDA, A., AND GESCHWIND, N. Dyslexia update. *Neurology and Neurosurgery Update Series,* 1982, *3,* 1–7.

GALABURDA, A., AND KEMPER, T.L. Observations cited by Geschwind, N. Specializations of the human brain. *Scientific American,* 1979, *241,* 180–199.

GALABURDA, A.M., LEMAY, M., KEMPER, T.L., AND GESCHWIND, N. Right-left asymmetries in the brain. *Science,* 1978, *199,* 852–856.

GALL, C., BRECHA, N., KARTEN, H.J., AND CHANG, K.-J. Localization of enkephalin-like immunoreactivity to identified axonal and neuronal populations of the rat hippocampus. *Journal of Comparative Neurology,* 1981, *198,* 335–350.

GALLAGHER, M., KAPP, B.S., FRYSINGER, R.C., AND RAPP, P.R. β-adrenergic manipulation in amygdala central nucleus alters rabbit heart rate conditioning. *Pharmacology, Biochemistry and Behavior,* 1980, *12,* 419–426.

GALLAGHER, M., KAPP, B.S., McNALL, C.L., AND PASCOE, J.P. Opiate effects in the amygdala central nucleus on heart rate conditioning in rabbits. *Pharmacology, Biochemistry and Behavior,* 1981, *14,* 497–505.

GALLISTEL, C.R. The incentive of brain stimulation reward. *Journal of Comparative and Physiological Psychology,* 1969, *69,* 713–721.

GALLISTEL, C.R., BOYTIM, M., GOMITA, Y., AND KLEBANOFF, L. Does pimozide block the reinforcing effect of brain stimulation? *Pharmacology, Biochemistry and Behavior,* 1982, *17,* 769–781.

GANDELMAN, R., AND SIMON, N.G. Spontaneous pup-killing by mice in response to large litters. *Developmental Psychobiology,* 1978, *11,* 235–241.

GANDELMAN, R., AND SIMON, N.G. Postpartum fighting in

the rat: Nipple development and the presence of young. *Behavioral and Neural Biology,* 1980, *28,* 350–360.

GANDELMAN, R., AND VOM SAAL, F.S. Exposure to early androgen attenuates androgen-induced pup-killing in male and female mice. *Behavioral Biology,* 1977, *20,* 252–260.

GANDELMAN, R., ZARROW, M.X., DENENBERG, V.H., AND MYERS, M. Olfactory bulb removal eliminates maternal behavior in the mouse. *Science,* 1971, *171,* 210–211.

GARCIA, J., AND KOELLING, R.A. Relation of cue to consequence in avoidance learning. *Psychonomic Science,* 1966, *4,* 123–124.

GAW, A.C., CHANG, L.W., AND SHAW, L.-C. Efficacy of acupuncture on osteoarthritic pain. *New England Journal of Medicine,* 1975, *293,* 375–378.

GEARY, N., AND SMITH, G.P. Pancreatic glucagon and postprandial satiety in the rat. *Physiology and Behavior,* 1982, *28,* 313–332.

GEBHARDT, G.F. Opiate and opioid peptide effects on brain stem neurons: Relevance to nociception and antinociceptive mechanisms. *Pain,* 1982, *12,* 93–140.

GERBINO, L., OLESHANSKY, M., AND GERSHON, S. Clinical use and mode of action of lithium. In *Psychopharmacology: A Generation of Progress,* edited by M.A. Lipton, A. DiMascio, and K.F. Killam. New York: Raven Press, 1978.

GERFEN, C.R., AND CLAVIER, R.M. Intracranial self-stimulation from the sulcal prefrontal cortex in the rat: The effect of 6-hydroxydopamine or kainic acid lesions at the site of stimulation. *Brain Research,* 1981, *224,* 291–304.

GERSHON, E.S., BUNNEY, W.E., JR., LECKMAN, J., VAN EERDEWEGH, M., AND DeBAUCHE, B. The inheritance of affective disorders: A review of data and hypotheses. *Behavior Genetics,* 1976, *6,* 227–261.

GESCHWIND, N. Disconnexion syndromes in animals and man. *Brain,* 1965, *88,* 237–294, 585–644.

GESCHWIND, N., AND BEHAN, P. Left-handedness: Association with immune disease, migraine, and developmental learning disorder. *Proceedings of the National Academy of Sciences (U.S.A.),* 1982, *79,* 5097–5100.

GESCHWIND, N., QUADFASEL, F.A., AND SEGARRA, J.M. Isolation of the speech area. *Neuropsychologia,* 1968, *6,* 327–340.

GESTELAND, R.C. The neural code: Integrative neural mechanisms. In *Handbook of Perception, Vol. VIA: Tasting and Smelling,* edited by E.C. Carterette and M.P. Friedman. New York: Academic Press, 1978.

GIBBS, J., YOUNG, R.C., AND SMITH, G.P. Cholecystokinin decreases food intake in rats. *Journal of Comparative and Physiological Psychology,* 1973a, *84,* 488–495.

GIBBS, J., YOUNG, R.C., AND SMITH, G.P. Cholecystokinin elicits satiety in rats with open gastric fistulas. *Nature,* 1973b, *245,* 323–325.

GLADUE, B.A., GREEN, R., AND HELLMAN, R.E. Neuroendocrine response to estrogen and sexual orientation. *Science,* 1984, *225,* 1496–1499.

GLENDENNING, K.K. Effects of septal and amygdaloid lesions on social behavior of the cat. *Journal of Comparative and Physiological Psychology,* 1972, *80,* 199–207.

GLICK, Z., TEAGUE, R.J., AND BRAY, G.A. Brown adipose tissue: thermic response increased by a single low protein, high carbohydrate meal. *Science,* 1981, *213,* 1125–1127.

GLOBUS, A., ROSENZWEIG, M.R., BENNETT, E.L., AND DIAMOND, M.C. Effects of differential experience on dendritic spine counts in rat cerebral cortex. *Journal of Comparative and Physiological Psychology,* 1973, *82,* 175–181.

GODDARD, G.V. Development of epileptic seizures through brain stimulation at low intensity. *Nature,* 1967, *214,* 1020–1021.

GODDARD, G.V., AND DOUGLAS, R.M. Does the engram of kindling model the engram of long term memory? *Canadian Journal of Neurological Science,* 1975, *2,* 385–394.

GODDARD, G.V., MCINTYRE, D.C., AND LEECH, C.K. A permanent change in brain function resulting from daily electrical stimulation. *Experimental Neurology,* 1969, *25,* 295–330.

GOLD, R.M. Hypothalamic obesity: The myth of the ventromedial nucleus. *Science,* 1973, *182,* 488–490.

GOLD, R.M., JONES, A.P., SAWCHENKO, P.E., AND KAPATOS, G. Paraventricular area: critical focus of a longitudinal neurocircuitry mediating food intake. *Physiology and Behavior,* 1977, *18,* 1111–1119.

GOLD, R.M., AND SIMSON, E.L. Perturbations of serum insulin, glucagon, somatostatin, epinephrine, norepinephrine and glucose after obesifying hypothalamic knife-cuts. In *The Neural Basis of Feeding and Reward,* edited by B.G. Hoebel and D. Novin. Brunswick, Maine: Haer Institute, 1982.

GOLDBERG, J.M., AND FERNANDEZ, C. Vestibular mechanisms. *Annual Review of Physiology,* 1975, *37,* 129–162.

GOLDFOOT, D.A. Olfaction, sexual behavior, and the pheromone hypothesis in rhesus monkeys: A critique. *American Zoologist,* 1981, *21,* 153–164.

GOLDFOOT, D.A., KREVETZ, M.A., GOY, R.W., AND FREEMAN, S.K. Lack of effect of vaginal lavages and aliphatic acids on ejaculatory responses in rhesus monkeys: Behavioral and chemical analyses. *Hormones and Behavior,* 1976, *7,* 1–28.

GOLDSTEIN, A., PRYOR, G.T., OTIS, L.S., AND LARSEN, F. On the role of endogenous opioid peptides: Failure of naloxone to influence shock escape threshold in the rat. *Life Sciences,* 1976, *18,* 599–604.

GOLDSTEIN, K. *Language and Language Disturbances.* New York: Grune & Stratton, 1948.

GOLGI, C. *Opera Omnia, Vols. I and II.* Milan: Hoepli, 1903.

GONZALEZ, M.F., AND DEUTSCH, J.A. Vagotomy abolishes cues of satiety produced by gastric distension. *Science,* 1981, *212,* 1283–1284.

GOODGLASS, H. Agrammatism. In *Studies of Neurolinguistics,* edited by H. Whitaker and H.A. Whitaker. New York: Academic Press, 1976.

GOODGLASS, H., AND KAPLAN, E. *Assessment of Aphasia and Related Disorders.* Philadelphia: Lea & Febiger, 1972.

GOODWIN, F.K., WIRZ-JUSTICE, A., AND WEHR, T.A. Evidence that the pathophysiology of depression and the mechanisms of action of antidepressant drugs both involve alterations in circadian rhythms. In *Typical and Atypical Antidepressants: Clinical Practice,* edited by E. Costa and G. Racagni. New York: Raven Press, 1982.

GORMEZANO, I. Classical conditioning. Investigations of defense and reward conditioning in the rabbit. In *Classical Conditioning II,* edited by A.H. Black and W.R. Prokasy. New York: Appleton-Century-Crofts, 1972.

GORSKI, R.A., GORDON, J.H., SHRYNE, J.E., AND SOUTHAM, A.M. Evidence for a morphological sex difference within the medial preoptic area of the rat brain. *Brain Research,* 1978, *148,* 333–346.

GOTSICK, J.E., AND MARSHALL, R.C. Time course of the septal rage syndrome. *Physiology and Behavior,* 1972, *9,* 685–687.

GOTTESMAN, I.I., AND SHIELDS, J. A critical review of recent adoption, twin, and family studies of schizophrenia: Behavioral genetics perspectives. *Schizophrenia Bulletin,* 1976, *2,* 360–401.

GOURAS, P. Identification of cone mechanisms in monkey ganglion cells. *Journal of Physiology (London),* 1968, *199,* 533–538.

GOY, R.W., AND GOLDFOOT, D.A. Hormonal influences on sexually dimorphic behavior. In *Handbook of Physiology, Section 7, Vol. 2, Part I,* edited by R.O. Green. Washington, D.C.: American Physiological Society, 1973.

GOY, R.W., AND KEMNITZ, J.W. Early, persistent, and delayed effects of virilizing substances delivered transplacentally to female rhesus fetuses. In *Applications of Behavioral Pharmacology in Toxicology,* edited by G. Zbinden. New York: Raven Press, 1983.

GOY, R.W., AND PHOENIX, C.H. The effects of testosterone propionate administered before birth on the development of behavior in genetic female rhesus monkeys. In *Steroid Hormones and Brain Function,* edited by C. Sawyer and R. Gorski. Berkeley: University of California Press, 1971.

GRANNEMAN, J., AND FRIEDMAN, M.I. Hepatic control of feeding and gastric acid secretion: Inhibition mediated by the hepatic vagus. Paper presented at the meeting of the Eastern Psychological Association, Philadelphia, 1978.

GRAY, J.A., WHITSETT, J.M., AND ZIESENIS, J.S. Hormonal regulation of aggression toward juveniles in female house mice. *Hormones and Behavior,* 1978, *11,* 310–322.

GREEN, J., CLEMENTE, C., AND DEGROOT, J. Rhinencephalic lesions and behavior in cats. *Journal of Comparative Neurology,* 1957, *108,* 505–545.

GREEN, J.D., AND ARDUINI, A.A. Hippocampal electrical activity in arousal. *Journal of Neurophysiology,* 1954, *17,* 533–557.

GREEN, J.P., AND MAAYANI, S. Tricyclic antidepressant drugs block histamine H2 receptor in brain. *Nature,* 1977, *269,* 163–165.

GREENBERG, R., PILLARD, R., AND PEARLMAN, C. The effect of dream (stage REM) deprivation on adaptation to stress. *Psychosomatic Medicine,* 1972, *34,* 257–262.

GREENOUGH, W.T., AND VOLKMAR, F.R. Pattern of dendritic branching in occipital cortex of rats reared in complex environments. *Experimental Neurology,* 1973, *40,* 491–504.

GREGORY, E., ENGLE, K., AND PFAFF, D. Male hamster preference for odors of female hamster vaginal discharges: Studies of experiential and hormonal determinants. *Journal of Comparative and Physiological Psychology,* 1975, *89,* 442–446.

GREISER, C., GREENBERG, R., AND HARRISON, R.H. The adaptive function of sleep: The differential effects of sleep and dreaming on recall. *Journal of Abnormal Psychology,* 1972, *80,* 280–286.

GRIFFITH, J.D., CAVANAUGH, J., HELD, N.N., AND OATES, J.A. Dextroamphetamine: Evaluation of psychotomimetic properties in man. *Archives of General Psychiatry,* 1972, *26,* 97–100.

GRIFFITHS, J.D., AND PAYNE, P.R. Energy expenditure in small children of obese and non-obese mothers. *Nature,* 1976, *260,* 698–700.

GROSS, C.G., ROCHA-MIRANDA, C.E., AND BENDER, D.B. Visual properties of neurons in inferotemporal cortex of the macaque. *Journal of Neurophysiology,* 1972, *35,* 96–111.

GROSS, M.D. Violence associated with organic brain disease. In *Dynamics of Violence,* edited by J. Fawcett. Chicago: American Medical Association, 1971.

GROSSMAN, S.P., GROSSMAN, L., AND WALSH, L. Functional organization of the rat amygdala with respect to avoidance behavior. *Journal of Comparative and Physiological Psychology,* 1975, *88,* 829–850.

GÜLDNER, F.-H. Synaptology of the rat suprachiasmatic nucleus. *Cell Tissue Research,* 1976, *165,* 509–544.

GÜLDNER, F.-H., AND WOLFF, H.R. Dendrodendritic synapses in the suprachiasmatic nucleus of the rat hypothalamus. *Journal of Neurocytology,* 1974, *3,* 245–250.

GULEVICH, G., DEMENT, W.C., AND JOHNSON, L. Psychiatric and EEG observations on a case of prolonged (264 hours) wakefulness. *Archives of General Psychiatry,* 1966, *15,* 29–35.

GUMULKA, W., SAMANIN, R., VALZELLI, L., AND CONSOLOS, S. Behavioural and biochemical effects following the stimulation of the nucleus raphis dorsalis on rats. *Journal of Neurochemistry,* 1971, *18,* 533–534.

HAEBERICH, F.J. Osmoreception in the portal system. *Federation Proceedings,* 1968, *27,* 1137–1141.

HALL, W.G. A remote stomach clamp to evaluate oral and gastric controls of drinking in the rat. *Physiology and Behavior,* 1973, *11,* 897–901.

HALL, W.G., AND BLASS, E.M. Orogastric determinants of drinking in rats: Interaction between absorptive and peripheral controls. *Journal of Comparative and Physiological Psychology,* 1977, *91,* 365–373.

HALMI, K.A. Anorexia nervosa: Recent investigations. *Annual Review of Medicine,* 1978, *29,* 137–148.

HARDING, C.F., AND LESHNER, A.I. The effects of adrenalectomy on the aggressiveness of differently housed mice. *Physiology and Behavior,* 1972, *8,* 437–440.

HARLAN, R.E., SHIVERS, B.D., KOW, L.-M., AND PFAFF, D.W. Intrahypothalamic colchicine infusions disrupt lordotic responsiveness in estrogen-treated female rats. *Brain Research,* 1982, *238,* 153–167.

HARMON, L.D., AND JULESZ, B. Masking in visual recognition: Effects of two-dimensional filtered noise. *Science,* 1973, *180,* 1194–1197.

HARRIS, G.W., AND JACOBSOHN, D. Functional grafts of the anterior pituitary gland. *Proceedings of the Royal Society (London), Series B,* 1951–1952, *139,* 263–267.

HART, B. Sexual reflexes and mating behavior in the male dog. *Journal of Comparative and Physiological Psychology,* 1967, *66,* 388–399.

HART, B. Gonadal hormones and sexual reflexes in the female rat. *Hormones and Behavior,* 1969, *1,* 65–71.

HART, B.L. Hormones, spinal reflexes, and sexual behaviour. In *Determinants of Sexual Behaviour,* edited by J.B. Hutchinson. Chichester, England: John Wiley & Sons, 1978.

HARTMANN, E. *The Biology of Dreaming.* Springfield, Ill.: Charles C Thomas, 1967.

HASELTINE, F.P., AND OHNO, S. Mechanisms of gonadal differentiation. *Science,* 1981, *211,* 1272–1277.

HATTON, G.I. Nucleus circularis: Is it an osmoreceptor in the brain? *Brain Research Bulletin,* 1976, *1,* 123–131.

HAWKE, C. Castration and sex crimes. *American Journal of Mental Deficiency,* 1951, *55,* 220–226.

HAWKINS, R.D., ABRAMS, T.W., CAREW, T.J., AND KANDEL, E.R. A cellular mechanism of classical conditioning in *Aplysia:* Activity-dependent amplification of presynaptic facilitation. *Science,* 1983, *219,* 400–405.

HEBB, D.O. *The Organization of Behaviour.* New York: Wiley-Interscience, 1949.

HEFFNER, T.G., ZIGMOND, M.J., AND STRICKER, E.M. Effects of dopaminergic agonists and antagonists on feeding in intact and 6-hydroxydopamine-treated rats. *Journal of Pharmacology and Experimental Therapeutics,* 1977, *201,* 386–399.

HEILMAN, K.M., ROTHI, L., AND KERTESZ, A. Localization of apraxia-producing lesions. In *Localization in Neuropsychology,* edited by A. Kertesz. New York: Academic Press, 1983.

HEILMAN, K.M., SCHOLES, R., AND WATSON, R.T. Auditory

affective agnosia: Disturbed comprehension of affective speech. *Journal of Neurology, Neurosurgery, and Psychiatry,* 1975, *38,* 69–72.

HEILMAN, K.M., WATSON, R.T., AND BOWERS, D. Affective disorders associated with hemispheric disease. In *Neuropsychology of Human Emotion,* edited by K.M. Heilman and P. Satz. New York: Guilford Press, 1983.

HEIMER, L., AND LARSSON, K. Impairment of mating behavior in male rats following lesions in the preoptic–anterior hypothalamic continuum. *Brain Research,* 1966/1967, *3,* 248–263.

HENDRICKSON, A.E., WAGONER, N., AND COWAN, W.M. Autoradiographic and electron microscopic study of retino-hypothalamic connections. *Zeitschrift für Zellforschung und Mikroskopische Anatomie,* 1972, *125,* 1–26.

HENRIKSEN, S., DEMENT, W., AND BARCHAS, J. The role of serotonin in the regulation of a phasic event of rapid eye movement sleep: The ponto-geniculo-occipital wave. *Advances in Biochemical Psychopharmacology,* 1974, *11,* 169–179.

HERZ, A., ALBUS, K., METYS, J., SCHUBERT, P., AND TESCHEMACHER, H. On the central sites for the antinociceptive action of morphine and fentanyl. *Neuropharmacology,* 1970, *9,* 539–551.

HESS, D.L., WILKINS, R.H., MOOSSY, J., CHANG, J.L., PLANT, T.M., McCORMACK, J.T., NAKAI, Y., AND KNOBIL, E. Estrogen-induced gonadotropin surges in decerebrated female rhesus monkeys with medial basal hypothalamic peninsulae. *Endocrinology,* 1977, *101,* 1264–1271.

HESTON, L.L. Psychiatric disorders in foster-home–reared children of schizophrenic mothers. *British Journal of Psychiatry,* 1966, *112,* 819–825.

HESTON, L.L., AND SHIELDS, J.S. Homosexuality in twins: A family study and a registry study. *Archives of General Psychiatry,* 1968, *18,* 819–825.

HETHERINGTON, A.W., AND RANSON, S.W. Experimental hypothalamohypophyseal obesity in the rat. *Proceedings of the Society for Experimental Biology and Medicine,* 1939, *41,* 465–466.

HEUSER, J.E. Synaptic vesicle exocytosis revealed in quick-frozen frog neuromuscular junctions treated with 4-aminopyridine and given a single electrical shock. In *Society for Neuroscience Symposia, Vol. II,* edited by W.M. Cowan and J.A. Ferrendelli. Bethesda, Md.: Society for Neuroscience, 1977.

HEUSER, J.E., AND REESE, T.S. Evidence for recycling of synaptic vesicle membrane during transmitter release at the frog neuromuscular function. *Journal of Cell Biology,* 1973, *57,* 315–344.

HEUSER, J.E., REESE, T.S., DENNIS, M.J., JAN, Y., JAN, L., AND EVANS, L. Synaptic vesicle exocytosis captured by quick freezing and correlated with quantal transmitter release. *Journal of Cell Biology,* 1979, *81,* 275–300.

HILTON, S.M., AND ZBROZYNA, A.W. Amygdaloid region for defense reactions and its afferent pathway to the brain stem. *Journal of Physiology (London),* 1963, *165,* 160–173.

HIMMS-HAGEN, J. Current status of nonshivering thermogenesis. In *Assessment of Energy Metabolism in Health and Disease,* edited by J.W. Kinney. Columbus, Ohio: Ross Laboratories, 1980.

HIRSCH, H.V.B., AND SPINELLI, D.N. Modification of the distribution of receptive field orientation in cats by selective visual exposure during development. *Experimental Brain Research,* 1971, *13,* 509–527.

HIRSCH, J., AND KNITTLE, J.L. Cellularity of obese and nonobese human adipose tissue. *Federation Proceedings,* 1970, *29,* 1516–1521.

HOEBEL, B.G. Inhibition and disinhibition of self-stimulation and feeding: Hypothalamic control and post-ingestional factors. *Journal of Comparative and Physiological Psychology,* 1968, *66,* 89–100.

HOEBEL, B.G., AND LEIBOWITZ, S.F. Brain monoamines in the regulation of self-stimulation, feeding and body weight. In *Brain, Behavior, and Bodily Disease,* edited by H. Weiner, M.A. Hofer, and A.J. Stunkard. New York: Raven Press, 1981.

HOEBEL, B.G., AND TEITELBAUM, P. Weight regulation in normal and hypothalamic hyperphagic rats. *Journal of Comparative and Physiological Psychology,* 1966, *61,* 189–193.

HOLADAY, J.W. Cardiovascular effects of endogenous opiate systems. *Annual Review of Pharmacology and Toxicology,* 1983, *23,* 541–594.

HOLADAY, J.W., WEI, E., LOH, H.H., AND LI, C.H. Endorphins may function in heat adaptation. *Proceedings of the National Academy of Sciences (U.S.A.),* 1978, *75,* 2923–2927.

HOLLIS, K.L. Pavlovian conditioning of signal-centered action patterns and autonomic behavior: A biological analysis of function. *Advances in the Study of Behavior,* 1982, *12,* 1–64.

HOLMAN, S.D., AND GOY, R.W. Behavioral and mammary responses of adult female rhesus to strange infants. *Hormones and Behavior,* 1980, *14,* 348–357.

HOLMES, G. The cerebellum of man. *Brain,* 1939, *62,* 21–30.

HOPKINS, D.A., AND HOLSTEGE, G. Amygdaloid projections to the mesencephalon, pons and medulla oblongata in the cat. *Experimental Brain Research,* 1978, *32,* 529–547.

HOREL, J.A. The neuroanatomy of amnesia. A critique of the hippocampal memory hypothesis. *Brain,* 1978, *101,* 403–445.

HORN, G. Neural mechanisms of learning: An analysis of imprinting in the domestic chick. *Proceedings of the Royal Society of London, Series B,* 1981, *213,* 101–137.

HORN, G., McCABE, B.J., AND BATESON, P.P.G. An autoradiographic study of the chick brain after imprinting. *Brain Research,* 1979, *168,* 361–374.

HOROWITZ, R.M., AND GENTILI, B. Dihydrochalcone sweeteners. In *Symposium: Sweeteners,* edited by G.E. Inglett. Westport, Conn.: Avi Publishing, 1974.

HORTON, J.C., AND HUBEL, D.H. Cytochrome oxidase stain preferentially labels intersection of ocular dominance and vertical orientation columns in macaque striate cortex. *Society for Neuroscience Abstracts,* 1980, *6,* 315.

HRDY, S.B. Infanticide as a primate reproductive strategy. *American Scientist,* 1977, *65,* 38–47.

HUANG, Y.H., AND ROUTTENBERG, A. Lateral hypothalamic self-stimulation pathways in *Rattus norvegicus. Physiology and Behavior,* 1971, *7,* 419–432.

HUBBELL, W.L., AND BOWNDS, M.D. Visual transduction in vertebrate photoreceptors. *Annual Review of Neuroscience,* 1979, *2,* 17–34.

HUBEL, D.H., AND LIVINGSTONE, M.S. Blobs and color vision. *Canadian Journal of Physiology and Pharmacology,* 1983, *61,* 1433–1441.

HUBEL, D.H., AND WIESEL, T.N. Functional architecture of macaque monkey visual cortex. *Proceedings of the Royal Society of London,* 1977, *198,* 1–59.

HUBEL, D.H., AND WIESEL, T.N. Brain mechanisms of vision. *Scientific American,* 1979, *241,* 150–162.

HUBEL, D.H., WIESEL, T.N., AND STRYKER, M.P. Anatomical demonstration of orientation columns in macaque monkeys. *Journal of Comparative Neurology,* 1978, *177,* 361–380.

HUDSPETH, A.J. Mechanoelectrical transduction by hair cells in the acousticolateralis sensory system. *Annual Review of Neuroscience,* 1983, *6,* 187–215.

HUDSPETH, A.J., AND JACOBS, R. Stereocilia mediate transduction in vertebrate hair cells. *Proceedings of the National Academy of Sciences, U.S.A.,* 1979, *76,* 1506–1509.

HUGHES, J., SMITH, T. W., KOSTERLITZ, H. W., FOTHERGILL, L. A., MORGAN, B. A., AND MORIS, H. R. Identification of two related pentapeptides from the brain with potent opiate agonist activity. *Nature,* 1975, *258,* 577–579.

HUMPHREY, A.L., AND HENDRICKSON, A.E. Radial zones of high metabolic activity in squirrel monkey striate cortex. *Society for Neuroscience Abstracts,* 1980, *6,* 315.

HUTCHINSON, R.R., AND RENFREW, J.W. Stalking attack and eating behavior elicited from the same sites in the hypothalamus. *Journal of Comparative and Physiological Psychology,* 1966, *61,* 300–367.

IBUKA, N., INOUYE, S.T., AND KAWAMURA, H. Analysis of sleep-wakefulness rhythms in male rats after suprachiasmatic nucleus lesions and ocular enucleation. *Brain Research,* 1977, *122,* 33–47.

IBUKA, N., AND KAWAMURA, H. Loss of circadian rhythm in sleep-wakefulness cycle in the rat by suprachiasmatic nucleus lesions. *Brain Research,* 1975, *96,* 76–81.

IGARASHI, M., CRANFORD, J.L., ALLEN, E.A., AND ALFORD, B.R. Behavioral auditory function after transection of crossed olivo-cochlear bundle in the cat. V. Pure-tone intensity discrimination. *Acta Otolaryngologica,* 1979, *87,* 429–433.

IGARASHI, M., CRANFORD, J.L., NAKAI, Y., AND ALFORD,

B.R. Behavioral auditory function after transection of crossed olivo-cochlear bundle in the cat. IV. Study on pure-tone frequency discrimination. *Acta Otolaryngologica,* 1979, *87,* 79–83.

IGGO, A., AND ANDRES, K.H. Morphology of cutaneous receptors. *Annual Review of Neuroscience,* 1982, *5,* 1–32.

INGELFINGER, F.J. The late effects of total and subtotal gastrectomy. *New England Journal of Medicine,* 1944, *231,* 321–327.

INOUYE, S.T., AND KAWAMURA, H. Persistence of circadian rhythmicity in mammalian hypothalamic "island" containing the suprachiasmatic nucleus. *Proceedings of the National Academy of Sciences (U.S.A.),* 1979, *76,* 5961–5966.

ISAACSON, R.L. *The Limbic System.* New York: Plenum Press, 1974.

ITO, M. Neuronal events in the cerebellar flocculus associated with an adaptive modification of the vestibulo-ocular reflex of the rabbit. In *Control of Gaze by Brain Stem Neurons, Developments in Neuroscience,* edited by R. Baker and A. Berthoz. Amsterdam: Elsevier, 1977.

IWAI, E., AND MISHKIN, M. Further evidence of the locus of the visual area in the temporal lobe of the monkey. *Experimental Neurology,* 1969, *25,* 585–594.

IWAI, E., OSAWA, Y., AND UMITSU, Y. Elevated visual pattern discrimination limen in monkeys with total removal of inferotemporal cortex. *Japanese Journal of Physiology,* 1979, *29,* 749–765.

JACKLET, J.W. Neuronal circadian rhythms: Phase shifting by protein synthesis inhibitor. *Science,* 1977, *198,* 69–71.

JACKLET, J.W. The cellular mechanisms of circadian clocks. *Trends in Neurosciences,* 1978, *1,* 117–119.

JACOBSON, C.D., CSERNUS, V.J., SHRYNE, J.E., AND GORSKI, R.A. The influence of gonadectomy, androgen exposure, or a gonadal graft in the neonatal rat on the volume of the sexually dimorphic nucleus of the preoptic area. *Journal of Neuroscience,* 1981, *1,* 1142–1147.

JACQUET, Y.F. Conditioned aversion during morphine maintenance in mice and rats. *Physiology and Behavior,* 1973, *11,* 527–541.

JAMES, W. *Principles of Psychology.* New York: Henry Holt, 1890.

JANKOWSKA, E., LUND, S., LUNDBERG, A., AND POMPEIANO, O. Inhibitory effects evoked through ventral reticulospinal pathways. *Archives Italiennes de Biologie,* 1968, *106,* 124–140.

JANOWITZ, H.D., AND GROSSMAN, M.I. Some factors affecting the food intake of normal dogs and dogs with esophagostomy and gastric fistula. *American Journal of Physiology,* 1949, *159,* 143–148.

JANOWITZ, H.D., AND HOLLANDER, F. Effect of prolonged intragastric feeding on oral ingestion. *Federation Proceedings,* 1953, *12,* 72.

JANOWSKY, A., STERANKA, L.R., AND SULSER, F. Role of neuronal signal input in the down-regulation of central noradrenergic receptor function by antidepressant drugs. Paper presented at the Annual Meeting of the Society for Neuroscience, 1981.

JARVIK, M.E. Effects of chemical and physical treatments on learning and memory. *Annual Review of Psychology,* 1972, *23,* 457–486.

JASPER, J.H., AND TESSIER, J. Acetylcholine liberation from cerebral cortex during paradoxical (REM) sleep. *Science,* 1969, *172,* 601–602.

JEWELL, P.A., AND VERNEY, E.B. An experimental attempt to determine the site of the neurohypophysial osmoreceptors in the dog. *Philosophical Transactions of the Royal Society,* 1957, *240B,* 197–324.

JOHNSON, A.K., AND BUGGY, J. A critical analysis of the site of action for the dipsogenic effect of angiotensin II. In *International Symposium of the Central Actions of Angiotensin and Related Hormones,* edited by J.P. Buckley and C. Ferrario. Oxford, England: Pergamon Press, 1977.

JOHNSON, R.N., DESISTO, M.J., AND KOENIG, A.B. Social and developmental experience and interspecific aggression in rats. *Journal of Comparative and Physiological Psychology,* 1972, *79,* 237–242.

JOHNSTONE, E.C., CROW, T.J., FRITH, C.D., HUSBAND, J., AND KREEL, L. Cerebral ventricular size and cognitive impairment in chronic schizophrenia. *Lancet,* 1976, *2,* 924–926.

JOHNSTONE, E.C., CROW, T.J., FRITH, C.D., STEVENS, M., KREEL, L., AND HUSBAND, J. The dementia of dementia praecox. *Acta Psychiatrica Scandinavica,* 1978, *57,* 305–324.

JONES, A.P., AND FRIEDMAN, M.I. Obesity and adipocyte abnormalities in offspring of rats undernourished during pregnancy. *Science,* 1982, *215,* 1518–1519.

JONES, B.E., BOBILLIER, P., AND JOUVET, M. Effets de la destruction des neurones contenant des catécholamines du mésencéphale sur le cycle veille-sommeils du chat. *Comptes Rendus de la Société de Biologie (Paris),* 1969, *163,* 176–180.

JONES, B.E., HARPER, S.T., AND HALARIS, A.E. Effects of locus coeruleus lesions upon cerebral monoamine content, sleep wakefulness states and the response to amphetamine in the cat. *Brain Research,* 1977, *124,* 473–496.

JONES, R. Anomalies of disparity in the human visual system. *Journal of Physiology,* 1977, *264,* 621–640.

JOUVET, M. Recherches sur les structures nerveuses et les mécanismes responsables des différentes phases du sommeil physiologique. *Archives Italiennes de Biologie,* 1962, *100,* 125–206.

JOUVET, M. Insomnia and decrease of cerebral 5-hydroxytryptamine after destruction of the raphe system in the cat. *Advances in Pharmacology,* 1968, *6,* 265–279.

JOUVET, M. The role of monoamines and acetylcholine-containing neurons in the regulation of the sleep-waking cycle. *Ergebnisse der Physiologie,* 1972, *64,* 166–307.

JOUVET, M., AND RENAULT, J. Insomnie persistante après lésions des noyaux du raphé chez le chat. *Comptes Rendus de la Société de Biologie (Paris),* 1966, *160,* 1461–1465.

JOUVET-MOUNIER, D., ASTIC, L., AND LACOTE, D. Ontogenesis of the states of sleep in rat, cat, and guinea pig during the first postnatal month. *Developmental Psychobiology,* 1970, *2,* 216–239.

JURKOWLANIEC, E., AND BIALOWAS, J. Rewarding effect of noradrenergic stimulation of the amygdala in food deprived rats. *Physiology and Behavior,* 1981, *27,* 27–31.

KALES, A., SCHARF, M.B., KALES, J.D., AND SOLDATOS, C.R. Rebound insomnia: A potential hazard following withdrawal of certain benzodiazepines. *Journal of the American Medical Association,* 1979, *241,* 1692–1695.

KALIVAS, P.W., JENNES, L., NEMEROFF, C.B., AND PRANGE, A.J. Neurotensin: Topographical distribution of brain sites involved in hypothermia and antinociception. *Journal of Comparative Neurology,* 1982, *210,* 235–238.

KANAMORI, N., SAKAI, K., AND JOUVET, M. Neuronal activity specific to paradoxical sleep in the ventromedial medullary reticular formation of unrestrained cats. *Brain Research,* 1980, *189,* 251–255.

KANDEL, E.R., AND SCHWARTZ, J.H. Molecular biology of learning: Modulation of transmitter release. *Science,* 1982, *218,* 433–443.

KANOF, P.D., AND GREENGARD, P. Brain histamine receptors as targets for antidepressant drugs. *Nature,* 1978, *272,* 329–333.

KAPP, B.S., FRYSINGER, R.C., GALLAGHER, M., AND HASELTON, J. Amygdala central nucleus lesions: Effects on heart rate conditioning in the rabbit. *Physiology and Behavior,* 1979, *23,* 1109–1117.

KAPP, B.S., GALLAGHER, M., APPLEGATE, C.D., AND FRYSINGER, R.C. The amygdala central nucleus: Contributions to conditioned cardiovascular responding during aversive Pavlovian conditioning in the rabbit. In *Conditioning: Representation of Involved Neural Functions,* edited by C.D. Woody. New York: Plenum Press, 1982.

KAPP, B.S., GALLAGHER, M., UNDERWOOD, M.D., MCNALL, C.L., AND WHITEHORN, D. Cardiovascular responses elicited by electrical stimulation of the amygdala central nucleus in the rabbit. *Brain Research,* 1981, *234,* 251–262.

KARACAN, I., SALIS, P.J., AND WILLIAMS, R.L. The role of the sleep laboratory in diagnosis and treatment of impotence. In *Sleep Disorders: Diagnosis and Treatment,* edited by R.J. Williams and I. Karacan. New York: John Wiley & Sons, 1978.

KARLI, P. The Norway rat's killing response to the white mouse. *Behavior,* 1956, *10,* 81–103.

KARLSON, P., AND LUSCHER, M. "Pheromones": A new term for a class of biologically active substances. *Nature,* 1959, *183,* 55–56.

KEBABIAN, J.W., AND CALNE, D.B. Multiple receptors for

dopamine. *Nature,* 1979, *277,* 197.

KEBABIAN, J.W., PETZOLD, G.L., AND GREENGARD, P. Dopamine-sensitive adenylate cyclase in caudate nucleus of rat brain and its similarity to the "dopamine receptor." *Proceedings of the National Academy of Science (U.S.A.),* 1972, *69,* 2145–2149.

KEELE, C.A. Measurement of responses to chemically induced pain. In *Touch, Heat, and Pain,* edited by A.V.S. deRenuck and J. Knight. Boston: Little, Brown, 1966.

KELLY, D.H., WALKER, A.M., CAHEN, L.A., AND SHANNON, D.C. Periodic breathing in siblings of SIDS victims. *Pediatric Research,* 1980, *14,* 645–650.

KEMBLE, E.D., AND NAGEL, J.A. Failure to form a learned taste aversion in rats with amygdaloid lesions. *Bulletin of the Psychonomic Society,* 1973, *2,* 155–156.

KERTESZ, A. *Aphasia and Associated Disorders: Taxonomy, Localization, and Recovery.* New York: Grune & Stratton, 1979.

KERTESZ, A. Personal communication, 1980.

KERTESZ, A. Anatomy of jargon. In *Jargonaphasia,* edited by J. Brown. New York: Academic Press, 1981.

KESSLER, S., GUILLEMINAULT, C., AND DEMENT, W.C. A family study of 50 REM narcoleptics. *Acta Neurologica Scandinavica,* 1974, *50,* 503–512.

KETY, S.S., ROSENTHAL, D., WENDER, P.H., AND SCHULSINGER, K.F. The types and prevalence of mental illness in the biological and adoptive families of adopted schizophrenics. In *The Transmission of Schizophrenia,* edited by D. Rosenthal and S.S. Kety. New York: Pergamon Press, 1968.

KEVERNE, E.B., AND MICHAEL, R.P. Sex-attractant properties of ether extracts of vaginal secretions from rhesus monkeys. *Journal of Endocrinology,* 1971, *51,* 313–322.

KIANG, N.Y.-S. Discharge patterns of single fibers in the cat's auditory nerve. Cambridge, Mass.: MIT Press, 1965.

KIEFER, S.W., AND RUSINIAK, K.W. Involvement of gustatory neocortex in the rat's neophobic and associative responses to taste and odor stimuli. *Society for Neuroscience Abstracts,* 1979, *5,* 129.

KIM, Y.K., AND UMBACH, W. Combined stereotaxic lesions for treatment of behavior disorders and severe pain. Paper presented at the Third World Congress of Psychosurgery. Cambridge, England, 1972. Cited by Valenstein, 1973.

KINSBOURNE, M., AND WARRINGTON, E.K. A variety of reading disabilities associated with right-hemisphere lesions. *Journal of Neurology, Neurosurgery and Psychiatry,* 1962, *25,* 339–344.

KLAUS, M.H., JERAULD, R., KRIEGER, N.C., MCALPINE, W., STEFFA, M., AND KENNELL, J.H. Maternal attachment: Importance of the first postpartum days. *New England Journal of Medicine,* 1972, *286,* 460–463.

KLEIN, M., AND KANDEL, E.R. Presynaptic modulation of voltage-dependent Ca^{2+} current: Mechanism for behavioral sensitization in *Aplysia californica. Proceedings of the National Academy of Sciences (U.S.A.),* 1978, *75,* 3512–3516.

KLEIN, M., AND KANDEL, E.R. Mechanism of calcium current modulation underlying presynaptic facilitation and behavioral sensitization in *Aplysia. Proceedings of the National Academy of Sciences (U.S.A.),* 1980, *77,* 6912–6916.

KLEITMAN, N. The nature of dreaming. In *The Nature of Sleep,* edited by G.E.W. Wolstenholme and M. O'Connor. London: J.&A. Churchill, 1961.

KLEITMAN, N. *Sleep and Wakefulness,* second edition. Chicago: University of Chicago Press, 1963.

KLEITMAN, N. Basic rest-activity cycle—22 years later. *Sleep,* 1982, *4,* 311–317.

KLING, A., LANCASTER, J., AND BENITONE, J. Amygdalectomy in the free-ranging vervet *(Cercopithecusalthiops). Journal of Psychiatric Research,* 1970, *7,* 191–199.

KLOPFER, P.H., ADAMS, D.J., AND KLOPFER, M.S. Maternal "imprinting" in goats. *Proceedings of the National Academy of Sciences (U.S.A.),* 1964, *52,* 911–914.

KLÜVER, H., AND BUCY, P.C. Preliminary analysis of functions of the temporal lobes in monkeys. *Archives of Neurology and Psychiatry (Chicago),* 1939, *42,* 979–1000.

KNITTLE, J.L., AND HIRSCH, J. Effect of early nutrition on the development of rat epididymal pads: Cellularity and metabolism. *Journal of Clinical Investigation,* 1968, *47,* 2001–2098.

KOLÁŘSKÝ, A., FREUND, K., MACHEK, J., AND POLÁK, O. Male sexual deviation. Association with early temporal lobe damage. *Archives of General Psychiatry,* 1967, *17,* 735–743.

KOMISARUK, B.R. Neural and hormonal interactions in the reproductive behavior of female rats. In *Reproductive Behavior,* edited by E. Montagna and W.A. Sadler. New York: Plenum Press, 1974.

KOOB, G.F., FRAY, P.J., AND IVERSEN, S.D. Tail-pinch stimulation: Sufficient motivation for learning. *Science,* 1976, *194,* 637–639.

KOOPMANS, H.S. The role of the gastrointestinal tract in the satiation of hunger. In *The Body Weight Regulatory System: Normal and Disturbed Mechanisms,* edited by L.A. Cioffi, W.P.T. James, and T.B. Van Italie. New York: Raven Press, 1981.

KORN, J.H., AND MOYER, K.E. Behavioral effects of isolation in the rat: The role of sex and time of isolation. *The Journal of Genetic Psychology,* 1968, *113,* 263–273.

KORNHUBER, H.H. Cerebral cortex, cerebellum, and basal ganglia: An introduction to their motor functions. In *The Neurosciences: Third Study Program,* edited by F.O. Schmitt and F.G. Worden. Cambridge: MIT Press, 1974.

KOVNER, R., AND STAMM, J.S. Disruption of short-term visual memory by electrical stimulation of inferotemporal cortex in the monkey. *Journal of Comparative and Physiological Psychology,* 1972, *81,* 163–172.

KOZLOWSKI, S., AND DRZEWIECKI, K. The role of osmoreception in portal circulation in control of water intake in dogs. *Acta Physiologica Polonica,* 1973, *24,* 325–330.

KRAEPELIN, E. *Dementia Praecox* (R.M. Barclay, trans.) Fascimile edition. New York: Krieger, 1919/1971.

KREUZ, L., AND ROSE, R. Assessment of aggressive behavior and plasma testosterone in a young criminal population. *Psychosomatic Medicine,* 1972, *34,* 321–332.

KRIEGER, M.S., CONRAD, L.C.A., AND PFAFF, D.W. An autoradiographic study of the efferent connections of the ventromedial nucleus of the hypothalamus. *Journal of Comparative Neurology,* 1979, *183,* 785–816.

KRIEGER, M.S., AND PFAFF, D.W. Projections from mesencephalic central grey in the rat. Unpublished paper, 1980. Cited by Pfaff, 1980.

KRUEGER, J.M., PAPPENHEIMER, J.R., AND KARNOVSKI, M.L. The composition of sleep-promoting factor isolated from human urine. *Journal of Biological Chemistry,* 1982, *257,* 1664–1669.

KUBIE, J.L., AND RANCK, J.B. Tonic and phasic firing of rat hippocampal complex–spike cells in three different situations: Context and place. In *Conditioning: Representation of Involved Neural Functions,* edited by C.D. Woody. New York: Plenum Press, 1982.

KUCHARCZYK, J., AND MOGENSON, G.J. Separate lateral hypothalamic pathways for extracellular and intracellular thirst. *American Journal of Physiology,* 1975, *228,* 295–301.

KUCHARCZYK, J., AND MOGENSON, G.J. Specific deficits in regulatory drinking following electrolytic lesions of the lateral hypothalamus. *Experimental Neurology,* 1976, *53,* 371–385.

KUCHARCZYK, J., AND MOGENSON, G.J. Effect of preoptic administration of angiotensin on lateral hypothalamic unit activity. *Physiology and Behavior,* 1977, *19,* 455–457.

KUFFLER, S.W. Neurons in the retina: Organization, inhibition and excitation problems. *Cold Spring Harbor Symposium on Quantitative Biology,* 1952, *17,* 281–292.

KUFFLER, S.W. Discharge patterns and functional organization of mammalian retina. *Journal of Neurophysiology,* 1953, *16,* 37–68.

KUKORELLI, T., AND JUHASZ, G. Sleep induced by intestinal stimulation in cats. *Physiology and Behavior,* 1977, *19,* 355–358.

KUPFER, D.J. REM latency: A psychobiologic marker for primary depressive disease. *Biological Psychiatry,* 1976, *11,* 159–174.

LABORIT, H. La thérapeutique neuro-végétate du choc et de la maladie post-traumatique. *Presse Medicale,* 1950, *58,* 138–140. Cited by Snyder, 1974.

LANCET, D. Molecular view of olfactory reception. *Trends in Neurosciences,* 1984, *7,* 35–36.

LAND, E.H. The retinex theory of color vision. *Scientific American,* 1977, *237,* 108–128.

LANGHANS, W., GEARY, N., AND SCHARRER, E. Liver glycogen content decreases during a meal. *American*

Journal of Physiology, 1982, *243,* R450–R453.

LANGHANS, W., ZIEGER, U., SCHARRER, E., AND GEARY, N. Stimulation of feeding in rats by intraperitoneal injection of antibodies to glucagon. *Science,* 1982, *218,* 894–896.

LARSSON, L.I., GOLTERMANN, N., MAGISTRIS, L.D., REHFIELD, J.F., AND SCHWARTZ, T.W. Somatostatin cell processes as pathways for paracrine secretion. *Science,* 1979, *205,* 1393–1395.

LASCHET, U. Antiandrogen in the treatment of sex offenders: Mode of action and therapeutic outcome. In *Contemporary Sexual Behavior: Critical Issues in the 1970's,* edited by J. Zubin and J. Money. Baltimore: Johns Hopkins University Press, 1973.

LASEK, R.J., GAINER, H., AND PRZYBYLSKI, R.J. Transfer of newly synthesized proteins from Schwann cells to the squid giant axon. *Proceedings of the National Academy of Sciences (U.S.A.),* 1974, *71,* 1188–1192.

LASHLEY, K. In search of the engram. *Society of Experimental Biology,* 1950, *Symposium 4,* 454–482.

LAVIE, P., PRATT, H., SCHARF, B., PELED, R., AND BROWN, J. Localized pontine lesion: Nearly total absence of REM sleep. *Neurology,* 1984, *34,* 1118–1120.

LAWRENCE, D.G., AND KUYPERS, G.J.M. The functional organization of the motor system in the monkey. I. The effects of bilateral pyramidal lesions. *Brain,* 1968a, *91,* 1–14.

LAWRENCE, D.G., AND KUYPERS, G.J.M. The functional organization of the motor system in the monkey. II. The effects of lesions of the descending brain-stem pathways. *Brain,* 1968b, *91,* 15–36.

LEDOUX, J.E., SAKAGUCHI, A., AND REIS, D.J. Cortical and subcortical efferent projections of the medial geniculate nucleus in rat. *Society for Neuroscience Abstracts,* 1983, *9,* 953.

LEE, K., SCHOTTLER, F., OLIVER, M., AND LYNCH, G. Brief bursts of high-frequency stimulation produce two types of structural change in rat hippocampus. *Journal of Neurophysiology,* 1980, *44,* 247–258.

LEE, T., AND SEEMAN, P. Elevation of brain neuroleptic/dopamine receptors in schizophrenia. *American Journal of Psychiatry,* 1980, *137,* 191–197.

LEGRENDE, R., AND PIÉRON, H. Recherches dur le besoin de sommeil consécutif a une veille prolongés. *Zeitschrift für Allgemeine Physiologie,* 1913, *14,* 235–362.

LEHMAN, M.N., AND WINANS, S.S. Vomeronasal and olfactory pathways to the amygdala controlling male hamster sexual behavior: Autoradiographic and behavioral analyses. *Brain Research,* 1982, *240,* 27–41.

LEIBOWITZ, S.F. Paraventricular nucleus: A primary site mediating adrenergic stimulation of feeding and drinking. *Pharmacology, Biochemistry and Behavior,* 1978, *8,* 163–175.

LEIBOWITZ, S.F. Neurochemical systems of the hypothalamus: Control of feeding and drinking behavior and water electrolyte excretion. In *Handbook of the Hypothalamus, Vol. 3, Part A,* edited by P.J. Morgane and J. Panksepp. New York: Marcel Dekker, 1980.

LEIBOWITZ, S.F. Hypothalamic catecholamine systems in relation to control of eating behavior and mechanisms of reward. In *The Neural Basis of Feeding and Reward,* edited by B.G. Hoebel and D. Novin. Brunswick, Maine: Haer Institute, 1982.

LEIBOWITZ, S.F. Hypothalamic catecholamine systems controlling eating behavior: A potential model for anorexia nervosa. *Anorexia Nervosa: Recent Developments in Research,* edited by P.L. Darby, P.E. Garfinkel, D.M. Garner, and D.V. Coscina. New York: A.R. Liss, 1983.

LEIBOWITZ, S.F., AND BROWN, L.L. Analysis of behavioral deficits produced by lesions in the dorsal and ventral midbrain tegmentum. *Physiology and Behavior,* 1980, *25,* 829–843.

LEIBOWITZ, S.F., HAMMER, N.J., AND CHANG, K. Hypothalamic paraventricular nucleus lesions produce overeating and obesity in the rat. *Physiology and Behavior,* 1981, *27,* 1031–1040.

LEMAGNEN, J., AND TALLEN, S. La periodicité spontanée de la prise d'aliments ad libitum du rat blanc. *Journal of Physiology (Paris),* 1966, *58,* 323–349.

LENARD, H.G., AND SCHULTE, F.J. Polygraph sleep study in cranipagus twins (where is the sleep transmitter?). *Journal of Neurology, Neurosurgery and Psychiatry,* 1972, *35,* 756–762.

LEONARD, B.E. On the mode of action of mianserin. In *Typical and Atypical Antidepressants: Molecular Mechanisms,* edited by E. Costa and G. Racagni. New York: Raven Press, 1982.

LESHNER, A.I. A model of hormones and agonistic behavior. *Physiology and Behavior,* 1975, *15,* 225–235.

LESHNER, A.I., WALKER, W.A., JOHNSON, A.E., KELLING, J.S., KREISLER, S.J., AND SVARE, B.B. Pituitary adrenocortical activity and intermale aggressiveness in isolated mice. *Physiology and Behavior,* 1973, *11,* 705–711.

LEVINE, D.N., AND SWEET, E. Localization of lesions in Broca's motor aphasia. In *Localization in Neuropsychology,* edited by A. Kertesz. New York: Academic Press, 1983.

LEVINE, J.D., GORDON, N.C., AND FIELDS, H.L. The role of endorphins in placebo analgesia. In *Advances in Pain Research and Therapy, Vol. 3,* edited by J.J. Bonica, J.C. Liebeskind, and D. Albe-Fessard. New York: Raven Press, 1979.

LEVY, W.B., AND STEWARD, O. Temporal contiguity requirements for long-term associative potentiation/depression in the hippocampus. *Neuroscience,* 1983, *8,* 791–797.

LEWIS, J.W., CANNON, J.T., AND LIEBESKIND, J.C. Opioid and non-opioid mechanisms of stress analgesia. *Science,* 1980, *208,* 623–625.

LEY, R.G., AND BRYDEN, M.P. Hemispheric differences in recognizing faces and emotions. *Brain and Language,* 1979, *7,* 127–138.

LEY, R.G., AND BRYDEN, M.P. A dissociation of right and left hemispheric effects for recognizing emotional tone and verbal content. *Brain and Cognition,* 1982, *1,* 3–9.

LIEBELT, R.A., BORDELON, C.B., AND LIEBELT, A.G. The adipose tissue system and food intake. In *Progress in Physiological Psychology,* edited by E. Stellar and J.M. Sprague. New York: Academic Press, 1973.

LINCOLN, J.S., MCCORMICK, D.A., AND THOMPSON, R.F. Ipsilateral lesions prevent learning of the classically conditioned nictitating membrane eyelid response. *Brain Research,* 1982, *242,* 190–193.

LIND, R.W., AND JOHNSON, A.K. Central and peripheral mechanisms mediating angiotensin-induced thirst. In *The Renin Angiotensin System in the Brain,* edited by D. Ganten, M. Printz, M.I. Phillips, and B.A. Schölkens. Berlin: Springer-Verlag, 1982.

LINDSLEY, D.B., SCHREINER, L.H., KNOWLES, W.B., AND MAGOUN, H.W. Behavioral and EEG changes following chronic brain stem lesions in the cat. *Electroencephalography and Clinical Neurophysiology,* 1950, *2,* 483–498.

LINDVALL, O. Dopamine pathways in the rat brain. In *The Neurobiology of Dopamine,* edited by A.S. Horn, J. Korb, and B.H.C. Westerink. New York: Academic Press, 1979.

LIPPA, A.S., ANTELMAN, S.M., FISHER, A.E., AND CANFIELD, D.R. Neurochemical mediation of reward: A significant role for dopamine? *Pharmacology, Biochemistry and Behavior,* 1973, *1,* 23–28.

LISK, R.D. The regulation of sexual "heat." In *Biological Determinants of Sexual Behaviour,* edited by J.B. Hutchison. New York: John Wiley & Sons, 1978.

LISK, R.D., PRETLOW, R.A., AND FRIEDMAN, S. Hormonal stimulation necessary for elicitation of maternal nest-building in the mouse *(Mus musculus). Animal Behaviour,* 1969, *17,* 730–737.

LIVINGSTONE, M.S., AND HUBEL, D.H. Thalamic inputs to cytochrome oxidase-rich regions in monkey visual cortex. *Proceedings of the National Academy of Sciences (U.S.A.),* 1982, *79,* 6098–6101.

LJUNGBERG, T., AND UNGERSTEDT, U. Sensory inattention produced by 6-hydroxydopamine-induced degeneration of ascending dopamine neurons in the brain. *Experimental Neurology,* 1976, *53,* 585–600.

LOEWENSTEIN, W.R., AND MENDELSON, M. Components of receptor adaptation in a Pacinian corpuscle. *Journal of Physiology (London),* 1965, *177,* 377–397.

LOEWENSTEIN, W.R., AND RATHKAMP, R. The sites for mechano-electric conversion in a Pacinian corpuscle. *Journal of General Physiology,* 1958, *41,* 1245–1265.

LØMO, T. Frequency potentiation of excitatory synaptic activity in the dentate area of the hippocampal formation. *Acta Physiologica Scandinavica,* 1966, *68* (Suppl. 227), 128.

LØMO, T. Patterns of activation in a monosynaptic cortical pathway: The perforant path input to the dentate area of the hippocampal formation. *Experimental Brain Research,* 1971, *12,* 18–45.

LORENZ, D.N., KREIELSHEIMER, G., AND SMITH, G.P. Effect of cholecystokinin, gastrin, secretin and GIP on sham feeding in the rat. *Physiology and Behavior,* 1979, *23,* 1065–1072.

LUND, J.S. Organization of neurons in the visual cortex,

area 17, of the monkey *(Macaca mulatta). Journal of Comparative Neurology,* 1973, *147,* 455–496.

LYDIC, R., SCHOENE, W.C., CZEISLER, C.A., AND MOORE-EDE, M.C. Suprachiasmatic region of the human hypothalamus: Homolog to the primate circadian pacemaker? *Sleep,* 1980, *2,* 355–361.

LYNCH, G., AND BAUDRY, M. The biochemical intermediates in memory formation: A new and specific hypothesis. *Science,* 1984, *224,* 1057–1063.

LYNCH, G., HALPAIN, S., AND BAUDRY, M. Effects of high-frequency synaptic stimulation of glutamate receptor binding studied with a modified in vitro hippocampal slice preparation. *Brain Research,* 1982, *244,* 101–111.

LYNCH, G., LARSON, J., KELSO, S., BARRIONUEVO, G., AND SCHOTTLER, F. Intracellular injections of EGTA block induction of long-term potentiation. *Nature,* 1984, *305,* 719–721.

LYNCH, G., ROSE, G., AND GALL, C.M. Anatomical and functional aspects of septo-hippocampal projections. In *Functions of the Septo-hippocampal System. Ciba Foundation Symposium,* 1978, *58* (new series), 5–24.

LYNDS, P.G. Olfactory control of aggression in lactating female housemice. *Physiology and Behavior,* 1976, *17,* 157–159.

MAAYANI, S., HOUGH, L.B., WEINSTEIN, H., AND GREEN, J.P. Response of the histamine H_2-receptor in brain to antidepressant drugs. In *Typical and Atypical Antidepressants: Molecular Mechanisms,* edited by E. Costa and G. Racagni. New York: Raven Press, 1982.

MACDONNELL, M.F., AND FLYNN, J.P. Control of sensory fields by stimulation of hypothalamus. *Science,* 1966, *152,* 1406–1408.

MACHNE, S., CALMA, I., AND MAGOUN, H.W. Unit activity of central cephalic brain stem in EEG arousal. *Journal of Neurophysiology,* 1955, *18,* 547–558.

MACKAY, A.V.P., IVERSEN, L.L., ROSSOR, M., SPOKES, P., BIRD, E., ARREGUI, A., CREESE, I., AND SNYDER, S.H. Increased brain dopamine and dopamine receptors in schizophrenia. *Archives of General Psychiatry,* 1982, *39,* 991–997.

MADDISON, S., ROLLS, B.J., ROLLS, E.T., AND WOOD, R.J. The role of gastric factors in drinking termination in the monkey. *Journal of Physiology (London),* 1980, *305,* 55–56P.

MAGNES, J., MORUZZI, G., AND POMPEIANO, O. Synchronization of the EEG produced by low-frequency electrical stimulation of the region of the solitary tract. *Archives Italiennes de Biologie,* 1961, *99,* 33–67.

MAGNI, F., MORUZZI, G., ROSSI, G.F., AND ZANCHETTI, A. EEG arousal following inactivation of the lower brain stem by selective injection of barbiturate into the vertebral circulation. *Archives Italiennes de Biologie,* 1959, *97,* 33–46.

MAIER, S.F., DRUGAN, R.C., AND GRAU, J.W. Controllability, coping behavior, and stress-induced analgesia in the rat. *Pain,* 1982, *12,* 47–56.

MALAMUT, B.L., SAUNDERS, R.C., AND MISHKIN, M. Successful object discrimination learning after combined amygdaloid-hippocampal lesions in monkeys de-

spite 24-hour intertrial intervals. *Society for Neuroscience Abstracts,* 1980, *6,* 191.

MALLOW, G.K. The relationship between aggression and cycle stage in adult female rhesus monkeys *(Macaca mulatta). Dissertation Abstracts,* 1979, *39,* 3194.

MALSBURY, C.W. Facilitation of male rat copulatory behavior by electrical stimulation of the medial preoptic area. *Physiology and Behavior,* 1971, *7,* 797–805.

MALVIN, R.L., MOUW, D., AND VANDER, A.J. Angiotensin: Physiological role in water-deprivation-induced thirst of rats. *Science,* 1977, *19,* 171–173.

MANN, F., BOWSHER, D., MUMFORD, J., LIPTON, S., AND MILES, J. Treatment of intractable pain by acupuncture. *Lancet,* 1973, *2,* 57–60.

MANN, M., BROIDA, J., MICHAEL, S.D., AND SVARE, B. Prolactin is not necessary for maternal aggression in mice. Paper presented at the meeting of the International Society for Developmental Psychobiology, Cincinnati, 1980.

MANTYH, P.W. Connections of midbrain periaqueductal gray in the monkey. II. Descending efferent projections. *Journal of Neurophysiology,* 1983, *49,* 582–594.

MARGOLIN, D.I., MARCEL, A.J., AND CARLSON, N.R. Common mechanisms in dysnomia and post-semantic surface dyslexia: Processing deficits and selective attention. In *Surface Dyslexia: Neuropsychological and Cognitive Studies of Phonological Reading,* edited by M. Coltheart. London: Lawrence Erlbaum Associates, 1985 (in press).

MARGOLIN, D.I., AND WALKER, J.A. Personal communication, 1981.

MARIN, O.V.M. Personal communication, 1982.

MARK, V.H., AND ERVIN, F.R. *Violence and the Brain.* New York: Harper & Row, 1970.

MARK, V.H., ERVIN, F.R., AND YAKOVLEV, P.I. The treatment of pain by stereotaxic methods. *Confina Neurologica,* 1962, *22,* 238–245.

MARK, V.H., SWEET, W.H., AND ERVIN, F.R. The effect of amygdalectomy on violent behavior in patients with temporal lobe epilepsy. In *Psychosurgery,* edited by E. Hitchcock, L. Laitinen, and K. Vernet. Springfield, Ill.: Charles C Thomas, 1972.

MARSHALL, J.C., AND NEWCOMBE, F. Patterns of paralexia: A psycholinguistic approach. *Journal of Psycholinguistic Research,* 1973, *2,* 175–199.

MARSHALL, J.F. Somatosensory inattention after dopamine-depleting intracerebral 6-OHDA injections: Spontaneous recovery and pharmacological control. *Brain Research,* 1979, *177,* 311–324.

MARTIN, G.E., AND BACINO, C.B. Action of intrahypothalamically-injected β-endorphin on the body temperature of the rat. *Society for Neuroscience Abstracts,* 1978, *4,* 411.

MARTIN, G.E., AND MYERS, R.D. Evoked release of [^{14}C]norepinephrine from the rat hypothalamus during feeding. *American Journal of Physiology,* 1975, *229,* 1547–1555.

MARTIN, J.R., NOVIN, D., AND VANDERWEELE, D.A. Loss of glucagon suppression of feeding after vagotomy in rats. *American Journal of Physiology,* 1978, *234,* E314–E315.

MARUNIAK, J., DESJARDINS, C., AND BRONSON, F. Dominant-subordinate relationships in castrated male mice bearing testosterone implants. *American Journal of Physiology,* 1977, *233,* 495–499.

MASSERMAN, J.H. *Principles of Dynamic Psychiatry.* Philadelphia: W.B. Saunders, 1961.

MASTERS, W.H., JOHNSON, V.E., AND KOLODNY, R.C. *Human Sexuality.* Boston: Little, Brown, 1982.

MATHEWS, D.F. Response patterns of single neurons in the tortoise olfactory epithelium and olfactory bulb. *Journal of General Physiology,* 1972, *60,* 166–180.

MAWSON, A.R. Anorexia nervosa and the regulation of intake: A review. *Psychological Medicine,* 1974, *4,* 289–308.

MAYER, C.H., AND STUMPF, C.H. Die Physostigminwirkung auf die Hippocampus-Tätigkeit nach Septumläsionen. *Naunyn-Schmiedebergs Archiv für Pharmakologie und Experimentelle Pathologie,* 1958, *234,* 490–500.

MAYER, D.J., AND LIEBESKIND, J.C. Pain reduction by focal electrical stimulation of the brain: An anatomical and behavioral analysis. *Brain Research,* 1974, *68,* 73–93.

MAYER, D.J., PRICE, D.D., RAFII, A., AND BARBER, J. Acupuncture hypalgesia: Evidence for activation of a central control system as a mechanism of action. In *Advances in Pain Research and Therapy, Vol. 1,* edited by J.J. Bonica, and D. Albe-Fessard. New York: Raven Press, 1976.

MAYER, J. Regulation of energy intake and the body weight: The glucostatic theory and the lipostatic hypothesis. *Annals of the New York Academy of Science,* 1955, *63,* 15–43.

MAZUR, A. Hormones, aggression, and dominance in humans. In *Hormones and Aggressive Behavior,* edited by B.B. Svare. New York: Plenum Press, 1983.

MAZUR, A., AND LAMB, T. Testosterone, status, and mood in human males. *Hormones and Behavior,* 1980, *14,* 236–246.

McCABE, B.J., HORN, G., AND BATESON, P.P.G. Effects of rhythmic hyperstriatal stimulation on chick's preferences for visual flicker. *Physiology and Behavior,* 1979, *23,* 137–140.

McCABE, B.J., HORN, G., AND BATESON, P.P.G. Effects of restricted lesions of the chick forebrain on the acquisition of filial preferences during imprinting. *Brain Research,* 1981, *205,* 29–37.

McCABE, J., AND LEIBOWITZ, S.F. Hindbrain catecholamine projections to the perifornical hypothalamus: Their role in the mediation of drug-induced anorexia and hyperphagia. *Neuroscience Abstracts,* 1980, *6,* 784.

McCLINTOCK, M.K. Menstrual synchrony and suppression. *Nature,* 1971, *229,* 244–245.

McCLINTOCK, M.K., AND ADLER, N.T. The role of the female during copulation in wild and domestic Nor-

way rats *(Rattus norvegicus).* *Behaviour,* 1978, *67,* 67–96.

McCORMICK, D.A., GUYER, P.E., AND THOMPSON, R.F. Superior cerebellar peduncle lesions selectively abolish the ipsilateral classically conditioned nictitating membrane/eyelid response of the rabbit. *Brain Research,* 1982, *244,* 347–350.

McCORMICK, D.A., AND THOMPSON, R.F. Possible neuronal substrate of classical conditioning within the mammalian CNS: Dentate and interpositus nuclei. *Society for Neuroscience Abstracts,* 1983, *9,* 643.

McCORMICK, D.A., AND THOMPSON, R.F. Cerebellum: Essential involvement in the classically conditioned eyelid response. *Science,* 1984, *223,* 296–299.

McDONALD, N. Living with schizophrenia. *Journal of the Canadian Medical Association,* 1960, *82,* 218–221.

McGINTY, D.J., AND STERMAN, M.B. Sleep suppression after basal forebrain lesions in the cat. *Science,* 1968, *160,* 1253–1255.

McGRATH, M.J., AND COHEN, D.B. REM sleep facilitation of adaptive waking behavior: A review of the literature. *Psychological Bulletin,* 1978, *85,* 24–57.

McNAMARA, J.O., BYRNE, M.C., DASHEIFF, R.M., AND FITZ, J.G. The kindling model of epilepsy: A review. *Progress in Neurobiology,* 1980, *15,* 139–159.

MEDDIS, R. *The Sleep Instinct.* London: Routledge & Kegan Paul, 1977.

MEDDIS, R., PEARSON, A., AND LANGFORD, G. An extreme case of healthy insomnia. *Electroencephalography and Clinical Neurophysiology,* 1973, *35,* 213–214.

MEFFORD, I.N., BAKER, T.L., BOEHME, R., FOUTZ, A.S., CIARANELLO, R.D., BARCHAS, J.D., AND DEMENT, W.C. Narcolepsy: Biogenic amine deficits in an animal model. *Science,* 1983, *220,* 629–632.

MELTZER, H.Y., AND ARORA, R.C. Skeletal muscle MAO activity in the major psychoses: Relationship with platelet and plasma MAO activities. *Archives of General Psychiatry,* 1980, *37,* 333–339.

MENDELSON, W.B., CAIN, M., COOK, J.M., PAUL, S.M., AND SKOLNICK, P. A benzodiazepine receptor antagonist decreases sleep and reverses the hypnotic actions of flurazepam. *Science,* 1983, *219,* 414–416.

MENNINGER, K.A. Influenza and schizophrenia. An analysis of post-influenzal "dementia praecox" as of 1918 and five years later. *American Journal of Psychiatry,* 1926, *5,* 469–529.

MILEDI, R. Acetylcholine sensitivity of partially denervated frog muscles. *Journal of Physiology (London),* 1959, *147,* 45–46P.

MILLER, G.A., AND TAYLOR, W.G. The perception of repeated bursts of noise. *Journal of the Acoustical Society of America,* 1948, *20,* 171–182.

MILLER, N.E., SAMPLINER, R.I., AND WOODROW, P. Thirst reducing effects of water by stomach fistula versus water by mouth, measured by both a consummatory and an instrumental response. *Journal of Comparative and Physiological Psychology,* 1957, *50,* 1–5.

MILLER, R.R., AND SPRINGER, A.D. Amnesia consolidation

and retrieval. *Psychological Review,* 1973, *80,* 69–70.

MILLER, V.M., AND BEST, P.J. Spatial correlates of hippocampal unit activity are altered by lesions of the fornix and entorhinal cortex. *Brain Research,* 1980, *194,* 311–323.

MILNER, B. Memory disturbance after bilateral hippocampal lesions. In *Cognitive Processes and the Brain,* edited by P. Milner and S. Glickman. Princeton, N.J.: Van Nostrand, 1965.

MILNER, B. Memory and the temporal regions of the brain. In *Biology of Memory,* edited by K.H. Pribram and D.E. Broadbent. New York: Academic Press, 1970.

MILNER, B., CORKIN, S., AND TEUBER, H.-L. Further analysis of the hippocampal amnesic syndrome: 14-year follow-up study of H.M. *Neuropsychologia,* 1968, *6,* 317–338.

MISELIS, R.R. New efferents and afferents of the subfornical organ: A strategic neural circuitry for the control of water balance behaviorally and physiologically. *Neuroscience Abstracts,* 1980, *6,* 32.

MISELIS, R.R., SHAPIRO, R.E., AND HAND, P.J. Subfornical organ efferents to neural systems for control of body water. *Science,* 1979, *205,* 1022–1025.

MISHKIN, M. Visual mechanisms beyond the striate cortex. In *Frontiers in Physiological Psychology,* edited by R.W. Russell. New York: Academic Press, 1966.

MISHKIN, M. Memory in monkeys severely impaired by combined but not by separate removal of amygdala and hippocampus. *Nature,* 1978, *273,* 297–298.

MISHKIN, M. A memory system in the monkey. *Philosophical Transactions of the Royal Society of London,* 1982, *298,* 85–95.

MITCHELL, W., FALCONER, M.A., AND HILL, D. Epilepsy and fetishism relieved by temporal lobectomy. *Lancet,* 1954, *2,* 626–630.

MOGENSON, G.J., AND YIM, C.Y. Electrophysiological and neuropharmacological-behavioral studies of the nucleus accumbens: Implications for its role as a limbic-motor interface. In *The Neurobiology of the Nucleus Accumbens,* edited by R.B. Chronister and J.F. DeFrance. Brunswick, Maine: Haer Institute, 1981.

MOHR, J.P., PESSIN, M.S., FINKELSTEIN, S., FUNKENSTEIN, H.H., DUNCAN, G.W., AND DAVIS, K.R. Broca aphasia: Pathologic and clinical aspects. *Neurology,* 1978, *28,* 311–324.

MOLDOFSKY, H., AND SCARISBRICK, P. Induction of neurasthenic musculoskeletal pain syndrome by selective sleep stage deprivation. *Psychosomatic Medicine,* 1976, *38,* 35–44.

MOLTZ, H., LUBIN, M., LEON, M., AND NUMAN, M. Hormonal induction of maternal behavior in the ovariectomized nulliparous rat. *Physiology and Behavior,* 1970, *5,* 1373–1377.

MOLTZ, H., ROBBINS, D., AND PARKS, M. Caesarian delivery and maternal behavior of primiparous and multiparous rats. *Journal of Comparative and Physiological Psychology,* 1966, *61,* 455–460.

MONEY, J. Components of eroticism in man: Cognitional rehearsals. In *Recent Advances in Biological Psychiatry,* edited by J. Wortis. New York: Grune & Stratton, 1960.

MONEY, J., AND EHRHARDT, A. *Man & Woman, Boy & Girl.* Baltimore: Johns Hopkins University Press, 1972.

MONEY, J., AND MATHEWS, D. Prenatal exposure to virilizing progestins: An adult follow-up study of twelve women. *Archives of Sexual Behavior,* 1982, *11,* 73–82.

MONNIER, M., DUDLER, L., GÄCHTER, R., MAIER, P.F., TOBLER, H.J., AND SCHOENENBERGER, G.A. The delta sleep inducing peptide (DSIP). Comparative properties of the original and synthetic nonapeptide. *Experientia,* 1977, *33/34,* 548–552.

MONNIER, M., AND HÖSLI, L. Dialysis of sleep and waking factors in blood of rabbit. *Science,* 1964, *146,* 796–798.

MONNIER, M., AND HÖSLI, L. Humoral regulation of sleep and wakefulness by hypnogenic and activating dialysable factors. *Progress in Brain Research,* 1965, *18,* 118–123.

MONNIER, M., KOLLER, T., AND GRABER, S. Humoral influences of induced sleep and arousal upon electrical brain activity of animals with crossed circulation. *Experimental Neurology,* 1963, *8,* 264–277.

MOORE, J.W., GOODELL, N.A., AND SOLOMON, P.R. Central cholinergic blockade by scopolamine and habituation, classical conditioning, and latent inhibition of the rabbit's nictitating membrane response. *Physiological Psychology,* 1976, *4,* 395–399.

MOORE, R.Y. Effects of some rhinencephalic lesions on retention of conditioned avoidance behavior in cats. *Journal of Comparative and Physiological Psychology,* 1964, *53,* 540–548.

MOORE, R.Y., AND BLOOM, F.E. Central catecholamine neuron systems: Anatomy and physiology of the dopamine systems. *Annual Review of Neuroscience,* 1978, *1,* 129–169.

MOORE, R.Y., AND BLOOM, F.E. Central catecholamine neuron systems: Anatomy and physiology of the norepinephrine and epinephrine systems. *Annual Review of Neuroscience,* 1979, *2,* 113–168.

MOORE, R.Y., CARD, J.P., AND RILEY, J.N. The suprachiasmatic hypothalamic nucleus: Neuronal ultrastructure. *Neuroscience Abstracts,* 1980, *6,* 758.

MOORE, R.Y., AND EICHLER, V.B. Loss of a circadian adrenal corticosterone rhythm following suprachiasmatic lesions in the rat. *Brain Research,* 1972, *42,* 201–206.

MOORE-EDE, M.C., SULZMAN, F.M., AND FULLER, C.A. *The Clocks That Time Us.* Cambridge, Mass.: Harvard University Press, 1982.

MORA, F., SANGUINETTI, A.M., ROLLS, E.T., AND SHAW, S.G. Differential effects of self-stimulation and motor behavior produced by microintracranial injections of a dopamine-receptor blocking agent. *Neuroscience Letters,* 1975, *1,* 179–184.

MORGANE, J.P. Alterations in feeding and drinking of rats with lesions in the globi pallidi. *American Journal of Physiology,* 1961, *201,* 420–428.

MORRELL, F. Physiology and histochemistry of the mirror focus. In *Basic Mechanisms of the Epilepsies,* edited by H.H. Jasper, A.A. Ward, and A. Pope. Boston: Little, Brown, 1969.

MORRELL, J.L., AND PFAFF, D.W. A neuroendocrine approach to brain function: Localization of sex steroid concentrating cells in vertebrate brains. *American Zoologist,* 1978, *18,* 447–460.

MORRIS, R.G.M., GARRUD, P., RAWLINS, J.N.P., AND O'KEEFE, J. Place navigation impaired in rats with hippocampal lesions. *Nature,* 1982, *297,* 681–683.

MORROW, L., URTUNSKI, P.B., KIM, Y., AND BOLLER, F. Arousal responses to emotional stimuli and laterality of lesion. *Neuropsychologia,* 1981, *19,* 65–72.

MORUZZI, G. The sleep-waking cycle. *Ergebnisse der Physiologie,* 1972, *64,* 1–165.

MORUZZI, G., AND MAGOUN, H.W. Brain stem reticular formation and activation of the EEG. *Electroencephalography and Clinical Neurophysiology,* 1949, *1,* 455–473.

MOSCOVITCH, M., AND OLDS, J. Asymmetries in emotional facial expressions and their possible relation to hemispheric specialization. *Neuropsychologia,* 1982, *20,* 71–81.

MOSS, R.L., URBAN, I., AND CROSS, A.B. Microelectrophoresis of cholinergic and aminergic drugs on paraventricular neurons. *American Journal of Physiology,* 1972, *223,* 310–318.

MOUNT, G.B., AND HOEBEL, B.G. Lateral hypothalamic reward decreased by intragastric feeding: Self-determined "threshold" technique. *Psychosomatic Science,* 1967, *9,* 265–266.

MOUNTCASTLE, V.B. Modality and topographic properties of single neurons of cat's somatic sensory cortex. *Journal of Neurophysiology,* 1957, *20,* 408–434.

MOUNTCASTLE, V.B., LYNCH, J.C., GEORGOPOULOS, A., SAKATA, H., AND ACUNA, C. Posterior parietal association cortex: Command functions for operations within extra-personal space. *Journal of Neurophysiology,* 1975, *38,* 871–908.

MOYER, K.E. *The Psychobiology of Aggression.* New York: Harper & Row, 1976.

MURRAY, E.A., AND MISHKIN, M. Severe tactual memory deficits in monkeys after combined removal of the amygdala and hippocampus. *Brain Research,* 1983, *270,* 340–344.

MYERS, R.D. An improved push pull cannula system for perfusing an isolated region of the brain. *Physiology and Behavior,* 1970, *5,* 243–246.

MYERS, R.D., AND MCCALEB, M.L. Feeding: Satiety signals from intestine trigger brain's noradrenergic mechanism. *Science,* 1980, *209,* 1035–1037.

NACHMAN, M., AND ASHE, J.H. Effects of basolateral amygdala lesions on neophobia, learned taste aversions, and sodium appetite in rats. *Journal of Comparative and Physiological Psychology,* 1974, *87,* 622–643.

NAFE, J.P., AND WAGONER, K.S. The nature of pressure adaptation. *Journal of General Psychology,* 1941, *25,* 323–351.

National Commission for the Protection of Human Subjects of Biomedical and Behavioral Research. *Report and Recommendations: Psychosurgery.* Washington, D.C.: U.S. Government Printing Office, 1977.

NAUTA, W.J.H. Hypothalamic regulation of sleep in rats. Experimental study. *Journal of Neurophysiology,* 1946, *9,* 285–316.

NEFF, W.D. The brain and hearing: Auditory discriminations affected by brain lesions. *Annals of Otology, Rhinology and Laryngology,* 1977, *86,* 500–506.

NICHOLS, D.G. Brown adipose tissue mitochondria. *Biochimica et Biophysica Acta,* 1979, *549,* 1–29.

NICOLAIDIS, S. Early systemic responses to orogastric stimulation in the regulation of food and water balance: Functional and electrophysiological data. *Annals of the New York Academy of Sciences (U.S.A.),* 1969, *151,* 1176–1203.

NICOLAIDIS, S., AND ROWLAND, N. Metering of intravenous versus oral nutrients and regulation of energy balance. *American Journal of Physiology,* 1976, *231,* 661–668.

NICOLL, R.A., ALGER, B.E., AND NICOLL, R.A. Enkephalin blocks inhibitory pathways in the vertebrate CNS. *Nature,* 1980, *287,* 22–25.

NIIJIMA, A. Afferent impulse discharge from glucoreceptors in the liver of the guinea pig. *Annals of the New York Academy of Science,* 1969, *157,* 690–700.

NIIJIMA, A. Glucose-sensitive afferent nerve fibers in the hepatic branch of the vagus nerve in the guinea pig. *Journal of Physiology,* 1982, *332,* 315–323.

NOCK, B.L., AND LESHNER, A.I. Hormonal mediation of the effects of defeat on agonistic responding in mice. *Physiology and Behavior,* 1976, *17,* 111–119.

NOIROT, E. Selective priming of maternal responses by auditory and olfactory cues from mouse pups. *Developmental Psychobiology,* 1972, *5,* 371–387.

NORGREN, R., AND GRILL, H. Brain-stem control of ingestive behavior. In *The Physiological Mechanisms of Motivation,* edited by D.W. Pfaff. New York: Springer-Verlag, 1982.

NORMAN, R.J., BUCHWALD, J.S., AND VILLABLANCA, J.R. Classical conditioning with auditory discrimination of the eye blink in decerebrate cats. *Science,* 1977, *196,* 551–553.

NOVIN, D., ROBINSON, B.A., CULBRETH, L.A., AND TORDOFF, M.G. Is there a role for the liver in the control of food intake? *American Journal of Clinical Nutrition,* 1983, *9,* 233–246.

NOVIN, D., VANDERWEELE, D.A., AND REZEK, M. Hepatic-portal 2-deoxy-D-glucose infusion causes eating: Evidence for peripheral glucoreceptors. *Science,* 1973, *181,* 858–860.

NOWLIS, G.H., AND FRANK, M. Qualities in hamster taste: Behavioral and neural evidence. In *Olfaction and*

Taste, Vol. 6, edited by J. LeMagnen and P. MacLeod. Washington, D.C.: Information Retrieval, 1977.

NUMAN, M. Medial preoptic area and maternal behavior in the female rat. *Journal of Comparative and Physiological Psychology,* 1974, *87,* 746–759.

NUMAN, M., AND CALLAHAN, E.C. The connections of the medial preoptic region and maternal behavior in the rat. *Physiology and Behavior,* 1980, *25,* 653–665.

NUMAN, M., MORRELL, J.I., AND PFAFF, D.W. Preoptic area connectivity relevant for maternal behavior in the rat. *Society for Neuroscience Abstracts,* 1983, *9,* 978.

NUMAN, M., ROSENBLATT, J.S., AND KOMISARUK, B.R. Medial preoptic area and onset of maternal behavior in the rat. *Journal of Comparative and Physiological Psychology,* 1977, *91,* 146–164.

NUMAN, M., AND SMITH, H.G. Maternal behavior in rats: Evidence for the involvement of preoptic projections to the ventral tegmental area. *Behavioral Neuroscience,* 1984, *98,* 712–727.

NUÑEZ, A.A., AND CASATI, M.J. The role of efferent connections of the suprachiasmatic nucleus in the control of circadian rhythms. *Behavioral and Neural Biology,* 1979, *25,* 263–267.

OAKLEY, K., AND TOATES, F.M. The passage of food through the gut of rats and its uptake of fluid. *Psychonomic Science,* 1969, *16,* 225–226.

O'KEEFE, J., AND CONWAY, D.H. On the trail of the hippocampal engram. *Physiological Psychology,* 1980, *8,* 229–238.

O'KEEFE, J., AND DOSTROVSKY, T. The hippocampus as a spatial map: Preliminary evidence from unit activity in the freely moving rat. *Brain Research,* 1971, *34,* 171–175.

O'KEEFE, J., AND NADEL, L. *The Hippocampus As a Cognitive Map.* New York: Oxford University Press, 1978.

OLDS, J. Commentary. In *Brain Stimulation and Motivation,* edited by E.S. Valenstein. Glenview, Ill.: Scott, Foresman, 1973.

OLDS, J., AND MILNER, P. Positive reinforcement produced by electrical stimulation of septal area and other regions of rat brain. *Journal of Comparative and Physiological Psychology,* 1954, *47,* 419–427.

OLDS, J., MINK, W.D., AND BEST, P.J. Single unit patterns during anticipatory behavior. *Electroencephalography and Clinical Neurophysiology,* 1969, *26,* 144–158.

OLDS, M.E., AND FOBES, J.L. The central basis of motivation: Intracranial self-stimulation studies. *Annual Review of Psychology,* 1981, *32,* 523–574.

OLDS, M.E., AND OLDS, J. Effects of lesions in medial forebrain bundle on self-stimulation behavior. *American Journal of Physiology,* 1969, *217,* 1253–1264.

OLINS, D.E., AND OLINS, A.L. Nucleosomes: The structural quantum in chromosomes. *American Scientist,* 1978, *66,* 704–711.

OLTON, D.S. Memory functions and the hippocampus. In *Neurobiology of the Hippocampus,* edited by W. Siefert. New York: Academic Press, 1983.

OLTON, D.S., COLLISON, C., AND WERZ, M.A. Spatial memory and radial arm maze performance in rats. *Learning and Motivation,* 1977, *8,* 289–314.

OLTON, D.S., AND FEUSTLE, W. Hippocampal function and nonspatial memory. *Experimental Brain Research,* 1981, *41,* 380–389.

OLTON, D.S., AND PAPAS, B.C. Spatial memory and hippocampal function. *Neuropsychologia,* 1979, *17,* 669–682.

OLTON, D.S., AND SAMUELSON, R.J. Remembrance of places past: Spatial memory in rats. *Journal of Experimental Psychology: Animal Behavior Processes,* 1976, *2,* 97–116.

OSWALD, I. Sleep as a restorative process: Human clues. In *Adaptive Capabilities of the Nervous System,* edited by P.S. McConnell, G.J. Boer, H.J. Romijn, N.E. van de Poll, and M.A. Corner. Amsterdam: Elsevier, 1980.

OWEN, F., CROSS, A.J., CROW, T.J., LONGDEN, M., POULTER, M., AND RILEY, G.J. Increased dopamine-receptor sensitivity in schizophrenia. *Lancet,* 1978, *2,* 223–226.

PANKSEPP, J. Aggression elicited by electrical stimulation of the hypothalamus in albino rats. *Physiology and Behavior,* 1971a, *6,* 321–329.

PANKSEPP, J. Drugs and stimulus-bound attack. *Physiology and Behavior,* 1971b, *6,* 317–320.

PANKSEPP, J., AND TROWILL, J.A. Intraoral self-injection. II. The simulation of self-stimulation phenomena with a conventional reward. *Psychonomic Science,* 1967, *9,* 407–408.

PAPEZ, J.W. A proposed mechanism of emotion. *Archives of Neurology and Psychiatry,* 1937, *38,* 725–744.

PATTERSON, K., AND KAY, J.A. How word-form dyslexics form words. Paper presented at the meeting of the British Psychological Society Conference on Reading, Exeter, England, 1980.

PATTERSON, K.E., AND MARCEL, A.J. Aphasia, dyslexia, and the phonological coding of written words. *Quarterly Journal of Experimental Psychology,* 1977, *29,* 307–318.

PATTERSON, P.H., AND CHUN, L.L.Y. The influence of nonneural cells on catecholamine and acetylcholine synthesis and accumulation in cultures of dissociated sympathetic neurons. *Proceedings of the National Academy of Sciences (U.S.A.),* 1974, *71,* 3607–3610.

PAUL, L., MILEY, W.M., AND BAENNINGER, R. Mouse killing by rats: Roles of hunger and thirst in its initiation and maintenance. *Journal of Comparative and Physiological Psychology,* 1971, *76,* 242–249.

PAVLOV, I.P. "Innere Hemmung" der bedingten Reflexe und der Schlaf—ein und derselbe Prozeß. *Skandinavisches Archiv für Physiologie,* 1923, *44,* 42–58.

PECK, J.W., AND BLASS, E.M. Localization of thirst and antidiuretic osmoreceptors by intracranial injections in rats. *American Journal of Physiology*, 1975, *5*, 1501–1509.

PENFIELD, W., AND JASPER, H. *Epilepsy and the Functional Anatomy of the Human Brain*. Boston: Little, Brown, 1954.

PENFIELD, W., AND MATHIESON, G. Memory: Autopsy findings and comments on the role of hippocampus in experiential recall. *Archives of Neurology*, 1974, *31*, 145–154.

PENFIELD, W., AND MILNER, B. Memory deficit produced by bilateral lesions in the hippocampal zone. *American Medical Association Archives of Neurological Psychiatry*, 1958, *79*, 475–497.

PENFIELD, W., AND RASMUSSEN, T. *The Cerebral Cortex of Man: A Clinical Study of Localization*. Boston: Little, Brown, 1950.

PERKEL, D.H., AND BULLOCK, T.H. Neural coding. *Neuroscience Research Progress Bulletin*, 1968, *6*, 221–347.

PERSKY, H. Reproductive hormones, moods, and the menstrual cycle. In *Sex Differences in Behavior*, edited by R.C. Friedman, R.M. Richart, and R.L. Vande Wiele. New York: John Wiley & Sons, 1974.

PERSKY, H., LIEF, H.I., STRAUSS, D., MILLER, W.R., AND O'BRIEN, C.P. Plasma testosterone level and sexual behavior of couples. *Archives of Sexual Behavior*, 1978, *7*, 157–173.

PERT, C.B, SNOWMAN, A.M., AND SNYDER, S.H. Localization of opiate receptor binding in presynaptic membranes of rat brain. *Brain Research*, 1974, *70*, 184–188.

PFAFF, D.W., AND KEINER, M. Atlas of estradiol-concentrating cells in the central nervous system of the female rat. *Journal of Comparative Neurology*, 1973, *151*, 121–158.

PFAFF, D.W., AND MCEWEN, B.S. Actions of estrogens and progestins on nerve cells. *Science*, 1983, *219*, 808–814.

PFAFF, D.W., AND SAKUMA, Y. Deficit in the lordosis reflex of female rats caused by lesions in the ventromedial nucleus of the hypothalamus. *Journal of Physiology*, 1979, *288*, 203–210.

PFAFF, D.W., AND ZIGMOND, R.E. Neonatal androgen effects on sexual and nonsexual behavior of adult rats tested under various hormone regimes. *Neuroendocrinology*, 1971, *7*, 129–145.

PFAFFMANN, C., FRANK, M., AND NORGREN, R. Neural mechanisms and behavioral aspects of taste. *Annual Review of Psychology*, 1979, *30*, 283–325.

PHILLIPS, A.G., AND LePIANE, F.G. Reward produced by microinjection of (D-ala$_2$)-met$_5$enkephalinamide into the ventral tegmental area. *Behavioural Brain Research*, 1982, *5*, 225–229.

PHILLIPS, M.I., AND FELIX, D. Specific angiotensin II receptive neurons in the cat subfornical organ. *Brain Research*, 1976, *109*, 531–540.

PHILLIPSON, O.T. Afferent projections to the ventral tegmental area of Tsai and interfascicular nucleus: A horseradish peroxidase study in the rat. *Journal of Comparative Neurology*, 1979, *187*, 117–143.

PIÉRON, H. *Le Problème Physiologique du Sommeil*. Paris: Masson, 1913.

PIJNENBURG, A.J.J., AND VAN ROSSUM, J.M. Stimulation of locomotor activity following injection of dopamine into the nucleus accumbens. *Journal of Pharmacy and Pharmacology*, 1973, *25*, 1003–1005.

POGGIO, G.F., AND FISCHER, B. Binocular interaction and depth sensitivity in striate and prestriate cortex of behaving rhesus monkey. *Journal of Neurophysiology*, 1977, *40*, 1392–1405.

POGGIO, G.F., AND POGGIO, T. The analysis of stereopsis. *Annual Review of Neuroscience*, 1984, *7*, 379–412.

POHL, C.R., AND KNOBIL, E. The role of the central nervous system in the control of ovarian function in higher primates. *Annual Review of Physiology*, 1982, *44*, 583–593.

POLC, P., AND MONNIER, M. An activating mechanism in the ponto-bulbar raphe system of the rabbit. *Journal of Pharmacology and Experimental Therapeutics*, 1966, *154*, 64–73.

POMPEIANO, O., AND SWETT, J.E. EEG and behavioral manifestations of sleep induced by cutaneous nerve stimulation in normal cats. *Archives Italiennes de Biologie*, 1962, *100*, 311–342.

POMPEIANO, O., AND SWETT, J.E. Action of graded cutaneous and muscular afferent volleys on brain stem units in the decerebrate cerebellectomized cats. *Archives Italiennes de Biologie*, 1963, *101*, 552–583.

POST, R.M., FINK, E., CARPENTER, W.T., AND GOODWIN, F.K. Cerebrospinal fluid amine metabolites in acute schizophrenia. *Archives of General Psychiatry*, 1975, *32*, 1063–1069.

POWELL, G.M., BERTHIER, N.E., AND MOORE, J.W. Efferent neuronal control of the nictitating membrane response in the rabbit *(Oryctolagus cuniculus):* A reexamination. *Physiology and Behavior*, 1979, *23*, 299–308.

POWERS, J.B., AND WINANS, S.S. Vomeronasal organ: Critical role in mediating sexual behavior of the male hamster. *Science*, 1975, *187*, 961–963.

PREMACK, D. Reinforcement theory. In *Nebraska Symposium on Motivation*, edited by D. Levine. Lincoln: University of Nebraska Press, 1965.

PRICE, J. The genetics of depressive behavior. *British Journal of Psychiatry*, 1968, *2*, 37–45.

PRISKO, L. Short term memory in cerebral damage. Unpublished Ph.D. dissertation, McGill University, 1963.

PUJOL, J.F., BUGUET, A., FROMENT, J.L., JONES, B., AND JOUVET, M. The central metabolism of serotonin in the cat during insomnia: A neurophysiological and biochemical study after p-chlorophenylalanine or destruction of the raphe system. *Brain Research*, 1971, *29*, 195–212.

PYCOCK, D.J., AND HORTON, R.W. Possible GABA-mediated control of dopamine-dependent behavioral effects from the nucleus accumbens of the rat. *Psychopharmacology*, 1976, *49*, 173–178.

QUABBE, H.-J. Chronobiology of growth hormone secretion. *Chronobiologica,* 1977, *4,* 217–246.

RACINE, R.J. Modification of seizure activity by electrical stimulation. II. Motor seizure. *Electroencephalography and Clinical Neurophysiology,* 1972, *32,* 281–291.

RACINE, R.J., MILGRAM, N.W., AND HAFNER, S. Long-term potentiation phenomena in the rat limbic forebrain. *Brain Research,* 1983, *260,* 217–233.

RAINBOW, R.C., PARSONS, B., AND McEWEN, B.S. Sex differences in rat brain oestrogen and progestin receptors. *Nature,* 1982, *300,* 648–649.

RAISMAN, G. Neuronal plasticity in the septal nuclei of the adult rat. *Brain Research,* 1969, *14,* 24–48.

RAKIC, P. Mode of cell migration to the superficial layers of fetal monkey neocortex. *Journal of Comparative Neurology,* 1972, *145,* 61–83.

RAMSAY, D.J., ROLLS, B.J., AND WOOD, R.J. Thirst following water deprivation in dogs. *American Journal of Physiology,* 1977, *232,* R93–R100.

RATCLIFF, G., AND NEWCOMBE, F. Object recognition: Some deductions from the clinical evidence. In *Normality and Pathology in Cognitive Functions,* edited by A.W. Ellis. London: Academic Press, 1982.

RAVELLI, G.P., STEIN, Z.A., AND SUSSER, M.W. Obesity in young men after famine exposure in utero and early infancy. *New England Journal of Medicine,* 1976, *295,* 349–353.

RAWLINS, J.N.P., FELDON, J., AND GRAY, J.A. Septo-hippocampal connections and the hippocampal theta rhythm. *Experimental Brain Research,* 1979, *37,* 49–63.

RAYBIN, J.B., AND DETRE, T.P. Sleep disorder and symptomatology among medical and nursing students. *Comprehensive Psychiatry,* 1969, *10,* 452–467.

RECHTSCHAFFEN, A., GILLILAND, M.A., BERGMANN, B.M., AND WINTER, J.B. Physiological correlates of prolonged sleep deprivation in rats. *Science,* 1983, *221,* 182–184.

RECHTSCHAFFEN, A., WOLPERT, E.A., DEMENT, W.C., MITCHELL, S.A., AND FISHER, C. Nocturnal sleep of narcoleptics. *Electroencephalography and Clinical Neurophysiology,* 1963, *15,* 599–609.

REES, H.D., BROGAN, L.L., ENTINGH, D.J., DUNN, A.J., SHINKMAN, P.G., DAMSTRA-ENTINGH, T., WILSON, J.E., AND GLASSMAN, E. Effect of sensory stimulation on the uptake and incorporation of radioactive lysine into protein of mouse brain and liver. *Brain Research,* 1974, *68,* 143–156.

REES, H.D., AND DUNN, A.J. The role of pituitary-adrenal system in the foot-shock-induced increase of [^{3}H]lysine incorporation into mouse brain and liver protein. *Brain Research,* 1977, *120,* 317–325.

REIFMAN, A., AND WYATT, R.J. Lithium: A brake in the rising cost of mental illness. *Archives of General Psychiatry,* 1980, *37,* 385–388.

REVELEY, M.A., GLOVER, V., SANDLER, M., AND SPOKES, E.G. Brain monoamine oxidase activity in schizophrenics and controls. *Archives of General Psychiatry,* 1981, *38,* 663–665.

REYNOLDS, D.V. Surgery in the rat during electrical analgesia induced by focal brain stimulation. *Science,* 1969, *164,* 444–445.

REYNOLDS, J., AND KEVERNE, E.B. The accessory olfactory system and its role in the pheromonally mediated suppression of oestrus in grouped mice. *Journal of Reproduction and Fertility,* 1979, *57,* 31–35.

RIBACK, C.E., AND PETERS, A. An autoradiographic study of the projections from the lateral geniculate body of the rat. *Brain Research,* 1975, *92,* 341–368.

RICHARDS, W. Selective stereoblindness. In *Spatial Contrast,* edited by H. Spekreijse and L.H. van der Tweel. Amsterdam: North Holland, 1977.

RICHTER, C.P. *Biological Clocks in Medicine and Psychiatry.* Springfield, Ill.: Charles C Thomas, 1965.

RICHTER, C.P. Sleep and activity: Their relation to the 24-hour clock. *Proceedings of the Association for Research on Nervous and Mental Disorders,* 1967, *45,* 8–27.

RINGLE, D.A., AND HERNDON, B.L. Plasma dialysates from sleep deprived rabbits and their effect on the electrocorticogram of rats. *Pflügers Archives,* 1968, *303,* 344–349.

RITTER, S., AND STEIN, L. Self-stimulation of noradrenergic cell group (A6) in locus coeruleus of rats. *Journal of Comparative and Physiological Psychology,* 1973, *85,* 443–452.

ROBBINS, M.J., AND MEYER, D.R. Motivational control of retrograde amnesia. *Journal of Experimental Psychology,* 1970, *84,* 220–225.

ROBERTS, D.C.S., CORCORAN, M.E., AND FIBIGER, H.C. On the role of ascending catecholaminergic systems in intravenous self-administration of cocaine. *Pharmacology, Biochemistry and Behavior,* 1977, *6,* 615–620.

ROBERTS, W.W., AND KIESS, H.O. Motivational properties of hypothalamic aggression in cats. *Journal of Comparative and Physiological Psychology,* 1964, *58,* 187–193.

ROBERTS, W.W., AND ROBINSON, T.C.L. Relaxation and sleep induced by warming of preoptic region and anterior hypothalamus in cats. *Experimental Neurology,* 1969, *25,* 282–294.

ROBERTS, W.W., STEINBERG, M.L., AND MEANS, L. Hypothalamic mechanisms for sexual, aggressive, and other motivational behaviors in the opossum, *Didelphis virginiana. Journal of Comparative and Physiological Psychology,* 1967, *64,* 1–15.

ROBERTSON, A., AND MOGENSON, G.J. Evidence for a role for dopamine in self-stimulation of the nucleus accumbens of the rat. *Canadian Journal of Psychology,* 1978, *68,* 67–76.

ROBINSON, T.E., VANDERWOLF, C.H., AND PAPPAS, B.A. Are the dorsal noradrenergic bundle projections from the locus coeruleus important for neocortical or hippocampal activation? *Brain Research,* 1977, *138,* 75–98.

RODGERS, R.J. Influence of intra-amygdaloid opiate injection on shock thresholds, tail flick latencies and open field behavior in rats. *Brain Research,* 1978, *153,* 211–216.

RODIECK, R.W. Visual pathways. *Annual Review of Neuroscience,* 1979, *2,* 193–226.

RODRIGUEZ-SIERRA, J.F., AND ROSENBLATT, J.S. Does prolactin have a role in estrogen-induced maternal behavior in rats: Apomorphine reduction of prolactin release. *Hormones and Behavior,* 1977, *9,* 1–7.

ROFFWARG, H.P., MUZIO, J.N., AND DEMENT, W.C. Ontogenesis development of human sleep-dream cycle. *Science,* 1966, *152,* 604–619.

ROGERS, R.C., AND NOVIN, D. The neurological aspects of hepatic osmoregulation. In *The Kidney in Liver Disease,* second edition, edited by M. Epstein. Amsterdam: Elsevier, 1983.

ROLDAN, E., ALVAREZ-PELAEZ, R., AND FERNANDEZ DeMOLINA, A. Electrographic study of the amygdaloid defense response. *Physiology and Behavior,* 1974, *13,* 779–787.

ROLLS, B.J., AND ROLLS, E.T. *Thirst.* Cambridge, England: Cambridge University Press, 1982.

ROLLS, E.T. Feeding and reward. In *The Neural Basis of Feeding and Reward,* edited by B.G. Hobel and D. Novin. Brunswick, Maine: Haer Institute, 1982.

ROLLS, E.T., ROLLS, B.J., KELLY, P.H., SHAW, S.G., WOOD, R.J., AND DALE, R. The relative attenuation of self-stimulation, eating and drinking produced by dopamine-receptor blockade. *Psychopharmacologia,* 1974, *38,* 219–230.

ROSE, G.A., AND WILLIAMS, R.T. Metabolic studies of large and small eaters. *British Journal of Nutrition,* 1961, *15,* 1–9.

ROSE, J.E., BRUGGE, J.F., ANDERSON, D.J., AND HIND, J.E. Phase-locked response to low-frequency tones in single auditory nerve fibers of the squirrel monkey. *Journal of Neurophysiology,* 1967, *30,* 769–793.

ROSE, R.M., BOURNE, P.G., POE, R.O., MOUGEY, E.H., COLLINS, D.R., AND MASON, J.W. Androgen responses to stress. II. Excretion of testosterone, epitestosterone, androsterone, and etiocholanolone during basic combat training and under attack. *Psychosomatic Medicine,* 1969, *31,* 418–436.

ROSÉN, I., AND ASANUMA, H. Peripheral inputs to the forelimb area of the monkey motor cortex: Input-output relations. *Experimental Brain Research,* 1972, *14,* 257–273.

ROSENBERG, K.M., DENENBERG, V.H., ZARROW, M.X., AND FRANK, B.L. Effects of neonatal castration and testosterone on the rat's pup-killing behavior and activity. *Physiology and Behavior,* 1971, *7,* 363–368.

ROSENBLATT, J.S. The development of maternal responsiveness in the rat. *Journal of Orthopsychiatry,* 1969, *39,* 36–56.

ROSENBLATT, J.S., AND ARONSON, L.R. The decline of sexual behavior in male cats after castration with special reference to the role of prior sexual experience. *Behaviour,* 1958a, *12,* 285–338.

ROSENBLATT, J.S., AND ARONSON, L.R. The influence of experience on the behavioural effects of androgen in prepuberally castrated male cats. *Animal Behaviour,* 1958b, *6,* 171–182.

ROSENBLATT, J.S., AND SIEGEL, H.I. Hysterectomy-induced maternal behavior during pregnancy in the rat. *Journal of Comparative and Physiological Psychology,* 1975, *89,* 685–700.

ROSENBLATT, J.S., SIEGEL, H.I., AND MAYER, A.D. Progress in the study of maternal behavior in the rat: Hormonal, nonhormonal, sensory, and developmental aspects. In *Advances in the Study of Behavior, Vol. 10,* edited by J.S. Rosenblatt, R.A. Hinde, E. Shaw, and C. Beer. New York: Academic Press, 1979.

ROSENFIELD, M.E., AND MOORE, J.W. Red nucleus lesions disrupt the classically conditioned membrane response in rabbits. *Behavioural Brain Research,* 1983, *10,* 393–398.

ROSENTHAL, D. A program of research on heredity in schizophrenia. *Behavioral Science,* 1971, *16,* 191–201.

ROSENZWEIG, M.R. Experience, memory, and the brain. *American Psychologist,* 1984, *39,* 365–376.

ROSS, E.D. The aprosodias: Functional-anatomic organization of the affective components of language in the right hemisphere. *Archives of Neurology,* 1981, *38,* 561–569.

ROTHWELL, N.J., AND STOCK, M.J. A role for brown adipose tissue in diet-induced thermogenesis. *Nature,* 1979, *281,* 31–35.

ROUTTENBERG, A., AND MALSBURY, C. Brainstem pathways of reward. *Journal of Comparative and Physiological Psychology,* 1969, *68,* 22–30.

ROUTTENBERG, A., AND SLOAN, M. Self-stimulation in the frontal cortex of *Rattus norvegicus. Behavioral Biology,* 1972, *7,* 567–572.

ROWLAND, N., AND ANTELMAN, S.M. Stress-induced hyperphagia and obesity in rats: A possible model for understanding human obesity. *Science,* 1976, *191,* 310–312.

RUBIN, B.S., AND BARFIELD, R.J. Priming of estrous responsiveness by implants of 17β-estradiol in the ventromedial hypothalamic nucleus of female rats. *Endocrinology,* 1980, *106,* 504–509.

RUSAK, B. The role of the suprachiasmatic nuclei in the generation of circadian rhythms in the golden hamster, *Mesocricetus auratus. Journal of Comparative Physiology,* 1977, *118,* 145–164.

RUSAK, B. Neural mechanisms for entrainment and generation of mammalian circadian rhythms. *Proceedings of the Federation of Experimental Biology (U.S.A.),* 1979, *38,* 2589–2595.

RUSAK, B., AND GROOS, G. Suprachiasmatic stimulation phase shifts rodent circadian rhythms. *Science,* 1982, *215,* 1407–1409.

RUSAK, B., AND MORIN, L.P. Testicular responses to photoperiod are blocked by lesions of the suprachiasmatic nuclei in golden hamsters. *Biology of Reproduction,* 1976, *15,* 366–374.

RUSINIAK, K.W., HANKINS, W.G., GARCIA, J., AND BRETT, L.P. Flavor-illness aversions: Potentiation of odor by taste in rats. *Behavioral and Neural Biology,* 1979, *25,* 1–17.

RUSSEK, M. Hepatic receptors and the neurophysiological mechanisms controlling feeding behavior. In *Neu-*

rosciences Research, Vol. 4, edited by S. Ehrenpreis. New York: Academic Press, 1971.

RUSSELL, M.J. Human olfactory communication. *Nature,* 1976, *260,* 520–522.

RUSSELL, M.J., SWITZ, G.M., AND THOMPSON, K. Olfactory influences on the human menstrual cycle. Paper presented at the meeting of the American Association for the Advancement of Science, San Francisco, June 1977.

RUSSELL, W.R., AND NATHAN, P.W. Traumatic amnesia. *Brain,* 1946, *69,* 280–300.

RUTTER, M., AND YULE, W. The concept of specific reading retardation. *Journal of the American Academy of Child Psychiatry,* 1975, *16,* 181–197.

RYBACK, R.S., AND LEWIS, O.F. Effects of prolonged bed rest on EEG sleep patterns in young, healthy volunteers. *Electroencephalography and Clinical Neurophysiology,* 1971, *31,* 395–399.

SAAYMAN, G.S. Aggressive behaviour in free-ranging chacma baboons *(Papio ursinus). Journal of Behavioral Science,* 1971, *1,* 77–83.

SACHAR, E.J., AND BARON, M. The biology of affective disorders. *Annual Review of Neuroscience,* 1979, *2,* 505–518.

SACKHEIM, H.A., AND GUR, R.C. Lateral asymmetry in intensity of emotional expression. *Neuropsychologia,* 1978, *16,* 473–482.

SAFFRAN, E.M., SCHWARTZ, M.F., AND MARIN, O.S.M. Evidence from aphasia: Isolating the components of a production model. In *Language Production,* edited by B. Butterworth. London: Academic Press, 1980.

SAITOH, K., MARUYAMA, N., AND KUDOH, M. Sustained response of auditory cortex units in the cat. In *Brain Mechanisms of Sensation,* edited by Y. Katsuki, R. Norgren, and M. Sato. New York: John Wiley & Sons, 1981.

SAKAGUCHI, A., LEDOUX, J.E., AND REIS, D.J. Medial geniculate but not auditory cortex lesions block emotional responses to auditory stimuli. *Society for Neuroscience Abstracts,* 1983, *9,* 637.

SAKAI, K. Some anatomical and physiological properties of ponto-mesencephalic tegmental neurons with special reference to the PGO waves and postural atonia during paradoxical sleep in the cat. In *The Reticular System Revisited,* edited by J.A. Hobson and M. Brazier. New York: Raven Press, 1980.

SAKUMA, Y., AND PFAFF, D.W. Facilitation of female reproductive behavior from mesencephalic central grey in the rat. *American Journal of Physiology,* 1979a, *237,* R278–R284.

SAKUMA, Y., AND PFAFF, D.W. Mesencephalic mechanisms for integration of female reproductive behavior in the rat. *American Journal of Physiology,* 1979b, *237,* R285–R290.

SAKUMA, Y., AND PFAFF, D.W. Convergent effects of lordosis-relevant somatosensory and hypothalamic influences on central gray cells in the rat mesencephalon. *Experimental Neurology,* 1980a, *70,* 269–281.

SAKUMA, Y., AND PFAFF, D.W. Excitability of female rat central gray cells with medullary projections:

Changes produced by hypothalamic stimulation and estrogen treatment. *Journal of Neurophysiology,* 1980b, *44,* 1012–1023.

SALLER, C.F., AND CHIODO, L.A. Glucose suppresses basal firing and haloperidol-induced increases in the firing rate of central dopaminergic neurons. *Science,* 1980, *210,* 1269–1271.

SASANUMA, S. Kana and kanji processing in Japanese aphasics. *Brain and Language,* 1975, *2,* 369–383.

SASSENRATH, E.N., POWELL, T.E., AND HENDRICKX, A.G. Perimenstrual aggression in groups of female rhesus monkeys. *Journal of Reproduction and Fertility,* 1973, *34,* 509–511.

SAVAGE, D.D., MENDELS, J., AND FRAZER, A. Decrease in [³H]- serotonin binding in rat brain produced by the repeated administration of either monoamine oxidase inhibitors or centrally acting serotonin agonists. *Neuropharmacology,* 1980a, *19,* 1036–1070.

SAVAGE, D.D., MENDELS, J., AND FRAZER, A. Monoamine oxidase inhibitors and serotonin uptake inhibitors: Differential effects on [³H]serotonin binding sites in rat brain. *Journal of Pharmacology and Experimental Therapeutics,* 1980b, *212,* 259–263.

SCHERSCHLICHT, R., POLC, P., SCHNEEBERGER, J., STEINER, M., AND HAEFELY, W. Selective suppression of rapid eye movement sleep (REMS) in cats by typical and atypical antidepressants. In *Typical and Atypical Antidepressants: Molecular Mechanisms,* edited by E. Costa and G. Racagni. New York: Raven Press, 1982.

SCHIFFMAN, P.L., WESTLAKE, R.E., SANTIAGO, T.V., AND EDELMAN, N.H. Ventilatory control in parents of victims of the sudden infant death syndrome. *New England Journal of Medicine,* 1980, *302,* 486–491.

SCHNEDORF, J.F., AND IVY, A.C. An examination of hypnotoxin theory of sleep. *American Journal of Physiology,* 1939, *125,* 491–505.

SCHREINER, L., AND KLING, A. Rhinencephalon and behavior. *American Journal of Physiology,* 1956, *184,* 486–490.

SCHWABER, J.S., KAPP, B.S., AND HIGGINS, G. The origin and extent of direct amygdala projections to the region of the dorsal motor nucleus of the vagus and the nucleus of the solitary tract. *Neuroscience Letters,* 1980, *20,* 15–20.

SCHWABER, J.S., KAPP, B.S., HIGGINS, G., AND RAPP, P.R. The origin, extent and terminal distribution of direct amygdala central nucleus projections to the dorsal motor nucleus and nucleus of the solitary tract. *Society for Neuroscience Abstracts,* 1980, *6,* 816.

SCHWARTZ, J.-C. Histaminergic mechanisms in brain. *Annual Review of Pharmacology and Toxicology,* 1977, *17,* 325–339.

SCHWARTZ, M.F., MARIN, O.S.M., AND SAFFRAN, E.M. Dissociations of language function in dementia: A case study. *Brain and Language,* 1979, *7,* 277–306.

SCHWARTZ, M.F., SAFFRAN, E.M., AND MARIN, O.S.M. The word order problem in agrammatism. I. Comprehension. *Brain and Language,* 1980, *10,* 249–262.

SCHWARTZ, W.J., AND GAINER H. Suprachiasmatic nucleus: Use of ^{14}C-labelled deoxyglucose uptake as a functional marker. *Science,* 1977, *197,* 1089–1091.

SCOVILLE, W.B., AND MILNER, B. Loss of recent memory after bilateral hippocampal lesions. *Journal of Neurology, Neurosurgery and Psychiatry,* 1957, *20,* 11–21.

SEDVALL, G., FYRÖ, B., GULLBERG, B., NYBÄCK, H., WIESEL, F.-A., AND WODE-HELGODT, B. Relationship in healthy volunteers between concentrations of monoamine metabolites in cerebrospinal fluid and family history of psychiatric morbidity. *British Journal of Psychiatry,* 1980, *136,* 366–374.

SEGAL, M., AND BLOOM, F.E. The action of norepinephrine in the rat hippocampus. III. Hippocampal cellular responses to locus coeruleus stimulation in the awake rat. *Brain Research,* 1976a, *107,* 499–511.

SEGAL, M., AND BLOOM, F.E. The action of norepinephrine in the rat hippocampus. IV. The effects of locus coeruleus stimulation on evoked hippocampal unit activity. *Brain Research,* 1976b, *107,* 513–525.

SEKULER, R. Spatial vision. *Annual Review of Psychology,* 1974, *25,* 195–232.

SERRA, G., ARGIOLAS, A., KLIMEK, V., FADDA, F., AND GESSA, G.L. Chronic treatment with antidepressants prevents the inhibitory effect of small doses of apomorphine on dopamine synthesis and motor activity. *Life Sciences,* 1979, *25,* 415–424.

SHAKOW, D. Segmental set: A theory of the formal psychological deficit in schizophrenia. *Archives of General Psychiatry,* 1962, *6,* 1–17.

SHALLICE, T., AND WARRINGTON, E.K. Single and multiple component central dyslexia syndromes. In *Deep Dyslexia,* edited by M. Coltheart, K. Patterson, and J.C. Marshall. London: Routledge & Kegan Paul, 1980.

SHAPIRO, C.M., BORTZ, R., MITCHELL, D., BARTEL, P., AND JOOSTE, P. Slow-wave sleep: A recovery period after exercise. *Science,* 1981, *214,* 1253–1254.

SHARP, P.E., MCNAUGHTON, B.L., AND BARNES, C.A. Spontaneous synaptic enhancement in hippocampi of rats exposed to a spatially complex environment. *Society for Neuroscience Abstracts,* 1983, *9,* 647.

SHERIDAN, P.J. The nucleus interstitialis striae terminalis and the nucleus amygdaloidus medialis: Prime targets for androgen in the rat forebrain. *Endocrinology,* 1979, *101,* 130–136.

SHIK, M.L., AND ORLOVSKY, G.N. Neurophysiology of locomotor automatism. *Physiological Review,* 1976, *56,* 465–501.

SHIMIZU, N., OOMURA, Y., NOVIN, D., GRIJALVA, C., AND COOPER, P.H. Functional correlations between lateral hypothalamic glucose-sensitive neurons and hepatic portal glucose-sensitive units in rat. *Brain Research,* 1983, *265,* 49–54.

SHIZGAL, P., BIELAJEW, C., AND KISS, I. Anodal hyperpolarization block technique provides evidence for rostro-caudal conduction of reward signals in the medial forebrain bundle. *Society for Neuroscience Abstracts,* 1980, *6,* 422.

SHRAGER, E.E., AND JOHNSON, A.K. Contributions of periventricular structures of the rostral third ventricle to the maintenance of drinking responses to humoral dipsogens and body fluid homeostasis. *Neuroscience Abstracts,* 1980, *6,* 128.

SIDMAN, M., STODDARD, L.T., AND MOHR, J.P. Some additional quantitative observations of immediate memory in a patient with bilateral hippocampal lesions. *Neuropsychologia,* 1968, *6,* 245–254.

SIEGAL, A., AND SKOG, D. Effect of electrical stimulation of the septum upon attack behavior elicited from the hypothalamus in the cat. *Brain Research,* 1970, *23,* 371–380.

SIEGEL, H.I., AND ROSENBLATT, J.S. Estrogen-induced maternal behavior in hysterectomized-ovariectomized virgin rats. *Physiology and Behavior,* 1975, *14,* 465–471.

SIEGEL, J.M. Behavioral functions of the reticular formation. *Brain Research Reviews,* 1979, *1,* 69–105.

SIEGEL, J.M. A behavioral approach to the analysis of reticular formation unit activity. In *Behavioral Approaches to Brain Research,* edited by T.E. Robinson. New York: Oxford University Press, 1983.

SIEGEL, J.M., AND MCGINTY, D.J. Pontine reticular formation neurons: Relationship of discharge to motor activity. *Science,* 1977, *196,* 678–680.

SIMAN, R., BAUDRY, M., AND LYNCH, G. A possible molecular mechanism for modification of dendritic spine shape. *Society for Neuroscience Abstracts,* 1983, *9,* 344.

SIMON, H., STINUS, L., TASSIN, J.P, LAVIELLE, S., BLANC, G., THIERRY, A.-M., GLOWINSKI, J., AND LEMOAL, M. Is the dopaminergic mesocorticolimbic system necessary for intracranial self-stimulation? *Behavioral and Neural Biology,* 1979, *27,* 125–145.

SIMPSON, J.B., EPSTEIN, A.N., AND CAMARDO, J.S., JR. The localization of dipsogenic receptors for angiotensin II in the subfornical organ. *Journal of Comparative and Physiological Psychology,* 1978, *92,* 581–608.

SIMS, E.A.H., AND HORTON, E.S. Endocrine metabolic adaptation to obesity and starvation. *American Journal of Clinical Nutrition,* 1968, *21,* 1455–1470.

SINCLAIR, D. *Cutaneous Sensation.* London: Oxford University Press, 1967.

SINCLAIR, D. *Mechanisms of Cutaneous Sensation.* Oxford, England: Oxford University Press, 1981.

SINGER, J. Hypothalamic control of male and female sexual behavior in female rats. *Journal of Comparative and Physiological Psychology,* 1968, *66,* 738–742.

SITARAM, N., MOORE, A.M., AND GILLIN, J.C. Experimental acceleration and slowing of REM ultradian rhythm by cholinergic agonist and antagonist. *Nature,* 1978, *274,* 490–492.

SITARAM, N., WEINGARTNER, H., AND GILLIN, J.C. Human serial learning: Enhancement with arecholine and choline and impairment with scopolamine. *Science,* 1978, *201,* 271–276.

SITARAM, N., WYATT, R.J., DAWSON, S., AND GILLIN, J.C. REM sleep induction by physostigmine infusion during sleep. *Science,* 1976, *191,* 1281–1283.

SKULTETY, F.M. Stimulation of periaqueductal gray and hypothalamus. *Archives of Neurology,* 1963, *8,* 608–620.

SLOTNICK, B.M. Disturbances of maternal behavior in the rat following lesions of the cingulate cortex. *Behaviour,* 1967, *29,* 203–236.

SLOTNICK, B.M., AND MCMULLEN, M.F. Intraspecific fighting in albino mice with septal forebrain lesions. *Physiology and Behavior,* 1972, *8,* 333–337.

SLOTNICK, B.M., MCMULLEN, M.F., AND FLEISCHER, S. Changes in emotionality following destruction of the septal area in albino mice. *Brain, Behavior and Evolution,* 1974, *8,* 241–252.

SMITH, G.P., GIBBS, J., AND KULKOSKY, P.J. Relationships between brain-gut peptides and neurons in the control of food intake. In *The Neural Basis of Feeding and Reward,* edited by B.G. Hoebel and D. Novin. Brunswick, Maine: Haer Institute, 1982.

SNYDER, S.H. *Madness and the Brain.* New York: McGraw-Hill, 1974.

SNYDER, S.H., BURT, D.R., AND CREESE, I. Dopamine receptor of mammalian brain: Direct demonstration of binding to agonist and antagonist states. *Neuroscience Symposia,* 1976, *1,* 28–49.

SOFRONIEW, M.V., AND WEINDL, A. Projections from the parvocellular vasopressin and neurophysin containing neurons of the SCN. *American Journal of Anatomy,* 1978, *153,* 391–430.

SOLCIA, E., POLAK, J.M., LARSSON, L.I., BUCHAN, A.M.G., AND CAPELLA, C. *Gut Hormones, Vol. II,* edited by S.R. Bloom and J.M. Polak. London: Churchill/Livingstone, 1980.

SOLOMON, P. Insomnia. *New England Journal of Medicine,* 1956, *255,* 755–760.

SOLOMON, P.R., AND MOORE, J.W. Latent inhibition and stimulus generalization of the classically conditioned nictitating membrane response in rabbits (*Oryctolagus cuniculus*) following dorsal hippocampal ablation. *Journal of Comparative and Physiological Psychology,* 1975, *89,* 1192–1203.

SOLOMON, P.R., SOLOMON, S.D., VANDER SCHAAF, E., AND PERRY, H.E. Altered activity in the hippocampus is more detrimental to classical conditioning than removing the structure. *Science,* 1983, *220,* 329–331.

SPEEDIE, L.J., ROTHI, L.J., AND HEILMAN, K.M. Spelling dyslexia: A form of cross-cuing. *Brain and Language,* 1982, *15,* 340–352.

SPINELLI, D.H., AND JENSEN, F.E. Plasticity: The mirror of experience. *Science,* 1979, *203,* 75–78.

SPINELLI, D.H., JENSEN, F.E., AND DiPRISCO, G.V. Early experience effect on dendritic branching in normally reared kittens. *Experimental Neurology,* 1980, *62,* 1–11.

SPOENDLIN, H. The innervation of the cochlear receptor. In *Basic Mechanisms in Hearing,* edited by A.R. Møeller. New York: Academic Press, 1973.

SPRAGUE, J.M., BERLUCCHI, G., AND RIZZOLATTI, G. The role of the superior colliculus and pretectum in vision and visually guided behavior. In *Handbook of Sensory Physiology, Vol. VII/3: Central Processing of Visual Information, Part B: Visual Centers in the Brain,* edited by R. Jung. Berlin: Springer, 1973.

SPYRAKI, C., FIBIGER, H.C., AND PHILLIPS, A.G. Attenuation by haloperidol of place preference conditioning using food reinforcement. *Psychopharmacology,* 1982a, *77,* 379–382.

SPYRAKI, C., FIBIGER, H.C., AND PHILLIPS, A.G. Dopaminergic substrates of amphetamine-induced place preference conditioning. *Brain Research,* 1982b, *253,* 185–193.

SPYRAKI, C., FIBIGER, H.C., AND PHILLIPS, A.C. Attenuation of heroin reward in rats by disruption of the mesolimbic dopamine system. *Psychopharmacology,* 1983, *79,* 278–283.

SQUIRE, L.R. Stable impairment in remote memory following electroconvulsive therapy. *Neuropsychologia,* 1974, *13,* 51–58.

SQUIRE, L.R. The neuropsychology of human memory. *Annual Review of Neuroscience,* 1982, *5,* 241–273.

SQUIRE, L.R., AND MOORE, R.Y. Dorsal thalamic lesions in a noted case of chronic memory dysfunction. *Annals of Neurology,* 1979, *6,* 503–506.

STACHOWIAK, M., BIALOWAS, J., AND JURKOWSKI, M. Catecholamines in some hypothalamic and telencephalic nuclei of food deprived rats. *Acta Neurobiologiae Experimentalis,* 1978, *38,* 157–165.

STEBBINS, W.C., MILLER, J.M., JOHNSSON, L.-G., AND HAWKINS, J.E. Ototoxic hearing loss and cochlear pathology in the monkey. *Annals of Otology, Rhinology and Laryngology,* 1969, *78,* 1007–1026.

STEFFENS, A.B. Influence of reversible obesity on eating behavior, blood glucose, and insulin in the rat. *American Journal of Physiology,* 1975, *228,* 1738–1744.

STEIN, G.S., STEIN, J.S., AND KLEINSMITH, L.J. Chromosomal proteins and gene regulation. *Scientific American,* 1975, *232,* 46–57.

STEIN, L. Self-stimulation of the brain and the central stimulant action of amphetamine. *Federation Proceedings,* 1964, *23,* 836–850.

STEIN, L. Chemistry of reward and punishment. In *Psychopharmacology: A Review of Progress,* edited by D.H. Efron. Washington, D.C.: U.S. Government Printing Office, 1968.

STEINHAUSEN, W. Über den experimentallen Nachweis der Ablenkung der Cupula terminalis in der intakten Bogengangsampulle des Labyrinths bei der thermischen und adäquäten rotatorischen Reizung. *Zeitschrift für Hals-, Nasen-und Ohrenheilkunde,* 1931, *29,* 211–216.

STEPHAN, F.K., AND NUÑEZ, A.A. Elimination of circadian rhythms in drinking activity, sleep, and temperature by isolation of the suprachiasmatic nuclei. *Behavioral Biology,* 1977, *20,* 1–16.

STEPHAN, F.K., AND ZUCKER, I. Circadian rhythms in

drinking behavior and locomotor activity of rats are eliminated by hypothalamic lesion. *Proceedings of the National Academy of Science (U.S.A.), 1972, 69,* 1583–1586.

STERMAN, M.B., AND CLEMENTE, C.D. Forebrain inhibitory mechanisms: Cortical synchronization induced by basal forebrain stimulation. *Experimental Neurology, 1962a, 6,* 91–102.

STERMAN, M.B., AND CLEMENTE, C.D. Forebrain inhibitory mechanisms: Sleep patterns induced by basal forebrain stimulation in the behaving cat. *Experimental Neurology,* 1962b, *6,* 103–117.

STERNBACH, R.A. *Pain: A Psychophysiological Analysis.* New York: Academic Press, 1968.

STEVENS, J.R. Neurology and neuropathology of schizophrenia. In *Schizophrenia As a Brain Disease,* edited by F.A. Henn and H.A. Nasrallah. New York: Oxford University Press, 1982a.

STEVENS, J.R. Neuropathology of schizophrenia. *Archives of General Psychiatry,* 1982b, *39,* 1131–1139.

STEVENS, S.S., AND NEWMAN, E.B. Localization of actual sources of sound. *American Journal of Psychology,* 1936, *48,* 297–306.

STEWART, W.B., KAUER, J.S., AND SHEPHERD, G.M. Functional organization of the rat olfactory bulb analysed by the 2-deoxyglucose method. *Journal of Comparative Neurology,* 1979, *185,* 715–734.

STONE, J., AND FUKUDA, Y. Properties of cat retinal ganglion cells: A comparison of W-cells with X- and Y-cells. *Journal of Neurophysiology,* 1974, *37,* 722–748.

STOYVA, J., AND METCALF, D. Sleep patterns following chronic exposure to cholinesterase-inhibiting organophosphate compounds. *Psychophysiology,* 1968, *5,* 206.

STRICKER, E.M. Thirst, sodium appetite, and complementary physiological contributions to the regulation of intravascular fluid volume. In *The Neuropsychology of Thirst: New Findings and Advances in Concepts,* edited by A.N. Epstein, H.R. Kissileff, and E. Stellar. Washington, D.C.: Winston, 1973.

STRICKER, E.M. The central control of food intake: A role for insulin. In *The Neural Basis of Feeding and Reward,* edited by B.G. Hoebel and D. Novin. Brunswick, Maine: Haer Institute, 1982.

STRICKER, E.M., ROWLAND, N., SALLER, C.F., AND FRIEDMAN, M.I. Homeostasis during hypoglycemia: Central control of adrenal secretion and peripheral control of feeding. *Science,* 1977, *196,* 79–81.

STRICKER, E.M., AND WOLF, G. The effects of hypovolemia on drinking in rats with lateral hypothalamic damage. *Proceedings of the Society for Experimental Biology and Medicine,* 1967, *124,* 816–820.

STUMPF, W.E., AND SAR, M. Autoradiographic localization of estrogen, androgen, progestin, and glucocorticosteriod in "target tissues" and "on-target tissues." In *Receptors and Mechanism of Action of Steroid Hormones,* edited by J. Pasqualini. New York: Marcel Dekker, 1976.

STURUP, G.K. Correctional treatment and the criminal

sexual offender. *Canadian Journal of Correction,* 1961, *3,* 250–265.

SULLIVAN, J.L., CAVENAR, J.O., STANFIELD, C.N., AND HAMMETT, E.B. Reduced MAO activity in platelets and lymphocytes of chronic schizophrenics. *American Journal of Psychiatry,* 1978, *135,* 597–598.

SULSER, F. Antidepressant drug research: Impact on neurobiology and psychobiology. In *Typical and Atypical Antidepressants: Molecular Mechanisms,* edited by E. Costa and G. Racagni. New York: Raven Press, 1982.

SVARE, B. Psychobiological determinants of maternal aggressive behavior. In *Aggressive Behavior: Genetic and Neural Approaches,* edited by E.C. Simmel, M.E. Hahn, and J.K. Walters. Hillsdale, N.J.: Lawrence Erlbaum Associates, 1983.

SVARE, B., BETTERIDGE, C., KATZ, D., AND SAMUELS, O. Some situational and experiential determinants of maternal aggression in mice. *Physiology and Behavior,* 1981, *26,* 253–258.

SVARE, B., AND GANDELMAN, R. Postpartum aggression in mice: Experiential and environmental factors. *Hormones and Behavior,* 1973, *4,* 323–334.

SVARE, B., AND GANDELMAN, R. Postpartum aggression in mice: The influence of suckling stimulation. *Hormones and Behavior,* 1976, *7,* 407–416.

SVEJDA, M.J., CAMPOS, J.J., AND EMDE, R.N. Mother-infant "bonding": failure to generalize. *Child Development,* 1980, *51,* 775–779.

SWANSON, L.W. Normal hippocampal circuitry: Anatomy. *Neurosciences Research Program Bulletin,* 1982, *20,* 624–634.

SWANSON, L.W., AND COWAN, W.M. The efferent connections of the suprachiasmatic nucleus of the hypothalamus. *Journal of Comparative Neurology,* 1975, *160,* 1–12.

SWANSON, L.W., KUCHARCZYK, J., AND MOGENSON, G.J. Autoradiographic evidence for pathways from the medial preoptic area to the midbrain involved in the drinking response to angiotensin II. *Journal of Comparative Neurology,* 1978, *178,* 645–660.

SWANSON, L.W., AND SAWCHENKO, P.E. Hypothalamic integration: Organization of the paraventricular and supraoptic nuclei. *Annual Review of Neuroscience,* 1983, *6,* 269–324.

TAKAHASHI, Y. Growth hormone secretion related to the sleep waking rhythm. In *The Functions of Sleep,* edited by R. Drucker-Colín, M. Shkurovich, and M.B. Sterman. New York: Academic Press, 1979.

TANABE, T., IINO, M., OOSHIMA, Y., AND TAKAGI, S.F. An olfactory area in the prefrontal lobe. *Brain Research,* 1974, *80,* 127–130.

TANABE, T., IINO, M., AND TAKAGI, S.G. Discrimination of odors in olfactory bulb, pyriform-amygdaloid areas, and orbitofrontal cortex of the monkey. *Journal of Neurophysiology,* 1975, *38,* 1284–1296.

TEITELBAUM, P., AND EPSTEIN, A.N. The lateral hypothalamic syndrome: Recovery of feeding and drinking after lateral hypothalamic lesions. *Psychological Review,* 1962, *69,* 74–90.

TEITELBAUM, P., AND STELLAR, E. Recovery from the failure to eat produced by hypothalamic lesions. *Science,* 1954, *120,* 894–895.

TERENIUS, L., AND WAHLSTRÖM, A. Morphine-like ligand for opiate receptors in human CSF. *Life Sciences,* 1975, *16,* 1759–1764.

TERRY, R.D., AND DAVIES, P. Dementia of the Alzheimer type. *Annual Review of Neuroscience,* 1980, *3,* 77–96.

THACH, W.T. Correlation of neural discharge with pattern and force of muscular activity, joint position, and direction of intended movement in motor cortex and cerebellum. *Journal of Neurophysiology,* 1978, *41,* 654–676.

THOMPSON, R.F., MAMOUNAS, L.A., LYNCH, G., AND BAUDRY, M. Increased glutamate receptor binding in hippocampus following classical conditioning of the rabbit eyelid response. *Society for Neuroscience Abstracts,* 1983, *9,* 830.

THORNDIKE, E.L. *The Elements of Psychology.* New York: Seiler, 1905.

TOOTELL, R.B., SILVERMAN, M.S., AND DE VALOIS, R.L. Spatial frequency columns in primary visual cortex. *Science,* 1981, *214,* 813–815.

TORDOFF, M.G., HOPFENBECK, J., AND NOVIN, D. Hepatic vagotomy (partial hepatic denervation) does not alter ingestive responses to metabolic challenges. *Physiology and Behavior,* 1982, *28,* 417–424.

TORREY, E.F., TORREY, B.B., AND PETERSON, M.R. Seasonality of schizophrenic births in the United States. *Archives of General Psychiatry,* 1977, *34,* 1065–1070.

TORREY, E.F., YOLKEN, R.H., AND WINFREY, C.J. Cytomegalovirus antibody in cerebrospinal fluid of schizophrenic patients detected by enzyme immunoassay. *Science,* 1982, *216,* 892–894.

TOURNEY, G. Hormones and homosexuality. In *Homosexual Behavior,* edited by J. Marmor. New York: Basic Books, 1980.

TRÄSKMANN, L., ÅSBERG, M., BERTILSSON, L., AND SJÖSTRAND, L. Monoamine metabolites in CSF and suicidal behavior. *Archives of General Psychiatry,* 1981, *38,* 631–636.

TRAYHURN, P., THURLBY, P.L., WOODWARD, C.J.H., AND JAMES, W.P.T. Thermoregulation in genetically obese rodents: The relationship to metabolic efficiency. In *Genetic Models of Obesity in Laboratory Animals,* edited by M.F.W. Festing. London: Macmillan, 1979.

TRULSON, M.E., AND JACOBS, B.L. Raphe unit activity in freely moving cats: Correlation with level of behavioral arousal. *Brain Research,* 1979, *163,* 135–150.

TRULSON, M.E., JACOBS, B.L., AND MORRISON, A.R. Raphe unit activity during REM sleep in normal cats and in pontine lesioned cats displaying REM sleep without atonia. *Brain Research,* 1981, *226,* 75–91.

TSOU, K., AND JANG, C.S. Studies on the site of analgesia action of morphine by intracerebral microinjection. *Scientia Sinica,* 1964, *13,* 1099–1109.

TUCKER, D.M., WATSON, R.T., AND HEILMAN, K.M. Affective discrimination and evocation in patients with right parietal disease. *Neurology,* 1977, *27,* 947–950.

TUNTURI, A.R. A difference in the representation of auditory signals for the left and right ears in the isofrequency contours of right middle ectosylvian auditory cortex in the dog. *American Journal of Physiology,* 1952, *168,* 712–727.

UNEMOTO, M., MURAI, Y., KODAMA, M., AND KIDO, R. Neuronal discharge patterns in conditioned emotional response. *Brain Research,* 1970, *24,* 347–351.

UNGERSTEDT, U. Stereotaxic mapping of the monoamine pathways in the rat. *Acta Physiologica Scandinavica,* 1971, *367,* 1–48.

URCA, G., AND NAHIN, R.L. Morphine-induced multiple unit changes in analgesic and rewarding brain sites. *Pain Abstracts,* 1978, *1,* 261.

UTTAL, W.R. *The Psychobiology of Sensory Coding,* New York: Harper & Row, 1973.

VALENSTEIN, E.S. The anatomical locus of reinforcement. In *Progress in Physiological Psychology, Vol. 1,* edited by E. Stellar and J. Sprague. New York: Academic Press, 1966.

VALENSTEIN, E.S. *Brain Control.* New York: John Wiley & Sons, 1973.

VALENSTEIN, E.S. *The Psychosurgery Debate: Scientific, Legal, and Ethical Perspectives.* San Francisco: W.H. Freeman, 1980.

VALENSTEIN, E.S., COX, V.C., AND KAKOLEWSKI, J.W. Reexamination of the role of the hypothalamus in motivation. *Psychological Review,* 1910, 77, 16–31.

VALLBO, Å.B. Muscle spindle response at the onset of isometric voluntary contractions in man. Time differences between fusimotor and skeletomotor effects. *Journal of Physiology (London),* 1971, *218,* 405–431.

VALLI, P., ZUCCA, G., AND CASELLA, C. Ionic composition of the endolymph and sensory transduction in labyrinthine organs. *Acta Otolaryngologica,* 1979, *87,* 466–471.

VAN DER LEE, S., AND BOOT, L.M. Spontaneous pseudopregnancy in mice. *Acta Physiologica et Pharmacologica Néerlandica,* 1955, *4,* 442–444.

VANDERWOLF, C.H. Hippocampal electrical activity and voluntary movement in the rat. *Electroencephalography and Clinical Neurophysiology,* 1969, *26,* 407–418.

VANDERWOLF, C.H., KRAMIS, R., GILLESPIE, L.A., AND BLAND, B.G. Hippocampal rhythmical slow activity and neocortical low voltage fast activity: Relations to behavior. In *The Hippocampus, Vol. 2: Neurophysiology and Behavior,* edited by R.L. Isaacson and K.H. Pribram. New York: Plenum Press, 1975.

VANDERWOLF, C.H., AND ROBINSON, T.E. Reticulo-cortical activity and behavior: A critique of the arousal theory and a new synthesis. *The Behavioral and Brain Sciences,* 1981, *4,* 459–514.

VAN DONGEN, P.A.M., BROEKKAMP, C.L.F., AND COOLS, A.R. Atonia after carbachol microinjections near the locus coeruleus in cats. *Pharmacology, Biochemistry and Behavior,* 1978, *8,* 527–532.

VAN ESSEN, D.C., AND ZEKI, S.M. The topographic organization of rhesus monkey prestriate cortex. *Journal of Physiology,* 1978, *277,* 193–226.

VAUGHAN, T., WYATT, R.J., AND GREEN, R. Changes in REM sleep of chronically anxious depressed patients given alpha-methyl-paratyrosine (AMPT). *Psychophysiology,* 1972, *9,* 96.

VERGNES, M. Déclenchement de réactions d'aggression interspécifique après lésion amygdalienne chez le rat. *Physiology and Behavior,* 1975, *14,* 271–276.

VERGNES, M. Contrôle amygdalien de comportements d'aggression chez le rat. *Physiology and Behavior,* 1976, *17,* 439–444.

VERNEY, E.B. The antidiuretic hormone and the factors which determine its release. *Proceedings of the Royal Society of London, Series B,* 1947, *135,* 25–106.

VICTOR, M., ADAMS, R.D., AND COLLINS, G.H. *The Wernicke-Korsakoff Syndrome.* Philadelphia: F.A. Davis, 1971.

VINCENT, J.D., ARNAULD, E., AND BIOULAC, B. Activity of osmosensitive single cells in the hypothalamus of the behaving monkey during drinking. *Brain Research,* 1972, *44,* 371–384.

VOCI, V.E., AND CARLSON, N.R. Enhancement of maternal behavior and nest behavior following systemic and diencephalic administration of prolactin and progesterone in the mouse. *Journal of Comparative and Physiological Psychology,* 1973, *83,* 388–393.

VOGEL, G.W., VOGEL, F., MCABEE, R.S., AND THURMOND, A.J. Improvement of depression by REM sleep deprivation: New findings and a theory. *Archives of General Psychiatry,* 1980, *37,* 247–253.

VOLICER, L., AND LOEW, C.G. Penetration of angiotensin II into the brain. *Neuropharmacology,* 1971, *10,* 631–636.

VOM SAAL, F.S. Prenatal exposure to androgen influences morphology and aggressive behavior of male and female mice. *Hormones and Behavior,* 1979, *12,* 1–11.

VOM SAAL, F.S. Models of early hormonal effects on intrasex aggression in mice. In *Hormones and Aggressive Behavior,* edited by B.B. Svare. New York: Plenum Press, 1983.

VOM SAAL, F.S., AND BRONSON, F.H. *In utero* proximity of female mouse fetuses to males: Effect on reproductive performance during later life. *Biology of Reproduction,* 1980a, *22,* 777–780.

VOM SAAL, F.S., AND BRONSON, F.H. Sexual characteristics of adult female mice are correlated with their blood testosterone levels during prenatal development. *Science,* 1980b, *208,* 597–599.

VON BÉKÉSY, G. Sweetness produced electrically on the tongue and its relation to taste theories. *Journal of Applied Physiology,* 1964, *19,* 1105–1113.

VON BONIN, G., AND BAILEY, P. *The Neocortex of Macaca*

Mulatta. Urbana: University of Illinois Press, 1947.

VON FREY, M. The distribution of afferent nerves in the skin. *Journal of the American Medical Association,* 1906, *47,* 645.

VON FRISCH, O. Herzfrequenzänderung bei Drückreaktion junger Nestflücher. *Zeitschrift für Tierpsychologie,* 1966, *23,* 497–500.

WADE, G.N., AND GRAY, J.M. Gonadal effects on food intake and adiposity: A metabolic hypothesis. *Physiology and Behavior,* 1979, *22,* 583–593.

WALINDER, J., SKOTT, A., CARLSSON, A., AND ROOS, B. Potentiation by metyrosine of thioridazine effects in chronic schizophrenics: A long term trial using double-blind cross-over technique. *Archives of General Psychiatry,* 1976, *33,* 501–505.

WALKER, W.A., AND LESHNER, A.I. The role of the adrenals in aggression. *American Zoologist,* 1962, *12,* 652.

WARD, A.A. The cingular gyrus: Area 24. *Journal of Neurophysiology,* 1948, *11,* 13–23.

WARD, I. Prenatal stress feminizes and demasculinizes the behavior of males. *Science,* 1972, *175,* 82–84.

WARD, I., AND WEISZ, J. Maternal stress alters plasma testosterone in fetal mice. *Science,* 1980, *207,* 328–329.

WARRINGTON, E.K., AND SHALLICE, T. Word-form dyslexia. *Brain,* 1980, *103,* 99–112.

WARRINGTON, E.K., AND WEISKRANTZ, L. The effect of prior learning on subsequent retention in amnesic patients. *Neuropsychologia,* 1974, *12,* 419–428.

WARRINGTON, E.K., AND WEISKRANTZ, L. Further analysis of the prior learning effect in amnesic patients. *Neuropsychologia,* 1978, *16,* 169–177.

WAXENBERG, S.E., DRELLICH, M.G., AND SUTHERLAND, A.M. The role of hormones in human behavior. I. Changes in female sexuality after adrenalectomy. *Journal of Clinical Endocrinology and Metabolism,* 1959, *19,* 193–202.

WEBB, W.B. *Sleep: The Gentle Tyrant.* Englewood Cliffs, N.J.: Prentice-Hall, 1975.

WEBB, W.B. Some theories about sleep and their clinical implications. *Psychiatric Annals,* 1982, *11,* 415–422.

WEINBERGER, D.R., BIGELOW, L.B., KLEINMAN, J.E., KLEIN, S.T., ROSENBLATT, J.E., AND WYATT, R.J. Cerebral ventricular enlargement in chronic schizophrenia: An association with poor response to treatment. *Archives of General Psychiatry,* 1980, *37,* 11–13.

WEINBERGER, D.R., CANNON-SPOOR, E., POTKIN, S.G., AND WYATT, R.J. Poor premorbid adjustment and CT scan abnormalities in chronic schizophrenia. *American Journal of Psychiatry,* 1980, *137,* 1410–1413.

WEINBERGER, D.R., DELISI, L.E., NEOPHYTIDES, A.N., AND WYATT, R.J. Familial aspects of CT abnormalities in chronic schizophrenic patients. *Psychiatry Research,* 1981, *4,* 65–71.

WEINBERGER, D.R., AND WYATT, R.J. Brain morphology in schizophrenia: *In vivo* studies. In *Schizophrenia as a Brain Disease,* edited by F.A. Henn and H.A.

Nasrallah. New York: Oxford University Press, 1982.

WEINBERGER, N.M. Sensory plasticity and learning: the magnocellular medial geniculate nucleus of the auditory system. In *Conditioning: Representation of Involved Neural Functions,* edited by C.D. Woody. New York: Plenum Press, 1982.

WEINGARTEN, H.P. Conditioned cues elicit feeding in sated rats: A role for learning in meal initiation. *Science,* 1983, *220,* 431–432.

WEINTRAUB, S., MESULAM, M.-M., AND KRAMER, L. Disturbances in prosody: A right-hemisphere contribution to language. *Archives of Neurology,* 1981, *38,* 742–744.

WEISZ, D.J., CLARK, G.A., YANK, B., THOMPSON, R.F., AND SOLOMON, P.R. Activity of dentate gyrus during NM conditioning in rabbit. In *Conditioning: Representation of Involved Neural Functions,* edited by C.D. Woody. New York: Plenum Press, 1982.

WEISZ, D.W., SOLOMON, P.R., AND THOMPSON, R.F. The hippocampus appears necessary for trace conditioning. *Bulletin of the Psychonomic Society,* 1980, *16* (Abstract).

WEITZMAN, E.D. Sleep and its disorders. *Annual Review of Neuroscience,* 1981, *4,* 381–418.

WENDER, P.H., ROSENTHAL, D., KETY, S., SCHULSINGER, F., AND WELNER, J. Cross fostering. *Archives of General Psychiatry,* 1974, *30,* 121–128.

WERNICKE, C. *Der Aphasische Symptomenkomplex.* Breslau, Poland: Cohn & Weigert, 1874.

WERSÄLL, J., FLOCK, A., AND LUNDQUIST, P. Structural basis for directional sensitivity in cochlear and vestibular sensory receptors. *Cold Spring Harbor Symposia on Quantitative Biology,* 1965, *30,* 115–132.

WETZEL, M.C. Self-stimulation aftereffects and runway performance in the rat. *Journal of Comparative and Physiological Psychology,* 1963, *56,* 673–678.

WEVER, E.G., AND BRAY, C.W. Present possibilities for auditory theory. *Psychological Review,* 1930, *37,* 365–380.

WHITEHEAD, R.G., ROWLAND, M.G.M., HUTTON, M., PRENTICE, A.M., MÜLLER, E., AND PAUL, A. Factors influencing lactation performance in rural Gambian mothers. *Lancet,* 1978, *2,* 178–181.

WHITEHOUSE, P.J., PRICE, D.L., STRUBLE, R.G., CLARK, A.W., COYLE, J.T., AND DeLONG, M.R. Alzheimer's disease and senile dementia: Loss of neurons in the basal forebrain. *Science,* 1982, *215,* 1237–1239.

WHITFIELD, I.C., AND EVANS, E.F. Responses of auditory cortical neurons to stimuli of changing frequency. *Journal of Neurophysiology,* 1965, *28,* 655–672.

WHITTEN, W.K. Occurrence of anestrus in mice caged in groups. *Journal of Endocrinology,* 1959, *18,* 102–107.

WIESEL, T.N. Postnatal development of the visual cortex and the influence of environment. *Nature,* 1982, *299,* 583–592.

WIESNER, B.P., AND SHEARD, N. *Maternal Behaviour in the Rat.* London: Oliver and Brody, 1933.

WIGSTRÖM, H., AND GUSTAFSSON, B. Facilitated induction of hippocampal long-lasting potentiation during blockade of inhibition. *Nature,* 1983, *301,* 603–604.

WILCOXON, H.C., DRAGOIN, W.B., AND KRAL, P.A. Illness-induced aversions in rat and quail: Relative salience of visual and gustatory cues. *Science,* 1971, *171,* 826–828.

WILDT, L., HAUSLER, A., HUTCHISON, J.S., MARSHALL, G., AND KNOBIL, E. Estradiol as a gonadotropin releasing hormone in the rhesus monkey. *Endocrinology,* 1981, *108,* 2011–2013.

WILSKA, A. Eine Methode zur Bestimmung der Horschwellenamplituden der Tromenfells bei verscheideden Frequenzen. *Skandinavisches Archiv für Physiologie,* 1935, *72,* 161–165.

WINANS, S.S., AND POWERS, J.B. Olfactory and vomeronasal deafferentation of male hamsters: Histological and behavioral analyses. *Brain Research,* 1977, *126,* 325–344.

WOLFE, B.B., HARDEN, T.K., SPORN, J.R., AND MOLINOFF, P.B. Presynaptic modulation of beta adrenergic receptors in rat cerebral cortex after treatment with antidepressants. *Journal of Pharmacology and Experimental Therapeutics,* 1978, *207,* 446–457.

WONG-RILEY, M. Personal communication, 1978. Cited by Livingstone and Hubel, 1982.

WOODRUFF, M.L., AND BOWNDS, M.D. Amplitude, kinetics, and reversibility of a light-induced decrease in guanosine $3',5'$-cyclic monophosphate in isolated frog receptor membranes. *Journal of General Physiology,* 1979, *73,* 629–653.

WOODRUFF, M.L., BOWNDS, M.D., GREEN, S.H., MORRISEY, J.L., AND SHEDLOVSKY, A. Guanosine $3',5'$-cyclic monophosphate and the in vitro physiology of frog photoreceptor membranes. *Journal of General Physiology,* 1977, *69,* 667–679.

WRIGHT, R.H. Predicting olfactory quality from far infrared spectra. *Annals of the New York Academy of Sciences,* 1974, *237,* 129–136.

WYATT, R.J. The serotonin-catecholamine dream bicycle: A clinical study. *Biological Psychiatry,* 1972, *5,* 33–64.

WYATT, R.J., POTKIN, S.G., AND MURPHY, D.L. Platelet monoamine oxidase activity in schizophrenia: A review of the data. *American Journal of Psychiatry,* 1979, *136,* 377–385.

WYSOCKI, C.J. Neurobehavioral evidence for the involvement of the vomeronasal system in mammalian reproduction. *Neuroscience and Biobehavioral Reviews,* 1979, *3,* 301–341.

YADIN, E., GUARINI, V., AND GALLISTEL, C.R. Unilaterally activated systems in rats self-stimulating at sites in the medial forebrain bundle, medial prefrontal cortex, or locus coeruleus. *Brain Research,* 1983, *266,* 39–50.

YAMAMOTO, T., YUYAMA, N., AND KAWAMURA, Y. Central processing of taste perception. In *Brain Mechanisms of Sensation,* edited by Y. Katsuki, R. Norgren, and M. Sato. New York: John Wiley & Sons, 1981.

YEO, C.H., HARDIMAN, M.J., AND GLICKSTEIN, M. Discrete lesions of cerebellar cortex abolish the classically conditioned nictitating membrane response of the rabbit. *Behavioural Brain Research,* 1984, *13,* 261–266.

YEO, C.H., HARDIMAN, M.J., GLICKSTEIN, M., AND STEELE-RUSSELL, I. Lesions of cerebellar nuclei abolish the classically conditioned nictitating membrane response. *Society for Neuroscience Abstracts,* 1982, *8,* 22.

YEOMANS, J.S. Quantitative measurement of neural post-stimulation excitability with behavioral methods. *Physiology and Behavior,* 1975, *15,* 593–602.

YEOMANS, J.S. The absolute refractory periods of self-stimulation neurons. *Physiology and Behavior,* 1979, *22,* 911–919.

YEUNG, J.C., AND RUDY, T. Sites of antinociceptive action of systemically injected morphine: Involvement of supraspinal loci as revealed by intracerebroventricular injection of naloxone. *Journal of Pharmacology and Experimental Therapeutics,* 1980, *215,* 626–632.

YOUNG, T. On the theory of light and colours. *Philosophical Transactions,* 1802, 12–48.

YOUNG, W.G., AND DEUTSCH, J.A. Rat brainstem responses to gastric signals of distention and nutrient as exam-ined with (^{14}C)-2-deoxy-D-glucose. *Society for Neuroscience Abstracts,* 1981, *7,* 656.

ZARCONE, V., GULEVICH, G., AND DEMENT, W.C. Sleep and electroconvulsive therapy. *Archives of General Psychiatry,* 1967, *16,* 567–577.

ZEKI, S.M. The cortical projections of foveal striate cortex in the rhesus monkey. *Journal of Physiology,* 1978a, *277,* 227–244.

ZEKI, S.M. The third visual complex of rhesus monkey prestriate cortex. *Journal of Physiology,* 1978b, *277,* 245–272.

ZEKI, S.M. Uniformity and diversity of structure and function in rhesus monkey prestriate visual cortex. *Journal of Physiology,* 1978c, *277,* 273–290.

ZEKI, S.M. The representation of colours in the cerebral cortex. *Nature,* 1980, *284,* 412–418.

ZIMEN, E. On the regulation of pack size in wolves. *Zeitschrift für Tierpsychologie,* 1976, *40,* 300–341.

ZOLA-MORGAN, S., SQUIRE, L.R., AND MISHKIN, M. The neuroanatomy of amnesia: Amygdala-hippocampus versus temporal stem. *Science,* 1982, *218,* 1337–1339.

ZUGER, D. Monozygotic twins discordant for homosexuality: Report of a pair and significance of the phenomenon. *Comprehensive Psychiatry,* 1976, *17,* 661–669.

Author Index

Subject Index

Neurotransmitters (*see* Transmitter substances)
Nialamide, 705
Nicotinic receptors, 70, 79
Nictitating membrane response, 583–588, 591–594, 606, 622
Nightmares, 326
Night terrors, 341
Nigrostriatal bundle, 311, 313, 467
Nigrostriatal system, 524
Nissl stains, 131–132
NMR (nuclear magnetic resonance) scanning, 141–142
Nocturnal emissions, 325
Nocturnal enuresis, 341
Nodes of Ranvier, 23, 46–48
Nonmatching-to-sample task, delayed, 547–548, 552
Nontheta behaviors, 579
Noradrenalin, 71
Norepinephrine (NE), 70–73, 122
  in depression, 702, 703–704
  in reinforcement, 523–524, 525–526
  in sleep and arousal, 355–356, 363
Nose, 280–281
Nuclear magnetic resonance (NMR) scanning, 141–142
Nucleolus, 17
Nucleus:
  of cell, 17
  in central nervous system, 103
Nucleus accumbens, 524, 525–526, 534–536
Nucleus basalis of Meynert, 631, 632–633
Nucleus circularis, 433
Nucleus of the diagonal band, 531
Nucleus of the solitary tract, 278, 279, 361–362
Nucleus raphe magnus, 271, 272
Nucleus reticularis magnocellularis, 366
Nucleus ruber, 109, 307, 593
Nutrients, storage and utilization of, 448–452
Nystagmus, 249

OA, 545–546
OB, 545–546
Obesity, 469–470, 473–475
OC, 545
Occipital lobes, 97, 99–100
Ocular dominance, 194–195, 216–217
Odor (*see* Olfaction)
Odor primaries, 282–284
Oleic acid, 451
Olfaction, 280–284
  in aggression, 490
  in eating, 446
  in maternal behavior, 412–413
  in sexual behavior, 386–390
Olfactory bulbs, 113–116, 280–281
  accessory, 387–388, 412, 490
Olfactory epithelium, 280
Olfactory glomeruli, 280
Oligodendroglia, 23–24
Operant conditioning, 508–514

Opiate(s):
  in conditioning, 530, 563–564
  endogenous, 77, 269–270, 274
  in learning, 634–635
  in pain perception, 269–274
Opsin, 176, 177, 209
Optic chiasm, 104, 181
Optic disk, 95–96, 173
Optic radiations, 179
Oral apraxia, 307, 645
Orbits, 171
Organic senses, 255, 257, 265
Organizational effects, 370
  on female sexual behavior, 405, 406
  on male sexual behavior, 384–386, 403–404
  on interfemale aggression, 493–494
  on intermale aggression, 489
  on sexual development, 374
  on sexual orientation, 398–399
Organ of Corti, 231
Organophosphates, 79
Orientation columns, 193–194, 195–197
Orienting response, 561, 563
Oscillograph, ink-writing, 155
Oscilloscope, 39, 151–155
Osmometric thirst, 439–441
Osmoreceptors, 431–434
Osmosis, 31–33
Osmotic pressure, 36–39, 424
Ossicles, 229
Otoconia, 251
Ova, 371–373, 379
Oval window, 229, 231, 232
Ovarian follicles, 378–379, 380–381
Ovaries, 121, 123, 379–381
Overtones, 242
Ovulation, 379, 380–381
Oxytocin, 121, 123

Pacemaker, of heart, 293
Pacemaker potentials, 292
Pacinian corpuscles, 258, 259, 260
Paleostriatum, 524
Palmitic acid, 451
Pancreas, 123, 447–448, 450, 452
Papillae:
  of skin, 258
  of tongue, 276–277
Parabrachial nucleus, 278
Parachlorophenylalanine (PCPA), 271, 359–361, 364
Paradoxical sleep (*see* REM sleep)
Parafascicular nucleus, 268, 269
Paranoid schizophrenia, 680
Paraphasic errors, 640
Parasympathetic division, 116–119
Parasympathetic ganglia, 119
Paraventricular nucleus, 429–430, 469–471
Parietal lobes, 97, 99–100
  damage to inferior, 647
  in movement control, 301, 310–311
Parkinson's disease, 73, 101–102, 311–313
Parturition, 410, 413
Passive avoidance task, 600–601

Patellar reflex, 293–294
Pavor nocturnus, 341
PCPA (parachlorophenylalanine), 271, 359–361, 364
Pelvic thrusting, 382–383, 400
Pepsin, 446
Peptide(s), 75
Peptide neurotransmitters, 75–76
Perforant path, 578
  in long-term potentiation, 613–614, 615, 621, 622
Perfusion, 129
Periaqueductal gray matter, 109
  in drinking, 444
  in female sexual behavior, 408
  in opiate-induced analgesia, 270–272
Perifornical region, 468–469
Perilymph, 234, 250
Peripheral nervous system (PNS):
  meninges covering, 92
  structure of, 86, 112–119
  supporting cells of, 25–27
Permeability, 31
Persistence, on oscilloscope, 153
PET (positron emission tomography), 141
PGO waves, 334
Phagocytosis, 23
Phase locking, 244–245
Phaseolamin, 460
Phasic response, 186
Pheromones, 386–390
Phosphodiesterase, 59
Phosphorylation, 59
Photons, 170–171
Photopigment, 176
Photoreceptors, 173
  in color vision, 209–210
  retinal circuitry of, 186–188
  structure and function of, 175–177
Physiological psychology:
  biological roots of, 6–9
  contributions of modern psychology to, 9–11
  philosophical roots of, 2–6
Physostigmine, 79, 364, 633
Pia mater, 92
Picrotoxin, 535, 536, 617
Piloerection, 292
Pimozide, 527, 528
Pineal body, 3–4
Pinna, 229
Pinocytosis, 54, 56
Pitch, 228, 239–240
Pituitary gland, 120
Pituitary hormones, 120–121, 123, 379–381
Pituitary stalk, 104
Placebo, 273–274
Placenta, 414
Planum temporale, 667–668
Plasma, 424, 430–431
Platelets, 638
Plexiform layers, 175
Plexuses, 113
PMS (premenstrual syndrome), 492
PNS (*see* Peripheral nervous system [PNS])
Poikilotherms, 422
Poisons, recognition of, 558–560
Polyethylene glycol, 435